W9-BJH-028

MCSA
Windows Server® 2012 R2
Complete Study Guide

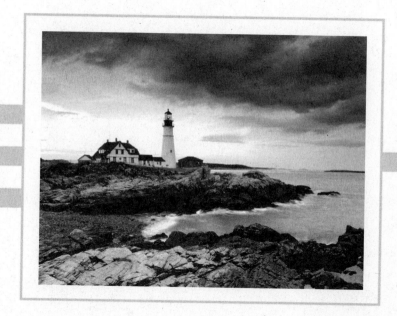

MCSA
Windows Server® 2012 R2
Complete Study Guide

William Panek

Senior Acquisitions Editor: Jeff Kellum
Development Editor: Gary Schwartz
Technical Editors: Rodney Fournier and Michael Rice
Production Editor: Eric Charbonneau
Copy Editor: Kim Wimpsett
Editorial Manager: Pete Gaughan
Production Manager: Kathleen Wisor
Professional Technology and Strategy Director: Barry Pruett
Associate Publisher: Jim Minatel
Media Project Manager 1: Laura Moss-Hollister
Media Associate Producer: Marilyn Hummel
Media Quality Assurance: Josh Frank
Book Designer: Judy Fung
Proofreader: Josh Chase, Word One New York
Indexer: Ted Laux
Project Coordinator, Cover: Patrick Redmond
Cover Designer: Wiley

Copyright © 2015 by John Wiley & Sons, Inc., Indianapolis, Indiana

Published simultaneously in Canada

ISBN: 978-1-118-85991-9

ISBN: 978-1-118-85969-8 (ebk.)

ISBN: 978-1-118-85990-2 (ebk.)

No part of this publication may be reproduced, stored in a retrieval system or transmitted in any form or by any means, electronic, mechanical, photocopying, recording, scanning or otherwise, except as permitted under Sections 107 or 108 of the 1976 United States Copyright Act, without either the prior written permission of the Publisher, or authorization through payment of the appropriate per-copy fee to the Copyright Clearance Center, 222 Rosewood Drive, Danvers, MA 01923, (978) 750-8400, fax (978) 646-8600. Requests to the Publisher for permission should be addressed to the Permissions Department, John Wiley & Sons, Inc., 111 River Street, Hoboken, NJ 07030, (201) 748-6011, fax (201) 748-6008, or online at www.wiley.com/go/permissions.

Limit of Liability/Disclaimer of Warranty: The publisher and the author make no representations or warranties with respect to the accuracy or completeness of the contents of this work and specifically disclaim all warranties, including without limitation warranties of fitness for a particular purpose. No warranty may be created or extended by sales or promotional materials. The advice and strategies contained herein may not be suitable for every situation. This work is sold with the understanding that the publisher is not engaged in rendering legal, accounting, or other professional services. If professional assistance is required, the services of a competent professional person should be sought. Neither the publisher nor the author shall be liable for damages arising herefrom. The fact that an organization or Web site is referred to in this work as a citation and/or a potential source of further information does not mean that the author or the publisher endorses the information the organization or Web site may provide or recommendations it may make. Further, readers should be aware that Internet Web sites listed in this work may have changed or disappeared between when this work was written and when it is read.

For general information on our other products and services or to obtain technical support, please contact our Customer Care Department within the U.S. at (877) 762-2974, outside the U.S. at (317) 572-3993 or fax (317) 572-4002.

Wiley publishes in a variety of print and electronic formats and by print-on-demand. Some material included with standard print versions of this book may not be included in e-books or in print-on-demand. If this book refers to media such as a CD or DVD that is not included in the version you purchased, you may download this material at http://booksupport.wiley.com. For more information about Wiley products, visit www.wiley.com.

Library of Congress Control Number: 2014948559

TRADEMARKS: Wiley, the Wiley logo, and the Sybex logo are trademarks or registered trademarks of John Wiley & Sons, Inc. and/or its affiliates, in the United States and other countries, and may not be used without written permission. Windows Server is a registered trademark of Microsoft Corporation. All other trademarks are the property of their respective owners. John Wiley & Sons, Inc. is not associated with any product or vendor mentioned in this book.

10 9 8 7 6 5 4

Dear Reader,

Thank you for choosing *MCSA: Windows Server 2012 R2 Complete Study Guide*. This book is part of a family of premium-quality Sybex books, all of which are written by outstanding authors who combine practical experience with a gift for teaching.

Sybex was founded in 1976. More than 30 years later, we're still committed to producing consistently exceptional books. With each of our titles, we're working hard to set a new standard for the industry. From the paper we print on to the authors we work with, our goal is to bring you the best books available.

I hope you see all that reflected in these pages. I'd be very interested to hear your comments and get your feedback on how we're doing. Feel free to let me know what you think about this or any other Sybex book by sending me an email at contactus@sybex. com. If you think you've found a technical error in this book, please visit http://sybex. custhelp.com. Customer feedback is critical to our efforts at Sybex.

Best regards,

Chris Webb
Associate Publisher
Sybex, an Imprint of Wiley

This book is dedicated to the three ladies of my life:
—Crystal, Alexandria, and Paige.

Acknowledgments

I would like to thank my wife and best friend, Crystal. She is always the light at the end of my tunnel. I want to thank my two daughters, Alexandria and Paige, for all of their love and support during the writing of all my books. They make it all worthwhile.

I want to thank my family, and especially my brothers, Rick, Gary, and Rob. They have always been there for me. I want to thank my father, Richard, who helped me become the man I am today, and my mother, Maggie, for all of her love and support.

I would like to thank all of my friends and co-workers, especially Vic, Catherine, Jeff, Stephanie, Don, Jason, Doug, Dave, Steve, Pat, Mike (all of them), Tommy, George, Greg, Becca, Deb, Jeri, Lisa, Scotty, and all of the field guys. I want to also thank my team and everyone who works with my group including Moe, Jimmy, Paul, Dana, Dean, Reanna, Todd, and Will F. Because of all of your hard work, you make me look good every day and make it a pleasure to go to work. Thanks to all of you for everything that you do.

I want to thank everyone on my Sybex team, especially my development editor, Gary Schwartz, who helped me make this the best book possible, and Rodney R. Fournier, who is the technical editor of many of my books. It's always good to have the very best technical guy backing you up.

I want to also thank Mike Rice, Winston McMiller, and Jeff Stokes for helping me update some of my chapters from Windows Server 2012 to Windows Server 2012 R2. Their hard work and knowledge helped finish this huge undertaking.

I want to thank Eric Charbonneau, who was my production editor, and my acquisitions editor, Jeff Kellum, who served as lead for the entire book. He has always been there for me, and it is always great to write for him.

Finally, I want to thank everyone else behind the scenes who helped make this book possible. It's truly an amazing thing to have so many people work on my books to help make them the very best. I can't thank you all enough for your hard work.

About the Authors

 William Panek holds the following certifications: MCP, MCP+I, MCSA, MCSA+ Security and Messaging, MCSE-NT (3.51 and 4.0), MCSE 2000 and 2003, MCSE+Security and Messaging, MCDBA, MCT, MCTS, MCITP, CCNA, and CHFI. Will is also a two time Microsoft MVP (he won in October 2013 and October 2014).

After many successful years in the computer industry and a degree in computer programming, Will decided that he could better use his talents and his personality as an instructor. He began teaching for schools such as Boston University, Clark University, and the University of Maryland, just to name a few. He has done consulting and training work for some of the biggest government and corporate companies in the world including the U.S. Secret Service, Cisco, the U.S. Air Force, and the U.S. Army.

In January 2015, Will is now teaching for StormWind (www.stormwind.com). He currently lives in New Hampshire with his wife and two daughters. Will was also a Representative in the New Hampshire House of Representatives from 2010 to 2012. In his spare time, he likes to golf, ski, shoot, and go snowmobiling. Will is also a commercially rated helicopter pilot.

Michael Allen Rice holds these certifications: MCP, MCTS, MCSA, MCSE, MCITP, CompTIA Network+, CompTIA Security+, VMware Certified Professional 5 - DCV, and NetApp Certified Data Management Administrator 7-mode.

Michael currently works as a Data Center Administrator for Intelligent Software Solutions, Inc., based in Colorado Springs. He lives there with his wife and two children. He specializes in leading the way for corporate infrastructure in the areas of virtualization, storage, and systems administration. Over the past decade as an IT professional, Michael has received numerous awards for his outstanding performance and dedication to excellence within the IT community.

Winston McMiller holds these certifications: MCP, MCP+I, MCSA, MCSE 2000, 2003, 2012/2012 R2, and ITIL. Winston is a Microsoft Premier Field Engineer.

After 18 years in the computer industry and a degree in information technology, Winston has done consulting and training for some of the largest companies in the world including General Electric, HP Enterprise services, Chrysler, and IBM.

He currently lives in the Seattle area. In his spare time, he likes to ski, do photography, and travel. He is an avid audiophile and songwriter.

Jeff Stokes holds these certifications: MCT, MCSA, MCSE 2003, and MCTS: Windows Internals. Jeff Stokes runs @WindowsPerf, a Windows Performance social networking property. He is a frequent guest on RunAsRadio and an avid blogger.

As a previous Premier Field Engineer at Microsoft, Jeff has worked in the Fortune 1000 space for the last eight years. After 21 years in the IT field, Jeff has established himself as a performance SME and a VDI pioneer in Microsoft technologies, including Windows optimization as a VDI guest. His work appears in VDI optimization guidance papers from Microsoft and other parties.

He currently lives in the Atlanta area. In his spare time, he analyzes performance traces, games, and mentors others in the IT field.

Contents at a Glance

Contents

Chapter 6 **Manage GPOs** **297**

<table>
<tr><td>**Part III**</td><td>**Exam 70-412: Configuring Advanced Windows Server 2012 R2 Services**</td><td>**817**</td></tr>
<tr><td>**Chapter 17**</td><td>**Configure and Manage High Availability**</td><td>**819**</td></tr>
</table>

Table of Exercises

Introduction

This book is drawn from more than 20 years of IT experience. I have taken that experience and translated it into a Windows Server 2012 R2 book that will help you not only prepare for the MCSA: Windows Server 2012 R2 exams but also develop a clear understanding of how to install and configure Windows Server 2012 R2 while avoiding all of the possible configuration pitfalls.

Many Microsoft books just explain the Windows operating system, but with *MCSA: Windows Server 2012 R2 Complete Study Guide*, I go a step further by providing many in-depth, step-by-step procedures to support my explanations of how the operating system performs at its best.

Microsoft Windows Server 2012 R2 is the newest version of Microsoft's server operating system software. Microsoft has taken the best of Windows Server 2003, Windows Server 2008, and Windows Server 2012 and combined them into the latest creation, Windows Server 2012 R2.

Windows Server 2012 R2 eliminates many of the problems that plagued the previous versions of Windows Server, and it includes a much faster boot time and shutdown. It is also easier to install and configure, and it barely stops to ask the user any questions during installation. In this book, I will show you what features are installed during the automated installation and where you can make changes if you need to be more in charge of your operating system and its features.

This book takes you through all the ins and outs of Windows Server 2012 R2, including installation, configuration, Group Policy Objects, auditing, backups, and so much more.

Windows Server 2012 R2 has improved on Microsoft's desktop environment, made networking easier, enhanced searching capability, and improved performance—and that's only scratching the surface.

When all is said and done, this is a technical book for IT professionals who want to take Windows Server 2012 R2 to the next step and get certified. With this book, not only will you learn Windows Server 2012 R2 and ideally pass the exams, you will also become a Windows Server 2012 R2 expert.

The Microsoft Certification Program

Since the inception of its certification program, Microsoft has certified more than 2 million people. As the computer network industry continues to increase in both size and complexity, this number is sure to grow—and the need for proven ability will also increase. Certifications can help companies verify the skills of prospective employees and contractors.

The Microsoft certification tracks for Windows Server 2012 R2 include the following:

MCSA: Windows Server 2012 R2   The MCSA is now the lowest-level certification you can achieve with Microsoft in relation to Windows Server 2012 R2. It requires passing three exams: 70-410, 70-411, and 70-412. Or, if you qualify, you can take the Upgrading exam: exam 70-417. This book assists in your preparation for all four exams.

MCSE: Server Infrastructure or MCSE: Desktop Infrastructure   The MCSE certifications, in relation to Windows Server 2012 R2, require that you become an MCSA first and then pass two additional exams. The additional exams will vary depending on which of the two MCSE tracks you choose. For more information, visit Microsoft's website at www.microsoft.com/learning.

MCSM: Directory Services   The MCSM certification takes things to an entirely new level. It requires passing a knowledge exam (in addition to having the MCSE in Windows Server 2012 R2) and a lab exam. This is now the elite-level certification in Windows Server 2012 R2.

How Do You Become Certified on Windows Server 2012 R2?

Attaining Microsoft certification has always been a challenge. In the past, students have been able to acquire detailed exam information—even most of the exam questions—from online "brain dumps" and third-party "cram" books or software products. For the new generation of exams, this is simply not the case.

Microsoft has taken strong steps to protect the security and integrity of its new certification tracks. Now prospective candidates must complete a course of study that develops detailed knowledge about a wide range of topics. It supplies them with the true skills needed, derived from working with the technology being tested.

The new generations of Microsoft certification programs are heavily weighted toward hands-on skills and experience. It is recommended that candidates have troubleshooting skills acquired through hands-on experience and working knowledge.

Fortunately, if you are willing to dedicate the time and effort to learn Windows Server 2012 R2, you can prepare yourself well for the exam by using the proper tools. By working through this book, you can successfully meet the requirements to pass the Windows Server 2012 R2 exams.

MCSA Exam Requirements

Candidates for MCSA certification on Windows Server 2012 R2 must pass at least the following three Windows Server 2012 R2 exams:

- 70-410: Installing and Configuring Windows Server 2012 R2
- 70-411: Administering Windows Server 2012 R2
- 70-412: Configuring Advanced Windows Server 2012 R2 Services

MCITP Exam Requirements

Candidates for MCITP certification on Windows Server 2012 R2 must pass one Windows Server 2012 R2 exams. This book will help you get ready for the 70-411: Administering Windows Server 2012 R2 exam.

Microsoft provides exam objectives to give you a general overview of possible areas of coverage on the Microsoft exams. Keep in mind, however, that exam objectives are subject to change at any time without prior notice and at Microsoft's sole discretion. Visit the Microsoft Learning website (www.microsoft.com/learning) for the most current listing of exam objectives. The published objectives and how they map to this book are listed later in this Introduction.

> For those who have a qualifying certification, they can take the Upgrading Your Skills to MCSA Windows Server 2012 R2 exam (exam 70-417). The objectives for this exam span the three individual exams. This book covers all of the objectives for the Upgrading exam. For details about the exam, visit Microsoft's website at www.microsoft.com/learning.

Microsoft provides exam objectives to give you a general overview of possible areas of coverage on the Microsoft exams. Keep in mind, however, that exam objectives are subject to change at any time without prior notice and at Microsoft's sole discretion. Visit the Microsoft Learning website (www.microsoft.com/learning) for the most current listing of exam objectives. The published objectives and how they map to this book are listed later in this introduction.

> For a more detailed description of the Microsoft certification programs, including a list of all of the exams, visit the Microsoft Learning website at: www.microsoft.com/learning.

Tips for Taking the Windows Server 2012 R2 Exams

Here are some general tips for achieving success on your certification exam:

- Arrive early at the exam center so that you can relax and review your study materials. During this final review, you can look over tables and lists of exam-related information.

- Read the questions carefully. Do not be tempted to jump to an early conclusion. Make sure that you know *exactly* what the question is asking.

- Answer all questions. If you are unsure about a question, mark it for review and come back to it at a later time.

- On simulations, do not change settings that are not directly related to the question. Also, assume the default settings if the question does not specify or imply which settings are used.

- For questions about which you're unsure, use a process of elimination to get rid of the obviously incorrect answers first. This improves your odds of selecting the correct answer when you need to make an educated guess.

Exam Registration

At the time this book was released, Microsoft exams are given using Prometric testing centers (800-755-EXAM [800-755-3926]). As of December 31, 2014, Microsoft will be ending its relationship with Prometric and all exams will be delivered through the more than 1,000 Authorized VUE Testing Centers around the world. For the location of a testing center near you, go to VUE's website at www.vue.com. If you are outside of the United States and Canada, contact your local VUE registration center.

Find out the number of the exam that you want to take and then register with the Prometric registration center nearest to you. At this point, you will be asked for advance payment for the exam. The exams are $125 each, and you must take them within one year of payment. You can schedule exams up to six weeks in advance, or as late as one working day prior to the date of the exam. You can cancel or reschedule your exam if you contact the center at least two working days prior to the exam. Same-day registration is available in some locations, subject to space availability. Where same-day registration is available, you must register a minimum of two hours before test time.

When you schedule the exam, you will be provided with instructions regarding appointment and cancellation procedures, ID requirements, and information about the testing center location. In addition, you will receive a registration and payment confirmation letter from Prometric.

Microsoft requires certification candidates to accept the terms of a nondisclosure agreement before taking certification exams.

Who Should Read This Book?

This book is intended for individuals who want to earn their MCSA: Windows Server 2012 R2 certification.

Not only will this book help anyone who is looking to pass the Microsoft exams, it will also help anyone who wants to learn the real ins and outs of the Windows Server 2012 R2 operating system.

What's Inside?

Here is a glance at what's in each chapter:

Chapter 1: Install Windows Server 2012 R2 The first chapter explains the requirements and steps required to install and configure Windows Server 2012 R2.

Chapter 2: Configure Network Services This chapter shows you how to install and configure DNS. It also explains the different types of DNS records and DNS zone types.

Chapter 3: Plan and Install Active Directory This chapter takes you through the advantages and benefits of Windows Server 2012 R2 Active Directory.

Chapter 4: Configure Windows Server 2012 R2 This chapter shows you how to manage file systems, print servers, and file and share access.

Chapter 5: Administer Active Directory This chapter takes you through the different ways to create and manage your users and groups on the Windows Server 2012 R2 operating system.

Chapter 6: Manage GPOs You will see how to configure different types of Group Policy objects (GPOs) in Active Directory.

Chapter 7: Manage Security This chapter shows you how to secure Windows Server 2012 R2.

Chapter 8: Configure TCP/IP This chapter shows you how to configure IPv4 and IPv6. You'll look at IPv4 subnetting and how to manage a TCP/IP network.

Chapter 9: Use Virtualization in Windows Server 2012 This chapter shows you how to implement and configure Windows Server Hyper-V and virtual machines. You will learn about virtual networking, virtual hard disks, migration types, and Integration Services.

Chapter 10: Manage and Maintain Servers This chapter explains the requirements and steps to deploy, manage, and maintain the Windows Server 2012 R2 system.

Chapter 11: Manage File Services This chapter shows you how to configure file and print services. You will learn how to set up a file server for faster response times and about the different ways to set up and configure print services.

Chapter 12: Configure DNS This chapter shows you the advantages and benefits of Windows Server 2012 R2 Network Services.

Chapter 13: Configure Routing and Remote Access This chapter shows you how to configure the different types of remote access and Windows routing protocols.

Chapter 14: Configure a Network Policy Server Infrastructure This chapter takes you through the different ways to create and manage your Windows Server 2012 R2 NPS server.

Chapter 15: Configure and Manage Active Directory   You will see how to configure and manage different types of objects in Active Directory.

Chapter 16: Configure and Manage Group Policy   This chapter shows you how to manage different parts of Windows policies by using the Group Policy Management Console. This chapter also explains how to install and configure software using GPOs.

Chapter 17: Configure and Manage High Availability   This chapter shows how to set up Windows Server 2012 R2 high availability. This includes clustering and failover systems.

Chapter 18: Configure File and Storage Solutions   This chapter shows you how to configure file and storage solutions. You will learn how to help your system run faster and give you better response times.

Chapter 19: Implement Business Continuity and Disaster Recovery   This chapter shows you how to protect yourself in the event of a system crash or a catastrophic failure.

Chapter 20: Configure Advanced Network Services   This chapter shows you how to configure the different types of network services and how to configure them properly.

Chapter 21: Configure the Active Directory Infrastructure   This chapter takes you through the different ways to create and manage your Windows Server 2012 R2 Active Directory infrastructure.

Chapter 22: Configure Access and Information Protection Solutions   You will see how to set up your Windows Server 2012 R2 system so that your information stays secure.

What's Included with the Book

This book includes many helpful items intended to prepare you for the MCSA: Windows Server 2012 R2 certification. These items include:

Assessment Test   There is an Assessment Test at the conclusion of the introduction that can be used to evaluate quickly where you are with Windows Server 2012 R2. This test should be taken prior to beginning your work in this book, and it should help you identify areas in which you are either strong or weak. Note that these questions are purposely simpler than the types of questions you may see on the exams.

Objective Map and Opening List of Objectives   Later in this introduction, you will find a detailed exam objective map showing you where each of the exam objectives is covered. Each chapter also includes a list of the exam objectives covered.

Helpful Exercises   Throughout the book are step-by-step exercises of some of the more important tasks that you should be able to perform. Some of these exercises have corresponding videos that can be downloaded from the book's website. Also, the following section has a recommended home lab setup that will be helpful in completing these tasks.

Exam Essentials   The end of each chapter also includes a listing of exam essentials. These are essentially repeats of the objectives, but remember that any objective on the exam blueprint could show up on the exam.

Chapter Review Questions   Each chapter includes review questions. These are used to assess your understanding of the chapter and are taken directly from the chapter. These questions are based on the exam objectives, and they are similar in difficulty to items you might actually receive on the MCSA: Windows Server 2012 R2 exams.

 You can obtain the Interactive Online Learning Environment, flashcards, videos, and glossary at www.sybex.com/go/mcsawin2012r2.

Interactive Online Learning Environment   You can access the Interactive Online Learning Environment, which includes the assessment test and chapter review questions. In addition, there are a total of three practice exams included with the Interactive Online Learning Environment: one each for exams 70-410, 70-411, and 70-412.

Flashcards   Flashcards are included for quick reference. They are a great tool for learning important facts quickly. You may even consider these as additional simple practice questions, which is essentially what they are.

Videos   Some of the exercises include corresponding videos. These videos show you how we do the exercises. There is also a video that shows you how to set up virtualization so that you can complete the exercises within a virtualized environment. This same video also shows you how to install Windows Server 2012 Datacenter on that virtualized machine.

PDF of Glossary of Terms   There is a glossary included that covers the key terms used in this book.

Recommended Home Lab Setup

To get the most out of this book, you will want to make sure you complete the exercises throughout the chapters. To complete the exercises, you will need one of two setups. First, you can set up a machine with Windows Server 2012 R2 and complete the labs using a regular Windows Server 2012 R2 machine.

The second way to set up Windows Server 2012 R2 (the way we set up Server 2012 R2) is by using virtualization. We set up Windows Server 2012 R2 as a virtual hard disk (VHD), and we did all the labs this way. The advantages of using virtualization are that you can always just wipe out the system and start over without losing a real server. Plus, you can set up multiple virtual servers and create a full lab environment on one machine.

We created a video for this book showing you how to set up a virtual machine and how to install Windows Server 2012 R2 onto that virtual machine.

How to Contact the Author/Sybex

Sybex strives to keep you supplied with the latest tools and information that you need for your work. Please check the website at www.sybex.com/go/mcsawin2012r2, where we'll post additional content and updates that supplement this book should the need arise.

You can contact Will Panek by going to www.willpanek.com.

Certification Objectives Maps

In addition to the book chapters, you will find coverage of exam objectives in the flashcards, practice exams, and videos on the book's companion website.

http://www.sybex.com/go/mcsawin2012r2

Exam objectives are subject to change at any time without prior notice and at Microsoft's sole discretion. Please visit Microsoft's website (www.microsoft.com/learning) for the most current listing of exam objectives.

Objectives

Part I: Exam 70-410: Installing and Configuring Windows Server 2014

Install servers, Chapter 1

Plan for a server installation

Plan for server roles

Plan for a server upgrade

Install Server Core

Optimize resource utilization by using Features on Demand

Migrate roles from previous versions of Windows Server

Configure servers, Chapter 1

    Configure Server Core

    Delegate administration

    Add and remove features in offline images

    Deploy roles on remote servers

    Convert Server Core to/from full GUI

    Configure services

    Configure NIC teaming

Configure local storage, Chapter 1

    Design storage spaces

    Configure basic and dynamic disks

    Configure MBR and GPT disks

    Manage volumes

    Create and mount virtual hard disks

    Configure storage pools and disk pools

Deploy and configure DNS service, Chapter 2

    Configure Active Directory integration of primary zones

    Configure forwarders

    Configure Root Hints

    Manage DNS cache

    Create A and PTR resource records

Deploy and configure Dynamic Host Configuration Protocol (DHCP) service, Chapter 2

    Create and configure scopes

    Configure a DHCP reservation

    Configure DHCP options

    Configure client and server for PXE boot

    Configure DHCP relay agent

    Authorize DHCP server

Install domain controllers, Chapter 3

    Add or remove a domain controller from a domain

    Upgrade a domain controller

    Install Active Directory Domain Services (AD DS) on a Server Core installation

    Install a domain controller from Install from Media (IFM)

    Resolve DNS SRV record registration issues

Create and manage Active Directory groups and organizational units (OUs), Chapter 5

    Configure group nesting

    Convert groups including security, distribution, universal, domain local, and domain global

    Manage group membership using Group Policy

    Enumerate group membership

    Delegate the creation and management of Active Directory objects

    Manage default Active Directory containers

    Create, copy, configure, and delete groups and OUs

Create Group Policy Objects (GPOs), Chapter 6

    Configure a Central Store

    Manage starter GPOs

    Configure GPO links

    Configure multiple local group policies

    Configure security filtering

Configure application restriction policies, Chapter 6

    Configure rule enforcement

    Configure applocker rules

    Configure Software Restriction Policies

Configuring security policies, Chapter 7

    Configure User Rights Assignment

    Configure Security Options settings

    Configure Security templates

    Configure Audit Policy

    Configure Local Users and Groups

    Configure User Account Control (UAC)

Configuring Windows Firewall, Chapter 7

    Configure rules for multiple profiles using Group Policy

    Configure connection security rules

    Configure Windows Firewall to allow or deny applications, scopes, ports, and users

    Configure authenticated firewall exceptions

    Import and export settings

Configure IPv4 and IPv6 addressing, Chapter 8

    Configure IP address options

    Configure IPv4 or IPv6 subnetting

Configure supernetting

Configure interoperability between IPv4 and IPv6

Configure ISATAP

Configure Teredo

Create and configure virtual machine settings, Chapter 9

Configure dynamic memory , Chapter 9

Configure smart paging, Chapter 9

Configure Resource Metering, Chapter 9

Configure guest integration services, Chapter 9

Create and configure Generation 1 and 2 virtual machines, Chapter 9

Configure and use extended session mode, Chapter 9

Configure remoteFX, Chapter 9

Create and configure virtual machine storage, Chapter 9

Create VHDs and VHDX

Configure differencing drives

Modify VHDs

Configure pass-through disks

Manage checkpoints

Implement a virtual Fibre Channel adapter

Configure storage Quality of Service

Create and configure virtual networks, Chapter 9

Configure Hyper-V virtual switches

Optimize network performance

Configure MAC addresses

Configure network isolation

Configure synthetic and legacy virtual network adapters

Configure NIC teaming in virtual machines

Part II: Exam 70-411: Administering Windows Server 2012

Deploy and manage server images, Chapter 10

Install the Windows Deployment Services (WDS) role

Configure and manage boot, install, and discover images

Update images with patches, hotfixes, and drivers

Configure file and disk encryption, Chapter 11

    Configure Bitlocker encryption

    Configure the Network Unlock feature

    Configure Bitlocker policies

    Configure the EFS recovery agent

    Manage EFS and Bitlocker certificates including backup and restore

Configure advanced audit policies, Chapter 11

    Implement auditing using Group Policy and AuditPol.exe

    Create expression-based

    Create removable device audit policies

Configure DNS zones, Chapter 12

    Configure primary and secondary zones

    Configure stub zones

    Configure conditional forwards

    Configure zone and conditional forward storage in Active Directory

    Configure zone delegation

    Configure zone transfer settings

    Configure notify settings

Configure DNS records, Chapter 12

    Create and configure DNS Resource Records (RR) including A, AAAA, PTR, SOA, NS, SRV, CNAME, and MX records

    Configure zone scavenging

    Configure record options including time to live (TTL) and weight

    Configure round robin

    Configure secure dynamic updates

Configure VPN and routing, Chapter 13

    Install and configure the Remote Access role

    Implement Network Address Translation (NAT)

    Configure VPN settings

    Configure remote dial-in settings for users

    Configure routing

    Configure Web Application proxy in passthrough mode

Configure DirectAccess, Chapter 13

    Implement server requirements

Implement client configuration

Configure DNS for DirectAccess

Configure certificates for DirectAccess

Configure Network Policy Server (NPS), Chapter 14

Configure a NPS server including RADIUS proxy

Configure RADIUS clients

Configure NPS templates

Configure RADIUS accounting

Configure certificates

Configure NPS policies, Chapter 14

Configure connection request policies

Configure network policies for VPN clients (multilink and bandwidth allocation, IP filters, encryption, IP addressing)

Import and export NPS policies

Configure Network Access Protection (NAP), Chapter 14

Configure System Health Validators (SHVs)

Configure health policies

Configure NAP enforcement using DHCP and VPN

Configure isolation and remediation of non-compliant computers using DHCP and VPN

Configure NAP client settings

Configure service authentication, Chapter 15

Create and configure Service Accounts

Create and configure Group Managed Service Accounts

Configure Kerberos delegation

Manage Service Principal Names (SPNS)

Configure virtual accounts

Configure Domain Controllers, Chapter 15

Transfer and seize operations master roles

Install and configure a read-only domain controller (RODC)

Configure domain controller cloning

Maintain Active Directory, Chapter 15

Back up Active Directory and SYSVOL

Manage Active Directory offline

Configure Group Policy Preferences (GPP), Chapter 16

> Configure GPP settings including printers, network drive mappings, power options, custom registry settings, Control Panel settings, Internet Explorer settings, file and folder deployment, and shortcut deployment
>
> Configure item-level targeting

Part III: Exam 70-412: Configuring Advanced Windows Server 2012 Services

Configure Network Load Balancing (NLB), Chapter 17

> This objective may include, but is not limited to:
>> Install NLB nodes
>> Configure NLB prerequisites
>> Configure affinity
>> Configure port rules
>> Configure cluster operation mode
>> Upgrade an NLB cluster

Configure failover clustering, Chapter 17

> This objective may include, but is not limited to:
>> Configure Quorum
>> Configure cluster networking
>> Restore single node or cluster configuration
>> Configure cluster storage
>> Implement cluster aware updating
>> Upgrade a cluster

Manage failover-clustering roles, Chapter 17

> This objective may include, but is not limited to:
>> Configure role-specific settings including continuously available shares
>> Configure VM monitoring
>> Configure failover and preference settings

Manage Virtual Machine (VM) Movement, Chapter 17

> This objective may include, but is not limited to:
>> Configure Virtual Machine network health protection
>> Configure drain on shutdown

Perform quick, live and storage migrations

Import/export/copy of VMS

Configure advanced file services, Chapter 18

Configure NFS data store

Configure BranchCache

Configure File Classification Infrastructure (FCI) using File Server Resource Manager (FSRM)

Configure file access auditing

Implement Dynamic Access Control (DAC), Chapter 18

Configure user and device claim types

Create and configure resource properties and lists

Create and configure Central Access Rules and Policies

Configure file classification

Implement policy changes and staging

Perform access-denied remediation

Configure and optimize storage, Chapter 18

Configure iSCSI Target and Initiator

Configure Internet Storage Name Server (iSNS)

Implement thin provisioning and trim

Manage server free space using Features on Demand

Configure tiered storage

Configure and manage backups, Chapter 19

Configure Windows Server backups

Configure Windows Azure backups

Configure role-specific backups

Manage VSS settings using VSSAdmin

Recover Servers, Chapter 19

Restore from backups

Perform a Bare Metal Restore (BMR)

Recover servers using Windows Recovery Environment (Win RE) and safe mode

Configure the Boot Configuration Data (BCD) store

Configure site-level fault tolerance, Chapter 19

Configure Hyper-V Replica including Hyper-V Replica Broker and VMs

Configure multi-site clustering including network settings, Quorum, and failover settings

Configure Hyper-V Replica extended replication

Configure Global Update Manager

Recover a multi-site failover cluster

Implement an advanced Dynamic Host Configuration Protocol (DHCP) solution, Chapter 20

Create and configure superscopes and multicast scopes

Implement DHCPv6

Configure high availability for DHCP including DHCP failover and split scopes

Configure DHCP Name Protection

Configure DNS registration

Implement an advanced DNS solution, Chapter 20

Configure security for DNS including DNSSEC, DNS Socket Pool, and cache locking

Configure DNS logging

Configure delegated administration

Configure recursion

Configure netmask ordering

Configure a GlobalNames zone

Analyze zone level statistics

Deploy and manage IPAM, Chapter 20

Provision IPAM manually or by using Group Policy

Configure server discovery

Create and manage IP blocks and ranges

Monitor utilization of IP address space

Migrate to IPAM

Delegate IPAM administration

Manage IPAM collections

Configure IPAM database storage

Configure a forest or a domain, Chapter 21

Implement multi-domain and multi-forest Active Directory environments including interoperability with previous versions of Active Directory

Upgrade existing domains and forests including environment preparation and functional levels

Configure multiple user principal name (UPN) suffixes

Configure Trusts, Chapter 21

Configure external, forest, shortcut, and realm trusts

Configure trust authentication

Assessment Test

1. Which of the following is a valid role for a Windows Server 2012 R2 computer?
   A. Stand-alone server
   B. Member server
   C. Domain controller
   D. All of the above

2. Which of the following is a benefit of using Active Directory? (Choose all that apply.)
   A. Hierarchical object structure
   B. Fault-tolerant architecture
   C. Ability to configure centralized and distributed administration
   D. Flexible replication

3. Which of the following features of the Domain Name System (DNS) can be used to improve performance? (Choose all that apply.)
   A. Caching-only servers
   B. DNS forwarding
   C. Secondary servers
   D. Zone delegation

4. Which of the following pieces of information should you have before you begin the Active Directory Installation Wizard? (Choose all that apply.)
   A. Active Directory domain name
   B. Administrator password for the local computer
   C. NetBIOS name for the server
   D. DNS configuration information

5. An Active Directory environment consists of three domains. What is the maximum number of sites that can be created for this environment?
   A. Two
   B. Three
   C. Nine
   D. Unlimited

6. Which of the following is *not* a valid Active Directory object?
   A. User
   B. Group

   C. Organizational unit

   D. Computer

   E. None of the above

7. Which of the following is *not* considered a security principal?

   A. Users

   B. Security groups

   C. Distribution groups

   D. Computers

8. Which of the following should play the *least* significant role in planning an OU structure?

   A. Network infrastructure

   B. Domain organization

   C. Delegation of permissions

   D. Group Policy settings

9. How can the Windows Server 2012 R2 file and printer resources be made available from within Active Directory?

   A. A system administrator can right-click the resource and select Publish.

   B. A system administrator can create Printer and Shared Folder objects that point to these resources.

   C. The Active Directory Domains and Trusts tool can be used to make resources available.

   D. Only resources on a Windows 2000 or newer server can be accessed from within Active Directory.

10. The process by which a higher-level security authority assigns permissions to other administrators is known as which of the following?

   A. Inheritance

   B. Delegation

   C. Assignment

   D. Trust

11. What is the minimum amount of information you need to create a Shared Folder Active Directory object?

   A. The name of the share

   B. The name of the server

   C. The name of the server and the name of the share

   D. The name of the server, the server's IP address, and the name of the share

12. Which of the following operations is not supported by Active Directory?

   A. Assigning applications to users

   B. Assigning applications to computers

   C. Publishing applications to users

   D. Publishing applications to computers

13. Which of the following filename extensions is used primarily for Windows Installer setup programs?

   A. `.msi`

   B. `.mst`

   C. `.zap`

   D. `.aas`

14. A system administrator wants to allow a group of users to add computer accounts to a specific organizational unit (OU). What is the easiest way to grant only the required permissions?

   A. Delegate control of a user account

   B. Delegate control at the domain level

   C. Delegate control of an OU

   D. Delegate control of a computer account

   E. Create a Group Policy object (GPO) at the OU level

15. A Group Policy object (GPO) at the domain level sets a certain option to Disabled, while a GPO at the OU level sets the same option to Enabled. All other settings are left at their default. Which setting will be effective for objects within the OU?

   A. Enabled

   B. Disabled

   C. No effect

   D. None of the above

16. Which of the following tools can be used to create Group Policy object (GPO) links to Active Directory?

   A. Active Directory Users and Computers

   B. Active Directory Domains and Trusts

   C. Active Directory Sites and Services

   D. Group Policy Management Console

17. To test whether a DNS server is answering queries properly, you can use which of the following tools?

   A. The `ping` tool

   B. The `nslookup` tool

C. The tracert tool

D. The ipconfig tool

18. Which of the following is true about the time to live (TTL) attached to a DNS record?

A. A resolver cannot use it; only servers making recursive queries can use it.

B. Only resolvers use it.

C. It is used to determine how long to cache retrieved results.

D. It is refreshed each time the record is modified.

19. Which of the following statements about Windows Server 2012 Dynamic DNS (DDNS) is true?

A. DDNS requires a Microsoft DHCP server to work.

B. The Windows Server 2012 DDNS server can interoperate with recent versions of BIND.

C. DDNS clients may not register their own addresses.

D. DDNS works only with Microsoft clients and servers.

20. You have been given a server that contains three HBAs. Each card can access the storage over a separate path. The application that runs on the server can exceed the usage of a single path. Which of the following MPIO options should be selected to provide the needed bandwidth as well as minimal redundancy?

A. Failover

B. Dynamic Least Queue Depth

C. Weighted path

D. Round robin

21. You need to stop an application from running in Task Manager. Which tab would you use to stop an application from running?

A. Performance

B. Users

C. Options

D. Details

22. As a network administrator, you are responsible for all client computers at the central corporate location. Your company has asked you to make sure that all of the client computers are secure. You need to use MBSA to scan your client computers, based on IP addresses, for possible security violations but you need to use the command-line version. Which of the following command-line commands would you use?

A. mdsacli.exe /hf -i *xxxx.xxxx.xxxx.xxxx*

B. mdsacli.exe /ip *xxxx.xxxx.xxxx.xxxx*

    C. `mbsa.exe /hf -ip xxxx.xxxx.xxxx.xxxx`

    D. `mbsa.exe /ip xxxx.xxxx.xxxx.xxxx`

23. You are the administrator of a new Windows Server 2012 R2 machine. You need to install DNS and create a primary zone. Which MMC snap-in would you use to install DNS?

    A. Add/Remove Programs

    B. Programs

    C. Server Manager

    D. Administrative Tools

24. You are the administrator for a large company that has purchased a new multifunction printer. You want to publish the printer to Active Directory. Where would you click in order to accomplish this task?

    A. The Sharing tab

    B. The Advanced tab

    C. The Device Settings tab

    D. The Printing Preferences button

25. Isabel is a system administrator for an Active Directory environment that is running in Native mode. Recently, several managers have reported suspicions about user activities and have asked her to increase security in the environment. Specifically, the requirements are as follows:

- The accessing of certain sensitive files must be logged.

- Modifications to certain sensitive files must be logged.

- System administrators must be able to provide information about which users accessed sensitive files and when they were accessed.

- All logon attempts for specific shared machines must be recorded.

Which of the following steps should Isabel take to meet these requirements? (Choose all that apply.)

    A. Enable auditing with the Computer Management tool.

    B. Enable auditing with Group Policy Objects.

    C. Enable auditing with the Active Directory Domains and Trusts tool.

    D. Enable auditing with the Event Viewer tool.

    E. View the audit log using the Event Viewer tool.

    F. View auditing information using the Computer Management tool.

    G. Enable failure and success auditing settings for specific files stored on NTFS volumes.

    H. Enable failure and success auditing settings for logon events on specific computer accounts.

26. You are the network administrator for a large widget distributor. Your company's network has 20 Windows 2012 R2 servers, and all of the clients are running either Windows 8 or Windows 7. All of your end users use laptops to do their work, and many of them work away from the office. What should you configure to help them work on documents when away from the office?

   A. Online file access

   B. Offline file access

   C. Share permissions

   D. NTFS permissions

27. Your company has decided to implement an external hard drive. The company IT manager before you always used FAT32 as the system partition. Your company wants to know whether it should move to NTFS. Which of the following are some advantages of NTFS? (Choose all that apply.)

   A. Security

   B. Quotas

   C. Compression

   D. Encryption

28. You have been hired by a small company to implement new Windows Server 2012 R2 systems. The company wants you to set up a server for users' home folder locations. What type of server would you be setting up?

   A. PDC server

   B. Web server

   C. Exchange server

   D. File server

29. GPOs assigned at which of the following level(s) will override GPO settings at the domain level?

   A. OU

   B. Site

   C. Domain

   D. Both OU and site

30. A system administrator wants to ensure that only the GPOs set at the OU level affect the Group Policy settings for objects within the OU. Which option can they use to do this (assuming that all other GPO settings are the defaults)?

   A. The Enforced option

   B. The Block Policy Inheritance option

   C. The Disable option

   D. The Deny permission

31. Mateo, a system administrator, is planning to implement Group Policy objects in a new Windows Server 2012 R2 Active Directory environment. To meet the needs of the organization, he decides to implement a hierarchical system of Group Policy settings. At which of the following levels is he able to assign Group Policy settings? (Choose all that apply.)

   A. Sites

   B. Domains

   C. Organizational units

   D. Local system

32. Ann is a system administrator for a medium-sized Active Directory environment. She has determined that several new applications that will be deployed throughout the organization use registry-based settings. She would like to do the following:

   ▪ Control these registry settings using Group Policy.

   ▪ Create a standard set of options for these applications and allow other system administrators to modify them using the standard Active Directory tools.

   Which of the following options can she use to meet these requirements? (Choose all that apply.)

   A. Implement the inheritance functionality of GPOs.

   B. Implement delegation of specific objects within Active Directory.

   C. Implement the No Override functionality of GPOs.

   D. Create administrative templates.

   E. Provide administrative templates to the system administrators who are responsible for creating Group Policy for the applications.

33. You are the network administrator for your organization. A new company policy has been released wherein if a user enters their password incorrectly three times within 5 minutes, they are locked out for 30 minutes. What three actions do you need to set to comply with this policy? (Choose all that apply.)

   A. Set Account Lockout Duration to 5 minutes.

   B. Set Account Lockout Duration to 30 minutes.

   C. Set the Account Lockout Threshold setting to 3 invalid logon attempts.

   D. Set the Account Lockout Threshold setting to 30 minutes.

   E. Set the Reset Account Lockout Counter setting to 5 minutes.

   F. Set the Reset Account Lockout Counter setting to 3 times.

34. You are teaching a Microsoft Active Directory class, and one of your students asks you, "Which of the following containers in the Active Directory Users and Computers tool is used when users from outside the forest are granted access to resources within a domain?" What answer would you give your student?

   A. Users

   B. Computers

   C. Domain Controllers

   D. Foreign Security Principals

35. Your manager has decided your organization needs to use an Active Directory application data partition. Which command can you use to create and manage application data partitions?

   A. `DCPromo.exe`

   B. `NTDSUtil.exe`

   C. `ADUtil.exe`

   D. `ADSI.exe`

36. Your network contains an Active Directory domain named Sybex.com. The domain contains a RADIUS server named Server1 that runs Windows Server 2012 R2. You add a VPN server named Server2 to the network. On Server1, you create several network policies. You need to configure Server1 to accept authentication requests from Server2. Which tool should you use on Server1?

   A. Set-RemoteAccessRadius

   B. CMAK

   C. NPS

   D. Routing and Remote Access

37. Your network contains an Active Directory domain named Sybex.com. The domain contains a server named Server1 that runs Windows Server 2012 R2. Server1 has the following role services installed:

   ■ DirectAccess and VPN (RRAS)

   ■ Network Policy Server

   Remote users have client computers that run Windows XP, Windows 7, or Windows 8. You need to ensure that only the client computers that run Windows 7 or Windows 8 can establish VPN connections to Server1. What should you configure on Server1?

   A. A vendor-specific RADIUS attribute of a Network Policy Server (NPS) connection request policy

   B. A condition of a Network Policy Server (NPS) network policy

   C. A condition of a Network Policy Server (NPS) connection request policy

   D. A constraint of a Network Policy Server (NPS) network policy

38. You are the network administrator for a large organization that contains an Active Directory domain named WillPanek.com. The domain contains a server named Server1 that runs Windows Server 2012 R2. Server1 has the Network Policy and Access Services server role installed. You plan to deploy 802.1x authentication to secure the wireless network.

You need to identify which Network Policy Server (NPS) authentication method supports certificate-based mutual authentication for the 802.lx deployment. Which authentication method should you identify?

A. PEAP-MS-CHAP v2

B. MS-CHAP v2

C. EAP-TLS

D. MS-CHAP

39. You have an Active Directory domain named WillPanek.com. The domain contains a server named ServerA that runs Windows Server 2012 R2. ServerA has the Network Policy and Access Services server role installed. Your company's security policy requires that certificate-based authentication must be used by some network services. You need to identify which Network Policy Server (NPS) authentication methods comply with the security policy. Which two authentication methods should you identify? Each correct answer presents part of the solution. (Choose two.)

A. MS-CHAP

B. PEAP-MS-CHAP v2

C. CHAP

D. EAP-TLS

E. MS-CHAP v2

40. You are the network administrator, and you have been asked to set up an accounting system so that each department is responsible for the cost of their use of network services. Your network contains a Network Policy Server (NPS) server named ServerA. The network contains a server named Database1 that has Microsoft SQL server installed. All servers run Windows Server 2012 R2. You configure NPS on ServerA to log accounting data to a database on Database1. You need to ensure that the accounting data is captured if Database1 fails. The solution must minimize cost. What should you do?

A. Implement Failover Clustering.

B. Implement database mirroring.

C. Run the Accounting Configuration Wizard.

D. Modify the SQL Server Logging properties.

41. In a secure environment, IPsec encryption should only be disabled for inter-node cluster communication (such as cluster heartbeat) under what circumstances?

A. Certificates use weak encryption methods such as DES

B. LowerQuorumPriorityNodeID is set on a node.

C. DatabaseReadWriteMode is set to 2

D. Group Policy Updates have a high processing latency

42. In Windows Server 2012 R2, Failover Clustering supports how many nodes?

   A. 8000

   B. 1024

   C. 64

   D. 1000

43. In Windows Server 2012 R2, what feature dynamically adjusts cluster node votes in order to maintain an odd vote count where no witness is being used?

   A. Witness Dynamic Weighting

   B. Tie Breaker for a 50% Node Split

   C. Lower Quorum Priority Node

   D. Force quorum resiliency

44. What authentication mechanism does Active Directory–detached clusters utilize?

   A. NTLM

   B. MIT Kerberos Realms

   C. AD Kerberos

   D. SSL

45. Shared virtual hard disks can be utilized by SQL Server and Exchange Server for virtualized workloads.

   A. True

   B. False

46. What is the default TCP port for iSCSI?

   A. 3389

   B. 21

   C. 1433

   D. 3260

47. You are a server administrator, and you are trying to save hard drive space on your Windows Server 2012 R2 machine. Which feature can help you save hard disk space?

   A. ADDS

   B. HDSaver.exe

   C. Features On Demand

   D. WinRM

48. Your company is headquartered in Colorado Springs and has a remote site location in Tampa. The Colorado Spring office has a file server named FS01. FS01 has the BranchCache for Network Files role service installed. Your Tampa Office has a file server named FS02. FS02 has been configured as a BranchCache-hosted cache server. You need to preload the data from the file shares on FS01 to the cache on FS02. You have already generated hashes for the file shares on FS01. Which cmdlet should you run next?

A. Set-BCCache

B. Publish-BCFileContent

C. Export-BCCachePackage

D. Add-BCDataCacheExtension

49. What command would be used to register an iSCSI initiator manually to an iSNS server?

A. iscsicli addisnsserver server_name

B. iscsicli listisnsservers server_name

C. iscsicli removeisnsserver server_name

D. iscsicli refreshisnsserver server_name

50. You have a Windows Server 2012 R2 file server named FS01. FS01 has the File Server Resource Manager role service installed. You attempt to delete a classification property, and you receive the error message "The classification property is in use and cannot be deleted." You need to delete the Contains Personal Information classification property. What should you do?

A. Clear the Contains Personal Information classification property value for all files.

B. Set files that have a Contains Personal Information classification property value of Yes to No.

C. Disable the classification rule that is assigned the Contains Personal Information classification property.

D. Delete the classification rule that is assigned the Contains Personal Information classification property.

51. After you update multiple drivers on your Windows Server 2012 R2 machine, the machine hangs at the logon screen, and you can't log into the machine. You need to get this computer up and running as quickly as possible. Which of the following repair strategies should you try first to correct your problem?

A. Restore your computer's configuration with your last backup.

B. Boot your computer with the Last Known Good Configuration option.

C. Boot your computer with the Safe Mode option.

D. Boot your computer to the Recovery Console and manually copy the old driver back to the computer.

52. You enable the Boot Logging option on the Advanced Boot Options menu. Where can you find the log file that is created?

A. \Windows\ntbtlog.txt

B. \Windows\System32\netlog.txt

C. \Windows\netlog.txt

D. \Windows\System32\netboot.log

53. You need to ensure that you can recover your Windows Server 2012 R2 configuration and data if the computer's hard drive fails. What should you do?

    A. Create a system restore point.

    B. Create a backup of all file categories.

    C. Perform an Automated System Recovery (ASR) backup.

    D. Create a complete PC Backup and Restore image.

54. You have a file server named FS01 that is running on a server core installation of Windows Server 2012 R2. You need to make sure that your users can access previous versions of files that are shared on FS01 using the Previous Versions tab. Which tool should you use?

    A. Wbadmin

    B. Vssadmin

    C. Ntsdutil.exe

    D. ADSI Editor

55. You are unable to boot your Windows Server 2012 R2 computer, so you decide to boot the computer to Safe Mode. Which of the following statements regarding Safe Mode is false?

    A. When the computer is booted to Safe Mode, there is no network access.

    B. Safe Mode loads all of the drivers for the hardware that is installed on the computer.

    C. When you run Safe Mode, boot logging is automatically enabled.

    D. When you run Safe Mode, the screen resolution is set to 800×600.

56. You are the network administrator for Stellacon Corporation. Stellacon has two trees in its Active Directory forest, stellacon.com and abc.com. Company policy does not allow DNS zone transfers between the two trees. You need to make sure that when anyone in abc.com tries to access the stellacon.com domain, all names are resolved from the stellacon.com DNS server. What should you do?

    A. Create a new secondary zone in abc.com for stellacon.com.

    B. Create a new secondary zone in stellacon.com for abc.com.

    C. Configure conditional forwarding on the abc.com DNS server for stellacon.com.

    D. Configure conditional forwarding on the stellacon.com DNS server for abc.com.

57. Your IT team has been informed by the compliance team that they need copies of the DNS Active Directory Integrated zones for security reasons. You need to give the Compliance department a copy of the DNS zone. How should you accomplish this goal?

    A. Run dnscmd /zonecopy.

    B. Run dnscmd /zoneinfo.

    C. Run dnscmd /zonefile.

    D. Run dnscmd /zoneexport.

58. You administer a network that assigns IP addresses via DHCP. You want to make sure that one of the clients always receives the same IP address from the DHCP server. You create an exclusion for that address, but you find that the computer isn't being properly configured at bootup. What's the problem?

    A. You excluded the wrong IP address.

    B. You must configure the client manually. You cannot assign the address via the DHCP server.

    C. You need to create a superscope for the address.

    D. You need to make a reservation for the client that ties the IP address to the computer's MAC address. Delete the exclusion.

59. You are the network administrator for a small company with two DNS servers: DNS1 and DNS2. Both DNS servers reside on domain controllers. DNS1 is set up as a standard primary zone, and DNS2 is set up as a secondary zone. A new security policy was written stating that all DNS zone transfers must be encrypted. How can you implement the new security policy?

    A. Enable the Secure Only setting on DNS1.

    B. Enable the Secure Only setting on DNS2.

    C. Configure Secure Only on the Zone Transfers tab for both servers.

    D. Delete the secondary zone on DNS2. Convert both DNS servers to use Active Directory Integrated zones.

60. You are the network administrator for a midsize computer company. You have a single Active Directory forest, and your DNS servers are configured as Active Directory Integrated zones. When you look at the DNS records in Active Directory, you notice that there are many records for computers that do not exist on your domain. You want to make sure that only domain computers register with your DNS servers. What should you do to resolve this issue?

    A. Set dynamic updates to None.

    B. Set dynamic updates to Nonsecure And Secure.

    C. Set dynamic updates to Secure Only.

    D. Set dynamic updates to Domain Users Only.

61. Which of the following does not need to be created manually when you are setting up a replication scenario involving three domains and three sites?

    A. Sites

    B. Site links

    C. Subnets

    D. Connection objects

62. You need to deactivate the UGMC option on some of your domain controllers. At which level in Active Directory would you deactivate UGMC?

   A. Server

   B. Forest

   C. Domain

   D. Site

63. Your network contains two Active Directory forests named contoso.com and fabrikam.com. Both forests contain multiple domains. All domain controllers run Windows Server 2012 R2. contoso.com has a one-way forest trust to fabrikam.com. A domain named paris.eu.contoso.com hosts several legacy Applications that use NTLM authentication. Users in a domain named london.europe.fabrikam.com report that it takes a long time to be authenticated when they attempt to access the legacy Applications hosted in paris.eu.contoso.com. You need to reduce how long it takes for the london.europe.fabrikam.com users to be authenticated in paris.eu.contoso.com. What should you do?

   A. Create an external trust

   B. Create a two-way transitive trust

   C. Disable SID filtering on the existing trust

   D. Create a shortcut trust

64. A system administrator suspects that there is an error in the replication configuration. How can the system administrator look for specific error messages related to replication?

   A. By going to Event Viewer ➢ Directory Service Log

   B. By using the Computer Management tool

   C. By going to Event Viewer ➢ System Log

   D. By using the Active Directory Sites and Services administrative tool

65. Which of the following services of Active Directory is responsible for maintaining the replication topology?

   A. File Replication Service

   B. Windows Internet Name Service

   C. Knowledge Consistency Checker

   D. Domain Name System

66. You are the administrator at Adacom. You need to make sure that you have daily backup of the AD CS database, logs, and private key. What command or commands should you run? (Choose all that apply.)

   A. Run certutil -backup.

   B. Run certutil -backupdb.

   C. Run Ntbackup /systemstate.

   D. Run certdb.ps1.

67. You are the new administrator at MMG Publishing. The previous administrator made a failed attempt to implement Active Directory. You attempt to implement AD RMS and receive an error that states, "The SCP is registered, but the root cluster cannot be contacted." You must remove the SCP. What tool should you use? (Choose all that apply.)

   A. Setspn

   B. Active Directory Sites and Services

   C. ADSI Edit

   D. Remove-SCP

68. ABC Company wants to allow external partners to log into a web application and run reports. What AD FS component does Company ABC need to configure for this access?

   A. Certificate exchange

   B. Transitive trust

   C. One-way trust

   D. Relying-party trust

69. Which TCP ports does AD RMS use to access the global catalog server?

   A. 445

   B. 1433

   C. 22

   D. 3268

Answers to the Assessment Test

1. **D.** Based on the business needs of an organization, a Windows 2012 R2 Server computer can be configured in any of the roles listed. See Chapter 1 for more information.

2. **A, B, C and D.** All of the options listed are benefits of using Active Directory. See Chapter 3 for more information.

3. **A, B, C and D.** One of the major design goals for DNS was support for scalability. All of the features listed can be used to increase the performance of DNS. See Chapter 2 for more information.

4. **A, B, C and D.** Before beginning the installation of a domain controller, you should have all of the information listed. See Chapter 3 for more information.

5. **D.** The number of sites in an Active Directory environment is independent of the domain organization. An environment that consists of three domains may have one or more sites, based on the physical network setup. See Chapter 3 for more information.

6. **E.** All of the choices are valid types of Active Directory objects, and all can be created and managed using the Active Directory Users and Computers tool. See Chapter 5 for more information.

7. **C.** Permissions and security settings cannot be made on distribution groups. Distribution groups are used only for sending email. See Chapter 4 for more information.

8. **A.** In general, you can accommodate your network infrastructure through the use of Active Directory sites. All of the other options should play a significant role when you design your OU structure. Permissions and Group Policy can both be applied at the domain or OU level. See Chapter 4 for more information.

9. **B.** Printer and Shared Folder objects within Active Directory can point to Windows Server 2012 R2 file and printer resources. See Chapter 4 for more information.

10. **B.** Delegation is the process by which administrators can assign permissions on the objects within an OU. This is useful when administrators want to give other users more control over administrative functions in Active Directory. See Chapter 4 for more information.

11. **C.** The name of the server and the name of the share make up the Universal Naming Convention (UNC) information required to create a Shared Folder object. See Chapter 4 for more information.

12. **D.** Applications cannot be published to computers, but they can be published to users and assigned to computers. See Chapter 5 for more information.

13. **A.** MSI files (.msi) are native Windows Installer files used with Windows Installer setup programs. The other file types do not apply to this situation. See Chapter 5 for more information.

14. E. To allow this permission at the OU level, the system administrator must create a GPO with the appropriate settings and link it to the OU. See Chapter 5 for more information.

15. A. Assuming that the default settings are left in place, the Group Policy setting at the OU level will take effect. See Chapter 5 for more information.

16. D. In Windows Server 2012 R2, you can create GPOs only by using the Group Policy Management Console. See Chapter 5 for more information.

17. B. The nslookup tool allows you to look up name and address information. See Chapter 2 for more information.

18. C. The TTL indicates how long the record may be safely cached; it may or may not be modified when the record is created. See Chapter 2 for more information on TTL.

19. B. DDNS works with BIND 8.2 and later. See Chapter 2 for more information on DDNS.

20. D. A round-robin configuration uses all of the available active paths and will distribute I/O in a balanced round-robin fashion. Failover uses only the primary and standby paths, allowing for link failure. Weighted path assigns requests to the path with the least weight value. Dynamic Least Queue Depth routes requests to the path with the least number of outstanding requests. See Chapter 2 for more information.

21. D. All of the applications that are running on the Windows Server 2012 R2 machine will show up under the Details tab. Right-click the application and end the process.

22. A. If you use MBSA from the command-line utility mdsacli.exe, you can specify several options. You type **mdsacli.exe/hf** (from the folder that contains Mdsacli.exe) and then customize the command execution with an option such as /i*xxxx.xxxx.xxxx.xxxx*, which specifies that the computer with the specified IP address should be scanned.

23. C. Server Manager is the one place where you install all roles and features for a Windows Server 2012 R2 system.

24. A. The Sharing tab contains a check box that you can use to list the printer in Active Directory.

25. B, E, G and H. The Active Directory Users and Computers tool allows system administrators to change auditing options and to choose which actions are audited. At the file system level, Isabel can specify exactly which actions are recorded in the audit log. She can then use Event Viewer to view the recorded information and provide it to the appropriate managers.

26. B. Offline files give you the opportunity to set up files and folders so that users can work on the data while outside the office.

27. A, B, C and D. Improved security, quotas, compression, and encryption are all advantages of using NTFS over FAT32. These features are not available in FAT32. The only security you have in FAT32 is shared folder permissions.

28. D.   File servers are used for storage of data, especially for users' home folders. Home folders are folder locations for your users to store data that is important and that needs to be backed up.

29. A.   GPOs at the OU level take precedence over GPOs at the domain level. GPOs at the domain level, in turn, take precedence over GPOs at the site level.

30. B.   The Block Policy Inheritance option prevents group policies of higher-level Active Directory objects from applying to lower-level objects as long as the Enforced option is not set.

31. A, B, C and D.   GPOs can be set at all of the levels listed. You cannot set GPOs on security principals such as users or groups.

32. D and E.   Administrative templates are used to specify the options available for setting Group Policy. By creating new administrative templates, Ann can specify which options are available for the new applications. She can then distribute these templates to other system administrators in the environment.

33. B, C and E.   The Account Lockout Duration setting states how long an account will be locked out if the password is entered incorrectly. The Account Lockout Threshold setting is the number of bad password attempts, and the Account Lockout Counter setting is the time in which the bad password attempts are made. Once the Account Lockout Counter setting reaches 0, the number of bad password attempts returns to 0.

34. D.   When resources are made available to users who reside in domains outside the forest, Foreign Security Principal objects are automatically created. These new objects are stored within the `Foreign Security Principals` container.

35. B.   The primary method by which systems administrators create and manage application data partitions is through the `ntdsutil` tool.

36. C.   The NPS snap-in allows you to set up RADIUS servers and designate which RADIUS server will accept authentication from other RADIUS servers. You can do your entire RADIUS configuration through the NPS snap-in.

37. C.   NPS allows you to set up policies on how your users could log into the network. NPS allows you to set up policies that systems need to follow, and if they don't follow these policies or rules, they will not have access to the full network.

38. C.   Windows Server 2012 R2 comes with *EAP-Transport Level Security (TLS)*. This EAP type allows you to use public key certificates as an authenticator. TLS is similar to the familiar Secure Sockets Layer (SSL) protocol used for web browsers and 802.1x authentication. When EAP-TLS is turned on, the client and server send TLS-encrypted messages back and forth. EAP-TLS is the strongest authentication method you can use; as a bonus, it supports smart cards. However, EAP-TLS requires your NPS server to be part of the Windows Server 2012 R2 domain.

39. B and D.   PEAP-MS-CHAP v2 is an EAP type protocol that is easier to deploy than Extensible Authentication Protocol with Transport Level Security (EAP-TLS). It is easier because user authentication is accomplished by using password-based credentials (user name and password) instead of digital certificates or smart cards. Both PEAP and EAP use certificates with their protocols.

40. C.   One advantage of NPS is that you can use the accounting part of NPS so that you can keep track of what each department does on your NPS server. This way, departments pay for the amount of time they use the SQL server database.

41. D.   Group Policy Updates have a high processing latency, because IPsec encryption is interrupted until updates to the Group Policies are complete. If the updates to Group Policy do not occur quickly, cluster heartbeat can be impacted (eg if the processing delay exceeds the heartbeat threshold).

42. C.   In Windows Server 2012, the number of cluster nodes increased to 64. 8000 is the number of VMs/Clustered Roles. 1024 is the maximum amount of VMs or Clustered Roles per cluster node, and 1000 is the maximum amount of VMs or Clustered Roles per cluster node in Windows Server 2008 R2.

43. B.   Witness Dynamic Weighting and Lower Quorum Priority Node are options in Power-Shell to modify Dynamic Quorum, but they are not a good answer. Force quorum resiliency is completely incorrect.

44. A.   NTLM is the only supported authentication mechanism that will utilize local security authorities (non-active directory integrated Windows Servers).

45. A.   Prior to Windows Server 2012 R2, shared virtual hard disks did not exist. At release of Windows Server 2012 R2, shared virtual disks were supported for file server roles as well as Exchange Server and SQL Server workloads.

46. D.   The iSCSI default port is TCP 3260. Port 3389 is used for RDP, port 1433 is used for MS SQL, and port 21 is used for FTP.

47. C.   Windows Server 2012 R2 Features On Demand allows an administrator not only to disable a role or feature but also to remove the role or feature's files completely from the hard drive.

48. C.   After generating hashes on the Colorado Springs file server that will be preloading Tampa's file server cache with file share data, the next logical step is to run the Export-BCCachePackage to get the data to FS02 from FS01.

49. A.   The `iscsicli addisnsserver server_name` command manually registers the host server to an iSNS server. `refreshisnsserver` refreshes the list of available servers. `removeisnsserver` removes the host from the iSNS server. `listisnsservers` lists the available iSNS servers.

50. D.   Since there is a classification rule that is currently configured and applied to company resources, you will be unable to delete the Contains Personal Information classification property manually because the classification rule controls the property. In this case, you have to delete the classification rule in order to be able to delete the classification property.

51. B.   If you need to get a stalled computer up and running as quickly as possible, you should start with the Last Known Good Configuration option. This option is used when you've made changes to your computer's hardware configuration and are having problems restarting but have not logged into the machine. The Last Known Good Configuration option will revert to the configuration used the last time the computer was successfully booted.

52. A.   When you enable boot logging, the file created is \Windows\ntbtlog.txt. This log file is used to troubleshoot the boot process.

53. D.   Using images allows you to back up and restore your entire Windows Server 2012 R2 machine instead of just certain parts of data.

54. B.   Out of the tools listed, remember that Vssadmin gives you the ability to use Shadow Copies, which in turn provides backups and previous versions of shared data. Wbadmin is used for Windows Server Backups, Ntsdutil.exe is used for Active Directory maintenance, and the ADSI Editor is used for extended Active Directory attribute management.

55. B.   When you run your computer in Safe Mode, you simplify your Windows Server 2012 R2 configuration. Only the drivers that are needed to get the computer up and running are loaded.

56. C.   Conditional forwarding allows you to send a DNS query to different DNS servers based on the request. Conditional forwarding lets a DNS server on a network forward DNS queries according to the DNS domain name in the query.

57. D.   The dnscmd /zoneexport command creates a file using the zone resource records. This file can then be given to the Compliance department as a copy.

58. D.   An exclusion just marks addresses as excluded; the DHCP server doesn't maintain any information about them. A reservation marks an address as reserved for a particular client.

59. D.   Active Directory Integrated zones give you many benefits over using primary and secondary zones including less network traffic, secure dynamic updates, encryption, and reliability in the event of a DNS server going down. The Secure Only option is for dynamic updates to a DNS database.

60. C.   The Secure Only option is for DNS servers that have an Active Directory Integrated zone. When a computer tries to register with DNS dynamically, the DNS server checks Active Directory to verify that the computer has an Active Directory account. If the computer that is trying to register has an account, DNS adds the host record. If the computer trying to register does not have an account, the record gets tossed away and the database is not updated.

61. D.   By default, Connection objects are automatically created by the Active Directory replication engine. You can choose to override the default behavior of Active Directory replication topology by manually creating Connection objects, but this step is not required.

62. D.   The NTDS settings for the site level are where you would activate and deactivate UGMC.

63. D.   Remember that a shortcut trust is used to eliminate multiple hops to and from certain domains within a multiforest, multidomain infrastructure. By configuring a shortcut trust between the two domains, you will reduce the slowness and authentication latency between them.

64. A.   The Directory Service event log contains error messages and information related to replication. These details can be useful when you are troubleshooting replication problems.

65. C.   The Knowledge Consistency Checker (KCC) is responsible for establishing the replication topology and ensuring that all domain controllers are kept up-to-date.

66. A and B.   `Certutil -backup` backs up the CA certificate including private key in the backup. `Certutil -backupdb` backs up only the certificate database and logs.

67. B and C.   Under AD Sites and Services, navigate to Services ➤ RightsManagementServices and remove the SCP object. This operation can also be done by using ADSI Edit.

68. D.   The relying party is the organization that receives and processes claims from a resource partner. The resource partner issues claims-based security tokens that contains published web-based applications that users in the account partner can access. This is accomplished through a relying-party trust. See Chapter 22 for more details.

69. D.   AD RMS contacts the global catalog through port 3268. See Chapter 22 for more details.

MCSA
Windows Server® 2012 R2
Complete Study Guide

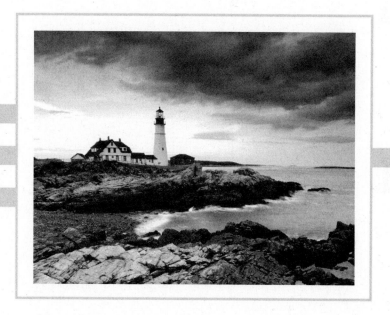

Exam 70-410: Installing and Configuring Windows Server 2012 R2

Chapter

1

Install Windows Server 2012 R2

THE FOLLOWING 70-410 EXAM OBJECTIVES ARE COVERED IN THIS CHAPTER:

✓ **Install servers**

- Plan for a server installation
- Plan for server roles
- Plan for a server upgrade
- Install Server Core
- Optimize resource utilization by using Features on Demand
- Migrate roles from previous versions of Windows Server
- Configure Server Core
- Add and remove features in offline images
- Deploy roles on remote servers
- Convert Server Core to/from full GUI
- Configure NIC teaming

✓ **Configure local storage**

- Design storage spaces
- Configure basic and dynamic disks
- Configure MBR and GPT disks
- Manage volumes
- Create and mount virtual hard disks
- Configure storage pools and disk pools

This chapter covers the installation of Windows Server 2012 R2. It shows how to install both the full version of Windows Server 2012 R2 and the Server Core version. It also shows you how to use some PowerShell commands in Windows Server 2012 R2 Server Core.

Let's dive right into the server by talking about some of the new features and advantages of Windows Server 2012 R2.

Features and Advantages of Windows Server 2012 and Server 2012 R2

Before I show how to install and configure Windows Server 2012 R2, let's take a look at some of the new features and the advantages it offers.

Since many of you will be upgrading from Windows Server 2003 and Windows Server 2008/2008 R2, these are the new features introduced by Microsoft since then. I will specifically identify any new features or advantages that are new to Windows Server 2012 R2 only.

I will talk about all of these features in greater detail throughout this book. What follows are merely brief descriptions.

Active Directory Certificate Services   *Active Directory Certificate Services (AD CS)* provides a customizable set of services that allow you to issue and manage *public key infrastructure (PKI) certificates*. These certificates can be used in software security systems that employ public key technologies.

Active Directory Domain Services   *Active Directory Domain Services (AD DS)* includes new features that make deploying domain controllers simpler and that let you implement them faster. AD DS also makes the domain controllers more flexible, both to audit and to authorize for access to files. Moreover, AD DS has been designed to make performing administrative tasks easier through consistent graphical and scripted management experiences.

Active Directory Rights Management Services   *Active Directory Rights Management Services (AD RMS)* provides management and development tools that let you work with industry security technologies, including encryption, certificates, and authentication. Using these technologies allows organizations to create reliable information protection solutions.

BitLocker *BitLocker* is a tool that allows you to encrypt the hard drives of your computer. By encrypting the hard drives, you can provide enhanced protection against data theft or unauthorized exposure of your computers or removable drives that are lost or stolen.

BranchCache *BranchCache* allows data from files and web servers on a wide area network (WAN) to be cached on computers at a local branch office. By using BranchCache, you can improve application response times while also reducing WAN traffic. Cached data can be either distributed across peer client computers (distributed cache mode) or centrally hosted on a server (hosted cache mode). BranchCache is included with Windows Server 2012 R2 and Windows 8.

> In this book, I will refer to *Windows 8*, which includes both Windows 8 and Windows 8.1. This is also true for *Windows Server 2008*. It will be used for both Windows Server 2008 and Windows Server 2008 R2. If, for some reason, both versions of Server 2008 did not cover an item, I will actually say 2008 R2.

DHCP *Dynamic Host Configuration Protocol (DHCP)* is an Internet standard that allows organizations to reduce the administrative overhead of configuring hosts on a TCP/IP-based network. Some of the new features are DHCP failover, policy-based assignment, and the ability to use Windows PowerShell for DHCP Server.

DNS *Domain Name System (DNS)* services are used in TCP/IP networks. DNS will convert a computer name or fully qualified domain name (FQDN) to an IP address. DNS also has the ability to do a reverse lookup and convert an IP address to a computer name. DNS allows you to locate computers and services through user-friendly names.

Failover Clustering *Failover Clustering* gives an organization the ability to provide high availability and scalability to networked servers. Failover clusters can include file share storage for server applications, such as Hyper-V and Microsoft SQL Server, and those that run on physical servers or virtual machines.

File Server Resource Manager *File Server Resource Manager* is a set of tools that allows administrators to manage and control the amount and type of data stored on the organization's servers. By using File Server Resource Manager, administrators have the ability to set up file management tasks, use quota management, get detailed reports, set up a file classification infrastructure, and configure file-screening management.

Hyper-V *Hyper-V* is one of the most changed features in Windows Server 2012 R2. Microsoft's new slogan is "Windows Server 2012 R2, built from the cloud up," and this has a lot to do with Hyper-V. It allows an organization to consolidate servers by creating and managing a virtualized computing environment. It does this by using virtualization technology that is built into Windows Server 2012 R2.

Hyper-V allows you to run multiple operating systems simultaneously on one physical computer. Each virtual operating system runs in its own virtual machine environment. I cover Hyper-V in detail in Chapter 9: "Use Virtualization in Windows Server 2012."

IPAM   *IP Address Management (IPAM)* is one of the features introduced with Windows Server 2012 R2. IPAM allows an administrator to customize and monitor the IP address infrastructure on a corporate network.

Kerberos Authentication   Windows Server 2012 R2 uses the *Kerberos authentication* (version 5) protocol and extensions for password-based and public key authentication. The Kerberos client is installed as a *security support provider (SSP)*, and it can be accessed through the *Security Support Provider Interface (SSPI)*.

Managed Service Accounts (gMSAs)   Stand-alone *managed service accounts*, originally created for Windows Server 2008 R2 and Windows 7, are configured domain accounts that allow automatic password management and *service principal names* (SPNs) management, including the ability to delegate management to other administrators.

Networking   There are many networking technologies and features in Windows Server 2012 R2, including BranchCache, Data Center Bridging (DCB), NIC Teaming, and many more.

Remote Desktop Services   Before Windows Server 2008, we used to refer to this as Terminal Services. *Remote Desktop Services* allows users to connect to virtual desktops, RemoteApp programs, and session-based desktops. Using Remote Desktop Services allows users to access remote connections from within a corporate network or from the Internet.

Security Auditing   *Security auditing* gives an organization the ability to help maintain the security of an enterprise. By using security audits, you can verify authorized or unauthorized access to machines, resources, applications, and services. One of the best advantages of security audits is to verify regulatory compliance.

Smart Cards   Using *smart cards* (referred to as *two-factor authentication*) and their associated *personal identification numbers (PINs)* is a popular, reliable, and cost-effective way to provide authentication. When using smart cards, the user not only must have the physical card but also must know the PIN to be able to gain access to network resources. This is effective because even if the smart card is stolen, thieves can't access the network unless they know the PIN.

TLS/SSL (Schannel SSP)   *Schannel* is a security support provider (SSP) that uses the *Secure Sockets Layer (SSL)* and *Transport Layer Security (TLS)* Internet standard authentication protocols together. The Security Support Provider Interface is an API used by Windows systems to allow security-related functionality, including authentication.

Windows Deployment Services   *Windows Deployment Services* allows an administrator to install Windows operating systems remotely. Administrators can use Windows Deployment Services to set up new computers by using a network-based installation.

Planning the Windows Server 2012 R2 Installation

Before you install Windows Server 2012 R2, you must first ask yourself these important questions: What type of server do I need? Will the server be a domain controller? What roles do I need to install on this server?

Once you have figured out what you need the server to do, you can make a game plan for the installation. So, let's start by looking at some of the server roles and technologies that can be installed on a Windows Server 2012 R2 computer.

Server Roles in Windows Server 2012 R2

When you install Windows Server 2012 R2, you have to decide which roles and features are going to be installed onto that server. This is an important decision in the computer world. Many administrators not only overuse a server but also underutilize servers in their organization.

For example, many administrators refuse to put any other roles or features on a domain controller. This may not be a good use of a server. Domain controllers help authenticate users onto the network, but after that the domain controllers are really not very busy all day long. Domain controllers have tasks that they must perform all day, but the server on which they reside is not heavily used when compared to a SQL Server machine or an Exchange mail server. This is where monitoring your server can be useful.

Now let's take a look at some of the roles and features you can install onto a Windows Server 2012 R2 machine. Knowing the different roles and features you can install will help you to design, deploy, manage, and troubleshoot technologies in Windows Server 2012 R2. Figure 1.1 shows the Add Roles And Features Wizard in Server Manager. It shows you just some of the roles that can be installed on a Windows Server 2012 R2 machine.

Roles and Features

Many of these features were discussed in the section "Features and Advantages of Windows Server 2012 and Server 2012 R2." I include them here again because they are also *roles* that can also be installed on Windows Server 2012 R2.

The following roles are available in Windows Server 2012 R2:

Active Directory Certificate Services   The AD CS server role in Windows Server 2012 R2 allows you to build a PKI and provide public key cryptography, digital certificates, and digital signature capabilities for your organization.

FIGURE 1.1   Available roles in Windows Server 2012 R2

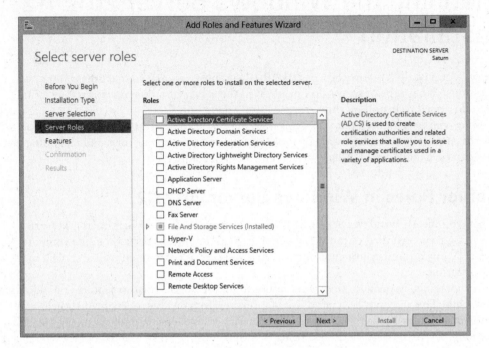

Feature   AD CS provides a customizable set of services that allows you to issue and manage PKI certificates. These certificates can be used in software security systems that employ public key technologies.

Role   AD CS in Windows Server 2012 R2 is the server role that allows you to build a PKI and provide public key cryptography, digital certificates, and digital signature capabilities for your organization.

Active Directory Domain Services   The AD DS server role allows you to create a scalable, secure, and manageable infrastructure for user and resource management and to provide support for directory-enabled applications, such as Microsoft Exchange Server.

Active Directory Federation Services   *Active Directory Federation Services (AD FS)* provides Internet-based clients with a secure identity access solution that works on both Windows and non-Windows operating systems. AD FS gives users the ability to do a *single sign-on (SSO)* and access applications on other networks without needing a secondary password.

Active Directory Lightweight Directory Services   *Active Directory Lightweight Directory Services (AD LDS)* is a *Lightweight Directory Access Protocol (LDAP)* directory service that provides flexible support for directory-enabled applications, without the dependencies and domain-related restrictions of AD DS.

Active Directory Rights Management Services   Active Directory Rights Management Services (AD RMS) in Windows Server 2012 R2 is the server role that provides you with management and development tools that work with industry security technologies including encryption, certificates, and authentication to help organizations create reliable information protection solutions.

Application Server   *Application Server* provides an integrated environment for deploying and running custom, server-based business applications.

Failover Clustering   The Failover Clustering feature provides a way to create, configure, and manage failover clusters for up to 4,000 virtual machines or up to 64 physical nodes.

File and Storage Services   *File and Storage Services* allows an administrator to set up and manage one or more file servers. These servers can provide a central location on your network where you can store files and then share those files with network users. If users require access to the same files and applications or if centralized backup and file management are important issues for your organization, administrators should set up network servers as a file server.

Group Policy   *Group policies* are a set of rules and management configuration options that you can control through the Group Policy settings. These policy settings can be placed on users' computers throughout the organization.

Hyper-V   The Hyper-V role allows administrators to create and manage a virtualized environment by taking advantage of the technology built into the Windows Server 2012 R2 operating system. When an administrator installs the Hyper-V role, all required virtualization components are installed.

Some of the required components include the Windows hypervisor, Virtual Machine Management Service, the virtualization WMI provider, the virtual machine bus (VMbus), the virtualization service provider (VSP), and the virtual infrastructure driver (VID).

Networking   This feature allows administrators to design, deploy, and maintain a Windows Server 2012 R2 network. The networking features include 802.1X authenticated wired and wireless access, BranchCache, Data Center Bridging, low-latency workload technologies, and many more.

Network Load Balancing   The *Network Load Balancing (NLB)* feature dispenses traffic across multiple servers by using the TCP/IP networking protocol. By combining two or more computers that are running applications in Windows Server 2012 R2 into a single virtual cluster, NLB provides reliability and performance for mission-critical servers.

Network Policy and Access Services   Use the *Network Policy and Access Services* server role to install and configure *Network Access Protection (NAP)*, secure wired and wireless access points, and RADIUS servers and proxies.

Print and Document Services   *Print and Document Services* allows an administrator to centralize print server and network printer tasks. This role also allows you to receive scanned documents from network scanners and route the documents to a shared network resource, Windows SharePoint Services site, or email addresses. Print and Document

Services also provides fax servers with the ability to send and receive faxes while also giving the administrator the ability to manage fax resources such as jobs, settings, reports, and fax devices on the fax server.

Remote Desktop Services   Remote Desktop Services allows for faster desktop and application deployments to any device, improving remote user effectiveness while helping to keep critical data secure. Remote Desktop Services allows for both a *virtual desktop infrastructure (VDI)* and session-based desktops, allowing users to connect from anywhere.

Security and Protection   Windows Server 2012 R2 has many new and improved security features for your organization. These security features include Access Control, AppLocker, BitLocker, Credential Locker, Kerberos, NTLM, passwords, security auditing, smart cards, and Windows Biometric Framework (WBF).

Telemetry   The *Telemetry* service allows the Windows Feedback Forwarder to send feedback to Microsoft automatically by deploying a Group Policy setting to one or more organizational units. Windows Feedback Forwarder is available on all editions of Windows Server 2012 R2, including Server Core.

Volume Activation   Windows Server 2012 R2 *Volume Activation* will help your organization benefit from using this service to deploy and manage volume licenses for a medium to large number of computers.

Web Server (IIS)   The *Web Server (IIS)* role in Windows Server 2012 R2 allows an administrator to set up a secure, easy-to-manage, modular, and extensible platform for reliably hosting websites, services, and applications.

Windows Deployment Services   Windows Deployment Services allows an administrator to install a Windows operating system over the network. Administrators do not have to install each operating system directly from a CD or DVD.

Windows Server Backup Feature   The *Windows Server Backup* feature gives an organization a way to back up and restore Windows servers. You can use Windows Server Backup to back up the entire server (all volumes), selected volumes, the system state, or specific files or folders.

Windows Server Update Services   *Windows Server Update Services (WSUS)* allows administrators to deploy application and operating system updates. By deploying WSUS, administrators have the ability to manage updates that are released through Microsoft Update to computers in their network. This feature is integrated with the operating system as a server role on a Windows Server 2012 R2 system.

Migrating Roles and Features to Windows Server 2012 R2

Once you decide on which roles and features you are going to install onto your Windows Server 2012 R2 system, then you either have to install those roles and features from scratch or migrate them from a previous version of Windows server.

Windows Server 2012 R2 includes a set of migration tools that administrators can use to help ease the process of migrating server roles, features, operating system settings, and data. Administrators can migrate this data from an existing server that is running Windows Server 2003, Windows Server 2003 R2, Windows Server 2008, Windows Server 2008 R2, or Windows Server 2012 R2 to a computer that is running Windows Server 2012 R2.

Using Windows Server Migration Tools to migrate roles, role services, and features can simplify the deployment of new servers. You can migrate roles and features on servers running the Server Core installation option of Windows Server 2012 R2 and virtual servers. By using Windows Server Migration Tools, an administrator can reduce migration downtime, increase the accuracy of the migration process, and help eliminate conflicts that could otherwise occur during the migration process.

One advantage of using the migration tools is that most of them support cross-architecture migrations (x86-based to x64-based computing platforms), migrations between physical and virtual environments, and migrations between both the full and Server Core installation options of the Windows Server operating system. In Windows Server 2012 R2, Windows Server Migration Tools also supports cross-subnet migrations.

To use Windows Server Migration Tools, the feature must be installed on both the source and destination computers. Windows Server Migration Tools installation and preparation can be divided into the following stages:

1. Installing Windows Server Migration Tools on destination servers that run Windows Server 2012 R2

2. Creating deployment folders on destination servers that run Windows Server 2012 R2 for copying to source servers

3. Copying deployment folders from destination servers to source servers

4. Registering Windows Server Migration Tools on source servers

If you plan to use Windows Server Migration Tools, you must be a member of the Administrators group on both the source and destination servers to install, remove, or set up the tools.

Administrators can install Windows Server Migration Tools by using either the Add Roles Or Features Wizard in Server Manager or Windows PowerShell deployment cmdlets for Server Manager.

To install Windows Server Migration Tools on a Server Core installation of Windows Server 2012 R2, you would complete the following steps:

1. Open a Windows PowerShell session by typing **powershell.exe** in the current command prompt session and then pressing Enter.

2. In the Windows PowerShell session, install Windows Server Migration Tools by using the Windows PowerShell `Install-WindowsFeature` cmdlet for Server Manager. In the Windows PowerShell session, type the following, and then press Enter. (Omit the `ComputerName` parameter if you are installing the Windows Server Migration Tools on the local server.)

```
Install-WindowsFeature Migration -ComputerName computer_name
```

Roles and Features That Have Been Reduced in Windows Server 2012 R2

One thing that we want to look at is which Roles and Features are being deprecated or removed from Windows Server 2012 and Windows Server 2012 R2. Table 1.1 was taken directly from Microsoft's website (http://technet.microsoft.com/en-us/library/dn303411.aspx), and this table may change at any time. Thus I would recommend that you go out to Microsoft's website to see the current list of Roles and Features.

Table 1.1 lists the features and functionalities in Windows Server 2012 and Windows Server 2012 R2 that either have been removed from the product in the current release or are planned for potential removal in subsequent releases (shown as *deprecated*).

TABLE 1.1   Roles and Features Updates

	Windows Server 2012		Windows Server 2012 R2	
	Removed	Deprecated	Removed	Deprecated
AD FS v1 Web Agent			X	
AD FS in-place upgrade from AD FS 1.0 or "out-of-the-box" AD FS 2.0	X			
AD FS support for "Resource Group"	X			
AD FS support for NT Token mode	X			
AD FS support for using AD LDS as an authentication store	X			
AD RMS license revocation				X
AD RMS SDK				X
Application Server role				X
Built-in drivers for tape drives				X
Cluster Automation Server COM API	X (Optional)		X (Optional)	
Cluster.exe command-line interface	X (Optional)		X (Optional)	

Feature			
CertObj COM and InetInfo interfaces of the Web Server role			X
Dcpromo.exe	X		
Dfscmd.exe			X
Drivers for Jet Red RDBMS and ODBC	X		X
File Replication Service			X
Internet Information Service (IIS) 6.0 Manager			X
Layered Service Providers	X		X
LPR/LPD protocol	X		X
Namespace for version 1.0 of WMI; WMIC (in WMI)	X	X	
NDIS version 5.0, 5.1, and 5.2 APIs	X	X	
Net DMA	X			
Network Access Protection (NAP)			X
Network Information Service (NIS) and Tools (in RSAT)			X
Nfsshare.exe			X
NFSv2 support			X
Oclist.exe	X			
ODBC support for 16- and 32-bit applications and drivers	X		X
ODBC/OLEDB support for Microsoft Oracle	X		
ODBC/OLEDB support for SQL beyond SQL Server 7 and SQL 2000	X		X

TABLE 1.1 Roles and Features Updates *(continued)*

	Windows Server 2012		Windows Server 2012 R2	
	Removed	Deprecated	Removed	Deprecated
Providers for SNMP, Win32_ ServerFeature API, Active Directory, MSClus WMI1.0 (in WMI)		X		X
Recovery disk creation			X	
Remote Data Service		X		
Role Collector (Ceiprole.exe) and associated API	X			
SCSIport host-bus adapter	X			
Servermanagercmd.exe		X	X	
SIS Limited API				X
Slmgr.vbs options			X	
SMB 1.0				X
SMB.sys	X			
SMTP and associated management tools		X		X
SQLXMLX		X		X
Storage Explorer snap-in for MMC	X			
Storage Manager for SANs snap-in for MMC	X			
Subsystem for UNIX-based applications		X	X	
Support for 32-bit cluster resource DLLs	X			
Support for hardware drivers for XDDM	X			

Feature				
Support for Microsoft SQL Server prior to 7.0	X			
Support for native VGA via the PC/AT BIOS or UEFI CSM	X			
Support for Static VMQ	X			
Support for Token Rings	X			
Support for Visual Studio Analyzer 2003 over ODBC, OLEDB, and ADO	X			
System Image Backup ("Windows 7 File Recovery")			X	
Telnet server				X
VM Chimney (also called TCP Offload) in Hyper-V	X			
Windows Server 2003 domain and functional levels of Active Directory				X
Windows Authorization Manager (AzMan)		X	X	
Windows Help executable (WinHlp32.exe)	X			
Windows Identity Foundation 3.5				X
Windows Server Resource Manager		X	X	
Winsock Direct		X	X	
WMI root/virtualization namespace v1 (in Hyper-V)		X	X	
XDR schema elements, XSI pattern feature of MSXML3 (in XML)		X		X

Deciding Which Windows Server 2012 R2 Versions to Use

You may be wondering which version of Windows Server 2012 R2 is best for your organization. After all, Microsoft offers the following four versions of Windows Server 2012 R2.

Windows Server 2012 R2 Datacenter   This version is designed for organizations that are looking to migrate to a highly virtualized, private cloud environment. Windows Server 2012 R2 Datacenter has full Windows Server functionality with unlimited virtual instances.

Windows Server 2012 R2 Standard   This version is designed for organizations with physical or minimally virtualized environments. Windows Server 2012 R2 Standard has full Windows Server functionality with two virtual instances.

Windows Server 2012 R2 Essentials   This version is ideal for small businesses that have as many as 25 users and 50 devices. Windows Server 2012 R2 Essentials has a simpler interface and preconfigured connectivity to cloud-based services but no virtualization rights.

Windows Server 2012 R2 Foundation   This version is designed for smaller companies that need a Windows Server experience for as few as 15 users. Windows Server 2012 R2 Foundation is a general-purpose server with basic functionality but no virtualization rights.

Once you choose what roles are going on your server, you must then decide how you're going to install Windows Server 2012 R2. There are two ways to install Windows Server 2012 R2. You can upgrade a Windows Server 2008 R2 with SP1 or Windows Server 2012 machine to Windows Server 2012 R2, or you can do a clean install of Windows Server 2012 R2. If you decide that you are going to upgrade, there are specific upgrade paths you must follow.

Your choice of Windows Server 2012 R2 version is dictated by how your current network is designed. If you are building a network from scratch, then it's pretty straightforward. Just choose the Windows Server 2012 R2 version based on your server's tasks. However, if you already have a version of Windows Server 2008 installed, you should follow the recommendations in Table 1.2, which briefly summarize the supported upgrade paths to Windows Server 2012 R2.

 If your version of Microsoft Windows Server is not listed in the left column, upgrading to Windows Server 2012 R2 is not supported. If there is more than one edition listed in the right column, you can then choose either edition.

TABLE 1.2   Supported Windows Server 2012 R2 upgrade path recommendations

Current System	Upgraded System
Windows Server 2008 R2 Datacenter with SP1	Windows Server 2012 R2 Datacenter
Windows Server 2008 R2 Enterprise with SP1	Windows Server 2012 R2 Standard or Windows Server 2012 R2 Datacenter

Windows Server 2008 R2 Standard with SP1	Windows Server 2012 R2 Standard or Windows Server 2012 R2 Datacenter
Windows Web Server 2008 R2 with SP1	Windows Server 2012 R2 Standard
Windows Server 2012 Datacenter	Windows Server 2012 R2 Datacenter
Windows Server 2012 Standard	Windows Server 2012 R2 Standard or Windows Server 2012 R2 Datacenter
Hyper-V Server 2012	Hyper-V Server 2012 R2
Windows Storage Server 2012 Standard	Windows Storage Server 2012 R2 Standard
Windows Storage Server 2012 Workgroup	Windows Storage Server 2012 R2 Workgroup

Deciding on the Type of Installation

One of the final choices you must make before installing Windows Server 2012 R2 is what type of installation you want. There are three ways to install Windows Server 2012 R2.

Windows Server 2012 R2 with the Graphical User Interface (GUI)   This is the version with which most administrators are familiar. This is the version that uses *Microsoft Management Console (MMC)* windows, and it is the version that allows the use of a mouse to navigate through the installation.

Windows Server 2012 R2 Server Core   This is a bare-bones installation of Windows Server 2012 R2. You can think of it this way: If Windows Server 2012 R2 is a top-of-the-line luxury car, then Windows Server 2012 R2 Server Core is the stripped-down model with no air-conditioning, manual windows, and cloth seats. It might not be pretty to look at, but it gets the job done.

Windows Server 2012 R2 MinShell   This is the best of both installation types mentioned previously. Minimum Shell (MinShell) gives you the advantage of using the GUI management tools, but MinShell does not actually install the GUI. It gives administrators the ability to use tools with which they are familiar but still provides a small attack surface and the advantages of Server Core.

In Windows Server 2012 R2, an administrator has the ability to remove the GUI shell after a GUI shell install has been completed. This removes Internet Explorer 10, Windows Explorer, the desktop, and the Start screen. Microsoft Management Console (MMC), Server Manager, and a subset of Control Panel are still present, giving you a MinShell installation plus PowerShell.

🌐 **Real World Scenario**

Server Core

Here is an explanation of Server Core that I have used ever since it was introduced in Windows Server 2008.

I am a *huge* sports fan. I love watching sports on TV, and I enjoy going to games. If you have ever been to a hockey game, you know what a hockey goal looks like. Between hockey periods, the stadium workers often bring out a huge piece of Plexiglas onto the ice. There is a tiny square cut out of the bottom of the glass. The square is just a bit bigger than a hockey puck itself.

Now they pick some lucky fan out of the stands, give them a puck at center ice, and then ask them to shoot the puck into the net with the Plexiglas in front of it. If they get it through that tiny little square at the bottom of the Plexiglas, they win a car or some such great prize.

Well, Windows Server 2012 R2 with the GUI is like regular hockey with a net, and Windows Server 2012 R2 Server Core is the Plexiglas version.

Server Core supports a limited number of roles.

- Active Directory Certificate Services (AD CS)
- Active Directory Domain Services (AD DS)
- Active Directory Federation Services (AD FS)
- Active Directory Lightweight Directory Services (AD LDS)
- Active Directory Rights Management Services (AD RMS)
- Application Server
- DHCP Server
- DNS Server
- Fax Server
- File and Storage Services
- BITS Server
- BranchCache
- Hyper-V
- Network Policy and Access Services
- Print and Document Services
- Remote Access
- Remote Desktop Services

- Volume Activation Services
- Web Server (IIS)
- Windows Deployment Services
- Windows Server Update Services
- .NET Framework 3.5 Features
- .NET Framework 4.5 Features
- Streaming Media Services
- Failover Clustering
- iSCSI
- Network Load Balancing
- MPIO
- qWave
- Telnet Server/Client
- Windows Server Migration Tools
- Windows PowerShell 4.0

Server Core does not have the normal Windows interface or GUI. Almost everything has to be configured via the command line or, in some cases, using the Remote Server Administration Tools from a full version of Windows Server 2012 R2. While this might scare off some administrators, it has the following benefits:

Reduced Management   Because Server Core has a minimum number of applications installed, it reduces management effort.

Minimal Maintenance   Only basic systems can be installed on Server Core, so it reduces the upkeep you would need to perform in a normal server installation.

Smaller Footprint   Server Core requires only 1GB of disk space to install and 2GB of free space for operations.

Tighter Security   With only a few applications running on a server, it is less vulnerable to attacks.

The prerequisites for Server Core are basic. It requires the Windows Server 2012 R2 installation media, a product key, and the hardware on which to install it.

After you install the base operating system, you use PowerShell or the remote administrative tools to configure the network settings, add the machine to the domain, create and format disks, and install roles and features. It takes only a few minutes to install Server Core, depending on the hardware.

One of the new things to keep in mind is that you can upgrade or downgrade to Server Core or MinShell. In Windows Server 2008 R2 and Windows Server 2008, if you wanted to switch your Windows Server GUI to Server Core, or vice versa, there was no way to convert to a full Windows Server installation or a Server Core installation without reinstalling the operating system. In Windows Server 2012 R2, the Server Core or GUI installation options are no longer an irreversible selection made during setup. An administrator now has the ability to convert between a Server Core installation and a full installation as needed.

 Real World Scenario

Better Security

When I started in this industry more than 20 years ago, I was a programmer. I used to program computer hospital systems. When I switched to the networking world, I continued to work under contract with hospitals and with doctors' offices.

One problem I ran into is that many doctors are affiliated with hospitals, but they don't actually have offices within the hospital. Generally, they have offices either near the hospital or, in some cases, right across the street.

Here is the issue: Do we put servers in the doctors' offices, or do we make the doctor log into the hospital network through a remote connection? Doctors' offices normally don't have computer rooms, and we don't want to place a domain controller or server on someone's desk. It's just unsafe!

This is where Windows Server 2012 R2 Server Core can come into play. Since it is a slimmed-down version of Windows and there is no GUI, it makes it harder for anyone in the office to hack into the system. Also, Microsoft introduced a new domain controller in Windows Server 2008 called a *read-only domain controller (RODC)*. As its name suggests, it is a read-only version of a domain controller (explained in detail later in this book).

With Server Core and an RODC, you can feel safer placing a server on someone's desk or in any office. Server Core systems allow you to place servers in areas that you would never have placed them before. This can be a great advantage to businesses that have small, remote locations without full server rooms.

If you have a server that is running Server Core, there may be a situation in which you need to use the graphical user interfaces available only in Windows Server 2012 R2 with a GUI mode. Windows Server 2012 and Windows Server 2012 R2 allow you to switch the Server Core system to a Server with a GUI mode, or vice versa.

To convert from a Windows 2012 or Windows Server 2012 R2 Server Core system to Server with a GUI mode, run this code snippet (a restart is required):

```
Install-WindowsFeature Server-Gui-Mgmt-Infra,Server-Gui-Shell -Restart
```

To convert from Server Core mode to Server with a GUI mode, follow these steps when the server is initially installed in Server Core mode:

1. Determine the index number for a server with a GUI image (for example, SERVERDATA-CENTER, not SERVERDATACENTERCORE) using this cmdlet:

    ```
    Get-WindowsImage -ImagePath path to wim\install.wim
    ```

2. Run this line of code:

    ```
    Install-WindowsFeature Server-Gui-Mgmt-Infra,Server-Gui-Shell -Restart
    -Source wim: path to wim\install.wim: Index # from step 1
    ```

    To install GUI to 12

3. Alternatively, if you want to use Windows Update as the source instead of a WIM file, use this Windows PowerShell cmdlet:

    ```
    Install-WindowsFeature Server-Gui-Mgmt-Infra,Server-Gui-Shell -Restart
    ```

After you have completed the management tasks, you can switch the server back to Server Core mode whenever it is convenient (a restart is required) with this Windows PowerShell cmdlet:

```
Uninstall-WindowsFeature Server-Gui-Mgmt-Infra -restart
```

NIC Teaming

NIC Teaming, also known as *load balancing and failover (LBFO)*, gives an administrator the ability to allow multiple network adapters on a system to be placed into a team. Independent hardware vendors (IHVs) have required NIC Teaming, but until Windows Server 2012, NIC Teaming was *not* part of the Windows Server Operating System.

To be able to use NIC Teaming, the computer system must have at least one Ethernet adapter. If you want to provide fault protection, an administrator must have a minimum of two Ethernet adapters. One advantage of Windows Server 2012 R2 is that an administrator can setup 32 network adapters in a NIC Team.

NIC Teaming is a very common practice when setting up virtualization. It is one way that you can have load balancing with Hyper-V.

NIC Teaming gives an administrator the ability to allow a virtual machine to use virtual network adapters in Hyper-V. The advantage of using NIC Teaming in Hyper-V is that the administrator can use it to connect to more than one Hyper-V switch. This allows Hyper-V to maintain connectivity even if the network adapter under the Hyper-V switch gets disconnected.

An administrator can configure NIC Teaming in either Server Manager or PowerShell.

Installing Windows Server 2012 R2

In the following sections, I am going to walk you through two different types of installs. I will show you how to do a full install of Windows 2012 Server with the GUI, and then I will show you how to install the Server Core version of the same software.

 For these labs, I am using the full release of Windows Server 2012 R2 Data-center, but you can use Windows Server 2012 R2 Standard.

Installing with the GUI

In Exercise 1.1, I will show you how to install Windows Server 2012 R2 Datacenter with the GUI. The GUI represents the Windows applications on the Desktop and the operating system functions that you can control and navigate with a mouse. The Server Core version is a command-line version only—you cannot use a mouse with Server Core unless you are going to use the mouse wheel for scrolling.

Windows Installation

At the time of this writing, I used the first full release of Windows Server 2012 R2 Data-center. For this reason, there may be screens that have changed somewhat since this book was published.

EXERCISE 1.1

Installing Windows Server 2012 R2 with the GUI

1. Insert the Windows Server 2012 R2 installation DVD, and restart the machine from the installation media.

2. At the first screen, Windows Server 2012 R2 will ask you to configure your language, time and currency, and keyboard. Make your selections, and click Next.

3. At the next screen, click Install Now.

4. Depending on what version of Windows Server 2012 R2 you have (MSDN, TechNet, and so on), you may be asked to enter a product key. If this screen appears, enter your prod-uct key and click Next. If this screen does not appear, just go to step 5.

5. The Select The Operating System That You Want To Install screen then appears. Choose the Windows Server 2012 R2 Datacenter (Server With A GUI) selection and click Next.

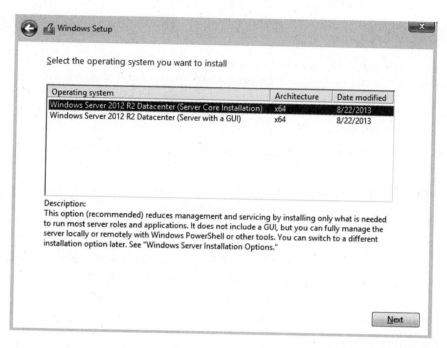

6. The license terms screen appears. After reading the Windows Server 2012 R2 license agreement, check the I Accept The License Terms check box and click Next.

7. On the Which Type Of Installation Do You Want? screen, choose Custom: Install Windows Only (Advanced).

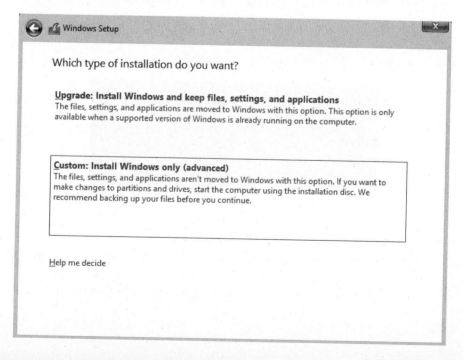

8. The next screen will ask you where you want to install Windows. If your hard disk is already formatted as NTFS, click the drive and then click Next. If the hard disk is not yet set up or formatted, choose the New link and create a partition. After creating the partition, click the Format link. Once the format is done, make sure you choose the new partition and click Next.

9. The Installing Windows screen will appear next. This is where the files from your media will be installed onto the system. The machine will reboot during this installation.

10. After the machine is finished rebooting, a screen requesting the administrator password will appear. Type in your password. (**P@ssword** is used in this exercise.) Your password must meet the password complexity requirements (one capitalized letter, one number, and/or one special character). Click Finish.

11. Next, log into the system. Press Ctrl+Alt+Del, and type in the administrator password. The machine will set up the properties of the administrator account.

12. Notice that the Server Manager dashboard automatically appears. Your Windows Server 2012 R2 installation is now complete.

13. Close Server Manager.

After you have logged into the Windows Server 2012 R2 Datacenter system, you will notice some big changes. The first is that the Start button in the lower-left corner of the screen has changed its look. Also, you can get to a Start button by clicking the Windows key (see Figure 1.2).

FIGURE 1.2   Windows key on a standard keyboard

Installing Windows Server 2012 R2 Server Core

In Exercise 1.2, you will learn how to install Windows Server 2012 R2 Server Core. You'll notice that the steps are similar to the ones in Exercise 1.1, with a couple of exceptions. As mentioned earlier, Server Core is a command-line configuration of Windows Server 2012 R2.

EXERCISE 1.2

Installing Windows Server 2012 R2 Using Server Core

1. Insert the Windows Server 2012 R2 installation DVD, and restart the machine from the installation media.

2. At the first screen, Windows Server 2012 R2 will prompt you to configure your language, time and currency, and keyboard. Make your selections, and click Next.

3. At the next screen, click Install Now.

4. Depending on what version of Windows Server 2012 R2 you have (MSDN, TechNet, and so on), you may be asked to enter a product key. If this screen appears, enter your product key and click Next. If this screen does not appear, just go to step 5.

5. The Select The Operating System That You Want To Install screen then appears. Choose the Windows Server 2012 R2 Datacenter (Server Core Installation) selection and click Next.

6. The license terms screen appears. After reading the Windows Server 2012 R2 license agreement, check the I Accept The License Terms check box and click Next.

7. At the Which Type Of Installation Do You Want? screen, choose Custom: Install Windows Only (Advanced).

8. The next screen will ask you where you want to install Windows. If your hard disk is already formatted as NTFS, click the drive and then click Next. If the hard disk is not set up or formatted, choose the New link and create a partition. After creating the partition, click the Format link. Once the format is done, make sure you choose the new partition and click Next.

9. The Installing Windows screen will appear next. This is where the files from your media will be installed onto the system. The machine will reboot during this installation.

10. After the machine is finished rebooting, a screen requesting the administrator password will appear. Type in your password. (**P@ssword** is used in this exercise.) Your password must meet the password complexity requirements (one capitalized letter, one number, and/or one special character).

11. Log into the system. Press Ctrl+Alt+Del, and type in the administrator password. The machine will set up the properties of the administrator account.

12. You will notice that the command prompt will automatically appear. Your Windows Server 2012 R2 Server Core installation is now complete.

13. To log out or turn off the machine, press Ctrl+Alt+Del and then click Sign Out.

After Windows Server 2012 R2 server is installed, you need to look at how to manage and configure the server. In the next section, you will learn how to manage a server remotely and with Windows PowerShell.

Using Windows Deployment Services

Another way that many IT departments deploy operating systems has been through the use of Windows Deployment Services (WDS). WDS allows an IT administrator to install a Windows operating system without using an installation disc. Using WDS allows you to deploy the operating system through a network installation. WDS can deploy Windows XP, Windows Server 2003, Windows Vista, Windows 7, Windows 8, Windows Server 2008/2008 R2, Microsoft Windows 2012, and Microsoft Windows Server 2012 R2.

The following are some of the advantages of using WDS for automated installation:

- You can remotely install Windows 7/Windows 8.
- The procedure simplifies management of the server image by allowing you to access Windows 7/8 distribution files from a distribution server.
- You can quickly recover the operating system in the event of a computer failure.

Here are the basic steps of the WDS process from a PXE-enabled WDS client:

1. The WDS client initiates a special boot process through the PXE network adapter (and the computer's BIOS configured for a network boot). On a PXE client, the user presses F12 to start the PXE boot process and to indicate that they want to perform a WDS installation.
2. A list of available Windows PE boot images is displayed. The user should select the appropriate Windows PE boot image from the boot menu.
3. The Windows Welcome screen is displayed. The user should click the Next button.
4. The WDS user is prompted to enter credentials for accessing and installing images from the WDS server.
5. A list of available operating system images is displayed. The user should select the appropriate image file to install.
6. The WDS user is prompted to enter the product key for the selected image.
7. The Partition And Configure The Disk screen is displayed. This screen provides the ability to install a mass storage device driver, if needed, by pressing F6.
8. The image copy process is initiated, and the selected image is copied to the WDS client computer.

The following sections describe how to set up the WDS server and the WDS clients and how to install Windows 7/8 through WDS.

Preparing the WDS Server

With the WDS server, you can manage and distribute Windows 7/8 operating system images to WDS client computers. The WDS server contains any files necessary for PXE booting, Windows PE boot images, and the Windows 7/8 images to be deployed.

The following steps for preparing the WDS server are discussed in the upcoming sections:

1. Make sure that the server meets the requirements for running WDS.
2. Install WDS.
3. Configure and start WDS.
4. Configure the WDS server to respond to client computers (if this was not configured when WDS was installed).

For WDS to work, the server on which you will install WDS must meet the requirements for WDS and be able to access the required network services.

WDS Server Requirements

The WDS server must meet these requirements:

- The computer must be a domain controller or a member of an Active Directory domain.
- At least one partition on the server must be formatted as NTFS.
- WDS must be installed on the server.
- The operating system must be Windows Server 2003, Windows Server 2008/2008 R2, Windows Server 2012, or Windows Server 2012 R2.
- A network adapter must be installed.

Network Services

The following network services must be running on the WDS server or be accessible to the WDS server from another network server:

- TCP/IP installed and configured.
- A DHCP server, which is used to assign DHCP addresses to WDS clients. (Ensure that your DHCP scope has enough addresses to accommodate all of the WDS clients that will need IP addresses.)
- A DNS server, which is used to locate the Active Directory controller.
- Active Directory, which is used to locate WDS servers and WDS clients as well as authorize WDS clients and manage WDS configuration settings and client installation options.

Installing the WDS Server Components

You can configure WDS on a Windows Server 2003/2008/2008 R2, Windows Server 2012, or Windows Server 2012 R2 computer by using the Windows Deployment Services Configuration Wizard or by using the WDSUTIL command-line utility. Table 1.3 describes the WDSUTIL command-line options.

TABLE 1.3 WDSUTIL command-line options

WDSUTIL Option	Description
/initialize-server	Initializes the configuration of the WDS server
/uninitialized-server	Undoes any changes made during the initialization of the WDS server
/add	Adds images and devices to the WDS server
/convert-ripimage	Converts Remote Installation Preparation (RIPrep) images to WIM images
/remove	Removes images from the server
/set	Sets information in images, image groups, WDS servers, and WDS devices
/get	Gets information from images, image groups, WDS servers, and WDS devices
/new	Creates new capture images or discover images
/copy- image	Copies images from the image store
/export-image	Exports to WIM files images contained within the image store
/start	Starts WDS services
/stop	Stops WDS services
/disable	Disables WDS services
/enable	Enables WDS services
/approve-autoadddevices	Approves Auto-Add devices
/reject-autoadddevices	Rejects Auto-Add devices
/delete-autoadddevices	Deletes records from the Auto-Add database
/update	Uses a known good resource to update a server resource

The first step in setting up WDS to deploy operating systems to the clients is to install the WDS role. You do this by using Server Manager.

One of the advantages of using the Windows deployment server is that WDS can work with Windows image (.wim) files. Windows image files can be created through the use of the Windows Sysprep utility.

One component to which you need to pay attention when using the Windows deployment server is *Preboot Execution Environment (PXE)* network devices. PXE boot devices are network interface cards (NICs) that can talk to a network without the need for an operating system. PXE boot NIC adapters are network adapters that have a set of preboot commands within the boot firmware.

This is important when using WDS because PXE boot adapters connect to a WDS server and request the data needed to load the operating system remotely. Remember, most of the machines for which you are using WDS do not have an operating system on the computer. You need NIC adapters that can connect to a network without the need for an operating system for WDS to work properly.

For the same reason, you must set up DHCP to accept PXE machines. Those machines need a valid TCP/IP address so that they can connect to the WDS server.

Preparing the WDS Client

The WDS client is the computer on which Windows 7/8 will be installed. WDS clients rely on a technology called PXE, which allows the client computer to boot remotely and connect to a WDS server.

To act as a WDS client, the computer must meet all of the hardware requirements for Windows 7/Windows 8 and have a PXE-capable network adapter installed, and a WDS server must be present on the network. Additionally, the user account used to install the image must be a member of the Domain Users group in Active Directory.

After the WDS server has been installed and configured, you can install Windows 7/Windows 8 on a WDS client that uses a PXE-compliant network card.

To install Windows 7/Windows 8 on the WDS client, follow these steps:

1. Start the computer. When prompted, press F12 for a network service boot. The Windows PE appears.

2. The Windows Welcome screen appears. Click the Next button to start the installation process.

3. Enter the username and password of an account that has permissions to access and install images from the WDS server.

4. A list of available operating system images stored on the WDS server appears. Select the image to install and click Next.

5. Enter the product key for the selected Windows 7/8 image and click Next.

6. The Partition And Configure The Disk screen appears. Select the desired disk-partitioning options, or click OK to use the default options.

7. Click Next to initiate the image-copying process. The Windows Setup process will begin after the image is copied to the WDS client computer.

Understanding Features On Demand

One of the problems in previous versions of Windows Server was how roles and features were stored on the hard disk. Before the introduction of Windows Server 2012, even if a server role or feature was disabled on a server, the binary files for that role or feature were still present on the disk. The problem with this approach is that, even if you disable the role, it still consumes space on your hard drive.

Features On Demand in Windows Server 2012 R2 solves this issue because not only can administrators disable a role or feature, they can also completely remove the role or feature's files.

Once this is done, a state of Removed is shown in Server Manager, or the state of Disabled With Payload Removed is shown in the Dism.exe utility. To reinstall a role or feature that has been completely removed, you must have access to the installation files.

If you want to remove a role or feature completely from the system, use –Remove with the Uninstall-WindowsFeature cmdlet of Windows PowerShell. For example, if you want to remove Windows Explorer, Internet Explorer, and all dependent components completely, run the following Windows PowerShell command:

```
Uninstall-WindowsFeature Server-Gui-Shell –Remove
```

If you want to reinstall a role or feature that has been removed completely, use the Windows PowerShell –Source option of the Install-WindowsFeature Server Manager cmdlet. Using the –Source option states the path where the WIM image files and the index number of the image will be located. If an administrator decides not to use the –Source option, Windows will use Windows Update by default.

When you're using the Features On Demand configuration, if feature files are not available on the server computer and the installation requires those feature files, Windows Server 2012 R2 can be directed to get those files from a side-by-side feature store, which is a shared folder that contains feature files. It is available to the server on the network, from Windows Update, or from installation media. This can be overwritten using the –Source option in the Windows PowerShell utility.

Source Files for Roles or Features

Offline virtual hard disks (VHDs) cannot be used as a source for installing roles or features that have been completely removed. Only sources for the same version of Windows Server 2012 R2 are supported.

To install a removed role or feature using a WIM image, follow these steps:

1. Run the following command:

   ```
   Get-windowsimage -imagepath \install.wim
   ```

In step 1, *imagepath* is the path where the WIM files are located.

2. Run the following command:

    ```
    Install-WindowsFeature featurename -Source wim: path:index
    ```

    In step 2, *featurename* is the name of the role or feature from `Get-WindowsFeature`.
    path is the path to the WIM mount point, and *index* is the index of the server image
    from step 1.

To add or remove a role or feature, you must have administrative rights to the Windows
Server 2012 R2 machine.

Storage in Windows Server 2012 R2

As an IT administrator, you'll need to ask many questions before you start setting up a
server. What type of disks should be used? What type of RAID sets should be made? What
type of hardware platform should be purchased? These are all questions you must ask when
planning for storage in a Windows Server 2012 R2 server. In the following sections, I will
answer these questions so that you can make the best decisions for storage in your network's environment.

Initializing Disks

To begin, I must first discuss how to add disk drives to a server. Once a disk drive has been
physically installed, it must be initialized by selecting the type of partition. Different types
of partition styles are used to initialize disks: *Master Boot Record (MBR)* and *GUID Partition Table (GPT)*.

MBR has a partition table that indicates where the partitions are located on the disk
drive, and with this particular partition style, only volumes up to 2TB (2,048GB) are
supported. An MBR drive can have up to four primary partitions or can have three
primary partitions and one extended partition that can be divided into unlimited logical
drives.

Windows Server 2012 R2 can only boot off an MBR disk unless it is based on the
Extensible Firmware Interface (EFI); then it can boot from GPT. An Itanium server is
an example of an EFI-based system. GPT is not constrained by the same limitations as
MBR. In fact, a GPT disk drive can support volumes of up to 18EB (18,874,368 million
terabytes) and 128 partitions. As a result, GPT is recommended for disks larger than
2TB or disks used on Itanium-based computers. Exercise 1.3 demonstrates the process of
initializing additional disk drives to an active computer running Windows Server 2012 R2.
If you're not adding a new drive, then stop after step 4. I am completing this exercise using
Computer Management, but you also can do this exercise using Server Manager.

EXERCISE 1.3

Initializing Disk Drives

1. Open Computer Management under Administrative Tools.

2. Select Disk Management.

3. After disk drives have been installed, right-click Disk Management and select Rescan Disks.

4. A pop-up box appears indicating that the server is scanning for new disks. If you did not add a new disk, go to step 9.

5. After the server has completed the scan, the new disk appears as Unknown.

6. Right-click the Unknown disk, and select Initialize Disk.

7. A pop-up box appears asking for the partition style. For this exercise, choose MBR.

8. Click OK.

9. Close Computer Management.

The disk will now appear online as a basic disk with unallocated space.

Configuring Basic and Dynamic Disks

Windows Server 2012 R2 supports two types of disk configurations: basic and dynamic. Basic disks are divided into partitions and can be used with previous versions of Windows. Dynamic disks are divided into volumes and can be used with Windows 2000 Server and newer releases.

When a disk is initialized, it is automatically created as a basic disk, but when a new fault-tolerant (RAID) volume set is created, the disks in the set are converted to dynamic disks. Fault-tolerance features and the ability to modify disks without having to reboot the server are what distinguish dynamic disks from basic disks.

Fault tolerance (RAID) is discussed in detail later in this chapter in the "Redundant Array of Independent Disks" section.

A basic disk can simply be converted to a dynamic disk without loss of data. When a basic disk is converted, the partitions are automatically changed to the appropriate volumes. However, converting a dynamic disk back to a basic disk is not as simple. First, all the data on the dynamic disk must be backed up or moved. Then, all the volumes on the dynamic disk have to be deleted. The dynamic disk can then be converted to a basic disk. Partitions and logical drives can be created, and the data can be restored.

The following are actions that can be performed on basic disks:

- Formatting partitions
- Marking partitions as active
- Creating and deleting primary and extended partitions
- Creating and deleting logical drives
- Converting from a basic disk to a dynamic disk

The following are actions that can be performed on dynamic disks:

- Creating and deleting simple, striped, spanned, mirrored, or RAID-5 volumes
- Removing or breaking a mirrored volume
- Extending simple or spanned volumes
- Repairing mirrored or RAID-5 volumes
- Converting from a dynamic disk to a basic disk after deleting all volumes

In Exercise 1.4, you'll convert a basic disk to a dynamic disk.

EXERCISE 1.4

Converting a Basic Disk to a Dynamic Disk

1. Open Computer Management under Administrative Tools.

2. Select Disk Management.

3. Right-click a basic disk that you want to convert and select Convert To Dynamic Disk.

4.   The Convert To Dynamic Disk dialog box appears. From here, select all of the disks that you want to convert to dynamic disks. In this exercise, only one disk will be converted.

5.   Click OK.

6.   The Convert To Dynamic Disk dialog box changes to the Disks To Convert dialog box and shows the disk/disks that will be converted to dynamic disks.

7.   Click Convert.

8.   Disk Management will warn that if you convert the disk to dynamic, you will not be able to start the installed operating system from any volume on the disk (except the current boot volume). Click Yes.

9.   Close Computer Management.

The converted disk will now show as Dynamic in Disk Management.

Managing Volumes

A *volume set* is created from volumes that span multiple drives by using the free space from those drives to construct what will appear to be a single drive. The following list includes the various types of volume sets and their definitions:

- *Simple volume* uses only one disk or a portion of a disk.

- *Spanned volume* is a simple volume that spans multiple disks, with a maximum of 32. Use a spanned volume if the volume needs are too great for a single disk.

- *Striped volume* stores data in stripes across two or more disks. A striped volume gives you fast access to data but is not fault tolerant, nor can it be extended or mirrored. If one disk in the striped set fails, the entire volume fails.

- *Mirrored volume* duplicates data across two disks. This type of volume is fault tolerant because if one drive fails, the data on the other disk is unaffected.

- *RAID-5 volume* stores data in stripes across three or more disks. This type of volume is fault tolerant because if a drive fails, the data can be re-created from the parity off of the remaining disk drives. Operating system files and boot files cannot reside on the RAID-5 disks.

Exercise 1.5 illustrates the procedure for creating a volume set.

Creating a Volume Set

1.   Open Computer Management under Administrative Tools.

2.   Select Disk Management.

3. Select and right-click a disk that has unallocated space. If there are no disk drives available for a particular volume set, that volume set will be grayed out as a selectable option. In this exercise, you'll choose a spanned volume set, but the process after the volume set selection is the same regardless of which kind you choose. The only thing that differs is the number of disk drives chosen.

4. The Welcome page of the New Spanned Volume Wizard appears and explains the type of volume set chosen. Click Next.

5. The Select Disks page appears. Select the disk that will be included with the volume set and click Add. Repeat this process until all of the desired disks have been added. Click Next.

6. The Assign Drive Letter Or Path page appears. From here you can select the desired drive letter for the volume, mount the volume in an empty NTFS folder, or choose not to assign a drive letter. The new volume is labeled as E. Click Next.

7. The Format Volume page appears. Choose to format the new volume. Click Next.

8. Click Finish.

9. If the disks have not been converted to dynamic, you will be asked to convert the disks. Click Yes.

The new volume will appear as a healthy spanned dynamic volume with the new available disk space of the new volume set.

Storage Spaces in Windows Server 2012 R2

Windows Server 2012 R2 includes a technology called *Storage Spaces*. Windows Server 2012 R2 allows an administrator to virtualize storage by grouping disks into storage pools. These storage pools can then be turned into virtual disks called *storage spaces*.

The Storage Spaces technology allows an administrator to have a highly available, scalable, low-cost, and flexible solution for both physical and virtual installations. Storage Spaces allows you to set up this advantage on either a single server or in scalable multinode mode. So, before going any further, let's look at these two terms that you must understand.

Storage Pools   *Storage pools* are a group of physical disks that allows an administrator to delegate administration, expand disk sizes, and group disks together.

Storage Spaces   *Storage spaces* allow an administrator to take free space from storage pools and create virtual disks called storage spaces. Storage spaces give administrators the ability to have precise control, resiliency, and storage tiers.

Storage spaces and storage pools can be managed by an administrator through the use of the Windows Storage Management API, Server Manager, or Windows PowerShell.

One of the advantages of using the Storage Spaces technology is the ability to set up resiliency. There are three types of Storage Space resiliency: mirror, parity, and simple (no resiliency).

Fault tolerance (RAID) is discussed in detail in the "Redundant Array of Independent Disks" section.

Now that you understand what storage spaces and storage pools do, let's take a look at some of the other advantages of using these features in Windows Server 2012 R2.

Availability   One advantage to the Storage Spaces technology is the ability to fully integrate the storage space with failover clustering. This advantage allows administrators to achieve service deployments that are continuously available. Administrators have the ability to set up storage pools to be clustered across multiple nodes within a single cluster.

Tiered Storage   The Storage Spaces technology allows virtual disks to be created with a two-tier storage setup. For data that is used often, you have an SSD tier; for data that is not used often, you use an HDD tier. The Storage Spaces technology will automatically transfer data at a subfile level between the two different tiers based on how often the data is used. Because of tiered storage, performance is greatly increased for data that is used most often, and data that is not used often still gets the advantage of being stored on a low-cost storage option.

Delegation   One advantage of using storage pools is that administrators have the ability to control access by using access control lists (ACLs). What is nice about this advantage is that each storage pool can have its own unique access control lists. Storage pools are fully integrated with Active Directory Domain Services.

Redundant Array of Independent Disks

The ability to support drive sets and arrays using *Redundant Array of Independent Disks (RAID)* technology is built into Windows Server 2012 R2. RAID can be used to enhance data performance, or it can be used to provide fault tolerance to maintain data integrity in case of a hard disk failure. Windows Server 2012 R2 supports three types of RAID technologies: RAID-0, RAID-1, and RAID-5.

RAID-0 (Disk Striping)   *Disk striping* is using two or more volumes on independent disks created as a single striped set. There can be a maximum of 32 disks. In a striped set, data is divided into blocks that are distributed sequentially across all of the drives in the set. With RAID-0 disk striping, you get very fast read and write performance because multiple blocks of data can be accessed from multiple drives simultaneously. However, RAID-0 does not offer the ability to maintain data integrity during a single disk failure. In other words, RAID-0 is not fault tolerant; a single disk event will cause the entire striped set to be lost, and it will have to be re-created through some type of recovery process, such as a tape backup.

RAID-1 (Disk Mirroring)   *Disk mirroring* is two logical volumes on two separate identical disks created as a duplicate disk set. Data is written on two disks at the same time; that way, in the event of a disk failure, data integrity is maintained and available. Although this fault tolerance gives administrators data redundancy, it comes with a price because it diminishes the amount of available storage space by half. For example, if an administrator wants to create a 300GB mirrored set, they would have to install two 300GB hard drives into the server, thus doubling the cost for the same available space.

RAID-5 Volume (Disk Striping with Parity) With a RAID-5 volume, you have the ability to use a minimum of three disks and a maximum of 32 disks. RAID-5 volumes allow data to be striped across all of the disks with an additional block of error-correction called parity. *Parity* is used to reconstruct the data in the event of a disk failure. RAID-5 has slower write performance than the other RAID types because the OS must calculate the parity information for each stripe that is written, but the read performance is equivalent to a stripe set, RAID-0, because the parity information is not read. Like RAID-1, RAID-5 comes with additional cost considerations. For every RAID-5 set, roughly an entire hard disk is consumed for storing the parity information. For example, a minimum RAID-5 set requires three hard disks, and if those disks are 300GB each, approximately 600GB of disk space is available to the OS and 300GB is consumed by parity information, which equates to 33.3 percent of the available space. Similarly, in a five-disk RAID-5 set of 300GB disks, approximately 1,200GB of disk space is available to the OS, which means that 20 percent of the total available space is consumed by the parity information. The words *roughly* and *approximately* are used when calculating disk space because a 300GB disk will really be only about 279GB of space. This is because vendors define a gigabyte as 1 billion bytes, but the OS defines it as 2^{30} (1,073,741,824) bytes. Also, remember that file systems and volume managers have overhead as well.

 Software RAID is a nice option for a small company, but hardware RAID is definitely a better option if the money is available.

Table 1.4 breaks down the various aspects of the supported RAID types in Window Server 2012 R2.

TABLE 1.4 Supported RAID-level properties in Windows Server 2012 R2

RAID Level	RAID Type	Fault Tolerant	Advantages	Minimum Number of Disks	Maximum Number of Disks
0	Disk striping	No	Fast reads and writes	2	32
1	Disk mirroring	Yes	Data redundancy and faster writes than RAID-5	2	2
5	Disk striping with parity	Yes	Data redundancy with less overhead and faster reads than RAID-1	3	32

Creating RAID Sets

Now that you understand the concepts of RAID and how to use it, you can look at the creation of RAID sets in Windows Server 2012 R2. The process of creating a RAID set is the same as the process for creating a simple or spanned volume set, except for the minimum disk requirements associated with each RAID type.

Creating a mirrored volume set is basically the same as creating a volume set, as shown in Exercise 1.6, except that you will select New Mirrored Volume. It is after the disk select wizard appears that you'll begin to see the difference. Since a new mirrored volume is being created, the volume requires two disks.

During the disk select process, if only one disk is selected, the Next button will be unavailable because the disk minimum has not been met. Refer to Figure 1.3 to view the Select Disks page of the New Mirrored Volume Wizard during the creation of a new mirrored volume, and notice that the Next button is not available.

FIGURE 1.3 Select Disks page of the New Mirrored Volume Wizard

To complete the process, you must select a second disk by highlighting the appropriate disk and adding it to the volume set. Once the second disk has been added, the Add button becomes unavailable, and the Next button is available to complete the mirrored volume set creation (see Figure 1.4).

FIGURE 1.4   Adding the second disk to complete a mirrored volume set

After you click Next, the creation of the mirrored volume set is again just like the rest of the steps in Exercise 1.5. A drive letter will have to be assigned, and the volume will need to be formatted. The new mirrored volume set will appear in Disk Management. In Figure 1.5, notice that the capacity of the volume equals one disk even though two disks have been selected.

FIGURE 1.5   Newly created mirrored volume set

To create a RAID-5 volume set, you use the same process that you use to create a mirrored volume set. The only difference is that a RAID-5 volume set requires that a minimum of three disks be selected to complete the volume creation. The process is simple: Select New RAID-5 Volume, select the three disks that will be used in the volume set, assign a drive letter, and format the volume. Figure 1.6 shows a newly created RAID-5 volume set in Disk Management.

FIGURE 1.6   Newly created RAID-5 volume set

Mount Points

With the ever-increasing demands of storage, mount points are used to surpass the limitation of 26 drive letters and to join two volumes into a folder on a separate physical disk drive. A *mount point* allows you to configure a volume to be accessed from a folder on another existing disk.

Through Disk Management, a mount point folder can be assigned to a drive instead of using a drive letter, and it can be used on basic or dynamic volumes that are formatted with NTFS. However, mount point folders can be created only on empty folders within a volume. Additionally, mount point folder paths cannot be modified; they can be removed only once they have been created. Exercise 1.6 shows the steps to create a mount point.

EXERCISE 1.6

Creating Mount Points

1. Open Server Manager.

2. Click and then expand Storage.

3. Select Disk Management.

4. Right-click the volume where the mount point folder will be assigned, and select Change Drive Letter And Paths.

5. Click Add.

6. Either type the path to an empty folder on an NTFS volume or click Browse to select or make a new folder for the mount point.

When you explore the drive, you'll see the new folder created. Notice that the icon indicates that it is a mount point.

Microsoft MPIO

Multipath I/O (MPIO) is associated with high availability because a computer will be able to use a solution with redundant physical paths connected to a storage device. Thus, if one path fails, an application will continue to run because it can access the data across the other path.

The MPIO software provides the functionality needed for the computer to take advantage of the redundant storage paths. MPIO solutions can also load-balance data traffic across both paths to the storage device, virtually eliminating bandwidth bottlenecks to the computer. What allows MPIO to provide this functionality is the new native *Microsoft Device Specific Module (Microsoft DSM)*. The Microsoft DSM is a driver that communicates with storage devices—iSCSI, Fibre Channel, or SAS—and it provides the chosen load-balancing policies. Windows Server 2012 R2 supports the following load-balancing policies:

Failover   In a failover configuration, there is no load balancing. There is a primary path that is established for all requests and subsequent standby paths. If the primary path fails, one of the standby paths will be used.

Failback   This is similar to failover in that it has primary and standby paths. However, with failback you designate a preferred path that will handle all process requests until it fails, after which the standby path will become active until the primary reestablishes a connection and automatically regains control.

Round Robin   In a round-robin configuration, all available paths will be active and will be used to distribute I/O in a balanced round-robin fashion.

Round Robin with a Subset of Paths   In this configuration, a specific set of paths will be designated as a primary set and another as standby paths. All I/O will use the primary set of paths in a round-robin fashion until all of the sets fail. Only at this time will the standby paths become active.

Dynamic Least Queue Depth   In a dynamic least queue depth configuration, I/O will route to the path with the least number of outstanding requests.

Weighted Path   In a weighted path configuration, paths are assigned a numbered weight. I/O requests will use the path with the least weight—the higher the number, the lower the priority.

Exercise 1.7 demonstrates the process of installing the Microsoft MPIO feature for Windows Server 2012 R2.

EXERCISE 1.7

Installing Microsoft MPIO

1. Choose Server Manager by clicking the Server Manager icon on the Taskbar.

2. Click number 2, Add Roles And Features.

3. Choose role-based or feature-based installation and click Next.

4. Choose your server and click Next.

5. Click Next on the Roles screen.

6. On the Select Features screen, choose the Multipath I/O check box. Click Next.

7. On the Confirm Installation Selections page, verify that Multipath I/O is the feature that will be installed. Click Install.

8. After the installation completes, the Installation Results page appears stating that the server must be rebooted to finish the installation process.

9. Click Close.

10. Restart the system.

Typically, most storage arrays work with the Microsoft DSM. However, some hardware vendors require DSM software that is specific to their products. Third-party DSM software is installed through the MPIO utility as follows:

1. Open Administrative Tools ➤ MPIO.

2. Select the DSM Install tab (see Figure 1.7).

FIGURE 1.7   The DSM Install tab in the MPIO Properties dialog box

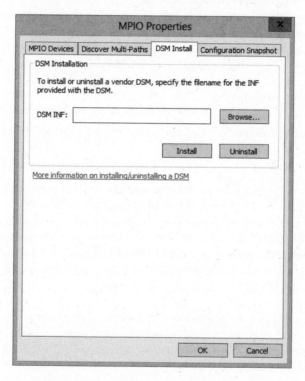

3. Add the path of the INF file and click Install.

iSCSI

Internet Small Computer System Interface (iSCSI) is an interconnect protocol used to establish and manage a connection between a computer (initiator) and a storage device (target). It does this by using a connection through TCP port 3260, which allows it to be used over a LAN, a WAN, or the Internet. Each initiator is identified by its iSCSI Qualified Name (iqn), and it is used to establish its connection to an iSCSI target.

iSCSI was developed to allow block-level access to a storage device over a network. This is different from using a network attached storage (NAS) device that connects through the use of Common Internet File System (CIFS) or Network File System (NFS).

Block-level access is important to many applications that require direct access to storage. Microsoft Exchange and Microsoft SQL are examples of applications that require direct access to storage.

By being able to leverage the existing network infrastructure, iSCSI was also developed as an alternative to Fibre Channel storage by alleviating the additional hardware costs associated with a Fibre Channel storage solution.

iSCSI also has another advantage over Fibre Channel in that it can provide security for the storage devices. iSCSI can use Challenge Handshake Authentication Protocol (CHAP or MS-CHAP) for authentication and Internet Protocol Security (IPsec) for encryption. Windows Server 2012 R2 is able to connect an iSCSI storage device out of the box with no additional software needing to be installed. This is because the Microsoft iSCSI initiator is built into the operating system.

Windows Server 2012 R2 supports two different ways to initiate an iSCSI session.

- Through the native Microsoft iSCSI software initiator that resides on Windows Server 2012 R2

- Using a hardware iSCSI host bus adapter (HBA) that is installed in the computer

Both the Microsoft iSCSI software initiator and iSCSI HBA present an iSCSI qualified name that identifies the host initiator. When the Microsoft iSCSI software initiator is used, the CPU utilization may be as much as 30 percent higher than on a computer with a hardware iSCSI HBA. This is because all of the iSCSI process requests are handled within the operating system. Using a hardware iSCSI HBA, process requests can be offloaded to the adapter, thus freeing the CPU overhead associated with the Microsoft iSCSI software initiator. However, iSCSI HBAs can be expensive, whereas the Microsoft iSCSI software initiator is free.

It is worthwhile to install the Microsoft iSCSI software initiator and perform load testing to see how much overhead the computer will have prior to purchasing an iSCSI HBA or HBAs, depending on the redundancy level. Exercise 1.8 explains how to install and configure an iSCSI connection.

EXERCISE 1.8

Configuring iSCSI Storage Connection

1. Click the Windows key or Start button in the left-hand corner ➢ Administrative Tools ➢ iSCSI Initiator.

2. If a dialog box appears, click Yes to start the service.

3. Click the Discovery tab.

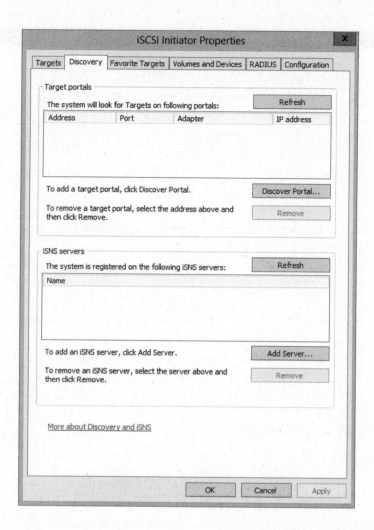

4.   In the Target Portals portion of the page, click Discover Portal.

5.   Enter the IP address of the target portal and click OK.

6. The IP address of the target portal appears in the Target Portals box.

7. Click OK.

To use the storage that has now been presented to the server, you must create a volume on it and format the space. Refer to Exercise 1.3 to review this process.

Internet Storage Name Service

Internet Storage Name Service (iSNS) allows for central registration of an iSCSI environment because it automatically discovers available targets on the network. The purpose of iSNS is to help find available targets on a large iSCSI network.

The Microsoft iSCSI initiator includes an iSNS client that is used to register with the iSNS. The iSNS feature maintains a database of clients that it has registered either through DCHP discovery or through manual registration. iSNS DHCP is available after the installation of the service, and it is used to allow iSNS clients to discover the location of the iSNS. However, if iSNS DHCP is not configured, iSNS clients must be registered manually with the `iscsicli` command.

To execute the command, launch a command prompt on a computer hosting the Microsoft iSCSI and type `iscsicli addisnsserver` *server_name*, where *server_name* is the name of the computer hosting iSNS. Exercise 1.9 walks you through the steps required to install the iSNS feature on Windows Server 2012 R2, and then it explains the different tabs in iSNS.

EXERCISE 1.9

Installing the iSNS Feature on Windows Server 2012 R2

1. Choose Server Manager by clicking the Server Manager icon on the Taskbar.

2. Click number 2 ➢ Add Roles And Features.

3. Choose role-based or featured-based installation and click Next.

4. Choose your server and click Next.

5. Click Next on the Roles screen.

6. On the Select Features screen, choose the iSNS Server Service check box. Click Next.

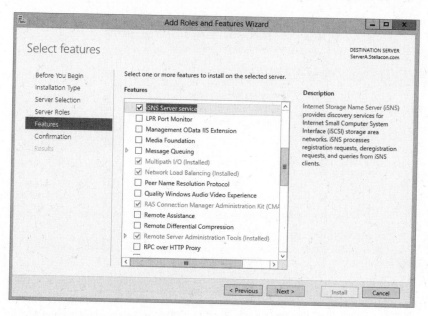

7. On the Confirmation screen, click the Install button.

8. Click the Close button. Close Server Manager and reboot.

9. Log in and open the iSNS server under Administrative Tools.

10. Click the General tab. This tab displays the list of registered initiators and targets. In addition to their iSCSI qualified name, it lists storage node type (Target or Initiator), alias string, and entity identifier (the Fully Qualified Domain Name [FQDN] of the machine hosting the iSNS client).

11. Click the Discovery Domains tab. The purpose of Discovery Domains is to provide a way to separate and group nodes. This is similar to zoning in Fibre Channel. The following options are available on the Discovery Domains tab:

- *Create* is used to create a new discovery domain.

- *Refresh* is used to repopulate the Discovery Domain drop-down list.

- *Delete* is used to delete the currently selected discovery domain.

- *Add* is used to add nodes that are already registered in iSNS to the currently selected discovery domain.

- *Add New* is used to add nodes by entering the iSCSI Qualified Name (iQN) of the node. These nodes do not have to be currently registered.

- *Remove Used* is used to remove selected nodes from the discovery domain.

12. Click the Discovery Domain Sets tab. The purpose of discovery domain sets is to separate further discovery domains. Discovery domains can be enabled or disabled, giving administrators the ability to restrict further the visibility of all initiators and targets. The options on the Discovery Domain Sets tab are as follows:

- The *Enable* check box is used to indicate the status of the discovery domain sets and to turn them off and on.

- *Create* is used to create new discovery domain sets.

- *Refresh* is used to repopulate the Discovery Domain Sets drop-down list.

- *Delete* is used to delete the currently selected discovery domain set.

- *Add* is used to add discovery domains to the currently selected discovery domain set.

- *Remove* is used to remove selected nodes from the discovery domain sets.

13. Close the iSNS server.

Fibre Channel

Fibre Channel storage devices are similar to iSCSI storage devices in that they both allow block-level access to their data sets and can provide MPIO policies with the proper hardware configurations. However, Fibre Channel requires a Fibre Channel HBA, fiber-optic cables, and Fibre Channel switches to connect to a storage device.

A *World Wide Name (WWN)* from the Fibre Channel HBA is used from the host and device so that they can communicate directly with each other, similar to using a NIC's MAC address. In other words, a logical unit number (LUN) is presented from a Fibre

Channel storage device to the WWN of the host's HBA. Fibre Channel has been the preferred method of storage because of the available connection bandwidth between the storage and the host.

Fibre Channel devices support 1Gb/s, 2Gb/s, and 4Gb/s connections, and they soon will support 8Gb/s connections, but now that 10Gb/s Ethernet networks are becoming more prevalent in many datacenters, iSCSI can be a suitable alternative. It is important to consider that 10Gb/s network switches can be more expensive than comparable Fibre Channel switches.

N-Port Identification Virtualization (NPIV) is a Fibre Channel facility allowing multiple n-port IDs to share a single physical N-Port. This allows multiple Fibre Channel initiators to occupy a single physical port. By using a single port, this eases hardware requirements in storage area network (SAN) design.

Network Attached Storage

The concept of a *network attached storage (NAS)* solution is that it is a low-cost device for storing data and serving files through the use of an Ethernet LAN connection. A NAS device accesses data at the file level via a communication protocol such as NFS, CIFS, or even HTTP, which is different from iSCSI or FC Fibre Channel storage devices that access the data at the block level. NAS devices are best used in file-storing applications, and they do not require a storage expert to install and maintain the device. In most cases, the only setup that is required is an IP address and an Ethernet connection.

Virtual Disk Service

Virtual Disk Service (VDS) was created to ease the administrative efforts involved in managing all of the various types of storage devices. Many storage hardware providers used their own applications for installation and management, and this made administering all of these various devices very cumbersome.

VDS is a set of application programming interfaces (APIs) that provides a centralized interface for managing all of the various storage devices. The native VDS API enables the management of disks and volumes at an OS level, and hardware vendor-supplied APIs manage the storage devices at a RAID level. These are known as software and hardware providers.

A *software provider* is host based, and it interacts with Plug and Play Manager because each disk is discovered and operates on volumes, disks, and disk partitions. VDS includes two software providers: basic and dynamic. The basic software provider manages basic disks with no fault tolerance, whereas the dynamic software providers manage dynamic disks with fault management. A hardware provider translates the VDS APIs into instructions specific to the storage hardware. This is how storage management applications are able to communicate with the storage hardware to create LUNs or Fibre Channel HBAs to view the WWN. The following are Windows Server 2012 R2 storage management applications that use VDS:

- The *Disk Management snap-in* is an application that allows you to configure and manage the disk drives on the host computer. You have already seen this application in use when you initialized disks and created volume sets.

- DiskPart is a command-line utility that configures and manages disks, volumes, and partitions on the host computer. It can also be used to script many of the storage management commands. DiskPart is a robust tool that you should study on your own because it is beyond the scope of this book. Figure 1.8 shows the various commands and their function in the DiskPart utility.

FIGURE 1.8 DiskPart commands

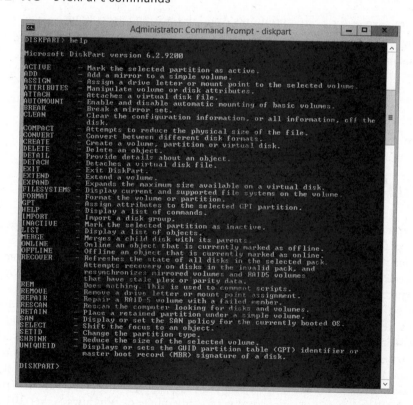

- DiskRAID is also a scriptable command-line utility that configures and manages hardware RAID storage systems. However, at least one VDS hardware provider must be installed for DiskRAID to be functional. DiskRAID is another useful utility that you should study on your own because it's beyond the scope of this book.

Booting from a VHD

Once you have installed each operating system, you can choose the operating system that you will boot to during the boot process. You will see a boot selection screen that asks you to choose which operating system you want to boot.

The Boot Configuration Data (BCD) store contains boot information parameters that were previously found in boot.ini in older versions of Windows. To edit the boot options in the BCD store, use the bcdedit utility, which can be launched only from a command prompt. To open a command prompt window, do the following:

1. Launch \Windows\system32\cmd.exe.

2. Open the Run command by pressing the Windows key plus the R key and then entering **cmd**.

3. Type **cmd.exe** in the Search Programs And Files box and press Enter.

After the command prompt window is open, type **bcdedit** to launch the bcdedit utility. You can also type **bcdedit /?** to see all of the different bcdedit commands.

 Virtualization is covered in greater detail in Chapter 9: "Use Virtualization in Windows Server 2012."

Summary

In this chapter, you studied the latest advantages of using Windows Server 2012 R2. You also learned about the different roles and features you can install on a Windows Server 2012 R2 machine. You also explored how to migrate those roles and features from a Windows Server 2008, 2008 R2, and Windows Server 2012 machine to a Windows Server 2012 R2 machine.

I discussed the different upgrade paths that are available and which upgrades are best for your current network setup. You learned that another important issue to decide when installing Windows Server 2012 R2 is whether to use Server Core or the GUI installation.

You learned how to install Windows Server 2012 R2 Datacenter with GUI, and you installed the Windows Server 2012 R2 Server Core. Remember, Server Core is a slimmed-down version of Windows Server. With no GUI desktop available, it's a safer alternative to a normal Windows install. As discussed, a nice advantage of Windows Server 2012 R2 is that you can change from Server Core to the GUI version and back again.

I discussed a feature called Features On Demand. This feature allows you to remove roles and features from the operating system and remove the associated files completely from the hard drive, thus saving disk space.

You examined the various aspects of Windows Server 2012 R2 storage services as well as the various types of storage technologies and native Windows Server 2012 R2 storage management tools. I started the chapter by discussing initializing disks and choosing a partition type: MBR or GPT. I then discussed the types of disk configurations, dynamic and basic, that are supported in Windows Server 2012 R2. You learned that various properties are associated with each type of configuration. Then I discussed the different types of RAID and the properties of each.

The next section explored storage technologies, namely, iSCSI, Fibre Channel, and NAS. I primarily focused on iSCSI because of the native support in Window Server 2012 R2. You learned how to configure an iSCSI initiator and a connection to an iSCSI target. After that, you looked at its iSNS server and how to configure it.

The chapter concluded by looking at Storage Manager for SANs and Storage Explorer, which are built-in management tools in Windows Server 2012 R2 for storage devices and firewall settings.

Exam Essentials

Understand the upgrade paths.   It's important to make sure you understand the different upgrade paths from Windows Server 2008 R2 with SP1 and Windows Server 2012 to Windows Server 2012 R2.

Understand Windows Server 2012 R2 server roles.   Understand what the Windows Server 2012 R2 server roles do for an organization and its users.

Understand Windows Server 2012 R2 GUI vs. Server Core.   Understand the difference between the Windows Server 2012 R2 GUI version and the Windows Server 2012 R2 Server Core version. Know the benefits of using Server Core, and know that you can convert between the two different versions.

Understand Features On Demand.   Understand the new feature called Features On Demand. Microsoft loves to ask exam questions about its new features, and this will be no exception. Understand how features and roles stay on the system until you physically remove them from the hard drive.

Know disk types.   Know how to initialize disks and the type of partitioning to choose. Also know the difference between dynamic and basic disks and when to use them.

Understand RAID.   Know the various RAID types, the requirements for each, and when it is appropriate to use each type.

Know storage technologies.   Understand how to use the storage technologies Fibre Channel, iSCSI, and NAS. Know how to configure an iSCSI initiator and how to establish a connection to a target. Know the various MPIO policies.

Understand how to manage storage.   Know what type of administrative features are available for Storage Manager for SANs and Storage Explorer.

Review Questions

1. You are the administrator for the ABC Company. You are looking to install Windows Server 2012 R2, and you need to decide which version to install. You need to install a version of Windows that is just for logon authentication and nothing else. You want the most secure option and cost is not an issue. What should you install?

   A. Windows Server 2012 R2 Datacenter with GUI

   B. Windows Server 2012 R2 Datacenter Server Core

   C. Windows Server 2012 R2 Standard with GUI

   D. Windows Server 2012 R2 Web Server Core

2. You are the IT manager for a large organization. One of your co-workers installed a new Windows Server 2012 R2 Datacenter Server Core machine, but now the IT team has decided that it should be a Windows Server 2012 R2 Datacenter with GUI. What should you do?

   A. Reinstall Windows Server 2012 R2 Datacenter Server Core on the same machine.

   B. Install a new machine with Windows Server 2012 R2 Datacenter Server Core.

   C. Convert the current Windows Server 2012 R2 Datacenter Server Core to the Windows Server 2012 R2 Datacenter with GUI version.

   D. Dual-boot the machine with both Windows Server 2012 R2 Datacenter Server Core and Windows Server 2012 R2 Datacenter with GUI.

3. You are the administrator for your company, and you are looking at upgrading your Windows Server 2008 web server to Windows Server 2012 R2. Which version of Windows Server 2012 R2 does Microsoft recommend you use?

   A. Windows Server 2012 R2 Datacenter

   B. Windows Server 2012 R2 Standard

   C. Windows Server 2012 R2 Essentials

   D. Windows Server 2012 R2 Foundation

4. You are looking at upgrading your Windows Server 2008 R2 Enterprise with SP2 machine to Windows Server 2012 R2. Your organization is considering virtualizing its entire server room, which has 25 servers. To which version of Windows Server 2012 R2 would you upgrade?

   A. Windows Server 2012 R2 Datacenter

   B. Windows Server 2012 R2 Standard

   C. Windows Server 2012 R2 Essentials

   D. Windows Server 2012 R2 Foundation

5. You have been hired to help a small company set up its first Windows network. It has had the same 13 users for the entire two years it has been open, and the company has no plans to expand. What version of Windows Server 2012 R2 would you recommend?

   A. Windows Server 2012 R2 Datacenter

   B. Windows Server 2012 R2 Standard

   C. Windows Server 2012 R2 Essentials

   D. Windows Server 2012 R2 Foundation

6. You have been hired to help a small company set up its Windows network. It has 20 users, and it has no plans to expand. What version of Windows Server 2012 R2 would you recommend?

   A. Windows Server 2012 R2 Datacenter

   B. Windows Server 2012 R2 Standard

   C. Windows Server 2012 R2 Essentials

   D. Windows Server 2012 R2 Foundation

7. Which of the following are benefits of using Windows Server 2012 R2 Server Core? (Choose all that apply.)

   A. Reduced management

   B. Minimal maintenance

   C. Smaller footprint

   D. Tighter security

8. You are a server administrator, and you are trying to save hard drive space on your Windows Server 2012 R2 Datacenter machine. Which feature can help you save hard disk space?

   A. HDSaver.exe

   B. Features On Demand

   C. ADDS

   D. WinRM

9. You have a server named SRV1 that runs Windows Server 2012 R2. You want to remove Windows Explorer, Windows Internet Explorer, and all components and files from this machine. Which command should you run?

   A. msiexec.exe /uninstall iexplore.exe /x

   B. msiexec.exe /uninstall explorer.exe /x

   C. Uninstall-WindowsFeature Server-Gui-Mgmt-Infra Remove

   D. Uninstall-WindowsFeature Server-Gui-Shell Remove

10. What type of domain controller would you install into an area where physical security is a concern?

    A. Primary domain controller

    B. Backup domain controller

    C. Read-only domain controller

    D. Locked-down domain controller

Chapter

2

Configure Network Services

THE FOLLOWING 70-410 EXAM OBJECTIVES ARE COVERED IN THIS CHAPTER:

✓ **Deploy and configure DNS service**

- Configure Active Directory integration of primary zones
- Configure forwarders
- Configure Root Hints
- Manage DNS cache
- Create A and PTR resource records

✓ **Deploy and configure Dynamic Host Configuration Protocol (DHCP) service**

- Create and configure scopes
- Configure a DHCP reservation
- Configure DHCP options
- Configure client and server for PXE boot
- Configure DHCP relay agent
- Authorize DHCP server

The Domain Name System (DNS) is one of the key topics that you'll need to understand if you plan to take any of the Microsoft Windows Server 2012 R2 administration exams (70-410, 70-411, 70-412, and so forth).

It's also imperative that you understand DNS to work with Active Directory because it requires DNS to function properly, and many important system functions (including Kerberos authentication and finding domain controllers) are handled through DNS lookups. Windows 2000, Windows XP, Windows Vista, Windows 7, and Windows 8 clients use DNS for name resolution and to find Kerberos key distribution centers (KDCs), global catalog servers, and other services that may be registered in DNS.

By the time you complete this chapter, you will have a deeper understanding of how DNS works and how to set up, configure, manage, and troubleshoot DNS in Microsoft Windows Server 2012 R2.

In this chapter, you'll also learn how to install and manage DHCP, including how to set up plain DHCP scopes, superscopes, and multicast scopes. You'll also learn how to set up integration between Dynamic DNS and DHCP and how to authorize a DHCP server to integrate with Active Directory.

There are two versions of DHCP: DHCP v4 and DHCP v6. In this chapter, I will just say "DHCP server" when referring to the physical DHCP server. If I am referring to a specific version of DHCP, I will specify the version.

Introducing DNS

The *Domain Name System (DNS)* is a service that allows you to resolve a hostname to an Internet Protocol (IP) address. One of the inherent complexities of operating in networked environments is working with multiple protocols and network addresses. Owing largely to the tremendous rise in the popularity of the Internet, however, most environments have transitioned to use *Transmission Control Protocol/Internet Protocol (TCP/IP)* as their primary networking protocol. Microsoft is no exception when it comes to supporting TCP/IP in its workstation and server products. All current versions of Microsoft's operating systems support TCP/IP, as do most other modern operating systems.

An easy way to understand DNS is to think about making a telephone call. If you wanted to call Microsoft and did not know the phone number, you could call information, tell them the name (Microsoft), and get the telephone number. You would then make the call. Now think about trying to connect to Server1. You don't know the TCP/IP number (the computer's telephone number), so your computer asks DNS (information) for the number of Server1. DNS returns the number, and your system makes the connection (call). DNS is your network's 411, or information, and it returns the TCP/IP data for your network.

TCP/IP is actually a collection of different technologies (protocols and services) that allow computers to function together on a single, large, and heterogeneous network. Some of the major advantages of this protocol include widespread support for hardware, software, and network devices; reliance on a system of standards; and scalability. TCP handles tasks such as sequenced acknowledgments. IP involves many jobs, such as logical subnet assignment and routing.

The Form of an IP Address

To understand DNS, you must first understand how TCP/IP addresses are formed. Because DNS is strictly on a network to support TCP/IP, understanding the basics of TCP/IP is extremely important.

 Microsoft exams cover TCP/IP. The TCP/IP material will be covered in Chapter 8, "Configure TCP/IP."

An *IP address* is a logical number that uniquely identifies a computer on a TCP/IP network. TCP/IP allows a computer packet to reach the correct host. Windows Server 2012 R2 works with two versions of TCP/IP: IPv4 and IPv6. An IPv4 address takes the form of four octets (eight binary bits), each of which is represented by a decimal number between 0 and 255. The four numbers are separated by decimal points. For example, all of the following are valid IP addresses:

- 128.45.23.17
- 230.212.43.100
- 10.1.1.1

The dotted decimal notation was created to make it easier for users to deal with IP addresses, but this idea did not go far enough. As a result, another abstraction layer was developed, which used names to represent the dotted decimal notation—the domain name. For example, the IP address 11000000 10101000 00000001 00010101 maps to 192.168.1.21, which in turn might map to `server1.company.org`, which is how the computer's address is usually presented to the user or application.

As stated earlier, IPv4 addresses are made up of octets, or the decimal (base 10) representation of 8 bits. It takes four octets to add up to the 32 bits required. IPv6 expands the address space to 128 bits. The address is usually represented in hexadecimal notation as follows:

```
2001:0DB8:0000:0000:1234:0000:A9FE:133E
```

You can tell that the implementation of DNS would make life a lot easier for everyone, even those of us who like to use alphanumeric values. (For example, some of us enjoy pinging the address in lieu of the name.) Fortunately, DNS already has the ability to handle IPv6 addresses using an AAAA record. An A record in IPv4's addressing space is 32 bits, and an AAAA record (4 *A*s) in IPv6's is 128 bits.

Nowadays, most computer users are quite familiar with navigating to DNS-based resources, such as www.microsoft.com. To resolve these "friendly" names to TCP/IP addresses that the network stack can use, you need a method for mapping them. Originally, ASCII flat files (often called HOSTS files, as shown in Figure 2.1) were used for this purpose. In some cases, they are still used today in small networks, and they can be useful in helping to troubleshoot name resolution problems.

FIGURE 2.1   HOSTS file

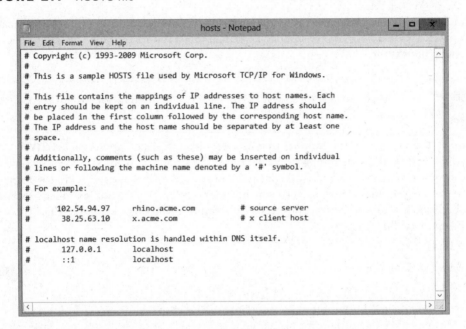

As the number of machines and network devices grew, it became unwieldy for administrators to manage all of the manual updates required to enter new mappings to a master HOSTS file and distribute it. Clearly, a better system was needed.

As you can see from the sample HOSTS file in Figure 2.1, you can conduct a quick test of the email server's name resolution as follows:

1. Open the HOSTS file: C:\Windows\Systems32\drivers\etc.

2. Add the IP-address-to-hostname mapping.

3. Try to ping the server using the hostname to verify that you can reach it using an easy-to-remember name.

Following these steps should drive home the concept of DNS for you because you can see it working to make your life easier. Now you don't have to remember 10.0.0.10; you only need to remember exchange03. However, you can also see how this method can become unwieldy if you have many hosts that want to use easy-to-remember names instead of IP addresses to locate resources on your network.

When dealing with large networks, users and network administrators must be able to locate the resources they require with minimal searching. Users don't care about the actual physical or logical network address of the machine; they just want to be able to connect to it using a simple name that they can remember.

From a network administrator's standpoint, however, each machine must have its own logical address that makes it part of the network on which it resides. Therefore, some scalable and easy-to-manage method for resolving a machine's logical name to an IP address and then to a domain name is required. DNS was created just for this purpose.

DNS is a hierarchically distributed database. In other words, its layers are arranged in a definite order, and its data is distributed across a wide range of machines, each of which can exert control over a portion of the database. DNS is a standard set of protocols that defines the following:

- A mechanism for querying and updating address information in the database

- A mechanism for replicating the information in the database among servers

- A schema of the database

 DNS is defined by a number of requests for comments (RFCs), though primarily by RFC 1034 and RFC 1035.

DNS was originally developed in the early days of the Internet (called ARPAnet at the time) when it was a small network created by the Department of Defense for research purposes. Before DNS, computer names, or hostnames, were manually entered into a HOSTS file located on a centrally administered server. Each site that needed to resolve hostnames outside of its organization had to download this file. As the number of computers on the Internet grew, so did the size of this HOSTS file—and along with it the problems of its management. The need for a new system that would offer features such as scalability, decentralized administration, and support for various data types became more and more obvious. DNS, introduced in 1984, became this new system.

With DNS, the hostnames reside in a database that can be distributed among multiple servers, decreasing the load on any one server and providing the ability to administer this naming system on a per-partition basis. DNS supports hierarchical names and allows for the registration of various data types in addition to the hostname-to-IP-address mapping used in HOSTS files. Database performance is ensured through its distributed nature as well as through caching.

The DNS distributed database establishes an inverted logical tree structure called the *domain namespace*. Each node, or domain, in that space has a unique name. At the top of the tree is the root. This may not sound quite right, which is why the DNS hierarchical model is described as being an inverted tree, with the root at the top. The root is represented by the null set "". When written, the root node is represented by a single dot (.).

Each node in the DNS can branch out to any number of nodes below it. For example, below the root node are a number of other nodes, commonly referred to as *top-level domains (TLDs)*. These are the familiar .com, .net, .org, .gov, .edu, and other such names. Table 2.1 lists some of these TLDs.

TABLE 2.1 Common top-level DNS domains

Common top-level domain names	Type of organization
com	Commercial (for example, stellacon.com for Stellacon Training Corporation).
edu	Educational (for example, gatech.edu for the Georgia Institute of Technology)
gov	Government (for example, whitehouse.gov for the White House in Washington, D.C.)
int	International organizations (for example, nato.int for NATO); this top-level domain is fairly rare
mil	Military organizations (for example, usmc.mil for the Marine Corps); there is a separate set of root name servers for this domain
net	Networking organizations and Internet providers (for example, hiwaay.net for HiWAAY Information Systems); many commercial organizations have registered names under this domain too
org	Noncommercial organizations (for example, fidonet.org for FidoNet)
au	Australia
uk	United Kingdom
ca	Canada
us	United States
jp	Japan

Each of these nodes then branches out into another set of domains, and they combine to form what we refer to as domain names, such as microsoft.com. A *domain name* identifies the domain's position in the logical DNS hierarchy in relation to its parent domain by separating each branch of the tree with a dot. Figure 2.2 shows a few of the top-level

domains, where the Microsoft domain fits, and a host called Tigger within the `microsoft`
`.com` domain. If someone wanted to contact that host, they would use the *fully qualified
domain name (FQDN)*, `tigger.microsoft.com`.

An FQDN includes the trailing dot (.) to indicate the root node, but it's commonly left
off in practice.

FIGURE 2.2   The DNS hierarchy

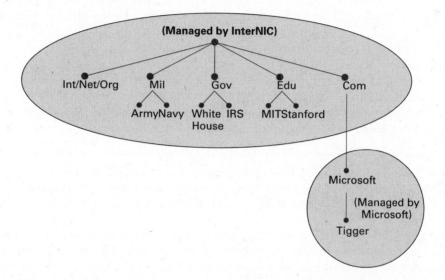

As previously stated, one of the strengths of DNS is the ability to delegate control
over portions of the DNS namespace to multiple organizations. For example, the Internet
Corporation for Assigned Names and Numbers (ICANN) assigns the control over TLDs
to one or more organizations. In turn, those organizations delegate portions of the DNS
namespace to other organizations. For example, when you register a domain name, let's
call it `example.com`, you control the DNS for the portion of the DNS namespace within
`example.com`. The registrar controlling the `.com` TLD has delegated control over the
`example.com` node in the DNS tree. No other node can be named `example` directly below
the `.com` within the DNS database.

Within the portion of the domain namespace that you control (`example.com`),
you could create host and other records (more on these later). You could also further
subdivide `example.com` and delegate control over those divisions to other organizations
or departments. These divisions are called *subdomains*. For example, you might create
subdomains named for the cities in which the company has branch offices and then delegate
control over those subdomains to the branch offices. The subdomains might be named
`losangeles.example.com`, `chicago.example.com`, `portsmouth.example.com`, and so on.

Each domain (or delegated subdomain) is associated with DNS name servers. In other
words, for every node in the DNS, one or more servers can give an authoritative answer to

queries about that domain. At the root of the domain namespace are the root servers. More on these later.

Domain names and hostnames must contain only characters a to z, A to Z, 0 to 9, and - (hyphen). Other common and useful characters, such as the & (ampersand), / (slash), . (period), and _ (underscore), are not allowed. This is in conflict with NetBIOS's naming restrictions. However, you'll find that Windows Server 2012 R2 is smart enough to take a NetBIOS name, like Server_1, and turn it into a legal DNS name, like server1.example.com.

DNS servers work together to resolve hierarchical names. If a server already has information about a name, it simply fulfills the query for the client. Otherwise, it queries other DNS servers for the appropriate information. The system works well because it distributes the authority over separate parts of the DNS structure to specific servers. A *DNS zone* is a portion of the DNS namespace over which a specific DNS server has authority (DNS zone types are discussed in detail later in this chapter).

There is an important distinction to make between DNS zones and Active Directory (AD) domains. Although both use hierarchical names and require name resolution, DNS zones do not map directly to AD domains.

Within a given DNS zone, resource records (RRs) contain the hosts and other database information that make up the data for the zone. For example, an RR might contain the host entry for www.example.com, pointing it to the IP address 192.168.1.10.

Understanding Servers, Clients, and Resolvers

You will need to know a few terms and concepts in order to manage a DNS server. Understanding these terms will make it easier to understand how the Windows Server 2012 R2 DNS server works.

DNS Server   Any computer providing domain name services is a *DNS name server*. No matter where the server resides in the DNS namespace, it's still a DNS name server. For example, 13 root name servers at the top of the DNS tree are responsible for delegating the TLDs. The *root servers* provide referrals to name servers for the TLDs, which in turn provide referrals to an authoritative name server for a given domain.

The Berkeley Internet Name Domain (BIND) was originally the only software available for running the root servers on the Internet. However, a few years ago the organizations responsible for the root servers undertook an effort to diversify the software running on these important machines. Today, root servers run multiple types of name server software. BIND is still primarily on Unix-based machines, and it is also the most popular for Internet providers. No root servers run Windows DNS.

Any DNS server implementation supporting Service Location Resource Records (see RFC 2782) and Dynamic Updates (RFC 2136) is sufficient to provide the name service for any operating system running Windows 2003 software and newer.

DNS Client   A *DNS client* is any machine that issues queries to a DNS server. The client hostname may or may not be registered in a DNS database. Clients issue DNS requests through processes called *resolvers*. You'll sometimes see the terms *client* and *resolver* used synonymously.

Resolver   *Resolvers* are software processes, sometimes implemented in software libraries that handle the actual process of finding the answers to queries for DNS data. The resolver is also built into many larger pieces of software so that external libraries don't have to be called to make and process DNS queries. Resolvers can be what you'd consider client computers or other DNS servers attempting to resolve an answer on behalf of a client (for example, Internet Explorer).

Query   A *query* is a request for information sent to a DNS server. Three types of queries can be made to a DNS server: recursive, inverse, and iterative. I'll discuss the differences between these query types in the section "DNS Queries," a bit later in the chapter.

Understanding the DNS Process

To help you understand the DNS process, I will start by covering the differences between Dynamic DNS and Non-Dynamic DNS. During this discussion, you will learn how Dynamic DNS populates the DNS database. You'll also see how to implement security for Dynamic DNS. I will then talk about the workings of different types of DNS queries. Finally, I will discuss caching and time to live (TTL). You'll learn how to determine the best setting for your organization.

Dynamic DNS and Non-Dynamic DNS

To understand Dynamic DNS and Non-Dynamic DNS, you must go back in time. (Here is where the TV screen always used to get wavy.) Many years ago when many of us worked on Windows NT 3.51 and Windows NT 4.0, almost all Microsoft networks used Windows Internet Name Service (WINS) to do their TCP/IP name resolution. Windows versions 95/98 and NT 4.0 Professional were all built on the idea of using WINS. This worked out well for administrators because WINS was dynamic (which meant that once it was installed, it automatically built its own database). Back then, there was no such thing as Dynamic DNS; administrators had to enter DNS records into the server manually. This is important to know even today. If you have clients still running any of these older operating systems (95/98 or NT 4), these clients cannot use Dynamic DNS.

Now let's move forward in time to the release of Windows Server 2000. Microsoft announced that DNS was going to be the name resolution method of choice. Many administrators (myself included) did not look forward to the switch. Because there was no such thing as Dynamic DNS, most administrators had nightmares about manually entering records. However, luckily for us, when Microsoft released Windows Server 2000, DNS had the ability to operate dynamically. Now when you're setting up Windows Server 2012 R2 DNS, you can choose what type of dynamic update you would like to use, if any. Let's talk about why you would want to choose one over the other.

The *Dynamic DNS (DDNS) standard*, described in RFC 2136, allows DNS clients to update information in the DNS database files. For example, a Windows Server 2012 R2 DHCP server can automatically tell a DDNS server which IP addresses it has assigned to what machines. Windows 2000, 2003, 2008, XP Pro, Vista, Windows 7, and Windows 8 DHCP clients can do this too. For security reasons, however, it's better to let the DHCP server do it. The result: IP addresses and DNS records stay in sync so that you can use DNS and DHCP together seamlessly. Because DDNS is a proposed Internet standard, you can even use the Windows Server 2012 R2 DDNS-aware parts with Unix/Linux-based DNS servers.

Non-Dynamic DNS (NDDNS) does not automatically populate the DNS database. The client systems do not have the ability to update to DNS. If you decide to use Non-Dynamic DNS, an administrator will need to populate the DNS database manually. Non-Dynamic DNS is a reasonable choice if your organization is small to midsized and you do not want extra network traffic (clients updating to the DNS server) or if you need to enter the computer's TCP/IP information manually because of strict security measures.

Dynamic DNS has the ability to be secure, and the chances are slim that a rogue system (a computer that does not belong in your DNS database) could update to a secure DNS server. Nevertheless, some organizations have to follow stricter security measures and are not allowed to have dynamic updates.

The major downside to entering records into DNS manually occurs when the organization is using the *Dynamic Host Configuration Protocol (DHCP)*. When using DHCP, it is possible for users to end up with different TCP/IP addresses every day. This means an administrator has to update DNS manually each day to keep it accurate.

If you choose to allow Dynamic DNS, you need to decide how you want to set it up. When setting up dynamic updates on your DNS server, you have three choices (see Figure 2.3).

None   This means your DNS server is Non-Dynamic.

Nonsecure and Secure   This means that any machine (even if it does not have a domain account) can register with DNS. Using this setting could allow rogue systems to enter records into your DNS server.

Secure Only   This means that only machines with accounts in Active Directory can register with DNS. Before DNS registers any account in its database, it checks Active Directory to make sure that account is an authorized domain computer.

FIGURE 2.3   Setting the Dynamic Updates option

How Dynamic DNS Populates the DNS Database

TCP/IP is the protocol used for network communications on a Microsoft Windows Server 2012 R2 network. Users have two ways to receive a TCP/IP number:

- Static (administrators manually enter the TCP/IP information)
- Dynamic (using DHCP)

When an administrator sets up TCP/IP, DNS can also be configured.

Once a client gets the address of the DNS server, if that client is allowed to update with DNS, the client sends a registration to DNS or requests DHCP to send the registration. DNS then does one of two things, depending on which Dynamic Updates option is specified:

- Check with Active Directory to see whether that computer has an account (Secure Only updates), and if it does, enter the record into the database.
- Enter the record into its database (Nonsecure and Secure updates).

What if you have clients that cannot update DNS? Well, there is a solution—DHCP. In the DNS tab of the IPv4 Properties window, check the option labeled "Dynamically update DNS A and PTR records for DHCP clients that do not request updates (for example, clients running Windows NT 4.0)," which is shown in Figure 2.4.

DHCP, along with Dynamic DNS clients, allows an organization to update its DNS database dynamically without the time and effort of having an administrator manually enter DNS records.

FIGURE 2.4   DHCP settings for DNS

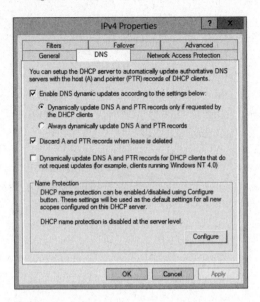

DNS Queries

As stated earlier, a client can make three types of queries to a DNS server: recursive, inverse, and iterative. Remember that the client of a DNS server can be a resolver (what you'd normally call a client) or another DNS server.

Iterative Queries

Iterative queries are the easiest to understand: A client asks the DNS server for an answer, and the server returns the best answer. This information likely comes from the server's cache. The server never sends out an additional query in response to an iterative query. If the server doesn't know the answer, it may direct the client to another server through a referral.

Recursive Queries

In a *recursive query*, the client sends a query to a name server, asking it to respond either with the requested answer or with an error message. The error states one of two things:

- The server can't come up with the right answer.
- The domain name doesn't exist.

In a recursive query, the name server isn't allowed just to refer the client to some other name server. Most resolvers use recursive queries. In addition, if your DNS server uses a forwarder, the requests sent by your server to the forwarder will be recursive queries.

Figure 2.5 shows an example of both recursive and iterative queries. In this example, a client within the Microsoft Corporation is querying its DNS server for the IP address for www.whitehouse.gov.

FIGURE 2.5 A sample DNS query

Here's what happens to resolve the request:

1. The resolver sends a recursive DNS query to its local DNS server asking for the IP address of www.whitehouse.gov. The local name server is responsible for resolving the name, and it cannot refer the resolver to another name server.

2. The local name server checks its zones, and it finds no zones corresponding to the requested domain name.

3. The root name server has authority for the root domain, and it will reply with the IP address of a name server for the .gov top-level domain.

4. The local name server sends an iterative query for www.whitehouse.gov to the Gov name server.

5. The Gov name server replies with the IP address of the name server servicing the whitehouse.gov domain.

6. The local name server sends an iterative query for www.whitehouse.gov to the whitehouse.gov name server.

7. The whitehouse.gov name server replies with the IP address corresponding to www.whitehouse.gov.

8. The local name server sends the IP address of www.whitehouse.gov back to the original resolver.

Inverse Queries

Inverse queries use pointer (PTR) records. Instead of supplying a name and then asking for an IP address, the client first provides the IP address and then asks for the name. Because there's no direct correlation in the DNS namespace between a domain name and its associated IP address, this search would be fruitless without the use of the in-addr.arpa domain. Nodes in the in-addr.arpa domain are named after the numbers in the dotted-octet representation of IP addresses. However, because IP addresses get more specific from left to right and domain names get less specific from left to right, the order of IP address octets must be reversed when building the in-addr.arpa tree. With this arrangement, administration of the lower limbs of the DNS in-addr.arpa tree can be given to companies as they are assigned their Class A, B, or C subnet address or delegated even further down thanks to Variable Length Subnet Masking (VLSM).

Once the domain tree is built into the DNS database, a special PTR record is added to associate the IP addresses with the corresponding hostnames. In other words, to find a hostname for the IP address 206.131.234.1, the resolver would query the DNS server for a PTR record for 1.234.131.206.in-addr.arpa. If this IP address is outside of the local domain, the DNS server will start at the root and sequentially resolve the domain nodes until arriving at 234.131.206.in-addr.arpa, which would contain the PTR record for the desired host.

Caching and Time to Live

When a name server is processing a recursive query, it may be required to send out several queries to find the definitive answer. Name servers, acting as resolvers, are allowed to cache all of the received information during this process; each record contains information called *time to live (TTL)*. The TTL specifies how long the record will be held in the local cache until it must be resolved again. If a query comes in that can be satisfied by this cached data, the TTL that's returned with it equals the current amount of time left before the data is flushed.

There is also a negative cache TTL. The *negative cache TTL* is used when an authoritative server responds to a query indicating that the record queried doesn't exist, and it indicates the amount of time that this negative answer may be held. Negative caching is quite helpful in preventing repeated queries for names that don't exist.

The administrator for the DNS zone sets TTL values for the entire zone. The value can be the same across the zone, or the administrator can set a separate TTL for each RR within the zone. Client resolvers also have data caches and honor the TTL value so that they know when to flush.

Choosing Appropriate TTL Values

For zones that you administer, you can choose the TTL values for the entire zone, for negative caching, and for individual records. Choosing an appropriate TTL depends on a number of factors, including the following:

- Amount of change you anticipate for the records within the zone

- Amount of time you can withstand an outage that might require changing an IP address

- Amount of traffic you believe the DNS server can handle

Resolvers query the name server every time the TTL expires for a given record. A low TTL, say 60 seconds, can burden the name server, especially for popular DNS records. (DNS queries aren't particularly intensive for a server to handle, but they can add up quickly if you mistakenly use 60 seconds instead of 600 seconds for the TTL on a popular record.) Set a low TTL only when you need to respond quickly to a changing environment.

A high TTL, say 604,800 seconds (that's one week), means that if you need to make a change to the DNS record, clients might not see the change for up to a week. This consideration is especially important when making changes to the network, and it's one that's all too frequently overlooked. I can't count the number of times I've worked with clients who had recently made a DNS change to a new IP for their email or website only to ask why it's not working for some clients. The answer can be found in the TTL value. If the record is being cached, then the only thing that can solve their problem is time.

You should choose a TTL that's appropriate for your environment. Take the following factors into account:

- The amount of time that you can afford to be offline if you need to make a change to a DNS record that's being cached

- The amount of load that a low TTL will cause on the DNS server

In addition, you should plan well ahead of any major infrastructure changes and change the TTL to a lower value to lessen the effect of the downtime by reducing the amount of time that the record(s) can be cached.

Introducing DNS Database Zones

As mentioned earlier in this chapter, a DNS zone is a portion of the DNS namespace over which a specific DNS server has authority. Within a given DNS zone, there are resource records (RRs) that define the hosts and other types of information that make up the database for the zone. You can choose from several different zone types. Understanding the characteristics of each will help you choose which is right for your organization.

The DNS zones discussed in this book are all Microsoft Windows Server 2012 / 2012 R2 zones. Non-Windows (for example, Unix) systems set up their DNS zones differently.

In the following sections, I will discuss the different zone types and their characteristics.

Understanding Primary Zones

When you're learning about zone types, things can get a bit confusing. But it's really not difficult to understand how they work and why you would want to choose one type of zone over the other. Zones are databases that store records. By choosing one zone type over another, you are basically just choosing how the database works and how it will be stored on the server.

The primary zone is responsible for maintaining all of the records for the DNS zone. It contains the primary copy of the DNS database. All record updates occur on the primary zone. You will want to create and add primary zones whenever you create a new DNS domain.

There are two types of primary zones:

- Primary zone
- Primary zone with Active Directory Integration (Active Directory DNS)

 From this point forward, I refer to a primary zone with Active Directory Integration as an *Active Directory DNS*. When I use only the term *primary zone*, Active Directory is not included.

To install DNS as a primary zone, you must first install DNS using the Server Manager MMC. Once DNS is installed and running, you create a new zone and specify it as a primary zone.

 The process of installing DNS and its zones will be discussed later in this chapter. In addition, there will be step-by-step exercises to walk you through how to install these components.

Primary zones have advantages and disadvantages. Knowing the characteristics of a primary zone will help you decide when you need the zone and when it fits into your organization.

Local Database

Primary DNS zones get stored locally in a file (with the suffix .dns) on the server. This allows you to store a primary zone on a domain controller or a member server. In addition, by loading DNS onto a member server, you can help a small organization conserve resources. Such an organization may not have the resources to load DNS on an Active Directory domain controller.

Unfortunately, the local database has many disadvantages:

Lack of Fault Tolerance   Think of a primary zone as a contact list on your smartphone. All of the contacts in the list are the records in your database. The problem is that, if you lose your phone or the phone breaks, you lose your contact list. Until your phone gets fixed or you swap out your phone card, the contacts are unavailable.

It works the same way with a primary zone. If the server goes down or you lose the hard drive, DNS records on that machine are unreachable. An administrator can install a secondary zone (explained later in the next section), and that provides temporary fault tolerance. Unfortunately, if the primary zone is down for an extended period of time, the secondary server's information will no longer be valid.

Additional Network Traffic   Let's imagine that you are looking for a contact number for John Smith. John Smith is not listed in your smartphone directory, but he is listed in your partner's smartphone. You have to contact your partner to get the listing. You cannot directly access your partner's phone's contacts.

When a resolver sends a request to DNS to get the TCP/IP address for Jsmith (in this case Jsmith is a computer name) and the DNS server does not have an answer, it does not have the ability to check the other server's database directly to get an answer. Thus it forwards the request to another DNS. When DNS servers are replicating zone databases with other DNS servers, this causes additional network traffic.

No Security   Staying with the smartphone example, let's say that you call your partner looking for John Smith's phone number. When your partner gives you the phone number over your wireless phone, someone with a scanner can pick up your conversation. Unfortunately, wireless telephone calls are not very secure.

Now a resolver asks a primary zone for the Jsmith TCP/IP address. If someone on the network has a packet sniffer, they can steal the information in the DNS packets being sent over the network. The packets are not secure unless you implement some form of secondary security. Also, the DNS server has the ability to be dynamic. A primary zone accepts all updates from DNS servers. You cannot set it to accept secure updates only.

Understanding Secondary Zones

In Windows Server 2012 R2 DNS, you have the ability to use secondary DNS zones. Secondary zones are noneditable copies of the DNS database. You use them for *load balancing* (also referred to as *load sharing*), which is a way of managing network overloads on a single server. A secondary zone gets its database from a primary zone.

A *secondary zone* contains a database with all of the same information as the primary zone, and it can be used to resolve DNS requests. Secondary zones have the following advantages:

- A secondary zone provides fault tolerance, so if the primary zone server becomes unavailable, name resolution can still occur using the secondary zone server.

- Secondary DNS servers can also increase network performance by offloading some of the traffic that would otherwise go to the primary server.

Secondary servers are often placed within the parts of an organization that have high-speed network access. This prevents DNS queries from having to run across slow wide area network (WAN) connections. For example, if there are two remote offices within the stellacon.com organization, you may want to place a secondary DNS server in each remote office. This way, when clients require name resolution, they will contact the nearest server for this IP address information, thus preventing unnecessary WAN traffic.

WARNING   Having too many secondary zone servers can actually cause an increase in network traffic because of replication (especially if DNS changes are fairly frequent). Therefore, you should always weigh the benefits and drawbacks and properly plan for secondary zone servers.

Understanding Active Directory Integrated DNS

Windows Server 2000 introduced *Active Directory Integrated DNS* to the world. This zone type was unique and was a separate choice during setup. In Windows Server 2003, this zone type became an add-on to a primary zone. In Windows Server 2012 R2, it works the same way. After choosing to set up a primary zone, you check the box labeled Store The Zone In Active Directory (see Figure 2.6).

FIGURE 2.6   Setting up an Active Directory Integrated zone

Disadvantages of Active Directory Integrated DNS

The main disadvantage of Active Directory Integrated DNS is that it has to reside on a domain controller because the DNS database is stored in Active Directory. As a result, you cannot load this zone type on a member server, and small organizations might not have the resources to set up a dedicated domain controller.

Advantages of Active Directory Integrated DNS

The advantages of using an Active Directory Integrated DNS zone well outweigh the disadvantage just discussed. The following are some of the major advantages to an Active Directory Integrated zone:

Full Fault Tolerance   Think of an Active Directory Integrated zone as a database on your server that stores contact information for all your clients. If you need to retrieve John Smith's phone number, as long as it was entered, you can look it up on the software.

If John Smith's phone number was stored only on your computer and your computer stopped working, no one could access John Smith's phone number. But since John Smith's phone number is stored in a database to which everyone has access, if your computer stops working, other users can still retrieve John Smith's phone number.

An Active Directory Integrated zone works the same way. Since the DNS database is stored in Active Directory, all Active Directory DNS servers can have access to the same data. If one server goes down or you lose a hard drive, all other Active Directory DNS servers can still retrieve DNS records.

No Additional Network Traffic   As previously discussed, an Active Directory Integrated zone is stored in Active Directory. Since all records are now stored in Active Directory, when a resolver needs a TCP/IP address for Jsmith, any Active Directory DNS server can access Jsmith's address and respond to the resolver.

When you choose an Active Directory Integrated zone, DNS zone data can be replicated automatically to other DNS servers during the normal Active Directory replication process.

DNS Security   An Active Directory Integrated zone has a few security advantages over a primary zone:

- An Active Directory Integrated zone can use secure dynamic updates.
- As explained earlier, the Dynamic DNS standard allows secure-only updates or dynamic updates, not both.
- If you choose secure updates, then only machines with accounts in Active Directory can register with DNS. Before DNS registers any account in its database, it checks Active Directory to make sure that it is an authorized domain computer.
- An Active Directory Integrated zone stores and replicates its database through Active Directory replication. Because of this, the data gets encrypted as it is sent from one DNS server to another.

Background Zone Loading   Background zone loading (discussed in more detail later in this chapter) allows an Active Directory Integrated DNS zone to load in the background. As a result, a DNS server can service client requests while the zone is still loading into memory.

Understanding Stub Zones

Stub zones work a lot like secondary zones—the database is a noneditable copy of a primary zone. The difference is that the stub zone's database contains only the information necessary (three record types) to identify the authoritative DNS servers for a zone (see Figure 2.7). You should not use stub zones to replace secondary zones, nor should you use them for redundancy and load balancing.

FIGURE 2.7 DNS stub zone type

Stub zone databases contain only three record types: name server (NS), start of authority (SOA), and glue host (A) records. Understanding these records will help you on the Microsoft certification exams. Microsoft asks many questions about stub zones on all DNS-related exams.

When to Use Stub Zones

Stub zones become particularly useful in a couple of different scenarios. Consider what happens when two large companies merge: example.com and example.net. In most cases, the DNS zone information from both companies must be available to every employee. You could set up a new zone on each side that acts as a secondary for the other side's primary zone, but administrators tend to be very protective of their DNS databases, and they probably wouldn't agree to this plan.

A better solution is to add to each side a stub zone that points to the primary server on the other side. When a client in example.com (which you help administer) makes a request for a name in example.net, the stub zone on the example.com DNS server would send the client to the primary DNS server for example.net without actually resolving the name. At this point, it would be up to example.net's primary server to resolve the name.

An added benefit is that, even if the administrators over at example.net change their configuration, you won't have to do anything because the changes will automatically replicate to the stub zone, just as they would for a secondary server.

Stub zones can also be useful when you administer two domains across a slow connection. Let's change the previous example a bit and assume that you have full control over example.com and example.net but that they connect through a 56Kbps line. In this case, you wouldn't necessarily mind using secondary zones because you personally administer the entire network. However, it could get messy to replicate an entire zone file across that slow line. Instead, stub zones would refer clients to the appropriate primary server at the other site.

GlobalName Zones

Earlier in this chapter, I talked about organizations using WINS to resolve NetBIOS names (also referred to as *computer names*) to TCP/IP addresses. Even today, many organizations still use WINS along with DNS for name resolution. Unfortunately, WINS is slowly becoming obsolete.

To help organizations move forward with an all-DNS network, Microsoft Windows Server 2012 R2 DNS supports *GlobalName zones*. These use single-label names (DNS names that do not contain a suffix such as .com, .net, and so on). GlobalName zones are not intended to support peer-to-peer networks and workstation name resolution, and they don't support dynamic DNS updates.

GlobalName zones are designed to be used with servers. Because GlobalName zones are not dynamic, an administrator has to enter the records into the zone database manually. In most organizations, the servers have static TCP/IP addresses, and this works well with the GlobalName zone design. GlobalName zones are usually used to map single-label CNAME (alias) resource records to an FQDN.

Zone Transfers and Replication

DNS is such an important part of the network that you should not just use a single DNS server. With a single DNS server, you also have a single point of failure, and in fact, many domain registrars encourage the use of more than two name servers for a domain. Secondary servers or multiple primary Active Directory Integrated servers play an integral role in providing DNS information for an entire domain.

As previously stated, secondary DNS servers receive their zone databases through zone transfers. When you configure a secondary server for the first time, you must specify the primary server that is authoritative for the zone and that will send the zone transfer. The primary server must also permit the secondary server to request the zone transfer.

Zone transfers occur in one of two ways: *full zone transfers (AXFR)* and *incremental zone transfers (IXFR)*.

When a new secondary server is configured for the first time, it receives a full zone transfer from the primary DNS server. The full zone transfer contains all of the information in the DNS database. Some DNS implementations always receive full zone transfers.

After the secondary server receives its first full zone transfer, subsequent zone transfers are incremental. The primary name server compares its zone version number with that of the secondary server, and it sends only the changes that have been made in the interim. This significantly reduces network traffic generated by zone transfers.

The secondary server typically initiates zone transfers when the refresh interval time for the zone expires or when the secondary or stub server boots. Alternatively, you can configure notify lists on the primary server that send a message to the secondary or stub servers whenever any changes to the zone database occur.

When you consider your DNS strategy, you must carefully consider the layout of your network. If you have a single domain with offices in separate cities, you want to reduce the number of zone transfers across the potentially slow or expensive WAN links, although this is becoming less of a concern because of continuous increases in bandwidth.

Active Directory Integrated zones do away with traditional zone transfers altogether. Instead, they replicate across Active Directory with all of the other AD information. This replication is secure and encrypted because it uses the Active Directory security.

How DNS Notify Works

Windows Server 2012 R2 supports DNS Notify. *DNS Notify* is a mechanism that allows the process of initiating notifications to secondary servers when zone changes occur (RFC 1996). DNS Notify uses a push mechanism for communicating to a select set of secondary zone servers when their zone information is updated. (DNS Notify does not allow you to configure a notify list for a stub zone.)

After being notified of the changes, secondary servers can then start a pull zone transfer and update their local copies of the database.

> Many different mechanisms use the push/pull relationship. Normally, one object pushes information to another, and the second object pulls the information from the first. Most applications push replication on a change value and pull it on a time value. For example, a system can push replication after 10 updates, or it can be pulled every 30 minutes.

To configure the DNS Notify process, you create a list of secondary servers to notify. List the IP address of the server in the primary master's Notify dialog box (see Figure 2.8). The Notify dialog box is located under the Zone Transfers tab, which is located in the zone Properties dialog box (see Figure 2.9).

FIGURE 2.8   DNS Notify dialog box

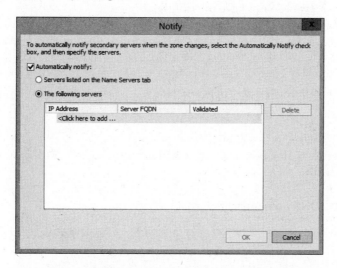

FIGURE 2.9   DNS Zone Transfers tab

Configuring Stub Zone Transfers with Zone Replication

In the preceding section, I talked about how to configure secondary server zone transfers. What if you wanted to configure settings for stub zone transfers? This is where zone replication scope comes in.

Only Active Directory–Integrated primary and stub zones can configure their replication scope. Secondary servers do not have this ability.

You can configure zone replication scope configurations in two ways. An administrator can set configuration options through the DNS snap-in or through a command-line tool called DNSCmd.

To configure zone replication scope through the DNS snap-in, follow these steps:

1. Click Start ➢ Administrative Tools ➢ DNS.

2. Right-click the zone you want to set up.

3. Choose Properties.

4. In the Properties dialog box, click the Change button next to Replication (see Figure 2.10).

FIGURE 2.10   DNS zone replication scope

5. Choose the replication scope that fits your organization.

Advantages of DNS in Windows Server 2012 R2

DNS in Microsoft Windows Server 2012 R2 has some great advantages over many other versions of Microsoft DNS. Here are some of the improvements of DNS in Windows Server 2012 R2 (some of these became available in Windows Server 2008, but they have been improved upon):

- Background zone loading
- Support for TCP/IP version 6 (IPv6)
- Read-only domain controllers
- GlobalName zone
- DNS Socket Pool
- DNS Cache Locking
- DNS Security Extensions (DNSSEC)
- DNS Devolution
- Zone Level Statistics
- Record Weighting
- Netmask Ordering
- DnsUpdateProxy Group
- Windows PowerShell Support

Background Zone Loading

If an organization had to restart a DNS server with an extremely large Active Directory Integrated DNS zones database in the past, DNS had a common problem with an Active Directory Integrated DNS zone. After the DNS restart, it could take hours for DNS data to be retrieved from Active Directory. During this time, the DNS server was unable to service any client requests.

Microsoft Windows Server 2008 DNS addressed this problem by implementing background zone loading, and Windows Server 2012 R2 has taken it a step further. As the DNS restarts, the Active Directory zone data populates the database in the background. This allows the DNS server to service client requests for data from other zones almost immediately after a restart.

Background zone loading accomplishes this task by loading the DNS zone using separate threads. This allows a DNS server to service requests while still loading the rest of the zone. If a client sends a request to the DNS server for a computer that has not yet loaded into memory, the DNS server retrieves the data from Active Directory and updates the record.

Support for IPv6 Addresses

Over the past few years, the Internet has starting running into a problem that was not foreseen when it was first created—it started running out of TCP/IP addresses. As you probably know, when the Internet was created, it was used for government and academic purposes only. Then, seemingly overnight, it grew to be the information superhighway. Nowadays, asking someone for his or her email address is almost as common as asking for their phone number.

Version 4 (IPv4) was the common version of TCP/IP. The release of TCP/IP version 6 (IPv6) has solved the lack-of-IP-addresses problem. IPv4 addresses are 32 bits long, but IPv6 addresses are 128 bits in length. The longer lengths allow for a much greater number of globally unique TCP/IP addresses.

Microsoft Windows Server 2012 R2 DNS has built-in support to accommodate both IPv4 and IPv6 address records. (DNS records are explained later in this chapter.) DHCP can also issue IPv6 addresses, which lets administrators allow DHCP to register the client with DNS, or the IPv6 client can register their address with the DNS server.

Support for Read-Only Domain Controllers

Windows Server 2008 introduced a new type of domain controller called the *read-only domain controller (RODC)*. This is a full copy of the Active Directory database without the ability to write to Active Directory. The RODC gives an organization the ability to install a domain controller in a location (onsite or offsite) where security is a concern.

Microsoft Windows Server 2012 R2 DNS has implemented a type of zone to help support an RODC. A primary read-only zone allows a DNS server to receive a copy of the application partition (including ForestDNSZones and DomainDNSZones) that DNS uses. This allows DNS to support an RODC because DNS now has a full copy of all DNS zones stored in Active Directory.

A primary, read-only zone is just what it says—a read-only zone; so to make any changes to it, you have to change the primary zones located on the Active Directory Integrated DNS server.

DNS Socket Pools

If your server is running Windows Server 2012 R2, you will be able to take advantage of DNS socket pools. *DNS socket pools* allow source port randomization to protect against DNS cache-poisoning attacks.

If you choose to use source port randomization, when the DNS service starts, the DNS server will randomly pick a source port from a pool of available sockets. This is an advantage because, instead of DNS using a well-known source port when issuing queries, the DNS server uses a random port selected from the socket pool. This helps guard against attacks because a hacker must correctly access the source port of the DNS query. The socket pool is automatically enabled in DNS with the default settings.

When using the DNS Socket Pool, the default size of the DNS socket pool is 2,500. When configuring the socket pool, you have the ability to choose a size value from 0 to 10,000. The larger the value, the greater the protection you will have against DNS spoofing attacks. If you decide to configure your socket pool size with a zero value, only a single socket for remote DNS queries will be used.

DNS Cache Locking

Windows Server 2012 R2 *DNS cache locking* allows cached DNS records to remain safe for the duration of the record's time to live (TTL) value. This means that the cached DNS records cannot be overwritten or changed. Because of this new DNS feature, it's tougher for hackers to perform cache-poisoning attacks against your DNS server.

DNS administrators can set how long a record will remain safe in cache. The configuration is based on a percent value. For example, if you set your cache locking value to 50 percent, then the cached records cannot be overwritten until half of the TTL has been reached. DNS cache locking is set to 100 percent by default. This means that the cached records never get overwritten.

DNS Security Extensions

One major issue that you must always look at is keeping your DNS safe. Think about it—DNS is a database of computer names and IP addresses. As a hacker, if I control DNS, I can control your company. In organizations that do not support extra security like IPsec, DNS security is even more important. This is where DNSSEC can help.

Windows Server 2012 R2 can use a suite of extensions that will help add security to DNS, and that suite is called *Domain Name System Security Extensions (DNSSEC)*, which was introduced in Windows Server 2008 R2. The DNSSEC protocol allows your DNS servers to be secure by validating DNS responses. DNSSEC secures your DNS resource records by accompanying the records with a digital signature.

To allow your DNS resource records to receive digital signatures, DNSSEC is applied to your DNS server by a procedure called *zone signing*. This process begins when a DNS resolver initiates a DNS query for a resource record in a signed DNS zone. When a response is returned, a digital signature (RRSIG) accompanies the response, and this allows the response to be verified. If the verification is successful, then the DNS resolver knows that the data has not been modified or tampered with in any way.

Once you implement a zone with DNSSEC, all of the records that are contained within that zone get individually signed. Since all of the records in the zone get individually signed, this gives administrators the ability to add, modify, or delete records without resigning the entire zone. The only requirement is to resign any updated records.

Trust Anchors

Trust anchors are an important part of the DNSSEC process because trust anchors allow the DNS servers to validate the DNSKEY resource records. *Trust anchors* are preconfigured public keys that are linked to a DNS zone. For a DNS server to perform validation, one or more trust anchors must be configured. If you are running an Active Directory Integrated zone, trust anchors can be stored in the Active Directory Domain Services directory partition of the forest. If you decide to store the trust anchors in the directory partition, then all DNS servers that reside on a domain controller get a copy of this trust anchor. On DNS servers that reside on stand-alone servers, trust anchors are stored in a file called TrustAnchors.dns.

If your servers are running Windows Server 2012 R2, then you can view trust anchors in the DNS Manager Console tree in the Trust Points container. You can also use Windows PowerShell or `Dnscmd.exe` to view trust anchors. Windows PowerShell is the recommended command-line method for viewing trust anchors. The following line is a PowerShell command to view the trust anchors for `Contoso.com`:

```
get-dnsservertrustanchor sec.contoso.com
```

DNSSEC Clients

Windows 7, Windows 8, Windows Server 2008/2008 R2, and Windows Server 2012/2012 R2 are all DNS clients that receive a response to a DNS query, examine the response, and then evaluate whether the response has been validated by a DNS server. The DNS client itself is nonvalidating, and the DNS client relies on the local DNS server to indicate that validation was successful. If the server doesn't perform validation, then the DNS client service can be configured to return no results.

If you are interested in learning how to set up DNSSEC in a lab environment, Microsoft has a website that explains all about DNSSEC and how to set up the lab environment. Visit http://technet.microsoft.com/en-us/library/hh831411.aspx.

DNS Devolution

Using *DNS devolution*, if a client computer is a member of a child namespace, the client computer will be able to access resources in the parent namespace without the need to provide explicitly the fully qualified domain name (FQDN) of the resource. DNS devolution removes the leftmost label of the namespace to get to the parent suffix. DNS devolution allows the DNS resolver to create the new FQDNs. DNS devolution works by appending the single-label, unqualified domain name with the parent suffix of the primary DNS suffix name.

Zone Level Statistics

DNS zone level server statistics are available in Windows Server 2012 R2 by using the Windows PowerShell cmdlet `Get-DnsServerStatistics`. This powerful Windows PowerShell cmdlet retrieves statistics and data for the DNS server. The following is an example of the `Get-DnsServerStatistics` cmdlet:

```
Get-DnsServerStatistics -ZoneName <String[]> [-AsJob][-CimSession
<CimSession[]> ][-Clear][-ComputerName <String> ][-ThrottleLimit <Int32> ]
[ <CommonParameters>]
```

The ZoneName parameter allows an administrator to get specific statistics for the DNS zone that you have specified. If the ZoneName parameter is not specified during the

PowerShell cmdlet, the server-level statistics are retrieved and shown. If an administrator uses the Clear parameter in the PowerShell cmdlet along with the ZoneName parameter, the statistics for the specified zone will be cleared. So, use this cmdlet carefully.

Record Weighting

Weighting DNS records will allow an administrator to place a value on DNS SRV records. Clients will then randomly choose SRV records proportional to the weight value assigned.

Netmask Ordering

If round robin is enabled, when a client requests name resolution, the first address entered in the database is returned to the resolver, and it is then sent to the end of the list. The next time a client attempts to resolve the name, the DNS server returns the second name in the database (which is now the first name) and then sends it to the end of the list, and so on. Round robin is enabled by default.

Netmask ordering is part of the round-robin process. When an administrator configures netmask ordering, the DNS server will detect the subnet of the querying client. The DNS server will then return a host address available for the same subnet. Netmask ordering is enabled through the DNS Manager console on the Advanced tab of the server Properties dialog box.

DnsUpdateProxy Group

As mentioned previously, the DHCP server can be configured to register host (A) and pointer (PTR) resource records dynamically on behalf of DHCP clients. Because of this, the DNS server can end up with stale resources. To help solve this issue, an administrator can use the built-in security group called *DnsUpdateProxy*.

To use the DnsUpdateProxy group, an administrator must first create a dedicated user account and configure the DHCP servers with its credentials. This will protect against the creation of unsecured records. Also, when you create the dedicated user account, members of the DnsUpdateProxy group will be able to register records in zones that allow only secured dynamic updates. Multiple DHCP servers can use the same credentials of one dedicated user account.

Now that you have looked at some of the new features of Windows Server 2012 R2 DNS, let's take a look at some of the DNS record types.

Windows PowerShell Support

Microsoft has more than 100 PowerShell cmdlets specifically for DNS. While in Windows PowerShell, you can list all of the DNS cmdlets that are available. To see the entire list, use the following PowerShell command:

```
Get-Command -Module DnsServer cmdlet.
```

For an entire list of all of the Windows PowerShell DNS cmdlets, go to `http://technet`
`.microsoft.com/en-us/library/jj649850.aspx`.

Introducing DNS Record Types

No matter where your zone information is stored, you can rest assured that it contains a
variety of DNS information. Although the DNS snap-in makes it unlikely that you'll ever
need to edit these files by hand, it's good to know exactly what data is contained there.

As stated previously, zone files consist of a number of resource records. You need to
know about several types of resource records to manage your DNS servers effectively. They
are discussed in the following sections.

Part of the resource record is its class. *Classes* define the type of network for the
resource record. There are three classes: Internet, Chaosnet, and Hesoid. By far, the
Internet class is the most popular. In fact, it's doubtful that you'll see either Chaosnet or
Hesoid classes in the wild.

 The following are some of the more important resource records in a
DNS database. For a listing of records in a Microsoft DNS database, visit
Microsoft's website at `http://technet.microsoft.com/en-us/library/`
`cc958958.aspx`.

Start of Authority Records

The first record in a database file is the *start of authority (SOA) record*. The SOA defines
the general parameters for the DNS zone, including the identity of the authoritative server
for the zone.

The SOA appears in the following format:

```
@ IN SOA primary_mastercontact_e-mailserial_number
refresh_timeretry_timeexpiration_timetime_to_live
```

Here is a sample SOA from the domain `example.com`:

```
@ IN SOA win2k3r2.example.com. hostmaster.example.com. (
                    5           ; serial number
                    900         ; refresh
                    600         ; retry
                    86400       ; expire
                    3600      ) ; default TTL
```

Table 2.2 lists the attributes stored in the SOA record.

TABLE 2.2   The SOA record structure

Field	Meaning
Current zone	The current zone for the SOA. This can be represented by an @ symbol to indicate the current zone or by naming the zone itself. In the example, the current zone is example.com. The trailing dot (.com.) indicates the zone's place relative to the root of the DNS.
Class	This will almost always be the letters *IN* for the Internet class.
Type of record	The type of record follows. In this case, it's SOA.
Primary master	The primary master for the zone on which this file is maintained.
Contact email	The Internet email address for the person responsible for this domain's database file. There is no @ symbol in this contact email address because @ is a special character in zone files. The contact email address is separated by a single dot (.). So the email address of root@example.com would be represented by root.example.com in a zone file.
Serial number	This is the "version number" of this database file. It increases each time the database file is changed.
Refresh time	The amount of time (in seconds) that a secondary server will wait between checks to its master server to see if the database file has changed and a zone transfer should be requested.
Retry time	The amount of time (in seconds) that a secondary server will wait before retrying a failed zone transfer.
Expiration time	The amount of time (in seconds) that a secondary server will spend trying to download a zone. Once this time limit expires, the old zone information will be discarded.
Time to live	The amount of time (in seconds) that another DNS server is allowed to cache any resource records from this database file. This is the value that is sent out with all query responses from this zone file when the individual resource record doesn't contain an overriding value.

Name Server Records

Name server (NS) records list the name servers for a domain. This record allows other name servers to look up names in your domain. A zone file may contain more than one name server record. The format of these records is simple:

```
example.com.    IN    NS    Hostname.example.com
```

Table 2.3 explains the attributes stored in the NS record.

TABLE 2.3   The NS record structure

Field	Meaning
Name	The domain that will be serviced by this name server. In this case, I used example.com.
AddressClass	Internet (IN)
RecordType	Name server (NS)
Name Server Name	The FQDN of the server responsible for the domain

Any domain name in the database file that is not terminated with a period will have the root domain appended to the end. For example, an entry that just has the name *sales* will be expanded by adding the root domain to the end, whereas the entry sales.example.com. won't be expanded.

Host Record

A *host record* (also called an *A record* for IPv4 and *AAAA record* for IPv6) is used to associate statically a host's name to its IP addresses. The format is pretty simple:

```
host_nameoptional_TTL IN  A   IP_Address
```

Here's an example from my DNS database:

```
www  IN  A  192.168.0.204
SMTP IN  A  192.168.3.144
```

The A or AAAA record ties a hostname (which is part of an FQDN) to a specific IP address. This makes these records suitable for use when you have devices with statically assigned IP addresses. In this case, you create these records manually using the DNS snap-in. As it turns out, if you enable DDNS, your DHCP server can create these for you. This automatic creation is what enables DDNS to work.

Notice that an optional TTL field is available for each resource record in the DNS. This value is used to set a TTL that is different from the default TTL for the domain. For example, if you wanted a 60-second TTL for the www A or AAAA record, it would look like this:

```
www 60 IN  A  192.168.0.204
```

Alias Record

Closely related to the host record is the *alias record*, or *canonical name (CNAME) record*. The syntax of an alias record is as follows:

```
aliasoptional_TTL  IN  CNAME  hostname
```

Aliases are used to point more than one DNS record toward a host for which an A record already exists. For example, if the hostname of your web server was actually chaos, you would likely have an A record such as this:

```
chaos IN A 192.168.1.10
```

Then you could make an alias or CNAME for the record so that www.example.com would point to chaos:

```
www IN CNAME chaos.example.com.
```

Note the trailing dot (.) on the end of the CNAME record. This means the root domain is not appended to the entry.

Pointer Record

A or AAAA records are probably the most visible component of the DNS database because Internet users depend on them to turn FQDNs like www.microsoft.com into the IP addresses that browsers and other components require to find Internet resources. However, the host record has a lesser-known but still important twin: the *pointer (PTR) record*. The format of a PTR record appears as follows:

```
reversed_address.in-addr.arpa. optional_TTL IN PTR targeted_domain_name
```

The A or AAAA record maps a hostname to an IP address, and the PTR record does just the opposite—mapping an IP address to a hostname through the use of the in-addr.arpa zone.

The PTR record is necessary because IP addresses begin with the least-specific portion first (the network) and end with the most-specific portion (the host), whereas hostnames begin with the most-specific portion at the beginning and the least-specific portion at the end.

Consider the example 192.168.1.10 with a subnet mask 255.255.255.0. The portion 192.168.1 defines the network and the final .10 defines the host, or the most-specific portion of the address. DNS is just the opposite: The hostname www.example.com. defines the most-specific portion, www, at the beginning and then traverses the DNS tree to the least-specific part, the dot (.), at the root of the tree.

Reverse DNS records, therefore, need to be represented in this most-specific-to-least-specific manner. The PTR record for mapping 192.168.1.10 to www.example.com would look like this:

```
10.1.168.192.in-addr.arpa. IN PTR www.example.com.
```

Now a DNS query for that record can follow the logical DNS hierarchy from the root of the DNS tree all the way to the most-specific portion.

Mail Exchanger Record

The *mail exchanger (MX) record* is used to specify which servers accept mail for this domain. Each MX record contains two parameters—a preference and a mail server, as shown in the following example:

```
domain IN MX preference mailserver_host
```

The MX record uses the preference value to specify which server should be used if more than one MX record is present. The preference value is a number. The lower the number, the more preferred the server. Here's an example:

```
example.com.    IN  MX  0  mail.example.com.
example.com.    IN  MX  10 backupmail.example.com.
```

In the example, `mail.example.com` is the default mail server for the domain. If that server goes down for any reason, emailers then use the `backupmail.example.com` mail server.

Service (SRV) Record

Windows Server 2012 R2 depends on some other services, like the Lightweight Directory Access Protocol (LDAP) and Kerberos. Using a service record, which is another type of DNS record, a Windows 2000, XP, Vista, Windows 7, Windows 8, and all Windows Server products can query DNS servers for the location of a domain controller. This makes it much easier (for both the client and the administrator) to manage and distribute logon traffic in large-scale networks. For this approach to work, Microsoft has to have some way to register the presence of a service in DNS. Enter the service (SRV) record.

Service (SRV) records tie together the location of a service (like a domain controller) with information about how to contact the service. SRV records provide seven items of information. Let's review an example to help clarify this powerful concept. (Table 2.4 explains the fields in the following example.)

```
ldap.tcp.example.com.  86400 IN SRV  10  100  389  hsv.example.com
ldap.tcp.example.com.  86400 IN SRV  20  100  389  msy.example.com
```

TABLE 2.4   The SRV record structure

Field	Meaning
Domain name	Domain for which this record is valid (`ldap.tcp.example.com.`).
TTL	Time to live (86,400 seconds).
Class	This field is always IN, which stands for Internet.

Record type	Type of record (SRV).
Priority	Specifies a preference, similar to the Preference field in an MX record. The SRV record with the lowest priority is used first (10).
Weight	Service records with equal priority are chosen according to their weight (100).
Port number	The port where the server is listening for this service (389).
Target	The FQDN of the host computer (hsv.example.com and msy.example.com).

 You can define other types of service records. If your applications support them, they can query DNS to find the services they need.

Configuring DNS

In the following sections, you'll begin to learn about the actual DNS server. You will start by installing DNS. Then I will talk about different zone configuration options and what they mean. Finally, you'll complete an exercise that covers configuring Dynamic DNS, delegating zones, and manually entering records.

DNS requires that you use a static IP address on the server. The reason for this is that clients access the DNS server by using its TCP/IP address, and that's why DNS servers need to install a static IP address.

If you are currently using DHCP on your server, change your DNS server to have a static IP address before completing this exercise. I know that most of you already know how to change your IP address, but for anyone new to Microsoft Server 2012 R2, click the Start button and go into Control Panel. Make sure that the VIEW BY in the upper-right corner is set to large icons, and then choose Network and Sharing Center. On the right side of the windows under Access Type, click the access type link you have (Ethernet, Wireless, and so forth). Choose Properties, and then click Internet Protocol Version 4 (TCP/IPv4) and choose Properties. Choose the radio button for Use The Following IP Address and enter your local TCP/IP settings. Click OK to change it from DHCP to a static TCP/IP address.

Installing DNS

Let's start by installing DNS. Installing DNS is an important part of running a network. Exercise 2.1 walks you through the installation of a DNS server.

EXERCISE 2.1

Installing and Configuring the DNS Service

1. Open Server Manager.

2. On the Server Manager dashboard, click the Add Roles And Features link.

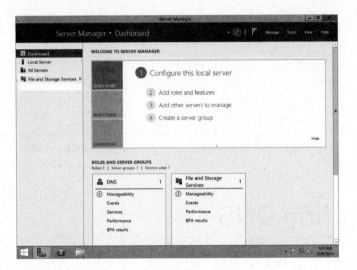

3. If a Before You Begin screen appears, click Next.

4. On the Selection type page, choose Role-Based Or Feature-Based Installation and click Next.

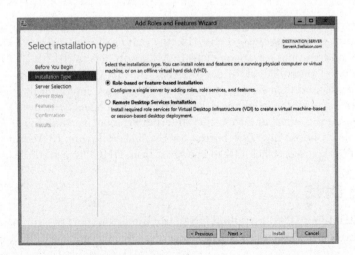

5. Click the Select A Server From The Server Pool radio button and choose the server under the Server Pool section. Click Next.

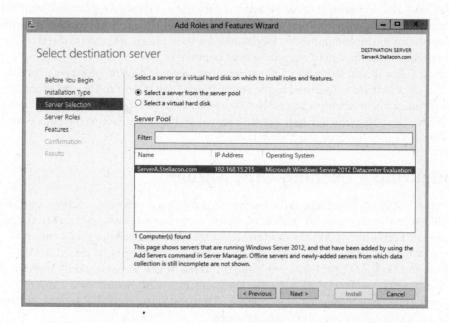

6. Click the DNS Server Item in the Server Role list. If a pop-up window appears telling you that you need to add additional features, click the Add Features button. If you did not give your system a static TCP/IP address, a window appears stating that you need a static TCP/IP address; just click the Continue button to bypass the error. Click Next to continue.

7. On the Add Features page, just click Next.

8. Click Next on the DNS Server information screen.

9. On the Confirm Installation screen, choose the Restart The Destination Server Automatically If Required check box and then click the Install button.

10. At the Installation progress screen, click Close after the DNS server is installed.

11. Close Server Manager.

Load Balancing with Round Robin

Like other DNS implementations, the Windows Server 2012 R2 implementation of DNS supports load balancing through the use of round robin. Load balancing distributes the network load among multiple network hosts if they are available. You set up round-robin load balancing by creating multiple resource records with the same hostname but different IP addresses for multiple computers. Depending on the options you select, the DNS server responds with the addresses of one of the host computers.

If round robin is enabled, when a client requests name resolution, the first address entered in the database is returned to the resolver and is then sent to the end of the list. The next time a client attempts to resolve the name, the DNS server returns the second name in the database (which is now the first name) and then sends it to the end of the list, and so on. Round robin is enabled by default.

Configuring a Caching-Only Server

Although all DNS name servers cache queries that they have resolved, caching-only servers are DNS name servers that only perform queries, cache the answers, and return the results. They are not authoritative for any domains, and the information that they contain is limited to what has been cached while resolving queries. Accordingly, they don't have any zone files, and they don't participate in zone transfers. When a caching-only server is first started, it has no information in its cache; the cache is gradually built over time.

Caching-only servers are easy to configure. After installing the DNS service, simply make sure the root hints are configured properly:

1. Right-click your DNS server and choose the Properties command.

2. When the Properties dialog box appears, switch to the Root Hints tab (see Figure 2.11).

FIGURE 2.11   The Root Hints tab of the DNS server's Properties dialog box

3. If your server is connected to the Internet, you should see a list of root hints for the root servers maintained by ICANN and the Internet Assigned Numbers Authority (IANA). If not, click the Add button to add root hints as defined in the cache.dns file.

You can obtain current cache.dns files on the Internet by using a search engine. Just search for *cache.dns* and download one. (I always try to get cache.dns files from a university or a company that manages domain names.)

Setting Zone Properties

There are six tabs on the Properties dialog box for a forward or reverse lookup zone. You only use the Security tab to control who can change properties and to make dynamic updates to records on that zone. The other tabs are discussed in the following sections.

Secondary zones don't have a Security tab, and their SOA tab shows you the contents of the master SOA record, which you can't change.

General Tab

The General tab includes the following:

- The Status indicator and the associated Pause button let you see and control whether this zone can be used to answer queries. When the zone is running, the server can use it to answer client queries; when it's paused, the server won't answer any queries it gets for that particular zone.

- The Type indicator and its Change button allow you to select the zone type. The options are Standard Primary, Standard Secondary, and AD-Integrated. (See "Introducing DNS Database Zones" earlier in this chapter.) As you change the type, the controls you see below the horizontal dividing line change too. For primary zones, you'll see a field that lets you select the zone filename; for secondary zones, you'll get controls that allow you to specify the IP addresses of the primary servers. But the most interesting controls are the ones you see for AD Integrated zones. When you change to the AD Integrated zones, you have the ability to make the dynamic zones Secure Only.

- The Replication indicator and its Change button allow you to change the replication scope if the zone is stored in Active Directory. You can choose to replicate the zone data to any of the following:

  - All DNS servers in the Active Directory forest

  - All DNS servers in a specified domain

  - All domain controllers in the Active Directory domain (required if you use Windows 2000 domain controllers in your domain)

  - All domain controllers specified in the replication scope of the application directory partition

- The Dynamic Updates field gives you a way to specify whether you want to support Dynamic DNS updates from compatible DHCP servers. As you learned earlier in the section "Dynamic DNS and Non-Dynamic DNS," the DHCP server or DHCP client must know about and support Dynamic DNS in order to use it, but the DNS server has to participate too. You can turn dynamic updates on or off, or you can require that updates be secured.

Start Of Authority (SOA) Tab

The options on the Start Of Authority (SOA) tab, shown in Figure 2.12, control the contents of the SOA record for this zone.

FIGURE 2.12   The Start Of Authority (SOA) tab of the zone Properties dialog box

- The Serial Number field indicates which version of the SOA record the server currently holds. Every time you change another field, you should increment the serial number so that other servers will notice the change and get a copy of the updated record.

- The Primary Server and Responsible Person fields indicate the location of the primary name server (NS) for this zone and the email address of the administrator responsible for the maintenance of this zone, respectively. The standard username for this is host-master.

- The Refresh Interval field controls how often any secondary zones of this zone must contact the primary zone server and get any changes that have been posted since the last update.

- The Retry Interval field controls how long secondary servers will wait after a zone transfer fails before they try again. They'll keep trying at the interval you specify (which should be shorter than the refresh interval) until they eventually succeed in transferring zone data.

- The Expires After field tells the secondary servers when to throw away zone data. The default of 1 day (24 hours) means that a secondary server that hasn't gotten an update in 24 hours will delete its local copy of the zone data.

- The Minimum (Default) TTL field sets the default TTL for all RRs created in the zone. You can assign specific TTLs to individual records if you want.

- The TTL For This Record field controls the TTL for the SOA record itself.

Name Servers Tab

The *name server (NS) record* for a zone indicates which name servers are authoritative for the zone. That normally means the zone primary server and any secondary servers you've configured for the zone. (Remember, secondary servers are authoritative read-only copies of the zone.) You edit the NS record for a zone using the Name Servers tab (see Figure 2.13). The tab shows you which servers are currently listed, and you use the Add, Edit, and Remove buttons to specify which name servers you want included in the zone's NS record.

FIGURE 2.13   The Name Servers tab of the zone Properties dialog box

WINS Tab

The WINS tab allows you to control whether this zone uses WINS forward lookups. These lookups pass on queries that DNS can't resolve to WINS for action. This is a useful setup if you're still using WINS on your network. You must explicitly turn this option on with the Use WINS Forward Lookup check box on the WINS tab for a particular zone.

Zone Transfers Tab

Zone transfers are necessary and useful because they're the mechanism used to propagate zone data between primary and secondary servers. For primary servers (whether AD Integrated or not), you can specify whether your servers will allow zone transfers and, if so, to whom.

You can use the following controls on the Zone Transfers tab to configure these settings per zone:

- The Allow Zone Transfers check box controls whether the server answers zone transfer requests for this zone at all; when it's not checked, no zone data is transferred. The Allow Zone Transfers selections are as follows:

  - To Any Server allows any server anywhere on the Internet to request a copy of your zone data.

  - Only To Servers Listed On The Name Servers Tab (the default) limits transfers to servers you specify. This is a more secure setting than To Any Server because it limits transfers to other servers for the same zone.

  - Only To The Following Servers allows you to specify exactly which servers are allowed to request zone transfers. This list can be larger or smaller than the list specified on the Name Servers tab.

- The Notify button is for setting up automatic notification triggers that are sent to secondary servers for this zone. Those triggers signal the secondary servers that changes have occurred on the primary server so that the secondary servers can request updates sooner than their normally scheduled interval. The options in the Notify dialog box are similar to those in the Zone Transfers tab. You can enable automatic notification and then choose either Servers Listed On The Name Servers Tab or The Following Servers.

Configuring Zones for Dynamic Updates

In Exercise 2.2, you will create and then modify the properties of a forward lookup zone. In addition, you'll configure the zone to allow dynamic updates. You are installing this DNS zone as a primary zone *without* AD integration. Even if you installed this DNS server onto a domain controller, do not choose the check box for AD integration.

EXERCISE 2.2

Configuring a Zone for Dynamic Updates

1. Open the DNS management snap-in by selecting Server Manager. Once in Server Manager, click DNS on the left side. In the Servers window (center screen), right-click your server name and choose DNS Manager.

2. Click the DNS server to expand it and then click the Forward Lookup Zones folder. Right-click the Forward Lookup Zones folder and choose New Zone.

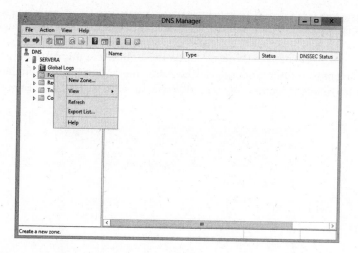

3. At the New Zone Welcome screen, click Next.

4. At the Zone Type screen, choose the Primary Zone option. Again, if your DNS server is also a domain controller, do not check the box to store the zone in Active Directory. Click Next when you are ready.

5. Enter a new zone name in the Zone Name field and click Next. (I used my last name—Panek.com.)

6. Leave the default zone filename and click Next.

7. Select the Do Not Allow Dynamic Updates radio button and click Next.

8. Click Finish to end the wizard.

9. Right-click the zone you just created and choose the Properties command.

10. Click the down arrow next to Dynamic Updates. Notice that there are only two options (None and Nonsecure And Secure). The Secure Only option is not available because you are not using Active Directory Integrated. Make sure Nonsecure And Secure is chosen.

11. Click OK to close the Properties box.

12. Close the DNS management snap-in.

13. Close the Server Manager snap-in.

Delegating Zones for DNS

DNS provides the ability to divide the namespace into one or more zones, which can then be stored, distributed, and replicated to other DNS servers. When deciding whether to divide your DNS namespace to make additional zones, consider the following reasons to use additional zones:

- A need to delegate management of part of your DNS namespace to another location or department within your organization.

- A need to divide one large zone into smaller zones for distributing traffic loads among multiple servers, for improving DNS name-resolution performance, or for creating a more fault-tolerant DNS environment.

- A need to extend the namespace by adding numerous subdomains at once, such as to accommodate the opening of a new branch or site.

Each newly delegated zone requires a primary DNS server just as a regular DNS zone does. When delegating zones within your namespace, be aware that for each new zone you create, you need to place delegation records in other zones that point to the authoritative DNS servers for the new zone. This is necessary both to transfer authority and to provide correct referral to other DNS servers and clients of the new servers being made authoritative for the new zone.

In Exercise 2.3, you'll create a delegated subdomain of the domain you created back in Exercise 2.2. Note that the name of the server to which you want to delegate the subdomain must be stored in an A or CNAME record in the parent domain.

EXERCISE 2.3

Creating a Delegated DNS Zone

1. Open the DNS management snap-in by selecting Server Manager. Once in Server Manager, click DNS on the left side. In the Servers window (center screen), right-click your server name and choose DNS Manager.

2. Expand the DNS server and locate the zone you created in Exercise 2.2.

3. Right-click the zone and choose the New Delegation command.

4. The New Delegation Wizard appears. Click Next to dismiss the initial wizard page.

5. Enter **ns1** (or whatever other name you like) in the Delegated Domain field of the Delegated Domain Name page. This is the name of the domain for which you want to delegate authority to another DNS server. It should be a subdomain of the primary domain (for example, to delegate authority for farmington.example.net, you'd enter **farmington** in the Delegated Domain field). Click Next to complete this step.

6. When the Name Servers page appears, click the Add button to add the name(s) and IP address(es) of the servers that will be hosting the newly delegated zone. For the purpose of this exercise, enter the server name you used in Exercise 2.2. Click the Resolve button to resolve this domain name's IP address automatically into the IP address field. Click OK when you are finished. Click Next to continue with the wizard.

7. Click the Finish button. The New Delegation Wizard disappears, and you'll see the new zone you just created appear beneath the zone you selected in step 3. The newly delegated zone's folder icon is drawn in gray to indicate that control of the zone is delegated.

DNS Forwarding

If a DNS server does not have an answer to a DNS request, it may be necessary to send that request to another DNS server. This is called *DNS forwarding*. You need to understand the two main types of forwarding:

External Forwarding   When a DNS server forwards an external DNS request to a DNS server outside of your organization, this is considered *external forwarding*. For example, a resolver requests the host www.microsoft.com. Most likely, your internal DNS server is not going to have Microsoft's web address in its DNS database. So, your DNS server is going to send the request to an external DNS (most likely your ISP).

Conditional Forwarding *Conditional forwarding* is a lot like external forwarding except that you are going to forward requests to specific DNS servers based on a condition. Usually, this is an excellent setup for internal DNS resolution. For example, let's say you have two companies, stellacon.com and stellatest.com. If a request comes in for Stellacon.com, it gets forwarded to the Stellacon DNS server, and any requests for Stellatest.com will get forwarded to the Stellatest DNS server. Requests are forwarded to a specific DNS server depending on the condition that an administrator sets up.

Manually Creating DNS Records

From time to time, you may find it necessary to add resource records manually to your Windows Server 2012 R2 DNS servers. Although Dynamic DNS frees you from the need to fiddle with A and PTR records for clients and other such entries, you still have to create other resource types (including MX records, required for the proper flow of SMTP email) manually. You can manually create A, PTR, MX, SRV, and many other record types.

There are only two important things to remember for manually creating DNS records:

- You must right-click the zone and choose either the New Record command or the Other New Records command.

- You must know how to fill in the fields of whatever record type you're using.

  For example, to create an MX record, you need three pieces of information (the domain, the mail server, and the priority). To create an SRV record, however, you need several more pieces of information.

In Exercise 2.4, you will manually create an MX record for a mailtest server in the zone you created in Exercise 2.2.

EXERCISE 2.4

Manually Creating DNS RRs

1. Open the DNS management snap-in by selecting Server Manager. Once in Server Manager, click DNS on the left side. In the Servers window (center screen), right-click your server name and choose DNS Manager.

2. Expand your DNS server, right-click its zone and choose New Host (A record).

3. Enter **mailtest** in the Name field. Enter a TCP/IP number in the IP Address field. (You can use any number for this exercise, for example, 192.168.1.254.) Click the Add Host button.

4. A dialog box appears stating that the host record was created successfully. Click OK. Click Done.

5. Right-click your zone name and choose New Mail Exchanger (MX).

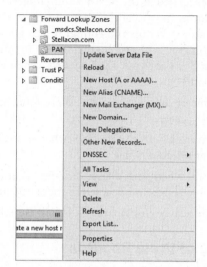

6. Enter `mailtest` in the Host Or Child Domain field and enter `mailtest.yourDomain`
`.com` (or whatever domain name you used in Exercise 2.2) in the Fully-Qualified Domain
Name (FQDN) Of Mail Server field; then click OK. Notice that the new record is already
visible.

7. Next create an alias (or CNAME) record to point to the mail server. (It is assumed that
you already have an A record for `mailtest` in your zone.) Right-click your zone, and
choose New Alias (CNAME).

8. Type `mail` into the Alias Name field.

9. Type `mailtest.yourDomain.com` into the Fully-Qualified Domain Name (FQDN) For Target Host field.

10. Click the OK button.

11. Close the DNS management snap-in.

DNS Aging and Scavenging

When using dynamic updates, computers (or DHCP) will register a resource record with
DNS. These records get removed when a computer is shut down properly. A major problem
in the industry is that laptops are frequently removed from the network without a proper
shutdown. Therefore, their resource records continue to live in the DNS database.

Windows Server 2012 R2 DNS supports two features called *DNS aging* and *DNS
scavenging*. These features are used to clean up and remove stale resource records of a
primary DNS zone. DNS aging and DNS scavenging flags old resource records that have

not been updated in a certain amount of time (determined by the scavenging interval). These stale records will be scavenged at the next cleanup interval. DNS uses time stamps on the resource records to determine how long they have been listed in the DNS database.

DNS allows an administrator to set up and configure aging and scavenging through the use of the DNS snap-in. DNS aging and scavenging allows an administrator to perform some of the following related tasks for your DNS servers and any of the Active Directory–Integrated zones that they load:

- Administrators can enable or disable the use of scavenging at a DNS server and/or for selected zones at the DNS server.

- You can modify the no-refresh/refresh interval, either as a server default or by specifying an overriding value at selected zones.

- Administrators can specify when periodic scavenging occurs automatically at the DNS server for any of its eligible zones and how often these operations are repeated.

- Manually initiate a single scavenging operation for all eligible zones at the DNS server.

Enabling Scavenging of Stale Records

When you install Windows Server 2012 R2 DNS aging and scavenging features on all DNS servers and any of their zones, administrators should consider the following settings before using these features:

Determine whether you should use aging and scavenging for server-wide settings.   When using these settings, you are choosing to affect every one of the zone-level properties for all Active Directory–Integrated zones that are loaded at the server.

Determine whether you should use aging and scavenging for zone settings.   When using these settings, you are choosing to use them for zone-specific properties for just the selected zones and not the entire server. These settings apply only to the applicable zone and its resource records, and they do not apply to any other zone on the DNS server. Unless these zone-level properties are otherwise configured, they inherit their defaults from comparable settings that are maintained in server aging and scavenging properties.

Enabling aging and scavenging for use with standard primary zones modifies the format of zone files. This change does not affect zone replication to secondary servers, but the modified zone files cannot be loaded by other versions of DNS servers.

Monitoring and Troubleshooting DNS

Now that you have set up and configured your DNS name server and created some resource records, you will want to confirm that it is resolving and replying to client DNS requests. A couple of tools allow you to do some basic monitoring and managing. Once you are able to monitor DNS, you'll want to start troubleshooting.

The simplest test is to use the ping command to make sure that the server is alive. A more thorough test would be to use nslookup to verify that you can actually resolve addresses for items on your DNS server.

In the following sections, you'll look at some of these monitoring and management tools and how to troubleshoot DNS.

Monitoring DNS with the DNS Snap-In

You can use the DNS snap-in to do some basic server testing and monitoring. More important, you use the snap-in to monitor and set logging options. On the Event Logging tab of the server's Properties dialog box (see Figure 2.14), you can pick which events you want logged. The more events you select, the more logging information you'll get. This is useful when you're trying to track what's happening with your servers, but it can result in a very large log file if you're not careful.

FIGURE 2.14   The Event Logging tab of the server's Properties dialog box

The Monitoring tab (see Figure 2.15) gives you some testing tools. When the check box labeled A Simple Query Against This DNS Server is checked, a test is performed that asks for a single record from the local DNS server. It's useful for verifying that the service is running and listening to queries, but not much else. When the check box labeled A Recursive Query To Other DNS Servers is checked, the test is more sophisticated—a recursive query checks whether forwarding is working okay. The Test Now button and the Perform Automatic Testing At The Following Interval check box allow you to run these tests now or later as you require.

FIGURE 2.15   The Monitoring tab of the server's Properties dialog box

Another tab in the server's properties that allows you to monitor the activity of the DNS server is the Debug Logging tab. The Debug Logging tab allows you to monitor all outbound and inbound DNS traffic, packet content, packet type, and which transport protocol (TCP or UDP) that you want to monitor on the DNS server.

If the simple query fails, check that the local server contains the zone 1.0.0.127.in-addr.arpa. If the recursive query fails, check that your root hints are correct and that your root servers are running.

In Exercise 2.5, you will enable logging, use the DNS MMC to test the DNS server, and view the contents of the DNS log.

EXERCISE 2.5

Simple DNS Testing

1. Open the DNS management snap-in by selecting Server Manager. Once in Server Manager, click DNS on the left side. In the Servers window (center screen), right-click your server name and choose DNS Manager.

2. Right-click the DNS server name on the top left and select Properties.

3. Switch to the Debug Logging tab, check all of the debug logging options except Filter Packets By IP Address, and enter a full path and filename in the File Path And Name field. Click the Apply button.

4. Switch to the Monitoring tab and check both A Simple Query Against This DNS Server and A Recursive Query To Other DNS Servers.

5. Click the Test Now button several times and then click OK.

6. Press the Windows key on the keyboard (left side between the Ctrl and Alt keys) and then choose Computer. Navigate to the folder that you specified in step 3 and use Word-Pad or Notepad to view the contents of the log file.

Troubleshooting DNS

When troubleshooting DNS problems, ask yourself the following basic questions:

- What application is failing? What works? What doesn't work?

- Is the problem basic IP connectivity, or is it name resolution? If the problem is name resolution, does the failing application use NetBIOS names, DNS names, or host-names?

- How are the things that do and don't work related?

- Have the things that don't work ever worked on this computer or network? If so, what has changed since they last worked?

Windows Server 2012 R2 provides several useful tools, discussed in the following sections, which can help you answer these questions:

- Nslookup is used to perform DNS queries and to examine the contents of zone files on local and remote servers.

- DNSLint is a command-line utility used for troubleshooting many common DNS issues.

- Ipconfig allows you to perform the following tasks:
    - View DNS client settings
    - Display and flush the resolver cache
    - Force a dynamic update client to register its DNS records
- The DNS log file monitors certain DNS server events and logs them for your edification.

Using *Nslookup*

Nslookup is a standard command-line tool provided in most DNS server implementations, including Windows Server 2012 R2. Windows Server 2012 R2 gives you the ability to launch nslookup from the DNS snap-in.

> When nslookup is launched from the DNS snap-in, a command prompt window opens automatically. You enter nslookup commands in this window.

Nslookup offers you the ability to perform query testing of DNS servers and to obtain detailed responses at the command prompt. This information can be useful for diagnosing and solving name resolution problems, for verifying that resource records are added or updated correctly in a zone, and for debugging other server-related problems. You can do a number of useful things with nslookup:

- Use it in noninteractive mode to look up a single piece of data
- Enter interactive mode and use the debug feature
- Perform the following from within interactive mode:
    - Set options for your query
    - Look up a name
    - Look up records in a zone
    - Perform zone transfers
    - Exit nslookup

> When you are entering queries, it is generally a good idea to enter FQDNs so that you can control what name is submitted to the server. However, if you want to know which suffixes are added to unqualified names before they are submitted to the server, you can enter nslookup in debug mode and then enter an unqualified name.

Using Nslookup on the Command Line

To use nslookup in plain-old command-line mode, enter the following in the command prompt window:

```
nslookup DNS_name_or_IP_address server_IP_address
```

This command will look up a DNS name or address using a server at the IP address you specify.

Using *Nslookup* in Interactive Mode

Nslookup is a lot more useful in interactive mode because you can enter several commands in sequence. Entering **nslookup** by itself (without specifying a query or server) puts it in interactive mode, where it will stay until you type **exit** and press Enter. Before that point, you can look up lots of useful stuff. The following are some of the tasks you can perform with nslookup in interactive mode:

Setting Options with the set **Command**   While in interactive mode, you can use the set command to configure how the resolver will carry out queries. Table 2.5 shows a few of the options available with set.

TABLE 2.5   Command-line options available with the set command

Option	Purpose
set all	Shows all the options available.
set d2	Puts nslookup in debug mode so that you can examine the query and response packets between the resolver and the server.
set domain=*domain name*	Tells the resolver what domain name to append for unqualified queries.
set timeout=*timeout*	Tells the resolver how long to keep trying to contact the server. This option is useful for slow links where queries frequently time out and the wait time must be lengthened.
set type=*record type*	Tells the resolver which type of resource records to search for (for example, A, PTR, or SRV). If you want the resolver to query for all types of resource records, type **settype=all**.

Looking Up a Name   While in interactive mode, you can look up a name just by typing it: **stellacon.com**. In this example, stellacon is the owner name for the record for which you are searching, and .com is the server you want to query.

You can use the wildcard character (*) in your query. For example, if you want to look for all resource records that have *k* as the first letter, just type **k*** as your query.

Looking Up a Record Type   If you want to query a particular type of record (for instance, an MX record), use the set type command. The command set type=mx tells nslookup you're interested only in seeing MX records that meet your search criteria.

Listing the Contents of a Domain   To get a list of the contents of an entire domain, use the `ls` command. To find all of the hosts in your domain, you'd type **`set type=a`** and then type **`ls -t yourdomain.com`**.

Troubleshooting Zone Transfers   You can simulate zone transfers by using the `ls` command with the `-d` switch. This can help you determine whether the server you are querying allows zone transfers to your computer. To do this, type **`ls -d domain__name`**.

Nslookup Responses and Error Messages

A successful `nslookup` response looks like this:

```
Server: Name_of_DNS_server
Address: IP_address_of_DNS_server
Response_data
```

Nslookup might also return an error message. Some common messages are listed in Table 2.6.

TABLE 2.6   Common `nslookup` error messages

Error message	Meaning
`DNS request timed out.` `Timeout was x seconds.` `*** Can't find server name for address` `IP_Address: Timed out` `*** Default servers are not available` `Default Server: Unknown` `Address: IP_address_of_DNS_server`	The resolver did not locate a PTR resource record (containing the hostname) for the server IP address you specified. Nslookup can still query the DNS server, and the DNS server can still answer queries.
`*** Request to Server timed-out`	A request was not fulfilled in the allotted time. This might happen, for example, if the DNS service was not running on the DNS server that is authoritative for the name.
`*** Server can't find Name_or_IP_` `address_queried_for: No response from` `server`	The server is not receiving requests on User Datagram Protocol (UDP) port 53.
`*** Server can't find Name_or_IP_` `address_queried_for: Non-existent` `domain`	The DNS server was unable to find the name or IP address in the authoritative domain. The authoritative domain might be on the remote DNS server or on another DNS server that this DNS server is unable to reach.

`*** Server can't find` *`Name_or_IP_`* `address_queried_for`: `Server failed`	The DNS server is running, but it is not working properly. For example, it might include a corrupted packet, or the zone in which you are querying for a record might be paused. However, this message can also be returned if the client queries for a host in a domain for which the DNS server is not authoritative. You will also receive the error if the DNS server cannot contact its root servers, it is not connected to the Internet, or it has no root hints.

In Exercise 2.6, you'll get some hands-on practice with the nslookup tool. You can run this exercise from Windows 7, Windows 8, and Windows Server 2012 R2.

EXERCISE 2.6

Using the nslookup Command

1. Click the Start button and in the Search Programs And Files box (above the Start button), type **CMD**. Then hit Enter.

2. Type **nslookup** and press the Enter key. (For the rest of the exercise, use the Enter key to terminate each command.)

3. Try looking up a well-known address: Type **www.microsoft.com**.

4. Try looking up a nonexistent host: Type **www.example.ccccc**. Notice that your server indicates that it can't find the address and times out. This is normal behavior.

5. Type **exit** at the prompt. Type **exit** again to leave the command prompt.

Using *DNSLint*

Microsoft Windows Server 2012 R2 DNS can use the DNSLint command-line utility to help diagnose some common DNS name-resolution issues and to help diagnose potential problems of incorrect delegation. You need to download DNSLint from the Microsoft Download Center.

DNSLint uses three main functions to verify DNS records and to generate a report in HTML:

dnslint/d   This function helps diagnose the reasons for "lame delegation" and other related DNS problems.

dnslint/ql   This function helps verify a user-defined set of DNS records on multiple DNS servers.

dnslint/ad   This function helps verify DNS records pertaining to Active Directory replication.

Here is the syntax for DNSLint:

```
dnslint /d domain_name | /ad [LDAP_IP_address] | /ql input_file
[/c [smtp,pop,imap]] [/no_open] [/r report_name]
[/t] [/test_tcp] [/s DNS_IP_address] [/v] [/y]
```

The following are some sample queries:

```
dnslint /d stellacon.com
dnslint /ad /s 192.168.36.201
dnslint /ql dns_server.txt
dnslint /ql autocreate
dnslint /v /d stellacon.com
dnslint /r newfile /d stellacon.com
dnslint /y /d stellacon.com
dnslint /no_open /d stellacon.com
```

Table 2.7 explains the command options.

TABLE 2.7 DNSLint command options

Command option	Meaning
/d	Domain name that is being tested.
/ad	Resolves DNS records that are used for Active Directory forest replication.
/s	TCP/IP address of host.
/ql	Requests DNS query tests from a list. This switch sends DNS queries specified in an input file.
/v	Turns on verbose mode.
/r filename	Allows you to create a report file.
/y	Overwrites an existing report file without being prompted.
/no_open	Prevents a report from opening automatically.

Using *Ipconfig*

You can use the command-line tool ipconfig to view your DNS client settings, to view and reset cached information used locally for resolving DNS name queries, and to register the resource records for a dynamic update client. If you use the ipconfig command with no parameters, it displays DNS information for each adapter, including the domain name and

DNS servers used for that adapter. Table 2.8 shows some command-line options available with ipconfig.

TABLE 2.8 Command-line options available for the ipconfig command

Command	What It Does
ipconfig /all	Displays additional information about DNS, including the FQDN and the DNS suffix search list.
ipconfig /flushdns	Flushes and resets the DNS resolver cache. For more information about this option, see the section "Configuring DNS" earlier in this chapter.
ipconfig /displaydns	Displays the contents of the DNS resolver cache. For more information about this option, see the section "Configuring DNS" earlier in this chapter.
ipconfig /registerdns	Refreshes all DHCP leases and registers any related DNS names. This option is available only on Windows 2000 and newer computers that run the DHCP client service.

You should know and be comfortable with the ipconfig commands related to DNS for the exam.

Using *DNSCmd*

DNSCmd allows you to display and change the properties of DNS servers, zones, and resource records through the use of command-line commands. The DNSCmd utility allows you to modify, create, and delete resource records and/or zones manually, and it allows you to force replication between two DNS servers.

Table 2.9 lists some of the DNSCmd commands and their explanations.

TABLE 2.9 DNSCmd command-line options

Command	Explanation
dnscmd /clearcache	Clears the DNS server cache
dnscmd /config	Resets DNS server or zone configuration
dnscmd /createdirectorypartition	Creates a DNS application directory partition
dnscmd /deletedirectorypartition	Deletes a DNS application directory partition
dnscmd /enumrecords	Shows the resource records in a zone

TABLE 2.9   DNSCmd command-line options *(continued)*

Command	Explanation
dnscmd /exportsettings	Creates a text file of all server configuration information
dnscmd /info	Displays server information
dnscmd /recordadd	Adds a resource record to a zone
dnscmd /recorddelete	Deletes a resource record from a zone
dnscmd /zoneadd	Creates a new DNS zone
dnscmd /zonedelete	Deletes a DNS zone
dnscmd /zoneexport	Creates a text file of all resource records in the zone
dnscmd /zoneinfo	Displays zone information
dnscmd /zonerefresh	Forces replication of the master zone to the secondary zone

Using the DNS Log File

You can configure the DNS server to create a log file that records the following information:

- Queries
- Notification messages from other servers
- Dynamic updates
- Content of the question section for DNS query messages
- Content of the answer section for DNS query messages
- Number of queries this server sends
- Number of queries this server has received
- Number of DNS requests received over a UDP port
- Number of DNS requests received over a TCP port
- Number of full packets sent by the server
- Number of packets written through by the server and back to the zone

The DNS log appears in systemroot\System32\dns\Dns.log. Because the log is in RTF format, you must use WordPad or Word to view it.

Once the log file reaches the maximum size, Windows Server 2012 R2 writes over the beginning of the file. You can change the maximum size of the log. If you increase the size value, data persists for a longer time period, but the log file consumes more disk space. If you decrease the value, the log file uses less disk space, but the data persists for a shorter time period.

WARNING   Do not leave DNS logging turned on during normal operation because it sucks up both processing and hard disk resources. Enable it only when diagnosing and solving DNS problems.

Troubleshooting the .*(root)* Zone

The *DNS root zone* is the top-level DNS zone in the DNS hierarchy. Windows Server 2012 R2-based DNS servers will build a .(root) zone when a connection to the Internet can't be found.

Because of this, the .(root) zone may prevent access to the Internet. The DNS forwarding option and DNS root hints will not be configurable. If you want your DNS to work as a DNS forwarder or you want to use root hints, you must remove the .(root) zone.

Issues with Non-Microsoft DNS Servers

Another troubleshooting problem that you may run into is working with both Microsoft DNS servers and non-Microsoft DNS servers. One of the most common non-Microsoft DNS servers is the Unix-based BIND DNS server.

If you need to complete a zone transfer from Microsoft DNS to a BIND DNS server, you need to enable BIND Secondaries on the Microsoft DNS server (see Figure 2.16).

FIGURE 2.16   Enabling BIND secondaries

If you need to enable Bind Secondaries, complete the following steps:

1. Open DNS management.
2. Right-click the server name and choose Properties.
3. Click the Advanced tab.
4. Check the Enable BIND Secondaries box.
5. Click OK.

Overview of DHCP

As you will see in Chapter 7, TCP/IP is the priority protocol for Windows Server 2012 R2. There are two ways to have clients and servers get TCP/IP addresses:

▪ You can manually assign the addresses.

▪ The addresses can be assigned automatically.

Manually assigning addresses is a fairly simple process. An administrator goes to each of the machines on the network and assigns TCP/IP addresses. The problem with this method arises when the network becomes midsized or larger. Think of an administrator trying to individually assign 4,000 TCP/IP addresses, subnet masks, default gateways, and all other configuration options needed to run the network.

DHCP's job is to centralize the process of IP address and option assignment. You can configure a DHCP server with a range of addresses (called a *pool*) and other configuration information and let it assign all of the IP parameters—addresses, default gateways, DNS server addresses, and so on.

 NOTE   DHCP is defined by a series of request for comments documents, notably 2131 and 2132.

Introducing the DORA Process

An easy way to remember how DHCP works is to learn the acronym DORA. *DORA* stands for Discover, Offer, Request, and Acknowledge. In brief, here is DHCP's DORA process:

1. *Discover*: When IP networking starts up on a DHCP-enabled client, a special message called a DHCPDISCOVER is broadcast within the local physical subnet.

2. *Offer*: Any DHCP server that hears the request checks its internal database and replies with a message called a DHCPOFFER, which contains an available IP address.

The contents of this message depend on how the DHCP server is configured—there are numerous options aside from an IP address that you can specify to pass to the client on a Windows Server DHCP server.

3. *Request*: The client receives one or more DHCPOFFERs (depending on how many DHCP servers exist on the local subnet), chooses an address from one of the offers, and sends a DHCPREQUEST message to the server to signal acceptance of the DHCPOFFER.

This message might also request additional configuration parameters.

Other DHCP servers that sent offers take the request message as an acknowledgment that the client didn't accept their offer.

4. *Acknowledge*: When the DHCP server receives the DHCPREQUEST, it marks the IP address as being in use (that is, usually, though it's not required). Then it sends a DHCPACK to the client.

The acknowledgment message might contain requested configuration parameters.

If the server is unable to accept the DHCPREQUEST for any reason, it sends a DHCPNAK message. If a client receives a DHCPNAK, it begins the configuration process over again.

5. When the client accepts the IP offer, the address is assigned to the client for a specified period of time, called a *lease*. After receiving the DHCPACK message, the client performs a final check on the parameters (sometimes it sends an ARP request for the offered IP address) and makes note of the duration of the lease. The client is now configured. If the client detects that the address is already in use, it sends a DHCPDECLINE.

If the DHCP server has given out all of the IP addresses in its pool, it won't make an offer. If no other servers make an offer, the client's IP network initialization will fail, and the client will use Automatic Private IP Addressing (APIPA).

DHCP Lease Renewal

No matter how long the lease period, the client sends a new lease request message directly to the DHCP server when the lease period is half over (give or take some randomness required by RFC 2131). This period goes by the name *T1* (not to be confused with the T1 type of network connection). If the server hears the request message and there's no reason to reject it, it sends a DHCPACK to the client. This resets the lease period.

If the DHCP server isn't available, the client realizes that the lease can't be renewed. The client continues to use the address, and once 87.5 percent of the lease period has elapsed (again, give or take some randomness), the client sends out another renewal request. This interval is known as *T2*. At that point, any DHCP server that hears the renewal can respond to this *DHCP request message* (which is a request for a lease renewal) with a DHCPACK and renew the lease. If at any time during this process the client gets a negative DHCPNACK message, it must stop using its IP address immediately and start the leasing process over from the beginning by requesting a new lease.

When a client initializes its IP networking, it always attempts to renew its old address. If the client has time left on the lease, it continues to use the lease until its end. If the client is unable to get a new lease by that time, all IP functions stop until a new, valid address can be obtained.

DHCP Lease Release

Although leases can be renewed repeatedly, at some point they might run out. Furthermore, the lease process is "at will." That is, the client or server can cancel the lease before it ends. In addition, if the client doesn't succeed in renewing the lease before it expires, the client loses its lease and reverts to APIPA. This release process is important for reclaiming extinct IP addresses used by systems that have moved or switched to a non-DHCP address.

Advantages and Disadvantages of DHCP

DHCP was designed from the start to simplify network management. It has some significant advantages, but it also has some drawbacks.

Advantages of DHCP

The following are advantages of DHCP:

- Configuration of large and even midsized networks is much simpler. If a DNS server address or some other change is necessary to the client, the administrator doesn't have to touch each device in the network physically to reconfigure it with the new settings.

- Once you enter the IP configuration information in one place—the server—it's automatically propagated to clients, eliminating the risk that a user will misconfigure some parameters and require you to fix them.

- IP addresses are conserved because DHCP assigns them only when requested.

- IP configuration becomes almost completely automatic. In most cases, you can plug in a new system (or move one) and then watch as it receives a configuration from the server. For example, when you install new network changes, such as a gateway or DNS server, the client configuration is done at only one location—the DHCP server.

- It allows a preboot execution environment (PXE) client to get a TCP/IP address from DHCP. PXE clients (also called Microsoft Windows Deployment Services [WDS] clients) can get an IP address without needing to have an operating system installed. This allows WDS clients to connect to a WDS server through the TCP/IP protocol and download an operating system remotely.

Disadvantages of DHCP

Unfortunately, there are a few drawbacks with DHCP:

- DHCP can become a single point of failure for your network. If you have only one DHCP server and it's not available, clients can't request or renew leases.

- If the DHCP server contains incorrect information, the misinformation will automatically be delivered to all of your DHCP clients.

- If you want to use DHCP on a multisegment network, you must put either a DHCP server or a relay agent on each segment, or you must ensure that your router can forward Bootstrap Protocol (BOOTP) broadcasts.

Ipconfig Lease Options

The `ipconfig` command-line tool is useful for working with network settings. Its `/renew` and `/release` switches make it particularly handy for DHCP clients. These switches allow you to request renewal of, or give up, your machine's existing address lease. You can do the same thing by toggling the Obtain An IP Address Automatically button in the Internet Protocol (TCP/IP) Properties dialog box, but the command-line option is useful especially when you're setting up a new network.

For example, I spend about a third of my time teaching MCSA or MCSE classes, usually in temporary classrooms set up at conferences, hotels, and so on. Laptops are used in these classes, with one brawny one set up as a DNS/DHCP/DC server. Occasionally, a client will lose its DHCP lease (or not get one, perhaps because a cable has come loose). The quickest way to fix it is to pop open a command-line window and type **ipconfig/renew**.

You can configure DHCP to assign options only to certain classes. *Classes*, defined by an administrator, are groups of computers that require identical DHCP options. The */setclassidclassID* switch of ipconfig is the only way to assign a machine to a class.

More specifically, the switches do the following:

ipconfig /renew Instructs the DHCP client to request a lease renewal. If the client already has a lease, it requests a renewal from the server that issued the current lease. This is equivalent to what happens when the client reaches the half-life of its lease. Alternatively, if the client doesn't currently have a lease, it is equivalent to what happens when you boot a DHCP client for the first time. It initiates the DHCP mating dance, listens for lease offers, and chooses one it likes.

ipconfig /release Forces the client to give up its lease immediately by sending the server a DHCP release notification. The server updates its status information and marks the client's old IP address as "available," leaving the client with no address bound to its network interface. When you use this command, most of the time it will be immediately followed by ipconfig renew. The combination releases the existing lease and gets a new one, probably with a different address. (It's also a handy way to force your client to get a new set of settings from the server before the lease expiration time.)

ipconfig /setclassidclassID Sets a new class ID for the client. You will see how to configure class options later in the section "Setting Scope Options for IPv4." For now, you should know that the only way to add a client machine to a class is to use this command. Note that you need to renew the client lease for the class assignment to take effect.

If you have multiple network adapters in a single machine, you can provide the name of the adapter (or adapters) upon which you want the command to work, including an asterisk (*) as a wildcard. For example, one of my servers has two network cards: an Intel EtherExpress (ELNK1) and a generic 100Mbps card. If you want to renew DHCP settings for both adapters, you can type `ipconfig /renew *`. If you just want to renew the Intel EtherExpress card, you can type `ipconfig /renew ELNK'`.

Understanding Scope Details

By now you should have a good grasp of what a lease is and how it works. To learn how to configure your servers to hand out those leases, however, you need to have a complete understanding of some additional topics: scopes, superscopes, exclusions, reservations, address pool, and relay agents.

Scope

Let's start with the concept of a *scope*, which is a contiguous range of addresses. There's usually one scope per physical subnet, and a scope can cover a Class A, Class B, or Class C network address or a TCP/IP v6 address. DHCP uses scopes as the basis for managing and assigning IP addressing information.

Each scope has a set of parameters, or scope options, that you can configure. *Scope options* control what data is delivered to DHCP clients when they're completing the DHCP negotiation process with a particular server. For example, the DNS server name, default gateway, and default network time server are all separate options that can be assigned. These settings are called *option types*. You can use any of the types provided with Windows Server 2012 R2, or you can specify your own.

Superscope

A *superscope* enables the DHCP server to provide addresses from more than one scope to clients on the same physical subnet. This is helpful when clients within the same subnet have more than one IP network and thus need IPs from more than one address pool. Microsoft's DHCP snap-in allows you to manage IP address assignment in the superscope, though you must still configure other scope options individually for each child scope.

Exclusions and Reservations

The scope defines what IP addresses could potentially be assigned, but you can influence the assignment process in two additional ways by specifying exclusions and reservations:

Exclusions These are IP addresses within the range that you never want automatically assigned. These excluded addresses are off-limits to DHCP. You'll typically use exclusions to tag any addresses that you never want the DHCP server to assign at all. You might use exclusions to set aside addresses that you want to assign permanently to servers that play a vital role in your organization.

Reservations These are IP addresses within the range for which you want a permanent DHCP lease. They essentially reserve a particular IP address for a particular device. The device still goes through the DHCP process (that is, its lease expires and it asks for a new one), but it always obtains the same addressing information from the DHCP server.

Exclusions are useful for addresses that you don't want to participate in DHCP at all. *Reservations* are helpful for situations in which you want a client to get the same settings each time they obtain an address.

An address cannot be simultaneously reserved and excluded. Be aware of this fact for the exam, possibly relating to a troubleshooting question.

 Real World Scenario

Using Reservations and Exclusions

Deciding when to assign a reservation or exclusion can sometimes be confusing. In practice, you'll find that certain computers in the network greatly benefit by having static IP network information. Servers such as DNS servers, the DHCP server itself, SMTP servers, and other low-level infrastructure servers are good candidates for static assignment. There are usually so few of these servers that the administrator is not overburdened if a change in network settings requires going out to reconfigure each individually. Chances are that the administrator would still need to reconfigure these servers manually (by using `ipconfig /release` and then `ipconfig /renew`), even if they did not have IP addresses reserved. Even in large installations, I find it preferable to manage these vital servers by hand rather than to rely on DHCP.

Reservations are also appropriate for application servers and other special but nonvital infrastructure servers. With a reservation in DHCP, the client device will still go through the DHCP process but will always obtain the same addressing information from the DHCP server. The premise behind this strategy is that these nonvital servers can withstand a short outage if DHCP settings change or if the DHCP server fails.

Address Pool

The range of IP addresses that the DHCP server can assign is called its *address pool*. For example, let's say you set up a new DHCP scope covering the 192.168.1 subnet. That gives you 255 IP addresses in the pool. After adding an exclusion from 192.168.1.240 to 192.168.1.254, you're left with 241 (255 – 14) IP addresses in the pool. That means (in theory, at least) that you can service 241 unique clients at a time before you run out of IP addresses.

DHCP Relay Agent

By design, DHCP is intended to work only with clients and servers on a single IP network to communicate. But RFC 1542 sets out how BOOTP (on which DHCP is based) should work in circumstances in which the client and server are on different IP networks. If no

DHCP server is available on the client's network, you can use a DHCP relay agent to forward DHCP broadcasts from the client's network to the DHCP server. The relay agent acts like a radio repeater, listening for DHCP client requests and retransmitting them through the router to the server.

Installing and Authorizing DHCP

Installing DHCP is easy using the Windows Server 2012/2012 R2 installation mechanism. Unlike some other services discussed in this book, the installation process installs just the service and its associated snap-in, starting it when the installation is complete. At that point, it's not delivering any DHCP service, but you don't have to reboot.

Installing DHCP

Exercise 2.7 shows you how to install DHCP Server using Server Manager. This exercise was completed on a Windows Server 2012 R2 Member Server since Active Directory is not installed yet.

EXERCISE 2.7

Installing the DHCP Service

1. Choose Server Manager by clicking the Server Manager icon on the taskbar.

2. Click Add Roles And Features.

3. Choose role-based or feature-based installation and click Next.

4. Choose your server and click Next.

5. Choose DHCP Server and click Next.

6. At the Features screen, click Next.

7. Click Next at the DHCP screen.

8. At the DHCP confirmation screen, click the Install button.

9. When the installation is complete, click the Close button.

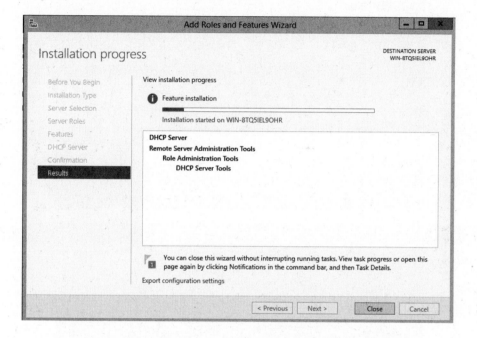

10. On the left side, click the DHCP link.

11. Click the More link next to Configuration Required For DHCP Server.

EXERCISE 2.7 *(continued)*

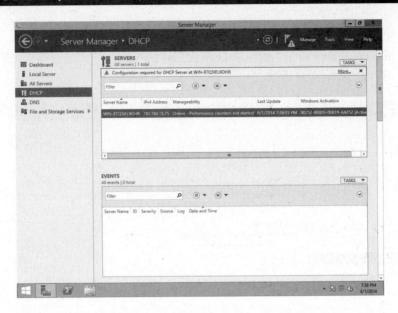

12. Under Action, click Complete DHCP Configuration.

13. At the DHCP Description page, click Commit.

14. Click Close at the Summary screen.

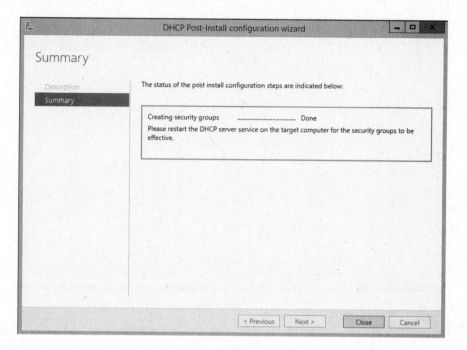

15. Close Server Manager.

Introducing the DHCP Snap-In

When you install the DHCP server, the DHCP snap-in is also installed. You can open it by selecting Administrative Tools ➢ DHCP. Figure 2.17 shows the snap-in.

As you can see, the snap-in follows the standard MMC model. The left pane displays IPv4 and IPv6 sections and which servers are available; you can connect to servers other than the one to which you're already connected. A Server Options folder contains options that are specific to a particular DHCP server. Each server contains subordinate items grouped into folders. Each scope has a folder named after the scope's IP address range. Within each scope, four subordinate views show you interesting things about the scope, such as the following:

- The Address Pool view shows what the address pool looks like.

- The Address Leases view shows one entry for each current lease. Each lease shows the computer name to which the lease was issued, the corresponding IP address, and the current lease expiration time.

FIGURE 2.17 DHCP snap-in

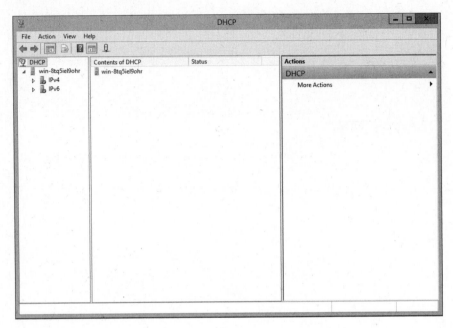

- The Reservations view shows the IP addresses that are reserved and which devices hold them.
- The Scope Options view lists the set of options you've defined for this scope.

Authorizing DHCP for Active Directory

Authorization creates an Active Directory object representing the new server. It helps keep unauthorized servers off your network. Unauthorized servers can cause two kinds of problems. They may hand out bogus leases, or they may fraudulently deny renewal requests from legitimate clients.

When you install a DHCP server using Windows Server 2012/2012 R2 and Active Directory is present on your network, the server won't be allowed to provide DHCP services to clients until it has been authorized. If you install DHCP on a member server in an Active Directory domain or on a stand-alone server, you'll have to authorize the server manually. When you authorize a server, you're adding its IP address to the Active Directory object that contains the IP addresses of all authorized DHCP servers.

You also have the ability to authorize a DHCP server during the installation of DHCP if you are installing DHCP onto an Active Directory machine.

At start time, each DHCP server queries the directory, looking for its IP address on the "authorized" list. If it can't find the list or if it can't find its IP address on the list, the DHCP service fails to start. Instead, it adds a message to the event log, indicating that it couldn't service client requests because the server wasn't authorized.

Exercise 2.8 and Exercise 2.9 show you how to authorize and unauthorize a DHCP server onto a network with Active Directory. If you installed DHCP onto a network with a domain, you can complete the following two exercises, but if you are still on a member server, you *cannot* do these exercises. These are here to show you how to do it after you have Active Directory on your network.

EXERCISE 2.8

Unauthorizing a DHCP Server

1. From Administrative Tools, choose DHCP to open the DHCP snap-in.

2. Right-click the server you want to unauthorize and choose the Unauthorize command.

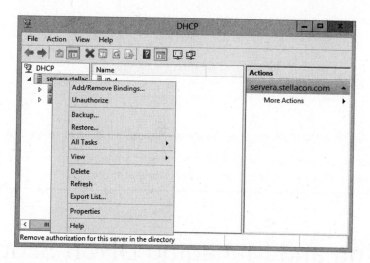

3. Click Yes on the dialog box asking if you are sure you want to complete this action.

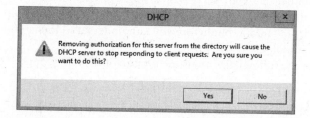

Authorizing a DHCP Server

1. From Administrative Tools, choose DHCP to open the DHCP snap-in.

2. Right-click the server you want to authorize and choose the Authorize command.

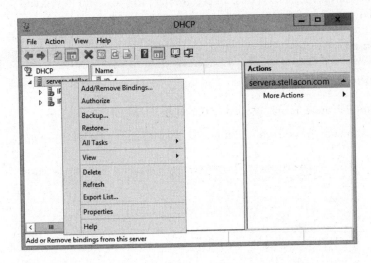

3. Wait a short time (30 to 45 seconds) to allow the authorization to take place.

4. Right-click the server again. Verify that the Unauthorize command appears in the pop-up menu. This indicates that the server is now authorized.

Creating and Managing DHCP Scopes

You can use any number of DHCP servers on a single physical network if you divide the range of addresses that you want assigned into multiple scopes. Each scope contains a number of useful pieces of data, but before you can understand them, you need to know some additional terminology.

You can perform the following management tasks on DHCP scopes:

- Create a scope

- Configure scope properties

- Configure reservations and exclusions

- Set scope options

- Activate and deactivate scopes
- Create a superscope
- Create a multicast scope
- Integrate Dynamic DNS and DHCP

I will cover each task in the following sections.

Creating a New Scope in IPv4

Like many other things in Windows Server 2012 R2, a wizard drives the process of creating a new scope. You will most likely create a scope while installing DHCP, but you may need to create more than one. The overall process is simple, as long as you know beforehand what the wizard is going to ask. If you think about what defines a scope, you'll be well prepared. You need to know the following:

- The IP address range for the scope you want to create.
- Which IP addresses, if any, you want to exclude from the address pool.
- Which IP addresses, if any, you want to reserve.
- Values for the DHCP options you want to set, if any. This item isn't strictly necessary for creating a scope. However, to create a useful scope, you'll need to have some options to specify for the clients.

To create a scope, under the server name, right-click the IPv4 option in the DHCP snap-in, and use the Action ➢ New Scope command. This starts the New Scope Wizard (see Figure 2.18). You will look at each page of the wizard in the following sections.

FIGURE 2.18   Welcome page of the New Scope Wizard

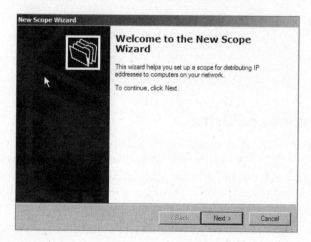

Setting the Screen Name

The Scope Name page allows you to enter a name and description for your scope. These will be displayed by the DHCP snap-in.

It's a good idea to pick sensible names for your scopes so that other administrators will be able to figure out the purpose of the scope. For example, the name DHCP is likely not very helpful, whereas a name like 1st Floor Subnet is more descriptive and can help in troubleshooting.

Defining the IP Address Range

The IP Address Range page (see Figure 2.19) is where you enter the start and end IP addresses for your range. The wizard does minimal checking on the addresses you enter, and it automatically calculates the appropriate subnet mask for the range. You can modify the subnet mask if you know what you're doing.

FIGURE 2.19 IP Address Range page of the New Scope Wizard

Adding Exclusions and Delay

The Add Exclusions And Delay page (see Figure 2.20) allows you to create exclusion ranges. Exclusions are TCP/IP numbers that are in the pool, but they do not get issued to clients. To exclude one address, put it in the Start IP Address field. To exclude a range, also fill in the End IP Address field. The delay setting is a time duration by which the server will delay the transmission of a DHCPOFFER message.

Although you can always add exclusions later, it's best to include them when you create the scope so that no excluded addresses are ever passed out to clients.

FIGURE 2.20 Add Exclusions And Delay page of the New Scope Wizard

Setting a Lease Duration

The Lease Duration page (see Figure 2.21) allows you to set how long a device gets to use an assigned IP address before it has to renew its lease. The default lease duration is eight days. You may find that a shorter or longer duration makes sense for your network. If your network is highly dynamic, with lots of arrivals, departures, and moving computers, set a shorter lease duration; if it's less active, make it longer.

FIGURE 2.21 Lease Duration page of the New Scope Wizard

Remember that renewal attempts begin when approximately half of the lease period is over (give or take a random interval), so don't set them too short.

Configuring Basic DHCP Options

The Configure DHCP Options page (see Figure 2.22) allows you to choose whether you want to set up basic DHCP options such as default gateway and DNS settings. The options are described in the following sections. If you choose not to configure options, you can always do so later. However, you should not activate the scope until you've configured the options you want assigned.

FIGURE 2.22 Configure DHCP Options page of the New Scope Wizard

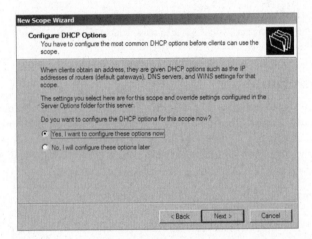

Configuring a Router

The first option configuration page is the Router (Default Gateway) page (see Figure 2.23), in which you enter the IP addresses of one or more routers (more commonly referred to as *default gateways*) that you want to use for outbound traffic. After entering the IP addresses of the routers, use the Up and Down buttons to order the addresses. Clients will use the routers in the order specified when attempting to send outgoing packets.

Providing DNS Settings

On the Domain Name And DNS Servers page (see Figure 2.24), you specify the set of DNS servers and the parent domain you want passed down to DHCP clients. Normally, you'll want to specify at least one DNS server by filling in its DNS name or IP address. You can also specify the domain suffix that you want clients to use as the base domain for all connections that aren't fully qualified. For example, if your clients are used to navigating based on server name alone rather than the fully qualified domain name (FQDN) of server.willpanek.com, then you'll want to place your domain here.

FIGURE 2.23 Router (Default Gateway) page of the New Scope Wizard

FIGURE 2.24 Domain Name And DNS Servers page of the New Scope Wizard

Providing WINS Settings

If you're still using Windows Internet Name Service (WINS) on your network, you can configure DHCP so that it passes WINS server addresses to your Windows clients. (If you want the Windows clients to honor it, you'll also need to define the WINS/NBT Node Type option for the scope.) As on the DNS server page, on the WINS Servers page (see Figure 2.25) you can enter the addresses of several servers and move them into the order in which you want clients to try them. You can enter the DNS or NetBIOS name of each server, or you can enter an IP address.

FIGURE 2.25   WINS Servers page of the New Scope Wizard

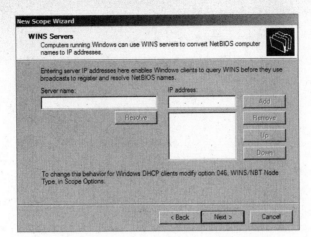

Here are some of the more common options you can set on a DHCP server:

003 Router   Used to provide a list of available routers or default gateways on the same subnet.

006 DNS Servers   Used to provide a list of DNS servers.

015 DNS Domain Name   Used to provide the DNS suffix.

028 Broadcast Address   Used to configure the broadcast address, if different than the default, based on the subnet mask.

44 WINS/NBNS Servers   Used to configure the IP addresses of WINS servers.

46 WINS/NBT Node Type   Used to configure the preferred NetBIOS name resolution method. There are four settings for node type:

B node (0x1)   Broadcast for NetBIOS resolution

P node (0x2)   Peer-to-peer (WINS) server for NetBIOS resolution

M node (0x4)   Mixed node (does a B node and then a P node)

H node (0x8)   Hybrid node (does a P node and then a B node)

051 Lease   Used to configure a special lease duration.

Activating the Scope

The Activate Scope page (see Figure 2.26) gives you the option to activate the scope immediately after creating it. By default, the wizard assumes that you want the scope activated unless you select the No, I Will Activate This Scope Later radio button, in which case the scope will remain dormant until you activate it manually.

FIGURE 2.26   Activate Scope page of the New Scope Wizard

WARNING   Be sure to verify that there are no other DHCP servers assigned to the address range you choose!

In Exercise 2.10, you will create a new scope for the 192.168.0.xprivate Class C network. First you need to complete Exercise 2.7 before beginning this exercise.

EXERCISE 2.10

Creating a New Scope

1. Open the DHCP snap-in by selecting Administrative Tools ➢ DHCP.

2. Right-click the IPv4 folder and choose New Scope. The New Scope Wizard appears.

3. Click the Next button on the welcome page.

4. Enter a name and a description for your new scope and click the Next button.

5. On the IP Address Range page, enter **192.168.0.2** as the start IP address for the scope and **192.168.0.250** as the end IP address. Leave the subnet mask controls alone (though when creating a scope on a production network, you might need to change them). Click the Next button.

6. On the Add Exclusions And Delay page, click Next without adding any excluded addresses or delays.

7. On the Lease Duration page, set the lease duration to 3 days and click the Next button.

8. On the Configure DHCP Options page, click the Next button to indicate you want to configure default options for this scope.

9. On the Router (Default Gateway) page, enter **192.168.0.1** for the router IP address and then click the Add button. Once the address is added, click the Next button.

10. On the Domain Name And DNS Servers page, enter the IP address of a DNS server on your network in the IP Address field (for example, you might enter **192.168.0.251**) and click the Add button. Click the Next button.

11. On the WINS Servers page, click the Next button to leave the WINS options unset.

12. On the Activate Scope page, if your network is currently using the 192.168.0.*x* range, select Yes, I Want To Activate This Scope Now. Click the Next button.

13. When the wizard's summary page appears, click the Finish button to create the scope.

Creating a New Scope in IPv6

Now that you have seen how to create a new scope in IPv4, I'll go through the steps to create a new scope in IPv6.

To create a scope, right-click the IPv6 option in the DHCP snap-in under the server name and select the Action ➤ New Scope command. This starts the New Scope Wizard. Just as with creating a scope in IPv4, the welcome page of the wizard tells you that you've launched the New Scope Wizard. You will look at each page of the wizard in the following sections.

Setting the Screen Name

The Scope Name page (see Figure 2.27) allows you to enter a name and description for your scope. These will be displayed by the DHCP snap-in.

FIGURE 2.27 IPv6 Scope Name page of the New Scope Wizard

It's a good idea to pick a sensible name for your scopes so that other administrators will be able to figure out what the scope is used for.

Scope Prefix

The Scope Prefix page (see Figure 2.28) gets you started creating the IPv6 scope. IPv6 has three types of addresses, which can be categorized by type and scope.

FIGURE 2.28   Scope Prefix page of the New Scope Wizard

Unicast Addresses   *One-to-one*. A packet from one host is delivered to another host. The following are some examples of IPv6 unicast:

- The unicast prefix for site-local addresses is FEC0::/48.
- The unicast prefix for link-local addresses is FE80::/64.

The 6to4 address allows communication between two hosts running both IPv4 and IPv6. The way to calculate the 6to4 address is by combining the global prefix 2002::/16 with the 32 bits of a public IPv4 address of the host. This gives you a 48-bit prefix. 6to4 is described in RFC 3056.

Multicast addresses   *One-to-many*. A packet from one host is delivered to multiple hosts (but not everyone). The prefix for multicast addresses is FF00::/8.

Anycast addresses   A packet from one host is delivered to the nearest of multiple hosts (in terms of routing distance).

Adding Exclusions

As with the IPv4 New Scope Wizard, the Add Exclusions page (see Figure 2.29) allows you to create exclusion ranges. *Exclusions* are TCP/IP numbers that are in the pool but do not get issued to clients. To exclude one address, put it in the Start IPv6 Address field. To exclude a range, also fill in the End IPv6 Address field.

FIGURE 2.29   Add Exclusions page of the New Scope Wizard

Setting a Lease Duration

The Scope Lease page (see Figure 2.30) allows you to set how long a device gets to use an assigned IP address before it has to renew its lease. You can set two different lease durations. The section labeled Non Temporary Address (IANA) is the lease time for your more permanent hosts (such as printers and server towers). The one labeled Temporary Address (IATA) is for hosts that might disconnect at any time, such as laptops.

Activating the Scope

The Completing The New Scope Wizard page (see Figure 2.31) gives you the option to activate the scope immediately after creating it. By default, the wizard will assume you want the scope activated. If you want to wait to activate the scope, choose No in the Activate Scope Now box.

Changing Scope Properties (IPv4 and IPv6)

Each scope has a set of properties associated with it. Except for the set of options assigned by the scope, you can find these properties on the General tab of the scope's Properties

FIGURE 2.30   Scope Lease page of the New Scope Wizard

FIGURE 2.31   Completing The New Scope Wizard page of the New Scope Wizard

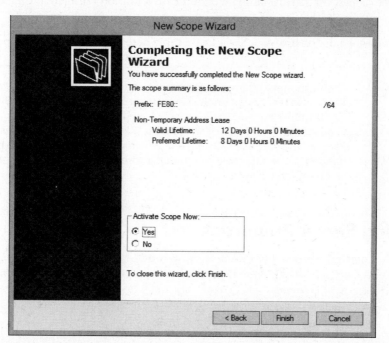

dialog box (see Figure 2.32). Some of these properties, such as the scope name and description, are self-explanatory. Others require a little more explanation.

FIGURE 2.32   General tab of the scope's Properties dialog box for an IPv4 scope

- The Start IP Address and End IP Address fields allow you to set the range of the scope.
- For IPv4 scopes, the settings in the section Lease Duration For DHCP Clients control how long leases in this scope are valid.

  The IPv6 scope dialog box includes a Lease tab where you set the lease properties.

When you make changes to these properties, they have no effect on existing leases. For example, say you create a scope from 172.30.1.1 to 172.30.1.199. You use that scope for a while and then edit its properties to reduce the range from 172.30.1.1 to 172.30.1.150. If a client has been assigned the address 172.30.1.180, which was part of the scope before you changed it, the client will retain that address until the lease expires but will not be able to renew it.

Changing Server Properties

Just as each scope has its own set of properties, so too does the server itself. You access the server properties by right-clicking the IPv4 or IPv6 object within the DHCP management console and selecting Properties.

IPv4 Server Properties

Figure 2.33 shows the IPv4 Properties dialog box.

FIGURE 2.33   General tab of the IPv4 Properties dialog box for the server

The IPv4 Properties dialog box has four tabs: General, DNS, Network Access Protection, and Advanced.

The Advanced tab, shown in Figure 2.34, contains the following configuration parameters:

- Audit Log File Path is where you enter the location for log files.

- Conflict Detection Attempts specifies how many ICMP echo requests (pings) the server sends for an address it is about to offer. The default is 0. Conflict detection is a way to verify that the DHCP server is not issuing IP addresses that are already being used on the network.

The Network Access Protection tab (see Figure 2.35) allows you to set up *Network Access Protection (NAP)*. With NAP, which is a Windows Server 2012 R2 service, an administrator can perform the following tasks:

- Carry out computer health policy validation

- Ensure ongoing compliance with health policies

- Optionally restrict the access of computers that do not meet the computer health requirements

FIGURE 2.34   The Advanced tab of the IPv4 Properties dialog box for the server

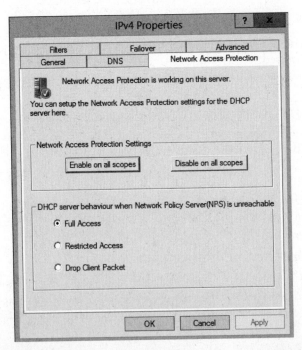

FIGURE 2.35   The Network Access Protection tab of the IPv4 Properties dialog box for the server

IPv6 Server Properties

The IPv6 Properties dialog box for the server has two tabs: General and Advanced. On the General tab (see Figure 2.36), you can configure the following settings:

- Frequency with which statistics are updated
- DHCP auditing

FIGURE 2.36 Server's IPv6 Properties, General tab

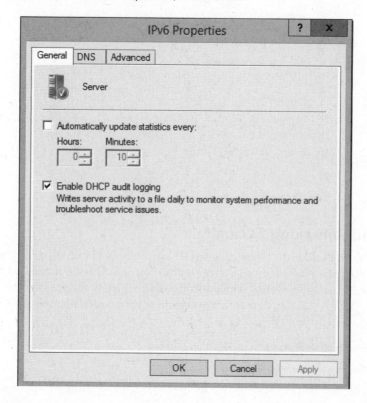

The Advanced tab (see Figure 2.37) allows you to configure the following settings:

- Database path for the audit log file path.
- Connection bindings.
- Registration credentials for dynamic DNS. The registration credential is the user account that DHCP will use to register clients with Active Directory.

Managing Reservations and Exclusions

After defining the address pool for your scope, the next step is to create reservations and exclusions, which reduce the size of the pool. In the following sections, you will learn how to add and remove exclusions and reservations.

FIGURE 2.37 Server's IPv6 Properties, Advanced tab

Adding and Removing Exclusions

When you want to exclude an entire range of IP addresses, you need to add that range as an exclusion. Ordinarily, you'll want to do this before you enable a scope because that prevents any of the IP addresses you want excluded from being leased before you have a chance to exclude them. In fact, you can't create an exclusion that includes a leased address—you have to get rid of the lease first.

Adding an Exclusion Range

Here's how to add an exclusion range:

1. Open the DHCP snap-in and find the scope to which you want to add an exclusion (either IPv4 or IPv6).

2. Expand the scope so that you can see its Address Pool item for IPv4 or the Exclusion section for IPv6.

3. Right-click the Address Pool or Exclusion section and choose the New Exclusion Range command.

4. When the Add Exclusion dialog box appears (see Figure 2.38), enter the IP addresses you want to exclude. To exclude a single address, type it in the Start IP Address field. To exclude a range of addresses, also fill in the End IP Address field.

5. Click the Add button to add the exclusion.

When you add exclusions, they appear in the Address Pool node, which is under the Scope section for IPv4 and under the Exclusion section of IPv6.

FIGURE 2.38 Add Exclusion dialog boxes for IPv4 and IPv6

IPv4 Add Exclusion dialog box   IPv6 Add Exclusion dialog box

Removing an Exclusion Range

To remove an exclusion, just right-click it and choose the Delete command. After confirming your command, the snap-in removes the excluded range and the addresses become immediately available for issuance.

Adding and Removing Reservations

Adding a reservation is simple as long as you have the MAC address of the device for which you want to create a reservation. Because reservations belong to a single scope, you create and remove them within the Reservations node beneath each scope.

Adding a Reservation

To add a reservation, perform the following tasks:

1. Right-click the scope and select New Reservation.

    This displays the New Reservation dialog box, shown in Figure 2.39.

FIGURE 2.39 New Reservation dialog boxes for IPv4 and IPv6

IPv4 New Reservation dialog box   IPv6 New Reservation dialog box

2. Enter the IP address and MAC address or ID for the reservation.

> To find the MAC address of the local computer, use the `ipconfig` command. To find the MAC address of a remote machine, use the `nbtstat -a`*computername* command.

3. If you want, you can also enter a name and description.

4. For IPv4, in the Supported Types section, choose whether the reservation will be made by DHCP only, BOOTP only (useful for remote-access devices), or both.

Removing a Reservation

To remove a reservation, right-click it and select Delete. This removes the reservation but does nothing to the client device.

> There's no way to change a reservation once it has been created. If you want to change any of the associated settings, you'll have to delete and re-create the reservation.

Setting Scope Options for IPv4

Once you've installed a server, authorized it in Active Directory, and fixed up the address pool, the next step is to set scope options that you want sent out to clients, such as router (that is, default gateway) and DNS server addresses. You must configure the options you want sent out before you activate a scope. If you don't, clients may register in the scope without getting any options, rendering them virtually useless. Thus, configure the scope options, along with the IP address and subnet mask that you configured earlier in this chapter.

In the following sections, you will learn how to configure and assign scope options on the DHCP server.

Understanding Option Assignment

You can control which DHCP options are doled out to clients in five (slightly overlapping) ways:

Predefined Options *Predefined options* are templates that are available in the Server, Scope, or Client Options dialog box.

Server Options *Server options* are assigned to all scopes and clients of a particular server. That means if there's some setting you want all clients of a DHCP server to have, no matter what scope they're in, this is where you assign it. Specific options (those that are set at the class, scope, or client level) will override server-level options. That gives you an escape valve; it's a better idea, though, to be careful about which options you assign if your server manages multiple scopes.

Scope Options   If you want a particular option value assigned only to those clients in a certain subnet, you should assign it as a *scope option*. For example, it's common to specify different routers for different physical subnets; if you have two scopes corresponding to different subnets, each scope would probably have a separate value for the router option.

Class Options   You can assign different options to clients of different types, that is, *class options*. For example, Windows 2000, XP, Vista, Windows 7, Windows 8, Server 2003, Server 2003 R2, Server 2008, Server 2008 R2, and Server 2012/2012 R2 machines recognize a number of DHCP options that Windows 98, Windows NT, and Mac OS machines ignore, and vice versa. By defining a Windows 2000 or newer class (using the ipconfig /setclassid command you saw earlier), you could assign those options only to machines that report themselves as being in that class.

Client Options   If a client is using DHCP reservations, you can assign certain options to that specific client. You attach *client options* to a particular reservation. Client options override scope, server, and class options. The only way to override a client option is to configure the client manually. The DHCP server manages client options.

> **NOTE**   Client options override class options, class options override scope options, and scope options override server options.

Assigning Options

You can use the DHCP snap-in to assign options at the scope, server, reserved address, or class level. The mechanism you use to assign these options is the same for each; the only difference is where you set the options.

When you create an option assignment, remember that it applies to all of the clients in the server or the scope from that point forward. Option assignments aren't retroactive, and they don't migrate from one scope to another.

Creating and Assigning a New Option

To create a new option and have it assigned, follow these steps:

1. Select the scope or server where you want the option assigned.

2. Select the corresponding Options node and choose Action ➤ Configure Options.

    To set options for a reserved client, right-click its entry in the Reservations node and select Configure Options.

    Then you'll see the Scope Options dialog box (see Figure 2.40), which lists all of the options that you might want to configure.

3. To select an individual option, check the box next to it and then use the controls in the Data Entry control group to enter the value you want associated with the option.

FIGURE 2.40 The Scope Options dialog box

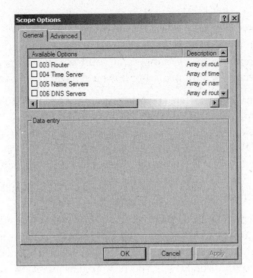

4. Continue to add options until you've specified all of the ones you want attached to the server or scope. Then click OK.

Configuring the DHCP Server for Classes

You saw how to assign classes to individual machines earlier in the chapter. Now you will learn how to configure the DHCP server to recognize your customized classes and configure options for them. In Exercise 2.11, you will create a new user class and configure options for the new class. Before you begin, make sure that the computers you want to use in the class have been configured with the `ipconfig /setclassid` command, as described in the section "Ipconfig Lease Options" earlier in this chapter.

EXERCISE 2.11

Configuring User Class Options

1. Open the DHCP snap-in by selecting Administrative Tools ➤ DHCP.

2. Right-click the IPv4 item and select Define User Classes.

3. Click the Add button in the DHCP User Classes dialog box.

4. In the New Class dialog box, enter a descriptive name for the class in the Display Name field. Enter a class ID in the ID field. (Typically, you will enter the class ID in the ASCII portion of the ID field.) When you have finished, click OK.

5. The new class appears in the DHCP User Classes dialog box. Click the Close button to return to the DHCP snap-in.

6. Right-click the Scope Options node and select Configure Options.

7. Click the Advanced tab. Select the class you defined in step 4 from the User Class pop-up menu.

8. Configure the options you want to set for the class. Click OK when you have finished. Notice that the options you configured (and the class with which they are associated) appear in the right pane of the DHCP window.

About the Default Routing and Remote Access Predefined User Class

Windows Server 2012/2012 R2 includes a predefined user class called the *Default Routing and Remote Access class*. This class includes options important to clients connecting to Routing and Remote Access, notably the 051 Lease option.

> Be sure to know that the 051 Lease option is included within this class and that it can be used to assign a shorter lease duration for clients connecting to Routing and Remote Access.

Activating and Deactivating Scopes

When you've completed the steps in Exercise 2.5 and you're ready to unleash your new scope so that it can be used to make client assignments, the final required step is activating the scope. When you activate a scope, you're just telling the server that it's OK to start handing out addresses from that scope's address pool. As soon as you activate a scope, addresses from its pool may be assigned to clients. Of course, this is a necessary precondition to getting any use out of your scope.

If you later want to stop using a scope, you can, but be aware that it's a permanent change. When you deactivate a scope, DHCP tells all clients registered with the scope that they need to release their leases immediately and renew them someplace else—the equivalent of a landlord who evicts tenants when the building is condemned!

> Don't deactivate a scope unless you want clients to stop using it immediately.

Creating a Superscope for IPv4

A *superscope* allows the DHCP server to provide multiple logical subnet addresses to DHCP clients on a single physical network. You create superscopes with the New Superscope command, which triggers the New Superscope Wizard.

NOTE   You can have only one superscope per server.

The steps in Exercise 2.12 take you through the process of creating a superscope.

EXERCISE 2.12

Creating a Superscope

1. Open the DHCP snap-in by selecting Administrative Tools ➤ DHCP.

2. Follow the instructions in Exercise 2.10 to create two scopes: one for 192.168.0.2 through 192.168.0.127 and one for 192.168.1.12 through 192.168.1.127.

3. Right-click IPv4 and choose the New Superscope command. The New Superscope Wizard appears. Click the Next button.

4. On the Superscope Name page, name your superscope and click the Next button.

5. The Select Scopes page appears, listing all scopes on the current server. Select the two scopes you created in step 2 and then click the Next button.

6. The wizard's summary page appears. Click the Finish button to create your scope.

7. Verify that your new superscope appears in the DHCP snap-in.

Deleting a Superscope

You can delete a superscope by right-clicking it and choosing the Delete command. A superscope is just an administrative convenience, so you can safely delete one at any time—it doesn't affect the "real" scopes that make up the superscope.

Adding a Scope to a Superscope

To add a scope to an existing superscope, find the scope you want to add, right-click it, and choose Action ➤ Add To Superscope. A dialog box appears, listing all of the superscopes known to this server. Pick the one to which you want the current scope appended and click the OK button.

Removing a Scope from a Superscope

To remove a scope from a superscope, open the superscope and right-click the target scope. The pop-up menu provides a Remove From Superscope command that will do the deed.

Activating and Deactivating Superscopes

Just as with regular scopes, you can activate and deactivate superscopes. The same restrictions and guidelines apply. You must activate a superscope before it can be used, and you must not deactivate it until you want all of your clients to lose their existing leases and be forced to request new ones.

To activate or deactivate a superscope, right-click the superscope name, and select Activate or Deactivate, respectively, from the pop-up menu.

Creating IPv4 Multicast Scopes

Multicasting occurs when one machine communicates to a network of subscribed computers rather than specifically addressing each computer on the destination network. It's much more efficient to multicast a video or audio stream to multiple destinations than it is to unicast it to the same number of clients, and the increased demand for multicast-friendly network hardware has resulted in some head scratching about how to automate the multicast configuration.

In the following sections, you will learn about MADCAP, the protocol that controls multicasting, and about how to build and configure a multicast scope.

Understanding the Multicast Address Dynamic Client Allocation Protocol

DHCP is usually used to assign IP configuration information for *unicast* (or one-to-one) network communications. With multicast, there's a separate type of address space assigned from 224.0.0.0 through 239.255.255.255. Addresses in this space are known as *Class D addresses*, or simply *multicast addresses*. Clients can participate in a multicast just by knowing (and using) the multicast address for the content they want to receive. However, multicast clients also need to have an ordinary IP address.

How do clients know what address to use? Ordinary DHCP won't help because it's designed to assign IP addresses and option information to one client at a time. Realizing this, the Internet Engineering Task Force (IETF) defined a new protocol: *Multicast Address Dynamic Client Allocation Protocol (MADCAP)*. MADCAP provides an analog to DHCP but for multicast use. A MADCAP server issues leases for multicast addresses only. MADCAP clients can request a multicast lease when they want to participate in a multicast.

DHCP and MADCAP have some important differences. First you have to realize that the two are totally separate. A single server can be a DHCP server, a MADCAP server, or both; no implied or actual relation exists between the two. Likewise, clients can use DHCP and/or MADCAP at the same time—the only requirement is that every MADCAP client has to get a unicast IP address from somewhere.

Remember that DHCP can assign options as part of the lease process but MADCAP cannot. The only thing MADCAP does is dynamically assign multicast addresses.

Building Multicast Scopes

Most of the steps you go through when creating a multicast scope are identical to those required for an ordinary unicast scope. Exercise 2.13 highlights the differences.

EXERCISE 2.13

Creating a New Multicast Scope

1. Open the DHCP snap-in by selecting Administrative Tools ➢ DHCP.

2. Right-click IPv4 and choose New Multicast Scope. The New Multicast Scope Wizard appears. Click the Next button on the welcome page.

3. In the Multicast Scope Name page, name your multicast scope (and add a description if you'd like). Click the Next button.

4. The IP Address Range page appears. Enter a start IP address of **224.0.0.0** and an end IP address of **224.255.0.0**. Adjust the TTL to 1 to make sure that no multicast packets escape your local network segment. Click the Next button when you're finished.

5. The Add Exclusions page appears; click its Next button.

6. The Lease Duration page appears. Since multicast addresses are used for video and audio, you'd ordinarily leave multicast scope assignments in place somewhat longer than you would with a regular unicast scope, so the default lease length is 30 days (instead of 8 days for a unicast scope). Click the Next button.

7. The wizard asks you if you want to activate the scope now. Click the No radio button and then the Next button.

8. The wizard's summary page appears; click the Finish button to create your scope.

9. Verify that your new multicast scope appears in the DHCP snap-in.

Setting Multicast Scope Properties

Once you create a multicast scope, you can adjust its properties by right-clicking the scope name and selecting Properties.

The Multicast Scope Properties dialog box has two tabs. The General tab (see Figure 2.41) allows you to change the scope's name, its start and end addresses, its Time To Live (TTL) value, its lease duration, and its description—in essence, all of the settings you provided when you created it in the first place.

The Lifetime tab (see Figure 2.42) allows you to limit how long your multicast scope will be active. By default, a newly created multicast scope will live forever, but if you're creating a scope to provide MADCAP assignments for a single event (or a set of events of limited duration), you can specify an expiration time for the scope. When that time is reached, the scope disappears from the server but not before making all of its clients give up their multicast address leases. This is a nice way to make sure that the lease cleans up after itself when you're finished with it.

FIGURE 2.41   General tab of the Multicast Scope Properties dialog box

FIGURE 2.42   Lifetime tab of the Multicast Scope Properties dialog box

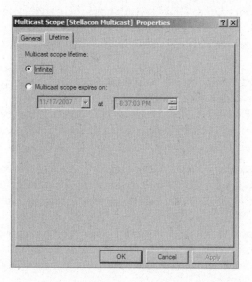

Integrating Dynamic DNS and IPv4 DHCP

DHCP integration with Dynamic DNS is a simple concept but powerful in action. By setting up this integration, you can pass addresses to DHCP clients while still maintaining the integrity of your DNS services.

The DNS server can be updated in two ways. One way is for the DHCP client to tell the DNS server its address. Another way is for the DHCP server to tell the DNS server when it registers a new client.

Neither of these updates will take place, however, unless you configure the DNS server to use Dynamic DNS. You can make this change in two ways:

- If you change it at the scope level, it will apply only to the scope.

- If you change it at the server level, it will apply to all scopes and superscopes served by the server.

Which of these options you choose depends on how widely you want to support Dynamic DNS; most of the sites I visit have enabled DNS updates at the server level.

To update the settings at either the server or scope level, you need to open the scope or server properties by right-clicking the appropriate object and choosing Properties. The DNS tab of the Properties dialog box (see Figure 2.43) includes the following options:

Enable DNS Dynamic Updates According To The Settings Below   This check box controls whether this DHCP server will attempt to register lease information with a DNS server. It must be checked to enable Dynamic DNS.

Dynamically Update DNS A And PTR Records Only If Requested By The DHCP Clients   This radio button (which is on by default) tells the DHCP server to register the update only if the DHCP client asks for DNS registration. When this button is active, DHCP clients that aren't hip to DDNS won't have their DNS records updated. However, Windows 2000, XP, Vista, Windows 7, Windows 8, Server 2003/2003 R2, Server 2008/2008 R2, and Server 2012/2012 R2 DHCP clients are smart enough to ask for the updates.

Always Dynamically Update DNS A And PTR Records   This radio button forces the DHCP server to register any client to which it issues a lease. This setting may add DNS registrations for DHCP-enabled devices that don't really need them, such as print servers. However, it allows other clients (such as Mac OS, Windows NT, and Linux machines) to have their DNS information automatically updated.

Discard A And PTR Records When Lease Is Deleted   This check box has a long name but a simple function. When a DHCP lease expires, what should happen to the DNS registration? Obviously, it would be nice if the DNS record associated with a lease vanished when the lease expired. When this check box is checked (as it is by default), that's exactly what happens. If you uncheck this box, your DNS will contain entries for expired leases that are no longer valid. When a particular IP address is reissued on a new lease, the DNS will be updated, but in between leases you'll have incorrect data in your DNS—something that's always best to avoid.

Dynamically Update DNS A And PTR Records For DHCP Clients That Do Not Request Updates   This check box lets you handle these older clients graciously by making the updates using a separate mechanism.

In Exercise 2.14, you will enable a scope to participate in Dynamic DNS updates.

FIGURE 2.43   DNS tab of the scope's IPv4 Properties dialog box

---

EXERCISE 2.14

Enabling DHCP-DNS Integration

1. Open the DHCP snap-in by selecting Administrative Tools ➢ DHCP.

2. Right-click the IPv4 item and select Properties.

3. The Server Properties dialog box appears. Click the DNS tab.

4. Verify that the check box labeled Enable DNS Dynamic Updates According To The Settings Below is checked and verify that the radio button labeled Dynamically Update DNS A And PTR Records Only If Requested By The DHCP Clients is selected.

5. Verify that the check box labeled Discard A And PTR Records When Lease Is Deleted is checked. If not, then check it.

6. Click the OK button to apply your changes and close the Server Properties dialog box.

Using Multiple DHCP Servers

DHCP can become a single point of failure within a network if there is only one DHCP server. If that server becomes unavailable, clients will not be able to obtain new leases or renew existing leases. For this reason, it is recommended that you have more than one DHCP server in the network. However, more than one DHCP server can create problems if they both are configured to use the same scope or set of addresses. Microsoft recommends the 80/20 rule for redundancy of DHCP services in a network.

Implementing the 80/20 rule calls for one DHCP server to make approximately 80 percent of the addresses for a given subnet available through DHCP while another server makes the remaining 20 percent of the addresses available. For example, with a /24 network of 254 addresses, say 192.168.1.1 to 192.168.1.254, you might have Server 1 offer 192.168.1.10 to 192.168.1.210 while Server 2 offers 192.168.1.211 to 192.168.254.

DHCP Load Sharing

Load sharing is the normal default way that you use multiple DHCP servers (as explained earlier). Both servers cover the same subnets (remember that a DHCP server can handle multiple subnets at the same time) simultaneously, and both servers assign IP addresses and options to clients on the assigned subnets. The client requests are load balanced and shared between the two servers.

This is a good option for a company that has multiple DHCP servers in the same physical location. The DHCP servers are set up in a failover relationship at the same site, and both servers respond to all DHCP client requests from the subnets to which they are associated. The DHCP server administrator can set the load distribution ratio between the multiple DHCP servers.

DHCP Hot Standby

When thinking of a DHCP hot standby setup, think of the old server failover cluster. You have two servers where one server does all of the work and the other server is a standby server in the event that the first server crashes or goes down.

In a DHCP hot standby situation, the two DHCP servers operate in a failover relationship where one server acts as an active server and is responsible for leasing IP addresses to all clients in a scope or subnet. The secondary DHCP server assumes the standby role, and it is ready to go in the event that the primary DHCP server becomes unavailable. If the primary server becomes unavailable, the secondary DHCP server is given the role of the primary DHCP server and takes over all the responsibilities of the primary DHCP server.

This failover situation is best suited to DHCP deployments where a company has DHCP servers in multiple locations.

To learn more about DHCP failover situations, please visit Microsoft at http://technet.microsoft.com/en-us/library/hh831385.aspx. Microsoft has been known for taking questions right off its websites, and this website is the perfect solution for doing this.

Working with the DHCP Database Files

DHCP uses a set of database files to maintain its knowledge of scopes, superscopes, and client leases. These files, which live in the *systemroot*\System32\DHCP folder, are always open when the DHCP service is running. DHCP servers use Joint Engine Technology (JET) databases to maintain their records.

> **WARNING**   You shouldn't modify or alter the DHCP database files when the service is running.

The primary database file is dhcp.mdb—it has all of the scope data in it.
The following files are also part of the DHCP database:

Dhcp.tmp   This is a backup copy of the database file created during reindexing of the database. You normally won't see this file, but if the service fails during reindexing, it may not remove the file when it should.

J50.log   This file (plus a number of files named J50*xxxxx*.log, where *xxxxx* stands for 00001, 00002, 00003, and so on) is a log file that stores changes before they're written to the database. The DHCP database engine can recover some changes from these files when it restarts.

J50.chk   This is a checkpoint file that tells the DHCP engine which log files it still needs to recover.

In the following sections, you will see how to manipulate the DHCP database files.

Removing the Database Files

If you're convinced that your database is corrupt because the lease information that you see doesn't match what's on the network, the easiest repair mechanism is to remove the database files and start over with an empty database.

> **TIP**   If you think the database is corrupt because the DHCP service fails at startup, you should check the event log.

To start over, follow these steps:

1. Stop the DHCP service by typing **net stop dhcpserver** at the command prompt.

2. Remove all of the files from the *systemroot*\system32\DHCP folder.

3. Restart the service (at command prompt type **net start dhcpserver**).

4. Reconcile the scope.

Changing the Database Backup Interval

By default, the DHCP service backs up its databases every 60 minutes. You can adjust this setting by editing the Backup Interval value under HKEY_LOCAL_MACHINE\SYSTEM\ CurrentControlSet\Services\DHCPServer\Parameters. This allows you to make backups either more frequently (if your database changes a lot or if you seem to have ongoing corruption problems) or less often (if everything seems to be on an even keel).

Moving the DHCP Database Files

You may find that you need to dismantle or change the role of your DHCP server and offload the DHCP functions to another computer. Rather than spend the time re-creating the DHCP database on the new machine by hand, you can copy the database files and use them directly. This is especially helpful if you have a complicated DHCP database with lots of reservations and option assignments.

By copying the files, you also minimize the amount of human error that could be introduced by reentering the information by hand.

Compacting the DHCP Database Files

There may be a time when you need to compact the DHCP database. Microsoft has a utility called jetpack.exe that allows you to compact the JET database. Microsoft JET databases are used for WINS and DHCP databases. If you wanted to use the jetpack command, the proper syntax is

```
JETPACK.EXE <database name><temp database name>
```

After you compact the database, you rename the temp database to dhcp.mdb.

Summary

DNS was designed to be a robust, scalable, and high-performance system for resolving friendly names to TCP/IP host addresses. This chapter presented an overview of the basics of DNS and how DNS names are generated. We then looked at the many new features available in the Microsoft Windows Server 2012 R2 version of DNS, and we focused on how to install, configure, and manage the necessary services. Microsoft's DNS is based on a widely accepted set of industry standards. Because of this, Microsoft's DNS can work with both Windows- and non-Windows-based networks.

This chapter also covered the DHCP lease process as it relates to TCP/IP configuration information for clients. The following stages were covered: IP discovery, IP lease offer, IP lease selection, and IP lease acknowledgment. You learned how to install and configure the DHCP server on Windows Server 2012 R2 and how to create and manage DHCP scopes and scope options. I also discussed the authorization of DHCP servers within Active Directory and scopes for IPv4 and IPv6 and showed how to create them. Finally, I covered superscopes as well as managing client leases with the options therein.

Exam Essentials

Understand the purpose of DNS. DNS is a standard set of protocols that defines a mechanism for querying and updating address information in the database, a mechanism for replicating the information in the database among servers, and a schema of the database.

Understand the different parts of the DNS database. The SOA record defines the general parameters for the DNS zone, including who is the authoritative server. NS records list the name servers for a domain; they allow other name servers to look up names in your domain. A host record (also called an address record or an A record) statically associates a host's name with its IP addresses. Pointer records (PTRs) map an IP address to a hostname, making it possible to do reverse lookups. Alias records allow you to use more than one name to point to a single host. The MX record tells you which servers can accept mail bound for a domain. SRV records tie together the location of a service (like a domain controller) with information about how to contact the service.

Know how DNS resolves names. With iterative queries, a client asks the DNS server for an answer, and the client, or resolver, returns the best kind of answer it has available. In a recursive query, the client sends a query to one name server, asking it to respond either with the requested answer or with an error. The error states either that the server can't come up with the right answer or that the domain name doesn't exist. With inverse queries, instead of supplying a name and then asking for an IP address, the client first provides the IP address and then asks for the name.

Understand the differences among DNS servers, clients, and resolvers. Any computer providing domain name services is a DNS server. A DNS client is any machine issuing queries to a DNS server. A resolver handles the process of mapping a symbolic name to an actual network address.

Know how to install and configure DNS. DNS can be installed before, during, or after installing the Active Directory service. When you install the DNS server, the DNS snap-in is installed too. Configuring a DNS server ranges from easy to difficult, depending on what you're trying to make it do. In the simplest configuration, for a caching-only server, you don't have to do anything except to make sure the server's root hints are set correctly. You can also configure a root server, a normal forward lookup server, and a reverse lookup server.

Know how to create new forward and reverse lookup zones. You can use the New Zone Wizard to create a new forward or reverse lookup zone. The process is basically the same for both types, but the specific steps and wizard pages differ somewhat. The wizard walks you through the steps, such as specifying a name for the zone (in the case of forward lookup zones) or the network ID portion of the network that the zone covers (in the case of reverse lookup zones).

Know how to configure zones for dynamic updates.   The DNS service allows dynamic updates to be enabled or disabled on a per-zone basis at each server. This is easily done in the DNS snap-in.

Know how to delegate zones for DNS.   DNS provides the ability to divide the namespace into one or more zones; these can then be stored, distributed, and replicated to other DNS servers. When delegating zones within your namespace, be aware that for each new zone you create, you need delegation records in other zones that point to the authoritative DNS servers for the new zone.

Understand the tools that are available for monitoring and troubleshooting DNS.   You can use the DNS snap-in to do some basic server testing and monitoring. More important, you use the snap-in to monitor and set logging options. Windows Server 2012 R2 automatically logs DNS events in the event log under a distinct DNS server heading. Nslookup offers the ability to perform query testing of DNS servers and to obtain detailed responses at the command prompt. You can use the command-line tool ipconfig to view your DNS client settings, to view and reset cached information used locally for resolving DNS name queries, and to register the resource records for a dynamic update client. Finally, you can configure the DNS server to create a log file that records queries, notification messages, dynamic updates, and various other bits of DNS information.

Know how to install and authorize a DHCP server.   You install the DHCP service using the Add/Remove Windows Components Wizard. You authorize the DHCP server using the DHCP snap-in. When you authorize a server, you're actually adding its IP address to the Active Directory object that contains a list of the IP addresses of all authorized DHCP servers.

Know how to create a DHCP scope.   You use the New Scope Wizard to create a new scope for both IPv4 and IPv6. Before you start, you'll need to know the IP address range for the scope you want to create; which IP addresses, if any, you want to exclude from the address pool; which IP addresses, if any, you want to reserve; and the values for the DHCP options you want to set, if any.

Understand how relay agents help with multiple physical network segments.   A question about relay agents on the exam may appear to be a DHCP-related question. Relay agents assist DHCP message propagation across network or router boundaries where such messages ordinarily wouldn't pass.

Understand the difference between exclusions and reservations.   When you want to exclude an entire range of IP addresses, you need to add that range as an exclusion. Any IP addresses within the range for which you want a permanent DHCP lease are known as reservations. Remember that exclusions are TCP/IP numbers in a pool that do not get issued and reservations are numbers in a TCP/IP pool that get issued only to the same client each time.

Review Questions

1. You are the network administrator for the ABC Company. Your network consists of two DNS servers named *DNS1* and *DNS2*. The users who are configured to use DNS2 complain because they are unable to connect to Internet websites. The following table shows the configuration of both servers:

DNS1	DNS2
`_msdcs.abc.comabc.com`	`.(root)_msdcs.abc.comabc.com`

   The users connected to DNS2 need to be able to access the Internet. What needs to be done?

   A. Build a new Active Directory Integrated zone on DNS2.

   B. Delete the `.(root)` zone from DNS2 and configure conditional forwarding on DNS2.

   C. Delete the current `cache.dns` file.

   D. Update your `cache.dns` file and root hints.

2. You are the network administrator for a large company that has one main site and one branch office. Your company has a single Active Directory forest, `ABC.com`. You have a single domain controller (ServerA) in the main site that has the DNS role installed. ServerA is configured as a primary DNS zone. You have decided to place a domain controller (ServerB) in the remote site and implement the DNS role on that server. You want to configure DNS so that, if the WAN link fails, users in both sites can still update records and resolve any DNS queries. How should you configure the DNS servers?

   A. Configure ServerB as a secondary DNS server. Set replication to occur every five minutes.

   B. Configure ServerB as a stub zone.

   C. Configure ServerB as an Active Directory Integrated zone and convert ServerA to an Active Directory Integrated zone.

   D. Convert ServerA to an Active Directory Integrated zone and configure ServerB as a secondary zone.

3. You are the network administrator for a midsize computer company. You have a single Active Directory forest, and your DNS servers are configured as Active Directory Integrated zones. When you look at the DNS records in Active Directory, you notice that there are many records for computers that do not exist on your domain. You want to make sure that only domain computers register with your DNS servers. What should you do to resolve this issue?

   A. Set dynamic updates to None.

   B. Set dynamic updates to Nonsecure And Secure.

   C. Set dynamic updates to Domain Users Only.

   D. Set dynamic updates to Secure Only.

4. Your company consists of a single Active Directory forest. You have a Windows Server 2012 R2 domain controller that also has the DNS role installed. You also have a Unix-based DNS server at the same location. You need to configure your Windows DNS server to allow zone transfers to the Unix-based DNS server. What should you do?

    A. Enable BIND secondaries.

    B. Configure the Unix machine as a stub zone.

    C. Convert the DNS server to Active Directory Integrated.

    D. Configure the Microsoft DNS server to forward all requests to the Unix DNS server.

5. You are the network administrator for Stellacon Corporation. Stellacon has two trees in its Active Directory forest, stellacon.com and abc.com. Company policy does not allow DNS zone transfers between the two trees. You need to make sure that when anyone in abc.com tries to access the stellacon.com domain, all names are resolved from the stellacon.com DNS server. What should you do?

    A. Create a new secondary zone in abc.com for stellacon.com.

    B. Configure conditional forwarding on the abc.com DNS server for stellacon.com.

    C. Create a new secondary zone in stellacon.com for abc.com.

    D. Configure conditional forwarding on the stellacon.com DNS server for abc.com.

6. You are the network administrator for your organization. A new company policy states that all inbound DNS queries need to be recorded. What can you do to verify that the IT department is compliant with this new policy?

    A. Enable Server Auditing – Object Access.

    B. Enable DNS debug logging.

    C. Enable server database query logging.

    D. Enable DNS Auditing – Object Access.

7. You are the network administrator for a small company with two DNS servers: DNS1 and DNS2. Both DNS servers reside on domain controllers. DNS1 is set up as a standard primary zone, and DNS2 is set up as a secondary zone. A new security policy was written stating that all DNS zone transfers must be encrypted. How can you implement the new security policy?

    A. Enable the Secure Only setting on DNS1.

    B. Enable the Secure Only setting on DNS2.

    C. Configure Secure Only on the Zone Transfers tab for both servers.

    D. Delete the secondary zone on DNS2. Convert both DNS servers to use Active Directory Integrated zones.

8. You are responsible for DNS in your organization. You look at the DNS database and see a large number of older records on the server. These records are no longer valid. What should you do?

    A. In the zone properties, enable Zone Aging and Scavenging.

    B. In the server properties, enable Zone Aging and Scavenging.

    C. Manually delete all of the old records.

    D. Set Dynamic Updates to None.

9. Your IT team has been informed by the compliance team that it needs copies of the DNS Active Directory Integrated zones for security reasons. You need to give the Compliance department a copy of the DNS zone. How should you accomplish this goal?

    A. Run dnscmd /zonecopy.

    B. Run dnscmd /zoneinfo.

    C. Run dnscmd /zoneexport.

    D. Run dnscmd /zonefile.

10. You are the network administrator for a Windows Server 2012 R2 network. You have multiple remote locations connected to your main office by slow satellite links. You want to install DNS into these offices so that clients can locate authoritative DNS servers in the main location. What type of DNS servers should be installed in the remote locations?

    A. Primary DNS zones

    B. Secondary DNS zones

    C. Active Directory Integrated zones

    D. Stub zones

Chapter

3

Plan and Install Active Directory

THE FOLLOWING 70-410 EXAM OBJECTIVES ARE COVERED IN THIS CHAPTER:

✓ **Install domain controllers**

- Add or remove a domain controller from a domain
- Upgrade a domain controller
- Install Active Directory Domain Services (AD DS) on a Server Core installation
- Install a domain controller from Install from Media (IFM)
- Resolve DNS SRV record registration issues
- Configure a global catalog server
- Deploy Active Directory iaas in Windows Azure

Now that you are familiar with Domain Name System (DNS), you need to verify that the computer you upgrade to a domain controller (DC) meets the basic file system and network connectivity requirements so that Active Directory runs smoothly and efficiently in your organization.

Next, you'll explore the concept of *domain functional levels*, which essentially determine what sorts of domain controllers you can use in your environment. For instance, in the Windows Server 2003 domain functional level, you can include Server 2012/2012 R2, Server 2008 R2, Server 2008, and Server 2003 domain controllers, but the functionality of the domain is severely limited.

Once you understand how to plan properly for your domain environment, you will learn how to install Active Directory, which you will accomplish by promoting a Windows Server 2012 R2 computer to a domain controller. I will also discuss a feature in Windows Server 2012 R2 called a *read-only domain controller (RODC)*.

After you become familiar with the initial Active Directory installation, you will learn how to install and configure Application Directory partitions. These partitions provide replicable data repositories using the Active Directory paradigm, but they don't actually store any security principals, such as users or groups. As the name implies, you use Application Directory partitions primarily to store data generated by applications that need to be replicated throughout your network environments independent of the rest of Active Directory.

The final section of this chapter deals with integrating DNS with Active Directory. You learned about DNS in Chapter 2, "Configure Network Services," but in this chapter I will review how DNS implements with Active Directory.

For these exercises, I assume you are creating a Windows Server 2012 R2 machine in a test environment and not on a live network. If this Windows Server 2012 R2 machine is being added into a Windows Server 2012 or 2008 R2 domain, you will need to prep the domain (explained in the section "Adprep" later in this chapter).

Verifying the File system

When you're planning your Active Directory deployment, the file system that the operating system uses is an important concern for two reasons. First, the file system can provide the ultimate level of security for all the information stored on the server itself. Second, it is responsible for managing and tracking all of this data. The Windows Server 2012 R2 platform supports two file systems:

- Windows NT File System (NTFS)

- Resilient File System (ReFS)

Although ReFS was new to Windows Server 2012, NTFS has been around for many years, and NTFS in Windows Server 2012 R2 has been improved for better performance.

If you have been working with servers for many years, you may have noticed a few changes to the server file system choices. For example, in Windows Server 2003, you could choose between FAT, FAT32, and NTFS. In Windows Server 2008 R2, you could choose between FAT32 and NTFS. In Windows Server 2012 R2, you will notice that all versions of FAT have been removed (see Figure 3.1).

FIGURE 3.1 Format options on Windows Server 2012 R2

Resilient File System (ReFS)

Windows Server 2012 R2 now includes a new file system called *Resilient File System (ReFS)*. ReFS was created to help Windows Server 2012 R2 maximize the availability of data and online operation. ReFS allows the Windows Server 2012 R2 system to continue to function despite some errors that would normally cause data to be lost or the system to go down. ReFS uses data integrity to protect your data from errors and also to make sure that all of your important data is online when that data is needed.

One of the issues that IT members have had to face over the years is the problem of rapidly growing data sizes. As we continue to rely more and more on computers, our data continues to get larger and larger. This is where ReFS can help an IT department. ReFS was designed specifically with the issues of scalability and performance in mind, which resulted in some of the following ReFS features:

Availability   If your hard disk becomes corrupt, ReFS has the ability to implement a salvage strategy that removes the data that has been corrupted. This feature allows the healthy data to continue to be available while the unhealthy data is removed. All of this can be done without taking the hard disk offline.

Scalability   One of the main advantages of ReFS is the ability to support volume sizes up to 2^{78} bytes using 16KB cluster sizes, while Windows stack addressing allows 2^{64} bytes. ReFS also supports file sizes of $2^{64}-1$ bytes, 2^{64} files in a directory, and the same number of directories in a volume.

Robust Disk Updating   ReFS uses a disk updating system referred to as an *allocate-on-write transactional model* (also known as *copy on write*). This model helps to avoid many hard disk issues while data is written to the disk because ReFS updates data using disk writes to multiple locations in an atomic manner instead of updating data in place.

Data Integrity   ReFS uses a check-summed system to verify that all data that is being written and stored is accurate and reliable. ReFS always uses allocate-on-write for updates to the data, and it uses checksums to detect disk corruption.

Application Compatibility   ReFS allows for most NTFS features and also supports the Win32 API. Because of this, ReFS is compatible with most Windows applications.

NTFS

Let's start with some of the features of NTFS. There are many benefits to using NTFS, including support for the following:

Disk Quotas   To restrict the amount of disk space used by users on the network, system administrators can establish *disk quotas*. By default, Windows Server 2012 R2 supports disk quota restrictions at the volume level. That is, you can restrict the amount of storage space that a specific user uses on a single disk volume. Third-party solutions that allow more granular quota settings are also available.

File System Encryption   One of the fundamental problems with network operating systems (NOSs) is that system administrators are often given full permission to view all files and data stored on hard disks, which can be a security and privacy concern. In some cases, this is necessary. For example, to perform backup, recovery, and disk management functions, at least one user must have all permissions. Windows Server 2012 R2 and NTFS address these issues by allowing for *file system encryption*. Encryption essentially scrambles all of the data stored within files before they are written to the disk. When an authorized user requests the files, they are transparently decrypted and provided. By using encryption, you can prevent the data from being used in case it is stolen or intercepted by an unauthorized user—even a system administrator.

Dynamic Volumes   Protecting against disk failures is an important concern for production servers. Although earlier versions of Windows NT supported various levels of Redundant Array of Independent Disks (RAID) technology, software-based solutions had some shortcomings. Perhaps the most significant was that administrators needed to perform server reboots to change RAID configurations. Also, you could not make some configuration changes without completely reinstalling the operating system. With Windows Server 2012 R2 support for *dynamic volumes*, system administrators can change RAID and other disk configuration settings without needing to reboot or reinstall the server. The result is greater data protection, increased scalability, and increased uptime. Dynamic volumes are also included with ReFS.

Mounted Drives   By using *mounted drives*, system administrators can map a local disk drive to an NTFS directory name. This helps them organize disk space on servers and increase manageability. By using mounted drives, you can mount the C:\Users directory to an actual physical disk. If that disk becomes full, you can copy all of the files to another, larger drive without changing the directory path name or reconfiguring applications.

Remote Storage   System administrators often notice that as soon as they add more space, they must plan the next upgrade. One way to recover disk space is to move infrequently used files to external hard drives. However, backing up and restoring these files can be quite difficult and time-consuming. System administrators can use the *remote storage* features supported by NTFS to off-load seldom-used data automatically to a backup system or other devices. The files, however, remain available to users. If a user requests an archived file, Windows Server 2012 R2 can automatically restore the file from a remote storage device and make it available. Using remote storage like this frees up system administrators' time and allows them to focus on tasks other than micromanaging disk space.

Self-healing NTFS   In previous versions of the Windows Server operating system, if you had to fix a corrupted NTFS volume, you used a tool called Chkdsk.exe. The disadvantage of this tool is that the Windows Server's availability was disrupted. If this server was your domain controller, that could stop domain logon authentication.

To help protect the Windows Server 2012 R2 NTFS file system, Microsoft now uses a feature called self-healing NTFS. *Self-healing NTFS* attempts to fix corrupted NTFS file systems without taking them offline. Self-healing NTFS allows an NTFS file system to be corrected without running the Chkdsk.exe utility. New features added to the NTFS kernel code allow disk inconsistencies to be corrected without system downtime.

Security   NTFS allows you to configure not only folder-level security but also file-level security. NTFS security is one of the biggest reasons most companies use NTFS. ReFS also allows folder- and file-level security.

Setting Up the NTFS Partition

Although the features mentioned in the previous section likely compel most system administrators to use NTFS, additional reasons make using it mandatory. The most important reason is that the Active Directory data store must reside on an NTFS partition. Therefore, before you begin installing Active Directory, make sure you have at least one NTFS partition available. Also, be sure you have a reasonable amount of disk space available (at least 4GB). Because the size of the Active Directory data store will grow as you add objects to it, also be sure that you have adequate space for the future.

Exercise 3.1 shows you how to use the administrative tools to view and modify disk configuration.

 WARNING Before you make any disk configuration changes, be sure you completely understand their potential effects; then perform the test in a lab environment and make sure you have good, verifiable backups handy. Changing partition sizes and adding and removing partitions can result in a total loss of all information on one or more partitions.

If you want to convert an existing partition from FAT or FAT32 to NTFS, you need to use the CONVERT command-line utility. For example, the following command converts the C: partition from FAT to NTFS:

```
CONVERT c: /fs:ntfs
```

EXERCISE 3.1

Viewing Disk Configuration

1. Press the Windows key on the keyboard (left side between the Ctrl and Alt keys) and then choose Administrative Tools.

2. Double-click Computer Management.

3. Under Storage, click Disk Management.

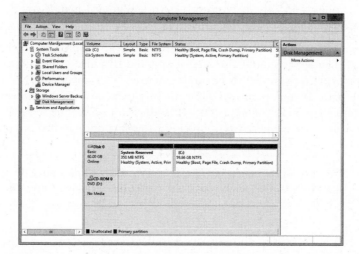

The Disk Management program shows you the logical and physical disks that are currently configured on your system. Note that information about the size of each partition is also displayed (in the Capacity column).

4. Use the View menu to choose various depictions of the physical and logical drives in your system.

5. To see the available options for modifying partition settings, right-click any of the disks or partitions. This step is optional.

6. Close Computer Management.

Verifying Network Connectivity

Although a Windows Server 2012 R2 computer can be used by itself without connecting to a network, you will not harness much of the potential of the operating system without network connectivity. Because the fundamental purpose of a network operating system is to provide resources to users, you must verify network connectivity.

Basic Connectivity Tests

Before you begin to install Active Directory, you should perform several checks of your current configuration to ensure that the server is configured properly on the network. You should test the following:

Network Adapter   At least one network adapter should be installed and properly configured on your server. A quick way to verify that a network adapter is properly installed is to use the Computer Management administrative tool. Under Device Manager, Network Adapters branch, you should have at least one network adapter listed. If you do not, use the Add Hardware icon in Control Panel to configure hardware.

TCP/IP   Make sure that TCP/IP is installed, configured, and enabled on any necessary network adapters. The server should also be given a valid IP address and subnet mask. Optionally, you may need to configure a default gateway, DNS servers, WINS servers, and other network settings. If you are using DHCP, be sure that the assigned information is correct. It is always a good idea to use a static IP address for servers because IP address changes can cause network connectivity problems if they are not handled properly.

 You must understand TCP/IP to use Windows Server 2012 R2 and Active Directory. TCP/IP will be covered in greater detail in Chapter 8, "Configure TCP/IP."

Internet Access   If the server should have access to the Internet, verify that it is able to connect to external web servers and other machines outside of the local area network (LAN). If the server is unable to connect, you might have a problem with the TCP/IP configuration.

LAN Access   The server should be able to view other servers and workstations on the network. If other machines are not visible, make sure that the network and TCP/IP configurations are correct for your environment.

Client Access   Network client computers should be able to connect to your server and view any shared resources. A simple way to test connectivity is to create a share and test whether other machines are able to see files and folders within it. If clients cannot access the machine, make sure that both the client and the server are configured properly.

Wide Area Network Access   If you're working in a distributed environment, you should ensure that you have access to any remote sites or users who will need to connect to this machine. Usually, this is a simple test that can be performed by a network administrator.

Tools and Techniques for Testing Network Configuration

In some cases, verifying network access can be quite simple. You might have some internal and external network resources with which to test. In other cases, it might be more complicated. You can use several tools and techniques to verify that your network configuration is correct.

Using the Ipconfig Utility   By typing **ipconfig/all** at the command prompt, you can view information about the TCP/IP settings of a computer. Figure 3.2 shows the types of information you'll receive.

FIGURE 3.2   Viewing TCP/IP information with the `ipconfig` utility

Using the `Ping` Command   The ping command was designed to test connectivity to other computers. You can use the command simply by typing **ping** and then an IP address or hostname at the command line. The following are some steps for testing connectivity using the ping command.

Ping Other Computers on the Same Subnet   You should start by pinging a known active IP address on the network to check for a response. If you receive one, then you have connectivity to the network.

Next check to see whether you can ping another machine using its hostname. If this works, then local name resolution works properly.

Ping Computers on Different Subnets   To ensure that routing is set up properly, you should attempt to ping computers that are on other subnets (if any exist) on your network. If this test fails, try pinging the default gateway. Any errors may indicate a problem in the network configuration or a problem with a router.

When You Don't Receive a Response

Some firewalls, routers, or servers on your network or on the Internet might prevent you from receiving a successful response from a ping command. This is usually for security reasons (malicious users might attempt to disrupt network traffic using excessive pings as well as redirects and smurf attacks). If you do not receive a response, do not assume that the service is not available. Instead, try to verify connectivity in other ways. For example, you can use the TRACERT command to demonstrate connectivity beyond your subnet, even if other routers ignore Internet Control Message Protocol (ICMP) responses. Because the display of a second router implies connectivity, the path to an ultimate destination shows success even if it does not display the actual names and addresses.

Browsing the Network To ensure that you have access to other computers on the network, be sure that they can be viewed by clicking Network. This verifies that your name resolution parameters are set up correctly and that other computers are accessible. Also, try connecting to resources (such as file shares or printers) on other machines.

 By default, Network Discovery is turned off. To browse the network, you must first enable Network Discovery from the Control Panel in the Network and Sharing Center ➢ Advanced Sharing settings.

Browsing the Internet You can quickly verify whether your server has access to the Internet by visiting a known website, such as www.microsoft.com. Success ensures that you have access outside of your network. If you do not have access to the Web, you might need to verify your proxy server settings (if applicable) and your DNS server settings.

By performing these simple tests, you can ensure that you have a properly configured network connection and that other network resources are available.

Understanding Domain and Forest Functionality

Windows Server 2012 R2 Active Directory uses a concept called *domain and forest functionality*. The functional level that you choose during the Active Directory installation determines which features your domain can use.

Windows Server 2008, Windows Server 2008 R2, Windows Server 2012, and Windows Server 2012 R2 include additional forest functionality compared to Windows Server 2003. Forest functionality applies to all of the domains within a forest.

About the Domain Functional Level

Windows Server 2012 R2 will support the following domain functional levels:

- Windows Server 2003
- Windows Server 2008
- Windows Server 2008 R2
- Windows Server 2012
- Windows Server 2012 R2

Which function level you use depends on the domain controllers you have installed on your network. This is an important fact to remember. You can use Windows Server 2003, Windows Server 2008/2008 R2, and Windows 2012 member servers in the Windows

Server 2012 R2 function level as long as all domain controllers are running Windows Server 2012 R2.

When you are deciding which function level you will use in your organization, you must choose the function level of your lowest domain controller. For example, if you have a Windows Server 2003 domain controller, your function levels should be Windows Server 2003. If you choose a higher level, the Windows Server 2003 domain controller will not function. Be careful—once a forest function level is upgraded, it cannot be downgraded lower than Windows Server 2008.

Table 3.1 shows the features available in Windows Server 2003, Windows Server 2008, Windows Server 2008 R2, Windows Server 2012, and Windows Server 2012 R2 domain function levels.

TABLE 3.1 Comparing domain functional levels

Domain functional feature	Windows Server 2003	Windows Server 2008	Windows Server 2008 R2	Windows Server 2012	Windows Server 2012 R2
Authentication assurance	Disabled	Disabled	Enabled	Enabled	Enabled
Fine-grained password policies	Disabled	Enabled	Enabled	Enabled	Enabled
Last interactive logon information	Disabled	Enabled	Enabled	Enabled	Enabled
Advanced Encryption Services (AES 128 and 256) support for the Kerberos protocol	Disabled	Enabled	Enabled	Enabled	Enabled
Distributed File System replication support for Sysvol	Disabled	Enabled	Enabled	Enabled	Enabled
Read-only domain controller (RODC)	Enabled	Enabled	Enabled	Enabled	Enabled
Ability to redirect the Users and Computers containers	Enabled	Enabled	Enabled	Enabled	Enabled
Ability to rename domain controllers	Enabled	Enabled	Enabled	Enabled	Enabled

TABLE 3.1   Comparing domain functional levels *(continued)*

Domain functional feature	Windows Server 2003	Windows Server 2008	Windows Server 2008 R2	Windows Server 2012	Windows Server 2012 R2
Logon time stamp updates	Enabled	Enabled	Enabled	Enabled	Enabled
Kerberos KDC key version numbers	Enabled	Enabled	Enabled	Enabled	Enabled
Passwords for InetOrgPerson objects	Enabled	Enabled	Enabled	Enabled	Enabled
Converts NT groups to domain local and global groups	Enabled	Enabled	Enabled	Enabled	Enabled
SID history	Enabled	Enabled	Enabled	Enabled	Enabled
Group nesting	Enabled	Enabled	Enabled	Enabled	Enabled
Universal groups	Enabled	Enabled	Enabled	Enabled	Enabled

About Forest Functionality

Windows Server 2012 R2 forest functionality applies to all of the domains in a forest. All domains have to be upgraded to Windows Server 2012 R2 before the forest can be upgraded to Windows Server 2012 R2.

There are five levels of forest functionality:

- Windows Server 2003
- Windows Server 2008
- Windows Server 2008 R2
- Windows Server 2012
- Windows Server 2012 R2

Windows Server 2003, Windows Server 2008, Windows Server 2008 R2, Windows Server 2012, and Windows Server 2012 R2 have many of the same forest features. Some of these features are described in the following list:

Global Catalog Replication Enhancements   When an administrator adds a new attribute to the global catalog, only those changes are replicated to other global catalogs in the forest. This can significantly reduce the amount of network traffic generated by replication.

Defunct Schema Classes and Attributes   You can never permanently remove classes and attributes from the Active Directory schema. However, you can mark them as defunct so that they cannot be used. With Windows Server 2003, Windows Server 2008, Windows Server 2008 R2, Windows Server 2012, and Windows Server 2012 R2 forest functionality, you can redefine the defunct schema attribute so that it occupies a new role in the schema.

Forest Trusts   Previously, system administrators had no easy way of granting permission on resources in different forests. Windows Server 2003, Windows Server 2008, Windows Server 2008 R2, Windows Server 2012, and Windows Server 2012 R2 resolve some of these difficulties by allowing trust relationships between separate Active Directory forests. Forest trusts act much like domain trusts, except that they extend to every domain in two forests. Note that all forest trusts are intransitive.

Linked Value Replication   Windows Server 2003, Windows Server 2008, Windows Server 2008 R2, Windows Server 2012, and Windows Server 2012 R2 use a concept called *linked value replication*. With linked value replication, only the user record that has been changed is replicated (not the entire group). This can significantly reduce network traffic associated with replication.

Renaming Domains   Although the Active Directory domain structure was originally designed to be flexible, there were several limitations. Because of mergers, acquisitions, corporate reorganizations, and other business changes, you may need to rename domains. In Windows Server 2003, Windows Server 2008, Windows Server 2008 R2, Windows Server 2012, and Windows Server 2012 R2 you can change the DNS and NetBIOS names for any domain. Note that this operation is not as simple as just issuing a rename command. Instead, there's a specific process that you must follow to make sure the operation is successful. Fortunately, when you properly follow the procedure, Microsoft supports domain renaming even though not all applications support it.

Other Features   Windows Server 2008, Windows Server 2008 R2, Windows Server 2012, and Windows Server 2012 R2 also support the following features:

- Improved replication algorithms and dynamic auxiliary classes are designed to increase performance, scalability, and reliability.

- *Active Directory Federation Services (AD FS)*, also known as *Trustbridge*, handles federated identity management. *Federated identity management* is a standards-based information technology process that enables distributed identification, authentication, and authorization across organizational and platform boundaries. The ADFS solution in Windows Server 2003 R2, Windows Server 2008, Windows Server 2008 R2, Windows Server 2012, and Windows Server 2012 R2 helps administrators address these challenges by enabling organizations to share a user's identity information securely.

- *Active Directory Lightweight Directory Services (AD LDS)* was developed for organizations that require flexible support for directory-enabled applications. AD LDS, which uses the Lightweight Directory Access Protocol (LDAP), is a directory service that adds flexibility and helps organizations avoid increased infrastructure costs.

- Active Directory Recycle Bin (Windows Server 2008 R2 Forest level or higher) provides administrators with the ability to restore deleted objects in their entirety while AD DS is running. Before this, if you deleted an Active Directory object, you needed to recover it from a backup. Now you can recover the object from the AD recycle bin.

NOTE   Many of the concepts related to domain and forest functional features are covered in greater detail later in this book.

Planning the Domain Structure

Once you have verified the technical configuration of your server for Active Directory, it's time to verify the Active Directory configuration for your organization. Since the content of this chapter focuses on installing the first domain in your environment, you really need to know only the following information prior to beginning setup:

- The DNS name of the domain
- The computer name or the NetBIOS name of the server (which will be used by previous versions of Windows to access server resources)
- In which domain function level the domain will operate
- Whether other DNS servers are available on the network
- What type of and how many DNS servers are available on the network

However, if you will be installing additional domain controllers in your environment or will be attaching to an existing Active Directory structure, you should also have the following information:

- If this domain controller will join an existing domain, you should know the name of that domain. You will also either require a password for a member of the Enterprise Administrators group for that domain or have someone with those permissions create a domain account before promotion.
- You should know whether the new domain will join an existing tree and, if so, the name of the tree it will join.
- You should know the name of a forest to which this domain will connect (if applicable).

Installing Active Directory

Installing Active Directory is an easy and straightforward process as long as you plan adequately and make the necessary decisions beforehand. There are many ways that you can install Active Directory. You can install Active Directory by using the Windows Server 2012 R2 installation disk (Install from Media (IFM)), using Server Manager, or using Windows PowerShell. But before you can do the actual installation, you must first make sure that your network is ready for the install.

In the following sections, you'll look at the required steps to install the first domain controller in a given environment.

Adprep

When you are adding a new user to Active Directory, you fill in fields such as First Name, Last Name, and so on. These fields are called *attributes*. The problem is that when you go to install Windows Server 2012 R2, its version of Active Directory has newer attributes than the previous versions of Active Directory. Thus, you need to set up your current version of Active Directory so that it can accept the installation of Windows Server 2012 R2 Active Directory. This is why you use Adprep. Adprep is required to run in order to add the first Windows Server 2012 R2 domain controller to an existing domain or forest.

You would need to run Adprep /forestprep to add the first Windows Server 2012 R2 domain controller to an existing forest. Adprep /forestprep must be run by an administrator who is a member of the Enterprise Admins group, the Schema Admins group, and the Domain Admins group of the domain that hosts the schema master.

You would need to run Adprep /domainprep to add the first Windows Server 2012 R2 domain controller to an existing domain. Again, to achieve this command, you must be a member of the Domain Admins group of the domain where you are installing the Windows Server 2012 R2 domain controller.

Adprep /rodcprep must be run to add the first Windows Server 2012 R2 RODC to an existing forest. The administrator who runs this command must be a member of the Enterprise Admins group.

One feature that is new to the Windows Server 2012 R2 Active Directory installation process is that, if needed, Adprep will automatically be executed during the normal Active Directory Domain Services installation.

Active Directory Prerequisites

Before you install Active Directory into your network, you must first make sure that your network and the server meet some minimum requirements. Table 3.2 will show you the requirements needed for Active Directory.

TABLE 3.2 Active Directory requirements

Requirement	Description
Adprep	When adding the first Windows Server 20012 R2 domain controller to an existing Active Directory domain, Adprep commands run automatically as needed.
Credentials	When installing a new AD DS forest, the administrator must be set to local Administrator on the first server. To install an additional domain controller in an existing domain, you need to be a member of the Domain Admins group.
DNS	Domain Name System needs to be installed for Active Directory to function properly. You can install DNS during the Active Directory installation.
NTFS	The Windows Server 2012 R2 drives that store the database, log files, and SYSVOL folder must be placed on a volume that is formatted with the NTFS file system.
RODCs	Read Only Domain Controllers can be installed as long as another domain controller (Windows Server 2008 or newer) already exists on the domain. Also the Forest functional level must be at least Windows Server 2003.
TCP/IP	You must configure the appropriate TCP/IP settings on your domain, and you must configure the DNS server addresses.

The Installation Process

Windows Server 2012 R2 computers are configured as either member servers (if they are joined to a domain) or stand-alone servers (if they are part of a workgroup). The process of converting a server to a domain controller is known as *promotion*. Through the use of a simple and intuitive wizard in Server Manager, system administrators can quickly configure servers to be domain controllers after installation. Administrators also have the ability to promote domain controllers using Windows PowerShell.

The first step in installing Active Directory is promoting a Windows Server 2012 R2 computer to a domain controller. The first domain controller in an environment serves as the starting point for the forest, trees, domains, and the operations master roles.

Exercise 3.2 shows the steps you need to follow to promote an existing Windows Server 2012 R2 computer to a domain controller. To complete the steps in this exercise, you must have already installed and configured a Windows Server 2012 R2 computer. You also need a DNS server that supports SRV records. If you do not have a DNS server available, the Active Directory Installation Wizard automatically configures one for you.

EXERCISE 3.2

Promoting a Domain Controller

1. Install the Active Directory Domain Services by clicking the Add Roles And Features link in Server Manager's Dashboard view.

2. At the Before You Begin screen, click Next.

3. The Select installation Type screen will be next. Make sure that the Role-Based radio button is selected and click Next.

4. At the Select Destination Server screen, choose the local machine. Click Next.

5. At the Select Server Roles screen, click the check box for Active Directory Domain Services.

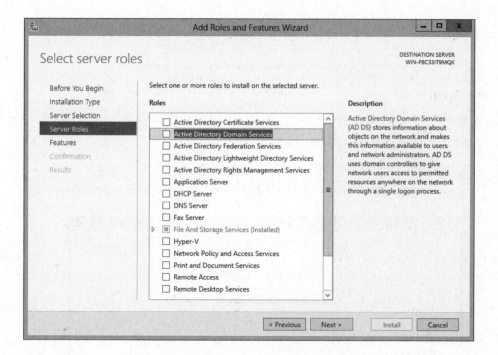

6. After you check the Active Directory Domain Services box, a pop-up menu will appear asking you to install additional features. Click the Add Features button.

7. Click Next.

8. At the Select Features screen, accept the defaults and click Next.

9. Click Next at the information screen.

10. Click the Install button at the Confirmation Installation screen.

11. The Installation Progress screen will show you how the installation is progressing.

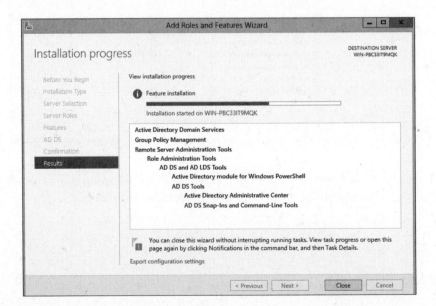

12. After the installation is complete, click the Close button.

13. On the left side window, click the AD DS link.

14. Click the More link next to Configuration Required for Active Directory Domain Services.

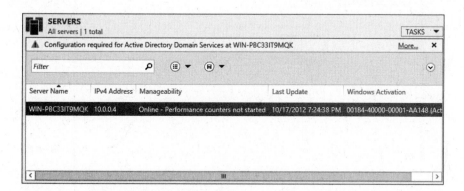

15. Under the Post-Deployment Configuration section, click the Promote This Server To A Domain Controller link.

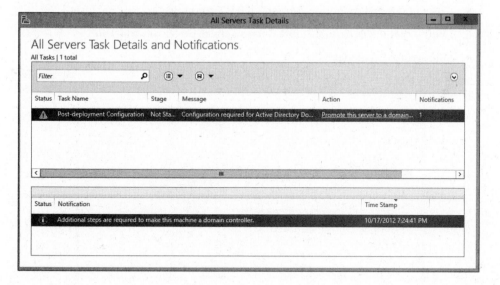

16. At this point, you will configure this domain controller. You are going to install a new domain controller in a new domain in a new forest. At the Deployment Configuration screen, choose the Add A New Forest radio button. You then need to add a root domain name. In this exercise, I will use Sybex.com. Click Next.

EXERCISE 3.2 *(continued)*

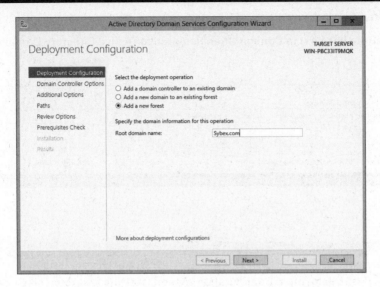

17. At the Domain Controller Options screen, set the following options:

    ▪ Function levels: Windows Server 2008 R2 (for both)

    ▪ Verify that the DNS and Global Catalog check boxes are checked

    ▪ Password: **P@ssw0rd**

    Then click Next.

18. At the DNS screen, click Next.

19. At the additional options screen, accept the default NetBIOS domain name and click Next.

20. At the Paths screen, accept the default file locations and click Next.

21. At the Review Options screen, verify your settings and click Next.

22. At the Prerequisites Check screen, click the Install button (as long as there are no errors).

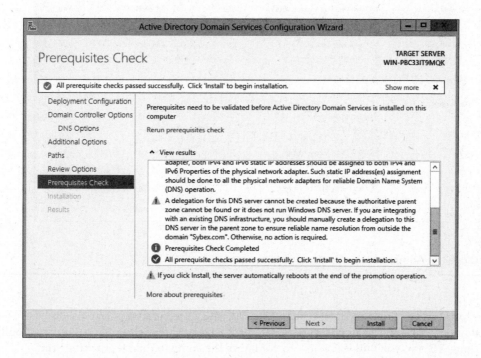

23. After the installation completes, the machine will automatically reboot. Log in as the administrator.

24. Close Server Manager.

25. Click the Start button on the keyboard and choose Administrative Tools.

26. You should see new MMC snap-ins for Active Directory.

EXERCISE 3.2 *(continued)*

27. Close the Administrative Tools window.

In Exercise 3.3, you will learn how to install Active Directory on a Server Core installation. You will use Windows Server 2012 R2 Datacenter Server Core. Before actually installing AD DS, you will learn how to configure the computer name, the time, the administrator password, and a static TCP/IP address, and then you will install DNS.

EXERCISE 3.3

Installing AD DS on Server Core

1. At the Server Core command prompt, type **cd\windows\system32** and press Enter.

2. Type **timedate.cpl** and set your date, local time zone, and time. Click OK.

3. Type **Netsh** and press Enter.

4. Type **Interface**, and press Enter.

5. Type **IPv4**, and press Enter.

6. Type **Show IP** and press Enter. This will show you the current TCP/IP address and the interface with which the TCP/IP address is associated.

7. As you can see, interface 12 is my Ethernet interface. To change this interface, type the following command and press Enter:

```
Set address name="12" source=static address=192.168.15.165
mask=255.255.255.0 gateway=192.168.15.1
```

I used 192.168.15.x for my address. You can replace the address, mask, and gateway based on your local settings.

8. Type **Show IP** and press Enter. You should see that the new address is now manual and set to the IP address you set.

EXERCISE 3.3 *(continued)*

9. Type **Exit** and press Enter.

10. Type **Net User Administrator** * and press Enter.

11. Type in your password and then confirm the password. I used P@ssw0rd for my password.

12. Type the following command and press Enter:

    Netdom renamecomputer %computername% /newname:ServerA

13. Type **Y** and press Enter.

14. Type **Shutdown /R /T 0** and press Enter. This will reboot the machine. After the reboot, log back into the system.

15. Type **PowerShell** and press Enter.

16. At the PowerShell prompt, type **Add-WindowsFeature DNS** and press Enter. This will add DNS to the server.

17. At the PowerShell prompt, type **Add-WindowsFeature AD-Domain-Services** and press Enter.

18. At the PowerShell prompt, type **Import-Module ADDSDeployment**.

19. At the PowerShell prompt, type **Install-ADDSForest**.

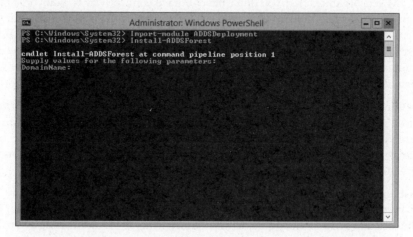

20. Type in your domain name and press Enter. I used Sybex.com.

21. Next you will be asked for your Safe mode administrator password. Type in **P@ssw0rd** and then confirm it.

22. Type **Y** and press Enter.

Active Directory will install, and the machine will automatically reboot.

Deploying Active Directory IaaS in Windows Azure

Well before I jump into this topic, I must first explain what I am talking about. Windows Azure is a Microsoft cloud platform that allows you to put your server data into the cloud. Deploying Active Directory with IaaS means you are using virtualization for the deployment.

So, to put this in a nutshell, when doing this type of install, it's actually not too far off from the install you already did. You create a virtual server and then install Active Directory. Then you upload that virtual server to the cloud.

I understand that I have not explained virtualization, but Hyper-V and virtualization will be covered in detail in Chapter 9, "Use Virtualization in Windows Server 2012 R2."

Now that you understand what this section is about, let's talk about some of the tasks that are different from the normal way you install Active Directory virtually. There are three main differences when installing Active Directory IaaS on Windows Azure.

Windows Azure virtual machines may need to have connectivity to the corporate network.   Microsoft states that you don't have to have connectivity to your on-site corporate network, but you will lose functionality. Thus, Microsoft recommends that you set up connectivity, and to do that, you must use Windows Azure Virtual Network. Windows Azure Virtual Network includes a site-to-site or site-to-point virtual private network (VPN) component capable of seamlessly connecting Windows Azure virtual machines and on-site machines.

Static IP addresses are *not* supported on Windows Azure virtual machines.   Normally, when setting up a server, we all use static IP addresses. This is actually required on a DHCP server, DNS server, and so on. But when you deploy Active Directory IaaS in Windows Azure, you must use Dynamic TCP/IP addressing, and this requires that you set up Windows Azure Virtual Network.

IP addresses for Windows Azure virtual machines are attached to Windows Azure Virtual Network, and that TCP/IP address persists for the lifetime of the virtual machine. Because of this, the Windows Server Active Directory requirements for IP addressing are met, and the requirements for DNS are also met if you want the server to have both roles.

Windows Azure allows for two distinct disk types for virtual machines.   As you will learn in Chapter 9, the selection of the virtual machine disk type is important when deploying domain controllers. Windows Azure allows both "operating system disks" and "data disks." Most of the time you will use data disks when installing Active Directory on the virtual machine. Data disks use write-through caching, guaranteeing durability of writes, and this is important to the integrity of any Windows Server active machine. There are some other factors of which you should be aware when choosing your disk type. Please check Microsoft's website for more details when choosing a disk type.

Verifying Active Directory Installation

Once you have installed and configured Active Directory, you'll want to verify that you have done so properly. In the following sections, you'll look at methods for doing this.

Using Event Viewer

The first (and perhaps most informative) way to verify the operations of Active Directory is to query information stored in the Windows Server 2012 R2 event log. You can do this using the Windows Server 2012 R2 Event Viewer. Exercise 3.4 walks you through this procedure. Entries seen with the Event Viewer include errors, warnings, and informational messages.

To complete the steps in Exercise 3.4, you must have configured the local machine as a domain controller.

EXERCISE 3.4

Viewing the Active Directory Event Log

1. Open Administrative tools by pressing the Windows key and choosing Administrative Tools.

2. Open the Event Viewer snap-in from the Administrative Tools program group.

3. In the left pane, under Applications And Services Logs, select Directory Service.

4. In the right pane, you can sort information by clicking column headings. For example, you can click the Source column to sort by the service or process that reported the event.

5. Double-click an event in the list to see the details for that item. Note that you can click the Copy button to copy the event information to the Clipboard. You can then paste the data into a document for later reference. Also, you can move between items using the up and down arrows. Click OK when you have finished viewing an event.

6. Filter an event list by right-clicking the Directory Service item in the left pane and selecting Filter Current Log. Note that filtering does not remove entries from the event logs—it only restricts their display.

7. To verify Active Directory installation, look for events related to the proper startup of Active Directory, such as Event ID 1000 (Active Directory Startup Complete) and 1394 (Attempts To Update The Active Directory Database Are Succeeding). Also, be sure to examine any error or warning messages because they could indicate problems with DNS or other necessary services.

8. When you've finished viewing information in the Event Viewer, close the application.

Gaining Insight Through Event Viewer

Despite its simple user interface and somewhat limited GUI functionality, the Event Viewer tool can be your best ally in isolating and troubleshooting problems with Windows Server 2012 R2. The Event Viewer allows you to view information that is stored in various log files that are maintained by the operating system. This includes information from the following logs:

Application Stores messages generated by programs running on your system. For example, SQL Server 2012 might report the completion of a database backup job within the Application log.

Security   Contains security-related information as defined by your auditing settings. For example, you could see when users have logged onto the system or when particularly sensitive files have been accessed.

System   Contains operating system-related information and messages. Common messages might include a service startup failure or information about when the operating system was last rebooted.

Directory Service   Stores messages and events related to how Active Directory functions. For example, you might find details related to replication here.

DNS Server   Contains details about the operations of the DNS service. This log is useful for troubleshooting replication or name-resolution problems.

Other Log Files   Contain various features of Windows Server 2012 R2 and the applications that may run on this operating system, which can create additional types of logs. These files allow you to view more information about other applications or services through the familiar Event Viewer tool.

Additionally, developers can easily send custom information from their programs to the Application log. Having all of this information in one place really makes it easy to analyze operating system and application messages. Also, many third-party tools and utilities are available for analyzing log files.

Although the Event Viewer GUI does a reasonably good job of letting you find the information you need, you might want to extract information to analyze other systems or applications. One especially useful feature of the Event Viewer is its ability to save a log file in various formats. You can access this feature by clicking Action ➢ Save As. You'll be given the option of saving in various formats, including tab- and comma-delimited text files. You can then open these files in other applications (such as Microsoft Excel) for additional data analysis.

Overall, in the real world, the Event Viewer can be an excellent resource for monitoring and troubleshooting your important servers and workstations.

In addition to providing information about the status of events related to Active Directory, the Event Viewer shows you useful information about other system services and applications. You should routinely use this tool.

Using Active Directory Administrative Tools

After a server has been promoted to a domain controller, you will see that various tools are added to the Administrative Tools program group, including the following:

Active Directory Administrative Center   This is a *Microsoft Management Console (MMC)* snap-in that allows you to accomplish many Active Directory tasks from one central location. This MMC snap-in allows you to manage your directory services objects, including doing the following tasks:

- Reset user passwords
- Create or manage user accounts
- Create or manage groups
- Create or manage computer accounts
- Create or manage organizational units (OUs) and containers
- Connect to one or several domains or domain controllers in the same instance of Active Directory Administrative Center
- Filter Active Directory data

Active Directory Domains and Trusts   Use this tool to view and change information related to the various domains in an Active Directory environment. This MMC snap-in also allows you to set up shortcut trusts.

Active Directory Sites and Services   Use this tool to create and manage Active Directory sites and services to map to an organization's physical network infrastructure. Sites and services are covered in detail in Chapter 5, "Administer Active Directory."

Active Directory Users and Computers   User and computer management is fundamental for an Active Directory environment. The Active Directory Users and Computers tool allows you to set machine- and user-specific settings across the domain. This tool is discussed throughout this book.

Active Directory Module for Windows PowerShell   *Windows PowerShell* is a command-line shell and scripting language. The Active Directory Module for Windows PowerShell is a group of cmdlets used to manage your Active Directory domains, Active Directory Lightweight Directory Services (AD LDS) configuration sets, and Active Directory Database Mounting Tool instances in a single, self-contained package.

A good way to make sure that Active Directory is accessible and functioning properly is to run the Active Directory Users and Computers tool. When you open the tool, you should see a configuration similar to that shown in Figure 3.3. Specifically, you should make sure the name of the domain you created appears in the list. You should also click the Domain Controllers folder and make sure that the name of your local server appears in the right pane. If your configuration passes these two checks, Active Directory is present and configured.

Testing from Clients

The best test of any solution is simply to verify that it works the way you had intended in your environment. When it comes to using Active Directory, a good test is to ensure that clients can view and access the various resources presented by Windows Server 2012 R2 domain controllers. In the following sections, you'll look at several ways to verify that Active Directory is functioning properly.

FIGURE 3.3 Viewing Active Directory information using the Active Directory Users and Computers tool

Verifying Client Connectivity

If you are unable to see the recently promoted server on the network, there is likely a network configuration error. If only one or a few clients are unable to see the machine, the problem is probably related to client-side configuration. To fix this, make sure that the client computers have the appropriate TCP/IP configuration (including DNS server settings) and that they can see other computers on the network.

If the new domain controller is unavailable from any of the other client computers, you should verify the proper startup of Active Directory using the methods mentioned earlier in this chapter. If Active Directory has been started, ensure that the DNS settings are correct. Finally, test network connectivity between the server and the clients by accessing the network or by using the ping command.

Joining a Domain

If Active Directory has been properly configured, clients and other servers should be able to join the domain. Exercise 3.5 outlines the steps you need to take to join a Windows 7 or Windows 8 computer to the domain.

To complete this exercise, you must have already installed and properly configured at least one Active Directory domain controller and a DNS server that supports SRV records in your environment. In addition to the domain controller, you need at least one other computer, not configured as a domain controller, running one of the following operating systems: Windows 2000, Windows XP Professional (Windows XP Home Edition cannot join a domain), Windows Vista, Windows 7, Windows 8, Windows Server 2003, Windows Server 2008, Windows Server 2008 R2, Windows Server 2012, or Windows Server 2012 R2.

Once clients are able to join the domain successfully, they should be able to view Active Directory resources using the Network icon. This test validates the proper functioning of Active Directory and ensures that you have connectivity with client computers.

 Exercise 3.5 is being done from a Windows 7 Enterprise computer.

EXERCISE 3.5

Joining a Computer to an Active Directory Domain

1. Right-click the Computer icon on the Start menu, and click Properties.

2. Go to the section called Computer Name. On the right side, click the Change Settings link.

3. Next to the section To Rename This Computer Or Change Its Domain Or Workgroup, click the Change button.

4. In the Member Of section, choose the Domain option. Type the name of the Active Directory domain that this computer should join. Click OK.

5. When prompted for the username and password of an account that has permission to join computers to the domain, enter the information for an administrator of the domain. Click OK to commit the changes. If you successfully joined the domain, you will see a dialog box welcoming you to the new domain.

6. You will be notified that you must reboot the computer before the changes take place. Select Yes when prompted to reboot.

Creating and Configuring Application Data Partitions

Organizations store many different kinds of information in various places. For the IT departments that support this information, it can be difficult to ensure that the right information is available when and where it is needed. Windows Server 2012 R2 uses a feature called *application data partitions*, which allows system administrators and application developers to store custom information within Active Directory. The idea behind application data partitions is that since you already have a directory service that can replicate all kinds of information, you might as well use it to keep track of your own information.

Developing distributed applications that can, for example, synchronize information across an enterprise is not a trivial task. You have to come up with a way to transfer data between remote sites (some of which are located across the world), and you have to ensure that the data is properly replicated. By storing application information in Active Directory, you can take advantage of its storage mechanism and replication topology. Application-related information stored on domain controllers benefits from having fault-tolerance features and availability.

Consider the following simple example to understand how this can work. Suppose your organization has developed a customer Sales Tracking and Inventory application. The company needs to make the information that is stored by this application available to all of its branch offices and users located throughout the world. However, the goal is to do this with the least amount of IT administrative effort. Assuming that Active Directory has already been deployed throughout the organization, developers can build support into the application for storing data within Active Directory. They can then rely on Active Directory to store and synchronize the information among various sites. When users request updated data from the application, the application can obtain this information from the nearest domain controller that hosts a replica of the Sales Tracking and Inventory data.

Other types of applications can also benefit greatly from the use of application data partitions. Now that you have a good understanding of the nature of application data partitions, let's take a look at how you can create and manage them using Windows Server 2012 R2 and Active Directory.

Creating Application Data Partitions

By default, after you create an Active Directory environment, you will not have any customer application data partitions. Therefore, the first step in making this functionality available is to create a new application data partition. You can use several tools to do this:

Third-Party Applications or Application-Specific Tools   Generally, if you are planning to install an application that can store information in the Active Directory database, you'll receive some method of administering and configuring that data along with the application. For example, the setup process for the application might assist you in the steps you need to take to set up a new application data partition and to create the necessary structures for storing data.

   Creating and managing application data partitions are advanced Active Directory–related functions. Be sure that you have a solid understanding of the Active Directory schema, Active Directory replication, LDAP, and your applications' needs before you attempt to create new application data partitions in a live environment.

Active Directory Service Interfaces   ADSI is a set of programmable objects that can be accessed through languages such as Visual Basic Scripting Edition (VBScript), Visual C#, Visual Basic .NET, and many other language technologies that support the Component Object Model (COM) standard. Through the use of ADSI, developers can create, access, and update data stored in Active Directory and in any application data partitions.

The LDP Tool   You can view and modify the contents of the Active Directory schema using LDAP-based queries. The LDP tool allows you to view information about application data partitions.

Ldp.exe is a graphical user interface (GUI) tool that allows an administrator to configure Lightweight Directory Access Protocol (LDAP) directory service. Administrators have the ability to use the LDP tool to administer an Active Directory Lightweight Directory Services (AD LDS) instance. To use the LDP tool, you must be an administrator or equivalent.

Figure 3.4 shows an example of connecting to a domain controller and browsing Active Directory information.

FIGURE 3.4   Using the LDP tool to view Active Directory schema information

Ntdsutil   The ntdsutil utility is the main method by which system administrators create and manage application data partitions on their Windows Server 2012 R2 domain controllers. This utility's specific commands are covered later in this chapter.

 Creating and managing application data partitions can be fairly complex. Such a project's success depends on the quality of the architecture design. This is a good example of where IT staff and application developers must cooperate to ensure that data is stored effectively and that it is replicated efficiently.

You can create an application data partition in one of three different locations within an Active Directory forest:

- As a new tree in an Active Directory forest
- As a child of an Active Directory domain partition

    For example, you can create an Accounting application data partition within the Finance.MyCompany.com domain.

- As a child of another application data partition

    This method allows you to create a hierarchy of application data partitions.

As you might expect, you must be a member of the Enterprise Admins or Domain Admins group to be able to create application data partitions. Alternatively, you can be delegated the appropriate permissions to create new partitions.

Now that you have a good idea of the basic ways in which you can create application data partitions, let's look at how replicas (copies of application data partition information) are handled.

Managing Replicas

A *replica* is a copy of any data stored within Active Directory. Unlike the basic information that is stored in Active Directory, application partitions cannot contain security principals. Also, not all domain controllers automatically contain copies of the data stored in an application data partition. System administrators can define which domain controllers host copies of the application data. This is an important feature because, if replicas are used effectively, administrators can find a good balance between replication traffic and data consistency. For example, suppose that three of your organization's 30 locations require up-to-date accounting-related information. You might choose to replicate the data only to domain controllers located in the places that require the data. Limiting replication of this data reduces network traffic.

Replication is the process by which replicas are kept up-to-date. Application data can be stored and updated on designated servers in the same way basic Active Directory information (such as users and groups) is synchronized between domain controllers. Application data partition replicas are managed using the *Knowledge Consistency Checker (KCC)*, which ensures that the designated domain controllers receive updated replica information. Additionally, the KCC uses all Active Directory sites and connection objects (covered in Chapter 5) that you create to determine the best method to handle replication.

Removing Replicas

When you perform a *demotion* on a domain controller, that server can no longer host an application data partition. If a domain controller contains a replica of application data partition information, you must remove the replica from the domain controller before you demote it. If a domain controller is the machine that hosts a replica of the application data partition, then the entire application data partition is removed and will be permanently lost. Generally, you want to do this only after you're absolutely sure that your organization no longer needs access to the data stored in the application data partition.

Using *ntdsutil* to Manage Application Data Partitions

The primary method by which system administrators create and manage application data partitions is through the ntdsutil command-line tool. You can launch this tool simply by entering **ntdsutil** at a command prompt. The ntdsutil command is both interactive and context sensitive. That is, once you launch the utility, you'll see an ntdsutil command prompt. At this prompt, you can enter various commands that set your context within the application. For example, if you enter the domain management command, you'll be able to use domain-related commands. Several operations also require you to connect to a domain, a domain controller, or an Active Directory object before you perform a command.

> For complete details on using ntdsutil, see the Windows Server 2012 R2 Help and Support Center.

Table 3.3 describes the domain management commands supported by the ntdsutil tool. You can access this information by typing in the following sequence of commands at a command prompt:

```
ntdsutil
domain management
Help
```

TABLE 3.3   ntdsutil domain management commands

ntdsutil domain management command	Purpose
Help or ?	Displays information about the commands that are available within the Domain Management menu of the ntdsutil command.
Connection or Connections	Allows you to connect to a specific domain controller. This will set the context for further operations that are performed on specific domain controllers.
Create NC *PartitionDistinguishedName DNSName*	Creates a new application directory partition.
Delete NC *PartitionDistinguishedName*	Removes an application data partition.
List NC Information *Partition DistinguishedName*	Shows information about the specified application data partition.
List NC Replicas *PartitionDistin-guishedName*	Returns information about all replicas for the specific application data partition.
Precreate *PartitionDistinguished NameServerDNSName*	Pre-creates cross-reference application data partition objects. This allows the specified DNS server to host a copy of the application data partition.
Remove NC Replica *PartitionDistin-guishedName DCDNSName*	Removes a replica from the specified domain controller.
Select Operation Target	Selects the naming context that will be used for other operations.

TABLE 3.3   ntdsutil domain management commands *(continued)*

ntdsutil domain management command	Purpose
Set NC Reference Domain *PartitionDistinguishedName DomainDistinguishedName*	Specifies the reference domain for an application data partition.
Set NC Replicate NotificationDelay *PartitionDistinguishedName FirstDCNotificationDelay OtherDCNotificationDelay*	Defines settings for how often replication will occur for the specified application data partition.

 The ntdsutil commands are all case insensitive. Mixed case was used in the table to make them easier to read. NC in commands stands for "naming context," referring to the fact that this is a partition of the Active Directory schema.

Figure 3.5 provides an example of working with ntdsutil. The following commands were entered to set the context for further operations:

```
ntdsutil
domain management
connections
connect to server localhost
connect to domain ADTest
quit
list
```

FIGURE 3.5   Viewing ntdsutil commands on the local domain controller

Configuring DNS Integration with Active Directory

There are many benefits to integrating Active Directory and DNS services:

- You can configure and manage replication along with other Active Directory components.

- You can automate much of the maintenance of DNS resource records through the use of dynamic updates.

- You will be able to set specific security options on the various properties of the DNS service.

Exercise 3.6 shows the steps that you must take to ensure that these integration features are enabled. You'll look at the various DNS functions that are specific to interoperability with Active Directory.

Before you begin this exercise, make sure that the local machine is configured as an Active Directory domain controller and that DNS services have been properly configured. If you instructed the Active Directory Installation Wizard to configure DNS automatically, many of the settings mentioned in this section may already be enabled. However, you should verify the configuration and be familiar with how the options can be set manually.

EXERCISE 3.6

Configuring DNS Integration with Active Directory

1. Open Administrative tools by pressing the Windows key and choosing Administrative Tools.

2. Open the DNS snap-in from the Administrative Tools program group.

3. Right-click the icon for the local DNS server and select Properties. Click the Security tab. Notice that you can now specify which users and groups have access to modify the configuration of the DNS server. Make any necessary changes and click OK.

EXERCISE 3.6 *(continued)*

4. Expand the local server branch and the Forward Lookup Zones folder.

5. Right-click the name of the Active Directory domain you created and select Properties.

6. On the General tab, verify that the type is Active Directory–Integrated and that the Data Is Stored In Active Directory message is displayed. If this option is not currently selected, you can change it by clicking the Change button next to Type and choosing the Store The Zone In Active Directory check box on the bottom.

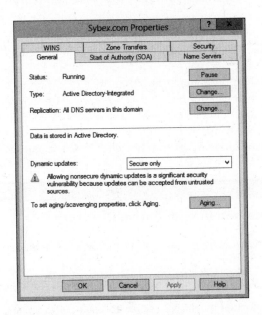

7. Verify that the Dynamic Updates option is set to Secure Only. This ensures that all updates to the DNS resource records database are made through authenticated Active Directory accounts and processes.

    The other options are Nonsecure And Secure (accepts all updates) and None (to disallow dynamic updates).

8. Finally, notice that you can define the security permissions at the zone level by clicking the Security tab. Make any necessary changes and click OK.

Summary

This chapter covered the basics of implementing an Active Directory forest and domain structure, creating and configuring application data partitions, and setting the functional level of your domain and forest.

You are now familiar with how you can implement Active Directory. We carefully examined all of the necessary steps and conditions that you need to follow to install Active Directory on your network. First you need to prepare for the Domain Name System because Active Directory cannot be installed without the support of a DNS server.

You also need to verify that the computer you upgrade to a domain controller meets some basic file system and network connectivity requirements so that Active Directory can run smoothly and efficiently in your organization. These are some of the most common things you will have to do when you deploy Active Directory.

The chapter also covered the concept of domain functional levels, which essentially determine the kinds of domain controllers you can use in your environment. For instance, in the Windows 2003 functional level, you can include Windows Server 2012 R2, Windows Server 2012, Windows Server 2008 R2, Windows Server 2008, and Windows Server 2003 domain controllers, but the functionality of the domain is severely limited.

In this chapter, you also learned how to install Active Directory, which you accomplish by promoting a Windows Server 2012 computer to a domain controller using Server Manager. You also learned how to verify the installation by testing Active Directory from a client computer.

This chapter was limited in scope to examining the issues related to installing and configuring the first domain in an Active Directory environment. In later chapters, you'll see how to create and manage more complex configurations.

Exam Essentials

Know the prerequisites for promoting a server to a domain controller.   You should understand the tasks that you must complete before you attempt to upgrade a server to a domain controller. Also, you should have a good idea of the information you need in order to complete the domain controller promotion process.

Understand the steps of the Active Directory Installation Wizard.   When you run the Active Directory Installation Wizard, you'll be presented with many different choices. You should understand the effects of the various options provided in each step of the wizard.

Be familiar with the tools that you will use to administer Active Directory.   Three main administrative tools are installed when you promote a Windows Server 2012 R2 to a domain controller. Be sure that you know which tools to use for which types of tasks.

Understand the purpose of application data partitions.   The idea behind application data partitions is that since you already have a directory service that can replicate all kinds of security information, you can also use it to keep track of application data. The main benefit of storing application information in Active Directory is that you can take advantage of its storage mechanism and replication topology. Application-related information stored on domain controllers benefits from having fault-tolerance features and availability.

Review Questions

1. You are the system administrator of a large organization that has recently implemented Windows Server 2012 R2. You have a few remote sites that do not have very tight security. You have decided to implement read-only domain controllers (RODCs). What forest and function levels does the network need for you to do the install? (Choose all that apply.)

    A. Windows 2000 Mixed

    B. Windows 2008 R2

    C. Windows 2003

    D. Windows 2008

2. What is the maximum number of domains that a Windows Server 2012 R2 computer configured as a domain controller may participate in at one time?

    A. Zero

    B. One

    C. Two

    D. Any number of domains

3. A system administrator is trying to determine which file system to use for a server that will become a Windows Server 2012 R2 file server and domain controller. The company has the following requirements:

    -   The file system must allow for file-level security from within Windows 2012 R2 Server.
    -   The file system must make efficient use of space on large partitions.
    -   The domain controller Sysvol must be stored on the partition.

    Which of the following file systems meets these requirements?

    A. FAT

    B. FAT32

    C. HPFS

    D. NTFS

4. For security reasons, you have decided that you must convert the system partition on your removable drive from the FAT32 file system to NTFS. Which of the following steps must you take in order to convert the file system? (Choose two.)

    A. Run the command CONVERT /FS:NTFS from the command prompt.

    B. Rerun Windows Server 2008 R2 Setup and choose to convert the partition to NTFS during the reinstallation.

   C. Boot Windows Server 2008 R2 Setup from the installation CD-ROM and choose Rebuild File System.

   D. Reboot the computer.

5. Windows Server 2012 R2 requires the use of which of the following protocols or services in order to support Active Directory? (Choose two.)

   A. DHCP

   B. TCP/IP

   C. NetBEUI

   D. IPX/SPX

   E. DNS

6. You are promoting a Windows Server 2012 R2 computer to an Active Directory domain controller for test purposes. The new domain controller will be added to an existing domain. While you are using the Active Directory Installation Wizard, you receive an error message that prevents the server from being promoted. Which of the following might be the cause of the problem? (Choose all that apply.)

   A. The system does not contain an NTFS partition on which the Sysvol directory can be created.

   B. You do not have a Windows Server 2012 R2 DNS server on the network.

   C. The TCP/IP configuration on the new server is incorrect.

   D. The domain has reached its maximum number of domain controllers.

7. Your network contains a single Active Directory domain. The domain contains five Windows Server 2008 R2 domain controllers. You plan to install a new Windows Server 2012 R2 domain controller. Which two actions would you need to perform? (Each correct answer presents part of the solution. Choose two.)

   A. Run `adprep.exe /rodcprep` at the command line.

   B. Run `adprep.exe /forestprep` at the command line.

   C. Run `adprep.exe /domainprep` at the command line.

   D. From Active Directory Domains and Trusts, raise the functional level of the domain.

   E. From Active Directory Users and Computers, prestage the RODC computer account.

8. You are the network administrator for a large company that creates widgets. Management asks you to implement a new Windows Server 2012 R2 system. You need to implement federated identity management. Which of the following will help you do this?

   A. Active Directory Federation Services

   B. Active Directory DNS Services

   C. Active Directory IIS Services

   D. Active Directory IAS Services

9. You are the system administrator responsible for your company's infrastructure. You think you have an issue with name resolution, and you need to verify that you are using the correct hostname. You want to test DNS on the local system and need to see whether the hostname server-1 resolves to the IP address 10.1.1.1. Which of the following actions provides a solution to the problem?

A. Add a DNS server to your local subnet.

B. Add the mapping for the hostname server-1 to the IP address 10.1.1.1 in the local system's HOSTS file.

C. Add an A record to your local WINS server.

D. Add an MX record to your local DNS server.

10. You have one Active Directory forest in your organization that contains one domain named Stellacon.com. You have two domain controllers configured with the DNS role installed. There are two Active Directory Integrated zones named Stellacon.com and Stellatest.com. One of your IT members (who is not an administrator) needs to be able to modify the Stellacon.com DNS server, but you need to prevent this user from modifying the Stellatest.com SOA record. How do you accomplish this?

A. Modify the permissions of the Stellacon.com zone from the DNS Manager snap-in.

B. Modify the permissions of the Stellatest.com zone from the DNS Manager snap-in.

C. Run the Delegation Of Control Wizard in Active Directory.

D. Run the Delegation Of Control Wizard in the DNS snap-in.

Chapter

4

Configure Windows Server 2012 R2

THE FOLLOWING 70-410 EXAM OBJECTIVES ARE COVERED IN THIS CHAPTER:

✓ **Configure file and share access**

- Create and configure shares
- Configure share permissions
- Configure offline files
- Configure NTFS permissions
- Configure access-based enumeration (ABE)
- Configure Volume Shadow Copy Service (VSS)
- Configure NTFS quotas
- Create and configure Work Folders

✓ **Configure print and document services**

- Configure the Easy Print print driver
- Configure Enterprise Print Management
- Configure drivers
- Configure printer pooling
- Configure print priorities
- Configure printer permissions

✓ **Configure servers for remote management**

- Configure WinRM
- Configure down-level server management
- Configure servers for day-to-day management tasks
- Configure multi-server management
- Configure Server Core
- Configure Windows Firewall
- Manage non-domain joined servers

This chapter explains how to set up your servers so that your network users have something to access. Before you can set up a server, you have to determine the purpose of it. Is it going to be a print server, a file storage server, a remote access server, or a domain controller?

After you have decided how the machine is going to help your network, you must implement your decision. In this chapter, I'll show you how to set up a print server and a file server. In addition, I will discuss how to set up permissions and security for these servers and how you can limit the amount of space your users can have on a server.

 Microsoft Windows Server 2012 and Windows Server 2012 R2 are used for all of the server types in this chapter. Although other operating systems can be used, this chapter refers only to Windows Server 2012 and Windows Server 2012 R2.

Understanding File Servers

Before you configure a file server, you must understand what a file server actually does. *File servers* are machines on your network that store data files to share among network clients. The same machine can be a file server and another type of server. For example, a machine can both host network files and run Exchange Server 2013. Such a machine would have both file server and application server functions. (*Application servers* are machines that host applications used by network clients.)

 Real World Scenario

Multiple Server Types on One Machine

More than ever, in today's world most IT departments have to worry about budgets. The problem is that the IT department often has the smallest budget in a company. You are typically stuck between a rock and a hard place because if your network is running well, people (including executives) forget about you. This makes it hard when you ask for anything that may impact the budget.

Because of the lack of funds, often you will leverage one machine to perform many server tasks. I have seen several companies where the IT department had to have the same machine running both as an application server and as a file server.

You must consider various factors before allowing a machine to run multiple server types. How many processors do you have? What are the processor speeds? How much RAM does the machine have? What is the hard drive speed? What type of applications will be hosted on the machine?

After you have gathered all of the information about the machine, then you can decide whether the machine can host multiple server types. Keep this one fact in mind, however—because of the requirements and demands on the computer system, it's always a good idea to host SQL Server on a dedicated machine.

When setting up a file server, one of the most important things you will do is to set up work and personal folders for your users. I have been consulting for many years, and one thing I always stress to all of my clients is to perform regular backups. After all, most organizations would not be able to recover after losing all of their data. Usually, companies back up only their servers, and this is why home folders are so important. *Home folders* are one of the most common file types on a file server; they are folders set up on the server for users to store information. Users have a location on the server to store their important data, and therefore that data will be backed up when the company does its regular backups.

Home folders are just one example of how to use work folders on a file server. I will be discussing other examples throughout this chapter.

Configuring File Servers

Now that you have an understanding of what a file server does, it's time to discuss how to configure these servers. Setting up a file server properly encompasses many steps. As always, one major concern is security. In the following sections, I will first describe how to share and publish online and offline files and folders. Then I will discuss the two types of security—shared permissions and NTFS security—that an administrator can set when sharing files or folders.

Sharing Folders

A file server is for sharing and storing data. To use one, you need to know how to set up a share, or a shared folder, on your server. A *shared folder* is exactly what it says; it's a folder that is shared on your network so that users can access the data within that folder. As an administrator, you have the ability to determine which users can access which files within a shared folder.

One of the main goals of Active Directory is to make resources easy to find. Active Directory also makes it easy to determine which files are available to users. That being said, I will explain how Active Directory manages to publish shared folders.

Making Active Directory Objects Available to Users

With Active Directory, a system administrator can control which objects users can see. The act of making an Active Directory object available is known as *publishing*. The two main publishable objects are Printer objects and Shared work folder objects. The reason I list Shared work folders here is because personal folders for users are not normally published in Active Directory. You publish an object in Active Directory because you want an easy way for everyone to find resources. Ordinarily, you don't want everyone accessing someone's home folder, and this is why you don't normally publish home folders.

The general process for creating server shares and shared printers has remained unchanged from previous versions of Windows. You create the various objects (printers or folders) and then enable them for sharing.

To make these resources available via Active Directory, however, there's an additional step: You must publish the resources. Once an object has been published in Active Directory, clients will be able to find it.

When you publish objects in Active Directory, you should know the server name and share name of the resource. This information, however, doesn't matter to your users. A system administrator can change the resource to which an object points without having to reconfigure or even notify clients. For example, if you move a share from one server to another, all you need to do is update the Shared Folder's object's properties to point to the new location. Active Directory clients still refer to the resource with the same path and name as they used before.

Exercise 4.1 will walk you through the steps for sharing and publishing a folder for use on your network.

EXERCISE 4.1

Creating and Publishing a Shared Work Folder

1. Create a new folder in the root directory of your C: partition, and name it **Test Share**.

2. Right-click the Test Share folder, and choose Share With ➤ Specific People.

3. In the File Sharing dialog box, enter the names of users with whom you want to share this folder. In the upper box, enter **Everyone** and then click Add. Note that Everyone appears in the lower box. Click in the Permission Level column next to Everyone, and choose Read/Write from the drop-down menu. Then click Share.

4. You see a message that your folder has been shared. Click Done.

5. Open the Active Directory Users and Computers tool. Expand the current domain. Select New ➢ Shared Folder.

6. In the New Object – Shared Folder dialog box, type **Shared Folder Test** for the name of the folder. Then type the UNC path to the share (for example, **\\serverA\Test Share**). Click OK to create the share.

One of the main benefits of having all of your resource information in Active Directory is that you can easily find the information that you're seeking using the Find dialog box. When setting up objects in Active Directory, I recommend you always enter as much information as possible for the objects you're creating. The extra effort will pay off when your users start doing searches for these objects. The more information you enter, the more users can search to find the appropriate resource they need.

Access-Based Enumeration

Access-Based Enumeration (ABE) is a feature included with Windows Server 2012/2012 R2. ABE allows your domain users to list only the files and folders to which they have access when browsing content on the file server.

ABE helps eliminate domain users' issues that are caused by users connecting to file servers and seeing large numbers of files and folders the user cannot connect. ABE allows users only to see files and folders to which they have access.

Knowing that ABE is working on the Windows Server helps you set up your permissions properly. If you need to give a user the ability to see files and folders that they might not be able to change, you need to allow them at least to read or view the directories. As an administrator, it's important that you understand that Access-Based Enumeration is working on the server and what you need to do to get a user around it when needed.

Configuring Offline Files

If you have been in this industry long enough, you have seen a major change in end-user computers. Years ago, only a few select users had laptops. They were big and bulky, and they weighed almost as much as today's desktop computers.

The pendulum has swung in the opposite direction. It probably seems like every one of your end users now has a laptop. As an IT administrator, this gives you a whole new set of challenges and problems to address.

One challenge that you have to address is how users can work on files while outside of the office. If you have a user who wants to work at home, how do you give them the files they need to get their work done?

The answer is *offline folders*. These folders contain data that can be worked on by users while outside the office. An IT administrator can set up offline folders through the use of *Group Policy objects (GPOs)*.

When you decide to make folders available for offline use, these folders need to synchronize with the laptops so that all of the data matches between both systems. As an administrator, one decision that you will need to make is when the offline folders will be synchronized. There are three synchronization options that you can set in a GPO (see Figure 4.1).

FIGURE 4.1   Synchronization options in a GPO

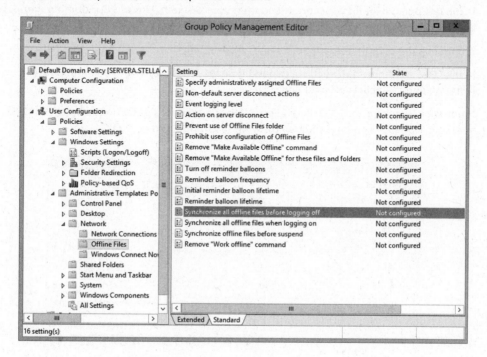

You can set up any combination of these options:

- When you select Synchronize All Offline Files Before Logging Off, offline folders are synchronized when the user logs off the network.

- When you select Synchronize All Offline Files When Logging On, offline folders are synchronized when the user logs on to the network.

- When you select Synchronize Offline Files Before Suspend, offline folders are synchronized before the user does a system suspend.

In Exercise 4.2, I will show you the steps necessary to configure offline folder options by using a GPO. This exercise uses the Group Policy Management Console (GPMC). If your GPMC is not installed, use the Server Manager MMC (under Features) to install it.

Group Policy objects will be covered in full detail in Chapter 6 "Manage GPOs."

EXERCISE 4.2

Configuring Offline Folder Options

1. Open the Group Policy Management Console.

2. In the left pane, expand your forest and then your domain. Under your domain name, there should be a default domain policy.

3. Right-click the default domain policy and choose Edit.

4. In the User Configuration section, expand Policies ➢ Administrative Templates ➢ Network and then click Offline Files.

5. Right-click Synchronize All Offline Files Before Logging Off and choose Edit. The GPO setting dialog box appears. Choose the Enabled option and click OK.

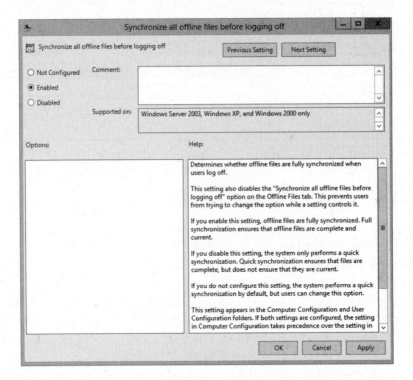

6. Right-click Synchronize All Offline Files When Logging On and choose Edit. The GPO setting dialog box appears. Choose the Enabled option and click OK.

7. Right-click Synchronize Offline Files Before Suspend and choose Edit. The GPO setting dialog box appears. Choose the Enabled option. In the Action drop-down box, make sure Quick is selected. Click OK.

8. Close the GPMC.

Now that you have set up a GPO for synchronization, it's time to share a folder for offline usage. In Exercise 4.3, you will set up a folder for offline access. You must complete Exercise 4.1 before doing this exercise.

EXERCISE 4.3

Configuring a Shared Network Folder for Offline Access

1. Right-click the Test Share folder that you created in Exercise 4.1 and choose Properties.

2. Click the Sharing tab and then click the Advanced Sharing button.

3. When the Advanced Sharing dialog box appears, click the Caching button.

4. When the Offline Settings dialog box appears, choose the All Files And Programs That Users Open From The Shares Will Be Automatically Available Offline option. Click OK.

5. Click OK twice more to close the Properties dialog box.

Volume Shadow Copy Services

Windows includes a feature that allows you to create a point-in-time image of one or more volumes. The *Volume Shadow Copy Service (VSS)* is the feature within Windows that allows an administrator take an image (shadow copy) of one or more volumes. Shadow copies have the ability to provide both file system and application.

Shadow copies allow an administrator to back up shared folders to a remote location. Shadow copies are designed to help recover files that were accidentally deleted, that were overwritten, or that have become corrupt. One major advantage to shadow copies is that open files can be backed up. This means that even if users are currently working on files in a shared folder that has shadow copies enabled, the shadow copies will continue to function.

Once administrators have configured and enabled shadow copies (using the Computer Management snap-in), network users can restore earlier versions of files. After the initial shadow copy of the shared folder is created, only changes are copied and not the entire file.

You can enable shadow copies of entire volumes.

The following are some of the settings that you can configure when setting up shadow copies:

Schedule   You have the ability to set the schedule of the shadow copies. You can set this schedule to run daily, weekly, monthly, once, at system startup, at logon, or when the system is idle. You can also set the time at which the shadow copy will run.

Storage Locations   An administrator needs to set the location of the shadow copy backup. If you are on a network, it is a good idea to place the shadow copy on a network drive.

Maximum Size   You can set a maximum size on your shadow copies, or you can specify that they have no size limit. One of the predetermined settings is 64 shadow copies per volume.

In Exercise 4.4, you'll set up a volume to make shadow copies every Monday at 7 a.m. To set up the shadow copies, you will use the Computer Management MMC snap-in.

EXERCISE 4.4

Configuring a Shadow Copy on a Volume

1. Open Computer Management by pressing the Windows key and selecting Administrative Tools ➢ Computer Management.

2. Expand Storage and then right-click Disk Management. Choose All Tasks ➢ Configure Shadow Copies.

3. When the Shadow Copies dialog box appears, click the Settings button.

4. When the Settings windows appears, click the Schedule button.

5. In the Schedule window, set the schedule task to weekly and the start time for 7 a.m. Uncheck all of the days-of-the-week boxes except Mon. Click OK.

6. When the Settings window reappears, click OK.

7. If the Enable button is enabled, click it. Then click OK.

8. Exit the Computer Management MMC.

To recover a previous version of a file from a shadow copy, you use the *server_name*\ *share_name* path. The operating system determines how you will gain access to the shared folders and shadow copies. Shadow copies are built into Windows XP (SP1), Windows Vista, Windows 7, Windows 8, Windows Server 2003, Windows Server 2008/2008 R2, and Windows Server 2012/2012 R2. If you are using a different Microsoft operating system, you need to download the Shadow Copy Client Pack from the Microsoft download center.

VssAdmin Command

Another way to create, configure, and manage shadow copies is by using the vssadmin.exe command-line utility. The vssadmin.exe command allows you to create, delete, list, and resize shadow copies and shadow storage.

One area where the VSS is very important is during backups. When you back up open files, the VSS copies the data and helps back up open files. For example, when you are backing up a Microsoft Exchange server using a Unitrends backup server, the VSS Exchange writer is used. To see if the VSS writers are functioning properly, you can open a command prompt (with administrative privileges) and type in the following statement:

VSSAdmin list writers

This command will show you all the different VSS service writers and how those VSS writers are functioning properly.

Table 4.1 describes the vssadmin.exe command and the different commands associated with the vssadmin utility.

TABLE 4.1 Vssadmin.exe commands

Command	Description
Add ShadowStorage	Adds a new volume shadow copy storage association
Create Shadow	Creates a new volume shadow copy
Delete Shadows	Deletes volume shadow copies
Delete ShadowStorage	Deletes the volume shadow copy storage associations
List Providers	Lists registered volume shadow copy providers
List Shadows	Lists existing volume shadow copies
List ShadowStorage	Lists volume shadow copy storage associations
List Volumes	Lists volumes eligible for shadow copies
List Writers	Lists subscribed volume shadow copy writers
Resize ShadowStorage	Resizes a volume shadow copy storage association
Revert Shadow	Reverts a volume to a shadow copy
Query Reverts	Queries the progress of in-progress revert operations

Configuring Permissions

You have gone through the steps necessary to set up a shared folder, publish it to Active Directory, and set it up for offline access. Now you will see how you can protect these files and folders by using permissions.

You can secure folders using permissions in two ways, and you can secure files in one way. You can set up permissions and security through NTFS or through sharing.

Understanding NTFS

NTFS is an option that you have when you are formatting a hard drive. You can format a hard drive for a Microsoft operating system in three ways.

- File Allocation Table (FAT) is supported on older operating systems only (Server 2003, Server 2000, XP, and so on).
- FAT32 is supported in Windows Server 2012 R2.
- NTFS is supported in Windows Server 2012 R2.

NTFS has many advantages over FAT and FAT32. They include the following:

Compression Compression helps compact files or folders to allow for more efficient use of hard drive space. For example, a file that usually takes up 20MB of space might use only 13MB after compression. To enable compression, just open the Advanced Attributes dialog box for a folder and check the Compress Contents To Save Disk Space box (see Figure 4.2).

FIGURE 4.2   Setting up compression on a folder

Quotas   *Quotas* allow you to limit how much hard drive space users can have on a server. Quotas are discussed in greater detail in the section "Configuring Disk Quotas."

Encryption   *Encrypting File System (EFS)* allows a user or administrator to secure files or folders by using encryption. Encryption employs the user's security identification

(SID) number to secure the file or folder. To implement encryption, open the Advanced Attributes dialog box for a folder and check the Encrypt Contents To Secure Data box (see Figure 4.3).

FIGURE 4.3 Setting up encryption on a folder

If files are encrypted using EFS and an administrator has to unencrypt the files, there are two ways to do this. First, you can log in using the user's account (the account that encrypted the files) and unencrypt the files. Second, you can become a recovery agent and manually unencrypt the files.

If you use EFS, it's best not to delete users immediately when they leave a company. Administrators have the ability to recover encrypted files, but it is much easier to gain access to the user's encrypted files by logging in as the user who left the company and unchecking the encryption box.

Security　One of the biggest advantages of NTFS is security. Security is one of the most important aspects of an IT administrator's job. An advantage of NTFS security is that the security can be placed on individual files and folders. It does not matter whether you are local to the share (in front of the machine where the data is stored) or remote to the share (coming across the network to access the data); the security is always in place with NTFS.

The default security permission is Users = Read on new folders or shares.

NTFS security is *additive*. In other words, if you are a member of three groups (Marketing, Sales, and R&D) and these three groups have different security settings, you get the highest level of permissions. For example, let's say you have a user by the name of wpanek who belongs to all three groups (Marketing, Sales, and R&D).

Figure 4.4 shows this user's permissions. The Marketing group has Read and Execute permissions to the Stellacon Documents folder. The Sales group has Read and Write, and the R&D group has Full Control. Since wpanek is a member of all three groups, wpanek would get Full Control (the highest level).

FIGURE 4.4 Security settings on the Stellacon Documents folder

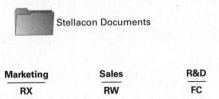

The only time this does not apply is with the Deny permission. Deny overrides any other group setting. Taking the same example, if Sales has Deny permission for the Stellacon Documents folder, the user wpanek would be denied access to that folder. The only way around this Deny is if you added wpanek directly to the folder and gave him individual permissions (see Figure 4.5). Individual permissions override a group Deny. In this example, the individual right of wpanek would override the Sales group's Deny. The user's security permission for the Stellacon Documents folder would be Full Control.

FIGURE 4.5 Individual permissions

Give users only the permissions necessary to do their jobs. Do not give them higher levels than they need.

Understanding Shared Permissions

When you set up a folder to be shared, you have the ability to assign that folder's permissions. *Shared permissions* can be placed only on the folder and not on individual files. Files have the ability to inherit their permissions from the parent folder.

Shared folder permissions are in effect only when users are remote to the shared data. In other words, if computer A shares a folder called Downloads and assigns that folder shared permissions, those permissions would apply only if you connected to that share from a machine other than computer A. If you were sitting in front of computer A, the shared permissions would not apply.

Like NTFS permissions (discussed in the previous section), shared permissions are additive, so users receive the highest level of permissions granted by the groups of which they are members.

Also, as with NTFS permissions, the Deny permission (see Figure 4.6) overrides any group permission, and an individual permission overrides a group Deny.

FIGURE 4.6   Setting up permissions on a shared folder

The default shared permission is Administrators = Full Control. The shared permissions going from lowest to highest are Read, Change, Full Control, and Deny. Table 4.2 compares the two different types of permissions and security.

TABLE 4.2   NTFS security vs. shared permissions

Description	NTFS	Shared
Folder-level security.	Yes	Yes
File-level security.	Yes	No
In effect when local to the data.	Yes	No
In effect when remote to the data.	Yes	Yes
Permissions are additive.	Yes	Yes
Group Deny overrides all other group settings.	Yes	Yes
Individual settings override group settings.	Yes	Yes

How NTFS Security and Shared Permissions Work Together

When you set up a shared folder, you need to set up shared permissions on that folder. If you're using NTFS, you will also need to set up NTFS security on the folder. Since both shared permissions and NTFS security are in effect when the user is remote, what happens when the two conflict?

These are the two basic rules of thumb:

- The local permission is the NTFS permission.

- The remote permission is the more restrictive set of permissions between NTFS and shared.

This is easy to do as long as you do it in steps. Let's look at Figure 4.7 and walk through the process of figuring out what wpanek has for rights.

FIGURE 4.7   NTFS security and shared permissions example

Shared permissions				Stellacon Documents		NTFS security		

Marketing	Sales	R&D				Marketing	Sales	R&D
R	R	R		Local = ?		RX	R	FC
				Remote = ?				

wpanek

Marketing
Sales
R&D

As you can see, wpanek belongs to three groups (Marketing, Sales, and R&D), and all three groups have settings for the Stellacon Documents folder. In the figure, you will notice that there are two questions: Remote = ? and Local = ? That's what you need to figure out—what are wpanek's effective permissions when he is sitting at the computer that shares the folder, and what are his effective permissions when he connects to the folder from another computer (remotely)? To figure this out, follow these steps:

1. Add up the permissions on each side separately.

   Remember, permissions and security are *additive*. You get the highest permission. So, if you look at each side, the highest shared permission is the Read permission. The NTFS security side should add up to equal Full Control. Thus, now you have Read permission on shared and Full Control on NTFS.

2. Determine the local permissions.

   Shared permissions do not apply when you are local to the data. Only NTFS would apply. Thus, the local permission would be Full Control.

3. Determine the remote permissions.

Remember, the remote permission is the most restrictive set of permissions between NTFS and shared. Since Read is more restrictive than Full Control, the remote permission would be Read.

Let's try another. Look at Figure 4.8, and see whether you can come up with wpanek's local and remote permissions.

FIGURE 4.8 NTFS security and shared permissions

Shared permissions   📁 Stellacon Documents   NTFS security

Marketing	Sales	R&D
R	R	FC

Local = ?
Remote = ?

Marketing	Sales	R&D
R	R	R

wpanek
Marketing
Sales
R&D

Your answer should match the following:

Local = Read

Remote = Read

Remember, first you add up each side to get the highest level of rights. NTFS would be Read, and shared would be Full Control. The local permission is always just NTFS (shared does not apply to local permissions), and remote permission is whichever permission (NTFS or shared) is the most restrictive (which would be Read on the NTFS side).

Exercise 4.5 walks you through the process of setting both NTFS and shared permissions. You must complete Exercise 4.1 before doing this exercise.

EXERCISE 4.5

Configuring Shared and NTFS Settings

1. Right-click the Test Share folder you created in Exercise 4.1 and choose Properties.

2. Click the Sharing tab and then click the Advanced Sharing button. (You will set the shared permissions first.)

3. Click the Permissions button. Click the Add button. When the Select User page appears, choose a group from Active Directory. (I used the Sales group.) Once you find your group, click OK.

EXERCISE 4.5 *(continued)*

4. The Permissions dialog box appears. With your group highlighted, click the Allow check box next to Full Control and click OK. (All of the other Allow check boxes will automatically become checked.)

5. On the Advanced Sharing page, click OK. Now click the Security tab. (This allows you to set the NTFS security settings.)

6. Click the Edit button. That takes you to the Permissions page. Now click the Add button. When the Select User page appears, choose a group from Active Directory. (I used the Everyone group.) Once you find your group, choose OK.

7. The Permissions dialog box appears. With your group highlighted, click the Allow check box next to Modify, and click OK. (All of the check boxes below Modify will automatically become checked.)

8. Click Close.

Configuring Disk Quotas

In this chapter so far, you have seen how to set up a share and publish it to Active Directory. You've also learned how to set up permissions and security and how NTFS and shared permissions work with each other. It's time to learn how to limit users' hard drive space on the servers.

Disk quotas give administrators the ability to limit how much storage space a user can have on a hard drive. As mentioned earlier in this chapter, disk quotas are an advantage of using NTFS over FAT32. If you decide to use FAT32 on a volume or partition, quotas will not be available.

You have a few options available to you when you set up disk quotas. You can set up disk quotas based on volume or on users.

 A good rule of thumb is to set up an umbrella quota policy that covers the entire volume and then let individual users exceed the umbrella as needed.

Setting Quotas by Volume   One way to set up disk quotas is by setting the quota by volume, on a per-volume basis. This means that if you have a hard drive with C:, D:, and E: volumes, you would have to set up three individual quotas—one for each volume. This is your umbrella. This is where you set up an entire disk quota based on the volume for all users.

Setting Quotas by User   You have the ability to set up quotas on volumes by user. Here is where you would individually let users have independent quotas that exceed your umbrella quota.

Specifying Quota Entries   You use quota entries to configure the volume and user quotas. You do this on the Quotas tab of the volume's Properties dialog box. (See Exercise 4.6.)

Creating Quota Templates   Quota templates are predefined ways to set up quotas. Templates allow you to set up disk quotas without needing to create a disk quota from scratch. One advantage of using a template is that when you want to set up disk quotas on multiple volumes (C:, D:, and E:) on the same hard drive, you do not need to re-create the quota on each volume.

Exercise 4.6 will show you how to set up an umbrella quota for all users and then have an individual account in your Active Directory exceed this quota.

EXERCISE 4.6

Configuring Disk Quotas

1. Open Windows Explorer.

2. Right-click the local disk (C:) and choose Properties.

3. Click the Quotas tab.

4. Check the Enable Quota Management check box. Also check the Deny Disk Space To Users Exceeding Quota Limit box.

5. Click the Limit Disk Space To option and enter **1000MB** in the box.

6. Enter **750MB** in the Set Warning Level To boxes.

7. Click the Apply button. If a warning box appears, click OK. This warning is just informing you that the disk may need to be rescanned for the quota.

8. Now that you have set up an umbrella quota to cover everyone, you'll set up a quota that exceeds the umbrella. Click the Quota Entries button.

9. The Quotas Entries for (C:) window appears. You will see some users already listed. These are users who are already using space on the volume. Click the Quota menu at the top and choose New Quota Entry.

   Notice the N/A entry in the Percent Used column. This belongs to the administrator account, which by default has no limit.

10. On the Select User page, choose a user that you want to allow to exceed the quota (for this example, I used the wpanek account). Click OK.

11. This opens the Add New Quota Entry dialog box. Click the Do Not Limit Disk Usage option and click OK.

12. You will notice that the new user has no limit. Close the disk quota tool.

Configuring Print Services

One of the most important components on a network is the printer. Printers today are almost as important as the computers themselves. Think about your network. What would your network be like without a printer? Even small networks or home networks have a printer today.

How many printers do you want on your network? It is not feasible to put a printer on every user's desk. What if some users need black and white while others need color? Do you give each user two printers? What if they need laser printing for reports but ink-jets will work fine for every other type of print job? These are all questions that you must answer before buying any printers for your networks.

This is also where network printers and print servers come into play. *Network printers* are printers that can be directly connected to the network through some form of network interface card. These printers usually have settings that can be configured for your network needs. For example, if your network uses DHCP, you can set the printer to be a DHCP client.

Print servers are servers that have a connected printer, where the server handles all printing issues. This is an excellent solution for printers that cannot directly connect to the network. Once the printer is connected to the network (through the use of a NIC or a server), the end user just connects to the printer and prints. To the end user, there is no real difference between the two options.

Before an end user can print to a network printer, an administrator must connect, set up, share, and publish the printer for use. An administrator must also set the permissions on the printer to allow users to print to that printer. The following sections will discuss these items in detail.

Creating and Publishing Printers

Once your printer is installed, you must share the printer and then publish the printer to Active Directory before users can print to it. Printers can be published easily within Active Directory. This makes them available to users in your domain.

Exercise 4.7 walks you through the steps you need to take to share and publish a Printer object by having you create and share a printer. To complete the printer installation, you need access to the Windows Server 2012 installation media (via the hard disk, a network share, or the CD/DVD drive). If you do not have a printer for this exercise, just choose one from the list and continue the exercise.

EXERCISE 4.7

Creating and Publishing a Printer

1. Press the Windows key and select ➢ Control Panel ➢ Devices and Printers ➢ Add Printer. This starts the Add Printer Wizard.

2. On the Add Printer page, click the link The Printer That I Want Isn't Listed.

3. Choose Add A Local Printer and click Next.

4. On the Choose A Printer Port page, select Use An Existing Port. From the drop-down list beside that option, make sure LPT1: (Printer Port) is selected. Click Next.

5. On the Install The Printer Driver page, select Generic for the manufacturer, and for the printer, highlight Generic/Text Only. Click Next.

6. If a driver page appears, choose Use The Driver That Is Currently Installed and click Next.

7. On the Type A Printer Name page, enter **Text Printer**. Uncheck the Set As The Default Printer box and then click Next.

8. The Installing Printer page appears. After the system is finished, the Printer Sharing page appears. Make sure the Share This Printer So That Others On Your Network Can Find And Use It box is selected, and accept the default share name of Text Printer.

9. In the Location section, type **Building 203**, and in the Comment section, add the following comment: **This is a text-only printer**. Click Next.

10. On the You've Successfully Added Text Printer page, click Finish.

11. Next you need to verify that the printer will be listed in Active Directory. Right-click the Text Printer icon, and select Text Printer Properties.

12. Next select the Sharing tab and make sure that the List In The Directory box is checked. Click OK to accept the settings.

13. Close the printer Properties box, and close Devices And Printers.

Note that when you create and share a printer this way, an Active Directory Printer object is not displayed within the Active Directory Users and Computers tool.

Configuring Printers

The printer has now been installed and published to Active Directory. It's time to set all of the different configuration options. To get to the options, right-click the Printer object and choose Properties.

The following are just some of the tabs you can configure:

The General Tab   The General tab (see Figure 4.9) allows you to set some basic printer attributes.

- The field at the top of the dialog box contains the display name of the Printer object.

- The Location field should contain text that helps users physically locate the printer. This allows users to search for printers based on location (location-aware printing).

- The Comment field allows an administrator to put in any additional information, such as the printer type.

- The Printing Preferences button takes you to controls that allow you to change the layout and paper type of the printer.

FIGURE 4.9   The General tab of the printer's Properties dialog box

The Sharing Tab   The Sharing tab (see Figure 4.10) allows you to configure your printer for sharing on your network. This is what allows users to use a network printer (if they have the proper permissions on the printer).

- The Share This Printer check box allows you to share the printer on the network.

- Share Name is the name your users will see on the network.

- When Render Print Jobs On Client Computers is checked, the client computer caches the print job until the printer is ready to print. If unchecked, the print server will cache the entire job before it prints to the printer.

- When List In The Directory is checked, users can search the directory for the printer.

- The Additional Drivers button allows you to load additional drivers for your clients. It is especially useful for giving access to drivers for older client systems. One advantage of a print server is that the server will automatically download drivers to client computers.

FIGURE 4.10   The Sharing tab of the printer's Properties dialog box

The Ports Tab   The Ports tab (see Figure 4.11) allows you to configure the port to which your printer is connected. You can add ports or configure existing ports.

- The Port check boxes allow you to choose to which port your printer is connected. Options are the printer port, serial port, local port, and print to file port.

- The Add Port button allows you to add a custom port (for example, a TCP/IP port).

- The Delete Port button allows you to remove a port from the Port list.

- The Configure Port button gives you settings to configure an existing port. For example, if you use TCP/IP, this button allows you to change the TCP/IP options.

- Enable Bidirectional Support allows your printer and computer to communicate back and forth. If this check box is disabled, your printer cannot support two-way communications.

- A *printer pool* allows two or more identical printers to share the print load. When a document is sent to the printer pool, the first available printer receives the print job and prints it. Enable Printer Pooling allows a large department or organization to get print jobs done faster. Users do not have to wait for one printer to get their print job. You should follow these rules when setting up a printer pool:

  - All printers in the pool need to be the same model and type.

  - All printers in the pool should be in the same physical location. Print jobs will be printed to the first available printer. If these printers are located all over the company, it may take a user too long to find their print job.

FIGURE 4.11   The Ports tab of the printer's Properties dialog box

The Advanced Tab   The Advanced tab (see Figure 4.12) is where you can set availability, priority, and many other options.

- The availability controls let you set the hours when this printer can be used. You can set it to be always available or available only between the hours you set.

- If multiple print shares are set up to go to the same printer, you can specify a printer priority with the Priority field for each share. The higher the number, the faster a print job sent to that share will access the printer. The highest priority is 99, and the default (lowest) is 1. If two users send jobs to the same printer at the same time, one with a 99 priority and the other with a 1 priority, the 99 priority would print first.

- Driver is the default printer driver that the printer is using.

- The print spooling controls let you decide how the print job will spool. You can choose to have the entire job spool first before printing (this ensures that the entire job is received by the print queue before printing), to start printing immediately while the job is still spooling, or to print directly to the printer without spooling. (The last option requires a printer with a large amount of RAM on the motherboard.)

- Hold Mismatched Documents allows the spooler to hold any print jobs that don't match the setup for the print device.

- Print Spooled Documents First allows a completely spooled printer job to be printed first even if it has a lower priority number than a job that is still spooling.

- Usually, after a print job has been printed, the print queue deletes the print job. If you check the Keep Printed Documents box, the print queue will not delete the print job after it is printed.

- Enable Advanced Printing Features allows you to set some advanced features such as the Page Order and Pages Per Sheet settings.

FIGURE 4.12   Advanced tab of the printer's Properties dialog box

The Color Management Tab   This tab allows you to adjust the color of your printing jobs.

The Security Tab   The Security tab (see Figure 4.13) is where you can set the permissions for your printer. This allows users to print, manage printers, manage documents, and take advantage of special permissions.

- The Add button allows you to add users and groups to the printer.

- The Remove button allows you to remove users and groups from the printer.

- The following controls, available in the Permissions For Everyone box, apply to everyone on your network:

  - Print gives everyone the right to print to this printer.

  - Manage Printers gives everyone the right to manage this printer, including deleting print jobs, setting priorities, setting availability, and so on.

  - Manage Documents gives everyone the right to manage print jobs.

  - Special Permissions allows you to set unique permissions such as Print, Manage Printers, Read permissions, Change permissions, and Take Ownership.

FIGURE 4.13   Security tab of the printer's Properties dialog box

Migrating Print Servers

In a network environment, an administrator may find it necessary to replace older print servers or to consolidate multiple print servers into one. To do this print server migration or replacement, you can use the Printer Migration Wizard or the Printbrm.exe command-line tool. These two utilities allow you to export print queues, printer settings, printer ports, and language monitors. These utilities then allow you to import these settings on another print server running Windows Server 2012 R2.

Printer Pooling

In a large organization, one issue that you may run into when you print a document to a print device is that you may have to wait a while for that document to print. If you have hundreds of print jobs being sent to a print device, it could take time until your print job appears on the print device. This is where printer pools can help.

A *printer pool* allows an administrator to associates multiple printers (identical print devices) with a single set of printer software. When you send a print job to a device, the print job will print to the first available device in the printer pool. This allows print jobs to print faster to multiple devices. For this to work, you must make sure that all devices are in the same physical area. You do not want a user traveling all over the company looking for their print job because they don't know which device printed the job.

To set up a printer to print to multiple devices, follow these steps:

1. Open Devices and Printers.

2. Right-click the printer you are using and then click Printer Properties.

3. On the Ports tab, select the Enable Printer Pooling check box.

4. Click each port where the printers you want to pool are connected.

Easy Print Driver

One printer configuration that is a little different from normal is when you are setting up a printer for a Remote Desktop server. However, Microsoft has included a feature to help. That feature is called the *Easy Print Driver.*

Remote Desktop Services gives you the ability to do printer redirection. What this means is Remote Desktop can route printing jobs from a server to a printer that is attached to a client computer. On an RD Session Host server, an administrator has the ability to use the Remote Desktop Easy Print printer driver to help simplify printer configuration.

The RD Session Host server first tries to use the Remote Desktop Easy Print driver, and if the RD client computer does not support this driver, the server looks for a matching printer driver on the server.

Configuring Remote Management

As an administrator, sometimes you might need to manage a server remotely. There are a few different tools you can use to do this task. You can use remote administration to help configure services on a Windows Server 2012 R2 system. The following sections cover Windows Remote Management and Windows PowerShell.

Windows PowerShell does not always have to be used remotely. For example, you can use Windows PowerShell when configuring a Windows Server 2012 R2 Server Core installation locally.

Windows Remote Management

The *Windows Remote Management (WinRM) utility* is Microsoft's version of the WS-Management protocol, an industry-standard protocol that allows different vendors' operating systems and hardware to work together. There are three main ways to access the WinRM utility:

- WinRM command-line tool
- WinRM scripting objects
- Windows Remote Shell command-line tool

The WinRM utility allows you to execute commands remotely and obtain management data from local and remote computers. You can use the WinRM utility on both Windows-based operating systems and non-Windows-based operating systems.

When using the WinRM utility, you can use the −machine switch to indicate the remote machine to which you are connecting. When connecting to a machine, you can connect using the localhost name, the NetBIOS name, the fully qualified domain name (FQDN), or the IP address of the remote machine. The following is an example of a WinRM command using a FQDN name on the secure port 443:

```
winrm get −machine:server.stellacon.local −port:443
```

Table 4.3 shows the command-line WinRM commands and descriptions of what each command does.

TABLE 4.3 WinRM commands and descriptions

Command	Description
WinRM g or WinRM get	Retrieves management information
WinRM s or WinRM set	Modifies management information
WinRM c or WinRM create	Creates a new instance on the managed resources
WinRM d or WinRM delete	Removes an instance from a managed resource
WinRM e or WinRM enumerate	Lists all instances of a managed resource
WinRM i or WinRM invoke	Executes a method on a managed resource
WinRM id or WinRM identity	Determines whether a WS-Management implementation is running on a remote machine

WinRM quickconfig	Configures a machine to accept WS-Management commands from a remote machine
WinRM configSDDL	Modifies an existing security descriptor for a Uniform Resource Identifier (URI)
WinRM helpmsg	Displays error messages for an error code

Now that you have looked at WinRM, let's take a look at how to use the Windows PowerShell utility.

Windows PowerShell

Windows PowerShell is a task-based, command-line scripting utility that allows you to execute commands locally or remotely on a Windows Server 2012 R2 machine. It was specifically designed for system administrators to allow for local or remote administration.

Microsoft asks a lot of questions on the exam about Windows PowerShell. Therefore, I will be discussing PowerShell throughout this book because of its importance on all of the Windows Server 2012 R2 exams.

Most operating system shells, including Cmd.exe and the SH, KSH, CSH, and BASH Unix shells, work by running a command or utility in a new process and then presenting the results to the user as text. These system shells also have commands that are built into the shell and execute in the shell process. In most system shells, because there are only a few built-in commands, many utilities have been created over the years to complete tasks.

Windows PowerShell contains an interactive prompt and a scripting environment that can be used independently or in combination. Unlike the previously mentioned system shells, which accept and return text, Windows PowerShell is built using the *.NET Framework common language runtime (CLR)* and the .NET Framework. Because of this, Windows PowerShell accepts and returns .NET Framework objects. This important change in the shell allows you to use entirely new tools and methods to manage and configure Windows.

Windows PowerShell introduced the concept of using cmdlets (pronounced "command-lets"). Cmdlets are simple, single-function command-line tools built into the shell. Administrators can use the cmdlets independently, or they can combine these tools to execute complex tasks and harness the true power of PowerShell. Windows PowerShell includes more than a hundred core cmdlets, but the true advantage of PowerShell is that anyone can write their own cmdlets and share them with other users.

Administrators often automate the management of their multicomputer environments by running sequences of long-running tasks, or *workflows*, which can affect multiple managed computers or devices at the same time. Windows PowerShell can help administrators accomplish workflows in a more effective way. Windows PowerShell includes some of the following advantages:

Windows PowerShell Scripting Syntax Administrators can use Windows PowerShell scripting expertise to create script-based tasks by using the extensible Windows PowerShell language. Windows PowerShell script-based tasks are easy to create, and IT members can share them easily by entering them into an email or publishing them on a web page.

Day-to-Day Management tasks Windows PowerShell allows administrators to configure and maintain servers. PowerShell allows you to pre-create scripts or use ready-to-use scripts to handle day-to-day tasks. This way, an administrator can just run a script to complete server configurations or management.

Multiserver Management Administrators can concurrently apply workflow tasks to hundreds of managed servers and computers. Windows PowerShell includes common parameters to set workflows automatically, such as PSComputerName, to enable multicomputer administrative scenarios.

Single Task to Manage Complex, End-to-End Processes Administrators can combine related scripts or commands that act upon an entire scenario into a single workflow. The status of activities within the workflow can be viewed at any time.

Automated Failure Recovery Using Windows PowerShell allows workflows to survive both planned and unplanned interruptions, such as computer restarts. Administrators have the ability to suspend workflow operations and then restart or resume the workflow from the exact point at which it was suspended. Administrators can then create checkpoints as part of their workflow process so that they can resume the workflow from the last persisted task (or checkpoint) instead of restarting the workflow from the beginning.

Activity Retries Administrators can create workflows that also specify activities that must rerun if the activity does not get completed on one or more managed computers (for example, if a target node was not online at the time the activity was running).

Connect and Disconnect Administrators can connect and disconnect from the node that is executing the workflow, but the workflow will continue to run.

Configuring Non-Domain Servers Another advantage of PowerShell is the ability to configure non-domain servers from a Windows Server 2012 R2 server (domain member). When you are running commands on the non-domain machine, you must have access to the non-domain machine's system administrator account. Another way to configure a non-domain server is to connect through remote desktop into the non-domain server and then configure the machine or run PowerShell commands while connected through remote desktop.

Task Scheduling Workflow tasks have the ability to be scheduled and started when specific conditions are met. This is also true for any other Windows PowerShell cmdlet or script.

Table 4.4 defines a few of the cmdlets available in Windows PowerShell. Again, there are hundreds of cmdlets, and the ones listed in the table are just some of the more common ones. You can retrieve a list of all the cmdlets starting here:

http://technet.microsoft.com/en-us/scriptcenter/dd772285.aspx

TABLE 4.4   Windows PowerShell cmdlets

Cmdlet	Definition
Clear-History	Deletes entries from the command history
Invoke-command	Runs commands on local or remote computers
Start-job	Starts a Windows PowerShell background job
Stop-job	Stops a Windows PowerShell background job
Remove-job	Deletes a Windows PowerShell background job
Import-Module	Adds modules to the current session
Receive-job	Gets the results of a Windows PowerShell background job
Format-table	Shows the results in a table format
Out-file	Sends the job results to a file
Get-Date	Gets the date and time
Set-Date	Sets the system time and date on a computer
Get-event	Gets an event in the event queue
New-event	Creates a new event
Trace-command	Configures and starts a trace of a command on a machine
Get-WindowsFeature	Gets a list of available and installed roles and features on the local server
Get-WindowsFeature -ServerName	Gets a list of available and installed roles and features on a remote server
Get-Help Install-WindowsFeature	Gets the syntax and accepted parameters for the Install-WindowsFeature cmdlet
Uninstall-WindowsFeature	Removes a role or feature
Get-NetIPAddress	Gets information about IP address configuration
Set-NetIPAddress	Modifies IP address configuration properties of an existing IP address
Set-NetIPv4Protocol	Modifies information about the IPv4 protocol configuration

---

Windows PowerShell Commands

I will show you Windows PowerShell commands throughout this book. If I show you how to install a role or feature in Server Manager, I will also include the Windows PowerShell equivalent.

Another advantage of Windows PowerShell is that it allows you to gain access to a file system on a computer and to access the registry, digital certificate stores, and other data stores.

Complete Exercise 4.8 to start the Windows PowerShell utility in the Windows Server 2012 R2 Server Core machine installed in the previous exercise.

EXERCISE 4.8

Starting the Windows PowerShell Utility

1. Type **Start PowerShell** at the Windows Server 2012 R2 Server Core command prompt.

2. When the Windows PowerShell utility starts, type **Help** and press Enter. This will show you the Windows PowerShell syntax and some of the commands included in Windows PowerShell.

3. At the Windows PowerShell command prompt, type **Get-Date**. This will show you the system's date and time.

4. At the Windows command prompt, type **Help** ✶. This will show you all of the cmdlets you can use.

5. Close the Windows PowerShell utility by typing **Exit**.

Configuring Down-Level Servers

As an administrator, sometimes you might have to configure a Windows Server 2008 R2 server from a Windows Server 2012 R2 machine. This is referred to as configuring a *down-level server*.

When you install Windows Server 2012 R2, Server Manager can be used to configure and manage a down-level server as long as that down-level server is running one of the following operating systems:

- Windows Server 2008 R2 SP1 (either full server or a Server Core installation)
- Windows Server 2008 SP2 (full server only)

To be able to configure the Windows Server 2008/2008 R2 servers remotely, you must first install Windows Management Framework 3.0 (WMF 3.0) and all of its prerequisites on the Windows Server 2008/2008 R2 servers. No special configuration is required on the Windows Server 2012 R2 server.

If you need to install WMF 3.0 on a Windows Server 2008 R2 Server Core installation, you can do this by using the Deployment Image Servicing and Management (DISM) commands. The command names that you would use for these features are as follows:

- MicrosoftWindowsPowerShell
- MicrosoftWindowsPowerShell-WOW64
- NetFx2-ServerCore
- NetFx2-ServerCore-WOW64

To run these commands, you would run the following in Server Core:

```
Dism /online /enable-feature: <Feature Name>
```

 It is important to remember that Dism is case-sensitive in the command shown here.

Configuring Server Core

When configuring servers remotely, an administrator may have to configure a Server Core system. Let's take a look at some of the Server Core commands that can be used to do some basic server configurations.

When configuring Server Core, you may need to set the system for a static TCP/IP address. Use the following Windows PowerShell commands:

- `Get-NetIPConfiguration` allows you to view your current network configuration.
- `Get-NetIPAddress` allows you to view the IP addresses you are currently using.

If you want to set your static TCP/IP address, do the following:

1. In Windows PowerShell, run `Get-NetIPInterface`.
2. Write down the number shown in the `IfIndex` column of the output for the IP interface or the `InterfaceDescription` string for the network adapter you want to change.
3. In Windows PowerShell, run `New-NetIPAddress -InterfaceIndex 10 -IPAddress -192.168.15.2 -PrefixLength 24 -DefaultGateway -192.168.15.1`.
   - `InterfaceIndex` is the value of `IfIndex` from step 2 (in this example, `10`).

- IPAddress is the static IP address you intend to set (in this example, 192.168.15.2).

- PrefixLength is the prefix length (another form of subnet mask) for the IP address you intend to set (in this example, 24).

- DefaultGateway is the default gateway (in this example, 192.168.15.1).

4. In Windows PowerShell, run Set-DNSClientServerAddress -InterfaceIndex 10 -ServerAddresses 192.168.15.4.

- InterfaceIndex is the value of IfIndex from step 2.

- ServerAddresses is the IP address of your DNS server.

5. To add multiple DNS servers, run Set-DNSClientServerAddress -InterfaceIndex 10 -ServerAddresses 192.168.15.4,192.168.15.5.

- In this example, 192.168.15.4 and 192.168.15.5 are both IP addresses of DNS servers.

Another Server Core task that you may need to configure is setting the server name. In PowerShell, run the following command to rename the server: Rename-Computer.

As an administrator, you may also want to run PowerShell commands on one system to run on another system. You can enable Windows PowerShell Remoting by using the Enable-PSRemoting command.

Configuring the Windows Firewall

The final item to examine is configuring Windows Firewall remotely. Microsoft Server 2012 R2 Windows Firewall will be discussed in full detail in Chapter 6, but since I am discussing remote administration, let's look at the commands needed to configure Windows Firewall remotely.

Netsh advfirewall is a command-line (with Administrator privileges) tool for Windows Firewall with Advanced Security that helps with the creation, administration, and monitoring of Windows Firewall and IPsec settings and provides an alternative to console-based management.

To enter into the netsh advfirewall prompt, you must first type **netsh**. After you enter the netsh prompt, you then type **advfirewall**, which will bring you to the netsh advfirewall prompt. When you enter netsh advfirewall, it enters you into a netsh advfirewall prompt that looks like the following:

netsh advfirewall> prompt

Once you are at the netsh firewall prompt, you can use the question mark to get a list of all available options (netsh advfirewall>?). Figure 4.14 shows you the list of available options.

FIGURE 4.14   Netsh advfirewall options

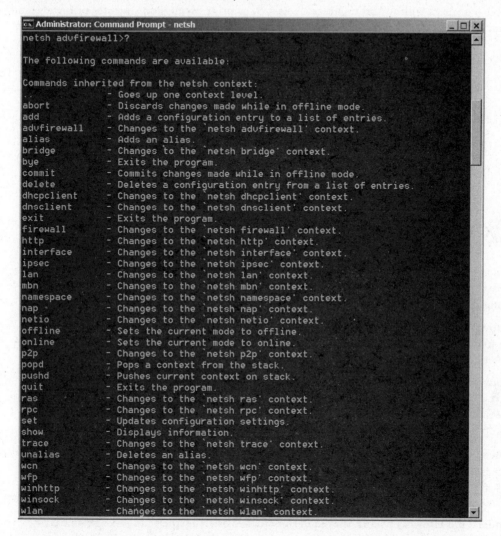

```
Administrator: Command Prompt - netsh                          _ □ X
netsh advfirewall>?

The following commands are available:

Commands inherited from the netsh context:
..                 - Goes up one context level.
abort              - Discards changes made while in offline mode.
add                - Adds a configuration entry to a list of entries.
advfirewall        - Changes to the `netsh advfirewall` context.
alias              - Adds an alias.
bridge             - Changes to the `netsh bridge` context.
bye                - Exits the program.
commit             - Commits changes made while in offline mode.
delete             - Deletes a configuration entry from a list of entries.
dhcpclient         - Changes to the `netsh dhcpclient` context.
dnsclient          - Changes to the `netsh dnsclient` context.
exit               - Exits the program.
firewall           - Changes to the `netsh firewall` context.
http               - Changes to the `netsh http` context.
interface          - Changes to the `netsh interface` context.
ipsec              - Changes to the `netsh ipsec` context.
lan                - Changes to the `netsh lan` context.
mbn                - Changes to the `netsh mbn` context.
namespace          - Changes to the `netsh namespace` context.
nap                - Changes to the `netsh nap` context.
netio              - Changes to the `netsh netio` context.
offline            - Sets the current mode to offline.
online             - Sets the current mode to online.
p2p                - Changes to the `netsh p2p` context.
popd               - Pops a context from the stack.
pushd              - Pushes current context on stack.
quit               - Exits the program.
ras                - Changes to the `netsh ras` context.
rpc                - Changes to the `netsh rpc` context.
set                - Updates configuration settings.
show               - Displays information.
trace              - Changes to the `netsh trace` context.
unalias            - Deletes an alias.
wcn                - Changes to the `netsh wcn` context.
wfp                - Changes to the `netsh wfp` context.
winhttp            - Changes to the `netsh winhttp` context.
winsock            - Changes to the `netsh winsock` context.
wlan               - Changes to the `netsh wlan` context.
```

Summary

In this chapter, I discussed file servers and how they can be effective on your network. I also discussed sharing folders for users to access, and then I discussed how to publish those shared folders to Active Directory.

You learned about NTFS security versus shared folder permissions and how to limit users' hard drive space by setting up disk quotas. The chapter also covered the Encrypting File System (EFS) and how users can encrypt and compress files.

I talked about print servers and configuring printers. I talked about how to share and publish printers within Active Directory as well as print permissions, printer priorities, and print pooling.

You then took a look at remote configuration and a few tools that allow you to configure servers.

- Windows Remote Management lets you configure a server remotely from another machine.

- PowerShell is an important tool in the Windows Server 2012 R2 arsenal. Microsoft has been moving the industry toward PowerShell, and there will be many questions on the exam about PowerShell.

- Netsh allows you to configure Windows Firewall remotely.

Exam Essentials

Learn How Resources Can Be Published   A design goal for Active Directory was to make network resources easier for users to find. With that in mind, you should understand how using published printers and shared folders can simplify network resource management.

Know How to Configure Offline Folders   Offline folders give you the opportunity to set up folders so that users can work on the data while outside the office and later synchronize it with a master copy. You can set up GPOs to help with offline folder synchronization.

Know How to Configure NTFS Security   One of the major advantages of using NTFS over FAT32 is access to additional security features. NTFS allows you to put security at the file and folder layers. NTFS security is in effect whether the user is remote or local to the computer with the data.

Know How to Configure Shared Permissions   Shared permissions allow you to determine the access a user will receive when connecting to a shared folder. Shared permissions are allowed only at the folder layer and are in effect only when the user is remote to the computer with the shared data.

Understand How NTFS and Shared Permissions Work Together   NTFS and shared permissions are individually additive—you get the highest level of security and permissions within each type. NTFS is always in effect, and it is the only security available locally. Shared permissions are in effect only when connecting remotely to access the shared data. When the two types of permissions meet, the most restrictive set of permissions applies.

Know How to Configure Disk Quotas   Disk quotas allow an organization to determine the amount of disk space that users can have on a volume of a server. An administrator can set up disk quotas based on volumes or by users. Each volume must have its own separate set of disk quotas.

Know How to Configure Printing   I discussed network printers versus print servers. Understand that when you create a printer, you want to publish the printer within Active Directory so that your users can find it throughout the domain. Understand the different printer permissions and how to install print drivers.

Understand Windows PowerShell   Understanding Windows PowerShell is not only important for the exam; it will also allow you to configure Server Core more efficiently. Windows PowerShell is a command-line utility that allows you run single cmdlets as well as run complex tasks to exploit the full power from PowerShell.

Review Questions

1. The company for which you work has a multilevel administrative team that is segmented by departments and locations. There are four major locations, and you are in the Northeast group. You have been assigned to the administrative group that is responsible for creating and maintaining network shares for files and printers in your region. The last place you worked had a large Windows Server 2003 network, where you had a much wider range of responsibilities. You are excited about the chance to learn more about Windows Server 2012 R2.

    For your first task, you have been given a list of file and printer shares that need to be created for the users in your region. You ask how to create them in Windows Server 2012 R2, and you are told that the process of creating a share is the same as with Windows Server 2003. You create the shares and use NETUSE to test them. Everything appears to work fine, so you send out a message that the shares are available. The next day, you start receiving calls from users who say they cannot see any of the resources you created. What is the most likely reason for the calls from the users?

    A. You forgot to enable NetBIOS for the shares.

    B. You need to force replication for the shares to appear in the directory.

    C. You need to publish the shares in the directory.

    D. The shares will appear within the normal replication period.

2. You want to publish a printer to Active Directory. Where would you click in order to accomplish this task?

    A. The Sharing tab

    B. The Advanced tab

    C. The Device Settings tab

    D. The Printing Preferences button

3. A system administrator creates a local Printer object, but it doesn't show up in Active Directory when a user executes a search for all printers. Which of the following are possible reasons for this? (Choose all that apply.)

    A. The printer was not shared.

    B. The printer is offline.

    C. The client does not have permission to view the printer.

    D. The printer is malfunctioning.

4. You are the network administrator for a midsize coffee bean distributor. Your company's network has four Windows 2012 R2 servers, and all of the clients are running either Windows 8 or Windows 7. Most of your end users use laptops to do their work, and many of them work away from the office. What should you configure to help them work on documents when away from the office?

    A. Online file access

    B. Offline file access

    C. Share permissions

    D. NTFS permissions

5. Your company has decided to implement a Windows 2012 R2 server. The company IT manager who came before you always used FAT32 as the system partition. Your company wants to know whether it should move to NTFS. Which of the following are some advantages of NTFS? (Choose all that apply.)

    A. Security

    B. Quotas

    C. Compression

    D. Encryption

6. Will, the IT manager for your company, has been asked to give Moe the rights to read and change documents in the `Stellacon Documents` folder. The following table shows the current permissions on the shared folder:

Group/User	NTFS	Shared
Sales	Read	Change
Marketing	Modify	Change
R&D	Deny	Full Control
Finance	Read	Read
Tylor	Read	Change

Moe is a member of the Sales and Finance groups. When Moe accesses the `Stellacon Documents` folder, he can read all of the files, but the system won't let him change or delete files. What do you need to do to give Moe the minimum amount of rights to do his job?

    A. Give Sales Full Control to shared permissions.

    B. Give Moe Full Control to NTFS security.

    C. Give Finance Change to shared permissions.

    D. Give Finance Modify to NTFS security.

    E. Give Moe Modify to NTFS security.

7. You are the administrator of your network, which consists of two Windows Server 2012 R2 systems. One of the servers is a domain controller, and the other server is a file server for data storage. The hard drive of the file server is starting to fill up. You do not have the ability to install another hard drive, so you decide to limit the amount of space everyone gets on the hard drive. What do you need to implement to solve your problem?

    A. Disk spacing

    B. Disk quotas

    C. Disk hardening

    D. Disk limitations

8. You are the IT manager for your company. You have been asked to give the Admin group the rights to read, change, and assign permissions to documents in the Stellacon Documents folder. The following table shows the current permissions on the Stellacon Documents shared folder:

Group/User	NTFS	Shared
Sales	Read	Change
Marketing	Modify	Change
R&D	Deny	Full Control
Finance	Read	Read
Admin	Change	Change

What do you need to do to give the Admin group the rights to do their job? (Choose all that apply.)

A. Give Sales Full Control to shared permissions.

B. Give Full Control to NTFS security.

C. Give Admin Full Control to shared permissions.

D. Give Finance Modify to NTFS security.

E. Give Admin Full Control to NTFS security.

9. You have been asked to configure a Windows Server 2012 R2 Datacenter Server Core machine. Which remote configuration applications can you use to configure this server from your machine? (Choose all that apply.)

A. Windows Remote Management

B. Command prompt

C. Windows PowerShell

D. Microsoft Remote Admin (MRA)

10. You have been hired by a small company to implement new Windows Server 2012 R2 systems. The company wants you to set up a server for users' home folder locations. What type of server would you be setting up?

A. PDC server

B. Web server

C. Exchange server

D. File server

Chapter

5

Administer Active Directory

THE FOLLOWING 70-410 EXAM OBJECTIVES ARE COVERED IN THIS CHAPTER:

✓ **Create and manage Active Directory users and computers**

- Automate the creation of Active Directory accounts
- Create, copy, configure, and delete users and computers
- Configure templates
- Perform bulk Active Directory operations
- Configure user rights
- Offline domain join
- Manage inactive and disabled accounts

✓ **Create and manage Active Directory groups and organizational units (OUs)**

- Configure group nesting
- Convert groups including security, distribution, universal, domain local, and domain global
- Manage group membership using Group Policy
- Enumerate group membership
- Delegate the creation and management of Active Directory objects
- Manage default Active Directory containers
- Create, copy, configure, and delete groups and OUs

In previous chapters, you learned how to install Domain Name System (DNS) and Active Directory, but you still haven't been introduced to the lower-level objects that exist in Active Directory. In this chapter, you will look at the structure of the various components within a domain. You'll see how an organization's business structure can be mirrored within Active Directory through the use of organizational units for ease of use and to create a seamless look and feel. Because the concepts related to organizational units are quite simple, some system administrators may underestimate their importance and not plan to use them accordingly. Make no mistake: one of the fundamental components of a successful Active Directory installation is the proper design and deployment of organizational units.

You'll also see in this chapter the actual steps you need to take to create common Active Directory objects and then learn how to configure and manage them. Finally, you'll look at ways to publish resources and methods for creating user accounts automatically.

An Overview of OUs

An *organizational unit (OU)* is a logical group of Active Directory objects, just as the name implies. OUs serve as containers within which Active Directory objects can be created, but they do not form part of the DNS namespace. They are used solely to create organization within a domain.

OUs can contain the following types of Active Directory objects:

- Users
- Groups
- Computers
- Shared Folder objects
- Contacts
- Printers
- InetOrgPerson objects
- Microsoft Message Queuing (MSMQ) Queue aliases
- Other OUs

Perhaps the most useful feature of OUs is that they can contain other OU objects. As a result, system administrators can hierarchically group resources and objects according to business practices. The OU structure is extremely flexible and, as you will see later in this chapter, can easily be rearranged to reflect business reorganizations.

Another advantage of OUs is that each can have its own set of policies. Administrators can create individual and unique Group Policy objects (GPOs) for each OU. GPOs are rules or policies that can apply to all of the objects within the OU. GPOs are discussed in detail in Chapter 6 "Manage GPOs."

Each type of object has its own purpose within the organization of Active Directory domains. Later in this chapter, you'll look at the specifics of User, Computer, Group, and Shared Folder objects. For now, let's focus on the purpose and benefits of using OUs.

The Purpose of OUs

OUs are mainly used to organize the objects within Active Directory. Before you dive into the details of OUs, however, you must understand how OUs, users, and groups interact. Most important, you should understand that OUs are simply containers that you can use to group various objects logically. They are not, however, groups in the classical sense. That is, they are not used for assigning security permissions. Another way of stating this is that the user accounts, computer accounts, and group accounts that are contained in OUs are considered security principals while the OUs themselves are not.

OUs do not take the place of standard user and group permissions. A good general practice is to assign users to groups and then place the groups within OUs. This enhances the benefits of setting security permissions and of using the OU hierarchy for making settings. Figure 5.1 illustrates this concept.

FIGURE 5.1   Relationships of users, groups, and OUs

An OU contains objects only from within the domain in which it resides. As you'll see in the section "Delegating Administrative Control" later in this chapter, the OU is the finest level of granularity used for group policies and other administrative settings.

Benefits of OUs

There are many benefits to using OUs throughout your network environment.

- OUs are the smallest unit to which you can assign directory permissions.
- You can easily change the OU structure, and it is more flexible than the domain structure.
- The OU structure can support many different levels of hierarchy.
- Child objects can inherit OU settings.
- You can set Group Policy settings on OUs.
- You can easily delegate the administration of OUs and the objects within them to the appropriate users and groups.

Now that you have a good idea of why you should use OUs, take a look at some general practices you can use to plan the OU structure.

Planning the OU Structure

One of the key benefits of Active Directory is the way in which it can bring organization to complex network environments. Before you can begin to implement OUs in various configurations, you must plan a structure that is compatible with business and technical needs. In this section, you'll learn about several factors that you should consider when planning for the structure of OUs.

Logical Grouping of Resources

The fundamental purpose of using OUs is to group resources (which exist within Active Directory) hierarchically. Fortunately, hierarchical groups are quite intuitive and widely used in most businesses. For example, a typical manufacturing business might divide its various operations into different departments as follows:

- Sales
- Marketing
- Engineering
- Research and Development
- Support
- Information Technology (IT)

Each of these departments usually has its own goals and mission. To make the business competitive, individuals within each of the departments are assigned to various roles. The following role types might be used:

- Managers
- Clerical staff
- Technical staff
- Planners

Each of these roles usually entails specific job responsibilities. For example, managers should provide direction to general staff members. Note that the very nature of these roles suggests that employees may fill many different positions. That is, one employee might be a manager in one department and a member of the technical staff in another. In the modern workplace, such situations are quite common.

All of this information helps you plan how to use OUs. First the structure of OUs within a given network environment should map well to the business's needs, including the political and logical structure of the organization as well as its technical needs. Figure 5.2 shows how a business organization might be mapped to the OU structure within an Active Directory domain.

FIGURE 5.2 Mapping a business organization to an OU structure

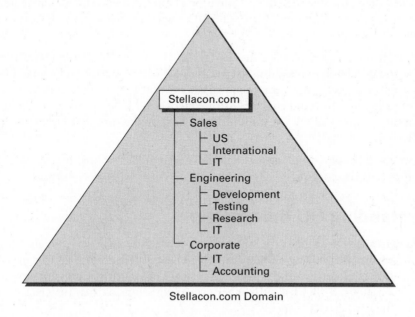

Stellacon.com Domain

When naming OUs for your organization, you should keep several considerations and limitations in mind:

Keep the Names and Descriptions Simple   The purpose of OUs is to make administering and using resources simple. Therefore, it's always a good idea to keep the names of your objects simple and descriptive. Sometimes, finding a balance between these two goals can be a challenge. For example, although a printer name like "The LaserJet located near Bob's cube" might seem descriptive, it is certainly difficult to type. Also, imagine the naming changes that you might have to make if Bob moves (or leaves the company)!

Pay Attention to Limitations   The maximum length for the name of an OU is 64 characters. In most cases, this should adequately describe the OU. Remember, the name of an OU does not have to describe the object uniquely because the OU is generally referenced only as part of the overall hierarchy. For example, you can choose to create an OU named "IT" within two different parent OUs. Even though the OUs have the same name, users and administrators are able to distinguish between them based on their complete pathname.

Pay Attention to the Hierarchical Consistency   The fundamental basis of an OU structure is its position in a hierarchy. From a design standpoint, this means you cannot have two OUs with the same name at the same level. However, you can have OUs with the same name at different levels. For example, you could create an OU named "Corporate" within the North America OU and another one within the South America OU. This is because the fully qualified domain name includes information about the hierarchy. When an administrator tries to access resources in a Corporate OU, they must specify which Corporate OU they mean.

For example, if you create a North America OU, the Canada OU should logically fit under it. If you decide that you want to separate the North America and Canada OUs into completely different containers, then you might want to use other, more appropriate names. For example, you could change North America to "U.S." Users and administrators depend on the hierarchy of OUs within the domain, so make sure that it remains logically consistent.

Based on these considerations, you should have a good idea of how best to organize the OU structure for your domain.

Understanding OU Inheritance

When you rearrange OUs within the structure of Active Directory, you can change several settings. When they are moving and reorganizing OUs, system administrators must pay careful attention to automatic and unforeseen changes in security permissions and other configuration options. By default, OUs inherit the permissions of their new parent container when they are moved.

By using the built-in tools provided with Windows Server 2012 R2 and Active Directory, you can move or copy OUs only within the same domain. You cannot use the Active

Directory Users and Computers tool to move OUs between domains. To do this, use the *Active Directory Migration Tool (ADMT)*. This is one of the many Active Directory support tools.

Delegating Administrative Control

I already mentioned that OUs are the smallest component within a domain to which administrative permissions and group policies can be assigned by administrators. Now you'll take a look specifically at how administrative control is set on OUs.

Real World Scenario

Delegation occurs when a higher security authority assigns permissions to a lesser security authority. As a real-world example, assume that you are the director of IT for a large organization. Instead of doing all of the work yourself, you would probably assign roles and responsibilities to other individuals. For example, if you worked within a multidomain environment, you might make one system administrator responsible for all operations within the Sales domain and another responsible for the Engineering domain. Similarly, you could assign the permissions for managing all printers and print queue objects within your organization to one individual user while allowing another individual user to manage all security permissions for users and groups. In this way, you can distribute the various roles and responsibilities of the IT staff throughout the organization.

Businesses generally have a division of labor that handles all of the tasks involved in keeping the company's networks humming. Network operating systems (NOSs), however, often make it difficult to assign just the right permissions; in other words, they do not support very granular permission assignments. Sometimes, fine granularity is necessary to ensure that only the right permissions are assigned. A good general rule of thumb is to provide users and administrators with the minimum permissions they require to do their jobs. This way, you can ensure that accidental, malicious, and otherwise unwanted changes do not occur.

You can use auditing to log events to the Security log in the Event Viewer. This is a way to ensure that if accidental, malicious, and otherwise unwanted changes do occur, they are logged and traceable.

In the world of Active Directory, you delegate to define responsibilities for OU adminis-trators. As a system administrator, you will occasionally be tasked with having to delegate responsibility to others—you can't do it all, although sometimes administrators believe that they can. You understand the old IT logic of doing all of the tasks yourself for job security, but this can actually make you look worse.

> You can delegate control only at the OU level and not at the object level within the OU.

If you do find yourself in a role where you need to delegate, remember that Windows Server 2012 R2 was designed to offer you the ability to do so. In its simplest definition, *del-egation* allows a higher administrative authority to grant specific administrative rights for containers and subtrees to individuals and groups. What this essentially does is to eliminate the need for domain administrators with sweeping authority over large segments of the user population. You can break up this control over branches within your tree, within each OU you create.

> To understand delegation and rights, you should first understand the con-cept of *access control entries (ACEs)*. ACEs grant specific administrative rights on objects in a container to a user or group. A container's access control list (ACL) is used to store ACEs.

When you are considering implementing delegation, keep these two concerns in mind:

Parent-Child Relationships   The OU hierarchy you create will be important when you consider the maintainability of security permissions. OUs can exist in a parent-child rela-tionship, which means that permissions and group policies set on OUs higher up in the hierarchy (parents) can interact with objects in lower-level OUs (children). When it comes to delegating permissions, this is extremely important. You can allow child containers to inherit the permissions set on parent containers automatically. For example, if the North America division of your organization contains 12 other OUs, you could delegate permis-sions to all of them at once (saving time and reducing the likelihood of human error) by placing security permissions on the North America division. This feature can greatly ease administration, especially in larger organizations, but it is also a reminder of the impor-tance of properly planning the OU structure within a domain.

Inheritance Settings   Now that you've seen how you can use parent-child relationships for administration, you should consider *inheritance*, the process in which child objects take on the permissions of a parent container. When you set permissions on a parent container, all of the child objects are configured to inherit the same permissions. You can override this behavior, however, if business rules do not lend themselves well to inheritance.

Applying Group Policies

One of the strengths of the Windows operating system is that it offers users a great deal of power and flexibility. From installing new software to adding device drivers, users can make many changes to their workstation configurations. However, this level of flexibility is also a potential problem. For instance, inexperienced users might inadvertently change settings, causing problems that can require many hours to fix.

In many cases (and especially in business environments), users require only a subset of the complete functionality the operating system provides. In the past, however, the difficulty associated with implementing and managing security and policy settings has led to lax security policies. Some of the reasons for this are technical—it can be tedious and difficult to implement and manage security restrictions. Other problems have been political—users and management might feel that they should have full permissions on their local machines, despite the potential problems this might cause.

That's where the idea of group policies comes in. Simply defined, *group policies* are collections of rules that you can apply to objects within Active Directory. Specifically, Group Policy settings are assigned at the site, domain, and OU levels, and they can apply to user accounts and computer accounts. For example, a system administrator can use group policies to configure the following settings:

- Restricting users from installing new programs
- Disallowing the use of the Control Panel
- Limiting choices for display and Desktop settings

Creating OUs

Now that you have looked at several different ways in which OUs can be used to bring organization to the objects within Active Directory, it's time to look at how you can create and manage them.

Through the use of the *Active Directory Users and Computers administrative tool*, also called the *MMC (Microsoft Management Console)*, you can quickly and easily add, move, and change OUs. This graphical tool makes it easy to visualize and create the various levels of hierarchy an organization requires.

Figure 5.3 shows a geographically based OU structure that a multinational company might use. Note that the organization is based in North America and that it has a corporate office located there. In general, the other offices are much smaller than the corporate office located in North America.

FIGURE 5.3   A geographically based OU structure

It's important to note that this OU structure could have been designed in several different ways. For example, I could have chosen to group all of the offices located in the United States within an OU named "U.S." However, because of the large size of these offices, I chose to place these objects at the same level as the Canada and Mexico OUs. This prevents an unnecessarily deep OU hierarchy while still logically grouping the offices.

One nice feature when creating an OU is the ability to protect the OU from being accidentally deleted. When you create an OU, you can check the Protect Container From Accidental Deletion check box. This check box protects against an administrator deleting the OU. To delete the OU, you must go into the advanced view of the OU and uncheck the box.

Exercise 5.1 walks you through the process of creating several OUs for a multinational business. You'll be using this OU structure in later exercises within this chapter.

To perform the exercises included in this chapter, you must have administrative access to a Windows Server 2012 R2 domain controller.

EXERCISE 5.1

Creating an OU Structure

1. Click the Windows key on the keyboard and choose Administrative Tools.

2. Open the Active Directory Users and Computers administrative tool.

3. Right-click the name of the local domain and choose New ➢ Organizational Unit. You will see the dialog box shown here. Notice that this box shows you the current context within which the OU will be created. In this case, you're creating a top-level OU, so the full path is simply the name of the domain.

4. Type **North America** for the name of the first OU. Uncheck the box Protect Container From Accidental Deletion and click OK to create this object.

5. Create the following top-level OUs by right-clicking the name of the domain and choosing New ➢ Organizational Unit. Also make sure to uncheck Protect Container From Accidental Deletion for all OUs in these exercises because you'll be deleting some of these OUs in later ones.

   Africa

   Asia

   Europe

   South America

   Note that the order in which you create the OUs is not important. In this exercise, you are simply using a method that emphasizes the hierarchical relationship.

6. Create the following second-level OUs within the North America OU by right-clicking the North America OU and selecting New ➢ Organizational Unit:

Austin

Boston

Canada

Chicago

Corporate

Los Angeles

Mexico

New York

San Francisco

7. Create the following OUs under the Asia OU:

China

India

Malaysia

Vietnam

8. Create the following OUs under the Europe OU:

France

Germany

Spain

UK

9. Create the following OUs under the South America OU:

Argentina

Brazil

Chile

Peru

10. Create the following third-level OUs under the India OU by right-clicking India within the Asia OU and selecting New ➢ Organizational Unit:

Bombay

New Delhi

11. Within the North America Corporate OU, create the following OUs:

Engineering

HR

Marketing

Research

Sales

12. When you have completed creating the OUs, you should have a structure that looks similar to the one in the left pane shown here.

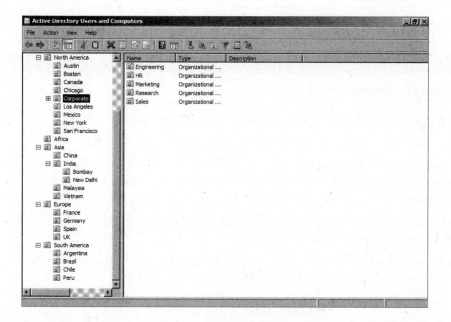

Managing OUs

Managing network environments would still be challenging, even if things rarely changed. However, in the real world, business units, departments, and employee roles change frequently. As business and technical needs change, so should the structure of Active Directory.

Fortunately, changing the structure of OUs within a domain is a relatively simple process. In the following sections, you'll look at ways to delegate control of OUs and make other changes.

Moving, Deleting, and Renaming OUs

The process of moving, deleting, and renaming OUs is a simple one. Exercise 5.2 shows how you can easily modify and reorganize OUs to reflect changes in the business organization. The specific scenario covered in this exercise includes the following changes:

- The Research and Engineering departments have been combined to form a department known as Research and Development (RD).

- The Sales department has been moved from the Corporate headquarters office to the New York office.

- The Marketing department has been moved from the Corporate headquarters office to the Chicago office.

This exercise assumes you have already completed the steps in Exercise 5.1.

EXERCISE 5.2

Modifying OU Structure

1. Click the Windows key on the keyboard and choose Administrative Tools.

2. Open the Active Directory Users and Computers administrative tool.

3. Right-click the Engineering OU (located within North America ➢ Corporate) and click Delete. When you are prompted for confirmation, click Yes. Note that if this OU contained objects, they would have all been automatically deleted as well.

4. Right-click the Research OU and select Rename. Type **RD** to change the name of the OU and press Enter.

5. Right-click the Sales OU and select Move. In the Move dialog box, expand the North America branch and click the New York OU. Click OK to move the OU.

6. You will use an alternate method to move the Marketing OU. Drag the Marketing OU and drop it onto the Chicago OU.

7. When you have finished, you should see an OU structure similar to the one shown here. Close the Active Directory Users and Computers administrative tool.

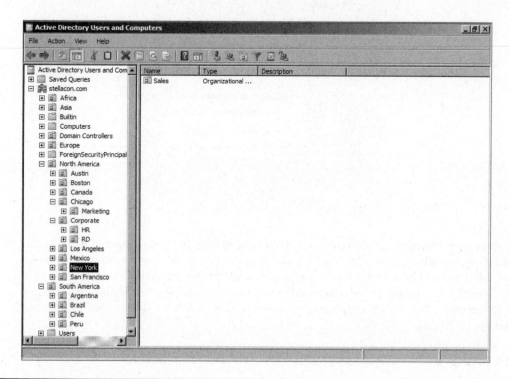

Administering Properties of OUs

Although OUs are primarily created for organizational purposes within the Active Directory environment, they have several settings that you can modify. To modify the properties of an OU using the Active Directory Users and Computers administrative tool, right-click the name of any OU and select Properties. When you do, the OU Properties dialog box appears. In the example shown in Figure 5.4, you'll see the options on the General tab.

FIGURE 5.4 The General tab of the OU's Properties dialog box

In any organization, it helps to know who is responsible for managing an OU. You can set this information on the Managed By tab (see Figure 5.5). The information specified on this tab is convenient because it is automatically pulled from the contact information on a user record. You should consider always having a contact for each OU within your organization so that other system administrators know whom to contact if they need to make any changes.

FIGURE 5.5 The Managed By tab of the OU's Properties dialog box

Delegating Control of OUs

In simple environments, one or a few system administrators may be responsible for managing all of the settings within Active Directory. For example, a single system administrator could manage all users within all OUs in the environment. In larger organizations, however, roles and responsibilities may be divided among many different individuals. A typical situation is one in which a system administrator is responsible for objects within only a few OUs in an Active Directory domain. Alternatively, one system administrator might manage User and Group objects while another is responsible for managing file and print services.

Fortunately, using the Active Directory Users and Computers tool, you can quickly and easily ensure that specific users receive only the permissions they need. In Exercise 5.3, you will use the Delegation of Control Wizard to assign permissions to individuals. To complete these steps successfully, first you must have created the objects in the previous exercises of this chapter.

EXERCISE 5.3

Using the Delegation of Control Wizard

1. Click the Windows key on the keyboard and choose Administrative Tools.

2. Open the Active Directory Users and Computers administrative tool.

3. Right-click the Corporate OU within the North America OU and select Delegate Control. This starts the Delegation of Control Wizard. Click Next to begin configuring security settings.

4. In the Users Or Groups page, click the Add button. In the Enter The Object Names To Select field, enter **Account Operators** and click the Check Names button. Click OK. Click Next to continue.

5. In the Tasks To Delegate page, select Delegate The Following Common Tasks and place a check mark next to the following items:

    Create, Delete, And Manage User Accounts

    Reset User Passwords And Force Password Change At Next Logon

    Read All User Information

    Create, Delete, And Manage Groups

    Modify The Membership Of A Group

6. Click Next to continue.

EXERCISE 5.3 *(continued)*

7. The Completing The Delegation Of Control Wizard page then provides a summary of the operations you have selected. To implement the changes, click Finish.

Although the common tasks available through the wizard are sufficient for many delegation operations, you may have cases in which you want more control. For example, you might want to give a particular system administrator permissions to modify only Computer objects. Exercise 5.4 uses the Delegation of Control Wizard to assign more granular permissions. To complete these steps successfully, you must have completed the previous exercises in this chapter.

EXERCISE 5.4

Delegating Custom Tasks

1. Click the Windows key on the keyboard and choose Administrative Tools.

2. Open the Active Directory Users and Computers administrative tool.

3. Right-click the Corporate OU within the North America OU and select Delegate Control. This starts the Delegation of Control Wizard. Click Next to begin making security settings.

4. In the Users Or Groups page, click the Add button. In the Enter The Object Names To Select field, enter **Server Operators** and click the Check Names button. Click OK and then click Next to continue.

5. In the Tasks To Delegate page, select the Create A Custom Task To Delegate radio button and click Next to continue.

6. In the Active Directory Object Type page, choose Only The Following Objects In The Folder and place a check mark next to the following items. (You will have to scroll down to see them all.)

User Objects

Computer Objects

Contact Objects

Group Objects

Organizational Unit Objects

Printer Objects

7. Click Next to continue.

8. In the Permissions page, place a check mark next to the General option and make sure the other options are not checked. Note that if the various objects within your Active Directory schema had property-specific settings, you would see those options here. Place a check mark next to the following items:

Create All Child Objects

Read All Properties

Write All Properties

This gives the members of the Server Operators group the ability to create new objects within the Corporate OU and the permissions to read and write all properties for these objects.

EXERCISE 5.4 *(continued)*

9. Click Next to continue.

10. The Completing The Delegation Of Control Wizard page provides a summary of the operations you have selected. To implement the changes, click Finish.

 Real World Scenario

Delegation: Who's Responsible for What?

You're the IT director for a large, multinational organization. You've been with the company for quite a while, that is, since the environment had only a handful of offices and a few network and system administrators. Times have changed, however. Now system administrators must coordinate the efforts of hundreds of IT staffers in 14 countries.

For years now, a debate has been raging among IT administrators on the question of when to create a new child domain and when to make it just an OU. For example, let's say you have a remote office in Concord, New Hampshire. Do you give the remote office its own domain (as a child domain), or do you just make the Concord office an OU? Well, it really depends on who you want to manage the resources in Concord. Do you want to create domains or OUs based on location?

Fortunately, through the proper use of OUs and delegation, you are given a lot of flexibility in determining how to handle the administration. You can structure the administration in several ways. First, if you choose to create OUs based on a geographic business structure, you could delegate control of these OUs based on the job functions of various system administrators. For example, you could use one user account to administer the

Concord OU. Within the Concord OU, this system administrator could delegate control of resources represented by the Printers and Scanners OUs.

Alternatively, the OU structure may create a functional representation of the business. For example, the Engineering OU might contain other OUs that are based on office locations such as New York and Paris. A system administrator of the Engineering domain could delegate permissions based on geography or job functions to the lower OUs. Regardless of whether you build a departmental, functional, or geographical OU model, keep in mind that each model excludes other models. This is one of the most important decisions you need to make. When you are making this decision or modifying previous decisions, your overriding concern is how it will affect the management and administration of the network. The good news is that, because Active Directory has so many features, the model you choose can be based on specific business requirements rather than imposed by architectural constraints.

Troubleshooting OUs

In general, you will find using OUs to be a relatively straightforward and painless process. With adequate planning, you'll be able to implement an intuitive and useful structure for OU objects.

The most common problems with OU configuration are related to the OU structure. When troubleshooting OUs, pay careful attention to the following factors:

Inheritance   By default, Group Policy and other settings are transferred automatically from parent OUs to child OUs and objects. Even if a specific OU is not given a set of permissions, objects within that OU might still get them from parent objects.

Delegation of Administration   If you allow the wrong user accounts or groups to perform specific tasks on OUs, you might be violating your company's security policy. Be sure to verify the delegations you have made at each OU level.

Organizational Issues   Sometimes, business practices do not easily map to the structure of Active Directory. A few misplaced OUs, user accounts, computer accounts, or groups can make administration difficult or inaccurate. In many cases, it might be beneficial to rearrange the OU structure to accommodate any changes in the business organization. In others, it might make more sense to change business processes.

If you regularly consider each of these issues when troubleshooting problems with OUs, you will be much less likely to make errors in the Active Directory configuration.

Creating and Managing Active Directory Objects

Now that you are familiar with the task of creating OUs, you should find creating and managing other Active Directory objects quite simple. The following sections will examine the details.

Overview of Active Directory Objects

When you install and configure a domain controller, Active Directory sets up an organizational structure for you, and you can create and manage several types of objects.

Active Directory Organization

When you are looking at your Active Directory structure, you will see objects that look like folders in Windows Explorer. These objects are containers, or *organizational units (OUs)*. The difference is that an OU is a container to which you can link a GPO. Normal containers cannot have a GPO linked to them. That's what makes an OU a special container.

By default, after you install and configure a domain controller, you will see the following organizational sections within the Active Directory Users and Computers tool (they look like folders):

Built-In   The *Built-In container* includes all of the standard groups that are installed by default when you promote a domain controller. You can use these groups to administer the servers in your environment. Examples include the Administrators group, Backup Operators group, and Print Operators group.

Computers   By default, the *Computers container* contains a list of the workstations in your domain. From here, you can manage all of the computers in your domain.

Domain Controllers   The *Domain Controllers OU* includes a list of all the domain controllers for the domain.

Foreign Security Principals   *Foreign security principals* containers are any objects to which security can be assigned and that are not part of the current domain. *Security principals* are Active Directory objects to which permissions can be applied, and they can be used to manage permissions in Active Directory.

Managed Service Accounts   The *Managed Service Accounts container* is a new Windows Server 2012 R2 container. Service accounts are accounts created to run specific services such as Exchange and SQL Server. Having a Managed Service Accounts container allows you to control the service accounts better and thus allows for better service account security.

Users   The *Users container* includes all the security accounts that are part of the domain. When you first install the domain controller, there will be several groups in this container.

For example, the Domain Admins group and the administrator account are created in this container.

You want to be sure to protect the administrator account. You should rename the admin account and make sure the password is complex. Protected admin accounts can make your network safer. Every hacker knows that there is an administrator account on the server by default. Be sure to make your network safer by protecting the admin account.

Active Directory Objects

You can create and manage several different types of Active Directory objects. The following are specific object types:

Computer   *Computer objects* represent workstations that are part of the Active Directory domain. All computers within a domain share the same security database, including user and group information. Computer objects are useful for managing security permissions and enforcing Group Policy restrictions.

Contact   *Contact objects* are usually used in OUs to specify the main administrative contact. Contacts are not security principals like users. They are used to specify information about individuals outside the organization.

Group   *Group objects* are logical collections of users primarily for assigning security permissions to resources. When managing users, you should place them into groups and then assign permissions to the group. This allows for flexible management without the need to set permissions for individual users.

InetOrgPerson   The *InetOrgPerson object* is an Active Directory object that defines attributes of users in Lightweight Directory Access Protocol (LDAP) and X.500 directories.

MSIMaging-PSPs   *MSIMaging-PSPs* is a container for all Enterprise Scan Post Scan Process objects.

MSMQ Queue Alias   An *MSMQ Queue Alias object* is an Active Directory object for the MSMQ-Custom-Recipient class type. The Microsoft Message Queuing (MSMQ) Queue Alias object associates an Active Directory path and a user-defined alias with a public, private, or direct single-element format name. This allows a queue alias to be used to reference a queue that might not be listed in Active Directory Domain Services (AD DS).

Organizational Unit   An *OU object* is created to build a hierarchy within the Active Directory domain. It is the smallest unit that can be used to create administrative groupings, and it can be used to assign group policies. Generally, the OU structure within a domain reflects a company's business organization.

Printer   *Printer objects* map to printers.

Shared Folder   *Shared Folder objects* map to server shares. They are used to organize the various file resources that may be available on file/print servers. Often, Shared Folder objects are used to give logical names to specific file collections. For example, system administrators might create separate shared folders for common applications, user data, and shared public files.

User A *User object* is the fundamental security principal on which Active Directory is based. User accounts contain information about individuals as well as password and other permission information.

Creating Objects Using the Active Directory Users and Computers Tool

Exercise 5.5 walks you through the steps necessary to create various objects within an Active Directory domain. In this exercise, you create some basic Active Directory objects. To complete this exercise, you must have access to at least one Active Directory domain controller, and you should have also completed the previous exercises in this chapter.

EXERCISE 5.5

Creating Active Directory Objects

1. Click the Windows key on the keyboard and choose Administrative Tools.

2. Open the Active Directory Users and Computers tool.

3. Expand the current domain to list the objects currently contained within it. For this exercise, you will use the second- and third-level OUs contained within the North America top-level OU, as shown here.

4. Right-click the Corporate OU and select New ➢ User. Fill in the following information:

    First Name: **Maria**

    Initial: **D**

    Last Name: **President**

    Full Name: (leave as default)

    User Logon Name: **mdpresident** (leave default domain)

    Click Next to continue.

5. Enter **P@ssw0rd** for the password for this user and then confirm it. Note that you can also make changes to password settings here. Click Next.

6. You will see a summary of the user information. Click Finish to create the new user.

7. Click the RD container and create another user in that container with the following information:

    First Name: **John**

    Initial: **Q**

    Last Name: **Adams**

    Full Name: (leave as default)

    User Logon Name: **jqadams** (leave default domain)

    Click Next to continue.

8. Assign the password **P@ssw0rd**. Click Next and then click Finish to create the user.

9. Right-click the RD OU and select New ➢ Contact. Use the following information to fill in the properties of the Contact object:

    First Name: **Jane**

    Initials: **R**

    Last Name: **Admin**

    Display Name: **jradmin**

    Click OK to create the new Contact object.

10. Right-click the RD OU and select New ➢ Shared Folder. Enter **Software** for the name and **\\server1\applications** for the network path (also known as the Universal Naming Convention [UNC] path). Note that you can create the object even though this resource (the physical server) does not exist. Click OK to create the Shared Folder object.

11. Right-click the HR OU and select New ➢ Group. Type **All Users** for the group name. Do not change the value in the Group Name (Pre–Windows 2000) field. For Group Scope, select Global, and for Group Type, select Security. To create the group, click OK.

12. Right-click the Sales OU and select New ➤ Computer. Type **Workstation1** for the name of the computer. Notice that the pre–Windows 2000 name is automatically populated and that, by default, the members of the Domain Admins group are the only ones who can add this computer to the domain. Place a check mark in the Assign This Computer Account As A Pre-Windows 2000 Computer box and then click OK to create the Computer object.

13. Close the Active Directory Users and Computers tool.

Configuring the User Principal Name

When you log into a domain, your logon name looks like an email address (for example, wpanek@willpanek.com). This is called your *user principal name (UPN)*. A UPN is the username followed by the @ sign and the domain name. At the time that the user account is created, the UPN suffix is generated by default. The UPN is created as *userName@Domain Name*, but an administrator can alter or change the default UPN. If your forest has multiple domains and you need to change the UPN to a different domain, you have that ability. To change the UPN suffix, in Active Directory Users and Computers, choose a user and go into their properties. Choose the Attribute Editor tab. Scroll down to the userPrincipalName attribute and make your changes. These changes then get replicated to the global catalog.

 If your organization has multiple forests set up by a trust, you can't change the UPN to a domain in the other forest. Global catalogs are used to log on users. Because UPNs get replicated to the local forest global catalog servers, you cannot log onto other forests using the UPN.

Using Templates

Now you are going to dive into user templates. *User templates* allow an Active Directory administrator to create a default account (for example, template_sales) and use that account to create all of the other users who match it (all the salespeople).

If you are creating multiple accounts, this can save you a lot of time and resources. For example, if you need to add 35 new salespeople to your company, you'll create one template for sales and use a copy of that template for all of the other new accounts. This saves you the trouble of filling out many of the same fields over and over again. When you copy a template, some of the information does *not* get copied over. This is because it is user-specific information. Here are some of the fields that do not get copied over from a template:

- Name
- Logon Name
- Password
- Email

- Phone Numbers
- Description
- Office
- Web Page

Many of the important fields such as Member Of (groups to which the user belongs), Profile Path, Department, and Company all get copied over. There is one important item that needs to be done when creating a template: the template account needs to be disabled after creation. You do not want anyone using this account to access your network. In Exercise 5.6, you will create a Sales template to use for your Sales department.

EXERCISE 5.6

Creating a User Template

1. Click the Windows key on the keyboard and choose Administrative Tools.

2. Open the Active Directory Users and Computers snap-in.

3. Expand the current domain to list the objects contained within it. For this exercise, you will use the Sales OU. Right-click the Sales OU and choose New ➢ User.

4. Use the following properties:

   First Name: **Sales**

   Last Name: **Template**

   Username: **sales_template**

   Password: **P@ssw0rd**

5. Click Next and then click Finish.

6. In the right window, double-click the Sales Template user to open the properties.

7. On the General tab, complete the following items:

   Description: **Template Account**

   Office: **Corporate**

   Telephone: **999-999-9999**

   Email: **Salet@abc.com**

   Web: **www.abc.com**

8. Click the Profile tab. In the Profile Path field, type **\\ServerA\%username%**.

9. On the Members Of tab, click the Add button. At the Enter The Object Name To Select box, type **Administrator** and click the Check Names button. (Normally you would not

add salespeople to the Administrators group, but you are doing so just for this exercise.) Click OK.

10. Click the Account tab. Scroll down in the Account Options box and check the Account Is Disabled check box.

11. Click OK in the user's Properties window to go back to the Sales OU.

12. Right-click the Sales Template account and choose Copy.

13. Enter the following information:

    First Name: **Jenny**

    Last Name: **Sales**

    Username: **jsales**

    Password: **P@ssw0rd**

    Uncheck the Account Is disabled check box.

14. In the right window, double-click the Jenny Sales user to open the properties.

15. Take a look at the Members Of tab, the General tab, and the Profile tab, and you will see that some of the fields are prefilled (including the Administrators group).

16. Close Jenny Sales Properties and exit Active Directory Users and Computers.

Importing Objects from a File

In Exercise 5.5, you created an account using the Active Directory Users and Computers tool. But what if you need to bulk import accounts? There are two main applications for doing bulk imports of accounts: the ldifde.exe utility and the csvde.exe utility. Both utilities import accounts from files.

The ldifde utility imports from line-delimited files. This utility allows an administrator to export and import data, thus allowing batch operations such as Add, Modify, and Delete to be performed in Active Directory. Windows Server 2012 R2 includes ldifde.exe to help support batch operations.

The csvde.exe utility performs the same export functions as ldifde.exe, but csvde.exe uses a comma-separated value file format. The csvde.exe utility does not allow administrators to modify or delete objects. It only supports adding objects to Active Directory.

Active Directory Migration Tool

Another tool that administrators have used in the past is *Active Directory Migration Tool (ADMT)*. ADMT allows an administrator to migrate users, groups, and computers from a previous version of the server to a current version of the server.

Administrators also used the ADMT to migrate users, groups, and computers between Active Directory domains in different forests (interforest migration) and between Active Directory domains in the same forest (intraforest migration).

At the time this book was written, Microsoft had not yet released a new version of ADMT that is supported by Windows Server 2012 R2. The reason I even mention it in this book is because Microsoft may be releasing a version of it soon, and I wanted you to understand what it can do. Continue to check the Microsoft website to see whether a new version has been released.

Offline Domain Join of a Computer

Offline domain join gives administrators the ability to preprovision computer accounts in the domain to prepare operating systems for deployments. At startup, computers can then join the domain without the need to contact a domain controller. This helps reduce the time it takes to deploy computers in a datacenter.

Let's say your datacenter needs to have multiple virtual machines deployed. This is where offline domain join can be useful. Upon initial startup after the operating system is installed, offline domain join allows the virtual machines to join the domain automatically. No additional steps or restart are needed.

The following are some of the benefits of using offline domain join:

- There is no additional network traffic for Active Directory state changes.
- There is no additional network traffic for computer state changes to the domain controller.
- Changes for both the Active Directory state and the computer state can be completed at a different times.

Managing Object Properties

Once you've created the necessary Active Directory objects, you'll probably need to make changes to their default properties. In addition to the settings you made when you were creating Active Directory objects, you can configure several more properties. You can also access object properties by right-clicking any object and selecting Properties from the pop-up menu.

Each object type contains a unique set of properties.

User Object Properties   The following list describes some of the properties of a User object:

General   General account information about this user

Address   Physical location information about this user

Account   User logon name and other account restrictions, such as workstation restrictions and logon hours

Profile   Information about the user's roaming profile settings

Telephones   Telephone contact information for the user

Organization   The user's title, department, and company information

Member Of   Group membership information for the user

Dial-In   Remote Access Service (RAS) permissions for the user

Environment   Logon and other network settings for the user

Sessions   Session limits, including maximum session time and idle session settings

Remote Control   Remote control options for this user's session

Remote Desktop Services Profile   Information about the user's profile for use with Remote Desktop Services

Personal Virtual Desktop   Allows you to assign a user a specific virtual machine to use as a personal virtual desktop

COM+   Specifies a COM+ partition set for the user

Computer Object Properties

Computer objects have different properties than User objects. Computer objects refer to the systems that clients are operating to be part of a domain. The following list describes some Computer object properties:

General   Information about the name of the computer, the role of the computer, and its description

(You can enable an option to allow the Local System account of this machine to request services from other servers. This is useful if the machine is a trusted and secure computer.)

Operating System   The name, version, and service pack information for the operating system running on the computer

Member Of   Active Directory groups of which this Computer object is a member

Delegation   Allows you to set services that work on behalf of another user

Location   A description of the computer's physical location

Managed By   Information about the User or Contact object that is responsible for managing this computer

Dial-In   Sets dial-in options for the computer

Setting Properties for Active Directory Objects

Now that you have seen the various properties that can be set for the Active Directory objects, let's complete an exercise on how to configure some of these properties. Exercise 5.7 walks you through how to set various properties for Active Directory objects. To complete the steps in this exercise, first you must have completed Exercise 5.5.

Although it may seem a bit tedious, it's always a good idea to enter as much information as you know about Active Directory objects when you create them. Although the name Printer1 may be meaningful to you, users will appreciate the additional information, such as location, when they are searching for objects.

EXERCISE 5.7

Managing Object Properties

1. Click the Windows key on the keyboard and choose Administrative Tools.

2. Open the Active Directory Users and Computers tool.

3. Expand the name of the domain and select the RD container. Right-click the John Q. Adams user account and select Properties.

4. Here you will see the various Properties tabs for the User account. Make some configuration changes based on your personal preferences. Click OK to continue.

5. Select the HR OU. Right-click the All Users group and click Properties. In the All Users Properties dialog box, you will be able to modify the membership of the group.

EXERCISE 5.7 *(continued)*

Click the Members tab and then click Add. Add the Maria D. President and John Q. Admin user accounts to the group. Click OK to save the settings and then OK to accept the group modifications.

6. Select the Sales OU. Right-click the Workstation1 Computer object. Notice that you can choose to disable the account or reset it (to allow another computer to join the domain under that same name). From the context menu, choose Properties. You'll see the properties for the Computer object.

   Examine the various options and make changes based on your personal preference. After you have examined the available options, click OK to continue.

7. Select the Corporate OU. Right-click the Maria D. President user account and choose Reset Password. You will be prompted to enter a new password, and then you'll be asked to confirm it. Note that you can also force the user to change this password upon the next logon, and you can also unlock the user's account from here. For this exercise, do not enter a new password; just click Cancel.

8. Close the Active Directory Users and Computers tool.

By now, you have probably noticed that Active Directory objects have a lot of common options. For example, Group and Computer objects both have a Managed By tab.

Windows Server 2012 R2 allows you to manage many User objects at once. For instance, you can select several User objects by holding down the Shift or Ctrl key while selecting. You can then right-click any one of the selected objects and select Properties to display the properties that are available for multiple users. Notice that not every user property is available because some properties are unique to each user. You can configure the Description field for multiple object selections that include both users and nonusers, such as computers and groups.

An important thing to think about when it comes to accounts is the difference between disabling an account and deleting an account. When you delete an account, the security ID (SID) gets deleted. Even if you later create an account with the same username, it will have a different SID number, and therefore it will be a different account. It is sometimes better to disable an account and place it into a nonactive OU called *Disabled*. This way, if you ever need to reaccess the account, you can do so.

Another object management task is the process of deprovisioning. *Deprovisioning* is the management of Active Directory objects in the container. When you remove an object from an Active Directory container, the deprovisioning process removes the object and synchronizes the container to stay current.

Understanding Groups

Now that you know how to create user accounts, it's time to learn how to create group accounts. As an instructor, I am always amazed when students (who work in the IT field) have no idea why they should use groups. This is something every organization should be using.

To illustrate their usefulness, let's say you have a Sales department user by the name of wpanek. Your organization has 100 resources shared on the network for users to access. Because wpanek is part of the Sales department, he has access to 50 of the resources. The Marketing department uses the other 50. If the organization is not using groups and wpanek moves from Sales to Marketing, how many changes do you have to make? The answer is 100. You have to move him out of the 50 resources he currently can use and place his account into the 50 new resources that he now needs.

Now let's say that you use groups. The Sales group has access to 50 resources, and the Marketing group has access to the other 50. If wpanek moves from Sales to Marketing, you need to make only two changes. You just have to take wpanek out of the Sales group and place him in the Marketing group. Once this is done, wpanek can access everything he needs to do his job.

Group Properties

Now that you understand why you should use groups, let's go over setting up groups and their properties. When you are creating groups, it helps to understand some of the options that you need to use.

Group Type   You can choose from two group types: security groups and distribution groups.

Security Groups   These groups can have rights and permissions placed on them. For example, if you want to give a certain group of users access to a particular printer, but you want to control what they are allowed to do with this printer, you'd create a security group and then apply certain rights and permissions to this group.

Security groups can also receive emails. If someone sent an email to the group, all users within that group would receive it (as long as they have a mail system that allows for mail-enabled groups, like Exchange).

Distribution Groups   These groups are used for email *only* (as long as they have a mail system that allows for mail-enabled groups, like Exchange). You cannot place permissions and rights for objects on this group type.

Group Scope   When it comes to group scopes, you have three choices.

Domain Local Groups   Domain local groups are groups that remain in the domain in which they were created. You use these groups to grant permissions within a single domain. For example, if you create a domain local group named HPLaser, you cannot use that group in any other domain, and it has to reside in the domain in which you created it.

Global Group   Global groups can contain other groups and accounts from the domain in which the group is created. In addition, you can give them permissions in any domain in the forest.

Universal Groups   Universal groups can include other groups and accounts from any domain in the domain tree or forest. You can give universal groups permissions in any domain in the domain tree or forest.

Creating Group Strategies

When you are creating a group strategy, think of this acronym that Microsoft likes to use in the exam: AGDLP (or AGLP). This acronym stands for a series of actions you should perform. Here is how it expands:

A   Accounts (Create your user accounts.)

G   Global groups (Put user accounts into global groups.)

DL   Domain local groups (Put global groups into domain local groups.)

P   Permissions (Assign permissions such as Deny or Apply on the domain local group.)

Another acronym that stands for a strategy you can use is AGUDLP (or AULP). Here is how it expands:

A   Accounts (Create your user accounts.)

G   Global groups (Put user accounts into global groups.)

U   Universal groups (Put the global groups into universal groups.)

DL   Domain local groups (Put universal groups into domain local groups.)

P   Permissions (Place permissions on the local group.)

Creating a Group

To create a new group, open the Active Directory Users and Computers snap-in. Click the OU where the group is going to reside. Right-click and choose New and then Group. After you create the group, just click the Members tab and choose Add. Add the users you want to reside in that group, and that's all there is to it.

Filtering and Advanced Active Directory Features

The Active Directory Users and Computers tool has a couple of other features that come in quite handy when you are managing many objects. You can access the Filter Options dialog box by clicking the View menu in the MMC and choosing Filter Options. You'll see a dialog box similar to the one shown in Figure 5.6. Here you can choose to filter objects by their specific types within the display. For example, if you are an administrator who works primarily with user accounts and groups, you can select those specific items by placing check marks in the list. In addition, you can create more complex filters by choosing Create Custom. Doing so provides you with an interface that looks similar to that of the Find command.

FIGURE 5.6   The Filter Options dialog box

Another option in the Active Directory Users and Computers tool is to view advanced options. You can enable the advanced options by choosing Advanced Features in the View menu. This adds some top-level folders to the list under the name of the domain. Let's take a look at a couple of the new top-level folders.

The System folder (shown in Figure 5.7) provides additional features that you can configure to work with Active Directory. You can configure settings for the Distributed File System (DFS), IP Security (IPSec) policies, the File Replication Service (FRS), and more. In addition to the System folder, you'll see the LostAndFound folder. This folder contains any files that may not have been replicated properly between domain controllers. You should check this folder periodically for any files so that you can decide whether you need to move them or copy them to other locations.

FIGURE 5.7   Advanced Features in the System folder of the Active Directory Users and Computers tool

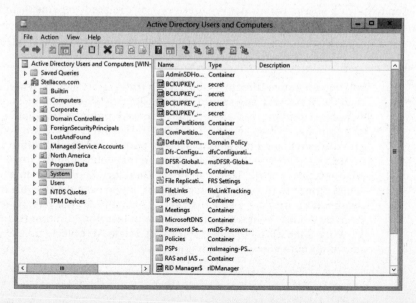

As you can see, managing Active Directory objects is generally a simple task. The Active Directory Users and Computers tool allows you to configure several objects. Let's move on to look at one more common administration function: moving objects.

Moving, Renaming, and Deleting Active Directory Objects

One of the extremely useful features of the Active Directory Users and Computers tool is its ability to move users and resources easily.

Exercise 5.8 walks you through the process of moving Active Directory objects. In this exercise, you will make several changes to the organization of Active Directory objects. To complete this exercise, first you must have completed Exercise 5.5.

EXERCISE 5.8

Moving Active Directory Objects

1. Click the Windows key on the keyboard and choose Administrative Tools.

2. Open the Active Directory Users and Computers tool and expand the name of the domain.

3. Select the Sales OU (under the New York OU), right-click Workstation1, and select Move. A dialog box appears. Select the RD OU and click OK to move the Computer object to that container.

4. Click the RD OU and verify that Workstation1 was moved.

5. Close the Active Directory Users and Computers tool.

In addition to moving objects within Active Directory, you can easily rename them by right-clicking an object and selecting Rename. Note that this option does not apply to all objects. You can remove objects from Active Directory by right-clicking them and choosing Delete.

WARNING   Deleting an Active Directory object is an irreversible action. When an object is destroyed, any security permissions or other settings made for that object are removed as well. Because each object within Active Directory contains its own security identifier (SID), simply re-creating an object with the same name does not place any permissions on it. Before you delete an Active Directory object, be sure that you will never need it again. Windows Server 2012 R2 has an Active Directory Recycle Bin to allow an administrator to retrieve a deleted object, but in case the Recycle Bin gets cleared, it's better to be safe than sorry. Also, the AD Recycle Bin is disabled by default, so it will be unavailable unless you turn that feature on. So, what is the moral of this story? Don't delete AD objects unless you are absolutely sure you want them gone.

Windows Server 2012 R2 has a check box called Protect Container From Accidental Deletion for all OUs. If this check box is checked, to delete or move an OU, you must go into the Active Directory Users and Computers advanced options. Once you are in the advanced options, you can uncheck the box to move or delete the OU.

Resetting an Existing Computer Account

Every computer on the domain establishes a discrete channel of communication with the domain controller at logon time. The domain controller stores a randomly selected password (different from the user password) for authentication across the channel. The password is updated every 30 days.

Sometimes the computer's password and the domain controller's password don't match, and communication between the two machines fails. Without the ability to reset the computer account, you wouldn't be able to connect the machine to the domain. Fortunately, you can use the Active Directory Users and Computers tool to reestablish the connection.

Exercise 5.9 shows you how to reset an existing computer account. You should have completed the previous exercises in this chapter before you begin this exercise.

EXERCISE 5.9

Resetting an Existing Computer Account

1. Click the Windows key on the keyboard and choose Administrative Tools.

2. Open the Active Directory Users and Computers tool and expand the name of the domain.

3. Click the RD OU and then right-click the Workstation1 computer account.

4. Select Reset Account from the context menu. Click Yes to confirm your selection. Click OK at the success prompt.

5. When you reset the account, you break the connection between the computer and the domain. So, after performing this exercise, reconnect the computer to the domain if you want it to continue working on the network.

Throughout this book, I have tried to show you the PowerShell way of doing a task shown previously using an MMC snap-in. Well, this is going to be no different.

This example shows you how to reset the secure connection between the local computer and the domain to which it is joined using a PowerShell command. In this example, the domain controller that performs the operation is specified as StellaDC1.Stellacon.com. To execute this PowerShell command, you must run this command on the local computer:

```
Test-ComputerSecureChannel -Repair -Server StellaDC1.Stellacon.com
```

Publishing Active Directory Objects

One of the main goals of Active Directory is to make resources easy to find. Two of the most commonly used resources in a networked environment are server file shares and printers. These are so common, in fact, that most organizations have dedicated file and print servers. When it comes to managing these types of resources, Active Directory makes it easy to determine which files and printers are available to users.

With that being said, take a look at how Active Directory manages to publish shared folders and printers.

Making Active Directory Objects Available to Users

An important aspect of managing Active Directory objects is that a system administrator can control which objects users can see. The act of making an Active Directory object available is known as *publishing*. The two main types of publishable objects are Printer objects and Shared Folder objects.

The general process for creating server shares and shared printers has remained unchanged from previous versions of Windows: you create the various objects (a printer or a file system folder) and then enable them for sharing. To make these resources available via Active Directory, however, there's an additional step: you must publish the resources. Once an object has been published in Active Directory, clients will be able to use it.

When you publish objects in Active Directory, you should know the server name and share name of the resource. When system administrators use Active Directory objects, they can change the resource to which the object points, without having to reconfigure or even notify clients. For example, if you move a share from one server to another, all you need to do is to update the Shared Folder object's properties to point to the new location. Active Directory clients still refer to the resource with the same path and name that they used before.

Publishing Printers

Printers can be published easily within Active Directory. This makes them available to users in your domain.

Exercise 5.10 walks you through the steps you need to take to share and publish a Printer object by having you create and share a printer. To complete the printer installation, you need access to the Windows Server 2012 R2 installation media (via the hard disk, a network share, or the CD-ROM drive).

EXERCISE 5.10

Creating and Publishing a Printer

1. Click the Windows key on the keyboard and choose Control Panel.

2. Click Devices And Printers ➢ Add A Printer. This starts the Add Printer Wizard. Then click the Next button.

3. In the Choose A Local Or Network Printer page, select Add A Local Printer. This should automatically take you to the next page. If it does not, click Next.

4. On the Choose A Printer Port page, select Use An Existing Port. From the drop-down list beside that option, make sure LPT1: (Printer Port) is selected. Click Next.

5. On the Install The Printer Driver page, select Generic for the manufacturer. For the printer, highlight Generic/Text Only. Click Next.

6. On the Type A Printer Name page, type **Text Printer**. Uncheck the Set As The Default Printer box and then click Next.

7. The Installing Printer screen appears. After the system is finished, the Printer Sharing page appears. Make sure the box labeled "Share this printer so that others on your network can find and use it" is selected, and accept the default share name of Text Printer.

8. In the Location section, type **Building 203**, and in the Comment section, add the following comment: **This is a text-only Printer**. Click Next.

9. On the You've Successfully Added Text Printer page, click Finish.

10. Next you need to verify that the printer will be listed in Active Directory. Right-click the Text Printer icon and select Printer Properties.

11. Select the Sharing tab and make sure that the List In The Directory box is checked. Note that you can also add additional printer drivers for other operating systems using this tab. Click OK to accept the settings.

Note that when you create and share a printer this way, an Active Directory Printer object is not displayed within the Active Directory Users and Computers tool. The printer is actually associated with the Computer object to which it is connected.

Publishing Shared Folders

Now that you've created and published a printer, you'll see how the same thing can be done to shared folders.

Exercise 5.11 walks through the steps required to create a folder, share it, and then publish it in Active Directory. This exercise assumes you are using the C: partition; however, you may want to change this based on your server configuration. This exercise assumes you have completed Exercise 5.5.

EXERCISE 5.11

Creating and Publishing a Shared Folder

1. Create a new folder in the root directory of your C: partition and name it Test Share. To do this, click the File Explorer link on the toolbar.

2. Right-click the Test Share folder. Choose Share With ➢ Specific People.

3. In the File Sharing dialog box, enter the names of users with whom you want to share this folder. In the upper box, enter **Everyone** and then click Add. Note that Everyone appears in the lower box. Click in the Permission Level column next to Everyone and choose Read/Write from the pop-up menu. Then click Share.

4. You'll see a message that your folder has been shared. Click Done.

5. Click the Windows key on the keyboard and choose Administrative Tools.

6. Open the Active Directory Users and Computers tool. Expand the current domain and right-click the RD OU. Select New ➤ Shared Folder.

7. In the New Object - Shared Folder dialog box, type **Shared Folder Test** for the name of the folder. Then type the UNC path to the share (for example, **\\server1\Test Share**). Click OK to create the share.

Once you have created and published the Shared Folder object, clients can use the My Network Places icon to find it. The Shared Folder object will be organized based on the OU in which you created it. When you use publication, you can see how this makes it easy to manage shared folders.

Querying Active Directory

So far you've created several Active Directory resources. One of the main benefits of having all of your resource information in Active Directory is that you can easily find what you're looking for using the Find dialog box. Recall that I recommended that you always enter as much information as possible when creating Active Directory objects. This is where that extra effort begins to pay off.

Exercise 5.12 walks you through the steps to find specific objects in Active Directory. To complete this exercise, you must have completed Exercise 5.5.

EXERCISE 5.12

Finding Objects in Active Directory

1. Click the Windows key on the keyboard and choose Administrative Tools.

2. Open the Active Directory Users and Computers tool.

3. Right-click the name of the domain and select Find.

4. In the Find Users, Contacts, And Groups dialog box, select Users, Contacts, And Groups from the Find drop-down list. For the In setting, choose Entire Directory. This searches the entire Active Directory environment for the criteria you enter.

   Note that if this is a production domain and there are many objects, searching the whole directory may be a time-consuming and network-intensive operation.

EXERCISE 5.12 *(continued)*

5. In the Name field, type **admin** and then click Find Now to obtain the results of the search.

6. Now that you have found several results, you can narrow down the list. Click the Advanced tab of the Find Users, Contacts, And Groups dialog box.

In the Field drop-down list, select User ➢ Last Name. For Condition, select Starts With, and for Value, type **admin**. Click Add to add this condition to the search criteria. Click Find Now. Now only the users that have the last name Admin are shown.

7. When you have finished searching, close the Find Users, Contacts, And Groups dialog box and exit the Active Directory Users and Computers tool.

Using the many options available in the Find dialog box, you can usually narrow down the objects for which you are searching quickly and efficiently. Users and system administrators alike find this tool useful in environments of any size. Now that you have seen how to create objects in Active Directory, let's take a look at a new Windows Server 2012 R2 feature called Active Directory Administrative Center.

Using the Active Directory Administrative Center

Windows Server 2012 R2 has a feature called the *Active Directory Administrative Center* (see Figure 5.8). This feature allows you to manage many Active Directory tasks from one central location (see Figure 5.9).

FIGURE 5.8   Active Directory Administrative Center

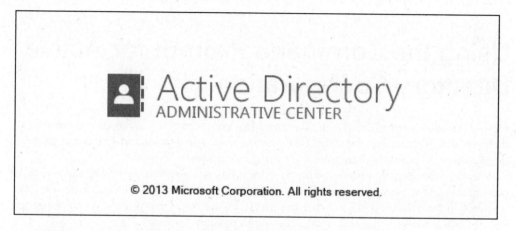

© 2013 Microsoft Corporation. All rights reserved.

FIGURE 5.9   Administrative Center Overview screen

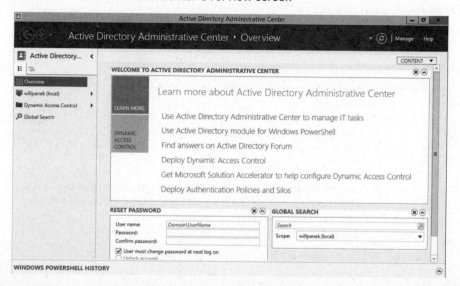

Using the Active Directory Administrative Center, here are some of the tasks that an administrator can perform:

- Reset passwords
- Create new objects
- Delete objects
- Move objects
- Perform global searches
- Configure properties for Active Directory objects

In Windows Server 2012 R2, the Active Directory Administrative Center is just another tool in your Active Directory tool belt. It does not matter which way you create your Active Directory objects as long as you have a good understanding of how to create them.

Using the Command Prompt for Active Directory Configuration

Many IT administrators like to use command-line commands to configure and maintain their Active Directory environment. One advantage of using command-line commands is the ability to do multiple changes at once using batch files.

Another advantage of knowing how to manipulate Active Directory using the command prompt is working with Windows Server 2012 R2 Server Core. Server Core is an installation of Windows Server 2012 R2 that has no GUI windows. One of the ways to configure Server Core is to use commands in the command prompt window.

Table 5.1 shows you many of the command prompt commands and explains how each command affects Active Directory.

TABLE 5.1 Command prompt commands

Command	Explanation
Csvde	This command allows you to import and export data from Active Directory. The data gets stored in a comma-separated value (CSV) format.
Dcdiag	This troubleshooting command checks the state of your domain controllers in your forest and sends back a report of any problems.

Djoin	This command allows a computer account to join a domain, and it runs an offline domain join when a computer restarts.
Dsacls	This command allows you to see and change permissions in the access control list for objects in Active Directory Domain Services (AD DS).
Dsadd	This command allows you to add an object to the AD DS directory.
Dsamain	This command shows the Active Directory data stored in either a snapshot or a backup as if it were in a Lightweight Directory Access Protocol (LDAP) server.
Dsdbutil	This command provides database utilities for Active Directory Lightweight Directory Services (AD LDS).
Dsget	This command shows the properties of an object in the AD DS directory.
Dsmgmt	This command gives an administrator management utilities for AD LDS.
Dsmod	This command allows you to modify an AD DS object.
Dsmove	This command allows you to move an object in an Active Directory domain from its current OU to a new OU within the same forest.
Dsquery	This command allows you to query AD DS.
Dsrm	This command removes an object from the AD DS directory.
Ldifde	This command allows you to import and export data from Active Directory. The data is stored as LDAP Data Interchange Format (LDIF).
Ntdsutil	This is one of the most important commands for Active Directory. It allows you to do maintenance on the Active Directory database.
Repadmin	This command allows administrators to diagnose Active Directory replication problems between domain controllers.

Summary

This chapter covered the fundamentals of administering Active Directory. The most important part of administering Active Directory is learning about how to work with OUs. Therefore, you should be aware of the purpose of OUs; that is, they help you to organize and manage the directory. For instance, think of administrative control. If you wanted to delegate rights to another administrator (such as a sales manager), you could delegate that authority to that user within the Sales OU. As the system administrator, you would retain the rights to the castle.

You also looked at how to design an OU structure from an example. The example showed you how to design a proper OU layout. You can also create, organize, and reorganize OUs if need be.

In addition, you took a look at groups and group strategies. There are different types of groups (domain local, global, and universal groups), and you should know when each group is available and when to use each group.

Finally, this chapter covered how to use the Active Directory Users and Computers tool to manage Active Directory objects. If you're responsible for day-to-day system administration, there's a good chance that you are already familiar with this tool; if not, you should be after reading this chapter. Using this tool, you learned how to work with Active Directory objects such as User, Computer, and Group objects. You also learned how to import users by doing a bulk import, and you studied the two different file types that work for bulk imports. Bulk imports allow you to import multiple users without the need to add one user at a time.

Exam Essentials

Understand the purpose of OUs.   OUs are used to create a hierarchical, logical organization for objects within an Active Directory domain.

Know the types of objects that can reside within OUs.   OUs can contain Active Directory User, Computer, Shared Folder, and other objects.

Understand how to use the Delegation of Control Wizard.   The Delegation of Control Wizard is used to assign specific permissions at the level of OUs.

Understand the concept of inheritance.   By default, child OUs inherit permissions and Group Policy assignments set for parent OUs. However, these settings can be overridden for more granular control of security.

Know groups and group strategies.   You can use three groups in Native mode: domain local, global, and universal. Understand the group strategies and when they apply.

Understand how Active Directory objects work.   Active Directory objects represent some piece of information about components within a domain. The objects themselves have attributes that describe details about them.

Understand how Active Directory objects can be organized.   By using the Active Directory Users and Computers tool, you can create, move, rename, and delete various objects.

Understand how to import bulk users.   You can import multiple accounts by doing a bulk import. Bulk imports use files to import the data into Active Directory. Know the two utilities (`ldifde.exe` and `csvde.exe`) you need to perform the bulk imports and how to use them.

Learn how resources can be published.   A design goal for Active Directory was to make network resources easier for users to find. With that in mind, you should understand how using published printers and shared folders can simplify network resource management.

Review Questions

1. You are the administrator of an organization with a single Active Directory domain. A user who left the company returns after 16 weeks. The user tries to log onto their old computer and receives an error stating that authentication has failed. The user's account has been enabled. You need to ensure that the user is able to log onto the domain using that computer. What do you do?

   A. Reset the computer account in Active Directory. Disjoin the computer from the domain and then rejoin the computer to the domain.

   B. Run the ADadd command to rejoin the computer account.

   C. Run the MMC utility on the user's computer, and add the Domain Computers snap-in.

   D. Re-create the user account and reconnect the user account to the computer account.

2. You are the administrator of an organization with a single Active Directory domain. One of your senior executives tries to log onto a machine and receives the error "This user account has expired. Ask your administrator to reactivate your account." You need to make sure that this doesn't happen again to this user. What do you do?

   A. Configure the domain policy to disable account lockouts.

   B. Configure the password policy to extend the maximum password age to 0.

   C. Modify the user's properties to set the Account Never Expires setting.

   D. Modify the user's properties to extend the maximum password age to 0.

3. You need to create a new user account using the command prompt. Which command would you use?

   A. dsmodify

   B. dscreate

   C. dsnew

   D. dsadd

4. Maria is a user who belongs to the Sales distribution global group. She is not able to access the laser printer that is shared on the network. The Sales global group has full access to the laser printer. How do you fix the problem?

   A. Change the group type to a security group.

   B. Add the Sales global group to the Administrators group.

   C. Add the Sales global group to the Printer Operators group.

   D. Change the Sales group to a local group.

5. You are a domain administrator for a large domain. Recently, you have been asked to make changes to some of the permissions related to OUs within the domain. To restrict security for the Texas OU further, you remove some permissions at that level. Later, a junior system administrator mentions that she is no longer able to make changes to objects within the Austin OU (which is located within the Texas OU). Assuming that no other changes have been made to Active Directory permissions, which of the following characteristics of OUs might have caused the change in permissions?

   A. Inheritance

   B. Group Policy

   C. Delegation

   D. Object properties

6. Isabel, a system administrator, created a new Active Directory domain in an environment that already contains two trees. During the promotion of the domain controller, she chose to create a new Active Directory forest. Isabel is a member of the Enterprise Administrators group and has full permissions over all domains. During the organization's migration to Active Directory, many updates were made to the information stored within the domains. Recently, users and other system administrators have complained about not being able to find specific Active Directory objects in one or more domains (although the objects exist in others). To investigate the problem, Isabel wants to check for any objects that have not been properly replicated among domain controllers. If possible, she would like to restore these objects to their proper place within the relevant Active Directory domains.

   Which two of the following actions should she perform to be able to view the relevant information? (Choose two.)

   A. Change Active Directory permissions to allow object information to be viewed in all domains.

   B. Select the Advanced Features item in the View menu.

   C. Promote a member server in each domain to a domain controller.

   D. Rebuild all domain controllers from the latest backups.

   E. Examine the contents of the LostAndFound folder using the Active Directory Users and Computers tool.

7. You are a consultant hired to evaluate an organization's Active Directory domain. The domain contains more than 200,000 objects and hundreds of OUs. You begin examining the objects within the domain, but you find that the loading of the contents of specific OUs takes a long time. Furthermore, the list of objects can be large. You want to do the following:

   ▪ Use the built-in Active Directory administrative tools and avoid the use of third-party tools or utilities.

   ▪ Limit the list of objects within an OU to only the type of objects that you're examining (for example, only Computer objects).

   ▪ Prevent any changes to the Active Directory domain or any of the objects within it.

Which one of the following actions meets these requirements?

A. Use the Filter option in the Active Directory Users and Computers tool to restrict the display of objects.

B. Use the Delegation of Control Wizard to give yourself permissions over only a certain type of object.

C. Implement a new naming convention for objects within an OU and then sort the results using this new naming convention.

D. Use the Active Directory Domains and Trusts tool to view information from only selected domain controllers.

E. Edit the domain Group Policy settings to allow yourself to view only the objects of interest.

8. You are the administrator for a small organization with four servers. You have one file server named Paniva that runs Windows Server 2012 R2. You have a junior administrator who needs to do backups on this server. You need to ensure that the junior admin can use Windows Server Backup to create a complete backup of Paniva. What should you configure to allow the junior admin to do the backups?

A. The local groups by using Computer Management

B. A task by using Authorization Manager

C. The User Rights Assignment by using the Local Group Policy Editor

D. The Role Assignment by using Authorization Manager

9. Miguel is a junior-level system administrator, and he has basic knowledge about working with Active Directory. As his supervisor, you have asked Miguel to make several security-related changes to OUs within the company's Active Directory domain. You instruct Miguel to use the basic functionality provided in the Delegation of Control Wizard. Which of the following operations are represented as common tasks within the Delegation of Control Wizard? (Choose all that apply.)

A. Reset passwords on user accounts.

B. Manage Group Policy links.

C. Modify the membership of a group.

D. Create, delete, and manage groups.

10. You are the primary system administrator for a large Active Directory domain. Recently, you have hired another system administrator upon whom you intend to offload some of your responsibilities. This system administrator will be responsible for handling help desk calls and for basic user account management. You want to allow the new employee to have permissions to reset passwords for all users within a specific OU. However, for security reasons, it's important that the user not be able to make permissions changes for objects within other OUs in the domain. Which of the following is the best way to do this?

A. Create a special administration account within the OU and grant it full permissions for all objects within Active Directory.

B. Move the user's login account into the OU that the new employee is to administer.

C. Move the user's login account to an OU that contains the OU (that is, the parent OU of the one that the new employee is to administer).

D. Use the Delegation of Control Wizard to assign the necessary permissions on the OU that the new employee is to administer.

Chapter

6

Manage GPOs

THE FOLLOWING 70-410 EXAM OBJECTIVES ARE COVERED IN THIS CHAPTER:

✓ **Create Group Policy Objects (GPOs)**

- Configure a Central Store

- Manage starter GPOs

- Configure GPO links

- Configure multiple local group policies

- Configure security filtering

✓ **Configure application restriction policies**

- Configure rule enforcement

- Configure applocker rules

- Configure Software Restriction Policies

For many years, making changes to computer or user environments was a time-consuming process. If you wanted to install a service pack or a piece of software, unless you had a third-party utility, you had to use the *sneakernet* (that is, you had to walk from one computer to another with a disk containing the software).

Installing any type of software or companywide security change was one of the biggest challenges faced by system administrators. It was difficult enough just to deploy and manage workstations throughout the environment. Combine this with the fact that users were generally able to make system configuration changes to their own machines, it quickly became a management nightmare!

For example, imagine that a user noticed that they did not have enough disk space to copy a large file. Instead of seeking assistance from the IT help desk, they may have decided to do a little cleanup on their own. Unfortunately, this cleanup operation may have resulted in deleting critical system files! Or, consider the case of users who changed system settings "just to see what they did." Relatively minor changes, such as modifying TCP/IP bindings or Desktop settings, could cause hours of support headaches. Now multiply these (or other common) problems by hundreds (or even thousands) of end users. Clearly, system administrators needed to have a secure way to limit the options available to users of client operating systems.

How do you prevent problems such as these from occurring in a Windows Server 2012 R2 environment? Fortunately, there's a readily available solution delivered with the base operating system that's easy to implement. Two of the most important system administration features in Windows Server 2012 R2 and Active Directory are *Group Policy* and *Security Policy*. By using *Group Policy objects (GPOs)*, administrators can quickly and easily define restrictions on common actions and then apply them at the site, domain, or organizational unit (OU) level. In this chapter, you will see how group and security policies work, and then you will look at how to implement them within an Active Directory environment.

Introducing Group Policy

One of the strengths of Windows-based operating systems is their flexibility. End users and system administrators can configure many different options to suit the network environment and their personal tastes. However, this flexibility comes at a price—generally, end users on a network should not change many of these options. For example, TCP/IP configuration and security policies should remain consistent for all client computers. In fact, end users really don't need to be able to change these types of settings in the first place because many of them do not understand the purpose of these settings.

Windows Server 2012 R2 *group policies* are designed to provide system administrators with the ability to customize end-user settings and to place restrictions on the types of actions that users can perform. Group policies can be easily created by system administrators and then later applied to one or more users or computers within the environment. Although they ultimately do affect registry settings, it is much easier to configure and apply settings through the use of Group Policy than it is to make changes to the registry manually. To make management easy, Microsoft has set up Windows Server 2008, Windows Server 2008 R2, Windows Server 2012, and Windows Server 2012 R2 so that Group Policy settings are all managed from within the Microsoft Management Console (MMC) in the Group Policy Management Console (GPMC).

Group policies have several potential uses. I'll cover the use of group policies for software deployment, and I'll also focus on the technical background of group policies and how they apply to general configuration management.

Let's begin by looking at how group policies function.

Understanding Group Policy Settings

Group Policy settings are based on *Group Policy administrative templates*. These templates provide a list of user-friendly configuration options and specify the system settings to which they apply. For example, an option for a user or computer that reads Require A Specific Desktop Wallpaper Setting would map to a key in the registry that maintains this value. When the option is set, the appropriate change is made in the registry of the affected users and computers.

By default, Windows Server 2012 R2 comes with several administrative template files that you can use to manage common settings. Additionally, system administrators and application developers can create their own administrative template files to set options for specific functionality.

Most Group Policy items have three different settings options:

Enabled   Specifies that a setting for this GPO has been configured. Some settings require values or options to be set.

Disabled   Specifies that this option is disabled for client computers. Note that disabling an option *is* a setting. That is, it specifies that the system administrator wants to disallow certain functionality.

Not Configured   Specifies that these settings have been neither enabled nor disabled. Not Configured is the default option for most settings. It simply states that this group policy will not specify an option and that other policy settings may take precedence.

The specific options available (and their effects) will depend on the setting. Often, you will need additional information. For example, when setting the Account Lockout policy, you must specify how many bad login attempts may be made before the account is locked out. With this in mind, let's look at the types of user and computer settings that can be managed.

Group Policy settings can apply to two types of Active Directory objects: User objects and Computer objects. Because both users and computers can be placed into groups and organized within OUs, this type of configuration simplifies the management of hundreds, or even thousands, of computers.

The main options you can configure within user and computer group policies are as follows:

Software Settings   The *Software Settings* options apply to specific applications and software that might be installed on the computer. System administrators can use these settings to make new applications available to end users and to control the default configuration for these applications.

Windows Settings   The *Windows Settings* options allow system administrators to customize the behavior of the Windows operating system. The specific options that are available here are divided into two types: user and computer. User-specific settings let you configure Internet Explorer (including the default home page and other settings). Computer settings include security options, such as Account Policy and Event Log options.

Administrative Templates   *Administrative templates* are used to configure user and computer settings further. In addition to the default options available, system administrators can create their own administrative templates with custom options.

Group Policy Preferences   The Windows Server 2012 R2 operating system includes *Group Policy preferences (GPPs)*, which give you more than 20 new Group Policy extensions. These extensions, in turn, give you a vast range of configurable settings within a Group Policy object. Included in the new Group Policy preference extensions are settings for folder options, mapped drives, printers, the registry, local users and groups, scheduled tasks, services, and the Start menu.

Besides providing easier management, Group Policy preferences give an administrator the ability to deploy settings for client computers without restricting the users from changing the settings. This gives an administrator the flexibility needed to decide which settings to enforce and which not to enforce.

Figure 6.1 shows some of the options you can configure with Group Policy.

ADMX Central Store   Another consideration in GPO settings is whether to set up an *ADMX Central Store*. GPO administrative template files are saved as ADMX (.admx) files and AMXL (.amxl) for the supported languages. To get the most benefit out of using administrative templates, you should create an ADMX Central Store.

You create the Central Store in the SYSVOL folder on a domain controller. The Central Store is a repository for all of your administrative templates, and the Group Policy tools check it. The Group Policy tools then use any ADMX files that they find in the Central Store. These files then replicate to all domain controllers in the domain.

If you want your clients to be able to edit domain-based GPOs by using the ADMX files that are stored in the ADMX Central Store, you must be using Windows Vista, Windows 7, Windows 8, Server 2008, Server 2008 R2, Server 2012, or Server 2012 R2.

Security Template   *Security templates* are used to configure security settings through a GPO. Some of the security settings that can be configured are settings for account policies, local policies, event logs, restricted groups, system services, and the registry.

FIGURE 6.1 Group Policy configuration options

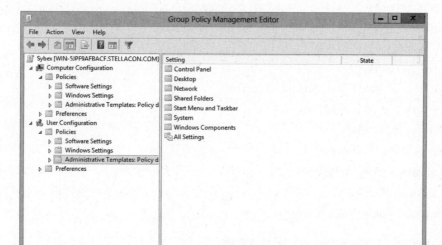

Starter GPOs *Starter Group Policy objects* give administrators the ability to store a collection of administrative template policy settings in a single object. Administrators then have the ability to import and export starter GPOs to distribute the GPOs easily to other environments. When a GPO is created from a starter GPO, as with any template, the new GPO receives the settings and values that were defined from the administrative template policy in the starter GPO.

WARNING Group Policy settings do not take effect immediately. You must run the gpupdate command at the command prompt or wait for the regular update cycle in order for the policy changes to take effect.

The Security Settings Section of the GPO

One of the most important sections of a GPO is the Security Settings section. The Security Settings section, under the Windows Settings section, allows an administrator to secure many aspects of the computer and user policies. The following are some of the configurable options for the Security Settings section:

Computer Section Only of the GPO

- Account Policies
- Local Policies
- Event Policies

- Restricted Groups
- System Services
- Registry
- File System
- Wired Network
- Windows Firewall with Advanced Security
- Network List Manager Policies
- Wireless Networks
- Network Access Protection
- Application Control Policies
- IP Security Policies
- Advanced Audit Policy Configuration

Computer and User Sections of the GPO

- Public Key Policies
- Software Restriction Policy

Restricted Groups

The *Restricted Groups* settings allow you to control group membership by using a GPO. The group membership I am referring to is the normal Active Directory groups (domain local, global, and universal). The settings offer two configurable properties: Members and Members Of.

The users on the Members list do not belong to the restricted group. The users on the Members Of list do belong to the restricted group. When you configure a Restricted Group policy, members of the restricted group that are not on the Members list are removed. Users who are on the Members list who are not currently a member of the restricted group are added.

Software Restriction Policy

Software restriction policies allow administrators to identify software and to control its ability to run on the user's local computer, organizational unit, domain, or site. This prevents users from installing unauthorized software. Software Restriction Policy is discussed in greater detail in this chapter in the "Implementing Software Deployment" section.

Group Policy Objects

So far, I have discussed what group policies are designed to do. Now it's time to drill down to determine exactly how you can set up and configure them.

To make them easier to manage, group policies may be placed in items called *Group Policy objects (GPOs)*. GPOs act as containers for the settings made within Group Policy files, which simplifies the management of settings. For example, as a system administrator, you might have different policies for users and computers in different departments. Based on these requirements, you could create a GPO for members of the Sales department and another for members of the Engineering department. Then you could apply the GPOs to the OU for each department. Another important concept you need to understand is that Group Policy settings are hierarchical; that is, system administrators can apply Group Policy settings at four different levels. These levels determine the GPO processing priority.

Local   Every Windows operating system computer has one Group Policy object that is stored locally. This GPO functions for both the computer and user Group Policy processing.

Sites   At the highest level, system administrators can configure GPOs to apply to entire sites within an Active Directory environment. These settings apply to all of the domains and servers that are part of a site. Group Policy settings managed at the site level may apply to more than one domain within the same forest. Therefore, they are useful when you want to make settings that apply to all of the domains within an Active Directory tree or forest.

Domains   Domains are the third level to which system administrators can assign GPOs. GPO settings placed at the domain level will apply to all of the User and Computer objects within the domain. Usually, system administrators make master settings at the domain level.

Organizational Units   The most granular level of settings for GPOs is the OU level. By configuring Group Policy options for OUs, system administrators can take advantage of the hierarchical structure of Active Directory. If the OU structure is planned well, you will find it easy to make logical GPO assignments for various business units at the OU level.

Based on the business need and the organization of the Active Directory environment, system administrators might decide to set up Group Policy settings at any of these four levels. Because the settings are cumulative by default, a User object might receive policy settings from the site level, from the domain level, and from the OUs in which it is contained.

 You can also apply Group Policy settings to the local computer (in which case Active Directory is not used at all), but this limits the manageability of the Group Policy settings.

Group Policy Inheritance

In most cases, Group Policy settings are cumulative. For example, a GPO at the domain level might specify that all users within the domain must change their password every 60 days, and a GPO at the OU level might specify the default desktop background for all users and computers within that OU. In this case, both settings apply, so users within the OU are forced to change their password every 60 days and have the default Desktop setting.

What happens if there's a conflict in the settings? For example, suppose you create a scenario where a GPO at the site level specifies that users are to use red wallpaper and another GPO at the OU level specifies that they must use green wallpaper. The users at the OU layer would have green wallpaper by default. Although hypothetical, this raises an important point about *inheritance*. By default, the settings at the most specific level (in this case, the OU that contains the User object) override those at more general levels. As a friend of mine from Microsoft always says, "Last one to apply wins."

Although the default behavior is for settings to be cumulative and inherited, system administrators can modify this behavior. They can set two main options at the various levels to which GPOs might apply.

Block Policy Inheritance   The *Block Policy Inheritance* option specifies that Group Policy settings for an object are not inherited from its parents. You might use this, for example, when a child OU requires completely different settings from a parent OU. Note, however, that you should manage blocking policy inheritance carefully because this option allows other system administrators to override the settings made at higher levels.

Force Policy Inheritance   The *Enforced option* (sometimes referred as *No Override*) can be placed on a parent object, and it ensures that all lower-level objects inherit these settings. In some cases, system administrators want to ensure that Group Policy inheritance is not blocked at other levels. For example, suppose it is corporate policy that all network accounts are locked out after five incorrect password attempts. In this case, you would not want lower-level system administrators to override the option with other settings.

System administrators generally use this option when they want to enforce a specific setting globally. For example, if a password expiration policy should apply to all users and computers within a domain, a GPO with the *Force Policy Inheritance* option enabled could be created at the domain level.

You must consider one final case: If a conflict exists between the computer and user settings, the user settings take effect. If, for instance, a system administrator applies a default desktop setting for the Computer policy and a different default desktop setting for the User policy, the one they specify in the User policy takes effect. This is because the user settings are more specific, and they allow system administrators to make changes for individual users regardless of the computer they're using.

Planning a Group Policy Strategy

Through the use of Group Policy settings, system administrators can control many different aspects of their network environment. As you'll see throughout this chapter, system administrators can use GPOs to configure user settings and computer configurations. Windows Server 2012 R2 includes many different administrative tools for performing these tasks. However, it's important to keep in mind that, as with many aspects of using Active Directory, a successful Group Policy strategy involves planning.

Because there are thousands of possible Group Policy settings and many different ways to implement them, you should start by determining the business and technical needs of your organization. For example, you should first group your users based on their work functions. You might find, for example, that users in remote branch offices require particular network configuration options. In that case, you might implement Group Policy settings best at the site level. In another instance, you might find that certain departments have varying requirements for disk quota settings. In this case, it would probably make the most sense to apply GPOs to the appropriate department OUs within the domain.

The overall goal should be to reduce complexity (for example, by reducing the overall number of GPOs and GPO links) while still meeting the needs of your users. By taking into account the various needs of your users and the parts of your organization, you can often determine a logical and efficient method of creating and applying GPOs. Although it's rare that you'll come across a right or wrong method of implementing Group Policy settings, you will usually encounter some that are either better or worse than others.

By implementing a logical and consistent set of policies, you'll also be well prepared to troubleshoot any problems that might come up or to adapt to your organization's changing requirements. Later in this chapter, you'll learn about some specific methods for determining effective Group Policy settings before you apply them.

Implementing Group Policy

Now that I've covered the basic layout and structure of group policies and how they work, let's look at how you can implement them in an Active Directory environment. In the following sections, you'll start by creating GPOs. Then you'll apply these GPOs to specific Active Directory objects, and you'll take a look at how to use administrative templates.

Creating GPOs

In Windows Server 2000 and Windows Server 2003, you could create GPOs from many different locations. For example, you could use Active Directory Users and Computers to create GPOs on your OUs along with other GPO tools. In Windows Server 2012 R2, things are simpler. You can create GPOs for OUs in only one location: the Group Policy Management Console (GPMC). You have your choice of three applications for setting up policies on your Windows Server 2012 R2 computers.

Local Computer Policy Tool   This administrative tool allows you to quickly access the Group Policy settings that are available for the local computer. These options apply to the local machine and to users who access it. You must be a member of the local Administrators group to access and make changes to these settings.

Administrators may need the ability to work on multiple local group policy objects (MLGPOs) at the same time. To do this, you would complete the following steps. (You can't configure MLGPOs on domain controllers.)

1. Open the MMC by typing **MMC** in the Run command box.
2. Click File and then click Add/Remove Snap-in.
3. From the available snap-ins list, choose Group Policy Object Editor and click Add.
4. In the Select Group Policy Object dialog box, click the Browse button.
5. Click the Users tab in the Browse For The Group Policy Object dialog box.
6. Click the user or group for which you want to create or edit a local Group Policy and click OK.
7. Click Finish and then click OK.
8. Configure the multiple policy settings.

Group Policy Management Console You must use the GPMC to manage Group Policy deployment. The GPMC provides a single solution for managing all Group Policy–related tasks, and it is also best suited to handle enterprise-level tasks, such as forest-related work.

The GPMC allows administrators to manage Group Policy and GPOs all from one easy-to-use console whether their enterprise solution spans multiple domains and sites within one or more forests or is local to one site. The GPMC adds flexibility, manageability, and functionality. Using this console, you can also perform other functions, such as backup and restore, importing, and copying.

Auditpol.exe Auditpol.exe is a command-line utility that works with Windows Vista, Windows 7, Windows 8, Windows Server 2008, Windows Server 2008 R2, Windows Server 2012, and Windows Server 2012 R2. An administrator has the ability to display information about policies and also to perform some functions to manipulate audit policies. Table 6.1 shows some of the switches available for auditpol.exe.

TABLE 6.1 Auditpol.exe switches

Switch	Description
/?	This is the Auditpol.exe help command.
/get	This allows you to display the current audit policy.
/set	This allows you to set a policy.
/list	This displays selectable policy elements.
/backup	This allows you to save the audit policy to a file.
/restore	This restores a policy from previous backup.
/clear	This clears the audit policy.
/remove	This removes all per-user audit policy settings and disables all system audit policy settings.
/ResourceSACL	This configures the Global Resource SACL.

WARNING You should be careful when making Group Policy settings because certain options might prevent the proper use of systems on your network. Always test Group Policy settings on a small group of users before you deploy them throughout your organization. You'll probably find that some settings need to be changed to be effective.

Exercise 6.1 walks you through the process of installing the Group Policy Management MMC snap-in for editing Group Policy settings and creating a GPO.

EXERCISE 6.1

Creating a Group Policy Object Using the GPMC

1. Click the Windows button and choose Administrative Tools ➢ Group Policy Management. The Group Policy Management tool opens.

2. Expand the Forest, Domains, *your domain name,* and North America containers. Right-click the Corporate OU and then choose Create A GPO In This Domain, And Link It Here.

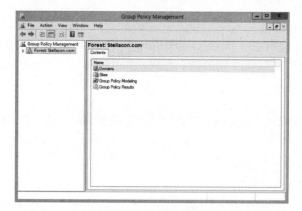

3. When the New GPO dialog box appears, type **Warning Box** in the Name field. Click OK.

4. The New GPO will be listed on the right side of the Group Policy Management window. Right-click the GPO and choose Edit.

5. In the Group Policy Management Editor, expand the following: Computer Configuration ➢ Policies ➢ Windows Settings ➢ Security Settings ➢ Local Policies ➢ Security Options. On the right side, scroll down and double-click Interactive Logon: Message Text For Users Attempting To Log On.

6. Click the box Define This Policy Setting In The Template. In the text box, type **Unauthorized use of this machine is prohibited** and then click OK. Close the GPO and return to the GPMC main screen.

7. Under the domain name (in the GPMC), right-click Group Policy Objects and choose New.

8. When the New GPO dialog box appears, type **Unlinked Test GPO** in the Name field. Click OK.

9. On the right side, the new GPO will appear. Right-click Unlinked Test GPO and choose Edit.

10. Under the User Configuration section, click Policies ➢ Administrative Templates ➢ Desktop. On the right side, double-click Hide And Disable All Items On The Desktop and then click Enabled. Click OK and then close the GPMC.

NOTE

Note that Group Policy changes may not take effect until the next user logs in (some settings may even require that the machine be rebooted). That is, users who are currently working on the system will not see the effects of the changes until they log off and log in again. GPOs are reapplied every 90 minutes with a 30-minute offset. In other words, users who are logged in will have their policies reapplied every 60 to 120 minutes. Not all settings are reapplied (for example, software settings and password policies).

Linking Existing GPOs to Active Directory

Creating a GPO is the first step in assigning group policies. The second step is to link the GPO to a specific Active Directory object. As mentioned earlier in this chapter, GPOs can be linked to sites, domains, and OUs.

Exercise 6.2 walks you through the steps that you must take to assign an existing GPO to an OU within the local domain. In this exercise, you will link the Test Domain Policy GPO to an OU. To complete the steps in this exercise, you must have completed Exercise 6.1.

EXERCISE 6.2

Linking Existing GPOs to Active Directory

1. Open the Group Policy Management Console.

2. Expand the Forest and Domain containers and right-click the Africa OU.

3. Choose Link An Existing GPO.

4. The Select GPO dialog box appears. Click Unlinked Test GPO and click OK.

5. Close the Group Policy Management Console.

Note that the GPMC tool offers a lot of flexibility in assigning GPOs. You can create new GPOs, add multiple GPOs, edit them directly, change priority settings, remove links, and delete GPOs all from within this interface. In general, creating new GPOs using the GPMC tool is the quickest and easiest way to create the settings you need.

To test the Group Policy settings, you can simply create a user account within the Africa OU that you used in Exercise 6.2. Then, using another computer that is a member of the same domain, you can log on as the newly created user.

Managing Group Policy

Now that you have implemented GPOs and applied them to sites, domains, and OUs within Active Directory, it's time to look at some ways to manage them. In the following sections, you'll look at how multiple GPOs can interact with one another and ways that you can provide security for GPO management. Using these features is an important part of working with Active Directory, and if you properly plan Group Policy, you can greatly reduce the time the help desk spends troubleshooting common problems.

Managing GPOs

One of the benefits of GPOs is that they're modular and can apply to many different objects and levels within Active Directory. This can also be one of the drawbacks of GPOs if they're not managed properly. A common administrative function related to using GPOs is finding all of the Active Directory links for each of these objects. You can do this when you are viewing the Linked Group Policy Objects tab of the site, domain, or OU in the GPMC (shown in Figure 6.2).

FIGURE 6.2   Viewing GPO links to an Active Directory OU

In addition to the common action of delegating permissions on OUs, you can set permissions regarding the modification of GPOs. The best way to accomplish this is to add users to the Group Policy Creator/Owners built-in security group. The members of this group are able to modify security policy. You saw how to add users to groups back in Chapter 5, "Administer Active Directory."

Windows Management Instrumentation

Windows Management Instrumentation (WMI) scripts are used to gather information or to help GPOs deploy better. The best way to explain this is to give an example. Let's say you wanted to deploy Microsoft Office 2013 to everyone in the company. You would first set up a GPO to deploy the Office package (explained later in the section "Deploying Software Through a GPO").

You can then place a WMI script on the GPO stating that only computers with 10GB of hard disk space actually deploy Office. Now if a computer has 10GB of free space, the Office GPO would get installed. If the computer does not have the 10GB of hard disk space, the GPO will not deploy. You can use WMI scripts to check for computer information such as MAC addresses. WMI is a powerful tool because if you know how to write scripts, the possibilities are endless. The following script is a sample of a WMI that is checking for at least 10GB of free space on the C: partition/volume:

```
Select * from Win32_LogicalDisk where FreeSpace > 10737418240 AND
Caption = "C:"
```

Security Filtering of a Group Policy

Another method of securing access to GPOs is to set permissions on the GPOs themselves. You can do this by opening the GPMC, selecting the GPO, and clicking the Advanced button in the Delegation tab. The Unlinked Test GPO Security Settings dialog box appears (see Figure 6.3).

FIGURE 6.3   A GPO's Security Settings dialog box

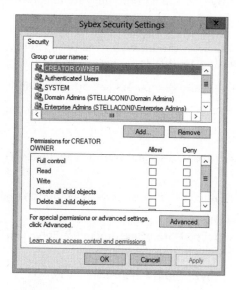

The following permissions options are available:

- Full Control

- Read

- Write

- Create All Child Objects
- Delete All Child Objects
- Apply Group Policy

You might have to scroll the Permissions window to see the Apply Group Policy item. Of these, the Apply Group Policy setting is particularly important because you use it to filter the scope of the GPO. *Filtering* is the process by which selected security groups are included or excluded from the effects of the GPOs. To specify that the settings should apply to a GPO, you should select the Allow check box for both the Apply Group Policy setting and the Read setting. These settings will be applied only if the security group is also contained within a site, domain, or OU to which the GPO is linked. To disable GPO access for a group, choose Deny for both of these settings. Finally, if you do not want to specify either Allow or Deny, leave both boxes blank. This is effectively the same as having no setting.

In Exercise 6.3, you will filter Group Policy using security groups. To complete the steps in this exercise, you must have completed Exercises 6.1 and 6.2.

EXERCISE 6.3

Filtering Group Policy Using Security Groups

1. Open the Active Directory Users and Computers administrative tool.

2. Create a new OU called **Group Policy Test**.

3. Create two new global security groups within the Group Policy Test OU and name them **PolicyEnabled** and **PolicyDisabled**.

4. Exit Active Directory Users and Computers and open the GPMC.

5. Right-click the Group Policy Test OU and select Link An Existing GPO.

6. Choose Unlinked Test GPO and click OK.

7. Expand the Group Policy Test OU so that you can see the GPO (Unlinked Test GPO) underneath the OU.

8. Click the Delegation tab and then click the Advanced button in the lower-right corner of the window.

9. Click the Add button and type **PolicyEnabled** in the Enter The Object Names To Select field. Click the Check Names button. Then click OK.

10. Add a group named **PolicyDisabled** in the same way.

11. Highlight the PolicyEnabled group and select Allow for the Read and Apply Group Policy permissions. This ensures that users in the PolicyEnabled group will be affected by this policy.

12. Highlight the PolicyDisabled group and select Deny for the Read and Apply Group Policy permissions. This ensures that users in the PolicyDisabled group will not be affected by this policy.

13. Click OK. You will see a message stating that you are choosing to use the Deny permission and that the Deny permission takes precedence over the Allow entries. Click the Yes button to continue.

14. When you have finished, close the GPMC tool.

Delegating Administrative Control of GPOs

So far, you have learned about how to use Group Policy to manage user and computer settings. What you haven't done yet is to determine who can modify GPOs. It's important to establish the appropriate security on GPOs themselves for two reasons.

- If the security settings aren't set properly, users and system administrators can easily override them. This defeats the purpose of having the GPOs in the first place.

- Having many different system administrators creating and modifying GPOs can become extremely difficult to manage. When problems arise, the hierarchical nature of GPO inheritance can make it difficult to pinpoint the problem.

Fortunately, through the use of delegation, determining security permissions for GPOs is a simple task. Exercise 6.4 walks you through the steps that you must take to grant the appropriate permissions to a user account. Specifically, the process involves delegating the ability to manage Group Policy links on an Active Directory object (such as an OU). To complete this exercise, you must have completed Exercises 6.1 and 6.2.

EXERCISE 6.4

Delegating Administrative Control of Group Policy

1. Open the Active Directory Users and Computers tool.

2. Expand the local domain and create a user named **Policy Admin** within the Group Policy Test OU.

3. Exit Active Directory Users and Computers and open the GPMC.

4. Click the Group Policy Test OU and select the Delegation tab.

5. Click the Add button. In the field Enter The Object Name To Select, type **Policy Admin** and click the Check Names button.

6. The Add Group Or User dialog box appears. In the Permissions drop-down list, make sure that the item labeled Edit Settings, Delete, Modify Security is chosen. Click OK.

EXERCISE 6.4 *(continued)*

7. At this point you should be looking at the Group Policy Test Delegation window. Click the Advanced button in the lower-right corner.

8. Highlight the Policy Admin account and check the Allow Full Control box. This user now has full control of these OUs and all child OUs and GPOs for these OUs. Click OK.

   If you just want to give this user individual rights, then, in the Properties window (step 8), click the Advanced button and then the Effective Permissions tab. This is where you can also choose a user and give them only the rights that you want them to have.

9. When you have finished, close the GPMC tool.

Understanding Delegation

Although I have talked about delegation throughout the book, it's important to discuss it again in the context of OUs, Group Policy, and Active Directory.

Once configured, Active Directory administrative delegation allows an administrator to delegate tasks (usually administration related) to specific user accounts or groups. What this means is that if you don't manage it all, the user accounts (or groups) you choose will be able to manage their portions of the tree.

It's important to be aware of the benefits of Active Directory Delegation (AD Delegation). *AD Delegation* will help you manage the assigning of administrative control over objects in Active Directory, such as users, groups, computers, printers, domains, and sites. AD Delegation is used to create more administrators, which essentially saves time.

For example, let's say you have a company whose IT department is small and situated in a central location. The central location connects three other smaller remote sites. These sites do not each warrant a full-time IT person, but the manager on staff (for example) at each remote site can become an administrator for their portion of the tree. If that manager administers the user accounts for the staff at the remote site, this reduces the burden on the system administrator of doing trivial administrative work, such as unlocking user accounts or changing passwords, and thus it reduces costs.

Controlling Inheritance and Filtering Group Policy

Controlling inheritance is an important function when you are managing GPOs. Earlier in this chapter, you learned that, by default, GPO settings flow from higher-level Active Directory objects to lower-level ones. For example, the effective set of Group Policy settings for a user might be based on GPOs assigned at the site level, at the domain level, and in the OU hierarchy. In general, this is probably the behavior you would want.

In some cases, however, you might want to block Group Policy inheritance. You can accomplish this easily by selecting the object to which a GPO has been linked. Right-click the object and choose Block Inheritance (see Figure 6.4). By enabling this option, you are effectively specifying that this object starts with a clean slate; that is, no other Group Policy settings will apply to the contents of this Active Directory site, domain, or OU.

FIGURE 6.4   Blocking GPO inheritance

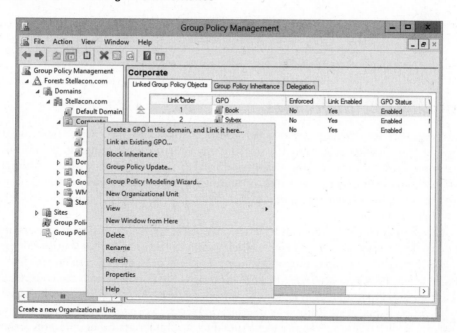

System administrators can also force inheritance. By setting the Enforced option, they can prevent other system administrators from making changes to default policies. You can set the Enforced option by right-clicking the GPO and choosing the Enforced item (see Figure 6.5).

FIGURE 6.5 Setting the Enforced GPO option

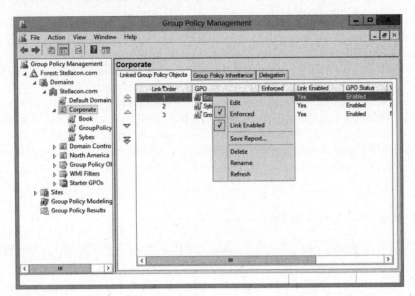

Assigning Script Policies

System administrators might want to make several changes and implement certain settings that would apply while the computer is starting up or the user is logging on. Perhaps the most common operation that logon scripts perform is mapping network drives. Although users can manually map network drives, providing this functionality within login scripts ensures that mappings stay consistent and that users only need to remember the drive letters for their resources.

Script policies are specific options that are part of Group Policy settings for users and computers. These settings direct the operating system to the specific files that should be processed during the startup/shutdown or logon/logoff processes. You can create the scripts by using the *Windows Script Host (WSH)* or with standard batch file commands. WSH allows developers and system administrators to create scripts quickly and easily using Visual Basic Scripting Edition (VBScript) or JScript (Microsoft's implementation of JavaScript). Additionally, WSH can be expanded to accommodate other common scripting languages.

To set script policy options, you simply edit the Group Policy settings. As shown in Figure 6.6, there are two main areas for setting script policy settings.

Startup/Shutdown Scripts These settings are located within the Computer Configuration ➤ Windows Settings ➤ Scripts (Startup/Shutdown) object.

Logon/Logoff Scripts These settings are located within the User Configuration ➤ Windows Settings ➤ Scripts (Logon/Logoff) object.

FIGURE 6.6 Viewing Startup/Shutdown script policy settings

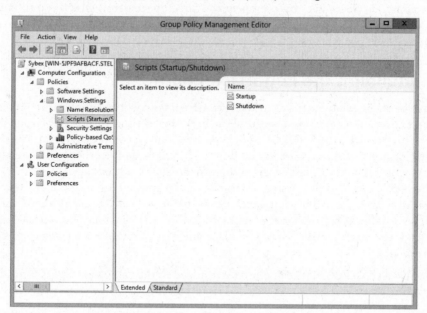

To assign scripts, simply double-click the setting, and its Properties dialog box appears. For instance, if you double-click the Startup setting, the Startup Properties dialog box appears (see Figure 6.7). To add a script filename, click the Add button. When you do, you will be asked to provide the name of the script file (such as MapNetworkDrives.vbs or ResetEnvironment.bat).

FIGURE 6.7 Setting scripting options

Note that you can change the order in which the scripts are run by using the Up and Down buttons. The Show Files button opens the directory folder in which you should store the Logon script files. To ensure that the files are replicated to all domain controllers, you should be sure you place the files within the SYSVOL share.

Understanding the Loopback Policy

There may be times when the user settings of a Group Policy object should be applied to a computer based on its location instead of the user object. Usually, the user Group Policy processing dictates that the GPOs be applied in order during computer startup based on the computers located in their organizational unit. User GPOs, on the other hand, are applied in order during logon, regardless of the computer to which they log on.

In some situations, this processing order may not be appropriate. A good example is a kiosk machine. You would not want applications that have been assigned or published to a user to be installed when the user is logged on to the kiosk machine. *Loopback Policy* allows two ways to retrieve the list of GPOs for any user when they are using a specific computer in an OU.

Merge Mode   The GPOs for the computer are added to the end of the GPOs for the user. Because of this, the computer's GPOs have higher precedence than the user's GPOs.

Replace Mode   In Replace mode, the user's GPOs are not used. Only the GPOs of the Computer object are used.

Managing Network Configuration

Group policies are also useful in network configuration. Although administrators can handle network settings at the protocol level using many different methods, such as Dynamic Host Configuration Protocol (DHCP), Group Policy allows them to set which functions and operations are available to users and computers.

Figure 6.8 shows some of the features that are available for managing Group Policy settings. The paths to these settings are as follows:

Computer Network Options   These settings are located within the Computer Configuration ➤ Administrative Templates ➤ Network ➤ Network Connections folder.

User Network Options   These settings are located within User Configuration ➤ Administrative Templates ➤ Network.

Here are some examples of the types of settings available:

- The ability to allow or disallow the modification of network settings.

  In many environments, the improper changing of network configurations and protocol settings is a common cause of help desk calls.

- The ability to allow or disallow the creation of Remote Access Service (RAS) connections.

FIGURE 6.8   Viewing Group Policy User network configuration options

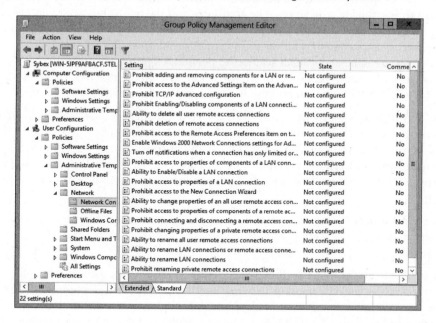

This option is useful, especially in larger networked environments, because the use of modems and other WAN devices can pose a security threat to the network.

- The ability to set offline files and folders options.

    This is especially useful for keeping files synchronized for traveling users, and it is commonly configured for laptops.

Each setting includes detailed instructions in the description area of the GPO Editor window. By using these configuration options, system administrators can maintain consistency for users and computers and avoid many of the most common troubleshooting calls.

Automatically Enrolling User and Computer Certificates in Group Policy

You can also use Group Policy to enroll user and computer certificates automatically, making the entire certificate process transparent to your end users. Before proceeding, you should understand what certificates are and why they are an important part of network security.

Think of a digital certificate as a carrying case for a public key. A certificate contains the public key and a set of attributes, including the key holder's name and email address.

These attributes specify something about the holder: their identity, what they're allowed to do with the certificate, and so on. The attributes and the public key are bound together because the certificate is digitally signed by the entity that issued it. Anyone who wants to verify the certificate's contents can verify the issuer's signature.

Certificates are one part of what security experts call a *public-key infrastructure (PKI)*. A PKI has several different components that you can mix and match to achieve the desired results. Microsoft's PKI implementation offers the following functions:

Certificate Authorities   CAs issue certificates, revoke certificates they've issued, and publish certificates for their clients. Big CAs like Thawte and VeriSign do this for millions of users. If you want, you can also set up your own CA for each department or workgroup in your organization. Each CA is responsible for choosing which attributes it will include in a certificate and what mechanism it will use to verify those attributes before it issues the certificate.

Certificate Publishers   They make certificates publicly available, inside or outside an organization. This allows widespread availability of the critical material needed to support the entire PKI.

PKI-Savvy Applications   These allow you and your users to do useful things with certificates, such as encrypt email or network connections. Ideally, the user shouldn't have to know (or even be aware of) what the application is doing—everything should work seamlessly and automatically. The best-known examples of PKI-savvy applications are web browsers such as Internet Explorer and Firefox and email applications such as Outlook.

Certificate Templates   These act like rubber stamps. By specifying a particular template as the model you want to use for a newly issued certificate, you're actually telling the CA which optional attributes to add to the certificate as well as implicitly telling it how to fill some of the mandatory attributes. Templates greatly simplify the process of issuing certificates because they keep you from having to memorize the names of all of the attributes you may potentially want to put in a certificate.

Learn More About PKI

When discussing certificates, it's also important to mention PKI and its definition. The exam doesn't go deeply into PKI, but I recommend you do some extra research on your own because it is an important technology and shouldn't be overlooked. PKI is actually a simple concept with a lot of moving parts. When broken down to its bare essentials, PKI is nothing more than a server and workstations utilizing a software service to add security to your infrastructure. When you use PKI, you are adding a layer of protection. The auto-enrollment Settings policy determines whether users and/or computers are automatically enrolled for the appropriate certificates when necessary. By default, this policy is enabled if a certificate server is installed, but you can make changes to the settings, as shown in Exercise 6.5.

In Exercise 6.5, you will learn how to configure automatic certificate enrollment in Group Policy. You must have first completed the other exercises in this chapter in order to proceed with Exercise 6.5.

EXERCISE 6.5

Configuring Automatic Certificate Enrollment in Group Policy

1. Open the Group Policy Management Console tool.

2. Right-click the North America OU that you created in the previous exercises in this book.

3. Choose Create A GPO In This Domain And Link It Here and name it **Test CA**. Click OK.

4. Right-click the Test CA GPO and choose Edit.

5. Open Computer Configuration ➢ Policies ➢ Windows Settings ➢ Security Settings ➢ Public Key Policies.

6. Double-click Certificate Services Client – Auto-Enrollment in the right pane.

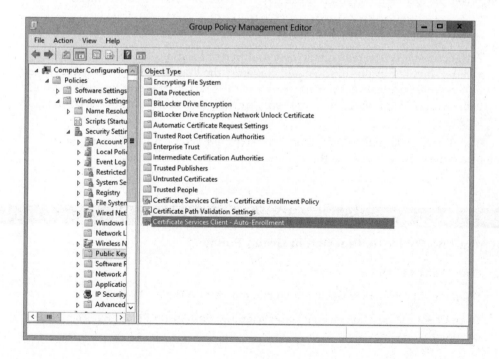

7. The Certificate Services Client – Auto-Enrollment Properties dialog box will appear.

8. For now, don't change anything. Just become familiar with the settings in this dialog box. Click OK to close it.

Redirecting Folders

Another set of Group Policy settings that you will learn about are the *folder redirection settings*. Group Policy provides a means for redirecting the Documents, Desktop, and Start Menu folders, as well as cached application data, to network locations. Folder redirection is particularly useful for the following reasons:

- When they are using roaming user profiles, a user's Documents folder is copied to the local machine each time they log on. This requires high bandwidth consumption and time if the Documents folder is large. If you redirect the Documents folder, it stays in the redirected location, and the user opens and saves files directly to that location.

- Documents are always available no matter where the user logs on.

- Data in the shared location can be backed up during the normal backup cycle without user intervention.

- Data can be redirected to a more robust server-side administered disk that is less prone to physical and user errors.

When you decide to redirect folders, you have two options: basic and advanced.

- Basic redirection redirects everyone's folders to the same location (but each user gets their own folder within that location).

- Advanced redirection redirects folders to different locations based on group membership. For instance, you could configure the Engineers group to redirect their folders to //Engineering1/Documents/ and the Marketing group to //Marketing1/Documents/. Again, individual users still get their own folder within the redirected location.

To configure folder redirection, follow the steps in Exercise 6.6. You must have completed the other exercises in this chapter to proceed with this exercise.

EXERCISE 6.6

Configuring Folder Redirection in Group Policy

1. Open the GPMC tool.

2. Open the North America OU and then edit the Test CA GPO.

3. Open User Configuration ➢ Policies ➢ Windows Settings ➢ Folder Redirection ➢ Documents.

4. Right-click Documents, and select Properties.

5. On the Target tab of the Documents Properties dialog box, choose the Basic – Redirect Everyone's Folder To The Same Location selection from the Settings drop-down list.

6. Leave the default option for the Target Folder Location drop-down list and specify a network path in the Root Path field.

7. Click the Settings tab. All of the default settings are self-explanatory and should typically be left at the default setting. Click OK when you have finished.

Folder Redirection Facts

Try not to mix up the concepts of *folder redirection* and *offline folders*, especially in a world with ever-increasing numbers of mobile users. Folder redirection and offline folders are different features.

Windows Server 2012 R2 folder redirection works as follows: The system uses a pointer that moves the folders you want to a location you specify. Users do not see any of this—it is transparent to them. One problem with folder redirection is that it does not work for mobile users (users who will be offline and who will not have access to files they may need).

Offline folders, however, are copies of folders that were local to you. Files are now available locally to you on the system you have with you. They are also located back on the server where they are stored. The next time you log in, the folders are synchronized so that both folders contain the latest data. This is a perfect feature for mobile users, whereas folder redirection provides no benefit for the mobile user.

Managing GPOs with Windows PowerShell Group Policy Cmdlets

As stated earlier in this book, *Windows PowerShell* is a Windows command-line shell and scripting language. Windows PowerShell can also help an administrator automate many of the same tasks that you perform using the Group Policy Management Console.

Windows Server 2012 R2 helps you perform many of the Group Policy tasks by providing more than 25 cmdlets. Each of these cmdlets is a simple, single-function command-line tool.

The Windows PowerShell Group Policy cmdlets can help you perform some of the following tasks for domain-based Group Policy objects:

- Maintain, create, remove, back up, and import GPOs

- Create, update, and remove GPO links to Active Directory containers

- Set Active Directory OUs and domain permissions and inheritance flags

- Configure Group Policy registry settings

- Create and edit Starter GPOs

The requirement for Windows PowerShell Group Policy cmdlets is Windows Server 2012 R2 on either a domain controller or a member server that has the GPMC installed. Windows 7 and Windows 8 also have the ability to use Windows PowerShell Group Policy cmdlets if they have Remote Server Administration Tools (RSAT) installed. RSAT includes the GPMC and its cmdlets. PowerShell is also a requirement.

Deploying Software Through a GPO

It's difficult enough to manage applications on a stand-alone computer. It seems that the process of installing, configuring, and uninstalling applications is never finished. Add in the hassle of computer reboots and reinstalling corrupted applications, and the reduction in productivity can be substantial.

Software administrators who manage software in network environments have even more concerns.

- First, they must determine which applications specific users require.

- Then, IT departments must purchase the appropriate licenses for the software and acquire any necessary media.

- Next, the system administrators need to install the applications on users' machines. This process generally involves help desk staff visiting computers, or it requires end users to install the software themselves. Both processes entail several potential problems, including installation inconsistency and lost productivity from downtime experienced when applications were installed.

- Finally, software administrators still need to manage software updates and remove unused software.

One of the key design goals for Active Directory was to reduce some of the headaches involved in managing software and configurations in a networked environment. To that end, Windows Server 2012 R2 offers several features that can make the task of deploying software easier and less error prone. Before you dive into the technical details, however, you need to examine the issues related to software deployment.

The Software Management Life Cycle

Although it may seem that the use of a new application requires only the installation of the necessary software, the overall process of managing applications involves many more steps. When managing software applications, there are three main phases to their life cycle, as follows:

Phase 1: Deploying Software   The first step in using applications is to install them on the appropriate client computers. Generally, some applications are deployed during the initial configuration of a PC, and others are deployed when they are requested. In the latter case, this often used to mean that system administrators and help desk staffs have to visit client computers and manually walk through the installation process. With Windows Server 2012 R2 and GPOs, the entire process can be automated.

Before You Install, Stop

It is important to understand that just because you can easily deploy software, it does not necessarily mean you have the right to do so. Before you install software on client computers, you must make sure you have the appropriate licenses for the software. Furthermore, it's important to take the time to track application installations. As many system administrators have discovered, it's much more difficult to inventory software installations after they've been performed. Another issue you may encounter is that you lack available resources (for instance, your system does not meet the minimum hardware requirements) and that you face problems such as limited hard disk space or memory that may not be able to handle the applications that you want to load and use. You may also find that your user account does not have the permission to install software. It's important to consider not only how you will install software but also whether you can.

Phase 2: Maintaining Software   Once an application is installed and in use on client computers, you need to ensure that the software is maintained. You must keep programs up-to-date by applying changes due to bug fixes, enhancements, and other types of updates. This is normally done with service packs, hot fixes, and updates. As with the initial software deployment, software maintenance can be tedious. Some programs require older versions to be uninstalled before updates are added. Others allow for automatically upgrading over existing installations. Managing and deploying software updates can consume a significant amount of the IT staff's time.

Using Windows Update

Make sure that you learn about Windows Update, a service that allows you to connect to Microsoft's website and download what your system may need to bring it up to compliance. This tool is helpful if you are running a stand-alone system, but if you want to deploy software across the enterprise, the best way to accomplish this is first to test the updates you are downloading and make sure you can use them and that they are not bug ridden. Then you can use a tool such as the Windows Server Update Service (WSUS), which was formerly called the Software Update Services (SUS).

You can check for updates at Microsoft's website (http://update.microsoft.com). Microsoft likes to ask many types of questions about WSUS on its certification exams. WSUS is described in detail in other Sybex certification books.

Phase 3: Removing Software   The end of the life cycle for many software products involves the actual removal of unused programs. Removing software is necessary when applications become outdated or when users no longer require their functionality. One of the traditional problems with uninstalling applications is that many of the installed files may not be removed. Furthermore, the removal of shared components can sometimes cause other programs to stop functioning properly. Also, users often forget to uninstall applications that they no longer need, and these programs continue to occupy disk space and consume valuable system resources.

The Microsoft Windows Installer (MSI) manages each of these three phases of the software maintenance life cycle. Now that you have an overview of the process, let's move forward to look at the steps involved in deploying software using Group Policy.

The *Microsoft Windows Installer* (sometimes referred to as Microsoft Installer or Windows Installer) is an application installation and configuration service. An instruction file (the Microsoft Installer package) contains information about what needs to be done to install a product. It's common to confuse the two.

The Windows Installer

If you've installed newer application programs (such as Microsoft Office 2013), you've probably noticed the updated setup and installation routines. Applications that comply with the updated standard use the *Windows Installer specification* and MSI software packages for deployment. Each package contains information about various setup options and the files required for installation. Although the benefits may not seem dramatic on the surface, there's a lot of new functionality under the hood.

The Windows Installer was created to solve many of the problems associated with traditional application development. It has several components, including the Installer service (which runs on Windows 2000, XP, Vista, Windows 7, Windows 8, Windows Server 2003, Windows Server 2008, Windows Server 2008 R2, Windows Server 2012, and Windows Server 2012 R2 computers), the Installer program (`msiexec.exe`) that is responsible for executing the instructions in a *Windows Installer package*, and the specifications third-party developers use to create their own packages. Within each installation package file is a relational structure (similar to the structure of tables in databases) that records information about the programs contained within the package.

To appreciate the true value of the Windows Installer, you'll need to look at some of the problems with traditional software deployment mechanisms and then at how the Windows Installer addresses many of them.

Application Installation Issues

Before the Windows Installer, applications were installed using a setup program that managed the various operations required for a program to operate. These operations included copying files, changing registry settings, and managing any other operating system changes that might be required (such as starting or stopping services). However, this method had several problems:

- The setup process was not robust, and aborting the operation often left many unnecessary files in the file system.

- The process included uninstalling an application (this also often left many unnecessary files in the file system) and remnants in the Windows registry and operating system folders. Over time, these remnants would result in reduced overall system performance and wasted disk space.

- There was no standard method for applying upgrades to applications, and installing a new version often required users to uninstall the old application, reboot, and then install the new program.

- Conflicts between different versions of *dynamic link libraries (DLLs)*—shared program code used across different applications—could cause the installation or removal of one application to break the functionality of another.

Benefits of the Windows Installer

Because of the many problems associated with traditional software installation, Microsoft created the *Windows Installer*. This system provides for better manageability of the software installation process and allows system administrators more control over the deployment process. Specifically, the Windows Installer provides the following benefits:

Improved Software Removal   The process of removing software is an important one because remnants left behind during the uninstall process can eventually clutter up the registry and file system. During the installation process, the Windows Installer keeps track of all of the changes made by a setup package. When it comes time to remove an application, all of these changes can then be rolled back.

More Robust Installation Routines   If a typical setup program is aborted during the software installation process, the results are unpredictable. If the actual installation hasn't yet begun, then the installer generally removes any temporary files that may have been created. However, if the file copy routine starts before the system encounters an error, it is likely that the files will not be automatically removed from the operating system. In contrast, the Windows Installer allows you to roll back any changes when the application setup process is aborted.

Ability to Use Elevated Privileges   Installing applications usually requires the user to have Administrator permissions on the local computer because file system and registry changes are required. When installing software for network users, system administrators have two options. First, they can log off of the computer before installing the software and then log back on as a user who has Administrator permissions on the local computer. This method is tedious and time-consuming. The second option is to give users Administrator permissions temporarily on their own machines. This method could cause security problems and requires the attention of a system administrator.

Through the use of the Installer service, the Windows Installer is able to use temporarily elevated privileges to install applications. This allows users, regardless of their security settings, to execute the installation of authorized applications. This saves time and preserves security.

Support for Repairing Corrupted Applications   Regardless of how well a network environment is managed, critical files are sometimes lost or corrupted. Such problems can prevent applications from running properly and can cause crashes. Windows Installer packages provide you with the ability to verify the installation of an application and, if necessary, replace any missing or corrupted files. This support saves time and lessens end-user headaches associated with removing and reinstalling an entire application to replace just a few files.

Prevention of File Conflicts   Generally, different versions of the same files should be compatible with each other. In the real world, however, this isn't always the case. A classic problem in the Windows world is the case of one program replacing DLLs that are used by several other programs. Windows Installer accurately tracks which files are used by certain programs and ensures that any shared files are not improperly deleted or overwritten.

Automated Installations   A typical application setup process requires end users or system administrators to respond to several prompts. For example, a user may be able to choose the program group in which icons will be created and the file system location to which the program will be installed. Additionally, they may be required to choose which options are installed. Although this type of flexibility is useful, it can be tedious when you are rolling out multiple applications. By using features of the Windows Installer, however, users are able to specify setup options before the process begins. This allows system administrators to ensure consistency in installations, and it saves users time.

Advertising and On-Demand Installations   One of the most powerful features of the Windows Installer is its ability to perform on-demand software installations. Prior to the

Windows Installer, application installation options were quite basic—either a program was installed or it was not. When setting up a computer, system administrators would be required to guess which applications the user might need and install all of them.

The Windows Installer supports a function known as advertising. *Advertising* makes applications appear to be available via the Start menu. However, the programs themselves may not actually be installed on the system. When a user attempts to access an advertised application, the Windows Installer automatically downloads the necessary files from a server and installs the program. The result is that applications are installed only when they are needed, and the process requires no intervention from the end user. We'll cover the details of this process later in this chapter.

To anyone who has managed many software applications in a network environment, all of these features of the Windows Installer are likely welcome ones. They also make life easier for end users and application developers; they can focus on the "real work" that their jobs demand.

Windows Installer File Types

When performing software deployment with the Windows Installer in Windows Server 2012 R2, you may encounter several different file types.

Microsoft Windows Installer Packages   To take full advantage of Windows Installer functionality, applications must include Microsoft Windows Installer packages. Third-party application vendors and software developers normally create these packages, and they include the information required to install and configure the application and any supporting files.

Microsoft Transformation Files   *Microsoft Transformation (MST) files* are useful when you are customizing the details of how applications are installed. When a system administrator chooses to assign or publish an application, they may want to specify additional options for the package. For example, if a system administrator wants to allow users to install only the Microsoft Word and Microsoft PowerPoint components of Office 2013, they could specify these options within a transformation file. Then, when users install the application, they will be provided only with the options related to these components.

Microsoft Patches   To maintain software, patches are often required. Patches may make registry and/or file system changes. *Patch files (MSP)* are used for minor system changes and are subject to certain limitations. Specifically, a patch file cannot remove any installed program components and cannot delete or modify any shortcuts created by the user.

Initialization Files   To provide support for publishing non-Windows Installer applications, *initialization files* can be used. These files provide links to a standard executable file that is used to install an application. An example might be \\server1\software\program1\ setup.exe. These files can then be published and advertised, and users can access the *Add Or Remove Programs* icon to install them over the network.

Application Assignment Scripts *Application assignment scripts (AAS)* store information regarding assigning programs and any settings that the system administrator makes. These files are created when Group Policy is used to create software package assignments for users and computers.

Each of these types of files provides functionality that allows the system administrator to customize software deployment. Windows Installer packages have special properties that you can view by right-clicking the file in Windows Explorer and choosing Properties (see Figure 6.9).

FIGURE 6.9 Viewing the properties of an MSI package file

Deploying Applications

The functionality provided by Windows Installer offers many advantages to end users who install their own software. However, that is just the beginning in a networked environment. As you'll see later in this chapter, the various features of Windows Installer and compatible packages allow system administrators to determine centrally applications that users will be able to install.

There are two main methods of making programs available to end users using Active Directory: assigning and publishing. Both assigning and publishing applications greatly ease the process of deploying and managing applications in a network environment.

In the following sections, you'll look at how the processes of assigning and publishing applications can make life easier for IT staff and users alike. The various settings for assigned and published applications are managed through the use of GPOs.

Assigning Applications

Software applications can be assigned to users and computers. *Assigning* a software package makes the program available for automatic installation. The applications advertise their availability to the affected users or computers by placing icons within the Programs folder of the Start menu for Windows 8 (and before) and Windows Server 2012, and within the Apps area on Windows 8.1 and Windows Server 2012 R2.

When applications are assigned to a user, programs will be advertised to the user regardless of which computer they are using. That is, icons for the advertised program will appear regardless of whether the program is installed on that computer. If the user clicks an icon for a program that has not yet been installed on the local computer, the application will automatically be accessed from a server and it will be installed.

When an application is assigned to a computer, the program is made available to any users of the computer. For example, all users who log on to a computer that has been assigned Microsoft Office 2013 will have access to the components of the application. If the user did not previously install Microsoft Office 2013, they will be prompted for any required setup information when the program first runs.

Generally, applications that are required by the vast majority of users should be assigned to computers. This reduces the amount of network bandwidth required to install applications on demand and improves the end-user experience by preventing the delay involved when installing an application the first time it is accessed. Any applications that may be used by only a few users (or those with specific job tasks) should be assigned to users.

Publishing Applications

When applications are *published*, they are advertised, but no icons are automatically created. Instead, the applications are made available for installation using the Add Or Remove Programs icon in Control Panel.

 NOTE Windows Vista, Windows 7, and Windows 8 do not have the Add Or Remove Programs feature. They use the Programs icon in Control Panel to install the software.

Implementing Software Deployment

So far, you have become familiar with the issues related to software deployment and management from a theoretical level. Now it's time to drill down into the actual steps required to deploy software using the features of Active Directory and the GPMC. In the following sections, you will walk through the steps required to create an application distribution share point, to publish and assign applications, to update previously installed applications, to verify the installation of applications, and to update Windows operating systems.

Preparing for Software Deployment

Before you can install applications on client computers, you must make sure that the necessary files are available to end users. In many network environments, system administrators create shares on file servers that include the installation files for many applications. Based on security permissions, either end users or system administrators can then connect to these shares from a client computer and install the needed software. The efficient organization of these shares can save the help desk from having to carry around a library of DVDs, and it allows you to install applications easily on many computers at once.

 One of the problems in network environments is that users frequently install applications whether or not they really need them. They may stumble upon applications that are stored on common file servers and install them out of curiosity. These actions can often decrease productivity and may violate software licensing agreements. You can help avoid this by placing all of your application installation files in hidden shares (for example, software$).

Exercise 6.7 walks you through the process of creating a software distribution share point. In this exercise, you will prepare for software deployment by creating a directory share and placing certain types of files in this directory. To complete the steps in this exercise, you must have access to the Microsoft Office 2010 or Microsoft Office 2013 installation files (via DVD or through a network share) and have 2,000MB of free disk space. For this exercise, I used Microsoft Office 2013.

EXERCISE 6.7

Creating a Software Deployment Share

1. Using Windows Explorer, create a folder called Software that you can use with application sharing. Be sure that the volume on which you create this folder has at least 2,000MB of available disk space.

2. Create a folder called Office 2013 within the Software folder.

3. Copy all of the installation files for Microsoft Office 2013 from the DVD or network share containing the files to the Office 2013 folder you created in step 2. If you prefer, you can use switches to install all of the Office 2013 installation files. You can find these switches at http://technet.microsoft.com/en-us/library/ee624360.aspx.

4. Right-click the Software folder (created in step 1) and select Share. In the Choose People On Your Network To Share With dialog box, type **Everyone**, and click the Add button. Next click the Share button. When you see a message that the sharing process is complete, click Done.

Once you have created an application distribution share, it's time to publish and assign the applications. This topic is covered next.

Software Restriction Policies

One of the biggest problems that we face as IT managers is users downloading and installing software. Many software packages don't cause any issues and are completely safe. Unfortunately, many software packages do have viruses and can cause problems. This is where software restriction policies can help. Software restriction policies help to identify software and to control its ability to run on a local computer, organizational unit, domain, or site.

Software restriction policies give administrators the ability to regulate unknown or untrusted software. Software restriction policies allow you to protect your computers from unwanted software by identifying and also specifying what software packages are allowed to be installed.

When configuring software restriction policies, an administrator is able to define a default security level of Unrestricted (software is allowed) or Disallowed (software is not allowed to run) for a GPO. Administrators can make exceptions to this default security level. They can create software restriction policy rules for specific software.

To create a software policy using the Group Policy Management Console, create a new GPO. In the GPO, expand the Windows Settings for either the user or computer configuration section, expand Security, right-click Software Restriction Policy, and choose New Software Restriction Policy. Set the policy for the level of security that you need.

Using AppLocker

AppLocker is a feature in Windows 7, Windows 8, Windows Server 2012, and Windows Server 2012 R2. It is the replacement for software restriction policies. *AppLocker* allows you to configure a Denied list and an Accepted list for applications. Applications that are configured on the Denied list will not run on the system, whereas applications on the Accepted list will operate properly.

The new capabilities and extensions of the AppLocker feature help reduce administrative overhead and help administrators control how users can access and use files, such as EXE files, scripts, Windows Installer files (MSI and MSP files), and DLLs.

Group Policy Slow Link Detection

When setting up GPOs, most of us assume that the connection speeds between servers and clients are going to be fast. In today's world, it is unlikely to see slow connections between locations, but they are still out there. Sometimes connection speeds can cause issues with the deployment of GPOs, specifically ones that are deploying software.

A setting in the Computer and User section of the GPO called *Group Policy Slow Link Detection* defines a slow connection for the purposes of applying and updating GPOs. If the data transfer rate from the domain controller providing the GPO to the computer is slower than what you have specified in this setting, the connection is considered to be a slow connection. If a connection is considered slow, the system response will vary depending on the policy. For example, if a GPO is going to deploy software and the connection is considered slow, the software may not be installed on the client computer. If you configure this option as 0, all connections are considered fast connections.

Publishing and Assigning Applications

As mentioned earlier in this section, system administrators can make software packages available to users by using publishing and assigning operations. Both of these operations allow system administrators to leverage the power of Active Directory and, specifically, GPOs to determine which applications are available to users. Additionally, OUs can provide the organization that can help group users based on their job functions and software requirements.

The general process involves creating a GPO that includes software deployment settings for users and computers and then linking this GPO to Active Directory objects.

Exercise 6.8 walks you through the steps required to publish and assign applications. In this exercise, you will create applications and assign them to specific Active Directory objects using GPOs. To complete the steps in this exercise, you must have completed Exercise 6.7.

EXERCISE 6.8

Publishing and Assigning Applications Using Group Policy

1. Open the Active Directory Users and Computers tool from the Administrative Tools program group (using the Windows key).

2. Expand the domain and create a new top-level OU called **Software**.

3. Within the Software OU, create a user named **Jane User** with a login name of **juser** (choose the defaults for all other options).

4. Exit Active Directory Users and Computers and open the Group Policy Management Console.

5. Right-click the Software OU and choose Create A GPO In This Domain And Link It Here.

6. For the name of the new GPO, type **Software Deployment**.

7. To edit the Software Deployment GPO, right-click it and choose Edit. Expand the Computer Configuration ➢ Policies ➢ Software Settings object.

8. Right-click the Software Installation item and select New ➢ Package.

9. Navigate to the Software share you created in Exercise 6.7.

10. Within the Software share, double-click the Office 2013 folder and select the appropriate MSI file depending on the version of Office 2013 you have. Office 2013 Professional is being used in this example, so you'll see that the OFFICEMUI.MSI file is chosen. Click Open.

11. In the Deploy Software dialog box, choose Advanced. (Note that the Published option is unavailable because applications cannot be published to computers.) Click OK to return to the Deploy Software dialog box.

12. To examine the deployment options of this package, click the Deployment tab. Accept the default settings by clicking OK.

13. Within the Group Policy Object Editor, expand the User Configuration ➢ Software Settings object.

14. Right-click the Software Installation item and select New ➢ Package.

15. Navigate to the Software share you created in Exercise 6.7.

16. Within the Software share, double-click the Office 2013 folder and select the appropriate MSI file. Click Open.

17. For the Software Deployment option, select Published in the Deploy Software dialog box and click OK.

18. Close the GPMC.

The overall process involved with deploying software using Active Directory is quite simple. However, you shouldn't let the intuitive graphical interface fool you—there's a lot of power under the hood of these software deployment features! Once you've properly assigned and published applications, it's time to see the effects of your work.

Applying Software Updates

The steps described in the previous section work only when you are installing a new application. However, software companies often release updates that you need to install on top of existing applications. These updates usually consist of bug fixes or other changes that are required to keep the software up-to-date. You can apply software updates in Active Directory by using the Upgrades tab of the software package Properties dialog box found in the Group Policy Object Editor.

In Exercise 6.9, you will apply a software update to an existing application. You should add the upgrade package to the GPO in the same way you added the original application in steps 8 through 12 of Exercise 6.8. You should also have completed Exercise 6.8 before attempting this exercise.

EXERCISE 6.9

Applying Software Updates

1. Open the Group Policy Management Console from the Administrative Tools program group.

2. Click the Software OU, right-click the Software Deployment GPO, and choose Edit.

3. Expand the Computer Configuration ➢ Policies ➢ Software Settings ➢ Software Installation object.

4. Right-click the software package and select Properties from the context menu to bring up the Properties dialog box.

5. Select the Upgrades tab and click the Add button.

6. Click the Current Group Policy Object (GPO) radio button in the Choose A Package From section of the dialog box or click the Browse button to select the GPO to which you want to apply the upgrade. Consult your application's documentation to see whether you should choose the Uninstall The Existing Package, Then Install The Upgrade Package radio button or the Package Can Upgrade Over The Existing Package radio button.

7. Click Cancel to close the Add Upgrade Package dialog box.

8. Click Cancel and exit the GPMC.

You should understand that not all upgrades make sense in all situations. For instance, if the Paniva 2010 files are incompatible with the Paniva 2013 application, then your Paniva 2010 users might not want you to perform the upgrade without taking additional steps to ensure that they can continue to use their files. In addition, users might have some choice about which version they use when it doesn't affect the support of the network.

Regardless of the underlying reason for allowing this flexibility, you should be aware that there are two basic types of upgrades that are available for administrators to provide to the users:

Mandatory Upgrade Forces everyone who currently has an existing version of the program to upgrade according to the GPO. Users who have never installed the program for whatever reason will be able to install only the new, upgraded version.

Nonmandatory Upgrade Allows users to choose whether they would like to upgrade. This upgrade type also allows users who do not have their application installed to choose which version they would like to use.

Verifying Software Installation

To ensure that the software installation settings you make in a GPO have taken place, you can log into the domain from a Windows 8, Windows 7, or Windows Vista computer that is within the OU to which the software settings apply. When you log in, you will notice two changes. First the application is installed on the computer (if it was not installed already). To access the application, a user needs to click one of the icons within the Program group of the Start menu. Note also that applications are available to any of the users who log on to this machine. Second, the settings apply to any computers that are contained within the OU and to any users who log on to these computers.

If you publish an application to users, the change may not be as evident, but it is equally useful. When you log on to a Windows 8, Windows 7, or Windows Vista computer that is a member of the domain, and when you use a user account from the OU where you published the application, you will be able to install any of the published applications automatically. On a Windows 8 or Windows 7 computer, you can do this by accessing the Programs icon in Control Panel. By clicking Add New Programs, you access a display of the applications available for installation. By clicking the Add button in the Add New Programs section of the Programs dialog box, you will automatically begin the installation of the published application.

Configuring Automatic Updates in Group Policy

So far you've seen the advantages of deploying application software in a group policy. Group policies also provide a way to install operating system updates across the network for Windows 2000, XP, Vista, Windows 7, Windows 8, Windows Server 2003, Windows Server 2008, Windows Server 2008 R2, Windows Server 2012, and Windows Server 2012 R2 machines using Windows Update in conjunction with Windows Server Update Service. WSUS is the newer version of SUS, and it is used on a Windows Server 2012 R2 system to update systems. As you may remember, WSUS and SUS are patch-management tools that help you deploy updates to your systems in a controlled manner.

Windows Update is available through the Microsoft website, and it is used to provide the most current files for Windows operating systems. Examples of updates include security fixes, critical updates, updated help files, and updated drivers. You can access Windows Update by clicking the Windows Update icon in the system tray.

WSUS is used to leverage the features of Windows Update within a corporate environment by downloading Windows updates to a corporate server, which in turn provides the updates to the internal corporate clients. This allows administrators to test and have full control over what updates are deployed within the corporate environment.

Within an enterprise network that is using Active Directory, you would typically see automatic updates configured through Group Policy. Group policies are used to manage configuration and security settings via Active Directory. Group Policy is also used to specify what server a client will use for automatic updates.

If the WSUS client were part of an enterprise network that is using Active Directory, you would configure the client via a group policy.

Configuring Software Deployment Settings

In addition to the basic operations of assigning and publishing applications, you can use several other options to specify the details of how software is deployed. In the following sections, you will examine the various options that are available and their effects on the software installation process.

The Software Installation Properties Dialog Box

The most important software deployment settings are contained in the Software Installation Properties dialog box, which you can access by right-clicking the Software Installation item and selecting Properties from the context menu. The following sections describe the features contained on the various tabs of the dialog box.

Managing Package Defaults

On the Deployment tab of the Software Installation Properties dialog box, you'll be able to specify some defaults for any packages that you create within this GPO. Figure 6.10 shows the Deployment options for managing software installation settings.

FIGURE 6.10   Deployment tab of the Software Installation Properties dialog box

The following options are used for managing software installation settings:

Default Package Location   This setting specifies the default file system or network location for software installation packages. This is useful if you are already using a specific share on a file server for hosting the necessary installation files.

New Packages   These settings specify the default type of package assignment that will be used when you add a new package to either the user or computer settings. If you'll be assigning or publishing multiple packages, you may find it useful to set a default here. Selecting the Advanced option (see Figure 6.11) enables Group Policy to display the package's Properties dialog box each time a new package is added.

FIGURE 6.11   Advanced Deployment dialog box

Installation User Interface Options   When installing an application, system administrators may or may not want end users to see all of the advanced installation options. If Basic is chosen, the user will be able to configure only the minimal settings (such as the installation location). If Maximum is chosen, all of the available installation options will be displayed. The specific installation options available will depend on the package itself.

Uninstall Applications When They Fall Out Of The Scope of Management   So far, you have seen how applications can be assigned and published to users or computers. But what happens when effective GPOs change? For example, suppose User A is currently located within the Sales OU. A GPO that assigns the Microsoft Office 2013 suite of applications is linked to the Sales OU. You decide to move User A to the Engineering OU, which has no software deployment settings. Should the application be uninstalled or should it remain?

If the Uninstall Applications When They Fall Out Of The Scope of Management option is checked, applications will be removed if they are not specifically assigned or published within GPOs. In this example, this means Office 2013 would be uninstalled for User A. If this box is left unchecked, however, the application will remain installed.

Managing File Extension Mappings

One of the potential problems associated with using many different file types is that it's difficult to keep track of which applications work with which files. For example, if you received a file with the filename extension .abc, you would have no idea which application you would need to view it.

Fortunately, through software deployment settings, system administrators can specify mappings for specific *filename extensions*. For example, you could specify that whenever users attempt to access a file with the extension .vsd, the operating system should attempt to open the file using Visio diagramming software. If Visio is not installed on the user's machine, the computer can automatically download and install it (assuming that the application has been properly advertised).

This method allows users to have applications automatically installed when they are needed. The following is an example of a sequence of events that might occur:

1. A user receives an email message that contains a PDF (.pdf) file attachment.

2. The computer realizes that the PDF file does not have the appropriate viewing application for this type of file installed. However, it also realizes that a filename extension mapping is available within the Active Directory software deployment settings.

3. The client computer automatically requests the PDF software package from the server, and it uses the Microsoft Windows Installer to install the application automatically.

4. The computer opens the attachment for the user.

Notice that all of these steps were carried out without any further interaction with the user.

You can manage filename extension mappings by right-clicking the Software Installation item, selecting Properties, and then clicking the File Extensions tab.

Creating Application Categories

In many network environments, the list of supported applications can include hundreds of items. For users who are looking for only one specific program, searching through a list of all of these programs can be difficult and time-consuming.

Fortunately, methods for categorizing the applications are available on your network. You can easily manage the application categories for users and computers by right-clicking the Software Installation item, selecting Properties, and then clicking the Categories tab.

Figure 6.12 shows you the categories tab of the Software Installation package. When creating categories, it is a good idea to use category names that are meaningful to users because it will make it easier for them to find the programs they're seeking.

Once the software installation categories have been created, you can view them by clicking the Programs or Programs And Features icon in Control Panel. When you click Add New Programs, you'll see that several options appear in the Category drop-down list. Now when you select the properties for a package, you will be able to assign the application to one or more of the categories.

FIGURE 6.12   The Categories tab of the Software Installation Properties dialog box

Removing Programs

As discussed in the beginning of the chapter, an important phase in the software management life cycle is the removal of applications. Fortunately, if you use the GPMC and the Windows Installer packages, the process is simple. To remove an application, you can right-click the package within the Group Policy settings and select All Tasks ➢ Remove (see Figure 6.13).

When choosing to remove a software package from a GPO, you have two options, shown here:

Immediately Uninstall The Software From Users And Computers   System administrators can choose this option to ensure that an application is no longer available to users who are affected by the GPO. When this option is selected, the program will be uninstalled automatically from users and/or computers that have the package. This option might be useful, for example, if the license for a certain application has expired or if a program is no longer on the approved applications list.

Allow Users To Continue To Use The Software, But Prevent New Installations   This option prevents users from making new installations of a package, but it does not remove the software if it has already been installed for users. This is a good option if the company has run out of additional licenses for the software but the existing licenses are still valid. Figure 6.14 shows these two removal options.

If you no longer require the ability to install or repair an application, you can delete it from your software distribution share point by deleting the appropriate Windows Installer package files. This will free up additional disk space for newer applications.

FIGURE 6.13   Removing a software package

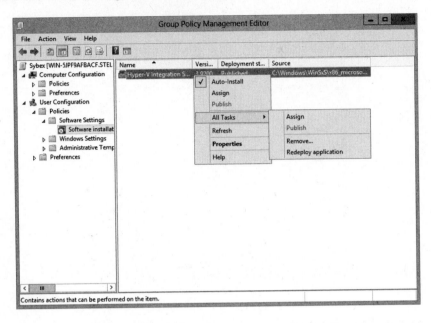

FIGURE 6.14   Software removal options

Microsoft Windows Installer Settings

Several options influence the behavior of the Windows Installer; you can set them within a GPO. You can access these options by navigating to User Configuration ➢ Administrative Templates ➢ Windows Components ➢ Windows Installer (see Figure 6.15).
The options are as follows:

Always Install With Elevated Privileges   This policy allows users to install applications that require elevated privileges. For example, if a user does not have the permissions necessary to modify the registry but the installation program must make registry changes, this policy will allow the process to succeed.

FIGURE 6.15 GPO settings for Windows Installer

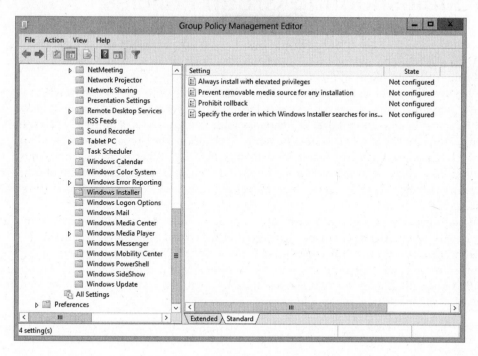

Prevent Removable Media Source For Any Install   This option disallows the installation of software using removable media (such as a CD-ROM or DVD-ROM). It is useful for ensuring that users install only approved applications.

Prohibit Rollback   When this option is enabled, the Windows Installer does not store the system state information that is required to roll back the installation of an application. System administrators may choose this option to reduce the amount of temporary disk space required during installation and to increase the performance of the installation operation. However, the drawback is that the system cannot roll back to its original state if the installation fails and the application needs to be removed.

Specify The Order In Which Windows Installer Searches   This setting specifies the order in which the Windows Installer will search for installation files. The options include *n* (for network shares), *m* (for searching removal media), and *u* (for searching the Internet for installation files).

With these options, system administrators can control how the Windows Installer operates for specific users who are affected by the GPO.

Troubleshooting Group Policies

Because of the wide variety of configurations that are possible when you are establishing GPOs, you should be aware of some common troubleshooting methods. These methods will help isolate problems in policy settings or GPO links.

One possible problem with GPO configuration is that logons and system startups may take a long time. This occurs especially in large environments when the Group Policy settings must be transmitted over the network and, in many cases, slow WAN links. In general, the number of GPOs should be limited because of the processing overhead and network requirements during logon. By default, GPOs are processed in a synchronous manner. This means that the processing of one GPO must be completed before another one is applied (as opposed to asynchronous processing, where they can all execute at the same time).

When a group policy gets processed on a Windows-based operating system, client-side extensions are the mechanisms that interpret the stored policy and then make the appropriate changes to the operating system environment. When an administrator is troubleshooting a given extension's application of policy, the administrator can view the configuration parameters for that extension in the operating system's registry. To view the extension in the registry, you would view the following key:

```
HKEY_LOCAL_MACHINE\Software\Microsoft\Windows \CurrentVersion\Group Policy
```

The most common issue associated with Group Policy is the unexpected setting of Group Policy options. In Windows Server 2000, administrators spent countless hours analyzing inheritance hierarchy and individual settings to determine why a particular user or computer was having policy problems. For instance, say a user named wpanek complains that the Run option is missing from his Start menu. The wpanek user account is stored in the New Hampshire OU, and you've applied group policies at the OU, domain, and site levels. To determine the source of the problem, you would have to sift through each GPO manually to find the Start menu policy as well as to figure out the applicable inheritance settings.

Windows Server 2012 R2 has a handy feature called *Resultant Set of Policy (RSoP)* that displays the exact settings that actually apply to individual users, computers, OUs, domains, and sites after inheritance and filtering have taken effect. In the example just described, you could run RSoP on the wpanek account and view a single set of Group Policy settings that represent the settings that apply to that account. In addition, each setting's Properties dialog box displays the GPO from which the setting is derived as well as the order of priority, the filter status, and other useful information, as you will see a bit later.

RSoP actually runs in two modes.

Logging Mode   *Logging mode* displays the actual settings that apply to users and computers, as shown in the example in the preceding paragraph.

Planning Mode *Planning mode* can be applied to users, computers, OUs, domains, and sites, and you use it before you apply any settings. As its name implies, planning mode is used to plan GPOs.

Additionally, you can run the command-line utility gpresult.exe to get a quick snapshot of the Group Policy settings that apply to a user and/or computer. Let's take a closer look at the two modes and the gpresult.exe command.

RSoP in Logging Mode

RSoP in logging mode can query policy settings only for users and computers. The easiest way to access RSoP in logging mode is through the Active Directory Users and Computers tool, although you can run it as a stand-alone MMC snap-in if you want.

To analyze the policy settings for wpanek from the earlier example, you would right-click the user icon in Active Directory Users and Computers and select All Tasks ➢ Resultant Set of Policy (Logging). The Group Policy Results Wizard appears. The wizard walks you through the steps necessary to view the RSoP for wpanek.

The Computer Selection page, shown in Figure 6.16, requires you to select a computer for which to display settings. Remember that a GPO contains both user and computer settings, so you must choose a computer to which the user is logged on in order to continue with the wizard. If the user has never logged on to a computer, then you must run RSoP in planning mode because there is no logged policy information yet for that user.

The User Selection page, shown in Figure 6.17, requires you to select a user account to analyze. Because I selected a user from the Active Directory Users and Computers tool, the username is filled in automatically. This page is most useful if you are running RSoP in MMC mode and don't have the luxury of selecting a user contextually.

FIGURE 6.16 The Computer Selection page of the Group Policy Results Wizard

FIGURE 6.17 The User Selection page of the Group Policy Results Wizard

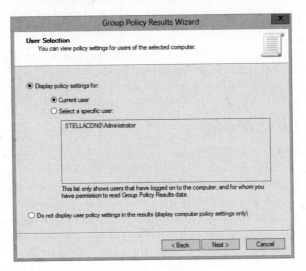

The Summary Of Selections page, shown in Figure 6.18, summarizes your choices and provides an option for gathering extended error information. If you need to make any changes before you begin to analyze the policy settings, you should click the Back button on the Summary screen. Otherwise, click Next.

FIGURE 6.18 The Summary Of Selections page of the Group Policy Results Wizard

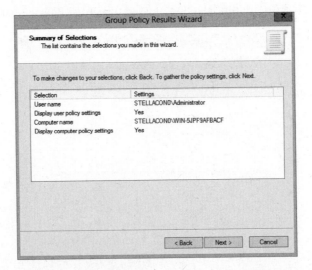

After the wizard is complete, you will see the window shown in Figure 6.19. This window displays only the policy settings that apply to the user and computer that you selected in the wizard. You can see these users and computers at the topmost level of the tree.

FIGURE 6.19 The User Selection page for the administrator on computer SERVER1

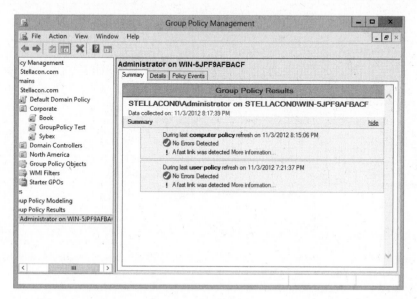

Any warnings or errors appear as a yellow triangle or red *X* over the applicable icon at the level where the warning or error occurred. To view more information about the warning or error, right-click the icon and select Properties, as shown in Figure 6.20.

You cannot make changes to any of the individual settings because RSoP is a diagnostic tool and not an editor, but you can get more information about settings by clicking a setting and selecting Properties from the context menu.

The Details tab of the user's Properties window, shown in Figure 6.21, displays the actual setting that applies to the user in question based on GPO inheritance.

RSoP in Planning Mode

Running RSoP in planning mode isn't much different from running RSoP in logging mode, but the RSoP Wizard asks for a bit more information than you saw earlier.

In the former example, wpanek couldn't see the Run option in the Start menu because his user account is affected by the New Hampshire GPO in the San Jose OU. As an administrator, you could plan to move his user account to the North America OU. Before doing so, you could verify his new policy settings by running RSoP in planning mode. Run the RSoP on the user wpanek under the scenario that you've already moved him from the San Jose OU to the North America OU. At this point, you haven't actually moved the user, but you can see what his settings would be if you did.

FIGURE 6.20   Details of event pertaining to the administrator account on computer SERVER1

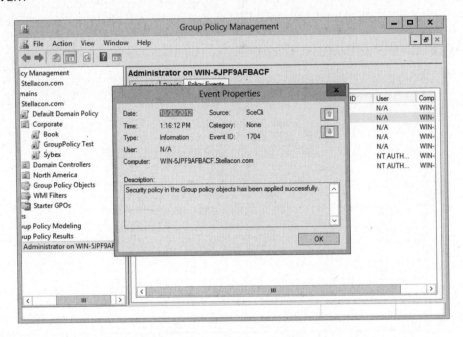

FIGURE 6.21   The Details tab of the object's Properties window

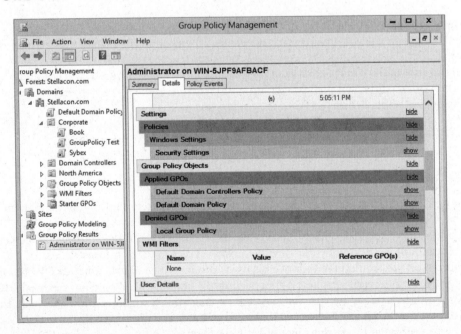

Using the *gpresult.exe* Command

The command-line utility gpresult.exe is included as part of the RSoP tool. Running the command by itself without any switches returns the following Group Policy information about the local user and computer:

- The name of the domain controller from which the local machine retrieved the policy information
- The date and time at which the policies were applied
- Which policies were applied
- Which policies were filtered out
- Group membership

You can use the switches shown in Table 6.2 to get information for remote users and computers and to enable other options.

Table 6.2 is not a complete list. To see a complete list of the gpresult.exe command, visit Microsoft at www.microsoft.com.

TABLE 6.2 gpresult switches

Switch	Description
/S systemname	Generates RSoP information for a remote computer name.
/USER username	Generates RSoP information for a remote username.
/x /h filename	Generates a report in either XML (/x) or HTML (/h) format. The filename and location is specified by the *filename* parameter.
/V	Specifies verbose mode, which displays more verbose information such as user rights information.
/Z	Specifies an even greater level of verbose information.
/SCOPE MACHINE	Displays maximum information about the computer policies applied to this system.
/SCOPE USER	Displays maximum information about the user policies applied to this system.
>textfile.txt	Writes the output to a text file.

For example, to obtain information about user wpanek in a system called STELLACON, you would use the command gpresult/S STELLACON/USERwpanek.

Through the use of these techniques, you should be able to track down even the most elusive Group Policy problems. Remember, however, that good troubleshooting skills do not replace planning adequately and maintaining GPO settings!

Summary

In this chapter, you examined Active Directory's solution to a common headache for many systems administrators: policy settings. Specifically, I discussed topics that covered Group Policy.

I covered the fundamentals of Group Policy including its fundamental purpose. You can use Group Policy to enforce granular permissions for users in an Active Directory environment. Group policies can restrict and modify the actions allowed for users and computers within the Active Directory environment.

Certain Group Policy settings may apply to users, computers, or both. Computer settings affect all users who access the machines to which the policy applies. User settings affect users regardless of the machines to which they log on.

You learned that you can link Group Policy objects to Active Directory sites, domains, or OUs. This link determines to which objects the policies apply. GPO links can interact through inheritance and filtering to result in an effective set of policies.

The chapter covered inheritance and how GPOs filter down. I showed you how to use the Enforced option on a GPO issued from a parent and how to block a GPO from a child.

You can also use administrative templates to simplify the creation of GPOs. There are some basic default templates that come with Windows Server 2012 R2.

In addition, administrators can delegate control over GPOs in order to distribute administrative responsibilities. Delegation is an important concept because it allows for distributed administration.

You can also deploy software using GPOs. This feature can save time and increase productivity throughout the entire software management life cycle by automating software installation and removal on client computers. The Windows Installer offers a more robust method for managing installation and removal, and applications that support it can take advantage of new Active Directory features. Make sure you are comfortable using the Windows Installer.

You learned about publishing applications via Active Directory and the difference between publishing and assigning applications. You can assign some applications to users and computers so that they are always available. You can also publish them to users so that the user can install them with minimal effort when required.

You also learned how to prepare for software deployment. Before your users can take advantage of automated software installation, you must set up an installation share and provide the appropriate permissions.

The final portion of the chapter covered the Resultant Set of Policy (RSoP) tool, which you can use in logging mode or planning mode to determine exactly which set of policies applies to users, computers, OUs, domains, and sites.

Exam Essentials

Understand the purpose of Group Policy.   System administrators use Group Policy to enforce granular permissions for users in an Active Directory environment.

Understand user and computer settings.   Certain Group Policy settings may apply to users, computers, or both. Computer settings affect all users that access the machines to which the policy applies. User settings affect users, regardless of which machines they log on to.

Know the interactions between Group Policy objects and Active Directory.   GPOs can be linked to Active Directory objects. This link determines to which objects the policies apply.

Understand filtering and inheritance interactions between GPOs.   For ease of administration, GPOs can interact via inheritance and filtering. It is important to understand these interactions when you are implementing and troubleshooting Group Policy.

Know how Group Policy settings can affect script policies and network settings.   You can use special sets of GPOs to manage network configuration settings.

Understand how delegation of administration can be used in an Active Directory environment.   Delegation is an important concept because it allows for distributed administration.

Know how to use the Resultant Set of Policy (RSoP) tool to troubleshoot and plan Group Policy.   Windows Server 2012 R2 includes the RSoP feature, which you can run in logging mode or planning mode to determine exactly which set of policies applies to users, computers, OUs, domains, and sites.

Identify common problems with the software life cycle.   IT professionals face many challenges with client applications, including development, deployment, maintenance, and troubleshooting.

Understand the benefits of the Windows Installer.   Using the Windows Installer is an updated way to install applications on Windows-based machines. It offers a more robust method for making the system changes required by applications, and it allows for a cleaner uninstall. Windows Installer–based applications can also take advantage of new Active Directory features.

Understand the difference between publishing and assigning applications.   Some applications can be assigned to users and computers so that they are always available.

Applications can be published to users so that the user may install the application with a minimal amount of effort when it is required.

Know how to prepare for software deployment. Before your users can take advantage of automated software installation, you must set up an installation share and provide the appropriate permissions.

Know how to configure application settings using Active Directory and Group Policy. Using standard Windows Server 2012 R2 administrative tools, you can create an application policy that meets your requirements. You can use automatic, on-demand installation of applications as well as many other features.

Create application categories to simplify the list of published applications. It's important to group applications by functionality or the users to whom they apply, especially in organizations that support a large number of programs.

Review Questions

1. You are the network administrator for a large organization that uses Windows Server 2012 R2 domain controllers and DNS servers. All of your client machines currently have the Windows XP operating system. You want to be able to have client computers edit the domain-based GPOs by using the ADMX files that are located in the ADMX Central Store. How do you accomplish this task? (Choose all that apply.)

   A. Upgrade your clients to Windows 8.

   B. Upgrade your clients to Windows 7.

   C. Add the client machines to the ADMX edit utility.

   D. In the ADMX store, choose the box Allow All Client Privileges.

2. You work for an organization with a single Windows Server 2012 R2 Active Directory domain. The domain has OUs for Sales, Marketing, Admin, R&D, and Finance. You need only the users in the Finance OU to get Windows Office 2013 installed automatically onto their computers. You create a GPO named OfficeApp. What is the next step in getting all of the Finance users Office 2013?

   A. Edit the GPO, and assign the Office application to the user's account. Link the GPO to the Finance OU.

   B. Edit the GPO, and assign the Office application to the user's account. Link the GPO to the domain.

   C. Edit the GPO, and assign the Office application to the computer account. Link the GPO to the domain.

   D. Edit the GPO, and assign the Office application to the computer account. Link the GPO to the Finance OU.

3. You are hired as a consultant to the ABC Company. The owner of the company complains that she continues to have desktop wallpaper that she did not choose. When you speak with the IT team, you find out that a former employee created 20 GPOs and they have not been able to figure out which GPO is changing the owner's desktop wallpaper. How can you resolve this issue?

   A. Run the RSoP utility against all forest computer accounts.

   B. Run the RSoP utility against the owner's computer account.

   C. Run the RSoP utility against the owner's user account.

   D. Run the RSoP utility against all domain computer accounts.

4. You are the network administrator for a large organization that has multiple sites and multiple OUs. You have a site named SalesSite that is for the sales building across the street. In the domain, there is an OU for all salespeople called Sales. You set up a GPO for the SalesSite, and you need to be sure that it applies to the Sales OU. The Sales OU GPOs cannot override the SalesSite GPO. What do you do?

    A. On the GPO, disable the Block Child Inheritance setting.

    B. On the GPO, set the Enforce setting.

    C. On the GPO, set the priorities to 1.

    D. On the Sales OU, set the Inherit Parent Policy settings.

5. You are the administrator for an organization that has multiple locations. You are running Windows Server 2012 R2, and you have only one domain with multiple OUs set up for each location. One of your locations, Boston, is connected to the main location by a 256Kbps ISDN line. You configure a GPO to assign a sales application to all computers in the entire domain. You have to be sure that Boston users receive the GPO properly. What should you do?

    A. Disable the Slow Link Detection setting in the GPO.

    B. Link the GPO to the Boston OU.

    C. Change the properties of the GPO to publish the application to the Boston OU.

    D. Have the users in Boston run the `GPResult/force` command.

6. To disable GPO settings for a specific security group, which of the following permissions should you apply?

    A. Deny Write

    B. Allow Write

    C. Enable Apply Group Policy

    D. Deny Apply Group Policy

7. GPOs assigned at which of the following level(s) will override GPO settings at the domain level?

    A. OU

    B. Site

    C. Domain

    D. Both OU and site

8. A system administrator wants to ensure that only the GPOs set at the OU level affect the Group Policy settings for objects within the OU. Which option can they use to do this (assuming that all other GPO settings are the defaults)?

    A. The Enforced option

    B. The Block Policy Inheritance option

    C. The Disable option

    D. The Deny permission

9. A system administrator is planning to implement Group Policy objects in a new Windows Server 2012 R2 Active Directory environment. In order to meet the needs of the organization, he decides to implement a hierarchical system of Group Policy settings. At which of the following levels is he able to assign Group Policy settings? (Choose all that apply.)

A. Sites

B. Domains

C. Organizational units

D. Local system

10. Ann is a system administrator for a medium-sized Active Directory environment. She has determined that several new applications that will be deployed throughout the organization use registry-based settings. She would like to do the following:

- Control these registry settings using Group Policy

- Create a standard set of options for these applications and allow other system administrators to modify them using the standard Active Directory tools

Which of the following options can she use to meet these requirements? (Choose all that apply.)

A. Implement the inheritance functionality of GPOs.

B. Implement delegation of specific objects within Active Directory.

C. Implement the No Override functionality of GPOs.

D. Create administrative templates.

E. Provide administrative templates to the system administrators who are responsible for creating Group Policy for the applications.

Chapter

7

Manage Security

THE FOLLOWING 70-410 EXAM OBJECTIVES ARE COVERED IN THIS CHAPTER:

✓ **Configuring security policies**

- ▪ Configure User Rights Assignment
- ▪ Configure Security Options settings
- ▪ Configure Security templates
- ▪ Configure Audit Policy
- ▪ Configure Local Users and Groups
- ▪ Configure User Account Control (UAC)

✓ **Configuring Windows Firewall**

- ▪ Configure rules for multiple profiles using Group Policy
- ▪ Configure connection security rules
- ▪ Configure Windows Firewall to allow or deny applications, scopes, ports, and users
- ▪ Configure authenticated firewall exceptions
- ▪ Import and export settings

As an IT Director and Microsoft Trainer, I can explain the importance of every chapter in this book, but some chapters are more important for real-world use. This is one of them.

Setting up security so that only people who need access to resources are the ones who get access to those resources is one of the most important jobs an IT member can have. This helps protect your data from hackers and, believe it or not, your own users.

In this chapter, you will learn how to protect data on your network. I will also discuss how to protect your individual system by using Windows Firewall.

Managing Security

One of the fundamental design goals for Active Directory is to define a single, centralized repository of users and information resources. Active Directory records information about all of the users, computers, and resources on your network. Each domain acts as a logical boundary, and members of the domain (including workstations, servers, and domain controllers) share information about the objects within them.

The information stored within Active Directory determines which resources are accessible to which users. Through the use of *permissions* that are assigned to Active Directory objects, you can control all aspects of network security.

You should be sure that you have implemented appropriate access control settings for the file system, network devices, and other resources. Let's look at the various components of network security, which include working with security principals and managing security and permissions, access control lists (ACLs), User Account Control (UAC), and access control entries (ACEs).

 When you are setting up a network, you should always keep in mind that 90 percent of all hacks on a network are internal. This means internal permissions and security (as well as external security) need to be as strong as possible while still allowing users to do their jobs.

Understanding Security Principals

Security principals are Active Directory objects that are assigned *security identifiers (SIDs)*. An SID is a unique identifier that is used to manage any object to which permissions can be assigned. Security principals are assigned permissions to perform certain actions and access certain network resources.

The following basic types of Active Directory objects serve as security principals:

User Accounts   User accounts identify individual users on your network by including information such as the user's name and their password. User accounts are the fundamental unit of security administration.

Groups   There are two main types of groups: *security groups* and *distribution groups.* Both types can contain user accounts. System administrators use security groups to ease the management of security permissions. They use distribution groups, on the other hand, solely to send email. Distribution groups are not security principals. You'll see the details of groups in the next section.

Computer Accounts   *Computer accounts* identify which client computers are members of particular domains. Because these computers participate in the Active Directory database, system administrators can manage security settings that affect the computer. They use computer accounts to determine whether a computer can join a domain and for authentication purposes. As you'll see later in this chapter, system administrators can also place restrictions on certain computer settings to increase security. These settings apply to the computer and, therefore, also apply to any user who is using it (regardless of the permissions granted to the user account).

Note that other objects, such as organizational units (OUs), do not function as security principals. What this means is that you can apply certain settings (such as Group Policy) on all of the objects within an OU; however, you cannot specifically set permissions with respect to the OU. The purpose of OUs is to organize other Active Directory objects logically based on business needs, add a needed level of control for security, and create an easier way to delegate.

You can manage security by performing the following actions with security principals:

- You can assign them permissions to access various network resources.
- You can give them user rights.
- You can track their actions through auditing (covered later in this chapter).

The major types of security principals—user accounts, groups, and computer accounts— form the basis of the Active Directory security architecture. As a system administrator, you will likely spend a portion of your time managing permissions for these objects.

It is important to understand that since a unique SID defines each security principal, deleting a security principal is an irreversible process. For example, if you delete a user account and then later re-create one with the same name, you'll need to reassign permissions and group membership settings for the new account. Once a user account is deleted, its SID is deleted.

Users and groups are two types of fundamental security principals employed for security administration. In the following sections, you'll learn how users and groups interact. You'll also learn about the different types of groups you can create.

Types of Groups

When dealing with groups, you should make the distinction between local security principals and domain security principals, as follows:

Local Users and Groups   You use *local users and groups* to assign the permissions necessary to access the local machine. For example, you may assign the permissions you need to reboot a domain controller to a specific domain local group.

Domain Users and Groups   *Domain users and groups*, on the other hand, are used throughout the domain. These objects are available on any of the computers within the Active Directory domain and between domains that have a trust relationship.

Here are the two main types of groups used in Active Directory:

Security Groups   *Security groups* are considered security principals. They can contain user accounts, computers, or groups. To make administration simpler, system administrators usually grant permissions to groups. This allows you to change permissions easily at the Active Directory level (instead of at the level of the resource on which the permissions are assigned).

You can also place Active Directory Contact objects within security groups, but security permissions will not apply to them.

Distribution Groups   Distribution groups are not considered security principals because they do not have SIDs. As mentioned earlier, they are used only for the purpose of sending email messages. You can add users to distribution groups just as you would add them to security groups. You can also place distribution groups within OUs so that they are easier to manage. You will find them useful, for example, if you need to send email messages to an entire department or business unit within Active Directory.

Understanding the differences between security and distribution groups is important in an Active Directory environment. For the most part, system administrators use security groups for the daily administration of permissions. On the other hand, system administrators who are responsible for maintaining email distribution lists generally use distribution groups to group members of departments and business units logically. (A system administrator can also email all of the users within a security group, but to do so, they would have to specify the email addresses for the accounts.)

When you are working in Windows Server 2003, Server 2008, Server 2008 R2, Windows Server 2012, or Windows Server 2012 R2 functional-level domains, you can convert security groups to or from distribution groups.

It is vital that you understand group types when you are getting ready to take the Microsoft exams. Microsoft likes to include trick questions about putting permissions on distribution groups. Remember, only security groups can have permissions assigned to them.

Group Scope

In addition to being classified by type, each group is given a specific scope. The scope of a group defines two characteristics. First, it determines the level of security that applies to a group. Second, it determines which users can be added to the group. *Group scope* is an important concept in network environments because it ultimately defines which resources users are able to access.

The three types of group scope are as follows:

Domain Local   The scope of *domain local groups* extends as far as the local domain. When you're using the Active Directory Users and Computers tool, domain local accounts apply to the computer for which you are viewing information. Domain local groups are used to assign permissions to local resources, such as files and printers. They can contain domain locals, global groups, universal groups, and user accounts.

Global   The scope of *global groups* is limited to a single domain. Global groups may contain any of the users who are a part of the Active Directory domain in which the global groups reside or other global groups. Global groups are often used for managing domain security permissions based on job functions. For example, if you need to specify permissions for the Engineering department, you could create one or more global groups (such as EngineeringManagers and EngineeringDevelopers). You could then assign security permissions to each group.

Universal   *Universal groups* can contain accounts or other universal groups from any domains within an Active Directory forest. Therefore, system administrators use them to manage security across domains. When you are managing multiple domains, it often helps to group global groups within universal groups. For instance, if you have an Engineering global group in the research.stellacon.com domain and an Engineering global group in the asia.stellacon.com domain, you can create a universal AllEngineers group that contains both of the global groups. Now whenever you must assign security permissions to all engineers within the organization, you need only assign permissions to the AllEngineers universal group.

For domain controllers to process authentication between domains, information about the membership of universal groups is stored in the global catalog (GC). Keep this in mind if you ever plan to place users directly into universal groups and bypass global groups because all of the users will be enumerated in the GC, which will impact size and performance.

Fortunately, universal group credentials are cached on domain controllers that universal group members use to log on. This process is called *universal group membership caching*. The domain controller obtains the cached data whenever universal group members log on, and then it is retained on the domain controller for eight hours by default. This is especially useful for smaller locations, such as branch offices, that run less expensive domain controllers. Most domain controllers at these locations cannot store a copy of the entire GC, and frequent calls to the nearest GC would require an inordinate amount of network traffic.

When you create a new group using the Active Directory Users and Computers tool, you must specify the scope of the group. Figure 7.1 shows the New Object – Group dialog box and the available options for the group scope.

Changing group scope, however, can be helpful when your security administration or business needs change. You can change group scope easily using the Active Directory Users and Computers tool. To do so, access the properties of the group. As shown in Figure 7.2, you can make a group scope change by clicking one of the options.

FIGURE 7.1   The New Object – Group dialog box

FIGURE 7.2   The Sales Security Group's Properties dialog box

Built-in Domain Local Groups

System administrators use built-in domain local groups to perform administrative functions on the local server. Because these have pre-assigned permissions and privileges, they allow system administrators to assign common management functions easily. Figure 7.3 shows the default built-in groups that are available on a Windows Server 2012 R2 domain controller.

FIGURE 7.3   Default built-in local groups

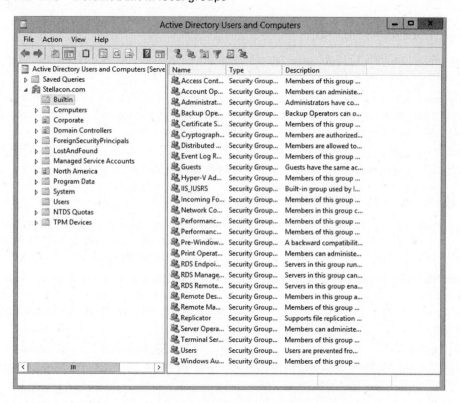

The list of built-in local groups includes some of the following:

Account Operators   These users can create and modify domain user and group accounts. Members of this group are generally responsible for the daily administration of Active Directory.

Administrators   By default, members of the Administrators group are given full permissions to perform any functions within the Active Directory domain and on the local computer. This means they can access all files and resources that reside on any server within the domain. As you can see, this is a powerful account.

In general, you should restrict the number of users who are included in this group because most common administration functions do not require this level of access.

Backup Operators   One of the problems associated with backing up data in a secure network environment is that you need to provide a way to bypass standard file system security so that you can copy files. Although you could place users in the Administrators group, doing so usually provides more permissions than necessary. Members of the Backup Operators group can bypass standard file system security for the purpose of backup and recovery only. They cannot, however, directly access or open files within the file system.

Generally, backup software applications and data use the permissions assigned to the Backup Operators group.

Certificate Service DCOM Access   Members of the Certificate Service DCOM Access group can connect to certificate authority servers in the enterprise.

Cryptographic Operators   Members of the Cryptographic Operators group are authorized to perform cryptographic operations. *Cryptography* allows the use of codes to convert data, which then allows a specific recipient to read it using a key.

Guests   Typically, you use the Guests group to provide access to resources that generally do not require security. For example, if you have a network share that provides files that should be made available to all network users, you can assign permissions to allow members of the Guests group to access those files.

Print Operators   By default, members of the Print Operators group are given permissions to administer all of the printers within a domain. This includes common functions such as changing the priority of print jobs and deleting items from the print queue.

Replicator   The Replicator group allows files to be replicated among the computers in a domain. You can add accounts used for replication-related tasks to this group to provide those accounts with the permissions they need to keep files synchronized across multiple computers.

Server Operators   A common administrative task is managing server configuration. Members of the Server Operators group are granted the permissions they need to manage services, shares, and other system settings.

Users   The Users built-in domain local group is used to administer security for most network accounts. Usually, you don't give this group many permissions, and you use it to apply security settings for most employees within an organization.

Windows Server 2012 R2 also includes many different default groups, which you can find in the Users folder. As shown in Figure 7.4, these groups are of varying scopes, including domain local, global, and universal groups. You'll see the details of these groups in the next section.

FIGURE 7.4   Contents of the default Users folder

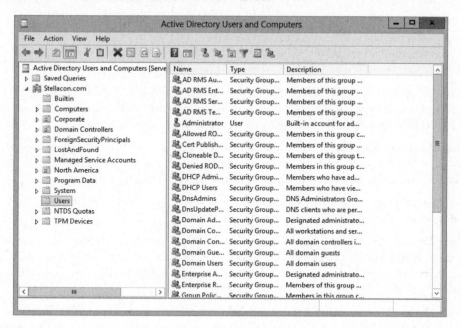

Three important user accounts are created during the promotion of a domain controller, described here:

Administrator Account   The Administrator account is assigned the password a system administrator provides during the promotion process, and it has full permissions to perform all actions within the domain.

Guest Account   The Guest account is disabled by default. The purpose of the *Guest account* is to provide anonymous access to users who do not have an individual logon and password to use within the domain. Although the Guest account might be useful in some situations, it is generally recommended that this account be disabled to increase security.

Krbtgt, or Key Distribution Center Service, Account   Only the operating system uses the *krbtgt*, or *Key Distribution Center Service, account* for Kerberos authentication while it is using DCPromo.exe. This account is disabled by default. Unlike other user accounts, the krbtgt account cannot be used to log on to the domain, and therefore it does not need to be enabled. Since only the operating system uses this account, you do not need to worry about hackers gaining access by using this account.

Predefined Global Groups

As mentioned earlier in this chapter, you use global groups to manage permissions at the domain level. Members of each of these groups can perform specific tasks related to managing Active Directory.

The following predefined global groups are installed in the Users folder:

Cert Publishers   Certificates are used to increase security by allowing for strong authentication methods. User accounts are placed within the *Cert Publishers group* if they must publish security certificates. Generally, Active Directory security services use these accounts.

Domain Computers   All of the computers that are members of the domain are generally members of the *Domain Computers group*. This includes any workstations or servers that have joined the domain, but it does not include the domain controllers.

Domain Admins   Members of the *Domain Admins group* have full permissions to manage all of the Active Directory objects for this domain. This is a powerful account; therefore, you should restrict its membership only to those users who require full permissions.

Domain Controllers   All of the domain controllers for a given domain are generally included within the *Domain Controllers group*.

Domain Guests   Generally, by default, members of the *Domain Guests group* are given minimal permissions with respect to resources. System administrators may place user accounts in this group if they require only basic access or temporary permissions within the domain.

Domain Users   The *Domain Users group* usually contains all of the user accounts for the given domain. This group is generally given basic permissions to resources that do not require higher levels of security. A common example is a public file share.

Enterprise Admins   Members of the *Enterprise Admins group* are given full permissions to perform actions within the entire forest. This includes functions such as managing trust relationships and adding new domains to trees and forests.

Group Policy Creator Owners   Members of the *Group Policy Creator Owners group* are able to create and modify Group Policy settings for objects within the domain. This allows them to enable security settings on OUs (and the objects they contain).

Schema Admins   Members of the *Schema Admins group* are given permissions to modify the Active Directory schema. As a member of Schema Admins, you can create additional fields of information for user accounts. This is a powerful function because any changes to the schema will be propagated to all the domains and domain controllers within an Active Directory forest. Furthermore, you cannot undo changes to the schema (although you can disable some).

In addition to these groups, you can create new ones for specific services and applications that are installed on the server. Specifically, services that run on domain controllers and servers will be created as security groups with domain local scope. For example, if a domain controller is running the DNS service, the DnsAdmins and DnsUpdateProxy groups become available. In addition, there are two read-only domain controller (RODC) local groups: the Allowed RODC Password Replication and the Denied RODC Password Replication groups. Similarly, if you install the DHCP service, it automatically creates the

DHCP Users and DHCP Administrators groups. The purpose of these groups depends on the functionality of the applications being installed.

Foreign Security Principals

In environments that have more than one domain, you may need to grant permissions to users who reside in multiple domains. Generally, you manage this using Active Directory trees and forests. However, in some cases, you may want to provide resources to users who belong to domains that are not part of the forest.

Active Directory uses the concept of *foreign security principals* to allow permissions to be assigned to users who are not part of an Active Directory forest. This process is automatic and does not require the intervention of system administrators. You can then add the foreign security principals to domain local groups for which, in turn, you can grant permissions for resources within the domain. You can view a list of foreign security principals by using the Active Directory Users and Computers tool. Figure 7.5 shows the contents of the ForeignSecurityPrincipals folder.

FIGURE 7.5 The ForeignSecurityPrincipals folder

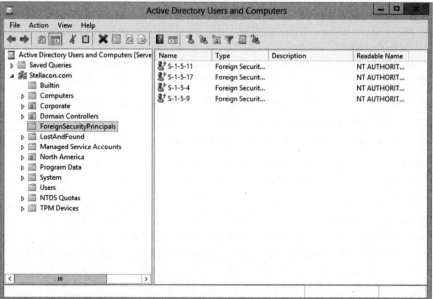

Managing Security and Permissions

Now that you understand the basic issues, terms, and Active Directory objects that pertain to security, it's time to look at how you can apply this information to secure your network resources. The general practice for managing security is to assign users to groups and then grant permissions and logon parameters to the groups so that they can access certain resources.

For management ease and to implement a hierarchical structure, you can place groups within OUs. You can also assign Group Policy settings to all of the objects contained within an OU. By using this method, you can combine the benefits of a hierarchical structure (through OUs) with the use of security principals. Figure 7.6 provides a diagram of this process.

FIGURE 7.6   An overview of security management

Users   Groups   Organizational Units (OUs)

The primary tool you use to manage security permissions for users, groups, and computers is the Active Directory Users and Computers tool. Using this tool, you can create and manage Active Directory objects and organize them based on your business needs. Common tasks for many system administrators might include the following:

- Resetting a user's password (for example, in cases where they forget their password)

- Creating new user accounts (when, for instance, a new employee joins the company)

- Modifying group memberships based on changes in job requirements and functions

- Disabling user accounts (when, for example, users will be out of the office for long periods of time and will not require network resource access)

Once you've properly grouped your users, you need to set the actual permissions that affect the objects within Active Directory. The actual permissions available vary based on the type of object. Table 7.1 provides an example of some of the permissions that you can apply to various Active Directory objects and an explanation of what each permission does.

TABLE 7.1   Permissions of Active Directory objects

Permission	Explanation
Control Access	Changes security permissions on the object
Create Child	Creates objects within an OU (such as other OUs)
Delete Child	Deletes child objects within an OU

Delete Tree	Deletes an OU and the objects within it
List Contents	Views objects within an OU
List Object	Views a list of the objects within an OU
Read	Views properties of an object (such as a username)
Write	Modifies properties of an object

Using ACLs and ACEs

Each object in Active Directory has an *access control list (ACL)*. The ACL is a list of user accounts and groups that are allowed to access the resource. For each ACL, there is an access control entry (ACE) that defines what a user or a group can actually do with the resource. Deny permissions are always listed first. This means that if users have Deny permissions through user or group membership, they will not be allowed to access the object, even if they have explicit Allow permissions through other user or group permissions. Figure 7.7 shows an ACL for the Sales OU.

FIGURE 7.7   The ACL for an OU named Sales

 The Security tab is enabled only if you selected the Advanced Features option from the View menu in the Active Directory Users and Computers tool.

Configuring User Account Control

One issue that many users have run into is as follows: When they log into their standard Windows user account and they need to make a change on their local machines or run a program that requires a higher level of security, they can't complete the task. This is where User Account Controls can help.

User Account Control (UAC) allows your domain users to log into their machines using their standard Windows user account and then execute processes that may require additional user group access.

Some applications may require additional security permissions to run successfully. These types of programs are normally referred to as *legacy applications*. Some applications, however, such as installing new software or making configuration changes, require more permissions than what is available to a standard user account. This is where UAC can help.

When an executable or program needs to function properly with more than just standard user rights, UAC can give that user's token additional user groups. This token allows the executable or program to function properly by giving the standard user account the rights to complete the task.

To configure the UAC, an administrator can go into the system's Control Panel and then User Accounts. Inside the User Accounts snap-in, choose Change User Account Control Settings.

Delegating Control of Users and Groups

A common administrative function related to the use of Active Directory involves managing users and groups. You can use OUs to group objects logically so that you can easily manage them. Once you have placed the appropriate Active Directory objects within OUs, you are ready to delegate control of these objects.

Delegation is the process by which a higher-level security administrator assigns permissions to other users. For example, if Admin A is a member of the Domain Admins group, they are able to delegate control of any OU within the domain to Admin B. You can access the Delegation Of Control Wizard through the Active Directory Users and Computers tool. You can use it to perform common delegation tasks quickly and easily. The wizard walks you through the steps of selecting the objects for which you want to perform delegation, what permission you want to allow, and which users will have those permissions.

Exercise 7.1 walks through the steps required to delegate control of OUs.

EXERCISE 7.1

Delegating Control of Active Directory Objects

1. Open the Active Directory Users and Computers tool.

2. Create a new user within the Engineering OU using the following information (use the default settings for any fields not specified):

First Name: **Robert**

Last Name: **Admin**

User Logon Name: **radmin**

Password: **P@ssw0rd**

3. Right-click the Sales OU and select Delegate Control. This starts the Delegation Of Control Wizard. Click Next.

4. To add users and groups to which you want to delegate control, click the Add button. In the Add dialog box, enter **Robert Admin** for the name of the user to add. Note that you can specify multiple users or groups using this option.

5. Click OK to add the account to the delegation list, which is shown in the Users Or Groups page. Click Next to continue.

6. On the Tasks To Delegate page, you must specify which actions you want to allow the selected user to perform within this OU. Select the Delegate The Following Common Tasks option and place a check mark next to the following options:

    Create, Delete, And Manage User Accounts

    Reset User Passwords And Force Password Change At Next Logon

    Read All User Information

    Create, Delete And Manage Groups

    Modify The Membership Of A Group

7. Click Next to continue. The wizard provides you with a summary of the selections that you have made on the Completing The Delegation Of Control Wizard page. To complete the process, click Finish to have the wizard commit the changes.

    Now when the user Robert Admin logs on (using *radmin* as his logon name), he will be able to perform common administrative functions for all the objects contained within the Sales OU.

8. When you have finished, close the Active Directory Users and Computers tool.

Understanding Dynamic Access Control

One of the advantages of Windows Server 2012 R2 is the ability to apply data governance to your file server. This will help control who has access to information and auditing. You get these advantages through the use of Dynamic Access Control (DAC). DAC allows you to identify data by using data classifications (both automatic and manual) and then to control access to these files based on these classifications.

DAC also gives administrators the ability to control file access by using a central access policy. This central access policy will also allow an administrator to set up audit access to files for reporting and forensic investigation.

DAC allows an administrator to set up Active Directory Rights Management Service (AD RMS) encryption for Microsoft Office documents. For example, you can set up encryption for any documents that contain financial information.

DAC gives an administrator the flexibility to configure file access and auditing to domain-based file servers. To do this, DAC controls claims in the authentication token, resource properties, and conditional expressions within permission and auditing entries.

Administrators have the ability to give users access to files and folders based on Active Directory attributes. For example, a user named Dana is given access to the file server share because in the user's Active Directory (department attribute) properties, the value contains the value Sales.

For DAC to function properly, an administrator must enable Windows 8 computers and Windows Server 2012/2012 R2 file servers to support claims and compound authentication.

Using Group Policy for Security

Through the use of Group Policy settings, system administrators can assign thousands of different settings and options for users, groups, and OUs. Specifically, in relation to security, you can use many different options to control how important features, such as password policies, user rights, and account lockout settings, can be configured.

The general process for making these settings is to create a Group Policy object (GPO) with the settings that you want and then link it to an OU or other Active Directory object.

Table 7.2 lists many Group Policy settings, which are relevant to creating a secure Active Directory environment. Note that this list is not comprehensive—many other options are available through Windows Server 2012 R2 administrative tools.

TABLE 7.2 Group Policy settings used for security purposes

Setting section	Setting name	Purpose
Account Policies ➢ Password Policy	Enforce Password History	Specifies how many passwords will be remembered. This option prevents users from reusing the same passwords whenever they're changed.
Account Policies ➢ Password Policy	Minimum Password Length	Prevents users from using short, weak passwords by specifying the minimum number of characters that the password must include.

Account Policies ➢ Account Lockout Policy	Account Lockout Threshold	Specifies how many bad password attempts can be entered before the account gets locked out.
Account Policies ➢ Account Lockout Policy	Account Lockout Duration	Specifies how long an account will remain locked out after too many bad password attempts have been entered. By setting this option to a reasonable value (such as 30 minutes), you can reduce administrative overhead while still maintaining fairly strong security.
Account Policies ➢ Account Lockout Policy	Reset Account Lockout Counter After	Specifies how long the Account Lockout Threshold counter will hold failed logon attempts before resetting to 0.
Local Policies ➢ Security Options	Accounts: Rename Administrator Account	Often, when trying to gain unauthorized access to a computer, individuals attempt to guess the administrator password. One method for increasing security is to rename this account so that no password allows entry using this logon.
Local Policies ➢ Security Options	Domain Controller: Allow Server Operators To Schedule Tasks	This option specifies whether members of the built-in Server Operators group are allowed to schedule tasks on the server.
Local Policies ➢ Security Options	Interactive Logon: Do Not Display Last User Name	Increases security by not displaying the name of the last user who logged onto the system.
Local Policies ➢ Security Options	Shutdown: Allow System To Be Shut Down Without Having To Log On	Allows system administrators to perform remote shutdown operations without logging on to the server.

Implementing an Audit Policy

One of the most important aspects of controlling security in networked environments is ensuring that only authorized users are able to access specific resources. Although system administrators often spend much time managing security permissions, it is almost always possible for a security problem to occur.

Sometimes, the best way to find possible security breaches is actually to record the actions that specific users take. Then, in the case of a security breach (the unauthorized shutdown of a server, for example), system administrators can examine the log to find the cause of the problem.

The Windows Server 2012 R2 operating system and Active Directory offer you the ability to audit a wide range of actions. In the following sections, you'll see how to implement auditing for Active Directory.

Overview of Auditing

The act of *auditing* relates to recording specific actions. From a security standpoint, auditing is used to detect any possible misuse of network resources. Although auditing does not necessarily prevent resources from being misused, it does help determine when security violations have occurred (or were attempted). Furthermore, just the fact that others know that you have implemented auditing may prevent them from attempting to circumvent security.

You need to complete several steps in order to implement auditing using Windows Server 2012 R2:

1. Configure the size and storage settings for the audit logs.

2. Enable categories of events to audit.

3. Specify which objects and actions should be recorded in the audit log.

Note that there are trade-offs to implementing auditing. First, recording auditing information can consume system resources. This can decrease overall system performance and use up valuable disk space. Second, auditing many events can make the audit log impractical to view. If too much detail is provided, system administrators are unlikely to scrutinize all of the recorded events. For these reasons, you should always be sure to find a balance between the level of auditing details provided and the performance-management implications of these settings.

Implementing Auditing

Auditing is not an all-or-none type of process. As is the case with security in general, system administrators must choose specifically which objects and actions they want to audit.

The main categories for auditing include the following:

- Audit account logon events
- Audit account management
- Audit directory service access
- Audit logon events
- Audit object access
- Audit policy change
- Audit privilege use
- Audit process tracking
- Audit system events

In this list of categories, four of the categories are related to Active Directory. Let's discuss these auditing categories in a bit more detail.

Audit Account Logon Events   You enable this auditing event if you want to audit when a user authenticates with a domain controller and logs onto the domain. This event is logged in the security log on the domain controller.

Audit Account Management   This auditing event is used when you want to watch what changes are being made to Active Directory accounts. For example, when another administrator creates or deletes a user account, it would be an audited event.

Audit Directory Service Access   This auditing event occurs whenever a user or administrator accesses Active Directory objects. Let's say that an administrator opens Active Directory and clicks a user account; even if nothing is changed on that account, an event is logged.

Audit Logon Events   Account logon events are created for domain account activity. For example, you have a user who logs on to a server so that they can access files; the act of logging onto the server creates this audit event.

Audit Object Access   Audit object access allows you to audit objects within your network such as folders, files, and printers. If you suspect someone is trying to hack into an object (for example, the finance folder), this is the type of auditing that you would use. You still would need to enable auditing on the actual object (for example, the finance folder).

Audit Policy Change   Audit policy change allows you to audit changes to user rights assignment policies, audit policies, or trust policies. This auditing allows you to see whether anyone changes any of the other audit policies.

Audit Privilege Use   Setting the audit privilege use allows an administrator to audit each instance of a user exercising a user right. For example, if a user changes the system time on a machine, this is a user right. Logging on locally is another common user right.

To audit access to objects stored within Active Directory, you must enable the Audit Directory Service Access option. Then you must specify which objects and actions should be tracked.

Exercise 7.2 walks through the steps you must take to implement auditing of Active Directory objects on domain controllers.

EXERCISE 7.2

Enabling Auditing of Active Directory Objects

1. Open the Local Security Policy tool (located in the Administrative Tools program group).

2. Expand Local Policies ➢ Audit Policy.

3. Double-click the setting for Audit Directory Service Access.

4. In the Audit Directory Service Access Properties dialog box, place check marks next to Success and Failure. Click OK to save the settings.

5. Close the Local Security Policy tool.

Using the *Auditpol.exe* Command

There may be a time when you need to look at your actual auditing policies set on a user or a system. This is where an administrator can use the Auditpol.exe command. *Auditpol* allows administrators the ability not only to view an audit policy but also to set, configure, modify, restore, and even remove an audit policy. Auditpol is a command-line utility, and there are multiple switches that can be used with Auditpol. The following is the syntax used with Auditpol; Table 7.3 describes some of the switches:

```
Auditpol command [<sub-command><options>]
```

Here's an example:

```
Auditpol /get /user:wpanek /category:"Detailed Tracking" /r
```

TABLE 7.3 Auditpol commands

Command	Description
/backup	Allows an administrator to save the audit policy to a file
/clear	Allows an administrator to clear an audit policy
/get	Gives administrators the ability to view the current audit policy
/list	Allows you to view selectable policy elements
/remove	Removes all per-user audit policy settings and disables all system audit policy settings
/restore	Allows an administrator to restore an audit policy from a file that was previously created by using auditpol /backup
/set	Gives an administrator the ability to set an audit policy
/?	Displays help

Features of Windows Server 2012 R2 Auditing

Microsoft continues to increase the level of detail in the security auditing logs. Microsoft has also simplified the deployment and management of auditing policies. The following list includes some of the features:

Global Object Access Auditing Administrators using Windows Server 2012 R2 and Windows 8 now have the ability to define computer-wide system access control lists (SACLs). Administrators can define SACLs for either the file system or the registry. After the specified SACL is defined, the SACL is then applied automatically to every object of that type. This can be helpful to administrators for verifying that all critical files, folders, and registry settings on a computer are protected. This is also helpful for identifying when an issue occurs with a system resource.

"Reason For Access" Reporting   When an administrator is performing auditing in Windows Server 2012 R2 and Windows 8, they can now see the reason why an operation was successful or unsuccessful. Previously, they lacked the ability to see the reason why an operation succeeded or failed.

Advanced Audit Policy Settings   In Windows Server 2012 R2, there are many new Advanced Audit Policy settings that can be used in place of the nine basic auditing settings. These advanced audit settings also help eliminate the unnecessary auditing activities that can make audit logs difficult to manage and decipher.

Expression-Based Audit Policies   Administrators have the ability, because of Dynamic Access Control, to create targeted audit policies by using expressions based on user, computer, and resource claims. For example, an administrator has the ability to create an audit policy that tracks all Read and Write operations for files that are considered high-business impact. Expression-based audit policies can be directly created on a file or folder or created through the use of a Group Policy.

Removable Storage Device Auditing   Administrators have the ability to monitor attempts to use a removable storage device on your network. If an administrator decides to implement this policy, an audit event is created every time one of your users attempts to copy, move, or save a network resource onto a removable storage device.

Configuring Windows Firewall Options

Another security aspect to look into is Windows Firewall. Before I can start talking about firewall options, you must first understand what a firewall does. A *firewall* is a software or hardware device that checks the information that is received from an outside (Internet) or external network and uses that information to determine whether the packet should be accepted or declined.

Depending on the firewall, you have the ability to check all potential remote users against Active Directory to verify that the remote user has an authorized domain account. This process is called *Active Directory account integration*.

Microsoft Windows Server 2012 R2 has a built-in firewall. The following are some of the configuration options included in the Windows Firewall Settings dialog box:

Domain Profile Tab   On the Domain Profile tab, you have the ability to turn the firewall on or off by using the Firewall State drop-down menu. When setting the Firewall State option on this tab, it's for turning the firewall on or off for the domain only. When turning the firewall on, you also have the ability to block inbound and outbound connections (see Figure 7.8). Administrators also have the ability to control the Windows Firewall behavior along with setting up logging.

FIGURE 7.8   Domain Profile tab of Windows Firewall Settings

Private Profile Tab   On the Private Profile tab, you have the ability to turn the firewall on or off by using the Firewall State drop-down menu. When setting the Firewall State in this tab, it's for turning the firewall on or off for the Private Profile only. When turning the firewall on, you also have the ability to block inbound and outbound connections (see Figure 7.9). Administrators also have the ability to control the Windows Firewall Private Profile behavior along with setting up logging.

FIGURE 7.9   Private Profile tab of Windows Firewall Settings

Public Profile   On the Public Profile tab, you have the ability to turn the firewall on or off by using the Firewall State drop-down menu. When setting the Firewall State in this tab, it's for turning the firewall on or off for the Public Profile only. When turning the firewall on, you also have the ability to block inbound and outbound connections (see Figure 7.10). Administrators also have the ability to control the Windows Firewall Public Profile behavior along with setting up logging.

FIGURE 7.10   Public Profile tab of Windows Firewall

IPsec Settings Tab   The IPsec Setting tab allows you to set up the IPsec defaults, IPsec exemptions, and IPsec tunnel authorization. The IPsec defaults button allows you to specify settings used by IPsec to establish secured connections. The IPsec exemptions allow you to set up ICMP exemptions from IPsec. Finally, you can set up IPsec tunnel authorization, which allows you to specify the users and computers that are authorized to establish an IPsec tunnel (see Figure 7.11).

Windows Server 2012 R2 takes firewalls a step further than just the normal firewall settings in Control Panel. An MMC snap-in called *Windows Firewall with Advanced Security* (see Figure 7.12) can block all incoming and outgoing connections based on its configuration.

One of the major advantages to using the Windows Firewall with Advanced Security snap-in is the ability to set firewall configurations on remote computers using group policies. Another advantage to using this MMC is the ability to set up firewalls using IPsec security. Windows Firewall with Advanced Security snap-in allows an administrator to set more in-depth rules for Microsoft Active Directory users and groups, source and destination Internet Protocol (IP) addresses, IP port numbers, ICMP settings, IPsec settings, specific types of interfaces, and services.

FIGURE 7.11   IPsec Settings tab of Windows Firewall Settings

FIGURE 7.12   Windows Firewall with Advanced Security snap-in

You can configure more advanced settings by configuring Windows Firewall with Advanced Security. To access Windows Firewall with Advanced Security, press the Windows key and choose Control Panel ➢ Large Icons View ➢ Windows Firewall, and click the Advanced Settings link.

The scope pane to the left shows that you can set up specific inbound and outbound rules, connection security rules, and monitoring rules. The central area shows an overview of the firewall's status as well as the current profile settings. Let's take a look at these in more detail.

Inbound and Outbound Rules

Inbound and outbound rules consist of many preconfigured rules that can be enabled or disabled. Obviously, inbound rules (see Figure 7.13) monitor inbound traffic, and outbound rules monitor outbound traffic. By default, many are disabled. Double-clicking a rule will bring up its Properties dialog box, as shown in Figure 7.14.

You can filter the rules to make them easier to view. Filtering can be performed based on the profile the rule affects or whether the rule is enabled or disabled or based on the rule group.

If you can't find a rule that is appropriate to your needs, you can create a new rule by right-clicking Inbound Rules or Outbound Rules in the scope pane and then selecting New Rule. The New Inbound (or Outbound) Rule Wizard will launch, and you will be asked whether you want to create a rule based on a particular program, protocol or port, predefined category, or custom settings.

FIGURE 7.13   Inbound rules

FIGURE 7.14 An inbound rule's Properties dialog box for WSUS

When setting up rules, you can also set up firewall exceptions. These exceptions allow you to work around a particular rule that you may be setting up. Firewall exceptions can be handy when an authenticated user or service needs to get around a firewall setting. These exceptions can be also set under the advanced firewall settings under the Connection Security Rules link.

Exercise 7.3 will walk you through the steps needed to create a new inbound rule that will allow only encrypted TCP traffic. In this exercise, you will have the ability to create a custom rule and then specify which authorized users and computers can connect using this rule.

EXERCISE 7.3

Configuring Windows Firewall

1. Press the Windows key and select Control Panel ➢ Large Icon View ➢ Windows Firewall.

2. Click Advanced Settings on the left side.

3. Right-click Inbound Rules and select New Rule.

4. Choose a rule type. For this exercise, choose Custom so that you can see all of the options available to you; then click Next.

5. Choose the programs or services that are affected by this rule. For this exercise, choose All Programs; then click Next.

6. Choose the protocol type as well as the local and remote port numbers that are affected by this rule. For this exercise, choose TCP and make sure All Ports is selected for both Local Port and Remote Port. Click Next to continue.

7. Choose the local and remote IP addresses that are affected by this rule. Choose Any IP Address for both local and remote; then click Next.

8. Specify whether this rule will allow the connection, allow the connection only if it is secure, or block the connection. Select the option Allow The Connection If It Is Secure; then click Next.

9. Specify whether connections should be allowed only from certain users. You can experiment with these options if you want. Then click Next to continue.

10. Specify whether connections should be allowed only from certain computers. Again, you can experiment with these options if you want. Then click Next to continue.

11. Choose those profiles that will be affected by this rule. Select one or more profiles; then click Next to continue.

12. Give your profile a name and description; then click Finish. Your custom rule will appear in the list of Inbound Rules, and the rule will be enabled.

13. Double-click your newly created rule. Notice that you can change the options you previously configured.

14. Disable the rule by right-clicking the rule and choosing Disable Rule.

15. Close Windows Firewall.

Now let's take a look at setting up Connection Security Rules through Windows Firewall with Advanced Security.

Configuring Windows Firewall with a GPO

If you wanted to configure Windows Firewall on all of your client machines, you have two options. You can either configure each machine manually or set up a GPO to configure the Windows Firewall. To set up the Windows Firewall using a GPO, configure the Computer section ➢ Windows Settings ➢ Security ➢ Windows Firewall With Advanced Security.

One of the advantages of using a GPO when configuring the Windows firewall is that you can configure multiple profiles and multiple firewall settings using the Group Policy.

Another even bigger advantage is being able to configure thousands of computers by setting just one GPO. It saves an IT administrator from going around the company from machine to machine to set up the firewall.

Import/Export Policies

One advantage of configuring Windows Firewall is the ability to export and import policy settings. For example, I set up a policy for 35 machines; I created the policy on one of the 35 machines and then exported the policy. I then imported the policy to the other

34 machines so that I did not have to re-create the policy over and over again. To export a policy, right-click Windows Firewall With Advanced Security and choose Export Policy. Choose Import Policy on the other machines to import the policy.

IPsec Policy Settings in Windows Firewall

When configuring options for Windows Firewall with Advanced Security, you have the ability to configure some IPsec policies. The three options are as follows:

IPsec Defaults   Specify settings used by IPsec to establish secure connections.

IPsec Exemptions   Exempting ICMP from all IPsec requirements can simplify troubleshooting of network connectivity issues.

IPsec Tunnel Authorization   Specify the computers or users authorized to establish IPsec tunnel connections to this computer.

Monitoring

The Monitoring section shows detailed information about the firewall configurations for the Domain Profile, Private Profile, and Public Profile settings. These network location profiles determine which settings are enforced for private networks, public networks, and networks connected to a domain.

 Real World Scenario

Firewalls

When I'm consulting, it always makes me laugh when I see small to midsize companies using Microsoft Windows Firewall and no other protection.

Microsoft Windows Firewall should be your *last* line of defense, not your only one. You need to make sure that you have good hardware firewalls that separate your network from the world.

Also watch Windows Firewall when it comes to printing. I have run into many situations where a printer that needs to talk to the operating system has issues when Windows Firewall is enabled. If this happens, make sure that the printer is allowed in the Allowed Programs section.

Summary

In this chapter, you examined server security and saw why it's one of the most important aspects of Windows Server 2012 R2. As a system administrator, Windows security is something that every administrator should be using but many don't know how it works properly.

I explained how to set up groups and group security as well as how to set up the permissions for those groups. I also covered auditing. I showed you how to set up and monitor auditing to see who has successfully, or unsuccessfully, accessed resources, machines, Active Directory, and all aspects of network security.

I finished the chapter by looking into Windows Firewall. I showed you how to configure the firewall and add exclusions and rules. I also showed you how to view and monitor the firewall results.

Exam Essentials

Understand group types and group scope.   The two major types of groups are security and distribution groups, and they have different purposes. Groups can be local, global, or universal. Domain local groups are used to assign permissions to local resources, such as files and printers. The scope of global groups is limited to a single domain. Universal groups can contain users from any domains within an Active Directory forest.

Understand the purpose and permissions of built-in groups.   The Active Directory environment includes several built-in local and global groups that are designed to simplify common system administration tasks. For instance, members of the Administrators group are given full permissions to perform any functions within the Active Directory domain and on the local computer.

Understand how to use Group Policy to manage security-related policies.   Through the use of Group Policy settings, you can configure password and account-related options. You can also specify to which users, groups, and OUs many of the settings apply.

Understand how to use auditing.   Through the use of auditing, an administrator can see who has been successfully and unsuccessfully accessing resources and Active Directory.

Understand Windows Firewall.   Windows Server 2012 R2 includes Windows Firewall. Windows Firewall gives you secure access to a machine by allowing or denying which applications or users can access a system.

Review Questions

1. You are the network administrator for your organization. A new company policy has been released wherein if a user enters their password incorrectly three times within five minutes, they are locked out for 30 minutes. What three actions do you need to set to comply with this policy? (Choose all that apply.)

   A. Set Account Lockout Duration to five minutes.

   B. Set Account Lockout Duration to 30 minutes.

   C. Set the Account Lockout Threshold setting to three invalid logon attempts.

   D. Set the Account Lockout Threshold setting to 30 minutes.

   E. Set the Reset Account Lockout Counter setting to five minutes.

   F. Set the Reset Account Lockout Counter setting to three times.

2. You create a GPO and link it to the Sales OU. You want to monitor users in the Sales OU who connect to the file server. What type of auditing do you enable?

   A. Audit Object Access

   B. Audit Logon Events

   C. Audit System Events

   D. Audit Process Tracking

3. Alexis is a system administrator for an Active Directory environment that contains four domains. Recently, several managers have reported suspicions about user activities and have asked her to increase security in the environment. Specifically, the requirements are as follows:

   - Audit changes to User objects that are contained within a specific OU.

   - Allow a special user account called Audit to view and modify all security-related information about objects in that OU.

   Which of the following steps should Alexis take to meet these requirements? (Choose all that apply.)

   A. Convert all volumes on which Active Directory information resides to NTFS.

   B. Enable auditing with the Active Directory Users and Computers tool.

   C. Create a new Active Directory domain and create restrictive permissions for the suspected users within this domain.

   D. Reconfigure trust settings using the Active Directory Domains and Trusts tool.

   E. Specify auditing options for the OU using the Active Directory Users and Computers tool.

   F. Use the Delegation of Control Wizard to grant appropriate permissions to view and modify objects within the OU to the Audit user account.

4. Crystal is a system administrator for an Active Directory environment that is running in Native mode. Recently, several managers have reported suspicions about user activities and have asked her to increase security in the environment. Specifically, the requirements are as follows:

- The accessing of certain sensitive files must be logged.

- Modifications to certain sensitive files must be logged.

- System administrators must be able to provide information about which users accessed sensitive files and when they were accessed.

- All logon attempts for specific shared machines must be recorded.

Which of the following steps should Crystal take to meet these requirements? (Choose all that apply.)

A. Enable auditing with the Computer Management tool.

B. Enable auditing with the Active Directory Users and Computers tool.

C. Enable auditing with the Active Directory Domains and Trusts tool.

D. Enable auditing with the Event Viewer tool.

E. View the audit log using the Event Viewer tool.

F. View auditing information using the Computer Management tool.

G. Enable failure and success auditing settings for specific files stored on NTFS volumes.

H. Enable failure and success auditing settings for logon events on specific computer accounts.

5. You create a GPO and link it to the Sales OU. You want to monitor users in the Sales OU who connect to the file server. What type of auditing do you enable?

A. Audit Object Access

B. Audit Logon Events

C. Audit System Events

D. Audit Process Tracking

Chapter

8

Configure TCP/IP

THE FOLLOWING 70-410 EXAM OBJECTIVES ARE COVERED IN THIS CHAPTER:

✓ **Configure IPv4 and IPv6 addressing**

- ▪ Configure IP address options
- ▪ Configure IPv4 or IPv6 subnetting
- ▪ Configure supernetting
- ▪ Configure interoperability between IPv4 and IPv6
- ▪ Configure ISATAP
- ▪ Configure Teredo

In this chapter, I will discuss the most important protocol used in a Microsoft Windows Server 2012 R2 network: *Transmission Control Protocol/Internet Protocol (TCP/IP)*.

TCP/IP is actually two sets of protocols bundled together: the Transmission Control Protocol (TCP) and the Internet Protocol (IP). TCP/IP is a suite of protocols developed by the U.S. Department of Defense's Advanced Research Projects Agency in 1969.

This chapter is divided into two main topics: First I'll talk about TCP/IP version 4, and then I'll discuss TCP/IP version 6. TCP/IP version 4 is still used in Windows Server 2012 R2, and it was the primary version of TCP/IP in all previous versions of Windows. However, TCP/IP version 6 is the new release of TCP/IP, and it has been incorporated into Windows Server 2012 R2.

Understanding TCP/IP

I mentioned that TCP/IP is actually two sets of protocols bundled together: TCP and IP. These protocols sit on a four-layer TCP/IP model.

Details of the TCP/IP Model

The four layers of the TCP/IP model are as follows (see Figure 8.1):

Application Layer The *Application layer* is where the applications that use the protocol stack reside. These applications include File Transfer Protocol (FTP), Trivial File Transfer Protocol (TFTP), Simple Mail Transfer Protocol (SMTP), and Hypertext Transfer Protocol (HTTP).

Transport Layer The *Transport layer* is where the two Transport layer protocols reside. These are TCP and the User Datagram Protocol (UDP). TCP is a connection-oriented protocol, and delivery is guaranteed. UDP is a connectionless protocol. This means that UDP does its best job to deliver the message, but there is no guarantee.

Internet Layer The *Internet layer* is where IP resides. *IP is a connectionless protocol that relies on the upper layer (Transport layer) for guaranteeing delivery. *Address Resolution Protocol (ARP)* also resides on this layer. ARP turns an IP address into a Media Access Control (MAC) address. All upper and lower layers travel through the IP protocol.

Link Layer The data link protocols like Ethernet and Token Ring reside in the *Link layer*. This layer is also referred to as the *Network Access layer*.

FIGURE 8.1   TCP/IP model

How TCP/IP Layers Communicate

When an application like FTP is called upon, the application moves down the layers and TCP is retrieved. TCP then connects itself to the IP protocol and gets released onto the network through the Link layer (see Figure 8.2). This is a connection-oriented protocol because TCP is the protocol that guarantees delivery.

When an application like TFTP gets called, the application moves down the layers and UDP is retrieved. UDP then connects itself to the IP protocol and gets released onto the network through the Link layer. This is a connectionless protocol because UDP does not have guaranteed delivery.

Understanding Port Numbers

TCP and UDP rely on port numbers assigned by the *Internet Assigned Numbers Authority (IANA)* to forward packets to the appropriate application process. Port numbers are 16-bit integers that are part of a message header. They identify the application software process with which the packet should be associated. For example, let's say that a client has a copy of Internet Explorer and a copy of Mail open at the same time. Both applications are sending TCP requests across the Internet to retrieve web pages and email, respectively. How does the computer know which return packets to forward to Internet Explorer and which packets to forward to Mail?

FIGURE 8.2 TCP/IP process

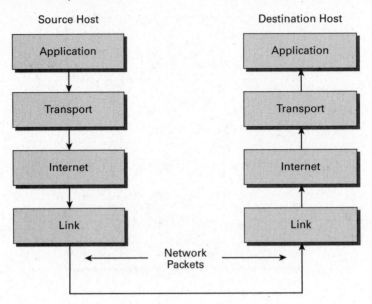

When making a connection, the client chooses a source port for the communication that is usually in the range 1024–65535 (or sometimes in the range 1–65535). This source port then communicates with a destination port of 80 or 110 on the server side. Every packet destined for Internet Explorer has a source port number of 80 in the header, and every packet destined for Mail has a source port number of 110 in the header.

Table 8.1 describes the most common port numbers (you might need to know these for the exam). You can visit www.iana.org to get the most current and complete list of port numbers. It's good to become familiar with specific port numbers because it's a benefit to be able to determine from memory the ports that, for example, allow or block specific protocols in a firewall. Allowing only port 80, for instance, does not ensure that all web traffic will be allowed. You must also allow port 443 for certain secure web traffic.

Simply because a port is "well known" doesn't mean that a given service must run on it. It's technically valid to run any service on any port, but doing so is usually a bad idea. For example, if you chose to run your web server on TCP port 25, clients would need to type www.example.com:25 to reach your website from most browsers.

TABLE 8.1 Common port numbers

Port number	Description
20	FTP data
21	FTP control
23	Telnet
25	Simple Mail Transfer Protocol (SMTP)
53	Domain Name System (DNS)
80	Hypertext Transfer Protocol (HTTP), Web
88	Kerberos
110	Post Office Protocol v3 (POP3)
443	Secure HTTP (HTTPS)

Understanding IP Addressing

Understanding IP addressing is critical to understanding how IP works. An IP address is a numeric identifier assigned to each device on an IP network. This type of address is a logical software address that designates the device's location on the network. It isn't the physical hardware address hard-coded in the device's network interface card.

In the following sections, you will see how IP addresses are used to identify uniquely every machine on the network (MAC address).

The Hierarchical IP Addressing Scheme

An IP address consists of 32 bits of information. These bits are divided into four sections (sometimes called *octets* or *quads*) containing 1 byte (8 bits) each. There are three common methods for specifying an IP address:

- Dotted-decimal, as in 130.57.30.56
- Binary, as in 10000010.00111001.00011110.00111000
- Hexadecimal, as in 82 39 1E 38

All of these examples represent the same IP address.

The 32-bit IP address is a structured, or hierarchical, address as opposed to a flat, or nonhierarchical, address. Although IP could have used either *flat addressing* or *hierarchical addressing*, its designers elected to use the latter for a very good reason, as you will now see.

 Real World Scenario

Why Hierarchical Addressing Is Used

What's the difference between flat and hierarchical addressing? A good example of a flat addressing scheme is a U.S. state driver's license number. There's no partitioning to it; the range of legal numbers isn't broken up in any meaningful way (say, by county of residence or date of issue). If this method had been used for IP addressing, every machine on the Internet would have needed a totally unique address, just as each driver's license number in a particular state is unique.

The good news about flat addressing is that it can handle a large number of addresses in 32 bits of data, namely, 4.3 billion. A 32-bit address space with two possible values for each position—either 0 (zero) or 1 (one)—gives you 2^{32} values, which equals approximately 4.3 billion.

The bad news—and the reason flat addressing isn't used in IP—relates to routing. If every address were totally unique, every router on the Internet would need to store the address of every other machine on the Internet. It would be fair to say that this would make efficient routing impossible, even if only a fraction of the possible addresses were used.

The solution to this dilemma is to use a hierarchical addressing scheme that breaks the address space into ordered chunks. Telephone numbers are a great example of this type of addressing. The first section of a U.S. telephone number, the area code, designates a very large area. The area code is followed by the prefix, which narrows the scope to a local calling area. The final segment, the customer number, zooms in on the specific connection. By looking at a number such as 603-766-xxxx, you can quickly determine that the number is located in the southern part of New Hampshire (area code 603) in the Portsmouth area (the 766 exchange).

IP Address Structure

IP addressing works the same way. Instead of the entire 32 bits being treated as a unique identifier, one part of the IP address is designated as the network address (or network ID) and the other part as a node address (or host ID), giving it a layered, hierarchical structure. Together, the IP address, the network address, and the node address uniquely identify a device within an IP network.

The network address—the first two sets of numbers in an IP address—uniquely identifies each network. Every machine on the same network shares that network address as part of its IP address, just as the address of every house on a street shares the same street name. In the IP address 130.57.30.56, for example, 130.57 is the network address.

The node address—the second two sets of numbers—is assigned to, and uniquely identifies, each machine in a network, just as each house on the same street has a different house number. This part of the address must be unique because it identifies a particular machine—an individual, as opposed to a network. This number can also be referred to as a *host address*. In the sample IP address 130.57.30.56, the node address is .30.56.

Understanding Network Classes

The designers of the Internet decided to create classes of networks based on network size. For the small number of networks possessing a very large number of nodes, they created the Class A network. At the other extreme is the Class C network, reserved for the numerous networks with small numbers of nodes. The class of networks in between the very large and very small ones is predictably called the Class B network.

The default subdivision of an IP address into a network and node address is determined by the class designation of your network. Table 8.2 summarizes the three classes of networks, which will be described in more detail in the following sections.

TABLE 8.2 Network address classes

Class	Mask bits	Leading bit pattern	Decimal range of first octet of IP address	Assignable networks	Maximum nodes per network
A	8	0	1–126	126	16,777,214
B	16	10	128–191	16,384	65,534
C	24	110	192–223	2,097,152	254

Classless Inter-Domain Routing (CIDR), explained in detail later in this chapter, has effectively done away with these class designations. You will still hear and should still know the meaning behind the class designations of addresses because they are important to understanding IP addressing. However, when you're working with IP addressing in practice, CIDR is more important to know.

To ensure efficient routing, Internet designers defined a mandate for the leading bits section of the address for each different network class. For example, because a router knows that a Class A network address always starts with a 0, it can quickly apply the default mask, if necessary, after reading only the first bit of the address. Table 8.2 illustrates how the leading bits of a network address are defined. When considering the subnet masking between network and host addresses, the number of bits to mask is important. For example, in a Class A network, 8 bits are masked, making the default subnet mask 255.0.0.0; in a Class C, 24 bits are masked, making the default subnet mask 255.255.255.0.

Some IP addresses are reserved for special purposes and shouldn't be assigned to nodes. Table 8.3 describes some of the reserved IP addresses. See RFC 3330 for others.

TABLE 8.3   Special network addresses

Address	Function
Entire IP address set to all 0s	Depending on the mask, this network (that is, the network or subnet of which you are currently a part) or this host on this network.
A routing table entry of all 0s with a mask of all 0s	Used as the default gateway entry. Any destination address masked by all 0s produces a match for the all 0s reference address. Because the mask has no 1s, this is the least desirable entry, but it will be used when no other match exists.
Network address 127	Reserved for loopback tests. Designates the local node, and it allows that node to send a test packet to itself without generating network traffic.
Node address of all 0s	Used when referencing a network without referring to any specific nodes on that network. Usually used in routing tables.
Node address of all 1s	Broadcast address for all nodes on the specified network, also known as a *directed broadcast*. For example, 128.2.255.255 means all nodes on the Class B network 128.2. Routing this broadcast is configurable on certain routers.
169.254.0.0 with a mask of 255.255.0.0	The "link-local" block used for autoconfiguration and communication between devices on a single link. Communication cannot occur across routers. Microsoft uses this block for Automatic Private IP Addressing (APIPA).
Entire IP address set to all 1s (same as 255.255.255.255)	Broadcast to all nodes on the current network; sometimes called a *limited broadcast* or an *all-1s broadcast*. This broadcast is not routable.
10.0.0.0/8 172.16.0.0 to 172.31.255.255 192.168.0.0/16	The private-use blocks for Classes A, B, and C. As noted in RFC 1918, the addresses in these blocks must never be allowed into the Internet, making them acceptable for simultaneous use behind NAT servers and non-Internet-connected IP networks.

In the following sections, you will look at the three network types.

Class A Networks

In a Class A network, the first byte is the network address, and the three remaining bytes are used for the node addresses. The Class A format is Network.Node.Node.Node.

For example, in the IP address 49.22.102.70, 49 is the network address, and 22.102.70 is the node address. Every machine on this particular network would have the distinctive network address of 49. Within that network, however, you could have a large number of machines.

There are 126 possible Class A network addresses. Why? The length of a Class A network address is 1 byte, and the first bit of that byte is reserved, so 7 bits in the first byte remain available for manipulation. This means that the maximum number of Class A networks is 128. (Each of the 7 bit positions that can be manipulated can be either a 0 or a 1, and this gives you a total of 2^7 positions, or 128.) But to complicate things further, it was also decided that the network address of all 0s (0000 0000) would be reserved. This means that the actual number of usable Class A network addresses is 128 minus 1, or 127. Also, 127 is a reserved number (a network address of 0 followed by all 1s [0111 1111], so you actually start with 128 addresses minus the 2 reserved, and you're left with 126 possible Class A network addresses.

Each Class A network has 3 bytes (24 bit positions) for the node address of a machine, which means that there are 2^{24}, or 16,777,216, unique combinations. Because addresses with the two patterns of all 0s and all 1s in the node bits are reserved, the actual maximum usable number of nodes for a Class A network is 2^{24} minus 2, which equals 16,777,214.

Class B Networks

In a Class B network, the first 2 bytes are assigned to the network address, and the remaining 2 bytes are used for node addresses. The format is Network.Network.Node. Node.

For example, in the IP address 130.57.30.56, the network address is 130.57, and the node address is 30.56.

The network address is 2 bytes, so there would be 2^{16} unique combinations. But the Internet designers decided that all Class B networks should start with the binary digits 10. This leaves 14 bit positions to manipulate; therefore, there are 16,384 (or 2^{14}) unique Class B networks.

This gives you an easy way to recognize Class B addresses. If the first 2 bits of the first byte can be only 10, that gives you a decimal range from 128 up to 191 in the first octet of the IP address. Remember that you can always easily recognize a Class B network by looking at its first byte, even though there are 16,384 different Class B networks. If the first octet in the address falls between 128 and 191, it is a Class B network, regardless of the value of the second octet.

A Class B network has 2 bytes to use for node addresses. This is 2^{16} minus the two patterns in the reserved-exclusive club (all 0s and all 1s in the node bits) for a total of 65,534 possible node addresses for each Class B network.

Class C Networks

The first 3 bytes of a Class C network are dedicated to the network portion of the address, with only 1 byte remaining for the node address. The format is Network.Network.Network.Node.

In the example IP address 198.21.74.102, the network address is 198.21.74, and the node address is 102.

In a Class C network, the first three bit positions are always binary 110. Three bytes, or 24 bits, minus 3 reserved positions leaves 21 positions. There are therefore 2^{21} (or 2,097,152) possible Class C networks.

The lead bit pattern of 110 equates to decimal 192 and runs through 223. Remembering our handy easy-recognition method, this means you can always spot a Class C address if the first byte is in the range 192–223, regardless of the values of the second and third bytes of the IP address.

Each unique Class C network has 1 byte to use for node addresses. This leads to 2^8, or 256, minus the two special patterns of all 0s and all 1s, for a total of 254 node addresses for each Class C network.

Class D networks, used for multicasting only, use the address range 224.0.0.0 to 239.255.255.255 and are used, as in broadcasting, as destination addresses only. Class E networks (reserved for future use at this point) cover 240.0.0.0 to 255.255.255.255. Addresses in the Class E range are considered within the experimental range.

Subnetting a Network

If an organization is large and has lots of computers or if its computers are geographically dispersed, it makes good sense to divide its colossal network into smaller ones connected by routers. These smaller networks are called *subnets*. The benefits of using subnets are as follows:

Reduced Network Traffic   We all appreciate less traffic of any kind, and so do networks. Without routers, packet traffic could choke the entire network. Most traffic will stay on the local network—only packets destined for other networks will pass through the router and to another subnet. This traffic reduction also improves overall performance.

Simplified Management   It's easier to identify and isolate network problems in a group of smaller networks connected together than within one gigantic one.

Understanding the Benefits of Subnetting

To understand one benefit of subnetting, consider a hotel or office building. Say that a hotel has 1,000 rooms with 75 rooms to a floor. You could start at the first room on the first floor and number it 1; then when you get to the first room on the second floor, you could number it 76 and keep going until you reach room 1,000. But someone looking for room 521 would have to guess on which floor that room is located. If you were to "subnet" the hotel, you would identify the first room on the first floor with the number 101 (1 = Floor 1 and 01 = Room 1), the first room on the second floor with 201, and so on. The guest looking for room 521 would go to the fifth floor and look for room 21.

An organization with a single network address (comparable to the hotel building mentioned in the sidebar "Understanding the Benefits of Subnetting") can have a subnet address for each individual physical network (comparable to a floor in the hotel building). Each subnet is still part of the shared network address, but it also has an additional identifier denoting its individual subnetwork number. This identifier is called a *subnet address*.

Subnetting solves several addressing problems:

- If an organization has several physical networks but only one IP network address, it can handle the situation by creating subnets.

- Because subnetting allows many physical networks to be grouped together, fewer entries in a routing table are required, notably reducing network overhead.

- These things combine collectively to yield greatly enhanced network efficiency.

The original designers of the Internet Protocol envisioned a small Internet with only tens of networks and hundreds of hosts. Their addressing scheme used a network address for each physical network. As you can imagine, this scheme and the unforeseen growth of the Internet created a few problems. The following are two examples:

Not Enough Addresses   A single network address can be used to refer to multiple physical networks, but an organization can request individual network addresses for each one of its physical networks. If all of these requests were granted, there wouldn't be enough addresses to go around.

Gigantic Routing Tables   If each router on the Internet needed to know about every physical network, routing tables would be impossibly huge. There would be an overwhelming amount of administrative overhead to maintain those tables, and the resulting physical overhead on the routers would be massive (CPU cycles, memory, disk space, and so on). Because routers exchange routing information with each other, an additional, related consequence is that a terrific overabundance of network traffic would result.

Although there's more than one way to approach these problems, the principal solution is the one that I'll cover in this book—subnetting. As you might guess, *subnetting* is the process of carving a single IP network into smaller logical subnetworks. This trick is achieved by subdividing the host portion of an IP address to create a subnet address. The actual subdivision is accomplished through the use of a subnet mask (covered later in the chapter).

In the following sections, you will see exactly how to calculate and apply subnetting.

Implementing Subnetting

Before you can implement subnetting, you need to determine your current requirements and plan on how best to implement your subnet scheme.

How to Determine Your Subnetting Requirements

Follow these guidelines to calculate the requirements of your subnet:

1. Determine the number of required network IDs: one for each subnet and one for each wide area network (WAN) connection.

2. Determine the number of required host IDs per subnet: one for each TCP/IP device, including, for example, computers, network printers, and router interfaces.

3. Based on these two data points, create the following:

    -   One subnet mask for your entire network

    -   A unique subnet ID for each physical segment

    -   A range of host IDs for each unique subnet

How to Implement Subnetting

Subnetting is implemented by assigning a subnet address to each machine on a given physical network. For example, in Figure 8.3, each machine on subnet 1 has a subnet address of 1.

The default network portion of an IP address can't be altered without encroaching on another administrative domain's address space, unless you are assigned multiple consecutive classful addresses. To maximize the efficient use of the assigned address space, machines on a particular network share the same network address. In Figure 8.3, you can see that all of the Widget Inc. machines have a network address of 130.57. That principle is constant. In subnetting, it's the host address that's manipulated—the network address doesn't change. The subnet address scheme takes a part of the host address and recycles it as a subnet address. Bit positions are stolen from the host address to be used for the subnet identifier. Figure 8.4 shows how an IP address can be given a subnet address.

FIGURE 8.3   A sample subnet

FIGURE 8.4   Network vs. host addresses

Because the Widget Inc. network is a Class B network, the first two bytes specify the network address and are shared by all machines on the network, regardless of their particular subnet. Here every machine's address on the subnet must have its third byte read 0000 0001. The fourth byte, the host address, is the unique number that identifies the actual host within that subnet. Figure 8.5 illustrates how a network address and a subnet address can be used together.

FIGURE 8.5   The network address and its subnet

When implementing subnetting, you need some type of hardware installed onto the network. Most of us will just use a router. But if you do not want to purchase an expensive router, there is another way.

One way that you can implement subnetting is by using a Windows Server 2012 R2 machine with multiple NIC adapters configured with routing enabled on the server. This type of router is called a *multihomed router*. This is an inexpensive way to set up a router using a Microsoft server, but it may not be the best way. Many companies specialize in routers, and these routers offer many more features and more flexibility than a multihomed router.

How to Use Subnet Masks

For the subnet address scheme to work, every machine on the network must know which part of the host address will be used as the network address. This is accomplished by assigning each machine a subnet mask.

The network administrator creates a 32-bit subnet mask comprising 1s and 0s. The 1s in the subnet mask represent the positions in the IP address that refer to the network and subnet addresses. The 0s represent the positions that refer to the host part of the address. Figure 8.6 illustrates this combination.

In the Widget Inc. example, the first two bytes of the subnet mask are 1s because Widget's network address is a Class B address, formatted as Network.Network.Node.Node. The third byte, normally assigned as part of the host address, is now used to represent the subnet address. Hence, those bit positions are represented with 1s in the subnet mask. The fourth byte is the only part of the example that represents the host address.

FIGURE 8.6 The subnet mask revealed

Subnet mask code

1s = Positions representing network or subnet addresses
0s = Positions representing the host address

Subnet mask for Widget, Inc.

1111 1111. 1111 1111. 1111 1111. 0000 0000

Network address   Subnet   Host
positions   positions   positions

The subnet mask can also be expressed using the decimal equivalents of the binary patterns. The binary pattern of 1111 1111 is the same as decimal 255. Consequently, the subnet mask in the example can be denoted in two ways, as shown in Figure 8.7.

FIGURE 8.7 Different ways to represent the same mask

Subnet mask in binary: 1111 1111. 1111 1111. 1111 1111. 0000 0000

Subnet mask in decimal: 255   .   255   .   255   .   0

(The spaces in the above example are only for illustrative purposes.
The subnet mask in decimal would actually appear as 255.255.255.0.)

Not all networks need to have subnets, and therefore they don't need to use custom subnet masks. In this case, they are said to have a *default* subnet mask. This is basically the same as saying that they don't have any subnets except for the one main subnet on which the network is running. Table 8.4 shows the default subnet masks for the different classes of networks.

TABLE 8.4 Default subnet masks

Class	Format	Default Subnet Mask
A	Network.Node.Node.Node	255.0.0.0
B	Network.Network.Node.Node	255.255.0.0
C	Network.Network.Network.Node	255.255.255.0

Once the network administrator has created the subnet mask and has assigned it to each machine, the IP software applies the subnet mask to the IP address to determine its subnet address. The word *mask* carries the implied meaning of "lens" in this case; that is, the IP software looks at its IP address through the lens of its subnet mask to see its subnet address. Figure 8.8 illustrates an IP address being viewed through a subnet mask.

FIGURE 8.8 Applying the subnet mask

In this example, the IP software learns through the subnet mask that, instead of being part of the host address, the third byte of its IP address is now going to be used as a subnet address. The IP software then looks in its IP address at the bit positions that correspond to the mask, which are 0000 0001.

The final step is for the subnet bit values to be matched up with the binary numbering convention and converted to decimal. In the Widget Inc. example, the binary-to-decimal conversion is simple, as illustrated in Figure 8.9.

FIGURE 8.9 Converting the subnet mask to decimal

Binary numbering convention

Position/value: ←—(continued)	128 64 32 16 8 4 2 1
Widget third byte:	0 0 0 0 0 0 0 1
Decimal equivalent:	0 + 1 = 1
Subnet address:	1

By using the entire third byte of a Class B address as the subnet address, it is easy to set and determine the subnet address. For example, if Widget Inc. wants to have a subnet 6, the third byte of all machines on that subnet will be 0000 0110 (decimal 6 in binary).

Using the entire third byte of a Class B network address for the subnet allows for a fair number of available subnet addresses. One byte dedicated to the subnet provides eight bit positions. Each position can be either a 1 or a 0, so the calculation is 2^8, or 256. Thus, Widget Inc. can have up to 256 total subnetworks, each with up to 254 hosts.

Although RFC 950 prohibits the use of binary all 0s and all 1s as subnet addresses, today almost all products actually permit this usage. Microsoft's TCP/IP stack allows it, as does the software in most routers (provided you enable this feature, which sometimes is not the case by default). This gives you two additional subnets. However, you should not use a subnet of 0 (all 0s) unless all the software on your network recognizes this convention.

How to Calculate the Number of Subnets

The formulas for calculating the maximum number of subnets and the maximum number of hosts per subnet are as follows:

$2 \times$ number of masked bits in subnet mask = maximum number of subnets

$2 \times$ number of unmasked bits in subnet mask $- 2 =$ maximum number of hosts per subnet

In the formulas, *masked* refers to bit positions of 1, and *unmasked* refers to bit positions of 0. The downside to using an entire byte of a node address as your subnet address is that you reduce the possible number of node addresses on each subnet. As explained earlier, without a subnet, a Class B address has 65,534 unique combinations of 1s and 0s that can be used for node addresses. The question then is why would you ever want 65,534 hosts on a single physical network?

The trade-off is acceptable to most who ask themselves this question. If you use an entire byte of the node address for a subnet, you then have only 1 byte for the host addresses, leaving only 254 possible host addresses. If any of your subnets are populated with more than 254 machines, you'll have a problem. To solve it, you would then need to shorten the subnet mask, thereby lengthening the number of host bits and increasing the number of host addresses. This gives you more available host addresses on each subnet. A side effect of this solution is that it shrinks the number of possible subnets.

Figure 8.10 shows an example of using a smaller subnet address. A company called Acme Inc. expects to need a maximum of 14 subnets. In this case, Acme does not need to take an entire byte from the host address for the subnet address. To get its 14 different subnet addresses, it needs to snatch only 4 bits from the host address ($2^4 = 16$). The host portion of the address has 12 usable bits remaining ($2^{12} - 2 = 4094$). Each of Acme's 16 subnets could then potentially have a total of 4,094 host addresses, and 4,094 machines on each subnet should be plenty.

FIGURE 8.10   An example of a smaller subnet address

Acme, Inc.

Network address: 132.8 (Class B; net.net.host.host)

Example IP address: 1000 0100. 0000 1000. 0001 0010. 0011 1100

Decimal: 132 .   8   . 18 .   60

Subnet Mask Code

1s = Positions representing network or subnet addresses
0s = Positions representing the host address

Subnet mask:
Binary: 1111 1111. 1111 1111. 1111 0000. 0000 0000
Decimal: 255 .   255 .   240 .   0
(The decimal 240 is equal to the binary 1111 0000.)

Positions relating to the subnet address

Subnet mask: 1111 1111. 1111 1111. 1111 0000. 0000 0000

IP address of a Acme machine: 1000 0100. 0000 1000. 0001 0010. 0011 1100
(Decimal: 132.8.18.60)

Bits relating to the subnet address

Binary-to-Decimal Conversions for Subnet Address

Subnet mask positions:	1	1	1	1	0	0	0	0
	↓	↓	↓	↓				
Position/value: ←—(continue)	128	64	32	16	8	4	2	1
Third byte of IP address:	0	0	0	1	0	0	1	0
Decimal equivalent:				0 + 16 = 16				
Subnet address for this IP address:				16				

An Easier Way to Apply Subnetting

Now that you have the basics of how to subnet down, you'll learn an easier way. If you
have learned a different way and it works for you, stick with it. It does not matter
how you get to the finish line, just as long as you get there. But if you are new to subnetting,
Figure 8.11 will make it easier for you.

This chart may look intimidating, but it's really simple to use once you have done it a
few times.

Remember that, on this chart, 1s equal subnets, and 0s equal hosts. If you
get this confused, you will get wrong answers in the following exercises.

FIGURE 8.11   TCP/IP v4 subnetting chart

$2^{(X)}-2=Y$	128	64	32	16	8	4	2	1
255	1	1	1	1	1	1	1	1
254	1	1	1	1	1	1	1	0
252	1	1	1	1	1	1	0	0
248	1	1	1	1	1	0	0	0
240	1	1	1	1	0	0	0	0
224	1	1	1	0	0	0	0	0
192	1	1	0	0	0	0	0	0
128	1	0	0	0	0	0	0	0
0	0	0	0	0	0	0	0	0

0 = Hosts, 1 = Subnets

X (POWER)			X		Y
2^x	3	=	8	–2	6
2^x	4	=	16	–2	14
2^x	5	=	32	–2	30
2^x	6	=	64	–2	62
2^x	7	=	128	–2	126
2^x	8	=	256	–2	254
2^x	9	=	512	–2	510
2^x	10	=	1024	–2	1022
2^x	11	=	2048	–2	2046
2^x	12	=	4096	–2	4094
2^x	13	=	8192	–2	8190
2^x	14	=	16384	–2	16382
2^x	15	=	32768	–2	32766
2^x	16	=	65536	–2	65534
2^x	17	=	131072	–2	131070

Watch the Y column on the lower end of the chart. This represents the number of addresses available to you after the two reserved addresses have been removed. The following exercises provide some examples.

SUBNET MASK EXERCISE 8.1

Class C, 10 Hosts per Subnet

You have a Class C address, and you require 10 hosts per subnet.

1. Write down the following:

    255.255.255.___

    The blank is the number you need to fill in.

2. Look under the Y column and choose the first number that is larger than 10 (the number of hosts per subnet you need). You should have come up with 14.

SUBNET MASK EXERCISE 8.1 *(continued)*

3. Move across the page and look at number in the X (Power) column. The power number is 4.

4. Go to the top of the chart and look for the row with exactly four 0s (hosts). Find the number at the beginning of the row.

The number at the beginning of the row is 240. That's your answer. The subnet mask should be 255.255.255.240.

SUBNET MASK EXERCISE 8.2

Class C, 20 Hosts per Subnet

You have a Class C address, and you need 20 hosts per subnet.

1. Write down the following:

    255.255.255.___

2. Look under the Y column and find the first number that covers 20. (This should be 30.)

3. Go across to the power number (5).

4. Go to the top part of the chart and find the row with exactly five 0s from right to left.

The number at the beginning of the row is 224. Your answer should be 255.255.255.224.

SUBNET MASK EXERCISE 8.3

Class C, Five Subnets

Now you have a Class C address, and you need five subnets. Remember that subnets are represented by 1s in the chart.

1. Write down the following:

    255.255.255.___

2. Look under the Y column and find the first number that covers 5. (This should be 6.)

3. Go across to the power number. (This should be 3.)

4. Go to the top part of the chart and find out which row has exactly three 1s (remember, 1s are for subnets) from left to right.

Your answer should be 255.255.255.224.

SUBNET MASK EXERCISE 8.4

Class B, 1,500 Hosts per Subnet

This one is a bit harder. You have a Class B address, and you need 1,500 hosts per subnet. Because you have a Class B address, you need to fill in the third octet of numbers. The fourth octet contains eight 0s.

1. Write down the following:

    255.255.___.0

2. Look at the Y column and find the first number that covers 1,500. (This should be 2,046.)

3. Go across and find the power number. (This should be 11.)

4. Remember, you already have eight 0s in the last octet. So, you need only three more. Find the row with three 0s.

You should come up with an answer of 255.255.248.0. This actually breaks down to 11111111. 11111111.11111000.00000000, and that's how you got the 11 zeros.

SUBNET MASK EXERCISE 8.5

Class B, 3,500 Hosts per Subnet

You have a Class B address, and you need 3,500 hosts per subnet.

1. Write down the following:

    255.255.___.0

2. Look at the Y column and find the first number that covers 3,500. (This should be 4,094.)

3. Go across and find the power number. (This should be 12.)

4. Remember, you already have eight 0s in the last octet, so you need only four more. Count for four zeros from right to left.

You should come up with an answer of 255.255.240.0. Again, this actually breaks down to 111 11111.11111111.11110000.00000000, and that's how you got the 12 zeros.

If you get a question that gives you both the hosts and the subnets, always figure out the larger number first. Then, depending on the mask you have decided to use, make sure that the lower number is also correct with that mask.

Now try some more subnet mask exercises using the data that follows:

Class B address	**Class B address**
1,000 hosts per subnet	25 subnets
Class C address	**Class B address**
45 hosts per subnet	4,000 hosts per subnet
192.168.0.0	**Class B address**
10 subnets	2,000 hosts per subnet
	25 subnets

Here are the answers. If any of your answers are wrong, follow the previous examples and try to work through them again.

Class B address	**Class B address**
1,000 hosts per subnet 255.255.252.0	25 subnets 255.255.248.0
Class C address	**Class B address**
45 hosts per subnet 255.255.255.192	4,000 hosts per subnet 255.255.240.0
192.168.0.0	**Class B address**
10 subnets 255.255.255.240	2,000 hosts per subnet
	25 subnets 255.255.248.0

Applying Subnetting the Traditional Way

Sometimes subnetting can be confusing. After all, it can be quite difficult to remember all of those numbers. You can step back a minute and take a look at the primary classes of networks and how to subnet each one. Let's start with Class C because it uses only 8 bits for the node address, so it's the easiest to calculate. In the following sections, I will explain how to subnet the various types of networks.

Subnetting Class C

If you recall, a Class C network uses the first 3 bytes (24 bits) to define the network address. This leaves you 1 byte (8 bits) with which to address hosts. So if you want to create subnets, your options are limited because of the small number of bits available.

If you break down your subnets into chunks smaller than the default Class C, then figuring out the subnet mask, network number, broadcast address, and router address can be confusing. To build a sturdy base for subnetting, study the following techniques for determining these special values for each subnet, but also learn and use the more efficient technique presented in the later section "Quickly Identifying Subnet Characteristics Using CIDR" and the earlier section "An Easier Way to Apply Subnetting." Table 8.5 summarizes how you can break down a Class C network into one, two, four, or eight smaller subnets, and it gives you the subnet masks, network numbers, broadcast addresses, and router addresses. The first three bytes have simply been designated x.y.z. (Note that the table assumes you can use the all-0s and all-1s subnets too.)

TABLE 8.5 Setting up Class C subnets

Number of desired subnets	Subnet mask	Network number	Router address	Broadcast address	Remaining number of IP addresses
1	255.255.255.0	x.y.z.0	x.y.z.1	x.y.z.255	253
2	255.255.255.128	x.y.z.0	x.y.z.1	x.y.z.127	125
	255.255.255.128	x.y.z.128	x.y.z.129	x.y.z.255	125
4	255.255.255.192	x.y.z.0	x.y.z.1	x.y.z.63	61
	255.255.255.192	x.y.z.64	x.y.z.65	x.y.z.127	61
	255.255.255.192	x.y.z.128	x.y.z.129	x.y.z.191	61
	255.255.255.192	x.y.z.192	x.y.z.193	x.y.z.255	61
8	255.255.255.224	x.y.z.0	x.y.z.1	x.y.z.31	29
	255.255.255.224	x.y.z.32	x.y.z.33	x.y.z.63	29
	255.255.255.224	x.y.z.64	x.y.z.65	x.y.z.95	29
	255.255.255.224	x.y.z.96	x.y.z.97	x.y.z.127	29
	255.255.255.224	x.y.z.128	x.y.z.129	x.y.z.159	29
	255.255.255.224	x.y.z.160	x.y.z.161	x.y.z.191	29
	255.255.255.224	x.y.z.192	x.y.z.193	x.y.z.223	29
	255.255.255.224	x.y.z.224	x.y.z.225	x.y.z.255	29

For example, suppose you want to chop up a Class C network, 200.211.192.*x*, into two subnets. As you can see in the table, you'd use a subnet mask of 255.255.255.128 for each subnet. The first subnet would have the network number 200.211.192.0, router address 200.211.192.1, and broadcast address 200.211.192.127. You could assign IP addresses 200.211.192.2 through 200.211.192.126—that's 125 additional different IP addresses.

Heavily subnetting a network results in the loss of a progressively greater percentage of addresses to the network number, broadcast address, and router address.

The second subnet would have the network number 200.211.192.128, router address 200.211.192.129, and broadcast address 200.211.192.255.

Why It's Best to Use Routers That Support Subnet 0

When subnetting a Class C network using the method in Table 8.5, if you use the $2^x - 2$ calculation, the subnet 128 in the table doesn't make sense. It turns out that there's a legitimate and popular reason to do it this way, however.

- Remember that using subnet 0 is not allowed according to the RFC standards, but by using it you can subnet your Class C network with a subnet mask of 128. This uses only 1 bit, and according to your calculator $2^1 - 2 = 0$, giving you zero subnets.

- By using routers that support subnet 0, you can assign 1–126 for hosts and 129–254 for hosts, as stated in the table. This saves a bunch of addresses! If you were to stick to the method defined by the RFC standards, the best you could gain is a subnet mask of 192 (2 bits), which allows you only two subnets ($2^2 - 2 = 2$).

Determining the Subnet Numbers for a Class C Subnet

The first subnet always has a 0 in the interesting octet. In the example, it would be 200.211.192.0, the same as the original nonsubnetted network address. To determine the subnet numbers for the additional subnets, first you have to determine the incremental value:

1. Begin with the octet that has an interesting value (other than 0 or 255) in the subnet mask. Then subtract the interesting value from 256. The result is the incremental value.

   If again you use the network 200.211.192.x and a mask of 255.255.255.192, the example yields the following equation: 256 – 192 = 64. Thus, 64 is your incremental value in the interesting octet—the fourth octet in this case. Why the fourth octet? That's the octet with the interesting value, 192, in the mask.

2. To determine the second subnet number, add the incremental value to the 0 in the fourth octet of the first subnet.

   In the example, it would be 200.211.192.64.

3. To determine the third subnet number, add the incremental value to the interesting octet of the second subnet number.

   In the example, it would be 200.211.192.128.

4. Keep adding the incremental value in this fashion until you reach the actual subnet mask number.

For example, 0 + 64 = 64, so your second subnet is 64. And 64 + 64 is 128, so your third subnet is 128. And 128 + 64 is 192, so your fourth subnet is 192. Because 192 is the subnet mask, this is your last subnet. If you tried to add 64 again, you'd come up with 256, an unusable octet value, which is always where you end up when you've gone too far. This means your valid subnets are 0, 64, 128, and 192.

The numbers between the subnets are your valid host and broadcast addresses. For example, the following are valid hosts for two of the subnets in a Class C network with a subnet mask of 192:

- The valid hosts for subnet 64 are in the range 65–126, which gives you 62 hosts per subnet.

  (You can't use 127 as a host because that would mean your host bits would be all 1s. The all-1s format is reserved as the broadcast address for that subnet.)

- The valid hosts for subnet 128 are in the range 129–190, with a broadcast address of 191.

As you can see, this solution wastes a few addresses—six more than not subnetting at all, to be exact. In a Class C network, this should not be hard to justify. The 255.255.255.128 subnet mask is an even better solution if you need only two subnets and expect to need close to 126 host addresses per subnet.

Calculating Values for an Eight-Subnet Class C Network

What happens if you need eight subnets in your Class C network?

By using the calculation of 2^x, where x is the number of subnet bits, you would need 3 subnet bits to get eight subnets ($2^3 = 8$). What are the valid subnets, and what are the valid hosts of each subnet? Let's figure it out.

11100000 is 224 in binary, and it would be the interesting value in the fourth octet of the subnet mask. This must be the same on all workstations.

You're likely to see test questions that ask you to identify the problem with a given configuration. If a workstation has the wrong subnet mask, the router could "think" that the workstation is on a different subnet than it actually is. When that happens, the misguided router won't forward packets to the workstation in question. Similarly, if the mask is incorrectly specified in the workstation's configuration, that workstation will observe the mask and send packets to the default gateway when it shouldn't.

To figure out the valid subnets, subtract the interesting octet value from 256 (256 – 224 = 32), so 32 is your incremental value for the fourth octet. Of course, the 0 subnet is your first subnet, as always. The other subnets would be 32, 64, 96, 128, 160, 192, and 224. The valid hosts are the numbers between the subnet numbers, except the numbers that equal all 1s in the host bits. These numbers would be 31, 63, 95, 127, 159, 191, 223, and 255. Remember that using all 1s in the host bits is reserved for the broadcast address of each subnet.

The valid subnets, hosts, and broadcasts are as follows:

Subnet	Hosts	Broadcast
0	1–30	31
32	33–62	63
64	65–94	95
96	97–126	127
128	129–158	159
160	161–190	191
192	193–222	223
224	225–254	255

You can add one more bit to the subnet mask just for fun. You were using 3 bits, which gave you 224. By adding the next bit, the mask now becomes 240 (11110000).

By using 4 bits for the subnet mask, you get 14 subnets because $2^4 = 16$. This subnet mask also gives you only 4 bits for the host addresses, or $2^4 - 2 = 14$ hosts per subnet. As you can see, the number of hosts per subnet gets reduced rather quickly for each host bit that gets reallocated for subnet use.

The first valid subnet for subnet 240 is 0, as always. Because $256 - 240 = 16$, your remaining subnets are then 16, 32, 48, 64, 80, 96, 112, 128, 144, 160, 176, 192, 208, 224, and 240. Remember that the actual interesting octet value also represents the last valid subnet, so 240 is the last valid subnet number. The valid hosts are the numbers between the subnets, except for the numbers that are all 1s—the broadcast address for the subnet.

Table 8.6 shows the numbers in the interesting (fourth) octet for a Class C network with eight subnets.

TABLE 8.6 Fourth octet addresses for a Class C network with eight subnets

Subnet	Hosts	Broadcast
0	1–14	15
16	17–30	31
32	33–46	47
48	49–62	63
64	65–78	79

80	81–94	95
96	97–110	111
112	113–126	127
128	129–142	143
144	145–158	159
160	161–174	175
176	177–190	191
192	193–206	207
208	209–222	223
224	225–238	239
240	241–254	255

Subnetting Class B

Because a Class B network has 16 bits for host addresses, you have plenty of available bits to play with when figuring out a subnet mask. Remember that you have to start with the leftmost bit and work toward the right. For example, a Class B network would look like x.y.0.0, with the default mask of 255.255.0.0. Using the default mask would give you one network with 65,534 hosts.

The default mask in binary is 11111111.11111111.00000000.00000000. The 1s represent the corresponding network bits in the IP address, and the 0s represent the host bits. When you're creating a subnet mask, the leftmost bit(s) will be borrowed from the host bits (0s will be turned into 1s) to become the subnet mask. You then use the remaining bits that are still set to 0 for host addresses.

If you use only 1 bit to create a subnet mask, you have a mask of 255.255.128.0. If you use 2 bits, you have a mask of 255.255.192.0, or 11111111.11111111.11000000.00000000.

As with subnetting a Class C address, you now have three parts of the IP address: the network address, the subnet address, and the host address. You figure out the subnet mask numbers the same way as you did with a Class C network (see the previous section, "Calculating Values for an Eight-Subnet Class C Network"), but you'll end up with a lot more hosts per subnet.

There are four subnets, because $2^2 = 4$. The valid third-octet values for the subnets are 0, 64, 128, and 192 (256 − 192 = 64, so the incremental value of the third octet is 64). However, there are 14 bits (0s) left over for host addressing. This gives you 16,382 hosts per subnet ($2^{14} − 2 = 16,382$).

The valid subnets and hosts are as follows:

Subnet	Hosts	Broadcast
x.y.0.0	x.y.0.1 through x.y. 63.254	x.y.63.255
x.y.64.0	x.y.64.1 through x.y.127.254	x.y.127.255
x.y.128.0	x.y.128.1 through x.y.191.254	x.y.191.255
x.y.192.0	x.y.192.1 through x.y.255.254	x.y.255.255

You can add another bit to the subnet mask, making it 11111111.11111111.11100000. 00000000, or 255.255.224.0. This gives you eight subnets ($2^3 = 8$) and 8,190 hosts. The valid subnets are 0, 32, 64, 96, 128, 160, 192, and 224 (256 − 224 = 32). The subnets, valid hosts, and broadcasts are listed here:

Subnet	Hosts	Broadcast
x.y.0.0	x.y.0.1 through x.y.31.254	x.y.31.255
x.y.32.0	x.y.32.1 through x.y.63.254	x.y.63.255
x.y.64.0	x.y.64.1 through x.y.95.254	x.y.95.255
x.y.96.0	x.y.96.1 through x.y.127.254	x.y.127.255
x.y.128.0	x.y.128.1 through x.y.159.254	x.y.159.255
x.y.160.0	x.y.160.1 through x.y.191.254	x.y.191.255
x.y.192.0	x.y.192.1 through x.y.223.254	x.y.223.255
x.y.224.0	x.y.224.1 through x.y.255.254	x.y.255.255

The following are the breakdowns for a 9-bit mask and a 14-bit mask:

- If you use 9 bits for the mask, it gives you 512 subnets (2^9). With only 7 bits for hosts, you still have 126 hosts per subnet ($2^7 − 2 = 126$). The mask looks like this:

    11111111.11111111.11111111.10000000, or 255.255.255.128

- If you use 14 bits for the subnet mask, you get 16,384 subnets (2^{14}) but only two hosts per subnet ($2^2 − 2 = 2$). The subnet mask would look like this:

    11111111.11111111.11111111.11111100, or 255.255.255.252

🌐 Real World Scenario

Subnet Mask Use in an ISP

You may be wondering why you would use a 14-bit subnet mask with a Class B address. This approach is actually very common. Let's say you have a Class B network and use a subnet mask of 255.255.255.0. You'd have 256 subnets and 254 hosts per subnet. Imagine also that you are an Internet service provider (ISP) and have a network with many WAN links, a different one between you and each customer. Typically, you'd have a direct connection between each site. Each of these links must be on its own subnet or network. There will be two hosts on these subnets—one address for each router port. If you used the mask described earlier (255.255.255.0), you would waste 252 host addresses per subnet. But by using the 255.255.255.252 subnet mask, you have more subnets available, which means more customers—each subnet with only two hosts, which is the maximum allowed on a point-to-point circuit.

You can use the 255.255.255.252 subnet mask only if you are running a routing algorithm such as Enhanced Interior Gateway Routing Protocol (EIGRP) or Open Shortest Path First (OSPF). These routing protocols allow what is called *variable-length subnet masking (VLSM)*. VLSM allows you to run the 255.255.255.252 subnet mask on your interfaces to the WANs and run 255.255.255.0 on your router interfaces in your local area network (LAN) using the same classful network address for all subnets. It works because these routing protocols transmit the subnet mask information in the update packets that they send to the other routers. Classful routing protocols, such as RIP version 1, don't transmit the subnet mask and therefore cannot employ VLSM.

Subnetting Class A

Class A networks have even more bits available than Class B and Class C networks. A default Class A network subnet mask is only 8 bits, or 255.0.0.0, giving you a whopping 24 bits for hosts to play with. Knowing which hosts and subnets are valid is a lot more complicated than it was for either Class B or Class C networks.

If you use a mask of 11111111.1111111.00000000.00000000, or 255.255.0.0, you'll have 8 bits for subnets, or 256 subnets (2^8). This leaves 16 bits for hosts, or 65,534 hosts per subnet ($2^{16} - 2 = 65534$).

If you split the 24 bits evenly between subnets and hosts, you would give each one 12 bits. The mask would look like this: 11111111.11111111.11110000.00000000, or 255.255.240.0. How many valid subnets and hosts would you have? The answer is 4,096 subnets each with 4,094 hosts ($2^{12} - 2 = 4094$).

The second octet will be somewhere between 0 and 255. However, you will need to figure out the third octet. Because the third octet has a 240 mask, you get 16

(256 – 240 = 16) as your incremental value in the third octet. The third octet must start with 0 for the first subnet, the second subnet will have 16 in the third octet, and so on. This means that some of your valid subnets are as follows (not in order):

Subnet	Hosts	Broadcast
x.0-255.0.0	x.0-255.0.1 through x.0-255.15.254	x.0-255.15.255
x.0-255.16.0	x.0-255.16.1 through x.0-255.31.254	x.0-255.31.255
x.0-255.32.0	x.0-255.32.1 through x.0-255.47.254	x.0-255.47.255
x.0-255.48.0	x.0-255.48.1 through x.0-255.63.254	x.0-255.63.255

They go on in this way for the remaining third-octet values through 224 in the subnet column.

Working with Classless Inter-Domain Routing

Microsoft uses an alternate way to write address ranges, called *Classless Inter-Domain Routing* (*CIDR*; pronounced "cider"). CIDR is a shorthand version of the subnet mask. For example, an address of 131.107.2.0 with a subnet mask of 255.255.255.0 is listed in CIDR as 131.107.2.0/24 because the subnet mask contains 24 1s. An address listed as 141.10.32.0/19 would have a subnet mask of 255.255.224.0, or 19 1s (the default subnet mask for Class B plus 3 bits). This is the nomenclature used in all Microsoft exams (see Figure 8.12).

FIGURE 8.12   Subnet mask represented by 1s

Subnet mask in binary: 1111 1111. 1111 1111. 1111 1111. 0000 0000

Subnet mask in decimal: 255   .   255   .   255   .   0

(The spaces in the above example are only for illustrative purposes.
The subnet mask in decimal would actually appear as 255.255.255.0.)

Let's say an Internet company has assigned you the following Class C address and CIDR number: 192.168.10.0/24. This represents the Class C address of 192.168.10.0 and a subnet mask of 255.255.255.0.

Again, CIDR represents the number of 1s turned on in a subnet mask. For example, a CIDR number of /16 stands for 255.255.0.0 (11111111.11111111.00000000.00000000).

The following is a list of all of the CIDR numbers (starting with a Class A default subnet mask) and their corresponding subnet masks:

CIDR	Mask	CIDR	Mask	CIDR	Mask
/8	255.0.0.0	/17	255.255.128.0	/25	255.255.255.128
/9	255.128.0.0	/18	255.255.192.0	/26	255.255.255.192
/10	255.192.0.0	/19	255.255.224.0	/27	255.255.255.224
/11	255.224.0.0	/20	255.255.240.0	/28	255.255.255.240
/12	255.240.0.0	/21	255.255.248.0	/29	255.255.255.248
/13	255.248.0.0	/22	255.255.252.0	/30	255.255.255.252
/14	255.252.0.0	/23	255.255.254.0	/31	255.255.255.254
/15	255.254.0.0	/24	255.255.255.0	/32	255.255.255.255
/16	255.255.0.0				

Quickly Identifying Subnet Characteristics Using CIDR

Given the limited time you have to dispatch questions in the structured environment of a Microsoft certification exam, every shortcut to coming up with the correct answer is a plus. The following method, using CIDR notation, can shave minutes off the time it takes you to complete a single question. Since you already understand the underlying binary technology at the heart of subnetting, you can use the following shortcuts, one for each address class, to come up with the correct answer without working in binary.

Identifying Class C Subnet Characteristics

Consider the host address 192.168.10.50/27. The following steps flesh out the details of the subnet of which this address is a member:

1. Obtain the CIDR-notation prefix length for the address by converting the dotted-decimal mask to CIDR notation.

   In this case, /27 corresponds to a mask of 255.255.255.224. Practice converting between these notations until it becomes second nature.

2. Using the closest multiple of 8 that is greater than or equal to the prefix length, compute the interesting octet (the octet that increases from one subnet to the next in increments other than 1 or 0). Divide this multiple by 8. The result is a number corresponding to the octet that is interesting.

   In this case, the next multiple of 8 greater than 27 is 32. Dividing 32 by 8 produces the number 4, pointing to the fourth octet as the interesting one.

3. To compute the incremental value in the interesting octet, subtract the prefix length from the next higher multiple of 8, which in this case is 32. The result (32 − 27) is 5. Raise 2 to the computed value ($2^5 = 32$). The result is the incremental value of the interesting octet.

4. Recall the value of the interesting octet from the original address (50 in this case). Starting with 0, increment by the incremental value until the value is exceeded. The values then are 0, 32, 64, and so on.

5. The subnet in question extends from the increment that is immediately less than or equal to the address's interesting octet value to the address immediately before the next increment. In this example, 192.168.10.50/27 belongs to the subnet 192.168.10.32, and this subnet extends to the address immediately preceding 192.168.10.64, which is its broadcast address, 192.168.10.63.

    Note that if the interesting octet is not the fourth octet, all octets after the interesting octet must be set to 0 for the subnet address.

6. The usable range of addresses for the subnet in question extends from one higher than the subnet address to one less than the broadcast address, making the range for the subnet in question 192.168.10.33 through 192.168.10.62. As you can see, 192.168.10.50/27 definitely falls within the subnet 192.168.10.32/27.

Identifying Class B Subnet Characteristics

Using the steps in the previous section, find the subnet in which the address 172.16.76.12 with a mask of 255.255.240.0 belongs.

1. The corresponding CIDR notation prefix length is /20.

2. The next multiple of 8 that is greater than 20 is 24. 24 × 8 = 3. Octet 3 is interesting.

3. 24 − 20 = 4, so the incremental value is $2^4 = 16$.

4. The increments in the third octet are 0, 16, 32, 48, 64, 80, and so on.

5. The increments of 64 and 80 bracket the address's third-octet value of 76, making the subnet in question 172.16.64.0, after setting all octets after the interesting octet to 0. This subnet's broadcast address is 172.16.79.255, which comes right before the next subnet address of 172.16.80.0.

6. The usable address range then extends from 172.16.64.1 through 172.16.79.254.

Identifying Class A Subnet Characteristics

Try it one more time with 10.6.127.255/14. Combine some of the related steps if possible:

1. The prefix length is 14. The next multiple of 8 that is greater than or equal to 14 is 16. 16 × 8 = 2, so the second octet is interesting.

2. 16 − 14 = 2, so the incremental value in the second octet is $2^2 = 4$.

3. The corresponding second-octet value of 6 in the address falls between the 4 and 8 increments. This means that the subnet in question is 10.4.0.0 (setting octets after the second one to 0) and its broadcast address is 10.7.255.255.

4. The usable address range is from 10.4.0.1 through 10.7.255.254.

Determining Quantities of Subnets and Hosts

The general technique described in the previous section is also useful when trying to determine the total number of subnets and hosts produced by a given mask with respect to the default mask of the class of address in question.

For example, consider the Class B address 172.16.0.0 with a subnet mask of 255.255.254.0.

This is a prefix length of 23 bits. When you subtract the default prefix length for a Class B address of 16 from 23, you get the value 7. Raising 2 to the 7th power results in the value 128, which is the number of subnets you get when you subnet a Class B address with the 255.255.254.0 mask.

Determining the number of hosts available in each of these 128 subnets is simple because you always subtract the prefix length that the subnet mask produces, 23 in this example, from the value 32, which represents the total number of bits in any IP address. The difference, 9, represents the remaining number of 0s, or host bits, in the subnet mask. Raising 2 to this value produces the total possible number of host IDs per subnet that this subnet mask allows. Remember to subtract 2 from this result to account for the subnet and broadcast addresses for each subnet. This gives you the actual number of usable host IDs per subnet. In this case, this value is $2^9 - 2 = 510$.

Repeated practice with this technique will reduce your time to obtain the desired answer to mere seconds, leaving time for the more challenging tasks in each question. You have a wealth of examples and scenarios in this chapter, as well as in the review questions, on which to try your technique and build your trust in this faster method.

Supernetting

Let's take a look at a different type of subnetting. Class B addresses give you 65,534 addresses, but let's say that you have 1,000 users. Would you really need a Class B address? Not if you use supernetting.

Supernetting allows you to have two or more blocks of contiguous subnetwork addresses. So what does that actually mean? Class C addresses give you 254 useable addresses. So if you needed 1,000 users, you could set up supernetting of 4 Class C addresses that are contiguous.

Example:
192.168.16.0
192.168.17.0
192.168.18.0
192.168.19.0

When you set up supernetting for a Class C, you would use a Class B subnet mask. When you set up supernetting for a Class B, you would use a Class A subnet mask. This allows you to use multiple classes to get a larger number of hosts without taking up an entire class.

So the subnet mask for the above example would be 255.255.252.0 or /22. The reason we used this subnet mask is because a 252 subnet mask allows for 4 subnets. Each of the above Class C numbers would equal one subnet on this network.

Understanding IPv6

Internet Protocol version 6 (IPv6) is the first major revamping of IP since RFC 791 was accepted in 1981. Yes, the operation of IP has improved, and there have been a few bells and whistles added (such as NAT, for example), but the basic structure is still being used as it was originally intended. IPv6 has actually been available to use in Microsoft operating systems since NT 4.0, but it always had to be manually enabled. Windows Vista was the first Microsoft operating system to have it enabled by default. It is also enabled by default in Windows 7, Windows 8, Windows Server 2008, Windows Server 2008 R2, and Windows Server 2012 R2, and it probably will be in all Microsoft operating systems from this point on.

TCP and UDP—as well as the IP applications, such as HTTP, FTP, SNMP, and the rest—are still being used in IPv4. So, you might ask, why change to the new version? What does IPv6 bring to your networking infrastructure? What is the structure of an IPv6 address? How is it implemented and used within Windows Server 2012 R2? I'll answer all of those questions and more in the following sections.

IPv6 History and Need

In the late 1970s, as the IP specifications were being put together, the vision of the interconnected devices was limited compared to what we actually have today. To get an idea of the growth of the Internet, take a look at Hobbes' Internet Timeline in RFC 2235 (www.faqs.org/rfcs/rfc2235.html). As you can see, in 1984, the number of hosts finally surpassed 1,000—two years after TCP and IP were introduced. With 32 bits of addressing available in IPv4, it handled the 1,000+ hosts just fine. And even with the number of hosts breaking the 10,000 mark in 1987 and then 100,000 in 1989, there were still plenty of IP addresses to go around. But when the number of hosts exceeded 2 million in 1992 and 3 million in 1994, concern in the industry started to build. So in 1994, a working group was formed to come up with a solution to the quickly dwindling usable address availability in the IPv4 space. Internet Protocol next generation (IPng) was started.

Have you heard of IP address depletion being a problem today? Probably not as much. When the working group realized that it could not have IPv6 standardized before the available addresses might run out, they developed and standardized *Network Address Translation (NAT)* as an interim solution. NAT, or more specifically an implementation of NAT called *Port Address Translation (PAT)*, took care of a big portion of the problem.

NAT works very well, but it does have some limitations, including issues of peer-to-peer applications with their IPv4 addresses embedded in the data, issues of end-to-end traceability, and issues of overlapping addresses when two networks merge. Because all devices in an IPv6 network will have a unique address and no network address translation will take place, the global addressing concept of IPv4 will be brought back (the address put on by the source device will stay all the way to the destination). Thus, with the new-and-improved functionality of IPv6, the drawbacks of NAT and the limitations of IPv4 will be eliminated.

New and Improved IPv6 Concepts

Several elements of the IPv4 protocol could use some enhancements. Fortunately, IPv6 incorporates those enhancements as well as new features directly into the protocol specification to provide better and additional functionality.

The following list includes new concepts and new implementations of old concepts in IPv6:

- Larger address space (128-bit vs. 32-bit).

- Autoconfiguration of Internet-accessible addresses with or without DHCP. (Without DHCP, it's called *stateless autoconfiguration*.)

- More efficient IP header (fewer fields and no checksum).

- Fixed-length IP header (the IPv4 header is variable length) with extension headers beyond the standard fixed length to provide enhancements.

- Built-in IP mobility and security. (Although available in IPv4, the IPv6 implementation is a much better implementation.)

- Built-in transition schemes to allow integration of the IPv4 and IPv6 spaces.

- ARP broadcast messages replaced with multicast request.

Here are more details about these features:

128-Bit Address Space   The new 128-bit address space will provide unique addresses for the foreseeable future. Although I would like to say that we will never use up all of the addresses, history may prove me wrong. The number of unique addresses in the IPv6 space is 2^{128}, or 3.4×10^{38}, addresses. How big is that number? It's enough for toasters and refrigerators (and maybe even cars) to all have their own addresses.

As a point of reference, the nearest black hole to Earth is 1,600 light years away. If you were to stack 4mm BB pellets from here to the nearest black hole and back, you would need 1.51×10^{22} BBs. This means you could uniquely address each BB from Earth to the black hole and back and still have quite a few addresses left over.

Another way to look at it is that the IPv6 address space is big enough to provide more than 1 million addresses per square inch of the surface area of the earth (oceans included).

Autoconfiguration and Stateless Autoconfiguration   Autoconfiguration is another added/improved feature of IPv6. We've used DHCP for a while to assign IP addresses to client machines. You should even remember that APIPA can be used to assign addresses automatically to Microsoft DHCP client machines in the absence of a DHCP server. The problem with APIPA is that it confines communication between machines to a local LAN (no default gateway). What if a client machine could ask whether there was a router on the LAN and what network it was on? If the client machine knew that, it could not only assign itself an address, it could also choose the appropriate network and default gateway. The stateless autoconfiguration functionality of IPv6 allows the clients to do this.

Improved IPv6 Header   The IPv6 header is more efficient than the IPv4 header because it is fixed length (with extensions possible) and has only a few fields. The IPv6 header consists of a total of 40 bytes:

32 bytes   Source and destination IPv6 addresses

8 bytes   Version field, traffic class field, flow label field, payload length field, next header field, and hop limit field

You don't have to waste your time with a checksum validation anymore, and you don't have to include the length of the IP header (it's fixed in IPv6; the IP header is variable length in IPv4, so the length must be included as a field).

IPv6 Mobility   IPv6 is only a replacement of the OSI layer 3 component, so you'll continue to use the TCP (and UDP) components as they currently exist. IPv6 addresses a TCP issue, though. Specifically, TCP is connection oriented, meaning that you establish an end-to-end communication path with sequencing and acknowledgments before you ever send any data, and then you have to acknowledge all of the pieces of data sent. You do this through a combination of an IP address, port number, and port type (socket).

If the source IP address changes, the TCP connection may be disrupted. But then how often does this happen? Well, it happens more and more often because more people are walking around with a wireless laptop or a wireless Voice over IP (VoIP) telephone. IPv6 mobility establishes a TCP connection with a home address and, when changing networks, it continues to communicate with the original endpoint from a care-of address as it changes LANs, which sends all traffic back through the home address. The handing off of network addresses does not disrupt the TCP connection state (the original TCP port number and address remain intact).

Improved Security   Unlike IPv4, IPv6 has security built in. *Internet Protocol Security (IPsec)* is a component used today to authenticate and encrypt secure tunnels from a source to a destination. This can be from the client to the server or between gateways. IPv4 lets you do this by enhancing IP header functionality (basically adding a second IP header while encrypting everything behind it). In IPv6, you add this as standard functionality by using extension headers. Extension headers are inserted into the packet only if they are needed. Each header has a "next header" field, which identifies the next piece of information. The extension headers currently identified for IPv6 are Hop-By-Hop Options, Routing, Fragment, Destination Options, Authentication, and Encapsulating Security Payload. The Authentication header and the Encapsulating Security Payload header are the IPsec-specific control headers.

IPv4 to IPv6 Interoperability   Several mechanisms in IPv6 make the IPv4-to-IPv6 transition easy.

- A simple dual-stack implementation where both IPv4 and IPv6 are installed and used is certainly an option. In most situations (so far), this doesn't work so well because most of us aren't connected to an IPv6 network and our Internet connection is not IPv6 even if we're using IPv6 internally. Therefore, Microsoft includes other mechanisms that can be used in several different circumstances.

- *Intra-Site Automatic Tunnel Addressing Protocol (ISATAP)* is an automatic tunneling mechanism used to connect an IPv6 network to an IPv4 address space (not using NAT). ISATAP treats the IPv4 space as one big logical link connection space.

- *6to4* is a mechanism used to transition to IPv4. This method, like ISATAP, treats the IPv4 address space as a logical link layer with each IPv6 space in transition using a 6to4 router to create endpoints using the IPv4 space as a point-to-point connection (kind of like a WAN, eh?). 6to4 implementations still do not work well through a NAT, although a 6to4 implementation using an Application layer gateway (ALG) is certainly doable.

- *Teredo* is a mechanism that allows users behind a NAT to access the IPv6 space by tunneling IPv6 packets in UDP.

Pseudo-interfaces are used in these mechanisms to create a usable interface for the operating system. Another interesting feature of IPv6 is that addresses are assigned to interfaces (or pseudo-interfaces), not simply to the end node. Your Windows Server 2012 R2 will have several unique IPv6 addresses assigned.

New Broadcast Methods   IPv6 has moved away from using broadcasting. The three types of packets used in IPv6 are unicast, multicast, and anycast. IPv6 clients then must use one of these types to get the MAC address of the next Ethernet hop (default gateway). IPv6 makes use of multicasting for this along with the new functionality called *neighbor discovery*. Not only does ARP utilize new functionality, but ICMP (also a layer 3 protocol) has been redone and is now known as ICMP6. *ICMP6* is used for messaging (packet too large, time exceeded, and so on) as it was in IPv4, but now it's also used for the messaging of IPv6 mobility. ICMP6 echo request and ICMP6 echo reply are still used for ping.

IPv6 Addressing Concepts

You need to consider several concepts when using IPv6 addressing. For starters, the format of the address has changed. Three types of addresses are used in IPv6 with some predefined values within the address space. You need to get used to seeing these addresses and be able to identify their uses.

IPv6 Address Format

For the design of IPv4 addresses, you present addresses as octets or the decimal (base 10) representation of 8 bits. Four octets add up to the 32 bits required. IPv6 expands the address space to 128 bits, and the representation is for the most part shown in hexadecimal (a notation used to represent 8 bits using the values 0–9 and A–F). Figure 8.13 compares IPv4 to IPv6.

A full IPv6 address looks like this example:

2001:0DB8:0000:0000:1234:0000:A9FE:133E

You can tell the implementation of DNS will make life a lot easier even for those who like to ping the address in lieu of the name. Fortunately, DNS already has the ability to handle IPv6 addresses with the use of an AAAA record. (*A* is short for *alias*.) An A record in IPv4's addressing space is 32 bits, so an AAAA record, or four *A*s, is 128 bits. The Windows Server 2012 R2 DNS server handles the AAAA and the reverse pointer (PTR) records for IPv6.

FIGURE 8.13 IPv4/IPv6 comparison

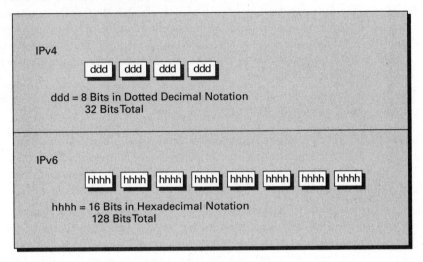

IPv6 Address Shortcuts

There are several shortcuts for writing an IPv6 address. These are described in the following list:

- :0: stands for :0000:.

- You can omit preceding 0s in any 16-bit word. For example, :DB8: and :0DB8: are equivalent.

- :: is a variable standing for enough zeros to round out the address to 128 bits. :: can be used only once in an address.

You can use these shortcuts to represent the example address 2001:0DB8:0000:0000:1234:0000:A9FE:133E, as shown here:

- Compress :0000: into :0::

  2001:0DB8:0000:0000:1234:0:A9FE:133E

- Eliminate preceding zeros:

  2001:DB8:0000:0000:1234:0:A9FE:133E

- Use the special variable shortcut for multiple 0s:

  2001:DB8::1234:0:A9FE:133E

You now also use prefix notation or slash notation when discussing IPv6 networks. For example, the network of the previous address can be represented as 2001:DB8:0000:0000:0000:0000:0000:0000. This can also be expressed as 2001:DB8:: /32. The /32 indicates 32 bits of network, and 2001:DB8: is 32 bits of network.

IPv6 Address Assignment

So, do you subnet IPv6? The answer depends on your definition of subnetting. If you are given 32 bits of network from your ISP, you have 96 bits with which to work. If you use some of the 96 bits to route within your network infrastructure, then you are subnetting. In this context, you do subnet IPv6. However, given the huge number of bits you have available, you will no longer need to implement VLSM. For example, Microsoft has a network space of 2001:4898:: /32. That gives the administrators a space of 96 bits (2^{96} = 79,228,162,514,264,337,593,543,950,336 unique addresses using all 96 bits) with which to work.

You can let Windows Server 2012 R2 dynamically/automatically assign its IPv6 address, or you can still assign it manually (see Figure 8.14). With dynamic/automatic assignment, the IPv6 address is assigned either by a DHCPv6 server or by the Windows Server 2012 R2 machine. If no DHCPv6 server is configured, the Windows Server 2012 R2 machine can query the local LAN segment to find a router with a configured IPv6 interface. If so, the server will assign itself an address on the same IPv6 network as the router interface and set its default gateway to the router interface's IPv6 address. Figure 8.14 shows that you have the same dynamic and manual choices as you do in IPv4; however, the input values for IPv6 must conform to the new format.

FIGURE 8.14 TCP/IPv6 Properties window

To see your configured IP addresses (IPv4 and IPv6), you can still use the `ipconfig` command. For example, I have configured a static IPv4 address and an IPv6 address on my server. The IPv6 address is the same as the one used in the earlier IPv6 example address. Figure 8.15 shows the result of this command on Windows Server 2012 R2 for my server.

FIGURE 8.15 IPv6 configuration as seen from the command prompt

```
Administrator: C:\Windows\system32\cmd.exe                                    _□×
Ethernet adapter Local Area Connection:

   Connection-specific DNS Suffix  . :
   Description . . . . . . . . . . . . : Intel 21140-Based PCI Fast Ethernet Adapt
er (Emulated)
   Physical Address. . . . . . . . . : 00-03-FF-11-02-CD
   DHCP Enabled. . . . . . . . . . . : No
   Autoconfiguration Enabled . . . . : Yes
   IPv6 Address. . . . . . . . . . . : 2001:db8::1234:0:a9fe:133e(Preferred)
   Link-local IPv6 Address . . . . . : fe80::a425:ab9d:7da4:ccba%10(Preferred)
   IPv4 Address. . . . . . . . . . . : 192.168.1.200(Preferred)
   Subnet Mask . . . . . . . . . . . : 255.255.255.0
   Default Gateway . . . . . . . . . : 2001:db8::1234:0:0:1
                                        0.0.0.0
                                        192.168.1.1
   DNS Servers . . . . . . . . . . . : ::1
                                        192.168.1.1
   NetBIOS over Tcpip. . . . . . . . : Enabled
```

IPv6 Address Types

As stated earlier, there are three types of addresses in IPv6: anycast, unicast, and multicast. A description of each of these types of IPv6 addresses follows.

> Note the absence of the broadcast type, which is included in IPv4. You can't use broadcasts in IPv6; they've been replaced with multicasts.

Anycast Addresses Anycast addresses are not really new. The concept of anycast existed in IPv4 but was not widely used. An *anycast address* is an IPv6 address assigned to multiple devices (usually different devices). When an anycast packet is sent, it is delivered to one of the devices, usually the closest one.

Unicast Addresses A *unicast packet* uniquely identifies an interface of an IPv6 device. The interface can be a virtual or pseudo-interface or a real (physical) interface.

Unicast addresses come in several types, as described in the following list:

Global Unicast Address As of this writing, the global unicast address space is defined as 2000:: /3. The 2001::/32 networks are the IPv6 addresses currently being issued to business entities. As mentioned, Microsoft has been allocated 2001:4898:: /32. A Microsoft DHCPv6 server would be set up with scopes (ranges of addresses to be assigned) within this address space. There are some special addresses and address formats that you will see in use as well. You'll find most example addresses listed as 2001:DB8:: /32; this space has been reserved for documentation. Do you remember the loopback address in IPv4, 127.0.0.1? In IPv6 the loopback address is ::1 (or 0:0:0:0:0:0:0:0001). You may also see an address with dotted-decimal used. A dual-stack Windows Server 2012 machine may also show you FE80::5EFE:192.168.1.200. This address form is used in an integration/ migration model of IPv6 (or if you just can't leave the dotted-decimal era, I suppose).

Link-Local Address Link-local addresses are defined as FE80:: /10. If you refer to Figure 8.15 showing the ipconfig command, you will see the link-local IPv6 address as fe80::a425:ab9d:7da4:ccba. The last 8 bytes (64 bits) are random to ensure a high probability of randomness for the link-local address. The link-local address is to be used on a single link (network segment) and should never be routed.

There is another form of the local-link IPv6 address called the *Extended User Interface 64-bit (EUI-64)* format. This is derived by using the MAC address of the physical interface and inserting an FFFE between the third and fourth bytes of the MAC. The first byte is also made 02 (this sets the universal/local or U/L bit to 1 as defined in IEEE 802 frame specification). Again looking at Figure 8.15, the EUI-64 address would take the physical (MAC) address 00-03-FF-11-02-CD and make the link-local IPv6 address FE80::0203:FFFF:FE11:02CD. (I've left the preceding zeros in the link-local IPv6 address to make it easier for you to pick out the MAC address with the FFFE inserted.)

AnonymousAddress   Microsoft Server 2012 R2 uses the random address by default instead of EUI-64. The random value is called the *AnonymousAddress* in Microsoft Server 2012 R2. It can be modified to allow the use of EUI-64.

Unique Local Address   The *unique local address* can be Fc00 or FD00, and it is used like the private address space of IPv4. RFC 4193 describes unique local addresses. They are not expected to be routable on the global Internet. They are used for private routing within an organization.

Multicast Address   *Multicast addresses* are one-to-many communication packets. Multicast packets are identifiable by their first byte (most significant byte, leftmost byte, leftmost 2 nibbles, leftmost 8 bits, and so on). A multicast address is defined as FF00::/8.

In the second byte shown (the 00 of FF00), the second 0 is what's called the *scope*. Interface-local is 01, and link-local is 02. FF01:: is an interface-local multicast.

There are several well-known (already defined) multicast addresses. For example, if you want to send a packet to all nodes in the link-local scope, you send the packet to FF02::1 (also shown as FF02:0:0:0:0:0:0:1). The all-routers multicast address is FF02::2.

You can also use multicasting to get the logical link layer address (MAC address) of a device with which you are trying to communicate. Instead of using the ARP mechanism of IPv4, IPv6 uses the ICMPv6 neighbor solicitation (NS) and neighbor advertisement (NA) messages. The NS and NA ICMPv6 messages are all part of the new *Neighbor Discovery Protocol (NDP)*. This new ICMPv6 functionality also includes router solicitation and router advertisements as well as redirect messages (similar to the IPv4 redirect functionality). Table 8.7 outlines the IPv6 address space known prefixes and some well-known addresses.

Unicast vs. Anycast

Unicast and anycast addresses look the same and may be indistinguishable from each other; it just depends on how many devices have the same address. If only one device has a globally unique IPv6 address, it's a unicast address. If more than one device has the same address, it's an anycast address. Both unicast and anycast are considered one-to-one communication, although you could say that anycast is one-to-"one of many."

TABLE 8.7   IPv6 address space known prefixes and addresses

Address Prefix	Scope of Use
2000:: /3	Global unicast space prefix
FE80:: /10	Link-local address prefix
FC00:: /7	Unique local unicast prefix
FD00:: /8	Unique local unicast prefix
FF00:: /8	Multicast prefix
2001:DB8:: /32	Global unicast prefix used for documentation
::1	Reserved local loopback address
2001:0000: /32	Teredo prefix (discussed later in this chapter)
2002:: /16	6to4 prefix

IPv6 Integration/Migration

It's time to get into the mind-set of integrating IPv6 into your existing infrastructure with the longer goal of migrating to IPv6. In other words, this is not going to be an "OK, Friday the Internet is changing over" rollout. You have to bring about the change as a controlled implementation. It could easily take three to five years before a solid migration occurs and probably longer. I think the migration will take slightly less time than getting the world to migrate to the metric system on the overall timeline. The process of integration/migration consists of several mechanisms.

Dual Stack   Simply running both IPv4 and IPv6 on the same network, utilizing the IPv4 address space for devices using only IPv4 addresses and utilizing the IPv6 address space for devices using IPv6 addresses

Tunneling   Using an encapsulation scheme for transporting one address space inside another

Address Translation   Using a higher-level application to change one address type (IPv4 or IPv6) to the other transparently so that end devices are unaware one address space is talking to another

I elaborate on these three mechanisms in the following sections.

IPv6 Dual Stack

The default implementation in Windows Server 2012 R2 is an enabled IPv6 configuration along with IPv4; this is dual stack. The implementation can be dual IP layer or dual TCP/IP stack. Windows Server 2012 R2 uses the dual IP layer implementation (see Figure 8.16). When an application queries a DNS server to resolve a hostname to an IP address, the DNS server may respond with an IPv4 address or an IPv6 address. If the DNS server responds with both, Windows Server 2012 R2 will prefer the IPv6 address. Windows Server 2012 R2 can use both IPv4 and IPv6 addresses as necessary for network communication. When looking at the output of the ipconfig command, you will see both address spaces displayed.

FIGURE 8.16   IPv6 dual IP layer diagram

IPv6 Tunneling

Windows Server 2012 R2 includes several tunneling mechanisms for tunneling IPv6 through the IPv4 address space. They include the following:

- Intra-Site Automatic Tunnel Addressing Protocol (ISATAP), which is used for unicast IPv6 communication across an IPv4 infrastructure. ISATAP is enabled by default in Windows Server 2012 R2.

- 6to4, which is used for unicast IPv6 communication across an IPv4 infrastructure.

- Teredo, which is used for unicast IPv6 communication with an IPv4 NAT implementation across an IPv4 infrastructure.

With multiple tunneling protocols available and enabled by default, you might ask, what's the difference, and why is one used over the others? They all allow you to tunnel IPv6 packets through the IPv4 address space (a really cool thing if you're trying to integrate/migrate). Here are the details of these tunneling mechanisms:

ISATAP   *Intra-Site Automatic Tunnel Addressing Protocol (ISATAP)* is the automatic tunnel addressing protocol providing IPv6 addresses based on the IPv4 address of the end interface (node). The IPv6 address is automatically configured on the local device, and the dual stack machine can use either its IPv4 or IPv6 address to communicate on the local network (within the local network infrastructure). ISATAP can use the neighbor discovery mechanism to determine the router ID and network prefix where the device is located, thus making intrasite communication possible even in a routed infrastructure.

The format of an ISATAP address is as follows:

[64bits of prefix] [32bits indicating ISATAP] [32bits IPv4 Address]

The center 32 bits indicating ISATAP are actually 0000:5EFE (when using private IPv4 addresses). The ISATAP address of the example Windows Server 2012 R2 machine using the link-local IPv6 address is FE80::5EFE:192.168.1.200. Each node participating in the ISATAP infrastructure must support ISATAP. If you're routing through an IPv4 cloud, a border router (a router transitioning from an IPv6 to IPv4 space) must support ISATAP. Windows Server 2012 R2 can be configured as a border router, and it will forward ISATAP packets. ISATAP is experimental and is defined in RFC 4214.

6to4   *6to4* specifies a procedure for IPv6 networks to communicate with each other through an IPv4 space without the IPv6 nodes having to know what's happening. The IPv6 nodes do not need to be dual stacked to make this happen. The border router is the device responsible for knowing about the IPv6-to-IPv4 transition. The IPv6 packets are encapsulated at the border router (and decapsulated at the other end or on the way back). There is an assigned prefix for the 6to4 implementation: 2002:: /16. 6to4 is defined in RFC 3056.

Teredo   *Teredo* (named after a kind of shipworm that drills holes in the wood of ships) is a protocol designed to allow IPv6 addresses to be available to hosts through one or more layers of NAT. Teredo uses a process of tunneling packets through the IPv4 space using UDP. The Teredo service encapsulates the IPv6 data within a UDP segment (packet) and uses IPv4 addressing to get through the IPv4 cloud. Having a layer 4 (Transport layer) available to use as translation functionality is what gives you the ability to be behind a NAT. Teredo provides host-to-host communication and dynamic addressing for IPv6 nodes (dual stack), allowing the nodes to have access to resources in an IPv6 network and the IPv6 devices to have access to the IPv6 devices that have only connectivity to the IPv4 space (like home users who have an IPv6-enabled operating system connecting to IPv6 resources while their home ISP has only IPv4 capabilities). Teredo is defined in RFC 4380.

In Windows Server 2012 R2, an IPv4 Teredo server is identified and configured (using the netsh command interface). The Teredo server provides connectivity resources (address) to the Teredo client (the node that has access to the IPv4 Internet and needs access to an IPv6 network/Internet). A Teredo relay is a component used by the IPv6 router to receive traffic destined for Teredo clients and forward the traffic appropriately. The defined prefix for Teredo address is 2001:0000:: /32. Teredo does add overhead like all the other implementations discussed. It is generally accepted that you should use the simplest model available. However, in the process of integration/migration for most of us behind a NAT, Teredo will be the process to choose.

From Windows Server 2012 R2, use the ipconfig /all command to view the default configurations including IPv4 and IPv6. You may notice a notation that I didn't discuss, the percent sign at the end of the IPv6 address (see Figure 8.17). The number after the percent sign is the virtual interface identifier used by Windows Server 2012 R2.

FIGURE 8.17   IPv6 interface identifier for ipconfig display

```
Link-local IPv6 Address . . . . . : fe80::a425:ab9d:7da4:ccba%10
```

Useful IPv6 Information Commands

You can use numerous commands to view, verify, and configure the network parameters of Windows Server 2012 R2. Specifically, you can use the netsh command set and the route command set as well as the standard ping and tracert functions.

Use the netsh command interface (as well as the provided dialog boxes, if you want) to examine and configure IPv6 functionality. The netsh command issued from the command interpreter changes into a network shell (netsh) where you can configure and view both IPv4 and IPv6 components.

Don't forget to use the ever-popular route print command to see the Windows Server 2012 R2 routing tables (IPv4 and IPv6). The other diagnostic commands are still available for IPv4 as well as IPv6. In previous versions of Microsoft operating systems, ping was the IPv4 command, and ping6 was the IPv6 command. This has changed in Windows Server 2012 R2; ping works for both IPv4 and IPv6 to test layer 3 connectivity to remote devices. The IPv4 tracert command was tracert6 for IPv6. The command is now tracert for both IPv4 and IPv6, and it will show you every layer 3 (IP) hop from source to destination. (This assumes that all of the administrators from here to there want you to see the hops and are not blocking ICMP. It also assumes that there are no IP tunnels, which your packets are traversing; you won't see the router hops in the tunnel either.)

Overall, the consortium of people developing the Internet and the Internet Protocol have tried to make all of the changes to communication infrastructures easy to implement. (This is a daunting task with the many vendors and various infrastructures currently in place.) The goal is not to daze and confuse administrators; it's designed to provide maximum flexibility with the greatest functionality. IPv6 is going to provide the needed layer 3 (Network layer, global addressing layer, logical addressing layer...call it what you like) functionality for the foreseeable future.

Subnetting with IPv6

Subnetting with IPv6 is a lot like subnetting with IPv4. You need to know how many bits you are going to use for the network mask to subnet it correctly.

For example, let's say you have an IPv6 prefix of 2001:DB8:BBCC:0000::/53 and you need to set up your network so that your IPv6 addressing scheme can handle 1,500 more subnets. How would you figure this out?

When determining any number of hosts or subnets, the calculation is 2 to the power (2^x). The first power number that is greater than or equal to the number you need is the power number that you add to the current network mask. Thus, in the previous question, to get to 1,500 subnets, you would need to determine which 2^x is the first one that is greater than or equal to 1,500. If you calculate your powers correctly, 2^{11} ($2^{11} = 2,048$) is the first one that is greater than or equal to 1,500. So, you would add the power of 11 to the /53 in the previous address, and you would now use /64 as your network mask. Table 8.8 shows you some of the power numbers for the power of 2.

TABLE 8.8 Powers of 2

Power	Equals
2^2	4
2^3	8
2^4	16
2^5	32
2^6	64
2^7	128
2^8	256
2^9	512
2^{10}	1024
2^{11}	2048
2^{12}	4096

Summary

Why TCP/IP is the primary protocol in use today is one of the important topics covered in this chapter. You also learned that the 32-bit IPv4 address is a structured and hierarchical one that is used to identify uniquely every machine on a network. You learned how to determine available IP addresses and implement subnetting. In addition, you learned how the new layer 3 IPv6 protocol is implemented, including the structure of the IPv6 address. Finally, I discussed the new functionality included in IPv6 addressing as well as several Windows Server 2012 R2 integration/migration implementations.

Exam Essentials

Understand what subnetting is and when to use it.   If an organization is large and has many computers or if its computers are geographically dispersed, it's sensible to divide its large network into smaller ones connected by routers. These smaller networks are called *subnets*. Subnetting is the process of carving a single IP network into smaller, logical subnetworks.

Understand subnet masks.   For the subnet address scheme to work, every machine on the network must know which part of the host address will be used as the subnet address. The network administrator creates a 32-bit subnet mask consisting of 1s and 0s. The 1s in the subnet mask represent the positions that refer to the network or subnet addresses. The 0s represent the positions that refer to the host portion of the address.

Understand IPv6.   Understand the structure of an IPv6 address and how it's displayed. Know the shortcuts and rules (such as for displaying 0s) for writing IPv6 addresses. Know the integration/migration components for IPv6 included in Windows Server 2012 R2, including tunneling and dual stack.

Review Questions

1. You are the network administrator for ABC Company. You have an IPv6 prefix of 2001:DB8:BBCC:0000::/53, and you need to set up your network so that your IPv6 addressing scheme can handle 1,000 more subnets. Which network mask would you use?

   A. /60

   B. /61

   C. /62

   D. /63

   E. /64

2. You are the network administrator for Stellacon Corporation. Stellacon has a Windows Server 2012 R2 machine that needs to be able to communicate with all of the computers on the internal network. Stellacon has decided to add 15 new segments to its IPv6 network. How would you configure the IPv6 address so that the server can communicate with all the segments?

   A. Configure the IPv6 address as fd00::2b0:e0ff:dee9:4143/8.

   B. Configure the IPv6 address as fe80::2b0:e0ff:dee9:4143/32.

   C. Configure the IPv6 address as ff80::2b0:e0ff:dee9:4143/64.

   D. Configure the IPv6 address as fe80::2b0:e0ff:dee9:4143/64.

3. You are the network administrator for a midsize organization that has installed Windows Server 2012 R2 onto the network. You are thinking of moving all machines to Windows 8 and IPv6. You decide to set up a test environment with four subnets. What type of IPv6 addresses do you need set up?

   A. Global addresses

   B. Link-local addresses

   C. Unique local addresses

   D. Site-local addresses

4. You have a large IP-routed network using the address 137.25.0.0; it is composed of 20 subnets, with a maximum of 300 hosts on each subnet. Your company continues on a merger-and-acquisitions spree, and your manager has told you to prepare for an increase to 50 subnets with some containing more than 600 hosts. Using the existing network address, which of the following subnet masks would work for the requirement set by your manager?

   A. 255.255.252.0

   B. 255.255.254.0

   C. 255.255.248.0

   D. 255.255.240.0

5. Your company is growing dramatically via acquisitions of other companies. As the network administrator, you need to keep up with the changes because they affect the workstations, and you need to support them. When you started, there were 15 locations connected via routers, and now there are 25. As new companies are acquired, they are migrated to Windows Server 2012 R2 and brought into the same domain as another site. Management says that they are going to acquire at least 10 more companies in the next two years. The engineers have also told you that they are redesigning the company's Class B address into an IP addressing scheme that will support these requirements and that there will never be more than 1,000 network devices on any subnet. What is the appropriate subnet mask to support this network when the changes are completed?

   A. 255.255.252.0

   B. 255.255.248.0

   C. 255.255.255.0

   D. 255.255.255.128

6. You work for a small printing company that has 75 workstations. Most of them run standard office applications such as word processing, spreadsheet, and accounting programs. Fifteen of the workstations are constantly processing huge graphics files and then sending print jobs to industrial-sized laser printers. The performance of the network has always been an issue, but you have never addressed it. You have now migrated your network to Windows 8 and Windows Server 2012 R2 and have decided to take advantage of the routing capability built into Windows Server 2012 R2. You choose the appropriate server and place two NICs in the machine, but you realize that you have only one network address, 201.102.34.0, which you obtained years ago. How should you subnet this address to segment the bandwidth hogs from the rest of the network while giving everyone access to the entire network?

   A. 255.255.255.192

   B. 255.255.255.224

   C. 255.255.255.252

   D. 255.255.255.240

7. You work for Carpathian Worldwide Enterprises, which has more than 50 administrative and manufacturing locations around the world. The size of these organizations varies greatly, with the number of computers per location ranging from 15 to slightly fewer than 1,000. The sales operations use more than 1,000 facilities, each of which contains 2 to 5 computers. Carpathian is also in merger talks with another large organization. If the merger materializes as planned, you will have to accommodate another 100 manufacturing and administrative locations, each with a maximum of 600 computers, as well as 2,000 additional sales facilities. You don't have any numbers for the future growth of the company, but you are told to keep growth in mind. You decide to implement a private addressing plan for the entire organization. More than half of your routers don't support variable-length subnet masking. Which subnet masks would work for this situation? (Choose all that apply.)

   A. 255.255.224.0

   B. 255.255.240.0

   C. 255.255.248.0

   D. 255.255.252.0

   E. 255.255.254.0

8. Which of the following subnet masks are represented with the CIDR of /27?

   A. 255.255.255.254

   B. 255.255.255.248

   C. 255.255.255.224

   D. 255.255.255.240

9. You are the administrator for a Windows Server 2012 R2 network that uses DHCP. You notice that your DHCP database is getting too large, and you want to reduce the size of the database. What should you do?

   A. From the folder containing the DHCP database, run `jetpack.exe dhcp.mdb temp.mdb`.

   B. From the folder containing the DHCP database, run `shrinkpack.exe dhcp.mdb temp.mdb`.

   C. From the folder containing the DHCP database, run `jetshrink.exe dhcp.mdb temp.mdb`.

   D. From the folder containing the DHCP database, run `shrinkjet.exe dhcp.mdb temp.mdb`.

10. You ask one of your technicians to get the IPv6 address of a new Windows Server 2012 R2 machine, and she hands you a note with FE80::0203:FFFF:FE11:2CD on it. What can you tell from this address? (Choose two.)

    A. This is a globally unique IPv6 address.

    B. This is a link-local IPv6 address.

    C. This is a multicast IPv6 address.

    D. In EUI-64 format, you can see the MAC address of the node.

    E. In EUI-64 format, you can see the IPv4 address of the node.

Chapter

9

Use Virtualization in Windows Server 2012

THE FOLLOWING 70-410 EXAM OBJECTIVES ARE COVERED IN THIS CHAPTER:

✓ **Create and configure virtual machine settings**

- Configure dynamic memory
- Configure smart paging
- Configure Resource Metering
- Configure guest integration services
- Create and configure Generation 1 and 2 virtual machines
- Configure and use extended session mode
- Configure remoteFX

✓ **Create and configure virtual machine storage**

- Create VHDs and VHDX
- Configure differencing drives
- Modify VHDs
- Configure pass-through disks
- Manage checkpoints
- Implement a virtual Fibre Channel adapter
- Configure storage Quality of Service

✓ **Create and configure virtual networks**

- Configure Hyper-V virtual switches
- Optimize network performance
- Configure MAC addresses
- Configure network isolation
- Configure synthetic and legacy virtual network adapters
- Configure NIC teaming in virtual machines

Hyper-V is a server role in Windows Server 2012 R2 that allows you to virtualize your environment and therefore run multiple virtual operating system instances simultaneously on a physical server. This not only helps you to improve server utilization but also helps you to create a more cost-effective and dynamic system.

In this chapter, you will learn the basic concepts and features of Hyper-V that a Windows Server 2012 R2 technical specialist must know. You will also get a solid understanding of what is important in virtualization and in what areas of your work life you can use it.

Hyper-V Overview

In the following sections, I'll introduce you to Hyper-V. To begin, you'll take a look at virtualization and what types of virtualization exist. I will then discuss Hyper-V features and the Hyper-V architecture before finishing up with the Hyper-V requirements for software and hardware.

What Is Virtualization?

Virtualization is a method for abstracting physical resources from the way that they interact with other resources. For example, if you abstract the physical hardware from the operating system, you get the benefit of being able to move the operating system between different physical systems.

This is called *server virtualization*. But there are also other forms of virtualization available, such as presentation virtualization, desktop virtualization, and application virtualization. I will now briefly explain the differences between these forms of virtualization:

Server Virtualization   This basically enables multiple servers to run on the same physical server. Hyper-V is a server virtualization tool that allows you to move physical machines to virtual machines and manage them on a few physical servers. Thus, you will be able to consolidate physical servers.

Presentation Virtualization   When you use *presentation virtualization*, your applications run on a different computer, and only the screen information is transferred to your computer. An example of presentation virtualization is Microsoft Remote Desktop Services in Windows Server 2012 R2.

Desktop Virtualization   *Desktop virtualization* provides you with a virtual machine on your desktop, comparable to server virtualization. You run your complete operating system and applications in a virtual machine so that your local physical machine just needs to run a very basic operating system. An example of this form of virtualization is Microsoft Virtual PC.

Application Virtualization   *Application virtualization* helps prevent conflicts between applications on the same PC. Thus, it helps you to isolate the application running environment from the operating system installation requirements by creating application-specific copies of all shared resources. It also helps reduce application-to-application incompatibility and testing needs. An example of an application virtualization tool is Microsoft Application Virtualization (App-V).

Hyper-V Features

As a lead-in to the virtualization topic and Hyper-V, I will start with a list of key features, followed by a list of supported guest operating systems. This should provide you with a quick, high-level view of this feature before you dig deeper into the technology.

Key Features of Hyper-V

The following are the key features of Hyper-V:

New Architecture   The hypervisor-based architecture, which has a 64-bit micro-kernel, provides a new array of device support as well as performance and security improvements.

Operating System Support   Both 32-bit and 64-bit operating systems can run simultaneously in Hyper-V. Also, different platforms like Windows, Linux, and others are supported.

Support for Symmetric Multiprocessors   Support for up to 64 processors in a virtual machine environment provides you with the ability to run applications as well as multiple virtual machines faster.

Network Load Balancing   Hyper-V provides support for *Windows Network Load Balancing (NLB)* to balance the network load across virtual machines on different servers.

New Hardware Architecture   Hyper-V's new architecture provides improved utilization of resources such as networking and disks.

Quick Migration   Hyper-V's *quick migration* feature provides you with the functionality to run virtual machines in a clustered environment with switchover capabilities when there is a failure. Thus, you can reduce downtime and achieve higher availability of your virtual machines.

Virtual Machine Snapshot   You can take snapshots of running virtual machines, which provides you with the capability to recover to any previous virtual machine snapshot state quickly and easily.

Resource Metering   Hyper-V *resource metering* allows an organization to track usage within the businesses departments. It allows an organization to create a usage-based billing solution that adjusts to the provider's business model and strategy.

Scripting   Using the Windows Management Instrumentation (WMI) interfaces and APIs, you can easily build custom scripts to automate processes in your virtual machines.

RemoteFX   Windows Server 2012 R2 Hyper-V RemoteFX allows for an enhanced user experience for RemoteFX desktops by providing a 3D virtual adapter, intelligent codecs, and the ability to redirect USB devices in virtual machines.

Fibre Channel   The virtual Fibre Channel feature allows you to connect to the Fibre Channel storage unit from within the virtual machine. *Virtual Fibre Channel* allows an administrator to use their existing Fibre Channel to support virtualized workloads. Hyper-V users have the ability to use Fibre Channel storage area networks (SANs) to virtualize the workloads that require direct access to SAN logical unit numbers (LUNs).

Enhanced Session Mode   *Enhanced Session Mode* enhances the interactive session of the Virtual Machine Connection for Hyper-V administrators who want to connect to their virtual machines. It gives administrators the same functionality as a remote desktop connection when the administrator is interacting with a virtual machine.

In previous versions of Hyper-V, the virtual machine connection gave you limited functionality while you connected to the virtual machine screen, keyboard, and mouse. An administrator could use an RDP connection to get full redirection abilities, but that would require a network connection to the virtual machine host.

Enhanced Session Mode gives administrators the following benefits for local resource redirection:

- Display configuration
- Audio
- Printers
- Clipboard
- Smart cards
- Drives
- USB devices
- Supported Plug and Play devices

Shared Virtual Hard Disk   Windows Server 2012 R2 Hyper-V has a new feature called Shared Virtual Hard Disk. *Shared Virtual Hard Disk* allows an administrator to cluster virtual machines by using shared virtual hard disk (VHDX) files.

Shared virtual hard disks allow an administrator to build a high availability infrastructure, which is important if you are setting up either a private cloud deployment or a cloud-hosted environment for managing large workloads. Shared virtual hard disks allow two or more virtual machines to access the same virtual hard disk (VHDX) file.

Automatic Virtual Machine Activation (AVMA)   *Automatic Virtual Machine Activation (AVMA)* is a new feature that allows administrators to install virtual machines on a properly activated Windows Server 2012 R2 system without the need to manage individual product keys for each virtual machine. When using AVMA, virtual machines get bound to the licensed Hyper-V server as soon as the virtual machine starts.

Network Isolation   One nice feature of using Microsoft Hyper-V network virtualization is the ability of Hyper-V to keep virtual networks isolated from the physical network infrastructure of the hosted system. Because administrators can set up Hyper-V software–defined virtualization policies, you are no longer limited by the IP address assignment or VLAN isolation requirements of the physical network. Hyper-V allows for built-in network isolation to keep the virtual network separated from the virtual network.

Dynamic Memory   *Dynamic Memory* is a feature of Hyper-V that allows it to balance memory automatically among running virtual machines. Dynamic Memory allows Hyper-V to adjust the amount of memory available to the virtual machines in response to the needs of the virtual machines. It is currently available for Hyper-V in Windows Server 2012 R2.

Supported Guest Operating Systems

The following guest operating systems have been successfully tested on Hyper-V and are hypervisor-aware. Table 9.1 shows all of the guest server operating systems and the maximum number of virtual processors. Table 9.2 shows all of the guest client operating systems and the maximum number of virtual processors.

TABLE 9.1   Hyper-V guest server operating systems

Guest Operating System (Server)	Maximum Number of Virtual Processors
Windows Server 2012 and Server 2012 R2	64
Windows Server 2008 R2 with Service Pack 1 (SP1)	64
Windows Server 2008 R2	64
Windows Server 2008 with Service Pack 2 (SP2)	8
Windows Home Server 2011	4
Windows Small Business Server 2011	Essentials edition: 2 Standard edition: 4
Windows Server 2003 R2 with Service Pack 2 (SP2)	2
Windows Server 2003 with Service Pack 2 (SP2)	2

TABLE 9.1 Hyper-V guest server operating systems *(continued)*

Guest Operating System (Server)	Maximum Number of Virtual Processors
Red Hat Enterprise Linux 5.7 and 5.8	64
Red Hat Enterprise Linux 6.0–6.3	64
SUSE Linux Enterprise Server 11 SP2	64
Open SUSE 12.1	64
Ubuntu 12.04	64

TABLE 9.2 Hyper-V guest client operating systems

Guest Operating System (Client)	Maximum Number of Virtual Processors
Windows 8	32
Windows 7 with Service Pack 1 (SP1)	4
Windows 7	4
Windows Vista with Service Pack 2 (SP2)	2
Windows XP with Service Pack 3 (SP3)	2
Windows XP x64 Edition with Service Pack 2 (SP2)	2
CentOS 5.7 and 5.8	64
CentOS 6.0–6.3	64
Red Hat Enterprise Linux 5.7 and 5.8	64
Red Hat Enterprise Linux 6.0–6.3	64
SUSE Linux Enterprise Server 11 SP2	64
Open SUSE 12.1	64
Ubuntu 12.04	64

The list of supported guest operating systems may always be extended. Please check the official Microsoft Hyper-V site to obtain a current list of supported operating systems: www.microsoft.com/virtualization.

Hyper-V Architecture

This section will provide you with an overview of the Hyper-V architecture (see Figure 9.1). I'll explain the differences between a hypervisor-aware and a non-hypervisor-aware child partition.

FIGURE 9.1   Hyper-V architecture

As you can see, Hyper-V is based on the new microkernel architecture. Hyper-V provides a virtualization layer called a *hypervisor* that runs directly on the system hardware. You can see that the hypervisor is similar to what the kernel is to Windows. It is a software layer responsible for the interaction with the core hardware and works in conjunction with an optimized instance of Windows Server 2012 R2 that allows running multiple operating systems on a physical server simultaneously. The Hyper-V architecture consists of the hypervisor and parent and child partitions.

The Windows Server 2012 R2 operating system runs in the parent partition, and it delivers the WMI provider for scripting as well as the VM service.

Virtual machines each run in their own child partitions. Child partitions do not have direct access to hardware resources; instead, they have a virtual view of the resources, which are called *virtual devices*.

If you're running a hypervisor-aware operating system like Windows Server 2003, Windows Server 2008, Windows Server 2008 R2, Windows Server 2012, or Windows Server 2012 R2 in your virtual machine, any request to the virtual devices is redirected via the high-speed bus to the devices in the parent partition, which will manage the requests.

By default, only Windows Server 2008 R2, Server 2012, and Server 2012 R2 are hypervisor-aware operating systems. Once you install Hyper-V Integration Components on an operating system other than Windows Server 2008 R2 and newer, it will be hypervisor-aware. Microsoft provides a hypervisor adapter to make Linux hypervisor aware.

Non-hypervisor-aware operating systems (for example, Windows NT 4.0) use an emulator to communicate with the Windows hypervisor, which is slower than molasses in the winter.

Hyper-V Requirements

The following sections will describe the hardware and software requirements for installing the Hyper-V server role. It is important to understand these requirements for obtaining your software license as well as for planning for server hardware. When you understand the requirements, you can design and configure a Hyper-V solution that will meet the needs of your applications.

Hardware Requirements

In addition to the basic hardware requirements for Windows Server 2012 R2, there are requirements for running the Hyper-V server role on your Windows server. They are listed in Table 9.3.

TABLE 9.3   Hardware requirements for Hyper-V

Requirement Area	Definition
CPU	x64-compatible processor with Intel VT or AMD-V technology enabled. Hardware Data Execution Prevention (DEP), specifically Intel XD bit (execute disable bit) or AMD NX bit (no execute bit), must be available and enabled. Minimum: 1.4GHz. Recommended: 2GHz or faster.
Memory	Minimum: 1GB RAM. Recommended: 2GB RAM or greater. (Additional RAM is required for each running guest operating system.) Maximum: 1TB.
Hard disk	Minimum: 8GB. Recommended: 20GB or greater. (Additional disk space needed for each guest operating system.)

The Add Roles Wizard in Server Manager additionally verifies the hardware requirements. A good starting point is to check your hardware against the Microsoft hardware list to make sure that Windows Server 2012 R2 supports your hardware. If you try to install the Hyper-V server role on a computer that does not meet the CPU requirements, you'll get a warning window that looks like Figure 9.2.

FIGURE 9.2   Warning window that Hyper-V cannot be installed

Software Requirements

To use virtualization in Windows Server 2012 R2, you need to consider the basic software requirements for Hyper-V. Hyper-V runs only on the following editions of the Windows Server 2012 R2 operating system:

- Windows Server 2012 R2 Standard edition
- Windows Server 2012 R2 Datacenter edition
- Microsoft Hyper-V Server 2012 R2 edition

Hyper-V Installation and Configuration

The following sections explain how to install the Hyper-V role using Server Manager in Windows Server 2012 R2 Full installation mode or the command line mode in Windows Server 2012 R2 Server Core. We will then take a look at Hyper-V as part of Server Manager before discussing how to use the Hyper-V Manager. Finally, we will look at the Hyper-V server settings and then cover two important areas for Hyper-V: virtual networks and virtual hard disks.

Install the Hyper-V Role

Now it's time to see how to install the Hyper-V server role on the two installation options of Windows Server 2012 R2, namely, a Full installation and a Server Core installation.

Installing Hyper-V in Full Installation Mode

You can install the Hyper-V server role on any Windows Server 2012 R2 installation for which the Full option was chosen. In addition, the server must meet both the hardware and software requirements. The installation process is simple, as Exercise 9.1 demonstrates.

EXERCISE 9.1

Installing Hyper-V in Full Installation Mode

1. Open Server Manager.

2. In Server Manager, choose option 2, Add Roles And Features.

3. At the Select Installation Type page, choose the role-based or feature-based installation. Click Next.

4. On the Select Destination Server screen, choose Select A Server From The Server Pool and choose the server to which you want to add this role. Click Next.

5. On the Select Server Roles screen, click the check box next to Hyper-V. When the Add Features dialog box appears, click the Add Features button. Then click Next.

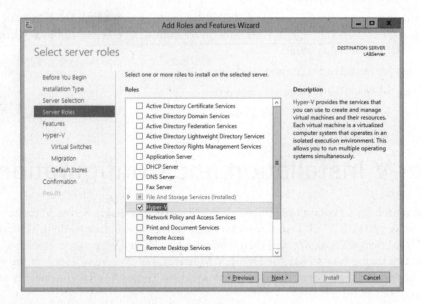

6. At the Select Features screen, click Next.

7. At the Hyper-V introduction screen, click Next.

8. At the Create Virtual Switches screen, choose your adapter and click Next.

9.   At the Virtual Machine Migration screen, click Next. You want to use migration only if you have multiple Hyper-V servers. Since we will have only one for this exercise, just skip this screen.

10. At the Default Stores screen, accept the defaults and click Next.

11. At the Confirmation screen, click the Install button.

12. After the installation is complete, click the Close button.

13. Restart your server.

Installing Hyper-V in Server Core

The Server Core installation option is introduced in Windows Server 2012 R2. It creates an operating system installation without a GUI shell. You can either manage the server remotely from another system or use the Server Core's command-line interface.

This installation option provides the following benefits:

- Reduces attack surface (because fewer applications are running on the server)
- Reduces maintenance and management (because only the required options are installed)
- Requires less disk space and produces less processor utilization
- Provides a minimal parent partition
- Reduces system resources required by the operating system as well as the attack surface

By using Hyper-V on a Server Core installation, you can fundamentally improve availability because the attack surface is reduced and the downtime required for installing patches is optimized. It will thus be more secure and reliable with less management.

To install Hyper-V for a Windows Server 2012 R2 installation, you must execute the following command in the command-line interface:

```
Dism /online /enable-feature /featurename:Microsoft-Hyper-V
```

Hyper-V in Server Manager

As with all of the other Windows Server 2012 R2 roles, the Hyper-V role neatly integrates into Server Manager. Server Manager filters the information just for the specific role and thus displays only the required information. As you can see in Figure 9.3, the Hyper-V Summary page shows related event log entries, the state of the system services for Hyper-V, and useful resources and support.

FIGURE 9.3 Hyper-V in Server Manager

Using Hyper-V Manager

Hyper-V Manager is the central management console to configure your server and create and manage your virtual machines, virtual networks, and virtual hard disks. Unlike Virtual Server 2005, where you managed all virtual machines through a web interface, Hyper-V Manager is managed through a Microsoft Management Console (MMC) snap-in. You can access it either in Server Manager or by using Administrative Tools ➢ Hyper-V Manager. Figure 9.4 shows how Hyper-V Manager looks once you start it.

FIGURE 9.4   Hyper-V Manager

Hyper-V Manager is available for the following operating systems:

- Windows Server 2012 R2
- Windows Server 2008 R2
- Windows Server 2008
- Windows 8
- Windows 7
- Windows Vista with Service Pack 1 (SP1)

Hyper-V Manager is installed on a Windows Server 2012 R2 machine only when you install Hyper-V on it. On Windows Server 2008/2008 R2, Server 2003, Windows Vista, Windows 7, or Windows 8, you will need to install the Hyper-V Manager MMC.

You can use Hyper-V Manager to connect to any Full or Server Core installation remotely. Besides Hyper-V Manager, you can use the WMI interface for scripting Hyper-V.

Configure Hyper-V Settings

In this section, you will get an overview of the available Hyper-V settings for the server. You configure all server-side default configuration settings like default locations of your configuration files or the release key. You can open the Hyper-V Settings page (see Figure 9.5) in Hyper-V Manager by clicking Hyper-V Settings in the Actions pane.

FIGURE 9.5 Hyper-V Settings

The Hyper-V Settings page includes the following settings:

Virtual Hard Disks   Specifies the default location of your virtual hard disk files (.vhd and .vdhx).

Virtual Machines   Specifies the default location of your virtual machine configuration files. It includes the Virtual Machine XML configuration files (part of the Virtual Machines folder) as well as related snapshots (part of the Snapshot folder).

Physical GPUs   This feature allows for graphical processing unit (GPU) accelerated video within a virtual machine. The GPU will allow you to support 3D GPU accelerated graphics.

NUMA Spanning   An administrator can configure Hyper-V to allow virtual machines to span nonuniform memory architecture (NUMA) nodes. When the physical computer has NUMA nodes, this setting provides virtual machines with additional computing resources. Spanning NUMA nodes can help you run more virtual machines at the same time. However, using NUMA can decrease overall performance.

Live Migrations   *Live migration* allows a Hyper-V administrator to relocate running virtual machines easily from one node of the failover cluster to another node in the same cluster. Live Migration is explained in more detail later in this chapter.

Storage Migrations   *Storage Migration* allows an administrator to move their virtual machine storage from one location to another. This setting allows you to specify how many storage migrations can be performed at the same time on this system.

Replication Configuration   This setting allows you to configure this computer as a Replica Server to another Hyper-V server. Hyper-V Replica allows administrators to replicate their Hyper-V virtual machines from one Hyper-V host at a primary site to another Hyper-V host at the Replica site.

Each node of the failover cluster that is involved in Replica must have the Hyper-V server role installed. One of the servers in the Hyper-V replication needs to be set up as a Replica Broker to allow the replication to work properly.

Keyboard   Defines how to use Windows key combinations. Options are Physical Computer, Virtual Machine, and Virtual Machine Only When Running Full Screen.

Mouse Release Key   Specifies the key combination to release the mouse in your virtual machine. Options are Ctrl+Alt+left arrow, Ctrl+Alt+right arrow, Ctrl+Alt+space, and Ctrl+Alt+Shift.

Reset Check Boxes   Resets any check boxes that hide pages and messages when checked. This will bring any window up again on which you checked the Do Not Show This Window Again check box.

Manage Virtual Switches

A *virtual network* provides the virtual links between nodes in either a virtual or physical network. Virtual networking in Hyper-V is provided in a secure and dynamic way because you can granularly define virtual network switches for their required usage. For example, you can define a private or internal virtual network if you don't want to allow your virtual machines to send packages to the physical network.

To allow your virtual machines to communicate with each other, you need virtual networks. Just like normal networks, virtual networks exist only on the host computer and allow you to configure how virtual machines communicate with each other, with the host, and with the network or the Internet. You manage virtual networks in Hyper-V using Virtual Switch Manager, as shown in Figure 9.6.

FIGURE 9.6   Virtual Network Manager

Using *Virtual Switch Manager*, you can create, manage, and delete virtual switches. You can define the network type as external, internal only, or private.

External   Any virtual machine connected to this virtual switch can access the physical network. You would use this option if you want to allow your virtual machines to access, for example, other servers on the network or the Internet. This option is used in production environments where your clients connect directly to the virtual machines.

Internal   This option allows virtual machines to communicate with each other as well as the host system but not with the physical network. When you create an internal network, it also creates a local area connection in Network Connections that allows the host machine to communicate with the virtual machines. You can use this if you want to separate your host's network from your virtual networks.

Private   When you use this option, virtual machines can communicate with each other but not with the host system or the physical network; thus, no network packets are hitting the wire. You can use this to define internal virtual networks for test environments or labs, for example.

On the external and internal-only virtual networks, you also can enable virtual LAN (VLAN) identification. You can use VLANs to partition your network into multiple subnets using a VLAN ID. When you enable virtual LAN identification, the NIC that is connected to the switch will never see packets tagged with VLAN IDs. Instead, all packets traveling from the NIC to the switch will be tagged with the access mode VLAN ID as they leave the switch port. All packets traveling from the switch port to the NIC will have their VLAN tags removed. You can use this if you are already logically segmenting your physical machines and also use it for your virtual ones.

Exercise 9.2 explains how to create an internal-only virtual switch.

EXERCISE 9.2

Creating an Internal Virtual Network

1.   Click the Windows Key ➢ Administrative Tools ➢ Hyper-V Manager.

2.   In Hyper-V Manager, in the Actions pane, choose Virtual Switch Manager.

3.   On the Virtual Switch page, select Private and click the Create Virtual Switch button.

4.   On the New Virtual Switch page, enter **Private Virtual Network** in the Name field.

5.   Click OK.

When you create the internal virtual switch, a network device is created in Network Connections, as shown in Figure 9.7.

FIGURE 9.7   Virtual network card

This is also the case when you create an external virtual network because it will replace the physical network card of the host machine to give the parent partition a virtual network card that is also used in the child partitions.

Unlike with Virtual Server 2005, Hyper-V binds the virtual network service to a physical network adapter only when an external virtual network is created. The benefit of this is that the performance is better if you do not use the external virtual network option. The downside, however, is that there will be a network disruption when you create or delete an external virtual network.

> Communication between the virtual machine and the local host computer is not configured automatically. Once you install a virtual machine, you need to make sure that the TCP/IP settings are in agreement with the settings you define in the virtual network card. Start with a ping from your host machine to the virtual machines to verify that communication is working.

Managing Virtual Hard Disks

In addition to virtual networks, you need to manage virtual hard disks that you attach to your virtual machines. A virtual hard disk in Hyper-V, apart from a pass-through disk, is a VHD or VHDX file that basically simulates a hard drive on your virtual machine.

The following sections will first show you what types of virtual hard disks are available and then show you how to create them. You will also learn about what options are available to manage virtual hard disks.

Types of Hard Disks

Depending on how you want to use the disk, Hyper-V offers various types, as described in Table 9.4.

TABLE 9.4   Virtual hard disks in Hyper-V

Type of disk	Description	When to use it
Dynamically expanding	This disk starts with a small VHD file and expands it on demand once an installation takes place. It can grow to the maximum size you defined during creation. You can use this type of disk to clone a local hard drive during creation.	This option is effective when you don't know the exact space needed on the disk and when you want to preserve hard disk space on the host machine. Unfortunately, it is the slowest disk type.

Fixed size	The size of the VHD file is fixed to the size specified when the disk is created. This option is faster than a dynamically expanding disk. However, a fixed-size disk uses up the maximum defined space immediately. This type is ideal for cloning a local hard drive.	A fixed-size disk provides faster access than dynamically expanding or differencing disks, but it is slower than a physical disk.
Differencing	This type of disk is associated in a parent-child relationship with another disk. The differencing disk is the child, and the associated virtual disk is the parent. Differencing disks include only the differences to the parent disk. By using this type, you can save a lot of disk space in similar virtual machines. This option is suitable if you have multiple virtual machines with similar operating systems.	Differencing disks are most commonly found in test environments and should not be used in production environments.
Physical (or pass-through disk)	The virtual machine receives direct pass-through access to the physical disk for exclusive use. This type provides the highest performance of all disk types and thus should be used for production servers where performance is the top priority. The drive is not available for other guest systems.	This type is used in high-end datacenters to provide optimum performance for VMs. It's also used in failover cluster environments.

Creating Virtual Hard Disks

To help you gain practice in creating virtual hard disks, the following three exercises will teach you how to create a differencing hard disk, how to clone an existing disk by creating a new disk, and how to configure a physical or pass-through disk to your virtual machine. First, in Exercise 9.3, you will learn how to create a differencing virtual hard disk.

EXERCISE 9.3

Creating a Differencing Hard Disk

1. Open Hyper-V Manager.

2. In Hyper-V Manager, on the Actions pane, choose New ➢ Hard Disk.

3. In the New Virtual Hard Disk Wizard, click Next on the Before You Begin page.

EXERCISE 9.3 *(continued)*

4. At the Choose Disk Format screen, choose VHDX and click Next. The size of your VHDs depends on which format you choose. If you're going to have a VHD larger than 2,040GB, use VHDX. If your VHD is less than 2,040GB, then you should use VHD.

5. On the Choose Disk Type page, select Fixed Size and click Next.

6. On the Specify Name And Location page, enter the new name of the child disk (for example, **newvirtualharddisk.vhd**). You can also modify the default location of the new VHD file if you want. Click Next to continue.

7. Next, on the Configure Disk page, you need to specify the size of the VHD file. Choose a size based on your hard disk and then click Next to continue. I used 60GB as our test size.

8. On the Completing The New Virtual Hard Disk Wizard page, verify that all settings are correct and click Finish to create the hard disk.

The process to add a physical or pass-through disk to a virtual machine is quite different. For this, first you need to create the virtual machine, and then you open the virtual machine settings to configure the physical disk. If you want to add a physical disk to a virtual machine, the physical disk must be set as Offline in Disk Management, as shown in Figure 9.8.

FIGURE 9.8   In Disk Management, you can set disks as Offline.

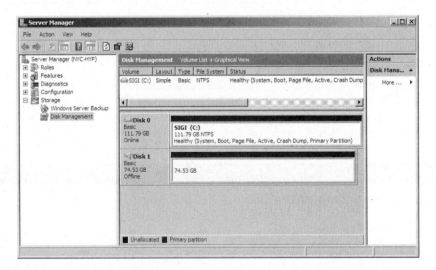

To access Disk Management, click the Windows key, choose Administrative Tools ➢ Computer Management, expand Storage in the left pane, and click Disk Management.

> You cannot share a physical disk among multiple virtual machines or with the host system.

Physical or pass-through disks might not be that important if your use of virtualization is based on test environments, but they become crucial when you need to plan for highly available virtual datacenters. This is especially true if you consider using failover clusters to provide the Quick Migration feature, which is when you should consider matching one logical unit number (LUN) from your enterprise storage system or storage area network (SAN) as one physical disk. This provides you with the optimum performance you need in such an environment.

Managing Virtual Hard Disks

Hyper-V also provides two tools to manage virtual hard disks: Inspect Disk and Edit Disk. These tools are available on the Actions pane in Hyper-V Manager.

Inspect Disk   This provides you with information about the virtual hard disk. It shows you not only the type of the disk but also information such as the maximum size for dynamically expanding disks and the parent VHD for differencing disks.

Edit Disk   This provides you with the Edit Virtual Hard Disk Wizard, which you can use to compact, convert, expand, merge, or reconnect hard disks. Figure 9.9 shows you the wizard's options when you select a dynamically expanding disk.

FIGURE 9.9   The Edit Virtual Hard Disk Wizard

![Edit Virtual Hard Disk Wizard screenshot showing the Convert Virtual Hard Disk page. The left navigation pane lists: Before You Begin, Locate Disk, Choose Action, Choose Disk Format, Choose Disk Type, Configure Disk, Summary. The main area asks "What type do you want to use for the converted virtual hard disk?" with two options: Fixed size ("This type of disk provides better performance and is recommended for workloads that are sensitive to disk performance. The virtual hard disk file that is created initially uses the size of the virtual hard disk and does not change when data is deleted or added.") and Dynamically expanding (selected) ("This type of disk provides better use of physical storage space. The virtual hard disk file that is created is small initially and changes as data is added."). Buttons at the bottom: Previous, Next, Finish, Cancel.]

Table 9.5 provides you with an overview of what you can do with the wizard.

TABLE 9.5 Edit Disk overview

Action	Description
Compact	Reduces the size of a dynamically expanding or differencing disk by removing blank space from deleted files.
Convert	Converts a dynamically expanding disk to a fixed disk or vice versa.
Expand	Increases the storage capacity of a dynamically expanding disk or a fixed virtual hard disk.
Merge	Merges the changes from a differencing disk into either the parent disk or another disk (applies to differencing disks only!).
Reconnect	If a differencing disk no longer finds its referring parent disk, this option can reconnect the parent to the disk.

Generation 1 vs. Generation 2 VHDs

Previous versions of Hyper-V had some pretty major drawbacks. One big drawback was that Hyper-V could not boot a virtual machine from a virtual hard drive that was SCSI. Believe it or not, SCSI controllers were not even recognized by Hyper-V unless you installed the Integration Services component.

Another issue that the previous versions of Hyper-V had was the inability to copy files from the Hyper-V host to the virtual machines without the use of a network connection in the virtual machine. The older versions of Hyper-V, prior to Windows Server 2012 R2, are now considered generation 1 versions. Why is it so important to know which generations of Hyper-V you should use or need to use?

Hyper-V generations help determine what functionality and what virtual hardware you can use in your virtual machine. Windows Server 2012 R2 Hyper-V now supports two different virtual machine generations: generation 1 and generation 2.

As already explained, previous versions of Hyper-V are considered generation 1, and this provides the same virtual hardware to the virtual machine as in previous versions of Hyper-V.

Generation 2 is now included with Windows Server 2012 R2, and it provides new functionality on the virtual machines including secure boot (which is enabled by default), the ability to boot from a SCSI virtual hard disk or boot from a SCSI virtual DVD, the ability to use a standard network adapter to PXE boot, and Unified Extensible Firmware

Interface (UEFI) firmware support. Generation 2 now gives you the ability to support UEFI firmware instead of BIOS-based firmware.

So when you create VHDs in Windows Server 2012 R2, one of your choices will be the ability to create the VHDs as a generation 1 or generation 2 VHD. If you need the ability to have your VHDs run on older versions of Hyper-V, make them a generation 1 VHD. If they are going to run only on Windows Server 2012 R2, make your VHDs generation 2 and take advantage of all the new features and functionality.

Configuring Virtual Machines

The following sections cover the topics of creating and managing virtual machines as well as how to back up and restore virtual machines using features such as Import and Export and Snapshot. You'll also briefly look at Hyper-V's Live Migration feature.

Creating and Managing Virtual Machines

It is important to learn how to create a virtual machine, how to change its configuration, and how to delete it. You will take a look at the Virtual Machine Connection tool and install the Hyper-V Integration Components onto a virtual machine.

Virtual Machines

Virtual machines define the child partitions in which you run operating system instances. Each virtual machine is separate and can communicate with the others only by using a virtual network. You can assign hard drives, virtual networks, DVD drives, and other system components to it. A virtual machine is similar to an existing physical server, but it no longer runs on dedicated hardware—it shares the hardware of the host system with the other virtual machines that run on the host.

Exercise 9.4 shows you how to create a new virtual machine.

EXERCISE 9.4

Creating a New Virtual Machine

1. Open Hyper-V Manager.

2. In Hyper-V Manager, on the Actions pane, choose New ➢ Virtual Machine.

3. In the New Virtual Machine Wizard, click Next on the Before You Begin page.

4. On the Specify Name And Location page, give your virtual machine a name and change the default location of the virtual machine configuration files. Click Next to continue.

EXERCISE 9.4 *(continued)*

5. On the Assign Memory page, define how much of your host computer's memory you want to assign to this virtual machine. Remember that once your virtual machine uses up all of your physical memory, it will start swapping to disk, thus reducing the performance of all virtual machines. Click Next to continue.

6. On the Configure Networking page, select the virtual network that you previously configured using Virtual Network Manager. Click Next to continue.

7. On the next page, you configure your virtual hard disk. You can create a new virtual hard disk, select an existing disk, or choose to attach the hard disk later. Be aware that you can create only a dynamically expanding virtual disk on this page; you cannot create a differencing, physical, or fixed virtual hard disk there. However, if you created the virtual hard disk already, you can, of course, select it. Click Next to continue.

8. On the Installation Options page, you can select how you want to install your operating system. You have the option to install an operating system later, install the operating system from a boot CD/DVD-ROM where you can select a physical device or an image file (ISO file), install an operating system from a floppy disk image (VFD file, or a virtual boot floppy disk), or install an operating system from a network-based installation server. The last option will install a legacy network adapter to your virtual machine so that you can boot from the network adapter. Select Install An Operating System Later and then click Next.

9. On the Completing The New Virtual Machine Wizard summary page, verify that all settings are correct. You also have the option to start the virtual machine immediately after creation. Click Next to create the virtual machine.

10. Repeat this process and create a few more virtual machines.

11. If you want to install an operating system on one of the VMs, start the VM, load a Windows Server 2012 R2 installation disk into the DVD drive, and then, under the Media menu, choose DVD and Capture. Then just do a normal install.

After completing Exercise 9.4, you will have a virtual machine available in Hyper-V Manager. Initially, the state of the virtual machine will be Off. Virtual machines can have the following states: Off, Starting, Running, Paused, and Saved. You can change the state of a virtual machine in the Virtual Machines pane by right-clicking the virtual machine's name, as shown in Figure 9.10, or by using the Virtual Machine Connection window.

Here is a list of some of the state options (when the VM is running) available for a virtual machine:

Start   Turn on the virtual machine. This is similar to pressing the power button when the machine is turned off. This option is available when your virtual machine is Off or in Saved state.

Turn Off   Turn off the virtual machine. This is similar to pressing the power-off button on the computer. This option is available when your virtual machine is in Running, Saved, or Paused state.

FIGURE 9.10 Options available when right-clicking a virtual machine

Shut Down   This option shuts down your operating system. You need to have the Hyper-V Integration Components installed on the operating system; otherwise, Hyper-V will not be able to shut down the system.

Save   The virtual machine is saved to disk in its current state. This option is available when your virtual machine is in Running or Paused state.

Pause   Pause the current virtual machine, but do not save the state to disk. You can use this option to release processor utilization quickly from this virtual machine to the host system.

Reset   Reset the virtual machine. This is like pressing the reset button on your computer. You will lose the current state and any unsaved data in the virtual machine. This option is available when your virtual machine is in Running or Paused state.

Resume   When your virtual machine is paused, you can resume it and bring it online again.

Changing Configuration on an Existing Virtual Machine

To change the configuration settings on an existing virtual machine, you right-click your virtual machine's name in the Virtual Machines pane in Hyper-V Manager and choose Settings. You can change settings such as memory allocation and hard drive configuration. All items that you can configure are described in the following list:

Add Hardware   Add devices to your virtual machine, namely, a SCSI controller, a network adapter, or a legacy network adapter. A legacy network adapter is required if you want to perform a network-based installation of an operating system.

BIOS This is the replacement of the virtual machine's BIOS. Because you can no longer enter the BIOS during startup, you need to configure it with this setting. You can turn Num Lock on or off and change the basic startup order of the devices.

Memory Change the amount of random access memory (RAM) allocated to the virtual machine.

Processor Change the number of logical processors this virtual machine can use and define resource control to balance resources among virtual machines by using a relative weight.

IDE Controller Add/change and remove devices from the IDE controller. You can have hard drives or DVD drives as devices. Every IDE controller can have up to two devices attached, and by default, you have two IDE controllers available.

Hard Drive Select a controller to attach to this device as well as to specify the media to use with your virtual hard disk. The available options are Virtual Hard Disk File (with additional buttons labeled New, Edit, Inspect, and Browse that are explained in the virtual hard disk section) and Physical Hard Disk. You can also remove the device here.

DVD Drive Select a controller to attach to this device and specify the media to use with your virtual CD/DVD drive. The available options are None, Image File (ISO Image), and Physical CD/DVD Drive Connected To The Host Computer. You also can remove the device here.

SCSI Controller Configure all hard drives that are connected to the SCSI controller. You can add up to 63 hard drives to each SCSI controller, and you can have multiple SCSI controllers available.

Network Adapter Specify the configuration of the network adapter or remove it. You can also configure the virtual network and MAC address for each adapter and enable virtual LAN identification.

COM1 and COM2 Configure the virtual COM port to communicate with the physical computer through a named pipe. You have COM1 and COM2 available.

Diskette Specify a virtual floppy disk file to use.

Name Edit the name of the virtual machine and provide some notes about it.

Integration Services Define what integration services are available to your virtual machine. Options are Operating System Shutdown, Time Synchronization, Data Exchange, Heartbeat, and Backup (Volume Snapshot).

Snapshot File Location Define the default file location of your snapshot files.

Smart Paging File Location This area allows you to set up a paging file for your virtual machine.

Windows Server 2012 R2 has a Hyper-V feature called *Smart Paging*. If you have a virtual machine that has a smaller amount of memory than what it needs for startup memory, when the virtual machine gets restarted, Hyper-V then needs additional memory to restart the virtual machine. Smart Paging is used to bridge the memory gap between minimum memory and startup memory. This allows your virtual machines to restart properly.

Automatic Start   Define what this virtual machine will do when the physical computer starts. Options are Nothing, Automatically Start If The Service Was Running, and Always Start This Virtual Machine. You also can define a start delay here.

Automatic Stop   Define what this virtual machine will do when the physical computer shuts down. Options are Save State, Turn Off, and Shut Down.

Please be aware that only some settings can be changed when the virtual machine's state is Running. It is best practice to shut down the virtual machine before you modify any setting.

Deleting Virtual Machines

You can also delete virtual machines using Hyper-V Manager. This deletes all of the configuration files, as shown in Figure 9.11.

FIGURE 9.11   Delete Virtual Machine warning window

Make sure you manually delete any virtual disks that were part of the virtual machines to free up disk space. Virtual disks are *not* deleted when you delete a virtual machine.

Virtual Machine Connection

Similar to the Virtual Machine Remote Control (VMRC) client that was available with Virtual Server 2005 R2 and previous versions, Hyper-V comes with Virtual Machine Connection to connect to virtual machines that run on a local or remote server.

You can use it to log onto the virtual machine and use your computer's mouse and keyboard to interact with the virtual machine. You can open Virtual Machine Connection in Hyper-V Manager by double-clicking a virtual machine or by right-clicking a virtual machine and selecting Connect. If your virtual machine is turned off, you might see a window similar to the one in Figure 9.12.

FIGURE 9.12   Virtual Machine Connection window when the machine is turned off

Virtual Machine Connection not only provides you with functionality similar to that of Hyper-V Manager, such as being able to change the state of a virtual machine, but it also provides you with additional features that are especially useful when you want to work with a virtual machine.

File Access Settings or Exit Virtual Machine Connection   Change the state of a virtual machine and create or revert a snapshot. Additionally, you have the options to send Ctrl+Alt+Delete to your virtual machine and Insert Integration Services Setup Disk.

Context-Sensitive Buttons Provide Quick Access to Key Features   These buttons are available under the menu bar to provide you with fast access to the most important features, as you can see in Figure 9.13. It shows the connection of a running VM, but the VM has not had an operating system installed yet, so the figure shows the Windows Setup screen.

NIC Teaming

NIC Teaming, also known as load balancing and failover (LBFO), gives an administrator the ability to allow multiple network adapters on a system to be placed into a team. Independent hardware vendors (IHVs) have required NIC Teaming, but until Windows Server 2012, NIC Teaming was *not* part of the Windows Server operating system.

To be able to use NIC Teaming, the computer system must have at least one Ethernet adapter. If you want to provide fault protection, an administrator must have a minimum of two Ethernet adapters. One advantage of Windows Server 2012 R2 is that an administrator can set up 32 network adapters in a NIC team.

FIGURE 9.13   Virtual Machine Connection window showing a running Windows Server 2012 virtual machine

NIC Teaming is a common practice when setting up virtualization. This is one way that you can have load balancing with Hyper-V.

NIC Teaming gives an administrator the ability to allow a virtual machine to use virtual network adapters in Hyper-V. The advantage of using NIC Teaming in Hyper-V is that the administrator can use NIC Teaming to connect to more than one Hyper-V switch. This allows Hyper-V still to have connectivity even if the network adapter under the Hyper-V switch gets disconnected.

An administrator can configure NIC Teaming in either Server Manager or PowerShell.

Storage Quality of Service

Windows Server 2012 R2 Hyper-V includes a new feature called *Storage Quality of Service (QoS)*. Storage QoS allows a Hyper-V administrator to manage how virtual machines access storage throughput for virtual hard disks.

Storage QoS gives an administrator the ability to guarantee that the storage throughput of a single VHD cannot adversely affect the performance of another VHD on the same host. It does this by giving administrators the ability to specify the maximum and minimum I/O loads based on I/O operations per second (IOPS) for each virtual disk in your virtual machines.

To configure Storage QoS, you would set the maximum IOPS values (or limits) and set the minimum values (or reserves) on virtual hard disks for virtual machines.

 If you are using shared virtual hard disks, Storage QoS will not be available.

Installing Hyper-V Integration Components

Hyper-V *Integration Components*, also called *Integration Services*, are required to make your guest operating system hypervisor-aware. Similar to the VM Additions that were part of Microsoft Virtual Server 2005, these components improve the performance of the guest operating system once they are installed. From an architectural perspective, virtual devices are redirected directly via the VMBus; thus, quicker access to resources and devices is provided.

If you do not install the Hyper-V Integration Components, the guest operating system uses emulation to communicate with the host's devices, which of course makes the guest operating system slower.

Exercise 9.5 shows you how to install Hyper-V Integration Components on one of your virtual machines running Windows Server 2012.

EXERCISE 9.5

Installing Hyper-V Integration Components

1. Open Hyper-V Manager.

2. In Hyper-V Manager, in the Virtual Machines pane, right-click the virtual machine on which you want to install Hyper-V Integration Components and click Start.

3. Right-click the virtual machine again and click Connect. Meanwhile, your virtual machine should already be booting.

4. If you need to log into the operating system of your virtual machine, you should do so.

5. Once the Windows Desktop appears, you need to select Insert Integration Services Setup Disk from the Actions menu of your Virtual Machine Connection window.

6. Once the Hyper-V Integration Components are installed, you are asked to perform a reboot.

After the reboot, Hyper-V Integration Components are installed on your operating system, and you will be able to use them.

Summary

Virtualization is quickly becoming a hot topic in information technology. The potential for consolidation is tremendous, and thus it will become more and more important.

After reading this chapter, you should have a good understanding of the Hyper-V architecture and what is required to install Hyper-V.

The section about installation and configuration covered various basic aspects of configuring the virtualization environment. You learned about the different types of virtual networks that are available, the options for installing the Hyper-V role, and the various types of virtual hard disks that you can use to optimize virtualization for your specific scenario.

You also learned how to configure virtual machines using the Hyper-V environment and how to create your own virtual datacenter on top of your Hyper-V machines. I showed you how to create and manage virtual machines, how to use Virtual Machine Connection to control a virtual machine remotely, and how to install Hyper-V Integration Components. You also learned how to export and import virtual machines as well as how to do snapshots of your virtual machine.

If you have never worked with virtualization software before, the information in this chapter may have been completely new to you. You should now be well prepared to try Hyper-V in your own environment.

Exam Essentials

Understand Hyper-V's architecture.   When you have a good understanding of Hyper-V's architecture, especially when an operating system in a virtual machine is hypervisor aware versus non-hypervisor aware, you have a solid understanding of what is important from an architectural perspective.

You should know about the Hyper-V Integration Components and how they change the behavior of a virtual machine. Also know for which operating systems the integration components are available.

Know Hyper-V's requirements and how to install it.   Know the hardware and software requirements as well as how to install Hyper-V. Hyper-V requires an x64-based processor and Data Execution Protection (DEP). Hardware-assisted virtualization must be enabled—don't forget this! Also remember that you can install Hyper-V two ways: using Server Manager or using the command line in Server Core.

Understand virtual networks and virtual hard disks.   Virtual networks and hard disks are the two most tested topics. You definitely should know the types of virtual networks available (that is, external, internal only, and private virtual network) as well as all types of virtual hard disks (namely, dynamically expanding, fixed size, differential, and physical or pass-through). You should be able to apply the correct one when needed. Don't forget the Edit Virtual Hard Disk Wizard, which is also a good source for questions in the exam.

Know how to create and manage virtual machines.   You should be able to explain how to create a virtual machine, what options are available to install an operating system in a virtual machine, and how to install the Hyper-V Integration Components on a virtual machine. Don't forget about the virtual machine states and the virtual machine settings!

Understand how to back up and restore virtual machines.   Have a good understanding of the concept of exporting and importing virtual machines, how snapshots work, and what lies behind a quick migration. Understand how you can export a virtual machine, what you should consider when moving it to a new host machine, and what happens after importing it to the import folder. The same applies to snapshots: You need to know what options you have available and what each option will do. Especially recognize the difference between applying and reverting a snapshot.

Review Questions

1. On which of the following x64 editions of Windows Server 2012 R2 does Hyper-V run? (Choose all that apply.)

    A. Windows Server 2012 R2 Web Edition

    B. Windows Server 2012 R2 Standard Edition

    C. Windows Server 2012 R2 Itanium Edition

    D. Windows Server 2012 R2 Datacenter Edition

2. You want to build a test environment based on virtual machines on a single Windows Server 2012 R2 machine, but you also want to make sure that the virtual machines communicate only with each other. What type of virtual network do you need to configure?

    A. External

    B. Internal only

    C. Private virtual machine network

    D. Public virtual machine network

3. Andy wants to change the memory of a virtual machine that is currently powered up. What does he need to do?

    A. Shut down the virtual machine, use the virtual machine's settings to change the memory, and start it again.

    B. Use the virtual machine's settings to change the memory.

    C. Pause the virtual machine, use the virtual machine's settings to change the memory, and resume it.

    D. Save the virtual machine, use the virtual machine's settings to change the memory, and resume it.

4. You want to make sure that the hard disk space for your virtual machines is occupied only when needed. What type of virtual hard disk would you recommend?

    A. Dynamically expanding disk

    B. Fixed-size disk

    C. Differencing disk

    D. Physical or pass-through disk

5. How do you add a physical disk to a virtual machine?

    A. Use the Virtual Hard Disk Wizard.

    B. Use the Edit Virtual Hard Disk Wizard.

    C. Use the virtual machine's settings.

    D. Use the New Virtual Machine Wizard.

6. Rich bought a new server with an Itanium IA-64 processor, 4GB RAM, and a SAN that provides 1TB hard disk space. After installing Windows Server 2012 R2 for Itanium-based systems, he wants to install Hyper-V on this server. Can Hyper-V be installed on this system?

A. Yes

B. No

7. What are the minimum CPU requirements for running Hyper-V on a machine? (Choose all that apply.)

A. An x64-based processor (Intel or AMD).

B. Hardware Data Execution Protection (DEP) must be enabled.

C. Hardware-assisted virtualization must be enabled.

D. The processor must at least have a dual core.

8. What is the command to install Hyper-V on a Windows Server 2008 machine that was installed in Server Core?

A. `start /w ocsetup Hyper-V`

B. `start /w ocsetup microsoft-hyper-v`

C. `start /w ocsetup Microsoft-Hyper-V`

D. `start /w ocsetup hyper-v`

9. On what operating systems can you install the Hyper-V Manager MMC? (Choose all that apply.)

A. Windows Server 2008 R2

B. Windows Server 2003

C. Windows XP SP3

D. Windows 7, Windows 8

10. What statement is correct for an external virtual network?

A. The virtual machines can communicate with each other and with the host machine.

B. The virtual machines can communicate with each other only.

C. The virtual machines can communicate with each other, with the host machine, and with an external network.

D. The virtual machines cannot communicate with each other.

Exam 70-411: Administering Windows Server 2012 R2

PART

II

Chapter

10

Manage and Maintain Servers

THE FOLLOWING 70-411 EXAM OBJECTIVES ARE COVERED IN THIS CHAPTER:

✓ **Deploy and manage server images**

- Install the Windows Deployment Services (WDS) role
- Configure and manage boot, install, and discover images
- Update images with patches, hotfixes, and drivers
- Install features for offline images
- Configure driver groups and packages

✓ **Implement patch management**

- Install and configure the Windows Server Update Services (WSUS) role
- Configure group policies for updates

✓ **Configure client-side targeting**

- Configure WSUS synchronization
- Configure WSUS groups
- Manage patch management in mixed environments

✓ **Monitor servers**

- Configure Data Collector Sets (DCS)
- Configure alerts
- Monitor real-time performance
- Monitor virtual machines (vms)
- Monitor events
- Configure event subscriptions
- Configure network monitoring
- Schedule performance monitoring

We have already discussed how to set up clients on a network and how to keep their systems running on that network. In this chapter, we will start the Windows Deployment Services. We will then turn the discussion to keeping your systems updated using Windows Server Update Services (WSUS).

Another important task of an IT team is to keep the network up and running quickly and efficiently. Keeping your network running at its peak performance is one way to make sure your end users continue to use the network and its resources without problems or interruptions. Remember, everyone has clients—salespeople have theirs, accountants have theirs, and so do we as system administrators. Our clients are the end users, and it's our job to make sure that our clients can do their jobs.

When you are working with servers, it is important you make sure that your system's information is safely backed up. Backups become useful when you lose data because of system failures, file corruptions, or accidental modifications of information. As consultants, we can tell you from experience that backups are among the most important tasks that an IT person performs daily.

Sometimes, performance optimization can feel like a luxury, especially if you can't get your domain controllers to the point where they are actually performing the services for which you intended them, such as servicing printers or allowing users to share and work on files. The Windows Server 2012 R2 operating system has been specifically designed to provide high-availability services solely intended to keep your mission-critical applications and data accessible, even in times of disaster. Occasionally, however, you might experience intermittent server crashes on one or more of the domain controllers or other computers in your environment.

The most common cause of such problems is a hardware configuration issue. Poorly written device drivers and unsupported hardware can cause problems with system stability. Failed hardware components (such as system memory) may do so as well. Memory chips can be faulty, electrostatic discharge can ruin them, and other hardware issues can occur. No matter what, a problem with your memory chip spells disaster for your server.

Third-party hardware vendors usually provide utility programs with their computers that can be used for performing hardware diagnostics on machines to help you find problems. These utilities are a good first step in resolving intermittent server crashes. When these utility programs are used in combination with the troubleshooting tips provided in this and other chapters of this book, you should be able to pinpoint most network-related problems that might occur.

In this chapter, I'll cover the tools and methods used for measuring performance and troubleshooting failures in Windows Server 2012 R2. Before you dive into the technical details, however, you should thoroughly understand what you're trying to accomplish and how you'll meet this goal.

> **Knowing How to Locate and Isolate Problems**
>
> In a book such as this, it would be almost impossible to cover everything that could go wrong with your Windows Server 2012 R2 system. This book covers many of the most common issues that you might come across, but almost anything is possible. Make sure you focus on the methodology used and the steps required to locate and isolate a problem—even if you are not 100 percent sure about the cause of the problem. Use online resources to help you locate and troubleshoot the problem, but don't believe everything you read (some things that are posted online can be wrong or misleading). Test your changes in a lab environment, and try to read multiple sources. Always use Microsoft Support (http://support.microsoft.com/) as one of your sources because this site is most likely the right source for information. You won't be able to find and fix everything, but knowing where to find critical information that will help you in your efforts never hurts. One of the tools that many of us in the industry use is *Microsoft TechNet*. The full version of TechNet (a paid subscription) is a resource that will help you find and fix many real-world issues.

Using Windows Deployment Services

In this section, you will look at how to install and configure *Windows Deployment Services (WDS)*. WDS is a utility that allows an administrator to deploy an operating system remotely. The client machine that is receiving the operating system needs to use a set of disks (WDS client disks) that will automatically initiate a network card, connect to the WDS server, and download the operating system.

WDS allows an IT administrator to install a Windows operating system without using a CD or DVD installation disc. Using WDS allows you to deploy the operating system through a network installation. WDS can deploy Windows XP, Windows Server 2003, Windows Vista, Windows 7, Windows 8, Windows Server 2008, Windows Server 2008 R2, Microsoft Windows 2012, and Microsoft Windows Server 2012 R2.

The following are some of the advantages of using WDS for automated installation:

- You can remotely install Windows 7 or Windows 8.

- The procedure simplifies management of the server image by allowing you to access Windows 7 or Windows 8 distribution files from a distribution server.

- You can quickly recover the operating system in the event of a computer failure.

Here are the basic steps of the WDS process from a PXE-enabled WDS client:

1. The WDS client initiates a special boot process through the PXE network adapter (and the computer's BIOS configured for a network boot). On a PXE client, the user presses F12 to start the PXE boot process and to indicate that they want to perform a WDS installation.

2. A list of available Windows PE boot images is displayed. The user should select the appropriate Windows PE boot image from the boot menu.

3. The Windows Welcome screen is displayed. The user should click the Next button.

4. The WDS user is prompted to enter credentials for accessing and installing images from the WDS server.

5. A list of available operating system images is displayed. The user should select the appropriate image file to install.

6. The WDS user is prompted to enter the product key for the selected image.

7. The Partition And Configure The Disk screen is displayed. This screen provides the ability to install a mass storage device driver, if needed, by pressing F6.

8. The image copy process is initiated, and the selected image is copied to the WDS client computer.

The following sections describe how to set up the WDS server and the WDS clients and how to install Windows 7 or Windows 8 through WDS.

Windows Server 2012 R2 WDS Functionality

Windows Server 2012 R2 allows you to use many new and improved features of WDS. Table 10.1 shows some of the highpoints of what WDS can do when installed onto a Windows Server 2012 or Windows Server 2012 R2 system.

Preparing the WDS Server

With the WDS server, you can manage and distribute Windows 7 or Windows 8 operating system images to WDS client computers. The WDS server contains any files necessary for PXE booting, Windows PE boot images, and the Windows 7 or Windows 8 images to be deployed.

The following steps for preparing the WDS server are discussed in the upcoming sections:

1. Make sure that the server meets the requirements for running WDS.

2. Install WDS.

3. Configure and start WDS.

4. Configure the WDS server to respond to client computers (if this was not configured when WDS was installed).

For WDS to work, the server on which you will install WDS must meet the requirements for WDS and be able to access the required network services.

WDS Server Requirements

WDS needs some services and requirements installed before it will work properly:

- Active Directory Domain Services must be present for WDS to function properly. The WDS server must be a domain controller or a member of the Active Directory domain.

- At least one partition on the server must be formatted as NTFS.

- The operating system must be Windows Server 2003, Windows Server 2008/2008 R2, Windows Server 2012, or Windows Server 2012 R2.

TABLE 10.1   WDS functionality with Windows Server 2012 R2

Feature	Description
OS deployed using WDS	Windows XP, Windows Server 2003, Windows Vista SP1, Windows Server 2008, Windows 7, Windows Server 2008 R2, Windows Server 2012, Windows 8, Windows 8.1, Windows Server 2012 R2.
Image types deployed	`.wim` and `.vhd` images are both supported. `.vhd` images can now be managed via the WDS management snap-in in addition to the command line. Also, .vhdx files, the new file format available since Windows Server 2012, are supported directly and over multicast.
Boot environment	Windows PE.
Administration options	MMC snap-in and WDSUTIL. Windows PowerShell cmdlets added in Windows Server 2012 R2.
Multicasting	IPv6 and DHCPv6 support for TFTP and multicasting along with improved multicast deployments.
Driver provisioning	Drivers are automatically detected and installed. Because of this, duplicate driver packages are prevented from being installed into the driver store.
PowerShell cmdlet scripting	Supported on Windows Server 2012 R2 only.

Network Services

Besides the server requirements, some networking requirements need to be installed for WDS. The following network services must be running on the WDS server or be accessible to the WDS server from another network server:

- TCP/IP installed and configured.

- A DHCP server, which is used to assign DHCP addresses to WDS clients. (Make sure your DHCP scope has enough addresses to accommodate all of the WDS clients that will need IP addresses.)

- A DNS server, which is used to locate the Active Directory controller.

- Active Directory, which is used to locate WDS servers and WDS clients as well as authorize WDS clients and manage WDS configuration settings and client installation options.

Installing the WDS Server Components

You can configure WDS on a Windows Server 2003/2008/2008 R2, Windows Server 2012, or Windows Server 2012 R2 computer by using the Windows Deployment Services Configuration Wizard or by using the WDSUTIL command-line utility. Table 10.2 describes the WDSUTIL command-line options.

TABLE 10.2   WDSUTIL command-line options

WDSUTIL option	Description
/initialize-server	Initializes the configuration of the WDS server
/uninitialized -server	Undoes any changes made during the initialization of the WDS server
/add	Adds images and devices to the WDS server
/convert-ripimage	Converts Remote Installation Preparation (RIPrep) images to WIM images
/remove	Removes images from the server
/set	Sets information in images, image groups, WDS servers, and WDS devices
/get	Gets information from images, image groups, WDS servers, and WDS devices
/new	Creates new capture images or discover images
/copy- image	Copies images from the image store
/export-image	Exports to WIM files images contained within the image store
/start	Starts WDS services
/stop	Stops WDS services
/disable	Disables WDS services
/enable	Enables WDS services
/approve-autoadddevices	Approves Auto-Add devices
/reject-autoadddevices	Rejects Auto-Add devices
/delete-autoadddevices	Deletes records from the Auto-Add database
/update	Uses a known good resource to update a server resource

The first step in setting up WDS to deploy operating systems to the clients is to install the WDS role. You do this by using Server Manager.

One of the advantages of using the Windows deployment server is that WDS can work with Windows image (.wim) files. Windows image files can be created through the use of the Windows Sysprep utility.

One component to which you need to pay attention when using the Windows deployment server is *Preboot Execution Environment (PXE)* network devices. PXE boot devices are network interface cards (NICs) that can talk to a network without the need for an operating system. PXE boot NIC adapters are network adapters that have a set of preboot commands within the boot firmware.

This is important when using WDS because PXE boot adapters connect to a WDS server and request the data needed to load the operating system remotely. Remember, most of these machines for which you are using WDS do not have an operating system on the computer. You need NIC adapters that can connect to a network without the need for an operating system for WDS to work properly.

For the same reason, you must set up DHCP to accept PXE machines. Those machines need a valid TCP/IP address so that they can connect to the WDS server.

Installing the WDS Services Using PowerShell

As we have stated multiple times throughout this book, we will show you how to do many of these tasks using the Windows PowerShell commands. Table 10.3 describes many of the WDS cmdlets that you can use in Windows Server 2012 R2.

 This table comes directly from Microsoft TechNet at http://technet .microsoft.com/library/dn283416.aspx.

TABLE 10.3 WDSUTIL command-line options

Cmdlet	Description
Add-WdsDriverPackage	Adds an existing driver package to a driver group or injects it into a boot image
Approve-WdsClient	Approves clients
Copy-WdsInstallImage	Copies install images within an image group
Deny-WdsClient	Denies approval for clients
Disable-WdsBootImage	Disables a boot image

TABLE 10.3 WDSUTIL command-line options *(continued)*

Cmdlet	Description
Disable-WdsDriverPackage	Disables a driver package in the Windows Deployment Services driver store
Disable-WdsInstallImage	Disables an install image
Disconnect-WdsMulticastClient	Disconnects a multicast client from a transmission or namespace
Enable-WdsBootImage	Enables a boot image
Enable-WdsDriverPackage	Enables a driver package in the Windows Deployment Services driver store
Enable-WdsInstallImage	Enables an install image
Export-WdsBootImage	Exports an existing boot image from an image store
Export-WdsInstallImage	Exports an existing install image from an image store
Get-WdsBootImage	Gets properties of boot images from the image store
Get-WdsClient	Gets client devices from the pending device database, or pre-staged devices from Active Directory or the standalone server device database.
Get-WdsDriverPackage	Gets properties of driver packages from the Windows Deployment Services driver store
Get-WdsInstallImage	Gets properties of install images from an image store
Get-WdsInstallImageGroup	Gets properties of install image groups
Get-WdsMulticastClient	Gets a list of clients connected to a multicast transmission or namespace
Import-WdsBootImage	Imports a boot image to the image store
Import-WdsDriverPackage	Imports a driver package into the Windows Deployment Services driver store
Import-WdsInstallImage	Imports an install image to an image store
New-WdsClient	Creates a prestaged client

`New-WdsInstallImageGroup`	Creates an install image group
`Remove-WdsBootImage`	Removes a boot image from the image store
`Remove-WdsClient`	Removes a prestaged client from AD DS or the stand-alone server device database or clears the Pending Devices database
`Remove-WdsDriverPackage`	Removes a driver package from a driver group or removes it from all driver groups and deletes it
`Remove-WdsInstallImage`	Removes an install image from an image store
`Remove-WdsInstallImageGroup`	Removes an install image group
`Set-WdsBootImage`	Modifies settings of a boot image
`Set-WdsClient`	Modifies a prestaged client device
`Set-WdsInstallImage`	Modifies the properties of an install image
`Set-WdsInstallImageGroup`	Modifies the name and access permissions of an install image group

Preparing the WDS Client

The WDS client is the computer on which Windows 7 or Windows 8 will be installed. WDS clients rely on PXE technology, which allows the client computer to remotely boot and connect to a WDS server.

To act as a WDS client, the computer must meet all of the hardware requirements for Windows 7 or Windows 8 and have a PXE-capable network adapter installed. In addition, a WDS server must be present on the network. Furthermore, the user account used to install the image must be a member of the Domain Users group in Active Directory.

After the WDS server has been installed and configured, you can install Windows 7 or Windows 8 on a WDS client that uses a PXE-compliant network card.

To install Windows 7 or Windows 8 on the WDS client, follow these steps:

1. Start the computer. When prompted, press F12 for a network service boot. The Windows PE appears.

2. The Windows Welcome screen appears. Click the Next button to start the installation process.

3. Enter the username and password of an account that has permissions to access and install images from the WDS server.

4. A list of available operating system images stored on the WDS server appears. Select the image to install and click Next.

5. Enter the product key for the selected Windows 7 or Windows 8 image and click Next.

6. The Partition And Configure The Disk screen appears. Select the desired disk-partitioning options or click OK to use the default options.

7. Click Next to initiate the image-copying process. The Windows Setup process will begin after the image is copied to the WDS client computer.

Configuring Windows Server Update Services

To keep your Windows operating systems up-to-date and secure, you can use Windows Update, Automatic Updates, WSUS, and the Microsoft Baseline Security Analyzer.

Windows Update This utility attaches to the Microsoft website through a user-initiated process, and it allows Windows users to update their operating systems by downloading updated files (critical and noncritical software updates).

Automatic Updates This utility extends the functionality of Windows Update by automating the process of updating critical files. With Automatic Updates, you can specify whether you want updates to be downloaded and installed automatically or whether you just want to be notified when updates are available.

Windows Server Update Services (WSUS) This utility is used to deploy a limited version of Windows Update to a corporate server, which in turn provides the Windows updates to client computers within the corporate network. This allows clients that are limited to what they can access through a firewall to be able to keep their Windows operating systems up-to-date.

Microsoft Baseline Security Analyzer (MBSA) You can download this utility from the Microsoft website to ensure you have the most current security updates.

In the following sections, you will learn how to use these tools.

Windows Update

Windows Update is available through the Microsoft website, and it is used to provide the most current files for Windows operating systems. Examples of updates include security fixes, critical updates, updated help files, and updated drivers.

You can download Windows Update through the Help And Support page on the Microsoft website. Once it's installed, click the Scan For Updates link on the Welcome To Windows Update screen to search for new updates.

The results of the Windows Update search will be displayed on the left side of the Windows Update screen. You will see the following options:

Pick Updates To Install   This lists what updates are available for your computer, and it includes the following categories:

- Critical Updates And Service Packs
- Windows Server 2012 R2 Family
- Driver Updates

Review And Install Updates   This allows you to view all of the updates that you have selected to install, and it installs the updates.

View Installation History   This allows you to track all of the updates that you have applied to your server.

Personalize Windows Update   This customizes what you see when you use Windows Update.

Get Help And Support   This displays help and support information about Windows Update.

Sometimes the updates that are installed require the computer to be restarted before they can take effect. In this event, Windows Update uses a technology called *chained installation*. With chained installation, all updates that require a computer restart are applied before the computer is restarted. This eliminates the need to restart the computer more than once.

 The information that is collected by Windows Update includes the operating system and version number, the Internet Explorer version, the software version information for any software that can be updated through Windows Update, the Plug and Play ID numbers for installed hardware, and the region and language settings. Windows Update will also collect the product ID and product key to confirm that you are running a licensed copy of Windows, but this information is retained only during the Windows Update session and it is not stored. No personal information that can be used to identify users of the Windows Update service is collected.

Windows Automatic Updates

The *Automatic Updates* application extends the functionality of Windows Update by automating the update process. With Automatic Updates, Windows Server 2012 R2 recognizes when you have an Internet connection and will automatically search for any updates for your computer from the Windows Update website.

If any updates are identified, they will be downloaded using *Background Intelligent Transfer Services (BITS)*. BITS is a bandwidth-throttling technology that allows downloads to occur using idle bandwidth only. This means that downloading automatic updates will not interfere with any other Internet traffic.

If Automatic Updates detects any updates for your computer, you will see an update icon in the notification area of the taskbar.

 To configure Automatic Updates, you must have local administrative rights to the computer on which Automatic Updates is being configured. Requiring administrative rights prevents users from specifying that critical security updates not be installed. In addition, Microsoft must digitally sign any updates that are downloaded.

You configure Automatic Updates by selecting Start ➢ Control Panel ➢ Windows Update. You will see the Check For Updates button shown in Figure 10.1.

FIGURE 10.1 Windows Update control panel

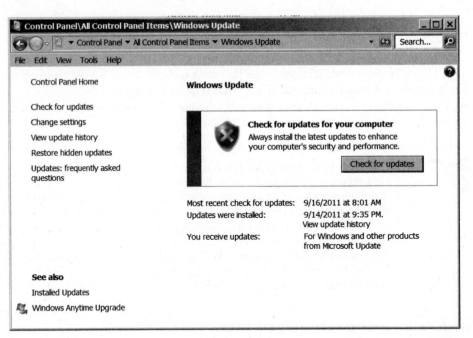

You enable Automatic Updates by clicking the Change Settings link. With this setting enabled, Windows Update software may be automatically updated prior to applying any other updates (see Figure 10.2).

FIGURE 10.2   Change Settings window of the Windows Update control panel

Using Windows Server Update Services

Windows Server Update Services (WSUS), formerly known as Software Update Services (SUS), is used to leverage the features of Windows Update within a corporate environment. WSUS downloads Windows updates to a corporate server, which in turn provides the updates to the internal corporate clients. This allows administrators to test and have full control over what updates are deployed within the corporate environment. WSUS is designed to work in medium-sized corporate networks that are not using System Center Essentials 2012 R2.

Advantages of Using WSUS

Using WSUS has many advantages:

- It allows an internal server within a private intranet to act as a virtual Windows Update server.

- Administrators have selective control over what updates are posted and deployed from the public Windows Update site. No updates are deployed to client computers unless an administrator first approves them.

- Administrators can control the synchronization of updates from the public Windows Update site to the WSUS server either manually or automatically.

- Administrators can configure Automatic Updates on client computers to access the local WSUS server as opposed to the public Windows Update site.

- WSUS checks each update to verify that Microsoft has digitally signed it. Any updates that are not digitally signed are discarded.

- Administrators can selectively specify whether clients can access updated files from the intranet or from Microsoft's public Windows Update site, which is used to support remote clients.

- Administrators can deploy updates to clients in multiple languages.

- Administrators can configure client-side targeting to help client machines get updates. Client-side targeting allows your organization's computers to automatically add themselves to the computer groups that were created in the WSUS console.

- Administrators can configure a WSUS statistics server to log update access, which allows them to track which clients have installed updates. The WSUS server and the WSUS statistics server can coexist on the same computer.

- Administrators can manage WSUS servers remotely using HTTP or HTTPS if their web browser is Internet Explorer 6.0 or newer.

WSUS Server Requirements

To act as a WSUS server, the server must meet the following requirements:

- It must be running Windows 2000 Server with Service Pack 4 or newer, Windows Server 2003 SP1 or greater, Windows Vista, Windows 7, Windows 8, Windows Server 2008, Windows Server 2008 R2, Windows Server 2012, or Windows Server 2012 R2.

- It must have all of the most current security patches applied.

- It must be running Internet Information Services (IIS) 6.0 or newer.

- It must be connected to the network.

- It must have an NTFS partition with 100MB free disk space to install the WSUS server software, and it must have 6GB of free space to store all of the update files.

- It must use BITS version 2.0.

- It must use Microsoft Management Console 3.0.

- It must use Microsoft Report Viewer Redistributable 2008.

If your WSUS server meets the following system requirements, it can support up to 15,000 WSUS clients:

- Pentium III 700MHz processor

- 512MB of RAM

Installing the WSUS Server

WSUS should run on a dedicated server, meaning that the server will not run any other applications except IIS, which is required. Microsoft recommends that you install a clean or new version of Windows Server 2003 SP1 or newer, Windows Server 2008, Windows Server 2008 R2, Windows Server 2012, or Windows Server 2012 R2 and apply any service packs or security-related patches.

Exercise 10.1 walks you through the installation process for WSUS.

EXERCISE 10.1

Installing a WSUS Server

1.   Choose Server Manager by clicking the Server Manager icon on the taskbar.

2.   Click option number 2, Add Roles And Features.

3.   Choose role-based or featured-based installation and click Next.

4.   Choose your server and click Next.

5.   Choose Windows Server Update Service. Click the Add Features button when the dialog box appears. Then click Next.

6.   At the Select features screen, just click Next.

7.   At the Windows Server Update Services screen, click Next.

8.   At the Select Role Services screen, make sure that WID Database and WSUS Services are both checked. Click Next.

9. At the Content Location Selection screen, uncheck the box Store Updates In The Following Location and click Next. When you uncheck this box, updates are not stored locally. They are downloaded from Microsoft only once they are approved. This will help save hard drive space.

10. At the Confirmation screen, click the Install button.

11. The installation will begin, and you will see the progress. Once the installation is complete, click Close.

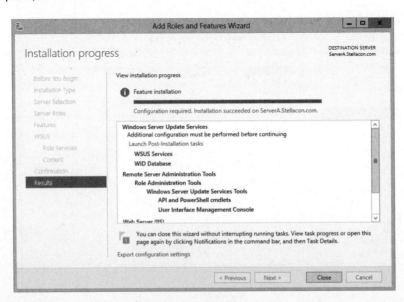

12. In Server Manager, click the WSUS link on the left side. Then click the More link next to Configuration Required For Windows Server Update Services.

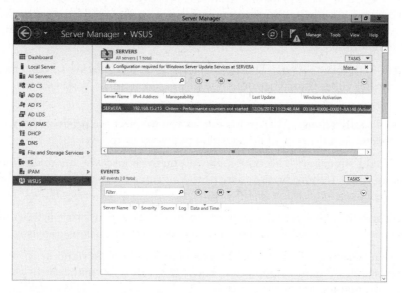

13. At the All Servers Task Details And Notifications screen, click the Launch Post-Installation Tasks link.

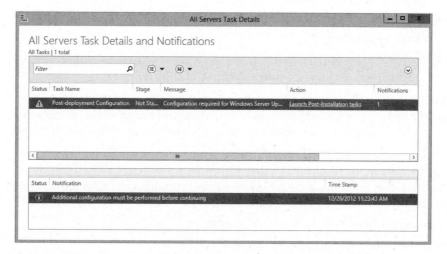

14. The installation process will automatically continue. Once it is finished, you will see Complete under Stage. Close the All Servers Task Details And Notifications screen.

15. Close Server Manager.

16. If a WSUS Configure Options box appears, just close it. You will set options in the next exercise.

Configuring a WSUS Server

Configuring a WSUS machine is a straightforward process. The easiest way to do it is to use the WSUS Server Configuration Wizard. This wizard walks you through the WSUS setup process, and it makes it easy to configure WSUS. When in the WSUS snap-in, you can configure different options.

Update Source And Proxy Server   This option allows you to configure whether this WSUS server synchronizes either from Microsoft Update or from another WSUS server on your network.

Products And Classifications   This option allows you to select the products for which you want to get updates and the type of updates that you want to receive.

Update Files And Languages   This option allows you to choose whether to download update files and where to store these update files. This option also allows you to choose which update languages you want downloaded.

Automatic Approvals   This option allows you to specify how to approve installation of updates automatically for selected groups and how to approve revisions to existing updates.

Synchronization Schedule   This option allows you to configure how and when you synchronize your updates. Administrators can choose to synchronize manually or to set up a schedule for daily automatic synchronization.

Computers   This option allows you to set computers to groups or use Group Policy or registry settings on the computer to receive updates.

Server Cleanup Wizard   This option allows you to clean out old computers, updates, and update files from your server.

Reporting Rollup   This option allows you to choose whether to have replica downstream servers roll up computer and update status to this WSUS server.

Email Notifications   This option allows you to set up email notifications for WSUS. You can be notified when new updates are synchronized, or you can get email status reports. This option also allows you to set up the email server's information on your WSUS server.

Microsoft Update Improvement Program   This option allows you to choose whether you want to participate in the Microsoft Update Improvement program. When you choose to participate in this program, your WSUS server will automatically send information to Microsoft about the quality of your updates. This following information is included:

- How many computers are in the organization
- How many computers successfully installed each update
- How many computers failed to install each update

Personalization   This option allows you to personalize the way that information is displayed for this server. This option also allows you to set up a to-do list for WSUS.

WSUS Server Configuration Wizard   This option allows you to set up many of the preceding options by just using this one setup wizard.

In Exercise 10.2, you will learn how to set up some of the WSUS server options. To complete this exercise, you need to have an Internet connection that can communicate with Microsoft.

EXERCISE 10.2

Setting WSUS Server Options

1. Open the Windows Server Update Services snap-in from Administrative Tools by pressing the Windows key on the keyboard and then choosing Administrative Tools. The Windows Server Update Services snap-in will be at the bottom of the list alphabetically.

2. On the left side, click the name of your server. Then, in the middle section under To Do, click the Options link.

EXERCISE 10.2 *(continued)*

3. A WSUS Server Configuration Wizard appears at the bottom of the options list. Click this link.

4. Click Next at the Before You Begin screen.

5. At the Join Microsoft Update Improvement Program screen, uncheck the Yes box and click Next.

6. At the Choose Upstream Server screen, choose Synchronize From Microsoft Update and click Next.

7. Fill in the information at the Specify Proxy Server screen if you need to use a proxy server. If you do not need a proxy server, just click Next.

8. At the Connect To Upstream Server screen, click the Start Connecting button. This step can take a few minutes depending on your connection speed. Once it's finished connecting, click Next.

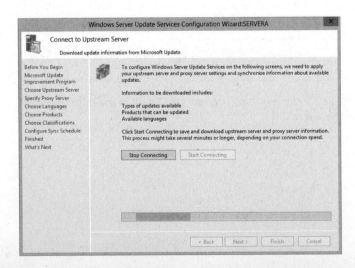

9. At the Choose Products screen, scroll down and choose the products for which you want to receive updates. Then click Next.

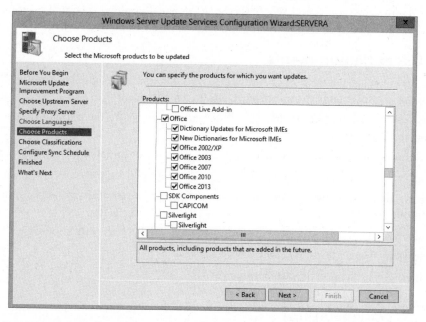

10. At the Choose Classifications screen, choose the classifications of updates you would like and click Next.

11. The Set Sync Schedule screen will appear next. At this screen, you can choose whether you want manual or automatic synchronizations. For this exercise, choose Synchronize Manually and click Next.

12. At the Finish screen, you can click Begin Initial Synchronization and click Finish. Be advised, this initial sync can take some time to finish. So if you don't have time to complete it now, you can always synchronize later.

13. Close WSUS.

Testing and Approving Updates

The administrator should test and approve updates before they are deployed to WSUS clients. The testing should be done on a test machine that is not used for daily tasks.

To approve updates, from the welcome screen, click Updates on the site's toolbar. Make your settings on the Updates page that appears.

Viewing the Synchronization Log

To view the synchronization log, click the Reports button on the site's toolbar from the welcome screen. The Reports page will appear. Click Synchronization Results to view the results.

Configuring a Disconnected Network

You have the ability to use WSUS on a disconnected network. To do so, you download the updates to the Internet-connected WSUS server. After the download is complete, you can export the updates and then import the updates to the disconnected network.

WSUS Client Requirements

WSUS clients run a special version of Automatic Updates that is designed to support WSUS. The following enhancements to Automatic Updates are included:

- Clients can receive updates from a WSUS server as opposed to the public Microsoft Windows Update site.

- The administrator can schedule when the downloading of updated files will occur.

- Clients can be configured via Group Policy or through editing the registry.

- Updates can occur when an administrative account or nonadministrative account is logged on.

The following client platforms are the only ones that WSUS currently supports:

- Windows XP Home Edition (with Service Pack 3)
- Windows XP Professional (with Service Pack 3)
- Windows Server 2003 (SP1 or newer)
- Windows Vista (all platforms)
- Windows 7 (all platforms)
- Windows 8 (all platforms)
- Windows Server 2008 and 2008 R2 (all platforms)
- Windows Server 2012 R2 (all platforms)

Configuring the WSUS Clients

You can configure WSUS clients in two ways. The method you use depends on whether you use Active Directory in your network.

In a nonenterprise network (not running Active Directory), you would configure Automatic Updates through the Control Panel using the same process that was defined in the section "Windows Automatic Updates" earlier in this chapter. Each client's registry would then be edited to reflect the location of the server providing the automatic updates.

Within an enterprise network, using Active Directory, you would typically see Automatic Updates configured through Group Policy. Group Policy is used to manage configuration and security settings via Active Directory. Group Policy is also used to specify what server a client will use for Automatic Updates. If Automatic Updates is configured through Group Policy, the user will not be able to change Automatic Updates settings by choosing Control Panel ➢ System (for XP) or Windows Update (for Windows 8, Windows 7, Windows Vista, Windows Server 2008, Windows Server 2008 R2, Windows Server 2012, and Windows Server 2012 R2).

Configuring a Client in a Non–Active Directory Network

The easiest way to configure the client to use Automatic Updates is through the control panel. However, you can also configure Automatic Updates through the registry. The registry is a database of all your server settings. You can access it by choosing Start ➢ Run and typing **regedit** in the Run dialog box. Automatic Updates settings are defined through HKEY_LOCAL_MACHINE\Software\Policies\Microsoft\Windows\WindowsUpdate\AU.

Table 10.4 lists some of the registry options that you can configure for Automatic Updates.

TABLE 10.4   Selected registry keys and values for Automatic Updates

Registry key	Options for values
NoAutoUpdate	0: Automatic Updates are enabled (default).
	1: Automatic Updates are disabled.
	2: Notify of download and installation.
	3: Autodownload and notify of installation.
	4: Autodownload and schedule installation.
	5: Automatic Updates is required, but end users can configure.
ScheduledInstallDay	1: Sunday.
	2: Monday.
	3: Tuesday.
	4: Wednesday.
	5: Thursday.
	6: Friday.
	7: Saturday.
UseWUServer	0: Use public Microsoft Windows Update site.
	1: Use server specified in WUServer entry.

To specify what server will be used as the Windows Update server, you edit two registry keys, which are found here:

`HKEY_LOCAL_MACHINE\Software\Policies\Microsoft\Windows\WindowsUpdate`

- The WUServer key sets the Windows Update server using the server's HTTP name—for example, `http://intranetSUS`.
- The WUStatusServer key sets the Windows Update intranet WSUS statistics server by using the server's HTTP name—for example, `http://intranetSUS`.

Configuring a Client in an Active Directory Network

If the WSUS client is part of an enterprise network using Active Directory, you would configure the client via Group Policy. In Exercise 10.3, we will walk you through the steps needed to configure the Group Policy object (GPO) for WSUS clients. The *Group Policy Management Console (GPMC)* needs to be installed to complete this exercise. If you don't have the GPMC installed, you can install it using the Server Manager utility.

EXERCISE 10.3

Configuring a GPO for WSUS

1. Open the GPMC by pressing the Windows key and selecting Administrative Tools ≻ Group Policy Management.

2. Expand the forest, domains, and your domain name. Under your domain name, click Default Domain Policy. Right-click and choose Edit.

3. Under the Computer Configuration section, expand Policies ≻ Administrative Templates ≻ Windows Components ≻ Windows Update.

4. In the right pane, double-click the Configure Automatic Updates option. The Configure Automatic Updates Properties dialog box appears. Click the Enabled button. Then, in the drop-down list, choose Auto Download And Notify For Install. Click OK.

5. Double-click Specify Intranet Microsoft Update Service Location Properties. This setting allows you to specify the server from which the clients will get the updates. Click Enabled. In the two server name boxes, enter **//servername** (the name of the server on which you installed WSUS in Exercise 10.1). Click OK.

6. To configure the rescheduling of automatic updates, double-click Reschedule Automatic Updates Scheduled Installations. You can enable and schedule the amount of time that Automatic Updates waits after system startup before it attempts to proceed with a scheduled installation that was previously missed. Click Enabled. Enter **10** in the Startup (Minutes) box. Click OK.

7. To configure auto-restart for scheduled Automatic Updates installations, double-click No Auto-Restart For Scheduled Automatic Updates Installations. When you enable this option, the computer is not required to restart after an update. Enable this option and click OK.

8. Close the GPMC.

Configuring Client-Side Targeting

Administrators can use a GPO to enable client-side targeting. Client machines can be automatically added into the proper computer group once the client computer connects to the WSUS server. Client-side targeting can be a very useful tool when an administrator has multiple client computers and the administrator needs to automate the process of assigning those computers to computer groups.

Administrators can enable client-side targeting on the WSUS server by clicking the Use Group Policy or registry settings on client computers option on the Computers Options page.

1. On the WSUS console toolbar, click Options and then click Computer Options.

2. In Computer Options, choose one of the following options:

   - If an administrator wants to create groups and assign computers through the WSUS console (server-side targeting), click Use The Move Computers Task In Windows Server Update Services.

   - If an administrator wants to create groups and assign computers by using Group Policy settings on the client computer (client-side targeting), click Use Group Policy Or Registry Settings On Computers.

3. Under Tasks, click the Save Settings button and then click OK.

Overview of Windows Server 2012 R2 Performance Monitoring

The first step in any performance optimization strategy is to measure performance accurately and consistently. The insight that you'll gain from monitoring factors such as network and system utilization will be extremely useful when you measure the effects of any changes.

The overall performance monitoring process usually involves the following steps:

1. Establish a baseline of current performance.

2. Identify the bottlenecks.

3. Plan for and implement changes.

4. Measure the effects of the changes.

5. Repeat the process based on business needs.

Note that the performance optimization process is never really finished because you can always try to gain more performance from your system by modifying settings and applying other well-known tweaks. Before you get discouraged, realize that you'll reach some level of performance that you and your network and system users consider acceptable and that it's not worth the additional effort it will take to optimize performance any further. Also note that as your network and system load increases (more users or users doing more), so too will the need to reiterate this process. By continuing to monitor, measure, and optimize, you will keep ahead of the pack and keep your end users happy.

Now that you have an idea of the overall process, let's focus on how changes should be made. It's important to keep in mind the following ideas when monitoring performance:

Plan Changes Carefully   Here's a rule of thumb that you should always try to follow: An hour of planning can save a week of work. When you are working in an easy-to-use GUI-based operating system like Windows Server 2012 R2, it's tempting to remove a check mark here or there and then retest the performance. You should resist the urge to do this because some changes can cause large decreases in performance or can impact functionality. Before you make haphazard changes (especially on production servers), take the time to learn about, plan for, and test your changes. Plan for outages and testing accordingly.

Utilize a Test Environment   Test in a test lab that simulates a production environment. Do not make changes on production environments without first giving warning. Ideally, change production environments in off-hours when fewer network and system users will be affected. Making haphazard changes in a production environment can cause serious problems. These problems will likely outweigh any benefits that you may receive from making performance tweaks.

Make Only One Change at a Time   The golden rule of scientific experiments is that you should always keep track of as many variables as possible. When the topic is server optimization, this roughly translates into making only one change at a time.

One of the problems with making multiple system changes is that although you may have improved overall performance, it's hard to determine exactly *which* change created the positive effects. It's also possible, for example, that changing one parameter increased performance greatly while changing another decreased it only slightly. Although the overall result was an increase in performance, you should identify the second, performance-reducing option so that the same mistake is not made again. To reduce the chance of obtaining misleading results, always try to make only one change at a time.

The main reason to make one change at a time, however, is that if you do make a mistake or create an unexpected issue, you can easily "back out" of the change. If you make two or three changes at the same time and are not sure which one created the problem, you will have to undo all of the changes and then make one alteration at a time to find the problem. If you make only one change at a time and follow that methodology every time, you won't find yourself in this situation.

WARNING   It's important to remember that many changes (such as registry changes) take place immediately; they do not need to be applied explicitly. Once the change is made, it's live. Be careful to plan your changes wisely.

Ensure Consistency in Measurements   When you are monitoring performance, consistency is extremely important. You should strive to have repeatable and accurate measurements. Controlling variables, such as system load at various times during the day, can help.

Assume, for instance, that you want to measure the number of transactions that you can simulate on the accounting database server within an hour. The results would be widely different if you ran the test during the month-end accounting close than if you ran the test on a Sunday morning. By running the same tests when the server is under a relatively static load, you will be able to get more accurate measurements.

Maintain a Performance History   In the introduction to this chapter, I mentioned that the performance optimization cycle is a continuous improvement process. Because many changes may be made over time, it is important to keep track of the changes that have been made and the results you have experienced. Documenting this knowledge will help solve similar problems if they arise. I understand that many IT professionals do not like to document, but documentation can make life much easier in the long run.

As you can see, you need to keep a lot of factors in mind when optimizing performance. Although this might seem like a lot to digest and remember, do not fear. As a system administrator, you will learn some of the rules you need to know to keep your system running optimally. Fortunately, the tools included with Windows Server 2012 R2 can help you organize the process and take measurements. Now that you have a good overview of the process, let's move on to look at the tools that can be used to set it in motion.

Using Windows Server 2012 R2 Performance Tools

Because performance monitoring and optimization are vital functions in network environments of any size, Windows Server 2012 R2 includes several performance-related tools.

Introducing Performance Monitor

The first and most useful tool is the Windows Server 2012 R2 *Performance Monitor*, which was designed to allow users and system administrators to monitor performance statistics for various operating system parameters. Specifically, you can collect, store, and analyze information about CPU, memory, disk, and network resources using this tool, and these are only a handful of the things that you can monitor. By collecting and analyzing performance values, system administrators can identify many potential problems.

You can use the Performance Monitor in the following ways:

Performance Monitor ActiveX Control   The Windows Server 2012 R2 Performance Monitor is an ActiveX control that you can place within other applications. Examples of applications that can host the Performance Monitor control include web browsers and client programs such as Microsoft Word or Microsoft Excel. This functionality can make it easy for applications developers and system administrators to incorporate the Performance Monitor into their own tools and applications.

Performance Monitor MMC For more common performance monitoring functions, you'll want to use the built-in Microsoft Management Console (MMC) version of the Performance Monitor.

System Stability Index The *System Stability Index* is a numerical value from 1 (least stable) to 10 (most stable) that represents the stability of your network. Performance Monitor calculates and creates the System Stability Index. You can view a graph of this index value. The graph can help a network administrator identify when the network started encountering problems. The System Stability Index also offers side-by-side comparisons. An administrator can view when system changes occurred (installing applications, devices, or drivers) and when system problems started to occur. This way, you can determine whether any system changes caused the problems that you are encountering.

Data Collector Sets Windows Server 2012 R2 Performance Monitor includes the Data Collector Set. This tool works with performance logs, telling Performance Monitor where the logs are stored and when the log needs to run. The Data Collector Sets also define the credentials used to run the set.

To access the Performance Monitor MMC, you open Administrative Tools and then choose Performance Monitor. This launches the Performance MMC and loads and initializes Performance Monitor with a handful of default counters.

You can choose from many different methods of monitoring performance when you are using Performance Monitor. A couple of examples are listed here:

- You can look at a snapshot of current activity for a few of the most important counters. This allows you to find areas of potential bottlenecks and monitor the load on your servers at a certain point in time.

- You can save information to a log file for historical reporting and later analysis. This type of information is useful, for example, if you want to compare the load on your servers from three months ago to the current load.

You'll get to take a closer look at this method and many others as you examine Performance Monitor in more detail.

In the following sections, you'll learn about the basics of working with the Windows Server 2012 R2 Performance Monitor and other performance tools. Then you'll apply these tools and techniques when you monitor the performance of your network.

 Your Performance Monitor grows as your system grows, and whenever you add services to Windows Server 2012 R2 (such as installing Exchange Server 2010), you also add to what you can monitor. You should make sure that, as you install services, you take a look at what it is you can monitor.

Deciding What to Monitor

The first step in monitoring performance is to decide *what* you want to monitor. In Windows Server 2012 R2, the operating system and related services include hundreds of performance statistics that you can track easily. For example, you may want to monitor IPsec by monitoring connection security rules. This is just one of many items that can be monitored. All performance statistics fall into three main categories that you can choose to measure:

Performance Objects   A *performance object* within Performance Monitor is a collection of various performance statistics that you can monitor. Performance objects are based on various areas of system resources. For example, there are performance objects for the processor and memory as well as for specific services such as web services.

Counters   *Counters* are the actual parameters measured by Performance Monitor. They are specific items that are grouped within performance objects. For example, within the Processor performance object, there is a counter for % Processor Time. This counter displays one type of detailed information about the Processor performance object (specifically, the amount of total CPU time all of the processes on the system are using). Another set of counters you can use will allow you to monitor print servers.

Instances   Some counters will have instances. An *instance* further identifies which performance parameter the counter is measuring. A simple example is a server with two CPUs. If you decide you want to monitor processor usage (using the Processor performance object)—specifically, utilization (the % Total Utilization counter)—you must still specify *which* CPU(s) you want to measure. In this example, you would have the choice of monitoring either of the two CPUs or a total value for both (using the Total instance).

To specify which performance objects, counters, and instances you want to monitor, you add them to Performance Monitor using the Add Counters dialog box. Figure 10.3 shows the various options that are available when you add new counters to monitor using Performance Monitor.

FIGURE 10.3   Adding a new Performance Monitor counter

The items that you will be able to monitor will be based on your hardware and software configuration. For example, if you have not installed and configured the IIS, the options available within the Web Server performance object will not be available. Or, if you have multiple network adapters or CPUs in the server, you will have the option of viewing each instance separately or as part of the total value.

Viewing Performance Information   The Windows Server 2012 R2 Performance Monitor was designed to show information in a clear and easy-to-understand format. Performance objects, counters, and instances may be displayed in each of three views. This flexibility allows system administrators to define quickly and easily the information they want to see once and then choose how it will be displayed based on specific needs. Most likely, you will use only one view, but it's helpful to know what other views are available depending on what it is you are trying to assess.

You can use the following main views to review statistics and information on performance:

Graph View   The *Graph view* is the default display that is presented when you first access the Windows Server 2012 R2 Performance Monitor. The chart displays values using the vertical axis and displays time using the horizontal axis. This view is useful if you want to display values over a period of time or see the changes in these values over that time period. Each point that is plotted on the graph is based on an average value calculated during the sample interval for the measurement being made. For example, you may notice overall CPU utilization starting at a low value at the beginning of the chart and then becoming much higher during later measurements. This indicates that the server has become busier (specifically, with CPU-intensive processes). Figure 10.4 provides an example of the Graph view.

FIGURE 10.4   Viewing information in Performance Monitor Graph view

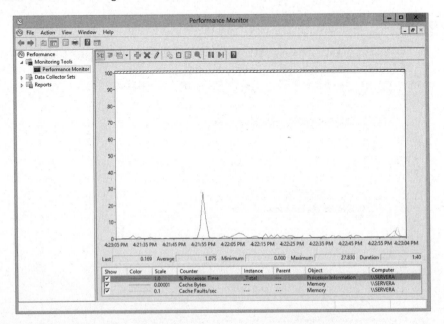

Histogram View   The *Histogram view* shows performance statistics and information using a set of relative bar charts. This view is useful if you want to see a snapshot of the latest value for a given counter. For example, if you were interested in viewing a snapshot of current system performance statistics during each refresh interval, the length of each of the bars in the display would give you a visual representation of each value. It would also allow you to compare measurements visually relative to each other. You can set the histogram to display an average measurement as well as minimum and maximum thresholds. Figure 10.5 shows a typical Histogram view.

FIGURE 10.5   Viewing information in Performance Monitor Histogram view

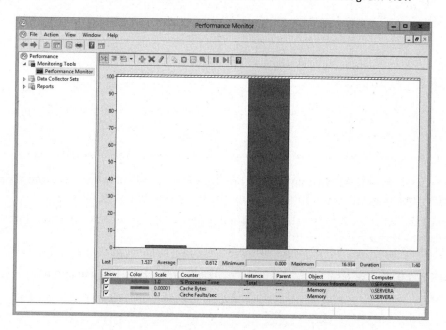

Report View   Like the Histogram view, the *Report view* shows performance statistics based on the latest measurement. You can see an average measurement as well as minimum and maximum thresholds. This view is most useful for determining exact values because it provides information in numeric terms, whereas the Chart and Histogram views provide information graphically. Figure 10.6 provides an example of the type of information you'll see in the Report view.

Managing Performance Monitor Properties

You can specify additional settings for viewing performance information within the properties of Performance Monitor. You can access these options by clicking the Properties button

FIGURE 10.6 Viewing information in Performance Monitor Report view

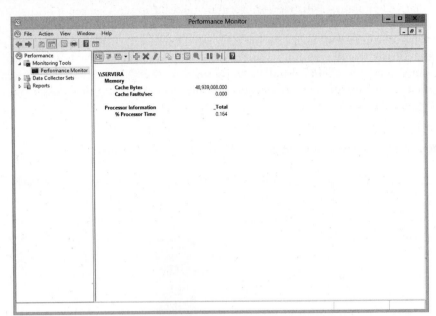

in the taskbar or by right-clicking the Performance Monitor display and selecting Properties. You can change these additional settings by using the following tabs:

General Tab On the General tab (shown in Figure 10.7), you can specify several options that relate to Performance Monitor views:

FIGURE 10.7 General tab of the Performance Monitor Properties dialog box

- You can enable or disable legends (which display information about the various counters), the value bar, and the toolbar.

- For the Report and Histogram views, you can choose which type of information is displayed. The options are Default, Current, Minimum, Maximum, and Average. What you see with each of these options depends on the type of data being collected. These options are not available for the Graph view because the Graph view displays an average value over a period of time (the sample interval).

- You can also choose the graph elements. By default, the display will be set to update every second. If you want to update less often, you should increase the number of seconds between updates.

Source Tab   On the Source tab (shown in Figure 10.8), you can specify the source for the performance information you want to view. Options include current activity (the default setting) or data from a log file. If you choose to analyze information from a log file, you can also specify the time range for which you want to view statistics. We'll cover these selections in the next section.

FIGURE 10.8   Source tab of the Performance Monitor Properties dialog box

Data Tab   The Data tab (shown in Figure 10.9) lists the counters that have been added to the Performance Monitor display. These counters apply to the Chart, Histogram, and Report views. Using this interface, you can also add or remove any of the counters and change the properties, such as the width, style, and color of the line and the scale used for display.

Graph Tab   On the Graph tab (shown in Figure 10.10), you can specify certain options that will allow you to customize the display of Performance Monitor views. First you can

FIGURE 10.9 The Data tab of the Performance Monitor Properties dialog box

specify what type of view you want to see (Line, Histogram, or Report). Then you can add a title for the graph, specify a label for the vertical axis, choose to display grids, and specify the vertical scale range.

FIGURE 10.10 The Graph tab of the Performance Monitor Properties dialog box

Appearance Tab   Using the Appearance tab (see Figure 10.11), you can specify the colors for the areas of the display, such as the background and foreground. You can also specify the fonts that are used to display counter values in Performance Monitor views. You can

FIGURE 10.11   The Appearance tab of the Performance Monitor Properties dialog box

change settings to find a suitable balance between readability and the amount of information shown on one screen. Finally, you can set up the properties for a border.

Now that you have an idea of the types of information Performance Monitor tracks and how this data is displayed, you'll take a look at another feature—saving and analyzing performance data.

Saving and Analyzing Data with Performance Logs and Alerts

One of the most important aspects of monitoring performance is that it should be done over a given period of time (referred to as a *baseline*). So far, I have shown you how you can use Performance Monitor to view statistics in real time. I have, however, also alluded to using Performance Monitor to save data for later analysis. Now let's take a look at how you can do this.

When viewing information in Performance Monitor, you have two main options with respect to the data on display:

View Current Activity   When you first open the Performance icon from the Administrative Tools folder, the default option is to view data obtained from current system information. This method of viewing measures and displays various real-time statistics on the system's performance.

View Log File Data   This option allows you to view information that was previously saved to a log file. Although the performance objects, counters, and instances may appear to be the same as those viewed using the View Current Activity option, the information itself was actually captured at a previous point in time and stored into a log file.

Log files for the View Log File Data option are created in the Performance Logs And Alerts section of the Windows Server 2012 R2 Performance tool.

Three items allow you to customize how the data is collected in the log files:

Counter Logs   *Counter logs* record performance statistics based on the various performance objects, counters, and instances available in Performance Monitor. The values are updated based on a time interval setting and are saved to a file for later analysis.

Circular Logging   In *circular logging*, the data that is stored within a file is overwritten as new data is entered into the log. This is a useful method of logging if you want to record information only for a certain time frame (for example, the past four hours). Circular logging also conserves disk space by ensuring that the performance log file will not continue to grow over certain limits.

Linear Logging   In *linear logging*, data is never deleted from the log files, and new information is added to the end of the log file. The result is a log file that continually grows. The benefit is that all historical information is retained.

Now that you have an idea of the types of functions that are supported by the Windows Server 2012 R2 Performance tools, you can learn how you can apply this information to the task at hand—monitoring and troubleshooting your Windows network.

 Real World Scenario

Real-World Performance Monitoring

In our daily jobs as system engineers and administrators, we come across systems that are in need of our help...and may even ask for it. You, of course, check your Event Viewer and Performance Monitor and perform other tasks that help you troubleshoot. But what is really the most common problem that occurs? From my experience, I'd say that you suffer performance problems many times if your Windows Server 2012 R2 operating system is installed on a subpar system. Either the server hardware isn't enterprise class or the minimum hardware requirements weren't addressed. Most production servers suffer from slow response times, lagging, and so on, because money wasn't spent where it should have been in the first place—on the server's hardware requirements.

Using Other Performance-Monitoring Tools

Performance Monitor allows you to monitor different parameters of the Windows Server 2012 R2 operating system and associated services and applications. However, you can also use three other tools to monitor performance in Windows Server 2012 R2. They are Network Monitor, Task Manager, and Event Viewer. All three of these tools are useful for monitoring different areas of overall system performance and for examining details related to specific system events. In the following sections, you'll take a quick look at these tools and how you can best use them.

The Network Monitor

Although Performance Monitor is a great tool for viewing overall network performance statistics, it isn't equipped for packet-level analysis and doesn't give you much insight into what types of network traffic are traveling on the wire. That's where the Network Monitor tool comes in. *Network Monitor* has two main components: the Network Monitor Agent and the Network Monitor tool.

The Network Monitor Agent is available for use with Windows XP, Windows Server 2003, Windows Vista, Windows 7, Windows 8, Windows Server 2008, Windows Server 2008 R2, Windows Server 2012, and Windows Server 2012 R2. The agent allows you to track network packets. When you install the Network Monitor Agent, you will also be able to access the Network Segment System Monitor counter.

On Windows Server 2012 R2 computers, you'll see the Network Monitor icon appear in the Administrative Tools program group. You can use the Network Monitor tool to capture data as it travels on your network.

 A version of Network Monitor is available for free with Windows Server 2012 R2. The full version of Network Monitor is available at Microsoft's download server. For more information, see www.microsoft.com/downloads/.

Once you have captured the data of interest, you can save it to a capture file or further analyze it using Microsoft Message Analyzer. Experienced network and system administrators can use this information to determine how applications are communicating and the types of data that are being passed via the network.

 For the exam, you don't need to understand the detailed information that Network Monitor displays, but you should be aware of the types of information that you can view and when you should use Network Monitor.

Task Manager

Performance Monitor is designed to allow you to keep track of specific aspects of system performance over time. But what do you do if you want to get a quick snapshot of what the local system is doing? Creating a System Monitor chart, adding counters, and choosing a view is overkill. Fortunately, the Windows Server 2012 R2 Task Manager has been designed to provide a quick overview of important system performance statistics without requiring any configuration. Better yet, it's always readily available.

You can easily access Task Manager in several ways:

- Right-click the Windows taskbar and then click Task Manager.
- Press Ctrl+Alt+Del and then select Task Manager.
- Press Ctrl+Shift+Esc.

Each of these methods allows you to access a snapshot of the current system performance quickly.

Once you access Task Manager, you will see the following five tabs:

Processes Tab   The Processes tab shows you all of the processes that are currently running on the local computer. By default, you'll be able to view how much CPU time and memory a particular process is using. By clicking any of the columns, you can quickly sort by the data values in that particular column. This is useful, for example, if you want to find out which processes are using the most memory on your server.

By accessing the performance objects in the View menu, you can add columns to the Processes tab. Figure 10.12 shows a list of the current processes running on a Windows Server 2012 R2 computer.

FIGURE 10.12   Viewing process statistics and information using Task Manager

Performance Tab   One of the problems with using Performance Monitor to get a quick snapshot of system performance is that you have to add counters to a chart. Most system administrators are too busy to take the time to do this when all they need is basic CPU and memory information. That's where the Performance tab of Task Manager comes in. Using the Performance tab, you can view details about how memory is allocated on the computer and how much of the CPU is utilized (see Figure 10.13).

FIGURE 10.13   Viewing CPU and memory performance information using Task Manager

Users Tab   The Users tab (see Figure 10.14) lists the currently active user accounts. This is particularly helpful if you want to see who is online and quickly log off or disconnect users. You can also send a console message to any remote user in the list by clicking the Send Message button. (The button is grayed out in Figure 10.14 because you cannot send a message to yourself. If you select a different user, the button will be available.)

FIGURE 10.14   Viewing user information using Task Manager

Details Tab The Details tab (see Figure 10.15) shows you what applications are currently running on the system. From this location, you can stop an application from running by right-clicking the application and choosing Stop. You also have the ability to set your affinity level here. By setting the affinity, you can choose which applications will use which processors on your system.

FIGURE 10.15 Viewing applications that are currently running using Task Manager

Name ▲	PID	Status	User name	CPU	Memory (p...	Description
certsrv.exe	1600	Running	SYSTEM	00	4,940 K	Microsoft® Certifica...
csrss.exe	340	Running	SYSTEM	00	968 K	Client Server Runtim...
csrss.exe	396	Running	SYSTEM	00	1,172 K	Client Server Runtim...
dfsrs.exe	1668	Running	SYSTEM	00	3,924 K	Distributed File Syste...
dfssvc.exe	1176	Running	SYSTEM	00	1,264 K	Windows NT Distrib...
dns.exe	1704	Running	SYSTEM	00	156,836 K	Domain Name Syste...
dsamain.exe	1412	Running	NETWORK...	00	6,880 K	Active Directory Lig...
dwm.exe	852	Running	DWM-1	00	20,300 K	Desktop Window M...
explorer.exe	3188	Running	Administra...	00	21,032 K	Windows Explorer
iexplore.exe	1348	Running	Administra...	00	4,836 K	Internet Explorer
iexplore.exe	3564	Running	Administra...	00	7,744 K	Internet Explorer
ifssvc.exe	2460	Running	SYSTEM	00	10,828 K	ADFS Web Agent Au...
inetinfo.exe	2340	Running	SYSTEM	00	14,160 K	Internet Information...
ismserv.exe	1776	Running	SYSTEM	00	1,040 K	Windows NT Intersit...
lsass.exe	500	Running	SYSTEM	00	15,936 K	Local Security Autho...
Microsoft.ActiveDire...	1456	Running	SYSTEM	00	14,936 K	Microsoft.ActiveDire...
Microsoft.IdentitySer...	3636	Running	NETWORK...	00	251,332 K	Microsoft.IdentitySe...
msdtc.exe	3824	Running	NETWORK...	00	2,292 K	Microsoft Distribute...
services.exe	492	Running	SYSTEM	00	3,816 K	Services and Control...
smss.exe	228	Running	SYSTEM	00	288 K	Windows Session M...
SMSvcHost.exe	1820	Running	LOCAL SE...	00	5,980 K	SMSvcHost.exe
spoolsv.exe	1384	Running	SYSTEM	00	3,784 K	Spooler SubSystem ...
sqlservr.exe	2128	Running	MSSQL$MI...	00	256,052 K	SQL Server Windows...

Services Tab The Services tab (see Figure 10.16) shows you what services are currently running on the system. From this location, you can stop a service from running by right-clicking the service and choosing Stop. The Open Services link launches the Services MMC.

These tabs can be different on Windows Client machines. For example, Windows 7 has six tabs, not five, and Windows 8 has seven tabs.

As you can see, Task Manager is useful for providing important information about the system quickly. Once you get used to using Task Manager, you won't be able to get by without it!

FIGURE 10.16   Viewing services information using Task Manager

Name	PID	Description	Status	Group
WSusCertServer		WSUS Certificate Server	Stopped	
WsusService	4048	WSUS Service	Running	
wmiApSrv		WMI Performance Adapter	Stopped	
WLMS	816	Windows Licensing Monitoring S...	Running	
WIDWriter	1960	Windows Internal Database VSS ...	Running	
VSS		Volume Shadow Copy	Stopped	
vds	2868	Virtual Disk	Running	
VaultSvc	500	Credential Manager	Running	
UI0Detect		Interactive Services Detection	Stopped	
TrustedInstaller		Windows Modules Installer	Stopped	
sppsvc		Software Protection	Stopped	
Spooler	1384	Print Spooler	Running	
SNMPTRAP		SNMP Trap	Stopped	
SamSs	500	Security Accounts Manager	Running	
RSoPProv		Resultant Set of Policy Provider	Stopped	
RpcLocator		Remote Procedure Call (RPC) Lo...	Stopped	
PerfHost		Performance Counter DLL Host	Stopped	
NtFrs		File Replication	Stopped	
NTDS	500	Active Directory Domain Services	Running	
NetTcpPortSharing	1820	Net.Tcp Port Sharing Service	Running	
NetTcpActivator	1820	Net.Tcp Listener Adapter	Running	
Netlogon	500	Netlogon	Running	
MSSQL$MICROSOFT##WID	2128	Windows Internal Database	Running	

Make sure that you use Task Manager and familiarize yourself with all that it can do; you can end processes that have become intermittent, kill applications that may hang the system, view NIC performance, and so on. In addition, you can access this tool quickly to get an idea of what could be causing you problems. Event Viewer, Network Monitor, and Performance Monitor are all great tools for getting granular information on potential problems.

Event Viewer

Event Viewer is also useful for monitoring network information. Specifically, you can use the logs to view any information, warnings, or alerts related to the proper functioning of the network. You can access Event Viewer by selecting Administrative Tools ➢ Event Viewer. Clicking any of the items in the left pane displays the various events that have been logged for each item. Figure 10.17 shows the contents of the Directory Service log.

Each event is preceded by a blue *i* icon. That icon designates that these events are informational and do not indicate problems with the network. Rather, they record benign events such as Active Directory startup or a domain controller finding a global catalog server.

FIGURE 10.17   Event Viewer

A yellow warning icon or a red error icon, both of which are shown in Figure 10.18, indicate problematic or potentially problematic events. Warnings usually indicate a problem that wouldn't prevent a service from running but might cause undesired effects with the service in question. For example, I was configuring a site with some fictional domain controllers and IP addresses. My local domain controller's IP address wasn't associated with any of the sites, and Event Viewer generated a warning. In this case, the local domain controller could still function as a domain controller, but the site configuration could produce undesirable results.

Error events almost always indicate a failed service, application, or function. For instance, if the dynamic registration of a DNS client fails, Event Viewer will generate an error. As you can see, errors are more severe than warnings because, in this case, the DNS client cannot participate in DNS at all.

Double-clicking any event opens the Event Properties dialog box, as shown in Figure 10.19, which displays a detailed description of the event.

Event Viewer can display thousands of different events, so it would be impossible to list them all here. The important points of which you should be aware are the following:

- Information events are always benign.

- Warnings indicate noncritical problems.

- Errors indicate show-stopping events.

FIGURE 10.18   Information, errors, and warnings in Event Viewer

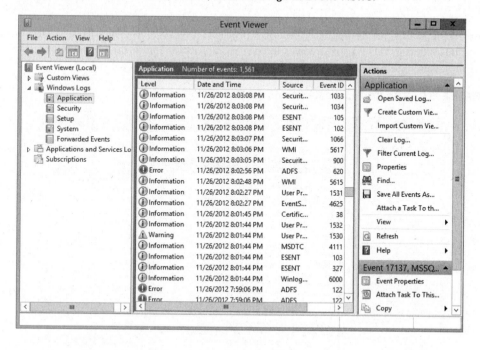

FIGURE 10.19   An Event Properties dialog box

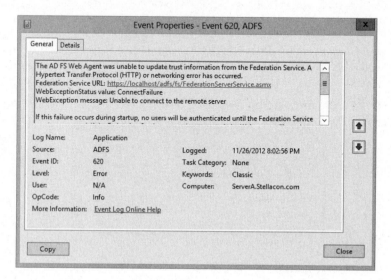

Let's discuss some of the logs and the ways you can view data:

Applications and Services   The *applications and services logs* are part of Event Viewer where applications (for example, Exchange) and services (DNS) log their events. DFS events would be logged in this part of Event Viewer. An important log in this section is the DNS Server log (see Figure 10.20). This is where all of your DNS events get stored.

FIGURE 10.20   The applications and services DNS Server log

Custom Views   *Custom views* allow you to filter events (see Figure 10.21) to create your own customized look. You can filter events by event level (critical, error, warning, and so

FIGURE 10.21   Create Custom View dialog box

on), by logs, and by source. You also have the ability to view events occurring within a specific timeframe. This allows you to look only at the events that are important to you.

Subscriptions   *Subscriptions* allow a user to receive alerts about events that you predefine. In the Subscription Properties dialog box (see Figure 10.22), you can define what type of events you want notifications about and the notification method. The Subscriptions section is an advanced alerting service to help you watch for events.

FIGURE 10.22   Subscription Properties dialog box

Microsoft Baseline Security Analyzer

The *Microsoft Baseline Security Analyzer (MBSA)* is a security assessment utility that you can download from the Microsoft website at the following location:

www.microsoft.com/en-us/download/details.aspx?id=19892

The filename of the download is mbsasetup.msi. It verifies whether your computer has the latest security updates and whether any common security violation configurations have been applied to your computer. MBSA can scan the following programs and operating systems:

- Windows 2000
- Windows XP
- Windows Vista
- Windows 7

- Windows 8
- Windows Server 2003
- Windows Server 2008
- Windows Server 2008 R2
- Windows Server 2012
- Windows Server 2012 R2
- IIS 5 or newer
- Internet Explorer, versions 6.0 and newer
- SQL Server 7 or newer
- Microsoft Office 2000 or newer
- Windows Media Player, versions 6.4 and newer

To use MBSA, the computer must meet the following requirements:

- It must be running Windows XP, Windows Vista, Windows 7, Windows 8, Windows Server 2003, Windows Server 2008, Windows Server 2008 R2, Windows Server 2012, or Windows Server 2012 R2.
- It must be running Internet Explorer 5.01 or newer.
- It must have an XML parser installed for full functionality.
- It must have the Workstation and Server services enabled.
- It must have Client for Microsoft Networks installed.

Using the GUI Version of MBSA

Once you have installed MBSA, you can access it by using the Windows key and choosing Microsoft Baseline Security Analyzer or by opening the command prompt and executing mbsa.exe. This opens the Baseline Security Analyzer utility. You can select from Scan A Computer, Scan More Than One Computer, and View Existing Security Reports.

When you click Scan A Computer, the Pick A Computer To Scan dialog box appears. You can specify that you want to scan a computer based on a computer name or IP address. You can also specify the name of the security report that will be generated.

The following are options for the security scan:

- Check For Windows Vulnerabilities
- Check For Weak Passwords
- Check For IIS Vulnerabilities
- Check For SQL Vulnerabilities
- Check For Security Updates

If you use the Check For Security Updates option and are using WSUS, you can specify the name of the WSUS server that should be checked for the security updates.

Once you have made your selections, click Start Scan. When the scan is complete, the security report will be automatically displayed. If you have scanned multiple computers, you can sort the security reports based on issue name or score (worst first or best first).

Using the MBSA Command-Line Utility *mbsacli.exe*

After Microsoft Baseline Security Analyzer has been installed, you can use the command-line utility mbsacli.exe. Enter **mbsacli.exe/hf** and then customize the command execution with any of the options defined in Table 10.5.

TABLE 10.5   mbsacli.exe /hf command-line options

Option	Description
-h *host name[, host name, . . .]*	Scans the specified host. You can specify that you want to scan multiple host computers by separating the hostnames with commas.
-fh *filename*	Scans the NetBIOS name of each computer that is to be scanned, and it saves the information as text within a file specified by *filename*.
-i *xxxx.xxxx.xxxx.xxxx [, xxxx.xxxx.xxxx.xxxx, . . .]*	Scans a computer based on the specified IP address. You can scan multiple computers by IP address by separating the IP addresses with commas.
-fip *filename*	Looks in the text file specified by *filename* for IP addresses and scans the computers with those IP addresses. The file can have up to a maximum of 256 IP addresses.
-d *domainname*	Scans the specified domain.
-n	Scans all of the computers on the local network.

Simple Network Management Protocol

The *Simple Network Management Protocol (SNMP)* is a TCP/IP protocol monitor. The SNMP service creates trap messages that are then sent to a trap destination. One way you might use SNMP is to trap messages that don't contain an appropriate hostname for a particular service.

When you set up SNMP, you set up communities. *Communities* are groupings of computers that help monitor each other.

Windows Server 2012 R2 includes SNMP with the operating system. To install the service, you must use Server Manager. In Exercise 10.4, you will walk through the process of installing the SNMP service.

EXERCISE 10.4

Installing SNMP

1. Open Server Manager by clicking the Server Manager icon on the taskbar.

2. Click option number 2, Add Roles And Features.

3. Choose role-based or feature-based installation and click Next.

4. Choose your server and click Next.

5. Click Next at the Select Server Roles screen.

6. When the Select Features window appears, click the SNMP Services check box. If an ADD Features dialog box appears, click the Add Features button. Click Next.

7. The Confirm Installation page appears. Click Install.

8. Click Close. Exit the Server Manager application.

Now that you have installed the SNMP service, you have to set up your community so that you can start trapping messages. As stated earlier, communities are a grouping of computers to help monitor each other. After you have created the initial community, you can add other computer systems to the community.

In Exercise 10.5, you will walk through the steps to set up the SNMP service and also set up your first community name. To complete this exercise, you must have completed Exercise 10.4.

EXERCISE 10.5

Configuring SNMP

1. Open Computer Management by pressing the keyboard's Windows Key and selecting Administrative Tools ➢ Computer Management.

2. Expand Services And Applications. Click Services. In the right pane, double-click SNMP Service.

3. The SNMP Service Properties window will open. Click the Traps tab. In the Community Name box, enter **Community1**. Click the Add To List button.

4. Click the General tab. Click the Start button to start the service. Click OK.

5. Close Computer Management.

Summary

This chapter began with a discussion of WSUS and what Windows Update can do for your network. You learned why you would want to use a WSUS server instead of having clients manually connect to the Internet to receive their updates.

The chapter also covered file server and print server optimization and reliability, including many tools that can help you monitor and manage your systems and the basics of troubleshooting the network in times of disaster.

Monitoring performance on servers is imperative to rooting out any issues that may affect your network. If your systems are not running at their best, your end users may experience issues such as latency, or worse, you may experience corruption in your network data. Either way, it's important to know how to monitor the performance of your servers. You also looked at ways system administrators can optimize the operations of servers to ensure that end users experience adequate performance.

You also examined how to use the various performance-related tools that are included with Windows Server 2012 R2. Tools such as Performance Monitor, Task Manager, Network Monitor, and Event Viewer can help you diagnose and troubleshoot system performance issues. These tools will help you find typical problems related to memory, disk space, and any other hardware-related issues you may experience. Knowing how to use tools to troubleshoot and test your systems is imperative, not only to passing the exam but also to performing your duties at work. To have a smoothly running network environment, it is vital that you understand the issues related to the reliability and performance of your network servers and domain controllers.

Exam Essentials

Understand WSUS.   Windows Server Update Services is one way to have your end users receive important updates from Microsoft. WSUS gives administrators the ability to download, test, and approve updates before they get released onto the network.

Understand the methodology behind troubleshooting performance.   By following a set of steps that involves making measurements and finding bottlenecks, you can systematically troubleshoot performance problems.

Be familiar with the features and capabilities of the Windows Server 2012 R2 Performance Monitor tool for troubleshooting performance problems.   The Performance Monitor administrative tool is a powerful method for collecting data about all areas of system performance. Through the use of performance objects, counters, and instances, you can choose to collect and record only the data of interest and use this information for pinpointing performance problems.

Know the importance of common performance counters.   Several important performance-related counters deal with general system performance. Know the importance of monitoring memory, print server, CPU, and network usage on a busy server.

Understand the role of other troubleshooting tools.   Windows Task Manager, Network Monitor, SNMP, Baseline Security Analyzer, and Event Viewer can all be used to diagnose and troubleshoot configuration- and performance-related issues.

Understand how to troubleshoot common sources of server reliability problems.   Windows Server 2012 R2 has been designed to be a stable, robust, and reliable operating system. Should you experience intermittent failures, you should know how to troubleshoot device drivers and buggy system-level software.

Review Questions

1. You need to stop an application from running in Task Manager. Which tab would you use to stop an application from running?

   A. Performance

   B. Users

   C. Options

   D. Details

2. You are the network administrator for a Fortune 500 company. You are responsible for all client computers at the central campus. You want to make sure that all of the client computers are secure. You decide to use MBSA to scan your client computers for possible security violations. You want to use the command-line version of MBSA to scan your computers based on IP address. Which of the following commands should you use?

   A. `mdsacli.exe /hf -i xxxx.xxxx.xxxx.xxxx`

   B. `mdsacli.exe /ip xxxx.xxxx.xxxx.xxxx`

   C. `mbsa.exe /hf -ip xxxx.xxxx.xxxx.xxxx`

   D. `mbsa.exe /ip xxxx.xxxx.xxxx.xxxx`

3. You are the network administrator for a Fortune 500 company. You are responsible for all client computers at the central campus. You want to make sure that all of the client computers have the most current software installed for their operating systems, including software in the categories Critical Updates and Service Packs, Windows Server 2012 R2 Family, and Driver Updates. You want to automate the process as much as possible, and you want the client computers to download the updates from a central server that you are managing. You decide to use Windows Server Update Services. The WSUS server software has been installed on a server called *WSUSServer*. You want to test the WSUS server before you set up group policies within the domain. You install Windows 8. Which of the following registry entries needs to be made for the client to specify that the client should use WSUSServer for Windows Update? (Choose all that apply.)

   A. Use `HKEY_LOCAL_MACHINE\Software\Policies\Microsoft\Windows\WindowsUpdate\AU\UseWUServer` and specify 0 data.

   B. Use `HKEY_LOCAL_MACHINE\Software\Policies\Microsoft\Windows\WindowsUpdate\AU\UseWUServer` and specify 1 for data.

   C. Use `HKEY_LOCAL_MACHINE\Software\Policies\Microsoft\Windows\WindowsUpdate\AU\WUServer` and specify `http://WSUSServer`.

   D. Use `HKEY_LOCAL_MACHINE\Software\Policies\Microsoft\Windows\WindowsUpdate\AU\WUServer` and specify WSUSServer.

   E. Use `HKEY_LOCAL_MACHINE\Software\Policies\Microsoft\Windows\WindowsUpdate\WUServer` and specify `http://WSUSServer`.

   F. Use `HKEY_LOCAL_MACHINE\Software\Policies\Microsoft\Windows\WindowsUpdate\WUServer` and specify WSUSServer.

4. You are the administrator of a new Windows Server 2012 R2 machine. You need to install WSUS. From where do you install WSUS?

    A. Add/Remove Programs

    B. Programs

    C. Server Manager

    D. Administrative Tools

5. You are a network administrator for your company. The network consists of a single Active Directory domain. All servers run Windows Server 2012 R2. Windows Server Update Services (WSUS) is installed on two servers, SERVERA and SERVERB. SERVERA receives software updates from Microsoft Windows Update servers. You manually synchronized SERVERB with the Windows Update servers, and now you need to complete the WSUS configuration on SERVERB. Which of the following is *not* a step that you might take to complete the configuration of WSUS on SERVERB?

    A. Approve the current updates.

    B. Set SERVERB to receive updates from SERVERA and automatically synchronize with approved updates on SERVERA.

    C. Set SERVERB to draw updates automatically from whichever sources that SERVERA is set to draw from.

    D. Set SERVERB to receive daily updates automatically at a given time.

6. You are the network administrator for your company. The network consists of a single Active Directory domain. All servers run Windows Server 2012 R2. All client computers run Windows 7. The company has 16 mobile sales representatives who are all members of the Power Users local group on their computers. From 6 p.m. until 7 a.m., the sales representatives' laptops are usually turned off and disconnected from the corporate network. The mobile sales representatives' computers must receive software updates every day with minimal user interaction. While verifying the recent updates on one of the laptops, you notice that the updates from the Windows Update servers were not applied. On the Automatic Updates tab of the System Properties dialog box of the mobile computer, what should you do to make sure that software updates are applied to the computer? (Choose three.)

    A. Set the scheduled time to every day at 12 a.m.

    B. Select the option Automatically Download The Updates, And Install Them On The Schedule That I Specify.

    C. Select the option Notify Me Before Downloading Any Updates And Notify Me Again Before Installing Them On My Computer.

    D. Select the Keep My Computer Up To Date check box.

    E. Select the option Download The Updates Automatically And Notify Me When They Are Ready To Be Installed.

    F. Set the scheduled time to every day at 12 p.m.

7. You are responsible for managing several Windows Server 2012 R2 domain controller computers in your environment. Recently, a single hard disk on one of these machines failed, and the Active Directory database was lost. You want to perform the following tasks:

- Determine which partitions on the server are still accessible.

- Restore as much of the system configuration (including the Active Directory database) as possible.

Which of the following could be used to help meet these requirements?

- **A.** Event Viewer

- **B.** Performance Monitor

- **C.** A hard disk from another server that is not configured as a domain controller

- **D.** A valid system state backup from the server

8. You have been hired as a consultant to research a network-related problem at a small organization. The environment supports many custom-developed applications that are not well documented. A manager suspects that some computers on the network are generating excessive traffic and bogging down the network. You want to do the following:

- Determine which computers are causing the problems.

- Record and examine network packets that are coming to/from specific machines.

- View data related only to specific types of network packets.

What tool should you use to accomplish all of the requirements?

- **A.** Task Manager

- **B.** Performance Monitor

- **C.** Event Viewer

- **D.** Network Monitor

9. You need to install Microsoft Baseline Security Analyzer. How do you need to do the install?

- **A.** Download MBSA from Microsoft's website.

- **B.** Install from Server Manager.

- **C.** Use Add/Remove Programs.

- **D.** Install from Programs.

10. While setting up WSUS, you need to configure the server from which you will be getting your Microsoft updates. Under which option would you set this up?

- **A.** Products And Classifications

- **B.** Update Files and Languages

- **C.** Update Source And Proxy Server

- **D.** Synchronization Schedule

Chapter

11

Manage File Services

THE FOLLOWING 70-411 EXAM OBJECTIVES ARE COVERED IN THIS CHAPTER:

✓ **Configure Distributed File System (DFS)**

- Install and configure DFS namespaces
- Configure DFS Replication Targets
- Configure Replication Scheduling
- Configure Remote Differential Compression settings
- Configure staging
- Configure fault tolerance
- Clone a DFS database
- Recover DFS databases
- Optimize DFS replication

✓ **Configure File Server Resource Manager (FSRM)**

- Install the FSRM role service
- Configure quotas
- Configure file screens
- Configure reports
- Configure file management tasks

✓ **Configure file and disk encryption**

- Configure Bitlocker encryption
- Configure the Network Unlock feature
- Configure Bitlocker policies
- Configure the EFS recovery agent
- Manage EFS and Bitlocker certificates including backup and restore

✓ **Configure advanced audit policies**

- Implement auditing using Group Policy and AuditPol.exe
- Create expression-based
- Create removable device audit policies

In this chapter, I will show you how to set up one of the more important server types: a file server. File servers are important because you
need storage allocation where you can store files on your server.

Microsoft Windows Server 2012 R2 is used for all the server types in this
chapter. Although other operating systems can be used, this chapter refers
only to Windows Server 2012 R2.

Configuring File Server Resource Manager

As an administrator, when you need to control and manage the amount and type of data
stored on your servers, Microsoft delivers the tools to help you do just that. The *File Server
Resource Manager (FSRM)* is a suite of tools that allows an administrator to place quotas
on folders or volumes, filter file types, and create detailed storage reports. These tools allow
an administrator to properly plan and implement policies on data as needed.

FSRM Features

Many of the advantages of using FSRM come from all of the included features, which allow
administrators to manage the data that is stored on their file servers. Some of the advantages included with FSRM are as follows:

Configure File Management Tasks   FSRM allows an administrator to apply a policy or
action to data files. Some of the actions that can be performed include the ability to encrypt
files or run a custom command.

Configure Quotas   Quotas give an administrator the ability to limit how much disk space
a user can use on a file server. Administrators have the ability to limit space to an entire
volume or to specific folders.

File Classification Infrastructure   Administrators can set file classifications and then manage
the data more effectively by using these classifications. Classifying files, and then setting
policies to those classifications, allows an administrator to set policies on those classifications.
These policies include restricting file access, file encryption, and file expirations.

Configure File Screens   Administrators can set file screening on a server and limit the types of files that are being stored on that server. For example, an administrator can set a file screen on a server so that any file ending in `.bmp` gets rejected.

Configure Reports   Administrators can create reports that show them how data is classified and accessed. They also have the ability to see which users are trying to save unauthorized file extensions.

Installing the FSRM Role Service

Installing FSRM is easy when using either Server Manager or PowerShell. To install using Server Manager, you go into Add Roles And Features and choose File And Storage Services ➢ File Services ➢ File Server Resource Manager. To install FSRM using PowerShell, you use the following command:

```
Install-WindowsFeature -Name FS-Resource-Manager -IncludeManagementTools
```

Configuring FSRM using the Windows GUI version is straightforward, but setting up FSRM using PowerShell is a bit more challenging. Table 11.1 describes some of the PowerShell commands for FSRM.

TABLE 11.1   PowerShell commands for FSRM

PowerShell cmdlet	Description
Get-FsrmAutoQuota	Gets auto-apply quotas on a server
Get-FsrmClassification	Gets the status of the running file classification
Get-FsrmClassificationRule	Gets classification rules
Get-FsrmFileGroup	Gets file groups
Get-FsrmFileScreen	Gets file screens
Get-FsrmFileScreenException	Gets file screen exceptions
Get-FsrmQuota	Gets quotas on the server
Get-FsrmSetting	Gets the current FSRM settings
Get-FsrmStorageReport	Gets storage reports
New-FsrmAutoQuota	Creates an auto-apply quota
New-FsrmFileGroup	Creates a file group
New-FsrmFileScreen	Creates a file screen

TABLE 11.1 PowerShell commands for FSRM *(continued)*

PowerShell cmdlet	Description
New-FsrmQuota	Creates an FSRM quota
New-FsrmQuotaTemplate	Creates a quota template
Remove-FsrmClassificationRule	Removes classification rules
Remove-FsrmFileScreen	Removes a file screen
Remove-FsrmQuota	Removes an FSRM quota from the server
Set-FsrmFileScreen	Changes the configuration settings of a file screen
Set-FsrmQuota	Changes the configuration settings for an FSRM quota

Configure File and Disk Encryption

Hardware and software encryption are some of the most important actions you can take as an administrator. You must make sure that if anyone steals hardware from your company or from your server rooms that the data they are stealing is secured and cannot be used. This is where BitLocker can help.

Using BitLocker Drive Encryption

To prevent individuals from stealing your computer and viewing personal and sensitive data found on your hard disk, some editions of Windows come with a new feature called *BitLocker Drive Encryption*. BitLocker encrypts the entire system drive. New files added to this drive are encrypted automatically, and files moved from this drive to another drive or computers are decrypted automatically.

Only Windows 7 Enterprise, Windows 7 Ultimate, Windows 8 Pro, Windows 8 Enterprise, Windows Server 2008, Windows Server 2008 R2, Windows Server 2012, and Windows Server 2012 R2 include BitLocker Drive Encryption, and only the operating system drive (usually C:) or internal hard drives can be encrypted with BitLocker. Files on other types of drives must be encrypted using BitLocker To Go. BitLocker To Go allows you to put BitLocker on removable media such as external hard disks or USB drives.

BitLocker uses a *Trusted Platform Module (TPM)* version 1.2 or newer to store the security key. A TPM is a chip that is found in newer computers. If you do not have a computer with a TPM, you can store the key on a removable USB drive. The USB drive will be required each time you start the computer so that the system drive can be decrypted.

If the TPM discovers a potential security risk, such as a disk error or changes made to the BIOS, hardware, system files, or startup components, the system drive will not be unlocked until you enter the 48-digit BitLocker recovery password or use a USB drive with a recovery key as a recovery agent.

BitLocker must be set up either within the Local Group Policy editor or through the BitLocker icon in the control panel. One advantage of using BitLocker is that you can prevent any unencrypted data from being copied onto a removable disk, thus protecting the computer.

BitLocker Recovery Password

The BitLocker recovery password is important. Do not lose it, or you may not be able to unlock the drive. Even if you do not have a TPM, be sure to keep your recovery password in case your USB drive becomes lost or corrupted.

BitLocker requires that you have a hard disk with at least two partitions, both formatted with NTFS. One partition will be the system partition that will be encrypted. The other partition will be the active partition that is used to start the computer. This partition will remain unencrypted.

Features of BitLocker

As with any version of Windows, Microsoft continues to improve on the technologies used in Windows Server 2012 R2 and Windows 8. The following sections cover some of the features of BitLocker.

BitLocker Provisioning

In previous versions of BitLocker (Windows Vista and Windows 7), BitLocker provisioning (system and data volumes) was completed during the postinstallation of the BitLocker utility. BitLocker provisioning was done through either the command-line interface (CLI) or the control panel. In the Windows 8/Windows Server 2012 R2 version of BitLocker, an administrator can choose to provision BitLocker before the operating system is even installed.

Administrators have the ability to enable BitLocker prior to the operating system deployment from the Windows Preinstallation Environment (WinPE). BitLocker is applied to the formatted volume, and BitLocker encrypts the volume prior to running the Windows setup process.

If an administrator wants to check the status of BitLocker on a particular volume, the administrator can view the status of the drive either in the BitLocker control panel applet or in Windows Explorer.

Used Disk Space–Only Encryption

Windows 7 BitLocker requires that all data and free space on the drive must be encrypted. Because of this requirement, the encryption process can take a long time on larger volumes.

In Windows 8 BitLocker, administrators have the ability to encrypt either the entire volume or just the space being used. When you choose the Used Disk Space Only option, only the section of the drive that contains data will be encrypted. Because of this, encryption is completed much faster.

Standard User PIN and Password Change

One issue that BitLocker has had in the past is that you need to be an administrator to configure BitLocker on operating system drives. This could become an issue in a large organization because deploying TPM + PIN to a large number of computers can be challenging.

Even with the new operating system changes, administrative privileges are still needed to configure BitLocker, but now your users have the ability to change the BitLocker PIN for the operating system or change the password on the data volumes.

When a user gets to choose their own PIN and password, they normally choose something that has meaning to them and something that is easy to remember. That is a good and bad thing at the same time. It's a good thing because when your users choose their own PIN and password, they normally don't need to write it down—they just know it. It's a bad thing because if anyone knows the user well, they can have an easier time figuring out the person's PIN and password. Even when you allow your users to choose their own PIN and password, make sure you set a GPO to require password complexity.

Network Unlock

One of the new features of BitLocker is called Network Unlock. *Network Unlock* allows administrators to easily manage desktop and servers that are configured to use BitLocker. Network Unlock allows an administrator to configure BitLocker to automatically unlock an encrypted hard drive during a system reboot when that hard drive is connected to their trusted corporate environment. For this to function properly on a machine, there has to be a DHCP driver implementation in the system's firmware.

If your operating system volume is also protected by the TPM + PIN protection, the administrator has to be sure to enter the PIN at the time of the reboot. This protection can actually make using Network Unlock more difficult to use, but they can be used in combination.

Support for Encrypted Hard Drives for Windows

One of the new advantages of using BitLocker is *Full Volume Encryption (FVE)*. BitLocker provides built-in encryption for Windows data files and Windows operating system files. The advantage of this type of encryption is that encrypted hard drives that use *Full Disk Encryption (FDE)* get each block of the physical disk space encrypted. Because each physical block gets encrypted, it offers much better encryption. The only downside to this is that because each physical block is encrypted, it degrades the hard drive speed somewhat. So, as an administrator, you have to decide whether you want better speed or better security on your hard disk.

Windows 7 and 2008 R2 vs. Windows 8 and 2012 R2

The real question is what's the difference between Windows 7/Windows 2008 R2 and Windows 8/Windows Server 2012 R2? Table 11.2 shows you many of the common features and how they work then and now.

TABLE 11.2 BitLocker then and now

Feature	Windows 7/Server 2008 R2	Windows 8/Server 2012 R2
Resetting the BitLocker PIN or password	The user's privileges must be set to an administrator if you want to reset the BitLocker PIN on an operating system drive and the password on a fixed or removable data drive.	Standard users now have the ability to reset the BitLocker PIN and password on operating system drives, fixed data drives, and removable data drives.
Disk encryption	When BitLocker is enabled, the entire disk is encrypted.	When BitLocker is enabled, users have the ability to choose whether to encrypt the entire disk or only the used space on the disk.
Hardware-encrypted drive support	Not supported.	If the Windows logo hard drive comes preencrypted from the manufacturer, BitLocker is supported.
Unlocking using a network-based key to provide dual-factor authentication	Not available.	If a computer is rebooted on a trusted corporate wired-network key protector, then this feature allows a key to unlock and skip the PIN entry.
Protection for clusters	Not available.	Windows Server 2012 R2 BitLocker includes the ability to support cluster-shared volumes and failover clusters as long as they are running in a domain that was established by a Windows Server 2012 R2 domain controller with the Kerberos Key Distribution Center Service enabled.
Linking a BitLocker key protector to an Active Directory account	Not available.	BitLocker allows a user, group, or computer account in Active Directory to be tied to a key protector. This key protector allows protected data volumes to be unlocked.

In Exercise 11.1, you will enable BitLocker on the Windows Server 2012 R2 system.

EXERCISE 11.1

Enabling BitLocker in Windows Server 2012 R2

1. Open Server Manager by selecting the Server Manager icon or running `servermanager.exe`.

2. Select Add Roles And Features from the dashboard.

3. Select Next at the Before you begin pane (if shown).

4. Select Role-based or feature-based installation and select Next to continue.

5. Select the Select a server from the server pool option and click Next.

6. At the Select Server Roles screen, click Next.

7. At the Select features screen, click the BitLocker Drive Encryption check box. When the Add Roles and Features dialog box appears, click the Add Features button. Then click Next.

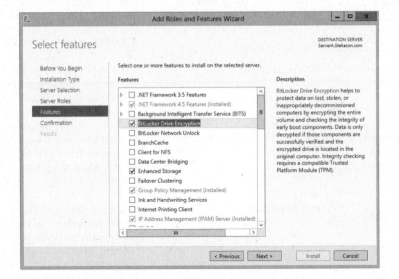

8. Select the Install button on the Confirmation pane of the Add Roles And Features Wizard to begin BitLocker feature installation. The BitLocker feature requires a restart to complete. Selecting the Restart The Destination Server Automatically If Required option in the Confirmation pane will force a restart of the computer after installation is complete.

9. If the Restart The Destination Server Automatically If Required check box is not selected, the Results pane of the Add Roles And Features Wizard will display the success or failure of the BitLocker feature installation. If required, a notification of additional action necessary to complete the feature installation, such as the restart of the computer, will be displayed in the results text.

You also can install BitLocker by using the Windows PowerShell utility. To install BitLocker, use the following PowerShell commands:

```
Install-WindowsFeature BitLocker –IncludeAllSubFeature –IncludeManagementTools
–Restart
```

Using EFS Drive Encryption

If you have been in the computer industry long enough, you may remember the days when only servers used NTFS. Years ago, most client systems used FAT or FAT32, but NTFS had some key benefits over FAT/FAT32. The main advantages were NTFS security, quotas, compression, and encryption. Encryption is available on a system because you are using a file structure (for example, NTFS) that allows encryption. Windows Server 2012 R2 NTFS allows administrators to use these four advantages including encryption.

Encrypting File System (EFS) allows a user or administrator to secure files or folders by using encryption. Encryption employs the user's security identification (SID) number to secure the file or folder. Encryption is the strongest protection that Windows provides to help you keep your information secure. Some key features of EFS are as follows:

- Encrypting is simple; just select a check box in the file or folder's properties to turn it on.

- You have control over who can read the files.

- Files are encrypted when you close them but are automatically ready to use when you open them.

- If you change your mind about encrypting a file, clear the check box in the file's properties.

To implement encryption, open the Advanced Attributes dialog box for a folder and check the Encrypt Contents To Secure Data box.

If files are encrypted using EFS and an administrator has to unencrypt the files, there are two ways to do this. You can log in using the user's account (the account that encrypted the files) and unencrypt the files using the Cipher command. Alternatively, you can become a recovery agent and manually unencrypt the files.

> If you use EFS, it's best not to delete users immediately when they leave a company. Administrators have the ability to recover encrypted files, but it is much easier to gain access to the user's encrypted files by logging in as the user who left the company and unchecking the encryption box.

Using the Cipher Command

The Cipher command is useful when it comes to EFS. Cipher is a command-line utility that allows you to change and/or configure EFS. When it comes to using the Cipher command, you should be aware of a few things:

- Administrators can decrypt files by running Cipher.exe in the Command Prompt window (advanced users).
- Administrators can use Cipher to modify an EFS-encrypted file.
- Administrators can use Cipher to import EFS certificates and keys.
- Administrators can also use Cipher to back up EFS certificates and keys.

Let's take a look at some of the different switches that you can use with Cipher. Table 11.3 describes many of the different Cipher switches you can use. This table comes from Microsoft's TechNet site. Microsoft continues to add and improve switches, so make sure you check Microsoft's website to see whether there are any changes.

TABLE 11.3 Using the cipher switches

Cipher switch	Description
/e	This switch allows an administrator to encrypt specified folders. With this folder encrypted, any files added to this folder will automatically be encrypted.
/d	This switch allows an administrator to decrypt specified folders.
/s: dir	By using this switch, the operation you are running will be performed in the specified folder and all subfolders.
/i	By default, when an error occurs, Cipher automatically halts. By using this switch, Cipher will continue to operate even after errors occur.
/f	The force switch (/f) will encrypt or decrypt all of the specified objects, even if the files have been modified by using encryption previously. Cipher, by default, does not touch files that have been encrypted or decrypted previously.

/q	This switch shows you a report about the most critical information of the EFS object.
/h	Normally, system or hidden files are not touched by encryption. By using this switch, you can display files with hidden or system attributes.
/k	This switch will create a new file encryption key based on the user currently running the Cipher command.
/?	This shows the Cipher help command.

Configuring Distributed File System

One problem that network administrators have is deciding how to share folders and communicating to end users how to find the shares. For example, if you share a folder called Stellacon Documents on server A, how do you make sure your users will find the folder and the files within it? The users have to know the server name and the share name. This can be a huge problem if you have hundreds of shares on multiple servers. If you want to have multiple copies of the folder called Stellacon Documents for fault tolerance and load balancing, the problem becomes even more complicated.

Distributed File System (DFS) in Windows Server 2012 R2 offers a simplified way for users to access geographically dispersed files. DFS allows you to set up a tree structure of virtual directories that allows users to connect to shared folders throughout the entire network.

Administrators have the ability to take shared folders that are located on different servers and transparently connect them to one or more DFS namespaces—virtual trees of shared folders throughout an organization. The advantage of using DFS is that if one of the folders becomes unavailable, DFS has failover capability that will allow your users to connect to the data on a different server.

Administrators can use the DFS tools to choose which shared folders will appear in the namespace and also to decide how the names of these shared folders will show up in the virtual tree listing.

Advantages of DFS

One of the advantages of DFS is that when a user views this virtual tree, the shared folders appear to be located on a single machine. These are some of the other advantages of DFS:

Simplified Data Migration   DFS gives you the ability to move data from one location to another without the user needing to know the physical location of the data. Because the users do not need to know the physical location of the shared data, administrators can simply move data from one location to another.

Security Integration   Administrators do not need to configure additional security for the DFS shared folders. The shared folders use the NTFS and shared folder permissions that an administrator has already assigned when the share was set up.

Access-Based Enumeration (ABE)   This DFS feature (disabled by default) displays only the files and folders that a user has permissions to access. If a user does not have access to a folder, Windows hides the folder from the user's DFS view. This feature is not active if the user is viewing the files and folders locally.

Types of DFS

The following are types of DFS:

DFS Replication   Administrators have the ability to manage replication scheduling and bandwidth throttling using the DFS management console. Replication is the process of sharing data between multiple machines. As explained earlier in the section, replicated shared folders allow you to balance the load and have fault tolerance. DFS also has read-only replication folders.

DFS Namespace   The DFS Namespace service is the virtual tree listing in the DFS server. An administrator can set up multiple namespaces on the DFS, allowing for multiple virtual trees within DFS. The DFS Namespace service was once known as *Distributed File System* in Windows 2000 Server and Windows Server 2003 (in case you still use Server 2003).

In Exercise 11.2, you will install the DFS Namespace service on the file server. You need to start the installation using the Server Manager MMC.

EXERCISE 11.2

Installing the DFS Namespace Service

1. Open Server Manager by selecting the Server Manager icon or running `servermanager.exe`.

2. Select Add Roles And Features from the dashboard.

3. Select Next at the Before You Begin pane (if shown).

4. Select Role-Based or Feature-Based installation and select Next to continue.

5. Select the Select A Server From The Server Pool option and click Next.

6. At the Select Server Roles screen, expand File And Storage Services and check the DFS Namespace and DFS Replication check boxes. Then click Next. If a dialog box appears, click the Add Features button.

7. At the Select Features screen, click Next.

8. At the Confirmation screen, click the Install button.

9. After the installation is complete, click the Close button.

10. Close Server Manager.

Once you have installed DFS, it's time to learn how to manage DFS with the DFS Management MMC. The DFS Management console (see Figure 11.1) gives you one place to do all of your DFS configurations. The DFS Management console allows you to set up DFS Replication and DFS Namespace. Another task you can do in the DFS Management console is to add a folder target—a folder that you add to the DFS namespace (the virtual tree) for all your users to share.

FIGURE 11.1   DFS Management console

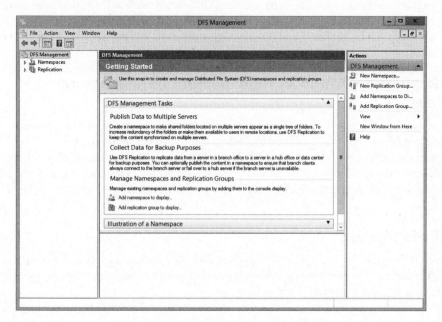

What's New in Windows Server 2012 R2

As with any new version of an operation system, Microsoft is trying to make each version of Windows Server better than the previous ones. This is also true with DFS. Microsoft has added many new features to DFS, and the following are just some of the major changes of Windows Server 2012 R2 DFS.

Windows PowerShell Module for DFS Replication

Windows PowerShell cmdlets for DFS replication modules can help administrators perform the majority of their DFS replication tasks. Administrators can use Windows PowerShell cmdlets to perform common administrative tasks such as creating, modifying, and removing DFS replication settings by using Window PowerShell scripts.

One of the nice new advantages of using Windows PowerShell for DFS is the ability to clone DFS replication databases and also to have the ability to restore those DFS databases in the event of an issue or crash.

Administrators have the ability to manage DFS management and replication through the use of the DNS Management and DFS Replication command-line utilities. Administrators who use the command-line tools are not doing anything incorrectly, but it is an inefficient way to do these tasks as well as being extremely time-consuming.

Administrators can use Windows PowerShell instead of command-line utilities and run hundreds of scripted commands, thus making their jobs easier and more efficient.

For an administrator who wants to use the Windows PowerShell cmdlets, the computer system installed with the DFS Management tools must be running Windows Server 2012 R2 or Windows 8.1 or newer. The DFS Management tools are part of the Remote Server Administration tools.

DFS Replication Windows Management Infrastructure Provider

In this book, I have spoken many times about using Windows Remote Management (WinRM) and how WinRM can help you administer a server remotely.

Introduced to Windows Server 2012 R2, the Windows Management Infrastructure (referred to as WMI v2) allows an administrator, using a properly configured firewall, to provide functionality and which provides programmatic access to manage DFS Replication.

Database Cloning

For the first time ever in DFS, Windows Server 2012 R2 includes a new DFS database cloning function. This new feature allows administrators to accelerate replication when creating folders, servers, or recovery systems.

Administrators will now have the ability to extract the DFS database from a single DFS server and then clone that database to multiple DFS servers.

Administrators can use PowerShell and the Export-DfsrClone cmdlet to export the volume that contains the DFS database and configuration .xml file settings. When executing this PowerShell cmdlet, a trigger is engaged that exports the DFS service, and the system will not proceed until the service is completed. Administrators would then use the PowerShell cmdlet Import-DfsrClone to import the data to a specific volume. The service will then validate that the replication was transferred completely.

Recovering a DFS Database

Windows Server 2012 R2 DFS database recovery is a feature that allows DFS to detect a corrupted database, thus allowing DFS to rebuild the database automatically and continue with normal operations of DFS replication. One advantage to this is that when DFS detects and fixes a corrupt database, it does so with no file conflicts.

Prior to this new feature, if a DFS database were determined to be corrupt, DFS Replication would delete the database and start again with an initial nonauthoritative sync process. This would cause newer file versions to be overwritten by older data causing real data loss.

DFS in Windows Server 2012 R2 uses local files and an update sequence number (USN) to fix a corrupt database, allowing for no loss of data.

Optimizing DFS

Windows Server 2012 R2 DFS allows an administrator to configure variable file staging sizes on individual DFS servers. This allows an administrator to set a minimum file size for a file to stage. This increases the staging size of files, and that in turn increases the performance of the replication.

Prior to Windows Server 2012 R2, DFS Replication used a hard-coded 256KB file size to determine staging requirements. If a file size were larger than 256KB, that file would be staged before it replicated. The more file staging that you have, the longer replication takes on a DFS system.

Remote Differential Compression

One issue that can arise occurs when files are changed. There has to be some mechanism that helps files stay accurate. That's where the *Remote Differential Compression (RDC)* feature comes into play. RDC is a group of application programming interfaces (APIs) that programs can use to determine whether files have changed. Once RDC determines that there has been a change, RDC then helps to detect which portions of the files contain the changes. RDC has the ability to detect insertions, removals, and rearrangements of data in files. This feature becomes helpful with limited-bandwidth networks when they replicate changes.

To install the RDC feature, use Server Manager and then run the Add Features Wizard, or type the following command at an elevated command prompt:

```
Servermanagercmd -Install Rdc
```

Implementing an Audit Policy

One of the most important aspects of controlling security in networked environments is ensuring that only authorized users are able to access specific resources. Although system administrators often spend much time managing security permissions, it is almost always possible for a security problem to occur.

Sometimes the best way to find possible security breaches is actually to record the actions that specific users take. Then, in the case of a security breach (the unauthorized shutdown of a server, for example), system administrators can examine the log to find the cause of the problem.

The Windows Server 2012 R2 operating system and Active Directory offer you the ability to audit a wide range of actions. In the following sections, you'll see how to implement auditing for Active Directory.

Overview of Auditing

The act of *auditing* relates to recording specific actions. From a security standpoint, auditing is used to detect any possible misuse of network resources. Although auditing does not necessarily prevent resources from being misused, it does help determine when security violations have occurred (or were attempted). Furthermore, just the fact that others know that you have implemented auditing may prevent them from attempting to circumvent security.

You need to complete several steps in order to implement auditing using Windows Server 2012 R2:

1. Configure the size and storage settings for the audit logs.

2. Enable categories of events to audit.

3. Specify which objects and actions should be recorded in the audit log.

Note that there are trade-offs to implementing auditing. First, recording auditing information can consume system resources. This can decrease overall system performance and use up valuable disk space. Second, auditing many events can make the audit log impractical to view. If too much detail is provided, system administrators are unlikely to scrutinize all of the recorded events. For these reasons, you should always be sure to find a balance between the level of auditing detail provided and the performance-management implications of these settings.

Implementing Auditing

Auditing is not an all-or-none type of process. As is the case with security in general, system administrators must choose specifically which objects and actions they want to audit.

The main categories for auditing include the following:

- Audit account logon events

- Audit account management

- Audit directory service access

- Audit logon events

- Audit object access

- Audit policy change

- Audit privilege use

- Audit process tracking

- Audit system events

In this list of categories, many of the categories are related to Active Directory. Let's discuss these auditing categories in more detail.

Audit Account Logon Events   You enable this auditing event if you want to audit when a user authenticates with a domain controller and logs onto the domain. This event is logged in the security log on the domain controller.

Audit Account Management   This auditing event is used when you want to watch what changes are being made to Active Directory accounts. For example, when another administrator creates or deletes a user account, it would be an audited event.

Audit Directory Service Access   This auditing event occurs whenever a user or administrator accesses Active Directory objects. Let's say an administrator opens Active Directory and clicks a user account; even if nothing is changed on that account, an event is logged.

Audit Logon Events   Account logon events are created for domain account activity. For example, you have a user who logs on to a server so that they can access files; the act of logging onto the server creates this audit event.

Audit Object Access   Audit object access allows you to audit objects within your network such as folders, files, and printers. If you suspect someone is trying to hack into an object (for example, the finance folder), this is the type of auditing that you would use. You still would need to enable auditing on the actual object (for example, the finance folder).

Audit Policy Change   Audit policy change allows you to audit changes to user rights assignment policies, audit policies, or trust policies. This auditing allows you to see whether anyone changes any of the other audit policies.

Audit Privilege Use   Setting the audit privilege use allows an administrator to audit each instance of a user exercising a user right. For example, if a user changes the system time on a machine, this is a user right. Log on locally is another common user right.

To audit access to objects stored within Active Directory, you must enable the Audit Directory Service Access option. Then you must specify which objects and actions should be tracked.

Exercise 11.3 walks through the steps you must take to implement auditing of Active Directory objects on domain controllers.

EXERCISE 11.3

Enabling Auditing of Active Directory Objects

1. Open the Local Security Policy tool (located in the Administrative Tools program group).

2. Expand Local Policies ➤ Audit Policy.

3. Double-click the setting for Audit Directory Service Access.

4. In the Audit Directory Service Access Properties dialog box, place check marks next to Success and Failure. Click OK to save the settings.

5. Close the Local Security Policy tool.

Viewing Auditing Information

One of the most important aspects of auditing is regularly monitoring the audit logs. If this step is ignored, as it often is in poorly managed environments, the act of auditing is useless. Fortunately, Windows Server 2012 R2 includes the *Event Viewer* tool, which allows system administrators to view audited events quickly and easily. Using the filtering capabilities of Event Viewer, they can find specific events of interest.

Exercise 11.4 walks you through the steps that you must take to generate some auditing events and to examine the data collected for these actions. In this exercise, you will perform some actions that will be audited, and then you will view the information recorded within the audit logs. To complete this exercise, you must first have completed the steps in Exercise 11.1 and Exercise 11.3.

EXERCISE 11.4

Generating and Viewing Audit Logs

1. Open the Active Directory Users and Computers tool.

2. Within the Engineering OU, right-click any user account and select Properties.

3. On the user's Properties dialog box, add the middle initial *A* for this user account and specify **Software Developer** in the Description box. Click OK to save the changes.

4. Within the Engineering OU, right-click the Robert Admin user account and select Properties.

5. In the Robert Properties dialog box, add the description **Engineering IT Admin** and click OK.

6. Close the Active Directory Users and Computers tool.

7. Open the Event Viewer tool from the Administrative Tools program group. Select the Security item under Windows Logs. You will see a list of audited events categorized under Directory Service Access. Note that you can obtain more details about a specific item by double-clicking it.

8. When you have finished viewing the security log, close the Event Viewer tool.

Using the *Auditpol.exe* Command

There may be a time when you need to look at your actual auditing policies set on a user or a system. This is where an administrator can use the Auditpol.exe command. *Auditpol* gives administrators the ability not only to view an audit policy but it also allows an administrator to set, configure, modify, restore, and even remove an audit policy. Auditpol is a command-line utility, and there are multiple switches that can be used with Auditpol. The following is the syntax used with Auditpol.

```
Auditpol command [<sub-command><options>]
```

Here's an example of using the command:

```
Auditpol /get /user:wpanek /category:"Detailed Tracking" /r
```

Table 11.4 describes some of the switches.

TABLE 11.4   Auditpol commands

Command	Description
/backup	Allows an administrator to save the audit policy to a file
/clear	Allows an administrator to clear an audit policy
/get	Gives administrators the ability to view the current audit policy
/list	Allows you to view selectable policy elements
/remove	Removes all per-user audit policy settings and disables all system audit policy settings
/restore	Allows an administrator to restore an audit policy from a file that was previously created using auditpol /backup
/set	Gives an administrator the ability to set an audit policy
/?	Displays help

Windows Server 2012 R2 Auditing Features

Auditing in Windows Server 2012 R2 and Windows 8 has been enhanced in many ways. Microsoft has increased the level of detail in the security auditing logs. Microsoft has also simplified the deployment and management of auditing policies. The following list includes some of the major enhancements:

Global Object Access Auditing   Administrators using Windows Server 2012 R2 and Windows 8 now have the ability to define computer-wide system access control lists (SACLs). Administrators can define SACLs for either the file system or the registry. After the specified SACL is defined, the SACL is then applied automatically to every single object of that type. This can be helpful to administrators in verifying that all critical files, folders, and registry settings on a computer are protected. This is also helpful for identifying when an issue occurs with a system resource.

"Reason for Access" Reporting   When an administrator is performing auditing in Windows Server 2012 R2 and Windows 8, they can now see the reason why an operation was successful or unsuccessful. Previously, they lacked the ability to see the reason why an operation succeeded or failed.

Advanced Audit Policy Settings   In Windows Server 2012 R2, there are hundreds of Advanced Audit Policy settings that can be used in place of the nine basic auditing settings. These advanced audit settings also help eliminate the unnecessary auditing activities that can make audit logs difficult to manage and decipher.

Expression-Based Audit Policies   Administrators have the ability, because of Dynamic Access Control, to create targeted audit policies by using expressions based on user, computer, and resource claims. For example, an administrator has the ability to create an audit policy that tracks all Read and Write operations for files that are considered high-business impact. Expression-based audit policies can be directly created on a file or folder or created through the use of a Group Policy.

Removable Storage Device Auditing   Administrators have the ability to monitor attempts to use a removable storage device on your network. If an administrator decides to implement this policy, an audit event is created every time one of your users attempts to copy, move, or save a network resource onto a removable storage device.

Making Active Directory Objects Available to Users

If you have been reading this book from the start, then this section will be familiar. But if you started this book with only exam 70-411 in mind, then you are about to learn how to make resources available to your users through the use of Active Directory.

With Active Directory, a system administrator can control which objects users can see. The act of making an Active Directory object available is known as *publishing*. The two main publishable objects are Printer objects and Shared Folder objects.

The general process for creating server shares and shared printers has remained unchanged from previous versions of Windows. You create the various objects (printers or file system folders) and then enable them for sharing.

To make these resources available via Active Directory, however, there's an additional step; you must publish the resources. Once an object has been published in Active Directory, clients will be able to find it.

When you publish objects in Active Directory, you should know the server name and share name of the resource. This information, however, doesn't matter to your users. A system administrator can change the resource to which an object points without having to reconfigure or even notify clients. For example, if you move a share from one server to another, all you need to do is update the Shared Folder object's properties to point to the new location. Active Directory clients still refer to the resource with the same path and name that they used previously.

Exercise 11.5 will walk you through the steps required for sharing and publishing a folder for use on your network.

EXERCISE 11.5

Creating and Publishing a Shared Network Folder

1. Create a new folder in the root directory of your C: partition and name it **Test Share**.

2. Right-click the Test Share folder and choose Share With ➤ Specific People.

3. In the File Sharing dialog box, enter the names of users with whom you want to share this folder. In the upper box, enter **Everyone** and then click Add. Note that Everyone appears in the lower box. Click in the Permission Level column next to Everyone and choose Read/Write from the drop-down menu. Then click Share.

4. You see a message that your folder has been shared. Click Done.

5. Open the Active Directory Users and Computers tool. Expand the current domain and right-click RD OU. Select New ➤ Shared Folder.

6. In the New Object – Shared Folder dialog box, type **Shared Folder Test** for the name of the folder. Then type the UNC path to the share (for example, **\\serverA\ Test Share**). Click OK to create the share.

One of the main benefits of having all of your resource information in Active Directory is that you can easily find the information you're seeking using the Find dialog box. When setting up objects in Active Directory, I recommend that you always enter as much information as possible for the objects you are creating. The extra effort will pay off when your users start doing searches for these objects. The more information you enter, the more that will be available for users to search to find the appropriate resource they need.

Configuring Offline Folders

If you have been in this industry long enough, you have seen a major change in end-user computers. Years ago, only a few select users had laptops. They were big and bulky, and they weighed almost as much as today's desktop computers.

The pendulum has swung in the opposite direction. It probably seems like every one of your end users now has a laptop. As an IT administrator, this gives you a whole new set of challenges and problems to address. One challenge that you have to address is how users can work on files while outside of the office. If you have a user who wants to work at home, how do you give them the files they need to get their work done? The answer is *offline folders*. These folders contain data that can be worked on by users while outside the office. An IT administrator can set up offline folders through the use of *Group Policy objects (GPOs)*.

When you decide to make folders available for offline use, these folders need to synchronize with the laptops so that all of the data matches between both systems. As an administrator, one decision that you will need to make is when the offline folders will be synchronized.

You can set up any combination of these three synchronization options in the GPO:

- When you select Synchronize All Offline Files Before Logging Off, offline folders are synchronized when the user logs off the network.

- When you select Synchronize All Offline Files When Logging On, offline folders are synchronized when the user logs on to the network.

- When you select Synchronize Offline Files Before Suspend, offline folders are synchronized before the user does a system suspend.

In Exercise 11.6, you will configure offline folder options by using a GPO. This exercise uses the Group Policy Management Console (GPMC). If your GPMC is not installed, use the Server Manager MMC (under Features) to install it.

EXERCISE 11.6

Configuring Offline Folder Options

1. Open the Group Policy Management Console.

2. In the left pane, expand your forest and then your domain. Under your domain name, there should be a default domain policy.

3. Right-click the default domain policy and choose Edit.

4. In the User Configuration section, expand Policies ➢ Administrative Templates ➢ Network and then click Offline Files.

5. Right-click Synchronize All Offline Files Before Logging Off and choose Edit. The GPO setting dialog box appears. Choose the Enabled option and click OK.

6. Right-click Synchronize All Offline Files When Logging On and choose Edit. The GPO setting dialog box appears. Choose the Enabled option and click OK.

7. Right-click Synchronize Offline Files Before Suspend and choose Edit. The GPO setting dialog box appears. Choose the Enabled option. In the Action drop-down box, make sure Quick is selected. Click OK.

8. Close the GPMC.

Now that you have set up a GPO for synchronization, it's time to share a folder for offline usage. In Exercise 11.7, you will set up a folder for offline access. You must complete Exercise 11.5 before doing this exercise.

EXERCISE 11.7

Configuring a Shared Network Folder for Offline Access

1. Right-click the Test Share folder you created in Exercise 11.5 and choose Properties.

2. Click the Sharing tab and then click the Advanced Sharing button.

3. When the Advanced Sharing dialog box appears, click the Caching button.

4. When the Offline Settings dialog box appears, choose the All Files And Programs That Users Open From The Shares Will Be Automatically Available Offline option. Click OK.

5. Click OK twice more to close the Properties dialog box.

Summary

This chapter took you through the use of many server tools and utilities such as DFS, BitLocker, and auditing. Distributed File System allows an administrator to set up a tree structure of virtual directories that allow users to connect to a shared folder anywhere throughout the entire network. You also looked at the new changes that have taken place with DFS in Windows Server 2012 R2.

You also learned about EFS and how to use Cipher to modify or configure EFS in a command window. Cipher is the best way to change encrypted directories and files.

This chapter also covered auditing. You looked at what needs to be audited if you are watching Active Directory and its objects. You looked at Auditpol and many of the switches that you would use when configuring Auditpol.

Finally, you learned how to publish share folders to Active Directory. By doing this, your users can search Active Directory to find resources they are looking for.

Exam Essentials

Know How to Configure DFS   Distributed File System in Windows Server 2012 R2 offers a simplified way for users to access geographically dispersed files. The DFS Namespace service allows you to set up a tree structure of virtual directories that lets users connect to shared folders throughout the entire network.

Understand EFS and Cipher   Users can encrypt their directories and files by using EFS. Understand how Cipher can help an administrator configure or modify an EFS object while in the command prompt.

Understand the Purpose and Function of Auditing   Auditing helps determine the cause of security violations and helps troubleshoot permissions-related problems.

Review Questions

1. The company for which you work has a multilevel administrative team that is segmented by departments and locations. There are four major locations, and you are in the Northeast group. You have been assigned to the administrative group that is responsible for creating and maintaining network shares for files and printers in your region. The last place you worked was a large Windows Server 2008 network, where you had a much wider range of responsibilities. You are excited about the chance to learn more about Windows Server 2012 R2.

   For your first task, you have been given a list of file and printer shares that need to be created for the users in your region. You ask how to create them in Windows Server 2012 R2, and you are told that the process of creating a share is the same as with Windows Server 2008. You create the shares and use NETUSE to test them. Everything appears to work fine, so you send a message that the shares are available. The next day, you start receiving calls from users who say they cannot see any of resources you created. What is the most likely reason for the calls from the users?

   A. You forgot to enable NetBIOS for the shares.

   B. You need to force replication for the shares to appear in the directory.

   C. You need to publish the shares in the directory.

   D. The shares will appear within the normal replication period.

2. You want to publish a printer to Active Directory. Where would you click in order to accomplish this task?

   A. The Sharing tab

   B. The Advanced tab

   C. The Device Settings tab

   D. The Printing Preferences button

3. Isabel is a system administrator for an Active Directory environment that is running in Native mode. Recently, several managers have reported suspicions about user activities and have asked her to increase security in the environment. Specifically, the requirements are as follows:

   - The accessing of certain sensitive files must be logged.

   - Modifications to certain sensitive files must be logged.

   - System administrators must be able to provide information about which users accessed sensitive files and when they were accessed.

   - All logon attempts for specific shared machines must be recorded.

   Which of the following steps should Isabel take to meet these requirements? (Choose all that apply.)

   A. Enable auditing with the Computer Management tool.

   B. Enable auditing with the Active Directory Users and Computers tool.

   C. Enable auditing with the Active Directory Domains and Trusts tool.

   D. Enable auditing with the Event Viewer tool.

E. View the audit log using the Event Viewer tool.

F. View auditing information using the Computer Management tool.

G. Enable failure and success auditing settings for specific files stored on NTFS volumes.

H. Enable failure and success auditing settings for logon events on specific computer accounts.

4. You are the network administrator for a midsize coffee bean distributor. Your company's network has four Windows 2012 servers, and all of the clients are running either Windows 8 or Windows 7. Most of your end users use laptops to do their work, and many of them work away from the office. What should you configure to help them work on documents when away from the office?

    A. Online file access

    B. Offline file access

    C. Share permissions

    D. NTFS permissions

5. Your company has decided to implement an external hard drive. The company IT manager before you always used FAT32 as the system partition. Your company wants to know whether it should move to NTFS. Which of the following are some advantages of NTFS? (Choose all that apply.)

    A. Security

    B. Quotas

    C. Compression

    D. Encryption

6. You are the administrator for a large organization that uses Windows Server 2012 R2. You have been asked by your manager to help protect his folders on his Windows 7 NTFS machine. Your manager wants to make sure he is the only person that can open his files. How do you protect his files?

    A. Use EFS.

    B. Use CDMA.

    C. Use FAT32 Security.

    D. Use the `Convert:FAT32/Encrypt` command.

7. You are the administrator of your network, which consists of two Windows Server 2012 R2 systems. One of the servers is a domain controller, and the other server is a file server for data storage. The hard drive of the file server is starting to fill up. You do not have the ability to install another hard drive, so you decide to limit the amount of space everyone gets on the hard drive. What do you need to implement to solve your problem?

    A. Disk spacing

    B. Disk quotas

    C. Disk hardening

    D. Disk limitations

8. You are the administrator for a large communications company. Your company uses Windows Server 2012 R2, and your user's files are encrypted using EFS. What command-line command would you use to change or modify the EFS files?

A. Convert

B. Cipher

C. Gopher

D. Encrypt

9. You are the administrator for a large organization. You have multiple Windows Server 2012 R2 systems that all contain files that need to be shared for all users. The files and folders constantly move among servers, and users are having a hard time finding files they need. What can you implement to help your users out?

A. Encrypting File System (EFS)

B. Distributed File System (DFS)

C. Shared File System (SFS)

D. Published File System (PFS)

10. You have been hired by a small company to implement new Windows Server 2012 R2 systems. The company wants you to set up a server for users' home folder locations. What type of server would you be setting up?

A. PDC server

B. Web server

C. Exchange server

D. File server

Chapter

12

Configure DNS

THE FOLLOWING 70-411 EXAM OBJECTIVES ARE COVERED IN THIS CHAPTER:

✓ **Configure DNS zones**

- Configure primary and secondary zones
- Configure stub zones
- Configure conditional forwards
- Configure zone and conditional forward storage in Active Directory
- Configure zone delegation
- Configure zone transfer settings
- Configure notify settings

✓ **Configure DNS records**

- Create and configure DNS Resource Records (RR) including A, AAAA, PTR, SOA, NS, SRV, CNAME, and MX records
- Configure zone scavenging
- Configure record options including time to live (TTL) and weight
- Configure round robin
- Configure secure dynamic updates

If you have been reading this book from cover to cover, then this chapter is going to look very familiar. DNS is covered heavily on both the 70-410 and 70-411 exams. I am repeating much of the same stuff from Chapter 2, "Configure Network Services," but if you are reading just Part 2 of this book to take exam 70-411, then I will cover everything that can be tested on that exam. If you have read Chapter 2, then this will be a great review, with a little extra material thrown in for exam 70-411.

The Domain Name System (DNS) is one of the most important networking services that you can put on your network, and it's also one of the key topics that you'll need to understand if you plan to take any of the Microsoft Windows Server 2012 R2 exams.

By the end of this chapter, you should have a deeper understanding of how DNS works, how to set it up properly, how to configure DNS, proper management of the DNS server, and how to troubleshoot DNS issues quickly and easily in Microsoft Windows Server 2012 R2.

Introducing DNS

The *Domain Name System (DNS)* is a service that allows you to resolve a hostname to an Internet Protocol (IP) address. One of the inherent complexities of operating in networked environments is working with multiple protocols and network addresses. Owing largely to the tremendous rise in the popularity of the Internet, however, most environments have transitioned to use *Transmission Control Protocol/Internet Protocol (TCP/IP)* as their primary networking protocol. Microsoft is no exception when it comes to supporting TCP/IP in its workstation and server products. All current versions of Microsoft's operating systems support TCP/IP, as do most other modern operating systems.

An easy way to understand DNS is to think about making a telephone call. If you wanted to call Microsoft and did not know the phone number, you could call information, tell the operator the name (Microsoft), and get the telephone number. You would then make the call. Now think about trying to connect to Server1. You don't know the TCP/IP number (the computer's telephone number), so your computer asks DNS (information) for the number of Server1. DNS returns the number, and your system makes the connection (call). DNS is your network's 411, or information, and it returns the TCP/IP data for your network.

TCP/IP is actually a collection of different technologies (protocols and services) that allow computers to function together on a single, large, and heterogeneous network. Some of the major advantages of this protocol include widespread support for hardware, software, and network devices; reliance on a system of standards; and scalability. TCP handles tasks such as sequenced acknowledgments. IP involves many jobs, such as logical subnet assignment and routing.

The Form of an IP Address

To understand DNS, you must first understand how TCP/IP addresses are formed. Because DNS is strictly on a network to support TCP/IP, understanding the basics of TCP/IP is extremely important.

 Microsoft exams cover TCP/IP. The TCP/IP material is covered in Chapter 8, "Configure TCP/IP."

An *IP address* is a logical number that uniquely identifies a computer on a TCP/IP network. TCP/IP allows a computer packet to reach the correct host. Windows Server 2012 R2 works with two versions of TCP/IP: IPv4 and IPv6. An IPv4 address takes the form of four octets (eight binary bits), each of which is represented by a decimal number between 0 and 255. The four numbers are separated by decimal points. For example, all of the following are valid IP addresses:

- 128.45.23.17
- 230.212.43.100
- 10.1.1.1

The dotted decimal notation was created to make it easier for users to deal with IP addresses, but this idea did not go far enough. As a result, another abstraction layer was developed, which used names to represent the dotted decimal notation—the domain name. For example, the IP address 11000000 10101000 00000001 00010101 maps to 192.168.1.21, which in turn might map to server1.company.org, which is how the computer's address is usually presented to the user or application.

As stated earlier, IPv4 addresses are made up of octets, or the decimal (base 10) representation of 8 bits. It takes four octets to add up to the 32 bits required. IPv6 expands the address space to 128 bits. The address is usually represented in hexadecimal notation as follows:

2001:0DB8:0000:0000:1234:0000:A9FE:133E

You can tell that the implementation of DNS would make life a lot easier for everyone; even those of us who like to use alphanumeric values. (For example, some of us enjoy pinging the address in lieu of the name.) Fortunately, DNS already has the ability to handle IPv6 addresses using an AAAA record. An A record in IPv4's addressing space is 32 bits, and an AAAA record (4 *A*s) in IPv6's is 128 bits.

Nowadays, most computer users are quite familiar with navigating to DNS-based resources, such as www.microsoft.com. To resolve these "friendly" names to TCP/IP addresses that the network stack can use, you need a method for mapping them. Originally, ASCII flat files (often called *HOSTS files*, as shown in Figure 12.1) were used for this

FIGURE 12.1 HOSTS file

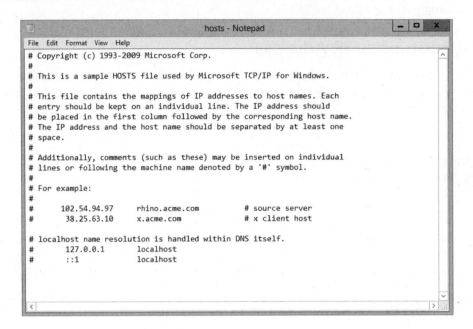

purpose. In some cases, they are still used today in small networks, and they can be useful in helping to troubleshoot name resolution problems.

As the number of machines and network devices grew, it became unwieldy for administrators to manage all of the manual updates required to enter new mappings to a master HOSTS file and distribute it. Clearly, a better system was needed.

As you can see from the sample HOSTS file in Figure 12.1, you can conduct a quick test of the email server's name resolution as follows:

1. Open the HOSTS file: `C:\Windows\Systems32\drivers\etc.`

2. Add the IP-address-to-hostname mapping.

3. Try to ping the server using the hostname to verify that you can reach it using an easy-to-remember name.

Following these steps should drive home the concept of DNS for you because you can see it working to make your life easier. Now you don't have to remember 10.0.0.10; you only need to remember exchange03. However, you can also see how this method can become unwieldy if you have many hosts that want to use easy-to-remember names instead of IP addresses to locate resources on your network.

When dealing with large networks, users and network administrators must be able to locate the resources they require with minimal searching. Users don't care about the actual physical or logical network address of the machine; they just want to be able to connect to it using a simple name that they can remember.

From a network administrator's standpoint, however, each machine must have its own logical address that makes it part of the network on which it resides. Therefore, some scalable and easy-to-manage method for resolving a machine's logical name to an IP address and then to a domain name is required. DNS was created just for this purpose.

DNS is a hierarchically distributed database. In other words, its layers are arranged in a definite order, and its data is distributed across a wide range of machines, each of which can exert control over a portion of the database. DNS is a standard set of protocols that defines the following:

- A mechanism for querying and updating address information in the database
- A mechanism for replicating the information in the database among servers
- A schema of the database

NOTE   DNS is defined by a number of requests for comments (RFCs), though primarily by RFC 1034 and RFC 1035.

DNS was originally developed in the early days of the Internet (called ARPAnet at the time) when it was a small network created by the Department of Defense for research purposes. Before DNS, computer names, or hostnames, were manually entered into a HOSTS file located on a centrally administered server. Each site that needed to resolve hostnames outside of its organization had to download this file. As the number of computers on the Internet grew, so did the size of this HOSTS file—and along with it the problems of its management. The need for a new system that would offer features such as scalability, decentralized administration, and support for various data types became more and more obvious. DNS, introduced in 1984, became this new system.

With DNS, the hostnames reside in a database that can be distributed among multiple servers, decreasing the load on any one server and providing the ability to administer this naming system on a per-partition basis. DNS supports hierarchical names and allows for the registration of various data types in addition to the hostname-to-IP-address mapping used in HOSTS files. Database performance is ensured through its distributed nature as well as through caching.

The DNS distributed database establishes an inverted logical tree structure called the *domain namespace*. Each node, or domain, in that space has a unique name. At the top of the tree is the root. This may not sound quite right, which is why the DNS hierarchical model is described as being an inverted tree, with the root at the top. The root is represented by the null set: "". When written, the root node is represented by a single dot (.).

Each node in the DNS can branch out to any number of nodes below it. For example, below the root node are a number of other nodes, commonly referred to as *top-level domains (TLDs)*. These are the familiar .com, .net, .org, .gov, .edu, and other such names. Table 12.1 lists some of these TLDs.

TABLE 12.1 Common top-level DNS domains

Domain name	Type of organization
com	Commercial (for example, `stellacon.com` for Stellacon Training Corporation)
edu	Educational (for example, `gatech.edu` for the Georgia Institute of Technology)
gov	Government (for example, `whitehouse.gov` for the White House in Washington, D.C.)
int	International organizations (for example, `nato.int` for NATO); this top-level domain is fairly rare
mil	Military organizations (for example, `usmc.mil` for the Marine Corps); there is a separate set of root name servers for this domain
net	Networking organizations and Internet providers (for example, `hiwaay.net` for HiWAAY Information Systems); many commercial organizations have registered names under this domain too
org	Noncommercial organizations (for example, `fidonet.org` for FidoNet)
au	Australia
uk	United Kingdom
ca	Canada
us	United States
jp	Japan

Each of these nodes then branches out into another set of domains, and they combine to form what we refer to as *domain names*, such as `microsoft.com`. A domain name identifies the domain's position in the logical DNS hierarchy in relation to its parent domain by separating each branch of the tree with a dot. Figure 12.2 shows a few of the top-level domains, where the Microsoft domain fits, and a host called Tigger within the `microsoft.com` domain. If someone wanted to contact that host, they would use the *fully qualified domain name (FQDN)*, `tigger.microsoft.com`.

An FQDN includes the trailing dot (.) to indicate the root node, but it's commonly left off in practice.

As previously stated, one of the strengths of DNS is the ability to delegate control over portions of the DNS namespace to multiple organizations. For example, the Internet Corporation for Assigned Names and Numbers (ICANN) assigns the control over TLDs

FIGURE 12.2 The DNS hierarchy

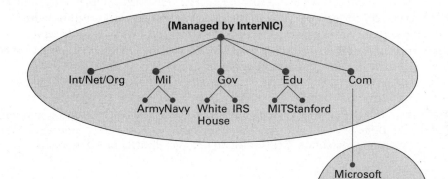

to one or more organizations. In turn, those organizations delegate portions of the DNS namespace to other organizations. For example, when you register a domain name, let's call it example.com, you control the DNS for the portion of the DNS namespace within example.com. The registrar controlling the .com TLD has delegated control over the example.com node in the DNS tree. No other node can be named example directly below the .com within the DNS database.

Within the portion of the domain namespace that you control (example.com), you could create host and other records (more on these later). You could also further subdivide example.com and delegate control over those divisions to other organizations or departments. These divisions are called *subdomains*. For example, you might create subdomains named for the cities in which the company has branch offices and then delegate control over those subdomains to the branch offices. The subdomains might be named losangeles.example.com, chicago.example.com, portsmouth.example.com, and so on.

Each domain (or delegated subdomain) is associated with DNS name servers. In other words, for every node in the DNS, one or more servers can give an authoritative answer to queries about that domain. At the root of the domain namespace are the root servers, which I'll cover later in the chapter.

Domain names and hostnames must contain only characters a to z, A to Z, 0 to 9, and − (hyphen). Other common and useful characters, such as the & (ampersand), / (slash), . (period), and _ (underscore) characters, are not allowed. This is in conflict with NetBIOS's naming restrictions. However, you'll find that Windows Server 2012 R2 is smart enough to take a NetBIOS name, like Server_1, and turn it into a legal DNS name, like server1.example.com.

DNS servers work together to resolve hierarchical names. If a server already has information about a name, it simply fulfills the query for the client. Otherwise, it queries other DNS servers for the appropriate information. The system works well because it distributes the authority over separate parts of the DNS structure to specific servers. A DNS zone is a portion of the DNS namespace over which a specific DNS server has authority. (DNS zone types are discussed in detail later in this chapter.)

> There is an important distinction to make between DNS zones and Active Directory (AD) domains. Although both use hierarchical names and require name resolution, DNS zones do not map directly to AD domains.

Within a given DNS zone, resource records (RRs) contain the hosts and other database information that make up the data for the zone. For example, an RR might contain the host entry for www.example.com, pointing it to the IP address 192.168.1.10.

Understanding Servers, Clients, and Resolvers

You will need to know a few terms and concepts in order to manage a DNS server. Understanding these terms will make it easier to understand how the Windows Server 2012 R2 DNS server works:

DNS Server Any computer providing domain name services is a *DNS name server*. No matter where the server resides in the DNS namespace, it's still a DNS name server. For example, 13 root name servers at the top of the DNS tree are responsible for delegating the TLDs. The *root servers* provide referrals to name servers for the TLDs, which in turn provide referrals to an authoritative name server for a given domain.

> The Berkeley Internet Name Domain (BIND) was originally the only software available for running the root servers on the Internet. However, a few years ago the organizations responsible for the root servers undertook an effort to diversify the software running on these important machines. Today, root servers run multiple types of name server software. BIND is still primarily on Unix-based machines, and it is also the most popular for Internet providers. None of the root servers run Windows DNS.

Any DNS server implementation supporting Service Location Resource Records (see RFC 2782) and Dynamic Updates (RFC 2136) is sufficient to provide the name service for any operating system running Windows 2003 software and newer.

DNS Client A *DNS client* is any machine that issues queries to a DNS server. The client hostname may or may not be registered in a DNS database. Clients issue DNS requests through processes called *resolvers*. You'll sometimes see the terms *client* and *resolver* used synonymously.

Resolver   *Resolvers* are software processes, sometimes implemented in software libraries, which handle the actual process of finding the answers to queries for DNS data. The resolver is also built into many larger pieces of software so that external libraries don't have to be called to make and process DNS queries. Resolvers can be what you'd consider client computers or other DNS servers attempting to resolve an answer on behalf of a client (for example, Internet Explorer).

Query   A *query* is a request for information sent to a DNS server. Three types of queries can be made to a DNS server: recursive, inverse, and iterative. I'll discuss the differences between these query types in the section "DNS Queries" a bit later in the chapter.

Understanding the DNS Process

To help you understand the DNS process, I will start by covering the differences between Dynamic DNS and Non-Dynamic DNS. During this discussion, you will learn how Dynamic DNS populates the DNS database. You'll also see how to implement security for Dynamic DNS. I will then talk about the workings of different types of DNS queries. Finally, I will discuss caching and time to live (TTL). You'll learn how to determine the best setting for your organization.

Dynamic DNS and Non-Dynamic DNS

To understand Dynamic DNS and Non-Dynamic DNS, you must go back in time (here is where the TV screen always used to get wavy). Many years ago when we all worked on NT 3.51 and NT 4.0, most networks used Windows Internet Name Service (WINS) to do their TCP/IP name resolution. Windows versions 95/98 and NT 4.0 Professional were all built on the idea of using WINS. This worked out well for administrators because WINS was dynamic (which meant that once it was installed, it automatically built its own database). Back then, there was no such thing as Dynamic DNS; administrators had to enter DNS records into the server manually. This is important to know even today. If you have clients still running any of these older operating systems (95/98 or NT 4), these clients cannot use Dynamic DNS.

Now let's move forward in time to the release of Windows Server 2000. Microsoft announced that DNS was going to be the name resolution method of choice. Many administrators (me included) did not look forward to the switch. Because there was no such thing as Dynamic DNS, most administrators had nightmares about manually entering records. However, luckily for us, when Microsoft released Windows Server 2000, DNS had the ability to operate dynamically. Now when you're setting up Windows Server 2012 R2 DNS, you can choose what type of dynamic update you would like to use, if any. Let's talk about why you would want to choose one over the other.

The *Dynamic DNS (DDNS) standard*, described in RFC 2136, allows DNS clients to update information in the DNS database files. For example, a Windows Server 2012 R2 DHCP server can automatically tell a DDNS server which IP addresses it has assigned to what machines. Windows 2000, 2003, 2008, XP Pro, Vista, Windows 7, and Windows 8 DHCP clients can do this too. For security reasons, however, it's better to let the DHCP server do it. The result: IP addresses and DNS records stay in sync so that you can use DNS and DHCP together seamlessly. Because DDNS is a proposed Internet standard, you can even use the Windows Server 2012 R2 DDNS-aware parts with Unix/Linux-based DNS servers.

Non-Dynamic DNS (NDDNS) does not automatically populate the DNS database. The client systems do not have the ability to update to DNS. If you decide to use Non-Dynamic DNS, an administrator will need to populate the DNS database manually. Non-Dynamic DNS is a reasonable choice if your organization is small-to-midsize and you do not want extra network traffic (clients updating to the DNS server) or if you need to enter the computer's TCP/IP information manually because of strict security measures.

Dynamic DNS has the ability to be secure, and the chances are slim that a rogue system (a computer that does not belong in your DNS database) could update to a secure DNS server. Nevertheless, some organizations have to follow stricter security measures and are not allowed to have dynamic updates.

The major downside to entering records into DNS manually occurs when the organization is using the *Dynamic Host Configuration Protocol (DHCP)*. When using DHCP, it is possible for users to end up with different TCP/IP addresses every day. This means that an administrator has to update DNS manually each day to keep it accurate.

If you choose to allow Dynamic DNS, you need to decide how you want to set it up. When setting up dynamic updates on your DNS server, you have three choices (see Figure 12.3).

FIGURE 12.3 Setting the Dynamic Updates option

None   This means your DNS server is Non-Dynamic.

Nonsecure and Secure   This means that any machine (even if it does not have a domain account) can register with DNS. Using this setting could allow rogue systems to enter records into your DNS server.

Secure Only   This means that only machines with accounts in Active Directory can register with DNS. Before DNS registers any account in its database, it checks Active Directory to make sure that account is an authorized domain computer.

How Dynamic DNS Populates the DNS Database

TCP/IP is the protocol used for network communications on a Microsoft Windows Server 2012 R2 network. Users have two ways to receive a TCP/IP number:

- Static (administrators manually enter the TCP/IP information)
- Dynamic (using DHCP)

When an administrator sets up TCP/IP, DNS can also be configured.

Once a client gets the address of the DNS server, if that client is allowed to update with DNS, the client sends a registration to DNS or requests DHCP to send the registration. DNS then does one of two things, depending on which Dynamic Updates option is specified:

- Check with Active Directory to see if that computer has an account (Secure Only updates) and, if it does, enter the record into the database.
- Enter the record into its database (nonsecure and secure updates).

What if you have clients that cannot update DNS? Well, there is a solution—DHCP. In the DNS tab of the IPv4 Properties window, check the option labeled "Dynamically update DNS A and PTR records for DHCP clients that do not request updates (for example, clients running Windows NT 4.0)," which is shown in Figure 12.4.

FIGURE 12.4   DHCP settings for DNS

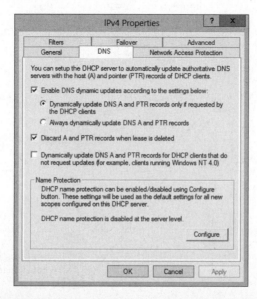

DHCP, along with Dynamic DNS clients, allows an organization to update its DNS database dynamically without the time and effort of having an administrator manually enter DNS records.

DNS Queries

As stated earlier, a client can make three types of queries to a DNS server: recursive, inverse, and iterative. Remember that the client of a DNS server can be a resolver (what you'd normally call a client) or another DNS server.

Iterative Queries

Iterative queries are the easiest to understand: A client asks the DNS server for an answer, and the server returns the best answer. This information likely comes from the server's cache. The server never sends out an additional query in response to an iterative query. If the server doesn't know the answer, it may direct the client to another server through a referral.

Recursive Queries

In a *recursive query*, the client sends a query to a name server, asking it to respond either with the requested answer or with an error message. The error states one of two things:

- The server can't come up with the right answer.

- The domain name doesn't exist.

In a recursive query, the name server isn't allowed to just refer the client to some other name server. Most resolvers use recursive queries. In addition, if your DNS server uses a forwarder, the requests sent by your server to the forwarder will be recursive queries.

Figure 12.5 shows an example of both recursive and iterative queries. In this example, a client within the Microsoft Corporation is querying its DNS server for the IP address for www.whitehouse.gov.

FIGURE 12.5 A sample DNS query

Here's what happens to resolve the request:

1. The resolver sends a recursive DNS query to its local DNS server asking for the IP address of www.whitehouse.gov. The local name server is responsible for resolving the name, and it cannot refer the resolver to another name server.

2. The local name server checks its zones, and it finds no zones corresponding to the requested domain name.

3. The root name server has authority for the root domain and will reply with the IP address of a name server for the .gov top-level domain.

4. The local name server sends an iterative query for www.whitehouse.gov to the Gov name server.

5. The Gov name server replies with the IP address of the name server servicing the whitehouse.gov domain.

6. The local name server sends an iterative query for www.whitehouse.gov to the whitehouse.gov name server.

7. The whitehouse.gov name server replies with the IP address corresponding to www.whitehouse.gov.

8. The local name server sends the IP address of www.whitehouse.gov back to the original resolver.

Inverse Queries

Inverse queries use pointer (PTR) records. Instead of supplying a name and then asking for an IP address, the client first provides the IP address and then asks for the name. Because there's no direct correlation in the DNS namespace between a domain name and its associated IP address, this search would be fruitless without the use of the in-addr.arpa domain. Nodes in the in-addr.arpa domain are named after the numbers in the dotted-octet representation of IP addresses. However, because IP addresses get more specific from left to right and domain names get less specific from left to right, the order of IP address octets must be reversed when building the in-addr.arpa tree. With this arrangement, administration of the lower limbs of the DNS in-addr.arpa tree can be given to companies as they are assigned their Class A, B, or C subnet address or delegated even further down thanks to variable-length subnet masking (VLSM).

Once the domain tree is built into the DNS database, a special PTR record is added to associate the IP addresses with the corresponding hostnames. In other words, to find a hostname for the IP address 206.131.234.1, the resolver would query the DNS server for a PTR record for 1.234.131.206.in-addr.arpa. If this IP address is outside the local domain, the DNS server will start at the root and sequentially resolve the domain nodes until arriving at 234.131.206.in-addr.arpa, which would contain the PTR record for the desired host.

Caching and Time to Live

When a name server is processing a recursive query, it may be required to send out several queries to find the definitive answer. Name servers, acting as resolvers, are allowed to cache all of the received information during this process; each record contains information called *time to live (TTL)*. The TTL specifies how long the record will be held in the local cache until it must be resolved again. If a query comes in that can be satisfied by this cached data, the TTL that's returned with it equals the current amount of time left before the data is flushed.

There is also a negative cache TTL. The *negative cache TTL* is used when an authoritative server responds to a query indicating that the record queried doesn't exist, and it indicates the amount of time that this negative answer may be held. Negative caching is quite helpful in preventing repeated queries for names that don't exist.

The administrator for the DNS zone sets TTL values for the entire zone. The value can be the same across the zone, or the administrator can set a separate TTL for each RR within the zone. Client resolvers also have data caches and honor the TTL value so that they know when to flush.

Choosing Appropriate TTL Values

For zones that you administer, you can choose the TTL values for the entire zone, for negative caching, and for individual records. Choosing an appropriate TTL depends on a number of factors, including the following:

- Amount of change you anticipate for the records within the zone

- Amount of time that you can withstand an outage that might require changing an IP address

- Amount of traffic that you believe the DNS server can handle

Resolvers query the name server every time the TTL expires for a given record. A low TTL, say 60 seconds, can burden the name server, especially for popular DNS records. (DNS queries aren't particularly intensive for a server to handle, but they can add up quickly if you mistakenly use 60 seconds instead of 600 seconds for the TTL on a popular record.) Set a low TTL only when you need to respond quickly to a changing environment.

A high TTL, say 604,800 seconds (that's one week), means that if you need to make a change to the DNS record, clients might not see the change for up to a week. This consideration is especially important when making changes to the network, and it's one that's all too frequently overlooked. I can't count the number of times I've worked with clients who have recently made a DNS change to a new IP for their email or website only to ask why it's not working for some clients. The answer can be found in the TTL value. If the record is being cached, then the only thing that can solve their problem is time.

You should choose a TTL that's appropriate for your environment. Take the following factors into account:

- The amount of time that you can afford to be offline if you need to make a change to a DNS record that's being cached

- The amount of load that a low TTL will cause on the DNS server

In addition, you should plan well ahead of any major infrastructure changes and change the TTL to a lower value to lessen the effect of the downtime by reducing the amount of time that the record(s) can be cached.

Introducing DNS Database Zones

As mentioned earlier in this chapter, a DNS zone is a portion of the DNS namespace over which a specific DNS server has authority. Within a given DNS zone, there are resource records that define the hosts and other types of information that make up the database for the zone. You can choose from several different zone types. Understanding the characteristics of each will help you choose which is right for your organization.

The DNS zones discussed in this book are all Microsoft Windows Server 2012/2012 R2 zones. Non-Windows (for example, Unix) systems set up their DNS zones differently.

In the following sections, I will discuss the different zone types and their characteristics.

Understanding Primary Zones

When you're learning about zone types, things can get a bit confusing. But it's really not difficult to understand how they work and why you would want to choose one type of zone over another. Zones are databases that store records. By choosing one zone type over another, you are basically just choosing how the database works and how it will be stored on the server.

The primary zone is responsible for maintaining all of the records for the DNS zone. It contains the primary copy of the DNS database. All record updates occur on the primary zone. You will want to create and add primary zones whenever you create a new DNS domain.

There are two types of primary zones:

- Primary zone

- Primary zone with Active Directory Integration (Active Directory DNS)

From this point forward, I refer to a primary zone with Active Directory Integration as an *Active Directory DNS*. When I use only the term *primary zone,* Active Directory is not included.

To install DNS as a primary zone, first you must install DNS using the Server Manager MMC. Once DNS is installed and running, you create a new zone and specify it as a primary zone.

The process of installing DNS and its zones will be discussed later in this chapter. In addition, there will be step-by-step exercises to walk you through how to install these components.

Primary zones have advantages and disadvantages. Knowing the characteristics of a primary zone will help you decide when you need the zone and when it fits into your organization.

Local Database

Primary DNS zones get stored locally in a file (with the suffix .dns) on the server. This allows you to store a primary zone on a domain controller or a member server. In addition, by loading DNS onto a member server, you can help a small organization conserve resources. Such an organization may not have the resources to load DNS on an Active Directory domain controller.

Unfortunately, the local database has many disadvantages:

Lack of Fault Tolerance   Think of a primary zone as a contact list on your smartphone. All of the contacts in the list are the records in your database. The problem is that if you lose your phone or the phone breaks, you lose your contact list. Until your phone gets fixed or you swap out your phone card, the contacts are unavailable.

It works the same way with a primary zone. If the server goes down or you lose the hard drive, DNS records on that machine are unreachable. An administrator can install a secondary zone (explained later in the next section), and that provides temporary fault tolerance. Unfortunately, if the primary zone is down for an extended period of time, the secondary server's information will no longer be valid.

Additional Network Traffic   Let's imagine that you are looking for a contact number for John Smith. John Smith is not listed in your cell phone directory, but he is listed in your partner's cell phone. You have to contact your partner to get the listing. You cannot directly access your partner's cell contacts.

When a resolver sends a request to DNS to get the TCP/IP address for Jsmith (in this case Jsmith is a computer name) and the DNS server does not have an answer, it does not have the ability to check the other server's database directly to get an answer. Thus, it forwards the request to another DNS. When DNS servers are replicating zone databases with other DNS servers, this causes additional network traffic.

No Security   Staying with the cell phone example, let's say that you call your partner look-ing for John Smith's phone number. When your partner gives you the phone number over your wireless phone, someone with a scanner can pick up your conversation. Unfortunately, wireless telephone calls are not very secure.

Now a resolver asks a primary zone for the Jsmith TCP/IP address. If someone on the net-work has a packet sniffer, they can steal the information in the DNS packets being sent over the network. The packets are not secure unless you implement some form of secondary security. Also, the DNS server has the ability to be dynamic. A primary zone accepts all updates from DNS servers. You cannot set it to accept secure updates only.

Understanding Secondary Zones

In Windows Server 2012 R2 DNS, you have the ability to use secondary DNS zones. Sec-ondary zones are noneditable copies of the DNS database. You use them for *load balanc-ing* (also referred to as *load sharing*), which is a way of managing network overloads on a single server. A secondary zone gets its database from a primary zone.

A *secondary zone* contains a database with all of the same information as the primary zone, and it can be used to resolve DNS requests. Secondary zones have the following advantages:

- A secondary zone provides fault tolerance, so if the primary zone server becomes unavailable, name resolution can still occur using the secondary zone server.

- Secondary DNS servers can also increase network performance by offloading some of the traffic that would otherwise go to the primary server.

Secondary servers are often placed within the parts of an organization that have high-speed network access. This prevents DNS queries from having to run across slow wide area network (WAN) connections. For example, if there are two remote offices within the stellacon.com organization, you may want to place a secondary DNS server in each remote office. This way, when clients require name resolution, they will contact the nearest server for this IP address information, thus preventing unnecessary WAN traffic.

 Having too many secondary zone servers can actually cause an increase in network traffic because of replication (especially if DNS changes are fairly frequent). Therefore, you should always weigh the benefits and drawbacks and properly plan for secondary zone servers.

Configure Zone Delegation

One advantage of DNS is the ability of turning a namespace into one or more zones. These zones can be replicated to each other or other DNS servers. As an administrator, you must decide when you want to break your DNS into multiple zones. When considering this option, there are a few things to think about:

- You want the management of your DNS namespace to be delegated by another location or department in your organization.

- You want to load-balance your traffic among multiple servers by turning a large zone into many smaller zones. This will help improve performance and create redundancy among your DNS servers.

- You have remote offices opening up, and you want to expand your DNS namespace.

To create a new zone delegation, you would complete the following steps:

1. Open the DNS console.

2. In the console tree, right-click the applicable subdomain and then click New Delegation.

3. Follow the instructions provided in the New Delegation Wizard to finish creating the newly delegated domain.

Understanding Active Directory Integrated DNS

Windows Server 2000 introduced *Active Directory Integrated DNS* to the world. This zone type was unique, and it was a separate choice during setup. In Windows Server 2003, this zone type became an add-on to a primary zone. In Windows Server 2012 R2, it works the same way. After choosing to set up a primary zone, you check the box Store The Zone In Active Directory (see Figure 12.6).

FIGURE 12.6   Setting up an Active Directory Integrated zone

Disadvantages of Active Directory Integrated DNS

The main disadvantage of Active Directory Integrated DNS is that it has to reside on a domain controller because the DNS database is stored in Active Directory. As a result, you cannot load this zone type on a member server, and small organizations might not have the resources to set up a dedicated domain controller.

Advantages of Active Directory Integrated DNS

The advantages of using an Active Directory Integrated DNS zone well outweigh the disadvantages just discussed. The following are some of the major advantages to an Active Directory Integrated zone:

Full Fault Tolerance   Think of an Active Directory Integrated zone as a database on your server that stores contact information for all your clients. If you need to retrieve John Smith's phone number, as long as it was entered, you can look it up on the software.

If John Smith's phone number was stored only on your computer and your computer stopped working, no one could access John Smith's phone number. But since John Smith's phone number is stored in a database to which everyone has access, if your computer stops working, other users can still retrieve John Smith's phone number.

An Active Directory Integrated zone works the same way. Since the DNS database is stored in Active Directory, all Active Directory DNS servers can have access to the same data. If one server goes down or you lose a hard drive, all other Active Directory DNS servers can still retrieve DNS records.

No Additional Network Traffic   As previously discussed, an Active Directory Integrated zone is stored in Active Directory. Since all records are now stored in Active Directory, when a resolver needs a TCP/IP address for Jsmith, any Active Directory DNS server can access Jsmith's address and respond to the resolver.

When you choose an Active Directory Integrated zone, DNS zone data can be replicated automatically to other DNS servers during the normal Active Directory replication process.

DNS Security   An Active Directory Integrated zone has a few security advantages over a primary zone:

- An Active Directory Integrated zone can use secure dynamic updates.

- As explained earlier, the Dynamic DNS standard allows secure-only updates or dynamic updates, not both.

- If you choose secure updates, then only machines with accounts in Active Directory can register with DNS. Before DNS registers any account in its database, it checks Active Directory to make sure that it is an authorized domain computer.

- An Active Directory Integrated zone stores and replicates its database through Active Directory replication. Because of this, the data gets encrypted as it is sent from one DNS server to another.

Background Zone Loading   Background zone loading (discussed in more detail later in this chapter) allows an Active Directory Integrated DNS zone to load in the background. As a result, a DNS server can service client requests while the zone is still loading into memory.

Understanding Stub Zones

Stub zones work a lot like secondary zones—the database is a noneditable copy of a primary zone. The difference is that the stub zone's database contains only the information necessary (three record types) to identify the authoritative DNS servers for a zone (see Figure 12.7). You should not use stub zones to replace secondary zones, nor should you use them for redundancy and load balancing.

FIGURE 12.7 DNS stub zone type

> **NOTE** Stub zone databases contain only three record types: name server (NS), start of authority (SOA), and glue host (A) records. Understanding these records will help you on the Microsoft certification exams. Microsoft asks many questions about stub zones on all DNS-related exams.

When to Use Stub Zones

Stub zones become particularly useful in a couple of different scenarios. Consider what happens when two large companies merge: example.com and example.net. In most cases, the DNS zone information from both companies must be available to every employee. You could set up a new zone on each side that acts as a secondary for the other side's primary zone, but administrators tend to be very protective of their DNS databases and probably wouldn't agree to this plan.

A better solution is to add to each side a stub zone that points to the primary server on the other side. When a client in example.com (which you help administer) makes a request for a name in example.net, the stub zone on the example.com DNS server would send the client to the primary DNS server for example.net without actually resolving the name. At this point, it would be up to example.net's primary server to resolve the name.

An added benefit is that, even if the administrators over at example.net change their configuration, you won't have to do anything because the changes will automatically replicate to the stub zone, just as they would for a secondary server.

Stub zones can also be useful when you administer two domains across a slow connection. Let's change the previous example a bit and assume that you have full control over example.com and example.net but they connect through a 56Kbps line. In this case, you wouldn't necessarily mind using secondary zones because you personally administer the entire network. However, it could get messy to replicate an entire zone file across that slow line. Instead, stub zones would refer clients to the appropriate primary server at the other site.

GlobalName Zones

Earlier in this chapter, I talked about organizations using WINS to resolve NetBIOS names (also referred to as *computer names*) to TCP/IP addresses. Even today, many organizations still use WINS along with DNS for name resolution. Unfortunately, WINS is slowly becoming obsolete.

To help organizations move forward with an all-DNS network, Microsoft Windows Server 2012 R2 DNS supports *GlobalName zones*. These use single-label names (DNS names that do not contain a suffix such as .com, .net, and so on). GlobalName zones are not intended to support peer-to-peer networks and workstation name resolution, and they don't support dynamic DNS updates.

GlobalName zones are designed to be used with servers. Because GlobalName zones are not dynamic, an administrator has to enter the records into the zone database manually. In most organizations, the servers have static TCP/IP addresses, and this works well with the GlobalName zone design. GlobalName zones are usually used to map single-label CNAME (alias) resource records to an FQDN.

Zone Transfers and Replication

DNS is such an important part of the network that you should not just use a single DNS server. With a single DNS server, you also have a single point of failure and, in fact, many domain registrars encourage the use of more than two name servers for a domain. Secondary servers or multiple primary Active Directory Integrated servers play an integral role in providing DNS information for an entire domain.

As previously stated, secondary DNS servers receive their zone databases through zone transfers. When you configure a secondary server for the first time, you must specify the primary server that is authoritative for the zone and will send the zone transfer. The primary server must also permit the secondary server to request the zone transfer.

Zone transfers occur in one of two ways: *full zone transfers (AXFR)* and *incremental zone transfers (IXFR)*.

When a new secondary server is configured for the first time, it receives a full zone transfer from the primary DNS server. The full zone transfer contains all of the information in the DNS database. Some DNS implementations always receive full zone transfers.

After the secondary server receives its first full zone transfer, subsequent zone transfers are incremental. The primary name server compares its zone version number with that of the secondary server, and it sends only the changes that have been made in the interim. This significantly reduces network traffic generated by zone transfers.

The secondary server typically initiates zone transfers when the refresh interval time for the zone expires or when the secondary or stub server boots. Alternatively, you can configure notify lists on the primary server that send a message to the secondary or stub servers whenever any changes to the zone database occur.

When you consider your DNS strategy, you must carefully consider the layout of your network. If you have a single domain with offices in separate cities, you want to reduce the number of zone transfers across the potentially slow or expensive WAN links, although this is becoming less of a concern because of continuous increases in bandwidth.

Active Directory Integrated zones do away with traditional zone transfers altogether. Instead, they replicate across Active Directory with all of the other AD information. This replication is secure and encrypted because it uses the Active Directory security.

How DNS Notify Works

Windows Server 2012 R2 supports DNS Notify. *DNS Notify* is a mechanism that allows the process of initiating notifications to secondary servers when zone changes occur (RFC 1996). DNS Notify uses a push mechanism for communicating to a select set of secondary zone servers when their zone information is updated. (DNS Notify does not allow you to configure a notify list for a stub zone.)

After being notified of the changes, secondary servers can then start a pull zone transfer and update their local copies of the database.

> Many different mechanisms use the push/pull relationship. Normally, one object pushes information to another, and the second object pulls the information from the first. Most applications push replication on a change value and pull it on a time value. For example, a system can push replication after 10 updates, or it can be pulled every 30 minutes.

To configure the DNS Notify process, you create a list of secondary servers to notify. List the IP address of the server in the primary master's Notify dialog box (see Figure 12.8). The Notify dialog box is located under the Zone Transfers tab, which is located in the zone Properties dialog box (see Figure 12.9).

FIGURE 12.8   DNS Notify dialog box

FIGURE 12.9   DNS Zone Transfers tab

Configuring Stub Zone Transfers with Zone Replication

In the preceding section, I talked about how to configure secondary server zone transfers. What if you wanted to configure settings for stub zone transfers? This is where zone replication scope comes in.

Only Active Directory–integrated primary and stub zones can configure their replication scope. Secondary servers do not have this ability.

You can configure zone replication scope configurations in two ways. An administrator can set configuration options through the DNS snap-in or through a command-line tool called DNSCmd.

To configure zone replication scope through the DNS snap-in, follow these steps:

1. Click Start ➢ Administrative Tools ➢ DNS.

2. Right-click the zone that you want to set up.

3. Choose Properties.

4. In the Properties dialog box, click the Change button next to Replication (see Figure 12.10).

FIGURE 12.10 DNS zone replication scope

5. Choose the replication scope that fits your organization.

Advantages of DNS in Windows Server 2012 R2

DNS in Microsoft Windows Server 2012 R2 has some great advantages over many other versions of Microsoft DNS. Here are some of the improvements of DNS in Windows Server 2012 R2 (some of these became available in Windows Server 2008):

- Background zone loading
- Support for TCP/IP version 6 (IPv6)
- Read-only domain controllers
- GlobalName zone
- DNS socket pools
- DNS cache locking
- DNS Security Extensions (DNSSEC)
- DNS devolution
- Record weighting
- Netmask ordering
- DnsUpdateProxy group

Background Zone Loading

If an organization had to restart a DNS server with an extremely large Active Directory Integrated DNS zones database in the past, DNS had a common problem with an Active Directory Integrated DNS zone. After the DNS restart, it could take hours for DNS data to be retrieved from Active Directory. During this time, the DNS server was unable to service any client requests.

Microsoft Windows Server 2008 DNS addressed this problem by implementing background zone loading, and Windows Server 2012 R2 has taken it a step further. As the DNS restarts, the Active Directory zone data populates the database in the background. This allows the DNS server to service client requests for data from other zones almost immediately after a restart.

Background zone loading accomplishes this task by loading the DNS zone using separate threads. This allows a DNS server to service requests while still loading the rest of the zone. If a client sends a request to the DNS server for a computer that has not yet loaded into memory, the DNS server retrieves the data from Active Directory and updates the record.

Support for IPv6 Addresses

Over the past few years, the Internet has starting running into a problem that was not foreseen when it was first created—it started running out of TCP/IP addresses. As you probably know, when the Internet was created, it was used for government and academic purposes only. Then, seemingly overnight, it grew to be the information superhighway. Nowadays, asking someone for their email address is almost more common as asking for their phone number.

Version 4 (IPv4) was the common version of TCP/IP. The release of TCP/IP version 6 (IPv6) has solved the lack-of-IP-addresses problem. IPv4 addresses are 32 bits long, but IPv6 addresses are 128 bits in length. The longer lengths allow for a much greater number of globally unique TCP/IP addresses.

Microsoft Windows Server 2012 R2 DNS has built-in support to accommodate both IPv4 and IPv6 address records (DNS records are explained later in this chapter). DHCP can also issue IPv6 addresses, which lets administrators allow DHCP to register the client with DNS, or the IPv6 client can register their address with the DNS server.

Support for Read-Only Domain Controllers

Windows Server 2008 introduced a new type of domain controller called the *read-only domain controller (RODC)*. This is a full copy of the Active Directory database without the ability to write to Active Directory. The RODC gives an organization the ability to install a domain controller in a location (onsite or offsite) where security is a concern.

Microsoft Windows Server 2012 R2 DNS has implemented a type of zone to help support an RODC. A primary read-only zone allows a DNS server to receive a copy of the application partition (including ForestDNSZones and DomainDNSZones) that DNS uses. This allows DNS to support an RODC because DNS now has a full copy of all DNS zones stored in Active Directory.

A primary, read-only zone is just what it says—a read-only zone; so to make any changes to it, you have to change the primary zones located on the Active Directory Integrated DNS server.

DNS Socket Pools

If your server is running Windows Server 2012 R2, you will be able to take advantage of DNS socket pools. *DNS socket pools* allow source port randomization to protect against DNS cache-poisoning attacks.

If you choose to use source port randomization, when the DNS service starts, the DNS server will randomly pick a source port from a pool of available sockets. This is an advantage because instead of DNS using a well-known source port when issuing queries, the DNS server uses a random port selected from the socket pool. This helps guard against attacks because a hacker must correctly access the source port of the DNS query. The socket pool is automatically enabled in DNS with the default settings.

When using the DNS socket pool, the default size of the DNS socket pool is 2,500. When configuring the socket pool, you have the ability to choose a size value from 0 to 10,000. The larger the value, the greater the protection you will have against DNS spoofing attacks. If you decide to configure your socket pool size with a zero value, only a single socket for remote DNS queries will be used.

DNS Cache Locking

Windows Server 2012 R2 *DNS cache locking* allows cached DNS records to remain safe for the duration of the record's time to live (TTL) value. This means that the cached DNS records cannot be overwritten or changed. Because of this new DNS feature, it's tougher for hackers to perform cache-poisoning attacks against your DNS server.

DNS administrators can set how long a record will remain safe in cache. The configuration is based on a percent value. For example, if you set your cache locking value to 50 percent, then the cached records cannot be overwritten until half of the TTL has been reached. DNS cache locking is set to 100 percent by default. This means that the cached records never get overwritten.

DNS Security Extensions

One major issue that you must always look at is keeping your DNS safe. Think about it: DNS is a database of computer names and IP addresses. As a hacker, if I control DNS, I can control your company. In organizations that do not support extra security like IPsec, DNS security is even more important. This is where *Domain Name System Security Extensions (DNSSEC)* can help.

Windows Server 2012 R2 can use a suite of extensions that will help add security to DNS, and that suite is called DNSSEC, which was introduced in Windows Server 2008 R2. The DNSSEC protocol allows your DNS servers to be secure by validating DNS responses. DNSSEC secures your DNS resource records by accompanying the records with a digital signature.

To allow your DNS resource records to receive digital signatures, DNSSEC is applied to your DNS server by a procedure called *zone signing*. This process begins when a DNS resolver initiates a DNS query for a resource record in a signed DNS zone. When a response is returned, a digital signature (RRSIG) accompanies the response, and this allows the response to be verified. If the verification is successful, then the DNS resolver knows that the data has not been modified or tampered with in any way.

Once you implement a zone with DNSSEC, all of the records that are contained within that zone get individually signed. Since all of the records in the zone get individually signed, this gives administrators the ability to add, modify, or delete records without re-signing the entire zone. The only requirement is to re-sign any updated records.

Trust Anchors

Trust anchors are an important part of the DNSSEC process because trust anchors allow the DNS servers to validate the DNSKEY resource records. *Trust anchors* are preconfigured public keys that are linked to a DNS zone. For a DNS server to perform validation, one or more trust anchors must be configured. If you are running an Active Directory Integrated zone, trust anchors can be stored in the Active Directory Domain Services directory partition of the forest. If you decide to store the trust anchors in the directory partition, then all DNS servers that reside on a domain controller get a copy of this trust anchor. On DNS servers that reside on stand-alone servers, trust anchors are stored in a file called TrustAnchors.dns.

If your servers are running Windows Server 2012 R2, then you can view trust anchors in the DNS Manager Console tree in the Trust Points container. You can also use Windows PowerShell or Dnscmd.exe to view trust anchors. Windows PowerShell is the recommended command-line method for viewing trust anchors. The following line is a PowerShell command to view the trust anchors for Contoso.com:

```
get-dnsservertrustanchor sec.contoso.com
```

DNSSEC Clients

Windows 7, Windows 8, Windows Server 2008/2008 R2, and Windows Server 2012/2012 R2 are all DNS clients that receive a response to a DNS query, examine the response, and then evaluate whether the response has been validated by a DNS server. The DNS client itself is nonvalidating, and the DNS client relies on the local DNS server to indicate that validation was successful. If the server doesn't perform validation, then the DNS client service can be configured to return no results.

DNS Devolution

Using *DNS devolution*, if a client computer is a member of a child namespace, the client computer will be able to access resources in the parent namespace without the need to explicitly provide the fully qualified domain name of the resource. DNS devolution removes the leftmost label of the namespace to get to the parent suffix. DNS devolution allows the DNS resolver to create the new FQDNs. DNS devolution works by appending the single-label, unqualified domain name with the parent suffix of the primary DNS suffix name.

Record Weighting

Weighting DNS records will allow an administrator to place a value on DNS SRV records. Clients will then randomly choose SRV records proportional to the weight value assigned.

Netmask Ordering

If round robin is enabled, when a client requests name resolution, the first address entered in the database is returned to the resolver, and it is then sent to the end of the list. The next time a client attempts to resolve the name, the DNS server returns the second name in the database (which is now the first name) and then sends it to the end of the list, and so on. Round robin is enabled by default.

Netmask ordering is a part of the round robin process. When an administrator configures netmask ordering, the DNS server will detect the subnet of the querying client. The DNS server will then return a host address available for the same subnet. Netmask ordering is enabled through the DNS Manager console on the Advanced tab of the server Properties dialog box.

DnsUpdateProxy Group

As mentioned previously, the DHCP server can be configured to register host (A) and pointer (PTR) resource records dynamically on behalf of DHCP clients. Because of this, the DNS server can end up with stale resources. To help solve this issue, an administrator can use the built-in security group called *DnsUpdateProxy*.

To use the DnsUpdateProxy group, an administrator must first create a dedicated user account and configure the DHCP servers with its credentials. This will protect against the creation of unsecured records. Also, when you create the dedicated user account, members of the DnsUpdateProxy group will be able to register records in zones that allow only secured dynamic updates. Multiple DHCP servers can use the same credentials of one dedicated user account.

Now that you have learned about some of the new features of Windows Server 2012 R2 DNS, let's take a look at some of the DNS record types.

Introducing DNS Record Types

No matter where your zone information is stored, you can rest assured that it contains a variety of DNS information. Although the DNS snap-in makes it unlikely that you'll ever need to edit these files by hand, it's good to know exactly what data is contained there.

As stated previously, zone files consist of a number of resource records. You need to know about several types of resource records to manage your DNS servers effectively. They are discussed in the following sections.

Part of the resource record is its class. *Classes* define the type of network for the resource record. There are three classes: Internet, Chaosnet, and Hesoid. By far, the Internet class is the most popular. In fact, it's doubtful that you'll see either Chaosnet or Hesoid classes in the wild.

 The following are some of the more important resource records in a DNS database. For a complete listing of records in a Microsoft DNS database, visit Microsoft's website at http://technet.microsoft.com/en-us/library/cc758321(v=WS.10).aspx.

Start of Authority (SOA) Records

The first record in a database file is the *start of authority (SOA) record*. The SOA defines the general parameters for the DNS zone, including the identity of the authoritative server for the zone.

The SOA appears in the following format:

```
@ IN SOA primary_mastercontact_e-mailserial_number
refresh_timeretry_timeexpiration_timetime_to_live
```

Here is a sample SOA from the domain example.com:

```
@ IN SOA win2k3r2.example.com. hostmaster.example.com. (
                5           ; serial number
                900         ; refresh
                600         ; retry
                86400       ; expire
                3600      ) ; default TTL
```

Table 12.2 lists the attributes stored in the SOA record.

TABLE 12.2 The SOA record structure

Field	Meaning
Current zone	The current zone for the SOA. This can be represented by an @ symbol to indicate the current zone or by naming the zone itself. In the example, the current zone is example.com. The trailing dot (.com.) indicates the zone's place relative to the root of the DNS.
Class	This will almost always be the letters *IN* for the Internet class.
Type of record	The type of record follows. In this case, it's SOA.
Primary master	The primary master for the zone on which this file is maintained.
Contact email	The Internet email address for the person responsible for this domain's database file. There is no @ symbol in this contact email address because @ is a special character in zone files. The contact email address is separated by a single dot (.). So, the email address of root@example.com would be represented by root.example.com in a zone file.
Serial number	This is the "version number" of this database file. It increases each time the database file is changed.
Refresh time	The amount of time (in seconds) that a secondary server will wait between checks to its master server to see whether the database file has changed and a zone transfer should be requested.
Retry time	The amount of time (in seconds) that a secondary server will wait before retrying a failed zone transfer.
Expiration time	The amount of time (in seconds) that a secondary server will spend trying to download a zone. Once this time limit expires, the old zone information will be discarded.
Time to live	The amount of time (in seconds) that another DNS server is allowed to cache any resource records from this database file. This is the value that is sent out with all query responses from this zone file when the individual resource record doesn't contain an overriding value.

Name Server Records

Name server (NS) records list the name servers for a domain. This record allows other name servers to look up names in your domain. A zone file may contain more than one name server record. The format of these records is simple:

```
example.com.    IN    NS    Hostname.example.com
```

Table 12.3 explains the attributes stored in the NS record.

TABLE 12.3 The NS record structure

Field	Meaning
Name	The domain that will be serviced by this name server. In this case I used example.com.
AddressClass	Internet (IN)
RecordType	Name server (NS)
Name Server Name	The FQDN of the server responsible for the domain

NOTE Any domain name in the database file that is not terminated with a period will have the root domain appended to the end. For example, an entry that just has the name *sales* will be expanded by adding the root domain to the end, whereas the entry sales.example.com. won't be expanded.

Host Record

A *host record* (also called an *A record* for IPv4 and *AAAA record* for IPv6) is used to associate statically a host's name to its IP addresses. The format is pretty simple:

```
host_nameoptional_TTL IN  A  IP_Address
```

Here's an example from my DNS database:

```
www  IN  A  192.168.0.204
SMTP IN  A  192.168.3.144
```

The A or AAAA record ties a hostname (which is part of an FQDN) to a specific IP address. This makes these records suitable for use when you have devices with statically assigned IP addresses. In this case, you create these records manually using the DNS snap-in. As it turns out, if you enable DDNS, your DHCP server can create these for you. This automatic creation is what enables DDNS to work.

Notice that an optional TTL field is available for each resource record in the DNS. This value is used to set a TTL that is different from the default TTL for the domain. For example, if you wanted a 60-second TTL for the www A or AAAA record, it would look like this:

```
www 60 IN  A  192.168.0.204
```

Alias Record

Closely related to the host record is the *alias record*, or *canonical name (CNAME) record*. The syntax of an alias record is as follows:

aliasoptional_TTL IN CNAME *hostname*

Aliases are used to point more than one DNS record toward a host for which an A record already exists. For example, if the hostname of your web server was actually chaos, you would likely have an A record such as this:

chaos IN A 192.168.1.10

Then you could make an alias or CNAME for the record so that www.example.com would point to chaos:

www IN CNAME chaos.example.com.

Note the trailing dot (.) on the end of the CNAME record. This means the root domain is not appended to the entry.

Pointer Record

A or AAAA records are probably the most visible component of the DNS database because Internet users depend on them to turn FQDNs like www.microsoft.com into the IP addresses that browsers and other components require to find Internet resources. However, the host record has a lesser-known but still important twin: the *pointer (PTR) record*. The format of a PTR record appears as follows:

reversed_address.in-addr.arpa. *optional_TTL* IN PTR *targeted_domain_name*

The A or AAAA record maps a hostname to an IP address, and the PTR record does just the opposite—mapping an IP address to a hostname through the use of the in-addr.arpa zone.

The PTR record is necessary because IP addresses begin with the least-specific portion first (the network) and end with the most-specific portion (the host), whereas hostnames begin with the most-specific portion at the beginning and the least-specific portion at the end.

Consider the example 192.168.1.10 with a subnet mask 255.255.255.0. The portion 192.168.1 defines the network and the final .10 defines the host, or the most-specific portion of the address. DNS is just the opposite: The hostname www.example.com. defines the most-specific portion, www, at the beginning and then traverses the DNS tree to the least-specific part, the dot (.), at the root of the tree.

Reverse DNS records, therefore, need to be represented in this most-specific-to-least-specific manner. The PTR record for mapping 192.168.1.10 to www.example.com would look like this:

```
10.1.168.192.in-addr.arpa. IN PTR www.example.com.
```

Now a DNS query for that record can follow the logical DNS hierarchy from the root of the DNS tree all the way to the most-specific portion.

Mail Exchanger Record

The *mail exchanger (MX) record* is used to specify which servers accept mail for this domain. Each MX record contains two parameters—a preference and a mail server, as shown in the following example:

```
domain IN MX preference mailserver_host
```

The MX record uses the preference value to specify which server should be used if more than one MX record is present. The preference value is a number. The lower the number, the more preferred the server. Here's an example:

```
example.com.    IN  MX  0  mail.example.com.
example.com.    IN  MX  10 backupmail.example.com.
```

In the example, `mail.example.com` is the default mail server for the domain. If that server goes down for any reason, the `backupmail.example.com` mail server is used by emailers.

Service Record

Windows Server 2012 R2 depends on some other services, like the Lightweight Directory Access Protocol (LDAP) and Kerberos. Using a service record, which is another type of DNS record, a Windows 2000, XP, Vista, Windows 7, or Windows 8 client can query DNS servers for the location of a domain controller. This makes it much easier (for both the client and the administrator) to manage and distribute logon traffic in large-scale networks. For this approach to work, Microsoft has to have some way to register the presence of a service in DNS. Enter the service (SRV) record.

Service (SRV) records tie together the location of a service (like a domain controller) with information about how to contact the service. SRV records provide seven items of information. Let's review an example to help clarify this powerful concept. (Table 12.4 explains the fields in the following example.)

```
ldap.tcp.example.com.  86400 IN SRV  10  100  389  hsv.example.com
ldap.tcp.example.com.  86400 IN SRV  20  100  389  msy.example.com
```

TABLE 12.4 The SRV record structure

Field	Meaning
Domain name	Domain for which this record is valid (`ldap.tcp.example.com.`).
TTL	Time to live (86,400 seconds).
Class	This field is always `IN`, which stands for Internet.
Record type	Type of record (`SRV`).
Priority	Specifies a preference, similar to the Preference field in an MX record. The SRV record with the lowest priority is used first (`10`).
Weight	Service records with equal priority are chosen according to their weight (`100`).
Port number	The port where the server is listening for this service (`389`).
Target	The FQDN of the host computer (`hsv.example.com` and `msy.example.com`).

You can define other types of service records. If your applications support them, they can query DNS to find the services they need.

Configuring DNS

In the following sections, you'll begin to learn about the actual DNS server. You will start by installing DNS. Then I will talk about different zone configuration options and what they mean. Finally, you'll complete an exercise that covers configuring Dynamic DNS, delegating zones, and manually entering records.

Installing DNS

If you have been reading this book since Chapter 1, then this exercise was done in Chapter 2. If you started reading this book with Part 2, then this chapter will show you how to install DNS. If DNS is already installed onto your server, you can skip this exercise. But if you have not installed DNS, let's start by installing DNS. Installing DNS is an important part of running a network. Exercise 12.1 walks you through the installation of a DNS server.

NOTE If you are using a Dynamic TCP/IP address, please change your TCP/IP number to static. If you are unsure how to assign your server a static TCP/IP address, please refer to Chapter 2.

EXERCISE 12.1

Installing and Configuring the DNS Service

1. Open Server Manager.

2. On the Server Manager dashboard, click the Add Roles And Features link.

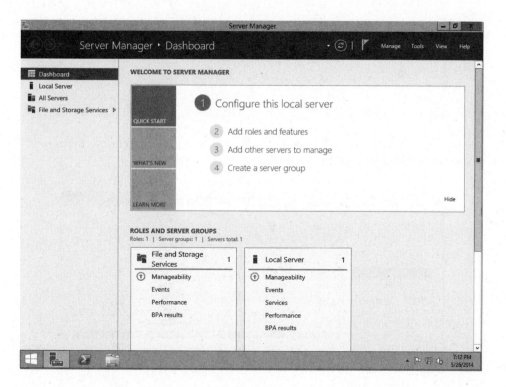

3. If a Before You Begin screen appears, click Next.

4. On the Selection type page, choose Role-Based Or Feature-Based Installation and click Next.

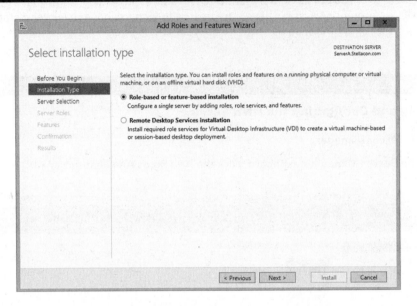

5. Click the Select A Server From The Server Pool radio button and choose the server under the Server Pool section. Click Next.

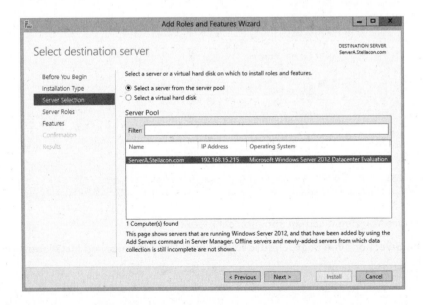

6. Click the DNS Server Item in the Server Role list. If a pop-up window appears telling you that you need to add additional features, click the Add Features button. Click Next to continue.

7. On the Add Features page, just click Next.

8. Click Next on the DNS Server information screen.

9. On the Confirm Installation screen, choose the Restart The Destination Server Automatically If Required check box and then click the Install button.

10. At the Installation progress screen, click Close after the DNS server is installed.

11. Close Server Manager.

Load Balancing with Round Robin

Like other DNS implementations, the Windows Server 2012 R2 implementation of DNS supports load balancing through the use of round robin. Load balancing distributes the network load among multiple network hosts if they are available. You set up round-robin load balancing by creating multiple resource records with the same hostname but different IP addresses for multiple computers. Depending on the options that you select, the DNS server responds with the addresses of one of the host computers.

If round robin is enabled, when a client requests name resolution, the first address entered in the database is returned to the resolver and is then sent to the end of the list. The next time a client attempts to resolve the name, the DNS server returns the second name in the database (which is now the first name) and then sends it to the end of the list, and so on. Round robin is enabled by default.

Configuring a Caching-Only Server

Although all DNS name servers cache queries that they have resolved, caching-only servers are DNS name servers that only perform queries, cache the answers, and return the results. They are not authoritative for any domains, and the information that they contain is limited to what has been cached while resolving queries. Accordingly, they don't have any zone files, and they don't participate in zone transfers. When a caching-only server is first started, it has no information in its cache; the cache is gradually built over time.

Caching-only servers are easy to configure. After installing the DNS service, simply make sure the root hints are configured properly.

1. Right-click your DNS server and choose the Properties command.

2. When the Properties dialog box appears, switch to the Root Hints tab (see Figure 12.11).

3. If your server is connected to the Internet, you should see a list of root hints for the root servers maintained by ICANN and the Internet Assigned Numbers Authority (IANA). If not, click the Add button to add root hints as defined in the cache.dns file.

FIGURE 12.11   The Root Hints tab of the DNS server's Properties dialog box

You can obtain current cache·dns files on the Internet by using a search engine. Just search for *cache.dns* and download one. (I always try to get cache·dns files from a university or a company that manages domain names.)

Setting Zone Properties

There are six tabs on the Properties dialog box for a forward or reverse lookup zone. You only use the Security tab to control who can change properties and to make dynamic updates to records on that zone. The other tabs are discussed in the following sections.

> Secondary zones don't have a Security tab, and their SOA tab shows you the contents of the master SOA record, which you can't change.

General Tab

The General tab includes the following:

- The Status indicator and the associated Pause button let you see and control whether this zone can be used to answer queries. When the zone is running, the server can use it to answer client queries; when it's paused, the server won't answer any queries it gets for that particular zone.

- The Type indicator and its Change button allow you to select the zone type. The options are Standard Primary, Standard Secondary, and AD-Integrated. (See "Introducing DNS Database Zones" earlier in this chapter.) As you change the type, the controls you see below the horizontal dividing line change too. For primary zones, you'll see a field that lets you select the zone filename; for secondary zones, you'll get controls that allow you to specify the IP addresses of the primary servers. But the most interesting controls are the ones you see for AD Integrated zones. When you change to the AD Integrated zones, you have the ability to make the dynamic zones Secure Only.

- The Replication indicator and its Change button allow you to change the replication scope if the zone is stored in Active Directory. You can choose to replicate the zone data to any of the following:

  - All DNS servers in the Active Directory forest

  - All DNS servers in a specified domain

  - All domain controllers in the Active Directory domain (required if you use Windows 2000 domain controllers in your domain)

  - All domain controllers specified in the replication scope of the application directory partition

- The Dynamic Updates field gives you a way to specify whether you want to support Dynamic DNS updates from compatible DHCP servers. As you learned earlier in the section "Dynamic DNS and Non-Dynamic DNS," the DHCP server or DHCP client must know about and support Dynamic DNS in order to use it, but the DNS server has to participate too. You can turn dynamic updates on or off, or you can require that updates be secured.

Start Of Authority (SOA) Tab

The following options in the Start Of Authority (SOA) tab, shown in Figure 12.12, control the contents of the SOA record for this zone.

FIGURE 12.12 The Start Of Authority (SOA) tab of the zone Properties dialog box

- The Serial Number field indicates which version of the SOA record the server currently holds. Every time you change another field, you should increment the serial number so that other servers will notice the change and get a copy of the updated record.

- The Primary Server and Responsible Person fields indicate the location of the primary name server for this zone and the email address of the administrator responsible for the maintenance of this zone, respectively. The standard username for this is hostmaster.

- The Refresh Interval field controls how often any secondary zones of this zone must contact the primary zone server and get any changes that have been posted since the last update.

- The Retry Interval field controls how long secondary servers will wait after a zone transfer fails before they try again. They'll keep trying at the interval you specify (which should be shorter than the refresh interval) until they eventually succeed in transferring zone data.

- The Expires After field tells the secondary servers when to throw away zone data. The default of 1 day (24 hours) means that a secondary server that hasn't gotten an update in 24 hours will delete its local copy of the zone data.

- The Minimum (Default) TTL field sets the default TTL for all RRs created in the zone. You can assign specific TTLs to individual records if you want.

- The TTL For This Record field controls the TTL for the SOA record itself.

Name Servers Tab

The *name server (NS) record* for a zone indicates which name servers are authoritative for the zone. That normally means the zone primary server and any secondary servers you've configured for the zone. (Remember, secondary servers are authoritative read-only copies of the zone.) You edit the NS record for a zone using the Name Servers tab (see Figure 12.13).

FIGURE 12.13   The Name Servers tab of the zone Properties dialog box

The tab shows you which servers are currently listed, and you use the Add, Edit, and Remove buttons to specify which name servers you want included in the zone's NS record.

WINS Tab

The WINS tab allows you to control whether this zone uses WINS forward lookups or not. These lookups pass on queries that DNS can't resolve to WINS for action. This is a useful setup if you're still using WINS on your network. You must explicitly turn this option on with the Use WINS Forward Lookup check box in the WINS tab for a particular zone.

Zone Transfers Tab

Zone transfers are necessary and useful because they're the mechanism used to propagate zone data between primary and secondary servers. For primary servers (whether AD Integrated or not), you can specify whether your servers will allow zone transfers and, if so, to whom.

You can use the following controls on the Zone Transfers tab to configure these settings per zone:

- The Allow Zone Transfers check box controls whether the server answers zone transfer requests for this zone at all—when it's not checked, no zone data is transferred. The Allow Zone Transfers selections are as follows:

  - To Any Server allows any server anywhere on the Internet to request a copy of your zone data.

  - Only To Servers Listed On The Name Servers Tab (the default) limits transfers to servers you specify. This is a more secure setting than To Any Server because it limits transfers to other servers for the same zone.

  - Only To The Following Servers allows you to specify exactly which servers are allowed to request zone transfers. This list can be larger or smaller than the list specified on the Name Servers tab.

- The Notify button is for setting up automatic notification triggers that are sent to secondary servers for this zone. Those triggers signal the secondary servers that changes have occurred on the primary server so that the secondary servers can request updates sooner than their normally scheduled interval. The options in the Notify dialog box are similar to those in the Zone Transfers tab. You can enable automatic notification and then choose either Servers Listed On The Name Servers Tab or The Following Servers.

Configuring Zones for Dynamic Updates

In Exercise 12.2, you will create and then modify the properties of a forward lookup zone. In addition, you'll configure the zone to allow dynamic updates.

EXERCISE 12.2

Configuring a Zone for Dynamic Updates

1. Open the DNS management snap-in by selecting Server Manager. Once in Server Manager, click DNS on the left side. In the Servers window (center screen), right-click your server name and choose DNS Manager.

2. Click the DNS server to expand it and then click the Forward Lookup Zones folder. Right-click the Forward Lookup Zones folder and choose New Zone.

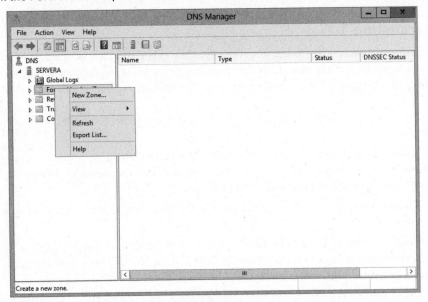

3. At the New Zone Welcome screen, click Next.

4. At the Zone Type screen, choose the Primary Zone option. If your DNS server is also a domain controller, do not check the box to store the zone in Active Directory. Click Next when you are ready.

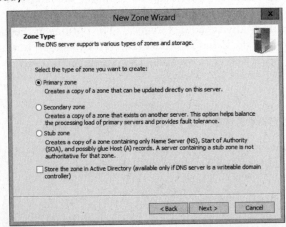

5. Enter a new zone name in the Zone Name field and click Next. (I used my last name—Panek.com.)

6. Leave the default zone filename and click Next.

7. Select the Do Not Allow Dynamic Updates radio button and click Next.

8. Click Finish to end the wizard.

9. Right-click the zone you just created and choose the Properties command.

10. Click the down arrow next to Dynamic Updates. Notice that there are only two options (None and Nonsecure And Secure). The Secure Only option is not available because you are not using Active Directory Integrated. Make sure Nonsecure And Secure is chosen.

11. Click OK to close the Properties box.

12. Close the DNS management snap-in.

13. Close the Server Manager snap-in.

Delegating Zones for DNS

DNS provides the ability to divide the namespace into one or more zones, which can then be stored, distributed, and replicated to other DNS servers. When deciding whether to divide your DNS namespace to make additional zones, consider the following reasons to use additional zones:

▪   A need to delegate management of part of your DNS namespace to another location or department within your organization

- A need to divide one large zone into smaller zones for distributing traffic loads among multiple servers, for improving DNS name-resolution performance, or for creating a more fault-tolerant DNS environment

- A need to extend the namespace by adding numerous subdomains at once, such as to accommodate the opening of a new branch or site

Each newly delegated zone requires a primary DNS server just as a regular DNS zone does. When delegating zones within your namespace, be aware that for each new zone you create, you need to place delegation records in other zones that point to the authoritative DNS servers for the new zone. This is necessary both to transfer authority and to provide correct referral to other DNS servers and clients of the new servers being made authoritative for the new zone.

In Exercise 12.3, you'll create a delegated subdomain of the domain you created in Exercise 12.2. Note that the name of the server to which you want to delegate the subdomain must be stored in an A or CNAME record in the parent domain.

EXERCISE 12.3

Creating a Delegated DNS Zone

1. Open the DNS management snap-in by selecting Server Manager. Once in Server Manager, click DNS on the left side. In the Servers window (center screen), right-click your server name and choose DNS Manager.

2. Expand the DNS server and locate the zone you created in Exercise 12.2.

3. Right-click the zone and choose the New Delegation command.

4. The New Delegation Wizard appears. Click Next to dismiss the initial wizard page.

5. Enter **ns1** (or whatever other name you like) in the Delegated Domain field of the Delegated Domain Name page. This is the name of the domain for which you want to delegate authority to another DNS server. It should be a subdomain of the primary domain (for example, to delegate authority for farmington.example.net, you'd enter **farmington** in the Delegated Domain field). Click Next to complete this step.

6. When the Name Servers page appears, click the Add button to add the names and IP addresses of the servers that will be hosting the newly delegated zone. For the purpose of this exercise, enter the server name you used in Exercise 12.2. Click the Resolve button to resolve this domain name's IP address automatically into the IP address field. Click OK when you are finished. Click Next to continue with the wizard.

7. Click the Finish button. The New Delegation Wizard disappears, and you'll see the new zone you just created appear beneath the zone you selected in step 3. The newly delegated zone's folder icon is drawn in gray to indicate that control of the zone is delegated.

DNS Forwarding

If a DNS server does not have an answer to a DNS request, it may be necessary to send that request to another DNS server. This is called *DNS forwarding*. You need to understand the two main types of forwarding:

External Forwarding When a DNS server forwards an external DNS request to a DNS server outside of your organization, this is considered *external forwarding*. For example, a resolver requests the host www.microsoft.com. Most likely, your internal DNS server is not going to have Microsoft's web address in its DNS database. So, your DNS server is going to send the request to an external DNS (most likely your ISP).

Conditional Forwarding *Conditional forwarding* is a lot like external forwarding except that you are going to forward requests to specific DNS servers based on a condition. Usually this is an excellent setup for internal DNS resolution. For example, let's say that you have two companies, stellacon.com and stellatest.com. If a request comes in for Stellacon.com, it gets forwarded to the Stellacon DNS server, and any requests for Stellatest.com will get forwarded to the Stellatest DNS server. Requests are forwarded to a specific DNS server depending on the condition that an administrator sets up.

Manually Creating DNS Records

From time to time you may find it necessary to add resource records manually to your Windows Server 2012 R2 DNS servers. Although Dynamic DNS frees you from the need to fiddle with A and PTR records for clients and other such entries, you still have to create other resource types (including MX records, required for the proper flow of SMTP email) manually. You can manually create A, PTR, MX, SRV, and many other record types.

There are only two important things to remember for manually creating DNS records:

- You must right-click the zone and choose either the New Record command or the Other New Records command.

- You must know how to fill in the fields of whatever record type you're using.

  For example, to create an MX record, you need three pieces of information (the domain, the mail server, and the priority). To create an SRV record, however, you need several more pieces of information.

In Exercise 12.4, you will manually create an MX record for a mailtest server in the zone you created in Exercise 12.2.

EXERCISE 12.4

Manually Creating DNS RRs

1. Open the DNS management snap-in by selecting Server Manager. Once in Server Manager, click DNS on the left side. In the Servers window (center screen), right-click your server name and choose DNS Manager.

EXERCISE 12.4 *(continued)*

2. Expand your DNS server, right-click its zone, and choose New Host (A record).

3. Enter **mailtest** in the Name field. Enter a TCP/IP number in the IP Address field. (You can use any number for this exercise, for example, 192.168.1.254.) Click the Add Host button.

4. A dialog box appears stating that the host record was created successfully. Click OK. Click Done.

5. Right-click your zone name and choose New Mail Exchanger (MX).

6. Enter **mailtest** in the Host Or Child Domain field and enter **mailtest.yourDomain.com** (or whatever domain name you used in Exercise 12.2) in the Fully-Qualified Domain Name (FQDN) Of Mail Server field and then click OK. Notice that the new record is already visible.

7. Next create an alias (or CNAME) record to point to the mail server. (It is assumed that you already have an A record for mailtest in your zone.) Right-click your zone and choose New Alias (CNAME).

8. Type **mail** into the Alias Name field.

9. Type **mailtest.yourDomain.com** into the Fully-Qualified Domain Name (FQDN) For Target Host field.

10. Click the OK button.

11. Close the DNS management snap-in.

DNS Aging and Scavenging

When using dynamic updates, computers (or DHCP) will register a resource record with DNS. These records get removed when a computer is shut down properly. A major problem in the industry is that laptops are frequently removed from the network without a proper shutdown. Therefore, their resource records continue to live in the DNS database.

Windows Server 2012 R2 DNS supports two features called *DNS aging* and *DNS scavenging.* These features are used to clean up and remove stale resource records. DNS zone or DNS server aging and scavenging flag old resource records that have not been updated in a certain amount of time (determined by the scavenging interval). These stale records will be scavenged at the next cleanup interval. DNS uses time stamps on the resource records to determine how long they have been listed in the DNS database.

Monitoring and Troubleshooting DNS

Now that you have set up and configured your DNS name server and created some resource records, you will want to confirm that it is resolving and replying to client DNS requests. A couple of tools allow you to do some basic monitoring and managing. Once you are able to monitor DNS, you'll want to start troubleshooting.

The simplest test is to use the ping command to make sure that the server is alive. A more thorough test would be to use nslookup to verify that you can actually resolve addresses for items on your DNS server.

In the following sections, you'll look at some of these monitoring and management tools and how to troubleshoot DNS.

Monitoring DNS with the DNS Snap-In

You can use the DNS snap-in to do some basic server testing and monitoring. More important, you use the snap-in to monitor and set logging options. On the Event Logging tab of the server's Properties dialog box (see Figure 12.14), you can pick which events you want logged. The more events you select, the more logging information you'll get. This is useful when you're trying to track what's happening with your servers, but it can result in a very large log file if you're not careful.

FIGURE 12.14 The Event Logging tab of the server's Properties dialog box

The Monitoring tab (see Figure 12.15) gives you some testing tools. When the check box labeled A Simple Query Against This DNS Server is checked, a test is performed that asks for a single record from the local DNS server. It's useful for verifying that the service is running and listening to queries, but not much else. When the check box labeled A Recursive Query To Other DNS Servers is checked, the test is more sophisticated—a recursive query checks whether forwarding is working okay. The Test Now button and the Perform Automatic Testing At The Following Interval check box allow you to run these tests now or later as you require.

FIGURE 12.15 The Monitoring tab of the server's Properties dialog box

Another tab in the server's properties that allows you to monitor the activity of the DNS server is the Debug Logging tab. The Debug Logging tab allows you to monitor all outbound and inbound DNS traffic, packet content, packet type, and which transport protocol (TCP or UDP) that you want to monitor on the DNS server.

> If the simple query fails, check that the local server contains the zone 1.0.0.127.in-addr.arpa. If the recursive query fails, check that your root hints are correct and that your root servers are running.

In Exercise 12.5, you will enable logging, use the DNS MMC to test the DNS server, and view the contents of the DNS log.

EXERCISE 12.5

Simple DNS Testing

1.   Open the DNS management snap-in by selecting Server Manager. Once in Server Manager, click DNS on the left side. In the Servers window (center screen), right-click your server name and choose DNS Manager.

2.   Right-click the DNS server name on the top left and select Properties.

3.   Switch to the Debug Logging tab, check all the debug logging options except Filter Packets By IP Address and enter a full path and filename in the File Path And Name field. Click the Apply button.

4.   Switch to the Monitoring tab and check both A Simple Query Against This DNS Server and A Recursive Query To Other DNS Servers.

5.   Click the Test Now button several times and then click OK.

6.   Press the Windows key on the keyboard (left side between the Ctrl and Alt keys) and then choose Computer. Navigate to the folder that you specified in step 3 and use Word-Pad or Notepad to view the contents of the log file.

Troubleshooting DNS

When troubleshooting DNS problems, ask yourself the following basic questions:

- What application is failing? What works? What doesn't work?

- Is the problem basic IP connectivity, or is it name resolution? If the problem is name resolution, does the failing application use NetBIOS names, DNS names, or host-names?

- How are the things that do and don't work related?

- Have the things that don't work ever worked on this computer or network? If so, what has changed since they last worked?

Windows Server 2012 R2 provides several useful tools, discussed in the following sections, which can help you answer these questions:

- Nslookup is used to perform DNS queries and to examine the contents of zone files on local and remote servers.

- DNSLint is a command-line utility used for troubleshooting many common DNS issues.

- Ipconfig allows you to perform the following tasks:

  - View DNS client settings

  - Display and flush the resolver cache

  - Force a dynamic update client to register its DNS records

- The DNS log file monitors certain DNS server events and logs them for your edification.

Using *Nslookup*

Nslookup is a standard command-line tool provided in most DNS server implementations, including Windows Server 2012 R2. Windows Server 2012 R2 gives you the ability to launch nslookup from the DNS snap-in.

> When nslookup is launched from the DNS snap-in, a command prompt window opens automatically. You enter nslookup commands in this window.

Nslookup offers you the ability to perform query testing of DNS servers and to obtain detailed responses at the command prompt. This information can be useful for diagnosing and solving name resolution problems, for verifying that resource records are added or updated correctly in a zone, and for debugging other server-related problems. You can do a number of useful things with nslookup:

- Use it in noninteractive mode to look up a single piece of data

- Enter interactive mode and use the debug feature

- Perform the following from within interactive mode:

  - Set options for your query

  - Look up a name

  - Look up records in a zone

- Perform zone transfers
- Exit nslookup

 When you are entering queries, it is generally a good idea to enter FQDNs so that you can control what name is submitted to the server. However, if you want to know which suffixes are added to unqualified names before they are submitted to the server, you can enter **nslookup** in debug mode and then enter an unqualified name.

Using *Nslookup* on the Command Line

To use nslookup in plain-old command-line mode, enter the following in the command prompt window:

    nslookup DNS_name_or_IP_address server_IP_address

This command will look up a DNS name or address using a server at the IP address you specify.

Using *Nslookup* in Interactive Mode

Nslookup is a lot more useful in interactive mode because you can enter several commands in sequence. Entering **nslookup** by itself (without specifying a query or server) puts it in interactive mode, where it will stay until you type **exit** and press Enter. Before that point, you can look up lots of useful stuff. The following are some of the tasks that you can perform with nslookup in interactive mode:

Setting Options with the set Command   While in interactive mode, you can use the set command to configure how the resolver will carry out queries. Table 12.5 shows a few of the options available with set.

TABLE 12.5 Command-line options available with the set command

Option	Purpose
set all	Shows all the options available.
set d2	Puts nslookup in debug mode so that you can examine the query and response packets between the resolver and the server.
set domain=*domain name*	Tells the resolver what domain name to append for unqualified queries.
set timeout=*timeout*	Tells the resolver how long to keep trying to contact the server. This option is useful for slow links where queries frequently time out and the wait time must be lengthened.
set type=*record type*	Tells the resolver which type of resource records to search for (for example, A, PTR, or SRV). If you want the resolver to query for all types of resource records, type **settype=all**.

Looking Up a Name   While in interactive mode, you can look up a name just by typing it: **stellacon.com**. In this example, stellacon is the owner name for the record for which you are searching, and .com is the server that you want to query.

You can use the wildcard character (*) in your query. For example, if you want to look for all resource records that have *k* as the first letter, just type **k*** as your query.

Looking Up a Record Type   If you want to query a particular type of record (for instance, an MX record), use the set type command. The command set type=mx tells nslookup that you're interested only in seeing MX records that meet your search criteria.

Listing the Contents of a Domain   To get a list of the contents of an entire domain, use the ls command. To find all the hosts in your domain, you'd type **set type=a** and then type **ls -t yourdomain.com**.

Troubleshooting Zone Transfers   You can simulate zone transfers by using the ls command with the -d switch. This can help you determine whether the server you are querying allows zone transfers to your computer. To do this, type the following: **ls -d domain_name**.

Nslookup Responses and Error Messages

A successful nslookup response looks like this:

```
Server: Name_of_DNS_server
Address: IP_address_of_DNS_server
Response_data
```

Nslookup might also return an error message. Some common messages are listed in Table 12.6.

TABLE 12.6   Common nslookup error messages

Error message	Meaning
DNS request timed out. Timeout was *x* seconds. *** Can't find server name for address *IP_Address*: Timed out *** Default servers are not available Default Server: Unknown Address: *IP_address_of_DNS_server*	The resolver did not locate a PTR resource record (containing the hostname) for the server IP address you specified. Nslookup can still query the DNS server, and the DNS server can still answer queries.
*** Request to Server timed-out	A request was not fulfilled in the allotted time. This might happen, for example, if the DNS service was not running on the DNS server that is authoritative for the name.

*** Server can't find *Name_or_IP_ address_queried_for*: `No response from server`	The server is not receiving requests on User Datagram Protocol (UDP) port 53.
*** Server can't find *Name_or_IP_ address_queried_for: `Non-existent domain`	The DNS server was unable to find the name or IP address in the authoritative domain. The authoritative domain might be on the remote DNS server or on another DNS server that this DNS server is unable to reach.
*** Server can't find *Name_or_IP_ address_queried_for*: `Server failed`	The DNS server is running, but it is not working properly. For example, it might include a corrupted packet, or the zone in which you are querying for a record might be paused. However, this message can also be returned if the client queries for a host in a domain for which the DNS server is not authoritative. You will also receive the error if the DNS server cannot contact its root servers, it is not connected to the Internet, or it has no root hints.

In Exercise 12.6, you'll get some hands-on practice with the `nslookup` tool.

EXERCISE 12.6

Using the `nslookup` Command

1. Press the Windows key on the keyboard and then choose Computer. Navigate to the `C:\Windows\System32` folder and double-click `CMD.exe`. (When you get to this file, you can right-click the file and choose Send To Desktop. The shortcut will then always be available on the desktop.)

2. Type **nslookup** and press the Enter key. (For the rest of the exercise, use the Enter key to terminate each command.)

3. Try looking up a well-known address: Type **www.microsoft.com**.

4. Try looking up a nonexistent host: Type **www.example.ccccc**. Notice that your server indicates that it can't find the address and times out. This is normal behavior.

5. Type **Exit** at the prompt. Type **Exit** again to leave the command prompt.

Using *DNSLint*

Microsoft Windows Server 2012 R2 DNS can use the DNSLint command-line utility to help diagnose some common DNS name-resolution issues and to help diagnose potential problems of incorrect delegation. You need to download DNSLint from the Microsoft Download Center.

DNSLint uses three main functions to verify DNS records and to generate a report in HTML:

dnslint /d This function helps diagnose the reasons for "lame delegation" and other related DNS problems.

dnslint /ql This function helps verify a user-defined set of DNS records on multiple DNS servers.

dnslint /ad This function helps verify DNS records pertaining to Active Directory replication.

Here is the syntax for DNSLint:

```
dnslint /d domain_name | /ad [LDAP_IP_address] | /ql input_file
[/c [smtp,pop,imap]] [/no_open] [/r report_name]
[/t] [/test_tcp] [/s DNS_IP_address] [/v] [/y]
```

The following are some sample queries:

```
dnslint /d stellacon.com
dnslint /ad /s 192.168.36.201
dnslint /ql dns_server.txt
dnslint /ql autocreate
dnslint /v /d stellacon.com
dnslint /r newfile /d stellacon.com
dnslint /y /d stellacon.com
dnslint /no_open /d stellacon.com
```

Table 12.7 explains the command options.

TABLE 12.7 DNSLint command options

Command option	Meaning
/d	Domain name that is being tested.
/ad	Resolves DNS records that are used for Active Directory forest replication.
/s	TCP/IP address of host.

/ql	Requests DNS query tests from a list. This switch sends DNS queries specified in an input file.
/v	Turns on verbose mode.
/r *filename*	Allows you to create a report file.
/y	Overwrites an existing report file without being prompted.
/no_open	Prevents a report from opening automatically.

Using *Ipconfig*

You can use the command-line tool ipconfig to view your DNS client settings, to view and reset cached information used locally for resolving DNS name queries, and to register the resource records for a dynamic update client. If you use the ipconfig command with no parameters, it displays DNS information for each adapter, including the domain name and DNS servers used for that adapter. Table 12.8 shows some command-line options available with ipconfig.

TABLE 12.8 Command-line options available for the **ipconfig** command

Command	What it does
ipconfig /all	Displays additional information about DNS, including the FQDN and the DNS suffix search list.
ipconfig /flushdns	Flushes and resets the DNS resolver cache. For more information about this option, see the section "Configuring DNS" earlier in this chapter.
ipconfig /displaydns	Displays the contents of the DNS resolver cache. For more information about this option, see "Configuring DNS" earlier in this chapter.
ipconfig /registerdns	Refreshes all DHCP leases and registers any related DNS names. This option is available only on Windows 2000 and newer computers that run the DHCP client service.

You should know and be comfortable with the ipconfig commands related to DNS for the exam.

Using *DNSCmd*

DNSCmd allows you to display and change the properties of DNS servers, zones, and resource records through the use of command-line commands. The DNSCmd utility allows you to modify, create, and delete resource records and/or zones manually, and it allows you to force replication between two DNS servers.

Table 12.9 lists some of the DNSCmd commands and their explanations.

TABLE 12.9 DNSCmd command-line options

Command	Explanation
dnscmd /clearcache	Clears the DNS server cache
dnscmd /config	Resets DNS server or zone configuration
dnscmd /createdirectorypartition	Creates a DNS application directory partition
dnscmd /deletedirectorypartition	Deletes a DNS application directory partition
dnscmd /enumrecords	Shows the resource records in a zone
dnscmd /exportsettings	Creates a text file of all server configuration information
dnscmd /info	Displays server information
dnscmd /recordadd	Adds a resource record to a zone
dnscmd /recorddelete	Deletes a resource record from a zone
dnscmd /zoneadd	Creates a new DNS zone
dnscmd /zonedelete	Deletes a DNS zone
dnscmd /zoneexport	Creates a text file of all resource records in the zone
dnscmd /zoneinfo	Displays zone information
dnscmd /zonerefresh	Forces replication of the master zone to the secondary zone

Using the DNS Log File

You can configure the DNS server to create a log file that records the following information:

- Queries
- Notification messages from other servers
- Dynamic updates
- Content of the question section for DNS query messages
- Content of the answer section for DNS query messages
- Number of queries this server sends
- Number of queries this server has received
- Number of DNS requests received over a UDP port
- Number of DNS requests received over a TCP port
- Number of full packets sent by the server
- Number of packets written through by the server and back to the zone

The DNS log appears in `systemroot\System32\dns\Dns.log`. Because the log is in RTF format, you must use WordPad or Word to view it.

Once the log file reaches the maximum size, Windows Server 2012 R2 writes over the beginning of the file. You can change the maximum size of the log. If you increase the size value, data persists for a longer time period, but the log file consumes more disk space. If you decrease the value, the log file uses less disk space, but the data persists for a shorter time period.

> **WARNING** Do not leave DNS logging turned on during normal operation because it sucks up both processing and hard disk resources. Enable it only when diagnosing and solving DNS problems.

Troubleshooting the .*(root)* Zone

The *DNS root zone* is the top-level DNS zone in the DNS hierarchy. Windows Server 2012 R2-based DNS servers will build a `.(root)` zone when a connection to the Internet can't be found.

Because of this, the `.(root)` zone may prevent access to the Internet. The DNS forwarding option and DNS root hints will not be configurable. If you want your DNS to work as a DNS forwarder or you want to use root hints, you must remove the `.(root)` zone.

Issues with Non-Microsoft DNS Servers

Another troubleshooting problem that you may run into is working with both Microsoft DNS servers and non-Microsoft DNS servers. One of the most common non-Microsoft DNS servers is the Unix-based BIND DNS server.

If you need to complete a zone transfer from Microsoft DNS to a BIND DNS server, you need to enable BIND Secondaries on the Microsoft DNS server (see Figure 12.16).

FIGURE 12.16 Enabling BIND Secondaries

If you need to enable Bind Secondaries, complete the following steps:

1. Open DNS management.

2. Right-click the server name and choose Properties.

3. Click the Advanced tab.

4. Check the Enable BIND Secondaries box.

5. Click OK.

Integrating Dynamic DNS and IPv4 DHCP

DHCP integration with Dynamic DNS is a simple concept but powerful in action. By setting up this integration, you can pass addresses to DHCP clients while still maintaining the integrity of your DNS services.

The DNS server can be updated in two ways. One way is for the DHCP client to tell the DNS server its address. Another way is for the DHCP server to tell the DNS server when it registers a new client.

Neither of these updates will take place, however, unless you configure the DNS server to use Dynamic DNS. You can make this change in two ways:

- If you change it at the scope level, it will apply only to the scope.

- If you change it at the server level, it will apply to all scopes and superscopes served by the server.

Which of these options you choose depends on how widely you want to support Dynamic DNS; most of the sites I visit have enabled DNS updates at the server level.

To update the settings at either the server or scope level, you need to open the scope or server properties by right-clicking the appropriate object and choosing Properties. The DNS tab of the Properties dialog box includes the following options:

Enable DNS Dynamic Updates According To The Settings Below   This check box controls whether this DHCP server will attempt to register lease information with a DNS server. It must be checked to enable Dynamic DNS.

> **Dynamically Update DNS A And PTR Records Only If Requested By The DHCP Clients**   This radio button (which is on by default) tells the DHCP server to register the update only if the DHCP client asks for DNS registration. When this button is active, DHCP clients that aren't hip to DDNS won't have their DNS records updated. However, Windows 2000, XP, Vista, Windows 7, Windows 8, Server 2003, Server 2008/2008 R2, and Server 2012/2012 R2 DHCP clients are smart enough to ask for the updates.

> **Always Dynamically Update DNS A And PTR Records**   This radio button forces the DHCP server to register any client to which it issues a lease. This setting may add DNS registrations for DHCP-enabled devices that don't really need them, such as print servers. However, it allows other clients (such as Mac OS, Windows NT, and Linux machines) to have their DNS information automatically updated.

Discard A And PTR Records When Lease Is Deleted   This check box has a long name but a simple function. When a DHCP lease expires, what should happen to the DNS registration? Obviously, it would be nice if the DNS record associated with a lease vanished when the lease expired. When this check box is checked (as it is by default), that's exactly what happens. If you uncheck this box, your DNS will contain entries for expired leases that are no longer valid. When a particular IP address is reissued on a new lease, the DNS will be updated, but in between leases you'll have incorrect data in your DNS—something that's always best to avoid.

Dynamically Update DNS A And PTR Records For DHCP Clients That Do Not Request Updates   This check box lets you handle these older clients graciously by making the updates using a separate mechanism.

In Exercise 12.7, you will enable a scope to participate in Dynamic DNS updates.

EXERCISE 12.7

Enabling DHCP-DNS Integration

1. Open the DHCP snap-in by selecting Administrative Tools ➢ DHCP.

2. Right-click the IPv4 item, and select Properties.

3. The Server Properties dialog box appears. Click the DNS tab.

4. Verify that the check box labeled Enable DNS Dynamic Updates According To The Settings Below is checked, and verify that the radio button labeled Dynamically Update DNS A And PTR Records Only If Requested By The DHCP Clients is selected.

5. Verify that the check box labeled Discard A And PTR Records When Lease Is Deleted is checked. If not, then check it.

6. Click the OK button to apply your changes and close the Server Properties dialog box.

Summary

DNS was designed to be a robust, scalable, and high-performance system for resolving friendly names to TCP/IP host addresses. This chapter presented an overview of the basics of DNS and how DNS names are generated. You then looked at the many new features available in the Microsoft Windows Server 2012 R2 version of DNS, and you learned how to install, configure, and manage the necessary services. Microsoft's DNS is based on a widely accepted set of industry standards. Because of this, Microsoft's DNS can work with both Windows- and non-Windows-based networks.

Exam Essentials

Understand the purpose of DNS. DNS is a standard set of protocols that defines a mechanism for querying and updating address information in the database, a mechanism for replicating the information in the database among servers, and a schema of the database.

Understand the different parts of the DNS database. The SOA record defines the general parameters for the DNS zone, including who is the authoritative server. NS records list the name servers for a domain; they allow other name servers to look up names in your domain. A host record (also called an address record or an A record) statically associates a host's name with its IP addresses. Pointer records (PTRs) map an IP address to a hostname, making it possible to do reverse lookups. Alias records allow you to use more than one name to point to a single host. The MX record tells you which servers can accept mail bound for a domain. SRV records tie together the location of a service (like a domain controller) with information about how to contact the service.

Know how DNS resolves names. With iterative queries, a client asks the DNS server for an answer, and the client, or resolver, returns the best kind of answer it has. In a recursive query, the client sends a query to one name server, asking it to respond either with the requested answer or with an error. The error states either that the server can't come up with the right answer or that the domain name doesn't exist. With inverse queries, instead of supplying a name and then asking for an IP address, the client first provides the IP address and then asks for the name.

Understand the differences among DNS servers, clients, and resolvers.   Any computer providing domain name services is a DNS server. A DNS client is any machine issuing queries to a DNS server. A resolver handles the process of mapping a symbolic name to an actual network address.

Know how to install and configure DNS.   DNS can be installed before, during, or after installing the Active Directory service. When you install the DNS server, the DNS snap-in is installed too. Configuring a DNS server ranges from easy to difficult, depending on what you're trying to make it do. In the simplest configuration, for a caching-only server, you don't have to do anything except to make sure that the server's root hints are set correctly. You can also configure a root server, a normal forward lookup server, and a reverse lookup server.

Know how to create new forward and reverse lookup zones.   You can use the New Zone Wizard to create a new forward or reverse lookup zone. The process is basically the same for both types, but the specific steps and wizard pages differ somewhat. The wizard walks you through the steps, such as specifying a name for the zone (in the case of forward lookup zones) or the network ID portion of the network that the zone covers (in the case of reverse lookup zones).

Know how to configure zones for dynamic updates.   The DNS service allows dynamic updates to be enabled or disabled on a per-zone basis at each server. This is easily done in the DNS snap-in.

Know how to delegate zones for DNS.   DNS provides the ability to divide the namespace into one or more zones; these can then be stored, distributed, and replicated to other DNS servers. When delegating zones within your namespace, be aware that for each new zone you create, you need delegation records in other zones that point to the authoritative DNS servers for the new zone.

Understand the tools that are available for monitoring and troubleshooting DNS.   You can use the DNS snap-in to do some basic server testing and monitoring. More important, you use the snap-in to monitor and set logging options. Windows Server 2012 R2 automatically logs DNS events in the event log under a distinct DNS server heading. Nslookup offers the ability to perform query testing of DNS servers and to obtain detailed responses at the command prompt. You can use the command-line tool ipconfig to view your DNS client settings, to view and reset cached information used locally for resolving DNS name queries, and to register the resource records for a dynamic update client. Finally, you can configure the DNS server to create a log file that records queries, notification messages, dynamic updates, and various other DNS information.

Review Questions

1. You are the network administrator for the ABC Company. Your network consists of two DNS servers named *DNS1* and *DNS2*. The users who are configured to use DNS2 complain because they are unable to connect to Internet websites. The following table shows the configuration of both servers:

DNS1	DNS2
_msdcs.abc.comabc.com	.(root)_msdcs.abc.comabc.com

   The users who are connected to DNS2 need to be able to access the Internet. What needs to be done?

   A. Build a new Active Directory Integrated zone on DNS2.

   B. Delete the .(root) zone from DNS2 and configure conditional forwarding on DNS2.

   C. Delete the current cache.dns file.

   D. Update your cache.dns file and root hints.

2. You are the network administrator for a large company that has one main site and one branch office. Your company has a single Active Directory forest, ABC.com. You have a single domain controller (ServerA) in the main site that has the DNS role installed. ServerA is configured as a primary DNS zone. You have decided to place a domain controller (ServerB) in the remote site and implement the DNS role on that server. You want to configure DNS so that if the WAN link fails, users in both sites can still update records and resolve any DNS queries. How should you configure the DNS servers?

   A. Configure ServerB as a secondary DNS server. Set replication to occur every 5 minutes.

   B. Configure ServerB as a stub zone.

   C. Configure ServerB as an Active Directory Integrated zone and convert ServerA to an Active Directory Integrated zone.

   D. Convert ServerA to an Active Directory Integrated zone and configure ServerB as a secondary zone.

3. You are the network administrator for a midsize computer company. You have a single Active Directory forest, and your DNS servers are configured as Active Directory Integrated zones. When you look at the DNS records in Active Directory, you notice that there are many records for computers that do not exist on your domain. You want to make sure that only domain computers register with your DNS servers. What should you do to resolve this issue?

   A. Set dynamic updates to None.

   B. Set dynamic updates to Nonsecure And Secure.

   C. Set dynamic updates to Domain Users Only.

   D. Set dynamic updates to Secure Only.

4. Your company consists of a single Active Directory forest. You have a Windows Server 2012 R2 domain controller that also has the DNS role installed. You also have a Unix-based DNS server at the same location. You need to configure your Windows DNS server to allow zone transfers to the Unix-based DNS server. What should you do?

    A. Enable BIND Secondaries.

    B. Configure the Unix machine as a stub zone.

    C. Convert the DNS server to Active Directory Integrated.

    D. Configure the Microsoft DNS server to forward all requests to the Unix DNS server.

5. You are the network administrator for Stellacon Corporation. Stellacon has two trees in its Active Directory forest, stellacon.com and abc.com. Company policy does not allow DNS zone transfers between the two trees. You need to make sure that when anyone in abc.com tries to access the stellacon.com domain, all names are resolved from the stellacon.com DNS server. What should you do?

    A. Create a new secondary zone in abc.com for stellacon.com.

    B. Configure conditional forwarding on the abc.com DNS server for stellacon.com.

    C. Create a new secondary zone in stellacon.com for abc.com.

    D. Configure conditional forwarding on the stellacon.com DNS server for abc.com.

6. You are the network administrator for your organization. A new company policy states that all inbound DNS queries need to be recorded. What can you do to verify that the IT department is compliant with this new policy?

    A. Enable Server Auditing – Object Access.

    B. Enable DNS debug logging.

    C. Enable server database query logging.

    D. Enable DNS Auditing – Object Access.

7. You are the network administrator for a small company with two DNS servers: DNS1 and DNS2. Both DNS servers reside on domain controllers. DNS1 is set up as a standard primary zone, and DNS2 is set up as a secondary zone. A new security policy was written stating that all DNS zone transfers must be encrypted. How can you implement the new security policy?

    A. Enable the Secure Only setting on DNS1.

    B. Enable the Secure Only setting on DNS2.

    C. Configure Secure Only on the Zone Transfers tab for both servers.

    D. Delete the secondary zone on DNS2. Convert both DNS servers to use Active Directory Integrated zones.

8. You are responsible for DNS in your organization. You look at the DNS database and see a large number of older records on the server. These records are no longer valid. What should you do?

    A. In the zone properties, enable Zone Aging and Scavenging.

    B. In the server properties, enable Zone Aging and Scavenging.

    C. Manually delete all of the old records.

    D. Set Dynamic Updates to None.

9. Your IT team has been informed by the compliance team that they need copies of the DNS Active Directory Integrated zones for security reasons. You need to give the Compliance department a copy of the DNS zone. How should you accomplish this goal?

    A. Run **dnscmd /zonecopy**.

    B. Run **dnscmd /zoneinfo**.

    C. Run **dnscmd /zoneexport**.

    D. Run **dnscmd /zonefile**.

10. You are the network administrator for a Windows Server 2012 R2 network. You have multiple remote locations connected to your main office by slow satellite links. You want to install DNS into these offices so that clients can locate authoritative DNS servers in the main location. What type of DNS servers should be installed in the remote locations?

    A. Primary DNS zones

    B. Secondary DNS zones

    C. Active Directory Integrated zones

    D. Stub zones

Chapter

13

Configure Routing and Remote Access

THE FOLLOWING 70-411 EXAM OBJECTIVES ARE COVERED IN THIS CHAPTER:

✓ **Configure VPN and routing**

- Install and configure the Remote Access role
- Implement Network Address Translation (NAT)
- Configure VPN settings
- Configure remote dial-in settings for users
- Configure routing
- Configure Web Application proxy in passthrough mode

✓ **Configure DirectAccess**

- Implement server requirements
- Implement client configuration
- Configure DNS for DirectAccess
- Configure certificates for DirectAccess

Now that you understand how routing works, it's time to discuss how clients connect using remote access. *Routing and Remote Access Services (RRAS)* includes some security features necessary to provide remote access effectively. For example, you'll probably want the ability to restrict user dial-up access by group membership, time of day, or other factors. You'll also need a way to specify the various callback, authentication, and encryption options that the protocols support.

In this chapter, you'll learn about *virtual private networks (VPNs),* which provide remote access to private networks across public connections. That is, using the Internet, clients can dial in to an Internet service provider (ISP) and connect to your private network. The main benefit of VPNs is reduced cost because it means that long-distance calls are unnecessary. VPNs are becoming more popular because of the increased popularity of high-speed Internet connections, such as cable and digital subscriber line (DSL) connections.

Many of the features included in Windows Server 2012 R2 are simply carried over from Windows Server 2008, with a few minor additions. This is the case with the Routing and Remote Access console.

Before I can get into the details of what these features do and how to configure them to provide remote access for your network, you need to understand some of the terms and concepts specific to RRAS. That's where you'll begin in this chapter, and then you'll move on to learning about the features and configuration settings that you need to understand to meet the exam objectives.

Overview of Dial-Up Networking

LANs provide relatively high-speed connectivity to attached machines, but where does that leave those of us who work from home, who travel, or who need to access data on a remote computer? Until wireless access is available worldwide, we have the option of using dial-up networking in which the client computer uses a modem to dial in and connect to a remote server. Once the connection is established, a variety of protocols and services make it possible for us to view web pages, transfer files and email, and do pretty much anything we could do with a hardwired LAN connection, albeit at a reduced speed.

In the following sections, you will learn more about what dial-up networking does and how it works by examining the specific technologies and protocols associated with remote access.

What DUN Does

At this point in the book, you should understand that Windows Server 2012 R2 network protocols are actually implemented as drivers. These drivers normally work with hardware network interfaces to get data from point A to point B. How do dial-up connections fit in? Many people may read this and say, "Who still uses dial-up?" Well, as a person who lives in New Hampshire, I can tell you that we still have many areas that can't get broadband or even satellite access.

Think back to the OSI model. Each layer has a function, and each layer serves as an intermediary between the layer above it and the one below it. By substituting one driver for another at some level in the stack, you can dramatically change how things work. That's exactly what the Windows Server 2012 R2's *Dial-Up Networking (DUN)* subsystem does. It makes the dial-up connection appear to be just another network adapter.

The DUN driver takes care of the task of making a slow asynchronous modem appear to work just like a fast LAN interface. Applications and services that use TCP/IP on your DUN connection never know the difference. In fact, you can configure Windows Server 2012 R2 to use your primary connection first and then to pass traffic over a secondary connection (such as a dial-up link) if the primary connection is down. This does not affect the applications with which you're working (except that they might run more slowly).

On the server side, DUN allows you to host one or more network users who dial into your Windows Server 2012 R2 machine. Windows XP Professional, Windows Vista, Windows 7, and Windows 8 all allow up to 10 concurrent dial-up connections, and Windows Server 2012 R2 allows up to 255. (Be aware that by the time you allow 255 concurrent connections, you'll probably be overloading your server.)

Depending on how you configure the DUN server, users who dial in can see the whole network or only specific resources on the server. You also get to control who can log on, when they can log on, and what they can do once they've logged on. As far as Windows Server 2012 R2 is concerned, a user connected via DUN is no different from one using resources over your LAN, so all the access controls and permissions you apply remain in force for DUN users.

How DUN Works

A lot of pieces are required to complete a dial-up call successfully from your computer to a server at another physical location. Understanding what these pieces are, how they work, and what they do for you is important. The following sections will cover the DUN infrastructure, how the *Point-to-Point Protocol (PPP)* helps with this connection, the relationship between PPP and the network protocols, and how multilink can be used to increase the speed and efficiency of your remote connections.

The DUN Infrastructure

This section covers the physical layer that underlies voice and data calls. Most of the following material will be familiar to anyone who has ever used a modem, but you should still understand the details you may not have considered before.

Plain Old Telephone Service

Plain Old Telephone Service (POTS) connections offer a theoretical maximum speed of 56Kbps; in practice, many users routinely get connections at 51Kbps or 52Kbps.

The word *modem* is actually short for *modulator-demodulator*. The original Bell System modems took digital data and modulated it into screechy analog audio tones suitable for use on regular phone lines. Because phone lines are purposely designed to pass only the low end of the audible frequency range that most can hear, the amount of data was limited. However, in the early 1990s, an engineer discovered that you could communicate much faster when the path between the sender and receiver was all digital.

An all-digital path doesn't have any analog components that induce signal loss, so it preserves the original signal quality faithfully. This in turn makes it possible to put more information into the original signal. As it happens, phone companies nationwide were in the process of making major upgrades to replace their analog equipment with newer and better digital equivalents. These upgrades made it possible for people in most areas to get almost 56Kbps speeds without changing any of the wiring in their homes or offices. The connection between the house and the phone office was still analog, but the connections between phone offices were digital, ensuring high-quality connections.

Integrated Services Digital Network

In the mid-1970s, *Integrated Services Digital Network (ISDN)* was designed. At the time, no one had any idea that you'd be able to get 56Kbps speeds out of an ordinary phone line. ISDN speeds of up to 128Kbps over a single pair of copper wires seemed pretty revolutionary. In addition, ISDN had features such as call forwarding, caller ID, and multiple directory numbers (so you could have more than one number, perhaps with different ringing patterns, associated with a single line).

Unfortunately, ISDN requires an all-digital signal path. It also requires special equipment on both ends of the connection. The phone companies were slow to promote ISDN as a faster alternative to regular dial-up service, so customers avoided it.

ISDN still has some advantages, though. Because it's all digital, call setup times are much shorter than they are for analog modems—it takes only about half a second to establish a new ISDN call. Modern ISDN adapters and ISDN-capable routers can seamlessly stitch together multiple ISDN channels to deliver bandwidth in 64Kbps increments. Because you can use ISDN lines for regular analog voice, data, and fax traffic, you can make a single ISDN act like two voice lines, a single 128Kbps data line, or a 64Kbps data line plus a voice line.

ISDN is quickly being replaced by faster broadband services such as DSL and cable modems. In fact, you should resort to ISDN only if these other solutions are not available in your area. Note that DSL (a misnomer because they are all digital) and cable modems do not use PPP (discussed later), so they are technically not considered dial-up connections.

Other Connection Methods

Any other on-demand connection that's established using the Point-to-Point Protocol can be thought of as a dial-up connection, and Windows Server 2012 R2 doesn't make any distinction between POTS, ISDN, and other dial-ups—they're all treated identically.

Connecting with PPP

The Point-to-Point Protocol enables any two devices to establish a TCP/IP connection over a serial link. That usually means a dial-up modem connection, but it could just as easily be a direct serial cable connection, an infrared connection, or any other type of serial connection. When one machine dials another, the machine that initiates the connection is referred to as a *client*, and the machine that receives the call is referred to as a *server*—even though PPP itself makes no such distinction.

PPP negotiation involves three phases that are required to establish a remote access connection. Actually, at least six distinct protocols run on top of PPP. Understanding what they do helps to make the actual PPP negotiation process clearer. These protocols are as follows:

The Link Control Protocol   The *Link Control Protocol (LCP)* handles the details of establishing and configuring the lowest-level PPP link. In that regard, you can think of LCP as if it were almost part of the Physical layer. When one PPP device calls another, the devices use LCP to agree that they want to establish a PPP connection.

The Challenge Handshake Authentication Protocol   *The Challenge Handshake Authentication Protocol (CHAP)*—as well as MS-CHAPv2 and PAP—allow the client to authenticate itself to the server. This authentication functions much like a regular network logon; once the client presents its logon credentials, the server can figure out what access to grant.

The Callback Control Protocol   The *Callback Control Protocol (CBCP)* is used to negotiate whether a callback is required, whether it's permitted, and when it happens. Once the client has authenticated itself, the server can decide whether it should hang up and call the client back. The client can also request a callback at a number it provides. Although this isn't as secure as having the server place a call to a predetermined number, it provides some additional flexibility. If a callback occurs, the connection is reestablished and reauthenticated, but the CBCP stage is skipped.

The Compression Control Protocol   The *Compression Control Protocol (CCP)* allows the two sides of the connection to determine what kind of compression, if any, they want to use on the network data. Because PPP traffic actually consists of wrapped-up IP datagrams and because IP datagram headers tend to be fairly compressible, negotiating effective compression can significantly improve overall PPP throughput.

The IP Control Protocol   At this point in the call, the two sides have agreed to authentication, compression, and a callback. They haven't yet agreed on what IP parameters to use for the connection. These parameters, which include the maximum packet size to be sent over the link (the *maximum transmission unit*, or *MTU*), have a great impact on the overall link performance, so the client and server use the *IP Control Protocol (IPCP)* to negotiate them based on the traffic they expect to be passed.

The Internet Protocol   Once the IPCP negotiation has been completed, each end has complete knowledge of how to communicate with its peer. That knowledge allows the two sides to begin exchanging Internet Protocol (IP) datagrams over the link, just as they would over a standard LAN connection.

The Relationship Between PPP and Network Protocols

Usually, when you hear about network communication, you hear about using TCP/IP on a hardwired LAN. How does this protocol fit in with PPP? In the case of TCP/IP, that's an easy question to answer: The client routes all (or some) of its outgoing TCP/IP traffic to its PPP peer, which can then inspect the IP datagrams it gets back from the PPP stack to analyze and route them properly.

Windows Server 2012 R2 supports only TCP/IP, so consider what has to happen when a client using AppleTalk needs to connect via dial-up. Because the server will not use those other protocols, it will drop the call or cause the client to warn its user (that's what Windows Server 2012 R2 does). After the other PPP setup steps are finished, the client and server can wrap other types of network traffic inside an IP datagram. This process, called *encapsulation*, allows the client to take a packet with some kind of private content, wrap it inside an IP datagram, and send it to the server. The server, in turn, processes the IP datagram, routing real datagrams normally and handling any encapsulated packets with the appropriate protocol. At that point, the client can communicate with the server without knowing that its non-TCP/IP packets are being encapsulated in any way—that detail is hidden deep in the layers of the OSI model.

Understanding the Benefits of Multilink

Many parts of the world don't have high-speed broadband access yet. In fact, many places don't have ISDN or even phone lines that support 56Kbps modems. The *multilink extensions* to the Point-to-Point Protocol provide a way to take several independent PPP connections and make them look like one line so that they act as a single connection.

For example, if you use two phone lines and modems to place a two-line multilink call to your ISP, instead of getting the usual 48Kbps connection, you would end up with an apparent bandwidth of 96Kbps. The multilink PPP software on your Windows Server 2012 R2 machine and on the ISP's router takes care of stringing all of the packets together to make this process seamless. Windows Server 2012's RRAS supports multilink PPP for inbound and outbound calls.

The primary drawback to multilink calls is that they take up more than one phone line apiece.

Overview of Virtual Private Networks

Private networks offer superior security. You own the wires, so you have control over what they're used for, who can use them, and what kind of data passes over them. However, they're not very flexible because they require you to configure and manage costly leased lines between remote locations. To make things worse, most private networks face a dilemma: Implementing enough capacity to handle peak loads almost guarantees that much of that capacity will remain idle much of the time, even though it still has to be paid for.

One way to work around this problem is to maintain private dial-up services. Such services allow, for example, a field rep in Chicago to dial into the home office in Boston. But dial-ups are expensive, and they have the same excess capacity problem as truly private networks. As an added detriment, someone has to pay long-distance or toll-free number charges.

Virtual private networks (VPNs) offer a solution. You get the security of a true private network with the flexibility, ubiquity, and low cost of the Internet. In the following sections, I will cover VPNs, including what they are used for and how they work (in general and with Windows Server 2012).

What VPNs Do

At any time, two parties can create a connection over the Internet. The idea behind a VPN is that you can use these connections to let two parties establish an *encrypted tunnel* between them using the Internet as a transportation medium. The VPN software on each end takes care of encrypting the VPN packets as they go; when the packets leave one end of the tunnel, their payloads are encrypted and encapsulated inside regular IP packets that cause them to be delivered to the remote machine. Figure 13.1 shows one way to conceptualize this process.

FIGURE 13.1   Drilling a tunnel through the Internet

As an example, let's say you're in the field at a client site. As long as you're somewhere that your ISP serves, you can dial into the client's local point of presence and get connected to the Internet. At that point, you can open a VPN connection back to the servers at your office and do whatever you could do when sitting in front of a regular desktop machine.

VPNs and Windows Server 2012 R2

Windows Server 2012 R2 includes support for Microsoft's proprietary *Point-to-Point Tunneling Protocol* and Layer 2 Tunneling Protocol. *Layer 2 Tunneling Protocol (L2TP)* provides a more generic tunneling mechanism than PPTP, and when combined with IPsec, L2TP also allows you to establish VPNs using a wide range of Microsoft or non-Microsoft hardware and software products, including routers and access devices from companies such as Cisco, Red Creek, and Nortel.

Windows Server 2012 R2's VPN support includes the following worthwhile features:

- You can set up account lockout policies for dial-up and VPN users. This capacity has existed for network and console users for some time.

- The *Extensible Authentication Protocol (EAP)* allows Microsoft or third parties to write modules that implement new authentication methods and retrofit them to servers. One example is the EAP-TLS module, which implements access control based on smart cards and certificates for VPN and dial-up users.

How you enable VPN support on your Windows Server 2012 R2 machine depends on whether you're using a server or a client (Windows XP, Windows Vista, Windows 7, Windows 8, and so on).

Client configuration is easy. Just install the Dial-Up Networking service and then use the Make New Connection Wizard to create a new VPN connection. On the server side, you'll need to install and configure RRAS and then enable it to accept incoming VPN connections.

How VPNs Work

The VPN client assumes that the VPN server is already connected to the Internet in some way. Here's how the VPN connection process works:

1. The client establishes a connection to the Internet. Dial-up networking or any other connection method can be used for this connection. The client must be able to send packets to the Internet.

2. The client sends a VPN connection request to the server. The exact format of the request varies, depending on whether the VPN is using PPTP, L2TP, or SSTP.

3. The client authenticates itself to the server. Again, the exact process varies according to the VPN protocol in use. If the client can't provide valid credentials, the connection is terminated.

4. The client and server negotiate parameters for the VPN session. This negotiation allows the two ends to agree on an encryption algorithm and strength.

5. The client and server go through the PPP negotiation process because both L2TP and PPTP depend on the lower-level PPP.

Because the contents of data passed around in step 2 and step 3 vary according to the tunneling protocol in use, I'll explain the differences. First, though, you should understand encapsulation and how VPNs use it to wrap one kind of data inside another.

An Encapsulation Primer

Most of yesterday's networks could carry only one kind of data. Each network vendor had its own protocol, and most of the time there was no way to intermingle data using different protocols on the same line. Over time, vendors began to find ways to allow a single network to carry many different types of traffic, resulting in the current assortment of traffic types found on most large networks. However, the Internet works only with IP, which is why it's called *Internet Protocol*. If you need to send other types of traffic, such as AppleTalk, across the Internet, you can encapsulate it within IP.

How does encapsulation work? Software at each level of the OSI model has to see header information to figure out where a packet is coming from and where it's going. However, the payload contents aren't important to most of those components, and the payload is what's encapsulated. By fabricating the right kind of header and prepending it for whatever you want in the payload, you can route foreign traffic types through IP networks with no trouble.

VPNs depend on encapsulation because their security method depends on being able to keep the payload information encrypted. The following steps demonstrate what happens to a typical packet as it goes from being a regular IP datagram to a PPTP packet (see Figure 13.2).

FIGURE 13.2   The encapsulation process

1. An application creates a block of data bound for a remote host. In this case, it's a web browser.

2. The client-side IP stack takes the application's data and turns it into an IP packet, first by adding a TCP header and then by adding an IP header. This is called the *IP datagram* because it contains all of the necessary addressing information to be delivered by IP.

3. The client is connected via PPP, so it adds a PPP header to the IP datagram. This PPP+IP combination is called a *PPP frame*.

4. If you are using PPP instead of a VPN protocol, the packet goes across the PPP link without further modification. When you are using a VPN (as in this example), the next step is for the VPN to encrypt the PPP frame, turning it into unreadable information to be transported over the Internet.

5. A *Generic Routing Encapsulation (GRE) header* is combined with the encrypted payload. GRE really is generic; in this case, the protocol ID field in the GRE header says that this is an encapsulated PPTP packet.

6. Now that there is a tag to tell you what's in the payload, the PPTP stack can add an IP header (specifying the destination address of the VPN server) and a PPP header.

7. Now the packet can be sent out over your PPP connection. The IP header specifies that it should be routed to the VPN server.

8. When the packet arrives at the VPN server, the server reverses steps 1 through 6 to extract the payload.

Encapsulation allows the use of VPN data inside ordinary-looking IP datagrams, which is part of what makes VPNs so powerful—you don't have to change any of your applications, routers, or network components (unless they have to be configured to recognize and pass GRE packets).

PPTP Tunneling

PPTP is a pretty straightforward protocol. It works by encapsulating packets using the mechanism described in the previous section, "An Encapsulation Primer," and performs encryption (step 4) using the *Microsoft Point-to-Point Encryption (MPPE) algorithm*. The encryption keys used to encrypt the packets are generated dynamically for each connection; in fact, the keys can be changed periodically during the connection.

When the client and server have successfully established a PPTP tunnel, the authorization process begins. This process is an exchange of credentials that allows the server to decide whether the client is permitted to connect:

1. The server sends a challenge message to the client.

2. The client answers with an encrypted response.

3. The server checks the response to see whether the answer is right. The challenge-response process allows the server to determine which account is trying to make a connection.

4. The server determines whether the user account is authorized to make a connection.

5. If the account is authorized, the server accepts the inbound connection; any access controls or remote access restrictions still apply.

L2TP/IPsec Tunneling

L2TP is much more flexible than PPTP, but it's also more complicated. It was designed to be a general-purpose tunneling protocol not limited to VPN use.

L2TP itself doesn't offer any kind of security. When you use L2TP, you're setting up an unencrypted, unauthenticated tunnel. Using L2TP by itself over the Internet, therefore, would be dangerous because anyone who wanted to could read your traffic.

The overall flow of an L2TP/IPsec tunnel session looks a little different from that of a PPTP session because IPsec security is different. Here's how the L2TP/IPsec combination works:

1. The client and server establish an IPsec security association using the ISAKMP and Oakley protocols. At this point, the two machines have an encrypted channel between them.

2. The client builds a new L2TP tunnel to the server. Because this happens after the channel has been encrypted, there's no security risk.

3. The server sends an authentication challenge to the client.

4. The client encrypts its answer to the challenge and returns it to the server.

5. The server checks the challenge response to see whether it's valid; if so, the server can determine which account is connecting. At this point, the server can accept the inbound connection, subject to whatever access policies you've put in place.

Note that steps 3 through 5 mirror the steps described for PPTP tunneling. This is because the authorization process is a function of the remote access server, not the VPN stack. All the VPN does is to provide a secure communications channel, and something else has to decide who gets to use it.

SSTP Tunneling

The *Secure Sockets Tunneling Protocol (SSTS)* is a secure way to make a VPN connection using the Secure Sockets Layer v.3 (SSL) port 443. The following steps show how SSTP operates and functions:

1. The client connects to the server through the Internet using port 443.

2. During the TCP session, SSL negotiation takes place.

3. During the SSL authentication phase, the client machine receives the server certificate.

4. The client machine will send HTTPS requests on top of the encrypted SSL session.

5. The client machine will then also send SSTP control packets on top of the HTTPS session.

6. PPP negotiation now takes place on both ends of the connection.

7. After PPP is finished, both ends are ready to send IP packets to each other.

Configuring Your Remote Access Server

Most of the configuration necessary for a remote access server happens at the server level. You use the server's Properties dialog box to control whether the server allows remote connections, what protocols and options it supports, and so forth. Because all of the protocols are carried via PPP, you can set some generic PPP options as well. I will cover these options in the following sections. You also have to configure settings for your users, which you'll read about in the next section, and you will install and configure the Remote Access role for the server in the first exercise.

Configuring PPP Options

You can use the PPP tab of the RRAS server's Properties dialog box (see Figure 13.3) to control the PPP layer options available to clients that call in. The settings you specify here control whether the related PPP options are available to clients; you can use remote access policies to control whether individual connections can use them.

FIGURE 13.3   The PPP tab of the RRAS server's Properties dialog box

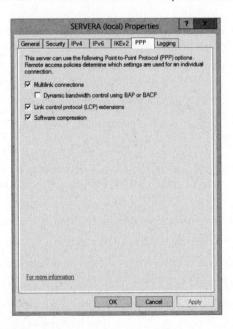

This tab has four check boxes:

- The Multilink Connections check box, which is selected by default, controls whether the server will allow clients to establish multilink connections when they call in.

- The Dynamic Bandwidth Control Using BAP Or BACP check box determines whether clients and servers are allowed to add or remove links dynamically during a multilink session. If you enable this feature, you can throttle the amount of available bandwidth up or down on demand. It's available only when the Multilink Connections check box is selected. (BAP stands for Bandwidth Allocation Protocol, and BACP stands for Bandwidth Allocation Control Protocol.)

- The Link Control Protocol (LCP) is used to establish a PPP link and negotiate its settings. A variety of LCP extensions are defined in various RFCs; these extensions allow a client and server to agree dynamically about which protocols are being passed back and forth, among other things. The Link Control Protocol (LCP) Extensions check box controls whether these extensions are available. Windows 9*x*, NT, 2000, Vista, XP, Windows 7, and Windows 8 clients depend on the LCP extensions, so you should leave this check box selected.

- The Software Compression check box controls whether RRAS will allow a remote client to use the Compression Control Protocol (CCP) to compress PPP traffic. In some cases, hardware compression at the modem level is more efficient, but not everyone has a compression-capable modem. You should leave this check box selected as well.

Configuring IP-Based Connections

TCP/IP is far and away the most commonly used remote access protocol; coincidentally, it's also the most configurable of the protocols that Windows Server 2012 R2 supports. Both of these facts are reflected in the IPv4 and IPv6 tabs of the server's Properties dialog box. Figure 13.4 shows the IPv4 tab.

FIGURE 13.4 The IPv4 tab of the RRAS server's Properties dialog box

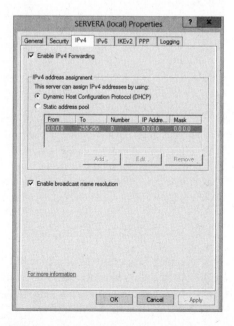

The controls on the IPv4 tab do the following:

- The Enable IPv4 Forwarding check box controls whether RRAS will route IPv4 packets between the remote client and other interfaces on your RRAS server. When this box is checked, as it is by default, remote clients' packets can go to the RRAS server or to any other host to which the RRAS server has a route. To allow clients to access resources on the RRAS server only, uncheck this box.

- The IP Address Assignment control group lets you specify how you want remote clients to get their IP addresses. The default settings here depend on what you told the RRAS Setup Wizard during setup:
    - If you want to use a DHCP server on your network as the source of IP addresses for remote clients, select the Dynamic Host Configuration Protocol (DHCP) radio button and make sure that you have the DHCP relay agent installed and running.
    - If you'd rather use static address allocation, select the Static Address Pool radio button. Then, in the list below, specify which IP address ranges you want issued to clients.
    - The Enable Broadcast Name Resolution option allows remote clients to resolve TCP/IP names without the use of a WINS or DNS server. This feature is enabled by default, and it is new for Windows Server 2012.

Figure 13.5 shows the IPv6 tab of the RRAS server's Properties dialog box. The controls on the IPv6 tab do the following:

FIGURE 13.5 The IPv6 tab of the RRAS Server's Properties dialog box

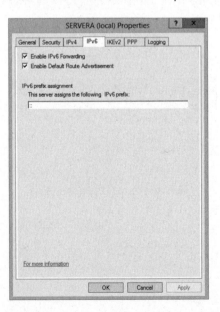

- The Enable IPv6 Forwarding check box controls whether RRAS will route IPv6 packets between the remote client and other interfaces on your RRAS server. When this box is checked, as it is by default, remote clients' packets can go to the RRAS server

or to any other host to which the RRAS server has a route. To allow clients to access resources on the RRAS server only, uncheck this box.

- The Enable Default Route Advertisement check box (enabled by default) makes the *Border Gateway Protocol (BGP)* routing protocol available. BGP can exchange routing information between Windows Server 2012 R2 routers. When this box is checked, your Windows Server 2012 R2 router can announce its route to other routers.

- On the IPv6 tab, you can also set up your IPv6 prefix assignment (assigning IPv6 prefixes were discussed in Chapter 9).

In Exercise 13.1, I will show you how to install and configure the Remote Access role onto your server. Just like many of our installations, you will use Server Manager to install the Remote Access role. This role also installs the DirectAccess role onto your server.

EXERCISE 13.1

Installing the Remote Access Role

1. Open Server Manager.

2. On the Server Manager dashboard, click the Add Roles And Features link (number 2).

3. If a Before You Begin screen appears, click Next.

4. On the Selection type page, choose a role-based or feature-based installation and click Next.

5. Click the top radio button, Select A Server From The Server Pool, and choose the server in the Server Pool section. Click Next.

6. On the Select Server Roles screen, click the Remote Access check box. If a pop-up window appears telling you that you need to add features, click the Add Features button. Click Next.

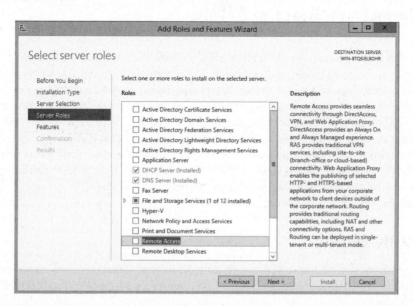

7. On the Add Features page, click Next.

8. On the Remote Access page, click Next.

9. On the Select role services page, choose the first two check boxes: DirectAccess and VPN (RAS) and Routing. If a pop-up window appears telling you that you need to add additional features, click the Add Features button. Click Next.

10. At the Web Server Role (IIS) page, click Next.

11. At the Select Role Services page, click Next.

12. At the Confirmation screen, click the Install button.

13. Open the Routing and Remote Access MMC in Administrative Tools.

14. Right-click your server name and choose Configure And Enable Routing And Remote Access.

15. At the Welcome Screen, click Next.

16. Choose the Custom Configuration radio button. Click Next.

17. Choose VPN access. Click Next.

18. Click Finish at the Completing screen.

19. Click the Start Service button.

Understanding a VPN

Conventional dial-up access works well, but as you saw earlier, it can be expensive to implement, painful to manage, and extremely slow by today's standards. VPNs offer a way around these problems by providing low initial and ongoing costs, easy management, and excellent speeds (depending on your connection). Windows Server 2012's RRAS component includes two complete VPN implementations: one using Microsoft's PPTP and one using a combination of the Internet-standard IPsec protocol and L2TP or SSTP.

The basic process of setting up a VPN is simple, but you need to think some things through before plunging ahead. Getting the VPN installation right may require small hardware or networking changes plus proper configuration of the VPN service. You will look at this process in the following sections.

How VPN Works

A VPN sits between your internal network and the Internet, accepting connections from clients in the outside world. In Figure 13.6, clients 1 and 2 are using different ISPs (probably because they're at different physical locations). For example, a packet from client 1 goes from its computer to its ISP and then through some route, unknown to you, that eventually delivers it to the VPN server, which transforms it into a packet suitable for use on the internal network.

Imagine a line around the internal network, and think of it as a security boundary. In general, you'll want your VPN server to be outside any firewalls or network security measures that you have in place. The most common configuration is to use two NICs: one connects to the Internet, and the other connects either to the private network or to an

FIGURE 13.6 VPNs provide private connections between clients and servers across the Internet

intermediate network that itself connects to the private network. Of course, you can use any type of Internet connection you want for the VPN server, such as cable modem, DSL, T1, satellite, or whatever.

The point behind giving the VPN its own network adapter is that your VPN clients need a public IP address to which they can connect, and you probably don't want them calling directly into your internal network. That also means that things will be easiest for your VPN users if the IP address for your VPN server's external interface is statically assigned so that it won't be changing on them when they least expect it.

Enabling RRAS as a VPN

If you're already using RRAS for IP routing or remote access, you can enable it as a VPN server without reinstalling.

The General tab of the server's Properties dialog box allows you to specify whether your RRAS server is a router, a remote access server, or both. The first step in converting your existing RRAS server to handle VPN traffic is to make sure that the IPv4 Remote Access Server or IPv6 Remote Access Server check box is selected on this tab.

Making this change requires you to stop and restart the RRAS service, but that's OK because the snap-in will do it for you. Then you must configure VPN ports, as shown in the following sections.

Configuring a VPN

VPN configuration is extremely simple, at least for PPTP. Either a server can accept VPN calls or it can't. If it can, it will have a certain number of VPN ports, all of which are configured identically. You don't have to change or tweak much to get a VPN server set up, but you can adjust a few things as you like.

Configuring VPN Ports

The biggest opportunity to configure your VPN server is to adjust the number and kind of VPN ports available for clients to use. You can enable or disable either PPTP or L2TP, depending on what you want your remote users to be able to access. You accomplish this through the Ports Properties dialog box.

For conventional remote access servers, this dialog box shows you a list of hardware ports, but for servers that support VPN connections, there are two WAN Miniport device selections: one for PPTP and one for L2TP. (These aren't really devices; they're actually virtual ports maintained by RRAS for accepting VPN connections.) You configure these ports by selecting one and clicking the Configure button, which displays the Configure Device – WAN Miniport (PPTP) dialog box (see Figure 13.7).

FIGURE 13.7 The Configure Device – WAN Miniport (PPTP) dialog box

Three controls are pertinent to a VPN configuration:

- The Remote Access Connections (Inbound Only) check box must be activated in order to accept VPN connections with this port type. To disable a VPN type (for instance, if you want to turn off L2TP), uncheck this box.

- The Demand-Dial Routing Connections (Inbound And Outbound) check box controls whether this VPN type can be used for demand-dial connections. By default, this box is checked; you'll need to uncheck it if you don't want to use VPN connections to link your network with other networks.

- The Maximum Ports control lets you set the number of inbound connections that this port type will support. By default, you get 5 PPTP and 5 L2TP ports when you install RRAS; you can use from 0 to 250 ports of each type by adjusting the number here.

You can also use the Phone Number For This Device field to enter the IP address of the public interface to which VPN clients connect. You might want to do this if your remote access policies accept or reject connections based on the number called by the client. Because you can assign multiple IP addresses to a single adapter, you can control VPN traffic by throttling which clients can connect to which addresses through a policy.

Troubleshooting VPNs

The two primary problems you might encounter with VPN are as follows:

- Inability to establish a connection at all
- Inability to reach some needed resource once connected

There's a lot of common ground between the process of troubleshooting a VPN connection and the process of troubleshooting an ordinary remote access connection.

The following are some extremely simple—but sometimes overlooked—things to check when your VPN clients can't connect. First, make sure your clients can make the underlying connection to their ISP; then, check the following:

- Is RRAS installed and configured on the server?
    - Is the server configured to allow remote access? Check the General tab of the server's Properties dialog box.
    - Is the server configured to allow VPN traffic? Check the Ports Properties dialog box to make sure that the appropriate VPN protocol is enabled and that the number of ports for that protocol is greater than 0.
    - Are there any available VPN ports? If you have 10 L2TP ports allocated, the 11th caller will not be able to connect.

- Do the client and server match?
    - Is the VPN protocol used by the client enabled on the server? Windows 2000 and newer clients will try L2TP first and switch to PPTP as a second choice. However, clients on other OSs (including Windows NT) can normally expect L2TP, PPTP, or SSTP (2008 or higher).

- Are the client and server authenticated correctly?
    - Are the username and password correct?
    - Does the user account in question have remote access permissions, either directly on the account or through a policy?
    - Do the authentication settings in the server's policies (if any) match the supported set of authentication protocols?

If you check all of the simple stuff and find nothing wrong, it's time to move on to checking more complex issues. These tend to affect more than one user, as opposed to the simple (and generally user-specific) issues just outlined. The problems include the following:

Policy Problems   If you're using a native-mode Windows Server 2012 R2 domain and you're using policies, those policies may cause some subtle problems that show up under some circumstances:

- Are there any policies whose Allow or Deny settings conflict with each other? Remember that all conditions of all policies must match to gain user access; if any condition of any policy fails or if there are any policies that deny access, the connection will be denied.
- Does the user match all of the necessary conditions that are in place, such as time and date?

Network Problems   If you're using dynamic IP addressing, are there any addresses left in the pool? If the VPN server can't assign an address, it won't accept the connection.

Domain Problems   Windows Server 2012 R2 RRAS servers can coexist with Windows NT RRAS servers, and both of them can interoperate with RADIUS servers from Microsoft and other vendors. Sometimes, though, this interoperation doesn't work exactly as you'd expect. Here are some questions to ask:

- Is the RRAS server's domain membership correct? Your RRAS servers don't have to be domain members unless you want to use native-mode features such as remote access policies.
- If you're in a domain, are the server's group memberships correct? The server account must be a member of the RAS group and Internet Authentication Servers security group.

Managing Your Remote Access Server

RRAS server management is generally pretty easy because, in most cases, there's not much to manage. You set up the server, and it answers calls. You'll probably find it necessary to monitor the server's ongoing activity, however, and you may find it necessary to log activity for accounting or security purposes.

You can monitor your server's activity in a number of ways, including having the server keep local copies of its logs or having it send logging data to a remote RADIUS server. In addition, you can monitor the current status of any of the ports on your system.

Microsoft's documentation distinguishes between event logging, which records significant things that happen such as the RRAS service starting up and shutting down, and authentication and accounting logging, which tracks things like when a user logged on and logged off. The settings for both types of logging are intermingled in the RRAS snap-in.

Managing Remote Users with a RADIUS Server

Remote Authentication Dial-In User Service (RADIUS) allows for maintaining and managing your remote users. A RADIUS server allows Remote Access Service (RAS) clients and dial-up routers to be authenticated.

Network Policy Server (NPS) is Microsoft's implementation of a RADIUS server in Windows Server 2012. NPS is replacing Windows Server 2003 Internet Authentication Service (IAS). NPS, working as a RADIUS server, allows for authentication, authorization, and accounting for wireless and VPN networks.

NPS allows a server to perform the duties of a RADIUS proxy. A RADIUS proxy allows the routing of RADIUS messages between RADIUS clients (RAS) and RADIUS servers. NPS also gives you the ability to record information about forwarded messages in an accounting log.

Monitoring Overall Activity

The Server Status node in the RRAS snap-in shows you a summary of all the RRAS servers known to the system. When you select the Server Status item, the right pane of the MMC will list each known RRAS server. Each entry in the list tells you whether the server is up, what kind of server it is, how many ports it has, how many ports are currently in use, and how long the server has been up. You can right-click any Windows Server 2012 R2 RRAS server in this view to start, stop, restart, pause, or resume its RRAS service; disable RRAS on the server; or remove the server's advertisement from Active Directory (provided, of course, that you're using Active Directory).

Controlling Remote Access Logging

A standard RRAS installation will always log some data locally, but that's pretty useless unless you know what gets logged and where it goes. Each RRAS server on your network has its own set of logs, which you manage through the Remote Access Logging folder. Within that folder, you'll usually see a single item labeled *Local File*, which is the log file stored on that particular server.

If you don't have Windows accounting or Windows authentication turned on, you won't have a local log file. Depending on whether you're using RADIUS accounting and logging, you may see additional entries.

Setting Server Logging Properties

You can control server logging at the server level. You use the Logging tab to control what level of detail you want in the server's event log.

These controls regulate all logging by RRAS, not just remote access log entries.

You have four choices for the level of logged detail:

- The Log Errors Only radio button instructs the server to log errors and nothing else. This gives you an adequate indication of problems after they happen, but it doesn't point out potential problems noted by warning messages.

- The Log Errors And Warnings radio button is the default choice. This forces the server to log error and warning messages to the event log, giving you a nice balance between information content and log volume.

- The Log All Events radio button causes the RRAS service to log mass quantities of messages, literally covering everything the server does. Although this voluminous output is useful for troubleshooting (or even for getting a better understanding of how remote access works), it's overkill for everyday use.

- The Do Not Log Any Events radio button turns off all event logging for RRAS.

Don't use the Do Not Log Any Events option. The service's logs are important in case of a problem.

The Log Additional Routing And Remote Access Information check box allows you to turn on the logging of all PPP negotiations and connections. This can provide valuable information when you're trying to figure out what's wrong, but it adds a lot of unnecessary bulk to your log files. Don't turn it on unless you're trying to pin down a problem.

Setting Log File Properties

By selecting an individual log file in the snap-in, you can change what events will be logged in that file. The Local Log File Properties dialog box has two tabs:

- The Settings tab controls what gets logged in the file:
  - Accounting Requests governs whether events related to the service will be logged (as well as accounting data). You should always leave this checked.

- Authentication Requests adjusts whether successful and failed logon requests are logged. You should always leave this checked.

- Periodic Status controls whether interim accounting packets are permanently stored on disk. You should usually leave this checked.

- Periodic Authentication Requests adjusts whether successful and failed logon requests are periodically logged. You should always leave this checked.

- The Log File tab (see Figure 13.8) controls the format of the file, specifically, how the log file is written to disk. You use this tab to designate three things:

  - The Directory field shows where the log file is stored. By default, each server logs its data in *systemroot*\system32\LogFiles. You can change this location to wherever you want.

  - The Format controls determine the format of the log file. By default, Windows Server 2000, 2003, 2008/2008 R2, and 2012/2012 R2 use the database-compatible file format. This format makes it easy for you to take log data and store it in a database, enabling more sophisticated postprocessing for things such as billing and chargebacks.

  - The Create A New Log File controls determine how often new log files are created. For example, some administrators prefer to start a new log file each week or each month, whereas others are content to let the log file grow without end. You can choose to have RRAS start new log files every day, week, month, never, or when the log file reaches a certain size.

FIGURE 13.8   The Log File tab

Having correct accounting and authorization data is critical to maintaining a good level of security. Exercise 13.2 walks you through configuring remote access logging.

EXERCISE 13.2

Changing Remote Access Logging Settings

1. Open the RRAS MMC snap-in by pressing the Windows key and selecting Administrative Tools ➤ Routing And Remote Access.

2. Navigate to the Remote Access Logging and Policies folder. Right-click the folder and select Launch NPS.

3. On the left pane, click Accounting. On the right side, click Change Log File Properties.

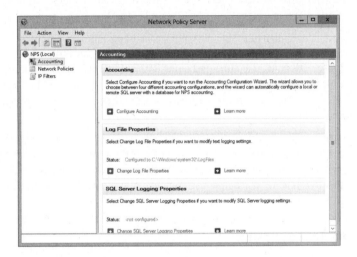

4. The Local File Logging dialog box appears. On the Settings tab, make sure that all check boxes are marked.

5. Switch to the Log File tab, and in the Create A New Log File controls, select the When Log File Reaches This Size option. Enter **50** to set the maximum size of the log file to 50MB.

6. Click the OK button. Close the Network Policy Server window.

Reviewing the Remote Access Event Log

You use the Log File tab to specify the format, size, and location of the log file. Once you have a log file, however, what do you do with the log information? Windows Server 2012 R2 online help has an exhaustive list of all of the fields logged for each connection attempt and accounting record. Because of the availability of online help, you don't need to have all of those fields memorized, and you don't have to remember exactly how to make sense of the log entries.

Why bother reviewing the logs? One nice feature is that each entry in the authentication log indicates which remote access policy was applied (either to accept or to reject the connection). This is a good way to identify problems with policies because sometimes multiple policies can combine to have an effect that you didn't expect.

Furthermore, if it's desirable in your environment, you can use the logged data to generate accounting reports to tell you things such as the average utilization of your dial-in ports, the top 10 users of dial-in connect time, or how much online time accounts or certain Windows groups use.

Monitoring Ports and Port Activity

You can monitor port status and activity from the RRAS snap-in. The Ports folder under the server contains one entry for each defined port. When you select the Ports folder, you'll see a list of the ports and their current status. The list indicates whether each port is a dial-in or VPN port and whether it's active, so you can get a quick summary of your server's workload at any time.

Double-clicking an individual port displays the Port Status dialog box (see Figure 13.9). This dialog box shows information such as a port's line speed (Line BPS), the amount of transmitted and received data (Bytes In and Bytes Out), and the network address for each protocol being carried on the port. This is a useful tool for verifying whether a port is in active use, and it gives you a count of the number of transmission and reception errors on the port.

FIGURE 13.9   The Port Status dialog box

Network Address Translation

Network Address Translation (NAT) provides an advantage with routing and tunneling. NAT (also referred to as network masquerading) allows a router to translate one IP address to another across the tunnel. This allows you to use private IP addressing internally but use pubic addresses between the tunnels.

The huge advantage of NAT is the ability for you to share a single public IP address and single Internet connection between multiple locations using private IP addressing schemes. The nodes on the private network use nonroutable private addresses. NAT maps the private addresses to the public address.

Implementing NAT

Implementing NAT is an easy process. I am going to show you the steps needed to implement NAT, but I am not going to do it as an exercise. To set up NAT in an exercise without a tunnel or without multiple networks is not always an easy thing to do. So, I will just show you how to implement NAT in case you need to do it at work. To run these steps, you must be a member of at least the local Administrators group or higher. The following steps show you how to implement NAT:

1. Start the Routing and Remote Access MMC snap-in (under Administrative Tools). Right-click your server name and choose Configure And Enable Routing And Remote Access.

2. At the Welcome Screen, click Next.

3. Choose the Custom Configuration radio button. Click Next.

4. Click NAT and click Next.

5. Start Service.

6. Expand your server name.

7. Expand IPv4.

At this point, you can configure NAT. If you need to install NAT, you must have a system with multiple NIC devices or a demand-dial setup.

NAT is also commonly used for Internet connections, but this is done through your firewall or router. For example, let's say you have an Internet service provider that issues you only four valid Internet TCP/IP addresses for you to use on your network. You can set up NAT and program it to use those four valid addresses. Then, when a user from the network wants to access the Internet, NAT swaps the user's internal IP address for one of the valid IP addresses.

Configuring a VPN Client

Dial-up RAS clients and VPN clients are similar. Almost all of the options that are available when you set up a RAS client are also available when you set up a VPN client. The main differences are as follows:

- VPN clients specify the server's IP address, whereas RAS clients specify the server's phone number.

- VPN clients require an underlying connection to the Internet.

Client configuration is not a focus of the exam, so in this chapter you will learn how to configure a VPN client but not a RAS client. Just remember that the RAS client configuration is extremely similar and that RAS clients are slowly fading away. Thus, here I will focus on VPN settings only.

VPN connections are almost always created on client workstations, so this section describes the settings in Windows 7 and Windows 8.

When you establish a virtual private network connection, you're actually building an encrypted tunnel between you and some other machine. The tunneled data is carried over an insecure network, such as the Internet.

Once you've created a connection, you can change its properties at any time by opening its Properties dialog box. The Dial-Up Connection Properties dialog box has a total of five tabs that you can use to adjust all of the pertinent settings for each connection.

Don't confuse these settings with the ones in the Local Area Connection Properties dialog box; they serve entirely different purposes.

The General Tab

The General tab of the Connection Properties dialog box (the box is called Dial-Up Connections or VPN Connections, depending on whether you're configuring dial-up RAS or VPN) is where you specify either the IP address of the VPN server or the modem and phone number to use with this particular connection. Some fields have been filled in already from when you used the Network Connection Wizard. Figure 13.10 shows the VPN settings.

FIGURE 13.10   General tab of the VPN Connection Properties dialog box

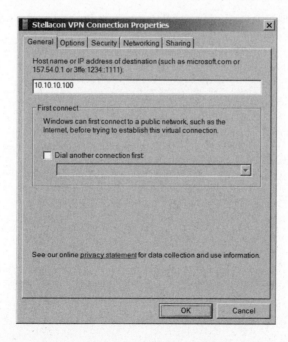

The General tab has a field where you enter the VPN server address or hostname. The First Connect group lets you specify which dial-up connection, if any, you want brought up before the VPN connection is established.

With the General tab, you can also do the following:

- Set VPN options:
    - Enter the VPN server address or hostname.
    - Specify whether to dial another connection automatically first and then specify the connection to dial.
- Set RAS options:
    - Change the modem this connection uses, or the settings for the modem you already have, with the Configure button.

 When configuring dial-up, you can also use the Phone And Modem Options control panel to adjust a broader range of modem settings.

The Options Tab

The Options tab holds settings that control how DUN dials and redials the connection. The controls in this dialog box are segregated into two groups. The Dialing Options group holds controls that govern DUN's interface behavior while dialing, and the Redialing Options group controls whether and how DUN will redial if it doesn't immediately connect (see Figure 13.11).

FIGURE 13.11   Options tab of the VPN Connection Properties dialog box

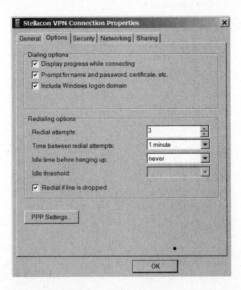

Dialing Options

Four dialing options are available in the Dialing Options group:

- The Display Progress While Connecting check box (selected by default) instructs DUN to keep you updated on its progress as it attempts to raise the connection.

- The Prompt For Name And Password, Certificate, Etc. check box is also selected by default. When it's on, Windows will prompt you for any credentials it needs to authenticate your connection to the remote server. This may be a username, a password, a public key certificate, or some combination of the three, depending on what the remote end requires.

- The Include Windows Logon Domain check box is unchecked by default. It forces DUN to include the domain name of the domain to which you're logged on as part of the authentication credential. Leave this unchecked unless you're dialing into a Windows NT/2000 network that has a trust relationship with your logon domain.

- For RAS connections, a Prompt For Phone Number check box tells DUN to display the phone number in the connection dialog box. This box is checked by default. This gives you a chance to edit the phone number before dialing; you may want to uncheck it if you (or your users) are prone to making accidental changes.

Redialing Options

The settings in the Redialing Options group control how DUN will attempt to redial the specified number if the remote end is busy or doesn't answer with a recognizable carrier tone. These settings are as follows:

- The Redial Attempts field controls how many attempts DUN will make to raise the other end before giving up. The default value is 3, but you can set any value from 0 (meaning that DUN won't attempt to redial) to 999,999,999.

- The Time Between Redial Attempts drop-down menu controls how long DUN will wait after each failed call before it tries again. Values in the drop-down menu range from 1 second all the way up to 10 minutes, with various increments in between.

- The Idle Time Before Hanging Up drop-down menu lets you specify an inactivity timer. If your connection is idle for longer than the specified period, your client will terminate the call. Note that the remote end may drop the call sooner than your client, depending on how it's configured. By default, this drop-down menu is set to Never, meaning that your client will never drop a call. If you want an inactivity timer, you can pick values ranging from 1 minute to 24 hours.

- The Redial If Line Is Dropped check box automatically redials the number if you are disconnected.

The Security Tab

How useful you find the Security tab will depend on whom you're calling. The default settings it provides will work fine with most Internet service providers and corporate dial-up facilities, but Windows 7 and Windows 8 have a broad range of security settings that you can change if you require. The Security Options group contains controls that directly affect the security of your connection. The Advanced (Custom Settings) radio button controls settings such as encryption and authentication protocols.

Security Options

The controls in the Security Options group are pretty straightforward. The security settings in effect for this connection are governed by your choice between the Typical (Recommended Settings) and Advanced (Custom Settings) radio buttons (see Figure 13.12).

FIGURE 13.12   Security tab of the VPN Connection Properties dialog box

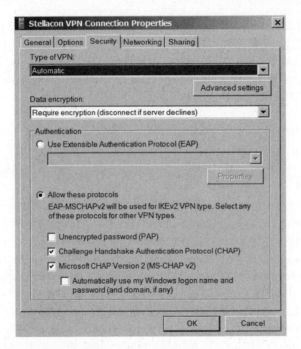

Typical (Recommended Settings)

Usually, it's best to stick with the Typical (Recommended Settings) option and use its subordinate controls to pick a canned setting that matches your needs. These subordinate controls are as follows:

- The Validate My Identity As Follows drop-down menu lets you choose among the following authentication methods:
    - Unsecured passwords (the default, and the only type of authentication that most networks support)

- Secured passwords

- Smart card authentication (useful only when calling another Windows 2000, 2003, 2008/2008 R2, or 2012/2012 R2 network)

- If you choose to require a secured password, the Automatically Use My Windows Logon Name And Password (And Domain If Any) check box instructs DUN to offer to the remote end the logon credentials you used to log on to the computer or domain. This is useful only if you're dialing into a network that has access to your domain authentication information.

- If you require a secured password or smart card authentication, the Require Encryption (Disconnect If None) check box allows you to have either an encrypted connection or none at all. If you check this box, your client and the remote server will attempt to negotiate a common encryption method. If they can't (perhaps because the remote end doesn't offer encryption), your client will hang up.

Advanced (Custom Settings)

If you select the Advanced (Custom Settings) radio button and then click the Settings button, you'll see the Advanced Security Settings dialog box. Its controls are more complex than the ones on the Security tab.

The first field is the Data Encryption drop-down menu. Windows 8 offers you the opportunity to encrypt both sides of network connections using IPsec. This capability extends to dial-up connections too. The drop-down menu gives you the following four choices:

- No Encryption Allowed means that the server will drop your call if it requires encryption because you can't provide it.

- Optional Encryption tells the client to request encryption but to continue the call if it's not available.

- Require Encryption tells the client to request encryption and to refuse to communicate with servers that don't support it.

- Maximum Strength Encryption tells the client to communicate only with servers that offer the same strength encryption it does. For example, with this setting in force, a North American Windows Server 2008 R2 machine running 3DES won't communicate with a French Windows XP machine because the French machine uses the weaker exportable encryption routines.

The Authentication section controls which authentication protocols this client can use. The default setting, Use Extensible Authentication Protocol (EAP), is for standard Windows authentication (using the MD5-Challenge method) or certificate-based authentication (using the Smart Card Or Other Certificate choice in the drop-down menu).

The Allow These Protocols radio button is followed by a long list of authentication protocols. Although the specifics of how they work are different, the basic idea behind all of these protocols is the same. Each provides a secure way for a client to prove its identity to a server. By selecting the appropriate check boxes, you can make your client use the same protocols as the remote end.

The Networking Tab

You use the Networking tab (see Figure 13.13) to control which protocols your client will attempt to use when communicating with other servers.

FIGURE 13.13   Networking tab of the VPN Connection Properties dialog box

The list box in the middle of the tab shows the network protocols installed on the client. Protocols marked with a check are available for use with this connection. Usually, when configuring RAS, you'll see TCP/IP and Client For Microsoft Networks marked, which indicates that those two protocols can be used over the connection.

The Install, Uninstall, and Properties buttons work just as they do in the Local Area Connection Properties dialog box. By using them, you can control which protocols are on your machine and their settings.

It's worth mentioning that selecting Internet Protocol (TCP/IP) in the protocols list and opening its Properties dialog box gives you access to a set of properties that are completely distinct from any TCP/IP settings that may apply to your LAN interfaces. Usually, the dial-up TCP/IP settings are configured to obtain an IP address and DNS information from the remote server, although if you need to, you can override these settings.

The Sharing Tab

Internet Connection Sharing allows other users to connect to the Internet through this machine. The machine on which you enable this feature works like a gateway to the Internet (see Figure 13.14).

FIGURE 13.14   Sharing tab of the VPN Connection Properties dialog box

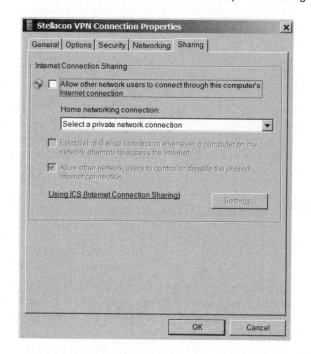

Configuring a Web Application Proxy

One of the new advantages of using the Remote Access role service in Windows Server 2012 R2 is the Web Application Proxy. Normally, your users access applications on the Internet from your corporate network. The *Web Application Proxy* reverses this feature, and it allows your corporate users to access applications from any device outside the network.

Administrators can choose which applications to provide reverse proxy features, and this allows administrators the ability to give access selectively to corporate users for the desired application that you want to set up for the Web Application Proxy service.

The Web Application Proxy feature allows applications running on servers inside the corporate network to be accessed by any device outside the corporate network. The process of allowing an application to be available to users outside of the corporate network is known as *publishing*.

Publishing Applications

One disadvantage to corporate networks are that the machines that access the network are normally devices issued by the organization. That's where Web Application Proxy publishing can help.

Web Application Proxy allows an administrator to publish an organization's applications, thus allowing corporate end users the ability to access the applications from their own devices. This is becoming a big trend in the computer industry called *bring your own device* (BYOD).

In today's technology world, users are buying and using many of their own devices, even for business work. Because of this, the users are comfortable with their own devices. Web Application Proxy allows an organization to set up applications and enable their corporate users to use these applications with the devices the users already own including computers, tablets, and smartphones.

The client side is easy to use as long as the end user has a standard browser or Office client. End users can also use apps from the Microsoft Windows Store that allow the client system to connect to the Web Application Proxy.

Configuring Pass-Through Authentication

Now when setting up the Web Application Proxy so that your users can access applications, you must have some kind of security or everyone with a device would be able to access and use your applications.

Because of this, Active Directory Federation Services (AD FS) must always be deployed with Web Application Proxy. AD FS gives you features such as single sign-on (SSO). *Single sign-on* allows you to log in one time with a set of credentials and use that set of credentials to access the applications over and over.

Pass-through authentication is truly a great benefit for your end users. Think of having a network where a user has to log in every time that user wants to access an application. The more times you make your end users log into an application, the more chances there are that the end user will encounter possible issues. Pass-through authentication works in the following way:

1. The client enters a URL address on their device, and the client system attempts to access the published web application.

2. The Web Application Proxy sends the request to the proxy server.

3. If the backend server needs the user to authenticate, the end user needs to enter their credentials only once.

4. After the server authenticates the credentials, the client has access to the published web application.

When an administrators sets up applications to use pass-through pre-authentication, additional features of AD FS will not function. For example, you will not be able to use AD FS Workplace Join, multifactor authentication (MFA), and multifactor access control.

Understanding DirectAccess

DirectAccess was a new technology that was introduced in the Windows Server 2008 R2 and Windows 7 operating systems. DirectAccess has been improved upon, and it is also available for Windows 8 and Windows Server 2012 R2.

DirectAccess allows a remote user to work on their corporate network when they are away from the office without the need for a VPN. As long as the remote user is connected to the Internet, DirectAccess will automatically connect the remote user to the corporate network without the need for any user intervention.

When a user's DirectAccess-enabled laptop is connected to the Internet, a bidirectional connection is automatically established with the user's corporate network. Because the connection is bidirectional, the IT administrator can also remotely manage the Windows 7 or Windows 8 machine while the machine is away from the network.

DirectAccess vs. VPNs

There really is no debate between VPN or DirectAccess—DirectAccess is the better way to go. The downside to DirectAccess is that it requires a great deal of time, resources, and knowledge to set it up properly.

There are a few problems with using VPNs to connect to a network. One issue is that when a user gets disconnected from their VPN connection, they must reestablish the VPN connection.

Another issue with VPNs is that many organizations filter VPN connection traffic. It may not be possible for an organization to open a firewall to allow VPN traffic. Also, if your intranet and your Internet connections are the same as your VPN connections, this can cause your Internet to be slower.

DirectAccess does not face the same limitations of a VPN. DirectAccess allows a laptop or desktop that is configured properly to connect automatically using a bidirectional connection between the client and the server.

To establish this connection, DirectAccess uses Internet Protocol Security (IPsec) and IPv6. IPsec provides a high level of security between the client and the server, and IPv6 is the protocol that the machines use.

Understanding the DirectAccess Process

Before you can set up the features and benefits of DirectAccess, there are some prerequisites that I must first go over. DirectAccess is great way to get your users to access the network from the road, but it is not the easiest thing to set up, and it must be done correctly.

DirectAccess Prerequisites

As with any software package, role, or feature, when you install any one of these, there are always prerequisites that you must deal with. DirectAccess is no different. The following is a list of DirectAccess Server with Advanced Settings prerequisites:

- A public key infrastructure must be deployed.

- ISATAP in the corporate network is not supported. If you are using ISATAP, you should remove it and use native IPv6.

- Computers that are running the following operating systems are supported as DirectAccess clients:

  - Windows Server 2012 R2

  - Windows 8.1 Enterprise

  - Windows Server 2012

  - Windows 8 Enterprise

  - Windows Server 2008 R2

  - Windows 7 Ultimate

  - Windows 7 Enterprise

- Force tunnel configuration is not supported with KerbProxy authentication.

- Changing policies by using a feature other than the DirectAccess management console or Windows PowerShell cmdlets is not supported.

- Separating NAT64/DNS64 and IPHTTPS server roles on another server is not supported.

The following is the list of prerequisites if you want to manage DirectAccess clients remotely:

- Windows Firewall must be enabled on all profiles.

- ISATAP in the corporate network is not supported. If you are using ISATAP, you should remove it and use native IPv6.

- Computers that are running the following operating systems are supported as DirectAccess clients:

  - Windows Server 2012 R2

  - Windows 8.1 Enterprise

  - Windows Server 2012

  - Windows 8 Enterprise

  - Windows Server 2008 R2

  - Windows 7 Ultimate

  - Windows 7 Enterprise

- Changing policies by using a feature other than the DirectAccess management console or Windows PowerShell cmdlets is not supported.

Understanding DirectAccess

To understand DirectAccess better, it helps to understand the process involved with how DirectAccess operates. The following steps, taken from the Microsoft white papers, show how DirectAccess operates.

1. The Windows 8 DirectAccess client determines whether the machine is connected to a network or the Internet.

2. The Windows 8 DirectAccess computer tries to connect to the web server specified during the DirectAccess setup configuration.

3. The Windows 8 DirectAccess client computer connects to the Windows Server 2012 R2 DirectAccess server using IPv6 and IPsec. Because most users connect to the Internet using IPv4, the client establishes an IPv6-over-IPv4 tunnel using 6to4 or Teredo.

4. If an organization has a firewall that prevents the DirectAccess client computer using 6to4 or Teredo from connecting to the DirectAccess server, the Windows 8 client automatically attempts to connect using the IP-HTTPS protocol.

5. As part of establishing the IPsec session, the Windows 8 DirectAccess client and server authenticate each other using computer certificates for authentication.

6. The DirectAccess server uses Active Directory membership, and the DirectAccess server verifies that the computer and user are authorized to connect using DirectAccess.

7. The DirectAccess server begins forwarding traffic from the DirectAccess client to the intranet resources to which the user has been granted access.

Now that you understand how DirectAccess works, let's look at the requirements for setting up DirectAccess on your network.

Knowing the DirectAccess Infrastructure Requirements

To set up DirectAccess, you must make sure that your network infrastructure meets some minimum requirements. The following are the requirements for setting up DirectAccess:

- Windows Server 2012 R2 configured to use DirectAccess. The Windows Server 2012 R2 machine will be set up as a multihomed system. This means your server will need two network adapters so that one adapter is connected directly to the Internet and a second adapter is connected to the intranet. Each network adapter will be configured with its own TCP/IP address.

- Windows 7 or Windows 8 client machines configured to use DirectAccess.

- Minimum of one domain controller and one Domain Name System (DNS) server running Windows Server 2008 SP2, Windows Server 2008 R2, Windows Server 2012, or Windows Server 2012 R2.

- Certificate authority (CA) server that will issue computer certificates, smart card certificates, or health certificates.
- IPsec policies to specify protection for traffic.
- IPv6 on the DirectAccess server that uses ISATAP, Teredo, or 6to4.

Summary

In this chapter, you learned how to install and configure Routing and Remote Access Services to handle dial-in connections, how to configure appropriate encryption and security settings so that communication between the client and server is encrypted and authenticated, how to install RRAS to provide VPN service using the PPTP and L2TP protocols, how to configure VPN services on the server and client, and, finally, how to troubleshoot common problems with VPNs.

Exam Essentials

Know how to install and configure RAS at the server level.   The RAS installation process is driven by the Routing and Remote Access Server Setup Wizard, which you use to set up a dial-up server. You can specify whether the server acts as a remote access server, specify what authentication providers and settings you want the server to use, control the settings applied to each protocol you have installed, specify which PPP protocols (including multilink) the clients on this server are allowed to use, and control what level of log detail is kept for incoming connections.

Know how to install and configure a VPN server.   If you don't have RRAS installed, you'll need to install it, activate it, and configure it as a VPN server. If you're already using RRAS for IP routing or remote access, you can enable it as a VPN server without reinstalling. VPN configuration is extremely simple, at least for PPTP. Either a server can accept VPN calls or it can't. If it can, it will have a certain number of VPN ports, all of which are configured identically.

Know how to configure an RRAS client.   Most client connections are made on Windows 8, Windows 7, Windows Vista, or Windows XP Professional workstations. Dial-in and VPN connections are configured similarly, but when creating a VPN connection, you must substitute an IP address for a phone number.

Review Questions

1. You have a local DHCP server for your dial-in clients, but you also want to use the DHCP relay agent to forward requests to a remote DHCP server if the local server doesn't answer a request. To do this, you must do which of the following?

   A. Add a static route to the remote server.

   B. Adjust the boot threshold on the DHCP relay agent interface for the remote network so that the local server has enough time to respond.

   C. Adjust the DHCP Forwarding Time parameter in the registry.

   D. Adjust the forwarding time in the DHCP Relay Agent Global Properties dialog box.

2. You are considering multilink PPP in order to increase bandwidth available for a dial-up client. Which of the following is not a benefit of multilink?

   A. Multilink can make the client experience faster by combining multiple phone lines and creating one logical PPP connection.

   B. Multilink enables the encryption of data between the client and the server.

   C. Multilink can be relatively low in cost and can utilize existing infrastructure.

   D. Multilink is easy to use and included in Windows Server 2012 R2 for both inbound and outbound calls.

3. Your company has offices in five locations around the country. Most of the users' activity is local to their own network. Occasionally, some of the users in one location need to send confidential information to one of the other four locations or to retrieve information from one of them. The communication between the remote locations is sporadic and relatively infrequent, so you have configured RRAS to use demand-dial lines to set up the connections. Management's only requirement is that any communication between the office locations be appropriately secured. Which of the following steps should you take to ensure compliance with this requirement? (Choose all that apply.)

   A. Configure CHAP on all the RRAS servers.

   B. Configure PAP on all the RRAS servers.

   C. Configure MPPE on all the RRAS servers.

   D. Configure L2TP on all the RRAS servers.

   E. Configure MS-CHAPv2 on all the RRAS servers.

4. Your small financial consulting company has a stand-alone Windows 2012 R2 server that provides a central location for your home-based consultants to upload and download spreadsheet files using Windows 8. A few of the consultants still use Windows XP Professional workstations. You want to set up VPN connections between the consultants and the RRAS server. The RRAS server is connected to a small peer-to-peer network of five Windows XP Professional workstations that use the network for storing files, including the files that the consultants are uploading and downloading. What authentication protocol should you use for the VPN?

    A. CHAP

    B. MS-CHAPv2

    C. EAP-TLS

    D. PAP

5. You recently migrated your company's Windows 2003 network to Windows Server 2012 R2. This migration includes 300 Windows 7 and Windows 8 workstations and 8 Windows Server 2012 R2 servers. Your company has just acquired another company with offices down the street. It has a Windows NT network that needs to be migrated to Windows Server 2012 R2 as well, and you have already begun to move the servers to the new operating system and associated services. Because you have a tight cap on expenses for network additions, you currently can't afford leased lines between the buildings. Until you can get support for them, you are going to create a VPN that is both encrypted and authenticated between the two facilities over the Internet connections that already exist. What do you need to implement to achieve this goal? (Choose all that apply.)

    A. L2TP

    B. PPTP

    C. IPsec

    D. RADIUS

    E. MS-CHAPv2

6. You have implemented VPNs to connect the various locations of your organization. These locations include offices in New York, Sacramento, Memphis, and Omaha, with a significant LAN in each one. The RRAS server is set up such that the users aren't aware of the intricacies of the connections. You are beginning to have problems with the connections between the offices and, as a result, the number of support calls is growing dramatically. What configurations could you use to troubleshoot the communication problems?

    A. L2TP using MPPE

    B. L2TP unencrypted

    C. L2TP using IPsec in transport mode

    D. L2TP using IPsec in tunnel mode

7. Your company's 450 sales reps are finally going to receive laptops so that they can communicate with the corporate office whenever they need information stored on the corporate network. The corporate network is fully upgraded to Windows Server 2012 R2, including the default configuration of the RRAS server for the remote connectivity over VPNs. You have installed Windows 8 with the default configuration on all of the laptops and have added the sales reps to a special group in Active Directory. After you test the laptops, everything appears to work fine. You ship them out and, as they reach the sales reps, you monitor their initial connections. During the next few days, you begin receiving support calls from people complaining they cannot connect to the network. What is the most likely cause of the problem?

    A. The Windows 8 clients are not configured to support a VPN.

    B. The default RRAS configuration does not support VPNs.

    C. The default RRAS configuration does not support enough VPN connections.

    D. The default RRAS configuration does not support L2TP.

    E. The Windows 8 client default configuration does not support L2TP.

8. You are the network administrator for a company with two offices; one is located on the East Coast and the other is located on the West Coast. Sales information needs to be sent from the East Coast to the West Coast office on a regular basis, and some payroll information and accounting reports need to be sent back to the East Coast. The owner of your company has been reading stories in the press about security problems on the Internet and refuses to allow any company information to travel through the Internet, regardless of how much you talk about securing those transmissions. The communications between the sites occur approximately once a week. What steps would you take to ensure secure authentication and secure transmission while not spending too much money? (Choose all that apply.)

    A. Configure PAP as the authentication method between the servers.

    B. Install RRAS on a server at each location and keep the line open with an ISDN connection that will always be available for the communication.

    C. Install RRAS on a server at each location and configure demand-dial to open the connection each time the transmission occurs.

    D. Configure CHAP as the authentication method between the servers.

    E. Configure MS-CHAPv2 as the authentication method between the servers.

    F. Configure IPsec as the encryption method between the servers.

    G. Configure MPPE as the encryption method between the servers.

    H. Configure L2TP as the encryption method between the servers.

9. You are using an RRAS server to manage remote access to your small Windows Server 2012 R2 network that serves a single location. RRAS provides access to several remote users and to the people who have machines on the local network but occasionally want to access the network from home or from hotels when on the road. Regardless of the category of user, everyone is authenticated through Active Directory. You haven't spent much time reviewing the use of this remote connectivity since you configured the system, but now there is a concern about unauthorized users as well as intermittent problems that remote users are experiencing when connecting to the network. You've been asked to prepare a report for management describing the extent of these problems in the company. You recall that when you set up the system, you configured the logging to track all connection attempts using local Windows accounting. Where will you find the logging information that you need for preparing your report?

A. The Performance Monitor log

B. Active Directory

C. The *systemroot*\System32\LogFiles folder

D. The system event log

E. The RRAS authentication log

10. Your area of responsibility at the All-Terrain Vehicle Rentals Company is to build, deploy, and maintain the remote access system for the Windows Server 2012 R2 network. The system consists of four RRAS servers that serve 200 users across the country. The users often travel from location to location, and they access different servers depending on where they call in. You put together a management station to monitor all of the RRAS servers so that you can keep an eye on this critical aspect of your network. What tool do you use to accomplish this?

A. The Server Monitor of the RRAS snap-in

B. The Server Status node of the RRAS snap-in

C. The System Monitor snap-in

D. The MMC

Chapter

14

Configure a Network Policy Server Infrastructure

THE FOLLOWING 70-411 EXAM OBJECTIVES ARE COVERED IN THIS CHAPTER:

✓ **Configure Network Policy Server (NPS)**

- Configure a NPS server including RADIUS proxy

- Configure RADIUS clients

- Configure NPS templates

- Configure RADIUS accounting

- Configure certificates

✓ **Configure NPS policies**

- Configure connection request policies

- Configure network policies for VPN clients (multilink and bandwidth allocation, IP filters, encryption, IP addressing)

- Import and export NPS policies

✓ **Configure Network Access Protection (NAP)**

- Configure System Health Validators (SHVs)

- Configure health policies

- Configure NAP enforcement using DHCP and VPN

- Configure isolation and remediation of non-compliant computers using DHCP and VPN

- Configure NAP client settings

In Chapter 13, "Configure Routing and Remote Access," you were introduced to VPNs and RADIUS. In this chapter, I will take that a step further. I will still talk about remote access, but I will get more into the security part of the access. I will talk about how to limit access to your users based on the rules and policies that you preset. When a user logs onto the domain from a remote location, if their system doesn't meet minimum requirements, you can limit how much, if any, access the user has on the network.

I will also cover Network Access Protection (NAP) to show you how to start to protect your network, and you will look into Network Policy Server (NPS). NPS allows you to set policies that your users must follow or get limited-to-no access to the domain.

Overview of Wireless Access

In today's computer world, it seems like everyone has a laptop. We all do a lot of traveling, and at any airport it seems like everyone is working on a laptop while waiting for a plane.

Because laptops have grown in popularity, IT professionals must account for them on their networks. Laptops offer IT administrators a unique set of challenges that must be dealt with on a day-to-day basis.

One major concern for IT administrators is security. Years ago, we never had to worry about users copying documents to a desktop computer and then walking out with the computer. However, today users can copy company documents to laptop computers and then walk out the door with the computer and the documents. So, I will discuss wireless networks, protocols, and security.

Windows 8, Windows 7, Windows Vista, Windows 2008/2008 R2, Windows Server 2012, and Windows Server 2012 R2 have enhanced the IEEE 802.11 wireless support to include some of the following changes:

- Single sign-on
- 802.11 wireless diagnostics
- WPA2 support
- Native Wi-Fi architecture
- User interface improvements for wireless connections
- Wireless Group Policy enhancements
- Changes in wireless auto-configuration
- Integration with Network Access Protection when using 802.1X authentication

- EAP host infrastructure
- Command-line support for configuring wireless settings
- Network location awareness and network profiles
- Next-generation TCP/IP stack enhancements for wireless environments

Configuring Wireless Access

Windows 8, Windows 7, Windows Vista, Windows XP, and Windows Server 2003, 2008/2008 R2, and 2012/2012 R2 provide built-in support for 802.11 wireless LAN networking. Inside the Network Connections folder, an installed 802.11 wireless LAN network adapter appears as a wireless network connection. The following are some of the items you can configure:

Operating Modes   There are two types of operating modes:

Infrastructure Mode   This mode uses at least one wireless access point (WAP) and/or a device that bridges the wireless computers to each other.

Ad Hoc Mode   Using this mode, wireless network computers connect directly to each other without the use of an access point (AP) or bridge.

Wired Equivalent Privacy   All of us (on a laptop) have tried to find a wireless network at one time or another. *Wired Equivalent Privacy (WEP)* is a wireless encryption that was originally defined in 802.11. WEP helps to prevent unauthorized wireless users from accessing your wireless network by the use of a shared secret key:

- If your wireless network is using the infrastructure mode, the WEP key must be configured on the wireless AP and all of the wireless clients.
- If your wireless network is using the ad hoc mode, the WEP key must be configured on all of the wireless clients.

The WEP key can be either 40-bit or 104-bit, depending on what your hardware can accommodate.

Wi-Fi Protected Access   An organization of wireless equipment vendors called the Wi-Fi Alliance created an interim standard called *Wi-Fi Protected Access (WPA)* while the IEEE 802.11i wireless LAN security standard was still being completed. WPA uses a strong encryption method called the *Temporal Key Integrity Protocol (TKIP)* to replace the weaker WEP standard. You have the ability to use the *Advanced Encryption Standard (AES)* for encryption that is provided by WPA.

WPA can be used in two different mode types:

WPA-Personal   This is used for a home office or small company. In the WPA-Personal model, you would use a preshared or passphrase code to gain authorization onto the network.

WPA-Enterprise   This was designed for a midsize to large organization. WPA-Enterprise has all of the same features as WPA-Personal, but it also includes the ability to use a 802.1X RADIUS server.

Wi-Fi Protected Access 2 Wi-Fi Protected Access 2 (WPA2) was officially designed to replace the WEP standard. WPA2 certifies that equipment used in a wireless network is compatible with the IEEE 802.11i standard. This certification is used to help standardize the use of the additional security features of the IEEE 802.11i standard that are not already included in WPA.

WPA2 can be used in two different mode types:

WPA2-Personal This is used for a home office or small company. In the WPA-Personal model, you would use a preshared or passphrase code to gain authorization onto the network.

WPA2-Enterprise This was designed for a midsize to large organization. WPA-Enterprise has all of the same features as WPA-Personal, but it also includes the ability to use a 802.1X RADIUS server.

Service Set Identifier To specify a wireless network by name, you specify the *service set identifier (SSID)*, also known as the *wireless network name*:

Infrastructure Mode The SSID is configured on the wireless access point.

Ad Hoc Mode The SSID is configured on the initial wireless client.

To help wireless clients discover and join the wireless network, the wireless AP or the initial wireless client periodically advertises the SSID. (This can be disabled for security.)

Group Policies for Wireless You have the ability to use Group Policy settings for Vista, Windows 7, Windows 8, Windows 2008/2008 R2, and Windows Server 2012/2012 R2 for WPA2. Group Policy settings allow you to configure WPA2 options at the server for all wireless clients.

Remote Access Security

In the past, remote access was seldom part of most companies' networks. It was too hard to implement, too hard to manage, and too hard to secure. It's reasonably easy to secure your networks from unauthorized physical access, but it was perceived to be much harder to do so for remote access. Recently, a number of security policies, protocols, and technologies have been developed to ease this problem. First I'll discuss the user authentication protocols.

User Authentication

One of the first steps in establishing a secure remote access connection involves allowing the user to present some credentials to the server. You can use any or all of the following authentication protocols that Windows Server 2012 R2 supports:

Password Authentication Protocol The *Password Authentication Protocol (PAP)* is the simplest authentication protocol. It transmits all authentication information in cleartext with no encryption, which makes it vulnerable to snooping if attackers can put themselves between the modem bank and the remote access server. However, this type of attack is unlikely in most networks. The security risk with PAP is largely overemphasized considering the difficulty of setting up a sniffer in between the modems and the remote access server. If an attacker has the ability to install a sniffer this deep in the network, you have larger problems to address. PAP is the most widely supported authentication protocol, and therefore you may find that you need to leave it enabled.

Microsoft CHAPv2   Microsoft created *Microsoft CHAPv2 (MS-CHAPv2)* as an extension of the CHAP protocol to allow the use of Windows authentication information. Version 2 is more secure than version 1, and version 1 is not supported by Windows Server 2008 and newer. Some other operating systems (besides Microsoft) support MS-CHAP version 1.

Extensible Authentication Protocol   The *Extensible Authentication Protocol (EAP)* doesn't provide any authentication itself. Instead, it relies on external third-party authentication methods that you can retrofit to your existing servers. Instead of hardwiring any one authentication protocol, a client-server pair that understands EAP can negotiate an authentication method. The computer that asks for authentication (the *authenticator*) is free to ask for several pieces of information, making a separate query for each one. This allows the use of almost any authentication method, including smart cards, secure access tokens such as SecurID, one-time password systems such as S/Key, or ordinary username/password systems.

Each authentication scheme supported in EAP is called an *EAP type*. Each EAP type is implemented as a plug-in module. Windows Server 2012 R2 can support any number of EAP types at once; the Routing and Remote Access Services (RRAS) server can use any EAP type to authenticate if you've allowed that module to be used and the client has the module in question.

Windows Server 2012 R2 comes with *EAP-Transport Level Security* (EAP-TLS). This EAP type allows you to use public key certificates as an authenticator. TLS is similar to the familiar Secure Sockets Layer (SSL) protocol used for web browsers. When EAP-TLS is turned on, the client and server send TLS-encrypted messages back and forth. EAP-TLS is the strongest authentication method you can use; as a bonus, it supports smart cards. However, EAP-TLS requires your RRAS server to be part of a Windows 2000, Windows Server 2003, Windows Server 2008/2008 R2, or Windows Server 2012 R2 domain.

EAP-RADIUS is another authentication method included with Windows Server 2012 R2. EAP-RADIUS is a fake EAP type that passes any incoming message to a Remote Authentication Dial-In User Service (RADIUS) server for authentication.

PEAP-MS-CHAP v2   This protocol is founded on the authenticated wireless access design, and it's based on Protected Extensible Authentication Protocol Microsoft Challenge Handshake Authentication Protocol version 2 (PEAP-MS-CHAP v2). This authentication protocol utilizes the user account credentials (username and password) stored in Active Directory Domain Services to authenticate wireless access clients instead of using smart cards or user and computer certificates for client authentication.

PEAP-MS-CHAP v2 is an EAP-type protocol that is easier to deploy than Extensible Authentication Protocol with Transport Level Security (EAP-TLS). It is easier because user authentication is accomplished by using password-based credentials (username and password) instead of digital certificates or smart cards. Only servers running Network Policy Server or PEAP-MS-CHAP v2 are required to have a certificate. The server certificate used by NPS can be issued by your organization's private trusted root CA deployed on your network or by a public CA that is already trusted by the client computer.

 Just in case you missed the very important line above, I will say it again: Servers that are running Network Policy Server or PEAP-MS-CHAP v2 are *required* to have a certificate.

TLS/SSL (Schannel)   *TLS/SSL (Schannel)* implements both the Secure Sockets Layer and Transport Layer Security Internet standard authentication protocols. Administrators can use TLS/SSL to authenticate servers and client computers. Administrators also have the ability to use the protocol to encrypt messages between the authenticated parties (client and server).

The Transport Layer Security protocol, Secure Sockets Layer protocol, Datagram Transport Layer Security (DTLS), and Private Communications Transport (PCT) protocol are all based on the public key cryptography. The Security Channel authentication protocol suite provides these protocols, and this protocol is based on the client-server model.

NTLMv2   *NTLMv2* (Windows NT LAN Manager) helps the authentication process for Windows NT 4 systems or earlier, and it allows for transactions between any two computers running these older systems. Networks that use NTLMv2 are referred to as *mixed mode.*

Kerberos   The *Kerberos authentication protocol* is used to perform Active Directory domain authentication. By default, all computers joined to a Windows Server 2012 R2 domain use the Kerberos authentication protocol. Kerberos allows for single sign-on to network resources on a domain or on a trusted domain. Administrators have the ability to control certain parameters through the Kerberos security settings of the account policies.

802.1X   The IEEE has a standard for wireless authentication called 802.1X. 802.1X allows wireless networks to authenticate onto wired Ethernet networks or wireless 802.11 networks. The IEEE 802.1X standard uses EAP for exchanging messages during the authentication process.

Connection Security

You can use some additional features to provide connection-level security for your remote access clients:

- The *Callback Control Protocol (CBCP)* allows your RRAS servers or clients to negotiate a callback with the other end. When CBCP is enabled, either the client or the server can ask the server at the other end to call the client back at a number supplied by the client or a prearranged number stored on the server.

- You can program the RRAS server to accept or reject calls based on the caller ID or automatic number identification (ANI) information transmitted by the phone company. For example, you can instruct your primary RRAS server to accept calls from only your home analog line. This means you can't call the server when you're on the road, and it also keeps the server from talking to strangers.

- You can specify various types and levels of encryption to protect your connection from interception or tampering.

 Real World Scenario

The Limits of Caller ID

It's risky to rely on ANI information for any type of authentication or caller verification. First, caller ID information can be forged. Therefore, if an attacker knows the telephone numbers from which your network accepted calls, they could make their ANI report as one of those numbers and be authenticated onto the network.

Another problem with relying on ANI for authentication is that not all telephone companies pass ANI information with the call. Therefore, if your users are in remote locations (which is why they'd be dialing in anyway), they might not be able to authenticate. Even when ANI information is sent, some telephone companies pass different pieces of the information, which can also result in authentication failures.

Finally, not all incoming line types support ANI. If your site uses a network access server or modem bank that doesn't receive this information based on the type of T1 connection used for incoming calls, the ANI information might not be there at all.

Access Control

Apart from the connection-level measures that you can use to prohibit outside callers from talking to your servers, you can restrict which users can make remote connections in a number of ways:

- You can allow or disallow remote access from individual user accounts. This is the same limited control you have in Windows NT, but it's just the start for Windows Server 2012 R2.

- You can use network access policies to control whether users can get access.

    Like group policies, network access policies give you an easy way to apply a consistent set of policies to groups of users. However, the policy mechanism is a little different: You create rules that include or exclude the users whom you want in the policy.

Unlike group policies, network access policies are available only in Windows 2000 native, Windows Server 2003, Windows Server 2008, and Windows Server 2008 R2 domain functional level (that is, in domains in which there are no Windows NT domain controllers present). This means you may not have the option to use network access policies until your Windows 2000, Windows Server 2003, Windows Server 2008/2008 R2, and Windows Server 2012 R2 deployment is further along.

In the next sections, you will learn how to configure user access control.

Configuring User Access

Now it's time to determine who can actually use the remote access services. You do this in two ways:

- By setting up remote access profiles on individual accounts
- By creating and managing network access policies that apply to groups of users

This distinction is subtle but important because you manage and apply profiles and policies in different places.

Setting Up User Profiles

Windows Server 2012 R2 stores a lot of information for each user account. Collectively, this information is known as the account's *profile*, and it's normally stored in Active Directory. Some settings in the user's profile are available through one of the two user-management snap-ins:

- If your RRAS server is part of an Active Directory domain, the user profile settings are in the Active Directory Users and Computers snap-in.

- If your RRAS server is *not* part of an Active Directory domain, the user profile settings are in the Local Users and Groups snap-in.

In either case, the interesting part of the profile is the Dial-In tab of the user's Properties dialog box (see Figure 14.1). This tab has a number of controls that regulate how the user account can be used for dial-in access.

These controls include the following:

Network Access Permission Control Group   The first, and probably most familiar, controls on this tab are in the Network Access Permission control group. These options control whether the user has dial-in permission. Windows Server 2012 R2 has a feature that, in addition to explicitly allowing or denying access, lets you control access through Network Access Protection.

Verify Caller-ID Check Box   RRAS can verify a user's caller ID information and use the results to allow or deny access. When you check the Verify Caller-ID check box and enter

FIGURE 14.1   The Dial-In tab of the user's Properties dialog box

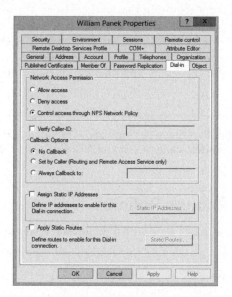

a phone number in the field, you're telling RRAS to reject a call from anyone who provides that username and password but whose caller ID information doesn't match what you enter. This means the user can call in only from a single phone number.

Callback Options Control Group   The Callback Options control group gives you three choices for regulating callback:

No Callback   This is the default setting. It means that the server will never honor callback requests from this account.

Set By Caller   This setting allows the calling system to specify a number at which it wants to be called back. The RRAS server will call the client back at that number.

Always Callback To   This setting allows you to enter a number that the server will call back no matter from where the client is actually calling. This option is less flexible but more secure than the Set By Caller option.

Assign Static IP Addresses Check Box   If you want this user always to get the same static IP address, you can arrange to do so by selecting the Assign Static IP Addresses check box and then entering the desired IP address. This allows you to set up nondynamic DNS records for individual users, guaranteeing that their machines will always have a valid DNS entry. On the other hand, this can be more prone to typographical errors on setup than the dynamic DNS-DHCP combination you could use instead.

Apply Static Routes Check Box   In an ordinary LAN, you don't have to do anything special to clients to enable them to route packets—just configure them with a default gateway, and the gateway handles the rest. For dial-up connections, though, you may want to define a list of static routes that will enable the remote client to reach hosts on your network, or elsewhere, without requiring that packets be sent to a gateway in between. Depending on the remote access server, though, the client may be able to use Address Resolution Protocol (ARP) for local devices too. If you want to define a set of static routes on the client, you'll have to do it manually. If you want to assign static routes on the server, select the Apply Static Routes check box and then use the Static Routes button to add and remove routes as necessary.

> Remember that these settings apply to individual users, so you can assign different routes, caller ID, or callback settings to each user.

Using Network Access Policies

Windows Server 2012 R2 includes support for additional configuration systems:

- Network access policies (which used to be called *remote access policy*).
- Remote access profiles.
- Network Policy Server (NPS) is the Microsoft implementation of a Remote Authentication Dial-in User Service (RADIUS) server and proxy in Windows Server 2012. NPS is the replacement for Internet Authentication Service (IAS) in Windows Server 2003.

Policies determine who can and cannot connect; you define rules with conditions that the system evaluates to see whether a particular user can connect.

You can have any number of policies in a native Windows Server 2012 R2 domain; each policy must have exactly one profile associated with it.

> Settings in an individual user's profile override settings in a network access policy.

You manage network access policies through the Remote Access Logging & Policies folder in the RRAS snap-in. Policies contain conditions that you pick from a list. When a caller connects, the policy's conditions are evaluated, one by one, to see whether the caller gets in. All of the conditions in the policy must match for the user to gain access. If there are multiple policies, they're evaluated according to an order you specify.

In the following sections, you will see how to create and configure network access policies.

Network Policy Attributes

To create a policy, right-click the Remote Access Logging & Policies folder and select Launch NPS (see Figure 14.2). Then right-click Network Policies and choose New.

FIGURE 14.2   The Launch NPS option in RRAS

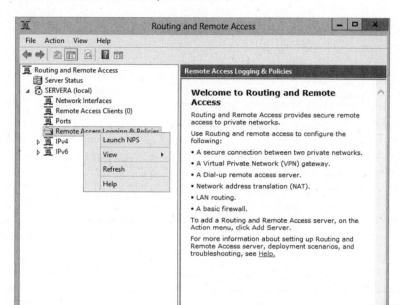

This command starts the New Network Policy Wizard, which uses a series of steps to help you define the policy.

The Select Condition dialog box (see Figure 14.3) is part of the New Network Policy Wizard. It lists the attributes you can evaluate in a policy. Table 14.1 describes the attributes that you can set. These attributes are drawn from the RADIUS standards, so you can (and in some cases, should) intermix your Windows Server 2012 R2 RRAS servers with RADIUS servers.

When setting up any policies, you must base your policy on company rules and standards. Remember, policies can allow or restrict users from remotely accessing your network. The needs of the organization determine the policy and when to use it.

Once you choose an attribute and click the Add button, its corresponding editor appears. You use the editor to set the value of the attribute. For example, if you select the Day And Time Restrictions attribute, you'll see the Time Of Day Constraints dialog box, which offers a calendar grid that lets you select which days and times are available for logging on.

FIGURE 14.3 Select Condition dialog box of New Network Policy Wizard

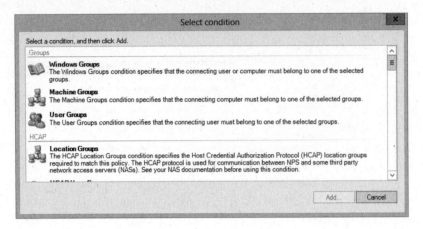

TABLE 14.1 Network access policy attributes

Attribute name	What it specifies
Authentication Type	Specifies the authentication methods required to match this policy.
Allowed EAP Types	Specifies the EAP types required for the client computer authentication method configuration to match this policy.
Called Station Id	Specifies the phone number of the remote access port called by the caller.
Calling Station Id	Specifies the caller's phone number.
Client Friendly Name	Specifies the name of the RADIUS server that's attempting to validate the connection.
Client IP Address (IPv4 and IPv6)	Specifies the IP address of the RADIUS server that's attempting to validate the connection.
Client Vendor	Specifies the vendor of the remote access server that originally accepted the connection. This is used to set different policies for different hardware.
Day And Time Restrictions	Specifies the weekdays and times when connection attempts are accepted or rejected.
Framed Protocol	Specifies the protocol to be used for framing incoming packets (for example, PPP, SLIP, and so on).

HCAP (Host Credential Authorization Protocol) User Groups	Used for communications between NPS and some third-party network access servers (NASs).
Location Groups	Specifies the HCAP location groups required to match this policy. This is used for communications between HCAP and some third-party network access servers (NASs).
MS RAS Vendor	Specifies the vendor identification number of the network access server (NAS) that is requesting authentication.
NAS Identifier	Specifies the friendly name of the remote access server that originally accepted the connection.
NAS IP Address (IPv4 and IPv6)	Specifies the IP address of the remote access server that originally accepted the connection.
NAS Port Type	Specifies the physical connection (for example, ISDN, POTS) used by the caller.
Service Type	Specifies Framed or Async (for PPP) or login (Telnet).
Tunnel Type	Specifies which tunneling protocol should be used (L2TP or PPTP).
Windows Groups	Specifies which Windows groups are allowed access.

After you select an attribute and give it a value, you can add more attributes or move to the next page by clicking the Next button on the Select Condition page.

Once you're finished setting attributes, you arrive at the Specify Access Permission page of the wizard. This page has only two radio buttons: Grant Remote Access Permissions and Deny Remote Access Permissions. These buttons specify whether the policy you create *allows* users to connect or *prevents* users from connecting. The page also includes an Access Is Determined By User Dial-In Properties check box. If this box is checked and there is a conflict between the network policy and user dial-in properties, the user dial-in properties take precedence.

Creating a Network Access Policy

In Exercise 14.1, you'll create an adjunct policy that adds time and day restrictions to the default policy. (An *adjunct policy* is one used in conjunction with another policy.) This exercise requires that you have completed the previous exercises in this chapter.

EXERCISE 14.1

Creating a Network Access Policy

1. Open the RRAS MMC snap-in by pressing the Windows key and selecting Administrative Tools ➢ Routing And Remote Access.

2. Expand the server you want to configure in the left pane of the MMC.

3. Right-click the Remote Access Logging And Policies folder.

4. Right-click and then select Launch NPS.

5. Once the Network Policy Server page appears, right-click Network Policies and then choose New.

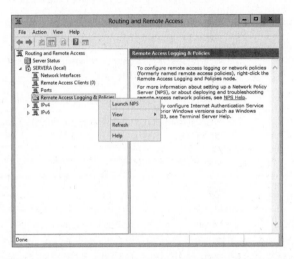

6. The New Network Policy Wizard starts. In the Policy Name box, enter **Test Policy** and then click Next (leave the other settings as they are).

7. On the Specify Conditions page, click the Add button.

8. In the Select Condition dialog box, scroll down and click Day And Time Restrictions. Click Add.

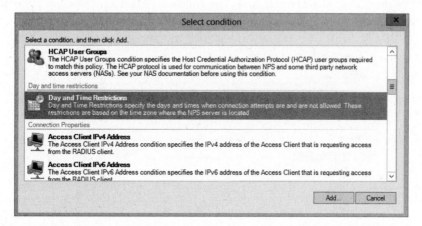

9. The Time Of Day Constraints dialog box appears. Use the calendar controls to allow remote access Monday through Saturday from 7 a.m. to 7 p.m. and then click the OK button.

10. The Select Conditions dialog box reappears, this time with the new condition listed. Click the Next button.

11. The Specify Access Permission page appears. Select the Access Granted radio button and click Next to continue.

12. The Configure Authentication Methods page appears next. This page is where you choose which authentication methods will be used for this connection. Make sure that MS-CHAP and MS-CHAPv2 are both checked, along with the check boxes associated with them. Click Next.

13. The Configure Constraints page appears. Under Constraints, click Session Timeout. On the right side, click the Disconnect After The Following Maximum Session Time box, and type **60** in the field (the value represents minutes). Click Next.

14. The Configure Settings page appears. This page allows you to configure any additional settings for this network policy. Click Next.

15. On the Completing New Network Policy page, click Finish.

NPS as a RADIUS Proxy Server

When a user tries to log into a domain through the use of a RADIUS server, the RADIUS server processes the connection request and helps the user log into the network.

RADIUS proxy servers work in a different way. When a connection request comes into a RADIUS proxy server, the RADIUS proxy server forwards the request to another RADIUS server for authentication onto the network. Servers that are running Network Policy Server can act both as a RADIUS server and as a RADIUS proxy.

When an administrator sets up NPS as a RADIUS server, NPS provides some of the following actions to help the RADIUS server work properly:

- RADIUS clients send an access request to the central authentication and authorization service. NPS uses Active Directory to authenticate the user's credentials. NPS accesses the Active Directories user's dial-in properties and policies to authorize the connection.

- When using NPS, the RADIUS server also records all accounting information on how much the RADIUS server is used. This is helpful when you have to bill other departments for the RADIUS use. Many organizations require that each department pay for its RADIUS use for its users, and using NPS allows an administrator to do this.

When you set up NPS as a RADIUS proxy, NPS provides all of the routing between all of the RADIUS servers and RADIUS clients. NPS is the main switching and routing service when you use RADIUS as a proxy server.

NPS Configuration

Now that you know that NPS can be set up as a RADIUS server, let's take a look at some of those details of how to do it. When an administrator sets up NPS as a RADIUS proxy, network access servers are then configured as the RADIUS clients. The RADIUS proxy server receives requests from the RADIUS clients, and then the RADIUS server forwards those requests to the appropriate servers. Using NPS to set up a RADIUS proxy should be done when the following conditions are needed:

- If you are the administrator of an organization that offers VPN or wireless network access to multiple clients, the RADIUS server can authenticate and authorize the user through their authentication server.

- If you are an administrator of a domain and you want users who are not members of your domain to authenticate into your domain, you can use an NPS server with a RADIUS proxy. To make this situation work, you must set up a two-way trust (two one-way trusts in opposite directions).

- Another great example of when to set up a RADIUS proxy server is when you are using a non-Microsoft-based database. RADIUS servers have the ability to communicate with different types of databases, allowing users still to be authenticated even when it's not a Microsoft authentication database; an example is a Novell Directory Services (NDS) database.

Another configuration that you may need to set when configuring NPS and RADIUS is the priority. The higher the RADIUS priority number, the less that the RADIUS server gets used. For example, if I have two RADIUS servers named Server1 and Server2 and I want Server2 used only when Server1 is unavailable, I would set the RADIUS priority from 1 to 10. This way it will get used only when Server1 is having issues or is unresponsive.

RADIUS Clients

Network access servers that are RADIUS RFC compliant (2865 and 2866) are considered RADIUS clients when used with NPS and a RADIUS server or proxy.

NPS allows an administrator to enable the use of wireless, switches, remote access, or VPN equipment as long as they are heterogeneous or homogenous sets. Network administrators can allow authentication and authorization through the use of NPS network connection requests as long as administrators deploy the following types of network access servers and technologies:

- Wired access with 802.1X-secured and RADIUS-compliant authenticating switches

- Wireless access with 802.1X-secured and RADIUS-compliant wireless access points

NPS Templates

Templates can be a valuable tool when used properly. Templates allow you to create something once and then use that template to create the same thing over and over again.

You can use templates when creating Active Directory users, when setting up GPOs, and now even when setting up NPS. NPS templates allow an administrator to save time and thus also save the cost required to manage and configure NPS on multiple servers. Multiple NPS templates are available in the Templates Management MMC for an administrator to configure:

- Shared Secrets
- RADIUS Clients
- Remote RADIUS Servers
- IP Filters
- Health Policies
- Remediation Server Groups

One advantage of creating a template is that once the template is created, there is no interference with the actual NPS server's performance. Creating templates does not affect an operational NPS server in any way. Once you load the template to the appropriate location, the template becomes active.

Creating Templates

To create a template in the Template Management MMC, right-click the template type you want to create (such as Health Policies) and click New. The New Template dialog box appears, and you just fill in all of your configuration information.

Importing and Exporting NPS Policies

Importing/exporting NPS is a pretty easy thing. It just happens to depend on which version of Windows you are exporting from. In the following examples, I will explain how to export from Windows Server 2008 R2 using the Windows MMC and how to import into Windows Server 2012 R2.

Exporting from Windows Server 2008 R2

To export NPS from Windows Server 2008 R2, follow these steps:

1. On the source server, open Server Manager.
2. In the Server Manager console tree, open Roles\Network Policy and Access Services\ NPS.
3. Right-click NPS and then click Export Configuration.
4. In the dialog box that appears, select the check box I Am Aware That I Am Exporting All Shared Secrets and then click OK.

5. For File Name, type **file.xml,** navigate to the migration store file location, and then click Save.

6. In the console tree, right-click Templates Management and then click Export Templates To A File.

7. For File Name, type **iastemplates.xml,** navigate to the migration store file location, and then click Save.

8. If you have configured SQL logging, you must manually record detailed SQL configuration settings.

   To record these settings, follow these steps:

   a. In the NPS console tree, click Accounting and then click Change SQL Server Logging Properties.

   b. Record the configuration settings on the Settings tab and then click Configure.

   c. Manually record all configuration settings from the Connection and Advanced tabs by copying them into the `sql.txt` file. Alternatively, you can click the All tab and enter Name and Value settings displayed on each line into the `sql.txt` file.

9. Copy the `file.xml`, `iastemplates.xml`, and `sql.txt` files to the migration store file location. This information will be required to configure the destination server.

Importing to Windows Server 2012 R2

To import NPS from Windows Server 2012 R2, follow these steps

1. Copy the configuration files `file.xml`, `iastemplates.xml`, and `sql.txt` that were exported to the migration store file location to the destination NPS server. Alternatively, you can import configuration settings directly from the migration store file location by supplying the appropriate path to the file in the import command. If you have custom settings that were recorded using the NPS Server Migration: Appendix A—Data Collection Worksheet, they must be configured manually on the destination server.

2. On the destination server, open Server Manager.

3. In the Server Manager console tree, click All Servers; then, from the list of servers in the right pane, right-click the relevant server and select Network Policy Server.

4. To import template configuration settings, complete the remaining steps in this list. If you do not have template settings, skip to step 7.

5. In the console tree, right-click Templates Management and then click Import Templates from a file.

6. Select the template configuration file `iastemplates.xml` that you copied from the source server and then click Open.

7. In the console tree, right-click NPS and then click Import Configuration.

8. Select the configuration file `file.xml` or `ias.txt` that you copied from the source server and then click Open.

9. Verify that a message appears indicating the import was successful.

10. Configure SQL accounting if required using the `sql.txt` file and the data collection worksheet. To configure SQL accounting, complete the remaining steps in this list.

11. In the NPS console tree, click Accounting and then click Change SQL Server Logging Properties in the details pane.

12. Modify the properties on the Settings tab if required and then click Configure to enter detailed settings.

13. Using information recorded in the `sql.txt` file, enter the required settings on the Connection and Advanced tabs and then click OK.

Using Remote Access Profiles

Remote access profiles are an integral part of network access policies. Profiles determine what happens during call setup and completion. Each policy has a profile associated with it; the profile determines what settings will be applied to connections that meet the conditions stated in the policy.

For security reasons, it's usually a good idea to limit access to the administrative accounts on your network. In particular, as a consultant, I usually tell clients to restrict remote access for the administrator account; that way, the potential exposure from a dial-up compromise is reduced. In Exercise 14.2, you will learn how to configure the administrator account's user profile to restrict dial-up access.

EXERCISE 14.2

Restricting a User Profile for Dial-In Access

1. Log on to your computer using an account that has administrative privileges.

2. If you're using an RRAS server that's part of an Active Directory domain, open the Active Directory Users and Computers snap-in by pressing the Windows key and selecting Administrative Tools ➢ Active Directory Users And Computers. If not, open the Local Users and Groups snap-in by pressing the Windows key and selecting Administrative Tools ➢ Computer Management ➢ Local Users And Groups.

3. Expand the tree to the Users folder. Right-click the Administrator account in the right pane and choose Properties. The Administrator Properties dialog box appears.

4. Switch to the Dial-In tab. On machines that participate in Active Directory, make sure the Control Access Through NPS Network Policy option (in the Permissions group) is selected.

5. Click the Deny Access radio button to prevent the use of this account over a dial-in connection.

6. Click the OK button.

You can create one profile for each policy. The profile contains settings that fit into specific areas. Each area has its own link in the profile's Properties dialog box.

The Constraints Tab

The Constraints tab has most of the settings that you think of when you consider dial-in access controls. The controls here allow you to adjust how long the connection can be idle before it gets dropped, how long it can be up, the dates and times for establishing the connection, and what dial-in port and medium can be used to connect.

Authentication Link

In the Authentication Methods pane (see Figure 14.4), you can specify which authentication methods are allowed on this specific policy. Note that these settings, like the other policy settings, will be useful only if the server's settings match. For example, if you turn EAP authentication off in the server's Properties dialog box, turning it on in the Authentication Methods pane of the profile's Properties dialog box will have no effect.

FIGURE 14.4   Authentication Methods settings

You'll notice that each authentication method has a check box. Check the appropriate boxes to control the protocols that you want this profile to use. If you enable EAP, you can also choose which specific EAP type you want the profile to support. You can also choose to allow totally unauthenticated access (which is unchecked by default).

Settings Tab

The Settings tab of the policy's Properties dialog box has several useful sections, which are described in the following list:

IP Settings Pane   The IP Settings pane (see Figure 14.5) gives you control over the IP-related settings associated with an incoming call. If you think back to the server-specific settings covered earlier, you'll remember that the server preferences include settings for protocols other than IP; this is not so in the network access profile. In this pane, you can specify where the client gets its IP address.

FIGURE 14.5   IP Settings pane of the Settings tab

Multilink And Bandwidth Allocation Protocol (BAP) Pane   The profile mechanism gives you a degree of control over how the server handles multilink calls. You exert this control through the Multilink And Bandwidth Allocation Protocol (BAP) pane of the profile Properties dialog box. Your first choice is to decide whether to allow multilink calls at all and, if so, how many ports you want to let a single client use at once. Normally, this setting is configured so that the server-specific settings take precedence, but you can override them.

Bandwidth Allocation Protocol Group   The Bandwidth Allocation Protocol control group gives you a way to control what happens during a multilink call when the bandwidth usage drops below a certain threshold. For example, why tie up three analog lines to provide 168Kbps of bandwidth when the connection is using only 56Kbps? You can tweak the capacity and time thresholds. By default, a multilink call will drop one line every time the bandwidth usage falls to less than 50 percent of the available bandwidth and stays there for two minutes. The Require BAP For Dynamic Multilink Requests check box allows you to refuse calls from clients that don't support BAP. This is an easy way to make sure that no client can hog your multilink bandwidth.

Encryption Pane   The Encryption pane of the Settings tab (see Figure 14.6) controls which type of encryption you want your remote users to be able to access.

FIGURE 14.6   Encryption pane of the Settings tab of the policy's Properties dialog box

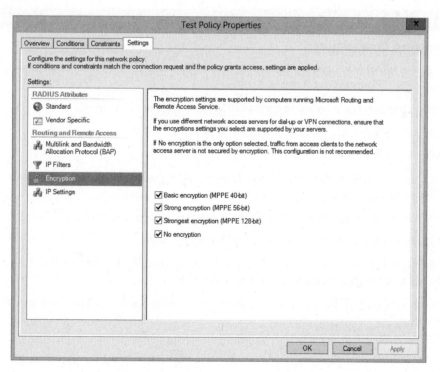

The following radio buttons are on the Encryption pane:

- Basic Encryption (MPPE 40-Bit) means single Data Encryption Standard (DES) for IPsec or 40-bit Microsoft Point-to-Point Encryption (MPPE) for Point-to-Point Tunneling Protocol (PPTP).

- Strong Encryption (MPPE 56-Bit) means 56-bit encryption (single DES for IPsec; 56-bit MPPE for PPTP).

- Strongest Encryption (MPPE 128-Bit) means triple DES for IPsec or 128-bit MPPE for PPTP connections.

- No Encryption allows users to connect using no encryption at all. Unless this button is selected, a remote connection must be encrypted, or it'll be rejected.

In Exercise 14.3, you'll force all connections to your server to use encryption. Any client that can't use encryption will be dropped. You must complete Exercise 14.1 before you do this exercise.

WARNING   Don't do this exercise on your production RRAS server unless you're sure that all of your clients are encryption-capable.

EXERCISE 14.3

Configuring Encryption

1. Open the RRAS MMC snap-in by pressing the Windows key and selecting Administrative Tools ➢ Routing And Remote Access.

2. Expand the server you want to configure in the left pane of the MMC.

3. Right-click the `Remote Access Logging & Policies` folder.

4. Select Launch NPS.

5. Once the Network Policy Server page appears, click the hours policy you created in Exercise 14.3. (I named mine Test Policy.)

6. Select Action ➢ Properties. The policy's Properties dialog box appears.

7. Click the Settings tab. Select Encryption in the left pane.

8. In the right pane, uncheck the No Encryption check box. Make sure that the Basic, Strong, and Strongest check boxes are all selected.

9. Click the OK button. When the policy Properties dialog box reappears, click the OK button.

Setting Up a VPN Network Access Policy

Earlier in this chapter, you learned how to use the Network Access Policy mechanism on a Windows Server 2012 R2 domain. Now it's time to apply what you've learned to a virtual private network (VPN). Recall that you have two ways to control which specific users can access a remote access server:

- You can grant and deny dial-up permission to individual users in each user's Properties dialog box.

- You can create a network access policy that embodies whatever restrictions you want to impose.

It turns out that you can do the same thing for VPN connections, but there are a few additional things to consider.

Granting and Denying Per-User Access

To grant or deny VPN access to individual users, all you have to do is make the appropriate change on the Dial-In tab of each user's Properties dialog box. Although this is the easiest method to understand, it gets tedious quickly if you need to change VPN permissions for more than a few users. Furthermore, this method offers you no way to distinguish between dial-in and VPN permissions.

Creating a Network Access Policy for VPNs

You may find it helpful to create network access policies that enforce the permissions that you want end users to have. You can accomplish this result in a number of ways; which one you use will depend on your overall use of network access policies.

The simplest way is to create a policy that allows all of your users to use a VPN. Earlier in this chapter, you learned how to create network access policies and specify settings for them; one thing you may have noticed was that there's a NAS-Port-Type attribute that you can use in the policy's conditions. That attribute is the cornerstone of building a policy that allows or denies remote access via VPN because you use it to accept or reject connections arriving over a particular type of VPN connection. For best results, you'll use the Tunnel-Type attribute in conjunction with the NAS-Port-Type attribute, as described in Exercise 14.4.

EXERCISE 14.4

Creating a VPN Network Access Policy

1. Open the RRAS MMC snap-in by pressing the Windows key and selecting Administrative Tools ➤ Routing And Remote Access.

2. Expand the server you want to configure in the left pane of the MMC.

3. Right-click the `Remote Access Logging & Policies` folder.

4. Select Launch NPS.

5. Once the Network Policy Server page appears, right-click Network Policies and choose New.

6. The New Network Policy Wizard starts. In the Policy Name box, enter **VPN Network Policy** and click Next (leave the other settings as they are).

7. On the Specify Conditions page, click the Add button.

8. On the Select Condition page, scroll down, click NAS-Port-Type Attribute, and click Add. When the NAS Port Type page appears, click Virtual VPN in the Common Dial-Up And VPN Tunnel Types box. Click OK and then click the Next button.

9. The Specify Conditions page reappears, this time with the new condition listed. Click the Next button.

10. The Specify Access Permission page appears. Select the Access Granted radio button and click Next to continue.

11. Next the Configure Authentication Methods page will appear. This page is where you choose which authentication methods will be used for this connection. Make sure that MS-CHAP and MS-CHAPv2 are both checked along with their associated check boxes. Click Next.

12. The Configure Constraints page appears. Under Constraints, click Session Timeout. On the right side, click the Disconnect After The Following Maximum Session Time box and type **60** in the box (the value specifies minutes). Click Next.

13. The Configure Settings page appears. This page allows you to configure any additional settings for this network policy. Click Next.

14. At the Completing New Network Policy page, click Finish.

If you don't want to grant VPN access to everyone, you can make some changes to the process in Exercise 14.6 to fine-tune it. First you'll probably want to move the VPN policy to the top of the list. (When you first add the policy described in the exercise, it is placed at the end of the policy list. Unless you move it, the default policies will take effect before the VPN-specific policy does.)

Next you can create an Active Directory group and put your VPN users in it. You can then create a policy using the two conditions outlined in Exercise 14.6 plus a condition that uses the Windows-Groups attribute to specify the new group. You can also use this process to allow everyone dial-up access and reserve VPN capability for a smaller group.

Connection Manager

To help administrators create and manage remote access connections, Microsoft includes a suite of components called Connection Manager within Windows Server 2012 R2. Connection Manager is not installed by default. You can install the Connection Manager using Server Manager ➢ Add Roles ➢ Network Access Services.

Connection Manager allows an administrator to create remote access connections called *service profiles*. These profiles then appear on client machines as network connections. You can use these network connections to connect client machines to VPNs or remote networks.

Configuring Security

When configuring remote access security, you must consider several aspects, the most fundamental of which involves configuring the types of authentication and encryption that the server will use when accepting client requests. You will look at each of these in the following sections.

Controlling Server Security

The Security tab of the server's Properties dialog box (see Figure 14.7) allows you to specify which authentication and accounting methods RRAS uses. You can choose one of two authentication providers by using the Authentication Provider drop-down list.

FIGURE 14.7   The Security tab of the RRAS server's Properties dialog box

Your choices include the following:

Windows Authentication This is a built-in authentication suite included with Windows Server 2012 R2.

RADIUS Authentication This authentication allows you to send all authentication requests heard by your server to a RADIUS server for approval or denial.

You can also use the Accounting Provider drop-down list on the Security tab to choose between the following:

Microsoft-Developed Accounting With this type of accounting, connection requests are maintained in the event log.

RADIUS Accounting In this type of accounting, all accounting events, such as call start and call stop, are sent to a RADIUS server for action.

RADIUS Authentication Settings

When you select the RADIUS Authentication option from the Authentication Provider drop-down menu, you are enabling a RADIUS client that passes authentication duties to a RADIUS server. This communication is sent via UDP on port 1645 or 1812, depending on the version of RADIUS being used.

Click the Configure button to open the RADIUS Authentication dialog box. From here, you can set the following options:

- Click the Add button to add the name or address of a RADIUS server to which the RAS server will pass authentication duties.

- You must also enter the correct secret, which is initially set by the RADIUS server.

- The Time-Out option determines how long the RRAS server will attempt to authenticate the remote user before giving up.

- The Initial Score option is similar to the cost value used by routers. The RAS server will attempt to authenticate users on the RADIUS server with the highest score first. If that attempt fails, the RAS server will use the RADIUS server with the next highest score, and so on.

- Although the Port option can be changed, the default setting is part of RFC 2866, "RADIUS Accounting," and it should not be altered unless extraordinary circumstances call for it.

The Internet Assigned Numbers Authority (IANA) is the official source for port number assignment. You can view current port number assignments and other valuable information at www.iana.org/assignments/port-numbers.

Windows Authentication Settings

Select the Windows Authentication option from the Authentication Provider drop-down menu if you want the local machine to authenticate your remote access users. To configure the server by telling it which authentication methods you want it to use, click the Authentication Methods button, which displays the Authentication Methods dialog box. If you look at the list of authentication protocols earlier in the chapter, you'll find that each one has a corresponding check box here: EAP, MS-CHAPv2, CHAP, and PAP. You can also turn on unauthenticated access by checking the Allow Remote Systems To Connect Without Authentication box, but that is not recommended because it allows anyone to connect to, and use, your server (and thus by extension your network).

There's actually a special set of requirements for using CHAP because it requires access to each user's encrypted password. Windows Server 2012 R2 normally doesn't store user passwords in a format that CHAP can use, so you have to take some additional steps if you want to use CHAP:

1. Enable CHAP at the server and policy levels.

2. Edit the default domain GPO's Password Policy object to turn on the Store Password Using Reversible Encryption policy setting.

3. Change or reset each user's password, which forces Windows Server 2012 R2 to store the password using reversible encryption.

After these steps are completed for an account, that account can be used with CHAP.

> These steps aren't required for MS-CHAPv2; for that protocol, you just enable MS-CHAPv2 at the server and policy levels.

Configuring Network Access Protection

Another way that you can have security is to allow users to access resources based on the identity of the client computer. This new security solution is called *Network Access Protection*. Determined by the client needs, network administrators now have the ability to define granular levels of network access using NAP. NAP also allows administrators to determine client access based on compliancy with corporate governance policies. The following are some of the NAP features:

Network Layer Protection   *Network layer protection* is the ability to secure communications at the Network layer of the OSI model.

All communications travel through the seven layers of the OSI model. Starting at the top (layer 7), the seven layers are the Application, Presentation, Session, Transport, Network, Data-Link, and Physical layers.

DHCP Enforcement   If a computer wants to receive unlimited IPv4 network access, the computer must be compliant with corporate governance policies. *DHCP enforcement* verifies that a computer is compliant before granting unlimited access. If a computer is noncompliant, the computer receives an IPv4 address that has limited network access and a default user profile. One advantage of using DHCP is that you can set up user classes so that specific machines (for example, noncompliant DHCP systems) can get specific rules or limited access to the network.

When a client computer attempts to receive an IP address from DHCP, the DHCP enforcement checks the health policy requirements of the system to make sure they meet the compliancy.

VPN Enforcement   *VPN enforcement* works a lot like DHCP enforcement, except that VPN enforcement verifies the compliancy of the system before the VPN connection is given full access to the network.

IPsec Enforcement   *IPsec enforcement* will allow a computer to communicate with other computers as long as the computers are IPsec compliant. You have the ability to configure the requirements for secure communications between the two compliant computer systems. You can configure the IPsec communications based on IP address or TCP/UDP port numbers.

802.1X Enforcement   For a computer system to have 802.1X unlimited access to network connections (Ethernet 802.11 or wireless access point), the computer system must be 802.1X compliant. *802.1X enforcement* verifies that the connecting system is 802.1X connection compliant. Noncompliant computers will obtain only limited access to network connections.

Flexible Host Isolation   *Flexible host isolation* allows a server and domain to isolate computers to help make it possible to design a layer of security between computers or networks. Even if a hacker gains access to your network using an authorized username and password, the server and domain isolation can stop the attack because the computer is not an authorized domain computer.

Multiconfiguration System Health Validator   This feature allows you to specify multiple configurations of a *system health validator (SHV)*. When an administrator configures a network policy for health evaluation, the administrator will select a specific health policy. Using this feature allows you to specify different network policies for different sets of health requirements based on a specific configuration of the SHV. For example, an administrator can create a network policy that specifies that all internal computers must have antivirus software enabled and a different network policy that specifies that VPN-connected computers must have their antivirus software enabled and signature files up-to-date.

NAP Monitoring

There may be many times when you will need to monitor how NAP is running and what NAP policies are being enforced. There are multiple ways that you can monitor NAP. You can use the Network Access Protection MMC snap-in to look at how things are running.

But there is another tool that you can use called Logman. Logman creates and manages Event Trace Session and Performance logs and allows an administrator to monitor many different applications through the use of the command line. Table 14.2 shows some of the different Logman switches you can use.

TABLE 14.2 Logman switches

Switch	Description
Logman create	Creates a counter, trace, configuration data collector, or API
Logman query	Queries data collector properties
Logman start | stop	Starts or stops data collection
Logman delete	Deletes an existing data collector
Logman update	Updates the properties of an existing data collector
Logman import | export	Imports a data collector set from an XML file or exports a data collector set to an XML file

Summary

In this chapter, I talked about the different ways that you can secure your remote access connections. You learned how to configure appropriate security settings so that communication between the client and server is secure because of NAP and NPS settings.

I talked about how to verify that client machines meet the minimum requirements in order to gain either full or limited access to your network.

I also discussed wireless networking and what types of security encryption you can use to help support your wireless network. You learned about the different components of wireless access and using group policies to configure wireless clients.

Exam Essentials

Understand what NAP can do for your network. Understand that NAP allows administrators to determine client access based on compliancy with corporate governance policies. Some of the settings are Network Layer Protection, DHCP Enforcement, VPN Enforcement, IPsec Enforcement, 802.1X Enforcement, Flexible Host Isolation, and Multi-configuration System Health Validator.

Understand what NPS can do for your network. Understand how to use NPS to manage network access centrally through a variety of network access servers, including RADIUS-compliant 802.1X-capable wireless access points, VPN servers, dial-up servers, and 802.1X-capable Ethernet switches.

Review Questions

1. You are the network administrator for a large Active Directory domain named Panek.com. The domain contains a server named Saturn that runs Windows Server 2012 R2. Saturn has the DHCP Server role installed. The network contains 400 client computers that run Windows 7 and Windows 8. All of the client computers are joined to the domain and are configured DHCP clients. You install a new server named Jupiter that runs Windows Server 2012 R2. On Jupiter, you install the Network Policy Server (NPS) role service, and you configure Network Access Protection (NAP) to use the DHCP enforcement method. You need to ensure that Saturn provides a valid default gateway only to computers that pass the system health validation. Which two actions should you perform? (Each correct answer presents part of the solution. Choose two.)

    A. From the DHCP console, configure the 016 Swap Server option.

    B. From the DHCP console, enable NAP on all scopes.

    C. From the NAP Client Configuration console, enable the DHCP Quarantine Enforcement client.

    D. From the DHCP console, create a new policy.

    E. From Server Manager, install the Network Policy Server role service.

2. Your network contains an Active Directory domain named Panek.com. The domain contains a server named Server1 that runs Windows Server 2012 R2. Server1 has the Network Policy Server (NPS) role service installed. You plan to configure Server1 as a Network Access Protection (NAP) health policy server for VPN enforcement by using the Configure NAP Wizard. You need to ensure that you can configure the VPN enforcement method on Server1 successfully. What should you install on Server1 before you run the Configure NAP Wizard?

    A. The Host Credential Authorization Protocol (HCAP)

    B. A system health validator (SHV)

    C. The Remote Access server role

    D. A computer certificate

3. You are a network administrator of an Active Directory domain named Stellacon.com. You have a server named Earth that runs Windows Server 2012 R2. Earth has the DHCP Server role and the Network Policy Server (NPS) role service installed. You enable Network Access Protection (NAP) on all of the DHCP scopes on Earth. You need to create a DHCP policy that will apply to all of the NAP noncompliant DHCP clients. Which criteria should you specify when you create the DHCP policy?

    A. The relay agent information

    B. The user class

    C. The vendor class

    D. The client identifier

4. Your network contains an Active Directory domain named contoso.com. Network Access Protection (NAP) is deployed to the domain. You need to create NAP event trace log files on a client computer. What should you run?

   A. Register-ObjectEvent

   B. Register-EngineEvent

   C. tracert

   D. logman

5. Your network contains four Network Policy Server (NPS) servers named ServerA, ServerB, ServerC, and ServerD. Server1 is configured as a RADIUS proxy that forwards connection requests to a remote RADIUS server group named Group1. You need to ensure that ServerB and ServerC receive connection requests. ServerD should receive connection requests only if both ServerB and ServerC are unavailable. How should you configure Group1?

   A. Change the weight of ServerB and ServerC to 10.

   B. Change the weight of ServerD to 10.

   C. Change the priority of ServerB and ServerC to 10.

   D. Change the priority of ServerD to 10.

6. Your network contains an Active Directory domain named Stellacon.com. The domain contains a RADIUS server named Server1 that runs Windows Server 2012 R2. You add a VPN server named Server2 to the network. On Server1, you create several network policies. You need to configure Server1 to accept authentication requests from Server2. Which tool should you use on Server1?

   A. Set-RemoteAccessRadius

   B. CMAK

   C. NPS

   D. Routing and Remote Access

7. Your network contains an Active Directory domain named Panek.com. The domain contains a server named Server1 that runs Windows Server 2012 R2. Server1 has the following role services installed:

   ▪ DirectAccess and VPN (RRAS)

   ▪ Network Policy Server

   Remote users have client computers that run either Windows XP, Windows 7, or Windows 8. You need to ensure that only the client computers that run Windows 7 or Windows 8 can establish VPN connections to Server1. What should you configure on Server1?

   A. A vendor-specific RADIUS attribute of a Network Policy Server (NPS) connection request policy

   B. A condition of a Network Policy Server (NPS) network policy

C. A condition of a Network Policy Server (NPS) connection request policy

D. A constraint of a Network Policy Server (NPS) network policy

8. You are the network administrator for a large organization that contains an Active Directory domain named Stellacon.com. The domain contains a server named Server1 that runs Windows Server 2012 R2. Server1 has the Network Policy and Access Services server role installed. You plan to deploy 802.1X authentication to secure the wireless network. You need to identify which Network Policy Server (NPS) authentication method supports certificate-based mutual authentication for the 802.lX deployment. Which authentication method should you identify?

A. PEAP-MS-CHAP v2

B. MS-CHAP v2

C. EAP-TLS

D. MS-CHAP

9. You are the administrator of a large organization that contains an Active Directory domain named Stellacon.com. The domain contains a server named ServerA that runs Windows Server 2012 R2. ServerA has the Network Policy and Access Services server role installed. Your company's security policy requires that certificate-based authentication be used by some network services. You need to identify which Network Policy Server (NPS) authentication methods comply with the security policy. Which two authentication methods should you identify? (Choose two.)

A. MS-CHAP

B. PEAP-MS-CHAP v2

C. CHAP

D. EAP-TLS

E. MS-CHAP v2

10. You are the network administrator, and you have been asked to set up an accounting system so each department is responsible for their cost of using network services. Your network contains a Network Policy Server (NPS) server named ServerA. The network contains a server named Database1 that has Microsoft SQL server installed. All servers run Windows Server 2012 R2. You configure NPS on ServerA to log accounting data to a database on Database1. You need to ensure that the accounting data is captured if Database1 fails. The solution must minimize cost. What should you do?

A. Implement Failover Clustering.

B. Implement database mirroring.

C. Run the Accounting Configuration Wizard.

D. Modify the SQL Server Logging properties.

Chapter
15

Configure and Manage Active Directory

THE FOLLOWING 70-411 EXAM OBJECTIVES ARE COVERED IN THIS CHAPTER:

✓ **Configure service authentication**

- Create and configure Service Accounts
- Create and configure Group Managed Service Accounts
- Configure Kerberos delegation
- Manage Service Principal Names (SPNS)
- Configure virtual accounts

✓ **Configure Domain Controllers**

- Transfer and seize operations master roles
- Install and configure a read-only domain controller (RODC)
- Configure domain controller cloning

✓ **Maintain Active Directory**

- Back up Active Directory and SYSVOL
- Manage Active Directory offline
- Optimize an Active Directory database
- Clean up metadata
- Configure Active Directory snapshots
- Perform object- and container-level recovery
- Perform Active Directory restore
- Configure and restore objects by using the Active Directory Recycle Bin

✓ **Configure account policies**

- Configure domain and local user password policy settings

- Configure and apply Password Settings Objects (PSOs)

- Delegate password settings management

- Configure account lockout policy settings

- Configure Kerberos policy settings

In this chapter, we will dive deeper into the Active Directory realm.

I have covered many important aspects of Active Directory. The most important aspect of any network, including Active Directory, is security. If your network is not secure, then hackers (internal or external) can make your life as a member of an IT department a living nightmare.

In this chapter, you'll learn how to implement security within Active Directory. By using Active Directory tools, you can quickly and easily configure the settings that you require in order to protect information.

Proper planning for security permissions is an important prerequisite of setting up Active Directory. Security is always one of the greatest concerns for an IT administrator.

You should have a security policy that states what is expected of every computer user in your company. Fine-tuning Active Directory to comply with your security policy and allowing end users to function without any issues should be your goals.

You should know how to use Active Directory to apply permissions to resources on the network, and you should pay particular attention to the evaluation of permissions when applied to different groups and the flow of permissions through the organizational units (OUs) via group policies. With all of this in mind, let's start looking at how you can manage security within Active Directory.

Some of the text in this chapter is repeated in Chapter 19 due to its relevancy and importance to both Exam 70-411 and Exam 70-412.

Active Directory Security Overview

One of the fundamental design goals for Active Directory is to define a single, centralized repository of users and information resources. Active Directory records information about all of the users, computers, and resources on your network. Each domain acts as a logical boundary, and members of the domain (including workstations, servers, and domain controllers) share information about the objects within them.

The information stored within Active Directory determines which resources are accessible to which users. Through the use of permissions that are assigned to Active Directory objects, you can control all aspects of network security.

Throughout this chapter, you'll learn the details of security as it pertains to Active Directory. Note, however, that Active Directory security is only one aspect of overall network security. You should also be sure that you have implemented appropriate access control settings for the file system, network devices, and other resources. Let's start by looking at the various components of network security, which include working with security principals and managing security and permissions, access control lists (ACLs), and access control entries (ACEs).

 When you are setting up a network, you should always keep in mind that 90 percent of all hacks on a network are internal. This means internal permissions and security (as well as external security) need to be as strong as possible while still allowing users to do their jobs.

Understanding Active Directory Features

I talked about many of these features in Part I, but just in case you are starting with Part II and exam 70-411, let's take a look at some of the Active Directory features and what each feature can do for you as an administrator.

Active Directory is the heart and soul of a Microsoft domain, and I can never talk enough about the roles and features included with Active Directory. Many of these features have already been discussed, but what follows will be a good review for the 70-411 exam:

Active Directory Certificate Services   Active Directory Certificate Services (AD CS) provides a customizable set of services that allows you to issue and manage public key infrastructure (PKI) certificates. These certificates can be used in software security systems that employ public key technologies.

Active Directory Domain Services   Active Directory Domain Services (AD DS) includes new features that make deploying domain controllers simpler and lets you implement them faster. AD DS also makes the domain controllers more flexible, both to audit and to authorize access to files. Moreover, AD DS has been designed to make performing administrative tasks easier through consistent graphical and scripted management experiences.

Active Directory Rights Management Services   Active Directory Rights Management Services (AD RMS) provides management and development tools that let you work with industry security technologies, including encryption, certificates, and authentication. Using these technologies allows organizations to create reliable information protection solutions.

Hyper-V   Hyper-V is one of the most changed features in Windows Server 2012 R2. Microsoft's new slogan is "Windows Server 2012 R2, built from the cloud up," and this has a lot to do with Hyper-V. It allows an organization to consolidate servers by creating and managing a virtualized computing environment. It does this by using virtualization technology that is built into Windows Server 2012 R2.

IPAM   IP Address Management (IPAM) was one of the new features introduced with Windows Server 2012. IPAM allows an administrator to customize and monitor the IP address infrastructure on a corporate network.

Kerberos Authentication   Windows Server 2012 R2 uses the Kerberos authentication (version 5) protocol and extensions for password-based and public-key authentication. The Kerberos client is installed as a security support provider (SSP), and it can be accessed through the Security Support Provider Interface (SSPI).

Managed Service Accounts   Stand-alone managed service accounts, originally created for Windows Server 2008 R2 and Windows 7, are configured domain accounts that allow automatic password management and service principal names (SPNs) management, including the ability to delegate management to other administrators.

Security Auditing   Security auditing gives an organization the ability to help maintain the security of an enterprise. By using security audits, you can verify authorized or unauthorized access to machines, resources, applications, and services. One of the best advantages of security audits is to verify regulatory compliance.

TLS/SSL (Schannel SSP)   Schannel is a security support provider (SSP) that uses the Secure Sockets Layer (SSL) and Transport Layer Security (TLS) Internet standard authentication protocols together. The Security Support Provider Interface (SSPI) is an API used by Windows systems to allow security-related functionality, including authentication.

Windows Deployment Services   Windows Deployment Services allows an administrator to install Windows operating systems remotely. Administrators can use Windows Deployment Services to set up new computers by using a network-based installation.

Understanding Security Principals

Security principals are Active Directory objects that are assigned *security identifiers (SIDs)*. An SID is a unique identifier that is used to manage any object to which permissions can be assigned. Security principals are assigned permissions to perform certain actions and access certain network resources.

The following basic types of Active Directory objects serve as security principals:

User Accounts   User accounts identify individual users on your network by including information such as the user's name and their password. User accounts are the fundamental unit of security administration.

Groups   There are two main types of groups: security groups and distribution groups. Both types can contain user accounts. System administrators use security groups to ease the management of security permissions. They use distribution groups, on the other hand, solely to send email. Distribution groups are not security principals. You'll see the details of groups in the next section.

Computer Accounts   Computer accounts identify which client computers are members of particular domains. Because these computers participate in the Active Directory database, system administrators can manage security settings that affect the computer.

They use computer accounts to determine whether a computer can join a domain and for authentication purposes. As you'll see later in this chapter, system administrators can also place restrictions on certain computer settings to increase security. These settings apply to the computer and, therefore, also apply to any user who is using it (regardless of the permissions granted to the user account).

Note that other objects—such as OUs—do not function as security principals. What this means is that you can apply certain settings (such as Group Policy) on all of the objects within an OU; however, you cannot specifically set permissions with respect to the OU itself. The purpose of OUs is to organize other Active Directory objects logically based on business needs, add a needed level of control for security, and create an easier way to delegate.

You can manage security by performing the following actions with security principals:

- You can assign them permissions to access various network resources.

- You can give them user rights.

- You can track their actions through auditing (covered later in this chapter).

The major types of security principals—user accounts, groups, and computer accounts—form the basis of the Active Directory security architecture. As a system administrator, you will likely spend a portion of your time managing permissions for these objects.

 It is important to understand that, since a unique SID defines each security principal, deleting a security principal is an irreversible process. For example, if you delete a user account and then later re-create one with the same name, you'll need to reassign permissions and group membership settings for the new account. Once a user account is deleted, its SID is deleted.

Users and groups are two types of fundamental security principals employed for security administration. In the following sections, you'll learn how users and groups interact and about the different types of groups you can create.

Types of Groups

When dealing with groups, you should make the distinction between local security principals and domain security principals:

Local Users and Groups   You use local users and groups to assign the permissions necessary to access the local machine. For example, you may assign the permissions you need to reboot a domain controller to a specific domain local group.

Domain Users and Groups   Domain users and groups, on the other hand, are used throughout the domain. These objects are available on any of the computers within the Active Directory domain and between domains that have a trust relationship.

Here are the two main types of groups used in Active Directory:

Security Groups   Security groups are considered security principals. They can contain user accounts, computers, or groups. To make administration simpler, system administrators usually grant permissions to groups. This allows you to change permissions easily at the Active Directory level (instead of at the level of the resource on which the permissions are assigned).

You can also place Active Directory contact objects within security groups, but security permissions will not apply to them.

Distribution Groups   Distribution groups are not considered security principals because they do not have SIDs. As mentioned earlier, they are used only for the purpose of sending email messages. You can add users to distribution groups just as you would add them to security groups. You can also place distribution groups within OUs so that they are easier to manage. You will find them useful, for example, if you need to send email messages to an entire department or business unit within Active Directory.

Understanding the differences between security and distribution groups is important in an Active Directory environment. For the most part, system administrators use security groups for the daily administration of permissions. On the other hand, system administrators who are responsible for maintaining email distribution lists generally use distribution groups to group members of departments and business units logically. (A system administrator can also email all of the users within a security group, but to do so, they would have to specify the email addresses for the accounts.)

When you are working in Windows Server 2003, Server 2008, Server 2008 R2, or Server 2012 functional-level domains, you can convert security groups to or from distribution groups. When group types are running in a Windows 2000 mixed domain functional level, you cannot change them.

It is vital that you understand group types when you are getting ready to take the Microsoft exams. Microsoft likes to include trick questions about putting permissions on distribution groups. Remember, only security groups can have permissions assigned to them.

Group Scope

In addition to being classified by type, each group is given a specific scope. The scope of a group defines two characteristics. First, it determines the level of security that applies to a group. Second, it determines which users can be added to the group. Group scope is an important concept in network environments because it ultimately defines which resources users are able to access.

The three types of group scope are as follows:

Domain Local   The scope of domain local groups extends as far as the local domain. When you're using the Active Directory Users and Computers tool, domain local accounts apply to the computer for which you are viewing information. Domain local groups are used to assign permissions to local resources, such as files and printers. They can contain domain locals, global groups, universal groups, and user accounts.

Global   The scope of global groups is limited to a single domain. Global groups may contain any of the users that are part of the Active Directory domain in which the global groups reside or may contain other global groups. Global groups are often used for managing domain security permissions based on job functions. For example, if you need to specify permissions for the Engineering department, you could create one or more global groups (such as EngineeringManagers and EngineeringDevelopers). You could then assign security permissions to each group.

Universal   Universal groups can contain accounts or other universal groups from any domains within an Active Directory forest. Therefore, system administrators use them to manage security across domains. When you are managing multiple domains, it often helps to group global groups within universal groups. For instance, if you have an Engineering global group in the research.stellacon.com domain and an Engineering global group in the asia.stellacon.com domain, you can create a universal AllEngineers group that contains both of the global groups. Now whenever you must assign security permissions to all engineers within the organization, you need only assign permissions to the AllEngineers universal group.

For domain controllers to process authentication between domains, information about the membership of universal groups is stored in the global catalog (GC). Keep this in mind if you ever plan to place users directly into universal groups and bypass global groups because all of the users will be enumerated in the GC, which will impact size and performance.

Fortunately, universal group credentials are cached on domain controllers that universal group members use to log on. This process is called *universal group membership caching*. The domain controller obtains the cached data whenever universal group members log on, and then it is retained on the domain controller for eight hours by default. This is especially useful for smaller locations, such as branch offices, which run less-expensive domain controllers. Most domain controllers at these locations cannot store a copy of the entire GC, and frequent calls to the nearest GC would require an inordinate amount of network traffic.

When you create a new group using the Active Directory Users and Computers tool, you must specify the scope of the group. Figure 15.1 shows the New Object – Group dialog box and the available options for the group scope.

However, changing group scope can be helpful when your security administration or business needs change. You can change group scope easily using the Active Directory Users and Computers tool. To do so, access the properties of the group. As shown in Figure 15.2, you can make a group scope change by clicking one of the options.

FIGURE 15.1   The New Object – Group dialog box

FIGURE 15.2   The Domain Admins Security Group's Properties dialog box

Built-in Service Account Groups

System administrators use built-in domain local groups to perform administrative functions on the local server. Because these have pre-assigned permissions and privileges, they allow system administrators to assign common management functions easily. Figure 15.3 shows the default built-in groups that are available on a Windows Server 2012 domain controller.

FIGURE 15.3   Default built-in local groups

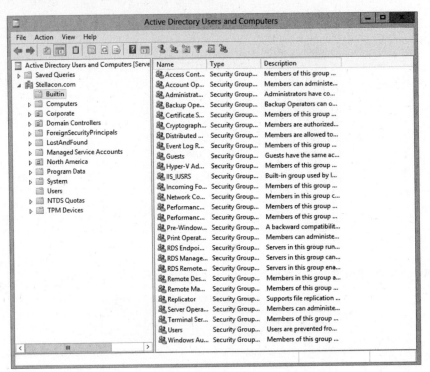

The list of built-in local groups includes some of the following:

Account Operators   These users can create and modify domain user and group accounts. Members of this group are generally responsible for the daily administration of Active Directory.

Administrators   By default, members of the Administrators group are given full permissions to perform any functions within the Active Directory domain and on the local computer. This means they can access all files and resources that reside on any server within the domain. As you can see, this is a powerful account.

In general, you should restrict the number of users who are included in this group because most common administration functions do not require this level of access.

Backup Operators   One of the problems associated with backing up data in a secure network environment is that you need to provide a way to bypass standard file system security so that you can copy files. Although you could place users in the Administrators group, doing so usually provides more permissions than necessary. Members of the Backup Operators group can bypass standard file system security for the purpose of backup and recovery only. They cannot, however, directly access or open files within the file system.

Generally, backup software applications and data use the permissions assigned to the Backup Operators group.

Certificate Service DCOM Access   Members of the Certificate Service DCOM Access group can connect to certificate authority servers in the enterprise.

Cryptographic Operators   Members of the Cryptographic Operators group are authorized to perform cryptographic operations. Cryptography allows the use of codes to convert data, which then allows a specific recipient to read it using a key.

Guests   Typically, you use the Guests group to provide access to resources that generally do not require security. For example, if you have a network share that provides files that should be made available to all network users, you can assign permissions to allow members of the Guests group to access those files.

Print Operators   By default, members of the Print Operators group are given permissions to administer all of the printers within a domain. This includes common functions such as changing the priority of print jobs and deleting items from the print queue.

Replicator   The Replicator group allows files to be replicated among the computers in a domain. You can add accounts used for replication-related tasks to this group to provide those accounts with the permissions they need to keep files synchronized across multiple computers.

Server Operators   A common administrative task is managing server configuration. Members of the Server Operators group are granted the permissions they need to manage services, shares, and other system settings.

Users   The Users built-in domain local group is used to administer security for most network accounts. Usually, you don't give this group many permissions, and you use it to apply security settings for most employees within an organization.

Windows Server 2012 also includes many different default groups, which you can find in the Users folder. As shown in Figure 15.4, these groups are of varying scopes, including domain local, global, and universal groups. You'll see the details of these groups in the next section.

Three important user accounts are created during the promotion of a domain controller:

- The *Administrator account* is assigned the password a system administrator provides during the promotion process, and it has full permissions to perform all actions within the domain.

- The Guest account is disabled by default. The purpose of the *Guest account* is to provide anonymous access to users who do not have an individual logon and password to use within the domain. Although the Guest account might be useful in some situations, it is generally recommended that this account be disabled to increase security.

- Only the operating system uses the *krbtgt*, or *Key Distribution Center Service account*, for Kerberos authentication. This account is disabled by default. Unlike other user accounts, the krbtgt account cannot be used to log on to the domain, and therefore it does not need to be enabled. Since only the operating system uses this account, you do not need to worry about hackers gaining access by using this account.

FIGURE 15.4 Contents of the default Users folder

Managed Service Account and Virtual Accounts

One issue that many administrators run into is how to handle application accounts. What I mean by this is, what type of account and what permissions are needed when installing an application such as Microsoft Exchange?

If you were the administrator for the local system, you could just configure Exchange to run as a Local Service. The problem with using these types of accounts is that they are normally used multiple times among different applications.

Another option that you could have is just to create a domain account for each application. For example, an administrator can create a specific domain account that Exchange could use. The problem with this option is that you have to remember to change the password frequency, and once you change that password, you have to remember which services you configured to use that account and change the passwords for each service. This is not an ideal way to set up an application service.

The two types of accounts available in Windows Server 2012 R2 are the managed service account and the virtual account. These two accounts were originally created in Windows Server 2008 R2 and Windows 7. These accounts are specifically designed for use with applications, and an administrator does not need to change the credentials manually every few months. These two domain accounts provide automatic password management and simplified service principal names management.

Virtual accounts even take it a step further because no password management is needed, and they can access the network using a computer identity from the domain environment.

To use the managed service account and the virtual account, your server needs to be running at least Windows Server 2008 R2 or Windows 7/8. When you are using managed service accounts, a managed service account can be used only for services on a single computer. You are not allowed to share managed service accounts between multiple computers. This also means you can't use managed service accounts in a server that is going to be part of a cluster.

To configure or manipulate your managed service account or virtual account on a server, you need to use Windows PowerShell cmdlets or any utility that allows you to work with these types of accounts (Dsacls.exe, Services snap-in mmc, SetSPN.exe, and so forth).

Predefined Global Groups

As mentioned earlier in this chapter, you use global groups to manage permissions at the domain level. Members of each of these groups can perform specific tasks related to managing Active Directory.

The following predefined global groups are installed in the Users folder:

Cert Publishers   Certificates are used to increase security by allowing for strong authentication methods. User accounts are placed within the *Cert Publishers group* if they must publish security certificates. Generally, Active Directory security services use these accounts.

Domain Computers   All of the computers that are members of the domain are generally members of the *Domain Computers group*. This includes any workstations or servers that have joined the domain, but it does not include the domain controllers.

Domain Admins   Members of the *Domain Admins group* have full permissions to manage all of the Active Directory objects for this domain. This is a powerful account; therefore, you should restrict its membership only to those users who require full permissions.

Domain Controllers   All of the domain controllers for a given domain are generally included within the *Domain Controllers group*.

Domain Guests   Generally, by default, members of the *Domain Guests group* are given minimal permissions with respect to resources. System administrators may place user accounts in this group if they require only basic access or temporary permissions within the domain.

Domain Users   The *Domain Users group* usually contains all of the user accounts for the given domain. This group is generally given basic permissions to resources that do not require higher levels of security. A common example is a public file share.

Enterprise Admins   Members of the *Enterprise Admins group* are given full permissions to perform actions within the entire forest. This includes functions such as managing trust relationships and adding new domains to trees and forests.

Group Policy Creator Owners   Members of the *Group Policy Creator Owners group* are able to create and modify Group Policy settings for objects within the domain. This allows them to enable security settings on OUs (and the objects that they contain).

Schema Admins   Members of the *Schema Admins group* are given permissions to modify the Active Directory schema. As a member of Schema Admins, you can create additional fields of information for user accounts. This is a powerful function because any changes to the schema will be propagated to all of the domains and domain controllers within an

Active Directory forest. Furthermore, you cannot undo changes to the schema (although you can disable some).

In addition to these groups, you can create new ones for specific services and applications that are installed on the server. (You'll notice that the list in Figure 15.4 includes more than just the ones in the preceding list.) Specifically, services that run on domain controllers and servers will be created as security groups with domain local scope. For example, if a domain controller is running the DNS service, the DnsAdmins and DnsUpdateProxy groups become available. In addition, there are two read-only domain controller (RODC) local groups: the Allowed RODC Password Replication and the Denied RODC Password Replication groups. Similarly, if you install the DHCP service, it automatically creates the DHCP Users and DHCP Administrators groups. The purpose of these groups depends on the functionality of the applications being installed.

Foreign Security Principals

In environments that have more than one domain, you may need to grant permissions to users who reside in multiple domains. Generally, you manage this using Active Directory trees and forests. However, in some cases, you may want to provide resources to users who belong to domains that are not part of the forest.

Active Directory uses the concept of *foreign security principals* to allow permissions to be assigned to users who are not part of an Active Directory forest. This process is automatic and does not require the intervention of system administrators. You can then add the foreign security principals to domain local groups for which, in turn, you can grant permissions for resources within the domain. You can view a list of foreign security principals by using the Active Directory Users and Computers tool. Figure 15.5 shows the contents of the ForeignSecurityPrincipals folder.

FIGURE 15.5 The ForeignSecurityPrincipals folder

Managing Security and Permissions

Now that you understand the basic issues, terms, and Active Directory objects that pertain to security, it's time to look at how you can apply this information to secure your network resources. The general practice for managing security is to assign users to groups and then grant permissions and logon parameters to the groups so that they can access certain resources.

For management ease and to implement a hierarchical structure, you can place groups within OUs. You can also assign Group Policy settings to all of the objects contained within an OU. By using this method, you can combine the benefits of a hierarchical structure (through OUs) with the use of security principals. Figure 15.6 provides a diagram of this process.

FIGURE 15.6   An overview of security management

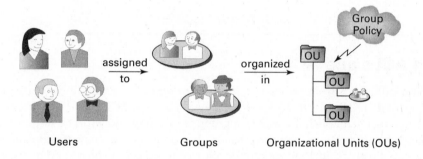

Users   Groups   Organizational Units (OUs)

The primary tool you use to manage security permissions for users, groups, and computers is the Active Directory Users and Computers tool. Using this tool, you can create and manage Active Directory objects and organize them based on your business needs. Common tasks for many system administrators might include the following:

- Resetting a user's password (for example, in cases where they forget their password)

- Creating new user accounts (when, for instance, a new employee joins the company)

- Modifying group memberships based on changes in job requirements and functions

- Disabling user accounts (when, for example, users will be out of the office for long periods of time and will not require network resource access)

Once you've properly grouped your users, you need to set the actual permissions that affect the objects within Active Directory. The actual permissions available vary based on the type of object. Table 15.1 provides an example of some of the permissions that you can apply to various Active Directory objects and an explanation of what each permission does.

TABLE 15.1   Permissions of Active Directory objects

Permission	Explanation
Control Access	Changes security permissions on the object
Create Child	Creates objects within an OU (such as other OUs)
Delete Child	Deletes child objects within an OU
Delete Tree	Deletes an OU and the objects within it
List Contents	Views objects within an OU
List Object	Views a list of the objects within an OU
Read	Views properties of an object (such as a username)
Write	Modifies properties of an object

Using ACLs and ACEs

Each object in Active Directory has an *access control list*. The ACL is a list of user accounts and groups that are allowed to access the resource. For each ACL, there is an access control entry that defines what a user or a group can actually do with the resource. Deny permissions are always listed first. This means that if users have Deny permissions through user or group membership, they will not be allowed to access the object, even if they have explicit Allow permissions through other user or group permissions. Figure 15.7 shows an ACL for the Sales OU.

FIGURE 15.7   The ACL for an OU named Sales

The Security tab is enabled only if you selected the Advanced Features option from the View menu in the Active Directory Users and Computers tool.

 Real World Scenario

Using Groups Effectively

You are a new system administrator for a medium-sized organization, and your network spans a single campus environment. The previous administrator had migrated the network from Windows 2003 to Windows Server 2012 R2, and everyone seems fine with the network and new workstations. As you familiarize yourself with the network, you realize that the previous administrator applied a very ad hoc approach. Many of the permissions to resources had been given to individual accounts on request. It seems that there was no particular strategy with regard to administration.

Management tells you that the company has acquired another company, ideally the first of several acquisitions. They tell you about these plans because they do not want any hiccups in the information system as necessary changes ensue.

You immediately realize that management practices of the past must be replaced with the best practices that have been developed for networks over the years. One of the fundamental practices that you need to establish for this environment is the use of groups to apply permissions and give privileges to users throughout the network.

It is quite simple to give permissions individually, and in some cases, it seems like overkill to create a group, give permissions to the group, and then add a user to the group. Using group-based permissions really pays off in the long run, however, regardless of how small your network is today.

One constant in the networking world is that networks grow. When they grow, it is much easier to add users to a well-thought-out system of groups and consistently applied policies and permissions than it is to patch these elements together for each individual user.

Don't get caught up in the "easy" way of dealing with each request as it comes down the pike. Take the time to figure out how the system will benefit from a more structured approach. Visualize your network as already large with numerous accounts, even if it is still small; this way, when it grows, you will be well positioned to manage the network as smoothly as possible.

Implementing Active Directory Security

So far, you have looked at many different concepts that are related to security within Active Directory. You began by exploring security principals and how they form the basis for administering Active Directory security. Then you considered the purpose and function of groups, how group scopes can affect how these groups work, and how to create a list of the predefined users and groups for new domains and domain controllers. Based on all of this information, it's time to see how you can implement Active Directory security.

In this section, you'll take a look at how you can create and manage users and groups. The most commonly used tool for working with these objects is the Active Directory Users and Computers tool. Using this tool, you can create new user and group objects within the relevant OUs of your domain, and you can modify group membership and group scope.

In addition to these basic operations, you can use some additional techniques to simplify the administration of users and groups. One method involves using user templates. Additionally, you'll want to be able to specify who can make changes to user and group objects. That's the purpose of delegation. Both of these topics are covered later in this section.

Let's start with the basics. In Exercise 15.1, you learn how to create and manage users and groups. If you went through Part I for exam 70-410, then you may have already completed this exercise, and you can use these same users for the rest of the exercises.

WARNING   This exercise involves creating new OUs and user accounts within an Active Directory domain. Be sure that you are working in a test environment to avoid any problems that might occur because of the changes you make.

EXERCISE 15.1

Creating and Managing Users and Groups

1. Open the Active Directory Users and Computers MMC snap-in by pressing the Windows key (on the keyboard) and choosing Administrative Tools ➢ Active Directory Users And Computers.

2. Create the following top-level OUs:

   Sales

   Marketing

   Engineering

   HR

3. Create the following User objects within the Sales container (use the defaults for all fields not listed):

   a.   First Name: **John**

   Last Name: **Sales**

   User Logon Name: **JSales**

   b.   First Name: **Linda**

   Last Name: **Manager**

   User Logon Name: **LManager**

4. Create the following User objects within the Marketing container (use the defaults for all fields not listed):

   a.   First Name: **Jane**

   Last Name: **Marketing**

   User Logon Name: **JMarketing**

   b.   First Name: **Monica**

   Last Name: **Manager**

   User Logon Name: **MManager**

5.   Create the following User object within the Engineering container (use the defaults for all fields not listed):

First Name: **Bob**

Last Name: **Engineer**

User Logon Name: **BEngineer**

6.   Right-click the HR container, and select New ➢ Group. Use the name **Managers** for the group and specify Global for the group scope and Security for the group type. Click OK to create the group.

7.   To assign users to the Managers group, right-click the Group object and select Properties. Change to the Members tab and click Add. Enter **Linda Manager** and **Monica Manager** and then click OK. You will see the group membership list. Click OK to finish adding the users to the group.

8.   When you have finished creating users and groups, close the Active Directory Users and Computers tool.

Notice that you can add users to groups regardless of the OU in which they're contained. In Exercise 15.1, for example, you added two user accounts from different OUs into a group that was created in a third OU. This type of flexibility allows you to manage user and group accounts easily based on your business organization.

The Active Directory Users and Computers tool also allows you to perform common functions simply by right-clicking an object and selecting actions from the context menu. For example, you could right-click a user account and select Add Members To Group to change group membership quickly. You even have the ability in Active Directory Users and Computers to drag users from one OU and drop them into another.

You may have noticed that creating multiple users can be a fairly laborious and a potentially error-prone process. As a result, you are probably ready to take a look at a better way to create multiple users—by using user templates, which is discussed in the next section.

Using User Templates

Sometimes you will need to add several users with the same security settings. Rather than creating each user from scratch and making configuration changes to each one manually, you can create one user template, configure it, and copy it as many times as necessary. Each copy retains the configuration, group membership, and permissions of the original, but you must specify a new username, password, and full name to make the new user unique.

In Exercise 15.2, you create a user template, make configuration changes, and create a new user based on the template. This exercise shows you that the new user you create will belong to the same group as the user template you copied it from. You must have completed Exercise 15.1 first before you begin this one.

EXERCISE 15.2

Creating and Using User Templates

1. Open the Active Directory Users and Computers tool.

2. Create the following User object within the Sales container (use the defaults for all fields not listed):

    First Name: **Sales User**

    Last Name: **Template**

    User Logon Name: **SalesUserTemplate**

3. Create a new global security group called Sales Users and add SalesUserTemplate to the group membership.

4. Right-click the SalesUserTemplate User object and select Copy from the context menu.

5. Enter the username, first name, and last name for the new user.

6. Click the Next button to move on to the password screen and enter the new user's password information. Close the Copy Object—User dialog box when you've finished.

7. Right-click the user that you created in step 5, select Properties, and click the Member Of tab.

8. Verify that the new user is a member of the Sales Users group.

Delegating Control of Users and Groups

A common administrative function related to the use of Active Directory involves managing users and groups. You can use OUs to group objects logically so that you can easily manage them. Once you have placed the appropriate Active Directory objects within OUs, you are ready to delegate control of these objects.

Delegation is the process by which a higher-level security administrator assigns permissions to other users. For example, if Admin A is a member of the Domain Admins group, Admin A is able to delegate control of any OU within the domain to Admin B. You can access the Delegation Of Control Wizard through the Active Directory Users and Computers tool. You can use it to perform common delegation tasks quickly and easily. The wizard walks you through the steps of selecting the objects for which you want to perform delegation, what permission you want to allow, and which users will have those permissions.

Exercise 15.3 walks through the steps required to delegate control of OUs. To complete the steps in this exercise, you must first have completed Exercise 15.1.

EXERCISE 15.3

Delegating Control of Active Directory Objects

1.   Open the Active Directory Users and Computers tool.

2.   Create a new user within the Engineering OU using the following information (use the default settings for any fields not specified):

   First Name: **Robert**

   Last Name: **Admin**

   User Logon Name: **radmin**

   Password: **P@ssw0rd**

3.   Right-click the Sales OU and select Delegate Control. This starts the Delegation Of Control Wizard. Click Next.

4.   To add users and groups to whom you want to delegate control, click the Add button. In the Add dialog box, enter **Robert Admin** for the name of the user to add. Note that you can specify multiple users or groups using this option.

5.   Click OK to add the account to the delegation list, which is shown in the Users Or Groups page. Click Next to continue.

6.   On the Tasks To Delegate page, you must specify which actions you want to allow the selected user to perform within this OU. Select the Delegate The Following Common Tasks option and place a check mark next to the following options:

   Create, Delete, And Manage User Accounts

   Reset User Passwords And Force Password Change At Next Logon

   Read All User Information

   Create, Delete And Manage Groups

   Modify The Membership Of A Group

7. Click Next to continue. The wizard summarizes the selections that you have made on the Completing The Delegation Of Control Wizard page. To complete the process, click Finish to have the wizard commit the changes.

    Now when the user Robert Admin logs on (using *radmin* as his logon name), he will be able to perform common administrative functions for all of the objects contained within the Sales OU.

8. When you have finished, close the Active Directory Users and Computers tool.

Understanding Dynamic Access Control

One of the advantages of Windows Server 2012 R2 is the ability to apply data governance to your file server. This will help control who has access to information and auditing. You get these advantages through the use of *Dynamic Access Control (DAC)*. Dynamic Access Control allows you to identify data by using data classifications (both automatic and manual) and then control access to these files based on these classifications.

DAC also gives administrators the ability to control file access by using a central access policy. This central access policy will also allow an administrator to set up audit access to files for reporting and forensic investigation.

DAC allows an administrator to set up Active Directory Rights Management Service encryption for Microsoft Office documents. For example, you can set up encryption for any documents that contain financial information.

Dynamic Access Control gives an administrator the flexibility to configure file access and auditing to domain-based file servers. To do this, DAC controls claims in the authentication token, resource properties, and conditional expressions within permission and auditing entries.

Administrators have the ability to give users access to files and folders based on Active Directory attributes. For example, a user named Dana is given access to the file server share because in the user's Active Directory (department attribute) properties, the value contains the value Sales.

 For DAC to function properly, an administrator must enable Windows 8 computers and Windows Server 2012 R2 file servers to support claims and compound authentication.

Using Group Policy for Security

As discussed in Chapter 6, "Manage GPOs," a useful and powerful feature of Active Directory is a technology known as a *Group Policy*. Through the use of Group Policy settings, system administrators can assign thousands of different settings and options for users, groups, and OUs. Specifically, in relation to security, you can use many different options to control how important features such as password policies, user rights, and account lockout settings can be configured.

The general process for making these settings is to create a *Group Policy object (GPO)* with the settings you want and then link it to an OU or other Active Directory object.

Table 15.2 lists many Group Policy settings, which are relevant to creating a secure Active Directory environment. Note that this list is not comprehensive—many other options are available through Windows Server 2012's administrative tools.

TABLE 15.2   Group Policy settings used for security purposes

Setting section	Setting name	Purpose
Account Policies ➢ Password Policy	Enforce Password History	Specifies how many passwords will be remembered. This option prevents users from reusing the same passwords whenever they're changed.
Account Policies ➢ Password Policy	Minimum Password Length	Prevents users from using short, weak passwords by specifying the minimum number of characters that the password must include.
Account Policies ➢ Account Lockout Policy	Account Lockout Threshold	Specifies how many bad password attempts can be entered before the account gets locked out.
Account Policies ➢ Account Lockout Policy	Account Lockout Duration	Specifies how long an account will remain locked out after too many bad password attempts have been entered. By setting this option to a reasonable value (such as 30 minutes), you can reduce administrative overhead while still maintaining fairly strong security.
Account Policies ➢ Account Lockout Policy	Reset Account Lockout Counter After	Specifies how long the Account Lockout Threshold counter will hold failed logon attempts before resetting to 0.
Local Policies ➢ Security Options	Accounts: Rename Administrator Account	Often, when trying to gain unauthorized access to a computer, individuals attempt to guess the administrator password. One method for increasing security is to rename this account so that no password allows entry using this logon.
Local Policies ➢ Security Options	Domain Controller: Allow Server Operators To Schedule Tasks	This option specifies whether members of the built-in Server Operators group are allowed to schedule tasks on the server.

Setting section	Setting name	Purpose
Local Policies ➢ Security Options	Interactive Logon: Do Not Display Last User Name	Increases security by not displaying the name of the last user who logged onto the system.
Local Policies ➢ Security Options	Shutdown: Allow System To Be Shut Down Without Having To Log On	Allows system administrators to perform remote shutdown operations without logging on to the server.

You can use several different methods to configure Group Policy settings using the tools included with Windows Server 2012. Exercise 15.4 walks through the steps required to create a basic group policy for the purpose of enforcing security settings. To complete the steps of this exercise, you must have completed Exercise 15.1.

EXERCISE 15.4

Applying Security Policies by Using Group Policy

1. Open the Group Policy Management Console tool.

2. Expand Domains and then click the domain name.

3. In the right pane, right-click the Default Domain Policy and choose Edit.

4. In the Group Policy Management Editor window, expand Computer Configuration ➢ Policies ➢ Windows Settings ➢ Security Settings ➢ Account Policies ➢ Password Policy.

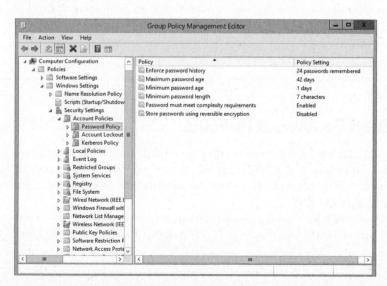

EXERCISE 15.4 *(continued)*

5. In the right pane, double-click the Minimum Password Length setting.

6. In the Security Policy Setting dialog box, make sure the box labeled Define This Policy Setting Option is checked. Increase the Password Must Be At Least value to eight characters.

7. Click OK to return to the Group Policy Management Editor window.

8. Expand User Configuration ➢ Policies ➢ Administrative Templates ➢ Control Panel. Double-click Prohibit Access To The Control Panel And PC settings, select Enabled, and then click OK.

9. Close the Group Policy window.

Fine-Grained Password Policies

The Windows 2012 R2 operating systems allow an organization to have different password and account lockout policies for different sets of users in a domain. In versions of Active Directory before 2008, an administrator could set up only one password policy and account lockout policy per domain.

The Default Domain policy for the domain is where these policy settings were configured. Because domains could have only one password and account lockout policy, organizations that wanted multiple password and account lockout settings had to either create a password filter or deploy multiple domains.

Fine-grained password policies allow you to specify multiple password policies within a single domain. Let's say you want administrators not to have to change their password as frequently as salespeople. Fine-grained password policies allow you to do just that.

Password Settings objects (PSOs) are created so that you can create fine-grained password policies. You create PSOs using the ADSI editor and then you can use those PSOs to create your fine-grained password policies.

Exercise 15.5 walks through the creation of a custom password policy using the ADSI Edit tool, and then you will link that policy to a group using Active Directory Users and Computers. Before completing this exercise, create a new global group named Passgroup in Active Directory Users and Computers.

EXERCISE 15.5

Fine-Grained Password Policy

1. Open ADSI Edit by pressing the Windows key and choosing ADSI Edit.

2. Right-click ADSI Edit and then choose Connect To.

3. When the Connection Settings dialog box appears, click OK.

4. In the window on the left, expand Default Naming Context ➢ DC=yourdomainname,DC=com ➢ CN=System ➢ CN=Password Settings Container.

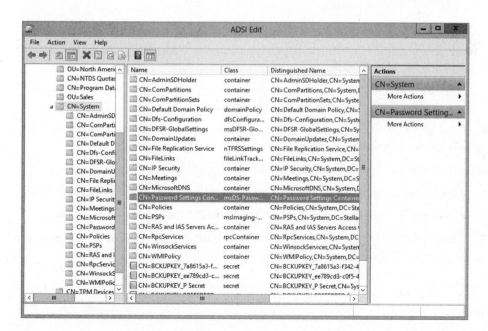

5. Right-click CN=Password Settings Container and choose New ➤ Object.

6. In the Select A Class box, choose msDS-PasswordSettings and click Next.

7. At the Common Name screen, type **CustomPolicy** and click Next.

8. At the Password Settings Precedence screen, enter **10** as the value. This works as a cost value. The lowest priority takes precedence.

9. At the Password Reversible Encryption Status For Users Accounts screen, set the value to False (recommended by Microsoft).

10. The Password History Length screen shows how many passwords are remembered before a password can be used again. You can set this for up to 1,024 remembered passwords. Set the value to **12**. Click Next.

11. At the Password Complexity screen, set the value to True.

12. The next screen will be the Minimum Password Length screen. Set the value to **8** and click Next.

13. At the Minimum Password Age screen, you must enter a value for the amount of time you want the password to be used at a minimum. Time is done in the I8 format, like so:

    –600000000 = 1 minute

    –36000000000 = 1 hour

    –864000000000 = 1 day

    So if you want the minimum to be 10 days, you must calculate –864000000000 × 10 (equaling –8640000000000).

    Enter **–8640000000000** (10 zeros) as your value for 10 days and click Next. You must put the – (minus) sign in the front of the value.

14. At the Maximum Password Age screen, set the value as **–51840000000000** (10 zeros). This value equals 60 days. Click Next.

15. At the Lockout Threshold screen, enter **3** and click Next.

16. At the Observation Window screen, enter **–3000000000** (5 minutes) and click Next.

17. At the Lockout Duration screen, enter **–18000000000** (30 minutes) and click Next.

18. Click Finished. If you received any errors, check all of your times to be sure the – (minus) sign appears in front of the number.

19. Close ADSI Edit.

20. Open the Active Directory Users and Computers snap-in.

21. On the View menu along the top, make sure Advanced Features is checked.

22. In the window on the left, expand Active Directory Users and Computers ➢ *yourdomain* ➢ System ➢ Password Settings Container.

23. In the details pane on the right side, right-click CustomPolicy and choose Properties.

24. Click the Attribute Editor tab.

25. Scroll down and select the `msDS-PsoAppliesTo` attribute. Click Edit.

26. In the Multi-valued Distinguished Name dialog box, click Add Windows Account.

27. Type in **Passgroup** (this is the group you created before the exercise) and click the Check Name button. Click OK.

28. Click OK twice more, and then you are finished. Close the Active Directory Users and Computers snap-in.

Managing Multiple Domains

You can easily manage most of the operations that must occur *between* domains by using the Active Directory Domains and Trusts administrative tool. On the other hand, if you want to configure settings *within* a domain, you should use the Active Directory MMC tools. In the following sections, you'll look at managing *single-master operations* (FSMO) roles.

Managing Single-Master Operations

For the most part, Active Directory functions in what is known as *multimaster replication*. That is, every domain controller within the environment contains a copy of the Active Directory database that is both readable and writable. This works well for most types of information. For example, if you want to modify the password of a user, you can easily do this on *any* of the domain controllers within a domain. The change is then automatically propagated to the other domain controllers.

However, some functions are not managed in a multimaster fashion. These operations are known as *operations masters*. You must perform single-master operations on specially designated domain controllers within the Active Directory forest. There are five main single-master functions: two that apply to an entire Active Directory forest and three that apply to each domain.

Forest Operations Masters

You use the Active Directory Domains and Trusts tool to configure forest-wide roles. The following single-master operations apply to the entire forest:

Schema Master   Earlier you learned that all of the domain controllers within a single Active Directory environment share the same schema. This ensures information consistency. However, developers and system administrators can modify the Active Directory schema by adding custom information. A trivial example might involve adding a field to employee information that specifies a user's favorite color.

When you need to make these types of changes, you must perform them on the domain controller that serves as the *Schema Master* for the environment. The Schema Master is then responsible for propagating all of the changes to all the other domain controllers within the forest.

Domain Naming Master   The purpose of the *Domain Naming Master* is to keep track of all the domains within an Active Directory forest. You access this domain controller whenever you need to add/remove new domains to a tree or forest.

Domain Operations Masters

You use the Active Directory Users and Computers snap-in to administer roles within a domain. Within each domain, at least one domain controller must fulfill each of the following roles:

Relative ID (RID) Master   Every security object within Active Directory must be assigned a unique identifier so that it is distinguishable from other objects. For example, if you have two OUs named IT that reside in different domains, you must have some way to distinguish easily between them. Furthermore, if you delete one of the IT OUs and then later re-create it, the system must be able to determine that it is not the same object as the other IT OU. The unique identifier for each object is made up of a domain identifier and a relative identifier (RID). RIDs are always unique within an Active Directory domain and are used for managing security information and authenticating users. The *RID Master* is responsible for creating these values within a domain whenever new Active Directory objects are created.

PDC Emulator Master   Within a domain, the *PDC Emulator Master* is responsible for maintaining backward compatibility with Windows 95, 98, and NT clients. The PDC emulator is also responsible for processing password changes between a domain user account and all of the domain controllers throughout the domain.

The PDC emulator is also the default time server for all of the domain controllers in the domain. This is why it's a good practice to make sure that your PDC emulator has the proper time. It's the system that all others will rely on for time accuracy.

The PDC Emulator Master serves as the default domain controller to process authentication requests if another domain controller is unable to do so. The PDC Emulator Master also receives preferential treatment whenever domain security changes are made. PDC emulators are also the preferred point of contact for many services and applications that run on the domain.

Infrastructure Master   Whenever a user is added to or removed from a group, all of the other domain controllers should be made aware of this change. The role of the domain controller that acts as an *Infrastructure Master* is to ensure that group membership information stays synchronized within an Active Directory domain.

Unless there is only one domain controller, you should not place the Infrastructure Master on a global catalog server. If the Infrastructure Master and global catalog are on the same domain controller, the Infrastructure Master will not function.

Another service that a server can control for the network is the Windows Time service. The Windows Time service uses a suite of algorithms in the Network Time Protocol (NTP). This helps ensure that the time on all computers throughout a network is as accurate as possible. All client computers within a Windows Server 2012 R2 domain are synchronized with the time of an authoritative computer.

Assigning Single-Master Roles

Now that you are familiar with the different types of single-master operations, take a look at Exercise 15.6. This exercise shows you how to assign these roles to servers within the Active Directory environment. In this exercise, you will assign single-master operations roles to various domain controllers within the environment. To complete the steps in this exercise, you need one Active Directory domain controller.

EXERCISE 15.6

Assigning Single-Master Operations

1. Open the Active Directory Domains and Trusts administrative tool.

2. Right-click Active Directory Domains And Trusts and choose Operations Masters.

3. In the Operations Masters dialog box, note that you can change the operations master by clicking the Change button. If you want to move this assignment to another computer, first you need to connect to that computer and then make the change. Click Close to continue without making any changes.

4. Close the Active Directory Domains and Trusts administrative tool.

5. Open the Active Directory Users and Computers administrative tool.

6. Right-click the name of a domain and select Operations Masters. This brings up the RID tab of the Operations Masters dialog box.

   Notice that you can change the computer that is assigned to the role. To change the role, first you need to connect to the appropriate domain controller. Notice that the PDC and Infrastructure roles have similar tabs. Click Close to continue without making any changes.

7. When you have finished, close the Active Directory Users and Computers tool.

Remember that you manage single-master operations with three different tools. You use the Active Directory Domains and Trusts tool to configure the Domain Name Master role, while you use the Active Directory Users and Computers snap-in to administer roles within a domain. Although this might not seem intuitive at first, it can help you remember which roles apply to domains and which apply to the whole forest. The third tool, the Schema Master role, is a bit different than these other two. To change the Schema Master role, you must install the Active Directory Schema MMS snap-in and change it there.

Seizing Roles

Changing roles from one domain controller to another is really simple. An administrator goes into Active Directory or PowerShell and changes an FSMO role from one machine to another. The problem happens when a machine with one of the roles crashes and goes down. You can't just switch the role from a machine that is not working.

So, what is an administrator to do? Well, at that point, what you need to do is seize control of the role. You do this through the use of PowerShell. Let's look at how to seize a role using PowerShell.

You may be familiar with seizing FSMO roles from previous versions of Windows Server. In previous versions, you would use the `NTDSUtil.exe` command-line utility, but in Windows Server 2012 R2 it needs to be done in PowerShell.

Normally, I would show you how to seize control of an FSMO role using an exercise, but since you probably don't have dozens of Microsoft Windows Server 2012 R2 domain controllers just lying around, I will show you how to seize control through a step-by-step process.

To show you how to set up a step-by-step process, you first have to know what FSMO roles are assigned to what FSMO numbers. The following roles each have a corresponding number:

FSMO role	Number
PDCEmulator	0
RIDMaster	1
InfrastructureMaster	2
SchemaMaster	3
DomainNamingMaster	4

Now that you know the role and the number associated to it, you just need to know the PowerShell commands to seize control of the role. The following is an example of how to use PowerShell commands to seize control of one of the FSMO roles.

I am using the `-Identity` switch to specify the target domain controller (I am calling my target domain controller DC1) and the `-OperationMasterRole` to specify which role to transfer. I've also used the `-Force` command because my current FSMO holder is offline. I will be moving all of the roles to the target domain controller, DC1.

1. On a domain controller, log in as an administrator and start PowerShell with elevated privileges.

2. In PowerShell, type the following command:

   ```
   Move-ADDirectoryServerOperationMasterRole -Identity DC1
   -OperationMasterRole 0,1,2,3,4 -Force
   ```

3. Either type **Y** on each role move prompt or type **A** to accept all prompts.

4. After a few minutes, all of the FSMO roles should be successfully moved.

Finally, I want to show you a couple of useful PowerShell commands so that you can view which domain controller owns which FSMO role.

```
Get-ADForest DomainName | FT SchemaMaster,DomainNamingMaster
Get-ADDomain DomainName | FT PDCEmulator,RIDMaster,InfrastructureMaster
```

Maintain Active Directory

If you have deployed Active Directory in your network environment, your users now depend on it to function properly in order to do their jobs. From network authentications to file access to print and web services, Active Directory has become a mission-critical component of your business. Therefore, the importance of backing up the Active Directory data store should be evident.

As I discussed in earlier chapters, it is important to have multiple domain controllers available to provide backup in case of a problem. The same goes for Active Directory itself—it too should be backed up by being saved. This way, if a massive disaster occurs in which you need to restore your directory services, you will have that option available to you.

Backups are just good common sense, but here are several specific reasons to back up data:

Protect Against Hardware Failures   Computer hardware devices have finite lifetimes, and all hardware eventually fails. We discussed this when we mentioned *Mean Time Between Failures (MTBF)* earlier. MBTF is the average time a device will function before it actually fails. There is also a rating derived from benchmark testing of hard disk devices that tells you when you may be at risk for an unavoidable disaster. Some types of failures, such as corrupted hard disk drives, can result in significant data loss.

Protect Against Accidental Deletion or Modification of Data   Although the threat of hardware failures is very real, in most environments, mistakes in modifying or deleting data are much more common. For example, suppose a systems administrator accidentally deletes all of the objects within a specific OU. Clearly, it's very important to be able to retrieve this information from a backup.

Keep Historical Information   Users and systems administrators sometimes modify files and then later find out that they require access to an older version of the file. Or a file is accidentally deleted, and a user does not discover that fact until much later. By keeping multiple backups over time, you can recover information from prior backups when necessary.

Protect Against Malicious Deletion or Modification of Data   Even in the most secure environments, it is conceivable that unauthorized users (or authorized ones with malicious intent!) could delete or modify information. In such cases, the loss of data might require valid backups from which to restore critical information.

Windows Server 2012 R2 includes a Backup utility that is designed to back up operating system files and the Active Directory data store. It allows for basic backup functionality, such as scheduling backup jobs and selecting which files to back up. Figure 15.8 shows the main screen of the Windows Server 2012 R2 Backup utility.

In the following sections, we'll look at the details of using the Windows Server 2012 R2 Backup utility and how you can restore Active Directory when problems do occur.

FIGURE 15.8   The main screen of the Windows Server 2012 Backup utility

Overview of the Windows Server 2012 R2 Backup Utility

Although the general purpose behind performing backup operations—protecting information—is straightforward, system administrators must consider many options when determining the optimal backup-and-recovery scenario for their environment. Factors include what to back up, how often to back up, and when the backups should be performed.

In this section, you'll see how the Windows Server 2012 R2 Backup utility makes it easy to implement a backup plan for many network environments.

> Although the Windows Server 2012 R2 Backup utility provides the basic functionality required to back up your files, you may want to investigate third-party products that provide additional functionality. These applications can provide options for specific types of backups (such as those for Exchange Server and SQL Server) as well as disaster recovery options, networking functionality, centralized management, and support for more advanced hardware.

Backup Types

One of the most important issues you will have to deal with when you are performing backups is keeping track of which files you have backed up and which files you need to back up. Whenever a backup of a file is made, the archive bit for the file is set. You can view the attributes of system files by right-clicking them and selecting Properties. By clicking the Advanced button in the Properties dialog box, you will access the Advanced Attributes dialog box. Here you will see the option Folder Is Ready For Archiving. Figure 15.9 shows an example of the attributes for a folder.

FIGURE 15.9   Viewing the Archive attributes for a folder

Although it is possible to back up all of the files in the file system during each backup operation, it's sometimes more convenient to back up only selected files (such as those that have changed since the last backup operation). When performing backups, you can back up to removable media (DVD) or to a network location.

It is recommended by Microsoft to do a backup to a network location. The reason for this is that if your company suffers from a disaster (fire, hurricane, and so forth), your data can all still be lost—including the backup. If you back up to a removable media source, a copy of the backup can be taken off-site. This protects against a major disaster. Several types of backups can be performed:

 Although Windows Server 2012 R2 does not support all of these backup types, it's very important that you understand the most common backup types. Most Administrators use third-party software for their backups. That's why it's important to know all of the different types.

Normal   Normal backups (also referred to as *system* or *full backups*) back up all of the selected files and then mark them as backed up. This option is usually used when a full system backup is made. Windows Server 2012 R2 supports this backup.

Copy   *Copy backups* back up all of the selected files but do not mark them as backed up. This is useful when you want to make additional backups of files for moving files offsite or you want to make multiple copies of the same data for archival purposes.

Incremental   *Incremental backups* copy any selected files that are marked as ready for backup (typically because they have not been backed up or they have been changed since the last backup) and then mark the files as backed up. When the next incremental backup is run, only the files that are not marked as having been backed up are stored. Incremental backups are used in conjunction with normal (full) backups.

The most common backup process is to make a full backup and then make subsequent incremental backups. The benefit to this method is that only files that have changed since the last full or incremental backup will be stored. This can reduce backup times and disk or tape storage space requirements.

When recovering information from this type of backup method, a system administrator must first restore the full backup and then restore each of the incremental backups.

Differential   *Differential backups* are similar in purpose to incremental backups with one important exception: Differential backups copy all of the files that are marked for backup but do not mark the files as backed up. When restoring files in a situation that uses normal and differential backups, you need only restore the normal backup and the latest differential backup.

Daily   *Daily backups* back up all of the files that have changed during a single day. This operation uses the file time/date stamps to determine which files should be backed up and does not mark the files as having been backed up.

Backing Up System State Data

When you are planning to back up and restore Active Directory, be aware that the most important component is known as the *System State data*. System State data includes the components upon which the Windows Server 2012 R2 operating system relies for normal operations. The Windows Server 2012 R2 Backup utility offers you the ability to back up the System State data to another type of media (such as a hard disk or network share). Specifically, it will back up the following components for a Windows Server 2012 R2 domain controller:

Active Directory   The *Active Directory data store* is at the heart of Active Directory. It contains all of the information necessary to create and manage network resources, such as users and computers. In most environments that use Active Directory, users and system administrators rely on the proper functioning of these services in order to do their jobs.

Boot Files   *Boot files* are the files required for booting the Windows Server 2012 R2 operating system and can be used in the case of boot file corruption.

COM+ Class Registration Database   The *COM+ Class Registration database* is a listing of all of the COM+ Class registrations stored on the computer. Applications that run on a Windows Server 2012 R2 computer might require the registration of various share code components. As part of the System State backup process, Windows Server 2012 R2 stores all of the information related to Component Object Model+ (COM+) components so that it can be quickly and easily restored.

Registry   The Windows Server 2012 R2 *Registry* is a central repository of information related to the operating system configuration (such as desktop and network settings), user settings, and application settings. Therefore, the Registry is absolutely vital to the proper functioning of Windows Server 2012 R2.

Sysvol **Directory**   The *Sysvol directory* includes data and files that are shared between the domain controllers within an Active Directory domain. Many operating system services rely on this information in order to function properly.

Bare Metal Backups and Restores

One of the options you have in Windows Server 2012 R2 is to do a *Bare Metal Restore (BMR)*. This is a restore of a machine after the machine has been completely wiped out and formatted. This type of restore is done usually after a catastrophic machine failure or crash.

Windows Server 2012 R2 gives you the ability to backup all of the files needed for a Bare Metal Restore by choosing the Bare Metal Recovery checkbox (see Figure 15.10).

FIGURE 15.10   Bare Metal Option

When you choose the Bare Metal Restore option in Windows Server 2012 R2, all of the sub-options (System State, System Reserved, and Local disk) automatically get checked.

When preparing your network for a Bare Metal Backup, you want to make sure that you have everything you need on hand to complete this type of restore. You may want to keep a copy of the server software, server drivers, and so forth on hand and ready to go, just in case you have to do a full restore.

Scheduling Backups

In addition to specifying which files to back up, you can schedule backup jobs to occur at specific times. Planning *when* to perform backups is just as important as deciding *what* to back up. Performing backup operations can reduce overall system performance; therefore, you should plan to back up information during times of minimal activity on your servers.

To add a backup operation to the schedule, you can simply click the Add button on the Specify Backup Time window.

Restoring System State Data

In some cases, the Active Directory data store or other System State data may become corrupt or unavailable. This could be due to many different reasons. A hard disk failure might, for example, result in the loss of data. Or the accidental deletion of an OU and all of its objects might require a restore operation to be performed.

The actual steps involved in restoring System State data are based on the details of what has caused the data loss and what effect this data loss has had on the system. In the best-case scenario, the System State data is corrupt or inaccurate but the operating system can still boot. If this is the case, all you must do is boot into a special *Directory Services Restore Mode (DSRM)* and then restore the System State data from a backup. This process will replace the current System State data with that from the backup. Therefore, any changes that have been made since the last backup will be completely lost and must be redone.

In a worst-case scenario, all of the information on a server has been lost or a hardware failure is preventing the machine from properly booting. If this is the case, here are several steps that you must take in order to recover System State data:

1. Fix any hardware problem that might prevent the computer from booting (for example, replace any failed hard disks).

2. Reinstall the Windows Server 2012 R2 operating system. This should be performed like a regular installation on a new system.

3. Reinstall any device drivers that may be required by your backup device. If you backed up information to the file system, this will not apply.

4. Restore the System State data using the Windows Server 2012 Backup utility.

I'll cover the technical details of performing restores later in this section. For now, however, you should understand the importance of backing up information and, whenever possible, testing the validity of backups.

Backing Up and Restoring Group Policy Objects

Group Policy Objects (GPOs) are a major part of Active Directory. When you back up Active Directory, GPOs can also get backed up. You also have the ability to back up GPOs through the Group Policy Management Console (GPMC). This gives you the ability to back up and restore individual GPOs.

To back up all GPOs, open the GPMC and right-click the Group Policy Objects container. You will see the option Back Up All. After you choose this option, a wizard will start asking you for the backup location. Choose a location and click Backup.

To back up an individual GPO, right-click the GPO (in the Group Policy Objects container) and choose Backup. Again, after you choose this option, a wizard will start asking you for the backup location. Choose a location and click Backup.

To restore a GPO, it's the same process as above except, instead of choosing Backup, you will either choose Manage Backups (to restore all GPOs) or Restore (for an individual GPO).

Setting Up an Active Directory Backup

The Windows Server 2012 R2 Backup utility makes it easy to back up the System data (including Active Directory) as part of a normal backup operation. We've already covered the ideas behind the different backup types and why and when they are used.

Exercise 15.7 walks you through the process of backing up the domain controller. In order to complete this exercise, the local machine must be a domain controller, and you must have a DVD burner or network location to back up the System State.

 The Windows Server 2012 R2 Backup utility is not installed by default. If you have already installed the Windows Server 2012 R2 Backup utility, skip to step 9.

EXERCISE 15.7

Backing Up Active Directory

1. To install the Windows Server 2012 R2 Backup utility, click the Start Key ➢ Administrative Tools ➢ Server Manager.

2. In the center console, click the link for Add Roles And Features.

3. At the Select Installation Type screen, choose role-based or feature-based installation and click Next.

4. The Select Destination Server screen appears. Choose Select A Server From The Server Pool, and choose your server under Server Pool. Click Next.

5. Click Next at the Select Server Roles screen.

6. At the Select Features screen, scroll down and check the box next to Windows Server Backup. Click Next.

7. At the Confirmation screen, click the checkbox to Restart the destination server automatically. This will bring up a dialog box. Click Yes, and then click the Install button.

8. Click the Close button when finished. Close Server Manager.

9. Open Windows Backup by clicking the Windows Key ➢ Administrative Tools ➢ Windows Server Backup.

10. On the left-hand side, click Local Backup. Then, under Actions, click Backup Once.

11. When the Backup Once Wizard appears, click Different Options and click Next.

12. At the Select Backup Configuration screen, choose Custom and click Next.

13. Click the Add Items button. Choose System State and click OK. Click Next.

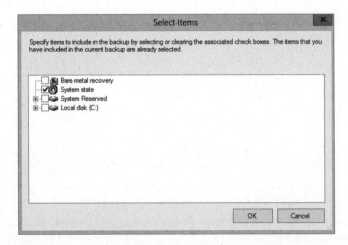

14. At the Specify Destination Type, choose Remote Shared Folder. Click Next.

15. Put in the shared path you want to use and click Next.

16. At the Confirmation screen, click the Backup button.

17. Once the backup is complete, close the Windows Server Backup utility.

Restoring Active Directory

Active Directory has been designed with fault tolerance in mind. For example, it is highly recommended by Microsoft that each domain have at least two domain controllers. Each of these domain controllers contains a copy of the Active Directory data store. Should one of the domain controllers fail, the available one can take over the failed server's functionality. When the failed server is repaired, it can then be promoted to a domain controller in the existing environment. This process effectively restores the failed domain controller without incurring any downtime for end users because all of the Active Directory data is replicated to the repaired server in the next scheduled replication.

In some cases, you might need to restore Active Directory from a backup. For example, suppose a system administrator accidentally deletes several hundred users from the domain and does not realize it until the change has been propagated to all of the other domain controllers. Manually re-creating the accounts is not an option because the objects' security identifiers will be different (and all permissions must be reset). Clearly, a method for restoring from backup is the best solution. You can elect to make the Active Directory restore authoritative or nonauthoritative, as described in the following sections.

Overview of Authoritative Restore

Restoring Active Directory and other System State data is an important process should system files or the Active Directory data store become corrupt or otherwise unavailable. Fortunately, the Windows Server 2012 R2 Backup utility allows you to restore data easily from a backup, should the need arise.

I mentioned earlier that in the case of the accidental deletion of information from Active Directory, you might need to restore the Active Directory from a recent backup. But what happens if there is more than one domain controller in the environment? Even if you did perform a restore, the information on this domain controller would be seen as outdated and it would be overwritten by the data from another domain controller. This data from the older domain controller is exactly the information you want to replace. The domain controller that was reloaded using a backup would have an older time stamp, and the other domain controllers would re-delete the information from the backup.

Fortunately, Windows Server 2012 R2 and Active Directory allow you to perform what is called an *authoritative restore*. The authoritative restore process specifies a domain controller as having the authoritative (or master) copy of the Active Directory data store. When other domain controllers communicate with this domain controller, their information will be overwritten with Active Directory data stored on the local machine.

Now that you have an idea of how an authoritative restore is supposed to work, let's move on to looking at the details of performing the process.

Performing an Authoritative Restore

When you are restoring Active Directory information on a Windows Server 2012 R2 domain controller, make sure that Active Directory services are not running. This is because the restore of System State data requires full access to system files and the Active Directory data store. If you attempt to restore System State data while the domain controller is active, you will see an error message.

In general, restoring data and operating system files is a straightforward process. It is important to note that restoring a System State backup will replace the existing Registry, Sysvol, and Active Directory files, so that any changes you made since the last backup will be lost.

In addition to restoring the entire Active Directory database, you can also restore only specific subtrees within Active Directory using the restoresubtree command in the ntdsutil utility. This allows you to restore specific information, and it is useful in case of accidental deletion of isolated material.

Following the authoritative restore process, Active Directory should be updated to the time of the last backup. Furthermore, all of the other domain controllers for this domain will have their Active Directory information overwritten by the results of the restore operation. The result is an Active Directory environment that has been recovered from media.

Overview of Nonauthoritative Restore

Now that you understand why you would use an authoritative restore and how it is performed, it's an easy conceptual jump to understand a *nonauthoritative restore*. Remember that by making a restore authoritative, you are simply telling other domain controllers in the domain to recognize the restored machine as the newest copy of Active Directory for replication purposes. If you only have one domain controller, the authoritative restore process becomes moot; you can simply skip the steps required to make the restore authoritative and begin using the domain controller immediately after the normal restore is complete.

If you have more than one domain controller in the domain and you need to perform a nonauthoritative restore, simply allow the domain controller to receive Active Directory database information from other domain controllers in the domain using normal replication methods.

Active Directory Recycle Bin

The Active Directory Recycle Bin is a great feature that allows an administrator to restore an active directory object that has been deleted.

Let's say that you have a junior administrator who has been making changes to Active Directory for hours. The junior admin then deletes an OU from Active Directory. You would then have to reload the OU from a tape backup, or even worse, you may have to reload the entire Active Directory (depending on your backup software), thus losing the hours of work the junior admin has completed.

The problem here is that when you delete a security object from Active Directory, the object's Security ID (SID) gets removed. All users' rights and permissions are associated with the users' SID number and not their account name. This is where the AD Recycle Bin can help.

The *Active Directory Recycle Bin* allows you to preserve and restore accidentally deleted Active Directory objects without the need of using a backup.

The Active Directory Recycle Bin works for both the Active Directory Domain Services (AD DS) and the Active Directory Lightweight Directory Services (AD LDS) environments.

By enabling (disabled by default) the Active Directory Recycle Bin, any deleted Active Directory objects are preserved and Active Directory objects can be restored, in their entirety, to the same condition that they were in immediately before deletion. This means that all group memberships and access rights that the object had before deletion will remain intact.

To enable the Active Directory Recycle Bin, you must do the following (you must be a member of the Schema Admins group):

- Run the `adprep /forestprep` command to prepare the forest on the server that holds the schema master to update the schema.

- Run the `adprep /domainprep /gpprep` command to prepare the domain on the server that holds the infrastructure operations master role.

- If a read-only domain controller (RODC) is present in your environment, you must also run the adprep /rodcprep command.
- Make sure that all domain controllers in your Active Directory forest are running Windows Server 2012 R2, Windows Server 2012, or Windows Server 2008 R2.
- Make sure that the forest functional level is set to Windows Server 2012 R2, Windows Server 2012, or Windows Server 2008 R2.

Restartable Active Directory

Administrators have the ability to stop and restart Active Directory in the Windows Server 2012 operating system without the need to reboot the entire system. Administrators can perform these actions either by using the Microsoft Management Console (MMC) snap-ins or the command line.

With *Restartable Active Directory Services*, an administrator has the ability to stop Active Directory Services so that updates and other tasks can be applied to a domain controller. One task that an administrator can perform while Active Directory is stopped is an offline defragmentation of the database.

One of the advantages of a Restartable Active Directory is that other services running on the same server do not depend on Active Directory to continue to function properly while Active Directory is stopped. An administrator has the ability to stop and restart the Active Directory Domain Services in the Local Services MMC snap-in.

Offline Maintenance

As you learned in the preceding section, there are times when you have to be offline to do maintenance. For example, you need to perform authoritative and nonauthoritative restores while the domain controller is offline. The main utility we use for offline maintenance is ntdsutil.

Ntdsutil.exe

The primary method by which system administrators can do offline maintenance is through the ntdsutil command-line tool. You can launch this tool by simply entering **ntdsutil** at a command prompt. For the commands to work properly, you must start the command prompt with elevated privileges. The ntdsutil command is both interactive and context sensitive. That is, once you launch the utility, you'll see an ntdsutil command prompt. At this prompt, you can enter various commands that set your context within the application. For example, if you enter **domain management**, you'll be able to enter domain-related commands. Several operations also require you to connect to a domain, a domain controller, or an Active Directory object before you perform a command.

Table 15.3 provides a list of some of the domain-management commands supported by the ntdsutil tool. You can access this functionality by typing the command at an elevated command prompt. Once you are in the ntdsutil prompt, you can use the question mark to see all of the commands available.

TABLE 15.3 Ntdsutil offline maintenance commands

Ntdsutil **Domain Management Command**	Purpose
Help or ?	Displays information about the commands that are available within the Domain Management menu of the ntdsutil utility.
Activate instance %s	Sets NTDS or a specific AD LDS instance as the active instance.
Authoritative restore	Sets the domain controller for the Authoritative restore of the Active Directory database.
Change service account	This allows an administrator to change the AD LDS service account to user name and password. You can use a "NULL" for a blank password, and you can use * to prompt the user to enter a password.
configurable settings	Allows an administrator to manage configurable settings.
DS behavior	Allows an administrator to view and modify AD DS or AD LDS behavior.
files	This command allows an administrator to manage the AD DS or AD LDS database files.
Group Membership Evaluation	Allows an administrator to evaluate the security IDs (SIDs) in a token for a given user or group.
LDAP policies	Administrators can manage the Lightweight Directory Access Protocol (LDAP) protocol policies.
metadata cleanup	Removes metadata from decommissioned domain controllers.
security account management	This command allows an administrator to manage SIDs.
Set DSRM Password	Resets the Directory Service Restore mode administrator account password.

Active Directory Database Mounting Tool

One issue that an administrator may run into when trying to restore Active Directory is the need to restore several backups to compare the Active Directory data that each backup contains. Windows Server 2012 R2 has a utility called the Active Directory database mounting tool (Dsamain.exe), which can resolve this issue.

The Dsamain.exe tool can help the recovery processes by giving you a way to compare data as it exists in snapshots (taken at different times) so that you have the ability to decide which Active Directory database to restore.

Creating snapshots on a regular basis will allow you to have enough data so that you can keep accurate records of how the Active Directory database changes over time. The ntdsutil utility allows you to take snapshots by using the ntdsutil snapshot operation.

 You are not required to run the ntdsutil snapshot operation to use Dsamain.exe. You have the ability to use a backup of the Active Directory database.

You must be a member of the Domain Admins group or the Enterprise Admins group to view any snapshots taken due to the fact that these snapshots contain sensitive Active Directory data.

Compact the Directory Database File (Offline Defragmentation)

One task that all of us having been doing for years is the process of defragging the operating systems that we run. We have used the defragmentation utility since Windows NT. Defragging a system helps return free space from data to the hard drive.

You can also use the defragmentation process to compact the Active Directory database while it's offline. Offline defragmentation helps return free disk space and check Active Directory database integrity.

To perform an offline defragmentation, you would use the ntdsutil command. When you perform a defragmentation of the Active Directory database, a new compacted version of the database is created. This new database file can be created on the same machine (if space permits) or on a network location. After the new file is created, copy the compacted Ntds.dit file back to the original location.

It is a good practice, if space allows, to maintain a copy of the older, original database file. You can either rename the older database file and keep it in its current location or copy the older database file to an alternate location.

Monitoring Replication

At times you may need to keep an eye on how your replication traffic is working on your domain controllers. We are going to examine the replication utility that you can use to help determine if there are problems on your domain.

Repadmin Utility

The Repadmin utility is included when you install Windows Server 2012 R2. This command-line tool helps administrators diagnose replication problems between Windows domain controllers.

Repadmin allows administrators to view the replication topology of each domain controller as seen from the domain controller's perspective. Administrators can also use Repadmin to create the replication topology manually. By manually creating the replication topology, administrators can force replication events between domain controllers and view the replication metadata vectors.

To access the Repadmin utility, open a command prompt using an elevated privilege (Run ➢ CMD). At the command prompt, type **Repadmin.exe**, and all of the available options will appear.

Using the ADSI Editor

Another utility (explained earlier in the chapter) that allows you to manage objects and attributes in Active Directory is the Active Directory Service Interfaces Editor (ADSI Edit). Earlier we used ADSI Edit (Adsiedit.msc) to create multiple password policies to allow for fine-grained password policies. ADSI Edit allows you to view every object and attribute in an Active Directory forest.

One advantage to using the Adsiedit.msc MMC snap-in is that this tool allows you to query, view, create, and edit attributes that are not exposed through other Active Directory Microsoft Management Console (MMC) snap-ins.

ADSI Edit allows you to administer an AD LDS instance. To do this, you must first connect and bind to the instance. After you connect and bind to the instance, you can administer the containers and objects within the instance by browsing to the containers or objects and then right-clicking them. To complete this task, you must be a member of the Administrators group for the AD LDS instance.

Wbadmin Command Line Utility

The wbadmin command allows you to back up and restore your operating system, volumes, files, folders, and applications from a command prompt.

You must be a member of the Administrators group to configure a backup schedule. You must be a member of the Backup Operators or the Administrators group (or you must have been delegated the appropriate permissions) to perform all other tasks using the wbadmin command.

To use the wbadmin command, you must run wbadmin from an elevated command prompt (to open an elevated command prompt, click Start, right-click Command Prompt, and then click Run As Administrator). Table 15.4 shows some of the wbadmin commands.

TABLE 15.4   Wbadmin commands

Command	Description
Wbadmin enable backup	Configures and enables a daily backup schedule.
Wbadmin disable backup	Disables your daily backups.
Wbadmin start backup	Runs a one-time backup.
Wbadmin stop job	Stops the currently running backup or recovery operation.
Wbadmin get items	Lists the items included in a specific backup.
Wbadmin start recovery	Runs a recovery of the volumes, applications, files, or folders specified.
Wbadmin get status	Shows the status of the currently running backup or recovery operation.
Wbadmin start systemstaterecovery	Runs a system state recovery.
Wbadmin start systemstatebackup	Runs a system state backup.
Wbadmin start sysrecovery	Runs a recovery of the full system state.

Summary

In this chapter, I talked about important items that pertain to security, such as which default groups are available after a base install of the operating system and how to secure the most vulnerable accounts.

I then covered how passwords and tokens work within Windows Server 2012 R2 and also how to create a separate password policy using the ADSI Edit utility. I discussed the different Operation Master roles (FSMO) and how to change or seize the role to another domain controller.

Finally, in this chapter, you also learned about how important it is to back up and restore a Windows Server 2012 R2 domain controller machine in the event of a hardware or software failure. I also explained how some of the features such as the Active Directory Recycle Bin and ntdsutil are part of Windows Server 2012 R2 domain controller and how these utilities make an administrator's life easier.

Exam Essentials

Understand the various backup types available with the Windows Server 2012 Backup utility. The Windows Server 2012 R2 Backup utility can perform full and incremental backup operations. Some third-party backup utilities also support differential and daily backups. You can use each of these operations as part of an efficient backup strategy.

Know how to back up Active Directory. The data within the Active Directory database on a domain controller is part of the system state data. You can back up the system state data to a file using the Windows Server 2012 R2 Backup utility.

Know how to restore Active Directory. Restoring the Active Directory database is considerably different from other restore operations. To restore some or the entire Active Directory database, you must first boot the machine into Directory Services Restore mode.

Understand the importance of an authoritative restore process. You use an authoritative restore when you want to restore earlier information from an Active Directory backup, and you want the older information to be propagated to other domain controllers in the environment.

Understand offline maintenance using ntdsutil. The ntdsutil command-line tool is a primary method by which system administrators perform offline maintenance. Understand how to launch this tool by entering **ntdsutil** at a command prompt.

Review Questions

1. You are the administrator of a large company, and you need to ensure that you can recover your Windows Server 2012 R2 Active Directory configuration and data if the computer's hard disk fails. What should you do?

    A. Create a complete PC Backup and Restore image.

    B. Create a backup of all file categories.

    C. Perform an automated system recovery (ASR) backup.

    D. Create a system restore point.

2. You need to back up the existing data on a computer before you install a new application. You also need to ensure that you are able to recover individual user files that are replaced or deleted during the installation. What should you do?

    A. Create a system restore point.

    B. Perform an automated system recovery (ASR) backup and restore.

    C. In the Windows Server Backup utility, click the Backup Once link.

    D. In the Backup And Restore Center window, click the Back Up Computer button.

3. You are the administrator of a large organization. While setting up your Windows Server 2012 R2 domain controller, you are creating a data recovery strategy that must meet the following requirements:

    - Back up all data files and folders in C:\Data.

    - Restore individual files and folders in C:\Data.

    - Ensure that data is backed up to and restored from external media.

    What should you do?

    A. Use the Previous Versions feature to restore the files and folders.

    B. Use the System Restore feature to perform backup and restore operations.

    C. Use the NTBackup utility to back up and restore individual files and folders.

    D. Use the Windows Server Backup to back up and restore files.

4. You are a network administrator, and you want to create multiple password policies for the users in your domain. What utility do you use to complete this task?

    A. MMC

    B. Schema Editor

    C. ADSI Edit

    D. Secedit.exe

5. You are the system administrator for a large organization with multiple Active Directory domain controllers. Currently, the environment supports many different domain controllers, some of which are running Windows 2008 and Windows Server 2012 R2. When you are running domain controllers in this type of environment, which of the following types of groups can you *not* use? (Choose all that apply.)

   A. Universal security groups

   B. Global groups

   C. Domain local groups

   D. None—you can use all group types

6. You are the network administrator for your organization. A new company policy has been released wherein if a user enters their password incorrectly three times within 5 minutes, they are locked out for 30 minutes. What three actions do you need to set to comply with this policy? (Choose all that apply.)

   A. Set Account Lockout Duration to 5 minutes.

   B. Set Account Lockout Duration to 30 minutes.

   C. Set the Account Lockout Threshold setting to 3 invalid logon attempts.

   D. Set the Account Lockout Threshold setting to 30 minutes.

   E. Set the Reset Account Lockout Counter setting to 5 minutes.

   F. Set the Reset Account Lockout Counter setting to 3 times.

7. You are teaching a Microsoft Active Directory class, and one of your students asks you which of the following folders in the Active Directory Users and Computers tool is used when users from outside the forest are granted access to resources within a domain? What answer would you give your student?

   A. Users

   B. Computers

   C. Domain Controllers

   D. Foreign Security Principals

8. Your manager has decided that your organization needs to use an Active Directory application data partition. Which command can you use to create and manage application data partitions?

   A. DCPromo.exe

   B. NTDSUtil.exe

   C. ADUtil.exe

   D. ADSI.exe

9. Robert is a system administrator who is responsible for performing backups on several servers. Recently, he has been asked to take over the operations of several new servers, including backup operations. He has the following requirements:

- The backup must finish as quickly as possible.

- The backup must use the absolute minimum amount of storage space.

- He must perform backup operations at least daily with a full backup at least weekly.

Robert decides to use the Windows Server 2012 R2 Windows Server Backup utility to perform the backups. He wants to choose a set of backup types that will meet all of these requirements. He decides to back up all files on each of these servers every week. Then he decides to store only the files that have changed since the last backup operation (regardless of type) during the weekdays. Which of the following types of backup operations should he use to implement this solution? (Choose two.)

A. Normal

B. Daily

C. Copy

D. Differential

E. Incremental

10. You are removing a domain controller from your network. This domain controller holds the forestwide operations master roles. Which roles would you need to transfer to another machine before you remove the domain controller? (Choose all that apply.)

A. PDC Emulator Master

B. Schema Master

C. RID Master

D. Domain Naming Master

E. Infrastructure Master

Chapter

16

Configure and Manage Group Policy

THE FOLLOWING 70-411 EXAM OBJECTIVES ARE COVERED IN THIS CHAPTER:

✓ **Configure Group Policy processing**

- Configure processing order and precedence
- Configure blocking of inheritance
- Configure enforced policies
- Configure security filtering and wmi filtering
- Configure loopback processing
- Configure and manage slow-link processing and group policy caching
- Configure client-side extension (CSE) behavior
- Force group policy update

✓ **Configure Group Policy settings**

- Configure settings including software installation, folder redirection, scripts, and administrative template settings
- Import security templates
- Import custom administrative template file
- Convert administrative templates using admx migrator
- Configure property filters for administrative templates

✓ **Manage Group Policy objects (GPOs)**

- Back up, import, copy, and restore GPOs
- Create and configure Migration Table
- Reset default GPOs
- Delegate Group Policy management

✓ **Configure Group Policy Preferences (GPP)**

- Configure GPP settings including printers, network drive mappings, power options, custom registry settings, Control Panel settings, Internet Explorer settings, file and folder deployment, and shortcut deployment

- Configure item-level targeting

One of the most important system administration features in Windows Server 2012 R2 and Active Directory is administering *Group Policy objects (GPOs)*. By using GPOs, administrators can quickly and easily define restrictions on common actions and then apply them at the site, domain, or organizational unit (OU) level. In this chapter, you will see how group policies work, and then you will look at how to implement them within an Active Directory environment.

This chapter will show Windows Server 2012 R2 administrators how to build, link, and deploy GPOs. GPOs are a great way to set policies throughout your entire forest. GPOs are one of the tools that many administrators never use, but once you start using them, you won't be able to stop. Not only can GPOs help you set policies for your users and computers, you can also install software and updates using GPOs.

If you have read this book from Chapter 1, you are familiar with the content of this chapter from Chapter 6, "Manage GPOs." But if you are just starting Part II to get ready for exam 70-411, then you will need to study all of this material. And if you have already taken and passed exam 70-410, then this chapter will be a good refresher with some added material and tips; this material will be on the 70-411 exam, so it will be best to take the extra time and go through the content again.

Introducing Group Policy Objects

Just like everything else, there are always pros and cons to whatever you are working on. Microsoft Windows-based operating systems have an advantage because of their flexibility and manageability. Administrators have the ability to lock down the Microsoft operating systems by placing some rules or policies onto the domain.

Administrators can configure many different options to suit the network environment and help follow corporate policies. However, having the flexibility to configure the network and the Windows operating system comes at a price—generally, end users on a network have the ability to configure many options that they should not be changing. For example, TCP/IP configuration and security policies should remain consistent for all client computers. In fact, end users really don't need to be able to change these types of settings in the first place because many end users do not understand the purpose of these settings.

Windows Server 2012 R2 *group policies* are designed to provide system administrators with the ability to customize end-user settings and to place restrictions on the types of actions those users can perform. Group policies can be easily created by system administrators and then later applied to one or more users or computers within the environment. Although they ultimately do affect registry settings, it is much easier to configure and apply settings through the use of Group Policy than it is to make changes to the registry manually. To make management easy, Microsoft has given administrators the ability to change all Group Policy settings from within one Microsoft Management Console (MMC) snap-in called the Group Policy Management Console (GPMC).

Group policies have several potential uses. I'll cover the use of group policies for software deployment, and I'll also focus on the technical background of group policies and how they apply to general configuration management.

Let's begin by looking at how group policies function.

Understanding Group Policy Settings

Group Policy settings are based on *Group Policy administrative templates*. These templates provide a list of user-friendly configuration options and specify the system settings to which they apply. For example, an option for a user or computer that reads Require A Specific Desktop Wallpaper Setting would map to a key in the registry that maintains this value. When the option is set, the appropriate change is made in the registry of the affected users and computers.

By default, Windows Server 2012 R2 comes with several administrative template files that you can use to manage common settings. Additionally, system administrators and applications developers can create their own administrative template files to set options for specific functionality.

Most Group Policy items have three different settings options:

Enabled   Specifies that a setting for this GPO has been configured. Some settings require values or options to be set.

Disabled   Specifies that this option is disabled for client computers. Note that disabling an option *is* a setting. That is, it specifies that the system administrator wants to disallow certain functionality.

Not Configured   Specifies that these settings have been neither enabled nor disabled. Not Configured is the default option for most settings. It simply states that this group policy will not specify an option and that other policy settings may take precedence.

The specific options available (and their effects) will depend on the setting. Often, you will need additional information. For example, when setting the Account Lockout policy, you must specify how many bad login attempts may be made before the account is locked out. With this in mind, let's look at the types of user and computer settings that can be managed.

Group Policy settings can apply to two types of Active Directory objects: User objects and Computer objects. Because both users and computers can be placed into groups and organized within OUs, this type of configuration simplifies the management of hundreds, or even thousands, of computers.

The main options you can configure within user and computer group policies are as follows:

Software Settings   *Software Settings* options apply to specific applications and software that might be installed on the computer. System administrators can use these settings to make new applications available to end users and to control the default configuration for these applications.

Windows Settings   *Windows Settings* options allow system administrators to customize the behavior of the Windows operating system. The specific options that are available here are divided into two types: user and computer. User-specific settings let you configure Internet Explorer (including the default home page and other settings). Computer settings include security options, such as Account Policy and Event Log options.

Administrative Templates   *Administrative Templates* options are used to configure user and computer settings further. In addition to the default options available, system administrators can create their own administrative templates with custom options.

Group Policy Preferences   The Windows Server 2012 R2 operating system includes *Group Policy Preferences (GPPs)* options, which give you more than 20 new Group Policy extensions. These extensions, in turn, give you a vast range of configurable settings within a Group Policy object. Included in the new Group Policy preference extensions are settings for folder options, mapped drives, printers, the registry, local users and groups, scheduled tasks, services, and the Start menu.

Besides providing easier management, Group Policy preferences give an administrator the ability to deploy settings for client computers without restricting the users from changing the settings. This gives an administrator the flexibility needed to decide which settings to enforce and which not to enforce.

Figure 16.1 shows some of the options that you can configure with Group Policy.

FIGURE 16.1   Group Policy configuration options

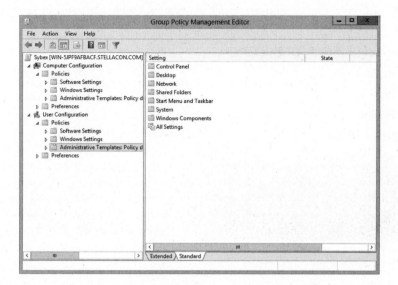

ADMX Central Store   Another consideration in GPO settings is whether to set up an *ADMX Central Store*. GPO administrative template files are saved as ADMX (.admx) files and AMXL (.amxl) for the supported languages. To get the most benefit out of using administrative templates, you should create an ADMX Central Store.

You create the Central Store in the SYSVOL folder on a domain controller. The Central Store is a repository for all of your administrative templates, and the Group Policy tools checks it. The Group Policy tools then use any ADMX files that they find in the Central Store. These files then replicate to all domain controllers in the domain.

If you want your clients to be able to edit domain-based GPOs by using the ADMX files that are stored in the ADMX Central Store, you must be using Windows Vista, Windows 7, Windows 8, Server 2008, Server 2008 R2, Server 2012, or Server 2012 R2.

Security Template   *Security templates* are used to configure security settings through a GPO. Some of the security settings that can be configured are settings for account policies, local policies, event logs, restricted groups, system services, and the registry.

Starter GPOs   *Starter Group Policy objects* give administrators the ability to store a collection of Administrative Template policy settings in a single object. Administrators then have the ability to import and export Starter GPOs to distribute the GPOs easily to other environments. When a GPO is created from a Starter GPO, as with any template, the new GPO receives the settings and values that were defined from the Administrative Template policy in the Starter GPO.

The Security Settings Section of the GPO

One of the most important sections of a GPO is the Security Settings section. The Security Settings section, under the Windows Settings section, allows an administrator to secure many aspects of the computer and user policies. The following are some of the configurable options for the Security Settings section:

Computer Section Only of the GPO

- Account Policies
- Local Policies
- Event Policies
- Restricted Groups
- System Services
- Registry
- File System
- Wired Network
- Windows Firewall with Advanced Security
- Network List Manager Policies

- Wireless Networks
- Network Access Protection
- Application Control Policies
- IP Security Policies
- Advanced Audit Policy Configuration

Computer and User Sections of the GPO
- Public Key Policies
- Software Restriction Policy

Restricted Groups   *Restricted Groups* allows you to control group membership by using a GPO. The group membership to which I am referring is the normal Active Directory groups (domain local, global, and universal). Restricted Groups offers two configurable properties: Members and Members Of.

The users on the Members list do not belong to the restricted group. The users on the Members Of list do belong to the restricted group. When you configure a Restricted Group policy, members of the restricted group that are not on the Members list are removed. Users who are on the Members list who are not currently a member of the restricted group are added.

Software Restriction Policy   *Software restriction policies* allow administrators to identify software and to control its ability to run on the user's local computer, organizational unit, domain, or site. This prevents users from installing unauthorized software. Software Restriction Policy is discussed in greater detail in this chapter in the "Implementing Software Deployment" section.

Group Policy Objects

So far, I have discussed what group policies are designed to do. Now it's time to drill down to determine exactly how you can set up and configure them.

To make them easier to manage, group policies may be placed in items called *Group Policy Objects (GPOs)*. GPOs act as containers for the settings made within Group Policy files, which simplifies the management of settings. For example, as a system administrator, you might have different policies for users and computers in different departments. Based on these requirements, you could create a GPO for members of the Sales department and another for members of the Engineering department. Then you could apply the GPOs to the OU for each department. Another important concept you need to understand is that Group Policy settings are hierarchical; that is, system administrators can apply Group Policy settings at four different levels. These levels determine the GPO processing priority:

Local   Every Windows operating system computer has one Group Policy object that is stored locally. This GPO functions for both the computer and user Group Policy processing.

Sites   At the highest level, system administrators can configure GPOs to apply to entire sites within an Active Directory environment. These settings apply to all of the domains and servers that are part of a site. Group Policy settings managed at the site level may apply to more than one domain within the same forest. Therefore, they are useful when you want to make settings that apply to all of the domains within an Active Directory tree or forest.

Domains   Domains are the third level to which system administrators can assign GPOs. GPO settings placed at the domain level will apply to all of the User and Computer objects within the domain. Usually, system administrators make master settings at the domain level.

Organizational Units   The most granular level of settings for GPOs is the OU level. By configuring Group Policy options for OUs, system administrators can take advantage of the hierarchical structure of Active Directory. If the OU structure is planned well, you will find it easy to make logical GPO assignments for various business units at the OU level.

Based on the business needs and the organization of the Active Directory environment, system administrators might decide to set up Group Policy settings at any of these four levels. Because the settings are cumulative by default, a User object might receive policy settings from the site level, from the domain level, and from the OUs in which it is contained.

 You can also apply Group Policy settings to the local computer (in which case Active Directory is not used at all), but this limits the manageability of the Group Policy settings.

Group Policy Inheritance

In most cases, Group Policy settings are cumulative. For example, a GPO at the domain level might specify that all users within the domain must change their password every 60 days, and a GPO at the OU level might specify the default desktop background for all users and computers within that OU. In this case, both settings apply, and users within the OU are forced to change their password every 60 days and have the default desktop setting.

So, what happens if there's a conflict in the settings? For example, suppose you create a scenario where a GPO at the site level specifies that users are to use red wallpaper and another GPO at the OU level specifies that they must use green wallpaper. The users at the OU layer would have green wallpaper by default. Although hypothetical, this raises an important point about *inheritance*. By default, the settings at the most specific level (in this case, the OU that contains the User object) override those at more general levels. As a friend of mine from Microsoft always says, "Last one to apply wins."

Although the default behavior is for settings to be cumulative and inherited, system administrators can modify this behavior. They can set two main options at the various levels to which GPOs might apply:

Block Policy Inheritance   The *Block Policy Inheritance* option specifies that Group Policy settings for an object are not inherited from its parents. You might use this, for example, when a child OU requires completely different settings from a parent OU. Note, however, that you should manage blocking policy inheritance carefully because this option allows other system administrators to override the settings made at higher levels.

Force Policy Inheritance   The *Enforced option* (sometimes referred as the *No Override*) can be placed on a parent object and ensures that all lower-level objects inherit these settings. In some cases, system administrators want to ensure that Group Policy inheritance is not blocked at other levels. For example, suppose it is corporate policy that all network accounts are locked out after five incorrect password attempts. In this case, you would not want lower-level system administrators to override the option with other settings.

System administrators generally use this option when they want to enforce a specific setting globally. For example, if a password expiration policy should apply to all users and computers within a domain, a GPO with the *Force Policy Inheritance* option enabled could be created at the domain level.

You must consider one final case: If a conflict exists between the computer and user settings, the user settings take effect. If, for instance, a system administrator applies a default Desktop setting for the Computer policy and a different default Desktop setting for the User policy, the one they specify in the User policy takes effect. This is because the user settings are more specific, and they allow system administrators to make changes for individual users regardless of the computer that they're using.

Planning a Group Policy Strategy

Through the use of Group Policy settings, system administrators can control many different aspects of their network environment. As you'll see throughout this chapter, system administrators can use GPOs to configure user settings and computer configurations. Windows Server 2012 R2 includes many different administrative tools for performing these tasks. However, it's important to keep in mind that, as with many aspects of using Active Directory, a successful Group Policy strategy involves planning.

Because there are hundreds of possible Group Policy settings and many different ways to implement them, you should start by determining the business and technical needs of your organization. For example, you should first group your users based on their work functions. You might find, for example, that users in remote branch offices require particular network configuration options. In that case, you might implement Group Policy settings best at the site level. In another instance, you might find that certain departments have varying requirements for disk quota settings. In this case, it would probably make the most sense to apply GPOs to the appropriate department OUs within the domain.

The overall goal should be to reduce complexity (for example, by reducing the overall number of GPOs and GPO links) while still meeting the needs of your users. By taking into account the various needs of your users and the parts of your organization, you can often determine a logical and efficient method of creating and applying GPOs. Although it's rare that you'll come across a right or wrong method of implementing Group Policy settings, you will usually encounter some that are either better or worse than others.

By implementing a logical and consistent set of policies, you'll also be well prepared to troubleshoot any problems that might come up or to adapt to your organization's changing requirements. Later in this chapter, you'll learn about some specific methods for determining effective Group Policy settings before you apply them.

Implementing Group Policy

Now that I've covered the basic layout and structure of group policies and how they work, let's look at how you can implement them in an Active Directory environment. In the following sections, you'll start by creating GPOs. Then you'll apply these GPOs to specific Active Directory objects, and you'll take a look at how to use administrative templates.

Creating GPOs

In Windows Server 2000 and 2003, you could create GPOs from many different locations. For example, in Windows Server 2003, you could use Active Directory Users and Computers to create GPOs on your OUs along with other GPO tools. In Windows Server 2012 R2, things are simpler. You can create GPOs for OUs in only one location: the Group Policy Management Console (GPMC). You have your choice of three applications for setting up policies on your Windows Server 2012 R2 computers:

Local Computer Policy Tool   This administrative tool allows you to access quickly the Group Policy settings that are available for the local computer. These options apply to the local machine and to users who access it. You must be a member of the local administrators group to access and make changes to these settings.

Group Policy Management Console   You must use the GPMC to manage Group Policy deployment. The GPMC provides a single solution for managing all Group Policy–related tasks, and it is also best suited to handle enterprise-level tasks, such as forest-related work.

The GPMC allows administrators to manage Group Policy and GPOs all from one easy-to-use console whether their enterprise solution spans multiple domains and sites within one or more forests or it is local to one site. The GPMC adds flexibility, manageability, and functionality. Using this console, you can also perform other functions, such as backup and restore, importing, and copying.

Auditpol.exe   Auditpol.exe is a command-line utility that works with Windows Vista, Windows 7, Windows 8, Windows Server 2008, Windows Server 2008 R2, Windows Server 2012, and Windows Server 2012 R2. An administrator has the ability to display information about policies and also to perform some functions to manipulate audit policies. Table 16.1 shows some of the switches available for auditpol.exe.

TABLE 16.1 Auditpol.exe switches

Switch	Explanation
/?	This is the auditpol.exe help command.
/get	Allows you to display the current audit policy.
/set	Allows you to set a policy.
/list	Displays selectable policy elements.
/backup	Allows you to save the audit policy to a file.
/restore	Restores a policy from previous backup.
/clear	Clears the audit policy.
/remove	Removes all per-user audit policy settings and disables all system audit policy settings.
/ResourceSACL	Configures the Global Resource SACL.

Exercise 16.1 walks you through the process of installing the Group Policy Management MMC snap-in for editing Group Policy settings and creating a GPO. If you started reading this book from Chapter 1, then this lab has been completed. I changed some of the parameters if you would like to create this GPO a bit differently.

You should be careful when making Group Policy settings because certain options might prevent the proper use of systems on your network. Always test Group Policy settings on a small group of users before you deploy them throughout your organization. You'll probably find that some settings need to be changed to be effective.

EXERCISE 16.1

Creating a Group Policy Object Using the GPMC

1. Press the Windows button and choose Administrative Tools ➢ Group Policy Management. The Group Policy Management tool opens.

2. Expand the Forest, Domains, *your domain name,* and North America containers. Right-click the Corporate OU and then choose Create A GPO In This Domain, And Link It Here.

EXERCISE 16.1 *(continued)*

3. When the New GPO dialog box appears, type **Logon Message** in the Name field. Click OK.

4. The New GPO will be listed on the right side of the Group Policy Management window. Right-click the GPO and choose Edit.

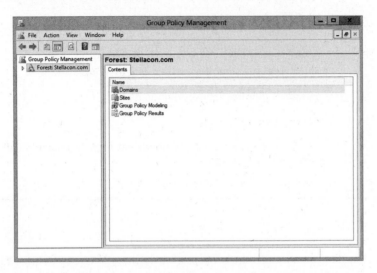

5. In the Group Policy Management Editor, expand the following: Computer Configuration ➢ Policies ➢ Windows Settings ➢ Security Settings ➢ Local Policies ➢ Security Options. On the right side, scroll down and double-click Interactive Logon: Message Text For Users Attempting To Log On.

6. Click the box labeled Define This Policy Setting In The Template. In the text box, type **Welcome to the domain. Domain members only are welcome** and then click OK. Close the GPO and return to the GPMC main screen.

7. Under the domain name (in the GPMC), right-click Group Policy Objects and choose New.

8. When the New GPO dialog box appears, type **Unlinked Test GPO** in the Name field. Click OK.

9. On the right side, the new GPO will appear. Right-click Unlinked Test GPO and choose Edit.

10. In the User Configuration section, click Policies ➢ Administrative Templates ➢ Desktop. On the right side, double-click Hide And Disable All Items On The Desktop and then click Enabled. Click OK and then close the GPMC.

Note that Group Policy changes may not take effect until the next user logs in (some settings may even require that the machine be rebooted). That is, users who are currently working on the system will not see the effects of the changes until they log off and log in again. GPOs are reapplied every 90 minutes with a 30-minute offset. In other words, users who are logged in will have their policies reapplied every 60 to 120 minutes. Not all settings are reapplied (for example, software settings and password policies).

Linking Existing GPOs to Active Directory

Creating a GPO is the first step in assigning group policies. The second step is to link the GPO to a specific Active Directory object. As mentioned earlier in this chapter, GPOs can be linked to sites, domains, and OUs.

Exercise 16.2 walks you through the steps you must take to assign an existing GPO to an OU within the local domain. In this exercise, you will link the Test Domain Policy GPO to an OU. To complete the steps in this exercise, you must have completed Exercise 16.1.

EXERCISE 16.2

Linking Existing GPOs to Active Directory

1. Open the Group Policy Management Console.

2. Expand the Forest and Domain containers and right-click the Africa OU.

3. Choose Link An Existing GPO.

4. The Select GPO dialog box appears. Click Unlinked Test GPO and click OK.

5. Close the Group Policy Management Console.

Note that the GPMC tool offers a lot of flexibility in assigning GPOs. You can create new GPOs, add multiple GPOs, edit them directly, change priority settings, remove links, and delete GPOs all from within this interface. In general, creating new GPOs using the GPMC tool is the quickest and easiest way to create the settings you need.

To test the Group Policy settings, you can simply create a user account within the Africa OU that you used in Exercise 16.2. Then, using another computer that is a member of the same domain, you can log on as the newly created user.

Forcing a GPO to Update

There will be times when you need a GPO to get processed immediately. If you are testing a GPO, you will not want to wait for the GPO to process in its own time or you may not want to have to log off the domain and log back onto the domain just to get the GPO processed.

Windows Server 2012 R2 has changed how GPOs get processed. In a Windows Server 2012 R2 domain, when a user logs onto the domain, the latest version of the Group Policy gets downloaded from the domain controller, and it writes that policy to the local store.

If you have your GPOs set up and running in synchronous mode, then the next time the computer restarts, it will use the most recently downloaded GPO from the local store and not download the GPO from the domain. This is a new feature in Windows Server 2012 R2, and it helps to reduce the time it takes to log onto the domain because the GPO policy doesn't need to be downloaded each time.

So, now that you understand how GPOs get processed in Windows Server 2012 R2, let's look at a few different ways that you can force a GPO to get processed immediately.

Forcing the GPO from the Server

Windows Server 2012 R2 has an MMC called Group Policy Management Console (GPMC), and by using this MMC, you can remotely refresh an organizational unit (OU) and force the GPO on all users and computers within that OU. The GPMC remote refresh automatically updates all settings, including security settings, which are configured in the GPO that is linked to the OU. In the OU's context menu, you can choose to refresh remotely the OU and the GPOs associated with that OU. When you remotely refresh an OU, the following steps occur:

1. Windows Server 2012 R2 does an Active Directory query, and that query returns a list of all users and computers that belong to the OU.

2. Windows Management Instrumentation (WMI) queries all users and computers that are currently logged into the domain and creates a list that will be used.

3. Using the list that was created in step 2, a remote scheduled task is created, and a GPUpdate.exe /force is executed on all of the users and computers that are logged into the domain. The remote scheduled task is then scheduled to execute with a 10-minute random delay to help decrease the load on network traffic.

 When you are using the GPMC to force a GPO update, you do not have the ability to change the 10-minute random delay, but if you force the GPO through the use of PowerShell, you have the ability to set the delay.

Another way that you can force a GPO to update immediately is to use Windows PowerShell. By using the PowerShell command Invoke-GPUpdate cmdlet, you cannot only force the GPO but also set the parameters to be more granular.

Forcing the GPO from the Client

As an administrator, you have the ability also to force a GPO onto a client machine on which you may be working. The GPUpdate.exe command allows you to run a GPO on a client machine. The GPUpdate command will run on all Windows client machines from Windows Vista to Windows Server 2012 R2. Table 16.2 shows some of the GPUpdate switches you can use.

TABLE 16.2   GPUpdate.exe switches

Switch	Description
/target:{Computer | User}	Updates only the User or Computer policy settings for the computer or user specified.
/force	Forces the GPO to reapply all policy settings. By default, only policy settings that have changed are applied.
/wait:<VALUE>	Determines the number of seconds that the system will wait after a policy is processed before returning to the command prompt.
/logoff	The domain user account will automatically log off the computer after the Group Policy settings are updated.
/boot	The computer will automatically restart after the Group Policy settings are applied.
/sync	This switch forces the next available foreground policy application to be done synchronously. Foreground policies are applied when the computer boots up and the user logs in.
/?	Displays help at the command prompt.

Managing Group Policy

Now that you have implemented GPOs and applied them to sites, domains, and OUs within Active Directory, it's time to look at some ways to manage them. In the following sections, you'll look at how multiple GPOs can interact with one another and ways that you can provide security for GPO management. Using these features is an important part of working with Active Directory, and if you properly plan Group Policy, you can greatly reduce the time the help desk spends troubleshooting common problems.

Managing GPOs

One of the benefits of GPOs is that they're modular and can apply to many different objects and levels within Active Directory. This can also be one of the drawbacks of GPOs if they're not managed properly. A common administrative function related to using GPOs is finding all of the Active Directory links for each of these objects. You can do this when you are viewing the Linked Group Policy Objects tab of the site, domain, or OU in the GPMC (shown in Figure 16.2).

FIGURE 16.2   Viewing GPO links to an Active Directory OU

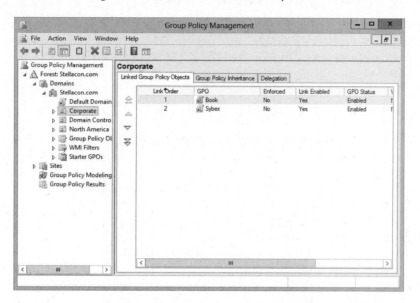

In addition to the common action of delegating permissions on OUs, you can set permissions regarding the modification of GPOs. The best way to accomplish this is to add users to the Group Policy Creator/Owners built-in security group. The members of this group are able to modify security policy.

Windows Management Instrumentation

Windows Management Instrumentation (WMI) scripts are used to gather information or to help GPOs deploy better. The best way to explain this is to give an example. Let's say you wanted to deploy Microsoft Office 2013 to everyone in the company. You would first set up a GPO to deploy the Office package (explained later in the section "Deploying Software Through a GPO").

You can then place a WMI script on the GPO stating that only computers with 10GB of hard disk space actually deploy Office. Now if a computer has 10GB of free space, the Office GPO would get installed. If the computer does not have the 10GB of hard disk space, the GPO will not deploy. You can use WMI scripts to check for computer information such as MAC addresses. WMI is a powerful tool because if you know how to write scripts, the possibilities are endless. The following script is a sample of a WMI that is checking for at least 10GB of free space on the C: partition/volume:

```
Select * from Win32_LogicalDisk where FreeSpace > 10737418240 AND
Caption = "C:"
```

Security Filtering of a Group Policy

Another method of securing access to GPOs is to set permissions on the GPOs themselves. You can do this by opening the GPMC, selecting the GPO, and clicking the Advanced button in the Delegation tab. The Unlinked Test GPO Security Settings dialog box appears (see Figure 16.3).

FIGURE 16.3   A GPO's Security Settings dialog box

The following permissions options are available:

- Full Control
- Read
- Write
- Create All Child Objects
- Delete All Child Objects
- Apply Group Policy

You might have to scroll the Permissions window to see the Apply Group Policy item. Of these, the Apply Group Policy setting is particularly important because you use it to filter the scope of the GPO. *Filtering* is the process by which selected security groups are included or excluded from the effects of the GPOs. To specify that the settings should apply to a GPO, you should select the Allow check box for both the Apply Group Policy setting and the Read setting. These settings will be applied only if the security group is also contained within a site, domain, or OU to which the GPO is linked. To disable GPO access for a group, choose Deny for both of these settings. Finally, if you do not want to specify either Allow or Deny, leave both boxes blank. This is effectively the same as having no setting.

In Exercise 16.3, you will filter Group Policy using security groups. To complete the steps in this exercise, you must have completed Exercises 16.1 and 16.2.

EXERCISE 16.3

Filtering Group Policy Using Security Groups

1. Open the Active Directory Users and Computers administrative tool.

2. Create a new OU called **Group Policy Test**.

3. Create two new global security groups within the Group Policy Test OU, and name them **PolicyEnabled** and **PolicyDisabled**.

4. Exit Active Directory Users and Computers and open the GPMC.

5. Right-click the Group Policy Test OU and select Link An Existing GPO.

6. Choose Unlinked Test GPO and click OK.

7. Expand the Group Policy Test OU so that you can see the GPO (Unlinked Test GPO) underneath the OU.

8. Click the Delegation tab and then click the Advanced button in the lower-right corner of the window.

9. Click the Add button and type **PolicyEnabled** in the Enter The Object Names To Select field. Click the Check Names button. Then click OK.

10. Add a group named **PolicyDisabled** in the same way.

11. Highlight the PolicyEnabled group and select Allow for the Read and Apply Group Policy permissions. This ensures that users in the PolicyEnabled group will be affected by this policy.

12. Highlight the PolicyDisabled group and select Deny for the Read and Apply Group Policy permissions. This ensures that users in the PolicyDisabled group will not be affected by this policy.

13. Click OK. You will see a message stating that you are choosing to use the Deny permission and that the Deny permission takes precedence over the Allow entries. Click the Yes button to continue.

14. When you have finished, close the GPMC tool.

Delegating Administrative Control of GPOs

So far, you have learned about how to use Group Policy to manage user and computer settings. What you haven't done yet is to determine who can modify GPOs. It's important to establish the appropriate security on GPOs themselves for two reasons:

- If the security settings aren't set properly, users and system administrators can easily override them. This defeats the purpose of having the GPOs in the first place.

- Having many different system administrators creating and modifying GPOs can become extremely difficult to manage. When problems arise, the hierarchical nature of GPO inheritance can make it difficult to pinpoint the problem.

Fortunately, through the use of delegation, determining security permissions for GPOs is a simple task. Exercise 16.4 walks you through the steps you must take to grant the appropriate permissions to a user account. Specifically, the process involves delegating the ability to manage Group Policy links on an Active Directory object (such as an OU). To complete this exercise, you must have completed Exercises 16.1 and 16.2.

EXERCISE 16.4

Delegating Administrative Control of Group Policy

1. Open the Active Directory Users and Computers tool.

2. Expand the local domain, and create a user named **Policy Admin** within the Group Policy Test OU.

3. Exit Active Directory Users and Computers and open the GPMC.

4. Click the Group Policy Test OU and select the Delegation tab.

5. Click the Add button. In the field labeled Enter The Object Name To Select, type **Policy Admin** and click the Check Names button.

6. The Add Group Or User dialog box appears. In the Permissions drop-down list, make sure that the item labeled Edit Settings, Delete, Modify Security is chosen. Click OK.

7. At this point, you should be looking at the Group Policy Test Delegation window. Click the Advanced button in the lower-right corner.

8. Highlight the Policy Admin account and check the Allow Full Control box. This user now has full control of these OUs and all child OUs and GPOs for these OUs. Click OK.

If you just want to give individual rights to this user, then in the Properties window (step 8), click the Advanced button and then the Effective Permissions tab. This is where you can also choose a user and give them only the rights that you want them to have.

9. When you have finished, close the GPMC tool.

Understanding Delegation

Although I have talked about delegation throughout the book, it's important to discuss it again in the context of OUs, Group Policy, and Active Directory.

Once configured, Active Directory administrative delegation allows an administrator to delegate tasks (usually administration related) to specific user accounts or groups. What this means is that if you don't manage it all, the user accounts (or groups) you choose will be able to manage their portions of the tree.

It's important to be aware of the benefits of Active Directory Delegation (AD Delegation). *AD Delegation* will help you manage the assigning of administrative control over objects in Active Directory, such as users, groups, computers, printers, domains, and sites. AD Delegation is used to create more administrators, which essentially saves time.

For example, let's say you have a company whose IT department is small and situated in a central location. The central location connects three other smaller remote sites. These sites do not each warrant a full-time IT person, but the manager on staff (for example) at each remote site can become an administrator for their portion of the tree. If the user accounts for the staff at the remote site are managed by that manager, this reduces the burden on the system administrator of trivial administrative work, such as unlocking user accounts or changing passwords, and thus it reduces costs.

Controlling Inheritance and Filtering Group Policy

Controlling inheritance is an important function when you are managing GPOs. Earlier in this chapter, you learned that, by default, GPO settings flow from higher-level Active Directory objects to lower-level ones. For example, the effective set of Group Policy settings for a user might be based on GPOs assigned at the site level, at the domain level, and in the OU hierarchy. In general, this is probably the behavior you would want.

In some cases, however, you might want to block Group Policy inheritance. You can accomplish this easily by selecting the object to which a GPO has been linked. Right-click the object and choose Block Inheritance (see Figure 16.4). By enabling this option, you are

FIGURE 16.4 Blocking GPO inheritance

effectively specifying that this object starts with a clean slate; that is, no other Group Policy settings will apply to the contents of this Active Directory site, domain, or OU.

System administrators can also force inheritance. By setting the Enforced option, they can prevent other system administrators from making changes to default policies. You can set the Enforced option by right-clicking the GPO and choosing the Enforced item (see Figure 16.5).

FIGURE 16.5 Setting the Enforced GPO option

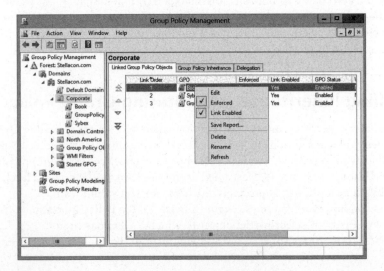

Assigning Script Policies

System administrators might want to make several changes and implement certain settings that would apply while the computer is starting up or the user is logging on. Perhaps the most common operation that logon scripts perform is mapping network drives. Although users can manually map network drives, providing this functionality within login scripts ensures that mappings stay consistent and that users only need to remember the drive letters for their resources.

Script policies are specific options that are part of Group Policy settings for users and computers. These settings direct the operating system to the specific files that should be processed during the startup/shutdown or logon/logoff processes. You can create the scripts by using the *Windows Script Host (WSH)* or with standard batch file commands. WSH allows developers and system administrators to create scripts quickly and easily using Visual Basic Scripting Edition (VBScript) or JScript (Microsoft's implementation of JavaScript). Additionally, WSH can be expanded to accommodate other common scripting languages.

To set script policy options, you simply edit the Group Policy settings. As shown in Figure 16.6, there are two main areas for setting script policy settings.

FIGURE 16.6   Viewing Startup/Shutdown script policy settings

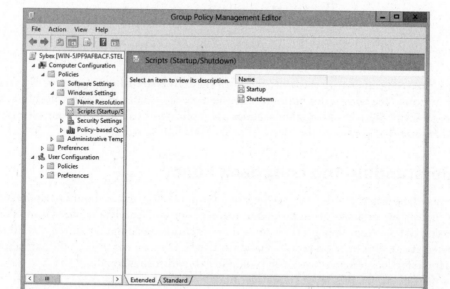

Startup/Shutdown Scripts   These settings are located within the Computer Configuration ➢ Windows Settings ➢ Scripts (Startup/Shutdown) object.

Logon/Logoff Scripts   These settings are located within the User Configuration ➢ Windows Settings ➢ Scripts (Logon/Logoff) object.

To assign scripts, simply double-click the setting and its Properties dialog box appears. For instance, if you double-click the Startup setting, the Startup Properties dialog box appears (see Figure 16.7). To add a script filename, click the Add button. When you do, you will be asked to provide the name of the script file (such as MapNetworkDrives.vbs or ResetEnvironment.bat).

FIGURE 16.7   Setting scripting options

Note that you can change the order in which the scripts are run by using the Up and Down buttons. The Show Files button opens the directory folder in which you should store the Logon script files. To ensure that the files are replicated to all domain controllers, you should be sure that you place the files within the SYSVOL share.

Understanding the Loopback Policy

There may be times when the user settings of a Group Policy object should be applied to a computer based on its location instead of the user object. Usually, the user Group Policy processing dictates that the GPOs be applied in order during computer startup based on the computers located in their organizational unit. User GPOs, on the other hand, are applied in order during logon, regardless of the computer to which they log on.

In some situations, this processing order may not be appropriate. A good example is a kiosk machine. You would not want applications that have been assigned or published to a user to be installed when the user is logged on to the kiosk machine. *Loopback Policy* allows two ways to retrieve the list of GPOs for any user when they are using a specific computer in an OU:

Merge Mode   The GPOs for the computer are added to the end of the GPOs for the user. Because of this, the computer's GPOs have higher precedence than the user's GPOs.

Replace Mode   In Replace mode, the user's GPOs are not used. Only the GPOs of the Computer object are used.

Managing Network Configuration

Group policies are also useful in network configuration. Although administrators can handle network settings at the protocol level using many different methods, such as Dynamic Host Configuration Protocol (DHCP), Group Policy allows them to set which functions and operations are available to users and computers.

Figure 16.8 shows some of the features that are available for managing Group Policy settings. The paths to these settings are as follows:

Computer Network Options   These settings are located within Computer Configuration ➢ Administrative Templates ➢ Network ➢ Network Connections folder.

User Network Options   These settings are located within User Configuration ➢ Administrative Templates ➢ Network.

FIGURE 16.8   Viewing Group Policy User network configuration options

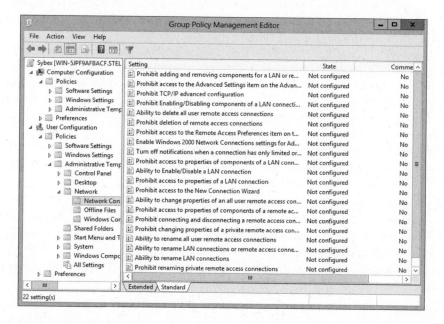

Here are some examples of the types of settings available:

- The ability to allow or disallow the modification of network settings.

   In many environments, the improper changing of network configurations and protocol settings is a common cause of help desk calls.

- The ability to allow or disallow the creation of Remote Access Service (RAS) connections.

  This option is very useful, especially in larger networked environments, because the use of modems and other WAN devices can pose a security threat to the network.

- The ability to set offline files and folders options.

  This is especially useful for keeping files synchronized for traveling users, and it is commonly configured for laptops.

Each setting includes detailed instructions in the description area of the GPO Editor window. By using these configuration options, system administrators can maintain consistency for users and computers and avoid many of the most common troubleshooting calls.

Automatically Enrolling User and Computer Certificates in Group Policy

You can also use Group Policy to enroll user and computer certificates automatically, making the entire certificate process transparent to your end users. Before proceeding further, you should understand what certificates are and why they are an important part of network security.

Think of a digital certificate as a carrying case for a public key. A certificate contains the public key and a set of attributes, including the key holder's name and email address. These attributes specify something about the holder: their identity, what they're allowed to do with the certificate, and so on. The attributes and the public key are bound together because the certificate is digitally signed by the entity that issued it. Anyone who wants to verify the certificate's contents can verify the issuer's signature.

Certificates are one part of what security experts call a *public-key infrastructure (PKI)*. A PKI has several components that you can mix and match to achieve the desired results. Microsoft's PKI implementation offers the following functions:

Certificate Authorities   CAs issue certificates, revoke certificates they've issued, and publish certificates for their clients. Big CAs like Thawte and VeriSign do this for millions of users. If you want, you can also set up your own CA for each department or workgroup in your organization. Each CA is responsible for choosing which attributes it will include in a certificate and what mechanism it will use to verify those attributes before it issues the certificate.

Certificate Publishers   They make certificates publicly available, inside or outside an organization. This allows widespread availability of the critical material needed to support the entire PKI.

PKI-Savvy Applications   These allow you and your users to do useful things with certificates, such as encrypt email or network connections. Ideally, the user shouldn't have to know (or even be aware of) what the application is doing—everything should work seamlessly and automatically. The best-known examples of PKI-savvy applications are web browsers such as Internet Explorer and Firefox and email applications such as Outlook and Outlook Express.

Certificate Templates   These act like rubber stamps. By specifying a particular template as the model you want to use for a newly issued certificate, you're actually telling the CA which optional attributes to add to the certificate as well as implicitly telling it how to fill some of the mandatory attributes. Templates greatly simplify the process of issuing certificates because they keep you from having to memorize the names of all the attributes that you may potentially want to put in a certificate.

Learn More About PKI

When discussing certificates, it's also important to mention PKI and its definition. The exam doesn't go deeply into PKI, but I recommend you do some extra research on your own because it is an important technology and shouldn't be overlooked. PKI is actually a simple concept with a lot of moving parts. When broken down to its bare essentials, PKI is nothing more than a server and workstations utilizing a software service to add security to your infrastructure. When you use PKI, you are adding a layer of protection. The auto-enrollment Settings policy determines whether users and/or computers are automatically enrolled for the appropriate certificates when necessary. By default, this policy is enabled if a certificate server is installed, but you can make changes to the settings, as shown in Exercise 16.5.

In Exercise 16.5, you will learn how to configure automatic certificate enrollment in Group Policy. You must have first completed the other exercises in this chapter in order to proceed with Exercise 16.5.

EXERCISE 16.5

Configuring Automatic Certificate Enrollment in Group Policy

1. Open the Group Policy Management Console tool.

2. Right-click the North America OU that you created in the previous exercises in this book.

3. Choose Create A GPO In This Domain And Link It Here and name it **Test CA**. Click OK.

4. Right-click the Test CA GPO and choose Edit.

5. Open Computer Configuration ➢ Policies ➢ Windows Settings ➢ Security Settings ➢ Public Key Policies.

6. Double-click Certificate Services Client – Auto-Enrollment in the right pane.

EXERCISE 16.5 *(continued)*

7. The Certificate Services Client – Auto-Enrollment Properties dialog box will appear.

8. For now, don't change anything. Just become familiar with the settings in this dialog box. Click OK to close it.

Redirecting Folders

Another set of Group Policy settings that you will learn about are the *folder redirection settings*. Group Policy provides a means for redirecting the Documents, Desktop, and Start Menu folders, as well as cached application data, to network locations. Folder redirection is particularly useful for the following reasons:

- When they are using roaming user profiles, a user's Documents folder is copied to the local machine each time they log on. This requires high-bandwidth consumption and time if the Documents folder is large. If you redirect the Documents folder, it stays in the redirected location, and the user opens and saves files directly to that location.

- Documents are always available no matter where the user logs on.

- Data in the shared location can be backed up during the normal backup cycle without user intervention.

- Data can be redirected to a more robust server-side administered disk that is less prone to physical and user errors.

When you decide to redirect folders, you have two options, basic and advanced:

- Basic redirection redirects everyone's folders to the same location (but each user gets their own folder within that location).

- Advanced redirection redirects folders to different locations based on group membership. For instance, you could configure the Engineers group to redirect their folders to //Engineering1/Documents/ and the Marketing group to //Marketing1/ Documents/. Again, individual users still get their own folder within the redirected location.

To configure folder redirection, follow the steps in Exercise 16.6. You must have completed the other exercises in this chapter to proceed with this exercise.

EXERCISE 16.6

Configuring Folder Redirection in Group Policy

1. Open the GPMC tool.

2. Open the North America OU and then edit the Test CA GPO.

3. Open User Configuration ➢ Policies ➢ Windows Settings ➢ Folder Redirection ➢ Documents.

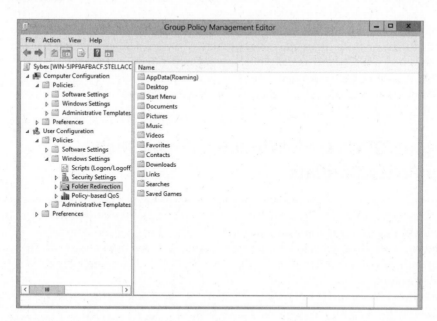

4. Right-click Documents and select Properties.

5. On the Target tab of the Documents Properties dialog box, choose the Basic – Redirect Everyone's Folder To The Same Location selection from the Settings drop-down list.

EXERCISE 16.6 *(continued)*

6. Leave the default option for the Target Folder Location drop-down list and specify a network path in the Root Path field.

7. Click the Settings tab. All of the default settings are self-explanatory and should typically be left at the defaults. Click OK when you have finished.

Folder Redirection Facts

Try not to mix up the concepts of *folder redirection* and *offline folders*, especially in a world with ever-increasing numbers of mobile users. Folder redirection and offline folders are different features.

Windows Server 2012 R2 folder redirection works as follows: The system uses a pointer that moves the folders you want to a location that you specify. Users do not see any of this—it is transparent to them. One problem with folder redirection is that it does not work for mobile users (users who will be offline and who will not have access to files that they may need).

Offline folders, however, are copies of folders that were local to you. Files are now available locally to you on the system you have with you. They are also located back on the server where they are stored. The next time you log in, the folders are synchronized so that both folders contain the latest data. This is a perfect feature for mobile users, whereas folder redirection provides no benefit for the mobile user.

Managing GPOs with Windows PowerShell Group Policy Cmdlets

As stated earlier in this book, *Windows PowerShell* is a Windows command-line shell and scripting language. Windows PowerShell can also help an administrator automate many of the same tasks that you perform using the Group Policy Management Console.

Windows Server 2012 R2 helps you perform many of the Group Policy tasks by providing more than 25 cmdlets. Each of these cmdlets is a simple, single-function command-line tool.

The Windows PowerShell Group Policy cmdlets can help you perform some of the following tasks for domain-based Group Policy objects:

- Maintain, create, remove, back up, and import GPOs.

- Create, update, and remove GPO links to Active Directory containers.

- Set Active Directory OUs and domain permissions and inheritance flags.

- Configure Group Policy registry settings.
- Create and edit Starter GPOs.

The requirement for Windows PowerShell Group Policy cmdlets is Windows Server 2012 R2 on either a domain controller or a member server that has the GPMC installed. Windows 7 and Windows 8 also have the ability to use Windows PowerShell Group Policy cmdlets if it has Remote Server Administration Tools (RSAT) installed. RSAT includes the GPMC and its cmdlets. PowerShell is also a requirement.

Item-Level Targeting

Administrators have the ability to apply individual preference items only to selected users or computers using a GPO feature called item-level targeting. *Item-level targeting* allows an administrator to select specific items that the GPO will look at and then apply that GPO only to the specific users or computers. Administrators have the ability to include multiple preference items, and each item can be customized for specific users or computers to use.

The target item has a value that belongs to it, and the value can be either true or false. Administrators can get even more granular by using the operation command of AND or OR while building this GPO, and this will allow an administrator to combine the targeted items with the preceding one. Once all of the conditions are executed, if the final value is false, then the GPO is not applied. If the final value is true, the GPO is applied to the users or computers that were previously determined. Administrators have the ability to item-target the following items:

- Battery Present Targeting
- Computer Name Targeting
- CPU Speed Targeting
- Date Match Targeting
- Disk Space Targeting
- Domain Targeting
- Environment Variable Targeting
- File Match Targeting
- IP Address Range Targeting
- Language Targeting
- LDAP Query Targeting
- MAC Address Range Targeting
- MSI Query Targeting
- Network Connection Targeting
- Operating System Targeting
- Organizational Unit Targeting

- PCMCIA Present Targeting
- Portable Computer Targeting
- Processing Mode Targeting
- RAM Targeting
- Registry Match Targeting
- Security Group Targeting
- Site Targeting
- Terminal Session Targeting
- Time Range Targeting
- User Targeting
- WMI Query Targeting

Administrators can easily set up item-level targeting by following these steps:

1. Open the Group Policy Management Console. Select the GPO that will contain the new preferences by right-clicking the GPO and then choose Edit.

2. In the console tree under Computer Configuration or User Configuration, expand the Preferences folder and then browse to the preference extension.

3. Double-click the node for the preference extension and then right-click the preference item and click Properties.

4. In the Properties dialog box, click the Common tab.

5. Select Item-Level Targeting and then click Targeting.

6. Click New Item. If you are configuring multiple targeted items, on the Item Option menu, click the logical operation (AND or OR). Then click OK when finished.

7. Click the OK button on the Properties dialog box, and you are all set.

Backup, Restore, Import, Copy, and Migration Tables

One of the biggest advantages of using the Group Policy Management Console is that it is a one-stop shopping utility. You can do everything you need to do for GPOs in one location. The GPMC not only allows you to create and link a GPO but also lets you backup, restore, import, copy, and use migration tables.

Backing Up a GPO

Since this book is about Windows Server 2012 R2 and everything you should do to set up the server properly, then you most likely already understand what backups can do for you.

The reason we back up data as an administrator is in the event of a crash or major error that requires us to reload data to the server. Backups should be done daily on all data that is important to your organization. Backups can be done either by using Windows Server 2012 R2's backup utility, or you can purchase third party software/hardware to back up your data.

I am an IT Director, and data recoverability is one of the most critical items that I deal with on a daily basis. I use a third-party hardware device from a company called Unitrends. This is just one of many companies that helps protect an organization's data.

This hardware device does hourly backups for all of my servers. One of the nice features of the Unitrends box is that it backs up onto the hardware device and then sends my data up to the cloud automatically for an offsite backup. This way, if I need to recover just one piece of data, I can grab it off the hardware device. But if I have a major issue, such as a fire that destroys the entire server room, I have an offsite backup from which I can retrieve my data.

It's the same for GPOs. You need to make sure you back up your GPOs in the event of an issue that requires you to do a reload. To back up your GPOs manually, you can go into the GPMC MMC and, under Group Policy Objects, you can right click and choose Backup All or right click on the specific GPO and choose Backup.

Restoring a GPO

There may be times when you have to restore a GPO that was previously backed up. There are normally two reasons why you have to restore a GPO—you accidently deleted the GPO, or you need to restore the GPO to a previous state. (This normally happens if you make changes and it causes an issue.) Restoring a GPO is simple.

1. Open the Group Policy Management Console.

2. In the console tree, right-click Group Policy Objects and choose Manage Backups.

3. Choose the backup you want to restore and click the Restore button.

Importing or Copying GPOs

As an administrator, there may be times when you need to import or copy a GPO from one domain to another domain. Administrators do this so that the second domain has the same settings as the first domain.

An administrator can use the import or copy-to-transfer settings from one GPO to another GPO within the same domain, to a GPO in another domain in the same forest, or to a GPO in a domain in a different forest.

Importing or copying a GPO is an easy process. To do this, an administrator completes the following steps:

1. Open the Group Policy Management Console.

2. In the console tree, right-click Group Policy Objects and choose either Import Settings or Copy.

Migration Tables

One issue that we run into when copying or moving a GPO from one system to another is that when some GPOs are built, they are domain specific. This can be a problem when they are moved to a system in another domain. This is where migration tables can help you out.

Migration tables will tell you how domain specific settings should be treated when the GPO is moved from the domain in which it was created to another domain.

Migration tables are files that are used to map previous domain information (such as users and groups) to the new domain's object-specific data. Migration tables have mapping entries that map the old data to the new data.

Migration tables store their mapping data in an XML format, and the migration tables have their own extension name, .migtable. If you want to create your own migration table, you can use the *Migration Table Editor (MTE)*. The MTE is an easy-to-use utility for configuring or just viewing migration tables.

It does not matter if you decide to copy or import a GPO, migration tables apply to any of the settings within the GPO. However, if you copy a GPO instead of move it, you have the option of bringing the Discretionary Access Control List (DACL) option over with the copy.

If you are looking at using migration tables, there are three settings that can be used:

Do Not Use A Migration Table   If an administrator chooses this option, the GPO is copied over exactly as is. All security objects and UNC paths are copied over without any modification.

Use A Migration Table   If an administrator chooses this option, the GPO has all of the options that can be in the migration table mapped.

Use A Migration Table Exclusively   If an administrator chooses this option, all security principals and UNC path information in the GPO are chosen. If any of this information is not included in the migration table, the operation will fail.

To open the Migration Table Editor, perform the following steps:

1.   Open the Group Policy Management Console.

2.   In the console tree, right-click Group Policy Objects and choose Open Migration Table Editor.

Resetting the Default GPO

There may be a time when you need to reset the default GPO to its original settings. This is easy to do as long as you understand how to use the DCGPOFix command-line utility. This command-line utility is just what it spells—it fixes the domain controller's GPO. To use this command, you would use the following syntax:

```
DCGPOFix [/ignoreschema] [/target: {Domain | DC | Both}] [/?]
```

So, let's take a look at the switches in the previous command. The /ignoreschema switch ignores the current version of the Active Directory Schema. The reason you use this switch is because this command works only on the same schema version as the Windows version in which the command was shipped. By using this switch, you don't need to worry about what schema you have on the system.

The next switch is [/target: {Domain | DC | Both}]. This switch specifies the GPO you are going to restore. An administrator has the ability to restore the Default Domain Policy GPO, the Default Domain Controllers GPO, or both. The final switch, /?, displays the help for this command.

Deploying Software Through a GPO

It's difficult enough to manage applications on a stand-alone computer. It seems that the process of installing, configuring, and uninstalling applications is never finished. Add in the hassle of computer reboots and reinstalling corrupted applications, and the reduction in productivity can be substantial.

Software administrators who manage software in network environments have even more concerns:

- First and foremost, they must determine which applications specific users require.

- Then IT departments must purchase the appropriate licenses for the software and acquire any necessary media.

- Next, the system administrators need to install the applications on users' machines. This process generally involves help desk staff visiting computers, or it requires end users to install the software themselves. Both processes entail several potential problems, including installation inconsistency and lost productivity from downtime experienced when the applications were installed.

- Finally, software administrators still need to manage software updates and remove unused software.

One of the key design goals for Active Directory was to reduce some of the headaches involved in managing software and configurations in a networked environment. To that end, Windows Server 2012 R2 offers several features that can make the task of deploying software easier and less error prone. Before you dive into the technical details, however, you need to examine the issues related to software deployment.

The Software Management Life Cycle

Although it may seem that the use of a new application requires only the installation of the necessary software, the overall process of managing applications involves many more steps. When managing software applications, there are three main phases to their life cycle:

Phase 1: Deploying Software   The first step in using applications is to install them on the appropriate client computers. Generally, some applications are deployed during the initial configuration of a PC, and others are deployed when they are requested. In the latter case, this often meant that system administrators and help desk staffs had to visit client computers and manually walk through the installation process. With Windows Server 2012 R2 and GPOs, the entire process can be automated.

Before You Install, Stop

It is important to understand that just because you can easily deploy software, it does not necessarily mean that you have the right to do so. Before you install software on client computers, you must make sure you have the appropriate licenses for the software. Furthermore, it's important to take the time to track application installations. As many system administrators have discovered, it's much more difficult to inventory software installations after they've been performed. Another issue you may encounter is that you lack available resources (for instance, your system does not meet the minimum hardware requirements) and face problems such as limited hard disk space or memory that may not be able to handle the applications that you want to load and use. You may also find that your user account does not have the permission to install software. It's important to consider not only how you will install software but also whether you can or not.

Phase 2: Maintaining Software   Once an application is installed and in use on client computers, you need to ensure that the software is maintained. You must keep programs up-to-date by applying changes due to bug fixes, enhancements, and other types of updates. This is normally done with service packs, hot fixes, and updates. As with the initial software deployment, software maintenance can be tedious. Some programs require older versions to be uninstalled before updates are added. Others allow for automatically upgrading over existing installations. Managing and deploying software updates can consume a significant amount of the IT staff's time.

Using Windows Update

Make sure you learn about Windows Update, a service that allows you to connect to Microsoft's website and download what your system may need to bring it up to compliance. This tool is helpful if you are running a stand-alone system, but if you want to deploy software across the enterprise, the best way to accomplish this is first to test the updates you are downloading and make sure you can use them and that they are not bug ridden. Then you can use a tool such as the Windows Server Update Service (WSUS), which was formerly called the Software Update Services (SUS).

You can check for updates at Microsoft's website (http://update.microsoft.com). Microsoft likes to ask many types of questions about WSUS on its certification exams. WSUS is described in detail in other Sybex certification series books.

Phase 3: Removing Software   The end of the life cycle for many software products involves the actual removal of unused programs. Removing software is necessary when applications become outdated or when users no longer require their functionality. One of the traditional problems with uninstalling applications is that many of the installed files may not be removed. Furthermore, removing shared components can sometimes cause other programs to stop functioning properly. Also, users often forget to uninstall applications that they no longer need, and these programs continue to occupy disk space and consume valuable system resources.

The Microsoft Windows Installer (MSI) manages each of these three phases of the software maintenance life cycle. Now that you have an overview of the process, let's move forward to look at the steps involved in deploying software using Group Policy.

 The *Microsoft Windows Installer* (sometimes referred to as Microsoft Installer or Windows Installer) is an application installation and configuration service. An instruction file (the Microsoft Installer package) contains information about what needs to be done to install a product. It's common to confuse the two.

The Windows Installer

If you've installed newer application programs (such as Microsoft Office 2013), you've probably noticed the updated setup and installation routines. Applications that comply with the updated standard use the *Windows Installer specification* and MSI software packages for deployment. Each package contains information about various setup options and the files required for installation. Although the benefits may not seem dramatic on the surface, there's a lot of new functionality under the hood.

The Windows Installer was created to solve many of the problems associated with traditional application development. It has several components, including the Installer service (which runs on Windows 2000, XP, Vista, Windows 7, Windows 8, Windows Server 2003, Windows Server 2008, Windows Server 2008 R2, and Windows Server 2012 R2 computers), the Installer program (msiexec.exe) that is responsible for executing the instructions in a *Windows Installer package*, and the specifications third-party developers use to create their own packages. Within each installation package file is a relational structure (similar to the structure of tables in databases) that records information about the programs contained within the package.

To appreciate the true value of the Windows Installer, you'll need to look at some of the problems with traditional software deployment mechanisms and then at how the Windows Installer addresses many of them.

Application Installation Issues

Before the Windows Installer, applications were installed using a setup program that managed the various operations required for a program to operate. These operations included copying files, changing registry settings, and managing any other operating system changes that might be required (such as starting or stopping services). However, this method had several problems:

- The setup process was not robust, and aborting the operation often left many unnecessary files in the file system.

- The process included uninstalling an application (this also often left many unnecessary files in the file system) and remnants in the Windows registry and operating system folders. Over time, these remnants would result in reduced overall system performance and wasted disk space.

- There was no standard method for applying upgrades to applications, and installing a new version often required users to uninstall the old application, reboot, and then install the new program.

- Conflicts between different versions of *dynamic link libraries (DLLs)*—shared program code used across different applications—could cause the installation or removal of one application to break the functionality of another.

Benefits of the Windows Installer

Because of the many problems associated with traditional software installation, Microsoft created the *Windows Installer*. This system provides for better manageability of the software installation process and gives system administrators more control over the deployment process. Specifically, the Windows Installer provides the following benefits:

Improved Software Removal   The process of removing software is an important one because remnants left behind during the uninstall process can eventually clutter up the registry and file system. During the installation process, the Windows Installer keeps track of all of the changes made by a setup package. When it comes time to remove an application, all of these changes can then be rolled back.

More Robust Installation Routines   If a typical setup program is aborted during the software installation process, the results are unpredictable. If the actual installation hasn't yet begun, then the installer generally removes any temporary files that may have been created. However, if the file copy routine starts before the system encounters an error, it is likely that the files will not be removed automatically from the operating system. In contrast, the Windows Installer allows you to roll back any changes when the application setup process is aborted.

Ability to Use Elevated Privileges   Installing applications usually requires the user to have Administrator permissions on the local computer because file system and registry changes are required. When installing software for network users, system administrators have two options. First they can log off of the computer before installing the software and then log back on as a user who has Administrator permissions on the local computer. This method is tedious and time-consuming. The second option is to give users Administrator permissions temporarily on their own machines. This method could cause security problems and requires the attention of a system administrator.

Through the use of the Installer service, the Windows Installer is able to use temporarily elevated privileges to install applications. This allows users, regardless of their security settings, to execute the installation of authorized applications. This saves time and preserves security.

Support for Repairing Corrupted Applications   Regardless of how well a network environment is managed, critical files are sometimes lost or corrupted. Such problems can prevent applications from running properly and can cause crashes. Windows Installer packages provide you with the ability to verify the installation of an application and, if necessary, replace any missing or corrupted files. This support saves time and lessens end-user headaches associated with removing and reinstalling an entire application to replace just a few files.

Prevention of File Conflicts   Generally, different versions of the same files should be compatible with each other. In the real world, however, this isn't always the case. A classic problem in the Windows world is the case of one program replacing DLLs that are used by several other programs. Windows Installer accurately tracks which files are used by certain programs and ensures that any shared files are not improperly deleted or overwritten.

Automated Installations   A typical application setup process requires end users or system administrators to respond to several prompts. For example, a user may be able to choose the program group in which icons will be created and the file system location to which the program will be installed. Additionally, they may be required to choose which options are installed. Although this type of flexibility is useful, it can be tedious when you are rolling out multiple applications. By using features of the Windows Installer, however, users are able to specify setup options before the process begins. This allows system administrators to ensure consistency in installations, and it saves users' time.

Advertising and On-Demand Installations   One of the most powerful features of the Windows Installer is its ability to perform on-demand software installations. Prior to the Windows Installer, application installation options were quite basic—either a program was installed or it was not. When setting up a computer, system administrators would be required to guess which applications the user might need and install all of them.

The Windows Installer supports a function known as advertising. *Advertising* makes applications appear to be available via the Start menu. However, the programs themselves may not actually be installed on the system. When a user attempts to access an advertised application, the Windows Installer automatically downloads the necessary files from a server and installs the program. The result is that applications are installed only when they are needed, and the process requires no intervention from the end user. We'll cover the details of this process later in this chapter.

To anyone who has managed many software applications in a network environment, all of these features of the Windows Installer are likely welcome ones. They also make life easier for end users and applications developers; they can focus on the "real work" that their jobs demand.

Windows Installer File Types

When performing software deployment with the Windows Installer in Windows Server 2012 R2, you may encounter several different file types:

Microsoft Windows Installer Packages   To take full advantage of Windows Installer functionality, applications must include Microsoft Windows Installer (MSI) packages. Third-party application vendors and software developers normally create these packages, and they include the information required to install and configure the application and any supporting files.

Microsoft Transformation Files   *Microsoft Transformation (MST) files* are useful when you are customizing the details of how applications are installed. When a system administrator chooses to assign or publish an application, they may want to specify additional options for the package. For example, if a system administrator wants to allow users to install only the Microsoft Word and Microsoft PowerPoint components of Office 2013, they could specify these options within a transformation file. Then, when users install the application, they will be provided only with the options related to these components.

Microsoft Patches   To maintain software, patches are often required. Patches may make registry and/or file system changes. *Patch files (MSP)* are used for minor system changes and are subject to certain limitations. Specifically, a patch file cannot remove any installed program components and cannot delete or modify any shortcuts created by the user.

Initialization Files   To provide support for publishing non–Windows Installer applications, *initialization files* can be used. These files provide links to a standard executable file that is used to install an application. An example might be \\server1\software\program1\ setup.exe. These files can then be published and advertised, and users can access the *Programs and Features* icon to install them over the network.

Application Assignment Scripts   *Application assignment scripts (AAS)* store information regarding assigning programs and any settings that the system administrator makes. These files are created when Group Policy is used to create software package assignments for users and computers.

Each of these types of files provides functionality that allows the system administrator to customize software deployment. Windows Installer packages have special properties that you can view by right-clicking the file in Windows Explorer and choosing Properties (see Figure 16.9).

FIGURE 16.9   Viewing the properties of an MSI package file

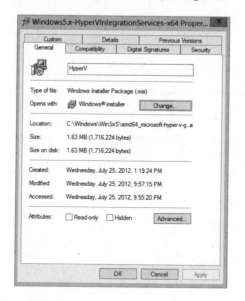

Deploying Applications

The functionality provided by Windows Installer offers many advantages to end users who install their own software. However, that is just the beginning in a networked environment. As you'll see later in this chapter, the various features of Windows Installer and compatible packages allow system administrators to determine centrally which applications users will be able to install.

There are two main methods of making programs available to end users using Active Directory: assigning and publishing. Both assigning and publishing applications greatly ease the process of deploying and managing applications in a network environment.

In the following sections, you'll look at how the processes of assigning and publishing applications can make life easier for IT staff and users alike. The various settings for assigned and published applications are managed through the use of GPOs.

Assigning Applications

Software applications can be assigned to users and computers. *Assigning* a software package makes the program available for automatic installation. The applications advertise their availability to the affected users or computers by placing icons within the Programs folder of the Start menu.

When applications are assigned to a user, programs will be advertised to the user regardless of which computer they are using. That is, icons for the advertised program will appear within the Start menu regardless of whether the program is installed on that computer. If the user clicks an icon for a program that has not yet been installed on the local computer, the application will automatically be accessed from a server and it will be installed.

When an application is assigned to a computer, the program is made available to any users of the computer. For example, all users who log on to a computer that has been assigned Microsoft Office 2013 will have access to the components of the application. If the user did not previously install Microsoft Office 2013, they will be prompted for any required setup information when the program first runs.

Generally, applications that are required by the vast majority of users should be assigned to computers. This reduces the amount of network bandwidth required to install applications on demand and improves the end-user experience by preventing the delay involved when installing an application the first time it is accessed. Any applications that may be used by only a few users (or those with specific job tasks) should be assigned to users.

Publishing Applications

When applications are *published*, they are advertised, but no icons are automatically created. Instead, the applications are made available for installation using the Add Or Remove Programs icon in Control Panel.

Windows Vista, Windows 7, and Windows 8 do not have the Add Or Remove Programs feature. They use the Programs and Features icon in Control Panel to install the software.

Implementing Software Deployment

So far, you have become familiar with the issues related to software deployment and management from a theoretical level. Now it's time to drill down into the actual steps required to deploy software using the features of Active Directory and the GPMC. In the following sections, you will walk through the steps required to create an application distribution share point, to publish and assign applications, to update previously installed applications, to verify the installation of applications, and to update Windows operating systems.

Preparing for Software Deployment

Before you can install applications on client computers, you must make sure that the necessary files are available to end users. In many network environments, system administrators create shares on file servers that include the installation files for many applications. Based on security permissions, either end users or system administrators can then connect to these shares from a client computer and install the needed software. The efficient organization of these shares can save the help desk from having to carry around a library of CD-ROMs, and it allows you to install applications easily on many computers at once.

One of the problems in network environments is that users frequently install applications whether or not they really need them. They may stumble upon applications that are stored on common file servers and install them out of curiosity. These actions can often decrease productivity and may violate software licensing agreements. You can help to avoid this by placing all of your application installation files in hidden shares (for example, software$).

Exercise 16.7 walks you through the process of creating a software distribution share point. In this exercise, you will prepare for software deployment by creating a directory share and placing certain types of files in this directory. To complete the steps in this exercise, you must have access to the Microsoft Office 2010 or Microsoft Office 2013 installation files (via CD-ROM or through a network share) and have 2000MB of free disk space. For this exercise, I used Microsoft Office 2010.

EXERCISE 16.7

Creating a Software Deployment Share

1. Using Windows Explorer, create a folder called Software that you can use with application sharing. Be sure that the volume on which you create this folder has at least 2000MB of available disk space.

2. Create a folder called Office 2010 within the Software folder.

3. Copy all the installation files for Microsoft Office 2010 from the CD-ROM or network share containing the files to the Office 2010 folder you created in step 2. If you prefer, you can use switches to install all the Office 2010 installation files. You can find these switches at http://technet.microsoft.com/en-us/library/ff521767.aspx.

4. Right-click the Software folder (created in step 1) and select Share. In the Choose People On Your Network To Share With dialog box, type **Everyone** and click the Add button. Next click the Share button. When you see a message that the sharing process is complete, click Done.

Once you have created an application distribution share, it's time to publish and assign the applications. This topic is covered next.

Software Restriction Policies

One of the biggest problems that we face as IT managers is that of users downloading and installing software. Many software packages don't cause any issues and are completely safe. Unfortunately, many software packages do have viruses and can cause problems. This is where software restriction policies can help. Software restriction policies help to identify software and to control its ability to run on a local computer, organizational unit, domain, or site.

Software restriction policies give administrators the ability to regulate unknown or untrusted software. Software restriction policies allow you to protect your computers from unwanted software by identifying and also specifying what software packages are allowed to be installed.

When configuring software restriction policies, an administrator is able to define a default security level of Unrestricted (software is allowed) or Disallowed (software is not allowed to run) for a GPO. Administrators can make exceptions to this default security level. They can create software restriction policy rules for specific software.

To create a software policy using the Group Policy Management Console, create a new GPO. In the GPO, expand the Windows Settings for either the user or computer configuration section, expand Security, right-click Software Restriction Policy, and choose New Software Restriction Policy. Set the policy for the level of security that you need.

Using AppLocker

AppLocker is a feature in Windows 7, Windows 8, and Windows Server 2012 R2. It is the replacement for Software Restriction Policies. *AppLocker* allows you to configure a Denied list and an Accepted list for applications. Applications that are configured on the Denied list will not run on the system, whereas applications on the Accepted list will operate properly.

The new capabilities and extensions of the AppLocker feature help reduce administrative overhead and help administrators control how users can access and use files, such as EXE files, scripts, Windows Installer files (MSI and MSP files), and DLLs.

Group Policy Slow Link Detection

When setting up GPOs, most of us assume that the connection speeds between servers and clients are going to be fast. In today's world, it is unlikely to see slow connections between locations, but they are still out there. Sometimes connection speeds can cause issues with the deployment of GPOs, specifically ones that are deploying software.

A setting in the Computer and User section of the GPO called *Group Policy Slow Link Detection* defines a slow connection for the purposes of applying and updating GPOs. If the data transfer rate from the domain controller providing the GPO to the computer is slower than what you have specified in this setting, the connection is considered to be a slow connection. If a connection is considered slow, the system response will vary depending on the policy. For example, if a GPO is going to deploy software and the connection is considered slow, the software may not be installed on the client computer. If you configure this option as 0, all connections are considered fast connections.

Publishing and Assigning Applications

As mentioned earlier in this section, system administrators can make software packages available to users by using publishing and assigning operations. Both of these operations allow system administrators to leverage the power of Active Directory and, specifically,

GPOs to determine which applications are available to users. Additionally, OUs can provide the organization that can help group users based on their job functions and software requirements.

The general process involves creating a GPO that includes software deployment settings for users and computers and then linking this GPO to Active Directory objects.

Exercise 16.8 walks you through the steps required to publish and assign applications. In this exercise, you will create applications and assign them to specific Active Directory objects using GPOs. To complete the steps in this exercise, you must have completed Exercise 16.7.

EXERCISE 16.8

Publishing and Assigning Applications Using Group Policy

1. Open the Active Directory Users and Computers tool from the Administrative Tools program group (using the Windows key).

2. Expand the domain and create a new top-level OU called **Software**.

3. Within the Software OU, create a user named **Jane User** with a login name of **juser** (choose the defaults for all other options).

4. Exit Active Directory Users and Computers and open the Group Policy Management Console.

5. Right-click the Software OU and choose Create A GPO In This Domain And Link It Here.

6. For the name of the new GPO, type **Software Deployment**.

7. To edit the Software Deployment GPO, right-click it and choose Edit. Expand the Computer Configuration ➢ Policies ➢ Software Settings object.

8. Right-click the Software Installation item and select New ➢ Package.

9. Navigate to the Software share you created in Exercise 16.7.

10. Within the Software share, double-click the Office 2010 folder and select the appropriate MSI file depending on the version of Office 2010 that you have. Office 2010 Professional is being used in this example, so you'll see that the OFFICEMUI.MSI file is chosen. Click Open.

11. In the Deploy Software dialog box, choose Advanced. (Note that the Published option is unavailable because applications cannot be published to computers.) Click OK to return to the Deploy Software dialog box.

12. To examine the deployment options of this package, click the Deployment tab. Accept the default settings by clicking OK.

13. Within the Group Policy Object Editor, expand the User Configuration ➢ Software Settings object.

EXERCISE 16.8 *(continued)*

14. Right-click the Software Installation item and select New ➢ Package.

15. Navigate to the Software share you created in Exercise 16.7.

16. Within the Software share, double-click the Office 2010 folder and select the appropriate MSI file. Click Open.

17. For the Software Deployment option, select Published in the Deploy Software dialog box and click OK.

18. Close the GPMC.

The overall process involved in deploying software using Active Directory is quite simple. However, you shouldn't let the intuitive graphical interface fool you—there's a lot of power under the hood of these software deployment features! Once you've properly assigned and published applications, it's time to see the effects of your work.

Applying Software Updates

The steps described in the previous section work only when you are installing a new application. However, software companies often release updates that you need to install on top of existing applications. These updates usually consist of bug fixes or other changes that are required to keep the software up-to-date. You can apply software updates in Active Directory by using the Upgrades tab of the software package Properties dialog box found in the Group Policy Object Editor.

In Exercise 16.9, you will apply a software update to an existing application. You should add the upgrade package to the GPO in the same way that you added the original application in steps 8 through 12 of Exercise 16.8. You should also have completed Exercise 16.8 before attempting this exercise.

EXERCISE 16.9

Applying Software Updates

1. Open the Group Policy Management Console from the Administrative Tools program group.

2. Click the Software OU, right-click the Software Deployment GPO, and choose Edit.

3. Expand the Computer Configuration ➢ Policies ➢ Software Settings ➢ Software Installation object.

4. Right-click the software package and select Properties from the context menu to bring up the Properties dialog box.

5. Select the Upgrades tab and click the Add button.

6. Click the Current Group Policy Object (GPO) radio button in the Choose A Package From section of the dialog box or click the Browse button to select the GPO to which you want to apply the upgrade. Consult your application's documentation to see whether you should choose the Uninstall The Existing Package, the Install The Upgrade Package radio button, or the Package Can Upgrade Over The Existing Package radio button.

7. Click Cancel to close the Add Upgrade Package dialog box.

8. Click Cancel and exit the GPMC.

You should understand that not all upgrades make sense in all situations. For instance, if the Stellacon 2010 files are incompatible with the Stellacon 2013 application, then your Stellacon 2012 users might not want you to perform the upgrade without taking additional steps to ensure that they can continue to use their files. In addition, users might have some choice about which version they use when it doesn't affect the support of the network.

Regardless of the underlying reason for allowing this flexibility, you should be aware that there are two basic types of upgrades that are available for administrators to provide to users:

Mandatory Upgrade   Forces everyone who currently has an existing version of the program to upgrade according to the GPO. Users who have never installed the program for whatever reason will be able to install only the new upgraded version.

Nonmandatory Upgrade   Allows users to choose whether they would like to upgrade. This upgrade type also allows users who do not have their application installed to choose which version they would like to use.

Verifying Software Installation

To ensure that the software installation settings you make in a GPO have taken place, you can log into the domain from a Windows 8, Windows 7, or Windows Vista computer that is within the OU to which the software settings apply. When you log in, you will notice two changes. First the application is installed on the computer (if it was not installed already). To access the application, a user needs to click one of the icons within the Program group of the Start menu. Note also that applications are available to any of the users who log on to this machine. Second, the settings apply to any computers that are contained within the OU and to any users who log on to these computers.

If you publish an application to users, the change may not be as evident, but it is equally useful. When you log on to a Windows 8, Windows 7, or Windows Vista computer that is a member of the domain, and when you use a user account from the OU where you published the application, you will be able to install any of the published applications automatically. On a Windows 8 or Windows 7 computer, you can do this by accessing the Programs icon in Control Panel. By clicking Add New Programs, you access a display of the applications available for installation. By clicking the Add button in the Programs and Features section of the Programs dialog box, you will automatically begin the installation of the published application.

Configuring Automatic Updates in Group Policy

So far you've seen the advantages of deploying application software in a group policy. Group policies also provide a way to install operating system updates across the network for Windows 2000, XP, Vista, Windows 7, Windows 8, Windows Server 2003, Windows Server 2008, Windows Server 2008 R2, and Windows Server 2012 R2 machines using Windows Update in conjunction with Windows Server Update Service. WSUS is the newer version of SUS, and it is used on a Windows Server 2012 R2 system to update systems. As you may remember, WSUS and SUS are patch-management tools that help you deploy updates to your systems in a controlled manner.

Windows Update is available through the Microsoft website, and it is used to provide the most current files for Windows operating systems. Examples of updates include security fixes, critical updates, updated help files, and updated drivers. You can access Windows Update by clicking the Windows Update icon in the system tray.

 We will discuss WSUS in greater detail in Chapter 10, "Manage and Maintain Servers."

WSUS is used to leverage the features of Windows Update within a corporate environment by downloading Windows updates to a corporate server, which in turn provides the updates to the internal corporate clients. This allows administrators to test and have full control over what updates are deployed within the corporate environment.

Within an enterprise network that is using Active Directory, you would typically see automatic updates configured through Group Policy. Group policies are used to manage configuration and security settings via Active Directory. Group Policy is also used to specify what server a client will use for automatic updates.

If the WSUS client is part of an enterprise network that is using Active Directory, you would configure the client via a group policy.

Configuring Software Deployment Settings

In addition to the basic operations of assigning and publishing applications, you can use several other options to specify the details of how software is deployed. In the following sections, you will examine the various options that are available and their effects on the software installation process.

The Software Installation Properties Dialog Box

The most important software deployment settings are contained in the Software Installation Properties dialog box, which you can access by right-clicking the Software Installation item and selecting Properties from the context menu. The following sections describe the features contained on the various tabs of the dialog box.

Managing Package Defaults

On the Deployment tab of the Software Installation Properties dialog box, you'll be able to specify some defaults for any packages that you create within this GPO. Figure 16.10 shows the Deployment options for managing software installation settings.

FIGURE 16.10   Deployment tab of the Software Installation Properties dialog box

The following options are used for managing software installation settings:

Default Package Location   This setting specifies the default file system or network location for software installation packages. This is useful if you are already using a specific share on a file server for hosting the necessary installation files.

New Packages   These settings specify the default type of package assignment that will be used when you add a new package to either the user or computer settings. If you'll be assigning or publishing multiple packages, you may find it useful to set a default here. Selecting the Advanced option enables Group Policy to display the package's Properties dialog box each time a new package is added (see Figure 16.11).

FIGURE 16.11 Advanced Deployment dialog box

Installation User Interface Options   When installing an application, system administrators may or may not want end users to see all of the advanced installation options. If Basic is chosen, the user will only be able to configure the minimal settings (such as the installation location). If Maximum is chosen, all of the available installation options will be displayed. The specific installation options available will depend on the package itself.

Uninstall Applications When They Fall Out of the Scope of Management   So far, you have seen how applications can be assigned and published to users or computers. But what happens when effective GPOs change? For example, suppose User A is currently located within the Sales OU. A GPO that assigns the Microsoft Office 2013 suite of applications is linked to the Sales OU. You decide to move User A to the Engineering OU, which has no software deployment settings. Should the application be uninstalled, or should it remain?

If the Uninstall This Application When It Falls Out Of The Scope Of Management option is checked, applications will be removed if they are not specifically assigned or published within GPOs. In this example, this means that Office 2013 would be uninstalled for User A. If this box is left unchecked, however, the application will remain installed.

Managing File Extension Mappings

One of the potential problems associated with using many different file types is that it's difficult to keep track of which applications work with which files. For example, if you received a file with the filename extension .abc, you would have no idea which application you would need to view it.

Fortunately, through software deployment settings, system administrators can specify mappings for specific *filename extensions*. For example, you could specify that whenever users attempt to access a file with the extension .vsd, the operating system should attempt to open the file using Visio diagramming software. If Visio is not installed on the user's machine, the computer can automatically download and install it (assuming that the application has been properly advertised).

This method allows users to have applications automatically installed when they are needed. The following is an example of a sequence of events that might occur:

1. A user receives an email message that contains a PDF (.pdf) file attachment.

2. The computer realizes that the PDF file does not have the appropriate viewing application for this type of file installed. However, it also realizes that a filename extension mapping is available within the Active Directory software deployment settings.

3. The client computer automatically requests the PDF software package from the server, and it uses the Microsoft Windows Installer to install the application automatically.

4. The computer opens the attachment for the user.

Notice that all of these steps were carried out without any further interaction with the user. You can manage filename extension mappings by right-clicking the Software Installation item, selecting Properties, and then clicking the File Extensions tab.

Creating Application Categories

In many network environments, the list of supported applications can include hundreds of items. For users who are looking for only one specific program, searching through a list of all of these programs can be difficult and time-consuming.

Fortunately, methods for categorizing the applications are available on your network. You can easily manage the application categories for users and computers by right-clicking the Software Installation item, selecting Properties, and then clicking the Categories tab.

Figure 16.12 shows you the categories tab of the Software Installation package. When creating categories, it is a good idea to use category names that are meaningful to users because it will make it easier for them to find the programs they're seeking.

FIGURE 16.12 The Categories tab of the Software Installation Properties dialog box

Once the software installation categories have been created, you can view them by clicking the Programs or Programs And Features icon in Control Panel. When you click Add New Programs, you'll see that several options appear in the Category drop-down list. Now when you select the properties for a package, you will be able to assign the application to one or more of the categories.

Removing Programs

As discussed in the beginning of the chapter, an important phase in the software management life cycle is the removal of applications. Fortunately, if you use the GPMC and the Windows Installer packages, the process is simple. To remove an application, you can right-click the package within the Group Policy settings and select All Tasks ➢ Remove (see Figure 16.13).

FIGURE 16.13   Removing a software package

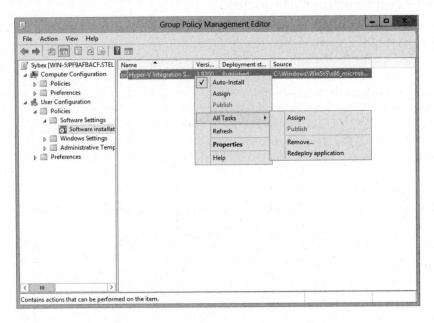

When choosing to remove a software package from a GPO, you have two options:

Immediately Uninstall The Software From Users And Computers   System administrators can choose this option to ensure that an application is no longer available to users who are affected by the GPO. When this option is selected, the program will be uninstalled automatically from users and/or computers that have the package. This option might be useful, for example, if the license for a certain application has expired or if a program is no longer on the approved applications list.

Allow Users To Continue To Use The Software, But Prevent New Installations   This option prevents users from making new installations of a package, but it does not remove the software if it has already been installed for users. This is a good option if the company has run out of additional licenses for the software, but the existing licenses are still valid.

Figure 16.14 shows these two removal options.

FIGURE 16.14   Software removal options

If you no longer require the ability to install or repair an application, you can delete it from your software distribution share point by deleting the appropriate Windows Installer package files. This will free up additional disk space for newer applications.

Microsoft Windows Installer Settings

Several options influence the behavior of the Windows Installer; you can set them within a GPO. You can access these options by navigating to User Configuration ➢ Administrative Templates ➢ Windows Components ➢ Windows Installer (see Figure 16.15). The options are as follows:

FIGURE 16.15   GPO settings for Windows Installer

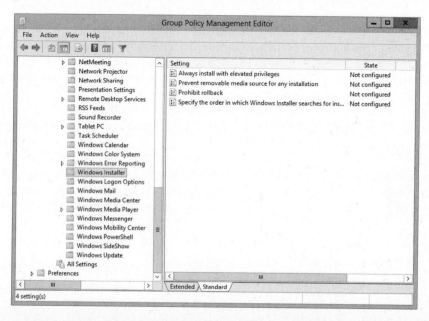

Always Install With Elevated Privileges   This policy allows users to install applications that require elevated privileges. For example, if a user does not have the permissions necessary to modify the registry but the installation program must make registry changes, this policy will allow the process to succeed.

Prevent Removable Media Source For Any Install   This option disallows the installation of software using removable media (such as CD-ROM or DVD-ROM). It is useful for ensuring that users install only approved applications.

Prohibit Rollback   When this option is enabled, the Windows Installer does not store the system state information that is required to roll back the installation of an application. System administrators may choose this option to reduce the amount of temporary disk space required during installation and to increase the performance of the installation operation. However, the drawback is that the system cannot roll back to its original state if the installation fails and the application needs to be removed.

Specify the Order In Which Windows Installer Searches   This setting specifies the order in which the Windows Installer will search for installation files. The options include n (for network shares), m (for searching removal media), and u (for searching the Internet for installation files).

With these options, system administrators can control how the Windows Installer operates for specific users who are affected by the GPO.

Troubleshooting Group Policies

Because of the wide variety of configurations that are possible when you are establishing GPOs, you should be aware of some common troubleshooting methods. These methods will help isolate problems in policy settings or GPO links.

One possible problem with GPO configuration is that logons and system startups may take a long time. This occurs especially in large environments when the Group Policy settings must be transmitted over the network and, in many cases, slow WAN links. In general, the number of GPOs should be limited because of the processing overhead and network requirements during logon. By default, GPOs are processed in a synchronous manner. This means that the processing of one GPO must be completed before another one is applied (as opposed to asynchronous processing, where they can all execute at the same time).

When a group policy gets processed on a Windows-based operating system, client-side extensions are the mechanisms that interpret the stored policy and then make the appropriate changes to the operating system environment. When an administrator is troubleshooting a given extension's application of policy, the administrator can view the configuration parameters for that extension in the operating system's registry. To view the extension in the registry, you would view the following key:

```
HKEY_LOCAL_MACHINE\Software\Microsoft\Windows CA
NT\CurrentVersion\Winlogon\GPExtensions
```

The most common issue associated with Group Policy is the unexpected setting of Group Policy options. In Windows Server 2000, administrators spent countless hours analyzing inheritance hierarchy and individual settings to determine why a particular user or computer was having policy problems. For instance, say a user named wpanek complains that the Run option is missing from his Start menu. The wpanek user account is stored in the New Hampshire OU, and you've applied group policies at the OU, domain, and site levels. To determine the source of the problem, you would have to sift through each GPO manually to find the Start menu policy as well as to figure out the applicable inheritance settings.

Windows Server 2012 R2 has a handy feature called *Resultant Set of Policy (RSoP)* that displays the exact settings that actually apply to individual users, computers, OUs, domains, and sites after inheritance and filtering have taken effect. In the example just described, you could run RSoP on the wpanek account and view a single set of Group Policy settings that represent the settings that apply to the wpanek account. In addition, each setting's Properties dialog box displays the GPO from which the setting is derived as well as the order of priority, the filter status, and other useful information, as you will see a bit later.

RSoP actually runs in two modes:

Logging Mode   *Logging mode* displays the actual settings that apply to users and computers, as shown in the example in the preceding paragraph.

Planning Mode   *Planning mode* can be applied to users, computers, OUs, domains, and sites, and you use it before you apply any settings. As its name implies, planning mode is used to plan GPOs.

Additionally, you can run the command-line utility gpresult.exe to get a quick snapshot of the Group Policy settings that apply to a user and/or computer. Let's take a closer look at the two modes and the gpresult.exe command.

RSoP in Logging Mode

RSoP in logging mode can query policy settings only for users and computers. The easiest way to access RSoP in logging mode is through the Active Directory Users and Computers tool, although you can run it as a stand-alone MMC snap-in if you want.

To analyze the policy settings for wpanek from the earlier example, you would right-click the user icon in Active Directory Users and Computers and select All Tasks ➢ Resultant Set of Policy (Logging). The Group Policy Results Wizard appears. The wizard walks you through the steps necessary to view the RSoP for wpanek.

The Computer Selection page, shown in Figure 16.16, requires you to select a computer for which to display settings. Remember that a GPO contains both user and computer settings, so you must choose a computer to which the user is logged on in order to continue with the wizard. If the user has never logged on to a computer, then you must run RSoP in planning mode because there is no logged policy information yet for that user.

FIGURE 16.16 The Computer Selection page of the Group Policy Results Wizard

The User Selection page, shown in Figure 16.17, requires you to select a user account to analyze. Because I selected a user from the Active Directory Users and Computers tool, the username is filled in automatically. This page is most useful if you are running RSoP in MMC mode and don't have the luxury of selecting a user contextually.

FIGURE 16.17 The User Selection page of the Group Policy Results Wizard

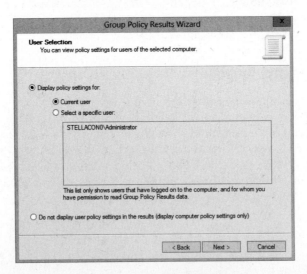

The Summary Of Selections page, shown in Figure 16.18, displays a summary of your choices and provides an option for gathering extended error information. If you need to make any changes before you begin to analyze the policy settings, you should click the Back button on the Summary screen. Otherwise, click Next.

FIGURE 16.18   The Summary Of Selections page of the Group Policy Results Wizard

After the wizard is complete, you will see the window shown in Figure 16.19. This window displays only the policy settings that apply to the user and computer that you selected in the wizard. You can see these users and computers at the topmost level of the tree.

FIGURE 16.19   The User Selection page for the administrator on computer SERVER1

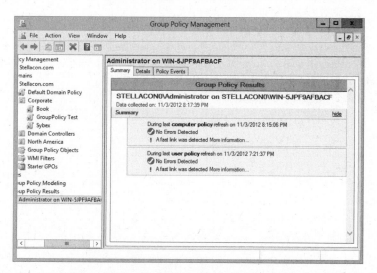

Any warnings or errors appear as a yellow triangle or red X over the applicable icon at the level where the warning or error occurred. To view more information about the warning or error, right-click the icon, select Properties, and select the Error Information tab. Figure 16.20 shows an error message.

FIGURE 16.20   Details of event pertaining to the administrator account on computer SERVER1

You cannot make changes to any of the individual settings because RSoP is a diagnostic tool and not an editor, but you can get more information about settings by clicking a setting and selecting Properties from the context menu.

The Details tab of the user's Properties window, shown in Figure 16.21, displays the actual setting that applies to the user in question based on GPO inheritance.

FIGURE 16.21   The Details tab of the object's Properties window

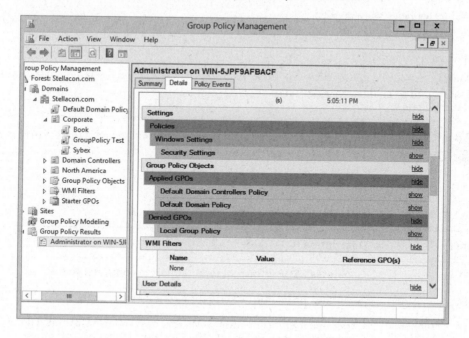

RSoP in Planning Mode

Running RSoP in planning mode isn't much different from running RSoP in logging mode, but the RSoP Wizard asks for a bit more information than you saw earlier.

In the former example, wpanek couldn't see the Run option in the Start menu because the New Hampshire GPO in the San Jose OU affects his user account. As an administrator, you could plan to move his user account to the North America OU. Before doing so, you could verify his new policy settings by running RSoP in planning mode. Run the RSoP on the user wpanek under the scenario that you've already moved him from the San Jose OU to the North America OU. At this point, you haven't actually moved the user, but you can see what his settings would be if you did.

Using the *gpresult.exe* Command

The command-line utility gpresult.exe is included as part of the RSoP tool. Running the command by itself without any switches returns the following Group Policy information about the local user and computer:

- The name of the domain controller from which the local machine retrieved the policy information

- The date and time in which the policies were applied
- Which policies were applied
- Which policies were filtered out
- Group membership

You can use the switches shown in Table 16.3 to get information for remote users and computers and to enable other options.

Table 16.3 is not a complete list. To see a complete list of the gpresult.exe switches, visit Microsoft at www.microsoft.com.

TABLE 16.3 gpresult switches

Switch	Description
/S systemname	Generates RSoP information for a remote computer name.
/USER username	Generates RSoP information for a remote username.
/x /h filename	Generates a report in either XML (/x) or HTML (/h) format. The filename and location is specified by the filename parameter.
/V	Specifies verbose mode, which displays more verbose information such as user rights information.
/Z	Specifies an even greater level of verbose information.
/SCOPE MACHINE	Displays maximum information about the computer policies applied to this system.
/SCOPE USER	Displays maximum information about the user policies applied to this system.
>textfile.txt	Writes the output to a text file.

For example, to obtain information about user wpanek in a system called STELLACON, you would use the command gpresult/S STELLACON/USERwpanek.

Through the use of these techniques, you should be able to track down even the most elusive Group Policy problems. Remember, however, that good troubleshooting skills do not replace planning adequately and maintaining GPO settings!

Summary

In this chapter, you examined Active Directory's solution to a common headache for many systems administrators: policy settings. Specifically, I discussed topics that covered Group Policy.

I covered the fundamentals of Group Policy, including its fundamental purpose. You can use Group Policy to enforce granular permissions for users in an Active Directory environment. Group policies can restrict and modify the actions allowed for users and computers within the Active Directory environment.

Certain Group Policy settings may apply to users, computers, or both. Computer settings affect all users who access the machines to which the policy applies. User settings affect users regardless of the machines to which they log on.

You learned that you can link Group Policy objects to Active Directory sites, domains, or OUs. This link determines to which objects the policies apply. GPO links can interact through inheritance and filtering to result in an effective set of policies.

The chapter covered inheritance and how GPOs filter down. I showed you how to use the Enforced option on a GPO issued from a parent and how to block a GPO from a child.

You can also use administrative templates to simplify the creation of GPOs. There are some basic default templates that come with Windows Server 2012 R2.

In addition, administrators can delegate control over GPOs in order to distribute administrative responsibilities. Delegation is an important concept because it allows for distributed administration.

You can also deploy software using GPOs. This feature can save time and increase productivity throughout the entire software management life cycle by automating software installation and removal on client computers. The Windows Installer offers a more robust method for managing installation and removal, and applications that support it can take advantage of new Active Directory features. Make sure you are comfortable using the Windows Installer.

You learned about publishing applications via Active Directory and the difference between publishing and assigning applications. You can assign some applications to users and computers so that they are always available. You can also publish them to users so that the user can install them with minimal effort when required.

You also learned how to prepare for software deployment. Before your users can take advantage of automated software installation, you must set up an installation share and provide the appropriate permissions.

The final portion of the chapter covered the Resultant Set of Policy (RSoP) tool, which you can use in logging mode or planning mode to determine exactly which set of policies apply to users, computers, OUs, domains, and sites.

Exam Essentials

Understand the purpose of Group Policy.   System administrators use Group Policy to enforce granular permissions for users in an Active Directory environment.

Understand user and computer settings.   Certain Group Policy settings may apply to users, computers, or both. Computer settings affect all users who access the machines to which the policy applies. User settings affect users, regardless of the machines to which they log on.

Know the interactions between Group Policy objects and Active Directory.   GPOs can be linked to Active Directory objects. This link determines to which objects the policies apply.

Understand filtering and inheritance interactions between GPOs.   For ease of administration, GPOs can interact via inheritance and filtering. It is important to understand these interactions when you are implementing and troubleshooting Group Policy.

Know how Group Policy settings can affect script policies and network settings.   You can use special sets of GPOs to manage network configuration settings.

Understand how delegation of administration can be used in an Active Directory environment.   Delegation is an important concept because it allows for distributed administration.

Know how to use the Resultant Set of Policy (RSoP) tool to troubleshoot and plan Group Policy.   Windows Server 2012 R2 includes the RSoP feature, which you can run in logging mode or planning mode to determine exactly which set of policies applies to users, computers, OUs, domains, and sites.

Identify common problems with the software life cycle.   IT professionals face many challenges with client applications, including development, deployment, maintenance, and troubleshooting.

Understand the benefits of the Windows Installer.   Using the Windows Installer is an updated way to install applications on Windows-based machines. It offers a more robust method for making the system changes required by applications, and it allows for a cleaner uninstall. Windows Installer–based applications can also take advantage of new Active Directory features.

Understand the difference between publishing and assigning applications.   Some applications can be assigned to users and computers so that they are always available. Applications can be published to users so that the user may install the application with a minimal amount of effort when it is required.

Know how to prepare for software deployment.   Before your users can take advantage of automated software installation, you must set up an installation share and provide the appropriate permissions.

Know how to configure application settings using Active Directory and Group Policy. Using standard Windows Server 2012 R2 administrative tools, you can create an application policy that meets your requirements. You can use automatic, on-demand installation of applications as well as many other features.

Create application categories to simplify the list of published applications. It's important to group applications by functionality or the users to whom they apply, especially in organizations that support a large number of programs.

Review Questions

1. The process of assigning permissions to set Group Policy for objects within an OU is known as:

   A. Promotion

   B. Inheritance

   C. Delegation

   D. Filtering

2. Which of the following statements is true regarding the actions that occur when a software package is removed from a GPO that is linked to an OU?

   A. The application will be automatically uninstalled for all users within the OU.

   B. Current application installations will be unaffected by the change.

   C. The system administrator may determine the effect.

   D. The current user may determine the effect.

3. You are the network administrator for your organization. You are working on creating a new GPO for the sales OU. You want the GPO to take effect immediately. Which command would you use?

   A. GPForce

   B. GPUpdate

   C. GPResult

   D. GPExecute

4. You are the network administrator for your organization. You are working on creating a new GPO for the Marketing OU. You want the GPO to take effect immediately, and you need to use Windows PowerShell. Which PowerShell cmdlet command would you use?

   A. Invoke-GPUpdate

   B. Invoke-GPForce

   C. Invoke-GPResult

   D. Invoke-GPExecute

5. You are the network administrator, and you have decided to set up a GPO with item-level targeting. Which of the following is *not* an option for item-level targeting?

   A. Battery Present Targeting

   B. Computer Name Targeting

   C. CPU Speed Targeting

   D. DVD Present Targeting

6. You are the network administrator for a large organization that uses Windows Server 2012 R2 domain controllers and DNS servers. All of your client machines currently have the Windows XP operating system. You want to be able to have client computers edit the domain-based GPOs by using the ADMX files that are located in the ADMX Central Store. How do you accomplish this task? (Choose all that apply.)

   A. Upgrade your clients to Windows 8.

   B. Upgrade your clients to Windows 7.

   C. Add the client machines to the ADMX edit utility.

   D. In the ADMX store, choose the box Allow All Client Privileges.

7. You work for an organization with a single Windows Server 2012 R2 Active Directory domain. The domain has OUs for Sales, Marketing, Admin, R&D, and Finance. You need the users in the Finance OU only to get Microsoft Office 2010 installed automatically onto their computers. You create a GPO named OfficeApp. What is the next step in getting all of the Finance users Office 2010?

   A. Edit the GPO, and assign the Office application to the user's account. Link the GPO to the Finance OU.

   B. Edit the GPO, and assign the Office application to the user's account. Link the GPO to the domain.

   C. Edit the GPO, and assign the Office application to the computer account. Link the GPO to the domain.

   D. Edit the GPO, and assign the Office application to the computer account. Link the GPO to the Finance OU.

8. You are hired as a consultant to the ABC Company. The owner of the company complains that she continues to have desktop wallpaper that she did not choose. When you speak with the IT team, you find out that a former employee created 20 GPOs and they have not been able to figure out which GPO is changing the owner's desktop wallpaper. How can you resolve this issue?

   A. Run the RSoP utility against all forest computer accounts.

   B. Run the RSoP utility against the owner's computer account.

   C. Run the RSoP utility against the owner's user account.

   D. Run the RSoP utility against all domain computer accounts.

9. You are the network administrator for a large organization that has multiple sites and multiple OUs. You have a site named SalesSite that is for the sales building across the street. In the domain, there is an OU for all salespeople called Sales. You set up a GPO for the SalesSite, and you need to be sure that it applies to the Sales OU. The Sales OU GPOs cannot override the SalesSite GPO. What do you do?

   A. On the GPO, disable the Block Child Inheritance setting.

   B. On the GPO, set the Enforce setting.

   C. On the GPO, set the priorities to 1.

   D. On the Sales OU, set the Inherit Parent Policy settings.

10. You are the administrator for an organization that has multiple locations. You are running Windows Server 2012 R2, and you have only one domain with multiple OUs set up for each location. One of your locations, Boston, is connected to the main location by a 256Kbps ISDN line. You configure a GPO to assign a sales application to all computers in the entire domain. You have to be sure that Boston users receive the GPO properly. What should you do?

    A. Disable the Slow Link Detection setting in the GPO.

    B. Link the GPO to the Boston OU.

    C. Change the properties of the GPO to publish the application to the Boston OU.

    D. Have the users in Boston run the GPResult/force command.

Exam 70-412: Configuring Advanced Windows Server 2012 R2 Services

PART III

Chapter

17

Configure and Manage High Availability

THE FOLLOWING 70-412 EXAM OBJECTIVES ARE COVERED IN THIS CHAPTER:

✓ **Configure Network Load Balancing (NLB)**

- ■ This objective may include, but is not limited to:
  - ■ Install NLB nodes
  - ■ Configure NLB prerequisites
  - ■ Configure affinity
  - ■ Configure port rules
  - ■ Configure cluster operation mode
  - ■ Upgrade an NLB cluster

✓ **Configure failover clustering**

- ■ This objective may include, but is not limited to:
  - ■ Configure Quorum
  - ■ Configure cluster networking
  - ■ Restore single node or cluster configuration
  - ■ Configure cluster storage
  - ■ Implement cluster aware updating
  - ■ Upgrade a cluster

✓ **Manage failover-clustering roles**

- ■ This objective may include, but is not limited to:
  - ■ Configure role-specific settings including continuously available shares

- Configure VM monitoring

- Configure failover and preference settings

✓ **Manage Virtual Machine (VM) Movement**

- This objective may include, but is not limited to:

  - Configure Virtual Machine network health protection

  - Configure drain on shutdown

  - Perform quick, live and storage migrations

  - Import/export/copy of VMS

The R2 update to Windows Server 2012 has improved upon the rich high availability capabilities already present in Windows Server 2012. The management, reporting, and ease of use of the feature set are all worth mentioning, but the expansion of features is the greatest benefit of the R2 update with regard to high availability.

The exam will cover the new features at a high level, and it will cover the basic configuration and operational functions for both a failover cluster and a network load balancer. This chapter will introduce how to achieve high availability with hardware and operational changes as well as how to use the high availability features of Windows Server 2012 R2.

Any discussion of high availability, network load balancers, and clustering would not be complete without a discussion of high availability in general. The chapter will first cover what it means, both from a purely technical perspective and from a business perspective.

Components of High Availability

High availability is a buzzword that many application and hardware vendors like to throw around to get you to purchase their products. Many different options are available to achieve high availability, and there also seems to be a number of definitions and variations that help vendors sell their products as high-availability solutions.

When it comes right down to it, however, high availability simply means providing services with maximum uptime by avoiding unplanned downtime. Often, *disaster recovery (DR)* is also closely lumped into discussions of high availability, but DR encompasses the business and technical processes that are used to recover once a disaster has happened.

Defining a high availability plan usually starts with a *service level agreement (SLA)*. At its most basic, an SLA defines the services and metrics that must be met for the availability and performance of an application or service. Often, an SLA is created for an IT department or service provider to deliver a specific level of service. An example of this might be an SLA for a Microsoft Exchange server. The SLA for an Exchange server might have uptime metrics on how much time during the month the mailboxes need to be available to end users, or it might define performance metrics for the amount of time it takes for email messages to be delivered.

When determining what goes into an SLA, two other factors need to be considered. However, you will often see them discussed only in the context of disaster recovery, even though they are important for designing a highly available solution. These factors are the *recovery point objective (RPO)* and the *recovery time objective (RTO)*.

An RTO is the length of time an application can be unavailable before service must be restored to meet the SLA. For example, a single component failure would have an RTO of less than five minutes, and a full-site failure might have an RTO of three hours. An RPO is essentially the amount of data that must be restored in the event of a failure. For example, in a single server or component failure, the RPO would be 0, but in a site failure, the RPO might allow for up to 20 minutes of lost data.

SLAs, on the other hand, are usually expressed in percentages of the time the application is available. These percentages are also often referred to by the number of nines the percentage includes, as shown in Table 17.1.

TABLE 17.1   Availability percentages

Availability rating	Allowed unplanned downtime/year
99 percent	3.7 days
99.9 percent	8.8 hours
99.99 percent	53 minutes
99.999 percent	5.3 minutes

Two important factors that affect an SLA are the *mean time between failure (MTBF)* and the *mean time to recovery (MTTR)*. To be able to reduce the amount of unplanned downtime, the time between failures must be increased, and the time it takes to recover must be reduced. Modifying these two factors will be addressed in the next several sections of this chapter.

Achieving High Availability

Windows Server 2012 R2 is the most secure and reliable Windows version to date. It also is the most stable, mature, and capable of any version of Windows. Although similar claims have been made for previous versions of Windows Server, you can rest assured that Windows Server 2012 R2 is much better than previous versions for a variety of reasons.

An honest look at the feature set and real-world use should prove that this latest version of Windows provides the most suitable foundation for creating a highly available solution. However, more than just good software is needed to be able to offer high availability for applications.

High Availability Foundation

Just as a house needs a good foundation, a highly available Windows server needs a stable and reliable hardware platform on which to run. Although Windows Server 2012 R2 will technically run on desktop-class hardware, high availability is more easily achieved with server-class hardware. What differentiates desktop-class from server-class hardware? *Server-class hardware* has more management and monitoring features built into it so that the health of the hardware is capable of being monitored and maintained.

Another large difference is that server-class hardware has redundancy options. Server-class hardware often has options to protect from drive failures, such as RAID controllers, and to protect against power supply failures, such as multiple power supplies. Enterprise-class servers have even more protection.

More needs to be done than just installing Windows Server 2012 R2 to ensure that the applications remain running with the best availability possible. Just as a house needs maintenance and upkeep to keep the structure in proper repair, so too does a server. In the case of a highly available server, this means *patch management.*

Installing Patches

Microsoft releases monthly updates to fix security problems with its software, both for operating system fixes and for applications. To ensure that your highly available applications are immune to known vulnerabilities, these patches need to be applied in a timely manner during a scheduled maintenance window. Also, to address stability and performance issues, updates and service packs are released regularly for many applications, such as Microsoft SQL Server, Exchange Server, and SharePoint Portal Server. Many companies have a set schedule—daily, weekly, or monthly—to apply these patches and updates after they are tested and approved.

Desired Configuration Manager (DCM), an option in Microsoft System Center Configuration Manager 2012 and newer, is a great tool for helping to validate that your cluster nodes are patched. It can leverage the SCCM client to collect installed patches and help reporting within the enterprise on compliancy with desired system states based on the software installed.

To continue with the house analogy, if you were planning to have the master bath remodeled, would you rather hire a college student on spring break looking to make some extra money to do the job or a seasoned artisan? Of course, you would want someone with experience and a proven record of accomplishment to remodel your master bath.

Likewise, with any work that needs to be done on your highly available applications, it's best to hire only decidedly qualified individuals. This is why obtaining a Microsoft certification is definitely an excellent start to becoming qualified to configure a highly available server properly. There is no substitute for real-life and hands-on experience. Working with highly available configurations in a lab and in production will help you know not only what configurations are available but also how the changes should be made.

For example, it may be possible to use Failover Clustering for a WINS server, but in practice WINS replication may be easier to support and require less expensive hardware in order to provide high availability. This is something you would know only if you had enough experience to make this decision.

As with your house, once you have a firm and stable foundation built by skilled artisans and a maintenance plan has been put into place, you need to ascertain what more is needed. If you can't achieve enough uptime with proper server configuration and mature operational processes, a cluster may be needed.

Windows Server 2012 R2 provides two types of clustering: *Failover Clustering* and *Network Load Balancing (NLB)*. Failover clustering is used for applications and services such as SQL Server and Exchange Server. Network Load Balancing is used for network-based services such as web and FTP servers. The remaining sections of this chapter will cover both of these clustering options in depth.

To Cluster or Not to Cluster

Clustering is often thrown into the mix when someone wants to achieve higher availability. This is a good step toward improved availability, but the return on the investment of a cluster doesn't always add up. Although Windows Server 2012 R2 greatly simplifies both the creation and management of a failover cluster, there is added complexity and cost in terms of hardware, software, and personnel.

How do you determine whether to cluster applications? Sometimes, even though it is possible to cluster applications, they perform worse when clustered. At other times, only a small improvement is made when a cluster is created. You have to balance the slight improvement over the increased hardware cost, complexity, and level of training required for administrators.

Configure Network Load Balancing

Network Load Balancing is a form of clustering where the nodes are highly available for a network-based service. This is typically a port listener configuration where a farm of, say, Microsoft Internet Information Services servers all listen on ports 80 and 443 for incoming web traffic from client endpoints. These nodes, while not fully clustered in a technical sense, are load balanced, where each node handles some of the distributed network traffic.

 Network Load Balancing at the software level (as I will discuss here) is generally reserved for light loads or loads in lower-budget environments, such as a test or QA environment, for example. Generally speaking, Network Load Balancing in large production environments relies on hardware-based solutions to front-end network load balancing and distributes it on a session-based load to multiple hosts. This type of configuration, however, is out of scope for this book.

Install NLB Nodes

You can install NLB nodes like any other server build. You want the host patched, provisioned with appropriate resources (typically with multiple network interface cards for capacity and responsiveness), and monitored for health and reliability. In Exercise 17.1, you'll install NLB nodes.

EXERCISE 17.1

Installing NLB Nodes

1. Once you have multiple hosts ready for the installation of NLB, simply run the Add Roles And Features Wizard and select Network Load Balancing in the Features area of the wizard.

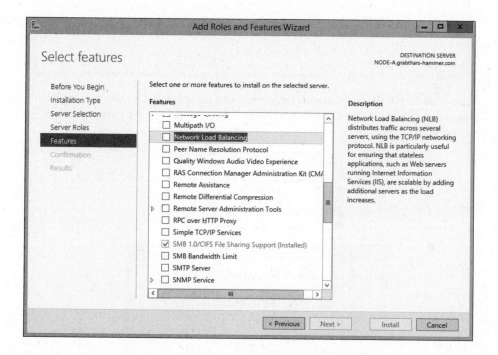

2. This wizard places a new application in your Start menu, the Network Load Balancing Manager (shown here), the execution of which loads the console.

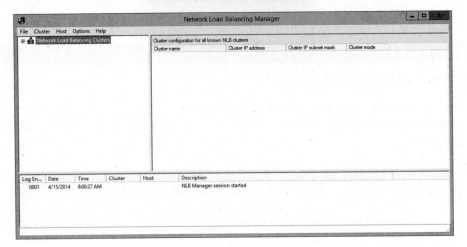

3. Right-click Network Load Balancing Clusters and select New Cluster. You are then presented with the connection wizard where you can specify the name of one of your hosts.

4. The next screen reveals a prompt to add any additional IPs and assign a priority level. You can do all this later, so hit Next.

5. The next wizard screen is where you specify the cluster IP address. This is the address that the endpoints or clients or users of the NLB cluster will contact. Typically the network team will assign a cluster IP address for this use.

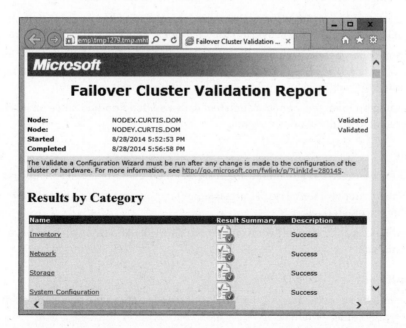

EXERCISE 17.1 *(continued)*

6. On the next screen, you configure the operation mode and specify a name.

With regard to the cluster operation modes, the differences between them are as follows:

Unicast

The cluster adapters for all nodes are assigned the same MAC address.

The outgoing MAC address for each packet is modified based on priority to prevent upstream switches from discovering that all nodes have the same MAC address.

Communication between cluster nodes (other than heartbeat and other administrative NLB traffic) is not possible unless there are additional adapters (because all nodes have the same MAC address).

Depending on load, this configuration can cause switch flooding since all inbound packets are sent to all ports on the switch.

Multicast

The cluster adapters for all nodes are assigned their own MAC unicast address.

The cluster adapters for all nodes are assigned a multicast MAC address (derived from the IP of the cluster).

Non-NLB network traffic between cluster nodes works fine since they all have their own MAC address.

IGMP Multicast

This is much like multicast, but the MAC traffic goes only to the switch ports of the NLB cluster, preventing switch flooding.

7. After selecting the appropriate settings, the next page is where port rules are configured. By default, it is set up to be wide open. Most implementations will limit NLB ports to just the ports needed for the application. For example, a web server would need port 80 enabled. It is also in this area where you can configure filtering mode.

The affinity sets a client's preference to a particular NLB host. It is not recommended to set affinity to None when UDP is an expected traffic type.

8. After clicking OK and finishing the wizard, you can add nodes to the NLB cluster by right-clicking and selecting Add Host To Cluster. Doing so presents a fairly straightforward wizard to add the host, specify a priority value, and then join the cluster. Shortly, your console will look similar to the one shown here.

Upgrading an NLB Cluster

Upgrading an NLB cluster is a fairly straightforward process. You execute a drainstop on the NLB cluster node or remove existing connections to the application on the local host, and then you can perform an in-place upgrade in a rolling manner.

Achieving High Availability with Failover Clustering

Taking high availability to the next level for enterprise services often means creating a failover cluster. In a failover cluster, all of the clustered application or service resources are assigned to one node or server in the cluster. Commonly clustered applications are SQL Server and Exchange Server; commonly clustered services are File and Print. Since the differences between a clustered application and a clustered service are primarily related to the number of functions or features, for simplicity's sake I will refer to both as *clustered applications*. Another, more frequently, clustered resource is a Hyper-V virtual machine.

If there is a failure of the primary node or if the primary node is taken offline for maintenance, the clustered application is started on another cluster node. The client requests are then automatically redirected to the new cluster node to minimize the impact of the failure.

How does Failover Clustering improve availability? By increasing the number of server nodes available on which the application or virtual machine can run, you can move the application or virtual machine to a healthy server if there is a problem, if maintenance needs to be completed on the hardware or the operating system, or if patches need to be applied. The clustered application being moved will have to restart on the new server regardless of whether the move was intentional. This is why the term *highly available* is used instead of *fault tolerant*. Virtual machines, however, can be moved from one node to another node using a process known as *live migration*. Live migration is where one or more virtual machines are intentionally moved from one node to another with their current memory state intact through the cluster network with no indicators to the virtual machine consumer that the virtual machine has moved from one server to another. However, in the event of a cluster node or virtual machine failure, the virtual machine will still fail and will then be brought online again on another healthy cluster node.

Figure 17.1 shows an example of SQL Server running on the first node of a Windows Server 2012 R2 failover cluster.

The clustered SQL Server in Figure 17.2 can be failed over to another node in the cluster and still service database requests. However, the database will be restarted.

Failover clustering is notorious for being complicated and expensive. Windows Server 2012 R2 makes strides in removing both of these concerns. Troubleshooting and other advanced concepts are outside of the scope of the Microsoft MCSA exams and thus this book, so I will cover only the basic requirements and concepts needed to configure a failover cluster.

FIGURE 17.1   Using Failover Clustering to cluster SQL Server

FIGURE 17.2   Failing the SQL Server service to another node

Failover Clustering Requirements

The Failover Clustering feature is available in the Datacenter, Standard, and Hyper-V editions of Windows Server 2012 R2.

To be able to configure a failover cluster, you must have the required components. A single failover cluster can have up to 64 nodes when using Windows Server 2012 R2, however, and the clustered service or application must support that number of nodes.

To create a failover cluster, an administrator must make sure that all the hardware involved meets the cluster requirements. To be supported by Microsoft, all hardware must be certified for Windows Server 2012 R2, and the complete failover cluster solution must pass all tests in the Validate A Configuration Wizard. Although the exact hardware will depend on the clustered application, a few requirements are standard:

- Server components must be marked with the "Certified for Windows Server 2012 R2" logo.
- Although not explicitly required, server hardware should match and contain the same or similar components.
- All of the Validate A Configuration Wizard tests must pass.

The requirements for Failover Clustering storage have changed from previous versions of Windows. For example, Parallel SCSI is no longer a supported storage technology for any of the clustered disks. There are, however, additional requirements that need to be met for the storage components:

- Disks available for the cluster must be Fibre Channel, iSCSI, or Serial Attached SCSI.
- Each cluster node must have a dedicated network interface card for iSCSI connectivity. The network interface card you use for iSCSI should not be used for network communication.
- Multipath software must be based on Microsoft's Multipath I/O (MPIO).
- Storage drivers must be based on storport.sys.
- Drivers and firmware for the storage controllers on each server node in the cluster should be identical.
- Storage components must be marked with the "Certified for Windows Server 2012 R2" logo.

In addition, there are network requirements that must be met for Failover Clustering:

- Cluster nodes should be connected to multiple networks for communication redundancy.
- Network adapters should be the same make, use the same driver, and have the firmware version in each cluster node.
- Network components must be marked with the "Certified for Windows Server 2012 R2" logo.

There are two types of network connections in a failover cluster. These should have adequate redundancy because total failure of either could cause loss of functionality of the cluster. The two types are as follows:

Public Network   This is the network through which clients are able to connect to the clustered service application.

Private Network   This is the network used by the nodes to communicate with each other.

To provide redundancy for these two network types, additional network adapters would need to be added to the node and configured to connect to the networks.

In previous versions of Windows Server, support was given only when the entire cluster configuration was tested and listed on the Hardware Compatibility List. The tested configuration listed the server and storage configuration down to the firmware and driver versions. This proved to be difficult and expensive from both a vendor and a consumer perspective to deploy supported Windows clusters.

When problems did arise and Microsoft support was needed, it caused undue troubleshooting complexity as well. With Windows Server 2012 R2 Failover Clustering and simplified requirements, including the "Certified for Windows Server 2012 R2" logo program and the Validate A Configuration Wizard, it all but eliminates the guesswork of getting the cluster components configured in a way that follows best practices and allows Microsoft support to assist you easily when needed.

Cluster Quorum

When a group of people sets out to accomplish a single task or goal, a method for settling disagreements and for making decisions is required. In the case of a cluster, the goal is to provide a highly available service in spite of failures. When a problem occurs and a cluster node loses communication with the other nodes because of a network error, the functioning nodes are supposed to try to bring the redundant service back online.

How, though, is it determined which node should bring the clustered service back online? If all the nodes are functional despite the network communications issue, each one might try. Just like a group of people with their own ideas, a method must be put in place to determine which idea, or node, to grant control of the cluster. Windows Server 2012 R2 Failover Clustering, like other clustering technologies, requires that a quorum exist between the cluster nodes before a cluster becomes available.

A *quorum* is a consensus of the status of each of the nodes in the cluster. Quorum must be achieved in order for a clustered application to come online by obtaining a majority of the votes available (see Figure 17.3). Windows Server 2012 R2 has four quorum models, or methods, for determining quorum and for adjusting the number and types of votes available:

- Node majority (no witness)
- Node majority with witness (disk or file share)
- Node and file share majority
- No majority (disk witness only)

FIGURE 17.3   Majority needed

When a majority of the nodes are communicating, the cluster is functional.

When a majority of the nodes are not communicating, the cluster stops.

Witness Configuration

Most administrators follow some basic rules. For example, when you configure a quorum, the voting components in the cluster should be an odd number. For example, if I set up a quorum for five elements and I lose one element, I continue to work. If I lose two elements, I continue to work. If I lose three elements, the cluster stops—as soon as it hits half plus 1, the cluster stops. This works well with an odd number.

If the cluster contains an even number of voting elements, an administrator should then configure a disk witness or a file share witness. The advantage of using a witness (disk or file share) is that the cluster will continue to run even if half of the cluster nodes simultaneously go down or are disconnected. The ability to configure a disk witness is possible only if the storage vendor supports read-write access from all sites to the replicated storage.

One of the advantages of Windows Server 2012 R2 is the advanced quorum configuration option. This option allows you to assign or remove quorum votes on a per-node basis. Administrators now have the ability to remove votes from nodes in certain configurations. For example, if your organization uses a multisite cluster, you may choose to remove votes from the nodes in the backup site. This way, those backup nodes would not affect your quorum calculations.

Dynamic Quorum Management

Another advantage in Windows Server 2012 R2 is dynamic quorum management. *Dynamic quorum management* automatically manages the vote assignment to nodes. With this feature enabled, votes are automatically added or removed from nodes when that node either joins or leaves a cluster. In Windows Server 2012 R2, dynamic quorum management is enabled by default.

Validating a Cluster Configuration

Configuring a failover cluster in Windows Server 2012 R2 is much simpler than in previous versions of Windows Server. Before a cluster can be configured, the Validate A Configuration Wizard should be run to verify that the hardware is configured in a fashion that is supportable. Before you can run the Validate A Configuration Wizard, however, the Failover Clustering feature needs to be installed using Server Manager. The account that is used to create a cluster must have administrative rights on each of the cluster nodes and have permissions to create a cluster name object in Active Directory. Follow these steps:

1. Prepare the hardware and software perquisites.

2. Install the Failover Clustering feature on each server.

3. Log in with the appropriate user ID and run the Validate A Configuration Wizard.

4. Create a cluster.

5. Install and cluster applications and services.

To install the Failover Clustering feature on a cluster node, follow the steps outlined in Exercise 17.2.

EXERCISE 17.2

Installing the Failover Cluster Feature

1. Press the Windows key and select Administrative Tools ➢ Server Manager.

2. Select number 2, Add Roles And Features.

3. At the Select Installation Type screen, choose a role-based or feature-based installation.

4. At the Select Destination Server screen, choose Select A Server From The Server Pool and click Next.

5. At the Select Server Roles screen, click Next.

6. At the Select Features screen, click the Failover Clustering check box. If the Add Features dialog box appears, click the Add Features button. Click Next.

7. At the Confirmation screen, click the Install button.

8. Once the installation is complete, click the Close button.

9. Close Server Manager.

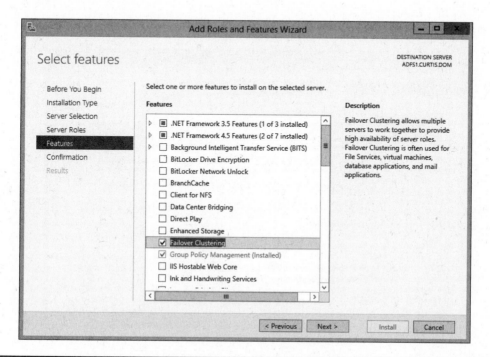

Using the Validate A Configuration Wizard before creating a cluster is highly recommended. This wizard validates that the hardware configuration and the software configuration for the potential cluster nodes are in a supported configuration. Even if the configuration passes the tests, take care to review all warnings and informational messages so that they can be addressed or documented before the cluster is created.

Running the Validate A Configuration Wizard does the following:

- Conducts four types of tests (software and hardware inventory, network, storage, and system configuration)

- Confirms that the hardware and software settings are supportable by Microsoft support staff

You should run the Validate A Configuration Wizard before creating a cluster or after making any major hardware or software changes to the cluster. Doing this will help you identify any misconfigurations that could cause problems with the failover cluster.

Running the Validate a Configuration Wizard

The Validate A Configuration Wizard, shown in Figure 17.4, is simple and straightforward to use, as its "wizard" name would suggest. It should be run after the Failover Clustering feature has been installed on each of the cluster nodes, and it can be run as many times as required.

FIGURE 17.4 The Validate A Configuration Wizard

When you are troubleshooting cluster problems or have changed the configuration of the cluster hardware, it is a good idea to run the Validate A Configuration Wizard again to help pinpoint potential cluster configuration problems.

If you already have a cluster configured and want to run the Validate A Configuration Wizard, you can do so; however, you will not be able to run all of the storage tests without taking the clustered resources offline. You will be prompted either to skip the disruptive tests or to take the clustered resources offline so that the tests can complete.

Exercise 17.3 shows the exact steps to follow to run the Validate A Configuration Wizard successfully on clusters named NODEA and NODEB, which are not yet clustered.

I am using NODEA and NODEB in the exercises. You need to replace these two nodes with your own two servers to complete these exercises.

EXERCISE 17.3

Running the Validate A Configuration Wizard

1. Press the Windows key and select Administrative Tools ➢ Failover Cluster Management.

2. In the Actions pane (right side of screen), click Validate Configuration.

3. At the Before You Begin screen, click Next.

4. Type **NODEA** in the Enter Name field and click Add.

5. Type **NODEB** in the Enter Name field and click Add.

EXERCISE 17.3 *(continued)*

6. Click Next.

7. Leave Run All Tests (Recommended) selected and click Next.

8. Click Next at the Confirmation screen.

9. Let the test complete, review the report in the Summary window, and then click Finish.

Addressing Problems Reported by the Validate A Configuration Wizard

After the Validate A Configuration Wizard has been run, it will show the results, as shown in Figure 17.5. This report can also be viewed in detail later using a web browser. The report is named with the date and time the wizard was run, and it is stored in %windir%\ cluster\Reports.

FIGURE 17.5   Validate A Configuration Wizard results

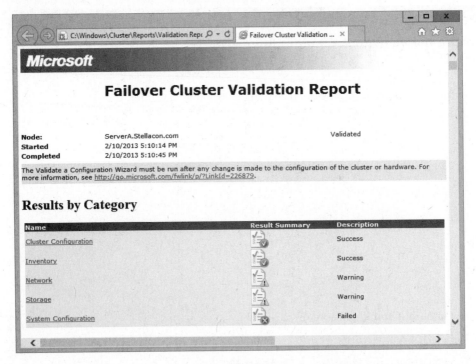

How should errors listed in the report be addressed? Often, the errors reported by the Validate A Configuration Wizard are self-explanatory; however, sometimes additional help is required. The following three guidelines should help troubleshoot the errors:

- Read all of the errors because multiple errors may be related.

- Use the checklists available in the Windows Server help files to ensure that all the steps have been completed.

- Contact the hardware vendor for updated drivers, firmware, and guidance for using the hardware in a cluster.

Multisite, Stretched, or Geographically Dispersed Clusters (Geoclustering)

One issue you may face is if you have multiple sites or if the cluster is geographically dispersed. If the failover cluster does not have a shared common disk, data replication between nodes might not pass the cluster validation "storage" tests.

Setting up a cluster in a multisite, stretched, or geocluster (these terms can be used interchangeably) configuration is a common practice. As long as the cluster solution does not require external storage to fail over, it will not need to pass the storage test to function properly.

Creating a Cluster

After you have successfully validated a configuration and the cluster hardware is in a supportable state, you can create a cluster. The process for creating a cluster is straightforward and similar to the process of running the Validate A Configuration Wizard. To create a cluster with two servers, follow the instructions in Exercise 17.4.

EXERCISE 17.4

Creating a Cluster

1. Open the Failover Cluster Management MMC.

2. In the Management section of the center pane, select Create A Cluster.

3. Read the Before You Begin information and click Next.

4. In the Enter Server Name box, type **NODEA** and then click Add.

5. Again, in the Enter Server Name box, type **NODEB** and then click Add. Click Next.

6. At the Validation screen, choose No for this exercise and then click Next.

7. In the Access Point For Administering The Cluster section, enter **Cluster1** for the cluster name.

8. Type an IP address and then click Next. This IP address will be the IP address of the cluster.

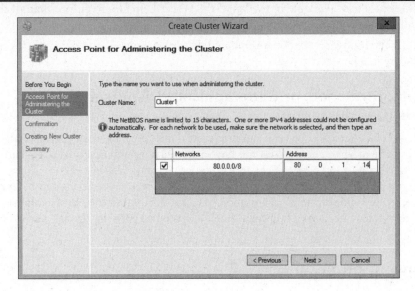

9. In the Confirmation dialog box, verify the information and then click Next.

10. On the Summary page, click Finish.

Working with Cluster Nodes

Once a cluster is created, a couple of actions are available. First you can add another node to the cluster by using the Add Node Wizard from the Failover Cluster Management Actions pane.

At this point, you also have the option to pause a node, which prevents resources from being failed over or moved to the node. You typically would pause a node when the node is involved in maintenance or troubleshooting. After a node is paused, it must be resumed to allow resources to be run on it again.

Another action available to perform on a node at this time is *evict*. Eviction is an irreversible process. Once you evict the node, it must be re-added to the cluster. You would evict a node when it is damaged beyond repair or is no longer needed in the cluster. If you evict a damaged node, you can repair or rebuild it and then add it back to the cluster using the Add Node Wizard.

Clustering Roles, Services, and Applications

Once the cluster is created, applications, services, and roles can be clustered. Windows Server 2012 R2 includes a number of built-in roles and features that can be clustered.

The following roles and features can be clustered in Windows Server 2012 R2 (see Figure 17.6):

FIGURE 17.6   High availability roles

- DFS Namespace Server
- DHCP Server
- Distributed Transaction Coordinator (DTC)
- File Server
- Generic Application
- Generic Script
- Generic Service
- Hyper-V Replica Broker
- iSCSI Target Server
- iSNS Server
- Message Queuing
- Other Server
- Virtual Machine
- WINS Server

In addition, other common services and applications can be clustered on Windows Server 2012 R2 clusters:

- Enterprise database services, such as Microsoft SQL Server
- Enterprise messaging services, such as Microsoft Exchange Server

To cluster a role or feature such as Print Services, the first step is to install the role or feature on each node of the cluster. The next step is to use the Configure A Service Or Application Wizard in the Failover Cluster Management tool. Exercise 17.5 shows you how to cluster the Print Services role once an appropriate disk has been presented to the cluster.

EXERCISE 17.5

Clustering the Print Services Role

1. Open the Failover Cluster Management MMC.

2. In the console tree, click the arrow next to the cluster name to expand the items underneath it.

3. Right-click Roles and choose Configure Role.

4. Click Next on the Before You Begin page.

5. Click Other Server on the Select Role screen and then click Next.

6. Type the name of the print server, such as **Print1**, and type in the IP address that will be used to access the print service, such as **80.0.0.34**. Then click Next.

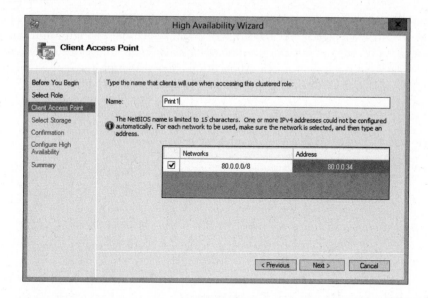

7. At the Select Storage page, just click Next.

8. Click Next at the Confirmation page.

9. After the wizard runs and the Summary page appears, you can view a report of the tasks the wizard performed by clicking View Report.

10. Close the report and click Finish.

The built-in roles and features all are configured in a similar fashion. Other applications, such as Microsoft Exchange Server 2013, have specialized cluster configuration routines that are outside the scope of this exam. Applications that are not developed to be clustered can also be clustered using the Generic Application, Generic Script, or Generic Service option in the Configure A Service Or Application Wizard, as shown in Figure 17.7.

FIGURE 17.7   Configuring a generic application

Clustered Application Settings

Windows Server 2012 R2 has options that allow an administrator to fine-tune the failover process to meet the needs of their business. These options will be covered in the next few sections.

Failover occurs when a clustered application or service moves from one node to another. The process can be triggered automatically because of a failure or server maintenance or can be done manually by an administrator. The failover process works as follows:

1. The cluster service takes all of the resources in the application offline in the order set in the dependency hierarchy.

2. The cluster service transfers the application to the node that is listed next on the application's list of preferred host nodes.

3. The cluster service attempts to bring all of the application's resources online, starting at the bottom of the dependency hierarchy.

   These steps can change depending on the use of Live Migration.

In a cluster that is hosting multiple applications, it may be important to set specific nodes to be primarily responsible for each clustered application. This can be helpful from a troubleshooting perspective since a specific node is targeted for hosting service. To set a preferred node and an order of preference for failover, use the General tab in the Properties dialog box of the clustered application.

Also, the order of failover is set in this same dialog box by moving the order in which the nodes are listed. If NODEA should be the primary node and NODEC should be the server that the application fails to first, NODEA should be listed first and selected as the preferred owner. NODEC should be listed second, and the remaining cluster nodes should be listed after NODEC.

As shown in Figure 17.8, a number of failover settings can be configured for the clustered service. The failover settings control the number of times a clustered application can fail in a period of time before the cluster stops trying to restart it. Typically, if a clustered application fails a number of times, some sort of manual intervention will be required to return the application to a stable state.

FIGURE 17.8   Clustered application failover settings

Specifying the maximum number of failures will keep the application from trying to restart until it is manually brought back online after the problem has been resolved. This is beneficial because if the application continues to be brought online and then fails, it may show as being functional to the monitoring system, even though it continues to fail. After the application is put in a failed state, the monitoring system will not be able to contact the application and should report it as being offline.

Figure 17.8 also shows the failback settings for Print1. Failback settings control whether and when a clustered application would fail back to the preferred cluster node once it becomes available. The default setting is Prevent Failback. If failback is allowed, two additional options are available, either to fail back immediately after the preferred node is available or to fail back within a specified time.

The time is specified in the 24-hour format. If you want to allow failback between 10 p.m. and 11 p.m., you would set the failback time to be between 22 and 23. Setting a failback time to off-hours is an excellent way to ensure that your clustered applications are running on the designated nodes and automatically scheduling the failover process for a time when it will impact the fewest users.

One tool that is valuable in determining how resources affect other resources is the dependency viewer. The *dependency viewer* visualizes the dependency hierarchy created for an application or service. Using this tool can help when troubleshooting why specific resources are causing failures and allow an administrator to visualize the current configuration better and adjust it to meet business needs. Exercise 17.6 will show you how to run the dependency viewer.

EXERCISE 17.6

Using the Dependency Viewer

1. Open the Failover Cluster Management MMC.

2. In the console tree, click the arrow to expand the cluster.

3. Click Roles.

4. Under the Roles section in the center of the screen, click one of the roles (such as Print1).

5. Right-click the role and under More Actions click Show Dependency Report.

6. Review the dependency report.

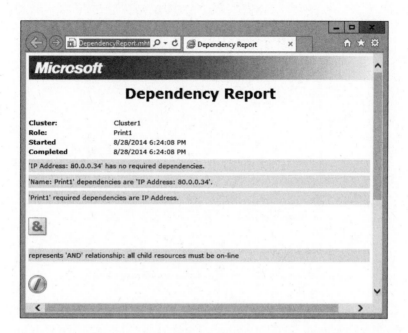

7. Close the Dependency Report and close the Failover Cluster Manager.

Exercise 17.6 generated a dependency report that shows how the print service is dependent on a network name and a clustered disk resource. The network name is then dependent on an IP address.

Resource Properties

Resources are physical or logical objects, such as a file share or IP address, which the failover cluster manages. They may be a service or application available to clients, or they may be part of the cluster. Resources include physical hardware devices such as disks and logical items such as network names. They are the smallest configurable unit in a cluster and can run on only a single node in a cluster at a time.

Like clustered applications, resources have a number of properties available for meeting business requirements for high availability. This section covers resource dependencies and policies.

Dependencies can be set on individual resources and control how resources are brought online and offline. Simply put, a dependent resource is brought online after the resources that it depends on, and it is taken offline before those resources. As shown in Figure 17.9, dependencies can be set on a specific resource, such as the print spooler.

FIGURE 17.9 Resource dependencies

Resource policies are settings that control how resources respond when a failure occurs and how resources are monitored for failures. Figure 17.10 shows the Policies tab of a resource's Properties dialog box.

FIGURE 17.10 Resource policies

The Policies tab sets configuration options for how a resource should respond in the event of a failure. The options available are as follows:

If Resource Fails, Do Not Restart   This option, as it would lead you to believe, leaves the failed resource offline.

If Resource Fails, Attempt Restart On Current Node   With this option set, the resource tries to restart if it fails on the node on which it is currently running. There are two additional options if this is selected so that the number of restarts can be limited. They set the number of times the resource should restart on the current node in a specified length of time. For example, if you specify 5 for Maximum Restarts In The Specified Period and 10:00 (mm:ss) for Period For Restarts, the cluster service will try to restart the resource five times during that 10-minute period. After the fifth restart, the cluster service will no longer attempt to restart the service on the active node.

If Restart Is Unsuccessful, Fail Over All Resources In This Service Or Application   If this option is selected, when the cluster service is no longer trying to restart the resource on the active node, it will fail the entire service or application to another cluster node. If you wanted to leave the application or service with a failed resource on the current node, you would clear this check box.

If All The Restart Attempts Fail, Begin Restarting Again After The Specified Period (hh:mm)   If this option is selected, the cluster service will restart the resource at a specified interval if all previous attempts have failed.

Pending Timeout   This option is used to set the amount of time in minutes and seconds that the cluster service should wait for this resource to respond to a change in states. If a resource takes longer than the cluster expects to change states, the cluster will mark it as having failed. If a resource consistently takes longer than this and the problem cannot be resolved, you may need to increase this value. Figure 17.11 shows the Advanced Policies tab.

FIGURE 17.11   Resource Advanced Policies

The options available on the Advanced Policies tab are as follows:

Possible Owners   This option allows an administrator to remove specific cluster nodes from running this resource. Using this option is valuable when there are issues with a resource on a particular node and the administrator wants to keep the applications from failing over to that node until the problem can be repaired.

Basic Resource Health Check Interval   This option allows an administrator to customize the health check interval for this resource.

Thorough Resource Health Check Interval   This option allows an administrator to customize the thorough health check interval for this resource.

Run This Resource In A Separate Resource Monitor   If the resource needs to be debugged by a support engineer or if the resource conflicts with other resources, this option may need to be used.

Windows Server 2012 R2 Clustering Features

Many new features are included in the Windows Server 2012 R2 release for clustering. It is a rich feature set of high availability with greatly improved flexibility based on the needs of IT organizations. The new features relate to quorum behavior, virtual machine hosting, Active Directory–detached clusters, and a new dashboard.

Windows PowerShell Cmdlets for Failover Clusters   As I have explained throughout this book, Windows PowerShell is a command-line shell and scripting tool. Windows Server 2012 R2 clustering has new cmdlets that provide powerful ways to script cluster configuration and management tasks. Windows PowerShell cmdlets have now replaced the Cluster.exe command-line interface.

Cluster Shared Volumes   *Cluster Shared Volumes (CSV)* allows for the configuration of clustered virtual machines. CSV allows you to do the following:

- Reduce the number of LUNs (disks) required for your virtual machines.
- Make better use of disk space. Any VHD file on that LUN can use the free space on a CSV volume.
- More easily track the paths to VHD files and other files used by virtual machines.
- Use a few CSV volumes to create a configuration that supports many clustered virtual machines.

CSV volumes also are utilized for the Scale-Out-File-Server cluster role.

Management of Large-Scale Clusters   One new advantage of Windows Server 2012 R2 clusters is the ability for Server Manager to discover and manage the nodes in a cluster. By starting the Failover Cluster Manager from Server Manager, you can do remote multiserver management and role and feature installation. Administrators now have the ability to manage a cluster from one convenient location.

Management and Mobility of Clustered Virtual Machines   As I have stated in previous chapters, Microsoft has built Windows Server 2012 R2 "from the cloud up." Microsoft, as well as the industry as a whole, is moving toward the cloud and virtualization. With that in mind, administrators can now configure settings such as prioritizing the starting or placement of virtual machines in the clustered workloads. This allows administrators to allocate resources efficiently to your cluster.

Cluster-Aware Updating   One issue that every administrator has dealt with is updating a system or application while it is running. For example, if you are running Microsoft Exchange and you want to do an Exchange update, when do you take the server offline to do the update? It always seems that someone is on the system 24 hours a day. Well, Windows Server 2012 R2 clustering has a solution. *Cluster-Aware Updating (CAU)* is a new automated feature that allows system updates to be applied automatically while the cluster remains available during the entire update process.

Scale-Out File Server for Application Data   By utilizing *Microsoft Storage Spaces*, you can create a highly available clustered file share that utilizes SMB 3.0 and CSV to provide scalable access to data.

Scale-out file servers are useful for storing the following application data:

- Hyper-V virtual machine storage
- SQL Server database files

Be aware that scale-out file servers are not useful at all for typical file share data because they benefit only from applications that require a persistent connection to their storage.

Shared Virtual Hard Disks   In the previous versions of Windows, Failover Cluster nodes running as virtual machines had to use iSCSI or virtual HBAs to connect directly to SAN-based storage. With Windows Server 2012 R2, you can set your Hyper-V virtualized cluster to use a shared VHDX virtual disk. Shared virtual hard disks can reside on the following:

- A scale-out file server failover cluster
- Cluster CSV volumes

Shared virtual hard disks are extremely useful in providing highly available shared storage for the following virtualized workloads:

- SQL Server
- Virtual Machine Manager
- Exchange Server

Virtual Machine Drain on Shutdown   When needing to perform maintenance on a Hyper-V failover cluster, you may have a lot of virtual machines on one node of a cluster. Inevitably, you will need to restart a cluster node for updates or shut it down for maintenance.

In previous versions of Windows, virtual machines running on the cluster would save their state, and then the cluster node would shut down. Windows Server 2012 R2 helps alleviate this issue by automatically draining the virtual machines running on a node before it shuts down or restarts. Windows does this by attempting to live migrate all virtual machines on the cluster node to other nodes in the cluster when at all possible.

This feature is turned on by default, but it can be disabled through PowerShell.

Active Directory–Detached Clusters   Previous versions of Windows Failover Clustering have depended on Active Directory to provide computer objects for the cluster name object as well as virtual computer objects. With Active Directory–detached failover clusters, communication to the cluster-form clients will use NTLM authentication rather than the normal Kerberos authentication. This is useful in maintaining high availability should a person accidently delete a virtual computer object in Active Directory that a clustered resource depends on for Kerberos authentication.

Dynamic Witness   Earlier in this chapter, I mentioned the Dynamic Quorum model and how votes were dynamically adjusted based on the number of nodes in a cluster. In Windows Server 2012 R2, there is a new feature called *dynamic witness* that is enabled by default when the cluster is configured to use a dynamic quorum. Since it is preferred to have an odd number of votes at any one time in a cluster, the dynamic witness will turn on or off the witness vote in order to ensure that there are an odd number of votes in the cluster.

Tie Breaker For 50% Node Split   Like the *dynamic witness* feature just described, the Tie Breaker For 50% Node Split option in Windows Server 2012 R2 dynamically adjusts cluster node votes in order to maintain an odd number of votes in a cluster where no witness is being used.

This is useful for a cluster in a multisite, stretched, or geocluster configuration.

Global Update Manager Mode   Since the first release of Microsoft Cluster Services appearing in Windows NT 4.0 Enterprise, all nodes in a cluster maintain a local database that keeps a copy of the cluster configuration. The *Global Update Manager (GUM)* is a component of the cluster that ensures that before a change is marked as being committed for the entire cluster, all nodes have received and committed that change to their local cluster database. If one or more nodes do not report back or commit a change, the cluster node is kicked out of being a member of the cluster. Another issue that can occur is that for various clustered applications, such as SQL and Exchange, their performance can be negatively impacted by the time it takes the GUM to coordinate with all the nodes of a cluster for any changes. The GUM is only as fast as the slowest node in the cluster.

With Windows Server 2012 R2, a new feature was added to Failover Clustering called *Global Update Manager mode*. This feature allows you to configure the GUM read-write modes manually in order to greatly speed up the processing of changes by the GUM and to improve the performance of certain clustered resources.

Turn Off IPsec Encryption For Inter-node Cluster Communications   In network environments where IPsec is used, slow Group Policy updates and other issues can cause

Active Directory Domain Services to be temporarily unavailable to cluster nodes. If the cluster intracluster communications protocol uses IPsec encryption, then these delays could cause cluster nodes to drop out of the cluster for failure to communicate in a timely manner with the rest of the nodes in the cluster. Windows Server 2012 R2 now provides a way to turn off IPsec encryption on the cluster communication network.

Cluster Dashboard   Starting with Windows Server 2012, Failover Clustering supports up to 64 nodes in a cluster. Keeping track of the status and resources on all of these nodes can be an administrative headache! Managing more than one failover cluster and determining what a certain cluster hosts can be painful as well. Fortunately, in Windows Server 2012 R2, the *Failover Cluster Manager*'s main dashboard has been updated to make it easier to see the status and health of multiple clusters.

Hyper-V Replica Broker   Starting with Windows Server 2012, Hyper-V supported continuous replication of virtual machines to another server or cluster for disaster recovery purposes. The Hyper-V Recovery Broker allows for virtual machines in a cluster to be replicated. The Hyper-V Recovery Broker keeps track of which cluster nodes virtual machines are residing on and ensures that replication is maintained.

Hyper-V Manager Integration into Failover Cluster Manager   In Windows Server 2012 R2, the Hyper-V Management Console is integrated with Failover Cluster Manager for managing virtual machines that are clustered. Normal Hyper-V operations such as configuring, exporting, importing, configuring replication, stopping, starting, and live migrating virtual machines are supported directly through Failover Cluster Manager.

Virtual Machine Monitoring   Starting with Windows Server 2012, Failover Clustering now supports Virtual Machine Monitoring for Windows Server 2012/2012 R2 virtual machines. Virtual Machine Monitoring monitors administrator-selected Windows services running within a virtual machine and will automatically restart a service if it should fail. If the service does not start for the configured number of restart attempts, the virtual machine will fail over to another node and then restart. For example, you can configure Failover Clustering to monitor the Print Spooler service on a Windows Server 2012 R2 virtual machine. If the Print Spooler service goes offline, then the cluster will attempt to restart the Print Spooler service within the virtual machine. If the service still fails, Failover Clustering will move the virtual machine to another node.

Summary

High availability is more than just clustering. It is achieved through improved hardware, software, and processes. This chapter focused on how to configure Failover Clustering and Network Load Balancing in order to achieve high availability and scalability.

High availability should be approached through proper hardware configuration, training, and operational discipline. Failover clustering provides a highly available base for many applications, such as databases and mail servers.

Network load-balanced clusters are used to provide high availability and scalability for network-based applications, such as VPNs and web servers. Network load balanced clusters can be configured with any edition of Windows Server 2012 R2 except for the Windows Server 2012 R2 Hyper-V Edition.

Exam Essentials

Know how to modify failover and failback settings.   These settings are set on the clustered service or application, but they can be modified by settings on the resources.

Know the hardware requirements for Failover Clustering and Network Load Balancing.   Failover clustering and Network Load Balancing have distinct hardware requirements. Know the differences.

Review Questions

1. Which of the following editions of Windows Server 2012 R2 can be configured in a failover cluster? (Choose all that apply.)

    A. Windows Server 2012 R2 Hyper-V edition

    B. Windows Server 2012 R2 Standard edition

    C. Windows Server 2012 R2 Foundation edition

    D. Windows Server 2012 R2 Datacenter edition

2. Which of the following editions of Windows Server 2012 can be configured in a Network Load Balancing cluster? (Choose all that apply.)

    A. Windows Server 2012 R2 Essentials edition

    B. Windows Server 2012 R2 Standard edition

    C. Windows Server 2012 R2 Hyper-V edition

    D. Windows Server 2012 R2 Datacenter edition

3. What is the maximum number of nodes that can participate in a Windows Server 2012 failover cluster?

    A. 2

    B. 4

    C. 16

    D. 64

4. Which of the following actions should be performed against an NLB cluster node if maintenance needs to be performed while not terminating current connections?

    A. Evict

    B. Drainstop

    C. Pause

    D. Stop

5. What is the maximum number of nodes that can participate in a Windows Server 2012 R2 NLB cluster?

    A. 4

    B. 8

    C. 16

    D. 32

6. Which of the following applications would be better suited on a failover cluster instead of a network load-balanced cluster? (Choose all that apply.)

   A. SQL Server

   B. Website

   C. Exchange Mailbox Server

   D. VPN services

7. Which of the following applications would be better suited on a Network Load Balancing cluster instead of a failover cluster? (Choose all that apply.)

   A. SQL Server

   B. Website

   C. Database servers

   D. Terminal Services

8. To configure an NLB cluster with unicast, what is the minimum number of network adapters required in each node?

   A. One

   B. Two

   C. Three

   D. Six

9. In a four-node cluster set to a Node And File Share Majority quorum model, how many votes can be lost before quorum is lost?

   A. One

   B. Two

   C. Three

   D. Four

10. In a three-node cluster set to a Node Majority quorum model, how many cluster nodes can be offline before quorum is lost?

   A. Zero

   B. One

   C. Two

   D. Three

Chapter

18

Configure File and Storage Solutions

THE FOLLOWING 70-412 EXAM OBJECTIVES ARE COVERED IN THIS CHAPTER:

✓ **Configure advanced file services**

- Configure NFS data store
- Configure BranchCache
- Configure File Classification Infrastructure (FCI) using File Server Resource Manager (FSRM)
- Configure file access auditing

✓ **Implement Dynamic Access Control (DAC)**

- Configure user and device claim types
- Create and configure resource properties and lists
- Create and configure Central Access Rules and Policies
- Configure file classification
- Implement policy changes and staging
- Perform access-denied remediation

✓ **Configure and optimize storage**

- Configure iSCSI Target and Initiator
- Configure Internet Storage Name Server (iSNS)
- Implement thin provisioning and trim
- Manage server free space using Features on Demand
- Configure tiered storage

Taking the time to understand and configure file and storage solutions fully is essential to managing an IT infrastructure efficiently. Companies will rely heavily on your ability as an administrator to properly manage their users and data. In this chapter, you will learn about some of the tools that will help to make you successful in controlling how data is accessed and stored, as well as how users will interact with that data throughout their environment.

Configure Advanced File Services

Windows Server has come a long way in terms of its file and storage capabilities. I have talked quite a bit about the new features and functionality provided in Windows Server 2012 R2. In this section, you will take a closer look at some of the advanced configuration options available in the Network File System (NFS), BranchCache, and the File Server Resource Manager (FSRM).

Configure the NFS Data Store

The NFS role service and feature set gives IT administrators the ability to integrate a Windows Server–based environment with Unix-based operating systems. Most corporate environments today consist of a mixed operating system infrastructure to some extent. Using a Windows NFS file server, you can configure file shares for use by multiple operating systems throughout the environment.

Windows Server 2012 R2 takes those capabilities even further by enabling you to integrate with platforms such as ESXi. ESXi is VMware's exclusive operating system–independent hypervisor. ESXi is referred to as a *bare-metal* operating system because once it is installed on server virtualization hardware, guest virtual machines can be installed without requiring the use of any other underlying operating system. With Windows Server 2012 R2, you can use an NFS share efficiently as an ESXi data store to house all of your guest virtual machines. Let's take a look at configuring an NFS data store in Exercise 18.1.

For this exercise, you will need the following:

- A Windows Server 2012 R2 server
- A VMware ESXi 5 server

EXERCISE 18.1

Configure the NFS Data Store

1. Open Server Manager on your Windows Server 2012 R2 machine.

2. Launch the Add Roles And Features Wizard from the dashboard.

3. Install the Server for NFS role on the server. A reboot is not required.

4. Create a new folder on your server named NFS_Datastore, right-click and select Properties, and then navigate to the NFS Sharing tab, as shown here.

5. Click the Manage NFS Sharing button to open the NFS Advanced Sharing page and then check the Share This Folder box, as shown here. Notice how enabling the share also enables the share's default settings. The share settings let you configure share authentication and user access further if the need arises. The default settings will work just fine for this exercise.

6. Click the Permissions tab to open the NFS Share Permissions page. This is where you
   will configure the type of access that will be allowed by machines accessing this NFS
   data store. By default, the NFS share permissions are set to Read-Only and do not
   include root access. For this exercise, you will need to change the type of access to
   Read-Write and check the box to allow root access, as shown here.

7. Click OK to close the NFS Share Permissions page and then click Apply and OK on the
   NFS Advanced Sharing page. Your new NFS share is now built, ready to be presented as
   an NFS data store to a VMware ESXi host. Be sure to record the network path displayed

on the NFS Sharing tab of the share's Properties page. You will need that information to perform a proper mount on the ESXi host.

8. Switch to your ESXi host and launch the Add Storage Wizard from the Configuration tab.

9. On the Select Storage Type page of the wizard, select the Network File System storage type; click Next to continue to the Locate Network File System page.

10. On this page of the wizard, you will fill in the server and folder information for the NFS share that you will be using as a vSphere data store. Using the information recorded from step 7, properly fill out the server and folder fields and then name your new data store as shown here.

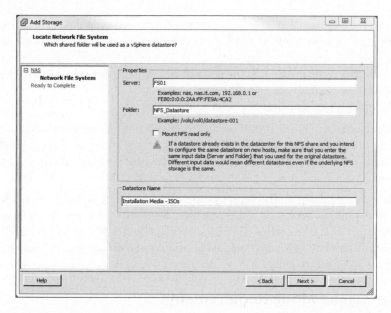

11. Click Next to continue to the Ready To Complete page of the wizard. Review the information and click Finish. Once the Create NAS data store task completes on the ESXi host, you are ready to use your Windows Server 2012 R2 shared folder as a vSphere ESXi data store. The graphic shown here confirms that the NFS share is mounted and available from the ESXi host.

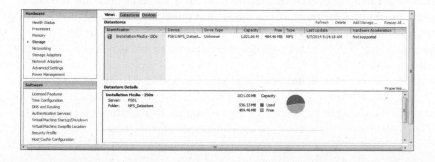

The previous exercise shows how versatile Windows Server 2012 R2 shares can be. The same principals can be applied to making Windows Server shares available to other Unix-based operating systems such as ESXi. Now that you have configured a NFS data store, let's take a look at what BranchCache has to offer.

Configure BranchCache

BranchCache is a technology that was introduced with Windows Server 2008 R2 and Windows 7. BranchCache allows an organization with slower links between offices to cache data so that downloads between offices do not have to occur each time a file is accessed.

For example, John comes into work and logs into the network. John accesses the corporate website and downloads a media file that takes four minutes to download. With BranchCache enabled, when Judy comes into work, connects to the corporate website, and tries to download the same media file, the file will be cached from the previous download and Judy will have immediate access to the file.

You can set up two types of BranchCache configurations:

Distributed Cache Mode   In the distributed cache mode configuration, all Windows 7 and Windows 8 client machines cache the files locally on the client machines. Thus, in the previous example, after John downloaded the media file, Judy would receive the cached media file from John's Windows 7 or Windows 8 machine.

Hosted Mode   In the hosted mode configuration, the cache files are cached on a local (within the site) Windows Server 2012 R2 machine. So, in the previous example, after John downloads the media file, the cached file would be placed on a Windows Server 2012 R2 machine by default, and all other users (Judy) would download the media file from the Windows Server 2012 R2 machine.

Distributed Cache Mode Requirements

If you decide to install BranchCache in the distributed cache mode configuration, a hosted cache server running Windows Server 2012 R2 is not required at the branch office. To set up distributed cache mode, the client machines must be running Windows 7 Enterprise, Windows 7 Ultimate, Windows 8 Pro, or Windows 8 Enterprise.

The Windows 7 or Windows 8 machines would download the data files from the content servers at the main branch office, and then these machines become the local cache servers. To set up distributed cache mode, you must install a Windows Server 2012 R2 content server at the main office first. After the content server is installed, physical connections (WAN or VPN connections) between the sites and branch offices must be established.

Client computers running Windows 7 and Windows 8 have BranchCache installed by default. However, you must enable and configure BranchCache and configure firewall exceptions. Complete Exercise 18.2 to configure BranchCache firewall rule exceptions.

EXERCISE 18.2

Configuring BranchCache Firewall Exceptions

1.   On a domain controller, open the Group Policy Management Console.

2.   In the Group Policy Management Console, expand the following path: Forest ➢ Domains ➢ Group Policy Objects. Make sure the domain you choose contains the BranchCache Windows 7/Windows 8 client computer accounts that you want to configure.

3.   In the Group Policy Management Console, right-click Group Policy Objects and select New. Name the policy **BranchCache Client** and click OK. Right-click BranchCache Client and click Edit. The Group Policy Management Editor console opens.

4.   In the Group Policy Management Editor console, expand the following path: Computer Configuration ➢ Policies ➢ Windows Settings ➢ Security Settings ➢ Windows Firewall With Advanced Security ➢ Windows Firewall With Advanced Security – LDAP ➢ Inbound Rules.

5.   Right-click Inbound Rules and then click New Rule. The New Inbound Rule Wizard opens.

6.   On the Rule Type screen, click Predefined, expand the list of choices, and then click BranchCache – Content Retrieval (Uses HTTP). Click Next.

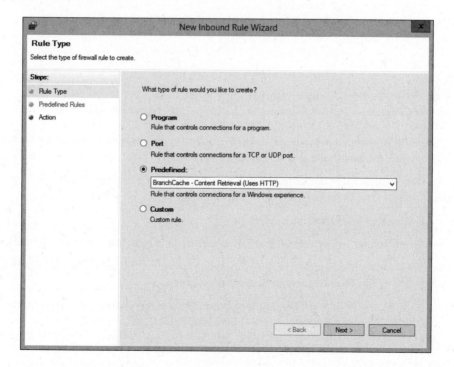

7. On the Predefined Rules screen, click Next.

8. On the Action screen, ensure that Allow The Connection is selected and then click Finish. You must select Allow The Connection for the BranchCache client to be able to receive traffic on this port.

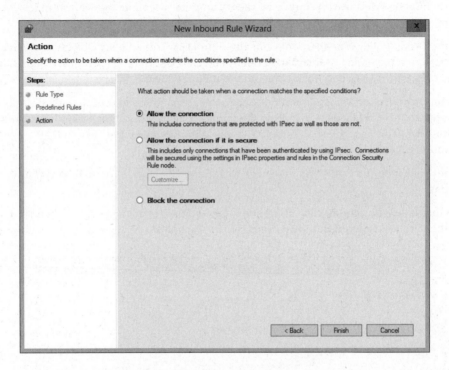

9. To create the WS-Discovery firewall exception, right-click Inbound Rules and click New Rule. The New Inbound Rule Wizard opens.

10. On the Rule Type screen, click Predefined, expand the list of choices, and then click BranchCache – Peer Discovery (Uses WSD). Click Next.

11. On the Predefined Rules screen, click Next.

12. On the Action screen, ensure that Allow The Connection is selected and then click Finish.

13. In the Group Policy Management Editor console, right-click Outbound Rules and then click New Rule. The New Outbound Rule Wizard opens.

14. On the Rule Type screen, click Predefined, expand the list of choices, and then click BranchCache – Content Retrieval (Uses HTTP). Click Next.

15. On the Predefined Rules screen, click Next.

16. On the Action screen, make sure that Allow The Connection is selected and then click Finish.

17. Create the WS-Discovery firewall exception by right-clicking Outbound Rules and then click New Rule. The New Outbound Rule Wizard opens.

18. On the Rule Type screen, click Predefined, expand the list of choices, and then click BranchCache – Peer Discovery (Uses WSD). Click Next.

19. On the Predefined Rules screen, click Next.

20. On the Action screen, make sure that Allow The Connection is selected and then click Finish.

Now that you have looked at the distributed cache mode configuration, let's take a look at the hosted mode configuration.

Hosted Mode Requirements

To set up a hosted mode BranchCache configuration, you must first set up a Windows Server 2012 R2 hosted cache server at the main and branch offices. You also need Windows 7 Enterprise, Windows 7 Ultimate, Windows 8 Pro, or Windows 8 Enterprise computers at the branch offices.

The Windows 7 or Windows 8 machines download the data from the main cache server, and then the hosted cache servers at the branch offices obtain a copy of the downloaded data for other users to access.

Your network infrastructure must also allow for physical connections between the main office and the branch offices. These connections can be VPNs or some type of WAN links. After these requirements are met, your cache server must obtain a server certificate so that the client computers in the branch offices can positively identify the cache servers.

Exercise 18.3 walks you through the process of installing the BranchCache feature on a Windows Server 2012 R2 machine. To begin this exercise, you must be logged into the Windows Server 2012 R2 machine as an administrator.

EXERCISE 18.3

Installing BranchCache on Windows Server 2012 R2

1. Open Server Manager by selecting the Server Manager icon or by running servermanager.exe.

2. Select Add Roles And Features.

3. Select Next at the Before You Begin pane (if shown).

4. Select Role-Based Or Feature-Based Installation and select Next to continue.

5. Select the Select A Server From The Server Pool option and click Next.

6. At the Select Server Roles screen, click Next.

EXERCISE 18.3 *(continued)*

7. At the Select Features screen, click the check box for BranchCache. Then click Next.

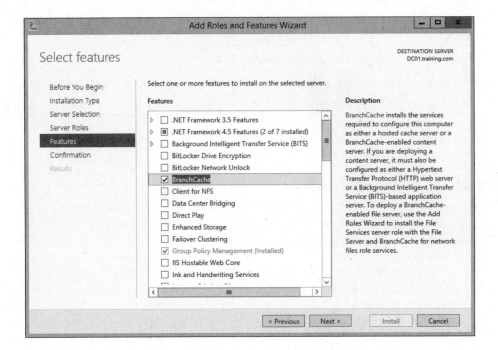

8. Check the Restart The Destination Server If Required box and then click the Install button. If a dialog box appears about restarting, click the Yes button. The system should restart.

9. After the system restarts, log in as the administrator.

Make sure to repeat this exercise on all branch office cache servers. One of the requirements for BranchCache is a physical connection between the main office and the branch offices.

BranchCache and PowerShell

As stated throughout this book, PowerShell is a command-line shell and scripting tool. BranchCache has many different PowerShell cmdlets that allow you to configure and maintain the BranchCache feature. Table 18.1 shows just some of the different PowerShell cmdlets for BranchCache.

TABLE 18.1 PowerShell cmdlets for BranchCache

Cmdlet	Description
Add-BCDataCache Extension	Increases the amount of cache storage space that is available on a hosted cache server by adding a new cache file
Clear-BCCache	Deletes all data in all data and hash files
Disable-BC	Disables the BranchCache service
Disable-BCDowngrading	Disables downgrading so that client computers that are running Windows 8 Consumer Preview do not request Windows 7–specific versions of content information from content servers
Enable-BCDistributed	Enables BranchCache and configures a computer to operate in distributed cache mode
Enable-BCHostedClient	Configures BranchCache to operate in hosted cache client mode
Enable-BCHostedServer	Configures BranchCache to operate in hosted cache server mode
Enable-BCLocal	Enables the BranchCache service in local caching mode
Export-BCCachePackage	Exports a cache package
Export-BCSecretKey	Exports a secret key to a file
Get-BCClient Configuration	Gets the current BranchCache client computer settings
Get-BCContent ServerConfiguration	Gets the current BranchCache content server settings
Get-BCDataCache	Gets the BranchCache data cache
Get-BCStatus	Gets a set of objects that provide BranchCache status and configuration information
Import-BCCachePackage	Imports a cache package into BranchCache
Import-BCSecretKey	Imports the cryptographic key that BranchCache uses for generating segment secrets
Set-BCAuthentication	Specifies the BranchCache computer authentication mode
Set-BCCache	Modifies the cache file configuration
Set-BCSecretKey	Sets the cryptographic key used in the generation of segment secrets

Enhanced Features in Windows Server 2012 R2 BranchCache

Microsoft continues to improve on many of the features of Windows Server, and BranchCache is no different. Microsoft has improved BranchCache in Windows Server 2012 R2 and Windows 8. The following list includes some of the enhanced features:

Office sizes and the number of branch offices are not limited.   Windows Server 2012 R2 BranchCache allows any number of offices along with any number of users once an administrator deploys hosted cache mode with multiple hosted cache servers.

There are no requirements for a Group Policy object (GPO) for each office location, streamlining deployment.   All that is required to deploy BranchCache is a single GPO that contains a small number of settings.

Client computer configuration is automatic.   Administrators have the ability to configure their clients through the use of a Group Policy object. If this is done, client configuration will automatically be configured through the GPO, and if a client can't find a hosted cache server, the client will automatically self-configure as a hosted cache mode client.

BranchCache is deeply integrated with the Windows file server.   BranchCache is automatically integrated with Windows file server technology. Because of this, the process of finding duplicate pieces in independent files is greatly improved.

Duplicate content is stored and downloaded only once.   BranchCache stores only one instance of the content on a hosted cache server or content server, and because of this, you get greater disk storage savings. Since client computers at the remote offices download only one instance of any content, your network saves on additional WAN bandwidth.

Small changes to large files produce bandwidth savings.   One advantage of BranchCache is the file server chunking system that helps divide files and web pages into smaller parts. Now when a file is changed, only the part of that file that has been changed gets replicated. This allows BranchCache to use lower bandwidth requirements.

Offline content creation improves performace.   When BranchCache is deployed as content or file servers, the data is calculated offline before a client even has the chance to request it. Because of this, the systems get faster performance and bandwidth.

Cache encryption is enabled automatically.   BranchCache stores its cached data as encrypted data. This guarantees data security without the need to encrypt the entire drive.

You can deploy multiple hosted cache servers.   In Windows 7 and Windows Server 2008 R2, BranchCache was able to deploy only one hosted cache server per office location. Windows Server 2012 R2 allows you to deploy as many hosted cache servers as are needed at a location.

Configure File Classification Infrastructure Using File Server Resource Manager

The *File Server Resource Manager (FSRM)* is a suite of tools that allows an administrator to place quotas on folders or volumes, filter file types, and create detailed storage reports. These tools allow an administrator to plan and implement policies on data properly and as needed.

One of the advantages of using FSRM is all of the included features that allow administrators to manage the data that is stored on their file servers. Some of the features included with FSRM are as follows:

File Management Tasks   FSRM allows an administrator to apply a policy or action to data files. Some of the actions that can be performed are encrypting files and running custom commands.

Quota Management   Quotas give an administrator the ability to limit how much disk space a user can use on a file server. Administrators have the ability to limit space to an entire volume or to specific folders.

File Classification Infrastructure   This feature uses rules to assign specific properties to files automatically and then performs tasks on those files based on the classification. A few examples of file classification properties are Country, Department, Birthday, and Social Security Number. The tasks performed using these classifications include restricting file access, implementing file encryption, and setting file expiration policies.

File Screening Management   Administrators can set up file screening on the server and limit what types of files can be stored on that server. For example, an administrator can set a file screen on the server so that any file ending in ·bmp gets rejected.

Storage Reports   Administrators can create reports that show them how data is classified and accessed. You also have the ability to see what users are trying to save unauthorized file extensions.

Installing FSRM is easy when using either Server Manager or PowerShell. To install using Server Manager, you go into Add Features and choose File And Storage Services ➢ File Services ➢ File Server Resource Manager. To install FSRM using PowerShell, use the following command:

```
Install-WindowsFeature -Name FS-Resource-Manager -IncludeManagementTools
```

Configuring FSRM using the Windows GUI version is straightforward, but setting up FSRM using PowerShell is a bit more challenging. Table 18.2 describes some of the PowerShell commands for FSRM.

TABLE 18.2   PowerShell commands for FSRM

PowerShell cmdlet	Description
Get-FsrmAutoQuota	Gets auto-apply quotas on a server
Get-FsrmClassification	Gets the status of the running file classification
Get-FsrmClassificationRule	Gets classification rules
Get-FsrmFileGroup	Gets file groups

TABLE 18.2 PowerShell commands for FSRM *(continued)*

PowerShell cmdlet	Description
Get-FsrmFileScreen	Gets file screens
Get-FsrmFileScreenException	Gets file screen exceptions
Get-FsrmQuota	Gets quotas on the server
Get-FsrmSetting	Gets the current FSRM settings
Get-FsrmStorageReport	Gets storage reports
New-FsrmAutoQuota	Creates an auto-apply quota
New-FsrmFileGroup	Creates a file group
New-FsrmFileScreen	Creates a file screen
New-FsrmQuota	Creates an FSRM quota
New-FsrmQuotaTemplate	Creates a quota template
Remove-FsrmClassificationRule	Removes classification rules
Remove-FsrmFileScreen	Removes a file screen
Remove-FsrmQuota	Removes an FSRM quota from the server
Set-FsrmFileScreen	Changes configuration settings of a file screen
Set-FsrmQuota	Changes configuration settings for an FSRM quota

Configure File Access Auditing

One of the most important aspects of controlling security in networked environments is ensuring that only authorized users are able to access specific resources. Although system administrators often spend much time managing security permissions, it is almost always possible for a security problem to occur.

Sometimes the best way to find possible security breaches is actually to record the actions that specific users take. Then, in the case of a security breach (the unauthorized shutdown of a server, for example), system administrators can examine the log to find the cause of the problem.

The Windows Server 2012 R2 operating system and Active Directory offer you the ability to audit a wide range of actions. In the following sections, you'll see how to implement auditing for Active Directory.

Overview of Auditing

The act of *auditing* relates to recording specific actions. From a security standpoint, auditing is used to detect any possible misuse of network resources. Although auditing does not necessarily prevent resources from being misused, it does help determine when security violations have occurred (or were attempted). Furthermore, just the fact that others know that you have implemented auditing may prevent them from attempting to circumvent security.

You need to complete several steps in order to implement auditing using Windows Server 2012 R2:

1. Configure the size and storage settings for the audit logs.

2. Enable categories of events to audit.

3. Specify which objects and actions should be recorded in the audit log.

Note that there are trade-offs to implementing auditing. First, recording auditing information can consume system resources. This can decrease overall system performance and use up valuable disk space. Second, auditing many events can make the audit log impractical to view. If too much detail is provided, system administrators are unlikely to scrutinize all of the recorded events. For these reasons, you should always be sure to find a balance between the level of auditing details provided and the performance-management implications of these settings.

Implementing Auditing

Auditing is not an all-or-none type of process. As is the case with security in general, system administrators must choose specifically which objects and actions they want to audit.

The main categories for auditing include the following:

Audit account logon events

Audit account management

Audit directory service access

Audit logon events

Audit object access

Audit policy change

Audit privilege use

Audit process tracking

Audit system events

In this list of categories, four of the categories are related to Active Directory. Let's discuss these auditing categories in a bit more detail.

Audit Account Logon Events   You enable this auditing event if you want to audit when a user authenticates with a domain controller and logs onto the domain. This event is logged in the security log on the domain controller.

Audit Account Management   This auditing event is used when you want to watch what changes are being made to Active Directory accounts. For example, when another administrator creates or deletes a user account, it would be an audited event.

Audit Directory Service Access   This auditing event occurs whenever a user or administrator accesses Active Directory objects. Let's say that an administrator opens Active Directory and clicks a user account; even if nothing is changed on that account, an event is logged.

Audit Logon Events   Account logon events are created for domain account activity. For example, you have a user who logs onto a server so that they can access files; the act of logging onto the server creates this audit event.

Audit Object Access   Audit object access allows you to audit objects within your network, such as folders, files, and printers. If you suspect that someone is trying to hack into an object (for example, the finance folder), this is the type of auditing you should use. You still would need to enable auditing on the actual object (the finance folder in this case).

Audit Policy Change   Audit policy change allows you to audit changes to user rights assignment policies, audit policies, or trust policies. This auditing allows you to see whether anyone changes any of the other audit policies.

Audit Privilege Use   Setting the audit privilege use allows an administrator to audit each instance of a user exercising a user right. For example, if a user changes the system time on a machine, this is a user right. Logging on locally is another common user right.

To audit access to objects stored within Active Directory, you must enable the Audit Directory Service Access option. Then you must specify which objects and actions should be tracked.

Exercise 18.4 walks you through the steps you must take to implement the auditing of Active Directory objects on domain controllers.

EXERCISE 18.4

Enabling Auditing of Active Directory Objects

1. Open the Local Security Policy tool (located in the Administrative Tools program group).

2. Expand Local Policies ➢ Audit Policy.

3. Double-click the Audit Directory Service Access setting.

4. In the Audit Directory Service Access Properties dialog box, place check marks next to Success and Failure. Click OK to save the settings.

5. Close the Local Security Policy tool.

Viewing Auditing Information

One of the most important aspects of auditing is regularly monitoring the audit logs. If this step is ignored, as it often is in poorly managed environments, the act of auditing is useless. Fortunately, Windows Server 2012 R2 includes the *Event Viewer* tool, which allows system administrators to view audited events quickly and easily. Using the filtering capabilities of Event Viewer, you can find specific events of interest.

Exercise 18.5 walks you through the steps that you must take in order to generate some auditing events and to examine the data collected for these actions. In this exercise, you will perform some actions that will be audited, and then you will view the information recorded within the audit logs.

EXERCISE 18.5

Generating and Viewing Audit Logs

1. Open the Active Directory Users and Computers tool.

2. Within an OU that has auditing enabled, right-click a user account and select Properties.

3. In the user's account Properties dialog box, add the middle initial **A** for this user account and enter **Software Developer** in the Description box. Click OK to save the changes.

4. Close the Active Directory Users and Computers tool.

5. Open the Event Viewer tool from the Administrative Tools program group. Select the Security item under Windows Logs. You will see a list of audited events categorized under Directory Service Access. Note that you can obtain more details about a specific item by double-clicking it.

6. When you have finished viewing the security log, close the Event Viewer tool.

Using the *Auditpol.exe* Command

There may be a time when you need to look at the auditing policies set on a user or system. This is where an administrator can use the Auditpol.exe command. Auditpol not only gives administrators the ability to view an audit policy but also lets them set, configure, modify, restore, and even remove an audit policy. Auditpol is a command-line utility, and there are multiple switches that can be used with Auditpol. The following is the syntax used with Auditpol, and table 18.3 describes some of the switches.

```
Auditpol command [<sub-command><options>]
```

Here's an example:

```
Auditpol /get /user:mrice /category:"Detailed Tracking" /r
```

TABLE 18.3   Auditpol commands

Command	Description
/backup	Allows an administrator to save the audit policy to a file
/clear	Allows an administrator to clear an audit policy
/get	Gives administrators the ability to view the current audit policy
/list	Allows you to view selectable policy elements
/remove	Removes all per-user audit policy settings and disables all system audit policy settings
/restore	Allows an administrator to restore an audit policy from a file that was previously created by using auditpol /backup
/set	Gives an administrator the ability to set an audit policy
/?	Displays help

Enhanced Features in Windows Server 2012 R2 Auditing

Auditing in Windows Server 2012 R2 and Windows 8 has been enhanced in many ways. Microsoft has increased the level of detail in the security auditing logs. Microsoft has also simplified the deployment and management of auditing policies. The following list includes some of the major enhancements:

Global Object Access Auditing   Administrators using Windows Server 2012 R2 and Windows 8 have the ability to define computer-wide system access control lists (SACLs). Administrators can define SACLs either for the file system or for the registry. After the specified SACL is defined, the SACL is then applied automatically to every object of that type. This can be helpful to administrators for verifying that all critical files, folders, and registry settings on a computer are protected. This is also helpful for identifying when an issue occurs with a system resource.

"Reason For Access" Reporting   When an administrator is performing auditing in Windows Server 2012 R2 and Windows 8, they can now see the reason why an operation was successful or unsuccessful. Previously, they lacked the ability to see the reason why an operation succeeded or failed.

Advanced Audit Policy Settings   In Windows Server 2012 R2, there are 53 advanced audit policy settings that can be used in place of the 9 basic auditing settings. These advanced audit settings also help eliminate the unnecessary auditing activities that can make audit logs difficult to manage and decipher.

Expression-Based Audit Policies   Administrators have the ability, because of Dynamic Access Control, to create targeted audit policies by using expressions based on user, computer, and resource claims. For example, an administrator has the ability to create an audit policy that tracks all Read and Write operations for files that are considered high-business impact. Expression-based audit policies can be directly created on a file or folder or created through the use of a Group Policy.

Removable Storage Device Auditing   Administrators have the ability to monitor attempts to use a removable storage device on your network. If an administrator decides to implement this policy, an audit event is created every time one of your users attempts to copy, move, or save a network resource onto a removable storage device.

Implement Dynamic Access Control

One of the advantages of Windows Server 2012 R2 is the ability to apply data governance to your file server. This will help control who has access to information and auditing. You get these advantages through the use of *Dynamic Access Control (DAC)*. Dynamic Access Control allows you to identify data by using data classifications (both automatic and manual) and then control access to these files based on these classifications.

DAC also gives administrators the ability to control file access by using a central access policy. This central access policy will also allow an administrator to set up audit access to files for reporting and forensic investigation.

DAC allows an administrator to set up Active Directory Rights Management Service (AD RMS) encryption for Microsoft Office documents. For example, you can set up encryption for any documents that contain financial information.

Dynamic Access Control gives an administrator the flexibility to configure file access and auditing to domain-based file servers. To do this, DAC controls claims in the authentication token, resource properties, and conditional expressions within permission and auditing entries.

Administrators have the ability to give users access to files and folders based on Active Directory attributes. For example, a user named Dana is given access to the file server share because in the user's Active Directory (department attribute) properties, the value contains the value Sales. Over the next few sections, you will take a deep dive into implementing Dynamic Access Control.

 For DAC to function properly, an administrator must enable Windows 8 computers and Windows Server 2012 R2 file servers to support claims and compound authentication.

Configure User and Device Claim Types

Dynamic Access Control is a must-have for any corporate environment. DAC takes folder and file permissions to a whole new level by enabling more granular methods of access and authentication within Active Directory. In this section, you will focus on configuring user and device claim types. Let's start off by enabling DAC (see Exercise 18.6).

EXERCISE 18.6

Enable Dynamic Access Control

1. On a domain controller, launch Server Manager and then navigate to the Group Policy Management Console under Tools.

2. Launch Group Policy Management and navigate to Default Domain Controllers Policy.

3. Right-click Default Domain Controllers Policy and select Edit to launch the Group Policy Management Editor.

4. Within the Group Policy Management Editor, navigate to Computer Configuration ➢ Policies ➢ Administrative Templates ➢ System ➢ KDC, as shown here.

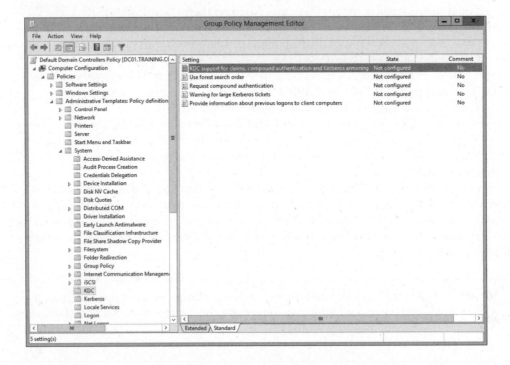

5. Double-click the KDC Support For Claims, Compound Authentication, And Kerberos Armoring policy, and select the Enabled radio button, as shown here.

6. Click Apply and OK to save the new policy setting.

That's all there is to it. Now you are ready to take a look at user and device claims. For the next exercise, you will need to have a functional Active Directory environment populated with multiple users across multiple departments. A simple lab environment consisting of a domain controller and a domain-joined file server will be sufficient.

Now that you have successfully enabled DAC within the environment, everything is managed from the Active Directory Administrative Center on a domain controller. You can now set what's referred to as *conditions* on your environment's folder and file server hierarchy. Conditions are user or device claims that you can set. For example, you could set a condition on a folder or file that limits user access to a specific department, or you could set a condition that allows a user to view folders and files from only a specific workstation. Setting these types of conditions will make managing your environment easier, and it will do so with enhanced security. Allowing file and folder access from only domain-joined machines bars users from connecting with an unsecured personal device. Also, setting conditions based upon the Active Directory department attribute makes user access available to those files and folders based on them being in that specific department. Let's put this into practice (see Exercise 18.7).

EXERCISE 18.7

Configure User and Device Claim Types

1. On a domain controller, launch Server Manager and then navigate to the Active Directory Administrative Center under Tools.

2. Launch the Active Directory Administrative Center and navigate to Dynamic Access Control, as shown here.

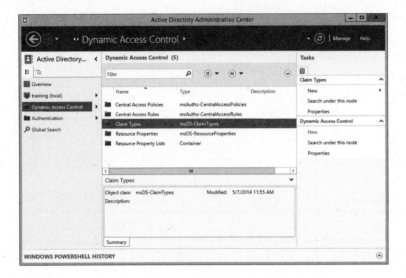

3. Select New ➢ Claim Type to open the Create Claim Type dialog box.

4. This is where you will choose what claims will be used to define permissions. You can filter claim types with the search field. Search for and select the Department claim type, as shown here. Notice how the Display Name, Description, User Claim Type, and Protect From Accidental Deletion fields are enabled by default.

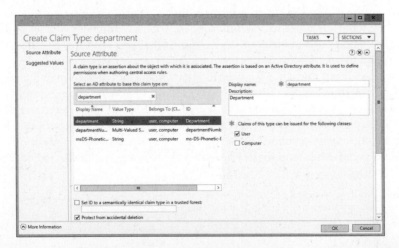

5. Click OK to finish creating the new claim type. You can now use the Active Directory department attribute as a condition for allowing access on file shares.

6. Navigate to a shared folder within the environment and open the Advanced Security Settings properties on that share.

7. Click the Add button to create a new permission entry.

8. Select a principal. A principal can be any Active Directory user or group. You must select a principal before the option Add A Condition becomes available.

9. Click Add A Condition to bring up the condition's parameters, as shown here. For this exercise, I have selected a user who belongs to the IT department. As long as that user remains in the IT department, the user will have full control over this file share.

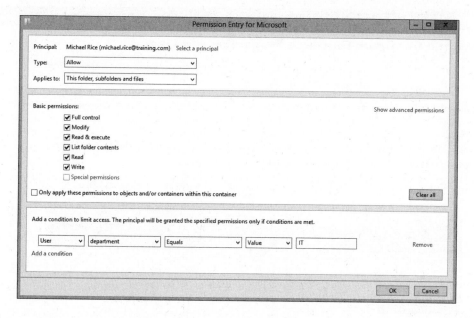

10. Click OK to save this new conditional permission entry.

That was just one example of how Dynamic Access Control can be used to control folder and file access. Spend some time configuring different user and device claims types. It is really handy to be able to change a user's department, country, or office location in Active Directory and have that change automatically affect what folders and files that user can access throughout the environment.

Create and Configure Resource Properties and Lists

Now that you have a practical understanding of configuring user and device claims, the next logical Dynamic Access Control configuration is to configure resource properties and lists. *Resource properties* are used to define additional properties that will appear on files and folders. These additional properties can be used for file access based on file classifications such as country or department. There are quite a few default resource properties already configured in DAC, and you can also create your custom resource properties as needed.

Once you have selected or created resource properties, they are added to the Global Resource Property List within DAC. The default resource properties have already been added for you. Note that any custom resource properties you create will also be added automatically to the Global Resource Property List. The list is then automatically pushed out via Group Policy and downloaded to all of the file servers within the environment. In Exercise 18.8, you will create and configure Resource Properties and Lists.

EXERCISE 18.8

Create and Configure Resource Properties and Lists

1. On a domain controller, launch Server Manager and then navigate to the Active Directory Administrative Center under Tools.

2. Launch the Active Directory Administrative Center and navigate to Dynamic Access Control.

3. Click and open Resource Properties. You will see that all of the default resource properties are listed, but they are all disabled by default.

4. Right-click and enable the Department resource property, as shown here.

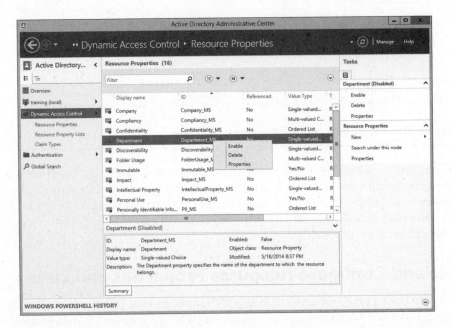

5. You'll also create a custom resource property. On the same page that you enabled the Department resource property, click New ➢ Resource Property.

6. Name the resource property **Country** and then click Add to list all of the countries that will be values of this resource property, as shown here.

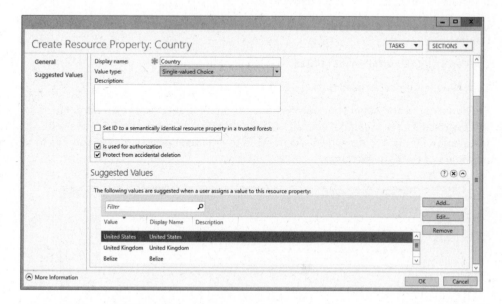

7. Click OK to create this new resource property.

8. Navigate to and open the global resource property list within the DAC management GUI to verify that both the Country and Department resource properties are enabled and ready to be downloaded to your file servers.

Now that you have defined resource properties, you can use those properties to create and configure central access rules and policies.

Create and Configure Central Access Rules and Policies

Central access rules are used to govern file and folder access based on the resource properties that have been previously defined, such as those you configured in the previous exercise. Let's say you wanted to limit access to a corporate software share to only corporate IT personnel. DAC uses central access rules and policies to accomplish this task. Once the rule has been created, Group Policy will be used to keep all of the environment's file servers up-to-date with all of your dynamic access control central access rules. Exercise 18.9 will demonstrate the configuration of Central Access Rules and Policies.

EXERCISE 18.9

Create and Configure Central Access Rules and Policies

1. On a domain controller, launch Server Manager and then navigate to the Active Directory Administrative Center under Tools.

2. Launch the Active Directory Administrative Center and navigate to Dynamic Access Control.

3. Click and open Central Access Rules. The list should be empty.

4. Click New ➢ Central Access Rule.

5. Provide a name and set proper permissions for the resource, as shown here. For this exercise, I have created a central access rule named Corporate IT Software & Installation Media Access, which will be used to limit user access to IT resources to only members of the IT department.

6. Click OK to create the new central access rule.

7. Navigate to and open Central Access Policies within the DAC management GUI.

8. Click New ➢ Central Access Policy. Note that a central access policy can contain multiple central access rules.

9. Name the central access policy and add the central access rule created in step 6 of this exercise. Your screen should look similar to what's shown here.

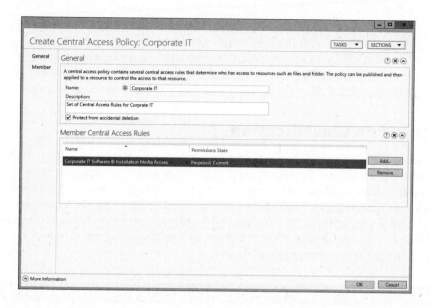

10. Now you can configure Group Policy in Active Directory to push out the new central access policy. Launch the Group Policy Manager on your domain controller and edit the default Domain Controllers Policy.

11. Drill down to Computer Configuration ➢ Policies ➢ Windows Settings ➢ Security Settings ➢ File System ➢ Central Access Policy and then right-click and select Manage Central Access Policies.

12. Add the central access policy, as shown here.

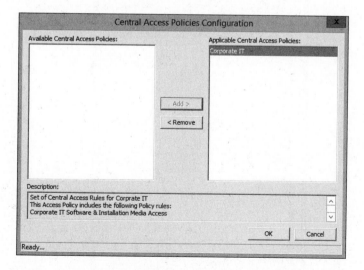

13. Click OK to save the new central access policy configuration.

By now, I'm sure you can see the power you have with Dynamic Access Control. By taking the time to configure central access rules and policies for your company's users and devices fully, you will enhance environmental security and ease of management significantly. Now that the new central access policy is applied to your environment, all you have to do to finish completely enabling DAC on your file shares is to configure file classification.

Configure File Classification

Administrators can set file classifications and then manage the data more effectively by using these classifications. By classifying files and then setting policies to those classifications, an administrator can set policies on those classifications that assist with managing environmental resources. These policies include restricting file access, file encryption, and file expirations. In Exercise 18.10, you will configure file classification through Dynamic Access Control and then test your work by using the Effective Access tab in the Advanced Security Settings of a file share.

EXERCISE 18.10

Configure File Classification

1. On a DAC-enabled file share, right-click and open Properties.

2. Select the Classification tab and enable values for both the Country and Department file classification properties, as shown here.

3. Click Apply to save the file classification.

4. Select the Security tab and click Advanced.

5. Select the Central Policy tab, making sure the central policy is set to the appropriate central access policy, as shown here. If you change the central access policy, make sure to click Apply before changing tabs.

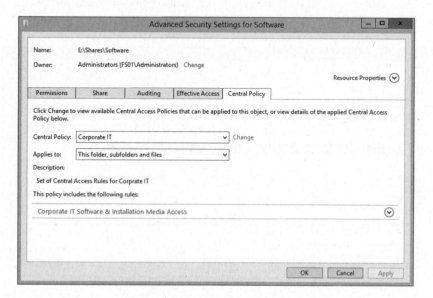

6. Select the Effective Access tab and test the effective access of a user to test your work.

Implement Policy Changes and Staging

One of the nice features of DAC is its ability to stage and test the effects of a new central access policy before actually implementing it. In Exercise 18.11, you will stage a central access policy and then test the effects of that policy on a file share.

EXERCISE 18.11

Implement Policy Stages and Staging

1. On a domain controller, launch Server Manager and then navigate to the Active Directory Administrative Center under Tools.

2. Launch the Active Directory Administrative Center and navigate to Dynamic Access Control.

3. Click Central Access Rules.

4. Right-click and open the properties of a central access policy.

5. Click the Proposed Permissions section, as shown here, to edit and stage the newly proposed permissions. For demonstration purposes, I have staged a policy change that would allow authenticated users to view the contents of the software library under the conditions that the user is a domain user who is logged into a domain computer.

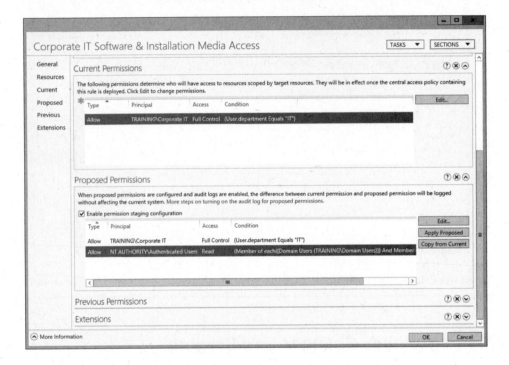

6. Click OK to set the new policy staging.

7. Switch to your file server and log in as an authenticated user.

8. Run a gpupdate /force from the command line to update the Group Policy settings on the file server.

9. As just an authenticated user, browse the share on which you staged your policy change. Notice how you have access as that authenticated user.

10. Now check the Event Viewer on the file server. Expand Windows Logs and then select Security. Under the Central Access Policy Staging task category, open the entries with Event ID 4818. You will notice how the authenticated user was allowed access to this share because of the staging policy.

11. Applying the staged policy is relatively straightforward. Switch to your domain controller and open the properties of the central access rule that was used in step 4 of this exercise. In the Proposed Permissions section, click Apply Proposed to save and enable the staged policy change, as shown here.

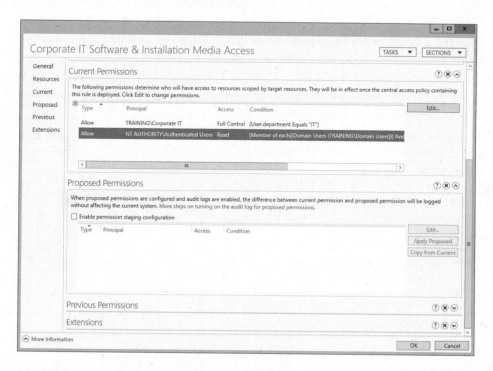

12. Verify that the current permissions reflect the applied proposed permissions and then click OK to close the Central Access Rules Properties dialog box.

Perform Access-Denied Remediation

One of the best features of Windows Server 2012 R2 is the ability to configure Access-Denied Assistance. With Access-Denied Assistance, you can set a preconfigured Windows error message to be displayed to users when they try to access resources to which they don't have proper permissions to access. The best part is that users can "request assistance" via the displayed error message. When a user requests assistance, an email notification can notify the administrator who is either on duty or on call that one of their users needs help accessing a resource. When the user requests assistance, they are provided with a dialog box that will be attached to the email sent to the administrator. Within the dialog box, the user can explain why they need access to the desired resource. In Exercise 18.12, you will configure and test Access-Denied Assistance using Group Policy.

EXERCISE 18.12

Configure Access-Denied Assistance

1. On a domain controller, launch Server Manager and then navigate to Group Policy Management under Tools.

2. Launch the Group Policy Management Tool and create a new GPO that targets both your file servers and domain-joined client machines.

3. Within the Group Policy Object Editor, navigate to Computer Configuration ➢ Policies ➢ Administrative Templates ➢ System ➢ Access-Denied Assistance and double-click Customize Message For Access Denied Errors.

4. Enable the policy, configure an access-denied message that will be displayed to users who are denied access, and check the box to enable users to request assistance, as shown here.

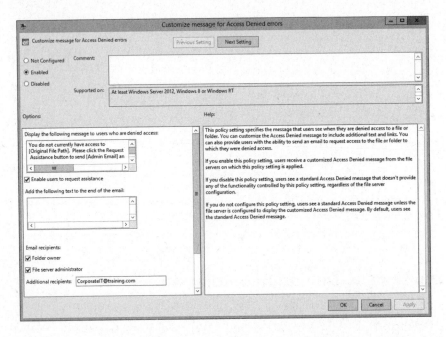

One of the great things about this policy is that it comes with preconfigured macros you can use to automate the access-denied message that will be displayed to users. Here are the four macros available within the access-denied message:

[Original File Path]: The original file path that was accessed by the user

[Original File Path Folder]: The parent folder of the original file path that was accessed by the user

[Admin Email]: The administrator email recipient list

[Data Owner Email]: The data owner email recipient list

For this exercise, I have configured the following access-denied message: "You do not currently have access to [*Original File Path*]. Please click the Request Assistance button to send [*Admin Email*] an email requesting assistance."

5. Click OK to save and close the policy.

6. Invoke the Enable Access-Denied Assistance On Client For All File Types policy here as well.

7. Launch the File Server Resource Manager on one of your file servers to configure the email notification settings for the access-denied assistance email service.

8. Within the File Server Resource Manager, click Configure Options to configure the SMTP server and email addresses that will be used for access-denied assistance email notifications, as shown here.

9. Click the Send Test Email button to verify your settings.

10. Click OK to save the configuration.

11. Test your work by trying to access a resource as a user who does not have permission for that resource and then use the Request Assistance feature to ask for help.

Configure and Optimize Storage

Disk storage is a requirement for just about every computer and application used in any corporate environment. Administrators have some familiarity with storage, whether it is internal storage, a locally attached set of disks, or network attached storage (NAS). In this section, you will examine the various aspects of Windows Server 2012 R2 file and storage solutions. Though I'll discuss the various types of file and storage technologies, this section will primarily focus on iSCSI because of the native features in Windows Server 2012 R2. You will also look at some of the advanced configuration options of implementing thin provisioning and trim, managing server free space, and configuring tiered storage.

Configure iSCSI Target and Initiator

Internet Small Computer System Interface (iSCSI) is an Internet protocol used to establish and manage a connection between a computer (initiator) and a storage device (target). It does this by using a connection through TCP port 3260, which allows it to be used over a LAN, a WAN, or the Internet. Each initiator is identified by its iSCSI Qualified Name (iqn), and it is used to establish its connection to an iSCSI target.

iSCSI was developed to allow block-level access to a storage device over a network. This is different from using a NAS device that connects through the use of Common Internet File System (CIFS) or NFS.

Block-level access is important to many applications that require direct access to storage. Microsoft Exchange and Microsoft SQL are examples of applications that require direct access to storage.

By being able to leverage the existing network infrastructure, iSCSI was also developed as an alternative to Fibre Channel storage by alleviating the additional hardware costs associated with a Fibre Channel storage solution.

iSCSI also has another advantage over Fibre Channel in that it can provide security for the storage devices. iSCSI can use Microsoft Challenge Handshake Authentication Protocol (CHAP or MS-CHAP) for authentication and Internet Protocol Security (IPsec) for encryption. Windows Server 2012 R2 is able to connect an iSCSI storage device out of the box with no additional software needing to be installed. This is because the Microsoft iSCSI initiator is built into the operating system.

Windows Server 2012 R2 supports two different ways to initiate an iSCSI session:

- Through the native Microsoft iSCSI software initiator that resides on Windows Server 2012 R2

- Using a hardware iSCSI host bus adapter (HBA) that is installed in the computer

Both the Microsoft iSCSI software initiator and iSCSI HBA present an iSCSI qualified name that identifies the host initiator. When the Microsoft iSCSI software initiator is used, the CPU utilization may be as much as 30 percent higher than on a computer with a hardware iSCSI HBA. This is because all of the iSCSI process requests are handled within the operating system. Using a hardware iSCSI HBA, process requests can be offloaded to the adapter, thus freeing the CPU overhead associated with the Microsoft iSCSI software initiator. However, iSCSI HBAs can be expensive, whereas the Microsoft iSCSI software initiator is free.

It is worthwhile installing the Microsoft iSCSI software initiator and performing load testing to see how much overhead the computer will have prior to purchasing an iSCSI HBA or HBAs, depending on the redundancy level. Exercise 18.13 explains how to install and configure an iSCSI connection.

EXERCISE 18.13

Configuring iSCSI Storage Connection

1. Press the Windows key or the Start button in the lower-left corner and select Administrative Tools ➢ iSCSI Initiator.

2. If a dialog box appears, click Yes to start the service.

3. Click the Discovery tab.

4. In the Target Portals portion of the page, click Discover Portal.

5. Enter the IP address of the target portal and click OK.

6. The IP address of the target portal appears in the Target Portals box.

7. Click OK.

   To use the storage that has now been presented to the server, you must create a volume on it and format the space.

Configure Internet Storage Name Server

Internet Storage Name Service (iSNS) allows for the central registration of an iSCSI environment because it automatically discovers available targets on the network. The purpose of iSNS is to help find available targets on a large iSCSI network.

The Microsoft iSCSI initiator includes an iSNS client that is used to register with the iSNS. The iSNS feature maintains a database of clients that it has registered either through DCHP discovery or through manual registration. iSNS DHCP is available after the installation of the service, and it is used to allow iSNS clients to discover the location of the iSNS. However, if iSNS DHCP is not configured, iSNS clients must be registered manually with the `iscsicli` command.

To execute the command, launch a command prompt on a computer hosting the Microsoft iSCSI and type **`iscsicli addisnsserver server_name`**, where `server_name` is the name of the computer hosting iSNS. Exercise 18.14 walks you through the steps required to install the iSNS feature on Windows Server 2012 R2, and then it explains the different tabs in iSNS.

EXERCISE 18.14

Installing the iSNS Feature on Windows Server 2012 R2

1. Open Server Manager.

2. Launch the Add Roles And Features Wizard.

3. Choose role-based or featured-based installation and click Next.

4. Choose your server and click Next.

5. Click Next at the Roles screen.

6. At the Select Features screen, choose the iSNS Server Service check box. Click Next.

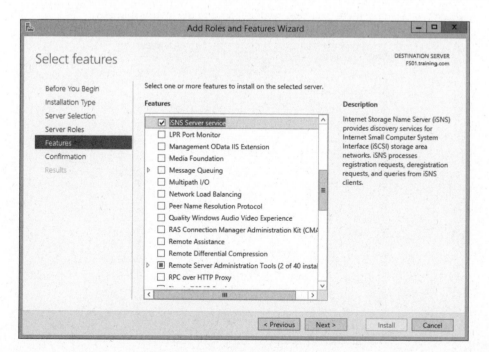

EXERCISE 18.14 *(continued)*

7. At the Confirmation screen, click the Install button.

8. Click the Close button. Close Server Manager and reboot.

9. Log in and open the iSNS server under Administrative Tools.

10. Click the General tab. This tab displays the list of registered initiators and targets. In addition to their iSCSI qualified names, it lists storage node type (Target or Initiator), alias string, and entity identifier (the fully qualified domain name [FQDN] of the machine hosting the iSNS client).

11. Click the Discovery Domains tab. The purpose of discovery domains is to provide a way to separate and group nodes. This is similar to zoning in Fibre Channel.

    The following options are available on the Discovery Domains tab:

    Create creates a new discovery domain.

    Refresh repopulates the Discovery Domain drop-down list.

    Delete deletes the currently selected discovery domain.

    Add adds nodes that are already registered in iSNS to the currently selected discovery domain.

    Add New adds nodes by entering the iSCSI qualified name of the node. These nodes do not have to be currently registered.

    Remove Used removes selected nodes from the discovery domain.

12. Click the Discovery Domain Sets tab. The purpose of discovery domain sets is to separate further discovery domains. Discovery domains can be enabled or disabled, giving administrators the ability to restrict further the visibility of all initiators and targets.

The options on the Discovery Domain Sets tab are as follows:

The *Enable* check box indicates the status of the discovery domain sets and turns them off and on.

Create creates new discovery domain sets.

Refresh repopulates the Discovery Domain Sets drop-down list.

Delete deletes the currently selected discovery domain set.

Add adds discovery domains to the currently selected discovery domain set.

Remove removes selected nodes from the discovery domain sets.

13. Close the iSNS server.

Implement Thin Provisioning and Trim

Thin provisioning and trim can be useful features that allow organizations to get the most out of their storage arrays. These solutions apply directly to a virtualized environment using virtual disks that are thin provisioned.

Thin provisioning is a way of providing what is known as just-in-time allocations. Blocks of data are written to disk only as they are used instead of zeroing out all of the blocks of data that have been allocated to the virtual disk configuration. Thin provisioning is tricky to manage properly because you could easily find yourself in a position where you have an over-provisioned environment because of over-allocation.

For example, you have 100 VMs that are all provisioned with 40GB thin-provisioned virtual disks. Each VM is currently utilizing only 20GB of the total 40GB that has been allocated. The problem is that you have only 2TB worth of storage. Without realizing it, you've over-provisioned your environment by 200 percent because of thin provisioning.

This is where trim comes in to help us manage thin provisioning. *Trim* automatically reclaims free space that is not being used. In addition to trim, Windows Server 2012 R2 provides standardized notifications that will alert administrators when certain storage thresholds are crossed.

Manage Server Free Space Using Features on Demand

Features on Demand was first introduced in Windows Server 2012. This feature lets you conserve disk space within the environment by installing only basic operating system components with every new installation of a Windows Server 2012 R2 or Windows 8 machine. Instead of loading unnecessary payload files, those files are stored in a central repository and used as needed to install roles and features. When I talk about *payload files*, I am talking about the binaries for all permissions, settings, and components of a feature. Features on Demand gives you the ability not only to disable Windows Server features but also to remove all of the payloads. This lets administrators keep a tighter security footprint at the operating system level, which is similar to a Server Core installation but without the limitation of not being able to control which source files are loaded during operating system installation.

Configure Tiered Storage

Tiered storage is an excellent new feature in Windows Server 2012 R2 that gives administrators the ability to use solid-state drives (SSDs) and conventional hard-disk drives (HDDs) within the same storage pool. You can configure virtual disks that span SSD and HDD tiers, which are presented as a single LUN. One of the really nice things about this feature is that with Windows Server 2012 R2, data is automatically saved to either an SSD or an HDD based on actual usage within the environment. Most frequently accessed data is stored on an SSD, and the less frequently accessed data is stored on an HDD.

Quite a few organizations these days use some sort of charge-back or show-back application to track and even charge for hosted solutions and services. Having the capability to tier storage gives users more options in selecting a plan that works for them. It also makes it possible for administrators to keep high I/O servers and applications on faster and better-performing drives without having to move data manually across multiple tiers of storage.

Summary

In this chapter, I discussed how configuring file and storage solutions can be highly effective within your organization. You now have a better understanding of how Windows Server 2012 R2 can provide you with extended functionality for effectively controlling corporate data. Quite a few of these solutions are essential to managing a Windows Server environment to the best of your ability. Take the time to complete each exercise thoroughly until you are comfortable with performing the majority of these tasks without documentation.

You learned how to configure and test some of the great features provided by Dynamic Access Control. Many of the exam questions will involve using both DAC and FSRM to manage and control shared resources. You will also want to focus heavily on auditing capabilities and the storage solutions talked about throughout the chapter. Configure and test the full extent of all of these applications and solutions to prepare appropriately for the exam.

Exam Essentials

Understand the purpose and function of auditing.   Auditing helps determine the cause of security violations and helps troubleshoot permissions-related problems. Configure and test the effects of auditing within a file share hierarchy in a lab environment.

Know storage technologies.   Understand how to use the Fibre Channel, iSCSI, and NAS storage technologies. Know how to configure an iSCSI initiator and how to establish a connection to a target. Practice configuring tiered storage and using thin provisioning and trim.

Understand the features and functionality of BranchCache.   BranchCache helps eliminate the problems of slow access and bandwidth issues when sharing data across multiple, geographically disparate locations. By syncing and caching data between sites, users can use company-wide shared resources more efficiently when slower site links exist between site locations.

Know how to configure Dynamic Access Control.   DAC has a wide array of features and functionality that will make an administrator's job of controlling file and folder access much easier. It will also provide tighter data security and data classification throughout the environment.

Understand file classification.   File classification is used when an administrator needs to manage and control both the type and the amount of data that is stored on their servers. You can use both Dynamic Access Control and the File Sever Resource Manager to implement file classification.

Review Questions

1. LaDonna is a system administrator for an Active Directory environment that is running in Native mode. Recently, several managers have reported suspicions about user activities and have asked her to increase security in the environment. Specifically, the requirements are as follows:

   - The accessing of certain sensitive files must be logged.

   - Modifications to certain sensitive files must be logged.

   - System administrators must be able to provide information about which users accessed sensitive files and when they were accessed.

   - All logon attempts for specific shared machines must be recorded.

   Which of the following steps should LaDonna take to meet these requirements? (Choose all that apply.)

   A. Enable auditing with the Computer Management tool.

   B. Enable auditing using the Group Policy Management Console.

   C. Enable auditing with the Active Directory Domains and Trusts tool.

   D. Enable auditing with the Event Viewer tool.

   E. View the audit log using the Event Viewer tool.

   F. View auditing information using the Computer Management tool.

   G. Enable failure and success auditing settings for specific files stored on NTFS volumes.

   H. Enable failure and success auditing settings for logon events on specific computer accounts.

2. What is the default TCP port for iSCSI?

   A. 3260

   B. 1433

   C. 21

   D. 3389

3. You create a GPO and link it to the Engineering OU. You want to monitor users in the Engineering OU who connect to the file server. What type of auditing do you enable?

   A. Audit object access

   B. Audit system events

   C. Audit logon events

   D. Audit process tracking

4. You have been hired by a small company to implement new Windows Server 2012 R2
    systems. The company wants you to set up a server for users' home folder locations. What
    type of server would you be setting up?

    A. File server

    B. Web server

    C. Exchange server

    D. PDC server

5. Your company has decided to implement a Windows 2012 R2 server. The company IT
    manager before you always used FAT32 as the system partition. Your company wants to
    know whether it should move to NTFS. Which of the following are some advantages of
    NTFS? (Choose all that apply.)

    A. Security

    B. Quotas

    C. Compression

    D. Encryption

6. What command would be used to register an iSCSI initiator manually to an iSNS server?

    A. `iscsicli refreshisnsserver server_name`

    B. `iscsicli listisnsservers server_name`

    C. `iscsicli removeisnsserver server_name`

    D. `iscsicli addisnsserver server_name`

7. You are a server administrator, and you are trying to save hard drive space on your
    Windows Server 2012 R2 machine. Which feature can help you save hard disk space?

    A. Features On Demand

    B. `HDSaver.exe`

    C. WinRM

    D. ADDS

8. You are an IT administrator who manages an environment that runs multiple Windows
    Server 2012 R2 servers from multiple site locations across the United States. Your
    Windows Server 2012 R2 machines use iSCSI storage. Other administrators report it is
    difficult to locate available iSCSI resources on the network. You need to make sure other
    administrators can easily access iSCSI resources using a centralized repository. What
    feature should you deploy?

    A. The iSCSI Target Storage Provider feature

    B. The Windows Standards-Based Storage Management feature

    C. The iSCSI Target Server role feature

    D. The iSNS Server service feature

9. Your company is headquartered in Colorado Springs and has a remote site location in Tampa. The Colorado Spring office has a file server named FS01. FS01 has the BranchCache for Network Files role service installed. Your Tampa Office has a file server named FS02. FS02 has been configured as a BranchCache hosted cache server. You need to preload the data from the file shares on FS01 to the cache on FS02. You have already generated hashes for the file shares on FS01. Which cmdlet should you run next?

   A. Export-BCCachePackage

   B. Publish-BCFileContent

   C. Set-BCCache

   D. Add-BCDataCacheExtension

10. You have a Windows Server 2012 R2 file server named FS01. FS01 has the File Server Resource Manager role service installed. You attempt to delete a classification property, and you receive the error message "The classification property is in use and cannot be deleted." You need to delete the Contains Personal Information classification property. What should you do?

   A. Clear the Contains Personal Information classification property value for all files.

   B. Delete the classification rule that is assigned the Contains Personal Information classification property.

   C. Disable the classification rule that is assigned the Contains Personal Information classification property.

   D. Set files that have a Contains Personal Information classification property value of Yes to No.

Implement Business Continuity and Disaster Recovery

THE FOLLOWING 70-412 EXAM OBJECTIVES ARE COVERED IN THIS CHAPTER:

✓ **Configure and manage backups**

- Configure Windows Server backups
- Configure Windows Azure backups
- Configure role-specific backups
- Manage VSS settings using VSSAdmin

✓ **Recover Servers**

- Restore from backups
- Perform a Bare Metal Restore (BMR)
- Recover servers using Windows Recovery Environment (Win RE) and safe mode
- Configure the Boot Configuration Data (BCD) store

✓ **Configure site-level fault tolerance**

- Configure Hyper-V Replica including Hyper-V Replica Broker and VMs
- Configure multi-site clustering including network settings, Quorum, and failover settings
- Configure Hyper-V Replica extended replication
- Configure Global Update Manager
- Recover a multi-site failover cluster

Throughout this book, I have stressed the importance of setting up your network properly. Once your network is set up and running properly, your users will get the most functionality out of the network. Your users will also become dependent on the network. Try taking a network offline for even 10 minutes, and your users will scream and complain.

Now that you have your users hooked, you must protect the network and the data. If your company loses their data, can they survive? Probably not. Most companies would go bankrupt if they lost all of their data and had no way to recover it. Data protection and recoverability is one of the most critical jobs you have as an administrator.

It is important to have multiple servers available to provide backup in case of a problem. The same goes for Active Directory itself—it too should be backed up. This way, if there is a massive disaster after which you need to restore your directory services, you will have that option available to you.

The process of reformatting a computer from scratch after a catastrophic system failure is a bare-metal restore and usually involves reinstalling the operating system and all of the system software.

In this chapter, you will learn about all the different ways to protect and recover your system.

 Some of the text in this chapter is repeated from Chapter 15 due to its relevancy and importance to both Exam 70-411 and Exam 70-412.

Protecting the System

One of the worst events you will experience is a computer that won't boot. But far worse is discovering that there is no recent backup for that computer.

The first step in preparing for disaster recovery is to expect that a disaster will happen at some point and to take proactive measures to plan for recovery before the failure occurs. Here are some of the preparations you can make:

- Keep your computer up-to-date with Windows Update.

- Perform regular system backups.

- Use current software to scan for malware (such as viruses, spyware, and adware) and make sure you have the most recent updates.

- Perform regular administrative functions, such as monitoring the logs in the Event Viewer utility.

If you can't start Windows Server 2012 R2, you can use several options and utilities to identify and resolve Windows errors. The following is a broad list of troubleshooting options:

- If you have recently made a change to your computer's configuration by installing a new device driver or application and Windows Server 2012 R2 will not load properly, you can use the Last Known Good Configuration, roll back the driver, or use System Restore to restore a previous system configuration.

- If you can boot your computer to Safe Mode and you suspect you have a system conflict, you can temporarily disable an application or processes, troubleshoot services, or uninstall software.

- If your computer will not boot to Safe Mode, you can use the Startup Repair tool to replace corrupted system files.

- If necessary, you can use the Windows Server Backup utility to restore files from backup media and to restore a complete image of your computer.

To safeguard your server, one of the most important functions is to protect Active Directory. Active Directory is the heart and soul of a Microsoft network, and losing your data would be a catastrophic event. So, let's start by discussing how to protect Active Directory.

Backup and Recovery of Active Directory

If you have deployed Active Directory in your network environment, your users now depend on it to function properly in order to do their jobs. From network authentications to file access to print and web services, Active Directory has become a mission-critical component of your business. Therefore, the importance of backing up the Active Directory data store should be evident.

As I discussed in earlier chapters, it is important to have multiple domain controllers available to provide backup in case of a problem. The same goes for Active Directory itself—it too should be backed up by being saved. This way, if a massive disaster occurs in which you need to restore your directory services, you will have that option available to you.

Backups are just good common sense, but here are several specific reasons to back up data:

Protect Against Hardware Failures Computer hardware devices have finite lifetimes, and all hardware eventually fails. I discussed this when I mentioned MTBF earlier in the book. *Mean Time Between Failures (MTBF)* is the average time a device will function before it actually fails. There is also a rating derived from benchmark testing of hard disk devices that tells you when you may be at risk for an unavoidable disaster. Some types of failures, such as corrupted hard disk drives, can result in significant data loss.

Protect Against Accidental Deletion or Modification of Data Although the threat of hardware failures is real, in most environments mistakes in modifying or deleting data are much more common. For example, suppose a system administrator accidentally deletes all of the objects within a specific OU. Clearly, it's important to be able to retrieve this information from a backup.

Keep Historical Information   Users and system administrators sometimes modify files and then later find out that they require access to an older version of the file. Or a file is accidentally deleted, and a user does not discover that fact until much later. By keeping multiple backups over time, you can recover information from prior backups when necessary.

Protect Against Malicious Deletion or Modification of Data   Even in the most secure environments, it is conceivable that unauthorized users (or authorized ones with malicious intent!) could delete or modify information. In such cases, the loss of data might require valid backups from which to restore critical information.

Windows Server 2012 R2 includes a Backup utility that is designed to back up operating system files and the Active Directory data store. It allows for basic backup functionality, such as scheduling backup jobs and selecting which files to back up. Figure 19.1 shows the main screen of the Windows Server 2012 R2 Backup utility.

FIGURE 19.1   The main screen of the Windows Server 2012 R2 Backup utility

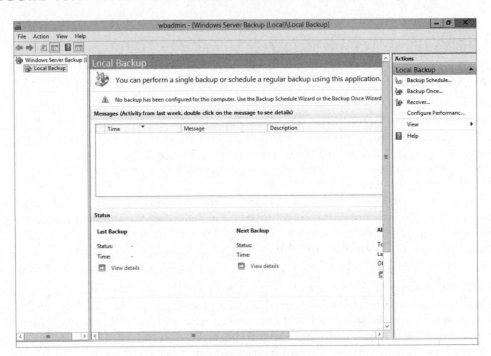

In the following sections, you'll learn about the details of using the Windows Server 2012 R2 Backup utility and how you can restore Active Directory when problems do occur.

Overview of the Windows Server 2012 R2 Backup Utility

Although the general purpose behind performing backup operations—protecting information—is straightforward, system administrators must consider many options when determining the optimal backup-and-recovery scenario for their environment. Factors include what to back up, how often to back up, and when the backups should be performed.

In this section, you'll see how the Windows Server 2012 R2 Backup utility makes it easy to implement a backup plan for many network environments.

> Although the Windows Server 2012 R2 Backup utility provides the basic functionality required to back up your files, you may want to investigate third-party products that provide additional functionality. These applications can provide options for specific types of backups (such as those for Exchange Server and SQL Server) as well as disaster recovery options, networking functionality, centralized management, and support for more advanced hardware.

Backup Types

One of the most important issues you will have to deal with when you are performing backups is keeping track of which files you have backed up and which files you need to back up. Whenever a backup of a file is made, the archive bit for the file is set. You can view the attributes of system files by right-clicking them and selecting Properties. By clicking the Advanced button in the Properties dialog box, you will access the Advanced Attributes dialog box. Here you will see the option Folder Is Ready For Archiving. Figure 19.2 shows an example of the attributes for a folder.

FIGURE 19.2   Viewing the archive attributes for a folder

Although it is possible to back up all of the files in the file system during each backup operation, it's sometimes more convenient to back up only selected files (such as those that have changed since the last backup operation). When performing backups, you can back up to removable media (DVD) or to a network location.

It is recommended by Microsoft to do a backup to a network location. The reason for this is that if your company suffers from a disaster (fire, hurricane, and so forth), your data can all still be lost—including the backup. If you back up to a removable media source, a copy of the backup can be taken offsite. This protects against a major disaster.

 Although Windows Server 2012 R2 does not support all of these backup types, it's important to understand the most common backup types. Most administrators use third-party software for their backups. That's why it's important to know all of the different types.

Several types of backups can be performed:

Normal   Normal backups (also referred to as *system* or *full backups*) back up all of the selected files and then mark them as backed up. This option is usually used when a full system backup is made. Windows Server 2012 R2 supports this backup.

Copy   *Copy backups* back up all of the selected files but do not mark them as backed up. This is useful when you want to make additional backups of files for moving files offsite or you want to make multiple copies of the same data for archival purposes.

Incremental   *Incremental backups* copy any selected files that are marked as ready for backup (typically because they have not been backed up or they have been changed since the last backup) and then mark the files as backed up. When the next incremental backup is run, only the files that are not marked as having been backed up are stored. Incremental backups are used in conjunction with normal (full) backups.

The most common backup process is to make a full backup and then make subsequent incremental backups. The benefit to this method is that only files that have changed since the last full or incremental backup will be stored. This can reduce backup times and disk or tape storage space requirements.

When recovering information from this type of backup method, a system administrator must first restore the full backup and then restore each of the incremental backups.

Differential   *Differential backups* are similar in purpose to incremental backups with one important exception: Differential backups copy all files that are marked for backup but do not mark the files as backed up. When restoring files in a situation that uses normal and differential backups, you need only restore the normal backup and the latest differential backup.

Daily   *Daily backups* back up all of the files that have changed during a single day. This operation uses the file time/date stamps to determine which files should be backed up and does not mark the files as having been backed up.

Backing Up System State Data

When you are planning to back up and restore Active Directory, be aware that the most important component is known as the *system state data*. System state data includes the components upon which the Windows Server 2012 R2 operating system relies for normal operations. The Windows Server 2012 R2 Backup utility offers you the ability to back up the system state data to another type of media (such as a hard disk or network share).

Specifically, it will back up the following components for a Windows Server 2012 R2 domain controller:

Active Directory   The *Active Directory data store* is at the heart of Active Directory. It contains all of the information necessary to create and manage network resources, such as users and computers. In most environments that use Active Directory, users and system administrators rely on the proper functioning of these services in order to do their jobs.

Boot Files   *Boot files* are the files required for booting the Windows Server 2012 R2 operating system and can be used in the case of boot file corruption.

COM+ Class Registration Database   The *COM+ class registration database* is a listing of all the COM+ class registrations stored on the computer. Applications that run on a Windows Server 2012 R2 computer might require the registration of various share code components. As part of the system state backup process, Windows Server 2012 R2 stores all of the information related to Component Object Model+ (COM+) components so that it can be quickly and easily restored.

Registry   The Windows Server 2012 R2 *registry* is a central repository of information related to the operating system configuration (such as desktop and network settings), user settings, and application settings. Therefore, the registry is absolutely vital to the proper functioning of Windows Server 2012 R2.

Sysvol Directory   The *Sysvol directory* includes data and files that are shared between the domain controllers within an Active Directory domain. Many operating system services rely on this information in order to function properly.

Bare-Metal Backups and Restores

One of the options you have in Windows Server 2012 R2 is to do a *bare-metal restore (BMR)*. This is a restore of a machine after the machine has been completely wiped out and formatted. This type of restore is done usually after a catastrophic machine failure or crash.

Windows Server 2012 R2 gives you the ability to back up all of the files needed for a bare-metal restore by choosing the Bare Metal Recovery check box (see Figure 19.3).

FIGURE 19.3   Bare Metal Recovery option

When you choose the Bare Metal Recovery option in Windows Server 2012 R2, all of the suboptions (System State, System Reserved, and Local Disk) automatically get checked.

When preparing your network for a bare-metal backup, you want to make sure you have everything you need on hand to complete this type of restore. You may want to keep a copy of the server software, server drivers, and so forth, on hand and ready to go, just in case you have to do a full restore.

Scheduling Backups

In addition to specifying which files to back up, you can schedule backup jobs to occur at specific times. Planning *when* to perform backups is just as important as deciding *what* to back up. Performing backup operations can reduce overall system performance; therefore, you should plan to back up information during times of minimal activity on your servers.

To add a backup operation to the schedule, you can simply click the Add button in the Specify Backup Time window.

Restoring System State Data

In some cases, the Active Directory data store or other system state data may become corrupt or unavailable. This could be because of many different reasons. A hard disk failure might, for example, result in the loss of data. Or the accidental deletion of an OU and all of its objects might require a restore operation to be performed.

The actual steps involved in restoring system state data are based on the details of what has caused the data loss and what effect this data loss has had on the system. In the best-case scenario, the system state data is corrupt or inaccurate, but the operating system can still boot. If this is the case, all you must do is boot into a special *Directory Services Restore Mode (DSRM)* and then restore the system state data from a backup. DSRM is available only on a domain controller. This process will replace the current system state data with that from the backup. Therefore, any changes that have been made since the last backup will be completely lost and must be redone.

In a worst-case scenario, all of the information on a server has been lost or a hardware failure is preventing the machine from properly booting. If this is the case, here are the steps you must take in order to recover system state data:

1. Fix any hardware problem that might prevent the computer from booting (for example, replace any failed hard disks).

2. Reinstall the Windows Server 2012 R2 operating system. This should be performed like a regular installation on a new system.

3. Reinstall any device drivers that may be required by your backup device. If you backed up information to the file system, this will not apply.

4. Restore the system state data using the Windows Server 2012 R2 Backup utility. When restoring the system state data on a domain controller, you must specify either an authoritative or nonauthoritative restore.

I'll cover the technical details of performing restores later in this chapter. For now, however, you should understand the importance of backing up information and, whenever possible, testing the validity of backups.

Backing Up and Restoring Group Policy Objects

Group Policy objects (GPOs) are a major part of Active Directory. When you back up Active Directory, GPOs can also get backed up. You also have the ability to back up GPOs through the Group Policy Management Console (GPMC). This gives you the ability to back up and restore individual GPOs.

To back up all GPOs, open the GPMC and right-click the Group Policy Objects container. You will see the option Back Up All. After you choose this option, a wizard will start asking you for the backup location. Choose a location and click Backup.

To back up an individual GPO, right-click the GPO (in the Group Policy Objects container) and choose Backup. Again, after you choose this option, a wizard will start asking you for the backup location. Choose a location and click Backup.

To restore a GPO, it's the same process, except instead of choosing Backup, you will choose either Manage Backups (to restore all GPOs) or Restore (for an individual GPO).

Configure the Boot Configuration Data Store

BCDEdit is another great command-line utility that is used primarily for managing boot configuration data (BCD) stores. A *BCD store* is a set of configuration files that describe an operating system's boot applications and settings. These files essentially replace the Boot.ini file in your local Windows directory. You will notice that the BCDEdit command-line utility is similar to the Bootcfg.exe utility used in earlier versions of Windows operating systems. You can effectively use BCDEdit to create new boot parameters for your Windows boot loader, modify the existing BCD stores, and create new BCD stores as needed. Please note that administrative permissions are required to use BCDEdit to modify a BCD store.

Setting Up an Active Directory Backup

The Windows Server 2012 R2 Backup utility makes it easy to back up the system data (including Active Directory) as part of a normal backup operation. I've already covered the ideas behind the different backup types and why and when they are used.

Exercise 19.1 walks you through the process of backing up the domain controller. To complete this exercise, the local machine must be a domain controller, and you must have a DVD burner or network location to back up the system state.

The Windows Server 2012 R2 Backup utility is not installed by default. If you have already installed the Windows Server 2012 R2 Backup utility, skip to step 9.

EXERCISE 19.1

Backing Up Active Directory

1. To install the Windows Server 2012 R2 Backup utility, press the Windows key and select Administrative Tools ➢ Server Manager.

2. In the center console, click the Add Roles And Features link.

3. At the Select Installation Type screen, choose a role-based or feature-based installation and click Next.

4. The Select Destination Server screen appears. Choose Select A Server From The Server Pool and choose your server under Server Pool. Click Next.

5. Click Next at the Select Server Roles screen.

6. At the Select Features screen, scroll down and check the box next to Windows Server Backup. Click Next.

7. At the Confirmation screen, click the check box to restart the destination server automatically. This will bring up a dialog box. Click Yes and then click the Install button.

8. Click the Close button when finished. Close Server Manager.

9. Open Windows Backup by pressing the Windows key and selecting Administrative Tools ➢ Windows Server Backup.

10. On the left side, click Local Backup. Then, under Actions, click Backup Once.

11. When the Backup Once Wizard appears, click Different Options and click Next.

EXERCISE 19.1 *(continued)*

12. At the Select Backup Configuration screen, choose Custom and click Next.

13. Click the Add Items button. Choose System State and click OK. Click Next.

14. At the Specify Destination Type, choose Remote Shared Folder. Click Next.

15. Put in the shared path you want to use and click Next.

16. At the Confirmation screen, click the Backup button.

17. Once the backup is complete, close the Windows Server Backup utility.

Restoring Active Directory

Active Directory has been designed with fault tolerance in mind. For example, it is highly recommended by Microsoft that each domain have at least two domain controllers. Each of these domain controllers contains a copy of the Active Directory data store. Should one of the domain controllers fail, the available one can take over the failed server's functionality. When the failed server is repaired, it can then be promoted to a domain controller in the existing environment. This process effectively restores the failed domain controller without incurring any downtime for end users because all of the Active Directory data is replicated to the repaired server in the next scheduled replication.

In some cases, you might need to restore Active Directory from a backup. For example, suppose a system administrator accidentally deletes several hundred users from the domain and does not realize it until the change has been propagated to all of the other domain controllers. Manually re-creating the accounts is not an option because the objects' security identifiers will be different (and all permissions must be reset). Clearly, a method for restoring from backup is the best solution. You can elect to make the Active Directory restore authoritative or nonauthoritative, as described in the following sections.

Overview of Authoritative Restore

Restoring Active Directory and other system state data is an important process should system files or the Active Directory data store become corrupt or otherwise unavailable. Fortunately, the Windows Server 2012 R2 Backup utility allows you to restore data easily from a backup, should the need arise.

I mentioned earlier that in the case of the accidental deletion of information from Active Directory, you might need to restore Active Directory from a recent backup. But what happens if there is more than one domain controller in the environment? Even if you did perform a restore, the information on this domain controller would be seen as outdated, and it would be overwritten by the data from another domain controller. This data from the older domain controller is exactly the information you want to replace. The domain controller that was reloaded using a backup would have an older timestamp, and the other domain controllers would re-delete the information from the backup.

Fortunately, Windows Server 2012 R2 and Active Directory allow you to perform what is called an *authoritative restore*. The authoritative restore process specifies a domain controller as having the authoritative (or master) copy of the Active Directory data store. When other domain controllers communicate with this domain controller, their information will be overwritten with Active Directory data stored on the local machine.

Now that you have an idea of how an authoritative restore is supposed to work, let's move on to looking at the details of performing the process.

Performing an Authoritative Restore

When you are restoring Active Directory information on a Windows Server 2012 R2 domain controller, make sure Active Directory services are not running. This is because the restore of system state data requires full access to system files and the Active Directory data store. If you attempt to restore system state data while the domain controller is active, you will see an error message.

In general, restoring data and operating system files is a straightforward process. It is important to note that restoring a system state backup will replace the existing registry, Sysvol, and Active Directory files so that any changes you made since the last backup will be lost.

In addition to restoring the entire Active Directory database, you can also restore only specific subtrees within Active Directory using the restoresubtree command in the ntdsutil utility. This allows you to restore specific information, and it is useful in case of accidental deletion of isolated material.

Following the authoritative restore process, Active Directory should be updated to the time of the last backup. Furthermore, all other domain controllers for this domain will have their Active Directory information overwritten by the results of the restore operation. The result is an Active Directory environment that has been recovered from media.

Overview of Nonauthoritative Restore

Now that you understand why you would use an authoritative restore and how it is performed, it's an easy conceptual jump to understand a *nonauthoritative restore*. Remember that by making a restore authoritative, you are simply telling other domain controllers in the domain to recognize the restored machine as the newest copy of Active Directory for replication purposes. If you have only one domain controller, the authoritative restore process becomes moot; you can simply skip the steps required to make the restore authoritative and begin using the domain controller immediately after the normal restore is complete.

If you have more than one domain controller in the domain and you need to perform a nonauthoritative restore, simply allow the domain controller to receive Active Directory database information from other domain controllers in the domain using normal replication methods.

Active Directory Recycle Bin

The Active Directory recycle bin is a great feature that allows administrators to restore an Active Directory object that has been deleted.

Let's say you have a junior administrator who has been making changes to Active Directory for hours. The junior admin then deletes an OU from Active Directory. You would then have to reload the OU from a tape backup, or even worse, you may have to reload the entire Active Directory (depending on your backup software), thus losing the hours of work the junior admin has completed.

The problem here is that when you delete a security object from Active Directory, the object's security ID (SID) gets removed. All users' rights and permissions are associated with the users' SID number and not their account name. This is where the AD recycle bin can help.

The *Active Directory recycle bin* allows you to preserve and restore accidentally deleted Active Directory objects without the need of using a backup.

The Active Directory recycle bin works for both the Active Directory Domain Services (AD DS) and Active Directory Lightweight Directory Services (AD LDS) environments.

By enabling (disabled by default) the Active Directory recycle bin, any deleted Active Directory objects are preserved, and Active Directory objects can be restored, in their entirety, to their same condition immediately before the deletion. This means all group memberships and access rights that the object had before deletion will remain intact.

To enable the Active Directory recycle bin, you must do the following (you must be a member of the Schema Admins group):

1. Run the adprep /forestprep command to prepare the forest on the server that holds the schema master to update the schema.

2. Run the adprep /domainprep /gpprep command to prepare the domain on the server that holds the infrastructure operations master role.

3. If a read-only domain controller (RODC) is present in your environment, you must also run the adprep /rodcprep command.

4. Make sure that all domain controllers in your Active Directory forest are running Windows Server 2012 R2 or at least Windows Server 2008 R2.

5. Make sure that the forest functional level is set to Windows Server 2012 R2 or at least Windows Server 2008 R2.

Restartable Active Directory

Administrators have the ability to stop and restart Active Directory in the Windows Server 2012 R2 operating system without the need to reboot the entire system. Administrators can perform these actions by using either the Microsoft Management Console (MMC) snap-ins or the command line.

With *Restartable Active Directory Services*, an administrator has the ability to stop Active Directory Services so that updates and other tasks can be applied to a domain controller. One task that an administrator can perform while Active Directory is stopped is an offline defragmentation of the database.

One of the advantages of a restartable Active Directory is that other services running on the same server do not depend on Active Directory to continue to function properly while Active Directory is stopped. An administrator has the ability to stop and restart the Active Directory Domain Services in the Local Services MMC snap-in.

Offline Maintenance

As mentioned, sometimes you have to be offline to do maintenance. For example, you need to perform authoritative and nonauthoritative restores while the domain controller is offline. The main utility administrators use for offline maintenance is ntdsutil.

Ntdsutil.exe

The primary method by which system administrators can do offline maintenance is through the ntdsutil command-line tool. You can launch this tool by simply entering **ntdsutil** at a command prompt. The ntdsutil command is both interactive and context sensitive. That is, once you launch the utility, you'll see an ntdsutil command prompt. At this prompt, you can enter various commands that set your context within the application. For example, if you enter **domain management**, you'll be able to enter domain-related commands. Several operations also require you to connect to a domain, a domain controller, or an Active Directory object before you perform a command.

Table 19.1 describes the domain-management commands supported by the ntdsutil tool. You can access this functionality by typing the command at a command prompt.

TABLE 19.1 Ntdsutil offline maintenance commands

Ntdsutil domain management command	Purpose
Help or ?	Displays information about the commands that are available within the Domain Management menu of the ntdsutil utility
compact to (at the file maintenance prompt)	Allows you to compact the Active Directory database (offline defragmentation)
metadata cleanup	Removes metadata from decommissioned domain controllers
Set DSRM Password	Resets the Directory Service Restore mode administrator account password

Active Directory Database Mounting Tool

One issue that an administrator may run into when trying to restore Active Directory is the need to restore several backups to compare the Active Directory data that each backup contains. Windows Server 2012 R2 has a utility called the Active Directory database mounting tool (Dsamain.exe) that can resolve this issue.

The Dsamain.exe tool can help the recovery processes by giving you a way to compare data as it exists in snapshots (taken at different times) so that you have the ability to decide which Active Directory database to restore.

Creating snapshots on a regular basis will allow you to have enough data so that you can keep accurate records of how the Active Directory database changes over time. The ntdsutil utility allows you to take snapshots by using the ntdsutil snapshot operation.

 You are not required to run the ntdsutil snapshot operation to use Dsamain.exe. You have the ability to use a backup of the Active Directory database.

You must be a member of the Domain Admins group or the Enterprise Admins group to view any snapshots taken because these snapshots contain sensitive Active Directory data.

Compact the Directory Database File (Offline Defragmentation)

One task you have probably done for years is defrag the operating systems that you run. Defragging a system helps return free space from data to the hard drive, and the defragmentation utility has been available since Windows NT.

You can also use the defragmentation process to compact the Active Directory database while it's offline. Offline defragmentation helps return free disk space and check Active Directory database integrity.

To perform an offline defragmentation, you use the ntdsutil command. When you perform a defragmentation of the Active Directory database, a new compacted version of the database is created. This new database file can be created on the same machine (if space permits) or on a network location. After the new file is created, copy the compacted Ntds.dit file to the original location.

It is a good practice, if space allows, to maintain a copy of the older, original database file. You can either rename the older database file and keep it in its current location or copy the older database file to an alternate location.

Monitoring Replication

At times you may need to keep an eye on how your replication traffic is working on your domain controllers. I will cover the replication utility that you can use to help determine whether there are problems on your domain.

Repadmin Utility

The Repadmin utility is included when you install Windows Server 2012 R2. This command-line tool helps administrators diagnose replication problems between Windows domain controllers.

Repadmin allows administrators to view the replication topology of each domain controller as seen from the domain controller's perspective. Administrators can also use Repadmin to create the replication topology manually. By manually creating the replication topology, administrators can force replication events between domain controllers and view the replication metadata vectors.

To access the Repadmin utility, open a command prompt using an elevated privilege (Run ➢ CMD). At the command prompt, type **Repadmin.exe**, and all of the available options will appear.

Using the ADSI Editor

Another utility that allows you to manage objects and attributes in Active Directory is the Active Directory Service Interfaces Editor (ADSI Edit). ADSI Edit allows you to view every object and attribute in an Active Directory forest.

One advantage to using the Adsiedit.msc MMC snap-in is that this tool allows you to query, view, create, and edit attributes that are not exposed through other Active Directory Microsoft Management Console (MMC) snap-ins.

ADSI Edit allows you to administer an AD LDS instance. To do this, you must first connect and bind to the instance. After you connect and bind to the instance, you can administer the containers and objects within the instance by browsing to the containers or objects and then right-clicking them. To complete this task, you must be a member of the Administrators group for the AD LDS instance.

Wbadmin Command-Line Utility

The wbadmin command allows you to back up and restore your operating system, volumes, files, folders, and applications from a command prompt.

You must be a member of the Administrators group to configure a backup schedule. You must be a member of the Backup Operators or the Administrators group (or you must have been delegated the appropriate permissions) to perform all other tasks using the wbadmin command.

To use the wbadmin command, you must run wbadmin from an elevated command prompt (to open an elevated command prompt, click Start, right-click Command Prompt, and then click Run As Administrator). Table 19.2 describes some of the wbadmin commands.

TABLE 19.2   Wbadmin commands

Command	Description
wbadmin enable backup	Configures and enables a daily backup schedule
wbadmin disable backup	Disables your daily backups
wbadmin start backup	Runs a one-time backup
wbadmin stop job	Stops the currently running backup or recovery operation
wbadmin get items	Lists the items included in a specific backup
wbadmin start recovery	Runs a recovery of the volumes, applications, files, or folders specified
wbadmin get status	Shows the status of the currently running backup or recovery operation
wbadmin start systemstaterecovery	Runs a system state recovery
wbadmin start systemstatebackup	Runs a system state backup
wbadmin start sysrecovery	Runs a recovery of the full system state

Configure Windows Azure Backups

Microsoft continues to offer robust cloud solutions to assist administrators with effective backup options. With Windows Server 2012 R2, you can integrate with Windows Azure Online Services to store short-term backup data to an off-premises location. This solution comes with additional costs for storing the data after the initial free trial. The cost model is relatively straightforward, and it is comparable to other cloud storage solutions that are currently available. To run backup jobs from your organization to the Microsoft Azure cloud solution, your environment must be running System Center 2012 with Data Protection Manager.

Data Protection Manager

System Center 2012 *Data Protection Manager (DPM)* is an application that runs on the server and allows disk-based and tape-based data protection and recovery. This recovery is for all the computers in the Active Directory domain. One of the nice features of DPM is that all replication, synchronization, and recovery point creation is done by DPM.

Because you are able to use DPM and set up recoverability for your computers, if a system needs to be recovered, DPM provides reliable protection and rapid recovery of the computer's data either by the system administrator and/or by end users.

DPM uses multiple features to help keep the computers in your network safe. These features include replication, the Volume Shadow Copy Service (VSS) infrastructure, and a policy-driven engine. DPM helps provide protection and fast data recovery for businesses of all sizes.

Windows Azure Backup Prerequisites

Before you can start using the Windows Azure backup services, you must first have a few prerequisites set up within your environment. The following are the deployment prerequisites that you will need to accomplish the task:

- A Windows Server 2012 R2 server running Data Protection Manager in System Center 2012 R2.

- An active Windows Azure account with the Windows Azure Backup feature enabled.

- The Windows Azure backup agent must be installed on the DPM servers that you want to back up, and the DPM servers must have at least 2.5GB of free space reserved for caching. At least 15GB to 20GB of free space is recommended.

- A management certificate that will be uploaded to the backup vault in Windows Azure Backup.

  Please note the following in regard to the certificate parameters:

  - To upload to the certificate to the vault, you must export it as a .cer format file that contains the public key.

  - The certificate should be an x.509 v3 certificate.

  - The key length should be at least 2,048 bits.

  - The certificate must have a valid ClientAuthentication EKU.

- The certificate should be valid currently, with a validity period that does not exceed 3 years.

- The certificate should reside in the Personal certificate store of your local computer.

- The private key should be included during installation of the certificate.

- You can create a self-signed certificate using the makecert tool or use any valid SSL certificate issued by a certification authority (CA) trusted by Microsoft whose root certificates are distributed via the Microsoft Root Certificate Program.

 Make sure to take full advantage of the Microsoft Azure free trial when preparing for your exam. You can start your free trial by following this web link: http://azure.microsoft.com/en-us/pricing/free-trial/.

Configure Backup Vaults for Windows Azure Backup

The Windows Azure backup vault is where your data will be stored in the cloud. After you obtain a Windows Azure account, you will be able to create and manage your cloud backups from the Windows Azure Management Portal. Before you can start storing data using Windows Azure, you must first configure the backup vault by following four easy configuration steps:

1. Obtain a management certificate that will be used by Windows Azure:

   - You can either use an existing management certificate or obtain one by using makecert.exe. If you want to register a server that was not used to run makecert. exe, you must export the .pfx file (containing the private key) from that server, copy it to the server that you want to register, and import it to the Personal certificate store on that computer.

2. Create a backup vault in Windows Azure:

   a. Log in to the Windows Azure Management Portal.

   b. Click Recovery Services and then click Create New. Point to Backup Vault and then click Quick Create.

   c. Name the Vault, specify the geographic region, enter your Windows Azure subscription, and then click Create Backup Vault. It usually takes only a few minutes for the backup vault to finish building. Notifications are provided at the bottom of the management portal.

3. Upload a management certificate to Windows Azure:

   a. Log in to the Windows Azure Management Portal.

   b. Click Recovery Services, click the backup vault you want to certify, and then open the Quick Start page by clicking the Quick Start icon.

   c. On the Quick Start page, click Manager Certificate. A dialog box will appear allowing you to browse your computer for the appropriate certificate that has been staged for upload. Select and upload that certificate.

4. Download and Install the Windows Azure Backup Agent onto each of your DPM servers that you want to back up:

    a. Log in to the Windows Azure Management Portal.

    b. Select Download Agent from the Quick Start page.

    c. Select the appropriate agent for your deployment to start the Agent Installation Wizard.

    d. Complete the installation wizard, keeping all defaults.

Register DPM Servers with the Backup Vault

Now that your Windows Azure Backup Vault is fully configured and all of your DPM servers have agents installed, it's time to register your DPM servers with the backup vault.

1. Launch the Windows Azure Backup application from one of your DPM servers.

2. Click the Register Server task in the Action pane to start the Register Server Wizard.

3. Follow the wizard, making appropriate selections suitable for your particular environment.

4. If the process is successful, a registration confirmation message is displayed, and you can close the wizard.

That's all there is to it. If you have completed these steps properly, you are ready to configure backup jobs to run from your DPM servers to your backup vault in Microsoft Azure. Make sure to spend lots of time running through all of the available options found in the Microsoft Azure Management Portal. The exam is likely to cover multiple scenarios surrounding the configuration and troubleshooting of backups using Microsoft Azure.

Understanding Shadow Copies

An excellent way to protect your shared folders is by using *shadow copies* (Volume Snapshot Service [VSS]). Shadow copies allow an administrator to back up shared folders to a remote location. Shadow copies are designed to help recover files that were accidentally deleted, that were overwritten, or that have become corrupt. One major advantage to shadow copies is that open files can be backed up. This means that even if users are currently working on files in a shared folder that has shadow copies enabled, the shadow copies will continue to function.

Once administrators have configured and enabled shadow copies (using the Computer Management snap-in), network users can restore earlier versions of files. After the initial shadow copy of the shared folder is created, only changes are copied and not the entire file.

You can enable shadow copies of entire volumes.

The following are some of the settings that you can configure when setting up shadow copies:

Schedule   You have the ability to set the schedule of the shadow copies. You can set this schedule to run daily, weekly, monthly, once, at system startup, at logon, or when the system is idle. You can also set the time at which the shadow copy will run.

Storage Locations   An administrator needs to set the location of the shadow copy backup. If you are on a network, it is a good idea to place the shadow copy on a network drive.

Maximum Size   You can set a maximum size on your shadow copies, or you can specify that they have no size limit. One of the predetermined settings is 64 shadow copies per volume.

In Exercise 19.2, you'll set up a volume to make shadow copies every Monday at 7 a.m. To set up the shadow copies, you will use the Computer Management MMC snap-in.

EXERCISE 19.2

Configuring a Shadow Copy on a Volume

1. Open Computer Management by pressing the Windows key and selecting Administrative Tools ➢ Computer Management.

2. Expand Storage and then right-click Disk Management. Choose All Tasks ➢ Configure Shadow Copies.

3. When the Shadow Copies dialog box appears, click the Settings button.

4. When the Settings windows appears, click the Schedule button.

5. In the Schedule window, set the schedule task to weekly and the start time for 7 a.m. Uncheck all of the days-of-the-week boxes except Mon. Click OK.

6. When the Settings window reappears, click OK.

7. If the Enable button is enabled, click it. Then click OK.

8. Exit the Computer Management MMC.

To recover a previous version of a file from a shadow copy, you use the \\servername\ sharename path. The operating system determines how you will gain access to the shared folders and shadow copies. Shadow copies are built into Windows XP (SP1), Windows Vista, Windows 7, Windows 8, Windows Server 2003, Windows Server 2008/2008 R2, Windows Server 2012, and Windows Server 2012 R2. If you are using a different Microsoft operating system, you need to download the Shadow Copy Client Pack from the Microsoft download center.

VssAdmin Command

Another way to create, configure, and manage shadow copies is by using the vssadmin.exe command-line utility (see Figure 19.4). The vssadmin.exe command allows you to create, delete, list, and resize shadow copies and shadow storage.

FIGURE 19.4 vssadmin.exe command-line utility

Table 19.3 describes the vssadmin.exe command and the different commands associated with the vssadmin utility.

TABLE 19.3 Vssadmin.exe commands

Command	Description
Add ShadowStorage	Adds a new volume shadow copy storage association
Create Shadow	Creates a new volume shadow copy
Delete Shadows	Deletes volume shadow copies
Delete ShadowStorage	Deletes the volume shadow copy storage associations
List Providers	Lists registered volume shadow copy providers
List Shadows	Lists existing volume shadow copies
List ShadowStorage	Lists volume shadow copy storage associations
List Volumes	Lists volumes eligible for shadow copies
List Writers	Lists subscribed volume shadow copy writers
Resize ShadowStorage	Resizes a volume shadow copy storage association
Revert Shadow	Reverts a volume to a shadow copy
Query Reverts	Queries the progress of in-progress revert operations

Using Advanced Boot Options

The Windows Server 2012 R2 advanced startup options can be used to troubleshoot errors that keep Windows Server 2012 R2 from successfully booting.

 To access the Windows Server 2012 R2 advanced startup options, start or reboot the computer and press the F8 key after the firmware POST process but before Windows Server 2012 R2 is loaded. This will bring up the Advanced Boot Options menu, which offers numerous options for booting Windows Server 2012 R2.

These advanced startup options are covered in the following three sections (see Figure 19.5).

FIGURE 19.5   Advanced Boot Options screen

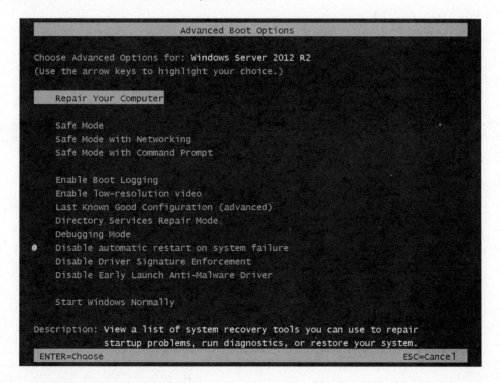

Starting in Safe Mode

When your computer will not start, one of the fundamental troubleshooting techniques is to simplify the configuration as much as possible. This is especially important when you do not know the cause of your problem and you have a complex configuration. After you have simplified the configuration, you can determine whether the problem is in the basic configuration or is a result of your complex configuration.

If the problem is in the basic configuration, you have a starting point for troubleshooting. If the problem is not in the basic configuration, you should proceed to restore each configuration option you removed, one at a time. This helps you to identify what is causing the error.

If Windows Server 2012 R2 will not load, you can attempt to load the operating system through *Safe Mode*. When you run Windows Server 2012 R2 in Safe Mode, you are simplifying your Windows configuration as much as possible. Safe Mode loads only the drivers needed to get the computer up and running.

The drivers that are loaded with Safe Mode include basic files and drivers for the mouse, monitor, keyboard, hard drive, standard video driver, and default system services. Safe Mode is considered a diagnostic mode, so you do not have access to all of the features and devices in Windows Server 2012 R2 that you have when you boot normally, including networking capabilities.

A computer booted to Safe Mode will show Safe Mode in the four corners of your desktop.

If you boot to Safe Mode, check all of your computer's hardware and software settings in Device Manager and try to determine why Windows Server 2012 R2 will not boot properly. After you take steps to fix the problem, try to boot to Windows Server 2012 R2 as you normally would.

In Exercise 19.3, you will boot your computer to Safe Mode.

EXERCISE 19.3

Booting Your Computer to Safe Mode

1. If your computer is currently running, restart the system.

2. During the boot process, press the F8 key to access the Advanced Boot Options menu.

3. Highlight Safe Mode and press Enter.

4. When Windows Server 2012 R2 starts, log in.

5. You will see a Help And Support dialog box letting you know what Safe Mode is. Exit Help And Support.

6. You should see that a network connection is not available in the lower-right corner.

7. Don't restart your computer yet; you will do this as a part of the next exercise.

Enabling Boot Logging

Boot logging creates a log file that tracks the loading of drivers and services. When you choose the Enable Boot Logging option from the Advanced Boot Options menu, Windows

Server 2012 R2 loads normally, not in Safe Mode. This allows you to log all of the processes that take place during a normal boot sequence.

This log file can be used to troubleshoot the boot process. When logging is enabled, the log file is written to \WINDOWS\Ntbtlog.txt (see Figure 19.6).

FIGURE 19.6 Ntbtlog.txt file

In Exercise 19.4, you will create and access a boot log file.

EXERCISE 19.4

Using Boot Logging

1. Restart your computer.

2. During the boot process, press the F8 key to access the Advanced Boot Options menu.

3. Highlight Enable Boot Logging and press Enter.

4. When Windows Server 2012 R2 starts, log in.

5. Click the Folders icon on the bottom left of the desktop and browse to C:\WINDOWS\ Ntbtlog.txt. Double-click this file.

6. Examine the contents of your boot log file.

7. Shut down your computer and restart it without using Advanced Boot Options.

The boot log file is cumulative. Each time you boot to Safe Mode, you are writing to this file. This enables you to make changes, reboot, and see whether you have fixed any problems. If you want to start from scratch, you should manually delete this file and reboot to an Advanced Boot Options menu selection that supports logging.

Using Other Advanced Boot Options Menu Modes

In this section, you will learn about additional Advanced Boot Options menu modes. These include the following:

Safe Mode With Networking   This is the same as the Safe Mode option, but it adds networking features. You might use this mode if you need networking capabilities to download drivers or service packs from a network location.

Safe Mode With Command Prompt   This starts the computer in Safe Mode, but after you log in to Windows Server 2012 R2, only a command prompt is displayed. This mode does not provide access to the desktop. Experienced troubleshooters use this mode.

Enable Low-Resolution Video (640×480)   This loads a standard VGA driver without starting the computer in Safe Mode. You might use this mode if you changed your video driver, did not test it, and tried to boot to Windows Server 2012 R2 with a bad driver that would not allow you to access video. The Enable VGA mode bails you out by loading a default driver, providing access to video so that you can properly install (and test!) the correct driver for your computer.

Safe Mode starts Windows Server 2012 R2 at a resolution of 800×600.

Last Known Good Configuration (Advanced)   This boots Windows Server 2012 R2 by using the registry information that was saved the last time the computer was successfully booted. You would use this option to restore configuration information if you improperly configured the computer and did not successfully reboot it. When you use the *Last Known Good Configuration* option, you lose any system configuration changes that were made since the computer last successfully booted.

Directory Services Restore Mode   This option is used for domain controllers only, and it is not relevant to Windows Server 2012 R2 unless it is a domain controller.

Debugging Mode   This runs the Kernel Debugger, if it is installed. The Kernel Debugger is an advanced troubleshooting utility.

Disable Automatic Restart On System Failure   This prevents Windows from restarting when a critical error causes Windows to fail. This option should be used only when Windows fails every time you restart so that you are not able to access the desktop or any configuration options.

Disable Driver Signature Enforcement   This allows drivers to be installed even if they do not contain valid signatures.

Start Windows Normally   This boots to Windows Server 2012 R2 in the default manner. This option is on the Advanced Boot Options menu in case you accidentally hit F8 during the boot process but really wanted to boot Windows Server 2012 R2 normally.

Windows Recovery Environment

When your Windows Server 2012 R2 machine fails to start, it will automatically enter into the *Windows Recovery Environment (Windows RE)*. This environment is an extensible recovery platform based on Windows Preinstallation Environment (Windows PE).

When your server starts in the Windows RE, the Startup Repair tool starts the diagnosis, and it will begin to help you repair the system. The Windows RE is also an environment in which you can use various tools to help you do a manual system recovery. The boot options for the Windows RE are as follows:

- Start recovery, troubleshooting, or diagnostic tools

- Boot from a device

- Access the Firmware menu

- Choose which operating system to boot, if multiple operating systems are installed on the same computer

Administrators also have the ability to configure a hardware button to run an alternate boot path that includes the Windows RE. This gives administrators the ability to help their users get to the Windows RE menus more easily, which allows your users to recover their PCs easily in the event of a corrupted system.

There are certain instances where Windows RE will automatically try to repair the system:

- Two successive failed attempts to start Windows

- Two successive unexpected shutdowns that occur within two minutes of boot completion

- A Secure Boot error (except for issues related to `Bootmgr.efi`)

- A BitLocker error on touch-only devices

Configure Site-Level Fault Tolerance

Disaster recovery is a key piece of maintaining a solid corporate infrastructure. Companies will rely heavily on the ability to configure fault tolerance, redundancy, and replication within the environment to ensure production uptime across the organization. Windows Server 2012 R2 has quite a few new features to help administrators accomplish these tasks in a failover clustered environment.

Hyper-V in Windows Server 2012 R2 gives you the power you need to be truly fault tolerant. Using the Hyper-V Replica feature, you can keep entire replicated copies of your virtual machines readily available to keep your production environment online when virtual machines fail. The nice thing about the replica VM is that it doesn't share storage with the primary VM like you are used to seeing with a traditional failover cluster. The replica starts off with a full cloned copy of the primary VM's virtual hard disk and then updates itself automatically through replication frequency from the primary VM. These automatic updates are configurable to occur anywhere from 30 seconds to 15 minutes.

To set up a Hyper-V replica properly, you must first configure the server-level replication settings for both physical Hyper-V hosts that will make up this failover configuration. One host will act as the primary, and the other will serve as the replica. You must enable replication on the replica host before you can replicate VMs from the primary host. These configuration settings are found in the Hyper-V Manager settings navigation pane under Replication Configuration. Check the box Enable This Computer As A Replica Server and then make your authentication, port, and storage selections, as shown in Figure 19.7. The authentication, port, and storage selections must be configured on both physical Hyper-V hosts.

FIGURE 19.7: Hyper-V settings

Once the Hyper-V hosts have been configured, you can enable replication on the VMs running on the primary Hyper-V host. Simply right-click a virtual machine running on the primary host and select the new Enable Replication option to start the Enable

Replication Wizard. Once you are finished configuring failover settings using the wizard, that VM is now considered to be fault tolerant between your two physical Hyper-V hosts. You should initiate a test failover action by launching the Hyper-V Manager on the replica host, right-clicking a replica VM, clicking Replication, and then clicking Test Failover. Testing failover is the only way you know for sure that your configuration settings are correct.

In addition to having the ability to create Hyper-V replicas, Windows Server 2012 R2 also has the ability to perform Hyper-V Extended Replication. Hyper-V Extended Replication is a new feature that allows administrators to extend the replication boundaries from the primary and replica hosts to an actual third site location. For example, you have a Hyper-V primary host in Denver replicating to a Hyper-V replica host in Tampa. Using Hyper-V Extended Replication, you can configure the Tampa replica host to replicate to a third Hyper-V host located at your London office. This feature gives you an added level of fault tolerance within your environment.

The component that manages how the cluster databases are updated within a failover cluster environment is known as the *Global Update Manager*. Whenever the state of the cluster changes, such as when a node goes down or offline, all of the other nodes in the cluster must acknowledge the change before those changes can be written to the cluster database. The Global Update Manager has three configurable settings available to you through Windows PowerShell using the following command:

```
(Get-Cluster).DatabaseReadWriteMode
```

The three configurable Global Update Manager settings are as follows:

0 = All (Write) And Local (Read)   This is the default setting in Windows Server 2012 R2 for all cluster workloads except Hyper-V. It requires that all of the cluster nodes acknowledge the update before the change is committed to the database. Database reads occur on the local node.

1 = Majority (Read And Write)   This is the default setting for Windows Server 2012 R2 Hyper-V failover clusters. It requires that only a majority of nodes acknowledge the update before the change is committed to the database. Database read involves comparing the most recent timestamp from the majority of available nodes and using the most recent data.

2 = Majority (Write) And Local (Read)   This mode also requires that the majority of the cluster nodes acknowledge the update before committing the change to the database. The difference is that database read occurs on the local node, which means the data may be stale.

Microsoft recommends that you use mode 0 only when you have a requirement to make sure that the cluster database is consistent between all nodes in the cluster. For example, you would want to use mode 0 only when using availability groups in a Microsoft Exchange Server 2013 or Microsoft SQL Server 2012 environment to ensure that all of the cluster nodes acknowledge the change before the update is committed to the database. You cannot afford mismatched or stale data within a SQL or Exchange failover clustered environment. Having this situation could result in serious performance issues within the cluster.

Using the Startup Repair Tool

If your Windows Server 2012 R2 computer will not boot because of missing or corrupted system files, you can use the *Startup Repair tool* to correct these problems. Startup Repair cannot repair hardware failures. Additionally, Startup Repair cannot recover personal files that have been corrupted, damaged by viruses, or deleted. To ensure that you can recover your personal files, you should use the Backup utility previously discussed in this chapter.

To use the Startup Repair tool, follow these steps:

1. Boot your computer using the Windows Server 2012 R2 media.

2. When the Install Windows dialog box appears, select the language, the time and currency format, and the keyboard or input method. Click Next to continue.

3. The Install Now button appears in the center of the screen. Click Repair Your Computer in the lower-left corner.

4. Select the operating system to recover and click Next. If you do not see your operating system, you might need to load your hard disk drivers by clicking the Load Drivers button.

5. The System Recovery Options dialog box appears. You can choose one of the following options:

   - Startup Repair
   - System Restore
   - Windows Complete PC Restore
   - Windows Memory Diagnostic Tool
   - Command Prompt
   - Choose Startup Repair to continue.

6. Startup Repair checks your computer for problems and attempts to repair them. After Startup Repair has finished, click Shut Down or Restart.

If you were not provided the Windows Server 2012 R2 media when you purchased your computer, the computer manufacturer might have placed the files on a recovery partition—or they might have replaced the Startup Repair tool with one of their own. Check with the manufacturer for more information.

If Startup Repair is unable to correct the problem, you might have to reinstall Windows Server 2012 R2. This should be done as a last resort. This is a reason why you should always back up your Windows Server 2012 R2 machine.

Summary

In this chapter, you learned about the different ways to recover and protect your Windows Server 2012 R2 machine from hardware and software issues. I discussed using the Advanced Boot Options, such as Last Known Good Configuration, Safe Mode, debugging mode, and VGA mode. You can use these Advanced Boot Options for troubleshooting multiple software and hardware related issues within your environment.

Other important items that need to be completed on a Windows Server 2012 R2 machine are backups and restores. Backing up a Windows Server 2012 R2 machine protects it in the event of a hardware or software failure. Don't find yourself caught in the situation where a machine fails, and you don't have a fresh backup copy to restore data from. Take the time to back up all of the data that you care about.

Another way to protect data is by the use of shadow copies. Shadow copies allow you to keep previous versions of data and revert to that previous version in the event of a problem. Shadow copies are very convenient when you need to restore a file quickly.

Exam Essentials

Understand the various backup types available with the Windows Server 2012 R2 Backup utility. The Windows Server 2012 R2 Backup utility can perform full and incremental backup operations. Some third-party backup utilities also support differential and daily backups. You can use each of these operations as part of an efficient backup strategy.

Know how to back up Active Directory. The data within the Active Directory database on a domain controller is part of the system state data. You can back up the system state data to a file using the Windows Server 2012 R2 Backup utility.

Know how to restore Active Directory. Restoring the Active Directory database is considerably different from other restore operations. To restore some or the entire Active Directory database, you must first boot the machine into Directory Services Restore mode.

Understand the importance of an authoritative restore process. You use an authoritative restore when you want to restore earlier information from an Active Directory backup and you want the older information to be propagated to other domain controllers in the environment.

Understand offline maintenance using ntdsutil. The ntdsutil command-line tool is a primary method by which system administrators perform offline maintenance. Understand how to launch this tool by entering **ntdsutil** at a command prompt.

Review Questions

1. You need to ensure that you can recover your Windows Server 2012 R2 configuration and data if the computer's hard disk fails. What should you do?

   A. Create a complete PC Backup.

   B. Create a backup of all file categories.

   C. Perform an automated system recovery (ASR) backup.

   D. Create a system restore point.

2. After you update multiple drivers on your Windows Server 2012 R2 machine, the machine hangs at the logon screen, and you can't log into the machine. You need to get this computer up and running as quickly as possible. Which of the following repair strategies should you try first to correct your problem?

   A. Restore your computer's configuration with your last backup.

   B. Boot your computer with the Safe Mode option.

   C. Boot your computer with the Last Known Good Configuration option.

   D. Boot your computer to the recovery console and manually copy the old driver back to the computer.

3. You are the system administrator for a large organization that uses Windows Server 2012 R2 and Windows 8. You have a Windows 8 machine that needs to be configured with a normal backup schedule to restore sensitive data in the event of a catastrophic failure. At a worst case interval, you need to be able to perform a full restore from within the last 24 hours of a failure. What type of backup should you schedule?

   A. Normal

   B. Differential

   C. Incremental

   D. Daily

4. You are the network administrator for a small company. You manage the computers for the Marketing department, all of which are running the Windows Server 2012 R2 operating system. You are making several configuration changes to the manager's computer to enhance performance. Before you make any changes, you want to create a restore point that can be used if any problems arise. How do you manually create a restore point?

   A. By using the System Restore utility

   B. By using the Shadow Copies tab of the System Properties dialog box

   C. By using the System Configuration utility

   D. By using the Startup Repair tool

5. Your computer uses a SCSI adapter that supports a SCSI drive, which contains your Windows 8 system and boot partitions. After updating the SCSI driver, you restart your computer, but Windows 8 will not load. You need to get this computer up and running as quickly as possible. Which of the following repair strategies should you try first to correct your problem?

    A. Restore your computer's configuration with your last backup.

    B. Boot your computer with the Last Known Good Configuration.

    C. Boot your computer with the Safe Mode option.

    D. Boot your computer to the recovery console and manually copy the old driver back to the computer.

6. You enable the Boot Logging option on the Advanced Boot Options menu. Where can you find the log file that is created?

    A. `\Windows\netlog.txt`

    B. `\Windows\System32\netlog.txt`

    C. `\Windows\ntbtlog.txt`

    D. `\Windows\System32\netboot.log`

7. After you updated Will's computer, his system files became corrupted because of a virus and now need to be restored. Which of the following processes should you use to fix the problem?

    A. Restore a backup.

    B. Restore an image.

    C. Use the Startup Repair tool.

    D. Boot to Safe Mode.

8. You are unable to boot your Windows Server 2012 R2 computer, so you decide to boot the computer to Safe Mode. Which of the following statements regarding Safe Mode is false?

    A. When the computer is booted to Safe Mode, there is no network access.

    B. Safe Mode loads all of the drivers for the hardware that is installed on the computer.

    C. When you run Safe Mode, boot logging is automatically enabled.

    D. When you run Safe Mode, the screen resolution is set to 800×600.

9. You need to back up the existing data on a computer before you install a new application. You also need to ensure that you are able to recover individual user files that are replaced or deleted during the installation. What should you do?

    A. Create a System Restore point.

    B. Perform an automated system recovery (ASR) backup and restore.

    C. In the Windows Server Backup utility, click the Backup Once link.

    D. In the Backup And Restore Center window, click the Back Up Computer button.

10. Your data recovery strategy must meet the following requirements:

- Back up all data files and folders in C:\Data.
- Restore individual files and folders in C:\Data.
- Ensure that data is backed up to and restored from external media.

What should you do?

A. Use the Previous Versions feature to restore the files and folders.

B. Use the System Restore feature to perform backup and restore operations.

C. Use the NTBackup utility to back up and restore individual files and folders.

D. Use the Windows Server Backup to back up and restore files.

Chapter

20

Configure Advanced Network Services

THE FOLLOWING 70-412 EXAM OBJECTIVES ARE COVERED IN THIS CHAPTER:

✓ **Implement an advanced Dynamic Host Configuration Protocol (DHCP) solution**

- Create and configure superscopes and multicast scopes
- Implement DHCPv6
- Configure high availability for DHCP including DHCP failover and split scopes
- Configure DHCP Name Protection
- Configure DNS registration

✓ **Implement an advanced DNS solution**

- Configure security for DNS including DNSSEC, DNS Socket Pool, and cache locking
- Configure DNS logging
- Configure delegated administration
- Configure recursion
- Configure netmask ordering
- Configure a GlobalNames zone
- Analyze zone level statistics

✓ **Deploy and manage IPAM**

- Provision IPAM manually or by using Group Policy
- Configure server discovery

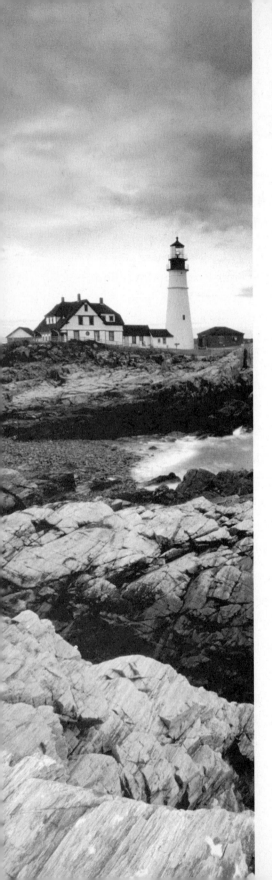

- Create and manage IP blocks and ranges
- Monitor utilization of IP address space
- Migrate to IPAM
- Delegate IPAM administration
- Manage IPAM collections
- Configure IPAM database storage

In this chapter, you will take a deep dive into configuring network services using the new features and functionality provided by Windows Server 2012 R2. You should be familiar with the basics of both DNS and DHCP from Chapter 2, "Configure Network Services." Unlike the 70-410 exam, the 70-412 exam will require that you have the skills and knowledge to configure advanced network configurations beyond just their initial installations and setup.

This chapter will discuss and demonstrate some of the most common advanced network configuration options that you will see both on the exam and in the field. Once you have completed this chapter, you will have a better understanding of how to configure advanced network services surrounding DHCP, DNS, and IPAM in a Windows Server 2012 R2 environment.

Working with Advanced DHCP Configuration Options

DHCP makes the life of an administrator easy when it comes to managing the IP addresses of devices within an organization. Could you imagine having to keep track of each device and that device's IP manually? With Windows Server 2012 R2's DHCP high availability and load balancing options available, life gets even easier. The next few sections will cover how to implement advanced DHCP solutions in detail.

Create and Configure Superscopes

A *superscope* enables the DHCP server to provide addresses from more than one scope to clients on the same physical subnet. This is helpful when clients within the same subnet have more than one IP network and thus need IPs from more than one address pool. Microsoft's DHCP Management Console allows you to manage IP address assignment in the superscope, though you must still configure other scope options individually for each child scope. In Exercise 20.1 you will configure a superscope from two preexisting scopes.

Remember that only one superscope can exist per server and that a super-scope requires at least two preconfigured scopes.

EXERCISE 20.1

Creating a Superscope

1. Open the DHCP Management Console.

2. Right-click IPv4 and choose the New Superscope command to launch the New Superscope Wizard. Click Next.

3. On the Superscope Name page, name your superscope and click the Next button.

4. The Select Scopes page appears, listing all scopes on the current server. Select the two scopes you want to use for a superscope and then click the Next button.

5. The wizard's summary page appears. Click the Finish button to create your scope.

6. Verify that your new superscope appears in the DHCP Management Console to complete this exercise.

Deleting a Superscope

You can delete a superscope by right-clicking it and choosing the Delete command. A superscope is just an administrative convenience, so you can safely delete one at any time—it doesn't affect the "real" scopes that make up the superscope.

Adding a Scope to a Superscope

To add a scope to an existing superscope, find the scope you want to add, right-click it, and choose Action ➢ Add To Superscope. A dialog box appears, listing all of the superscopes known to this server. Pick the one to which you want the current scope appended and click the OK button.

Removing a Scope from a Superscope

To remove a scope from a superscope, open the superscope and right-click the target scope. The pop-up menu provides a Remove From Superscope command that will do the deed.

Activating and Deactivating Superscopes

Just as with regular scopes, you can activate and deactivate superscopes. The same restrictions and guidelines apply. You must activate a superscope before it can be used, and you must not deactivate it until you want all of your clients to lose their existing leases and be forced to request new ones.

To activate or deactivate a superscope, right-click the superscope name and select Activate or Deactivate, respectively, from the pop-up menu.

Create and Configure Multicast Scopes

Multicasting occurs when one machine communicates to a network of subscribed computers rather than specifically addressing each computer on the destination network.

It's much more efficient to *multicast* a video or audio stream to multiple destinations than it is to unicast it to the same number of clients, and the increased demand for multicast-friendly network hardware has resulted in some head scratching about how to automate the multicast configuration.

In the following sections, you will learn about MADCAP, the protocol that controls multicasting, and about how to build and configure a multicast scope.

Understanding the Multicast Address Dynamic Client Allocation Protocol

DHCP is usually used to assign IP configuration information for *unicast* (or one-to-one) network communications. With multicast, there's a separate type of address space assigned from 224.0.0.0 through 239.255.255.255. Addresses in this space are known as *Class D addresses*, or simply *multicast addresses*. Clients can participate in a multicast just by knowing (and using) the multicast address for the content they want to receive. However, multicast clients also need to have an ordinary IP address.

How do clients know what address to use? Ordinary DHCP won't help because it's designed to assign IP addresses and option information to one client at a time. Realizing this, the Internet Engineering Task Force (IETF) defined a new protocol: *Multicast Address Dynamic Client Allocation Protocol (MADCAP)*. MADCAP provides an analog to DHCP but for multicast use. A MADCAP server issues leases for multicast addresses only. MADCAP clients can request a multicast lease when they want to participate in a multicast.

DHCP and MADCAP have some important differences. First you have to realize that the two are totally separate. A single server can be a DHCP server, a MADCAP server, or both; no implied or actual relation exists between the two. Likewise, clients can use DHCP and/or MADCAP at the same time—the only requirement is that every MADCAP client has to get a unicast IP address from somewhere.

Remember that DHCP can assign options as part of the lease process, but MADCAP cannot. The only thing MADCAP does is to assign multicast addresses dynamically.

Building Multicast Scopes

Building a multicast scope is similar to building a unicast scope, but it requires a few different configuration settings when going through the wizard. Exercise 20.2 walks you through creating and activating a new multicast scope.

EXERCISE 20.2

Creating and Activating a New Multicast Scope

1. Open the DHCP Management Console.

2. Right-click IPv4 and choose New Multicast Scope to launch the New Multicast Scope Wizard. Click the Next button on the welcome page.

3. On the Multicast Scope Name page, provide a name and description for your multicast scope. Click Next.

4. The IP Address Range page appears. Enter a start IP address of **224.0.0.0** and an end IP address of **224.255.0.0**. Adjust the TTL to 1 to make sure no multicast packets escape your local network segment. Click Next.

5. On the Add Exclusions page of the wizard, add any IP Exclusions or leave this page blank. Click Next.

6. Keep the defaults on the Lease Duration page. Click Next.

7. Ensure the Activate Scope Now radio button is toggled to Yes. Click Finish to complete the creation and activation of your new multicast scope.

8. Verify that your new multicast scope appears in the DHCP Management Console to complete this exercise.

Setting Multicast Scope Properties

Once you create a multicast scope, you can adjust its properties by right-clicking the scope name and selecting Properties.

The Multicast Scope Properties dialog box has two tabs. The General tab (see Figure 20.1) allows you to change the scope's name, its start and end addresses, its Time To Live (TTL) value, its lease duration, and its description—in essence, all of the settings you provided when you created it in the first place.

FIGURE 20.1   General tab of the Multicast Scope Properties dialog box

The Lifetime tab (see Figure 20.2) allows you to limit how long your multicast scope will be active. By default, a newly created multicast scope will live forever, but if you're creating a scope to provide MADCAP assignments for a single event (or a set of events of limited duration), you can specify an expiration time for the scope. When that time is reached, the scope disappears from the server but not before making all of its clients give up their multicast address leases. This is a nice way to make sure the lease cleans up after itself when you're finished with it.

FIGURE 20.2   Lifetime tab of the Multicast Scope Properties dialog box

Implement DHCPv6

In Windows Server 2012 R2, administrators can create and manage both IPv4 and IPv6 DHCP scopes for their organization. Even though they are managed separately, they have the same capabilities of being able to configure reservations, exclusions, and other DHCP options. Unlike an IPv4 client, a DHCPv6 client uses a device unique identifier (DUID) instead of a MAC address to get an IP address from the DHCP server.

DHCPv6 supports both stateful address configuration and stateless address configuration. An easy way to think of the difference between a stateful configuration and a stateless configuration is that, with a stateful configuration, the DHCPv6 client receives its IPv6 address and its additional DHCP options from the DHCPv6 server. With a stateless configuration, the IPv6 client can automatically assign itself an IPv6 address without ever having to communicate with the DHCPv6 server. The stateless configuration process is also known as *DHCPv6 autoconfiguration*. Exercise 20.3 will walk you through the process of creating and activating a new DHCPv6 scope.

EXERCISE 20.3

Creating and Activating a New DHCPv6 Scope

1. Open the DHCP Management Console.

2. Right-click IPv6 and choose the New Scope command. The New Scope Wizard appears. Click the Next button.

3. On the Welcome to the New Scope Wizard page, click the Next button.

4. On the Scope Name page, provide a name and description for your new DHCPv6 scope. Click the Next button.

5. On the Scope Prefix page, input the corresponding prefix for your organization's IPv6 network settings. In the event that you have more than one DHCPv6 server, you can set a preference value that will indicate your server priority. The lower the preference value, the higher the server priority. Click Next.

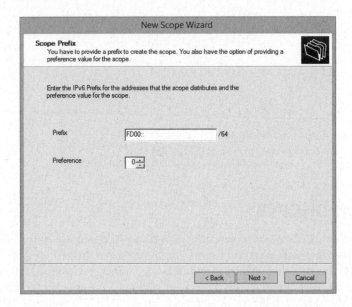

6. On the Add Exclusions page of the wizard, you can configure either a single IP exclusion or a range of IPs to exclude from obtaining an address automatically. Exclusions should include any device or range of devices that have been manually set with a static IP on that particular scope. Click Next.

7. Keep the default selections on the Scope Lease page. Click Next.

8. Make sure the Activate Scope Now radio button is toggled to Yes. Click Finish to complete the creation and activation of your new DHCPv6 scope.

9. Verify that your new scope appears in the DHCP Management Console to complete this exercise.

Configure High Availability for DHCP Including DHCP Failover and Split Scopes

DHCP failover provides load balancing and redundancy for DHCP services, enabling administrators to deploy a highly resilient DHCP service for their organization. The idea is to share your DHCP IPV4 scopes between two Windows Server 2012 R2 servers so that if one of the failover partners goes down, then the other failover partner will continue providing DHCP services throughout the environment. DHCP failover supports large-scale DHCP deployments without the challenges of a split-scope DHCP environment.

Here are a few of the benefits that DHCP failover provides:

Multisite   DHCP failover supports a deployment architecture that includes multiple sites. DHCP failover partner servers do not need to be located at the same physical site.

Flexibility   DHCP failover can be configured to provide redundancy in hot standby mode; or, with load balancing mode, client requests can be distributed between two DHCP servers.

Seamless   DHCP servers share lease information, allowing one server to assume the responsibility for servicing clients if the other server is unavailable. DHCP clients can keep the same IP address when a lease is renewed, even if a different DHCP server issues the lease.

Simplicity   A wizard is provided to create DHCP failover relationships between DHCP servers. The wizard automatically replicates scopes and settings from the primary server to the failover partner.

Configuring DHCP Failover

One of the nice things about DHCP failover is that the configured scope is replicated between both clustered DHCP nodes whether or not you are running the cluster in hot standby or load balancing mode. If one server fails, the other can manage the entire pool of IP addresses on behalf of the environment. Exercise 20.4 provides step-by-step DHCP failover configuration in Windows Server 2012 R2.

EXERCISE 20.4

Configuring DHCP Failover

1. Open the DHCP Management Console.

2. Right-click IPv4 and choose the Configure Failover command to launch the Configure Failover Wizard. Click Next on the Introduction page.

3. On the Specify The Partner Server To Use For Failover page, select your partner DHCP server from the drop-down menu or by browsing the Add Server directory. Click Next.

4. On the Create A New Failover Relationship page, provide a relationship name, select the Load Balance mode from the drop-down, and provide a shared secret password that will be used to authenticate the DHCP failover relationship between the two servers in the failover cluster. Click Next.

5. Review your configuration settings and click the Finish button to configure your new DHCP failover configuration. Click Close upon successful completion.

6. After the wizard successfully completes on the primary DHCP server, verify that the new failover scope has been created and activated on the secondary DHCP server in the DHCP Management Console to complete this exercise.

You can always go back in and change the properties of the failover scope if you want. Test both hot standby and load balancing modes to decide which deployment configuration option best suits your organization's needs. Expect to see exam scenarios discussing both DHCP failover configuration modes and the differences between them.

DHCP Split Scopes

Even though you have the capabilities of DHCP failover in Windows Server 2012 R2, for exam purposes you will need to understand how DHCP split scopes work. Split scopes are configurable only on IPv4 IP addresses and cannot be configured on IPv6 scopes. The idea of DHCP split scopes is to have two stand-alone DHCP servers that are individually responsible for only a percentage of the IP addresses on a particular subnet.

For example, DHCP Server 1 would be responsible for 70 percent of the IP addresses, and DHCP Server 2 would be responsible for the other 30 percent of IP addresses. The two DHCP servers in a split-scope configuration do not share any lease information between one another, and they do not take over for one another in the event that one of the two DHCP servers fail. As you can see, a split-scope configuration is less fault tolerant than a full DHCP failover configuration. However, a split scope configuration does split the load of DHCP leases and renewals between two servers providing a basic level of native load balancing in a Windows Server 2012 R2 environment.

DHCP Allow and Deny Filtering

One of the nice things about DHCP is that administrators can use allow or deny filtering to control which devices get an IP address and which devices do not on your network. DHCP filtering is controlled by recording a client's MAC address in a list and then enabling either the Allow or Deny filter. One thing to keep in mind about DHCP filtering is that by enabling the allow list, you automatically deny DHCP addresses to any client computer not on the list. In Exercise 20.5, you will configure DHCP filtering by adding a client machine to the Deny filter by MAC address.

EXERCISE 20.5

Configuring DHCP Filtering

1. Open the DHCP Management Console.

2. Expand IPv4 until you reach the Deny filter object in your DHCP hierarchy.

3. Right-click the Deny filter object and select New Filter.

4. Enter the MAC address of the device you want to exclude from your network, provide a description such as **Unwanted Device**, click Add, and then click Close.

5. Right-click the Deny filter and select Enable to complete this exercise.

One of the good things about these filters is that you can move devices from one filter to the other quite easily at any time by right-clicking the device in the list and selecting either Move To Allow or Move To Deny. Test both Allow and Deny filters thoroughly while preparing for the exam. You will most likely see multiple scenarios surrounding DHCP filtering.

Configure DHCP Name Protection

DHCP name protection is an additional configuration option that administrators should consider when working DHCP within their environment. Name protection protects a DHCP leased machine's name from being overwritten by another machine with the same name during DNS dynamic updates so that you can configure a Windows 2012 R2 DHCP server to verify and update the DNS records of a client machine during the lease renewal process. If the DHCP server detects that a machine's DNS A and PTR records already exist in the environment when a DHCP update occurs, then that DHCP update will fail on that client machine, making sure not to overwrite the existing server name. There are just a few simple steps needed in order to configure DHCP name protection. Exercise 20.6 will walk you through these steps.

EXERCISE 20.6

Enabling DHCP Name Protection

1. Open the DHCP Management Console.

2. Right-click IPv4 and select Properties.

3. The Server Properties dialog box appears. Click the DNS tab.

4. Verify that Enable DNS Dynamic Updates According To The Settings Below is checked, and verify that the radio button labeled Dynamically Update DNS A And PTR Records Only If Requested By The DHCP Clients is selected.

5. Verify that Discard A And PTR Records When Lease Is Deleted is checked. If not, then check it.

6. Click Configure under Name Protection, and select Enable Name Protection.

7. Click OK twice to complete this exercise.

Configure DNS Registration

Another great feature of Windows Server 2012 R2 DHCP server is the ability to perform registration of DNS records with the DNS server on behalf of its clients. The DHCP server has the flexibility to register DNS clients based on Host A records only instead of being forced to use PTR records during DNS registration. This functionality reduces the number of registration failures that are directly due to the absence of suitable reverse and forward lookup zones on the DNS server.

In addition, you can now also create a DHCP policy that will register only certain clients that match a specific DNS suffix. Together, these new Windows Server 2012 R2 features further integrate DNS and DHCP so that administrators have cleaner control over how clients are registered on their networks. Exercise 20.7 will demonstrate disabling dynamic updates for DNS PTR records in DHCP.

EXERCISE 20.7

Disabling Dynamic Updates

1. Open the DHCP Management Console.

2. Right-click IPv4 and select Properties.

3. Navigate to the DNS tab.

4. Check the box Disable Dynamic Updates For DNS PTR Records.

5. Click Apply and OK to complete this exercise.

All of the new DHCP features provided to you by Windows Server 2012 R2 are worth examining. DHCP failover is a big win for administrators. I'm quite sure that many Windows customers will be changing their DHCP infrastructure from split scopes to a load balanced or hot standby configuration in the near future.

The Ins and Outs of DNS

You learned quite a bit about DNS in Chapter 2. This chapter will expand on what you have already learned over the course of the next few sections. It will focus on hardening your environment with DNS security options, DNS logging and analysis, and a few other advanced configuration options that you will most likely see on the 70-412 exam. DNS is a core network service about which every administrator should have a full understanding. Make it a point to be able to complete each lab from memory to prepare fully for your test.

DNS Security

Security is a main focal point for almost every organization. Since DNS is a core network service that has its hands in every piece of your infrastructure, it is extremely important that you take the time to make sure this environment's DNS is as secure as possible. Let's take a look at few major configuration options for securing DNS on your network.

DNSSEC

Domain Name System Security Extensions (DNSSEC) is a suite of extensions that add security to the Domain Name System (DNS) protocol by enabling DNS responses to be validated. DNSSEC works by securing a DNS zone with a process called *zone signing*. When a client machine queries a record in a zone that is signed by DNSSEC, the DNS server returns both the record and the record's digital signature. When you sign a DNS zone using DNSSEC, the following new resource records become available within the environment:

Resource Record Signature (RRSIG) Record   This is the additional record that is returned to a client for validity upon a DNS query. This record is stored in the DNSSEC signed zone.

Next Secure (NSEC/NSEC3) Record   This record provides proof that a queried record does not exist in the zone. If a client queries a nonexistent record, then the DNS server returns a NSEC record.

DNSKEY   This record is used for cryptographic verification of the RRSIG records.

DNSSEC is usually used in high-security environments. The main security advantage of DNSSEC is that it prevents attacks where clients on your network are fed false DNS information. In addition to the new resource records, when you deploy DNSSEC, the following cryptographic keys are created within the environment:

Zone Signing Key (ZSK)   This cryptographic key is used to sign individual host records within a DNSSEC-implemented DNS zone.

Key Signing Key (KSK)   This cryptographic key is used to sign all DNSKEY records.

Trust Anchor   This cryptographic key is used to validate the DNSKEY record in a DNSSEC protected zone. The trust anchor is replicated to all domain controllers in the forest when you deploy DNSSEC with an Active Directory Integrated zone.

Together, these records and keys provide administrators with enhanced security on their DNS networks. The first DNS server within your environment that you implement with DNSSEC is referred to as the *DNSSEC key master*. It's the key master's job to generate and manage the keys that are signed within a DNSSEC protected zone. Using Group Policy, administrators can set client rules that will ensure that those clients will accept records only from a DNSSEC protected zone. In Exercise 20.8, you will use DNSSEC to sign a zone.

EXERCISE 20.8

Configuring DNSSEC

1.   Open DNS Manager.

2.   Right-click a forward lookup zone, scroll down to DNSSEC, and click Sign The Zone to launch the Zone Signing Wizard.

3.   On the DNS Security Extensions (DNSSEC) page, click Next.

4.   On the Signing Options page, select Use Default Settings To Sign The Zone and click Next.

5. On the DNS Security Extensions (DNSSEC) page, click Next.

6. On the Signing the Zone page, click Finish.

7. Verify that the new DNSSEC records and keys have been generated in the zone to complete this exercise.

DNS Socket Pool

DNS socket pooling is another great security technology that helps reduce cache-tampering and spoofing attacks by randomizing which source port is used when issuing DNS queries to remote DNS servers. Port randomization makes it difficult for an attacker to spoof the DNS server with an invalid record. By default, Windows Server 2012 R2 uses a socket pool of 2,500. The maximum configuration is 10,000. Administrators can use the dnscmd command-line utility to adjust the DNS socket pool size within their environment. The following is an example of expanding the pool to 5,000 via the command line. Make sure to restart the DNS service after making a change.

```
dnscmd /config /socketpoolsize 5000
```

DNS Cache Locking

DNS cache locking allows an administrator to control when the information stored in the DNS server's cache can be overwritten. When a DNS record is queried, that query is cached by the DNS server based on that record's Time To Live settings. If that same record is queried again before the TTL has expired, the cached information on the DNS server is overwritten. If DNS cache locking is enabled, the DNS server will not overwrite the cached information on new queries of the same record. The feature protects DNS from cache poisoning attacks.

DNS cache locking is configured as a percent value. For example, let's say you configure DNS cache locking at a defined value of 80 percent. This means the DNS server will not overwrite a record's cached information for 80 percent of the duration of that record's TTL. Just like DNS socket pools, DNS cache locking can be configured using the dnscmd command-line utility. By default, DNS cache locking is set to 100 percent. The following is an example of changing the default DNS cache locking percentage to 80 percent via the command line. Make sure and restart the DNS service after making a change.

```
dnscmd /config /cachelockingpercent 80
```

Having all of these additional DNS security tools at your disposal will greatly assist you in hardening your environment and making your network more secure overall.

Configure DNS Logging

Since DNS is such a crucial piece of every organization's infrastructure, it has a dedicated event log that tracks all of the actions that are completed by the DNS Server service, as shown in Figure 20.3. By default, in Windows Server 2012 R2, the DNS Server event logs automatically track audit events correlated to the DNS Server service. An audit event is logged each time DNS settings are changed. A few examples of audit events include zone transfers, zone signing, and dynamic updates.

Windows Server 2012 R2 comes with a new set of enhanced DNS Logging and Diagnostic Tools that provide administrators with Analytical and Debug logs in addition to the Audit logs enabled already. Analytical and Debug logs enable activity tracking that logs an event every time the DNS server sends or receives information. A few examples of Analytical log events include response success, response failure, and internal lookup CNAME.

To take full advantage of these additional tools, you must first install a Windows hotfix that will add change auditing and query logging to your DNS server. Analytical and Debug logs are not enabled by default. You can download and install the hotfix from the following location: http://support.microsoft.com/kb/2956577.

Once you have successfully installed the Windows hotfix, you can enable Analytical and Debug logs in the Window Event Viewer. Exercise 20.9 will demonstrate the process on enabling these additional DNS logs.

FIGURE 20.3 DNS Server Event Viewer log

EXERCISE 20.9

Enabling DNS Diagnostic Logging

1. Open Event Viewer.

2. Navigate to Applications And Services Logs ➢ Microsoft ➢ Windows ➢ DNS-Server.

3. Right-click and change your view to Show Analytic And Debug Logs. The Analytical log will be displayed.

4. Right-click the Analytical log and select Properties.

5. On the Log Properties page, select the Do Not Overwrite Events radio button, check the box to enable logging, and then click Apply.

EXERCISE 20.9 *(continued)*

6. Click OK to close log properties. You should now see detailed DNS Analytical events populate in the log.

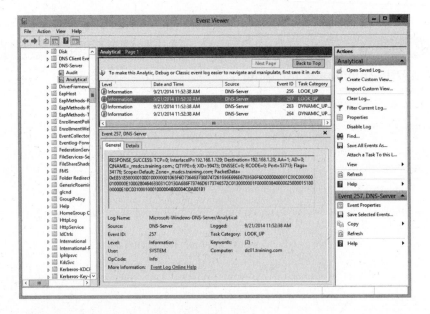

7. Close the Event Viewer to complete this exercise.

DNS logging is a great way to manage and troubleshoot what DNS is doing on your network. Administrators can easily isolate and fix most DNS related issues by checking the event logs. It's even easier when you have the enhanced DNS diagnostic tools enabled.

Configure Delegated Administration

As you are well aware, DNS is highly integrated with Active Directory Domain Services (ADDS). Since the relationship between these two technologies is so close, Active Directory has a built-in security group called DNS Admins to help delegate DNS administration within an environment without having to expose full Domain Admins level privileges to a user account. An administrator would use this security group to separate roles and responsibilities between users.

For example, let's say you have an administrator who is required to manage DNS records, but it is not their responsibility to manage user accounts. Instead of just throwing that administrator in the Domain Admins security group and granting them permissions they don't need, place that administrator's user account in the DNSAdmins security group. This will ensure that you are managing environmental permissions properly, and it will eliminate the possibility of that administrator making changes to things not within their responsibility. You can then use the DNSAdmins group to restrict/allow access to DNS servers on your network just like any other security group.

Configure Recursion

DNS recursion is automatically configured by default in Windows Server 21012 R2. When a client asks a DNS server for a record that isn't stored in a zone that is hosted by that particular DNS server, the DNS server performs a recursive query by going out and finding the result of that query and passing it back to the client if it can be found. This is a nice service for the DNS server to perform, but unfortunately it leaves your network open to denial-of-service (DoS) attacks. In a DoS attack, false or invalid record requests are repeatedly sent to the DNS server, causing it to become increasingly slowed down and even crash completely if it gets too overburdened by requests. To avoid such attacks, it is recommended that DNS recursion be turned off. Exercise 20.10 will walk you through disabling DNS recursion on a DNS server.

EXERCISE 20.10

Disabling DNS Recursion

1.   Open DNS Manager.

2.   Right-click a DNS server of your choice and click Properties.

3.   Navigate to the Advanced tab of the Properties window.

4.   Check the box to disable recursion.

EXERCISE 20.10 *(continued)*

5. Click Apply and OK to complete this exercise.

Configure Netmask Ordering

Netmask ordering is another DNS feature that comes automatically enabled by default on Windows Server 2012 R2. Basically, this feature makes sure that if a client requests a host record from the DNS server, the DNS server will always return a host record from that client's subnet if one lives there. The DNS server will examine the first three octets of the client's IP address against the record request, assuming that the closest available response would come from that client's subnet.

DNS uses a round-robin rotation to load balance traffic between multiple server IP addresses that happen to share a single DNS name. For example, you have a hostname of www.stellacon.com that maps to three different servers across multiple subnets to help load-balance requests and improve performance within your environment. The IP addresses to each server are as follows:

172.100.10.10

172.100.20.10

172.100.30.10

A client machine with an IP of 172.100.10.150 submits a record request to the DNS server for a lookup on www.stellacon.com. Because of netmask ordering, the DNS server will return the IP of 172.100.10.10 for that client to use. Without netmask ordering enabled, the DNS server could have returned IPs for either of the other two servers, depending on where the next request would fall in this round-robin rotation.

Imagine if the other two servers in the previous example were physically located halfway around the world. Your client's connection could be severely degraded compared to the connection you would have on your local subnet. DNS netmask ordering ensures that your clients get the best possible connection available. Verifying that netmask ordering is enabled is done on the same advanced properties page as disabling DNS recursion (shown in Exercise 20.10).

Configure a GlobalNames Zone

A *GlobalNames zone* is a DNS zone in which the host records that live in that zone use short, single-labeled names instead of a fully qualified domain name (FQDN) to communicate on the network. This is similar to the way administrators use Windows Internet Name Service (WINS) as a name resolution protocol alternative to DNS. GlobalName zones are not intended to support peer-to-peer networks and workstation name resolution, and they don't support dynamic DNS updates. In Exercise 20.11, you will configure a DNS GlobalNames zone.

EXERCISE 20.11

Configuring a GlobalNames Zone

1. Open DNS Manager.

2. Right-click one of your DNS servers and click New Zone to start the New Zone Wizard.

3. Click Next on the Welcome page.

4. On the Zone Type page, make sure that Primary Zone and the Store Zone in Active Directory (available only if DNS server is a writeable domain controller) are selected and then click Next.

5. Click To All DNS Servers In This Forest and then click Next.

6. Click Forward Lookup Zone and then click Next.

7. In Zone Name, type **GlobalNames** and then click Next.

8. Click Do Not Allow Dynamic Updates and then click Next.

9. Click Finish to create the GlobalNames zone and complete this exercise.

Analyze Zone-Level Statistics

Windows Server 2012 R2 introduces a set of new features for gathering and analyzing DNS server statistics. Having this level of granularity for DNS statistics is useful for troubleshooting DNS-related issues. Using PowerShell, an administrator can now easily get the following statistics on every authoritative zone within the environment.

Zone Update Statistics   Provides information on zone dynamic update transactions

DynamicUpdateReceived   The total number of dynamic update requests received by the DNS server

DynamicUpdateRejected   The total number of dynamic updates rejected by the DNS server

Zone Query Statistics   Provides the following information

QueriesReceived   The number of queries received

QueriesResponded   The number of queries responded successfully (with a valid DNS response)

QueriesFailure   The number of queries not responded successfully

QueriesNameError   The number of queries that responded with an NXDOMAIN or EMPTY AUTH response

Zone Transfer Statistics   Provides information about the zone transfer transactions

RequestReceived   The total number of zone transfer requests received by the DNS Server service when operating as a primary server for a specific zone

RequestSent   The total number of zone transfer requests sent by the DNS Server service when operating as a secondary server for a specific zone

ResponseReceived   The total number of zone transfer requests received by the DNS Server service when operating as a secondary server for a specific zone

SuccessReceived   The total number of zone transfers received by the DNS Server service when operating as a secondary server for a specific zone

SuccessSent   The total number of zone transfers successfully sent by the DNS Server service when operating as a master server for a specific zone

Use the following PowerShell syntax to analyze and view complete DNS zone-level statistics within your environment:

```
Get-DnsServerStatistics –ZoneName yourdomain.com
```

IPAM Administration 101

One of the great features of Windows Server 2012 R2 is the *IP Address Management (IPAM)* utility. IPAM is a built-in utility that allows an administrator to discover, monitor, audit, and manage the TCP/IP schema used on your network. IPAM provides an administrator with the ability to observe and administer the servers that are running the Dynamic Host Configuration Protocol (DHCP) and the Domain Name System. IPAM includes some of the following advantages:

Automatic IP Address Infrastructure Discovery   IPAM has the ability to discover automatically the domain's DHCP servers, DNS servers, and domain controllers. IPAM can do the discovery for any of the domains you specify. Administrators also have the ability to enable or disable management of these servers using the IPAM utility.

Management of DHCP and DNS Services   IPAM gives administrators the capability to monitor and manage Microsoft DHCP and DNS servers across an entire network using the IPAM console.

Custom IP Address Management   Administrators now have the ability to customize the display of IP addresses and tracking and utilization data. IPAM allows the IP address space to be organized into IP address blocks, IP address ranges, and individual IP addresses. To help you organize the IP address space further, built-in or user-defined fields are also assigned to the IP addresses.

Auditing and Tracking of IP Address   IPAM allows administrators to track and audit IP addresses through the use of the IPAM console. IPAM allows IP addresses to be tracked using DHCP lease events and user logon events. These events are collected from the Network Policy Server (NPS) servers, domain controllers, and DHCP servers. Administrators can track IP data by following the IP address, client ID, hostname, or username.

   As an administrator, you should understand a few things before installing the IPAM feature. When setting up an IPAM server, you must *not* install IPAM on a domain controller. There are three main methods to deploy an IPAM server.

Distributed   This method allows an IPAM server deployment at every site in an enterprise network.

Centralized   This method allows only one IPAM server in an enterprise network.

Hybrid   This method uses a central IPAM server deployment along with dedicated IPAM servers at each site in the enterprise network.

    Remember, when installing IPAM in any of the scenarios mentioned, you cannot install the IPAM feature on an Active Directory domain controller.

Provision IPAM Manually or by Using Group Policy

If configured, IPAM automatically communicates on your domain. IPAM will try to locate your DNS servers, DHCP servers, and domain controllers as long as those servers are within the searching scope that you have configured. An administrator can configure whether the servers (DNS, DHCP, and domain controllers) are managed by IPAM or unmanaged. Please note that this will work only with Microsoft products; it won't find Infoblox or Unix-based DNS/DHCP.

If you want your servers to be managed by IPAM, you must make sure you set up the network and the servers properly. For example, you will need to configure the security settings and firewall ports properly on the servers (DNS, DHCP, and domain controllers) in order to allow IPAM to access these servers and perform its configuration and monitoring. You can configure these server settings in one of two ways: manually or automatically through the use of a Group Policy object (GPO).

Exercise 20.12 will show you how to install the IPAM feature. You will install and configure the IPAM feature using Server Manager. This exercise has to be done on a member server.

EXERCISE 20.12

Installing the IPAM Feature

1. Open Server Manager.

2. Click the number 2 link, Add Roles And Features.

3. Choose a role-based or feature-based installation and click Next.

4. Choose your server and click Next.

5. On the Roles screen, just click Next.

6. On the Features screen, click the box for the IP Address Management (IPAM) server. Click the Add Features button when the box appears. Click Next.

7.   At the Confirmation screen, click the Install button.

8.   Once the installation is complete, click the Close button.

9.   While in Server Manager, click the IPAM link on the left side. This opens the IPAM Overview page.

10. Click number 2, Provision The IPAM Server.

11. Click Next at the Before You Begin screen.

12. Make your database selection on the Configure Database screen and click Next.

13. At the Select Provisioning Method screen, choose GPO and put in a GPO suffix name. I used IPAM1 for the GPO suffix name. This is a unique name to help identify the IPAM.

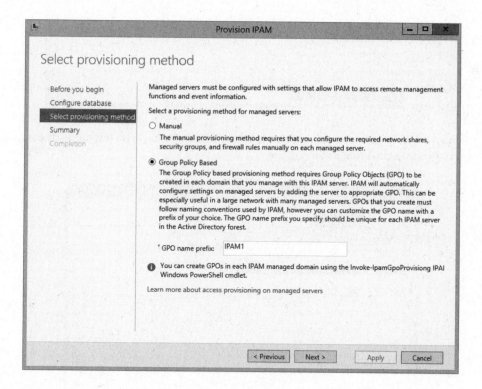

14. At the Summary screen, click the Apply button.

15. Once the process is completed, click the Close button.

16. Under Manage on the IPAM overview screen, choose Add Server.

EXERCISE 20.12 *(continued)*

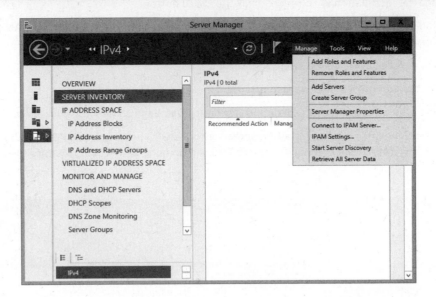

17. In the Add Servers box, click the DNS tab. In the search box, type the name of your DNS server and click the magnifying glass.

18. Under Name, double-click the server name. The server will be added to the right-side box. Click OK. Close Server Manager.

Configure Server Discovery

Once you have successfully installed and provisioned the IPAM feature on your Windows Server 2012 R2 machine, you can begin server discovery. One of the great things about IPAM is that you can define multiple domains within the same forest to be managed by a single IPAM server. Once initiated, server discovery will automatically search for all of the machines running on the specified domain. Administrator privileges are required for the domain against which you are running server discovery. Exercise 20.13 will walk you through the server discovery process.

EXERCISE 20.13

Configuring IPAM Server Discovery

1. Open Server Manager and select IPAM.

2. On the IPAM Overview page, select option 3, Configure Server Discovery.

3. On the Configure Server Discovery page, select and add the domains you want to discover and click OK.

4. On the IPAM Overview page, select option 4, Start Server Discovery. The task will run in the background. You will receive notification once server discovery has completed.

5. On the IPAM home page, select Server Inventory to review the now-completed server discovery of the requested domain. Servers found by server discovery will be in a blocked status until those servers have applied the GPO configured from Exercise 20.12.

Create and Manage IP Blocks and Ranges

In IPAM, IP address space is divided into addresses, ranges, and blocks. Blocks are groups of ranges, and ranges are groups of IPs. Here you will find a breakdown of each IP Management space found within IPAM:

IP Addresses   Individual IP addresses map to a single IP address range. When you map an IP address to a range, it enables actions to be taken on a range that affect all IP addresses in the range, such as adding, updating, or deleting IP address fields.

IP Address Ranges   IP address ranges are smaller chunks of IP addresses that typically correspond to a DHCP scope. IP address ranges are contained within, or "mapped to," IP address blocks. IP address ranges cannot map to multiple IP address blocks, and ranges that map to the same block cannot overlap.

IP Address Blocks   IP address blocks are large chunks of IP addresses that are used to organize address space at a high level. For example, you might use one IP address block for all private IP addresses in your organization and another block for public IP addresses. You can think of IP address blocks as containers that hold IP address ranges. IP address blocks are not deployed and managed on the network like IP address ranges or individual IP addresses.

When you have an IPAM managed DHCP server, the IP address ranges found within the scopes of that DHCP server are automatically entered into the IPAM database during the discovery process. Individual IP addresses and IP blocks are not automatically added to the IPAM database. Exercise 20.14 will demonstrate how to add an IP address space manually.

EXERCISE 20.14

Manually Add IPAM IP Address Space

1. Open Server Manager and select IPAM.

2. Select IP Address Inventory.

3. Right-click IPv4 and select Add IP Address.

4. Enter the IP address of the device that is to be managed by IPAM. Keep all other defaults.

5.   Click Apply.

6.   On the Summary page, verify that the task completed successfully.

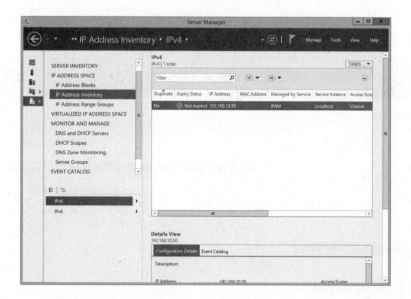

7.   Click OK to complete this exercise. Your new IP address is now managed by IPAM. You can now both create and delete DHCP reservations and DNS records for this IP address space from inside the IPAM management console. Similar steps are used to create IP address ranges and blocks. Find the wizard for each under the Tasks menu in the IPAM navigation window.

Monitor Utilization of IP Address Space

It is essential for network administrators to be able to monitor and manage their IP address infrastructure well. This grows increasingly difficult as your network gets bigger and becomes more complex. Unfortunately, quite a few administrators still rely on spreadsheets and basic database applications for IP tracking and usage. The problem is that manual tracking is time-consuming and prone to error.

IPAM tracks the service status of the DNS and DHCP servers on the network. By aggregating multiple DHCP servers, the multiserver management (MSM) module enables an administrator to perform editing and configuration of important properties on multiple DHCP servers and scopes. It also facilitates surveillance and tracking of DHCP service status and utilization of DHCP scopes. IPAM allows for monitoring the condition of a DNS zone on multiple DNS servers by exposing the collected status of a zone across all authoritative DNS servers.

IPAM also comes with its own event catalog that allows administrators to track both DHCP and DNS correlated events. The nice thing about this event log is that you can easily search by client hostname, client ID, username, or IP address for a full list of both DNS- and DHCP-related events on that client. You can also export these event logs to an Excel workbook. The Event Catalog is found toward the bottom of the IPAM hierarchical navigation window, as shown in Figure 20.4.

FIGURE 20.4   IPAM event catalog

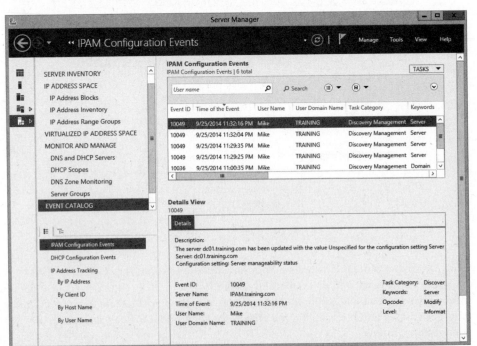

Migrate to IPAM

The situation may arise in which you must migrate your IPAM database infrastructure either from a Windows Internal Database (WID) to a Microsoft SQL database or from one SQL server to another. New to Windows Server 2012 R2, IPAM comes with the functionality to migrate an IPAM database via PowerShell. The `Move-IpamDatabase` cmdlet is used to complete this operation. When this cmdlet is run, a new IPAM schema is created, and then all of the IP address information is copied over. You can also use the `Get-IpamDatabase` cmdlet to review and compare pre- and postdatabase configuration settings during an IPAM database migration.

Delegate IPAM Administration

The delegation of IPAM administration is similar to the delegation of DNS. When IPAM is installed and provisioned, new security groups become available to administrators to configure role-based administration within your IPAM infrastructure. The five new security groups for IPAM administration are as follows:

IPAM Administrators   Members of this group have full permissions to manage and administer an IPAM infrastructure.

IPAM IP Audit Administrators   Members of this group can perform common IPAM management tasks and can carry out IPAM audits.

IPAM ASM Administrators   Members of this group can perform tasks related to IP address space management (ASM) functionality.

IPAM MSM Administrator   Members of this group can perform tasks across multiple IPAM servers through the IPAM multiserver management (MSM) functionality.

IPAM Users   Members of this group can only view information about server discovery, ASM, and MSM in IPAM. They can also view operational events, but they have no access to tracking or auditing information.

In addition to these new security groups, IPAM comes with a new Access Control feature, which allows administrators to get even more granular with IPAM permissions by using up to eight different preconfigured roles. You can also create your own custom IPAM administration roles for full IPAM permissions flexibility within your environment. Figure 20.5 illustrates the new Access Control panel for IPAM delegation of administration. Take the time to add and remove users from each of these groups and roles to get used to IPAM permission sets.

FIGURE 20.5 IPAM Access Control

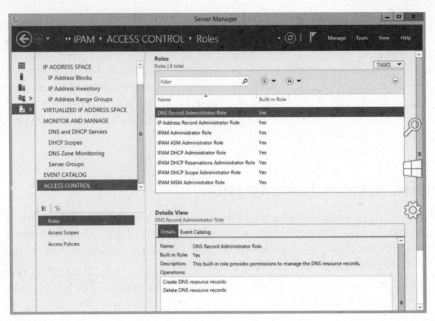

Manage IPAM Collections

In IPAM, server groups are logical groups used to organize managed DHCP and DNS servers. Servers are members of a server group based on values of custom fields that are assigned to the server. Having servers of the same type sorted into their own IPAM collections makes it easier to manage your server lists within the IPAM Management Console. Drop-down menus will allow you to filter server and task lists by IPAM service categories such as DNS or DHCP servers.

Configure IPAM Database Storage

There are two possible IPAM database storage solutions. An administrator can use either a Windows Internal Database (WID) or a dedicated Microsoft SQL Server Instance for their IPAM configuration. For smaller networks, a WID back end will work just fine for the initial IPAM deployment. If in the future the need arises to expand past a WID to a SQL database, then you already know that IPAM comes with migration functionality just for that situation. The database configuration options are chosen during the provisioning steps of an IPAM deployment.

Fully deploy and test the capabilities of the IPAM feature set to help track and forecast IP address utilization within your organization. IPAM is great way to discover, monitor, and manage all of the TCP/IP devices on your network.

Summary

This chapter talked about the advanced configuration options of DHCP, DNS, and IPAM. You learned step-by-step how to configure core network services and features. These features allow administrators to manage network devices easily in a large or complex environment. Understanding how DHCP, DNS, and IPAM all work together is essential for ensuring success when taking the exam. Focus your attention on completing the labs found within the chapter and learning the ins and outs of each management console for DHCP, DNS, and IPAM administration.

Exam Essentials

Understand DHCP Failover   DHCP failover (and load sharing) is one of the hottest new features in Windows Server 2012 R2. It is easy to deploy, and it provides an added level of redundancy when compared to using a DHCP split-scope configuration.

Know How to Configure DHCP Name Protection   DHCP name protection protects DNS Host A records from being overwritten by other client's Host A records during DNS dynamic updates. DHCP name protection is configured using the DHCP Management Console.

Understand IP Address Management   IPAM allows administrators to track and audit IP addresses through the use of the IPAM console. IPAM allows IP addresses to be tracked using DHCP lease events and user logon events.

Know How to Provision IPAM and Configure Server Discovery   IPAM is managed and monitored in Server Manager. Know that there are two separate provisioning models— manual and GPO—and know how to configure each. Know how to configure IPAM server discovery.

Understand Security for DNS   Hardening your DNS infrastructure is important. Know how to configure and use DNSSEC, socket pooling, and cache locking to make your network more secure.

Know How to Configure and Use DNS Logging   DNS logging gives administrators a more granular inside view at what DNS is actually doing on the network. DNS logging helps administrators troubleshoot DNS issues within the environment.

Know How to Analyze DNS Zone-Level Statistics   Administrators can use PowerShell to troubleshoot DNS-related issues further. You can generate and export multiple reports that will help you analyze DNS queries, requests, and dynamic updates.

Know How to Delegate Both DNS and IPAM Administration   Active Directory has specific security groups for delegating DNS administration, and IPAM has its own internal delegation of administration. A user does not need to be a member of the Domain Admins group in order to manage these services.

Review Questions

1. You are the network administrator for a midsize computer company. You have a single Active Directory forest, and you have a requirement to implement DHCP for the organization. You need to ensure that your DHCP deployment configuration is both fault-tolerant and redundant. Out of the options provided, which is the most reliable DHCP configuration that you could implement?

   A. DHCP split scope

   B. DHCP multicast scope

   C. DHCP failover

   D. DHCP super scope

2. You are a systems administrator for a large computer company. You have a multidomain Active Directory forest, and you have a requirement to implement advanced DNS security options for the organization. Which three security options could you configure to make DNS more secure on your network? (Choose three.)

   A. DNSSEC

   B. DNS registration

   C. DNS cache locking

   D. DNS socket pooling

3. You are the network administrator for a software development company. Your DNS infrastructure consists of multiple DNS servers that are geographically disparate. You need to ensure that when clients perform DNS queries, those queries will always be sent to the closest DNS server for lookup services. What must be enabled for this to take place on your network?

   A. DNS logging

   B. DNS delegated administration

   C. DNS recursion

   D. DNS netmask ordering

4. You are an IT manager for an enterprise storage solutions company. You have just hired a new team member to your network staff with the primary responsibility of managing DNS for your organization. It will not be this administrator's responsibility to manage any other active directory services for the company. Which security group would best fit this administrator's responsibilities?

   A. Domain Admins

   B. Enterprise Admins

   C. Schema Admins

   D. DNSAdmins

5. You are the network administrator for a toy company. Your DHCP infrastructure includes the use of DNS dynamic updates. You need to ensure that DNS host A records are not over-written by new DNS devices with the same hostname during DNS dynamic updates. Which DHCP configuration option would fulfill this requirement?

A. Configure DNS Registration

B. Configure DHCP Name Protection

C. Configure DHCP High Availability

D. Implement A DHCPv6 Scope

6. You are the infrastructure team lead for a high-tech hardware development company. You need to delegate some of the teams IPAM administration responsibilities between team members. You decide that Noelle will be managing IPAM address spaces, but she will not be managing IP address tracking and auditing. Which IPAM security group would best fit Noelle's new responsibilities?

A. IPAM Administrators

B. IPAM Users

C. IPAM ASM Administrators

D. IPAM MSM Administrators

7. You are the network administrator for a large communications company. You have recently decided to implement IPAM within your organization with the release of Windows Server 2012 R2. You want to set up your IPAM infrastructure so that one primary server can manage your entire enterprise. Which IPAM deployment method would fulfill this require-ment?

A. Isolated

B. Centralized

C. Hybrid

D. Distributed

8. You are the systems administrator for an advanced space exploration research facility. Your DNS infrastructure needs to accommodate the use of short, single-labeled DNS hostnames instead of the usual FQDN. Which advanced network configuration option would accom-modate this requirement?

A. Configure DNS Recursion

B. Configure DHCP Name Protection

C. Configure IPAM Server Discovery

D. Configure A GlobalNames Zone

9. You are the lead network administrator for a web hosting company. You have recently made the decision to implement IPAM within your organization. You have already installed and provisioned the IPAM feature on your dedicated Windows Server 2012 R2 server. What is the next logical step in your IPAM deployment?

    A.   Create a new IP block

    B.   Delegate IPAM administration

    C.   Configure server discovery

    D.   Create a new IP range

10. You are a systems administrator for the Stellacon Corporation. Because of the unusual growth of TCP/IP devices on your corporate network over the last year, you need to scale out your IPAM database capabilities. You are currently using a Windows Internal Database (WID) for your IPAM infrastructure, and you want to migrate your IPAM database to a Microsoft SQL Server. Which PowerShell cmdlet would you use to verify current IPAM database configuration settings?

    A.   `Get-IpamDatabase`

    B.   `Show-IpamDatabaseConfig`

    C.   `Show-IpamStatistics`

    D.   `Get-IpamMigrationSettings`

Chapter

21

Configure the Active Directory Infrastructure

THE FOLLOWING 70-412 EXAM OBJECTIVES ARE COVERED IN THIS CHAPTER:

✓ **Configure a forest or a domain**

  ▪ Implement multi-domain and multi-forest Active Directory environments including interoperability with previous versions of Active Directory

  ▪ Upgrade existing domains and forests including environment preparation and functional levels

  ▪ Configure multiple user principal name (UPN) suffixes

✓ **Configure Trusts**

  ▪ Configure external, forest, shortcut, and realm trusts

  ▪ Configure trust authentication

  ▪ Configure SID filtering

  ▪ Configure name suffix routing

✓ **Configure Sites**

  ▪ Configure sites and subnets

  ▪ Create and configure site links

  ▪ Manage site coverage

  ▪ Manage registration of SRV records

  ▪ Move domain controllers between sites

✓ **Manage Active Directory and SYSVOL replication**

- Configure replication to Read-Only Domain Controllers (RODCs)

- Configure Password Replication Policy (PRP) for RODCs

- Monitor and manage replication

- Upgrade SYSVOL replication to Distributed File System Replication (DFSR)

Microsoft has designed Active Directory to be an enterprise-wide solution for managing network resources. In previous chapters, you saw how to create Active Directory objects based on an organization's logical design. Domain structure and organizational unit (OU) structure, for example, should be designed based primarily on an organization's business needs.

Now it's time to learn how Active Directory can map to an organization's *physical* requirements. Specifically, you must consider network connectivity between sites and the flow of information between domain controllers (DCs) under less-than-ideal conditions. These constraints determine how domain controllers can work together to ensure that the objects within Active Directory remain synchronized no matter how large and geographically dispersed the network.

Fortunately, through the use of the Active Directory Sites and Services administrative tool, you can quickly and easily create the various components of an Active Directory replication topology. Using this tool, you can create objects called *sites*, place servers in sites, and create connections between sites. Once you have configured Active Directory replication to fit your current network environment, you can sit back and allow Active Directory to make sure that information remains consistent across domain controllers.

This chapter covers the features of Active Directory, which allow system administrators to modify the behavior of replication based on their physical network design. Through the use of sites, system and network administrators will be able to leverage their network infrastructure best to support Windows Server 2012 R2 and Active Directory.

So far, you have learned the steps necessary to install the Domain Name System (DNS) and to implement the first Active Directory domain. Although I briefly introduced multidomain Active Directory structures earlier, I focused on only a single domain and the objects within it.

Many businesses find that using a single domain provides an adequate solution to meet their business needs. By working with *trees* and *forests*, however, large organizations can use multiple domains to organize their environments better.

Overview of Network Planning

Before I discuss sites and replication, you need to understand some basic physical and network concepts.

The Three Types of Networks

When designing networks, system and network administrators use the following terms to define the types of connectivity between locations and servers:

Local Area Networks   A *local area network (LAN)* is usually characterized as a high-bandwidth network. Generally, an organization owns all of its LAN network hardware and software. Ethernet is by far the most common networking standard. Ethernet speeds are generally at least 10Mbps and can scale to multiple gigabits per second. Currently, the standard for Ethernet is the 10 Gigabit Ethernet, which runs at 10 times the speed of Gigabit Ethernet (1GB). Several LAN technologies, including routing and switching, are available to segment LANs and to reduce contention for network resources.

Wide Area Networks   The purpose of a *wide area network (WAN)* is similar to that of a LAN, that is, to connect network devices. Unlike LANs, however, WANs are usually leased from third-party telecommunications carriers and organizations known as *Internet service providers (ISPs)*. Although extremely high-speed WAN connections are available, they are generally costly for organizations to implement through a distributed environment. Therefore, WAN connections are characterized by lower-speed connections and, sometimes, nonpersistent connections.

The Internet   The *Internet* is a worldwide public network infrastructure based on the *Internet Protocol (IP)*. Access to the Internet is available through Internet service providers (ISPs). Because it is a public network, there is no single "owner" of the Internet. Instead, large network and telecommunications providers constantly upgrade the infrastructure of this network to meet growing demands.

Organizations use the Internet regularly to sell and market their products and services. For example, it's rare nowadays to see advertisements that don't direct you to one website or another. Through the use of technologies such as *virtual private networks (VPNs)*, organizations can use encryption and authentication technology to enable secure communications across the Internet.

Exploring Network Constraints

In an ideal situation, a high-speed network would connect all computers and networking devices. In such a situation, you would be able to ensure that any user of your network, regardless of location, would be able to access resources quickly and easily. When you are working in the real world, however, you have many other constraints to keep in mind, including network bandwidth and network cost.

Network Bandwidth

Network bandwidth generally refers to the amount of data that can pass through a specific connection in a given amount of time. For example, in a WAN situation, a T1 may have 1.544Mbps (megabits per second), while a DSL might have a bandwidth of 56Kbps or 57.6Kbps (kilobits per second) or more. On the other hand, your LAN's Ethernet connection may have a bandwidth of 100Mbps. Different types of networks work at different speeds. Therefore, it's imperative that you always consider network bandwidth when thinking about how to deploy domain controllers in your environment.

Network Cost

Cost is perhaps the single largest factor in determining a network design. If cost were not a constraint, organizations would clearly elect to use high-bandwidth connections for all of their sites. Realistically, trade-offs in performance must be made for the sake of affordability. Some factors that can affect the cost of networking include the distance between networks and the types of technology available at locations throughout the world. In remote or less-developed locations, you may not even be able to get access through an ISP or telecom beyond a satellite connection or dial-up, and what is available can be quite costly. Network designers must keep these factors in mind, and they must often settle for less-than-ideal connectivity.

You have considered the monetary value of doing business. Now let's consider another aspect of cost. When designing and configuring networks, you can require certain devices to make data-transport decisions automatically based on an assigned network cost. These devices are commonly known as *routers*, and they use routing protocols to make routing decisions. One of the elements a router uses to configure a routing protocol is its ability to adjust the cost of a route. For example, a router may have multiple ways to connect to a remote site, and it may have multiple interfaces connected to it, each with different paths out of the network to which it is connected locally. When two or more routes are available, you can set up a routing protocol that states that the route with the lower cost is automatically used first.

Another cost is personnel. Do you have the personnel to do the job, or do you need to hire a consultant? Remember that even if you use individuals already on staff, they will be spending time on these projects. When your IT team is working on a project, this is a cost because they cannot also be working on day-to-day tasks.

All of these factors play an important role when you make your Active Directory implementation decisions.

Overview of Active Directory Replication and Sites

Now I need to address two topics that not only are covered heavily on the Microsoft exams but are two areas that all IT administrators should understand. Understanding Active Directory replication and sites can help you fine-tune a network to run at peak performance.

Replicating Active Directory

Regardless of the issues related to network design and technological constraints, network users have many different requirements and needs that must be addressed. First, network resources, such as files, printers, and shared directories, must be made available.

Similarly, the resources stored within Active Directory, and its security information in particular, are required for many operations that occur within domains.

With these issues in mind, take a look at how you can configure Active Directory to reach connectivity goals using replication.

Active Directory was designed as a scalable, distributed database that contains information about an organization's network resources. In previous chapters, you saw how you can create and manage domains and how you can use domain controllers to store Active Directory databases.

Even in the simplest of network environments, you generally need more than one domain controller. The major reasons for this are *fault tolerance* (if one domain controller fails, others can still provide services as needed) and performance (the workload can be balanced between multiple domain controllers). Windows Server 2012 R2 domain controllers have been designed to contain read-write copies as well as read-only copies of the Active Directory database. However, the domain controllers must also remain current when objects are created or modified on other domain controllers.

To keep information consistent between domain controllers, you use *Active Directory replication*. Replication is the process by which changes to the Active Directory database are transferred between domain controllers. The result is that all of the domain controllers within an Active Directory domain contain up-to-date information and achieve convergence. Keep in mind that domain controllers may be located very near to each other (for example, within the same server rack), or they may be located across the world from each other. Although the goals of replication are quite simple, the real-world constraints of network connections between servers cause many limitations that you must accommodate. If you have a domain controller on your local LAN, you may find that you have Gigabit Ethernet, which runs at 1000Mbps between your server connections, whereas you may have a domain controller on the other side or a WAN where the network link runs at a fraction of a T1, 56Kbps. Replication traffic must traverse each link to ensure convergence no matter what the speed or what bandwidth is available.

Throughout this chapter, you will study the technical details of Active Directory replication. You will also learn how to use the concept of sites and site links to map the logical structure of Active Directory to a physical network topology to help it work efficiently, no matter the type of link with which you are working.

Understanding Active Directory Site Concepts

One of the most important aspects of designing and implementing Active Directory is understanding how it allows you to separate the logical components of the directory service from the physical components.

The logical components—Active Directory domains, OUs, users, groups, and computers—map to the organizational and business requirements of a company.

The physical components, on the other hand, are designed based on the technical issues involved in keeping the network synchronized (that is, making sure that all parts of the network have the same up-to-date information). Active Directory uses the concept of sites to map to an organization's physical network. Stated simply, a *site* is a collection of well-connected subnets. The technical implications of sites are described later in this chapter.

It is important to understand that no specified relationship exists between Active Directory domains and Active Directory sites. An Active Directory site can contain many domains. Alternatively, a single Active Directory domain can span multiple sites. Figure 21.1 illustrates this very important characteristic of domains and sites.

FIGURE 21.1   Potential relationships between domains and sites

One Site,
Multiple Domains

One Domain,
Multiple Sites

There are two main reasons to use Active Directory sites: service requests and replication.

Service Requests

Clients often require the network services of a domain controller. One of the most common reasons for this is that they need the domain controller to perform network authentication. If your Active Directory network is set up with sites, clients can easily connect to the domain controller that is located closest to them. By doing this, they avoid many of the inefficiencies associated with connecting to distant domain controllers or to those that are located on the other side of a slow network connection. For example, by connecting to a local domain controller, you can avoid the problems associated with a saturated network link that might cause two domain controllers to be out of sync with each other.

Replication

As mentioned earlier, the purpose of Active Directory replication is to ensure that the information stored on all domain controllers within a domain remains synchronized. In environments with many domains and domain controllers, multiple communication paths usually connect them, which makes the synchronization process more complicated. A simple method of transferring updates and other changes to Active Directory involves all of the servers communicating directly with each other as soon as a change occurs; they can all update with the change and reach convergence again. This is not ideal, however, because it places high requirements on network bandwidth and is inefficient for many network environments that use slower and more costly WAN links, especially if all environments update at the same time. Such simultaneous updating could cause the network connection at the core of your network to become saturated and decrease the performance of the entire WAN.

Using sites, Active Directory can automatically determine the best methods for performing replication operations. Sites take into account an organization's network infrastructure, and Active Directory uses these sites to determine the most efficient method for synchronizing information between domain controllers. System administrators can make their physical network design map to Active Directory objects. Based on the creation and configuration of these objects, the Active Directory service can then manage replication traffic in an efficient way.

Whenever a change is made to the Active Directory database on a domain controller, the change is given an update sequence number. The domain controller can then propagate these changes to other domain controllers based on replication settings.

Windows Server 2012 R2 uses a feature called *linked value replication* that is active only when the domain is in the Windows Server 2003, Windows Server 2008, Windows Server 2008 R2, Windows Server 2012, or Windows Server 2012 R2 domain functional level. With linked value replication, only the group member is replicated. This greatly enhances replication efficiency and cuts down on network traffic utilization. Linked value replication is automatically enabled in Windows Server 2003, Windows Server 2008, Windows Server 2008 R2, Windows Server 2012, and Windows Server 2012 R2 functional-level domains.

Planning Your Sites

Much of the challenge of designing Active Directory is related to mapping a company's business processes to the structure of a hierarchical data store. So far, you've seen many of these requirements. What about the existing network infrastructure, however? Clearly, when you plan for and design the structure of Active Directory, you must take into account your LAN and WAN characteristics. Let's see some of the ways that you can use Active Directory sites to manage replication traffic.

Synchronizing Active Directory is extremely important. To keep security permissions and objects within the directory consistent throughout the organization, you must use replication. The Active Directory data store supports *multimaster replication*; that is, data can be modified at any domain controller within the domain because replication ensures that information remains consistent throughout the organization.

Ideally, every site within an organization has reliable, high-speed connections with the other sites. A much more realistic scenario, however, is one in which bandwidth is limited and connections are sometimes either sporadically available or completely unavailable.

Using sites, network and system administrators can define which domain controllers are located on which areas of the network. These settings can be based on the bandwidth available between the areas of the network. Additionally, these administrators can define *subnets*—logically partitioned areas of the network—between areas of the network. Subnets are designed by subdividing IP addresses into usable blocks for assignment, and they are also objects found within the Sites and Services Microsoft Management Console (MMC) in the Administrative Tools folder. Windows Server 2012 R2 Active Directory services use this information to decide how and when to replicate data between domain controllers.

Directly replicating information between all domain controllers might be a viable solution for some companies. For others, however, this might result in a lot of traffic traveling over slow or undersized network links. One way to synchronize data efficiently between sites that have slow connections is to use a *bridgehead server*. Bridgehead servers are designed to accept traffic between two remote sites and then to forward this information to the appropriate servers. Figure 21.2 provides an example of how a bridgehead server can reduce network bandwidth requirements and improve performance. Reduced network bandwidth requirements and improved performance can also be achieved by configuring replication to occur according to a predefined schedule if bandwidth usage statistics are available.

FIGURE 21.2 Using a bridgehead server

Bridgehead servers do not fit a normal hub-and-spoke WAN topology. Such a topology usually involves a core site (for example, company headquarters) with remote sites as links one off from the core. However, you can use a bridgehead server design to fit a distributed star, where you have a hub-and-spoke topology design with additional spokes coming out of the first set of spokes. Doing so would make some of your spoke sites into smaller core sites. It is at these sites that you would place your bridgehead servers. In Figure 21.2, you can see that your Asia headquarters site is also where you can connect to India, China, and Hong Kong, thus making the Asia headquarters the ideal site for the bridgehead server.

In addition to managing replication traffic, sites offer the advantage of allowing clients to access the nearest domain controller. This prevents problems with user authentication across slow network connections, and it can help find the shortest and fastest path to resources such as files and printers. Therefore, Microsoft recommends that you place at least one domain controller at each site that contains a slow link. Preferably, this domain controller also contains a copy of the global catalog so that logon attempts and resource search queries do not occur across slow links. The drawback, however, is that deploying more copies of the global catalog to servers increases replication traffic.

Through proper planning and deployment of sites, organizations can best use the capabilities of the network infrastructure while keeping Active Directory synchronized.

Understanding Distributed File System Replication

DFS Replication (DFSR) was created to replace the File Replication Service (FRS) that was introduced in the Windows 2000 Server operating systems. DFSR is a state-based, multimaster replication engine that supports replication scheduling and bandwidth throttling. DFSR has the ability to detect insertions, removals, and rearrangements of data in files. This allows DFS Replication to replicate only the changed file blocks when files are updated.

The DFS Replication component uses many different processes to keep data synchronized on multiple servers. To understand the DFSR process, it is helpful to understand some of the following concepts:

- DFSR is a multimaster replication engine, and changes that occur on one of the members are then replicated to all of the other members of the replication group.

- DFSR uses the update sequence number (USN) journal to detect changes on the volume, and then DFSR replicates the changes only after the file is closed.

- Before sending or receiving a file, DFSR uses a staging folder to stage the file.

- When a file is changed, DFSR replicates only the changed blocks and not the entire file. The RDC protocol is what helps determine the blocks that have changed in the file.

- One of the advantages of DFSR is that it is self-healing and can automatically recover from USN journal wraps, USN journal loss, or loss of the DFS Replication database.

- Windows Server 2012 R2 DFSR includes the ability to add a failover cluster as a member of a replication group.

- Windows Server 2012 R2 DFSR allows for read-only replicated folders on a particular member in which users cannot add or change files.

- In Windows Server 2012 R2, it is possible to make changes to the SYSVOL folder of an RODC.

The Dfsrdiag.exe command-line tool includes three Windows Server 2012 R2 command-line switches that provide enhanced diagnostic capabilities for DFSR:

Dfsrdiag.exe ReplState   When you use the ReplState switch, a summary of the replication status across all connections on the specified replication group member is provided. The ReplState switch takes a snapshot of the internal state of the DFSR service, and the updates that are currently being processed (downloaded or served) by the service are shown in a list.

Dfsrdiag.exe IdRecord   When replicating a file or folder, the DFSR service creates an ID record, and an administrator can use this ID record to determine whether a file has replicated properly to a specific member. The IdRecord switch returns the DFSR ID record for the file or folder that you specify by using its path or its unique identifier (UID).

Dfsrdiag.exe FileHash   The FileHash switch, when used against a particular file, will compute and display the hash value that is generated by the DFSR service. An administrator can then look at the hash values to compare two files. If the hash values for the two files are the same, then the two files are the same.

Implementing Sites and Subnets

Now that you have a good idea of the goals of replication, take a look at the following quick overview of the various Active Directory objects that are related to physical network topology.

The basic objects that are used for managing replication include the following:

Subnets   A *subnet* is a partition of a network. As I started to discuss earlier, subnets are logical IP blocks usually connected to other IP blocks through the use of routers and other network devices. All of the computers that are located on a given subnet are generally well connected with each other.

> It is extremely important to understand the concepts of TCP/IP and the routing of network information when you are designing the topology for Active Directory replication. TCP/IP is covered in detail in Chapter 8, "Configure TCP/IP."

Sites   An Active Directory site is a logical object that can contain servers and other objects related to Active Directory replication. Specifically, a *site* is a grouping of related subnets. Sites are created to match the physical network structure of an organization. Sites are primarily used for slow WAN links. If your network is well connected (using fiber optics, Category 5 Ethernet, and so on), then sites are not needed.

Site Links   A *site link* is created to define the types of connections that are available between the components of a site. Site links can reflect a relative cost for a network connection and can also reflect the bandwidth that is available for communications.

All of these components work together to determine how information is used to replicate data between domain controllers. Figure 21.3 provides an example of the physical components of Active Directory.

FIGURE 21.3   Active Directory replication objects

Many issues are related to configuring and managing sites, and all of them are covered in this chapter. Overall, using sites allows you to control the behavior of Active Directory replication between domain controllers. With this background and goal in mind, let's look at how you can implement sites to control Active Directory replication so that it is efficient and in sync.

If you do not have replication set up properly, after a while you will experience problems with your domain controllers. An example of a common replication problem is Event Log event ID 1311, which states that the Windows NT Directory Services (NTDS) Knowledge Consistency Checker (KCC) has found (and reported) a problem with Active Directory replication. This error message states that the replication configuration information in Active Directory does not accurately reflect the physical topology of the network. This error is commonly found on ailing networks that have replication problems for one reason or another.

Creating Sites

The primary method for creating and managing Active Directory replication components is to utilize the Active Directory Sites and Services tool or the MMC found within the Administrative Tools folder. Using this administrative component, you can graphically create and manage sites in much the same way that you create and manage OUs.

Exercise 21.1 walks you through the process of creating Active Directory sites. For you to complete this exercise, the local machine must be a domain controller. Also, this exercise assumes that you have not yet changed the default domain site configuration.

Do not perform any testing on a production system or network. Make sure you test site configuration in a lab setting only.

EXERCISE 21.1

Creating Sites

1. Open the Active Directory Sites and Services tool from the Administrative Tools program group.

2. Expand the Sites folder.

3. Right-click the Default-First-Site-Name item and choose Rename. Rename the site **CorporateHQ**.

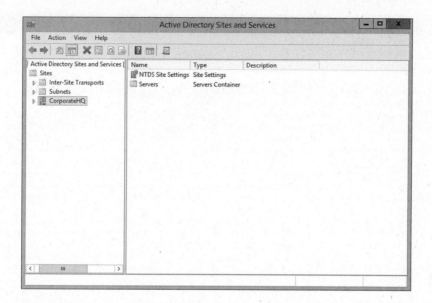

4. Create a new site by right-clicking the Sites object and selecting New Site.

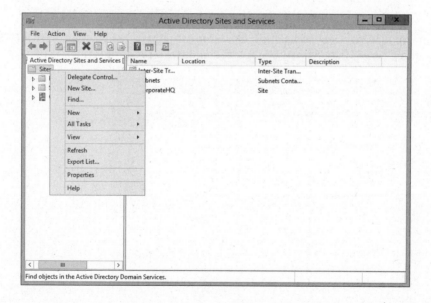

5. In the New Object – Site dialog box, type **Farmington** for the site name. Click the DEFAULTIPSITELINK item, and an information screen pops up. Then click OK to create the site. Note that you cannot include spaces or other special characters in the name of a site.

6.   Notice that the Farmington site is now listed under the Sites object.

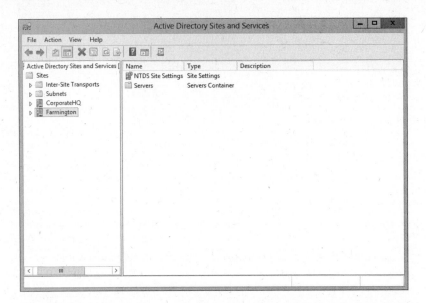

7.   Create another new site and name it **Portsmouth**. Again, choose the DEFAULTIPSITE-
     LINK item. Notice that the new site is listed under the Sites object.

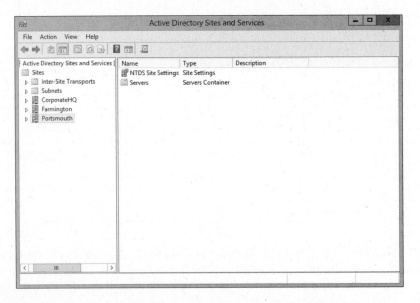

8.   When you have finished, close the Active Directory Sites and Services tool.

Creating Subnets

Once you have created the sites that map to your network topology, it's time to define the subnets that define the site boundaries.

Subnets are based on TCP/IPv4 or TCP/IPv6 address information. For example, the IPv4 address may be 10.10.0.0, and the subnet mask may be 255.255.0.0. This information specifies that all of the TCP/IP addresses that begin with the first two octets are part of the same TCP/IP subnet. All of the following TCP/IP addresses would be within this subnet:

- 10.10.1.5

- 10.10.100.17

- 10.10.110.120

The Active Directory Sites and Services tool expresses these subnets in a somewhat different notation. It uses the provided subnet address and appends a slash followed by the number of bits in the subnet mask. In the example in the previous paragraph, the subnet would be defined as 10.1.0.0/16.

Remember that sites typically represent distinct physical locations, and they almost always have their own subnets. The only way for a domain controller in one site to reach a DC in another site is to add subnet information about the remote site. Generally, information regarding the definition of subnets for a specific network environment will be available from a network designer. Exercise 21.2 walks you through the steps that you need to take to create subnets and assign subnets to sites. To complete the steps in this exercise, you must have completed Exercise 21.1.

EXERCISE 21.2

Creating Subnets

1. Open the Active Directory Sites and Services tool from the Administrative Tools program group.

2. Expand the Sites folder. Right-click the Subnets folder and select New Subnet.

3. In the New Object – Subnet dialog box, you are prompted for information about the IPv4 or IPv6 details for the new subnet. For the prefix, type **10.10.1.0/24** (you are staying with the more commonly used IPv4). This actually calculates out to 10.10.1.0 with the mask of 255.255.255.0. Click the Farmington site and then click OK to create the subnet.

EXERCISE 21.2 *(continued)*

4. In the Active Directory Sites and Services tool, right-click the newly created 10.10.1.0/24 subnet object and select Properties.

5. On the subnet's Properties dialog box, type **Farmington 100MB LAN** for the description. Click OK to continue.

6. Create a new subnet using the following information:

Address: **160.25.0.0/16**

Site: **Portsmouth**

Description: **Portsmouth 100Mbit LAN**

7. Finally, create another subnet using the following information:

Address: **176.33.0.0/16**

Site: **CorporateHQ**

Description: **Corporate 100Mbit switched LAN**

8. When finished, close the Active Directory Sites and Services tool.

So far, you have created the basic components that govern Active Directory sites and subnets. You also linked these two components by defining which subnets belong in which sites. These two steps—creating sites and creating subnets—form the basis of mapping the physical network infrastructure of an organization to Active Directory. Now look at the various settings that you can make for sites.

Configuring Sites

Once you have created Active Directory sites and have defined which subnets they contain, it's time to make some additional configuration settings for the site structure. Specifically, you'll need to assign servers to specific sites and configure the site-licensing options. By placing servers in sites, you tell Active Directory replication services how to replicate information for various types of servers. Later in this chapter, you'll examine the details of working with replication within and between sites.

In Exercise 21.3, you will add servers to sites and configure CorpDC1 options. To complete the steps in this exercise, you must have completed Exercise 21.1 and Exercise 21.2.

EXERCISE 21.3

Configuring Sites

1. Open the Active Directory Sites and Services tool from the Administrative Tools program group.

2. Expand the Sites folder and click and expand the Farmington site.

3. Right-click the Servers container in the Farmington site and select New ➢ Server. Type **FarmingtonDC1** for the name of the server and then click OK.

EXERCISE 21.3 *(continued)*

4. Create a new Server object within the CorporateHQ site and name it **CorpDC1**. Note that this object also includes the name of the local domain controller.

5. Create two new Server objects within the Portsmouth site and name them **PortsmouthDC1** and **PortsmouthDC2**.

6. Right-click the CorpDC1 server object and select Properties. On the General tab of the CorpDC1 Properties box, select SMTP in the Transports Available For Inter-site Data Transfer box and click Add to make this server a preferred IP bridgehead server. Click OK to accept the settings.

7. When you have finished, close the Active Directory Sites and Services tool.

With the configuration of the basic settings for sites out of the way, it's time to focus on the real details of the site topology—creating site links and site link bridges.

Configuring Replication

Sites are generally used to define groups of computers that are located within a single geographic location. In most organizations, machines that are located in close physical proximity (for example, within a single building or branch office) are well connected. A typical example is a LAN in a branch office of a company. All of the computers may be connected using Ethernet, and routing and switching technology may be in place to reduce network congestion.

Often, however, domain controllers are located across various states, countries, and even continents. In such a situation, network connectivity is usually much slower, less reliable, and more costly than that for the equivalent LAN. Therefore, Active Directory replication must accommodate this situation accordingly. When managing replication traffic within Active Directory sites, you need to be aware of two types of synchronization:

Intrasite *Intrasite replication* refers to the synchronization of Active Directory information between domain controllers that are located in the same site. In accordance with the concept of sites, these machines are usually well connected by a high-speed LAN.

Intersite *Intersite replication* occurs between domain controllers in different sites. Usually, this means there is a WAN or other type of low-speed network connection between the various machines. Intersite replication is optimized for minimizing the amount of network traffic that occurs between sites.

In the following sections, you'll look at ways to configure both intrasite and intersite replication. Additionally, you'll see features of Active Directory replication architecture that you can use to accommodate the needs of almost any environment.

Intrasite Replication

Intrasite replication is generally a simple process. One domain controller contacts the others in the same site when changes to its copy of Active Directory are made. It compares the update sequence numbers in its own copy of Active Directory with those of the other domain controllers; then the most current information is chosen by the DC in question, and all domain controllers within the site use this information to make the necessary updates to their database.

Because you can assume that the domain controllers within an Active Directory site are well connected, you can pay less attention exactly to when and how replication takes place. Communications between domain controllers occur using the *Remote Procedure Call (RPC) protocol*. This protocol is optimized for transmitting and synchronizing information on fast and reliable network connections. The RPC protocol provides for fast replication at the expense of network bandwidth, which is usually readily available because most LANs today are running on Fast Ethernet (100Mbps) at a minimum.

Intersite Replication

Intersite replication is optimized for low-bandwidth situations and network connections that have less reliability. Intersite replication offers several features that are tailored toward these types of connections. To begin with, two different protocols may be used to transfer information between sites:

RPC over IP   When connectivity is fairly reliable, IP is a good choice. IP-based communications require you to have a live connection between two or more domain controllers in different sites and let you transfer Active Directory information. RPC over IP was originally designed for slower WANs in which packet loss and corruption may often occur.

Simple Mail Transfer Protocol   *Simple Mail Transfer Protocol (SMTP)* is perhaps best known as the protocol that is used to send and receive email messages on the Internet. SMTP was designed to use a store-and-forward mechanism through which a server receives a copy of a message, records it to disk, and then attempts to forward it to another email server. If the destination server is unavailable, it holds the message and attempts to resend it at periodic intervals.

This type of communication is extremely useful for situations in which network connections are unreliable or not always available. For example, if a branch office in Peru were connected to the corporate office through a dial-up connection that is available only during certain hours, SMTP would be a good choice for communication with that branch.

SMTP is an inherently insecure network protocol. Therefore, if you would like to ensure that you transfer replication traffic securely and you use SMTP for Active Directory replication, you must take advantage of Windows Server 2012's Certificate Services functionality.

Other intersite replication characteristics are designed to address low-bandwidth situations and less-reliable network connections. These features give you a high degree of flexibility in controlling replication configuration. They include the following:

- Compression of Active Directory information. This compression is helpful because changes between domain controllers in remote sites may include a large amount of information and also because network bandwidth tends to be less available and more costly.

- Site links and site link bridges help determine intersite replication topology.

- Replication can occur based on a schedule defined by system administrators.

You can configure intersite replication by using the Active Directory Sites and Services tool. Select the name of the site for which you want to configure settings. Then right-click the NTDS Site Settings object in the right window pane and select Properties. By clicking the Change Schedule button in the NTDS Site Settings Properties dialog box, you'll be able to configure how often replication occurs between sites (see Figure 21.4).

FIGURE 21.4   Configuring intersite replication schedules

    You will see how to set the replication schedule in Exercise 21.4.

In the following sections, you will see how to configure site links and site link bridges as well as how to manage connection objects and bridgehead servers.

Creating Site Links and Site Link Bridges

The overall topology of intersite replication is based on the use of site links and site link bridges. *Site links* are logical connections that define a path between two Active Directory sites. Site links can include several descriptive elements that define their network characteristics. *Site link bridges* are used to connect site links so that the relationship can be transitive. Figure 21.5 provides an example of site links and site link bridges.

FIGURE 21.5 An example of site links and site link bridges

Both of these types of logical connections are used by Active Directory services to determine how information should be synchronized between domain controllers in remote sites. The Knowledge Consistency Checker (KCC) uses this information, which forms a replication topology based on the site topology created. The KCC service is responsible for determining the best way to replicate information within sites.

When creating site links for your environment, you'll need to consider the following factors:

Transporting Information   You can choose to use either RPC over IP or SMTP for transferring information over a site link. You will need to determine which is best based on your network infrastructure and the reliability of connections between sites.

Assigning a Cost Value   You can create multiple site links between sites and assign site links a cost value based on the type of connection. The system administrator determines the cost value, and the relative costs of site links are then used (by the system) to determine the optimal path for replication. The lower the cost, the more likely the link is to be used for replication.

For example, a company may primarily use a T1 link between branch offices, but it may also use a slower and circuit-switched dial-up ISDN connection for redundancy (in case the T1 fails). In this example, a system administrator may assign a cost of 25 to the T1 line and a cost of 100 to the ISDN line. This ensures that the more reliable and higher-bandwidth T1 connection is used whenever it's available but that the ISDN line is also available.

Determining a Replication Schedule   Once you've determined how and through which connections replication will take place, it's time to determine when information should be replicated. Replication requires network resources and occupies bandwidth. Therefore, you need to balance the need for consistent directory information with the need to conserve bandwidth. For example, if you determine that it's reasonable to have a lag time of six hours between when an update is made at one site and when it is replicated to all others, you might schedule replication to occur once in the morning, once during the lunch hour, and more frequently after normal work hours.

Based on these factors, you should be able to devise a strategy that allows you to configure site links.

Exercise 21.4 walks you through the process of creating site links and site link bridges. To complete the steps in this exercise, you must have completed Exercises 21.1, 21.2, and 21.3.

EXERCISE 21.4

Creating Site Links and Site Link Bridges

1. Open the Active Directory Sites and Services tool from the Administrative Tools program group.

2. Expand the Sites, Inter-site Transports, and IP objects. Right-click the DEFAULTIPSITE-LINK item in the right pane and select Rename. Rename the object **CorporateWAN**.

3. Right-click the CorporateWAN link and select Properties. In the General tab of the CorporateWAN Properties dialog box, type **T1 Connecting Corporate and Portsmouth Offices** for the description. Remove the Farmington site from the link by highlighting Farmington in the Sites In This Site Link box and clicking Remove. For the Cost value, type **50** and specify that replication should occur every **60** minutes. To create the site link, click OK.

4. Right-click the IP folder and select New Site Link. In the New Object – Site Link dialog box, name the link **CorporateDialup**. Add the Farmington and CorporateHQ sites to the site link and then click OK.

5. Right-click the CorporateDialup link and select Properties. In the General tab of the CorporateDialup Properties dialog box, type **ISDN Dialup between Corporate and Farmington** for the description. Set the Cost value to **100** and specify that replication should occur every **120** minutes. To specify that replication should occur only during certain times of the day, click the Change Schedule button.

6. In the Schedule For Corporate Dialup dialog box, highlight the area between 8:00 a.m. and 6:00 p.m. for the days Monday through Friday and click the Replication Not Available option. This will ensure that replication traffic is minimized during normal work hours.

7. Click OK to accept the new schedule and then click OK again to create the site link.

8. Right-click the IP object and select New Site Link Bridge. In the New Object – Site Link Bridge dialog box, name the site link bridge **CorporateBridge**. Note that the CorporateDialup and CorporateWAN site links are already added to the site link bridge. Because there must be at least two site links in each bridge, you will not be able to remove these links. Click OK to create the site link bridge.

9. When finished, close the Active Directory Sites and Services tool.

Creating Connection Objects

Generally, it is a good practice to allow Active Directory's replication mechanisms to schedule and manage replication functions automatically. In some cases, however, you may want to have additional control over replication. Perhaps you want to replicate certain changes on demand (for example, when you create new accounts). Or you may want to specify a custom schedule for certain servers.

Connection objects provide you with a way to set up these different types of replication schedules. You can create connection objects with the Active Directory Sites and Services tool by expanding a server object, right-clicking the NTDS Settings object, and selecting New Active Directory Domain Services Connection (see Figure 21.6).

FIGURE 21.6   Creating a new Active Directory Domain Services connection

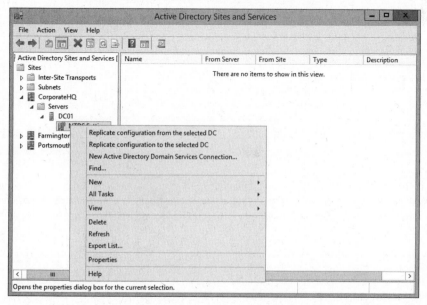

Within the properties of the connection object, which you can see in the right pane of the Active Directory Sites and Services tool, you can specify the type of transport to use for replication (RPC over IP or SMTP), the schedule for replication, and the domain controllers that participate in the replication. Additionally, you can right-click the connection object and select Replicate Now.

Moving Server Objects between Sites

Using the Active Directory Sites and Services tool, you can easily move servers between sites. To do this, simply right-click the name of a domain controller and select Move. You can then select the site to which you want to move the domain controller object.

Figure 21.7 shows the Move Server dialog box. After the server is moved, all replication topology settings are updated automatically. If you want to choose custom replication settings, you'll need to create connection objects manually (as described earlier).

FIGURE 21.7   Choosing a new site for a specific server

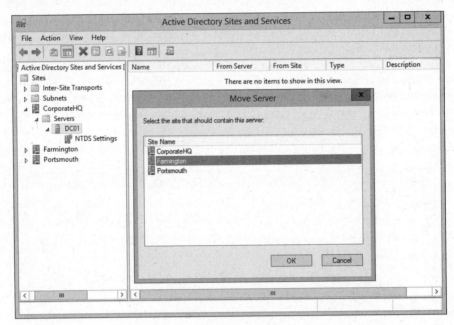

In Exercise 21.5, you move a server object between sites. To complete the steps in this exercise, you must have completed the previous exercises in this chapter.

EXERCISE 21.5

Moving Server Objects Between Sites

1. Open the Active Directory Sites and Services administrative tool.

2. Right-click the server named PortsmouthDC1 and select Move.

3. In the Move Server dialog box, select the Farmington site and then click OK. This moves this server to the Farmington site.

4. To move the server back, right-click PortsmouthDC1 (now located in the Farmington site) and then click Move. Select Portsmouth for the destination site.

5. When finished, close the Active Directory Sites and Services administrative tool.

Creating Bridgehead Servers

By default, all of the servers in one site communicate with all of the servers in another site. You can, however, further control replication between sites by using bridgehead servers. As mentioned earlier in the chapter, using bridgehead servers helps minimize replication traffic, especially in larger distributed star network topologies, and it allows you to dedicate machines that are better connected to receive replicated data. Figure 21.8 provides an example of how bridgehead servers work.

FIGURE 21.8   A replication scenario using bridgehead servers

You can use a bridgehead server to specify which domain controllers are preferred for transferring replication information between sites. Different bridgehead servers can be selected for RPC over IP and SMTP replication, thus allowing you to balance the load. To create a bridgehead server for a site, simply right-click a domain controller and select Properties, which brings up the bridgehead server's Properties dialog box (see Figure 21.9). To make the server a bridgehead server, just select one or both replication types (called *transports*) from the left side of the dialog box and click the Add button to add them to the right side of the dialog box.

FIGURE 21.9   Specifying a bridgehead server

RODCs and Replication

I have talked quite a bit about read-only domain controllers (RODCs) throughout the book. It's important that you understand that since RODCs don't actually commit changes against the Active Directory Domain Services (ADDS) database within your environment, then replication to and from your primary domain controller (PDC) and your RODCs can occur only one way. This is referred to as *unidirectional replication*. Any writable domain controller that serves as a replication partner to one of your RODCs will never pull changes from that RODC by design. This helps ensure that no malicious or corrupt changes that are made from an RODC are replicated throughout your entire forest. The RODC performs normal inbound replication for AD DS and Sysvol changes. Any other shares on an RODC that you configure to replicate using DFS Replication would still use bidirectional replication.

RODCs come with additional configuration settings like the *Password Replication Policy (PRP)*. The PRP is used to determine which user's credentials can be cached locally on a specific RODC. By default, an RODC will not cache an Active Directory user's credentials. That would defeat the purpose of an RODC. When a user wants to authenticate to an RODC, the authentication request is forwarded to a writable domain controller for authentication. If the request succeeds, it is then passed back to the RODC, and then that user will be able to log in to the domain.

Nonetheless, it is possible to allow certain user credentials to be cached on an RODC by configuring the PRP. Once a user has been added to the Allowed RODC Password Replication group, then that user's credentials will be cached, and that RODC would be able to authenticate that user locally again in the future. Because the RODC maintains only a subset of user credentials, if the RODC is compromised or stolen, only the user accounts that had been cached on the RODC must have their passwords changed. To configure an RODC PRP, open the properties of an RODC computer object in Active Directory and select the Password Replication Policy tab.

Configuring Server Topology

When you are using environments that require multiple sites, you must carefully consider where you place your servers. In doing so, you can greatly improve performance and end user experience by reducing the time they must spend performing common operations, such as authentication or searching Active Directory for resources.

There are two main issues to consider when you are designing a distributed Active Directory environment. The first is how you should place domain controllers within the network environment. The second is how to manage the use of global catalog servers. Finding the right balance between servers, server resources, and performance can be considered an art form for network and system administrators. In the following sections, you'll look at some of the important considerations that you must take into account when you design a replication server topology.

Placing Domain Controllers

Microsoft highly recommends that you have at least two domain controllers in each domain of your Active Directory environment. As mentioned earlier in this chapter, using additional domain controllers provides the following benefits:

- Increased network performance:
  - The servers can balance the burden of serving client requests.
  - Clients can connect to the server closest to them instead of performing authentication and security operations across a slow WAN link.
- Fault tolerance (in case one domain controller fails, the other still contains a valid and usable copy of the Active Directory database).
- In Windows Server 2012 R2, RODCs help increase security when users connect to a domain controller in an unsecured remote location.

Placing Global Catalog Servers

A *global catalog (GC)* server is a domain controller that contains a copy of all of the objects contained in the forest-wide domain controllers that compose the Active Directory database. Making a domain controller a GC server is simple, and you can change this setting quite easily. That brings us to the harder part—determining which domain controllers should also be GC servers.

Where you place domain controllers and GC servers and how many you deploy are important network planning decisions. Generally, you want to make GC servers available in every site that has a slow link. This means the most logical places to put GC servers are in every site and close to the WAN link for the best possible connectivity. However, having too many GC servers is a bad thing. The main issue is associated with replication traffic—you must keep each GC server within your environment synchronized with the other servers. In a very dynamic environment, using additional GC servers causes a considerable increase in network traffic. Therefore, you will want to find a good balance between replication burdens and GC query performance in your own large multidomain environment.

To create a GC server, simply expand the Server object in the Active Directory Sites and Services tool, right-click NTDS Settings, and select Properties to bring up the NTDS Settings Properties dialog box (see Figure 21.10). To configure a server as a GC server, simply place a check mark in the Global Catalog box.

FIGURE 21.10   Enabling the global catalog on an Active Directory domain controller

⊕ Real World Scenario

Accommodating a Changing Environment

You're a system administrator for a medium-sized business that consists of many offices located throughout the world. Some of these offices are well connected because they use high-speed, reliable links, while others are not so fortunate. Overall, things are going well until your CEO announces that the organization will be merging with another large company and that the business will be restructured. The restructuring will involve opening new offices, closing old ones, and transferring employees to different locations. Additionally, changes in the IT budget will affect the types of links that exist between offices. Your job as the system administrator is to ensure that the network environment and, specifically, Active Directory keep pace with the changes and ultimately outperform them.

An important skill for any technical professional is the ability to adapt quickly and efficiently to a changing organization. When a business grows, restructures, or forms relationships with other businesses, often many IT-related changes must also occur. You may have to create new network links, for example.

Fortunately, Active Directory was designed with these kinds of challenges in mind. For example, you can use the Active Directory Sites and Services administrative tool to reflect physical network changes in Active Directory topology. If a site that previously had 64Kbps of bandwidth is upgraded to a T1 connection, you can change those characteristics for the site link objects. Conversely, if a site that was previously well connected is reduced to a slow, unreliable link, you can reconfigure the sites, change the site link transport mechanisms (perhaps from IP to SMTP to accommodate a nonpersistent link), and create connection objects (which would allow you to schedule replication traffic to occur during the least busy hours).

Suppose further that many of your operations move overseas to a European division. This might call for designating specific domain controllers as preferred bridgehead servers to reduce the amount of replication traffic over costly and slow overseas links.

Sweeping organizational changes inevitably require you to move servers between sites. For example, an office may close and its domain controllers may move to another region of the world. Again, you can accommodate this change by using Active Directory administrative tools. You may change your OU structure to reflect new logical and business-oriented changes, and you can move server objects between sites to reflect physical network changes.

Rarely can the job of mapping a physical infrastructure to Active Directory be "complete." In most environments, it's safe to assume that you will always need to make changes based on business needs. Overall, however, you should feel comfortable that the physical components of Active Directory are at your side to help you accommodate these changes.

Using Universal Group Membership Caching

To understand how Universal Group Membership Caching (UGMC) works, you must first understand how authentication works. When a user tries to authenticate with a domain controller, the first action that takes place is that the domain controller checks with the global catalog to see to which domain the user belongs.

If the domain controller (the one to which the user is trying to authenticate) is not a GC, then the domain controller sends a request to the GC to verify the user's domain. The GC responds with the user's information, and the domain controller authenticates the user (if the user belongs to the same domain as the domain controller).

There are two ways to speed up the authentication process. First, you can make all of the domain controllers global catalogs. But then you end up with a lot of GC replication traffic. This becomes even more of an issue if you have multiple sites. Now replication traffic can be too large for your site link connections.

Thus, if you have a slower site link connection or multiple domains, you can use Universal Group Membership Caching. If you are using UGMC, after a domain controller communicates with the global catalog, the domain controller will then cache the user's credentials for eight hours by default. Now if the user logs off the domain and then logs back into the domain, the domain controller will use the cached credentials and not ask the global catalog. The downside to using UGMC is that it is for authentication only. Global catalogs help speed up Active Directory searches, and they work with Directory Service–enabled applications (applications that have to work with Active Directory) such as Exchange and SQL.

Domain Controller Cloning

Throughout the book, I have talked about why so many organizations are switching to virtualization in their server rooms. Virtualization allows an administrator to take one physical server and turn it into multiple virtual servers by using Windows Server 2012 R2.

In Windows Server 2012 R2, administrators can now easily and safely create replica domain controllers by copying an existing virtual domain controller. Before Windows Server 2012, an administrator would have to deploy a server image that they prepared by using sysprep.exe. After going through the process of using sysprep.exe, the administrator would have to promote this server to a domain controller and then complete additional configuration requirements for deploying each replica domain controller.

Domain controller cloning allows an administrator to deploy rapidly a large number of domain controllers. To set up domain controller cloning, you must be a member of the Domain Admins group or have the equivalent permissions. The administrator must then run Windows PowerShell from an elevated command prompt.

Only Windows Server 2012 or Windows Server 2012 R2 domain controllers that are hosted on a VM-compatible hypervisor can be used as a source for cloning. You should also make sure that the domain controller that you choose to clone is in a healthy state (use computer management to see the computer's state).

The following example is used to create a clone domain controller named TestClone with a static IP address of 10.0.0.5 and a subnet mask of 255.255.0.0. This command also configures the DNS Server and WINS server configurations.

```
New-ADDCCloneConfigFile -CloneComputerName "TestClone" -Static -IPv4Address
"10.0.0.5" -IPv4DNSResolver "10.0.0.1" -IPv4SubnetMask "255.255.0.0" -
PreferredWinsServer "10.0.0.1" -AlternateWinsServer "10.0.0.2"
```

 When you are ready to clone a domain controller, I recommend you visit Microsoft's TechNet site for all of the PowerShell commands needed to complete this entire process.

Monitoring and Troubleshooting Active Directory Replication

For the most part, domain controllers handle the replication processes automatically. However, system administrators still need to monitor the performance of Active Directory replication because failed network links and incorrect configurations can sometimes prevent the synchronization of information between domain controllers.

You can monitor the behavior of Active Directory replication and troubleshoot the process if problems occur.

About System Monitor

The Windows Server 2012 R2 System Monitor administrative tool was designed so that you can monitor many performance statistics associated with using Active Directory. Included within the various performance statistics that you can monitor are counters related to Active Directory replication.

Troubleshooting Replication

A common symptom of replication problems is that information is not updated on some or all domain controllers. For example, a system administrator creates a user account on one domain controller, but the changes are not propagated to other domain controllers. In most environments, this is a potentially serious problem because it affects network security and can prevent authorized users from accessing the resources they require.

You can take several steps to troubleshoot Active Directory replication. These steps are discussed in the following sections.

Verifying Network Connectivity

For replication to work properly in distributed environments, you must have network connectivity. Although ideally all domain controllers would be connected by high-speed LAN links, this is rarely the case for larger organizations. In the real world, dial-up connections and slow connections are common. If you have verified that your replication topology is set up properly, you should confirm that your servers are able to communicate. Problems such as a failed dial-up connection attempt can prevent important Active Directory information from being replicated.

Verifying Router and Firewall Configurations

Firewalls are used to restrict the types of traffic that can be transferred between networks. They are mainly used to increase security by preventing unauthorized users from transferring information. In some cases, company firewalls may block the types of network access that must be available for Active Directory replication to occur. For example, if a specific router or firewall prevents data from being transferred using SMTP, replication that uses this protocol will fail.

Examining the Event Logs

Whenever an error in the replication configuration occurs, the computer writes events to the Directory Service and File Replication Service event logs. By using the Event Viewer administrative tool, you can quickly and easily view the details associated with any problems in replication. For example, if one domain controller is unable to communicate with another to transfer changes, a log entry is created.

Verifying That Information Is Synchronized

It's often easy to forget to perform manual checks regarding the replication of Active Directory information. One of the reasons for this is that Active Directory domain controllers have their own read-write copies of the Active Directory database. Therefore, if connectivity does not exist, you will not encounter failures while creating new objects.

It is important to verify periodically that objects have been synchronized between domain controllers. This process might be as simple as logging on to a different domain controller and looking at the objects within a specific OU. This manual check, although it might be tedious, can prevent inconsistencies in the information stored on domain controllers, which, over time, can become an administration and security nightmare.

Verifying Authentication Scenarios

A common replication configuration issue occurs when clients are forced to authenticate across slow network connections. The primary symptom of the problem is that users complain about the amount of time it takes them to log on to Active Directory (especially during a period when there's a high volume of authentications, such as at the beginning of the workday).

Usually, you can alleviate this problem by using additional domain controllers or reconfiguring the site topology. A good way to test this is to consider the possible scenarios for the various clients that you support. Often, walking through a configuration, such as "A client in Domain1 is trying to authenticate using a domain controller in Domain2, which is located across a slow WAN connection," can be helpful in pinpointing potential problem areas.

Verifying the Replication Topology

The Active Directory Sites and Services tool allows you to verify that a replication topology is logically consistent. You can quickly and easily perform this task by right-clicking NTDS Settings within a Server object and choosing All Tasks ➢ Check Replication. If any errors are present, a dialog box alerts you to the problem.

Another way to verify replication is by using the command-line utility Repadmin. Table 21.1 shows some of the Repadmin commands.

TABLE 21.1   Repadmin commands

Command	Description
Repadmin Bridgeheads	Lists the bridgehead servers for a specified site.
Repadmin dsaguid	Returns a server name when given a GUID.
Repadmin failcache	Shows a list of failed replication events.
Repadmin istg	Returns the server name of the Inter-Site Topology Generator (ISTG) server for a specified site. The ISTG manages the inbound replication connection objects for the bridgehead servers in a site.
Repadmin kcc	Forces the Knowledge Consistency Checker (KCC) to recalculate replication topology for a specified domain controller. The KCC modifies data in the local directory in response to system-wide changes.
Repadmin latency	Shows the amount of time between replications.
Repadmin queue	Shows tasks waiting in the replication queue.
Repadmin querysites	Uses routing information to determine the cost of a route from a specified site to another specified site or to other sites.
Repadmin replicate	Starts a replication event for the specified directory partition between domain controllers.
Repadmin replsummary	Displays the replication state and relative health of a forest.
Repadmin showrepl	Displays replication partners for each directory partition on a specified domain controller.

Reasons for Creating Multiple Domains

Before you look at the steps that you must take to create multiple domains, become familiar with the reasons an organization might want to create them.

In general, you should always try to reflect your organization's structure within a single domain. By using organizational units (OUs) and other objects, you can usually create an accurate and efficient structure within one domain. Creating and managing a single domain is usually much simpler than managing a more complex environment consisting of multiple domains.

That being said, you should familiarize yourself with some real benefits and reasons for creating multiple domains and some drawbacks of using them.

Reasons for Using Multiple Domains

You might need to implement multiple domains for several reasons. These reasons include the following considerations:

Scalability   Although Microsoft has designed Active Directory to accommodate millions of objects, this may not be practical for your current environment. Supporting thousands of users within a single domain requires more disk space, greater central processing unit (CPU) usage, and additional network burdens on your domain controllers (computers containing Active Directory security information). To determine the size of the Active Directory domain your network can support, you need to plan, design, test, and analyze within your own environment.

Reducing Replication Traffic   All of the domain controllers in a domain must keep an up-to-date copy of the entire Active Directory database. For small to medium-sized domains, this is generally not a problem. Windows Server 2012 R2 and Active Directory manage all of the details of transferring the database behind the scenes. Other business and technical limitations might, however, affect Active Directory's ability to perform adequate replication. For example, if you have two sites that are connected by a slow network link (or a sporadic link or no link at all), replication is not practical. In this case, you would probably want to create separate domains to isolate replication traffic. Sporadic coverage across the wide area network (WAN) link would come from circuit-switching technologies such as Integrated Services Digital Network (ISDN) technologies. If you didn't have a link at all, then you would have a service provider outage or some other type of disruption. Separate domains mean separate replication traffic, but the amount of administrative overhead is increased significantly.

Because it's common to have WAN links in your business environment, you will always need to consider how your users authenticate to a domain controller (DC). DCs at a remote site are commonly used to authenticate users locally to their local area network (LAN). The most common design involves putting a DC at each remote site to keep authentication traffic from traversing the WAN. If it is the other way around, the authentication traffic may cause users problems if WAN utilization is high or if the link is broken and no other way to the central site is available. The design you are apt to see most often is one in which each server replicates its database of information to each other's server so that the network and its systems converge.

However, it's important to realize that the presence of slow WAN links alone is *not* a good reason to break an organization into multiple domains. The most common solution is to set up site links with the Sites and Services Microsoft Management Console (MMC). When you use this MMC, you can manage replication traffic and fine-tune independently of the domain architecture.

You would want to use a multidomain architecture, such as when two companies merge through an acquisition, for the following reasons:

Meeting Business Needs   Several business needs might justify the creation of multiple domains. Business needs can be broken down even further into organizational and political needs.

One of the organizational reasons for using multiple domains is to avoid potential problems associated with the Domain Administrator account. At least one user needs to have permissions at this level. If your organization is unable or unwilling to trust a single person to have this level of control over all business units, then multiple domains may be the best answer. Because each domain maintains its own security database, you can keep permissions and resources isolated. Through the use of trusts, however, you can still share resources.

A political need for separate domains might arise if you had two companies that merged with two separate but equal management staffs and two sets of officers. In such a situation, you might need to have Active Directory split into two separate databases to keep the security of the two groups separate. Some such organizations may need to keep the internal groups separate by law. A multidomain architecture provides exactly this type of pristinely separate environment.

Many Levels of Hierarchy   Larger organizations tend to have complex internal and external business structures that dictate the need for many different levels of organization. For example, two companies might merge and need to keep two sets of officers who are managed under two different logical groupings. In Chapter 5, "Administer Active Directory," I showed you that you can use OUs to help group different branches of the company so that you can assign permissions, delegations, or whatever else you can think of without affecting anyone else. Managing data becomes much easier when you're using OUs, and if you design them correctly, OUs will help you control your network right from one console. You may need only one level of management—your company may be small enough to warrant the use of the default OU structure you see when Active Directory is first installed. If, however, you find that you need many levels of OUs to manage resources (or if large numbers of objects exist within each OU), it might make sense to create additional domains. Each domain would contain its own OU hierarchy and serve as the root of a new set of objects.

Decentralized Administration   Two main models of administration are commonly used: a centralized administration model and a decentralized administration model. In the centralized administration model, a single IT organization is responsible for managing all of the users, computers, and security permissions for the entire organization. In the decentralized administration model, each department or business unit might have its own IT department. In both cases, the needs of the administration model can play a significant role in whether you decide to use multiple domains.

Consider, for example, a multinational company that has a separate IT department for offices in each country. Each IT department is responsible for supporting only the users and computers within its own region. Because the administration model is largely decentralized, creating a separate domain for each of these major business units might make sense from a security and maintenance standpoint.

Multiple DNS or Domain Names   Another reason you may need to use a multidomain architecture is if you want or plan to use multiple DNS names within your organization. If you use multiple DNS names or domain names, you must create multiple Active Directory domains. Each AD domain can have only one *fully qualified domain name (FQDN)*. An FQDN is the full name of a system that consists of a local host, a second-level domain name, and a top-level domain (TLD). For example, corp.stellacon.com is an FQDN, .com is the TLD, www is the host, and stellacon is the second-level domain name.

Legality   One final reason you may need to use a multidomain architecture is legality within your organization. Some corporations have to follow state or federal regulations and laws. For this reason, they may need to have multiple domains.

Drawbacks of Multiple Domains

Although there are many reasons why it makes sense to have multiple domains, there are also reasons why you should not break an organizational structure into multiple domains, many of which are related to maintenance and administration. Here are some of the drawbacks to using multiple domains:

Administrative Inconsistency   One of the fundamental responsibilities of most system administrators is implementing and managing security. When you are implementing Group Policy and security settings in multiple domains, you want to be careful to ensure that the settings are consistent. In Windows Server 2012 R2, security policies can be different between and within the same domains. If this is what the organization intended, then it is not a problem. However, if an organization want to make the same settings apply to all users, then each domain requires a separate GPO with similar security settings.

Increased Management Challenges   Managing servers, users, and computers can become a considerable challenge when you are also managing multiple domains because many more administrative units are required. In general, you need to manage all user, group, and computer settings separately for the objects within each domain. The hierarchical structure provided by OUs, on the other hand, provides a much simpler and easier way to manage permissions.

Decreased Flexibility   Creating a domain involves the *promotion* of a DC to the new domain. Although the process is quite simple, it is much more difficult to rearrange the domain topology within an Active Directory environment than it is simply to reorganize OUs. When planning domains, you should ensure that the domain structure will not change often, if at all.

Now that you have examined the pros and cons related to creating multiple domains, it is time to see how to create trees and forests.

Creating Domain Trees and Forests

So far, this chapter has covered some important reasons for using multiple domains in a single network environment. Now it's time to look at how to create multidomain structures such as domain trees and domain forests.

Regardless of the number of domains you have in your environment, you always have a tree and a forest. This might surprise those of you who generally think of domain trees and forests as belonging only to Active Directory environments that consist of multiple domains. However, recall that when you install the first domain in an Active Directory environment, that domain automatically creates a new forest and a new tree.

In the following sections, you will learn how to plan trees and forests and how to promote domain controllers to establish a tree and forest environment.

Planning Trees and Forests

You have already seen several reasons why you might want to have multiple domains within a single company. What you haven't yet seen is how multiple domains can be related to each other and how their relationships can translate into domain forests and trees.

A fundamental commonality between the various domains that exist in trees and forests is that they all share the same Active Directory global catalog (GC). This means that if you modify the Active Directory schema, these changes must be propagated to all of the domain controllers in all of the domains. This is an important point because adding and modifying the structure of information in the GC can have widespread effects on replication and network traffic. Also, you need to ensure that any system you use in the GC role can handle it—you might need to size up the system's hardware requirements. This is especially true if there are multiple domains.

Every domain within an Active Directory configuration has its own unique name. For example, even though you might have a sales domain in two different trees, the complete names for each domain will be different (such as `sales.stellacon1.com` and `sales.stellacon2.com`).

In the following sections, you'll look at how you can organize multiple Active Directory domains based on business requirements.

Using a Single Tree

The concept of domain trees was created to preserve the relationship between multiple domains that share a common contiguous namespace. For example, you might have the following DNS domains (based on Internet names):

- `mycompany.com`
- `sales.mycompany.com`
- `engineering.mycompany.com`
- `europe.sales.mycompany.com`

Note that all of these domains fit within a single contiguous namespace. That is, they are all direct or indirect children of the `mycompany.com` domain. In this case, `mycompany.com` is called the *root domain*. All of the direct children (such as `sales.mycompany.com` and `engineering.mycompany.com`) are called *child domains*. Finally, *parent domains* are the domains that are directly above one domain. For example, `sales.mycompany.com` is the parent domain of `europe.sales.mycompany.com`. Figure 21.11 provides an example of a domain tree.

FIGURE 21.11   A domain tree

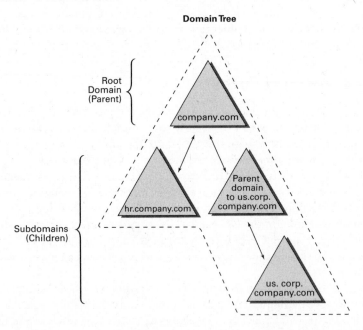

To establish a domain tree, you must first create the root domain for the tree. Then you can add child domains off this root. These child domains can then serve as parents for further subdomains. Each domain must have at least one domain controller, and domain controllers can participate in only one domain at a time. However, you can move a domain controller from one domain to another. To do this, you must first demote a domain controller to a member server and then promote it to a domain controller in another domain.

 You will learn how to demote a domain controller later in this chapter in the section "Demoting a Domain Controller."

Domains are designed to be logical boundaries. The domains within a tree are, by default, automatically bound together using a two-way transitive trust relationship, which allows resources to be shared among domains through the use of the appropriate user and group assignments. Because trust relationships are transitive, all of the domains within the tree trust each other. Note, however, that a trust by itself does not automatically grant any security permissions to users or objects between domains. Trusts are designed only to *allow* resources to be shared; you must still go through the process of sharing and managing them. Enterprise administrators must explicitly assign security settings to resources before users can access resources between domains.

Using a single tree makes sense when your organization maintains only a single contiguous namespace. Regardless of the number of domains that exist within this environment and how different their security settings are from each other, they are related by a common name. Although domain trees make sense for many organizations, in some cases the network namespace may be considerably more complicated. You'll look at how forests address these situations next.

Using a Forest

Active Directory forests are designed to accommodate multiple noncontiguous namespaces. That is, they can combine domain trees into logical units. An example might be the following tree and domain structure:

- Tree: `Organization1.com`
  - `Sales.Organization1.com`
  - `Marketing.Organization1.com`
  - `Engineering.Organization1.com`
  - `NorthAmerica.Engineering.Organization1.com`
- Tree: `Organization2.com`
  - `Sales.Organization2.com`
  - `Engineering.Organization2.com.`

Figure 21.12 provides an example of how multiple trees can fit into a single forest. Such a situation might occur in the acquisition and merger of companies or if a company is logically divided into two or more completely separate and autonomous business units.

FIGURE 21.12   A single forest consisting of multiple trees

All of the trees within a forest are related through a single forest root domain. This is the first domain that was created in the Active Directory environment. The root domain in each tree creates a transitive trust with the forest root domain. The result is a configuration in which all of the trees within a domain and all of the domains within each tree trust each other. Again, as with domain trees, the presence of a trust relationship does not automatically signify that users have permissions to access resources across domains. It allows only objects and resources to be shared. Authorized network administrators must set up specific permissions.

All of the domains within a single Active Directory forest have the following features in common:

Schema   The *schema* is the Active Directory structure that defines how the information within the data store is structured. For the information stored on various domain controllers to remain compatible, all of the domain controllers within the entire Active Directory environment must share the same schema. For example, if you add a field for an employee benefit plan number, all domain controllers throughout the environment need to recognize this information before you can share information among them.

Global Catalog   One of the problems associated with working in large network environments is that sharing information across multiple domains can be costly in terms of network and server resources. Fortunately, Active Directory uses the global catalog (GC), which serves as a repository for information about a subset of all objects within *all* Active Directory domains in a forest. System administrators can determine what types of information should be added to the defaults in the GC. Generally, they decide to store commonly used information, such as a list of all of the printers, users, groups, and computers. In addition, they can configure specific domain controllers to carry a copy of the GC. Now if you have a question about where to find all of the color printers in the company, for example, all you need to do is to contact the nearest GC server.

Configuration Information   Some roles and functions must be managed for the entire forest. When you are dealing with multiple domains, this means that you must configure certain domain controllers to perform functions for the entire Active Directory environment. I will discuss some specifics of this later in this chapter.

The main purpose of allowing multiple domains to exist together is to allow them to share information and other resources. Now that you've seen the basics of domain trees and forests, take a look at how domains are actually created.

The Promotion Process

A domain tree is created when a new domain is added as the child of an existing domain. This relationship is established during the promotion of a Windows Server 2012 R2 computer to a domain controller. Although the underlying relationships can be quite complicated in larger organizations, the Server Manager's Active Directory Installation Wizard makes it easy to create forests and trees.

Using the Active Directory Installation Wizard, you can quickly and easily create new domains by promoting a Windows Server 2012 R2 stand-alone server or a member server to a domain controller. When you install a new domain controller, you can choose to make it part of an existing domain, or you can choose to make it the first domain controller in a new domain. In the following sections and exercises, you'll become familiar with the exact steps you need to take to create a domain tree and a domain forest when you promote a server to a domain controller.

Creating a Domain Tree

In previous chapters, you learned how to promote the first domain controller in the first domain in a forest, also known as the root. If you don't promote any other domain controllers, then that domain controller simply controls that one domain and only one tree is created. To create a new domain tree, you need to promote a Windows Server 2012 R2 computer to a domain controller. In the Active Directory Installation Wizard, you select the option that makes this domain controller the first machine in a new domain that is a child of an existing domain. As a result, you will have a domain tree that contains two domains—a parent and a child, or two trees if you don't create a child domain.

Before you can create a new child domain, you need the following information:

- The name of the parent domain (for the exercises, you'll use the one you created in the previous chapter.)
- The name of the child domain (the one you are planning to install)
- The file system locations for the Active Directory database, logs, and shared system volume

- DNS configuration information
- The NetBIOS name for the new server
- A domain administrator username and password

Exercise 21.6 walks you through the process of creating a new child domain using Server Manager. This exercise assumes you have already created the parent domain and you are using a server in the domain that is not a domain controller.

EXERCISE 21.6

Creating a New Subdomain

1. Open Server Manager.

2. Click item 2, Add Roles And Features.

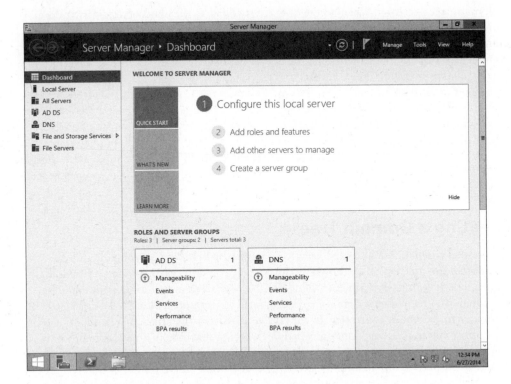

3. Make sure that the Role-Based Or Feature-Based Installation button is selected and click Next.

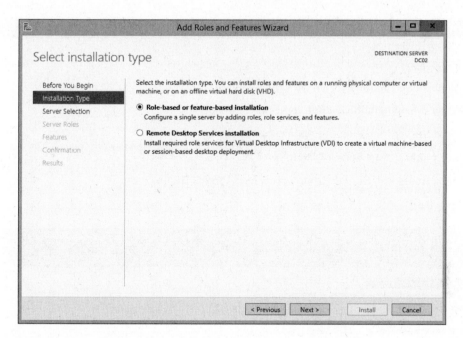

4. At the Select Destination screen, click Next.

5. At the Select Server Roles screen, check the Active Directory Domain Services check box. A box will appear stating that you need to install additional roles. Click the Add Features button. Then click Next.

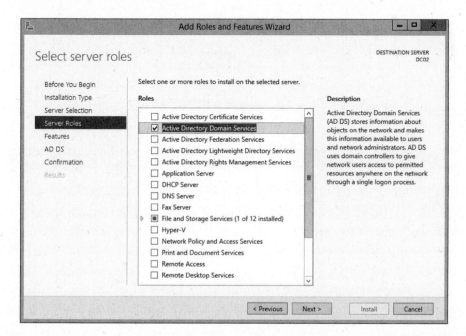

6. At the Add Roles And Features Wizard screen, click Next.

7. At the Confirmation screen, click the Install button.

8. When the installation is complete, click the Close button.

9. Close Server Manager and restart the machine.

10. Log in and restart Server Manager.

11. In the Roles And Server Groups area, click the AD DS link.

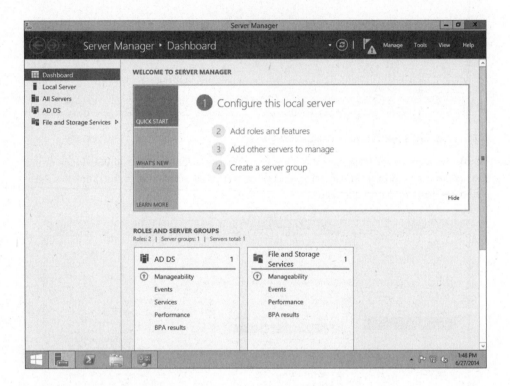

12. In the Servers section, click the More link next to Configuration Required For Active Directory Domain Services.

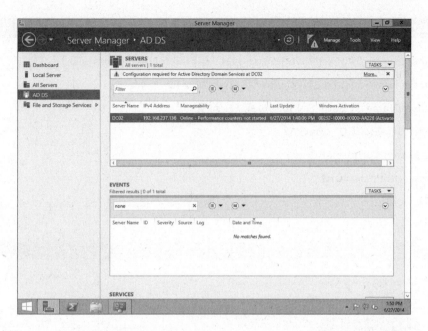

13. At the All Servers Task Details screen, click the Promote This Server To A Domain Controller link.

14. At the Deployment Configuration screen, click the radio button Add A New Domain To An Existing Forest. In the Select Domain Type drop-down, chose Child Domain and then choose your parent domain. In the New Domain Name box, type in the name of your new domain. I used NewHampshire. Click the Next button.

EXERCISE 21.6 *(continued)*

15. At the Domain Controller Options screen, I set the following options:

Domain Functional Level: Windows Server 2012 R2

Domain Name System (DNS) Server: Checked

Global Catalog (GC): Checked

Site Name: CorporateHQ

Password: **P@ssw0rd**

Click Next.

16. At the DNS screen, click Next.

17. At the Additional Options screen, accept the default NetBIOS domain name and click Next.

18. At the Paths screen, accept the default file locations and click Next.

19. At the Review Options screen, verify your settings and click Next.

20. At the Prerequisites Check screen, click the Install button (as long as there are no errors).

21. After the installation completes, the machine will automatically reboot. Log in as the administrator.

22. Close Server Manager.

Joining a New Domain Tree to a Forest

A *forest* is one or more trees that do not share a contiguous namespace. For example, you could join the `organization1.com` and `organization2.com` domains together to create a single Active Directory environment.

Any two trees can be joined together to create a forest, as long as the second tree is installed after the first and the trees have noncontiguous namespaces. (If the namespaces were contiguous, you would actually need to create a new domain for an existing tree.) The process of creating a new tree to form or add to a forest is as simple as promoting a server to a domain controller for a new domain that does *not* share a namespace with an existing Active Directory domain.

 The command-line tool `adprep.exe` is used to prepare a Microsoft Windows 2003, 2008, or 2008 R2 forest or a Windows 2003, 2008, or 2008 R2 domain for the installation of Windows Server 2012 R2 domain controllers.

To add a new domain to an existing forest, you must already have at least one other domain, which is the root domain. Keep in mind that the entire forest structure is destroyed if the original root domain is ever removed entirely. Therefore, you should have at least two domain controllers in the Active Directory root domain; the second serves as a backup in case you have a problem with the first, and it can also serve as a backup solution for disaster recovery and fault tolerance purposes. Such a setup provides additional protection for the entire forest in case one of the domain controllers fails.

Adding Additional Domain Controllers

In addition to the operations you've already performed, you can use the Active Directory Installation Wizard to create additional domain controllers for any of your domains. There are two main reasons to create additional domain controllers:

Fault Tolerance and Reliability   You should always consider the theory of *disaster recovery (DR)* and have a plan, sometimes referred to as a *disaster recovery plan (DRP)*. If you're part of one of those organizations that rely upon their network directory services infrastructures, you need Active Directory to provide security and resources for all users.

For this reason, downtime and data loss are very costly. Through the use of multiple domain controllers, you can ensure that if one of the servers goes down, another one is available to perform the necessary tasks, such as user authentication and resource browsing. Additionally, data loss (perhaps from hard disk drive failure) will not result in the loss or unavailability of network security information because you can easily recover Active Directory information from the remaining, still-functional domain controller.

Performance   The burden of processing login requests and serving as a repository for security permissions and other information can be quite extensive, especially in larger businesses. By using multiple domain controllers, you can distribute this load across multiple systems. Additionally, by strategically placing domain controllers, you can greatly increase response times for common network operations, such as authentication and browsing for resources.

As a rule of thumb, you should always plan and design your infrastructure to have at least two domain controllers per domain. For many organizations, this provides a good balance between the cost of servers and the level of reliability and performance. For larger or more distributed organizations, however, additional domain controllers greatly improve performance.

Demoting a Domain Controller

In addition to being able to promote member servers to domain controllers, the Active Directory Installation Wizard can do the exact opposite, that is, demote domain controllers. You might choose to demote a domain controller for a couple of reasons. First, if you have determined that the role of a server should change (for example, from a domain controller to a member or stand-alone server that you might make into a web server), you can easily demote it to make this happen. Another common reason to demote a domain controller is if you want to move the machine from one domain to another. You cannot do this in a single step: First you need to demote the existing domain controller to remove it from the current domain and then promote it into a new domain. The result is that the server is now a domain controller for a different domain.

To demote a domain controller, you simply access the Active Directory Installation Wizard. The wizard automatically notices that the local server is a domain controller, and it asks you to verify each step you take, as with most things you do in Windows. You are prompted to decide whether you really want to remove this machine from the current domain. Note that if the local server is a global catalog server, you will be warned that at least one copy of the GC must remain available so that you can perform logon authentication.

By default, at the end of the demotion process, the server is joined as a member server to the domain for which it was previously a domain controller. If you demote the last domain controller in the domain, the server becomes a stand-alone server.

 Real World Scenario

Planning for Domain Controller Placement

You are the senior system administrator for a medium-sized Active Directory environment. Currently the environment consists of only one Active Directory domain. Your company's network is spread out over 40 different sites throughout North America. Recently, you've received complaints from users and other system administrators about the performance of Active Directory–related operations. For example, users report that it takes several minutes to log on to their machines between 9 a.m. and 10 a.m., when activity is at its highest. Simultaneously, system administrators complain that updating user information within the OUs for which they are responsible can take longer than expected.

Fortunately, Active Directory's distributed domain controller architecture allows you to optimize performance for this type of situation without making dramatic changes to your environment. You decide that the quickest and easiest solution is to deploy additional domain controllers throughout the organization. The domain controllers are generally placed within areas of the network that are connected by slow or unreliable links. For example, a small branch office in Des Moines, Iowa, receives its own domain controller. The process is quite simple: You install a new Windows Server 2012 R2 computer and then run the Active Directory Installation Wizard in Server Manager to make the new machine a domain controller for an existing domain. Once the initial directory services data is copied to the new server, it is ready to service requests and updates of your domain information.

Note that there are potential drawbacks to this solution; for instance, you have to manage additional domain controllers and the network traffic generated from communications between the domain controllers. It's important that you monitor your network links to ensure that you've reached a good balance between replication traffic and overall Active Directory performance. In later chapters, you'll see how you can configure Active Directory sites to map Active Directory operations better to your physical network structure.

WARNING   Removing a domain from your environment is not an operation that you should take lightly. Before you plan to remove a domain, make a list of all of the resources that depend on the domain and the reasons why the domain was originally created. If you are sure that your organization no longer requires the domain, then you can safely continue. If you are not sure, think again, because the process cannot be reversed, and you could lose critical information!

Managing Multiple Domains

You can easily manage most of the operations that must occur *between* domains by using the Active Directory Domains and Trusts administrative tool. On the other hand, if you want to configure settings *within* a domain, you should use the Active Directory Users and Computers tool. In the following sections, you'll look at ways to perform two common domain management functions with the tools just mentioned: managing *single-master operations* and managing *trusts*. You'll also look at ways to manage UPN suffixes in order to simplify user accounts, and you'll examine GC servers in more detail.

Managing Single-Master Operations

For the most part, Active Directory functions in what is known as *multimaster* replication. That is, every domain controller within the environment contains a copy of the Active Directory database that is both readable and writable. This works well for most types of information. For example, if you want to modify the password of a user, you can easily do this on *any* of the domain controllers within a domain. The change is then automatically propagated to the other domain controllers.

However, some functions are not managed in a multimaster fashion. These operations are known as *operations masters*. You must perform single-master operations on specially designated domain controllers within the Active Directory forest. There are five main single-master functions: two that apply to an entire Active Directory forest and three that apply to each domain.

Forest Operations Masters

You use the Active Directory Domains and Trusts tool to configure forest-wide roles. The following single-master operations apply to the entire forest:

Schema Master   Earlier you learned that all of the domain controllers within a single Active Directory environment share the same schema. This ensures information consistency. However, developers and system administrators can modify the Active

Directory schema by adding custom information. A trivial example might involve adding a field to employee information that specifies a user's favorite color.

When you need to make these types of changes, you must perform them on the domain controller that serves as the *Schema Master* for the environment. The Schema Master is then responsible for propagating all of the changes to all of the other domain controllers within the forest.

Domain Naming Master   The purpose of the *Domain Naming Master* is to keep track of all of the domains within an Active Directory forest. You access this domain controller whenever you need to add/remove new domains to a tree or forest.

Domain Operations Masters

You use the Active Directory Users and Computers snap-in to administer roles within a domain. Within each domain, at least one domain controller must fulfill each of the following roles:

Relative ID (RID) Master   Every security object within Active Directory must be assigned a unique identifier so that it is distinguishable from other objects. For example, if you have two OUs named IT that reside in different domains, you must have some way to distinguish easily between them. Furthermore, if you delete one of the IT OUs and then later re-create it, the system must be able to determine that it is not the same object as the other IT OU. The unique identifier for each object consists of a domain identifier and a relative identifier (RID). RIDs are always unique within an Active Directory domain and are used for managing security information and authenticating users. The *RID Master* is responsible for creating these values within a domain whenever new Active Directory objects are created.

PDC Emulator Master   Within a domain, the *PDC Emulator Master* is responsible for maintaining backward compatibility with Windows 95, 98, and NT clients. It is also responsible for processing account lockouts, performing password changes, and validating failed logon authentications within the domain. If a user's logon authentication fails to a bad password on a domain controller, then that domain controller passes the authentication request to the PDC Emulator Master to check and see whether the password that was used matches the password that is most current for that user.

The PDC Emulator Master serves as the default domain controller to process authentication requests if another domain controller is unable to do so. The PDC Emulator Master also receives preferential treatment whenever domain security changes are made.

Infrastructure Master   Whenever a user is added to or removed from a group, all of the other domain controllers should be made aware of this change. The role of the domain controller that acts as an *Infrastructure Master* is to ensure that group membership information stays synchronized within an Active Directory domain.

Unless there is only one domain controller, you should not place the Infrastructure Master on a global catalog server. If the Infrastructure Master and global catalog are on the same domain controller, the Infrastructure Master will not function. If you have only one domain, then all DCs are GCs.

Another service that a server can control for the network is the Windows Time service. The Windows Time service uses a suite of algorithms in the Network Time Protocol (NTP). This helps ensure that the time on all computers throughout a network is as accurate as possible. All client computers within a Windows Server 2012 R2 domain are synchronized with the time of an authoritative computer.

Assigning Single-Master Roles

Now that you are familiar with the different types of single-master operations, take a look at Exercise 21.7. This exercise shows you how to assign these roles to servers within the Active Directory environment. In this exercise, you will assign single-master operations roles to various domain controllers within the environment. To complete the steps in this exercise, you need one Active Directory domain controller.

EXERCISE 21.7

Assigning Single-Master Operations

1. Open the Active Directory Domains and Trusts administrative tool.

2. Right-click Active Directory Domains And Trusts and choose Operations Masters.

3. In the Operations Masters dialog box, note that you can change the operations master by clicking the Change button. If you want to move this assignment to another computer, first you need to connect to that computer and then make the change. Click Close to continue without making any changes.

4. Close the Active Directory Domains and Trusts administrative tool.

5. Open the Active Directory Users and Computers administrative tool.

6. Right-click the name of a domain and select Operations Masters. This brings up the RID tab of the Operations Masters dialog box.

   Notice that you can change the computer that is assigned to the role. To change the role, first you need to connect to the appropriate domain controller. Notice that the PDC and Infrastructure roles have similar tabs. Click Close to continue without making any changes.

7. When you have finished, close the Active Directory Users and Computers tool.

Remember that you manage single-master operations with three different tools. You use the Active Directory Domains and Trusts tool to configure the Domain Name Master role, while you use the Active Directory Users and Computers snap-in to administer roles within a domain. Although this might not seem intuitive at first, it can help you remember which roles apply to domains and which apply to the whole forest. The third tool, the Schema Master role, is a bit different from these other two. To change the Schema Master role, you must install the Active Directory Schema MMS snap-in and change it there.

Managing Trusts

Trust relationships make it easier to share security information and network resources between domains. As was already mentioned, standard transitive two-way trusts are automatically created between the domains in a tree and between each of the trees in a forest. Figure 21.13 shows an example of the default trust relationships in an Active Directory forest.

FIGURE 21.13 Default trusts in an Active Directory forest

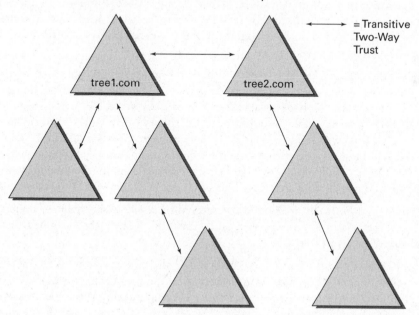

When configuring trusts, you need to consider two main characteristics:

Transitive Trusts   By default, Active Directory trusts are *transitive trusts*. The simplest way to understand transitive relationships is through this example: If Domain A trusts Domain B and Domain B trusts Domain C, then Domain A implicitly trusts Domain C. If you need to apply a tighter level of security, trusts can be configured as intransitive.

One-Way vs. Two-Way   Trusts can be configured as one-way or two-way relationships. The default operation is to create *two-way trusts* or *bidirectional trusts*. This makes it easier to manage trust relationships by reducing the trusts you must create. In some cases, however, you might decide against two-way trusts. In one-way relationships, the trusting domain allows resources to be shared with the trusted domain but not the other way around.

When domains are added together to form trees and forests, an automatic transitive two-way trust is created between them. Although the default trust relationships work well for most organizations, there are some reasons you might want to manage trusts manually:

- You may want to remove trusts between domains if you are absolutely sure you do not want resources to be shared between domains.

- Because of security concerns, you may need to keep resources isolated.

In addition to the default trust types, you can configure the following types of special trusts:

External Trusts   You use *external trusts* to provide access to resources on a Windows NT 4 domain or forest that cannot use a forest trust. Windows NT 4 domains cannot benefit from the other trust types that are used in Windows Server 2012 R2. Thus, in some cases, external trusts could be your only option. External trusts are always nontransitive, but they can be established in a one-way or two-way configuration.

Default SID Filtering on External Trusts   When you set up an external trust, remember that it is possible for hackers to compromise a domain controller in a trusted domain. If this trust is compromised, a hacker can use the security identifier (SID) history attribute to associate SIDs with new user accounts, granting themselves unauthorized rights (this is called an *elevation-of-privileges attack*). To help prevent this type of attack, Windows Server 2012 R2 automatically enables SID filter quarantining on all external trusts. SID filtering allows the domain controllers in the trusting domain (the domain with the resources) to remove all SID history attributes that are not members of the trusted domain.

Realm Trusts   *Realm trusts* are similar to external trusts. You use them to connect to a non-Windows domain that uses Kerberos authentication. Realm trusts can be transitive or nontransitive, one-way or two-way.

Cross-Forest Trusts   *Cross-forest trusts* are used to share resources between forests. They have been used since Windows Server 2000 domains and cannot be nontransitive, but you can establish them in a one-way or a two-way configuration. Authentication requests in either forest can reach the other forest in a two-way cross-forest trust. If you want one forest to trust another forest, you must set it (at a minimum) to at least the forest function level of Windows Server 2003.

Selective Authentication vs. Forest-wide Authentication   Forest-wide authentication on a forest trust means that users of the trusted forest can access all of the resources of the trusting forest. Selective authentication means that users cannot authenticate to a domain controller or resource server in the trusting forest unless they are explicitly allowed to do so. Exercise 21.8 will show you the steps necessary to change forest-wide authentication to selective authentication.

Shortcut Trusts   In some cases, you may actually want to create direct trusts between two domains that implicitly trust each other. Such a trust is sometimes referred to as a *shortcut trust*, and it can improve the speed at which resources are accessed across many different domains. Let's say you have a forest, as shown in Figure 21.14.

FIGURE 21.14   Example of a forest

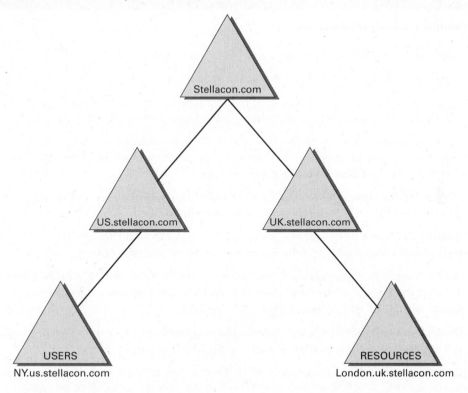

Users in the NY.us.stellacon.com domain can access resources in the London.
uk.stellacon.com domain, but the users have to authenticate using the parent domains to gain access (NY.us.stellacon.com to us.stellacon.com to stellacon.com to uk.stellacon.com to finally reach London.uk.stellacon.com). This process can be slow.

An administrator can set up a one-way trust from London.uk.stellacon.com (trusting domain) to NY.us.stellacon.com (trusted domain) so that the users can access the resources directly.

> Perhaps the most important aspect to remember regarding trusts is that creating them only *allows* you to share resources between domains. The trust does not grant any permissions between domains by itself. Once a trust has been established, however, system administrators can easily assign the necessary permissions.

Exercise 21.8 walks you through the steps necessary to manage trusts. In this exercise, you will see how to assign trust relationships between domains. To complete the steps in this exercise, you must have domain administrator access permissions.

EXERCISE 21.8

Managing Trust Relationships

1. Open the Active Directory Domains and Trusts administrative tool.

2. Right-click the name of a domain and select Properties.

3. Select the Trusts tab. You will see a list of the trusts that are currently configured. To modify the trust properties for an existing trust, highlight that trust and click Properties.

4. The Properties window for the trust displays information about the trust's direction, transitivity, and type along with the names of the domains involved in the relationship. Click Cancel to exit without making any changes.

5. To create a new trust relationship, click the New Trust button on the Trusts tab. The New Trust Wizard appears. Click Next to proceed with the wizard.

6. On the Trust Name page, you are prompted for the name of the domain with which the trust should be created. Enter the name of the domain and click Next.

7. On the Trust Type page, you would normally choose the Trust With A Windows Domain option if you know that the other domain uses a Windows domain controller. Choose Realm Trust. Click Next when you have finished.

8. On the Transitivity Of Trust page, you choose whether the trust is transitive or nontransitive. Choose the Nontransitive option and click Next to continue.

9. On the Direction Of Trust page, you select the direction of the trust. If you want both domains to trust each other, you select the Two-Way option. Otherwise, you select either One-Way: Incoming or One-Way: Outgoing, depending on where the affected users are located. For the sake of this exercise, choose One-Way: Incoming and then click Next.

10. On the Trust Password page, you need to specify a password that should be used to administer the trust. Type **P@ssw0rd** and confirm it. Note that if there is an existing trust relationship between the domains, the passwords must match. Click Next to continue.

11. Now you see the Trust Selections Complete page that recaps the selections you have made. Because this is an exercise, you don't actually want to establish this trust. Click Cancel to cancel the wizard without saving the changes.

12. Exit the trust properties for the domain by clicking Cancel.

To Enable Selective Authentication

1. In the console tree, right-click the name of a domain and select Properties.

2. Select the Trusts tab. Under either Domains Trusted By This Domain (Outgoing Trusts) or Domains That Trust This Domain (Incoming Trusts), click the forest trust that you want to administer and then click Properties.

3. On the Authentication tab, click Selective Authentication and then click OK.

Managing UPN Suffixes

User principal name (UPN) suffixes are the part of a user's name that appears after the @ symbol. For example, the UPN suffix of wpanek@stellacon.com would be stellacon.com. By default, the UPN suffix is determined by the name of the domain in which the user is created. In this example, the user wpanek was created in the domain stellacon.com, so the two pieces of the UPN logically fit together. However, you might find it useful to provide an alternative UPN suffix to consolidate the UPNs forest wide.

For instance, if you manage a forest that consists of stellacon.com and stellacon2.com, you might want all of your users to adopt the more generally applicable stellacon.com UPN suffix. By adding additional UPN suffixes to the forest, you can easily choose the appropriate suffix when it comes time to create new users. Exercise 21.9 shows you how to add additional suffixes to a forest.

EXERCISE 21.9

Adding a UPN Suffix

1. Open the Active Directory Domains and Trusts administrative tool.

2. Right-click Active Directory Domains And Trusts in the left side of the window and select Properties.

3. On the UPN Suffixes tab of the Active Directory Domains And Trusts Properties dialog box, enter an alternative UPN suffix in the Alternative UPN Suffixes field. Click the Add button to add the suffix to the list.

4. To remove a UPN suffix, select its name in the list and click the Remove button.

Name Suffix Routing

Name Suffix Routing is a mechanism that is used to manage how authentication requests are routed across Active Directory forests that are joined together by forest trusts. To simplify the administration of authentication requests, when you create a forest trust, all unique name suffixes are routed by default. A *unique name suffix* is a name suffix within a forest, such as a user principal name (UPN) suffix, service principal name (SPN) suffix, or Domain Name System forest, or a domain tree name that is not subordinate to any other name suffix. Name Suffix Routing is managed from the Active Directory Domains and Trusts Administrative Console.

Managing Global Catalog Servers

One of the best features of a distributed directory service like Active Directory is that you can store different pieces of information in different places within an organization. For example, a domain in Japan might store a list of users who operate within a company's Asian operations business unit, while one in New York would contain a list of users who operate within its North American operations business unit. This architecture allows system administrators to place the most frequently accessed information on domain controllers in different domains, thereby reducing disk space requirements and replication traffic.

However, you may encounter a problem when you deal with information that is segmented into multiple domains. The issue involves querying information stored within Active Directory. For example, what would happen if a user wanted a list of all the printers available in all domains within the Active Directory forest? In this case, the search would normally require information from at least one domain controller in each of the domains within the environment. Some of these domain controllers may be located across slow WAN links or may have unreliable connections. The result would include an extremely long wait while retrieving the results of the query, that is, if any results came up without the query timing out.

Fortunately, Active Directory has a mechanism that speeds up such searches. You can configure any number of domain controllers to host a copy of the GC. The GC contains all of the schema information and a subset of the attributes for all domains within the Active Directory environment. Although a default set of information is normally included with the GC, system administrators can choose to add additional information to this data store if it is needed. To help reduce replication traffic and to keep the GC's database small, only a limited subset of each object's attributes is replicated. This is called the *partial attribute set (PAS)*. You can change the PAS by modifying the schema and marking attributes for replication to the GC.

Servers that contain a copy of the GC are known as *GC servers*. Now whenever a user executes a query that requires information from multiple domains, they need only contact the nearest GC server for this information. Similarly, when users must authenticate across domains, they do not have to wait for a response from a domain controller that may be located across the world. The result is that the overall performance of Active Directory queries improves.

Exercise 21.10 walks you through the steps that you need to take to configure a domain controller as a GC server. Generally, GC servers are useful only in environments that use multiple Active Directory domains.

EXERCISE 21.10

Managing GC Servers

1. Open the Active Directory Sites and Services administrative tool.

2. Find the name of the local domain controller within the list of objects, typically under Default First Site Name ➢ Servers, and expand this object. Right-click NTDS Settings, and select Properties.

3. In the NTDS Settings Properties dialog box, type **Primary GC Server for Domain** in the Description field. Note that there is a check box that determines whether this computer contains a copy of the global catalog. If the box is checked, then this domain controller contains a subset of information from all other domains within the Active Directory environment. Select the Global Catalog check box and then click OK to continue.

4. When you have finished, close the Active Directory Sites and Services administrative tool.

Managing Universal Group Membership Caching

Many networks run into problems with available network bandwidth and server hardware limitations. For this reason, it may not be wise to install a GC in smaller branch offices. Windows Server 2012 R2 can help these smaller sites by deploying domain controllers that use *Universal Group Membership Caching (UGMC)*.

Once enabled, Universal Group Membership Caching stores information locally when a user attempts to log on for the first time. With the use of a GC, the domain controller retains the universal group membership for that logged-on user.

The next time that user attempts to log on, the authenticating domain controller running Windows Server 2012 R2 will obtain the universal group membership information from its local cache without the need to contact a GC. By default, the universal group membership information is retained on the domain controller for eight hours.

There are several advantages of using Universal Group Membership Caching:

Faster Logon Times   Because the domain controller does not need to contact a global catalog, logon authentication is faster.

Reduced Network Bandwidth   The domain controller does not have to handle object replication for all of the objects located in the forest.

Ability to Use Existing Hardware   There is no need to upgrade hardware to support a GC.

Exercise 21.11 shows you the steps necessary to configure Universal Group Membership Caching.

EXERCISE 21.11

Managing Universal Group Membership Caching

1. Open the Active Directory Sites and Services administrative tool.

2. Click Sites and then click CorporateHQ. In the right pane, right-click NTDS Settings and choose Properties.

3. In the NTDS Site Settings Properties dialog box, check the box Enable Universal Group Membership Caching and then click OK to continue.

4. When you have finished, close the Active Directory Sites and Services administrative tool.

Upgrading Existing Domains and Forests

Now that you have a new operating system to which you can upgrade, it's important that you take some time to talk about the different ways you can get your infrastructure up-to-date. There are quite a few upgrade paths to consider. Table 21.2 illustrates the most commonly used in-place upgrade paths for upgrading your domain controllers from Windows Server 2008 to Windows Server 2012 R2. The in-place upgrades hold true only for 64-bit versions of Server 2008 to Server 2012 R2. You cannot in-place upgrade domain controllers that run either Windows Server 2003 or a 32-bit version of Windows Server 2008. If your current environmental configurations fall outside of the possibility of an in-place upgrade, then you will need to install new domain controllers on the most up-to-date Windows Server OS and then delete the old ones.

TABLE 21.2   Supported domain controller in-place upgrade paths

If you are running these editions...	You can upgrade to these editions...
Windows Server 2008 Standard with SP2 or Windows Server 2008 Enterprise with SP2	Windows Server 2012 R2 Standard or Windows Server 2012 R2 Datacenter
Windows Server 2008 Datacenter with SP2	Windows Server 2012 R2 Datacenter
Windows Web Server 2008	Windows Server 2012 R2 Standard

Windows Server 2008 R2 Standard with SP1 or	Windows Server 2012 R2 Standard or
Windows Server 2008 R2 Enterprise with SP1	Windows Server 2012 R2 Datacenter
Windows Server 2008 R2 Datacenter with SP1	Windows Server 2012 R2 Datacenter
Windows Web Server 2008 R2	Windows Server 2012 Standard

When preparing for your domain controller upgrade, make sure you make a full backup of your Active Directory environment prior to the performing the task. If you have never actually performed a full backup and restore of your Active Directory environment, then I recommend doing so by following the instructions in Chapter 19 of this book. You never know if a backup actually works until you perform the restore, and you should never make infrastructure changes without a backup of your current configuration.

In addition to knowing the proper upgrade path and having full backups of your environment, you will also want to take into account domain and forest functional levels. Windows Server 2012 R2 requires a forest functional level of at least Windows Server 2003. This essentially means you cannot add a Windows Server 2012 R2 domain controller to a forest that contains a Windows 2000 machine. You would need to upgrade or eliminate any Windows 2000 machine and then raise the forest functional level to at least Windows Server 2003 in order to accommodate a Windows Server 2012 R2 domain controller. It may seem old, but you'd be surprised how many government organizations still have Windows Server 2000 and Windows Server 2003 running legacy applications in a production environment. You will notice that the issue is far less frequent in commercial settings.

Summary

In this chapter, I discussed the purpose of Active Directory replication. As you have learned, replication is used to keep domain controllers synchronized, and it is important in Active Directory environments of all sizes. Replication is the process by which changes to the Active Directory database are transferred between domain controllers.

This chapter also covered the concepts of sites, site boundaries, and subnets. In addition to learning how to configure them, you learned that subnets define physical portions of your network environment and that sites are defined as collections of well-connected IP subnets. Site boundaries are defined by the subnet or subnets that you include in your site configuration.

I also covered the basics of replication and the differences between intrasite and intersite replication. Additionally, I covered the purpose and use of bridgehead servers in depth. Although replication is a behind-the-scenes type of task, the optimal configuration of sites in distributed network environments results in better use of bandwidth and faster response by network resources. For these reasons, you should be sure you thoroughly understand the concepts related to managing replication for Active Directory.

I covered the placement of domain controllers and global catalog servers in the network and how, when placed properly, they can increase the performance of Active Directory operations.

I also showed how to monitor and troubleshoot replication. The Windows Server 2012 R2 System Monitor administrative tool was designed so that you can monitor many performance statistics associated with using Active Directory.

The chapter also covered the basics of linking multiple domains in trees and forests. You now know why you would want to plan for them and the benefits and drawbacks of using only one domain or of having a multidomain environment. For example, you might decide to have multiple domains if you have an acquisitions-and-mergers situation where you need to keep multiple administrators. In addition, by using multiple domains, organizations can retain separate security databases; however, in such cases, they are also able to share resources between domains.

You can use multiple domains to provide two major benefits for the network directory services—security and availability. These benefits are made possible through Active Directory and the administrative tools that can be used to access it.

System administrators can simplify operations while still ensuring that only authorized users have access to their data. Multiple domains can interact to form Active Directory trees and forests, and you can use the Active Directory Installation Wizard to create new Active Directory trees and forests.

Exam Essentials

Understand the reasons for using multiple domains.   There are seven primary reasons for using multiple domains: They provide additional scalability, they reduce replication traffic, they help with political and organizational issues, they provide many levels of hierarchy, they allow for decentralized administration, they preserve legality, and they allow for multiple DNS or domain names.

Understand the drawbacks of using multiple domains.   With multiple domains, maintaining administrative consistency is more difficult. The number of administrative units multiplies as well, which makes it difficult to keep track of network resources. Finally, it is much more difficult to rearrange the domain topology within an Active Directory environment than it is simply to reorganize OUs.

Know how to create a domain tree.   To create a new domain tree, you need to promote a Windows Server 2012 R2 computer to a domain controller, select the option that makes this domain controller the first machine in a new domain, and make that domain the first domain of a new tree. The result is a new domain tree.

Know how to join a domain tree to a forest.   Creating a new tree to form or add to a forest is as simple as promoting a server to a domain controller for a new domain that does *not* share a namespace with an existing Active Directory domain. To add a domain to an existing forest, you must already have at least one other domain. This domain serves as the root domain for the entire forest.

Understand how to manage single-master operations.   Single-master operations must be performed on specially designated machines within the Active Directory forest. There are five main single-master functions: two that apply to an entire Active Directory forest (Schema Master and Domain Naming Master) and three that apply to each domain (RID Master, PDC Emulator Master, and Infrastructure Master).

Understand how to manage trusts.   When configuring trusts, you'll need to consider two main characteristics: transitivity and direction. The simplest way to understand transitive relationships is through this example: If Domain A trusts Domain B and Domain B trusts Domain C, then Domain A implicitly trusts Domain C. Trusts can be configured as nontransitive so that this type of behavior does not occur. In one-way relationships, the trusting domain allows resources to be shared with the trusted domain. In two-way relationships, both domains trust each other equally. Special trusts include external trusts, realm trusts, cross-forest trusts, and shortcut trusts.

Understand how to manage UPN suffixes.   By default, the name of the domain in which the user is created determines the UPN suffix. By adding additional UPN suffixes to the forest, you can easily choose more manageable suffixes when it comes time to create new users.

Understand how to manage global catalog servers.   You can configure any number of domain controllers to host a copy of the global catalog. The GC contains all of the schema information and a subset of the attributes for all domains within the Active Directory environment. Servers that contain a copy of the GC are known as GC servers. Whenever a user executes a query that requires information from multiple domains, they need only contact the nearest GC server for this information. Similarly, when users must authenticate across domains, they will not have to wait for a response from a domain controller that may be located across the world. The result is increased overall performance of Active Directory queries.

Understand universal group membership caching.   You can enable a domain controller as a Universal Group Membership Caching server. The Universal Group Membership Caching machine will then send a request for the logon authentication of a user to the GC server. The GC will then send the information back to the Universal Group Membership Caching server to be cached locally for eight hours (by default). The user can then authenticate without the need to contact the GC again.

Understand the purpose of Active Directory replication.   Replication is used to keep domain controllers synchronized, and it is important in Active Directory environments of all sizes. Replication is the process by which changes to the Active Directory database are transferred between domain controllers.

Understand the concept of sites, site boundaries, and subnets.   Subnets define physical portions of your network environment. Sites are defined as collections of well-connected IP subnets. Site boundaries are defined by the subnet or subnets that you include in your site configuration.

Understand the differences between intrasite and intersite replication.   Intrasite replication is designed to synchronize Active Directory information to machines that are located in the same site. Intersite replication is used to synchronize information for domain controllers that are located in different sites.

Understand the purpose of bridgehead servers.   Bridgehead servers are designed to accept traffic between two remote sites and then to forward this information to the appropriate servers. One way to synchronize data between sites efficiently that are connected with slow connections is to use a bridgehead server.

Implement site links, site link bridges, and connection objects.   You can use all three of these object types to finely control the behavior of Active Directory replication and to manage replication traffic. Site links are created to define the types of connections that are available between the components of a site. Site links can reflect a relative cost for a network connection and can reflect the bandwidth that is available for communications. You can use site link bridges to connect site links so that the relationship can be transitive. Connection objects provide you with a way to set up special types of replication schedules such as immediate replication on demand or specifying a custom schedule for certain servers.

Configure replication schedules and site link costs.   You can create multiple site links between sites, and you can assign site links a cost value based on the type of connection. The system administrator determines the cost value, and the relative costs of site links are then used to determine the optimal path for replication. The lower the cost, the more likely the link is to be used for replication. Once you've determined how and through which connections replication will take place, it's time to determine *when* information should be replicated. Replication requires network resources and occupies bandwidth. Therefore, you need to balance the need for consistent directory information with the need to conserve bandwidth.

Determine where to place domain controllers and global catalog servers based on a set of requirements.   Where you place domain controllers and global catalog servers can positively affect the performance of Active Directory operations. However, to optimize performance, you need to know the best places to put these servers in a network environment that consists of multiple sites.

Monitor and troubleshoot replication.   The Windows Server 2012 R2 System Monitor administrative tool is designed so that you can monitor many performance statistics associated with using Active Directory. In addition to this monitoring, you should always verify basic network connectivity and router and firewall connections and also examine the event logs.

Review Questions

1. You need to deactivate the UGMC option on some of your domain controllers. At which level in Active Directory would you deactivate UGMC?

   A. Server

   B. Site

   C. Domain

   D. Forest

2. You work for an organization with a single domain forest. Your company has one main location and two branch locations. All locations are configured as Active Directory sites, and all sites are connected with the DEFAULTIPSITELINK object. Your connections are running slower than company policy allows. You want to decrease the replication latency between all domain controllers in the various sites. What should you do?

   A. Decrease the Replication interval for the DEFAULTIPSITELINK object.

   B. Decrease the Replication interval for the site.

   C. Decrease the Replication schedule for the site.

   D. Decrease the Replication schedule for all domain controllers.

3. You need to enable three of your domain controllers as global catalog servers. Where would you configure the domain controllers as global catalogs?

   A. Forest, NTDS settings

   B. Domain, NTDS settings

   C. Site, NTDS settings

   D. Server, NTDS settings

4. Daniel is responsible for managing Active Directory replication traffic for a medium-sized organization that has deployed a single Active Directory domain. Currently, the environment is configured with two sites and the default settings for replication. Each site consists of 15 domain controllers. Recently, network administrators have complained that Active Directory traffic is using a large amount of available network bandwidth between the two sites. Daniel has been asked to meet the following requirements:

   - Reduce the amount of network traffic between domain controllers in the two sites.

   - Minimize the amount of change to the current site topology.

   - Require no changes to the existing physical network infrastructure.

   Daniel decides that it would be most efficient to configure specific domain controllers in each site that will receive the majority of replication traffic from the other site. Which of the following solutions meets the requirements?

   A. Create additional sites that are designed only for replication traffic and move the existing domain controllers to these sites.

   B. Create multiple site links between the two sites.

   C. Create a site link bridge between the two sites.

   D. Configure one server at each site to act as a preferred bridgehead server.

5. Which of the following does not need to be created manually when you are setting up a replication scenario involving three domains and three sites?

A. Sites

B. Site links

C. Connection objects

D. Subnets

6. Which of the following services of Active Directory is responsible for maintaining the replication topology?

A. File Replication Service

B. Knowledge Consistency Checker

C. Windows Internet Name Service

D. Domain Name System

7. A system administrator for an Active Directory environment that consists of three sites wants to configure site links to be transitive. Which of the following Active Directory objects is responsible for representing a transitive relationship between sites?

A. Additional sites

B. Additional site links

C. Bridgehead servers

D. Site link bridges

8. You have configured your Active Directory environment with multiple sites and have placed the appropriate resources in each of the sites. You are now trying to choose a protocol for the transfer of replication information between two sites. The connection between the two sites has the following characteristics:

- The link is generally unavailable during certain parts of the day because of an unreliable network provider.

- The replication transmission must be attempted whether the link is available or not. If the link was unavailable during a scheduled replication, the information should automatically be received after the link becomes available again.

- Replication traffic must be able to travel over a standard Internet connection.

Which of the following protocols meets these requirements?

A. IP

B. SMTP

C. RPC

D. DHCP

9. A system administrator suspects that there is an error in the replication configuration. How can the system administrator look for specific error messages related to replication?

    A. By using the Active Directory Sites and Services administrative tool

    B. By using the Computer Management tool

    C. By going to Event Viewer ➤ System Log

    D. By going to Event Viewer ➤ Directory Service Log

10. Christina is responsible for managing Active Directory replication traffic for a medium-sized organization. Currently, the environment is configured with a single site and the default settings for replication. The site contains more than 50 domain controllers, and the system administrators are often making changes to the Active Directory database. Recently, network administrators have complained that Active Directory traffic is consuming a large amount of network bandwidth between portions of the network that are connected by slow links. Ordinarily, the amount of replication traffic is reasonable, but recently users have complained about slow network performance during certain hours of the day.

    Christina has been asked to alleviate the problem while meeting the following requirements:

    - Be able to control exactly when replication occurs.

    - Be able to base Active Directory replication on the physical network infrastructure.

    - Perform the changes without creating or removing any domain controllers.

    Which two of the following steps can Christina take to meet these requirements? (Choose two.)

    A. Create and define Connection objects that specify the hours during which replication will occur.

    B. Create multiple site links.

    C. Create a site link bridge.

    D. Create new Active Directory sites that reflect the physical network topology.

    E. Configure one server at each of the new sites to act as a bridgehead server.

Chapter

22

Configure Access and Information Protection Solutions

THE FOLLOWING 70-412 EXAM OBJECTIVES ARE COVERED IN THIS CHAPTER:

✓ **Install and configure Active Directory Certificate Services (AD CS)**

- Describe and explain the new features in Windows Server 2012 Active Directory Certificate Services

- Install and configure Active Directory Certificate Services using Server Manager and Windows PowerShell

- Manage Active Directory Certificate Services using management consoles and Windows PowerShell

- Configure CRL distribution points

- Install and configure Online Responder

- Implement administrative role separation

- Configure CA Disaster recovery

- Manage certificates

- Manage certificate templates

- Implement and manage certificate deployment, validation, and revocation

- Manage certificate renewal

- Manage certificate enrollment and renewal to computers and users using Group Policies

- Configure and manage key archival and recovery

- Manage trust between organizations including Certificate Trust List (CTL)
- Managing Cross certifications and bride CAs
- Monitoring CA Health

✓ **Install and Configure Active Directory Federation Services (AD FS)**

- Implement claims-based authentication including Relying Party Trusts
- Configure authentication policies
- Configure Workplace Join
- Configure multi-factor authentication

✓ **Install and configure Active Directory Rights Management Services (AD RMS)**

- Install a licensing or certificate AD RMS server
- Manage AD RMS Service Connection Point (SCP)
- Manage RMS templates
- Configure Exclusion Policies
- Backup and restore AD RMS

In this chapter, I will discuss certificate services and the importance of securing the corporate *public key infrastructure (PKI)* environment. The Windows 2012 PKI implementation resides in Active Directory Certificate Services. PKI is the collection of technology, protocols, services, standards, and policies that control the issuing and management of public and private keys using digital certificates, which are the core of PKI. Encryption is used to protect data messages. While certificates provide a certain level of security, they are still vulnerable.

Next, I will cover federation services and how to set up relying party trusts with certificates. Finally, I will discuss rights management, which Microsoft created to further protect documents, email, and web pages from unauthorized copying, printing, forwarding, editing, deleting, and so forth.

What's New in Windows Server 2012 R2 with Active Directory Certificate Services?

Active Directory Certificate Services is a server role included in Windows Server 2012 R2. AD CS allows administrators to customize, issue, and manage public key certificates. AD CS issues digital certificates for authentication, encryption and decryption, and signing.

The following are the new features regarding Active Directory Certificate Services (AD CS) in Windows Server 2012 R2:

Server Core and Minimal Server Interface Support   You can install and deploy any of the six AD CS role services to any version of Windows Server 2012 R2, including Server Core and Minimal Server Interface. The Minimal Server Interface looks and feels like a Server Core installation with most of the GUI management utilities intact. Windows Server 2012 R2 Minimal Server Interface reduces the attack surface and lowers the footprint by removing components such as Windows Explorer and Internet Explorer and their supporting libraries.

Site-Aware Certificate Enrollment   Windows 8/8.1 and Windows Server 2012 R2 computers default to using certificate authorities within their sites when requesting certificates. However, you must configure site information on the certificate authorities' objects within Active Directory for the site-awareness feature to be worthwhile. Once configured, computers running Windows 8/8.1 and Windows Server 2012 R2 request certificates from a certificate authority running in the same site as the computer.

Automatic Certificate Renewal for Non-Domain-Joined Computers   Certificate Enrollment Web Services (CES) allows non-domain-joined computers and computers not directly connected to the corporate network to request and retrieve certificates. AD CS in Windows Server 2012 R2 includes the ability for these clients to renew certificates automatically for non-domain-joined computers.

Enforcement of Certificate Renewal with the Same Key   In earlier versions of Windows, clients that received certificates from templates that were configured for renewal with the same key had to renew their certificates using the same key, or renewal would fail.

With Windows 8/8.1 or Windows Server 2012 R2, you can continue this behavior, or you can configure certificate templates to give higher priority to Trusted Platform Module (TPM)–based KSPs for generating keys. Moreover, using renewal with the same key, administrators can rest assured that the key remains on TPM after renewal.

This feature allows you to enforce renewal with the same key, which can reduce administrative costs (when keys are renewed automatically) and increase key security (when keys are stored using TPM-based KSPs).

Internationalized Domain Names (IDNs)   International languages often contain characters that cannot be represented using ASCII encoding, which limits the function of these languages when enrolling for a certificate. Windows Server 2012 R2 now includes support for international domain names.

Default Security Increased on the Certificate Authority Role Service   Certificate authorities running on Windows Server 2012 R2 include increased RPC security. Increased RPC security on the CA requires that all clients must encrypt the RPC communication between themselves and the CA when requesting certificates.

Active Directory Certificate Services Roles

The Active Directory Certificate Services role provides six role services to issue and manage public key certificates in an enterprise environment. These roles are listed in Table 22.1 and described in the following sections.

TABLE 22.1   AD CS roles

Role service	Description
Certificate Authority (CA)	The CA service includes root and subordinate CAs for issuing certificates to users, computers, and services. This role service also manages certificate validity.
Web Enrollment	This is a web-based interface to enable users to enroll, request, and retrieve certificates as well as retrieve certificate revocation lists from a CA using a web browser.

Online Responder (OCSP)	The Online Responder service retrieves revocation status requests for specific certificates and the status of these certificates, and it returns a signed response with the requested certificate status information.
Network Device Enrollment Service (NDES)	NDES enables routers and other non-domain-joined network devices to acquire certificates.
Certificate Enrollment Policy Web Server (CEP)	CEP enables users and computers to inquire about certificate enrollment policy information.
Certificate Enrollment Web Services (CES)	CES enables users and computers to enroll for certificates with the HTTPS protocol. CEP and CES can be used together to support certificate enrollment for non-domain-joined computers and computers not directly connected to the corporate network.

Planning the Certificate Authority Hierarchy

A *certification authority (CA)* is a trusted server designed to grant certificates to individuals, computers, or organizations to certify the identity and other attributes of the certificate subject.

A CA receives a certificate request, verifies the requester's identity data according to the policy of the CA, and uses its private key to apply its digital signature to the certificate. The CA issues the certificate to the subject of the certificate as a security credential within a PKI environment. A CA is also responsible for revoking certificates and publishing a *certificate revocation list (CRL)*.

A CA can be a third-party issuer, such as VeriSign, or you can create your own CA by installing Active Directory Certificate Services. Every CA also has a certificate confirming its identity, issued by another trusted CA or root CAs.

Cryptography

The Cryptography options for a certificate authority provide increased deployment flexibility to those with a more advanced understanding of cryptography. You can implement cryptographic options by using cryptographic service providers (CSPs) or key storage providers (KSPs).

CSPs are hardware and software components of Windows operating systems that provide generic cryptographic functions. CSPs can provide a variety of encryption and signature algorithms. Key storage providers can provide strong key protection on computers running Windows Server 2012/2012 R2, Windows Server 2008/2008 R2, Windows Vista, Windows 7, or Windows 8. Figure 22.1 shows some of the Cryptography options in the AD CS installation.

FIGURE 22.1 Cryptography for CA screen

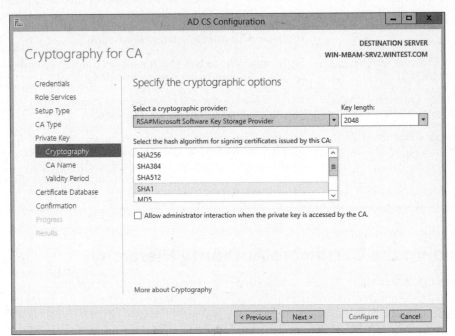

Here are the options:

Select a Cryptographic Provider   Windows Server 2012 R2 provides many CSPs and KSPs, and you can install additional CSPs or KSPs provided by third parties. In Windows Server 2012 R2, the algorithm name is listed in the provider list. All providers with a number sign (#) in the name are cryptography next-generation (CNG) providers. CNG providers can support multiple asymmetric algorithms. CSPs implement only a single algorithm.

Key Length   Each CSP and KSP supports different character lengths for cryptographic keys. Configuring a longer key length hardens against an attack by a hacker to decrypt the key and also degrades the performance of cryptographic operations.

Select The Hash Algorithm For Signing Certificates Used By This CA   The CA uses hash algorithms to sign CA certificates and issues certificates to ensure that an external identity has not tampered with a certificate. Each CSP can support different hash algorithms.

Make sure that your applications, your devices, and all operating systems that may request certificates from this certificate authority support the selected hash algorithm.

Allow Administrator Interaction When The Private Key Is Accessed By The CA   Use this option to help secure the CA and its private key by requiring an administrator to enter a password before every cryptographic operation.

> Exercise caution with this setting because this requires user interaction each time the certificate authority accesses the private key. A certificate authority signs each issued certificate. To sign the issued certificate, the certificate authority must access the private key.

Private Key

A certificate authority uses its assigned certificate to generate and issue certificates. The certificate used by the CA includes a public key and a private key. The private key should be available only to the owner. The public key is publicly available to other entities on the network.

For example, a user's public key can be published within a certificate in a folder so that it is accessible to other people in the organization. The sender of a message can retrieve the user's certificate from Active Directory Domain Services, obtain the public key from the certificate, and then encrypt the message by using the recipient's public key.

Data encrypted with a public key can be decrypted only with the mathematically paired private key. Certificate authorities use their private key to create a digital signature in the certificate when issuing certificates.

Enterprise Certificate Authorities

Enterprise certificate authorities (CAs) publish certificates and CRLs to Active Directory. Enterprise CAs access domain data stored in Active Directory. Enterprise CAs engage certificate templates when issuing certificates. The enterprise CA uses default configuration data in the certificate template to create a certificate with the appropriate attributes for that certificate type.

If you want to enable automatic certificate approval and automatic user certificate enrollment, use enterprise CAs to issue certificates. These features are available only when the CA infrastructure is integrated with Active Directory. Additionally, only enterprise CAs can issue certificates that enable smart card logon because this process requires the CA to map the user account in Active Directory to the smart card certificates.

A *root CA*, sometimes called a *root authority*, is the most trusted CA type in an organization's PKI. The root CA is the only CA that signs its own certificate. The physical security and the certificate issuance policy of a root CA should be tightly reinforced. If the root CA is compromised or if it issues a certificate to an unauthorized identity, any certificate-based security in your organization is compromised by the exposed private key. The best practice is to deploy a second PKI tier to issue certificates from other CAs, called *subordinate CAs* (see Figure 22.2).

FIGURE 22.2 Two-tier PKI hierarchy model

Root Certificate Authority

Subordinate Certificate
Authority 1

Subordinate Certificate
Authority 2

A *subordinate CA* is one that has received its signing certificate by a root CA, third-party CA, or stand-alone CA in your organization. Subordinate CAs normally issue certificates for specific purposes, such as secure email, SSL, Wireless 801.x security, or smart card authentication. Subordinate CAs can also issue certificates to other, more subordinate CAs. A root CA, the subordinate CAs certified by the root, and subordinate CAs certified by other subordinate CAs form a certification hierarchy.

Stand-alone certificate authorities are not integrated into Active Directory and do not support certificate templates. If you deploy stand-alone CAs, you must include all the information about the requested certificate type in the certificate request. By default, all submitted certificate requests to a stand-alone CA are placed in a pending queue, awaiting a CA administrator's approval. Stand-alone CAs can issue certificates automatically upon request, but this is not recommended because the requests are not authenticated.

Because stand-alone CAs are not Active Directory integrated, a stand-alone CA would seem like a less appropriate choice for an enterprise. However, stand-alone root CAs offer a layer of protection when a powered-down stand-alone CA is less likely to be compromised and does not have a footprint in Active Directory. More organizations are deploying *offline stand-alone root CAs* that are brought online only temporarily for re-issuing signing certificates to subordinate CAs. Some organizations permanently keep the offline stand-alone root CA disconnected from the network and distribute signing certificates only via removable media such as CDs, DVDs, or USB flash drives. Offline root CAs have the following characteristics:

- Deployed as a stand-alone root CA

- Deployed on a non-domain-joined server to avoid being offline or powered down for long periods without requiring computer password synchronizations

Real World Scenario

Protect the Offline Root CA

Best practice strongly recommends you securely store and back up the offline stand-alone root CA. A large Medical center implemented their offline stand-alone root CA solution by installing their root CA on a laptop. They routinely kept the laptop in the datacenter until a new administrator discovered and returned laptop to the help desk for repurposing. Needless to say, the laptop was re-imaged, and the entire PKI infrastructure was wiped out. No one was aware until the subordinate CA's certificate had expired a year later and certificates could no longer be issued. You can avoid this catastrophic scenario by securely storing and backing up the offline stand-alone CA.

Two-Tier and Three-Tier Models

It's acceptable for a single enterprise to have multiple PKIs. Multiple PKIs result in one root CA for each PKI and possibly multiple subordinate CAs that chain to their respective roots.

Organizations also may choose a third-tier CA hierarchy model, which involves adding a CA policy server. CA policy servers are designed to implement specific certificate policies that can include certificate life cycle, encryption type, key length, and some approval workflow.

Validity Period

All certificates issued by a certification authority have a validity period. The *validity period* is a time range that specifies how long PKI clients can accept the certificate as an authoritative credential based on the identity stated in the subject of the certificate. This assertion presumes the certificate is not revoked before the validity period ends and the issuing CA remains trusted. The validity period limits the time in which an issued certificate is exposed to the possibility of being compromised (http://technet.microsoft.com/en-us/library/cc740209(v=WS.10).aspx).

All CAs have an expiration date based on its CA certificate's validity ending period. This rule affects the CA's ability to issue certificates and not the validity period of its CA certificate. Because of this rule, organizations must plan for the renewal of every certificate issued to a CA in the certification hierarchy to ensure the existing trust chains and to extend the lifetimes of CAs.

Active Directory Certificate Services enforces a rule that a CA never issues a certificate past the expiration date of its own certificate. Because of this behavior, when a CA's certificate reaches the end of its validity period, all certificates issued by the CA will also expire. Certificates issued by the now-expired CA will not be honored as valid security credentials.

Active Directory Certificate Services allows for the maximum validity periods shown in Table 22.2, which are based on the type of certificate. You configure these validity periods using certificate templates.

TABLE 22.2   AD CS maximum validity periods

Certificate type	Maximum validity period
Root certificate authority	Determined during CA deployment
Subordinate CA Internet Protocol Security Enrollment agent Domain controller	Up to five years, but never more than the root CA's or the issuing CA's validity period
All other certificates	One year, but never more than the root CA's or issuing CA's validity period

Certificate Validation

PKI trust requires a certificate to be validated for both for its expiration and its overall chain of trust. When a certificate user leaves the company, you will want to make sure that no one can use that certificate for authentication and revoke the certificate. Revocation checking is one of the key components of PKI.

Certificate revocation uses certificate revocation lists. CRLs contain a list of certificates that are no longer valid, and the CRL can become large. To solve this, you can access a delta CRL that contains changes or new revocations.

CRLs are accessed through *CRL distribution points (CDPs)*, which are part of a CA role in Windows Server 2012. HTTP, FTP, LDAP, or file-based addresses may be used as URLs. Only newly issued certificates will recognize new changes in the CRL URL; old certificates will use the old URL for revocation list operations.

Online Responders

When a new certificate is issued, the computer queries the issuing CA to find out whether the certificate has been revoked. Traditionally, certificate revocation checking can be done by retrieving certificate revocation lists that are published in Lightweight Directory Access Protocol (LDAP) or Hypertext Transfer Protocol (HTTP) or by using a newer HTTP method named the Online Certificate Status Protocol (OCSP).

OCSP is a lightweight HTTP protocol that responds faster and more efficiently than downloading a traditional CRL. An *online responder* is a trusted server that receives and responds to individual client requests for the status of a certificate. An OCSP responder retrieves CRLs and provides digitally signed real-time certificate revocation status responses to clients based on a given certificate authority's CRL. The amount of data retrieved per request remains constant regardless of the number of revoked certificates.

Online responders process certificate status requests more efficiently than direct access to CRLs in several scenarios (`http://technet.microsoft.com/en-us/library/cc725958 .aspx`):

- When clients have slow VPN connections or do not have the high-speed connections required to download large CRLs

- When network utilization peaks because revocation-checking activity is high, such as when large numbers of users log on or send signed email simultaneously

- When revocation data for certificates is needed from a non-Microsoft certification authority

- When revocation data is needed to verify individual certificate status requests rather than all revoked or suspended certificates

Installing AD CS

Server Manager provides a graphical user interface to install Active Directory Certificate Services on local and remote computers running Windows Server 2012 R2. The Remote Server Administration Tools for Windows Server 2012 R2 also includes Server Manager, which allows you to run Server Manager on a computer running Windows 8/8.1. In Exercise 22.1, you'll install an AD CS role on the local computer using Server Manager.

EXERCISE 22.1

Installing AD CS Through Server Manager

1. Start Server Manager.

2. Click Manage and click Add Roles And Features

3. The Add Roles And Features Wizard shows the Before You Begin screen. Click Next.

4. Click Role-Based Or Feature-Based Installation on the Select Installation Type screen. Click Next.

5. Click the server on which you want to install Active Directory Certificate Services from the Server Pool list on the Select Destination Server screen. Click Next.

6. Select the Active Directory Certificate Services check box on the Select Server Roles screen.

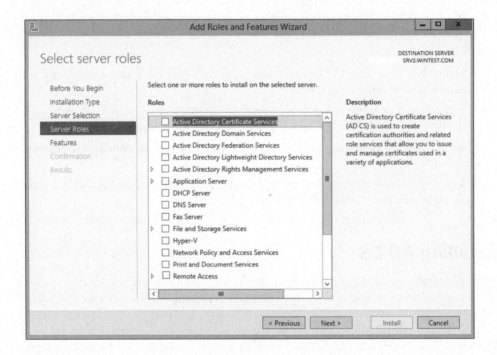

Server Manager prompts you to add more features associated with this role, such as management tools. Leave the default selections. Click Add Features to close the dialog. Click Next on the Select Server Roles screen.

7. Click Next on the Select Features screen.

8. Server Manager displays the Active Directory Certificate Services screen. This screen provides a simple role introduction and noteworthy information, such as that the name of the certificate authority cannot be changed. Click Next.

9. From the Select Role Services screen, select the check boxes next to the AD CS role services you want to install on the computer. Click Next.

10. Read the Confirm Installation Selections screen. This screen provides a list of roles, role services, and features that the current installation prepares on the computer. Click Install to start the installation.

Installation Using Windows PowerShell

A major benefit gained from basing Windows Server 2012 R2's Server Manager on Windows PowerShell is consistency of installation. Server Manager relies on its Windows PowerShell foundation as the underlying engine responsible for installing any of the Active Directory Certificate Services role services. However, you cannot use Server Manager to install roles and features on a Windows Server 2012 R2 core installation.

The Server Manager module for Windows PowerShell provides cmdlets to install, view, and remove features and roles included in Windows Server 2012 R2. You can use these cmdlets on any installation of Windows Server 2012 R2 because it provides Windows PowerShell in all installation types. Also, these cmdlets can install, view, and uninstall Active Directory Certificate Services role services from remote computers running Windows Server 2012 R2.

To view the installation state of Active Directory Certificate Services using Windows PowerShell, follow these steps:

1. Open an elevated Windows PowerShell console. (On Server Core installations, type **PowerShell** in the command console.)

2. In the Windows PowerShell console, type the following command and press Enter:

```
Get-WindowsFeature | where {$_.name -like "adcs*" -or $_.name -like "ad-c*"}
```

The Windows PowerShell cmdlet outputs three columns of information: Display Name, Name, and Install State. The Display Name column is a user-friendly name that describes the feature or service role's use. The Name column represents the name of the component. You use this name with the Install-WindowsFeature and Remove-WindowsFeature cmdlets. Use the Install State column to determine the installation state of the role or service role.

Typically, the Install State column shows one of three install states: Removed, Available, and Installed. The Removed install state designates that its associated role or feature is not included in the current installation of Windows. You cannot install the associated role or feature without the installation media or Internet connectivity to Windows Update if the feature or role is removed. The Available installation state indicates that the role or feature is staged in the current installation of Windows; however, it is currently not installed. The Installed installation state indicates that the role or feature is installed on the current installation of the computer and is ready, or it has been deployed or configured.

The Active Directory Certificate Services entry from the cmdlet's output represents the parent role. Six child role services appear underneath the parent role. A lowercase *x* appears between the opening and closing square brackets in the parent role if any of the six child role services are installed. The cmdlet also places a lowercase *x* between the opening and closing square brackets for any installed child role service. You should interpret entries without a lowercase *x* between the opening and closing square brackets as not installed. Check the install state to determine whether the role or role service is staged on your installation of Windows.

To install Active Directory Certificate Services using Windows PowerShell, follow these steps:

1. Open an elevated Windows PowerShell console.

2. Use the `Get-WindowsFeature` cmdlet to ensure the Active Directory Certificate Services role's installation state is Available.

3. In the Windows PowerShell console, type the following command and press Enter:

   `Install-WindowsFeature adcs-cert-authority -IncludeManagementTools`

4. Use the `Get-WindowsFeature` cmdlet to verify the installation (see Figure 22.1).

The preceding command instructs the Server Manager module of Windows PowerShell to take the staged binaries for the Certificate Authority role service and install them to the current computer.

It's important to remember the `-IncludeManagementTools` argument when installing a feature using Windows PowerShell. The Server Manager module for Windows PowerShell does not install a feature or role management tool by default. The `Install-WindowsFeature` cmdlet does not install the role management tool without this argument. The Server Manager GUI automatically selects installing the role management tool for you, and it gives you a choice of not to install it before completing the installation.

You can install any of the other child role services using the `Install-WindowsFeature` cmdlet simply by replacing the `adcs-cert-authority` argument with the associated name of the child role service. The following example installs the Active Directory Certificate Services Web Enrollment role service:

`Install-WindowsFeature adcs-web-enrollment -IncludeManagementTools`

> The role and feature installation experience is consistent on Windows Server 2012 R2 using the Server Manager module for Windows Power-Shell. You can use the same syntax to install a feature or role listed using Get-WindowsFeature.

Configuring Active Directory Certificate Services

You begin the Active Directory Certificate Services deployment by starting the AD CS Configuration Wizard (Exercise 22.2). To start the wizard, click the Configure Active Directory Certificate Services On The Destination Server link shown in the Action Flag dialog. The wizard shows the current destination for the role deployment in the Destination Server portion of the screen.

EXERCISE 22.2

Configuring AD CS Through Server Manager

1. After the AD CS installation is successful, click the Configure Active Directory Certificate Services On The Destination Server link.

2. The Credentials screen of the AD CS Configuration Wizard displays the required credentials to perform specific AD CS role services deployment. The wizard shows your current credentials in the Credentials portion of the screen. Click Change if your current credentials do not match the credentials needed for the current role service deployment. Otherwise, continue by clicking Next.

3. Select the check boxes for the Certification Authority and Online Responder role services.

4. The Setup Type screen of the AD CS Configuration Wizard shows the two types of certificate authorities you can configure with Active Directory Certificate Services: enterprise or stand-alone. An enterprise certificate authority must run on domain-joined computers and typically remains online to issue certificates or certificate policies. Select Enterprise and click Next.

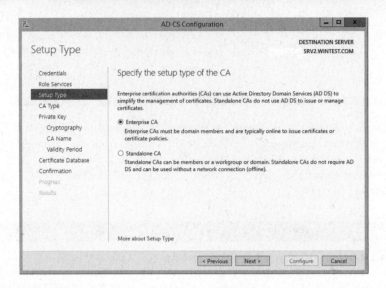

5. In the Setup Type dialog box, select Enterprise CA and click Next.

6. In the CA Type dialog box, click Root CA and click Next.

7. In the Private Key dialog box, verify that Create A New Private Key is selected and click Next.

8. Select the RSA# Microsoft Software Key Storage Provider.

9. Windows Server 2012 includes a number of CSPs and KSPs, and you can install additional CSPs or KSPs provided by third parties. In Windows Server 2012 R2, the provider list includes the name of the algorithm. All providers with a number sign (#) in the name are CNG providers. CNG providers can support multiple asymmetric algorithms. CSPs implement only a single algorithm.

10. Select a key length of 2048.

11. Each CSP and KSP supports different character lengths for cryptographic keys. Configuring a longer key length can enhance security by making it more difficult for a hacker or disgruntled employee to decrypt the key, but it can also slow down the performance of cryptographic operations.

12. Select the SHA1 hash algorithm and click Next.

13. Enter a name for the root CA Server and click Next.

14. In the Certificate Request dialog box, verify that Save A Certificate Request To File On The Target Machine is selected and click Next.

15. In the CA Database dialog box, verify the location for the log files in the Certificate Database Log Location box and click Next.

16. In the Confirmation dialog box, click Configure.

17. In the Results dialog box, click Close.

The CA uses hash algorithms to sign CA certificates and issues certificates to ensure that an external identity has not tampered with a certificate. Each CSP can support different hash algorithms. Make sure your applications, devices, and all operating systems that may request certificates from this certificate authority support the selected hash algorithm.

Use the Create A New Private Key option when creating or reinstalling a certificate authority.

Certificate Authority Name

Names for CAs cannot exceed 64 characters in length. You can create a name by using any Unicode character, but you might want the ANSI character set if interoperability is a concern.

In Active Directory Domain Services (AD DS), the name you specify when you configure a server as a CA (Figure 22.3) becomes the common name of the CA, and this name is reflected in every certificate the CA issues. Because of this behavior, it is important that you do not use the fully qualified domain name (FQDN) for the common name of the CA. Hackers can acquire a copy of a certificate and use the FQDN of the CA to compromise security.

FIGURE 22.3 Specifying the name of the CA

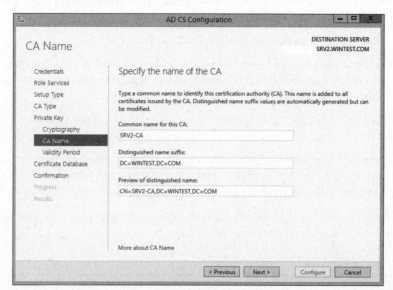

The CA name does not have to be the computer's name. Changing the name after installing Active Directory Certificate Services (AD CS) will invalidate every certificate issued by the CA.

Group Policy Certificate Auto-enrollment

Many certificates can be distributed without the client interaction. These can include most types of certificates issued to computers and services, as well as many certificates issued to users.

To enroll clients automatically for certificates in a domain environment, you must do the following:

- Configure a certificate template with auto-enroll permissions
- Configure an auto-enrollment policy for the domain

Membership in Domain Admins or Enterprise Admins, or equivalent, is the minimum required to complete this procedure. In Exercise 22.3 we are going to configure a group policy to support the auto-enrollment feature.

EXERCISE 22.3

Configure an Auto-enrollment Group Policy for a Domain

1. On a domain controller running Windows Server 2008 R2 or Windows Server 2008, click Start ➢ Administrative Tools ➢ Group Policy Management.

2. In the console tree, double-click Group Policy Objects in the forest and domain containing the Default Domain Policy Group Policy object (GPO) that you want to edit.

3. Right-click the Default Domain Policy GPO and click Edit.

4. In the Group Policy Management Console (GPMC), go to User Configuration ➢ Windows Settings ➢ Security Settings and click Public Key Policies.

5. Double-click Certificate Services Client – Auto-Enrollment.

6. Select the Enroll Certificates Automatically check box to enable auto-enrollment. If you want to block auto-enrollment from occurring, select the Do Not Enroll Certificates Automatically check box.

7. If you are enabling certificate auto-enrollment, you can select the following check boxes:

   "Renew expired certificates, update pending certificates, and remove revoked certificates enables auto-enrollment for certificate renewal, issuance of pending certificate requests, and the automatic removal of revoked certificates from a user's certificate store."

   "Update certificates that use certificate templates enables auto-enrollment for issuance of certificates that supersede issued certificates."

8. Click OK to accept your changes.

Key-Based Renewal for Non-Domain-Joined Computers

Windows Server 2012 R2 combines automatic certificate renewal with AD CS Certificate Enrollment Web Services to enable non-domain-joined computers to renew their certificates automatically before they expire like Internet-facing web servers.

Many organizations and service providers maintain servers that require SSL certificates. These servers are not typically joined to the same domain as an issuing certificate authority, and they do not have identity records or accounts in the organization's Active Directory. This means they cannot benefit from today's automatic certificate renewal, which is based on secured certificate templates in Active Directory. As a result, these organizations manage and renew SSL certificates manually, a time-intensive and error-prone process. Neglecting to renew a single SSL certificate can cause a massive and costly system outage.

Currently, Certificate Enrollment Web Services supports three types of server-side authentication modes:

- Windows integrated (Kerberos)
- Certificate-based
- Username and password

These authentication mode options, however, are not viable choices when the client is not joined to a domain and the enterprise certificate authority makes authorization decisions using templates that are based on the Active Directory group membership of the requestor.

Consider the following authentication options for automatic renewal:

Windows Integrated   This authentication option is not suitable for auto renewal because the two domains to which the certificate authority and the requesting server belong do not have a trust relationship between them or the requesting server is not joined to any domain.

Certificate-Based   The initially enrolled server certificate is not suitable for authentication because it contains no identity information within it that can be mapped to a directory account object.

Username And Password   Usernames and passwords can be cached within the system's identity vault and used for authentication to the enrollment server. However, passwords usually have shorter lifetimes than server SSL certificates. (Both default and recommended settings for passwords are shorter than the default and recommended certificate lifetime.) Thus, by the time renewal happens, the password will likely have changed.

Anonymous   This authentication option is not suitable since MS CEP and CES do not support this option, making automatic renewal impossible for these targeted server systems.

Enforcement of Certificate Renewal with Same Key

Windows 8/8.1 and Windows Server 2012 R2 provide an efficient mechanism to increase the security of renewing hardware-based certificates. This is accomplished by enforcing the certificate renewal to occur for the same key. This guarantees the same assurance level for the key throughout its life cycle. Additionally, Windows Server 2012 R2's Certificate

Template Management Console supports CSP/KSP ordering that clients may choose for generating a private/public key pair. This way, you can give a higher priority to hardware-based keys (Trusted Platform Module or smart card) over software-based keys.

Cryptographic Service Provider/Key Service Provider Ordering

Another problem addressed in Windows Server 2012 R2 is GUI support for CSP/KSP ordering. With increased interest in the deployment of Trusted Platform Module in enterprise scenarios, providing a mechanism for prioritizing TPM-based keys over other types of keys has become a "must-have" for certificate enrollment based on certificate templates. This is important from the client perspective when enrolling for a non-exportable key. You want to have assurance that the non-exportable keys are generated in the TPM and are not software-based (assuming that no malware is involved and the user is not malicious).

Currently this prioritization is captured as an attribute of a certificate template object in Active Directory; however, a user interface does not exist for modifying such properties, and Microsoft does not support it. Windows Server 2012 R2's Certificate Template Management Console fully supports CSP/KSP ordering.

Managing Certificate Authority: Certificate Templates Overview

Enterprise certificate authorities issue certificates from certificate templates, a preconfigured list of certificate settings. This allows administrators to enroll users and computers for certificates without the need to create complex certificate requests. Windows Server 2012 AD CS does include a minor user interface change and the Active Directory Certificate Services Administration module for Windows PowerShell. The new Compatibility tab in the Certificate Templates Management Console lets you identify incompatible certificate template settings between different versions of Windows-based certificate recipients and the certificate authority. The AD CS Administration module for Windows PowerShell lets you manage common AD CS management tasks using Windows PowerShell.

Certificate Template Compatibility

Multiple versions of certificate templates have been released for the family of Windows Server products. New certificate template versions include settings that control the features relevant to each new certificate authority. However, not all features are compatible with all certificate authorities and certificate requests. Therefore, it can be difficult to determine which certificate templates are compatible with different versions of certificate authorities and different Windows-based certificate requestors.

Version 2 certificate templates are customizable certificate templates that are supported with Windows Server 2008 Enterprise CAs or Windows Server 2003 Enterprise edition CAs. Version 2 certificate templates enable advanced CA features, such as key archiving and recovery and certificate auto-enrollment.

To use version 2 templates, Active Directory must be upgraded to support Windows Server 2008 or Windows Server 2003 schema changes. Standard editions of Windows Server 2008 and Windows Server 2003 support only version 1 certificate templates, which are not customizable and do not support key archival or automatic enrollment.

Version 3 certificate templates were new to Windows Server 2008. Version 3 certificate templates function similarly to version 2 templates, and they support new Active Directory Certificate Services features available in Windows Server 2008. These features include CNG, which introduces support for Suite B cryptographic algorithms such as elliptic curve cryptography (ECC).

The Windows Server 2012 R2 Certificate Template Management Console includes a new certificate template Compatibility tab that lets you select the Windows operating system of the certificate authority and the Windows operating system of the certificate recipient. The Certificate Template Management Console determines incompatible settings between the selections and shows a list of template settings that the management console adds or removes from template selection.

You view the compatibility table from the Certificate Template Management Console. You can launch the Certificate Template Management Console by typing `certtmpl.msc` in the Run dialog or on the Start screen and pressing Enter.

Creating Certificate Templates

When creating a new certificate template, you copy an existing template similar to the configuration defaults needed for your particular application. It is best to review the default list of certificate template and find the template that best matches your application's requirements.

The Request Handling tab (Figure 22.4) in the Certificate Templates Management console has the Renew With Same Key Certificate Template Configuration option. This certificate template option becomes visible in the user interface when you configure the Certification Authority and the Certificate Recipient options to Windows Server 2012 R2 and Windows 8/8.1, respectively.

You will create an example certificate template in Exercise 22.4.

EXERCISE 22.4

Creating a Certificate Template

1. Start the Certificate Templates snap-in, read through the certificate templates titles, and choose the Computer Template.

2. In the details pane, right-click an existing certificate and click Duplicate Template.

3. Choose to duplicate the template as a Windows Server 2008–based template.

4. On the General tab, enter the template display name and the template name and click OK.

5. Define any additional attributes for the newly created certificate template.

FIGURE 22.4 Request Handling tab of the Certificate Templates Management console

Publishing the Certificate Template

After creating a certificate template and applying the proper security permissions, you will want to deploy the new certificate template by publishing to the Active Directory where it can be shared with other Enterprise CAs. The following exercise will take us through the steps to perform the task.

In Exercise 22.5, you will deploy a certificate template.

EXERCISE 22.5

Publishing a Certificate Template

1. In Server manager, click Tools and then Certification Authority

2. In the Certification Authority MMC, expand the CA Server Name

3. Select the Certificate Templates container.

4. Right-click Certificate Templates container and then click New Certificate Template To Issue.

5. In the Enable Certificate Templates dialog box, select the certificate template or templates that you want the CA server to issue and click OK. The newly selected certificate template or templates should appear in the right side details pane.

If a certificate template is not displayed in the Enable Certificate Templates dialog box, the replication of the certificate template may not have finished on all domain controllers in the forest.

Certificate Revocation

Revocation renders a certificate invalid and lists the revoked certificate in the CRL. You can revoke a certificate in the Certificate Authority snap-in with the steps shown in Exercise 22.6.

EXERCISE 22.6

Revoking a Certificate

1. Start the Certification Authority snap-in.

2. In the console tree, click the Issuing certificate container.

3. In the right pane, select and right-click the target certificate.

4. Select All Tasks.

5. Select Revoke Certificate.

6. In Certificate Revocation dialog box, you must select one of the following reason codes:

    Unspecified: Default reason code. This lacks information during future audits.
    Key Compromise: Select this when you think the key has been compromised.
    CA Compromise: Select this when you suspect the issuing CA of being compromised.
    Change of Affiliation: Select this when the person has exited the organization or changed roles.
    Superseded: Select this when issuing a new certificate to replace an existing certificate.
    Cease of Operation: Select this when the issuing device or server has been decommissioned.
    Certificate Hold: Select this to suspend an existing certificate temporarily.

7. Click OK.

Display the Current Site Name for Certificate Authorities

Enter the following command to display current site names for one or more certificate authorities:

```
Certutil -ping caDnsName, [caDnsName, …]
```

The command utilizes the DsGetSiteName API on each named certificate authority. After determining the site for all the certificate authorities, certutil.exe uses the DsQuerySitesByCost API to obtain the client's site costs for all the name certificate authorities.

CA Policy Auditing

PKI auditing logging is not enabled on the Windows 2012 R2 CA server by default. After the auditing is enabled, all the events will be logged in the Security log.

Exercise 22.7 covers the steps that the CA administrator must complete to enable auditing.

EXERCISE 22.7

Configuring CA Policy Auditing

1. Enable Object Access/Success Auditing in the CA machine's local security policy.

   a. Start mmc.exe.

   b. Add the snap-in Group Policy Object Editor and select the Local Computer GPO.

   c. Under the path Computer Configuration\Windows Settings\Security Settings\Local Policies\Audit Policy, enable success auditing for Object Access.

2. Enable auditing on the CA.

   a. Start the CA Management snap-in.

   b. Open the CA Properties dialog.

   c. On the Auditing tab, check the Change CA Configuration and Change CA Security Settings options.

Backing Up the Certificate Authority Server

The AD CS certificate authority deployment creates a database. The CA records certificates issued by the CA, private keys archived by the CA, revoked certificates, and all certificate requests to the database regardless of issuance status.

Configure the database location on an NTFS partition on the server's disk drives to provide the best security possible for the database file. Specify the location for the database in the Certificate Database Location box. By default, the wizard configured the database location to systemroot\system32\certlog. The name of the database file uses the CA's name, with an .edb extension.

The certificate database uses a transaction log to ensure the integrity of the database. The CA records its transactions in its configured log files. The CA then commits each transaction from the log file into the database. The CA then updates the last committed transaction in the database, and the process continues.

The CA database logs are selected when restoring the CA from a backup. If a CA is restored from a backup that is one month old, then the CA database can be updated with more recent activity recorded in the log to restore the database to its most current state. When you back up a CA, the existing certificate database logs are truncated in size because they are no longer needed to restore the certificate database to its most current state.

The recommended method to back up a CA is to leverage the native Backup utility (included with the operating system) to back up the entire server, including the system state, which contains the CA's data. However, the Certificate Authority snap-in can be used to back up and restore the CA, but this backup method is intended only in cases where you want to migrate CA data to different server hardware. The public key and private key are backed up or restored using the PKCS #12 PFX format.

The Backup Or Restore Wizard will ask you to supply a password when backing up the public and private keys and CA certificates. This password will be needed to restore the CA.

Start the Certificate Authority snap-in for Exercise 22.8, which explains how to back up a CA.

EXERCISE 22.8

Backing Up the Certificate Authority Server

1. Start the Certification Authority MMC.

2. In the left pane, right-click the name of the server; then choose All Tasks > Back Up CA.

3. When the Certification Authority Backup Wizard appears, click Next.

4. At the Items To Back Up screen, click the Private Key And CA Certificate check box. Next to the Back Up To This Location field, click the Browse button. Choose a location for your backup and click OK. Click Next.

5. At the Select A Password screen, enter and confirm a password. For this exercise, enter **P@ssw0rd**. Click Next.

Configuring and Managing Key Archive and Recovery

The key archive stores a certificate's subject name, public key, private key, and supported cryptographic algorithms in its CA database. This procedure can be performed manually or automatically, depending on the configuration. If the certificate template requires key archiving, then the process requires no manual intervention. However, key archiving can also be performed manually if the private key is exported and then sent to an administrator for import into the CA database.

There is also a Key Recovery Agent template available in the standard templates within Active Directory Certificate Services. The Key Recovery Agent template enables Domain Admins and Enterprise Admins to export private keys. Additionally, you can add other accounts and groups to have the necessary permissions (Read and Enroll) through the Security tab of the template.

The Key Recovery Agent template also needs to be enabled, as with other certificate templates, through the Certification Authority tool by selecting Certificate Template To Issue. See "Publishing a Certificate Template" earlier in this chapter for more details on enabling a certificate template on a CA.

With the Key Recovery Agent template in place, the following process must take place for key archiving and recovery:

1. Request a key recovery agent certificate using the Certificates snap-in.

2. Issue the key recovery agent certificate using the Certification Authority tool.

3. Retrieve the enrolled certificate using the Certificates snap-in.

4. Configure the CA for key archiving and recovery.

The final step, configuring the CA for key archiving and recovery, takes place in the Properties dialog box of each CA that will need to archive and recover keys. Specifically, the Recovery Agents tab configures the behavior of the CA when a request includes key archiving.

Each Key Recovery Agent certificate should be added using the Add button on the Recovery Agents tab.

Implement Active Directory Federation Services

Active Directory Federation Services (AD FS) demands a great deal of preparation and planning to ensure a successful implementation. The type of certificate authority used to sign the AD FS server's certificate must be planned. The SSL encryption level must be negotiated with the partnering organization. For instance, how much Active Directory information should be shared with the partnering organization? What should the DNS structure look like to support federation communications? You must explore all of these questions before implementing AD FS. In this section, I will discuss how to deploy AD FS and the configurations used to set up a federated partnership between businesses.

What Is a Claim?

A *claim* is an identifiable element (email address, username, password, and so on) that a trusted source asserts about an identity, for example, the SID of a user or computer. An identity can contain more than one claim, and any combination of those claims can be used to authorize access to resources.

Windows Server 2012 R2 extends the authorization identity beyond using the SID for identity and enables administrators to configure authorization based on claims published in Active Directory.

Today, the claims-based identity model brings us to cloud-based authentication. One analogy to the claim-based model is the old airport check-in procedure.

1. You first check in at the ticket counter.

2. You present a suitable form of ID (driver's license, passport, credit card, and so on). After verifying that your picture ID matches your face (authentication), the agent pulls up your flight information and verifies that you've paid for a ticket (authorization).

3. You receive a boarding pass (token). The boarding pass lets the gate agents know your name and frequent flyer number (authentication and personalization), your flight number and seating priority (authorization), and more. The boarding pass has bar-code information (certificate) with a boarding serial number proving that the boarding pass was issued by the airline and not a (self-signed) forgery.

Active Directory Federation Service is Microsoft's claims-based identity solution providing browser-based clients (internal or external to your network) with transparent access to one or more protected Internet-facing applications.

When an application is hosted in a different network than the user accounts, users are occasionally prompted for secondary credentials when they attempt to access the application. These secondary credentials represent the identity of the users in the domain where the application is hosted. The web server hosting the application usually requires these credentials to make the most proper authorization decision.

AD FS makes secondary accounts and their credentials unnecessary by providing trust relationships that send a user's digital identity and access rights to trusted partners. In a federated environment, each organization continues to manage its own identities, but each organization can also securely send and accept identities from other organizations. This seamless process is referred to as *single sign-on (SSO)*.

Windows Server 2012 R2 AD FS federation servers can extract Windows authorization claims from a user's authorization token that is created when the user authenticates to the AD FS federation server. AD FS inserts these claims into its claim pipeline for processing. You can configure Windows authorization claims to pass through the pipeline as is, or you can configure AD FS to transform Windows authorization claims into a different or well-known claim type.

Claims Provider

A *claims provider* is a federation server that processes trusted identity claims requests. A federation server processes requests to issue, manage, and validate security tokens. Security tokens consist of a collection of identity claims, such as a user's name or role or an anonymous identifier. A federation server can issue tokens in several formats. In addition, a federation server can protect the contents of security tokens in transmission with an X.509 certificate.

For example, when a Stellacon Corporation user needs access to Fabrikam's web application, the Stellacon Corporation user must request claims from the Stellacon Corporation AD FS server claim provider. The claim is transformed into an encrypted security token, which is then sent to Fabrikam's AD FS server.

Relying Party

A *relying party* is a federation server that receives security tokens from a trusted federation partner claims provider. In turn, the relying party issues new security tokens that a local relying party application consumes. In the prior example, Fabrikam is the relying party that relies on the Stellacon's claim provider to validate the user's claim. By using a relying-party federation server in conjunction with a claims provider, organizations can offer web single sign-on to users from partner organizations. In this scenario, each organization manages its own identity stores.

Endpoints

Endpoints provide access to the federation server functionality of AD FS, such as token issuance, information card issuance, and the publishing of federation metadata. Based on the type of endpoint, you can enable or disable the endpoint or control whether the endpoint is published to AD FS proxies.

Table 22.3 describes the property fields that distinguish the various built-in endpoints that AD FS exposes. The table includes the types of endpoints and their methods of client authentication. Table 22.4 describes the AD FS security modes.

TABLE 22.3   AD FS Endpoints

Name	Description
WS-Trust 1.3	An endpoint built on a standard Simple Object Access Protocol (SOAP)–based protocol for issuing security tokens.
WS-Trust 2005	An endpoint built on a prestandard, SOAP-based protocol for issuing security tokens.
WS-Federation Passive/ SAML Web SSO	An endpoint published to support protocols that redirect web browser clients to issue security tokens.
Federation Metadata	A standard-formatted endpoint for exchanging metadata about a claims provider or a relying party.
SAML Artifact Resolution	An endpoint built on a subset of the Security Assertion Markup Language (SAML) version 2.0 protocol that describes how a relying party can access a token directly from a claims provider.
WS-Trust WSDL	An endpoint that publishes WS-Trust Web Services Definition Language (WSDL) containing the metadata that the federation service must be able to accept from other federation servers.
SAML Token (Asymmetric)	The client accepts a SAML token with an asymmetric key.

TABLE 22.4   AD FS Security Modes

Name	Description
Transport	The client credentials are included at the transport layer. Confidentiality is preserved at the transport layer (Secure Sockets Layer [SSL]).
Mixed	The client credentials are included in the header of a SOAP message. Confidentiality is preserved at the transport layer (SSL).
Message	The client credentials are included in the header of a SOAP message. Confidentiality is preserved by encryption inside the SOAP message.

Claim Descriptions

Claim descriptions are claim types based on an entity's or user's attribute like a user's email address, common name or UPN. AD FS publishes these claims types in the federation metadata and most common claim descriptions are pre-configured in the AD FS Management snap-in.

The claim descriptions are published to federation metadata which is stored in the AD FS configuration database. The claim descriptions include a claim type URI, name, publishing state, and description.

Claim Rules

Claim rules define how AD FS processes a claim. The most common rule is using a user's email address as a valid claim. The email address claim is validated through the partner's Active Directory email attribute for the user's account. If there is a match, the claim is accepted as valid.

Claim rules can quickly evolve into more complex rules with more attributes such as a user's employee ID or department. The key goal of claim rules is to process the claim in a manner that validates the user's claim and to assemble a user's profile information based on a sufficient number of attributes to place the user into a role or group.

The Attribute Store

Attribute stores are the repositories containing claim values. AD FS natively supports Active Directory by default as an attribute store. SQL Server, AD LDS, and custom attribute stores are also supported.

AD FS Role Services

The AD FS server role includes federation, proxy, and web agent services. These services enable the following:

- Web SSO
- Federated web-based resources

- Customizing the access experience
- Managing authorization to access applications

Based on your organization's requirements, you can deploy servers running any one of the following AD FS role services:

Active Directory Federation Service   Microsoft federation solution for accepting and issuing claims based token for users to experience a single sign-on to a partnered web application.

Federation Service Proxy   The Federation Service Proxy forwards user claims over the internet or DMZ using WS-Federation Passive Requestor Profile (WS-F PRP) protocols to the internal ADFS farm. Only the user credential data is forwarded to the Federation Service. All other datagram packets are dropped.

Claims-Aware Agent   The claims-aware agent resides on a web server with a claims-aware application to enable the Microsoft ASP.NET application to accept AD FS security token claims.

Windows Token-Based Agent   The Windows token-based agent resides on a web server with a Windows NT token-based application to translate an AD FS security token to an impersonation-level Windows NT token-based authentication.

What's New for AD FS in Windows Server 2012 R2?

The Active Directory Federation Services role in Windows Server 2012 R2 introduces the following new features:

- HTTP.SYS
- Server Manager integration
- AD FS deployment cmdlets in the AD FS module for Windows PowerShell
- Interoperability with Windows authorization claims
- Web proxy service

HTTP.SYS

Prior AD FS versions relied on IIS components for the AD FS claim functions. Microsoft has improved the overall claims handling performance and SSO customization by building the AD FS 3.0 code on top of the standard kernel mode driver—HTTP.SYS. This approach also avoids the huge security "no-no" of hosting IIS on a domain controller.

The classic netsh HTTP command can be entered to query and configure HTTP.SYS. AD FS proxy server introduces interesting deployment nuisances and "gotchas" with HTTP.SYS, which I will discuss in the "Web Proxy Service" section.

Improved Installation Experience

The installation experience for Active Directory Federation Services 3.0 was cumbersome, requiring multiple hotfixes, as well as .NET Framework 3.5, Windows PowerShell, and the

Windows Identity Foundation SDK. Windows Server 2012 R2's AD FS role includes all of the software you need to run AD FS for an improved installation experience.

Web Proxy Service

The kernel mode (HTTP.SYS) in Windows Server 2012 R2 includes server name indication (SNI) support configuration. I strongly recommend verifying that your current load balancer/reverse proxy firmware supports SNI. This prerequisite is a sore spot for most AD FS 3.0 upgrade projects in the field. Therefore, it's worthwhile checking the following:

- Your preferred load balancer/device needs to support SNI.

- Clients and user agents need to support SNI and should not become locked out of authentication.

- All SSL termination endpoints vulnerable to the recent heartbleed bug (http://heartbleed.com) need to be patched, exposing OpenSSL libraries and certificates.

AD FS Dependency Changes in Windows Server 2012 R2

Active Directory Federation Services was built on a claim-based identity framework called *Windows Identity Foundation (WIF)*. Prior to Windows Server 2012 R2, WIF was distributed in a software development kit and the .NET runtime. WIF is currently integrated into version 4.5 of the .NET Framework, which ships with Windows Server 2012 R2.

Windows Identity Foundation

WIF is a set of .NET Framework classes; it is a framework for implementing claims-based identity for applications. Any web application or web service that uses .NET Framework version 4.5 or newer can run WIF.

New Claims Model and Principal Object

Claims are at the core of .NET Framework 4.5. The base claim classes (Claim, ClaimsIdentity, ClaimsPrincipal, ClaimTypes, and ClaimValueTypes) all live directly in mscorlib. Interfaces are no longer necessary to plug claims in the .NET identity system. WindowsPrincipal, GenericPrincipal, and RolePrincipal now inherit from ClaimsPrincipal, WindowsIdentity, and GenericIdentity, and FormsIdentity now inherit from ClaimsIdentity. In short, every principal class will now serve claims. The integration classes and interfaces (WindowsClaimsIdentity, WindowsClaimsPrincipal, IClaimsPrincipal, and IClaimsIdentity) have thus been removed. The ClaimsIdentity object model also contains various improvements, which makes it easier to query the identity's claims collection.

As you climb further up "Mount Federation," you will realize that not all vendor SAML flavors are compatible, and configuration challenges can bring even the most seasoned system integrators to their knees. SAML deserves an entire book, so to avoid this chapter reaching encyclopedia size, I will touch on just a few pointers.

AD FS negotiates SAML authentication in order of security strength from the weakest to the strongest, as shown in Table 22.5. The default mode, Kerberos, is considered the strongest method. The authentication precedence can be tuned by executing the PowerShell command Set-AD FSProperties -AuthenticationContextOrder to select an order to meet your organization's security requirements.

TABLE 22.5 SAML-supported authentication methods

Authentication method	Authentication context class URI
Username/password	urn:oasis:names:tc:SAML:3.0:ac:classes: Password
Password-protected transport	urn:oasis:names:tc:SAML:3.0:ac:classes: PasswordProtectedTransport
Transport Layer Security (TLS) Client	urn:oasis:names:tc:SAML:3.0:ac:classes:TLSC lient
X.509 certificate	urn:oasis:names:tc:SAML:3.0:ac:classes:X509
Integrated Windows authentication	urn:federation:authentication:windows
Kerberos	urn:oasis:names:tc:SAML:3.0:classes:Kerberos

Active Directory Federation Services Installation

This section describes how to install and deploy Active Directory Federation Services roles on computers running Windows Server 2012 R2 (see Exercise 22.9). You will learn about the following:

- Deploying AD FS role services using Windows PowerShell
- Supporting upgrade scenarios for AD FS

EXERCISE 22.9

Installing the AD FS Role on a Computer Using Server Manager

1. Start Server Manager.

2. Click Manage and click Add Roles And Features. Click Next.

3. The Add Roles And Features Wizard shows the Before You Begin screen. Click Next.

4. Click Role-Based Or Feature-Based Installation on the Select Installation Type screen. Click Next.

5. Click the server on which you want to install Active Directory Federation Services from the Server Pool list on the Select Destination Server screen. Click Next.

6. Select the Active Directory Federation Services check box on the Select Server Roles screen. Server Manager will prompt you to add other features associated with this role, such as management tools. Leave the default selections. Click Add Features to close the dialog.

7. Click Next on the Select Server Roles screen.

8. Click Next on the Select Features screen.

9. Server Manager shows the Active Directory Federation Services screen. This screen displays simple role introduction and important AD FS configuration information. Click Next.

10. From the Select Server Roles screen, select the check box next to the AD FS role services to install on the computer. Click Next.

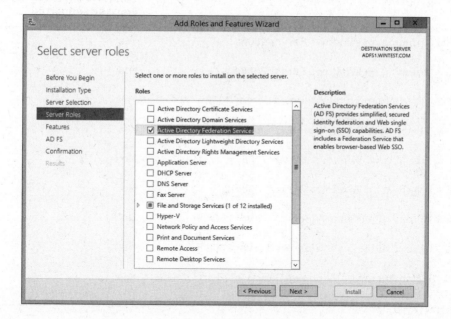

11. Server Manager prompts you to add other features associated with this role, such as management tools. Leave the default selections. Click Add Features to close the dialog.

12. Read the Confirm Installation Selections screen. This screen provides a list of roles, role services, and features that the current installation prepares on the computer. Click Install to begin the installation.

Role Installation Using Windows PowerShell

To view the installation state of AD FS using Windows PowerShell, open an elevated Windows PowerShell console, type the following command, and press Enter:

```
Get-WindowsFeature "adfs*","*fed*"
```

Upgrading to Windows AD FS 2012 R2

Windows Server 2012 R2's AD FS role supports upgrading version 3.0 of Active Directory Federation Services. You cannot upgrade versions of AD FS prior to version 3.0 using Windows Server 2012 R2.

Table 22.6 represents the support upgrade matrix for the AD FS role in Windows Server 2012 R2.

TABLE 22.6 Support upgrade matrix for the AD FS role in Windows Server 2012 R2

AD FS and operating system version	Windows Server 2012 R2 upgrade supported
AD FS 3.0 running on Windows Server 2008	Yes
AD FS 3.0 running on Windows Server 2008 R2	Yes
AD FS 3.0 Proxy running on Windows Server 2008	Yes
AD FS 3.0 Proxy running on Windows Server 2008 R2	Yes
AD FS 1.1 running on Windows Server 2008	No
AD FS 1.1 running on Windows Server 2008 R2	No
AD FS 1.1 Proxy running on Windows Server 2008	No
AD FS 1.1 Proxy running on Windows Server 2008 R2	No
AD FS 1.1 Web Agents on Windows Server 2008 or Windows Server 2008 R2	Yes

Configuring Active Directory Federation Services

Windows Server 2012 R2 delineates role installation and role deployment. Role installations make staged role services and features available for deployment. Role deployment enables you to configure the role service, which enables the role service in your environment. AD FS in Windows Server 2012 R2 uses the same deployment tools as AD FS 3.0. However, an entry point to start these tools is included in Server Manager. Server Manager indicates that one or more role services are eligible for deployment by showing an exclamation point inside a yellow triangle on the Action Flag notification. Click the action flag to show the role services you can deploy (see Figure 22.5).

FIGURE 22.5   Alert for role services eligible for deployment in Server Manager

AD FS Graphical Deployment

The Run The AD FS Management snap-in link in Windows Server 2012 R2 Server Manager is how you perform the initial configuration for the AD FS roles using the graphical interface. Alternatively, you can start the AD FS management console using the AD FS Management tile on the Start screen. The Start screen tile points to the Microsoft. IdentityServer.msc file located in the c:\windows\adfs folder.

To configure AD FS, select Start ➢ Run and type **FsConfigWizard.exe**; alternatively, click the FsConfigWizard.exe file located in the c:\windows\adfs folder.

Exercise 22.10 uses the AD FS Federation Server Configuration Wizard. To complete this exercise, you'll need an active SSL certificate assigned to the server and a managed service account for AD FS service.

EXERCISE 22.10

Configuring the AD FS Role on the Computer Using Server Manager

1. Select Create The First Federation Server In The Federation Server Farm.

2. Select the administrative account with permissions to configure the AD FS server and click Next.

3. Select the server certificate from the SSL certificate drop-down list.

4. Select the AD FS service name from the drop-down list.

5. Type **ADFS-Test** in the federation service's Display Name field and click Next.

EXERCISE 22.10 *(continued)*

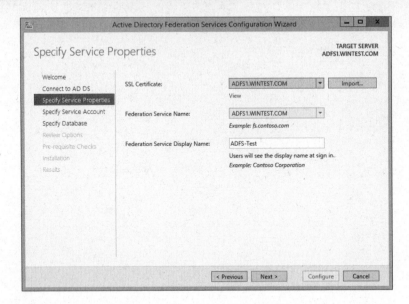

6. Select Create A Database On This Server Using Windows Internal Database and click Next.

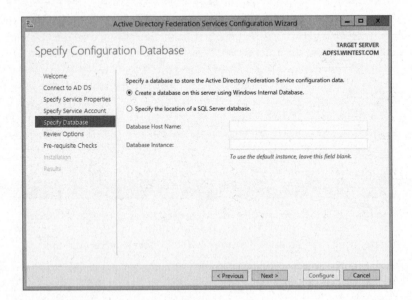

7. Click Next on the Review Options screen.

8. If the prerequisites check is successful, click Configure on the Prerequisite Check screen.

9. If the Result screen displays "This Server was successfully configured," you can click Close.

Deployment Using Windows PowerShell

Windows Server 2012 R2 includes the Active Directory Federation Services module for Windows PowerShell when you install the AD FS role using Server Manager. The AD FS module for Windows PowerShell includes five new cmdlets to deploy the AD FS role.

- `Add-AdfsProxy`
- `Add-AdfsFarmNode`
- `Export-AdfsDeploymentSQLScript`
- `Install-AdfsStand-alone`
- `Install-AdfsFarm`

 These AD FS cmdlets provide the same functionality as the command-line version of the AD FS Federation Server Configuration Wizard, `fsconfig.exe`. The AD FS role in Windows Server 2012 R2 includes `fsconfig.exe` to remain compatible with previously authored deployment scripts. New deployments should take advantage of the deployment cmdlets included in the AD FS module for Windows PowerShell.

Add-AdfsProxy   Configures a server as a federation server proxy.

FederationServiceName   Specifies the name of the federation service for which a server proxies requests.

FederationServiceTrustCredentials   Specifies the credentials of the Active Directory identity that is authorized to register new federation server proxies. By default, this is the account under which the federation service runs or an account that is a member of the Administrators group on the federation server.

ForwardProxy   Specifies the DNS name and port of an HTTP proxy that this federation server proxy uses to obtain access to the federation service.

Add-AdfsFarmNode   Adds this computer to an existing federation server farm.

CertificateThumbprint   Specifies the value of the certificate thumbprint of the certificate that should be used in the SSL binding of the default website in IIS. This value should match the thumbprint of a valid certificate in the Local Computer certificate store.

OverwriteConfiguration   Must be used to remove an existing AD FS configuration database and overwrite it with a new database.

SQLConnectionString   Specifies the SQL Server database that will store the AD FS configuration settings. If not specified, AD FS uses Windows Internal Database to store configuration settings.

ServiceAccountCredential   Specifies the Active Directory account under which the AD FS service runs. All nodes in the farm must have the same service account.

PrimaryComputerName Specifies the name of the primary federation server in the farm that this computer will join.

PrimaryComputerPort Specifies the value of the HTTP port that this computer uses to connect with the primary computer in order to synchronize configuration settings. Specify a value for this parameter only if the HTTP port on the primary computer is not 80.

Active Directory Federation Services Certificates

There are three types of certificates used by an AD FS implementation:

- Service communications
- Token decrypting
- Token signing

The service communications certificate is required for communication with web clients over SSL and with web application proxy services using Windows Communication Foundation (WCF) components. This certificate is specified at configuration time for AD FS.

The token decrypting certificate is required to decrypt claims and tokens received by the federation service. The public key for the decrypting certificate is usually shared with relying parties and others to encrypt the claims and tokens using the certificate.

The token signing certificate is required to sign all claims and tokens created by the server. You can have multiple token encrypting and signing certificates for an implementation, and new ones can be added within the AD FS management tool, shown in Figure 22.6.

FIGURE 22.6 Active Directory Federation Certificate Console screen

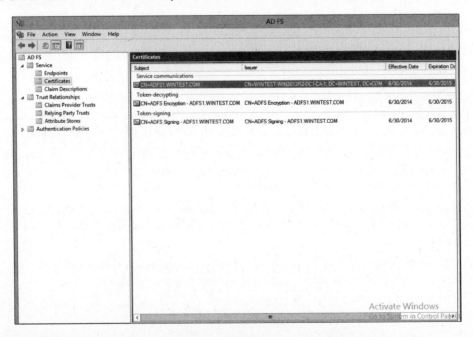

Relying-Party Trust

The federation service name originates from the SSL certificate used for AD FS. The SSL certificate can be template-based and needs to be enrolled and used by IIS.

The next step in setting up AD FS is to configure a relying-party trust. A relying-party trust can be configured with a URL acquired from the relying party. The URL contains the federation metadata used to complete the federation trust configuration. The federation metadata may also be exported to a file that can then be imported into the relying-party trust. There is also a manual option for configuring a relying-party trust.

See Table 22.7 for the Federation Metadata fields.

TABLE 22.7 Federation Metadata Fields

Field	Description
Display Name	This is the friendly display name given to this relying party trust.
Profile	Select AD FS Profile for the standard Windows Server 2012 AD FS, or select AD FS 1.0 And 1.1 Profile for AD FS configurations that need to work with older versions of AD FS.
Certificate	This is the optional certificate file from the relying party for token encryption.
URL	This is the URL for the relying party. WS-Federation Passive Protocol URL or SAML 2.0 WebSSO protocols are supported.
Identifiers	This is the unique identifier used for this trust.
Authorization Rules	Selecting this permits all users to access the relying party or denies all users access to the relying party, depending on the needs of this trust.

Configuring Claims Provider and Transform Claims Rules

Claims provider trust rules are configured within the AD FS management console and are configured on a per-trust basis. Planning claims rules involves determining what claims are needed by the relying party to complete the authentication and authorization process and which users will need access to the relying-party trust. The relying party determines what claims need to be received and trusted from the claims provider.

Trust rules start with templates as the basis for the rule. There are different types of claims templates depending on the type of rule being used. The claims rule templates for transforms are described in Table 22.8.

TABLE 22.8 Transform claims rule templates

Template	Description
Send LDAP Attributes as Claims	Attributes found in an LDAP directory (such as Active Directory) can be used as part of the claim.
Send Group Membership as Claim	The group memberships of the logged-in user are sent as part of the claim.
Transform an Incoming Claim	This is used for configuring a rule to change an incoming claim. Changes include both the type and the value of an incoming claim.
Pass Through or Filter an Incoming Claim	This performs an action such as pass-through or filter on an incoming claim based on certain criteria, as defined in the rule.
Send Claims Using a Custom Rule	This creates a rule that's not covered by a predefined template, such as an LDAP attribute generated with a custom LDAP filter.

Defining Windows Authorization Claims in AD FS

Windows Server 2012 R2 stores information that describes Windows authorization claims in the configuration partition of Active Directory. Windows refers to this information as *claim types*; however, Active Directory Federation Services typically refers to this information as claim descriptions (see Figure 22.7). There are more than 40 new claims descriptions available in the AD FS Windows Server 2012 R2 release.

The Active Directory Federation Services role included in Windows Server 2012 R2 lets you configure AD FS to include Windows authorization claims in the AD FS claim pipeline. To simplify this configuration, you can create *claim descriptions* in AD FS. Claim types in Windows authorization claims are analogous to claim descriptions in AD FS. The Windows authorization claim ID maps to the AD FS claim description's claim identifier (see Figure 22.8).

To simplify AD FS configuration using Windows authorization claims, create a claim description in AD FS for each Windows authorization claim you intend to deploy in AD FS.

Create Claim Pass-Through and Transformation Rules

You need to configure a claim rule with the Active Directory Claims Provider Trusts Wizard to insert Windows authorization claims into the AD FS claims pipeline.

Creating a claim description makes it easier to select the incoming claim type. Alternatively, you can type the claim type ID directly in the Incoming Claim Type list. A *pass-through claim rule* enables the Windows authorization claim to enter the AD FS claim

FIGURE 22.7   AD FS claim descriptions

FIGURE 22.8   Adding a claim description

pipeline. A pass-through claim leaves the claim type ID intact. Therefore, the pass-through claim ID begins with ad://ext, whereas most claim description URIs begin with http://. In addition, you can create a claim transformation claim rule on the Active Directory Claim Provider Trust Wizard to transform a Windows authorization claim into a well-known claim description (see Figure 22.9).

FIGURE 22.9 Claim transformation claim rule

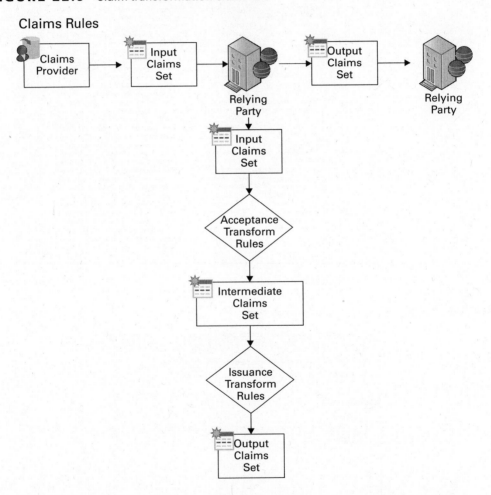

Creating a claim provider trust claim rule enables the Windows authorization claim to enter the AD FS claim pipeline. However, this does not ensure that AD FS sends the Windows authorization claim. AD FS claim processing begins with the claim provider. This allows the claim to enter the pipeline. Claim processing continues for the targeted relying party—first with the issuance authorization rules and then with the issuance transform rules.

You can configure Windows authorization claims in claims rules configured on a relying party. By default, a relying party does not have any issuance transform rules. Therefore, AD FS drops all claims in the pipeline destined for a relying party when the relying party does not have any rules that pass incoming claims. Additionally, issuance authorization rules determine whether a user can receive claims for a relying party and, therefore, access the relying party.

Choose the claims types from the list of inbound rules created in the Active Directory claim provider trust that you want to send to the designated relying party. Then create rules that continue to pass the selected claim types through the pipeline to the relying party. Alternatively, you can create a rule that passes all the inbound claims to the relying party (see Figure 22.10).

FIGURE 22.10   Editing the claims rules

The AD FS role in Windows Server 2012 R2 cannot provide claim information when the incoming authentication is not Kerberos. Clients must authenticate to AD FS using Kerberos authentication. If Windows authorization claims are not entering the AD FS claim pipeline, then make sure the client authenticates to AD FS using Kerberos and the correct service principal name is registered on the computer/service account.

Enabling AD FS to Use Compound Authentication for Device Claims: Compound Authentication

Windows Server 2012 R2 enhances Kerberos authentication by introducing compound authentication. Compound authentication enables a Kerberos TGS request to include two identities: the identity of the user and the identity of the user's device. Windows accomplishes compound authentication by extending Kerberos Flexible Authentication Secure Tunneling (FAST) or Kerberos armoring.

During normal Kerberos authentication, the Kerberos client requesting authentication for a service sends the ticket-granting service (TGS) a request for that service. Using Kerberos armoring, the TGS exchange is armored using the user's ticket-granting ticket (TGT). Prior to sending the ticket-granting service reply (TGS-REP) to the client, the KDC checks the 0x00020000 bit in the value of the msDS-SupportedEncryptionTypes attribute of the security principal's object running the service. An enabled bit means that the service can accept compound authentication. The KDC sends the TGS-REP, which includes the service's ability to support compound authentication.

The Kerberos client receives the ticket-granting service TGS-REP that includes compound authentication information. The Kerberos client then sends another ticket-granting service request (TGS-REQ), with the difference being that this TGS-REQ is armored with the device's TGT rather than the user. This allows the KDC to retrieve authentication information about the principal and the device.

The Active Directory Federation Services role included in Windows Server 2012 R2 automatically enables compound authentication when creating an AD FS web farm. During the creation of the first node in the farm, the AD FS configuration wizard enables the compound authentication bit on the msDS-SupportedEncryptionTypes attribute on the account that you designate to run the AD FS service. If you change the service account, then you must manually enable compound authentication by running the Set-ADUser -compoundIdentitySupported:$true Windows PowerShell cmdlet.

In Exercise 22.11, you will learn how to configure multifactor authentication.

EXERCISE 22.11

Configuring Multifactor Authentication

1. In the AD FS Management Console, traverse to Trust Relationships And Relying Party Trusts.

2. Select the relying party trust that represents your sample application (claimapp) and then either by using the Actions pane or by right-clicking this relying party trust, select Edit Claim Rules.

3. In the Edit Claim Rules For Claimapp window, select the Issuance Authorization Rules tab and click Add Rule.

4. In the Add Issuance Authorization Claim Rule Wizard, on the Select Rule Template screen, select Permit Or Deny Users Based On An Incoming Claim Rule Template and click Next.

5. On the Configure Rule screen, complete all of the following tasks and click Finish.

   a. Enter a name for the claim rule, for example **TestRule**.

   b. Select Group SID As Incoming Claim Type.

   c. Click Browse, type in **Finance** for the name of your AD test group, and resolve it for the Incoming Claim Value field.

   d. Select the Deny Access To Users With This Incoming Claim option.

   e. In the Edit Claim Rules For Claimapp window, make sure to delete the Permit Access To All Users rule that was created by default when you created this relying party trust.

Verify Multifactor Access Control Mechanism

In this phase, you will verify the multifactor access control policy that you set up in the previous phase. You can use the following procedure to verify that a test AD user can access your sample application because the test account belongs to the Finance group. Conversely, you will use the procedure to verify that AD users who do not belong to the Finance group cannot access the sample application.

1. On your client computer, open a browser window and navigate to your sample application: `https://webserv1.contoso.com/claimapp`. This action automatically redirects the request to the federation server, and you are prompted to sign in with a username and password.

2. Type in the credentials of a test AD account to be granted access to the application.

3. Type in the credentials of another test AD account that does not belong to the Finance group.

At this point, because of the access control policy that you set up in the previous steps, an access denied message is displayed for an AD account that does not belong to the Finance group. The default message text is "You are not authorized to access this site. Click here to sign out, and sign in again or contact your administrator for permissions." However, this text is fully customizable.

Workplace Join

Today's employees are mobile and remote, working across a plethora of consumer platforms. The age of bring your own device (BYOD) is here to stay. CIOs, IT security workers, and administrators cringe at the idea of storing company data on unmanaged devices. The Workplace Join feature adds a safety measure to ensure that only registered devices have access to company data.

For Workplace Join to work, a certificate is placed on the mobile device. AD FS challenges the device as a claims-based authentication to applications or other resources without requiring administrative control of the device.

Device Registration Service

Workplace Join is supported by the Device Registration Service (DRS) included with the Active Directory Federation Services role in Windows Server 2012 R2. When a device is set up with Workplace Join, the DRS registers a device as an object in Active Directory and sets a certificate on the consumer device that is used to represent the device identity. The DRS is meant to be both internal and external facing.

DRS requires at least one global catalog server in the forest root domain. The global catalog server is needed to run the PowerShell cmdlet -Initialize-ADDeviceRegistration during AD FS authentication.

Workplace Join Your Device

For Workplace Join to succeed, the client computer must trust the AD FS SSL certificate. It must also be able to access and validate revocation information for the certificate from the CRL.

In Exercise 22.12, you will configure the DRS.

EXERCISE 22.12

Workplace Joining a Device

1. Start a Windows PowerShell command window and type **Initialize-ADDevice Registration**.

2. When prompted for a service account, type **contoso\fsgmsa$**. Now run the Windows PowerShell cmdlet.

   ```
   Enable-AdfsDeviceRegistration
   ```

3. On the AD FS server, in the AD FS Management console, navigate to the Authentication Policies tab. Select Edit Global Primary Authentication. Select the Enable Device Authentication check box and click OK.

   Finally, you will need to make sure you have the following DNS records for the DRS.

Entry	Type	Address
adfs1	A	IP address of the AD FS server
enterpriseregistration	Alias (CNAME)	adfs1.contoso.com

4. Log on to the client with your Microsoft account.

5. On the Start screen, start the Charms bar and then select the Settings charm. Select Change PC Settings.

6. On the PC Settings screen, select Network and click Workplace.

7. In the Enter Your UserID To Get Workplace Access Or Turn On Device Management box, type the user's UPN or email address—for example, **RobertM@contoso.com**—and click Join.

8. When prompted for credentials, type the user's UPN or email address—for example, **roberth@contoso.com**—and a password such as **P@ssword**. Click OK.

9. You should now see the message "This device has joined your workplace network."

Active Directory Rights Management Services

Active Directory Rights Management Services (AD RMS), included with Microsoft Windows Server 2012 R2, helps safeguard sensitive information created and distributed using AD RMS–enabled applications such as Word, Outlook, or InfoPath, similar to Adobe Acrobat's permissions for print, save, fill-form, and copy functions. Unlike traditional file permission methods, RMS rights stay with the content and ensure exclusive access to the intended recipient.

Application developers may enable their applications to work with RMS extensions. AD RMS uses policies managed from the RMS server to provide a consistent experience for users across the enterprise.

You can enforce AD RMS usage policy templates directly to protect confidential information. You can install AD RMS easily using Server Manager, and you can administer it through the MMC snap-in. These three new administrative roles allow you to delegate AD RMS responsibilities:

- AD RMS Enterprise Administrators
- AD RMS Template Administrators
- AD RMS Auditors

AD RMS integrates with AD FS, which allows two organizations to share information without requiring AD RMS in both organizations.

Self-enrollment AD RMS server enrollment allows for the creation and signing of a server licensor certificate (SLC). This SLC enables the AD RMS server to issue certificates and licenses whenever required.

Considerations and Requirements for AD RMS

Before installing Active Directory Rights Management Services on Windows Server 2012 R2 for the first time, you must meet several requirements:

AD RMS Server   Install the AD RMS server as a member server in the same Active Directory domain as the user accounts that will be using rights-protected content.

AD RMS Service Account   Create a domain user account that has no additional permissions that can be used as the AD RMS service account. I recommend using a group-managed service account to ensure that the account password is managed by Active Directory and that it does not require a manual password change by an administrator.

If you are registering the AD RMS service connection point during installation, the user account installing AD RMS must be a member of the AD DS Enterprise Admins group or equivalent.

Which database AD RMS Will Store Configuration Data   Microsoft SQL Server 2008 or newer and WID are supported databases for the AD RMS configuration data. Windows Internal Database is more suitable for small and/or test environments. If you are using an external SQL database server for the AD RMS databases, the user account installing AD RMS must have the right to create new databases.

AD RMS URL   Reserve a URL for the AD RMS cluster that will be available throughout the lifetime of the AD RMS installation. Make sure the reserved URL differs from the computer name.

Cryptographic Mode   Mode 1 is composed of RSA 1024-bit keys and SHA-1 hashes. Mode 2 includes RSA 2048-bit keys and SHA-256 hashes for a more secure and recommended option.

Location for Cluster Key Storage   By default, the cluster key is stored within AD RMS. You may also deploy a cryptographic service provider to store the cluster key. However, you will have to distribute the key manually when installing additional AD RMS servers.

Cluster Key Password   The Cluster Key password helps to encrypt the cluster key, and it must be provided when adding AD RMS servers to the cluster. The Cluster Key password must also be provided when recovering an AD RMS cluster from backup.

Cluster Name   Choose the fully qualified domain name to be hosted on the AD RMS server. An SSL certificate should be configured with the FQDN of the AD RMS server. The cluster address and port cannot be changed after AD RMS is deployed. A non-SSL address can be configured, but you will lose the AD RMS with Identity Federation functionality.

AD RMS Add-on for Internet Explorer

The Windows Rights Management Add-on (RMA) for Internet Explorer enables rights-protected content to be viewed only. Because you can only view and not alter these restricted files, this prevents sensitive documents, web-based information, and email messages from being forwarded, edited, or copied by unauthorized individuals. For you to run RMA for Internet Explorer successfully, you must first install the Windows Rights Management (RM) client. The Extensible Rights Markup Language (XrML) is the XML verbiage used by AD RMS to express usage rights for rights-protected content.

AD RMS Requirements

AD RMS requires an AD RMS–enabled client. Windows Vista, Windows 7, and Windows 8/8.1 include the AD RMS client by default. If you are not using Windows Vista, Windows 7, Windows 8/8.1, Windows Server 2008, Windows Server 2008 R2, or Windows Server 2012 R2, you can download the AD RMS client for previous versions of Windows from Microsoft's Download Center.

File System: The NTFS file system is recommended.

Messaging: Message Queuing.

Web Services: Internet Information Services (IIS). ASP.NET must be enabled.

Active Directory Domain Services

AD RMS must be installed in an Active Directory domain in which the domain controllers are running Windows Server 2008, Windows Server 2008 R2, or Windows Server 2008 R2. All users and groups that use AD RMS to acquire licenses and publish content require an email address configured in Active Directory.

Database Server: AD RMS requires a SQL database server. Microsoft SQL Server 2005, 2008, and 2012 are supported SQL versions.

The new AD RMS administrative roles are as follows:

AD RMS Service Group   When the AD RMS role is installed onto a server, a local AD RMS service account is created and added to the local AD RMS service group. The server uses the service account to start services at system startup and cannot be the same account used to install the service.

AD RMS Enterprise Administrators   The AD RMS policies and settings are managed by members of the local AD RMS Enterprise Administrators group. When AD RMS is installed onto the server, the user account installing the role is added to the AD RMS Enterprise Administrators group. Only administrators who manage RMS should be added to this group.

AD RMS Template Administrators   Users who belong to the local AD RMS Templates Administrators group are allowed to manage rights policy templates. AD RMS template administrators have the rights to read cluster data, list rights policy templates, create new rights policy templates, modify existing rights policy templates, and export rights policy templates.

AD RMS Auditors   The local AD RMS Auditors role allows administrators who have this right to manage logs and reports. The AD RMS Auditors role is a read-only role that is restricted to running reports available on the AD RMS cluster, reading cluster information, and reading logging settings.

Installing AD RMS

AD RMS deployment is described as a root cluster, which is not used in terms of failover or network balancing clustering. An AD RMS root cluster manages all of the AD RMS licensing and certificate provisions for the forest. There can be only one AD RMS root cluster per AD forest. After a root cluster is deployed, there is the option of installing additional licensing-only clusters, which issue licenses to clients for publishing their content.

Now that you have a basic understanding of AD RMS, let's take the next step and install it. In Exercise 22.13, you will install AD RMS using the Server Manager MMC.

EXERCISE 22.13

Installing an AD RMS Role on the Local Computer Using Server Manager

1. Start Server Manager. Click Manage and then click Add Roles And Features.

2. The Add Roles And Features Wizard shows the Before You Begin screen. Click Next.

3. Select the Active Directory Rights Management Services Role and click Next.

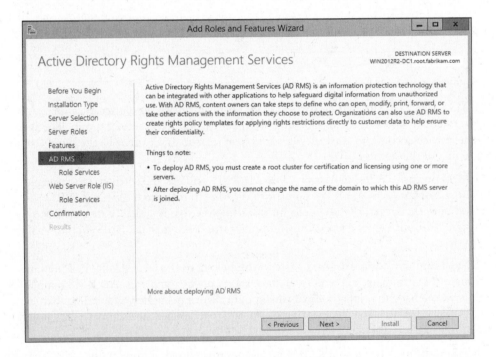

4. Add the required Active Directory Rights Management Services by default and click Add Features.

5. Click Next.

6. On the screen that explains ADRMS, click Next.

7. On the Select Role Services screen, by default Active Directory Rights Management Server is selected. Identity Federation Support uses AD FS federated trust between organizations to establish user identities and provide access to the RMS-protected content across the federation. Click Next.

8. Click Next on the Web Server (IIS) screen.

9. At the confirmation screen, click Install.

10. Once the installation is complete, click Close.

11. While still in Server Manager, click the AD RMS link on the left side.

12. Click the More About The AD RMS Service Account link next to Configuration Required For Active Directory Rights Management Service.

13. Under Action, click the Perform Additional Configuration link.

14. At the AD RMS introduction screen, click Next.

15. On the Create Or Join An AD RMS Cluster screen, choose Create A New AD RMS Cluster. (The other choice will not be available because you are installing the first AD RMS server and must start the cluster.) Click Next.

16. AD RMS uses a database to store configuration and policy information. At the Select Configuration Database screen, choose Use Windows Internal Database on this server. (The other option is to use a third-party database engine or MSSQL.) Click Next.

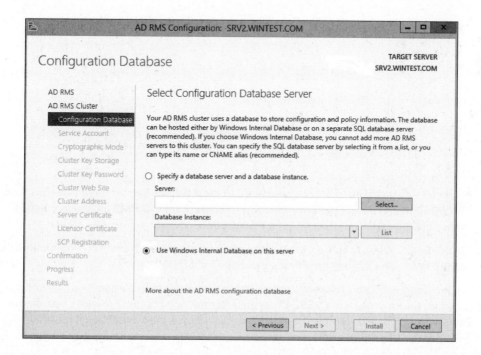

EXERCISE 22.13 *(continued)*

17. On the Specify Service Account screen, choose the service account that AD RMS will use. Click the Specify button and type in an administrator account and password other than the ones with which you are currently logged in. Click Next.

18. At the Cryptographic Mode screen, choose Cryptographic Mode 2 (RSA 2048-bit keys/SHA-256 hashes) and click Next.

19. At the Configure AD RMS Cluster Key Storage screen, choose Use AD RMS Centrally Managed Key Storage and click Next.

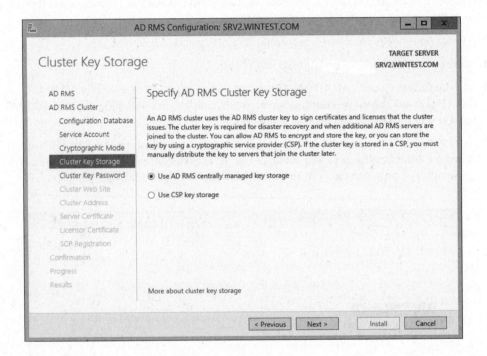

20. Next you will be asked to enter a password in the AD RMS Cluster Key Password field. The AD RMS cluster key password is used to encrypt the AD RMS cluster key that is stored in the AD RMS database. Type **P@ssw0rd**, confirm it, and click Next.

21. On the Select Website screen, click default website and click Next. AD RMS needs to be hosted in IIS. This will set up a default website for AD RMS.

22. On the Specify Cluster Address screen, choose whether to use a secure or a nonsecure website. Choose the Use An SSL-Encrypted Connection (https://) check box. In the Internal Address box, type in the server name and click the Validate button. After the address is verified, click Next.

23. The Choose A Server Authentication Certificate For SSL Encryption screen appears. If you receive a message stating the certificate for this server is already created, just click Next. If the message doesn't appear, choose one of your certificates and click Next.

24. The Name The Server Licensor Certificate screen appears. Accept the default server and click Next.

25. You have the option to register AD RMS now or later. If you register the server now, AD RMS will take effect immediately. If you register the server later, AD RMS will not work until you register. You will not register during this exercise. Choose Register Later and click Next.

26. At the Configure Identity Federation Support screen, specify the name of the web server that Identity Federation will use and click the Validate button. The Next button will become available once the server is validated. If an error appears during validation, it will not affect this exercise. Click Next.

27. At the Confirm Installation Selections screen, verify all of your settings and click Install.

28. The install progress screen appears. When the install is complete, click Close.

29. Close the Server Manager MMC.

Managing AD RMS: AD RMS Service Connection Point

The *service connection point (SCP)* is used to store the URL of the AD RMS cluster. The SCP is stored as an object in Active Directory. The SCP can be configured when AD RMS is being installed or later through the Active Directory Rights Management Services console. Only one SCP can exist in an Active Directory forest.

The AD RMS SCP can be registered automatically during AD RMS installation, or it can be registered after installation has finished. To register the SCP, you must be a member of the local AD RMS Enterprise Administrators group and the Active Directory Domain Services (AD DS) Enterprise Admins group, or you must have been given the appropriate authority.

Managing the SCP is accomplished on the SCP tab of the AD RMS cluster's Properties dialog box.

If a client computer is not located within the Active Directory forest, you must use registry keys to point the AD RMS client to the AD RMS cluster. These registry keys are created in HKEY_Local_Machine\Software\ Microsoft\MSDRM\ServiceLocation. Create a key called Activation with the value of http(s)://<your_cluster>/_wmcs/certification, where <your_cluster> is the URL of the root cluster used for certification.

AD RMS Templates

As you know, a template is a mold that you can use over and over again. AD RMS templates are no different. Before you start creating AD RMS templates, you must first create a shared directory where the templates can be stored. An administrator can then create AD RMS rights policy templates on the AD RMS cluster and export those templates to the shared directory. If your users are connected to the company intranet and they are using AD RMS–enabled applications, they can access the AD RMS templates right from the shared directory as long as they have read access to the shared folder. If your users are not connected to the company intranet, just copy the template to their computers, and this will allow AD RMS–enabled applications to continue to function properly.

When publishing protected content, the author selects the rights policy template to apply from the templates that are available on the local computer. Visibility of the templates is controlled via NTFS permissions. If the user does not have NTFS read access, the respective template will not be visible in an RMS-aware application.

When a user attempts to use protected content, the RMS-enabled application obtains the latest version of the rights policy template that was used to publish the content from the configuration database. The RMS-enabled application then applies its settings to the content. When the rights policy template is modified on the RMS server, RMS updates the template accordingly, in both the configuration database and the shared folder.

If a rights policy template is deleted, it is removed from the configuration database and also from the shared folder (that is specified as the file location for storing copies of templates) location when the template is deleted.

When working with rights policy templates, perform the following tasks:

1. Create and edit rights policy templates.

2. When creating a rights policy template, define the users and rights that apply. Also define how the rights policy template is to be applied to content.

3. Edit the rights policy templates later when they need to be updated.

4. Create as many rights policy templates as are required to manage rights in the organization, but consider that some applications are limited in the number of templates that can be displayed in the application's user interface. If more than a few templates are created in a cluster, you might want to scope the different templates to different groups of users by modifying NTFS permissions.

5. When a template is no longer appropriate, archive the rights policy template and update the distribution of the rights policy templates to the clients so that users do not try to protect content with the retired template. Users attempting to use content protected with the template will still be able to do so because the archived template is still accessible to the RMS servers issuing licenses.

6. If usage of all documents protected with a template is no longer desired, you can delete the template instead of archiving it. If users attempt to use content that was published by using the deleted rights policy template, they will not be issued licenses to do so.

See Table 22.9 for a description of the RMS template rights.

TABLE 22.9   Description of rights in RMS templates

Right	Description
Full control	If established, this right enables a user to exercise all rights in the license, whether or not the rights are specifically established to that user.
View	If this right is established, the AD RMS client enables protected content to be decrypted. Usually, when this right is established, the RMS-aware application will allow the user to view protected content.
Edit	If this right is established, the AD RMS client enables protected content to be decrypted and re-encrypted by using the same content key. Usually, when this right is established, the RMS-aware application will allow the user to change protected content and then save it to the same file. This right is effectively identical to the Save right.
Save	If this right is established, the AD RMS client enables protected content to be decrypted and then re-encrypted by using the same content key. Usually, when this right is established, the RMS-aware application will allow the user to change protected content and then save it to the same file. This right is effectively identical to the Edit right.
Export (Save As)	If this right is established, the AD RMS client enables protected content to be decrypted and then re-encrypted by using the same content key. Usually, when this right is established, the RMS-aware application will allow the user to use the Save As feature to save protected content to a new file.
Print	Usually when this right is established, the RMS-aware application will allow the user to print protected content.
Forward	Usually when this right is established, the RMS-aware application will allow an email recipient to forward a protected message.
Reply	Usually when this right is established, the RMS-aware application will allow an email recipient to reply to a protected message and include a copy of the original message.
Reply All	Usually when this right is established, the RMS-aware application will allow an email recipient to reply to all recipients of a protected message and include a copy of the original message.
Extract	Usually when this right is established, the RMS-aware application will allow the user to copy and paste information from protected content.
Allow Macros	Usually when this right is established, the RMS-aware application will allow the user to run macros in the document or use an editor to modify macros in the document.
View Rights	If this right is established, the AD RMS client enables a user to view the user rights that are assigned by the license.
Edit Rights	If this right is established, the AD RMS client enables a user to edit the user rights that are assigned by the license.

Backing Up AD RMS

Follow these steps to allow you to recover from any AD rights management server failure:

1. Record your cluster key password and store it in a safe manner.

2. Export the trusted publishing domain (see Exercise 22.18).

3. Create database backups.

Record and Store Your Cluster Key Password

During installation, take note of the cluster key password and securely store it. If you inherited the AD RMS server and the cluster key password hasn't been documented, you should change it before backup. To accomplish this, start the Active Directory Rights Management Services console under ServerName ➢ Security Policies ➢ Cluster Key Password. Click Change Cluster Key Password.

Create a Backup of the AD RMS Database

AD RMS uses three databases in the database server:

Configuration Database   This is a critical component of an AD RMS installation. The database stores, shares, and retrieves all configuration data and other data that the service requires to manage account certification, licensing, and publishing services for a whole cluster.

Directory Services Database   This contains information about users, identifiers (such as email addresses), security IDs, group membership, and alternate identifiers. This information is a cache of directory services data.

Logging Database   This is all of the historical data about client activity and license acquisition. For each root or licensing-only cluster, by default AD RMS installs a logging database in the same database server instance hosting the configuration database.

In Exercise 22.14, we will perform a backup of the RMS database.

EXERCISE 22.14

Backing Up an AD RMS Database

1. Log on to the SQL server.

2. Click Start ➢ All Programs ➢ Microsoft SQL Server 2008 or 2012 and select SQL Server Management Studio. The Connect To Server dialog box will appear. Verify the server name is correct and that authentication is set for Windows Authentication.

3. Click Connect.

4. Expand the Databases node.

5. Right-click DRMS_Config_rms_domain_com_443, select Tasks, and then select Back Up.

6. Click Add in the Destination section and select the location.

7. Click OK to finish the backup.

8. Repeat these steps to back up the logging and directory services cache database.

 If you cannot restore the configuration database, you can recover your AD RMS infrastructure with the exported TPD and the cluster key password.

AD RMS Trust Policies

Trust policies are implemented to define how content licensing requests are processed throughout the enterprise, including rights-protected content from other AD RMS clusters. Trust policies are defined as follows:

Trusted User Domains   A trusted user domain (TUD) is the boundary mechanism for the AD RMS root cluster to process client licensor certificates or use licenses from users whose rights account certificates (RACs) were issued by another AD RMS root cluster. You must import the server licensor certificate of the AD RMS cluster to be trusted, to define your TUD.

Trusted Publishing Domains   A trusted publishing domain (TPD) is another boundary type for one AD RMS cluster to issue licenses against publishing licenses issued by another AD RMS cluster. You must also import the server licensor certificate and private key of the server to be trusted, to define the TPD.

Windows Live ID   Microsoft offers an online RMS service for an AD RMS user to send rights-protected content to another user with their Windows Live ID. The Windows Live ID recipient is then able to read rights-protected content from the originating AD RMS cluster registered through Microsoft's online RMS service. This extended AD RMS implantation does not allow the Windows Live ID user to create rights-protected content from the on-premise AD RMS cluster.

Federated Trust   With a federated trust established between AD forests, users from one organization can share rights-protected content with another organization without requiring AD RMS implementation on both sides of the trust.

Microsoft Federation Gateway   Microsoft also offers federated trust through the Microsoft Federation Gateway, which is essentially a trusted broker between organizations. Microsoft Federation Gateway handles all of the identity verifications with all participating Microsoft federated organizations. Microsoft federated organizations can take advantage of this gateway by filtering lists to select which domains can receive certificates or licenses from the on-premise AD RMS cluster.

Managing Trusted User Domains   Trusted user domains enable trust between domains running AD RMS, and they are often used to connect users between forests. TUD management is accomplished in the AD RMS Management console. TUD information is exported to a `.bin` file and then subsequently imported using the Import Trusted User Domain dialog box.

Adding a Trusted User Domain   By default, Active Directory Rights Management Services (AD RMS) will not process requests from users whose rights account certificate was issued by a different AD RMS installation. However, you can add user domains to the list of trusted user domains, which allows AD RMS to process such requests.

For each TUD, you can also add and remove specific users or groups of users. In addition, you can remove a TUD; however, you cannot remove the root cluster for this Active Directory forest from the list of TUDs. Every AD RMS server trusts the root cluster in its own forest. In Exercise 22.15 we'll add a TUD into the test domain.

EXERCISE 22.15

Adding a Trusted User Domain

Before getting started, the TUD of the AD RMS installation should already be exported and available.

1. Start the Active Directory Rights Management Services console and expand the AD RMS cluster.

2. In the console tree, expand Trust Policies and click Trusted User Domains.

3. In the Actions pane, click Import Trusted User Domain.

4. In the Trusted User Domain File dialog box, type the path to the exported server licensor certificate of the user domain to trust or click Browse to locate it.

5. In Display Name, type a name to identify this trusted user domain. If you would like to extend this trust to federated users, select Extend Trust To Federated Users Of The Imported Server.

7. Click Finish.

Exporting the Trusted User Domain

TUDs allow an AD RMS cluster to issue licenses to users whose rights account certificate was established by another server in an AD RMS cluster. Exporting a TUD's key and importing it into another AD RMS cluster allows the cluster to process requests for use licenses from users whose rights account certificates are in a different cluster.

Membership in the local **AD RMS Enterprise Admins group,** or equivalent, is the minimum required to complete this procedure. In Exercise 22.16, we will export the TUD and store the data in a location you provide.

EXERCISE 22.16

Exporting the Trusted User Domain

1. Start the Active Directory Rights Management Services console and expand the AD RMS cluster.

2. In the console tree, expand Trust Policies and click Trusted User Domains.

3. In the Actions pane, click Export Trusted User Domain.

4. The Save As dialog box appears. I recommend you modify the .bin file name to include the name of your server, such as `ADRMS_Cluster1_LicensorCert.bin`.

5. Click Save to save the file with the name and location you specified.

Exporting the Trusted Publishing Domain

Unlike a trusted user domain, a trusted publishing domain enables an AD RMS cluster to issue licenses as if it was a different AD RMS cluster. To accomplish this, both the certificate and the private key need to be imported. This is different from a TUD scenario, where only the certificate is imported.

Importing a TPD is accomplished within the AD RMS Management console using the Import Trusted Publishing Domain dialog box. Saving a copy of the trusted publishing domain can be done from within the AD RMS administration console. In the Exercise 22.17, we will export the TPD.

EXERCISE 22.17

Exporting the Trusted Publishing Domain

1. Start the AD RMS administration console.

2. In the console tree view, select Trusted Publishing Domains node.

3. In the details pane on the right, select Export Trusted Publishing Domain. The Export Trusted Publishing Domain dialog box will appear.

4. From the Export Trusted Publishing Domain dialog box, click Save As. The Export Trusted Publishing Domain File Save As dialog box will appear. On the left pane, select the folder you want to save the trusted publishing domain.

5. In File Name enter a filename; then verify the XML File (*.xml) type is selected for Save As Type.

6. Click Save. This will close the Export Trusted Publishing Domain As dialog box.

7. In the Export Trusted Publishing Domain dialog box, enter a password in the Password box.

8. Enter a password again in the Confirm Password dialog box.

9. Click Finish.

Adding a Trusted Publishing Domain

Exercise 22.18 assumes you have exported the trusted publishing domain of another AD RMS cluster (as described in the preceding section). Membership in the local AD RMS Enterprise Admins group, or equivalent, is the minimum required to complete this procedure.

EXERCISE 22.18

Adding the Trusted Publishing Domain

1. Start the Active Directory Rights Management Services console and expand the AD RMS cluster.

2. In the console tree, expand Trust Policies and click Trusted Publishing Domains.

3. In the Actions pane, click Import Trusted Publishing Domain.

4. In the Trusted Publishing Domain File dialog box, type the path to the trusted publishing domain file or click Browse to locate it. This file contains the licensor certificate, private key (if the key is stored in software), and rights policy templates. This file is encrypted.

5. In Password, type the password required to decrypt this file.

6. In Display Name, type a name to identify this trusted user domain.

7. Click Finish.

Managing Distributed and Archived Rights Policy Templates

Rights policy templates are managed in the AD RMS Management console. Planning and overviews of rights policies are available here:

http://technet.microsoft.com/en-us/library/ee221094

http://technet.microsoft.com/en-us/library/dd996658

You can designate the location for the templates as well as set whether the templates can be exported by using the properties of the Rights Policy Template tab.

Summary

In this chapter, I discussed the certificate authority role and some of the new features in Microsoft Windows Server 2012 R2, including additional management options, new certificate templates, and better support for globalized organizations with limited IDN support. I also covered the details of the same-key certificate renewal requirement and the effects of the new increased default security settings on the CA role service.

I also discussed Active Directory Federation Services, which provides Internet-based clients with a secure identity access solution that works on both Windows and non-Windows operating systems.

Finally, I talked about Active Directory Rights Management Services. I explained that AD RMS is included with Microsoft Windows Server 2012 R2 and discussed how it allows administrators or users to determine what access to give other users in an organization.

Exam Essentials

Understand the concepts behind certificate authority.   Certificate authority servers manage certificates. Make sure you understand why companies use certificate servers and how they work.

Understand certificate enrollment.   You need to understand the many different ways to issue certificates to users and computers. You also need to understand the differences between installing certificates using GPOs, auto-enrollment, and web enrollment.

Understand Active Directory Federation Service.   Active Directory Federation Service gives users the ability to do a single sign-on and access applications on other networks without needing a secondary password. Organizations can set up trust relationships with other trusted organizations so that a user's digital identity and access rights can be accepted without a secondary password.

Know how to install Active Directory Rights Management Services.   Active Directory Rights Management Services, included with Microsoft Windows Server 2012 R2, allows administrators and users to determine what access (open, read, modify, and so on) they give to other users in an organization. This access can be used to secure email messages, internal websites, and documents.

Review Questions

1. Channel Fishing Company wants to configure a CA server in the DMZ to issue certificates to remote users. How would you accomplish this? (Choose all that apply.)

   A. You should consider having the Certificate Enrollment Policy Web Server role included in the solution.

   B. You should consider having the online responder included in the solution.

   C. You should consider having the Network Device Enrollment Service included in the solution.

   D. You should consider having the web service included in the solution.

   E. You should consider having the Certificate Enrollment Web Service included in the solution.

   F. You should consider having the Web Enrollment service included in the solution.

2. The certificate revocation list (CRL) polling begins to consume bandwidth. What steps should you consider to reduce network traffic?

   A. You should consider implementing the Certificate Enrollment Policy Web Server role and Certificate Enrollment Web Services role.

   B. You should consider implementing an online responder.

   C. You should consider implementing an online issuing CA and a root CA.

   D. You consider publishing more CRLs.

3. ABC Industries wants configuration modifications of the Certification Authority role service to be logged. How would you implement this? (Choose all that apply.)

   A. You should consider enabling auditing of system events.

   B. You should consider enabling logging.

   C. You should consider enabling auditing of object access.

   D. You should consider enabling auditing of privilege use.

   E. You should consider enabling auditing of process tracking.

4. Federation proxy services are installed through which of the following?

   A. Separate Active Directory Federation Proxy install download

   B. Server Manager ➤ Remote Access ➤ Web Proxy

   C. Server Manager ➤ Active Directory Federation Services ➤ Active Directory Proxy services

   D. Windows PowerShell ➤ Install-Windows-Feature Web Proxy

5. The new Workplace Join feature supports which of following? (Choose all that apply.)

   A. Federates an iPhone to the corporate intranet

   B. Allows Windows 8 clients to process claim-based trusts

   C. Allows Windows 8 clients to form claim-based trusts automatically with the home domain

   D. None of the above

6. You install and configure four Windows Server 2012 R2 servers as an AD FS server farm. The AD FS configuration database is stored in a Microsoft SQL Server 2012 database. You need to ensure that AD FS will continue to function in the event of an AD FS server failure. You also need to ensure that all four servers in the AD FS farm will actively perform AD FS functions. What should you include in your solution?

   A. Windows Failover Clustering

   B. Windows Identity Foundation 3.5

   C. Network Load Balancing

   D. Web Proxy Server

7. Your network contains an Active Directory domain named contoso.com. You plan to deploy a Windows 2012 R2 Active Directory Federation Services (AD FS) farm that will contain eight federation servers. You need to identify which technology or technologies must be deployed on the network before you install the federation servers. Which technology or technologies should you identify? (Choose all that apply.)

   A. Network Load Balancing

   B. Microsoft Forefront Identity Manager 2010

   C. Windows Internal Database feature

   D. Microsoft SQL Server 2012 R2

   E. The Windows Identity Foundation 3.5 feature

8. You are the system administrator at JavaCup, which hosts a web RMS-aware application that the JavaCup forest and Boston Tea Company forest users need to access. You deploy a single AD FS server in the JavaCup forest. Which of the following is a true statement about your AD FS implementation? (Choose all that apply.)

   A. You will configure a relying-party server on the JavaCup AD FS server.

   B. The AD FS server in the Boston Tea Company forest functions as the claims provider.

   C. The AD FS server in the Boston Tea Company forest functions as the relying-party server.

   D. You will configure a claims provider trust on the JavaCup AD FS server.

9. You store AD FS servers in an OU named Federation Servers. You want to auto-enroll the certificates used for AD FS. Which certificates should you add to the GPO?

    A. The CA certificate of the forest

    B. The third-party (VeriSign, Entrust) CA certificate

    C. The SSL certificate assigned to the AD FS servers

    D. The Token Signing certificate assigned to the AD FS Servers

10. You plan to implement Active Directory Rights Management Services (AD RMS) across the enterprise. You need to plan the AD RMS cluster installations for the forest. Users in all domains will access AD RMS–protected documents. You need to minimize the number of AD RMS clusters. Which of the following will help you determine how many AD RMS root clusters you require?

    A. You need at least one AD RMS root cluster for the enterprise.

    B. You need at least one AD RMS root cluster per forest.

    C. You need at least one AD RMS root cluster per domain.

    D. You need at least one AD RMS root cluster per Active Directory site.

    E. An AD RMS root cluster is not required.

Appendix A

Answers to Review Questions

Chapter 1: Install Windows Server 2012 R2

1. B. Windows Server 2012 R2 Server Core is a more secure, slimmed-down version of Windows Server. Web versions of Windows Server 2012 R2 are not available. You would use Windows Server 2012 R2 Standard as a web server.

2. C. One of the new advantages of Windows Server 2012 R2 is that you can convert Server Core and GUI versions without the need to reinstall the operating system files completely.

3. B. Microsoft recommends that you upgrade your Windows Server 2008 or Windows Server 2008 R2 web server to Windows Server 2012 R2 Standard.

4. A. Windows Server 2012 R2 Datacenter was designed for organizations that are seeking to migrate to a highly virtualized, private cloud environment. Windows Server 2012 R2 Datacenter has full Windows Server functionality with unlimited virtual instances.

5. D. Windows Server 2012 R2 Foundation was designed for smaller companies that need a Windows Server experience for as few as 15 users. Windows Server 2012 R2 Foundation is general-purpose server with basic server functionality and no virtualization rights.

6. C. Windows Server 2012 R2 Essentials is ideal for small businesses that have as many as 25 users and 50 devices. It has a simple interface, preconfigured connectivity to cloud-based services, and no virtualization rights.

7. A, B, C and D. All four answers are advantages of using Windows Server 2012 R2 Server Core. Server Core is a smaller installation of Windows Server, and therefore all four answers apply.

8. B. Windows Server 2012 R2 Features On Demand allows an administrator not only to disable a role or feature but also to remove the role or feature's files completely from the hard disk.

9. D. New to Windows Server 2012 R2, an administrator has the ability to turn a Windows GUI installation into a Server Core installation.

10. C. Windows Server 2012 R2 has a type of domain controller called a read-only domain controller (RODC). This gives an organization the ability to install a domain controller in an area or location (onsite or offsite) where security is a concern.

Chapter 2: Configure Network Services

1.   B. Because of the .(root) zone, users will not be able to access the Internet. The DNS forwarding option and DNS root hints will not be configurable. If you want your users to access the Internet, you must remove the .(root) zone.

2.   C. Active Directory Integrated zones store their records in Active Directory. Because this company has only one Active Directory forest, it's the same Active Directory that both DNS servers are using. This allows ServerA to see all of the records of ServerB and ServerB to see all the records of ServerA.

3.   D. The Secure Only option is for DNS servers that have an Active Directory Integrated zone. When a computer tries to register with DNS dynamically, the DNS server checks Active Directory to verify that the computer has an Active Directory account. If the computer that is trying to register has an account, DNS adds the host record. If the computer trying to register does not have an account, the record gets tossed away, and the database is not updated.

4.   A. If you need to complete a zone transfer from Microsoft DNS to a BIND (Unix) DNS server, you need to enable BIND secondaries on the Microsoft DNS server.

5.   B. Conditional forwarding allows you to send a DNS query to different DNS servers based on the request. Conditional forwarding lets a DNS server on a network forward DNS queries according to the DNS domain name in the query.

6.   B. On a Windows Server 2012 R2 DNS machine, debug logging is disabled by default. When it is enabled, you have the ability to log DNS server activity, including inbound and outbound queries, packet type, packet content, and transport protocols.

7.   D. Active Directory Integrated zones give you many benefits over using primary and secondary zones including less network traffic, secure dynamic updates, encryption, and reliability in the event of a DNS server going down. The Secure Only option is for dynamic updates to a DNS database.

8.   A. Windows Server 2012 R2 DNS supports two features called DNS Aging and DNS Scavenging. These features are used to clean up and remove stale resource records. DNS zone or DNS server aging and scavenging flags old resource records that have not been updated in a certain amount of time (determined by the scavenging interval). These stale records will be scavenged at the next cleanup interval.

9.   C. The dnscmd /zoneexport command creates a file using the zone resource records. This file can then be given to the Compliance department as a copy.

10.   D. Stub zones are useful for slow WAN connections. These zones store only three types of resource records: NS records, glue host (A) records, and SOA records. These three records are used to locate authoritative DNS servers.

Chapter 3: Plan and Install Active Directory

1. **B, C and D.** The forest and function levels have to be Windows 2003 or newer to install an RODC.

2. **B.** A domain controller can contain Active Directory information for only one domain. If you want to use a multidomain environment, you must use multiple domain controllers configured in either a tree or a forest setting.

3. **D.** NTFS has file-level security, and it makes efficient usage of disk space. Since this machine is to be configured as a domain controller, the configuration requires at least one NTFS partition to store the Sysvol information.

4. **A and D.** To convert the system partition to NTFS, you must first use the CONVERT command-line utility and then reboot the server. During the next boot, the file system will be converted.

5. **B and E.** The use of LDAP and TCP/IP is required to support Active Directory. TCP/IP is the network protocol favored by Microsoft, which determined that all Active Directory communication would occur on TCP/IP. DNS is required because Active Directory is inherently dependent on the domain model. DHCP is used for automatic address assignment and is not required. Similarly, NetBEUI and IPX/SPX are not available network protocols in Windows Server 2012 R2.

6. **A and C.** The Sysvol directory must be created on an NTFS partition. If such a partition is not available, you will not be able to promote the server to a domain controller. An error in the network configuration might prevent the server from connecting to another domain controller in the environment.

7. **B and C.** You need to run the Adprep command when installing your first Windows Server 2012 R2 domain controller onto a Windows Server 2008 R2 domain. Adprep /rodcprep actually gets the network ready to install a read-only domain controller and not a GUI version.

8. **A.** You'll need to use Active Directory Federation Services (AD FS) in order to implement federated identity management. Federated identity management is a standards-based and information technology process that will enable distributed identification, authentication, and authorization across organizational and platform boundaries. The AD FS solution in Windows Server 2012 R2 helps administrators address these challenges by enabling organizations to share a user's identity information securely.

9. **B.** The HOSTS file is a text-file-based database of mappings between hostnames and IP addresses. It works like a file-based version of DNS. DNS resolves a hostname to an IP address.

10. **A.** You only need to give them rights to the Stellacon.com zone using the DNS snap-in. If they do not have any rights to the Stellatest.com zone, they will not be able to configure this zone in any way.

Chapter 4: Configure Windows Server 2012 R2

1. C. You need to publish shares in the directory before they are available to the users of the directory. If NetBIOS is still enabled on the network, the shares will be visible to the NetBIOS tools and clients, but you do not have to enable NetBIOS on shares. Although replication must occur before the shares are available in the directory, it is unlikely that the replication will not have occurred by the next day. If this is the case, then you have other problems with the directory as well.

2. A. The Sharing tab contains a check box that you can use to list the printer in Active Directory.

3. A and C. A printer may not show up within Active Directory if the printer has not been shared or if the client does not have permission to view the printer. The printer will appear as an object in Active Directory even if it is offline or malfunctioning.

4. B. Offline files give you the opportunity to set up files and folders so that users can work on the data while outside the office.

5. A, B, C and D. Improved security, quotas, compression, and encryption are all advantages of using NTFS over FAT32. These features are not available in FAT32. The only security you have in FAT32 is shared folder permissions.

6. E. By giving Moe Modify on the NTFS security setting, you're giving him just enough to do his job. You could also give Sales or Finance the Modify permission, but then everyone in those groups would be able to delete, change, and do more than they all need to do. Also, Moe does not need Full Control to change or delete files.

7. B. Disk quotas allow you to limit the amount of space on a volume or partition. You can set an umbrella quota for all users and then implement individual users' quotas to bypass the umbrella quota.

8. C and E. The Admin group needs Full Control on the NTFS security and shared permission settings in order to do their job. To be able to give other users permissions, you must have the Full Control permission.

9. A and C. Windows Remote Management and Windows PowerShell allow an administrator to configure a Windows Server 2012 R2 machine remotely. The command prompt is used locally on a Windows Server 2012 R2 Server Core system, and there is no application called Microsoft Remote Admin (MRA).

10. D. File servers are used for storage of data, especially for users' home folders. Home folders are folder locations for your users to store data that is important and that needs to be backed up.

Chapter 5: Administer Active Directory

1. A. A computer account and the domain authenticate each other by using a password. The password resets every 30 days. Since the machine has not connected to the domain for 16 weeks, the computer needs to be rejoined to the domain.

2. C. Checking the box Account Never Expires will prevent this user's account from expiring again.

3. D. The dsadd command allows you to add an object (user's account) to the Active Directory database.

4. A. Distribution groups are for emails only, and distribution groups cannot be assigned rights and permissions to objects.

5. A. Inheritance is the process by which permissions placed on parent OUs affect child OUs. In this example, the permissions change for the higher-level OU (Texas) automatically caused a change in permissions for the lower-level OU (Austin).

6. B and E. Enabling the Advanced Features item in the View menu will allow Isabel to see the LostAndFound and System folders. The LostAndFound folder contains information about objects that could not be replicated among domain controllers.

7. A. Through the use of filtering, you can choose which types of objects you want to see using the Active Directory Users and Computers tool. Several of the other choices may work, but they require changes to Active Directory settings or objects.

8. A. To allow the junior admin to do backups, their account needs to be part of the Backup Operators local group. To add their account to the local group, you need to use Computer Management.

9. A, B, C and D. All of the options listed are common tasks presented in the Delegation of Control Wizard.

10. D. The Delegation of Control Wizard is designed to allow administrators to set up permissions on specific Active Directory objects.

Chapter 6: Manage GPOs

1. A and B. If you want your clients to be able to edit domain-based GPOs by using the ADMX files that are stored in the ADMX Central Store, you must be using Windows Vista, Windows 7, Windows 8, or Windows Server 2003/2008/2008 R2/2012/2012 R2.

2.   D. If you assign an application to a user, the application does not get automatically installed. To have an application installed automatically, you must assign the application to the computer account. Since Finance is the only OU that should receive this application, you would link the GPO to Finance only.

3.   C. The Resultant Set of Policy (RSoP) utility displays the exact settings that apply to individual users, computers, OUs, domains, and sites after inheritance and filtering have taken effect. Desktop wallpaper settings are under the User section of the GPO, so you would run the RSoP against the user account.

4.   B. The Enforced option can be placed on a parent GPO, and this option ensures that all lower-level objects inherit these settings. Using this option ensures that Group Policy inheritance is not blocked at other levels.

5.   A. If the data transfer rate from the domain controller providing the GPO to the computer is slower than what you have specified in the slow link detection setting, the connection is considered to be a slow connection and the application will not install properly.

6.   D. To disable the application of Group Policy on a security group, you should deny the Apply Group Policy option. This is particularly useful when you don't want GPO settings to apply to a specific group, even though that group may be in an OU that includes the GPO settings.

7.   A. GPOs at the OU level take precedence over GPOs at the domain level. GPOs at the domain level, in turn, take precedence over GPOs at the site level.

8.   B. The Block Policy Inheritance option prevents group policies of higher-level Active Directory objects from applying to lower-level objects as long as the Enforced option is not set.

9.   A, B, C and D. GPOs can be set at all of the levels listed. You cannot set GPOs on security principals such as users or groups.

10. D and E. Administrative templates are used to specify the options available for setting Group Policy. By creating new administrative templates, Ann can specify which options are available for the new applications. She can then distribute these templates to other system administrators in the environment.

Chapter 7: Manage Security

1.   B, C and E. The Account Lockout Duration setting states how long an account will be locked out if the password is entered incorrectly. Account Lockout Threshold is the number of bad password attempts, and Account Lockout Counter is the time in which the bad password attempts are made. Once the Account Lockout Counter value reaches 0, the number of bad password attempts returns to 0.

2.   B. Account logon events are created for domain account activity. For example, you have a user who logs onto a server so that they can access files; the act of logging onto the server creates this audit event.

3. B, E and F. The first step is to enable auditing. With auditing enabled, Alexis can specify which actions are recorded. To give permissions to the Audit user account, she can use the Delegation of Control Wizard.

4. B, E, G and H. The Active Directory Users and Computers tool allows system administrators to change auditing options and to choose which actions are audited. At the file system level, Crystal can specify exactly which actions are recorded in the audit log. She can then use Event Viewer to view the recorded information and provide it to the appropriate managers.

5. B. Account logon events are created for domain account activity. For example, you have a user who logs on to a server so that they can access files; the act of logging on to the server creates this audit event.

Chapter 8: Configure TCP/IP

1. D. To calculate the network mask, you need to figure out which power number (2^x) is greater than or equal to the number you need. Since you are looking for 1000, $2^{10} = 1024$. You then add the power (10) to the current network mask (53 + 10 = 63).

2. A. When you look at an IPv6 address, the first sections tell you the IPv6 address space prefix. Fd00:: /8 is the unique local unicast prefix, and this allows the server to communicate with all local machines within your intranet.

3. C. The unique local address can be FC00 or FD00, and it is used like the private address space of IPv4. Unique local addresses are not expected to be routable on the global Internet, but they are used for private routing within an organization.

4. A. A Class B address with a default subnet mask of 255.255.0.0 will support up to 65,534 hosts. To increase the number of networks that this network will support, you need to subnet the network by borrowing bits from the host portion of the address. The subnet mask 255.255.252.0 uses 6 bits from the host's area, and it will support 64 subnets while leaving enough bits to support 1,022 hosts per subnet. The subnet mask 255.255.248.0 uses 5 bits from the hosts and will support 32 subnetworks while leaving enough bits to support 2,046 hosts per subnet. 255.255.252.0 is the better answer because it leaves quite a bit of room for further growth in the number of networks while still leaving room for more than 1,000 hosts per subnet, which is a fairly large number of devices on one subnet. The subnet mask 255.255.254.0 uses 7 bits from the host's area and will support more than 120 networks, but it will leave only enough bits to support 500 hosts per subnet. The subnet mask 255.255.240.0 uses 4 bits from the hosts and will support only 16 subnetworks, even though it will leave enough bits to support more than 4,000 hosts per subnet.

5. A. The network mask applied to an address determines which portion of that address reflects the number of hosts available to that network. The balance with subnetting is always between the number of hosts and individual subnetworks that can be uniquely represented within one encompassing address. The number of hosts and networks that are made available depends on the number of bits that can be used to represent them. This scenario requires more than 35 networks and fewer than 1,000 workstations on each network. If you convert the subnet masks as described in the chapter, you will see that the mask in option A allows for more than 60 networks and more than 1,000 hosts. All of the other options are deficient in either the number of networks or the number of hosts that they represent.

6.   A. The subnet mask 255.255.255.192 borrows 2 bits from the hosts, which allows you to build four separate networks that you can route through the Windows server. This will allow you to have 62 hosts on each segment. A mask of 255.255.255.128 would have been even better, with two subnets of 126 hosts each, but that wasn't an option, and this solution gives you room for growth in the number of subnets. The subnet mask 255.255.255.224 borrows 3 bits from the hosts. This allows you to create 8 networks, which you don't need, and it leaves only enough bits for 30 hosts. The subnet mask 255.255.255.252 borrows 6 bits from the hosts. This allows you to create more than 60 networks, which you don't need, and it leaves only enough bits for 2 hosts. The subnet mask 255.255.255.240 borrows 4 bits from the hosts. This allows you to create 16 networks, which you don't need, and it leaves only enough bits for 14 hosts per subnet.

7.   B, C and D. When you add up the locations that currently need to be given a network address, the total is 3,150, and the maximum number of hosts at any one of these locations is fewer than 1,000. The subnet masks need to support those requirements. Assuming that you choose the Class A private address space 10.0.0.0/8, the subnet masks given in options B, C, and D will provide the address space to support the outlined requirements. The subnet mask 255.255.240.0 supports more than 4,000 subnets and more than 4,000 hosts. The subnet mask 255.255.248.0 supports more than 8,000 subnets and more than 2,000 hosts. The subnet mask 255.255.252.0 supports more than 16,000 subnets and more than 1,000 hosts. Although each of these subnet masks will work, at the rate that this company is growing, 255.255.252.0 is probably the best mask to prepare for the future. It's unlikely that there will ever be more than 1,000 hosts on any given network. In fact, that number would probably cause performance problems on that subnet. Therefore, it's better to have more subnets available to deploy as the company grows. The subnet mask 255.255.224.0 supports more than 2,000 subnets—an insufficient number to cover the locations. The subnet mask 255.255.254.0 supports more than 32,000 subnets, but only 500 hosts per subnet, which are not enough hosts to cover all of the locations.

8.   C. The CIDR /27 tells you that 27 1s are turned on in the subnet mask. Twenty-seven 1s equals 11111111.11111111.11111111.11100000. This would then equal 255.255.255.224.

The network address 192.168.11.192 with a subnet mask of 255.255.255.224 is perfect for Subnet A because it supports up to 30 hosts. The network address 192.168.11.128 with a subnet mask of 255.255.255.192 is perfect for Subnet B because it supports up to 62 hosts. The network address 192.168.11.0 with a subnet mask of 255.255.255.128 is perfect for Subnet C because it supports up to 126 hosts.

9.   A. Microsoft's jetpack.exe utility allows you to compact a JET database. Microsoft JET databases are used for WINS and DHCP databases.

10.   B and D. If the first word of an IPv6 address is FE80 (actually the first 10 bits of the first word yields 1111 1110 10 or FE80:: /10), then the address is a link-local IPv6 address. If it's in EUI-64 format, then the MAC address is also available (unless it's randomly generated). The middle FF:FE is the filler and indicator of the EUI-64 space, with the MAC address being 00:03:FF:11:02:CD. Remember also the 00 of the MAC becomes 02 in the link-local IPv6 address, flipping a bit to call it local.

Chapter 9: Use Virtualization in Windows Server 2012

1. B and D. Hyper-V can be installed on the Standard or Datacenter Editions of Windows Server 2012 R2. Itanium, x86, and Web Editions are not supported.

2. C. The external virtual network type will allow the virtual machine to communicate with the external network as it would with the Internet, so A is wrong. The internal-only network type allows communication between the virtual machines and the host machine. Because the question says that only communication between the virtual machines should be allowed, the only valid answer is private virtual machine network. The last option, public virtual machine network, does not exist in Hyper-V.

3. A. This question focuses on the fact that you cannot change the memory if the virtual machine is running, paused, or saved. The only valid answer is to shut it down and then change the memory.

4. A. The only virtual hard disk that increases in size is the dynamically expanding disk. Thus, this is the only valid answer to this question. The fixed-size disk creates a disk of the size you specify, the differencing disk is a special disk that stores only the differences between it and a parent disk, and the physical disk uses a physical drive and makes it available to the virtual machine.

5. C. Physical hard disks cannot be configured using the Virtual Hard Disk Wizard, the Edit Virtual Hard Disk Wizard, or the New Virtual Machine Wizard. You can configure and attach a physical disk only by using the virtual machine's settings.

6. B. Hyper-V is not supported on Itanium-based systems; thus, he cannot install it.

7. A, B and C. The minimum CPU requirement for running Hyper-V is a x64-based processor (Itanium is not supported), hardware Data Execution Protection must be enabled, and hardware-assisted virtualization must be enabled. There is no minimum requirement for a dual-core processor.

8. C. This question relates to the setup command used to install the Hyper-V server role on a Windows Server 2008 Server Core machine. It's important to remember that these commands are case sensitive and that the correct command is start /wocsetup Microsoft-Hyper-V, which is option C. All of the other commands will fail to install Hyper-V on a Server Core machine. If you were using a Windows Server 2012 R2 machine, you would use the DISM command.

9. A and D. The Hyper-V Manager is available only for Windows Server 2008, Windows 7, and Windows 8. There is no version available that runs on Windows Server 2003 or on Windows XP SP3.

10. C. The virtual network type in which the machines communicate with each other and with the host machine is called *internal only*. In a private virtual network, the virtual machines can communicate only with each other, not with the network or the host machine. The external network type defines a network where the virtual machines can communicate with each other, with the host machine, and with an external network like the Internet.

Chapter 10: Manage and Maintain Servers

1. **D.** All of the applications that are running on the Windows Server 2012 R2 machine will show up on the Details tab. Right-click the application and end the process.

2. **A.** If you use MBSA from the command-line utility `mdsacli.exe`, you can specify several options. You type **mdsacli.exe/hf** (from the folder that contains `mdsacli.exe`) and then customize the command execution with an option such as */ixxxx.xxxx.xxxx.xxxx*, which specifies that the computer with the specified IP address should be scanned.

3. **B and E.** You can set the registry key `HKEY_LOCAL_MACHINE\Software\Policies\Microsoft\Windows\WindowsUpdate\AU\UseWUServer` to 0 to use the public Windows Update server, or you can set it to 1, which means that you will specify the server for Windows Update in the `HKEY_LOCAL_MACHINE\Software\Policies\Microsoft\Windows\WindowsUpdate` key. The WUServer key sets the Windows Update server using the server's HTTP name, for example, `http://intranetSUS`.

4. **C.** Server Manager is the one place where you install all roles and features for a Windows Server 2012 R2 system.

5. **C.** All options are valid steps to complete the configuration except option C because SERVERB cannot automatically draw updates from whichever sources are on SERVERA.

6. **B, D, and F.** Option A schedules the updates to occur at a time when the computers are generally not connected to the corporate network. Options C and E require more user interaction than would be considered minimal. By setting updates to occur with no user interaction at noon, you satisfy the requirements.

7. **D.** You can recover system state data from a backup, which always includes the Active Directory database. In this case, Event Viewer and System Monitor wouldn't help you recover the database, but they might help you determine why the hard drive crashed in the first place.

8. **D.** By using the Network Monitor, you can view all of the network packets that are being sent to or from the local server. Based on this information, you can determine the source of certain types of traffic, such as pings. The other types of monitoring can provide useful information, but they do not allow you to drill down into the specific details of a network packet, and they don't allow you to filter the data that has been collected based on details about the packet.

9. **A.** Microsoft Baseline Security Analyzer is a free download that you can get from Microsoft's website.

10. **C.** The Update Source And Proxy Server option allows you to specify where you will be receiving your updates (from Microsoft or another WSUS server) and your proxy settings if a proxy server is needed.

Chapter 11: Manage File Services

1. C. You need to publish shares in the directory before they are available to the users of the directory. If NetBIOS is still enabled on the network, the shares will be visible to the NetBIOS tools and clients, but you do not have to enable NetBIOS on shares. Although replication must occur before the shares are available in the directory, it is unlikely that the replication will not have occurred by the next day. If this is the case, then you have other problems with the directory as well.

2. A. The Sharing tab contains a check box that you can use to list the printer in Active Directory.

3. B, E, G and H. The Active Directory Users and Computers tool allows system administrators to change auditing options and to choose which actions are audited. At the file system level, Isabel can specify exactly which actions are recorded in the audit log. She can then use Event Viewer to view the recorded information and provide it to the appropriate managers.

4. B. Offline files give you the opportunity to set up files and folders so that users can work on the data while outside the company walls. Offline files allows a user to work on files while at home without the need to be logged into the network.

5. A, B, C and D. Improved security, quotas, compression, and encryption are all advantages of using NTFS over FAT32. These features are not available in FAT32. The only security you have in FAT32 is shared folder permissions.

6. A. Encrypting File System (EFS) allows a user or administrator to secure files or folders by using encryption. Encryption employs the user's security identification (SID) number to secure the file or folder. Encryption is the strongest protection that Windows provides.

7. B. Disk quotas allow you to limit the amount of space on a volume or partition. You can set an umbrella quota for all users and then implement individual users' quotas to bypass the umbrella quota.

8. B. Cipher is a command-line utility that allows you to configure or change EFS files and folders.

9. B. The Distributed File System (DFS) Namespace service in Windows Server 2012 R2 offers a simplified way for users to access geographically dispersed files. DFS allows you to set up a tree structure of virtual directories to allow users to connect to shared folders throughout the entire network.

10. D. File servers are used for storage of data, especially for users' home folders. Home folders are folder locations for your users to store data that is important and that needs to be backed up.

Chapter 12: Configure DNS

1. B. Because of the .(root) zone, users will not be able to access the Internet. The DNS forwarding option and DNS root hints will not be configurable. If you want your users to access the Internet, you must remove the .(root) zone.

2. C. Active Directory Integrated zones store their records in Active Directory. Because this company has only one Active Directory forest, it's the same Active Directory that both DNS servers are using. This allows ServerA to see all of the records of ServerB and allows ServerB to see all the records of ServerA.

3. D. The Secure Only option is for DNS servers that have an Active Directory Integrated zone. When a computer tries to register with DNS dynamically, the DNS server checks Active Directory to verify that the computer has an Active Directory account. If the computer that is trying to register has an account, DNS adds the host record. If the computer trying to register does not have an account, the record gets tossed away and the database is not updated.

4. A. If you need to complete a zone transfer from Microsoft DNS to a BIND (Unix) DNS server, you need to enable BIND Secondaries on the Microsoft DNS server.

5. B. Conditional forwarding allows you to send a DNS query to different DNS servers based on the request. Conditional forwarding lets a DNS server on a network forward DNS queries according to the DNS domain name in the query.

6. B. On a Windows Server 2012 R2 DNS machine, debug logging is disabled by default. When it is enabled, you have the ability to log DNS server activity, including inbound and outbound queries, packet type, packet content, and transport protocols.

7. D. Active Directory Integrated zones give you many benefits over using primary and secondary zones including less network traffic, secure dynamic updates, encryption, and reliability in the event of a DNS server going down. The Secure Only option is for dynamic updates to a DNS database.

8. A. Windows Server 2012 R2 DNS supports two features called DNS Aging and DNS Scavenging. These features are used to clean up and remove stale resource records. DNS zone or DNS server aging and scavenging flags old resource records that have not been updated in a certain amount of time (determined by the scavenging interval). These stale records will be scavenged at the next cleanup interval.

9. C. The dnscmd /zoneexport command creates a file using the zone resource records. This file can then be given to the Compliance department as a copy.

10. D. Stub zones are useful for slow WAN connections. These zones store only three types of resource records: NS records, glue host (A) records, and SOA records. These three records are used to locate authoritative DNS servers.

Chapter 13: Configure Routing and Remote Access

1. B. The boot threshold for an interface controls how long the relay agent will wait before forwarding DHCP requests it hears on that interface.

2. B. Multilink PPP has nothing to do with encryption of data. Multilink is easy to set up, relatively low in cost, and it makes the connection faster.

3. C and E. MS-CHAPv2 provides encrypted and mutual authentication between the respective RRAS locations. MPPE works with MS-CHAPv2 and provides encryption for all of the data between the locations. CHAP provides encrypted authentication, but MS-CHAPv2 is needed for MPPE to work. PAP is the lowest level of authentication providing passwords, but it sends passwords in cleartext, which is not the most secure solution. L2TP needs to team up with IPsec to provide the data encryption for the secure transfer of information between the locations.

4. B. MS-CHAPv2 authentication allows you to create VPN connections with a stand-alone server using PPTP and MPPE. MPPE employs keys that are created via MS-CHAPv2 or EAP-TLS authentication. EAP-TLS is not the correct answer because only domain controllers or member servers support EAP-TLS. Stand-alone servers support only MPPE. Neither PAP nor CHAP is supported with MPPE.

5. A and C. L2TP connections can be used to authenticate both sides of the VPN. L2TP needs IPsec to provide the encryption for the connection. These two together will provide the secure and authenticated transmission of data across the Internet between the two sites. PPTP connections provide encryption using only MPPE, but they don't provide authentication between the machines. RADIUS is a service that provides dial-in connectivity. MS-CHAPv2 is an authentication protocol for clients accessing the network.

6. B. L2TP and IPsec each has its own negotiation procedure for making a connection. If you remove the IPsec portion of the connection and the problem is alleviated, it is likely that IPsec is the problem, and you can then focus on IPsec. If the problem remains, you can work on the L2TP portion of the connection. IPsec has two modes: tunnel mode and transport mode. But because L2TP is a tunneling protocol, there is no sense in using IPsec tunneling. IPsec transport mode is used with L2TP and should be set aside for troubleshooting, as discussed. The L2TP implementation in Windows Server 2012 R2 doesn't support MPPE.

7. C. The default configuration for RRAS supports 5 PPTP ports and 5 L2TP ports. There are up to 150 sales reps trying to connect to the server, but only the first 10 will be able to connect. You can increase the number of ports available, up to 1,000, by using the Ports Properties dialog box. The Windows 8 clients are, by default, ready to support VPNs; they will first try L2TP and then switch over to PPTP if ports are unavailable.

8. C, E and G. Because the communication is not a continuous or frequent occurrence, it doesn't make sense to have the line always available, so RRAS with demand-dial will be less expensive than ISDN, which is always up. MS-CHAPv2 provides encryption and

a mutual authentication process. The MPPE provides the encryption of the actual data that travels across the connection. PAP is a cleartext authentication method, and CHAP provides only one-way authentication. L2TP doesn't provide any encryption by itself.

9. C. When you use Windows accounting, the local Windows account logs are found in the `systemroot\System32\LogFiles` folder. These logs can be stored in one of two formats for later analysis—Open Database Connectivity (ODBC) or Internet Authentication Service. The Performance Monitor utility that came with Windows NT has been replaced with the system event log. This keeps track of global service errors such as initialization failures and service starts and stops. There is no RRAS authentication log. You do have RADIUS logging available; when it's used, the log files are stored on the RADIUS servers. This is useful when you have multiple RRAS servers because you can centralize RRAS authentication requests. Active Directory is not used to log events from the various services in Windows Server 2012 R2.

10. B. The Server Status node in the RRAS snap-in shows you a summary of all the RRAS servers known to the system. Each server entry displays whether the server is up, what kind of server it is, how many ports it has, how many ports are currently in use, and how long the server has been up.

Chapter 14: Configure a Network Policy Server Infrastructure

1. B and E. By setting the Network Policy Server, you can force your DHCP users to use NAP on all of the DHCP scopes. This ensures that client systems meet minimum requirements to connect to a domain network.

2. D. Servers that are running Network Policy Server (NPS) are required to have a certificate installed on the NPS server.

3. B. One advantage of using NAP for DHCP is that you can set up user classes so that specific machines (for example, noncompliant DHCP systems) can get specific rules or limited access to the network.

4. D. Logman creates and manages Event Trace Session and Performance logs, and it allows an administrator to monitor many different applications through the use of the command line.

5. D. The higher the RADIUS priority number, the less that the RADIUS server gets used. To make sure that RADIUS ServerD is used only when ServerB and ServerC is unavailable, you would set the RADIUS priority from 1 to 10. This way it will get used only when ServerB and ServerC are having issues or are unresponsive.

6. C. The NPS snap-in allows you to set up RADIUS servers and specify which RADIUS server would accept authentication from other RADIUS servers. You can do your entire RADIUS configuration through the NPS snap-in.

7. C. NPS allows you to set up policies on how your users could log into the network. NPS allows you to set up policies that systems needs to follow, and if they don't follow these policies or rules, they will not have access to the full network.

8. C. Windows Server 2012 R2 comes with Extensible Authentication Protocol with Transport Level Security (EAP-TLS). This EAP type allows you to use public key certificates as an authenticator. TLS is similar to the familiar Secure Sockets Layer (SSL) protocol used for web browsers and 802.1X authentication. When EAP-TLS is turned on, the client and server send TLS-encrypted messages back and forth. EAP-TLS is the strongest authentication method you can use; as a bonus, it supports smart cards. However, EAP-TLS requires your NPS server to be part of the Windows Server 2012 R2 domain.

9. B and D. PEAP-MS-CHAP v2 is an EAP-type protocol that is easier to deploy than Extensible Authentication Protocol with Transport Level Security (EAP-TLS). It is easier because user authentication is accomplished by using password-based credentials (username and password) instead of digital certificates or smart cards. Both PEAP and EAP both use certificates with their protocols.

10. C. One advantage of NPS is that you can use the accounting part of NPS so that you can keep track of what each department does on your NPS server. This way, departments pay for the amount of time they use on the SQL server database.

Chapter 15: Configure and Manage Active Directory

1. A. Using images allows you to back up and restore your entire Windows Server 2012 R2 machine instead of just certain parts of data.

2. C. The Backup Once link allows you to start a backup on the Windows Server 2012 R2 system.

3. D. If you need to back up and restore your Windows Server 2012 R2 machine, you need to use the Windows Server Backup MMC.

4. C. To create multiple password policies, you would use ADSI Edit (or adsiedit.msc).

5. D. Universal security groups, global groups, and domain local groups are all available when you are running a Windows 2008 and Windows 2012 domain functional level.

6. B, C and E. The Account Lockout Duration setting states how long an account will be locked out if the password is entered incorrectly. The Account Lockout Threshold setting is the number of bad password attempts, and the Account Lockout Counter setting is the time in which the bad password attempts are made. Once Account Lockout Counter reaches 0, the number of bad password attempts returns to 0.

7. D. When resources are made available to users who reside in domains outside the forest, foreign security principal objects are automatically created. These new objects are stored within the `Foreign Security Principals` folder.

8. B. The primary method by which systems administrators create and manage application data partitions is through the `ntdsutil` tool.

9. A and E. To meet the requirements, Robert should use the normal backup type to create a full backup every week and the incremental backup type to back up only the data that has been modified since the last full or incremental backup operation.

10. B and D. You would need to transfer the two forestwide operations master roles: Schema Master and Domain Naming Master. This means that there can only be one Schema Master and only one Domain Naming Master per forest. The PDC Emulator Master, RID Master, and Infrastructure Master are all domain-based operations master roles. (Each domain in the forest must have a domain controller with these three roles installed.)

Chapter 16: Configure and Manage Group Policy

1. C. The Delegation of Control Wizard can be used to allow other system administrators permission to add GPO links.

2. C. The system administrator can specify whether the application will be uninstalled or whether future installations will be prevented.

3. B. You would use `GPUpdate.exe /force`. The `/force` switch forces the GPO to reapply all policy settings. By default, only policy settings that have changed are applied.

4. A. You would use the Windows PowerShell `Invoke-GPUpdate` cmdlet. This PowerShell cmdlet allows you to force the GPO to reapply the policies immediately.

5. D. DVD Present Targeting is not one of the options that you may consider when using item-level targeting.

6. A and B. If you want your clients to be able to edit domain-based GPOs by using the ADMX files that are stored in the ADMX Central Store, you must be using Windows Vista, Windows 7, Windows 8, or Windows Server 2003/2008/2008 R2/2012/2012 R2.

7. D. If you assign an application to a user, the application does not get automatically installed. To have an application automatically installed, you must assign the application to the computer account. Since Finance is the only OU that should receive this application, you would link the GPO to Finance only.

8. C. The Resultant Set of Policy (RSoP) utility displays the exact settings that apply to individual users, computers, OUs, domains, and sites after inheritance and filtering have taken effect. Desktop wallpaper settings are under the User section of the GPO, so you would run the RSoP against the user account.

9. B. The Enforced option can be placed on a parent GPO, and this option ensures that all lower-level objects inherit these settings. Using this option ensures that Group Policy inheritance is not blocked at other levels.

10. A. If the data transfer rate from the domain controller providing the GPO to the computer is slower than what you have specified in the slow link detection setting, the connection is considered to be a slow connection, and the application will not install properly.

Chapter 17: Configure and Manage High Availability

1. A, B and D. Only the Standard, Datacenter, and Hyper-V editions of Windows Server 2012 R2 can participate in a failover cluster.

2. A, B and D. All versions of Windows Server 2012 R2 can participate in an NLB cluster except for the Windows Server 2012 R2 Hyper-V edition.

3. D. A Windows Server 2012 R2 cluster can contain up to 64 nodes.

4. B. Drainstop is the function that allows the current session to end before stopping the cluster on the node. Evict is used to remove a node completely from a failover cluster. Pause is used to keep resources from failing over to a failover cluster node. Stop will immediately end the cluster service on the NLB cluster node, not allowing the current sessions to complete.

5. D. A Windows Server 2012 R2 NLB cluster can contain up to 32 nodes.

6. A and C. SQL Server and Exchange Server are supported only on failover clusters. Websites and VPN services are network-based services, so they are better suited for NLB clusters.

7. B and D. Websites and Terminal Services are all designed to work with NLB clusters. Database servers such as SQL Server do not work on NLB clusters.

8. B. To use unicast communication between NLB cluster nodes, each node must have a minimum of two network adapters.

9. B. Up to two votes can be lost before quorum can no longer be achieved. These votes can come from the file share witness or a cluster node.

10. B. In a three-node cluster, only one node can be offline before quorum is lost; a majority of the votes must be available to achieve quorum.

Chapter 18: Configure File and Storage Solutions

1. **B, E, G and H.** The Group Policy Management Console allows system administrators to change auditing options and to choose which actions are audited. At the file system level, LaDonna can specify exactly which actions are recorded in the audit log. She can then use Event Viewer to view the recorded information and provide it to the appropriate managers.

2. **A.** The iSCSI default port is TCP 3260. Port 3389 is used for RDP, port 1433 is used for Microsoft SQL, and port 21 is used for FTP.

3. **C.** Account logon events are created for domain account activity. For example, you have a user who logs onto a server so that they can access files; the act of logging onto the server creates this audit event.

4. **A.** File servers are used for storage of data, especially for users' home folders. Home folders are folder locations for your users to store data that is important and that needs to be backed up.

5. **A, B, C and D.** Improved security, quotas, compression, and encryption are all advantages of using NTFS over FAT32. These features are not available in FAT32. The only security you have in FAT32 is shared folder permissions.

6. **D.** The `iscsicli addisnsserver server_name` command manually registers the host server to an iSNS server. `refreshisnsserver` refreshes the list of available servers. `removeisnsserver` removes the host from the iSNS server. `listisnsservers` lists the available iSNS servers.

7. **A.** Windows Server 2012 R2 Features On Demand allows an administrator not only to disable a role or feature but also to remove the role or feature's files completely from the hard disk.

8. **D.** The iSNS feature is used to provide for the automatic discovery of iSCSI targets that are available on the network. This is a useful feature within a larger environment. Note that without iSNS DHCP configured, iSNS clients must be registered manually with the `iscsicli` command.

9. **A.** After generating hashes on the Colorado Springs file server that will be preloading Tampa's file server cache with file share data, the next logical step is to run `Export-BCCachePackage` to get the data to FS02 from FS01.

10. **B.** Since there is a classification rule that is currently configured and applied to company resources, you will be unable to delete the Contains Personal Information classification property manually because the Classification Rule controls the property. In this case, you have to delete the Classification Rule in order to be able to delete the classification property.

Chapter 19: Implement Business Continuity and Disaster Recovery

1. A. Using images allows you to back up and restore your entire Windows Server 2012 R2 machine instead of just certain parts of data.

2. C. If you need to get a stalled computer up and running as quickly as possible, you should start with the Last Known Good Configuration option. This option is used when you've made changes to your computer's hardware configuration and are having problems restarting but have not logged into the machine. Last Known Good Configuration will revert to the configuration used the last time the computer was successfully booted.

3. D. Daily backups back up all of the files that have changed during a single day. This operation uses the file time/date stamps to determine which files should be backed up and does not mark the files as having been backed up.

4. B. To create a restore point manually or to restore your computer to a previous restore point, you use the Shadow Copies tab of the System Properties dialog box. Although System Restore uses restore points, you do not use the System Restore utility to create a restore point.

5. B. You should start with the Last Known Good Configuration option. This option is used when you've made changes to your computer's hardware configuration and are having problems restarting. The Last Known Good Configuration will revert to the configuration used the last time the computer was successfully booted. Although this option helps overcome configuration errors, it will not help when there are hardware errors.

6. C. When you enable boot logging, the file created is \Windows\ntbtlog.txt. This log file is used to troubleshoot the boot process.

7. C. To repair the system files quickly, you can use the Startup Repair tool. You can restore an image by using the Backup and Repair Center, but it is faster to use the Startup Repair tool. Additionally, you will not lose any personal files by using the Startup Repair tool. Alternatively, you could try to use System Restore to go back to a previous checkpoint.

8. B. When you run your computer in Safe Mode, you simplify your Windows Server 2012 R2 configuration. Only the drivers that are needed to get the computer up and running are loaded.

9. C. The Backup Once link allows you to start a backup on the Windows Server 2012 R2 system.

10. D. If you need to back up and restore your Windows Server 2012 R2 machine, you need to use the Windows Server Backup MMC.

Chapter 20: Configure Advanced Network Services

1. C. Out of the possible answers provided, the only DHCP configuration option that would be both fault-tolerant and redundant is DHCP failover.

2. B, C and D. DNS registration is an advanced DHCP configuration. All three other options provide additional security for DNS on your network.

3. D. DNS netmask ordering is the only way to ensure that clients will get the closest DNS server to their subnet when performing DNS queries on your network. If DNS netmask ordering were not enabled, requests would go through a round-robin approach from all of the DNS servers available to provide lookup services. You could end up with a poor connection depending on which DNS server responds to your client's requests.

4. D. The DNSAdmins security group is the best fit for this administrator's responsibilities. If you were to place this administrator in either the Domain Admins or Enterprise Admins security group, that individual would have too many unnecessary permissions granted within the environment, making their Active Directory account a security vulnerability. The Schema Admins group does not pertain to this question.

5. B. DHCP name protection ensures that DNS host A records are never overwritten during DNS dynamic updates. The other three possible answers would not fulfill this question's requirements.

6. C. The IPAM ASM Administrators group is specifically designed for the delegation of IPAM Address Space Management. The IPAM Administrators group would give her domain account way to much access within the environment, and the other two possible answers would not provide her with enough permissions to perform her required responsibilities.

7. B. Out of the three real possible deployment methods—Distributed, Centralized, and Hybrid—only the Centralized deployment method allows one primary IPAM server to manage the entire enterprise. The Distributed method places an IPAM server at each site location, and the Hybrid method uses a primary server with an additional IPAM server at each site location within the enterprise.

8. D. The only way to accommodate the use of short, single-labeled host names within your DNS infrastructure is to implement a GlobalNames zone.

9. C. After you have successfully installed and provisioned your IPAM server, the next logical step in the IPAM deployment configuration is to configure and run server discovery. Be sure to follow the step-by-step configuration guide found on the IPAM Overview page in Server Manager when going through your IPAM test deployment.

10. A. The proper PowerShell syntax to display current IPAM database configuration settings is `Get-IpamDatabase`. The other possible answers are not valid PowerShell cmdlets.

Chapter 21: Configure the Active Directory Infrastructure

1. B. The NTDS settings for the site level are where you would activate and deactivate UGMC.

2. A. By decreasing the Replication interval for the DEFAULTIPSITELINK object, you will decrease the replication latency for all sites using the DEFAULTIPSITELINK.

3. D. In the Active Directory Sites and Services console, the Server NTDS settings are where you would activate and deactivate global catalogs.

4. D. Preferred bridgehead servers receive replication information for a site and transmit this information to other domain controllers within the site. By configuring one server at each site to act as a preferred bridgehead server, Daniel can ensure that all replication traffic between the two sites is routed through the bridgehead servers and that replication traffic will flow properly between the domain controllers.

5. C. By default, connection objects are automatically created by the Active Directory replication engine. You can choose to override the default behavior of Active Directory replication topology by manually creating connection objects, but this step is not required.

6. B. The Knowledge Consistency Checker (KCC) is responsible for establishing the replication topology and ensuring that all domain controllers are kept up-to-date.

7. D. Site link bridges are designed to allow site links to be transitive. That is, they allow site links to use other site links to transfer replication information between sites. By default, all site links are bridged. However, you can turn off transitivity if you want to override this behavior.

8. B. Simple Mail Transfer Protocol was designed for environments in which persistent connections may not always be available. SMTP uses the store-and-forward method to ensure that information is not lost if a connection cannot be made.

9. D. The Directory Service event log contains error messages and information related to replication. These details can be useful when you are troubleshooting replication problems.

10. A and D. By creating new sites, Christina can help define settings for Active Directory replication based on the environment's network connections. She can use connection objects to define further the details of how and when replication traffic will be transmitted between the domain controllers.

Chapter 22: Configure Access and Information Protection Solutions

1. **A and E.** Certificate Enrollment Web Service with the Certificate Enrollment Policy Web Server role is the preferred Microsoft solution for issuing certificates through the internet.

2. **B.** The online responder uses a lightweight HTTP protocol that responds faster and more efficiently than downloading a traditional CRL.

3. **B and C.** To enable AD FS 3.0 auditing, you must check the boxes for Success Audits and Failure Audits on the Events tab of the Federation Service Properties dialog box. You must also enable Object Access Auditing in Local Policy or Group Policy.

4. **B.** Federation Proxy Services are installed under Remote Access as a web application proxy server in Windows Server 2012.

5. **A, B and C.** By using Workplace Join, information workers can join their personal devices with their company's workplace computers to access company resources and services. When you join your personal device to your workplace, it becomes a known device and provides seamless second-factor authentication and single sign-on to workplace resources and applications. Windows Server 2012 R2, Windows 8.1, and iOS devices can be joined by using Workplace Join.

6. **C.** Network Load Balancing (NLB) is the only support Microsoft solution for providing high availability across an ADFS server farm. Windows Failover Clustering does not currently support ADFS as one master server is allowed to write to the configuration database per farm.

7. **D.** The AD FS configuration database stores all of the configuration data. It contains information that a federation service requires to identify partners, certificates, attribute stores, claims, and so forth. You can store this configuration data in either a Microsoft SQL Server 2005 or newer database or the Windows Internal Database feature that is included with Windows Server 2008, Windows Server 2008 R2, and Windows Server 2012 R2. The Windows Internal Database supports only up to five federation servers in a farm.

8. **A and B.** The relying-party server is a member of the Active Directory forest that hosts resources that a user in the partner organization wants to access. In this case, the relying party server should be the JavaCup AD FS server. A claims provider provides users with claims. These claims are stored within digitally encrypted and signed tokens. In this case, Boston Tea Party is the claims provider.

9. **A.** The Forest CA certificate is the only certificate that is automatically trusted, does not require user interaction and digital signature does not change in this scenario.

10. **B.** Licensing Server/Cluster is the component in charge of delivering publishing and use licenses. Several clusters can be installed per forest depending on the technical needs (servers' workload and bandwidth constraints).

Appendix B

About the Additional Study Tools

IN THIS APPENDIX:

- Additional Study Tools
- System requirements
- Using the Study Tools
- Troubleshooting

Additional Study Tools

The following sections are arranged by category and summarize the software and other goodies you'll find from the companion website. If you need help with installing the items, refer to the installation instructions in the "Using the Study Tools" section of this appendix.

> The additional study tools can be found at www.sybex.com/go/mcsawin2012r2. Here, you will get instructions on how to download the files to your hard drive.

Sybex Test Engine

The files contain the Sybex test engine, which includes two bonus practice exams, as well as the Assessment Test and the Chapter Review Questions, which are also included in the book itself.

Electronic Flashcards

These handy electronic flashcards are just what they sound like. One side contains a question, and the other side shows the answer.

PDF of Glossary of Terms

We have included an electronic version of the Glossary in .pdf format. You can view the electronic version of the Glossary with Adobe Reader.

Adobe Reader

We've also included a copy of Adobe Reader so you can view PDF files that accompany the book's content. For more information on Adobe Reader or to check for a newer version, visit Adobe's website at www.adobe.com/products/reader/

System Requirements

Make sure your computer meets the minimum system requirements shown in the following list. If your computer doesn't match up to most of these requirements, you may have problems using the software and files. For the latest and greatest information, please refer to the ReadMe file located in the downloads.

- A PC running Microsoft Windows 98, Windows 2000, Windows NT4 (with SP4 or later), Windows Me, Windows XP, Windows Vista, or Windows 7

- An Internet connection

Using the Study Tools

To install the items, follow these steps:

1. Download the .ZIP file to your hard drive, and unzip to an appropriate location. Instructions on where to download this file can be found here: www.sybex.com/go/mcsawin2012r2

2. Click the Start.EXE file to open up the study tools file.

3. Read the license agreement, and then click the Accept button if you want to use the study tools.

The main interface appears. The interface allows you to access the content with just one or two clicks.

Troubleshooting

Wiley has attempted to provide programs that work on most computers with the minimum system requirements. Alas, your computer may differ, and some programs may not work properly for some reason.

The two likeliest problems are that you don't have enough memory (RAM) for the programs you want to use or you have other programs running that are affecting installation or running of a program. If you get an error message such as "Not enough memory" or "Setup cannot continue," try one or more of the following suggestions and then try using the software again:

Turn off any antivirus software running on your computer. Installation programs sometimes mimic virus activity and may make your computer incorrectly believe that it's being infected by a virus.

Close all running programs. The more programs you have running, the less memory is available to other programs. Installation programs typically update files and programs; so if you keep other programs running, installation may not work properly.

Have your local computer store add more RAM to your computer. This is, admittedly, a drastic and somewhat expensive step. However, adding more memory can really help the speed of your computer and allow more programs to run at the same time.

Customer Care

If you have trouble with the book's companion study tools, please call the Wiley Product Technical Support phone number at (800) 762-2974. 74, or email them at `http://sybex .custhelp.com/`

Index

Note to the Reader: Throughout this index **boldfaced** page numbers indicate primary discussions of a topic. *Italicized* page numbers indicate illustrations.

O

V

Free Interactive Online Study Environment

Register on Sybex.com to gain access to our interactive learning environment and study tools to help you study for your MCSA Windows Server 2012 R2 certification.

Our Superior Study Tools include:

- Assessment Test to help you focus your study to specific objectives
- Chapter Tests to reinforce what you learned
- Three Practice Exams to test your knowledge of the material
- Electronic Flashcards to reinforce your learning and give you that last-minute test prep before the exam
- Searchable Glossary gives you instant access to the key terms you'll need to know for the exam

Visit www.sybex.com/go/mcsawin2012r2, type in your PIN and instantly gain access to our interactive learning environment.